ART LAW

ASPEN CASEBOOK SERIES

ART LAW
Cases and Materials

SECOND EDITION

Leonard D. DuBoff
The DuBoff Law Group, LLC

Michael D. Murray
University of Kentucky College of Law

Wolters Kluwer

To contact Customer Service, e-mail customer.service@wolterskluwer.com, call 1-800-234-1660, fax 1-800-901-9075, or mail correspondence to:

>   Wolters Kluwer
>   Attn: Order Department
>   PO Box 990
>   Frederick, MD 21705

Printed in the United States of America.

1 2 3 4 5 6 7 8 9 0

ISBN 978-1-4548-7663-2

Library of Congress Cataloging-in-Publication Data

Names: DuBoff, Leonard D., author. | Murray, Michael D., 1965- author.
Title: Art law : cases and materials / Leonard D. DuBoff, The DuBoff Law
    Group, LLC, Michael D. Murray, University of Kentucky College of Law.
Description: Second edition. | New York : Wolters Kluwer, [2017] | Series:
    Aspen casebook series
Identifiers: LCCN 2017004256 | ISBN 9781454876632
Subjects: LCSH: Law and art — United States — Cases. | Artists — Legal status,
    laws, etc. — United States — Cases.
Classification: LCC KF4288 .D799 2017 | DDC 344.73/097 — dc23
LC record available at https://lccn.loc.gov/2017004256

About Wolters Kluwer Legal & Regulatory U.S.

Wolters Kluwer Legal & Regulatory U.S. delivers expert content and solutions in the areas of law, corporate compliance, health compliance, reimbursement, and legal education. Its practical solutions help customers successfully navigate the demands of a changing environment to drive their daily activities, enhance decision quality and inspire confident outcomes.

Serving customers worldwide, its legal and regulatory portfolio includes products under the Aspen Publishers, CCH Incorporated, Kluwer Law International, ftwilliam.com and MediRegs names. They are regarded as exceptional and trusted resources for general legal and practice-specific knowledge, compliance and risk management, dynamic workflow solutions, and expert commentary.

Leonard DuBoff would like to dedicate this book to his
partner in law and in life — Mary Ann Crawford DuBoff — for
her love of art, her knowledge of law, and her ability
to meld the two.

Michael Murray dedicates this book to Denise, Olivia,
and Dennis, who show patience and love as I pursue
my dream, and to Donald King, who greatly helped
make it all happen.

SUMMARY OF CONTENTS

TABLE OF CONTENTS

PART II ART MARKETS

PREFACE

Greatness in art, similar to immortality in literature, may be measured by its long-term impact on the lives of human beings. Just as children and adults continue to read the plays of Shakespeare 500 years after their creation, people throughout the world still revere the art works of Michelangelo, Rembrandt, and van Dyck. An even more supreme era of art creation took place during the life of Ramses the II, the pharaoh who oversaw the rise of Egyptian empire between 304 and 237 BCE. The lasting impact of this period can be measured in the infinite treasures that tell the story of Egypt's artistic soul in museums from New York to Cairo and from London to Tokyo.

Great art may be timeless, yet just as an artist's work changes during his or her lifetime, art has undergone many transformations throughout history. Art does not grow in a vacuum. As the ideas of mankind change, so does their mode of expression. Today, anything from bread wrappers and abstract paintings to tea kettles and skyscrapers can be art. The urge to portray "color suspended in air" has driven some artists to fashion their art with the use of spray paint.[1] Others utilize a can of paint to express their artistic feelings in a more traditional manner — graffiti. Yet it is not beyond comprehension to imagine the argument in support of defining either form of expression as art. An artist may contribute nothing more of herself than a signature and a date to a piece of garbage, and call the result art. *Id.* Applying the label "art" is a judgment one makes for oneself, whether the subject matter is rubbish, spray paint on a wall, or replicas of currency drawn on paper, cleverly exchanged by the artist for goods and services and subsequently exhibited along with receipts and other paraphernalia representing the transactions.[2]

Judging art changes with contemporary standards. Works considered poor at one time may at another time be acknowledged as masterpieces.

---

1. *Vasari Diary*, ARTnews, Apr. 1988, at 11-12.
2. Weschler, *Onward and Upward with the Arts: Value*, New Yorker, Jan. 18, 1988.

Witness the furor associated with the development of abstract painting. What we call art, in part, may be a product of what survives the passage of time. In fact, "[i]n the long run [it could be that] any artifact will be art . . . [and in] a thousand years the art of this century will be ceramic sinks and toilets because that's all that will survive the wars and the developers."[3] Art itself is a critic of the culture that produced it and serves as a historic record for future civilizations. Even after much time has elapsed, we can learn a great deal about other people by studying their art forms.

The search for a universal definition of art has produced an array of responses and little agreement. Of those artists, philosophers, and art historians who have attempted to define the term, few have settled on any single meaning or even a single common component. The suggested definitions run the gamut from the simple and familiar "art is experience," to the more complex "a work of art . . . is an organic complex presented in sensuous medium, which complex is composed of elements, their expressive characteristics and the relations obtaining them."[4]

For the purposes of this text, it may be less important to define what art is than to determine what art does. Art communicates. It transmits aspects of human experience that often cannot be expressed in words. R.G. Collingwood suggests that art is expression, and it cannot arise until men have something to express.[5] John Dewey viewed art as the most universal and freest form of communication.[6] What it communicates is inextricably interwoven with and depends upon a mesh of the creator, the creator's culture and society, the viewer, and the viewer's culture and society.

Moreover, art feeds the soul. Paintings can make us laugh, cry, and ponder the meaning of life. Sculpture can fill us with hope for humanity or disgust over the degradation of human beings. A photograph can move us to political action or stop us in our tracks. Even glasswork observed from seats in churches, mosques, synagogues, and temples sends our minds wandering on new journeys and adventures.

Art affects us. We buy visual art for our homes and offices so we can enjoy the images over moments in our day. We visit unobtainable art in museums to see products of artistic imagination over the centuries. We peruse galleries to discover the output of contemporary artists.

Art can evoke passionate responses centuries, even millennia, after creation. An Egyptian cab driver complained to University of New Mexico law

3. Judd, *A Long Discussion Not About Masterpieces But Why There Are So Few of Them*, Art in Am., Oct. 1984, at 9.
4. Morris Weitz, Philosophy of the Arts 44 (1950) (quoted in Joseph Margolis, The Language of Art & Art Criticism 40 (1965)). *See also* Karlen, *What Is Art?: A Sketch for a Legal Definition*, 94 L.Q. Rev. 383 (1978) (discussing the legal definition of art in the United Kingdom).
5. R.G. Collingwood, Essays in the Philosophy of Art (1964).
6. John Dewey, Art as Experience 270 (1934).

professor Sherri Burr on a trip from Manhattan to La Guardia airport about Hitler having placed the Bust of Nefertiti in his office. "How dare such an evil man possess something so precious to the Egyptian soul?" he wanted to know.

Unbeknownst to the cab driver, the Germans counted the Bust of Nefertiti among their assets. On Sunday, April 8, 1945, Josef Goebbels, Hitler's Minister of Information, wrote in his diary, "Our entire gold reserve amounting to hundreds of tons and vast art treasures, including the bust of Nefertiti, have fallen into American hands." Even in 2009, the German possession of the Bust of Nefertiti remained a hot button issue in Egypt as it sought repatriation of the item.

Greek students wailed about the fact that England had the marbles of the Parthenon (aka Elgin Marbles) and refused to give them back. When Professor Burr asked these students in 1997 whether their country would be a different place if the marbles of the Parthenon had never been taken, the Greek students responded, "We would be so much stronger today."

It is moments like these that inspired the authors to research and write this book. We write for all the students we've taught in our U.S. classes and lectured to throughout the world. We write for the gallery owners and museum personnel who have shared so much about art over the decades with our students or called us with their legal issues. We write for the Egyptian cab driver who cared about others looking at and touching art created millennia before his birth.

We hope that you enjoy reading and thinking about art law issues as much as we have taken pleasure in writing this book. We wish you a happy journey into the world of art law.

Leonard D. DuBoff
Michael D. Murray

April 2017

ACKNOWLEDGMENTS

Adler, Amy. Inverting the First Amendment, 149 U. Penn. L. Rev. 921 (Apr. 2001). Copyright © 2001 by Amy Adler. Reproduced with permission. All rights reserved.

Adler, Amy. What's Left?: Hate Speech, Pornography, and the Problem for Artistic Expression, 84 Cal. L. Rev. 1499 (Dec. 1996). Copyright © 1996 by Amy Adler. Reproduced with permission. All rights reserved.

Burr, Sheila L. The Acclaim and Hazards of Being an International Artist, Author Interview with Bill Arms (2004). Copyright © 2004 by Sheila L. Burr. Reproduced with permission. All rights reserved.

Burr, Sheila L. Conversing with the Picasso of Indian Artists, Author Interview with R.C. Gorman (2004). Copyright © 2004 by Sheila L. Burr. Reproduced with permission. All rights reserved.

Burr, Sheila L. Creating Public Art, Evoking Emotional Responses, Author Interview with Betty Sabo (2004) Copyright © 2004 by Sheila L. Burr. Reproduced with permission. All rights reserved.

Burr, Sheila L. Introducing Art Law, 37 Copyright World 22, 28-29 (1994) Copyright © 1994 by Sheila L. Burr. Reproduced with permission. All rights reserved.

Burr, Sheila L. Photographing Nudes in Black and White, Author Interview with Chris McDonald. Copyright © 2004, 2016 by Sheila L. Burr. Reproduced with permission. All rights reserved.

Toobin, Jeffrey. The Battle for the Barnes, The New Yorker, Jan. 21, 2002, at 34. Copyright © 2002 by Condé Nast. Reproduced with permission. All rights reserved.

Wu, Jeffrey C. Art Resale Rights and the Art Resale Market: A Follow-Up Study, 46 J. Copr. Soc. 531 (Summer 1999). Copyright © 1999 by Jeffrey C. Wu. Reproduced with permission. All rights reserved.

TABLE OF PHOTOGRAPHS AND IMAGES

Chapter-Image #	Author-Owner, Date	Title or Description	Page #
2 – 3	Michael D. Murray, 2009	Collage of two revised and resized images derived from the trial exhibits in *Mannion v. Coors Brewing Co.*, 377 F. Supp. 2d 444 (S.D.N.Y. 2005)	43
2 – 4	Michael D. Murray, 2016	Cropped, revised, and resized thumbnail image derived from the photograph "Place de l'Europe. Gare Saint Lazare" by Henri Cartier-Bresson (1932)	48
2 – 5	Michael D. Murray, 2014	Revised and resized thumbnail image derived from a public domain chromolithographic circus poster, the subject of *Bleistein v. Donaldson Lithographing Co.*, 188 U.S. 239 (1903)	50 Top
2 – 6	Michael D. Murray, 2014	Revised and resized thumbnail image derived from a public domain chromolithographic circus poster, the subject of *Bleistein v. Donaldson Lithographing Co.*, 188 U.S. 239 (1903)	50 Bottom
2 – 7	Michael D. Murray, 2016	Revised and resized thumbnail image of tribal-style tattoo created by tattoo artist Victor Whitmill on the face of former boxing champion Mike Tyson, the subject of *Whitmill vs. Warner Bros., the Producers of the Motion Picture "The Hangover Part II"* (2014)	52 Left
2 – 8	Michael D. Murray, 2016	Revised and resized thumbnail image of actor Ed Helms wearing a tribal-style tattoo in the style of a design by tattoo artist Victor Whitmill, the subject of *Whitmill vs. Warner Bros., the Producers of the Motion Picture "The Hangover Part II"* (2014)	52 Right
2 – 9	Michael Murray, 2014	Cropped, revised, and resized thumbnail image derived from the image of Kelley's Plan for Wildflower Works, at http://www.rarin.org/index.php/File:KelleyChicagoAerial.JPG, the subject of *Kelley v. Chicago Park Dist.*, 635 F.3d 290 (7th Cir. 2011)	54 Left

Chapter-Image #	Author-Owner, Date	Title or Description	Page #
2 – 10	Michael D. Murray, 2014	Cropped, revised, and resized thumbnail image derived from a photograph of the Wildflower Works installation, the subject of *Kelley v. Chicago Park Dist.*, 635 F.3d 290 (7th Cir. 2011)	54 Right
2 – 11	Michael D. Murray, 2009	Cropped, revised, and resized image of a Satava sculpture derived from the exhibits to the Ninth Circuit's opinion in *Satava v. Lowry*, 323 F.3d 805 (9th Cir. 2003)	60 Left
2 – 12	Michael D. Murray, 2009	Cropped, revised, and resized image of a Lowry sculpture derived from the exhibits to the Ninth Circuit's opinion in *Satava v. Lowry*, 323 F.3d 805 (9th Cir. 2003)	60 Right
2 – 13	Michael D. Murray, 2014	Collage of cropped, revised, and resized thumbnail images derived from photographs of common features of doll faces, to illustrate the facts of *Mattel, Inc. v. Goldberger Doll Mfg. Co.*, 365 F.3d 133 (2d Cir. 2004)	66
2 – 14	Michael D. Murray, 2014	Collage of cropped, revised, and resized thumbnail images derived from photographs of doll faces, to illustrate the facts of *Mattel, Inc. v. Goldberger Doll Mfg. Co.*, 365 F.3d 133 (2d Cir. 2004)	67 Top
2 – 15	Michael D. Murray, 2007	Cropped, revised, and resized photograph by Michael Murray (2007) depicting two actual Mattel Barbie dolls and one Italian counterfeit "Barbie" doll, to illustrate the facts of *Mattel, Inc. v. Goldberger Doll Mfg. Co.*, 365 F.3d 133 (2d Cir. 2004)	67 Bottom
2 – 16	Michael D. Murray, 2004	Cropped, revised, and resized image of the Esquire Lamp whose design was litigated in *Esquire, Inc. v. Ringer*, 591 F.2d 796 (D.C. Cir. 1978), *cert. denied*, 449 U.S. 908 (1979)	72
2 – 17	Michael D. Murray, 2016	Cropped, revised, and resized thumbnail images derived from exhibits depicting Varsity Brand cheerleading uniform designs, at issue in *Varsity Brands, Inc. v. Star Athletica, LLC*, 799 F.3d 468 (6th Cir. 2015)	74

Chapter-Image #	Author-Owner, Date	Title or Description	Page #
2 – 18	Michael D. Murray, 2016	Cropped, revised, and resized thumbnail images derived from exhibits depicting Home Legend's "Distressed Maple Mendocino" design and Mannington Mills' "Glazed Maple" design, at issue in *Home Legend, LLC v. Mannington Mills, Inc.*, 784 F.3d 1404 (11th Cir. 2015)	75 Top
2 – 19	Michael D. Murray, 2016	Cropped, revised, and resized thumbnail images derived from exhibits depicting Inhale, Inc.'s and Starbuzz Tobacco's hookah water container designs, at issue in *Inhale, Inc. v. Starbuzz Tobacco, Inc.*, 755 F.3d 1038 (9th Cir. 2014)	75 Bottom
2 – 20	Michael D. Murray, 2016	Cropped, revised, and resized thumbnail image derived from an exhibit depicting Klauber's lace design, at issue in *Klauber Bros., Inc. v. Target Corp.*, 2015 Copr. L. Dec. P 30, 795, 116 U.S.P.Q.2d 1165 (S.D.N.Y. 2015)	76
2 – 21	Michael D. Murray, 2009	Cropped, revised, and resized thumbnail images derived from photographs depicting statuettes used as lamp bases, derived from exhibits to the U.S. Supreme Court's opinion in *Mazer v. Stein*, 347 U.S. 201 (1954)	78
2 – 22	Michael D. Murray, 2016	Cropped, revised, and resized thumbnail image derived from an exhibit depicting Jack Kirby's most famous characters in Marvel Comics: Captain America, X-Men, Fantastic Four, Hulk, and Spider-man, at issue in *Marvel Characters, Inc. v Kirby*, 726 F.3d 119 (2d Cir. 2013)	96
2 – 23	Michael D. Murray, 2014	Cropped, revised, and resized thumbnail image derived from an exhibit depicting the High Museum of Art poster of the Ringgold story quilt at issue in *Ringgold v. Black Entm't Television, Inc.*, 126 F.3d 70 (2d Cir. 1997)	111

Chapter-Image #	Author-Owner, Date	Title or Description	Page #
2 – 24	Michael D. Murray, 2016	Cropped, revised, and resized thumbnail image derived from a single frame of video of Los Angeles News Service coverage of South Central Los Angeles riots litigated in *Los Angeles News Serv. v. KCAL-TV Channel 9*, 108 F.3d 1119 (9th Cir. 1997)	127
2 – 25	Michael D. Murray, 2014	Cropped, revised, and resized thumbnail image derived from Daniel Morel's Photograph of Haiti earthquake victim at issue in the litigation of *Morel v. AFP, Getty Images, and the Washington Post* (2010)	128 Top
2 – 26	Michael D. Murray, 2014	Collage of cropped, revised, and resized thumbnail images derived from newspaper covers depicting Daniel Morel's photograph of Haiti earthquake victim at issue in the litigation of *Morel v. AFP, Getty Images, and the Washington Post* (2010)	128 Bottom
2 – 27	Michael D. Murray, 2016	Cropped, revised, and resized thumbnail image derived from frame 312 of the film taken by Abraham Zapruder of the assassination of President John F. Kennedy on November 22, 1963	129
2 – 28	Michael D. Murray, 2014	Cropped, revised, and resized thumbnail images derived from exhibits depicting the cover of Gerald Ford's Biography, "A Time to Heal," and the cover of Nation Magazine's article excerpting Gerald Ford's biography, "A Time to Heal," the subject of *Harper & Row Publishers, Inc. v. Nation Enters.*, 471 U.S. 539 (1985)	130
2 – 29	Michael D. Murray, 2015	Cropped, revised, and resized thumbnail image derived from a single frame from NBC's 1977 Saturday Night Live television skit, "I Love Sodom," the subject of *Elsmere Music, Inc. v. National Broadcasting Co.*, 482 F. Supp. 741, 747 (S.D.N.Y. 1980)	132 Top

Chapter-Image #	Author-Owner, Date	Title or Description	Page #
2 – 30	Michael D. Murray, 2014	Cropped, revised, and resized thumbnail images derived from exhibits depicting the Vanity Fair cover with Annie Leibovitz's photograph of Demi Moore, and the Naked Gun 33 1/3 Movie Poster depicting Leslie Neilson in a pose reminiscent of Demi Moore on Vanity Fair, both of which are the subject of *Leibovitz v. Paramount Pictures Corp.*, 137 F.3d 109, 110 (2d Cir. 1998)	132 Bottom
2 – 31	Michael D. Murray, 2014	Collage of cropped, revised, and resized thumbnail images derived from exhibits, including excerpt of Blanch's "Silk Sandals" photograph, excerpt from Koon's "Niagara" painting, and grayscale comparison of Blanch's feet to Koon's treatment of the feet, all of which are the subject of *Blanch v. Koons*, 467 F.3d 244 (2d Cir. 2006)	135
2 – 32	Michael D. Murray, 2016	Collage of cropped, revised, and resized thumbnail images derived from exhibits depicting Richard Prince's "Canal Zone" work incorporating in part the photographs of Patrick Cariou from his book, "Yes Rasta," which are the subject of *Cariou v. Prince*, 714 F.3d 694 (2d Cir.), *cert. denied*, 134 S. Ct. 618 (2013)	137
2 – 33	Michael D. Murray, 2016	Collage of cropped, revised, and resized thumbnail images derived from exhibits depicting Richard Prince's "Canal Zone" images next to the original photographs of Patrick Cariou from his book, "Yes Rasta," which reflect two of the Prince images remanded by the court in *Cariou v. Prince*, 714 F.3d 694 (2d Cir.), *cert. denied*, 134 S. Ct. 618 (2013), for further consideration of their "transformative" nature	138
2 – 34	Michael D. Murray, 2016	Cropped, revised, and resized thumbnail image derived from Dereck Seltzer's "Scream Icon" (2003), the subject of *Seltzer v. Green Day, Inc.*, 725 F.3d 1170 (9th Cir. 2013)	139 Left

Chapter-Image #	Author-Owner, Date	Title or Description	Page #
2 – 40	Michael D. Murray, 2007	Cropped, revised, and resized thumbnail image derived from exhibits depicting characters from "The Cat Not in the Hat," juxtaposed with original Dr. Seuss "Cat in the Hat" characters, as displayed in the exhibits to the court opinion in *Dr. Seuss Enters. v. Penguin Books*, 109 F.3d 1394 (9th Cir. 1997)	147
2 – 41	Michael D. Murray, 2007	Cropped and resized images derived from two Michael Murray photographs of Sacré-Coeur Basilica in Paris, France (2007)	149
2 – 42	Michael D. Murray, 2014	Cropped, revised, and resized thumbnail images derived from four Michael Murray photographs of Dale Chihuly "Macchia" glass sculptures displayed at the Missouri Botanical Gardens, St. Louis, MO (2006)	150
3 – 1	Michael D. Murray, 2016	Collage of Revised and Resized Thumbnail Images of 18 Trademark Logos (2016), derived from *Fabrily Campaigns: Trademark vs. Copyright*, https://fabrily.wordpress.com/2014/06/26/fabrily-campaigns-trademark-vs-copyright/ (2014)	159
3 – 2	Michael D. Murray, 2014	Collage of three cropped, revised, resized thumbnail images of Michael Murray, a Murray lawnmower, and a Murray bicycle	172 Top
3 – 3	Michael Murray, 2014	Collage of cropped, revised, and resized thumbnail images derived from images depicting non-trademarkable seals, flags, symbols, coats of arms, and slogans	172 Bottom
3 – 4	Michael D. Murray, 2014	Composite diagram with cropped, revised, and resized thumbnail images derived from images of Tiger Woods wearing Nike and TW brand golf attire and using a Nike golf club, shown next to a ProStaff golf ball to simulate a false endorsement scenario	186

Chapter-Image #	Author-Owner, Date	Title or Description	Page #
3 – 5	Michael D. Murray, 2014	Collage of cropped, revised, and resized thumbnail images derived from images of product knockoffs or counterfeits for J Crew, Nike (Nkie), M & Ms (S & Ms)	187
3 – 6	Michael D. Murray, 2014	Collage of revised and resized thumbnail images derived from geographic indication logos	188
3 – 7	Michael D. Murray, 2014	Cropped, revised, and resized images derived from excerpts of exhibits depicting the Mutual of Omaha logo and the Novak "Mutant of Omaha" logo, the subject of *Mutual of Omaha Ins. Co. v. Novak*, 836 F. 2d 397 (8th Cir. 1987)	197
3 – 8	Michael D. Murray, 2007	Revised and resized images derived from excerpts of exhibits depicting Anheuser Busch Michelob Dry and A & Eagle logos, and the Balducci "Michelob Oily" spoof ad, the subject of *Anheuser-Busch, Inc. v. Balducci Publications*, 28 F.3d 769 (8th Cir. 1994)	198
3 – 9	Michael D. Murray, 2014	Cropped, revised, and resized images derived from excerpts of exhibits depicting Samara's children's clothing compared to Wal-Mart's children's clothing, the subject of *Wal-Mart Stores, Inc. v. Samara Brothers, Inc.*, 529 U.S. 205 (2000)	208
3 – 10	Michael D. Murray, 2014	Collage of cropped, revised, and resized thumbnail images derived from images of Dolce & Gabbana products to show the non-functionality of the DG logo	209 Top
3 – 11	Michael D. Murray, 2014	Collage of cropped, revised, and resized thumbnail images derived from images of Chanel clothing to show the non-functionality of the Chanel designs	209 Bottom
3 – 12	Michael D. Murray, 2014	Collage of cropped, revised, and resized thumbnail images derived from photographs of Christian Louboutin shoes compared to Yves Saint Laurent shoes, the subject of *Christian Louboutin S.A. v. Yves Saint Laurent America Holdings, Inc.*, 696 F.3d 206 (2d Cir. 2012)	210 Top

Chapter-Image #	Author-Owner, Date	Title or Description	Page #
3 – 13	Michael D. Murray, 2016	Cropped, revised, and resized thumbnail excerpt of an exhibit depicting Qualitex's dry cleaning pad, the subject of *Qualitex Co. v. Jacobson Products Co., Inc.*, 514 U.S. 159 (1995)	210 Bottom
3 – 14a, 3 – 14b, 3 – 14c, 3 – 14d, 3 – 14e, 3 – 14f	Michael D. Murray, 2009	Collage of cropped, revised, and resized thumbnail images of exhibits depicting Itzchak Tarkay "Women in Cafes" paintings, and Patricia Govezensky paintings, the subject of *Romm Art Creations Ltd. v. Simcha Int'l, Inc.*, 786 F. Supp. 1126 (E.D.N.Y. 1992)	215-216
3 – 15	Michael D. Murray, 2016	Cropped, revised, and resized thumbnail images derived from exhibits depicting Hormel Foods Corp.'s Spam product and the Spa'am Muppet Character, at issue in *Hormel Foods Corp. v. Jim Henson Prods., Inc.*, 73 F.3d 497 (2d Cir. 1996)	221
4 – 1	Michael D. Murray, 2014	Cropped, revised, and resized thumbnail excerpt of an exhibit depicting the attempted restoration of James Abbott McNeill Whistler's overpainted portrait of Lady Eden, the subject of *Eden c. Whistler*, [1898] Recueil Periodique et Critique, II.4.65 (Civ. Trib. Seine) [1900] S.II.201 (Cour d'Appel, Paris), [1900] Recueil Periodique Sirey [hereinafter S. Jur.] I.490 (Cass. Civ.)	227
4 – 2	Michael D. Murray, 2015	Cropped, revised, and resized thumbnail images derived from two photographs depicting Jean Dubuffet and his model for an installation at Renault Headquarters, the subject of *Dubuffet v. Régie Nationales des Usines Renault*, Judgment of Jan. 8, 1980, Cass. civ. Ire, R.I.D.A. April 1980, at 154, A. Francon obs./ Judgment of March 16, 1983, Cass. civ. Ire, R.I.D.A. July 1983, at 80.	229

Chapter-Image #	Author-Owner, Date	Title or Description	Page #
4 – 10	Michael D. Murray, 2014	Collage of three cropped, revised, and resized thumbnail images derived from photographs depicting Richard Serra's "Tilted Arc" sculpture in Foley Square, New York City, the subject of *Serra v. United States Gen. Servs. Admin.*, 847 F.2d 1045 (2d Cir. 1988)	267
4 – 11	Michael D. Murray, 2014	Cropped, revised, and resized image derived from a photograph of David Phillips' Eastport Park installation, the subject of *Phillips v. Pembroke Real Estate, Inc.*, 288 F. Supp. 2d 89 (D. Mass. 2003), *aff'd*, 459 F.3d 128 (1st Cir. 2006)	268
4 – 12	Michael D. Murray, 2014	Collage of three cropped, revised, and resized thumbnail images derived from photographs of Chapman Kelley's "Wildflower Works" Art Installation in Chicago, the subject of *Kelley v. Chicago Park Dist.*, 635 F.3d 290 (7th Cir. 2011)	269 Top
4 – 13	Michael D. Murray, 2014	Collage of three cropped, revised, and resized thumbnail images derived from photographs depicting the changes to Chapman Kelley's "Wildflower Works" Art Installation in Chicago, the subject of *Kelley v. Chicago Park Dist.*, 635 F.3d 290 (7th Cir. 2011)	269 Bottom
4 – 14	Michael D. Murray, 2016	Two cropped, revised, and resized thumbnail images derived from photographs depicting Shepard Fairey's "Duality of Humanity 4 Pike Street" mural in Cincinnati, and a man painting over that same mural	280
4 – 15	Michael D. Murray, 2014	Cropped, revised, and resized thumbnail image derived from a photograph of Kent Twitchell's mural, "Portrait of artist, Ed Ruscha" (1978), located on a building in Los Angeles	282 Top
4 – 16	Michael D. Murray, 2014	Cropped, revised, and resized thumbnail image derived from a photograph of Alexander Calder's Pittsburgh mobile, restored to its original colors and mobility, the subject of Calder's dispute with Allegheny County, PA	282 Bottom

Chapter-Image #	Author-Owner, Date	Title or Description	Page #
4 – 17	Michael D. Murray, 2016	Collage of three cropped, revised, and resized thumbnail images derived from photographs relating to the destruction of 5Poinz, the subject of *Cohen v. G & M Realty L.P.*, 988 F. Supp. 2d 212 (E.D.N.Y. 2013)	304
4 – 18	Michael D. Murray, 2015	Cropped, revised, and resized thumbnail images derived from a photographs depicting the newly unveiled "Tiger Spot" sculpture at the University of Missouri (2001), and a photograph depicting a dejected Paul Jackson inspecting his damaged "Tiger Spot" sculpture (2006)	305
4 – 19	Michael D. Murray, 2014	Four cropped, revised, and resized thumbnail images derived from "before and after" photographs depicting the alterations to David Ascalon's Holocaust Memorial	307
5 – 1	Michael D. Murray, 2009	Composite image of soccer ball bearing a cropped, revised, and resized thumbnail image of soccer player, David Beckham surrounded by ironic words (2009)	325
5 – 2	Michael D. Murray, 2014	Collage of three cropped, revised, and resized thumbnail images derived from photographs depicting Human Cannonball Hugo Zacchini (2014), the claimant in *Zacchini v. Scripps-Howard Broadcasting Co.*, 433 U.S. 562 (1977)	326
5 – 3	Michael D. Murray, 2009	Two cropped, revised, and resized thumbnail images derived from photographs of Cheryl Tiegs and a Mihail Simeonov bust (2009), the subject of *Simeonov v. Tiegs*, 602 N.Y.S.2d 1014 (N.Y. City Civ. Ct. 1993)	336
5 – 4	Michael D. Murray, 2016	Cropped, revised, and resized image of the Three Stooges (2016) that was derived from a still from the motion picture, *You Natzy Spy*, that was used a reference for Gary Saderup's work at issue in *Comedy III Productions, Inc. v. Gary Saderup, Inc.*, 21 P.3d 797 (Cal. 2001)	340 Top

Chapter-Image #	Author-Owner, Date	Title or Description	Page #
5 – 17	Michael D. Murray, 2014	Composite of two cropped, revised, and resized thumbnail excerpts of exhibits depicting hockey player Tony Twist, and cover art of the Spawn comic, featuring the character, Tony Twist, at issue in *Doe v. TCI Cablevision*, 110 S.W.3d 363 (Mo. 2003).	375
5 – 18	Michael D. Murray, 2007	Cropped, revised, and resized thumbnail excerpt of exhibit depicting OutKast's "Rosa Parks" single release, the subject of *Parks v. LaFace Records*, 329 F.3d 437 (6th Cir. 2003).	378
5 – 19	Michael D. Murray, 2014	Cropped, revised, and resized thumbnail excerpts of exhibits depicting Kierin Kirby, better known as Lady Miss Kier, and the Sega video game character, Ulala, the subjects of the case, *Kirby v. Sega of Am.*, Inc., 50 Cal. Rptr. 3d 607 (Ct. App. 2006).	380
5 – 20	Michael D. Murray, 2015	Cropped, revised, and resized thumbnail excerpt of exhibit (2015) depicting a single frame taken from the video recording by westfesttv, "Tupac Hologram Snoop Dogg and Dr. Dre Perform Coachella Live 2012," https://www.youtube.com/watch?v=TGbrFmPBV0Y (Apr. 17, 2012)	382 Top
5 – 21	Michael D. Murray, 2015	Cropped, revised, and resized thumbnail excerpt of exhibit (2015) depicting the modern version of the old "Pepper's Ghost" illusion used at the Coachella 2012 concert to allow the virtual performance of the deceased Tupac Shakur; Original Source: Musion Systems Ltd; Original Graphic by Alberto Cervantes for the Wall Street Journal (2012)	382 Bottom
6 – 1	Michael D. Murray, 2009	Cropped, revised, resized photograph by Michael D. Murray of the Satyr "Anapauomenos" Sculpture, Palazzo Medici Riccardi, Florence (2009)	392

Chapter-Image #	Author-Owner, Date	Title or Description	Page #
6 – 2	Michael D. Murray, 2014	Cropped, revised, resized photograph of children saluting the American flag as discussed in *West Virginia State Board of Education v. Barnette*, 319 U.S. 624 (1943)	395
6 – 3	Michael D. Murray, 2014	Composite of two cropped, revised, and resized thumbnail excerpts of photographs depicting Mary Beth Tinker, the named litigant in the case, *Tinker v. Des Moines Independent Community School Dist.*, 393 U.S. 503 (1969)	397
6 – 4	Michael D. Murray, 2014	Cropped, revised, and resized thumbnail excerpt of an exhibit depicting the "Bong Hits 4 Jesus" Banner that was the subject of *Morse v. Frederick*, 551 U.S. 393 (2007)	400
6 – 5	Michael D. Murray, 2015	Cropped, revised, and resized thumbnail excerpt of an exhibit depicting the poster art for "Les Amants," the subject of *Jacobellis v. Ohio*, 378 U.S. 184 (1964)	409 Top
6 – 6	Michael D. Murray, 2016	Cropped, revised, and resized thumbnail excerpt of an exhibit depicting the cover of the Wordsworth Classics edition of John Cleland's book, "Memoirs of a Woman of Pleasure," the subject of *Memoirs v. Massachusetts*, 383 U.S. 413, 418 (1966)	409 Bottom
6 – 7	Michael D. Murray, 2012	Cropped, revised, and resized thumbnail excerpt of an exhibit depicting a portion of the Danish newspaper, Morgenavisen Jyllands-Posten, KulturWeekend section (Sep. 30, 2005), featuring "Muhammeds Ansigt" cartoons	447
6 – 8	Michael D. Murray, 2007	Cropped, revised, and resized thumbnail excerpt from the Government's trial exhibits depicting O'Brien and others burning their draft cards, at issue in *United States v. O'Brien*, 391 U.S. 367 (1968)	448

Chapter-Image #	Author-Owner, Date	Title or Description	Page #
6 – 9	Michael D. Murray, 2007	Cropped, revised, and resized thumbnail excerpt from the Government's trial exhibits depicting the burnt remains of O'Brien's draft card, at issue in *United States v. O'Brien*, 391 U.S. 367 (1968)	449
6 – 10	Michael D. Murray, 2007	Cropped, revised, and resized thumbnail excerpts of exhibits depicting Richard Serra's "Tilted Arc" sculpture in Manhattan, the subject of *Serra v. U.S. General Services Admin.*, 847 F.2d 1045 (2d Cir. 1988)	453
6 – 11	Michael D. Murray, 2007	Cropped, revised, and resized thumbnail excerpt of an exhibit depicting Claudio's "Sex, Laws, and Coathangers" work, the subject of *Claudio v. United States*, 836 F. Supp. 1230 (E.D.N.C. 1993)	459
6 – 12	Michael D. Murray, 2015	Cropped, revised, and resized thumbnail excerpt of an exhibit depicting Kara Walker's work, "The Moral Arc of History," the subject of censorship by the Newark Public Library	464
6 – 13	Michael D. Murray, 2015	Cropped, revised, and resized thumbnail excerpt of a public domain photograph of Speaker's Corner at Hyde Park in London (2015)	465
6 – 14	Michael D. Murray, 2014	Cropped, revised, and resized thumbnail excerpt of an exhibit depicting the Ten Commandments monument in a Pleasant Grove City Park (2014), the subject matter of *Pleasant Grove City, Utah v. Summum*, 555 U.S. 460 (2009)	466 Top
6 – 15	Michael D. Murray, 2015	Cropped, revised, and resized thumbnail excerpt of an exhibit (2015) depicting three panels of Judy Taylor's "Mural of the History of Maine's Labor Movement," at issue in *Newton v. LePage*, 700 F.3d 595 (1st Cir. 2012)	466 Bottom5

Chapter-Image #	Author-Owner, Date	Title or Description	Page #
6 – 23	Michael D. Murray, 2015	Cropped, revised, and resized thumbnail excerpt of an exhibit depicting Ryan and Laetitia Coleman (2015), the plaintiffs in *Coleman v. City of Mesa*, 284 P.3d 863 (Ariz. 2012)	474
6 – 24	Michael D. Murray, 2007	Cropped, revised, and resized thumbnail excerpt of an exhibit depicting Chris Ofili, "Holy Virgin Mary" (1996), at issue in *Brooklyn Institute of Arts and Sciences v. City of New York*, 64 F. Supp. 2d 184 (E.D.N.Y. 1999)	483
6 – 25	Michael D. Murray, 2007	Cropped, revised, and resized thumbnail excerpt of an exhibit depicting Damien Hirst, "Some Comfort Gained from the Acceptance of the Inherent Lies in Everything" (1996), at issue in *Brooklyn Institute of Arts and Sciences v. City of New York*, 64 F. Supp. 2d 184 (E.D.N.Y. 1999)	484
6 – 26	Michael D. Murray, 2007	Cropped, revised, and resized thumbnail excerpt (2007) of an exhibit depicting Alma Lopez, "Our Lady" (1999), the subject of a private censorship campaign by residents of Santa Fe, NM	504
6 – 27	Michael D. Murray, 2007	Cropped, revised, and resized thumbnail excerpt (2007) of an exhibit depicting David Nelson, "Mirth and Girth" (1988), the subject of *Nelson v. Streeter*, 16 F.3d 145 (7th Cir. 1994)	505
6 – 28	Michael D. Murray, 2007	Cropped, revised, and resized thumbnail excerpt (2007) of an exhibit depicting Chicago aldermen carrying David Nelson's painting, "Mirth and Girth" (1988) away from the Art Institute of Chicago, at issue in *Nelson v. Streeter*, 16 F.3d 145 (7th Cir. 1994)	506
7 – 1	Michael D. Murray, 2007	Cropped, revised, and resized thumbnail excerpt of a Michael D. Murray photograph (2007) of the public domain sculpture by Michelangelo, "Self-Portrait as Nicodemus in The Florence Pietà" or "The Deposition of Christ," Florence, Italy (1547-1555)	517

Chapter-Image #	Author-Owner, Date	Title or Description	Page #
7 – 2	Michael D. Murray, 2016	Cropped, revised, and resized thumbnail excerpt of an exhibit depicting forger David Stein and one of his forgeries, the subject of *State of New York v. Wright Hepburn Webster Gallery, Limited*, 64 Misc. 2d 423, 314 N.Y.S.2d 661 (Sup. Ct. N.Y. County 1970)	521
7 – 3	Michael D. Murray, 2009	Cropped, revised, and resized thumbnail excerpt of an exhibit depicting Barbara Grygutis, "Cruising San Mateo" (1991), the subject of vocal community disapproval in Albuquerque, New Mexico	555
9 – 1	Sherri Burr, 2009	Cropped, revised, and resized thumbnail excerpt of a Sherri Burr photograph of "Venus" by Koto Bolofo, Tenniseum, Roland Garros, France (2009)	633
10 – 1	Michael D. Murray, 2016	Cropped, revised, and resized thumbnail excerpts (2016) of exhibits depicting the two panels of "Adam and Eve" by Lucas Cranach the Elder (1530), at issue in *Von Saher v. Norton Simon Museum of Art at Pasadena*, 754 F.3d 712 (9th Cir. 2014)	717
11 – 1	Sherri Burr, 1997	Cropped, revised, and resized thumbnail excerpt of a Sherri Burr photograph of the Erechtheum of the Acropolis of Athens (1997)	741
11 – 2	Sherri Burr, 1997	Cropped, revised, and resized thumbnail excerpt of a Sherri Burr photograph of the Sphinx and the Pyramid of Khafre, Giza, Egypt (1997)	763
12 – 1	Sherri Burr, 2016	Cropped, revised, and resized thumbnail excerpt of a Jim Garton photograph (2010) of an R.C. Gorman poster of a seated Navajo woman, from the collection of Sherri Burr	833

ART LAW

1   LEGAL AND OTHER DEFINITIONS OF ART

The term art has many dimensions that vary according to the context in which the word is used. In broad strokes, art is associated with the human ability to create things from imagination and skill. Because human thoughts remain unlimited, the definition of art expands with technical and other innovations.

The arts tend to be divided into two primary forms of visual arts, such as paintings, drawings, architecture, ceramics, sculpture, and photography, or performing arts like drama, dance, and music. Yet some art types, like film and literature, comprise both elements. Books can be physically held and observed, but they may also be performed in a poetry slam or other dramatic reading. Some people even frame the covers of books they find artistically intriguing. Presently, people collect movies and play them in DVD or Blu-ray machines as they might assemble a group of oil paintings and display them on their office walls.

This book focuses on the legal protection of the visual arts. Although there may be some references to the literary and performing arts throughout this text, the primary intent is to teach law students and lawyers how to protect the rights of visual artists and collectors.

A. General Definitions of Art

What Is Art?

http://www.merriam-webster.com/dictionary/art

- something that is created with imagination and skill and that is beautiful or that expresses important ideas or feelings
- works created by artists: paintings, sculptures, etc., that are created to be beautiful or to express important ideas or feelings
- the methods and skills used for painting, sculpting, drawing, etc.

PROBLEM 1-1

Please read the quotes below from established artists defining art and then answer the questions that follow.

Quotes

"Art is either plagiarism or revolution."
Paul Gauguin, painter
http://www.brainyquote.com/quotes/authors/p/paul_gauguin.html

"A good painter has two main objects to paint, man and the intention of his soul. The former is easy, the latter hard as he has to represent it by the attitude and movement of the limbs."
Leonardo da Vinci, painter and sculptor
http://www.artquotes.net/masters/leonardo_quotes.htm

"Art is not an end in itself, but a means of addressing humanity."
Modest Mussorgsky, conductor
http://www.brainyquote.com/quotes/quotes/m/modestmuss309507.html

"Work doesn't become art until some rich person comes along and buys it."
Alfred Stieglitz, photographer
Georgia O'Keeffe, Lifetime Original Movie, Sept. 19, 2009

Questions

1. DaVinci references art to the soul. Does this mark the essence of what is art? Some people think that a painting or sculpture has to be beautiful to be considered valid. But since beauty is so often in the eye of the beholder, would this qualify every painting or sculpture as art so long as one person defined it as attractive?
2. Gauguin implies that artists are either plagiarizing each other or creating the truly revolutionary. Is there something in between?
3. Modest Mussorgsky was a Russian composer who lived from 1839 to 1881. How does his famous quote, "Art is not an end in itself, but a means of addressing humanity" apply to the visual arts?
4. Do you agree with Stieglitz's definition of art? Is the value defined by the price or the personal regard towards the work?

Sherri L. Burr, Photographing Nudes in Black and White

Author Interview with Chris McDonald*

Photographer Robert Mapplethorpe often spoke about his search for the perfect moment, when lighting and subject come together.

Hawaii photographer Chris McDonald has also experienced a "perfect moment" in his work. McDonald says, "I shot like a thousand photographs, maybe 3000, and I have a run of five photographs, boom, boom, boom, shot within maybe 30 seconds. They were exquisite, my best pieces. Everything was right. My mood was right. The lighting was right. Everything was just perfect. I just moved the camera a little bit, and they all turned out to be totally different photographs."

Like Mapplethorpe, McDonald photographs nude individuals, often using a female companion or himself as models. There is no sexual conduct shown in his work and he does not display the pubic region. Michelangelo's David, which depicts a full frontal naked man, is more explicit than any of McDonald's work. Nevertheless, he has received a negative reaction to his photographs of full backsides, breasts and buttocks.

McDonald prefers to shoot in black and white "because it allows people to fill in their own color. People put in their own emotion."

To show his work, McDonald and his friend Henry Paoa produced a video called "Black and White in Color." McDonald says he did the video "out of his heart, out of his spirit." The video begins with "Viewer Discretion Advised: Adults or Parents please be aware that the following program deals with black & white nude photography."

McDonald says he put the disclaimer in because he had experienced problems displaying his photographs in Honolulu. "People wouldn't show them because they called them 'pornography.' A lot of art shops refused to hang them on the wall. They considered them vulgar. We took a shot at putting my work on TV. We showed the video to people who suggested we put that clip (Viewer Discretion Advised) in the beginning and let it run."

Given the response to his nude photographs, McDonald says, "I don't know what's happening in the world we live in. This is something that the Greeks have done. Throughout time, people have explored the human form, because it's the purest form of art, the closest thing we can touch. . . . I look at the human form and I feel it. I illuminate the face because I don't want the thoughts to become too distracted."

In reading about his favorite photographer, McDonald found that Alfred Stieglitz removed the pubic region because he didn't "want the focus to be swayed from the form." Says McDonald, "Stieglitz has a photograph of Georgia O'Keeffe, where she's lying in a lake. It looks ice cold. It is the most beautiful photograph I ever saw. You can feel the goose bumps on her skin. She's totally naked. The photograph is so strong, it's incredible."

---

* Copyright © 2004, 2016 by Sherri Burr.

Like Stieglitz, McDonald often uses the female he is involved with as a model because he feels closer to and more involved with the subject. "I've had some girls model for me," he says, and "I don't have any feeling from it. If I'm involved with the model, I understand the form because I've touched it. I understand the feeling and I want to relay it on a picture. My photographs are sculptural."

He sees art in imperfection. "I would rather have a woman model for me who is about 70 or 80 years old. I would love to find the beauty that is still there. I would have a hard time shooting a swimsuit model. I'm looking for a model who is more pure at heart, simpler in mind, and uncomplicated. That actually reads on the photograph."

"Art is a form of meditation. . . . It's like taking all the noise out of life."

Note and Questions

1. Would Chris McDonald's description of his art fall within the *Webster's Dictionary* definition of art or that of the other artists? Can photography be considered part of the fine arts?
2. When individuals react to an artist's work, does that indicate that the artist may be on to something because she has caused her audience to feel her work?

B. Customs Definition of Art in Historical Context

In this chapter, the legal definition of the term "art" is reviewed and analyzed in the historical setting of customs court litigation. The authors chose customs law because it provides a record of the ways courts have struggled to define art in particular cases. Art has been subject to no import duties, thus creating an incentive to litigate and attempt to prove that certain objects are art. Please note that other legal definitions of art are presented throughout this text and some of them are quite different from those discussed here.

United States v. Perry

146 U.S. 71 (1892)

[This case arose out of the importation of stained glass windows containing images of saints and other biblical subjects. These windows were imported and entered the United States on November 24, 1890, as "paintings" upon glass for the use of the Convent of the Sacred Heart, located in Philadelphia. The windows consisted of pieces of variously colored glass cut into irregular shapes, and fastened together by strips of lead. They were to be used for decorative purposes in churches. The lead strips are placed upon the interior of the window frame, and backed by an outer window of ordinary white glass. The outer window is necessary for the proper exhibition of a transmitted light. Artists of superior merit, especially trained for the work, had executed these paintings. They did not come to this country in a completed state, but in fragments to be put together in the form of windows.

Customs officers levied and collected a duty of 45 per cent imposed by paragraph 122 of the Tariff Act of October 1, 1890, 26 Stat. 573, c. 1244, upon "stained or painted window glass and stained or painted glass windows, ... wholly or partly manufactured, and not specially provided for in this act." The respondent protested against this classification, claiming the articles were exempt from duty as "paintings ... specially imported in good faith for the use of any society or institution ... established for religious ... purposes, ... and not intended for sale," under paragraph 677.

A hearing was held before the board of general appraisers, who overruled the protest and affirmed the action of the customs officers. Respondent thereupon filed a petition in the circuit court for the Southern District of New York, praying for a review of the decision of the general appraisers, as provided in section 15 of the Act of June 10, 1890, 26 Stat. 138, c. 407. The circuit court reversed the decision of the board of appraisers, and held the paintings to be entitled to free entry. *In re Perry*, 47 F. 110. From this decision the United States appealed to the Supreme Court.]

Mr. Justice BROWN delivered the opinion of the court.

It is insisted by the defendants that the painted glass windows in question, having been executed by artists of superior merit, specially trained for the work, should be regarded as works of art, and still exempted from duty as "paintings," and that the provision in paragraph 122, for "stained or painted window glass and stained or painted glass windows," applies only to such articles as are the work of an artisan, the product of handicraft, and not to memorial windows which attain to the rank of works of art. Those who are familiar with the painted windows of foreign cathedrals and churches will indeed find it difficult to deny them the character of works of art; but they would nevertheless be reluctant to put them in the same category with the works of Raphael, Rembrandt, Murillo, and other great masters of the art of painting. While they are artistic in the sense of being beautiful, and requiring a high degree of artistic merit for their production, they are ordinarily classified in foreign exhibits as among the decorative and industrial rather than among the fine arts. And in the catalogues of manufacturers and dealers in stained glass, including the manufacturers of these very importations, no distinction is made between these windows and other stained or painted glass windows, which, by paragraph 757, are specially excepted from the exemption of pictorial paintings on glass.

For most practical purposes works of art may be divided into four classes:

1. The fine arts, properly so called, intended solely for ornamental purposes, and including paintings in oil and water, upon canvas, plaster, or other material, and original statuary of marble, stone or bronze. These are subject to a duty of 15 per cent.
2. Minor objects of art, intended also for ornamental purposes, such as statuettes, vases, plaques, drawings, etchings, and the thousand and one

articles which pass under the general name of bric-a-brac, and are susceptible of an indefinite reproduction from the original.

3. Objects of art, which serve primarily an ornamental, and incidentally a useful, purpose, such as painted or stained glass windows, tapestry, paper hangings, etc.

4. Objects primarily designed for a useful purpose, but made ornamental to please the eye and gratify the taste, such as ornamented clocks, the higher grade of carpets, curtains, gas-fixtures, and household and table furniture.

No special favor is extended by Congress to either of these classes except the first, which is alone recognized as belonging to the domain of high art. It seems entirely clear to us that in paragraph 757, Congress intended to distinguish between "pictorial paintings on glass" which subserve a purely ornamental purpose, and stained or painted glass windows which also subserve a useful purpose, and moved doubtless by a desire to encourage the new manufacture, determined to impose a duty of 45 per cent upon the latter, while the former were admitted free. As new manufactures are developed, the tendency of each tariff act is to nicer discriminations in favor of particular industries. . . .

The judgment of the circuit court must, therefore, be reversed, and the case remanded for further proceedings in conformity to this opinion.

Notes and Questions

1. Here is an example of the type of stain glass window at issue in *In re Perry* from the Metropolitan Museum of Art.

Stained glass windows at the Metropolitan Museum of Art[1]

Do you agree with *Perry* that the definition of art should be limited to fine arts as distinguished from the useful or mechanical and industrial arts? In other words, because something decorative is also useful, like a window, should it be robbed of its definition of art?

---

1. Sherri Burr, Image derived from a photograph by Sherri Burr (2009) of public domain stained glass windows at the Metropolitan Museum of Art.

2. A Rhode Island court employed a similar definition of art in a non-customs case shortly before the *In re Perry* decision. *Almy v. Jones*, 17 R.I. 265, 21 A. 616 (1891), involved a decedent's bequest of a fund to be used for the aid of an art institute. The institute had not yet been established, and the donor had apparently hoped to persuade the public to do so with his bequest. The bequest was upheld against challenges on several grounds, including one directed at the vagueness of the term art. The court held, among other things, that art is not a word of indeterminate meaning. Although often used very broadly, the term, when used without any qualifying adjective, signifies art in its higher manifestations, or art as represented by the works of those who are denominated artists. The word art designates the fine arts, as distinguished from the useful or mechanical and industrial arts.

3. Even in the late 1800s, one case departed from the conservative view of art taken in *In re Perry*. In *Tiffany v. United States*, 66 F. 736 (C.C.S.D.N.Y. 1895), the imported items were silk and bone fans upon which professional artists had executed watercolor paintings. The court rejected the government's assessment of them as manufactures of silk, holding that a painting need not be suitable for framing and hanging on a wall to be a work of art. The essential element was that the item be beautiful and have its chief value imparted by the work of an artist.

United States v. Olivotti & Co.

T.D. 36309, 7 Ct. Cust. App. 46 (1916)

SMITH, Judge.

A marble font . . . and two marble seats imported at the port of New York were classified by the collector of customs as manufactures of marble. . . . The importers protested that the several articles which were so classified and assessed by the collector were dutiable at [the lower] 15 per cent ad valorem under the provisions of paragraph 376 of said act, which said paragraph reads as follows:

> 376. Works of art, including paintings in oil or water colors, pastels, pen-and-ink drawings, or copies, replicas or reproductions of any of the same, statuary, sculptures, or copies, replicas or reproductions thereof, and etchings and engravings, not specially provided for in this section, 15 per centum ad valorem. . . .

The board held that the marble font and marble seats were works of art within the meaning of paragraph 376 as interpreted by the board in the matter of the protest of Downing & Co. (T.D. 35564). In that case the board decided that if the so-called Greek temple involved was a work of art at all it was such by reason of the fact that it was a sculpture, and from that we assume that the board must have concluded that the marble font and seats here in controversy were sculptures, and therefore held them to be works of art and dutiable under paragraph 376, apparently because they were copies of original sculptures not provided for in paragraph 652.

From the decision of the board the government appealed and now contends that its appeal should be sustained on the ground that the font and marble seats are not sculptures at all, and that they are not works of art as that term is used in paragraph 376.

... [T]he font is a plain marble basin, supported by a long, slender, tapering column, which is sustained by a short, round pillar of smaller diameter. .... The surface of the long, tapering column is ornamented by carvings suggestive of leaves. The font was made by Molonari, a sculptor, and was copied by him from an original found in one of the churches of Italy; but whether the original was the work of a sculptor does not appear. The production is the work of a sculptor. It is fashioned from the solid marble. It may be conceded that it is artistic and beautiful. Nevertheless, those conditions, or, better said, those distinguishing features of the article, are not sufficient of themselves to constitute a sculpture.

Sculpture as an art is that branch of the free fine arts which chisels or carves out of stone or other solid material or models in clay or other plastic substance for subsequent reproduction by carving or casting, imitations of natural objects, chiefly the human form, and represents such objects in their true proportions of length, breadth, and thickness, or of length and breadth only. Standard Dictionary; Century Dictionary; United States v. Downing & Co. (6 Ct. Cust. Appls., 545; T.D. 36197); Stern v. United States (3 Ct. Cust. Appls., 124, 126; T.D. 32381); United States v. Baumgarten (2 Ct. Cust. Appls., 321, 322; T.D. 32052). It cannot be said that the font, considered as an entirety, portrays any natural object. The surface of the tapering column which supports the plain marble basin is carved, it is true, with a representation suggestive of leaves, but that representation is so plainly ornamental and so clearly incidental that it can scarcely be regarded as sculpture and much less as giving that status to the whole article. Indeed, as appears from the photograph in evidence and the testimony in the case, that which makes the font artistic and beautiful is the purity of its lines and its just proportions, and not the carving on the column, which we think must be regarded, at best, as decorative and not sculptural art.

Finding, as we do, that the font is not sculpture, the next question which arises is, can it, because of its beauty and artistic character, be classified as a work of art within the meaning of paragraph 376? We think not. In our opinion, the expression "works of art" as used in paragraph 376 was not designed by Congress to cover the whole range of the beautiful and artistic, but only those productions of the artist which are something more than ornamental or decorative and which may be properly ranked as examples of the free fine arts, or possibly that class only of the free fine arts imitative of natural objects as the artist sees them, and appealing to the emotions through the eye alone. The potter, the glassmaker, the goldsmith, the weaver, the needlewoman, the lace maker, the wood-worker, the jeweler, all produce things which are both artistic and beautiful. It can hardly be seriously contended, however, that it was the legislative purpose to include such things, beautiful and artistic though they may be, in a provision which, as shown by its history and the enumeration therein contained, was intended to favor that particular kind of art of which painting and sculpture are the types. See Lazarus v. United States (2 Ct. Cust. Appls., 508, 509; T.D. 32247); United States v. Downing (6 Ct. Cust. Appls., 545; T.D. 36197).

That everything artistic and beautiful cannot be classed as fine art was well established in United States v. Perry. . . . As we are of the opinion that the carved marble seats are not sculptures or works of art within the intention of paragraph 376, we must hold that they are not dutiable as found by the board, and that the assessment of the collector should be sustained.

Notes

1. For an early holding radically different from that of *Olivotti, see Stern v. United States*, T.D. 32381, 3 Ct. Cust. App. 124 (1912), which involved the tariff classification of a variety of stone jardinières, vases, and figures under the Tariff Act of 1909. The objects were embellished with carvings of leaves, animals, human figures, and composites. The court in *Stern* rejected the government's assertion of the representation test relied on in *Olivotti* and upheld the importer's contention that the items should be classified as sculpture. In so doing, the court's opinion read:

   > We are not prepared to assent to the doctrine that sculpture is confined to a representation of human or animal figures or statues alone. It is notably true that some of the most magnificent productions of professional sculptors which have attracted the attention and admiration of the world were found in the buildings and museums of countries the beliefs of which teach it is a sacrilege to portray human forms. [*Id.* at 126.]

2. One problem with the implementation of legal standards of artwork that involve terms such as "artistic" or "beautiful" is that judges — not art critics or art experts — ultimately must make the decisions as to what qualifies as "art." Justice Oliver Wendell Holmes lamented this problem in the following passage from *Bleistein v. Donaldson Lithographing Co.*, 188 U.S. 239, 251 (1903):

   > It would be a dangerous undertaking for persons trained only to the law to constitute themselves final judges of the worth of pictorial illustrations, outside of the narrowest and most obvious limits. At the one extreme, some works of genius would be sure to miss appreciation. Their very novelty would make them repulsive until the public had learned the new language in which their author spoke.

Brancusi v. United States

54 Treas. Dec. 428 (Cust. Ct. 1928)

WAITE, Judge.

The importation in this case is invoiced as a bronze bird and mentioned in the record as "Bird in Flight." It was entered as a work of art in the form of a sculpture and claimed to be entitled to entry free of duty under paragraph 1704 of the Tariff Act of 1922. It was assessed by the collector of customs at 40 percent ad valorem as a manufacture of metal under paragraph 399 of the same law. . . .

The piece is characterized . . . as a bird. Without the exercise of rather a vivid imagination it bears no resemblance to a bird except, perchance, with such imagination it may be likened to the shape of the body of a bird. It has neither head nor feet nor feathers portrayed in the piece. . . . [I]t is entirely smooth on its exterior, which is a polished and burnished surface.

There is no question in the mind of the court but that the man who produced the importation is a professional sculptor, as is shown by his reputation and works and the manner in which he is considered by those competent to judge upon that subject. We also find it is an original production.

The requirements of the paragraph under which this is claimed to be entitled to free entry provide for original sculptures, the works of a professional sculptor, with the further proviso that the term shall not be understood to include any articles of utility. . . .

Having found that this is the work of a professional sculptor, and that it is original, the question then for us to determine is as to whether it conforms to the definition given under the law for works of art. It must be conceded that what have been determined to be works of art under the decisions of recent years, would, under the more remote decisions of the courts, not only the customs courts but the United States Supreme Court, have been rejected as not falling within that term. We think that under the earlier decisions this importation would have been rejected as a work of art, or, to be more accurate, as a work within the classification of high art.

Constantin Brancusi, Bird in Space (1923), The Metropolitan Museum of Art, New York, NY[2]

2. Michael D. Murray, Image derived from a photograph by Michael Murray (2009) of the public domain sculpture, "Bird in Space" by Constantine Brancusi (1923), as displayed at the Metropolitan Museum of Art.

Under the influence of the modern schools of art the opinion previously held has been modified with reference to what is necessary to constitute art within the meaning of the statute, and it has been held by the Court of Customs Appeals that drawings or sketches, designs for wall paper and textiles, are works of art, although they were intended for a utilitarian purpose. (See American Colortype Co. v. United States, 9 Ct. Cust. Appls. 212, T.D. 38046; MacLoughlin v. United States, 10 Ct. Cust. Appls. 37, T.D. 38261; Cheney Bros. v. United States, 12 Ct. Cust. Appls. 195, T.D. 40172.)

Government counsel in support of the contention that this importation is not sculpture, cites the case of United States v. Olivotti (7 Ct. Cust. Appls. 46; T.D. 36309). . . . This decision was handed down in 1916. In the meanwhile there has been developing a so-called new school of art, whose exponents attempt to portray abstract ideas rather than to imitate natural objects. Whether or not we are in sympathy with these newer ideas and the schools which represent them, we think the fact of their existence and their influence upon the art world as recognized by the courts must be considered.

The object now under consideration is shown to be for purely ornamental purposes, its use being the same as that of any piece of sculpture of the old masters. It is beautiful and symmetrical in outline, and while some difficulty might be encountered in associating it with a bird, it is nevertheless pleasing to look at and highly ornamental, and as we hold under the evidence that it is the original production of a professional sculptor and is in fact a piece of sculpture and a work of art according to the authorities above referred to, we sustain the protest and find that it is entitled to free entry under paragraph 1704, supra. Let judgment be entered accordingly.

Notes and Questions

1. How did court definitions of art evolve from *In re Perry* in 1892 to *Olivotti* in 1916 to *Brancusi* in 1928? The full implications of the liberal position adopted in *Brancusi* were not realized for almost thirty years. Until the 1958 amendments to the tariff laws, courts continued to struggle with many subtle and somewhat arbitrary distinctions between art and non-art. These distinctions often penalized innovative forms.

   For instance, many art works were subject to higher tariffs because they were not executed in any of the media specifically enumerated in the statutes. *United States v. Wanamaker*, 19 C.C.P.A. 229 (1931), involved "wool embroidered linen bands" that were reproductions of the *Queen Mathilda Tapestries* on display at the Art Library in Bayeux, Normandy. The court held that the customs collector had properly assessed these items as "manufactures of wool" because not even the original tapestries would have been considered works of art under the restrictions of the Tariff Act of 1922. In *United States v. Ehrich*, 22 C.C.P.A. 1 (1934), vases crafted by a noted French sculptor by shaping molten glass with a spatula suffered a similar fate. They were treated as decorative or ornamental glassware.

2. Should mosaic pictures be classified as art? In *Petry Co. v. United States*, 11 Ct. Cust. App. 525 (1923), the court held that mosaic pictures should be classified as manufactures of marble. It stated that "mosaic articles, while often beautiful and artistic, are the fabrications of artificers rather than the productions of artists, and not within the domain of the fine arts," *Id.* at 527.

   The *Petry* view of mosaics was followed in two other leading cases: *United States v. Colombo Co.*, 21 C.C.P.A. 177, *cert. denied*, 290 U.S. 673 (1933), and *Frei Art Glass Co. v. United States*, 15 Ct. Cust. App. 132 (1927). *Colombo* involved a mosaic copy of the oil painting "Disputa," one of the works of Raphael that hangs at the Vatican. The mosaic copy itself was designed, produced, and installed by professional artists. In *Frei*, Judge Smith vigorously dissented, arguing that art should be defined as anything "conceived, designed, produced, or reproduced by an artist, or under his immediate supervision and control." 15 Ct. Cust. App. at 139.

3. Bear in mind that some art may not enter the United States at all. As discussed in Chapters 10 and 11, the international community is making attempts to halt the movement of looted art. Political pressure has also prompted import bans.

PROBLEM 1-2

Given the cases above, would the courts classify the following item as a work of art?

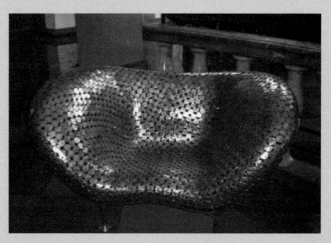

This chair,[3] consisting of 1,500 Kennedy half dollars, was selling for $59,000 at the Museum of American Finance in New York in

---

3. Sherri Burr, Image derived from a photograph by Sherri Burr (2009) of a chair consisting of 1,500 Kennedy half dollars as displayed at the Museum of American Finance in New York.

September 2009. In the television film *Georgia O'Keeffe*, photographer Alfred Stiglitz tells his wife, "Work doesn't become art until some rich person comes along and buys it." Is that what it would take for this chair? Or is it already art?

C. Artist vs. Artisan

Consmiller v. United States

3 Ct. Cust. App. 298 (1912)

SMITH, Judge.

This case involves the tariff classification of marble mantel pieces which were imported at the port of New York and assessed for duty by the collector of customs as manufactures of marble under the provisions of paragraph 112 of the Tariff Act of 1909. . . .

The importer protested that the mantels were improperly classified, and as grounds for his protest alleged, first, that the goods were works or objects of art exempt from duty under paragraph 717 of the free list, and, second, that if not exempt the merchandise was dutiable as sculptures at 15 per cent ad valorem under the provisions of paragraph 470. . . .

The Board of General Appraisers overruled the protest and the importers appealed. . . .

[O]ur attention will be confined to the one remaining issue tendered by the protest, namely, "Are the mantels sculptures within the meaning of the provision of paragraph 470?" The importer had the affirmative of that proposition, and it was incumbent upon him to establish by a preponderance of credible evidence that the mantels were sculptures, cut, carved, or otherwise wrought by hand, and the professional production of a sculptor only.

In that behalf the testimony of Ernest Plancon, foreman of the shops which produced the goods, was offered by the importer. This witness stated that he was a sculptor and marble mason and that he had followed that profession since he was first apprenticed to the trade in 1885. He said that he had served his apprenticeship as a sculptor in the shops of Mr. Jean Joseph Rousseau, at Antwerp, with whom he remained for nine years and from whom he acquired his knowledge of ornamental sculpture. Subsequent to his service with Mr. Rousseau, Mr. Plancon worked for two years as an ornamental sculptor at Brussels and finally became the foreman of the workshops in which the mantels under consideration were made.

During the period of his apprenticeship Mr. Plancon attended the morning and evening classes at the Royal Academy of Fine Arts, but he never took any diploma or degree conferred by any institution having for its purpose the instruction of students in art and sculpture. He admitted that no object of sculpture produced by him had ever been displayed in any art gallery or public institution and, so far as the record discloses, he never at any time executed an original work of sculptural art, unless a monument designed by him for the market place at Wattignies, France, can be so considered. That monument was worked out in granite, a stone not usually selected for the sculptor's chisel, and whether sculpture was a feature of it or whether it depended upon its proportions to impress does not appear.

Giving due weight to all that Mr. Plancon said of himself, it is difficult to avoid the conclusion that he is a highly skilled artisan rather than a capable artist and that his occupation is not a profession but a trade which was largely acquired as an apprentice in a shop and not as a student in a studio. His own description of his calling and his record of accomplishment does not warrant his recognition as a professional sculptor, but rather establishes him as an ornamentalist whose specialty is the decoration of stonework. Though sculptor and decorator may both work in stone, between them there is a very wide gulf and the domain of the one is seldom, if ever, invaded by the other. Ordinarily the ornamentalist in stone imitates that which he actually sees and his work goes no farther than to please the eye. The sculptor, on the other hand, reproduces that which is pictured by his imagination and his production appeals not only to the eye, but to the emotions as well. . . .

Mr. Plancon's testimony may not have done him full justice, but in our opinion it fell considerably short of showing that he was a professional sculptor. But even if he were a professional sculptor, the mantels themselves and the method and manner of their production do not justify us in holding that they are sculptures. It does not appear that any of the mantels or any part of them is the original creation of a sculptor. Indeed, it appears affirmatively that they are executed by a purely commercial firm and that most of them are made from stock models.

That a copy of a sculpture may itself rank as a sculpture it must be something more than a mere facsimile reproduction of the original. To be a sculpture a copy must be the work of a sculptor and a production which is stamped with some of the artistic individuality and genius of the artist by whom it is produced. Some of the mantels are ornamented with moldings, fluted columns or pillars, and the conventional garland, vase, disk, Grecian border, or spray of leaves. The flutings and moldings on the mantels ornamented in this way were executed by marble masons, and the conventional ornamentation, such as garlands, disks, sprays, and Grecian borders by ornamentalists, or, if by sculptors, then by sculptors doing nothing higher than ornamental work. Mantels of such a character are unquestionably artistic, esthetic, and all that, but they certainly can not be classed as sculptures without doing violence to the term.

One of the mantels has fluted columns and a frieze ornamented with garlands and a panel on which is carved two children playing with a basket of fruit. Another of the mantels has garlanded jambs bearing a carved head at the top. The frieze of the mantel is ornamented at the ends with carved cupids and a paneled center on which is chiseled in relief a small figure carrying a torch and tendering a dove to a reclining cupid. The figures on both of these mantels are declared by Plancon to be, and they appear to be, the work of a sculptor. If the panels containing these figures were separate entities they might be considered as sculpture, but, as it is, they are incidental parts of the mantels and nothing more. Possibly the inspiration of a sculptor might be so chiseled on a marble mantel that the identity and especially the utilitarian nature of the latter would be practically forgotten in the motif and artistic beauty of the sculptural work, in which event the marble mantel would become a piece of sculpture, but it can hardly be said that the small figures carved on the two mantels referred to accomplish that result or anything approaching it.

All the goods imported call attention to themselves as mantels, not as sculptures. They are artistic in the sense that they appeal to the finer tastes. Possibly they are even works of art, but if they are, they are works of architectural, not sculptural, art.

The decision of the Board of General Appraisers is affirmed.

Mayers, Osterwald & Muhlfeld, Inc. v. Bendler

18 C.C.P.A. 117 (1930), *cert. denied*, 283 U.S. 828 (1931)

GRAHAM, Judge.

The only question presented for our determination is whether the imported diamond is properly dutiable as a "diamond, cut but not set, and suitable for use in the manufacture of jewelry," or free as an "artistic antiquity, . . . produced more than one hundred years prior to the date of importation."

That it is a diamond, cut but not set, and suitable for use in the manufacture of jewelry, is conceded. If it be also an artistic antiquity, produced more than 100 years prior to the date of its importation, the question would then arise as to the comparative specificity of the two provisions of the law.

That the diamond before us is an antiquity, no one will deny. But one question therefore remains: Is it artistic, within the meaning of the statute? This at once suggests the inquiry: What more has been done to this diamond than has been done to any diamond, cut but not set, and suitable for jewelry uses? The stone was cut and faceted by artisans, diamond cutters, first in remote times in some Indian workshop, and then by European workmen. In cutting it, nothing was done but that which is always done in cutting a diamond, namely, to so cut it as to refract and reflect the rays of light properly and thus add to its beauty and brilliancy. No special design was used except such as has been known to the art since time immemorial. It was the conventional cutting required by the shape of the stone. The Congress indicated by a statutory provision, paragraph 1429, that cut diamonds should be dutiable. If this diamond, cut in the ordinary way, is to be treated as artistic, where shall we say the line of demarcation is between dutiable cut diamonds and free artistically cut diamonds, having in mind, of course, diamonds which have been produced more than 100 years prior to importation? Certainly not in the size of the stone, for the law has made no such distinction. Certainly not in the beauty of the stone, for the law has made no such distinction. But one test is proposed by the law, namely, that it shall be artistic.

It is very evident, from a consideration of said paragraph 1708, that by the term "artistic antiquities" the Congress had in mind something more than the mere ordinary work of an artisan. Associated as the term is with works of art, collections in illustration of the progress of the arts, works in bronze, etc., and other objects of art, it is the reasonable deduction that the Congress intended by the word "artistic" to include only antiquities which were the production of artists and which had an aesthetic appeal. In the congressional hearings on H.R. 7456, which afterwards became the Tariff Act of 1922, such showing as was made before the Senate Committee on Finance seemed to be upon the theory that the articles named in said paragraph 1708 were assumed to be the work of artists, as contra-distinguished from that of artisans. (Senate Hearings, Part VI, at 5011-28).

Webster's New International Dictionary, 1925, thus defines the adjective "artistic":

> artistic. a. Of or pertaining to art or artists; made in the manner of an artist; conforming to, or characterized by, art; showing taste or skill.

One of the meanings attached to the word "artist" by the same lexicographer is:

> artist. 3. One who professes and practices an art in which imagination and taste preside over the execution, esp. a fine art.

It is true that the same author also defines the word "artist" as having a meaning including one who practices some mechanical art or craft. It is equally true that in the ordinary use of the term in the language of the people, singers, actors, and others are alluded to as artists. We are convinced, however, that it was in the sense given by the above-quoted definitions that the Congress intended to use the word "artistic." This being true, something more is required to make an antiquity artistic, under this paragraph, than mere mechanical skill. . . .

It does not necessarily follow that the inclusion of this element must make them works of the fine arts, but in order to be "artistic," as that word is used in paragraph 1708, there must be in the production of the article a mental concept resulting in an aesthetic expression of the producer, or, applied to this case, the cutter of the diamond. If his work was merely that of a cutter following well-established rules, and involving no aesthetic expression originating in his own mind and thought, it is not artistic, however beautiful it may be. . . .

While these authorities announce the rule that there may be articles which cannot be classified as belonging to the fine arts, and which yet are artistic, they also indicate, in a marked degree, the elements which are usually taken in account in concluding that an object is or is not artistic. In every instance there was the work of the artist, the artistic concept, which added originality to the work and gave it a distinctive appeal to the artistic sensibilities. The skilled craftsman, the lapidary, the stone cutter, the cabinetmaker, each can produce objects of beauty by the practice of his craft. It is only, however, when he leaves the beaten paths of his trade, and, as a result of a mental concept, constructs something original with him, which appeals to the artistic eye and mind, that his work ceases to be that of an artisan and becomes that of an artist.

What is or is not artistic depends largely upon the degree of mental perception of the individual. To the Alaskan Indian a totem pole is artistic and also a work of art. As our mental and aesthetic comprehension increases, our ideas of what constitutes an artistic creation develop and change. But one thing we do know, that a thing, to be artistic, must be something more than the common product of a utilitarian art or trade. Divesting our minds of the glamour and romance of the history of this diamond, we have nothing left but a large diamond, cut in an ordinary way. . . .

The judgment of the Customs Court is reversed and the cause remanded for further proceedings in conformity herewith.

Notes and Questions

1. One criterion that has been used in determining whether an item may be classified as art, or merely as a utilitarian achievement typical of an artisan, is whether the item was made according to the inspiration of the artist or the instructions of the purchaser. This problem was clearly presented in *United States v. Oberlaender*, T.D. 48475, 25 C.C.P.A. 24 (1937), which involved porcelain plates that had been hand-painted in mineral colors. The importer protested when they were not classified as works of art. His protest was overruled. In order to be classified as a work of art, the court held, an item must embody not only the professional skill, but the artistic conception and imagination of the artist as well.

2. Training, education, and development of artistic skills traditionally has meant a great deal to artists and, more generally, to museums, gallery owners, and other "gatekeepers" whose recognition and approval are sought by artists. But not so much with the art-buying, art-investing, and art-consuming crowd. Witness Thierry Guetta, also known as "Mr. Brainwash," and his meteoric rise to fame and prominence in the art world and art auction business, without a shred of evidence that he has had any art training — or even time to "develop" his artistic abilities. *See* xbimolx YouTube Channel, *Mr. Brainwash finds accidental fame with 'Exit Through the Gift Shop'*, https://www.youtube.com/watch?v=HAwmovplwec (August 20, 2011). Should a self-declared artist with accidental fame be regarded as a true artist producing bona fide art, or should the standard be higher?

D. Art Reproductions and Replicas

Gregory v. United States

32 Cust. Ct. 228 (1954)

EKWALL, Judge.

This is a protest against the collector's assessment of duty on a bronze statue imported from France at 20 per centum ad valorem under the provision in paragraph 1547(a) of the Tariff Act of 1930 for "statuary, sculptures, or copies, replicas, or reproductions thereof," not specially provided for. It is claimed that the article is entitled to free entry under the provision in paragraph 1807 for "original sculptures or statuary, including not more than two replicas or reproductions of the same," or, in the alternative, under paragraph 1773 as sculpture imported for use as models or for art educational purposes, or under paragraph 1809 as a work of art, imported for exhibition at a fixed place by an institution established for the encouragement of the arts and not intended for sale. . . .

The first question before us is whether the imported statue is entitled to free entry under paragraph 1807 of the Tariff Act of 1930. Under the applicable provision thereof, the article must be an original sculpture or one of not more than two replicas or reproductions of the same, the professional production of a sculptor only, and not an article of utility or for industrial use. From the record, it appears that the statue herein was produced from a model created by a recognized professional sculptor; that it was cast after the death of the sculptor, but under the supervision of his wife, a professional sculptress; that it was the 10th casting made, but the second imported into the United States; and that it is not an article of utility or for industrial use.

Plaintiff claims that it is, therefore, entitled to free entry under paragraph 1807. Defendant contends, on the contrary, that the statue is not covered by said paragraph, on the ground that it was produced after the death of the sculptor who created the original and on the further ground that only the first and second replicas or reproductions produced are included under paragraph 1807, whereas the imported article is the tenth.

Two questions of construction are involved herein: First, whether the "reproductions" provided for in paragraph 1807 must be the work of the sculptor who created the original, and, second, whether such reproductions must be the first or second produced.

The provisions now found in paragraph 1807 and paragraph 1547 of the Tariff Act of 1930 first appeared in the Tariff Act of 1913 (paragraphs 652 and 376). Under these provisions, free entry is granted to original works of art, but other artistic objects, including copies, are dutiable. In the case of statuary, however, two replicas or reproductions are also free of duty. It is, therefore, necessary to determine what is meant by "replica" and "reproduction," as distinguished from "copy."

It was held under the Tariff Act of 1913 in *Wm. Baumgarten & Co. v. United States*, 29 Treas. Dec. 67, T.D. 35597, that a sculpture, consisting of a group of human figures executed in marble by modern artists, a copy of part of a fountain made by Giovanni di Bologna in the 16th century, was not entitled to free entry under paragraph 652 as a replica or reproduction of an original sculpture. The court stated that a replica must be a duplicate of the original produced by the same artist and that the word "reproduction" covered the same class of articles as that described by the term "replica."

In *United States v. Downing & Co.*, 6 Ct. Cust. Appls. 545, T.D. 36197 (1916), it was held that parts of a marble temple were not classifiable as "sculptures" since there was no evidence that they were the professional productions of sculptors. In the course of the opinion, the court referred to definitions of the word "replica" as a duplicate executed by the artist making the original, of the word "reproduction" as a thing reproduced, and of the word "copy" as a thing as near like the original as the copyist has the power to make it. The court added that the word "copy" has a wider meaning than "reproduction," but may not correctly include "replica." The court did not, however, attempt to define the exact scope of the words "copy" and "reproduction." . . .

These words were used in reference to sculptures and statuary. Sculpture has been created traditionally in several ways: By carving, from marble, stone, alabaster, or wood; by casting in bronze or other metal or substance; and by modeling in clay or wax. The Encyclopedia Americana, volume 24, page 458; Collier's Encyclopedia, volume 17, page 430; *United States v. Olivotti & Co.*, 7 Ct. Cust. Appls. 46, T.D. 36309. These types were specifically provided for in paragraph 1807 and its predecessors. It seems to us that in using the word "reproduction" Congress had in mind the method of producing sculptures by casting. By that method, a model first made in a soft substance is afterwards cast or reproduced in a more permanent material. It is actually the model which comes from the hand of the sculptor and upon which his individual conception is stamped, the statue in bronze or other metal or substance being but the final embodiment of his idea in durable material. The final form is achieved by making a mold from the model and pouring the molten metal therein. See description of methods of casting in *Encyclopaedia Britannica*, volume 20, page 229, and *Collier's Encyclopedia*, volume 17, page 431. . . .

While lexicographers agree that the word "replica" means a duplicate or copy made by the artist who made the original, the word "reproduction" does not have that limitation. Because of the method by which one class of statuary is produced, we believe that Congress used the word "reproductions" to cover sculpture which was not, strictly speaking, a replica of the original, but which was more than a copy, since it embodied all of the artistic conception of the sculptor, although the casting and verification of the final form may have been done by or under the supervision of another artist.

We conclude, therefore, that the word "reproduction," as used in paragraph 1807 of the Tariff Act of 1930, and its predecessors, refers to sculptures which have been produced by casting and that the term includes castings made from a model created by a professional sculptor, where the casting has been done by or under the supervision of a professional sculptor, either the one who created the model or another.

The next question is whether such reproduction must be the first and second produced or may be one of any two imported into the United States. The statute itself uses the words "not more than two replicas or reproductions of the same." In construing these words, it is to be kept in mind that the paragraph was intended primarily to cover original works of fine art and not commercial objects produced in great numbers. *United States v. Downing & Co.*, supra; *Wm. S. Pitcairn Corp. v. United States*, 39 C.C.P.A. (Customs) 15, C.A.D. 458 (1951). Where 10 or 100 reproductions are made, the sculptures become articles of trade, which, while still works of art, do not belong to that class of fine art of a rare and special genius which is covered by paragraph 1807. Therefore, only the first and second replicas or reproductions are entitled to free entry under that paragraph. This conclusion is supported by the administrative practice since the enactment of the Tariff Act of 1913, and . . . by judicial decision. . . .

In our view, the statue involved herein is not entitled to free entry under the provision in paragraph 1807 for "original sculptures or statuary, including not more than two replicas or reproductions of the same," since it is not a first or second replica or reproduction. . . .

We hold, on the record presented, that the statue is properly dutiable as assessed by the collector at 20 per centum ad valorem under the provision in paragraph 1547(a) of the Tariff Act of 1930 for "statuary, sculptures, or copies, replicas, or reproductions thereof," not specially provided for.

The protest is overruled and judgment will be rendered for the defendant.

Notes

1. The rule announced in *Gregory* was applied in *Ward Eggleston Galleries v. United States*, C.D. 1670, 34 Cust. Ct. 19 (1955), upholding the collector's tariff assessment of a bronze sculpture under paragraph 1547(a) of the Tariff Act of 1930, rather than allowing it free entry under paragraph 1807, where there was no evidence that it was the original or first or second reproduction. The bronze was made by individually casting the parts and then fastening them together. The fastening was performed by the sculptor using bronze pins. The sculptor then touched up the entire work with a file. The fine details of each cast, such as fingernails, were applied by the artist after the work came out of the mold. The individual castings were given different colored finishes, or patina. Each time a cast was made, the mold would be damaged in some way so that it was necessary for the sculptor to clean and rework it in order to make the next casting as much like the original as possible.

   The court stated that "[in its] view, any retouching, difference in coloring, or other work on a sculpture which does not affect the original idea of the artist does not make a second, third, or fifth casting an 'original,' within the meaning of the statute." *Id.* at 23; cf. *Thannhauser v. United States*, C.D. 912, 14 Cust. Ct. 62 (1945). According to the facts in *Thannhauser,* seventy-three wax sculptures were found in the studio of a French sculptor after his death. The heirs had twenty-two reproductions cast from each. The court found the reproductions eligible for entry under paragraph 1547(a), but ineligible under paragraph 1807.

2. The 1958 amendments to the Tariff Act modified the *Gregory* holding. This legislation allowed the first ten castings free. *See* 73 Stat. 549, 19 U.S.C. "1201 (1959) (amended by 76 Stat. 72, 19 U.S.C." 1202). Under the amendments, the classification was not affected by the fact that the castings were made after the artist's death. The reasons for the change were explained before the Senate's Committee of Finance, July 16, 1959, by Dorothy H. Dudley, then Registrar of the Museum of Modern Art and Chairman of the American Association of Museums' Committee on Customs:

> Sculpture is customarily cast from molds in strictly limited editions of usually no more than 10 replicas. Each unit is finished by hand, and the first is not more valuable or more original than the last. In exceptional cases an edition is completed by associates after the death or incapacity of the sculptor. In addition to the edition (of 10 replicas) one sculptor's model made by hand, in less permanent material, is often preserved. This too is considered an original work of art. Such editions are a normal feature of professional production of sculpture and do not constitute mass-produced commercial reproductions. The practice is traditional and not a recent innovation.

Derenberg & Baum, *Congress Rehabilitates Modern Art*, 34 N.Y.U. L. Rev. 1228, 1250 (1959).

Elder & Co. v. United States

C.D. 3525, 61 Cust. Ct. 50 (1968)

RICHARDSON, Judge.

The merchandise of this protest consists of a mosaic panel invoiced as *Pannello Acenzione* which was produced in and exported from Italy. The mosaic was classified in liquidation as a work of art not specially provided for under 19 U.S.C., section 1001, paragraph 1547(a) (paragraph 1547(a), Tariff Act of 1930) and assessed for duty at the rate of 20 per centum ad valorem. It is claimed by the plaintiff-importer that the mosaic is properly classifiable as an "original mosaic" under the duty free provision therefore in 19 U.S.C., section 1201, paragraph 1807(a) (paragraph 1807(a), Tariff Act of 1930, as amended by the Public Law 86-262). . . .

It appears from the evidence that the importer commissioned Messrs. Ferrari and Bacci to produce a mosaic panel of the "Ascension" for placement in the Cypress Gardens cemetery, selecting a religious theme on the basis of the oil painting of the "Ascension" by La Farge located in the Church of the Ascension in New York City. To this end the importer sent or caused to be delivered to the mosaicists a transparency of La Farge's "Ascension". . . . [T]here seems to be no dispute over the fact that the only exposure which the mosaicists had to LaFarge's painting was by way of the transparency. And the mosaicists maintained that the transparency only gave them an idea as to how to create the mosaic panel. . . .

If the imported mosaic is actually like it is depicted in plaintiffs' exhibits 2 and 4 (and there is no evidence that it is not) we must conclude, from a lay point of view, that the mosaic appears to be a work of fine quality and high artistic talent which we have no hesitancy in calling a work of art. The evidence shows without contradiction that the mosaic panel in question was solicited by the importer as an art form, that it was produced by recognized and accomplished artists for exhibition purposes, and that there is no utilitarian or industrial usage here involved.

The question before the court is whether the subject mosaic is "original." Both parties maintain and we find that the test of originality under the tariff statutes is whether or not the artist exercised his own aesthetic imagination and conception in creating the work. Plaintiffs contend that the involved mosaic is original, citing principally the case of *Forest Lawn Memorial Park v. United States*, 39 Cust. Ct. 224, C.D. 1472 (1952). And defendant contends that the mosaic is a copy of La Farge's painting of the "Ascension," citing *American Express Co. v. United States*, 31 Treas. Dec. 344, T.D. 36765. Neither case involved mosaic art works. . . .

In two cases decided subsequent to the decision in the *Baldwin* case the Court of Customs and Patent Appeals took the view that the originality of an artist's work is not diminished by virtue of the fact that he has received suggestions from others. *See Pitt & Scott v. United States*, 18 CCPA 326, T.D. 44584, and *Wm. S. Pitcairn Corp. v. United States*, 39 CCPA 15, 35, C.A.D. 458. Thus, in view of the holdings in *Baldwin*, which we find to have overruled the *American Express Co.* case by implication, and in the *Pitt & Scott* and *Pitcairn* cases, it would appear that neither the furnishing by the importer of the transparency nor the projection of its ideas relative to an ethereal and celestial expression precludes a finding of "originality" in the artists' creation of the involved mosaic panel if the completed work is otherwise the product of the artists' imagination and conception.

We do not believe that the creators of the mosaic at bar can be adjudged to have "copied" La Farge's "Ascension" on the basis of such meager evidence as this record presents of their exposure to the famous oil painting. Cf. *United States v. Columbo Co.*, 21 CCPA 177, T.D. 46510. Neither of the mosaicists Ferrari and Bacci saw the painting. And their uncontradicted testimony is to the effect that they exercised their own original creative conception in developing the imported mosaic from the ideas they derived from the transparency. In the *Columbo* case our appeals court held that a mosaic representation of Raphael's oil painting *Disputa*, which is painted upon a wall of one of the chapels of the Vatican at Rome, was not a "copy" of the *Disputa* within the meaning of the word "copies" as used in paragraph 1547(a) of the 1930 Act, the common meaning of which term the court construed to be broader than the associated words "replicas" or "reproductions". The appeals court deemed the mosaic in *Columbo* to be a work of art in fact, but concluded that the mosaic could not be deemed a work of art within the meaning of the tariff statutes, citing, among other cases, *United States v. Olivotti & Co.*, 7 Ct. Cust. Appls. 46, T.D. 36309. And it is to be noted that in the Columbo case great pains were taken to reproduce the *Disputa* colorings exactly, that the artist went to the Vatican and personally made color sketches of the painting, and that during the progress of the work, which took about 3 years for completion of the mosaic, the artist personally attended to the making of corrections in order to carry out the proper color scheme. . . .

Consequently, for the reasons stated, we find upon the evidence that the importer has established its burden of proving that the imported mosaic is an "original mosaic" within the meaning of paragraph 1807(a). The instant protest is, therefore, sustained.

Judgment will be entered accordingly.

Note

1. In *United States v. Baumgarten & Co.*, 2 Ct. Cust. App. 321 (1911), the court considered whether a carved marble vase, a copy of one in the Borghese collection at Rome, qualified for treatment under the Tariff Act as a sculpture, or whether it should be subject to the higher duty for manufactures of marble. The court affirmed the decision that the vase qualified for treatment as a work of art not specially provided for, holding that the work showed "the application of personal study upon the part of the artist and proves the professional character and ability of its author" and was "obviously no mere mechanical effort at a reproduction of the original." *Id.* at 322.

PROBLEM 1-3

Consider these chairs which were on display in the Metropolitan Museum of Art in September 2009.[4] Are they art? Does the classification depend on whether they function only for utilitarian purposes (to sit on) or for display purposes (to admire)?

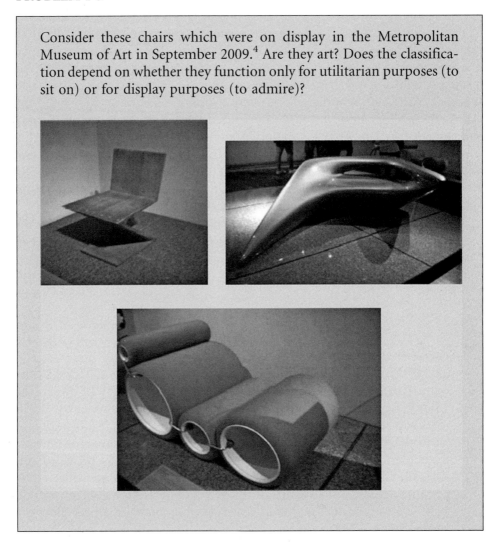

ASSESSMENT

1. Arthur Artist is a Spanish artist who creates original paintings using found objects as canvases. His most popular paintings are those painted on old doors from the streets of Madrid. His paintings have been so highly valued that Arthur wants to sell them in the United States, but he is worried he will be subject to high duties under the Tariff Act. Based on the U.S. Supreme Court's definition of Fine Art in *United States v. Perry,*

which of the following is the most accurate statement of his ability to import the items as art?

(A) The paintings will not be subject to duties under the tariff act because they are beautiful and pleasing to look at, which classifies them as "high art"
(B) They will not be allowed into the United States at all because they can be created by anyone with some paint and a paintbrush
(C) Because the doors were originally created to serve a useful purpose, they are subject to a duty under the tariff act
(D) Both (A) and (B)
(E) Both (A) and (C)

2. Wynona Weaver is a student at the National Weaver's Academy. She began weaving under the instruction of her grandmother, who was a world famous tapestry weaver. She worked under, and learned from, her grandmother for six years and then decided to start a weaving business on her own. She ran the business for two years, and then decided that she wanted to attend classes to learn about basket weaving.

After a year at the Academy, Wynona began displaying her basket weavings in her store. One fortunate day, pop singer Lady Gaga happened to stop into her store and fall in love with Wynona's circus animal basket, which she then bought for five million dollars. A few weeks later, the local newspaper published a story about the five million dollar sale of the circus animal and criticized the fact that someone would buy such an item at that price, especially since the creator was not even a true artist, but simply an artisan.

Consider photographer Alfred Steiglitz's definition of art on page 2 of this chapter. Which of the following would be Wynona's strongest argument that she is an artist, as opposed to merely an artisan, using Steiglitz's definition?

(A) She is an artist because Lady Gaga bought her circus animal baskets for five million dollars
(B) She learned weaving from her grandmother, who is a famous artist, therefore she is an artist as well
(C) She is an artist because she is one credit away from receiving her degree in basket weaving from NWA; her baskets are original works, created from her own imagination, that have been displayed in small galleries around the United States; and her baskets create an emotional response in the people who observe them
(D) She is not an artisan because she owns her own weaving store and her baskets are well known for being aesthetically pleasing
(E) She is not an artisan because she doesn't define herself as such

3. **(Same facts as in Question 2)** Wynona Weaver was so thrilled that she sold her circus animal basket to Lady Gaga that she decided to make 50 more using her original design. Before beginning production of the new baskets Wynona broke her arm. Unfortunately, although she used the same design she used for the first one, the other baskets did not end up looking the same. Instead of lions and clowns, the new images on the baskets looked more like blobs and stick figures.

     The 50 circus animal baskets, made from Wynona's original design, are best described as:

  (A) Copies because they do not look as good as the original and she made 50 of them
  (B) Replicas because Wynona created them and she is the creator of the original design
  (C) Failed pieces of art that should be thrown away
  (D) Replications because, although the original artist recreated them, another famous artist who would have made them look better could have created them
  (E) Both (C) and (D)

4. Harry Hirer asked a famous artist, Pamela Potter, to create a designer ceramic pot for the centerpiece of his garden. Harry was a big fan of Edgar Degas' various depictions of ballet dancers and wanted the ceramic pot to incorporate these depictions. Pamela Potter had never heard of Degas or his work on ballet dancers, so Harry did a rough sketch of how the dancers were depicted and explained to Pamela Potter how the paintings looked. Harry was a much better artist than he gave himself credit for and his drawing was an almost perfect copy of Degas' "Ballet Rehearsal" painting. From the drawing, Pamela Potter created a beautiful ceramic pot depicting ballet dancers at a rehearsal.

     Under the test created in *Elder & Co. v. United States*, which of the following best describes Pamela Potter's creation?

  (A) A copy because Pamela did not think of the idea of the ballerinas herself
  (B) A garden centerpiece that will bring much joy and happiness to those who view it
  (C) "High art" because it is only meant for ornamental purposes and creates an emotional reaction in those who view it
  (D) An original creation because Pamela had never seen the Degas paintings and her only exposure to them was through the drawing by Harry, and the ceramic pot was the product of her own imagination and conception
  (E) Both (B) and (C)

5. In *Mayers*, the court was faced with the question of whether a cut diamond could be considered artistic. The court ultimately held that

the diamond was not art. Which of the following reasons did the court give to support their holding?

(A) A cut diamond is merely a common product of a utilitarian art or trade
(B) Diamond cutting is an aesthetic expression that comes from the diamond cutters' own imagination
(C) The diamond is not beautiful enough and too ordinary to be considered artistic
(D) All of the above
(E) (A) and (B) only

ASSESSMENT ANSWERS

1. Arthur Artist is a Spanish artist who creates original paintings using found objects as canvases. His most popular paintings are those painted on old doors from the streets of Madrid. His paintings have been so highly valued that Arthur wants to sell them in the United States, but he is worried he will be subject to high duties under the Tariff Act. Based on the U.S. Supreme Court's definition of Fine Art in *United States v. Perry*, which of the following is the most accurate statement of his ability to import the items as art?

   (A) The paintings will not be subject to duties under the tariff act because they are beautiful and pleasing to look at, which classifies them as "high art"
   (B) They will not be allowed into the United States at all because they can be created by anyone with some paint and a paintbrush
   (C) Because the doors were originally created to serve a useful purpose, they are subject to a duty under the tariff act
   (D) Both (A) and (B)
   (E) Both (A) and (C)

   ANSWER: Answer (C) is correct. Remember that the question asks you to apply the definition in the *Perry* case. Because the doors were originally created to serve a useful purpose, under *Perry*, they are subject to a duty under the tariff act. Answer (A) is not correct because the *Perry* case dealt with "Fine Art" and not "High Art," and being beautiful and pleasing does not fully address the issue here. Answer (B) is not correct because the paintings may be allowed into the United States, but would be subject to duty because they also have a utilitarian function. Neither answers (D) nor (E) can be correct because they both assume answer (A) is correct when it is not.

2. Wynona Weaver is a student at the National Weaver's Academy. She began weaving under the instruction of her grandmother, who was a

world famous tapestry weaver. She worked under, and learned from, her grandmother for six years, and then decided to start a weaving business on her own. She ran the business for two years, and then decided that she wanted to attend classes to learn about basket weaving.

After a year at the Academy, Wynona began displaying her basket weavings in her store. One fortunate day, pop singer Lady Gaga happened to stop into her store and fall in love with Wynona's circus animal basket, which she then bought for five million dollars. A few weeks later, the local newspaper published a story about the five million dollar sale of the circus animal and criticized the fact that someone would buy such an item at that price, especially since the creator was not even a true artist, but simply an artisan.

Consider photographer Alfred Steiglitz's definition of art on page 2. Which of the following would be Wynona's strongest argument that she is an artist, as opposed to merely an artisan, using Steiglitz's definition?

(A) She is an artist because Lady Gaga bought her circus animal baskets for five million dollars

(B) She learned weaving from her grandmother, who is a famous artist, therefore she is an artist as well

(C) She is an artist because she is one credit away from receiving her degree in basket weaving from NWA; her baskets are original works, created from her own imagination, that have been displayed in small galleries around the United States; and her baskets create an emotional response in the people who observe them

(D) She is not an artisan because she owns her own weaving store and her baskets are well known for being aesthetically pleasing

(E) She is not an artisan because she doesn't define herself as such

ANSWER: Answer (A) is correct because Stieglitz said, "Work doesn't become art until some rich person comes along and buys it. In Question 2, Wynona Weaver would thus be considered an artist because Lady Gaga bought her circus animal baskets for five million dollars. The other answers — (B), (C), (D), and (E) — do not take into account Stieglitz's definition of when a work becomes art.

3. **(Same facts as in Question 2).** Wynona Weaver was so thrilled that she sold her circus animal basket to Lady Gaga that she decided to make 50 more using her original design. Before beginning production of the new baskets Wynona broke her arm. Unfortunately, although she used the design she used for the first one, the other baskets did not end up looking the same. Instead of lions and clowns, the new images on the baskets looked more like blobs and stick figures.

The 50 circus animal baskets, made from Wynona's original design, are best described as:

(A) Copies because they do not look as good as the original and she made 50 of them

(B) Replicas because Wynona created them and she is the creator of the original design
(C) Failed pieces of art that should be thrown away
(D) Replications because, although the original artist recreated them, another famous artist who would have made them look better could have created them
(E) Both (C) and (D)

ANSWER: Answer (B) is the best answer because the court in *Gregory* defined replica as a "duplicate or copy made by the same artist who made the original." Here Wynona Weaver created her own baskets and she is the creator of the original design. None of the other answers provides a better definition of the works than the official definition of a replica.

4. Harry Hirer asked a famous artist, Pamela Potter, to create a designer ceramic pot for the centerpiece of his garden. Harry was a big fan of Edgar Degas' various depictions of ballet dancers and wanted the ceramic pot to incorporate these depictions. Pamela Potter had never heard of Degas or his work on ballet dancers, so Harry did a rough sketch of how the dancers were depicted and explained to Pamela Potter how the paintings looked. Harry was a much better artist than he gave himself credit for and his drawing was an almost perfect copy of Degas' "Ballet Rehearsal" painting. From the drawing, Pamela Potter created a beautiful ceramic pot depicting ballet dancers at a rehearsal.

   Under the test created in *Elder & Co. v. United States*, which of the following best describes Pamela Potter's creation?

   (A) A copy because Pamela did not think of the idea of the ballerinas herself
   (B) A garden centerpiece that will bring much joy and happiness to those who view it
   (C) "High art" because it is only meant for ornamental purposes and creates an emotional reaction in those who view it
   (D) An original creation because Pamela had never seen the Degas paintings and her only exposure to them was through the drawing by Harry, and the ceramic pot was the product of her own imagination and conception
   (E) Both (B) and (C)

ANSWER: Answer (D) is correct. In *Elder & Co. v. United States*, the court stated, "The test of originality under the tariff statutes is whether or not the artist exercised his own aesthetic imagination and conception in creating the work." Thus, Pamela Potter's work is an original creation because she had never seen the Degas paintings, her only exposure to them was through the drawing by Harry, and the ceramic pot was the product of her own imagination and conception.

5. In *Mayers,* the court was faced with the question of whether a cut diamond could be considered artistic. The court ultimately held that the diamond was not art. Which of the following reasons did the court give to support their holding?

(A) A cut diamond is merely a common product of a utilitarian art or trade

(B) Diamond cutting is an aesthetic expression that comes from the diamond cutters' own imagination

(C) The diamond is not beautiful enough and too ordinary to be considered artistic

(D) All of the above

(E) A and B only

ANSWER: Answer (E) is the best answer because the Court said both (A) a cut diamond is merely a common product of a utilitarian art or trade; and (B) diamond cutting is an aesthetic expression that comes from the diamond cutter's own imagination. Nothing was said concerning (C), that the diamond was not beautiful or rare enough to be called art.

2 | COPYRIGHTS

A. Historical Overview

In *Standard Oil Co. v. Clark*,[1] the court described all property as conceptually consisting of "a bundle of rights." A work of art is personal property and, as such, has many attributes, both tangible and intangible. Tangible attributes include color, size, shape and a myriad of other qualities that contribute to the aesthetic appreciation of a piece. Intangible attributes may be thought of as the rights of an owner or possessor with respect to the creation. For the visual artist, one of the most important parts of that bundle of rights is the copyright. Copyright is a term that refers to an intangible set of rights that protect the owner's right to control the duplication, distribution, performance, and exploitation of a creative work.

The founding fathers perceived the importance of this right and provided for it in the Constitution: "To promote the Progress of Science and useful Arts, by securing for limited Times to Authors and Inventors the exclusive Right to their respective Writings and Discoveries."[2] Pursuant to this constitutional power, the first Congress enacted the Copyright Law of 1790. Subsequent Congresses revised and refined this legislation at approximately 40-year intervals, with this evolutionary process continuing until 1909, when Title 17 of the United States Code was enacted.

Author or Artist?

Copyright law uses the term "**author**" to mean anyone who creates things in expressive media. So, author can be used to mean artist, composer, playwright, photographer, cinematographer, or musician.

---

1. *Standard Oil Co. v. Clark*, 163 F.2d 917, 930 (1947).
2. U.S. Const. art. I, § 8, cl. 8.

The Copyright Revision Act of 1976 [hereinafter 1976 Act], effective on January 1, 1978, is the current copyright law of the United States, and is applicable to works created or published on or after that date.[3] The creation of copyright in all works published prior to January 1, 1978, is governed by the 1909 Act.[4] Rights other than creation, such as duration, infringement penalties, and infringement remedies are governed by the 1976 Act.

Many of the provisions of the 1976 Act have been amended numerous times. Two of the most important of these amendments are the Berne Convention Implementation Act of 1988,[5] which, among other things, modified notice requirements, and the Visual Artists Rights Act of 1990, which protects rights of attribution and integrity for certain types of works of visual art.[6] The Berne Convention Implementation Act is discussed more fully in later sections of this chapter, while the Visual Artists Rights Act is discussed more fully in Chapter 4, "Moral Rights and the Visual Artists Rights Act."

B. Copyrightable Subject Matter — 17 U.S.C. § 102

The Constitution authorizes Congress to provide protection for a limited time to "authors" for their "writings." An author, from the point of view of copyright law, is a creator — be it a photographer, sculptor, writer, painter, or the like. Congress, nevertheless, has avoided use of the word "writings" in describing the scope of copyright protection. Instead, 17 U.S.C. § 102 grants copyright protection to "original works of authorship fixed in any tangible medium of expression."[7] Legislative comments on this section suggest that Congress chose to use this wording rather than "writings" in order to have more leeway to legislate in the copyright field.[8]

Section 102(b) expressly exempts from copyright protection "any idea, procedure, process, system, method of operation, concept, principle, or discovery."[9] In short, a copyright extends only to the "expression" of creations of the mind, not to the ideas themselves.[10] No one can obtain a copyright on the

---

3. Pub. L. No. 94-553, 90 Stat. 2541 (codified at 17 U.S.C. §§ 101 et seq.).

4. 17 U.S.C. §§ 1 et seq.

5. Pub. L. No. 100-568, 102 Stat. 2853 (1988). Author Leonard D. DuBoff discussed the benefits of United States accession to the Berne Convention in an article that was influential in the United States' decision to become a party to Berne. DuBoff, Winter, Flacks & Keplinger, *Out of UNESCO and into Berne: Has the United States' Participation in the Berne Convention for International Copyright Protection Become Essential?* Symposium, 4 CARDOZO ARTS & ENT. L.J. 203 (1985).

6. Pub. L. No. 101-650, 104 Stat. 5089 (1990).

7. *See Darden v. Peters*, 488 F.3d 277 (4th Cir. 2007) (author's additions to preexisting census maps were not original enough to be copyrightable), *cert. denied*, 552 U.S. 1230 (2008).

8. R. Anthony Reese, *Copyrightable Subject Matter in the "Next Great Copyright Act"*, 29 BERKELEY TECH. L.J. 1489, 1533 and n. 108 (2014).

9. 17 U.S.C. § 102.

10. *See, e.g., Feist Publications, Inc. v. Rural Tel. Serv. Co.*, 499 U.S. 340, 346 (1991); *Boisson v. Banian, Ltd*, 273 F.3d 262, 268 (2d Cir. 2001).

idea of painting the Grand Canyon from the North Rim, nor even the idea of painting the Grand Canyon from the North Rim in oil on a 24X30 inch stretched canvas. What is protected from unauthorized copying is the artist's particular rendition of this scene. Frequently, there is no clear line of division between an idea and its expression, a problem that is discussed throughout the first half of this chapter. For now, it is sufficient to note that a pure idea, such as a theme, cannot be copyrighted no matter how original or creative it is.[11]

C. Obtaining a Copyright: Expression and Fixation

Obtaining a copyright is not complicated. All a person needs to do is write something, paint something, or do something that creates something. At the moment that person is finished, the copyright attaches. Copyright protects works in every expressive media. Writings, paintings, sculptural works, drawings, musical compositions and musical recordings, literature, plays, poems, motion pictures, pantomimes, and computer programs all are covered by copyright protection.[12]

The substantive parts that matter to copyright are: **Expression** and **Fixation in Media**. "Expression" means the work has to have some communicative potential for one of the senses. What must the artist or author be trying to communicate?—It really doesn't matter, the work just needs to communicate the *idea* of something.

Copyright is broad. It only is looking for an author to communicate a concept that can exist as an idea in the mind of the author and be communicated to the mind of someone else through some communicative media. And "fixation in media" means that it has to be in some form in which it can be perceived by one of the senses for long enough that we can tell what the creation is and receive its communication. The law defines "fixed" as:

> authorship fixed in any tangible medium of expression, now known or later developed, from which [the works] can be perceived, reproduced, or otherwise communicated, either directly or with the aid of a machine or device.[13]

If a person conceives of a work, and fixes it in some perceptible media so that it can be communicated to others, then that person has a copyright over that work—whatever it is that was created.

The procedural requirements for copyright are minimal. Registration of a copyright with the Library of Congress is not required under current law,

---

11. *See Feist Publications*, 499 U.S. at 345; *Ets-Hokin v. Skyy Spirits, Inc.*, 225 F.3d 1068, 1076 (9th Cir. 2000).
12. *See generally* 17 U.S.C. § 101 (definitions of works).
13. 17 U.S.C. § 101 (definition of "fixed").

although there are advantages to registration.[14] However, the important proviso regarding registration is that registration is required if the owner wants to sue someone over a copyright in United States federal court.[15] And that is an important thing to remember, because a copyright owner cannot sue anyone over a copyright dispute in a state court. Copyright law is federal law, an area of complete federal preemption.[16]

The owner also gets another special benefit for registering copyrighted works promptly: the owner can sue for what are called "statutory damages," which are recoverable from anyone who copies the works after registration, and these damages are preset amounts that are generous.[17] Statutory damages often are regarded as a superior option to having to prove actual damages.[18] In addition, the court may order the infringer to reimburse the owner's attorneys' fees if the infringement occurs after registration.[19]

D. What Can't You Protect with a Copyright?

The Copyright Act, § 102(b) states, "In no case does copyright protection . . . extend to any idea, procedure, process, system, method of operation, concept,

---

14. Although registration is not required to create a copyright, the 1976 Act provides several incentives for registration:

First, if the registration is made within five years after the first publication of the work, there is a presumption of the validity of the copyright and of the facts stated in the Certificate of Registration. § 410. This presumption applies in "any judicial proceedings."

Second, registration is a prerequisite to certain remedies for infringement. Statutory damages and attorneys' fees may be available for the infringement of an unpublished work, if the work was registered prior to the commencement of the infringement. § 412(1). In the case of an infringement occurring after a work is first published, statutory damages and attorneys' fees are available only if the work is registered prior to the infringement.

Third, if the work is registered within three months after the first publication, registration is deemed to have been made as of the date of first publication. § 412(2).

It has been held that, in a series of ongoing discrete infringements, the infringement "commences" at the time when the first infringement occurs. *Harper House, Inc. v. Thomas Nelson, Inc.*, 1988 Copy. L. Rep. (CCH) ¶26,203 (C.D. Cl. 1987). *Harper House* involved a "special verdict on which the jury found twelve (12) separate acts of infringement," some of which occurred prior to registration and some of which occurred after. Plaintiff argued that defendants' post-registration acts constituted separate acts of infringement upon which a claim for attorneys' fees may be based. The court, applying the policy that encourages prompt registration, found that § 412 precluded an award of attorneys' fees because an infringement occurred prior to the date of registration. *See also Johnson v. Univ. of Virginia*, 606 F. Supp. 321 (D. Va. 1985); *Whelan Assocs., Inc. v. Jaslow Dental Laboratories*, 609 F. Supp. 1325, 1331 (E.D. Pa. 1985), *aff'd*, 797 F.2d 1222 (3d Cir. 1986). Prompt registration is, therefore, advisable.

15. 17 U.S.C. § 411(a).

16. 17 U.S.C. § 301. *See Ryan v. Editions Ltd. West, Inc.*, 786 F.3d 754 (9th Cir. 2015); *Rosciszewski v. Arete Associates, Inc.*, 1 F.3d 225 (4th Cir. 1993).

17. *See* 17 U.S.C. § 504(c).

18. *See, e.g., Yellow Pages Photos, Inc. v. Ziplocal, LP*, 795 F.3d 1255, 1284 (11th Cir. 2015); Ralph S. Brown, *Civil Remedies for Intellectual Property Invasions: Themes and Variations*, Law & Contemp. Probs. 45, 53 (Spring 1992).

19. 17 U.S.C. § 505.

principle, or discovery, regardless of the form in which it is described, explained, illustrated, or embodied in such work."[20]

Intellectual Property, Public Policy

Artists seek intellectual property law protection as a way to protect their very livelihood. Government enacts and enforces intellectual property laws as a way to enrich and improve the lives of members of the general public. If you noticed that the two aims are not directly connected, this is the beginning of the understanding of the definition and scope of coverage of the intellectual property laws. The American intellectual property system is not an artist-incentive, or artist-reward based system. It is a public policy, public benefit system. So, the laws define and protect the subjects of protection with an eye to what best benefits the public at large, not what seems best to help artists live, thrive, and survive.

This is a long list. Why? Because copyright law is a public-policy driven set of laws, and the policy is: benefit the general public. Note that statement— copyright is intended to benefit the general public directly, not artists and authors directly.[21]

Ideas and concepts are free, they can be copied.[22] Processes, procedures, and methods are useful, and they are to be repeated and republished without the limitations of copyright.[23] Discoveries are not the stuff of copyright. First, discoveries and inventions are interpreted as "ideas" in copyright law, and useful, practical ideas will not be locked up in the monopoly of copyright for the lifetime and seventy more years after the death of a single person. And second, among the intellectual property protections, patent law exists to protect truly inventive, innovative, and useful ideas, processes, inventions, and discoveries.[24] Patent law has strict requirements for true inventions that were not obvious to persons skilled in the prior art,[25] and only locks the information up for twenty years.[26]

Copyright, on the other hand, protects *expressions* of ideas,[27] communication of concepts, writings, descriptions, and depictions of processes,

---

20. 17 U.S.C. § 102(b).

21. *Twentieth Century Music Corp. v. Aiken*, 422 U.S. 151, 156 (1975); *Veeck v. Southern Bldg. Code Cong. Int'l Inc.*, 241 F.3d 398, 402 (5th Cir. 2001).

22. *Golan*, 132 S. Ct. at 890; *Eldred v. Ashcroft*, 537 U.S. 186, 219 (2003); *Feist*, 499 U.S. at 349-50; *Harper & Row Publishers, Inc. v. Nation Enterprises*, 471 U.S. 539, 556 (1985).

23. *See* 37 C.F.R. § 202.1(b); Copyright Office Circular 31; *CCC Info. Servs., Inc. v. Maclean Hunter Mkt. Reports, Inc.*, 44 F.3d 61, 72 (2d Cir. 1994).

24. *Bilski v. Kappos*, 561 U.S. 593, 631-32 (2010).

25. 35 U.S.C. § 103; *KSR Int'l Co. v. Teleflex Inc.*, 550 U.S. 398, 399 (2007); *Graham v. John Deere Co. of Kansas City*, 383 U.S. 1, 12-13 (1966).

26. 35 U.S.C. § § 154(a)(1) and (2); *Kimble v. Marvel Entm't, LLC*, 135 S. Ct. 2401, 2415 (2015).

27. 17 U.S.C. § 102(b); *Golan*, 132 S. Ct. at 890.

procedures, and methods. It protects the communicative form that was created, and its particular wording, arrangement, or depiction.

E. Creativity and Originality

The formal requirement of copyright is that the expression is fixed in a tangible medium. Copyright also has two basic conceptual requirements:

(1) original
(2) creations[28]

The words "original" and "creations" in copyright are legal terms of art. **Original** means one thing: *not copied.*[29] It does not mean unique, clever, ingenious, or inventive. It only means that the work is the work of the artist, not copied from another artist's work. And **creation** means that the author created the work as a conception and "work of the mind," which is then produced and fixed by the author in some observable, perceptible media.[30] Creation, creative, or creativity in copyright law also do not mean unique, clever, ingenious, or inventive.[31] Creative means "created by the author," not found, not borrowed, and not naturally occurring.[32]

What is the *work* in a copyright situation?

Note that the work protected by copyright is not the subject matter of the painting, sculpture, or photograph. The work is the composition, arrangement, and scene conceived of and created by the artist. It is the expression of the subject matter that counts, not the actual ideas or subjects expressed.

What these two concepts together mean is that the artist must think up and create the work without taking or copying it from some other thing. Things found in nature are not included — the artist didn't think these up and didn't create them. The artist can conceive of a way to arrange and depict naturally occurring or already existing things,[33] but then the work protected is only the expression of the subjects as conceived of and depicted by the artist. Other artists can take the same subject matter and think of their own way of arranging

---

28. *See Feist Publications*, 499 U.S. at 345-51.
29. *Id.*
30. *See id.* at 346; *Boisson*, 273 F.3d at 268.
31. *See Feist Publications*, 499 U.S. at 346.
32. *See id.* at 345-47; *Oracle Am., Inc. v. Google Inc.*, 750 F.3d 1339, 1354 (Fed. Cir. 2014), *cert. denied*, 135 S. Ct. 2887 (2015).
33. *Feist Publications*, 499 U.S. at 346-47 (facts, which are not created or conceived of by the author, may still be arranged in a manner that is conceived of and created by the author, and this arrangement is potentially copyrightable).

and depicting the subjects and receive copyright protection for their own original, creative expression of the subjects.

Case Study: Photography

Ambrotypists and Daguerreotypists (early photographers) were not characterized as artists, and their works were not eligible for copyright protection. In 1865, Congress wrote photographs into the list of items that could potentially be copyrighted,[34] but still the usefulness of this inclusion was illusory. Courts were reluctant to recognize photography as a copyrightable art form because they viewed photography as a purely mechanical production that took objects in the world and exposed them to a photo-chemical plate that reproduced them fairly and accurately in all their features created by God or Mother Nature. That last phrase is the kicker: created by God — not created by the artist. What was left for copyright? What could the photographer bring to a photograph that would look like an original creation of the mind produced in a fixed and tangible form by the photographer? The *Burrows-Giles Lithographic Company v. Sarony* case in 1884 addressed these questions.[35]

Burrow-Giles Lithographic Co. v. Sarony

111 U.S. 53 (1884)*

MILLER, Justice.

This is a writ of error to the circuit court for the southern district of New York. Plaintiff is a lithographer, and defendant a photographer, with large business in those lines in the city of New York. The suit was commenced by an action at law in which Sarony was plaintiff and the lithographic company was defendant, the plaintiff charging the defendant with violating his copyright in regard to a photograph, the title of which is "Oscar Wilde, No. 18". . . and that said plaintiff made the same at his place of business in said city of New York, and within the United States, entirely from his own original mental conception, to which he gave visible form by posing the said Oscar Wilde in front of the camera, selecting and arranging the costume, draperies, and other various accessories in said photograph, arranging the subject so as to present graceful outlines, arranging and disposing the light and shade, suggesting and evoking the desired expression, and from such disposition, arrangement, or representation, made entirely by the plaintiff, he produced the picture in suit. . . .

We entertain no doubt that the constitution is broad enough to cover an act authorizing copyright of photographs, so far as they are representatives of original intellectual conceptions of the author. But it is said that an engraving, a painting, a print, does embody the intellectual conception of its author, in

---

34. Copyright Act of 1865, ch. 126, 13 Stat. 540. *See* Christine Haight Farley, *The Lingering Effects of Copyright's Response to the Invention of Photography*, 65 U. PITT. L. REV. 385, 456 (2004).

35. *Burrow-Giles Lithographic Co. v. Sarony*, 111 U.S. 53 (1884).

* Citations omitted.

36

which there is novelty, invention, originality, and therefore comes within the purpose of the constitution in securing its exclusive use or sale to its author, while a photograph is the mere mechanical reproduction of the physical features or outlines of some object, animate or inanimate, and involves no originality of thought or any novelty in the intellectual operation connected with its visible reproduction in shape of a picture. That while the effect of light on the prepared plate may have been a discovery in the production of these pictures, and patents could properly be obtained for the combination of the chemicals, for their application to the paper or other surface, for all the machinery by which the light reflected from the object was thrown on the prepared plate, and for all the improvements in this machinery, and in the materials, the remainder of the process is merely mechanical, with no place

36. Michael D. Murray, Revised and resized image derived from the public domain photograph "Oscar Wilde No. 18" by Napoleon Sarony (1882), the subject of *Burrow-Giles Lithographic Co. v. Sarony*, 111 U.S. 53 (1884).

for novelty, invention, or originality. It is simply the manual operation, by the use of these instruments and preparations, of transferring to the plate the visible representation of some existing object, the accuracy of this representation being its highest merit. This may be true in regard to the ordinary production of a photograph, and that in such case a copyright is no protection. On the question as thus stated we decide nothing.

In regard, however, to the kindred subject of patents for invention, they cannot, by law, be issued to the inventor until the novelty, the utility, and the actual discovery or invention by the claimant have been established by proof before the commissioner of patents; and when he has secured such a patent, and undertakes to obtain redress for a violation of his right in a court of law, the question of invention, of novelty, of originality is always open to examination. Our copyright system has no such provision for previous examination by a proper tribunal as to the originality of the book, map, or other matter offered for copyright. A deposit of two copies of the article or work with the librarian of congress, with the name of the author and its title page, is all that is necessary to secure a copyright. It is therefore much more important that when the supposed author sues for a violation of his copyright, the existence of those facts of originality, of intellectual production, of thought, and conception on the part of the author should be proved than in the case of a patent-right. In the case before us we think this has been done.

The third finding of facts says, in regard to the photograph in question, that it is a "useful, new, harmonious, characteristic, and graceful picture, and that plaintiff made the same . . . entirely from his own original mental conception, to which he gave visible form by posing the said Oscar Wilde in front of the camera, selecting and arranging the costume, draperies, and other various accessories in said photograph, arranging the subject so as to present graceful outlines, arranging and disposing the light and shade, suggesting and evoking the desired expression, and from such disposition, arrangement, or representation, made entirely by plaintiff, he produced the picture in suit." These findings, we think, show this photograph to be an original work of art, the product of plaintiff's intellectual invention, of which plaintiff is the author, and of a class of inventions for which the constitution intended that congress should secure to him the exclusive right to use, publish, and sell, as it has done by § 4952 of the Revised Statutes.

Kaplan v. Stock Market Photo Agency, Inc.

133 F. Supp. 2d 317 (S.D.N.Y. 2001)*

SCHWARTZ, District Judge.

This action relates to two photographs, one published by plaintiff and one by defendants, which depict a frequently portrayed metropolitan scene: a businessperson contemplating a leap from a tall building onto the bustling city

---

* Footnotes and most inner citations omitted.

street below.[37] Plaintiff brings claims for copyright infringement under 17 U.S.C. §§ 101 et seq. and for unfair competition arising out of defendants' publication of their photograph. Defendants move for summary judgment on the ground that the photographs are not substantially similar. For the reasons set forth below, the motions are granted. . . .

The determination of which elements of a work are protectable is also an inexact science, and is case-specific. It is a fundamental principal of copyright law that a copyright does not protect an idea or concept but only the expression of that idea or concept. Similarly, the doctrine of *scenes a faire* holds that sequences of events necessarily resulting from the choice of setting or situation, *Walker v. Time Life Films*, Inc., 784 F.2d 44, 50 (2d Cir. 1986), or "incidents, characters or settings which are as a practical matter indispensable, or at least standard, in the treatment of a given topic," *Hoehling v. Universal City Studios*, Inc., 618 F.2d 972, 979 (2d Cir. 1980), are not protectable under the copyright laws. The distinction between an idea and its expression is "elusive" and is often an "impenetrable inquiry." While there is no firm gauge to enable the Court to determine when an "imitator has gone beyond copying the 'idea,' and has borrowed its 'expression,' the inquiry often turns on the level of abstraction or generalization of the works being compared." The Court is guided in this task by the oft-cited passage of Learned Hand in *Nichols v. Universal Pictures Corp.*, 45 F.2d 119, 121 (2d Cir. 1930):

> Upon any work, . . . a great number of patterns of increasing generality will fit equally well, as more and more of the incident is left out. The last may perhaps be no more than the most general statement of what the [work] is about, and at times might consist only of its title; but there is a point in this series of abstractions where they are no longer protected, since otherwise the [author]

---

37. Michael D. Murray, Collage of two revised and resized images derived from the trial exhibits in *Kaplan v. Stock Market Photo Agency, Inc.*, 133 F. Supp. 2d 317 (S.D.N.Y. 2001).

could prevent the use of his "ideas," to which, apart from their expression, his property is never extended.

With regard to photographs in particular, a copyright derives from "the photographer's original conception of his subject, not the subject itself." Protectable elements "may include posing the subjects, lighting, angle, selection of film and camera, [and] evoking the desired expression," along with other variants. . . .

Turning to the two photographs in the instant case, the Court finds that nearly all the similarities between the works arise from noncopyrightable elements, thus rendering the works not substantially similar. The subject matter of both photographs is a businessperson contemplating a leap from a tall building onto the city street below. As the photograph's central idea, rather than Kaplan's expression of the idea, this subject matter is unprotectable in and of itself. Moreover, as the situation of a leap from a tall building is standard in the treatment of the topic of the exasperated businessperson in today's fast-paced work environment, especially in New York, the subject matter of the photographs is also rendered unprotectable by the doctrine of *scenes a faire*. Kaplan, like other artists before and after him, has chosen to express a businessperson's frustration with the world by portraying him at the top of a building; his contemplation of a leap from the edge of that building is the necessary sequence of events that follows from the chosen setting.

Drawing on Judge Hand's conceptual framework as set out in Nichols, Kaplan argues that the concept of a "distraught businessman standing on the ledge of a tall city building" misdefines his photograph's central idea by selecting "too concrete a level of abstraction." Instead, he suggests that the idea "might be expressed" at a higher level, namely, by "the depiction of a person contemplating a leap from a city building." The Court acknowledges, as defendants do, that the concept of Kaplan's photograph "may" be expressed more generally, at the level of the person, and that such idea may itself be unprotectable under the doctrine of scenes a faire; however, this idea is clearly not the most accurate characterization of the concept embraced by the photographs at issue in this case. By suggesting this higher level of abstraction, Kaplan merely overgeneralizes the concept embraced by his photograph. . . .

In this case, almost all of the similarities in expression between the two photographs are unprotectable elements or themes that flow predictably from the underlying subject matter. Let us begin by examining the businessperson. Both photographs depict him standing on the roof or ledge of a tall building, with his shoes partially extended over the edge. However, such positioning is essential to the businessperson's contemplation of a suicide leap; it would be impossible to depict the photograph's subject matter without portraying him in this pose. The Court concludes that the similarities relating to pose are clearly encompassed by the unprotectable subject matter of the photographs.

Second, each businessperson is dressed in similar attire, a pinstripe suit and wing-tip shoes, although the suits and shoes in the respective photographs are different in color. Such is the businessperson's typical garb, and therefore might reasonably be expected to appear in any expression of the unprotectable idea in question here. In his opposition papers, Kaplan does not dispute defendants' characterization of his subject's wardrobe as generic; in fact, one of the images he claims is a noninfringing work depicts a businessman dressed exactly the same way. Thus, the wardrobe depicted in both photographs does not support a finding of substantial similarity.

Third, both photographs are taken from a similar angle or viewpoint, namely, that of the businessperson looking down at the street below. In arguing for a finding of substantial similarity, Kaplan alleges that Benvenuto misappropriated the "particular expression" of "the lower pant legs and shoes, the sheer side of the building, and the traffic below." However, while there are parallels in such details, there are also substantial differences: Kaplan's photograph shows only the very bottom of the pants legs, while Benvenuto's photograph shows the legs from about the knees down; the photographs are taken from different locations, depicting different buildings, roads and vehicles. In addition, as defendants point out, in order to most accurately express the idea of a businessperson's contemplation of a leap, the photograph must be taken from the "jumper's" own viewpoint, which would (i) naturally include the sheer side of the building and the traffic below, and (ii) logically restrict the visible area of the businessperson's body to his shoes and a certain portion of his pants legs, depending on the angle from which the businessperson observes the scene below, i.e., how far he is bending over. Thus, the angle and viewpoint used in both photographs are essential to, commonly associated with, and naturally flow from the photograph's unprotectable subject matter.

There may be, as Kaplan suggests, many other angles from which to depict the scene, e.g., by shooting "the person on top of the building from other viewpoints, such as from either side, the rear, a three-quarter view, or a view from slightly above and to the side." He further states that "it is also easy to conceive of a particularly dramatic treatment of the idea that could be done from somewhere below the person leaning over the building edge with the camera looking upward." However, the most common, and most effective, viewpoint from which to convey the idea of the "jumper" — whether he is merely a "person" or a "businessperson" — remains that of the "jumper" himself. . . .

Thus, the Court concludes that any similarities between the protected elements of Kaplan's and Benvenuto's photographs "are of small import quantitatively and qualitatively," such that a rational trier of fact would not be able to find they are substantially similar. In designing his photograph, Benvenuto added his own originality to the underlying, unprotectable idea of a businessperson on contemplating a leap from a tall building to the street below, and his expression of that idea is not infringing as a matter of law. Accordingly, summary judgment must be awarded to defendants on Kaplan's copyright claim.

Mannion v. Coors Brewing Co.

377 F. Supp. 2d 444 (S.D.N.Y. 2005)*

KAPLAN, District Judge.

The parties dispute whether a photograph used in billboard advertisements for Coors Light beer infringes the plaintiff's copyright in a photograph of a basketball star.[38] The defendants almost certainly imitated the plaintiff's photograph. The major question is whether and to what extent what was copied is protected. The case requires the Court to consider the nature of copyright protection in photographs. The matter is before the Court on cross motions for summary judgment. . . .

Appendix

The Garnett Photograph

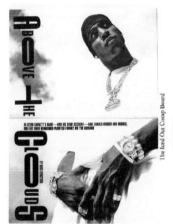 

1. PROTECTIBLE ELEMENTS OF PHOTOGRAPHS

It is well-established that "[t]he sine qua non of copyright is originality" and, accordingly, that "copyright protection may extend only to those components of a work that are original to the author." "Original" in the copyright context "means only that the work was independently created by the author (as opposed to copied from other works), and that it possesses at least some minimal degree of creativity."

It sometimes is said that "copyright in the photograph conveys no rights over the subject matter conveyed in the photograph." But this is not always true. It of course is correct that the photographer of a building or tree or other pre-existing object has no right to prevent others from photographing the same thing. That is because originality depends upon independent creation, and the photographer did not create that object. By contrast, if a photographer

---

* Footnotes omitted.

38. Michael D. Murray, Collage of two revised and resized images derived from the trial exhibits in *Mannion v. Coors Brewing Co.*, 377 F. Supp. 2d 444 (S.D.N.Y. 2005).

arranges or otherwise creates the subject that his camera captures, he may have the right to prevent others from producing works that depict that subject.

Almost any photograph "may claim the necessary originality to support a copyright." Indeed, ever since the Supreme Court considered an 1882 portrait by the celebrity photographer Napoleon Sarony of the 27-year-old Oscar Wilde, courts have articulated lists of potential components of a photograph's originality. These lists, however, are somewhat unsatisfactory. Even these lists are not complete. They omit such features as the amount of the image in focus, its graininess, and the level of contrast.

First, they do not deal with the issue, alluded to above, that the nature and extent of a photograph's protection differs depending on what makes that photograph original.

Second, courts have not always distinguished between decisions that a photographer makes in creating a photograph and the originality of the final product. Several cases, for example, have included in lists of the potential components of photographic originality "selection of film and camera," "lens and filter selection," and "the kind of camera, the kind of film, [and] the kind of lens." Having considered the matter fully, however, I think this is not sufficiently precise. Decisions about film, camera, and lens, for example, often bear on whether an image is original. But the fact that a photographer made such choices does not alone make the image original. "Sweat of the brow" is not the touchstone of copyright. Protection derives from the features of the work itself, not the effort that goes into it. . . .

a. Rendition

First, "there may be originality which does not depend on creation of the scene or object to be photographed . . . and which resides [instead] in such specialties as angle of shot, light and shade, exposure, effects achieved by means of filters, developing techniques etc." We will refer to this type of originality as originality in the rendition because, to the extent a photograph is original in this way, copyright protects not what is depicted, but rather how it is depicted. . . .

b. Timing

A photograph may be original in a second respect. "[A] person may create a worthwhile photograph by being at the right place at the right time." We will refer to this type of originality as originality in timing. . . .

c. Creation of the Subject

The principle that copyright confers no right over the subject matter has an important limitation. A photograph may be original to the extent that the photographer created "the scene or subject to be photographed." . . .

To conclude, the nature and extent of protection conferred by the copyright in a photograph will vary depending on the nature of its originality.

Insofar as a photograph is original in the rendition or timing, copyright protects the image but does not prevent others from photographing the same object or scene. . . . [T]o the extent that a photograph is original in the creation of the subject, copyright extends also to that subject. Thus, an artist who arranges and then photographs a scene often will have the right to prevent others from duplicating that scene in a photograph or other medium.

2. ORIGINALITY OF THE GARNETT PHOTOGRAPH

There can be no serious dispute that the Garnett Photograph is an original work. The photograph does not result from slavishly copying another work and therefore is original in the rendition. Mannion's relatively unusual angle and distinctive lighting strengthen that aspect of the photograph's originality. His composition — posing man against sky — evidences originality in the creation of the subject. Furthermore, Mannion instructed Garnett to wear simple and plain clothing and as much jewelry as possible, and "to look 'chilled out.'" His orchestration of the scene contributes additional originality in the creation of the subject.

Of course, there are limits to the photograph's originality and therefore to the protection conferred by the copyright in the Garnett Photograph. For example, Kevin Garnett's face, torso, and hands are not original with Mannion, and Mannion therefore may not prevent others from creating photographic portraits of Garnett. Equally obviously, the existence of a cloudy sky is not original, and Mannion therefore may not prevent others from using a cloudy sky as a backdrop.

The defendants, however, take this line of reasoning too far. They argue that it was Garnett, not Mannion, who selected the specific clothing, jewelry, and pose. In consequence, they maintain, the Garnett Photograph is not original to the extent of Garnett's clothing, jewelry, and pose. They appear to be referring to originality in the creation of the subject. . . .

3. THE IDEA / EXPRESSION DIFFICULTY

Notwithstanding the originality of the Garnett Photograph, the defendants argue that the Coors Billboard does not infringe because the two, insofar as they are similar, share only "the generalized idea and concept of a young African American man wearing a white T-shirt and a large amount of jewelry. . . ."

The "idea" (if one wants to call it that) postulated by the defendants does not even come close to accounting for all the similarities between the two works, which extend at least to angle, pose, background, composition, and lighting. It is possible to imagine any number of depictions of a black man wearing a white T-shirt and "bling bling" that look nothing like either of the photographs at issue here. This alone is sufficient to dispose of the defendants' contention that Mannion's claims must be rejected because he seeks to protect an idea rather than its expression. But the argument reveals an analytical difficulty in the case law about which more ought to be said. . . .

To be sure, the difficulty of distinguishing between idea and expression long has been recognized. Judge Learned Hand famously observed in 1930 [in Nichols v. Universal Pictures Corp., 45 F.2d 119, 121 (2d Cir. 1930) (citation omitted)]:

> "Upon any work, and especially upon a play, a great number of patterns of increasing generality will fit equally well, as more and more of the incident is left out. The last may perhaps be no more than the most general statement of what the play is about, and at times might consist only of its title; but there is a point in this series of abstractions where they are no longer protected, since otherwise the playwright could prevent the use of his 'ideas,' to which, apart from their expression, his property is never extended. Nobody has ever been able to fix that boundary, and nobody ever can."

The idea/expression distinction arose in the context of literary copyright. For the most part, the Supreme Court has not applied it outside that context. The classic Hand formulations reviewed above also were articulated in the context of literary works. And it makes sense to speak of the idea conveyed by a literary work and to distinguish it from its expression. To take a clear example, two different authors each can describe, with very different words, the theory of special relativity. The words will be protected as expression. The theory is a set of unprotected ideas.

In the visual arts, the distinction breaks down. For one thing, it is impossible in most cases to speak of the particular "idea" captured, embodied, or conveyed by a work of art because every observer will have a different interpretation. Furthermore, it is not clear that there is any real distinction between the idea in a work of art and its expression. An artist's idea, among other things, is to depict a particular subject in a particular way. As a demonstration, a number of cases from this Circuit have observed that a photographer's "conception" of his subject is copyrightable. By "conception," the courts must mean originality in the rendition, timing, and creation of the subject — for that is what copyright protects in photography. But the word "conception" is a cousin of "concept," and both are akin to "idea." In other words, those elements of a photograph, or indeed, any work of visual art protected by copyright, could just as easily be labeled "idea" as "expression." . . .

For all of these reasons, we think little is gained by attempting to distinguish an unprotectible "idea" from its protectible "expression" in a photograph or other work of visual art. It remains, then, to consider just what courts have been referring to when they have spoken of the "idea" in a photograph. . . .

[T]he Court concludes that it is immaterial whether the ordinary or more discerning observer test is used here because the inquiries would be identical. The cases agree that the relevant comparison is between the protectible elements in the Garnett Photograph and the Coors Billboard, but that those elements are not to be viewed in isolation.

The Garnett Photograph is protectible to the extent of its originality in the rendition and creation of the subject. Key elements of the Garnett Photograph that are in the public domain — such as Kevin Garnett's likeness — are not replicated in the Coors Billboard. Other elements arguably in the public domain — such as the existence of a cloudy sky, Garnett's pose, his white T-shirt, and his specific jewelry — may not be copyrightable in and of themselves, but their existence and arrangement in this photograph indisputably contribute to its originality. Thus the fact that the Garnett Photograph includes certain elements that would not be copyrightable in isolation does not affect the nature of the comparison. The question is whether the aesthetic appeal of the two images is the same.

The two photographs share a similar composition and angle. The lighting is similar, and both use a cloudy sky as backdrop. The subjects are wearing similar clothing and similar jewelry arranged in a similar way. The defendants, in other words, appear to have recreated much of the subject that Mannion had created and then, through imitation of angle and lighting, rendered it in a similar way. The similarities here thus relate to the Garnett Photograph's originality in the rendition and the creation of the subject and therefore to its protected elements. . . .

The parties have catalogued at length and in depth the similarities and differences between these works. In the last analysis, a reasonable jury could find substantial similarity either present or absent. . . .

The defendants' motion for summary judgment dismissing the complaint (docket item 18) is granted to the extent that the complaint seeks relief for violation of the plaintiff's exclusive right to prepare derivative works and otherwise denied. The plaintiff's cross motion for summary judgment is denied.

SO ORDERED.

Notes and Questions

1. *Burrow-Giles Lithographic Co. v. Sarony* answered the question whether photographs could be "writings" and copyrightable "works of authorship" in the affirmative. Do you agree with this determination? Is there not an obvious difference between the work of an artist engraver or painter, and a photographer?

2. *Burrow-Giles* made a distinction between the "ordinary production of photographs" and posed and arranged photographs, such as the one at issue in the case. What was the "ordinary production of photographs" referred to in the case? What qualities of originality and creativity may be found that would render photographs copyrightable? Consider *Latimer v. Roaring Toyz, Inc.*, 574 F. Supp. 2d 1265 (M.D. Fla. 2008), *Gentieu v. Tony Stone Images/Chicago, Inc.*, 255 F. Supp. 2d 838 (N.D. Ill. 2003), and *Kaplan* and *Mannion* excerpted above.

3. The French photographer Henri Cartier-Bresson, known as a pioneer of modern snap-shooting photography, is best known for his black and white snapshots of scenes of daily life capturing, in his words and those

of his admirers, the "decisive moment" of the scene.[39] Since there obviously is no posing, staging, or arrangement of lights and subject matter in these scenes, and the equipment used is a standard 35mm rangefinder camera and 50mm lens, what would Monsieur Cartier-Bresson claim as the copyrightable original and creative elements of these photographs?

Henri Cartier-Bresson, Place de l'Europe. Gare Saint Lazare (1932)

4. Is the digital production of photographs any more or less creative and original than the analog production of photographs? In digital photography, don't you simply take natural light reflected off of natural objects and manipulate it with mathematical algorithms and computer coding? Consider *Tiffany Design, Inc. v. Reno-Tahoe Specialty, Inc.*, 55 F. Supp. 2d 1113 (D. Nev. 1999).

F. Standard of Creativity and Originality

The standard of creativity in copyright is a very low standard, and this is intentional.[40] "Creative" simply means created by the author. A work must also be original in order to obtain copyright protection, but "original" means that the work is independently created, or not copied, rather than unique or one of a kind.[41] It follows that if, by strange coincidence, a work is, in all respects, identical to an earlier one, but it was not copied from the earlier one, the latter work will be independently eligible for copyright protection.[42] This result is not changed if the earlier article is copyrighted or in the public domain.[43] Similarly, if two people independently create identical maps at the same time, each will be entitled to his or her own copyright and neither will infringe on the other's copyright.[44] It is for this reason that many cartographers intentionally include a minor error in their creations. If the identical mistake

---

39. Michael D. Murray, Cropped, revised, and resized thumbnail image derived from the photograph "Place de l'Europe. Gare Saint Lazare" by Henri Cartier-Bresson (1932).

40. *See id.*

41. *See Feist Publications,* 499 U.S. 340.

42. 1 Melville B. Nimmer & David Nimmer, Nimmer § 2.01[A] (2006); *Mazer v. Stein,* 347 U.S. 201, *reh'g denied,* 347 U.S. 949 (1954).

43. 1 Nimmer & Nimmer, *supra* at § 2.01[A]; *Millworth Converting Corp. v. Slifka,* 276 F.2d 443 (2d Cir. 1960).

44. *Fred Fisher, Inc. v. Dillingham,* 298 F. 145, 151 (S.D.N.Y. 1924).

appears in another alleged original, it may be shown as prima facie evidence of copying.

Q. and A. Originality and Creativity

Q. Is a telephone directory copyrightable?

A. Not unless some creative, original selection or arrangement of the names or numbers is made. Just listing the existing names and numbers in alphabetical or numeric order has been done before; it is not a creative, original arrangement. *See Feist Publications*, 499 U.S. at 345-47.

Q. What if the author has picked out and listed only businesses that speak Chinese?

A. Picking out and publishing only the businesses that speak Chinese is a creative, original arrangement of otherwise unprotectable data that could qualify for copyright protection. Only the arrangement and compilation would be protected, not the actual names and numbers of the individual businesses (which are data). *Key Publications, Inc. v. Chinatown Today Pub. Enterprises, Inc.*, 945 F.2d 509, 512-13 (2d Cir. 1991).

Copyright is concerned with encouraging creativity, not specifically rewarding time and effort.[45] No matter how much sweat equity goes into obtaining or compiling non-copyrightable facts, the effort does not render the research copyrightable.[46] In *Feist Publications, Inc. v. Rural Tel. Serv. Co.*,[47] the Court held that copyright protection did not extend to a telephone directory's white pages because a mere alphabetical arrangement of otherwise non-copyrightable names and numbers was not sufficiently creative to satisfy the originality requirements of the 1976 Act and the U.S. Constitution. The arrangement of material in an obvious way through "the sweat of one's brow" will not entitle the material or its arrangement to copyright protection. However, compilations of facts and derivative works may be copyrightable under 17 U.S.C. § 103 if the material is gathered and arranged in a new or original form. Copyright in a 'new version' covers only the material added by the later author, and has no effect one way or the other on the copyright or public domain status of the preexisting material."[48]

The law and the courts generally avoid using the copyright law to arbitrate the public's taste. Thus, a work is not denied a copyright even if it makes no pretense to aesthetic or academic merit. The only requirements are that a work be original and show some creativity. Courts, however, have been reluctant to

---

45. *CDN Inc. v. Kapes*, 197 F.3d 1256, 1260 (9th Cir. 1999).

46. *See id.*

47. 499 U.S. 340, 361 (1991).

48. H. Rep. No. 1476, 94th Cong., 2d Sess. 55 (1976), p. 57 [hereinafter H.R. 94-1476]. *See, e.g., Estate of Burne Hogarth v. Edgar Rice Burroughs, Inc.*, 342 F.3d 149, 165-66 & n.19 (2d Cir. 2003), *cert. denied*, 541 U.S. 937 (2004).

impose a strict standard of creativity for works of art as the effect would be to exclude many items from copyright protection.

Bleistein v. Donaldson Lithographing Co.

188 U.S. 239 (1903)*

HOLMES, Justice.

This case comes here from the United States circuit court of appeals for the sixth circuit by writ of error. . . . It is an action brought by the plaintiffs in error to recover the penalties prescribed for infringements of copyrights. . . . The alleged infringements consisted in the copying in reduced form of three chromolithographs prepared by employees of the plaintiffs for advertisements of a circus owned by one Wallace. . . . The circuit court directed a verdict for the defendant on the ground that the chromolithographs were not within the protection of the copyright law, and this ruling was sustained by the circuit court of appeals. . . .[49]

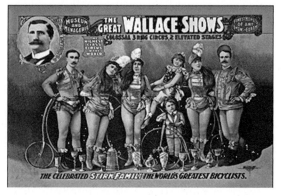

We shall do no more than mention the suggestion that painting and engraving, unless for a mechanical end, are not among the useful arts, the progress of which Congress is empowered by the Constitution to promote. The Constitution does not limit the useful to that which satisfies immediate bodily needs. . . . It is obvious also that the plaintiff's case is not affected by the fact, if it be one, that the pictures represent actual groups — visible things. They seem from the testimony to have been composed from hints or description, not from sight of a performance. But even if they had been drawn from the life, that fact would not deprive them of protection. The opposite proposition would mean

---

* Citations omitted.

49. Michael D. Murray, Two revised and resized thumbnail images derived from public domain chromolithographic circus posters, the subject of *Bleistein v. Donaldson Lithographing Co.*, 188 U.S. 239 (1903).

that a portrait by Velasquez or Whistler was common property because others might try their hand on the same face. Others are free to copy the original. They are not free to copy the copy. . . . The copy is the personal reaction of an individual upon nature. Personality always contains something unique. It expresses its singularity even in handwriting, and a very modest grade of art has in it something irreducible, which is one man's alone. That something he may copyright unless there is a restriction in the words of the act. . . .

There is no reason to doubt that these prints in their ensemble and in all their details, in their design and particular combinations of figures, lines, and colors, are the original work of the plaintiffs' designer. . . . [T]he act, however construed, does not mean that ordinary posters are not good enough to be considered within its scope. The antithesis to 'illustrations or works connected with the fine arts' is not works of little merit or of humble degree, or illustrations addressed to the less educated classes; it is 'prints or labels designed to be used for any other articles of manufacture.' Certainly works are not the less connected with the fine arts because their pictorial quality attracts the crowd, and therefore gives them a real use, — if use means to increase trade and to help to make money. A picture is none the less a picture, and none the less a subject of copyright, that it is used for an advertisement. And if pictures may be used to advertise soap, or the theatre, or monthly magazines, as they are, they may be used to advertise a circus. . . .

It would be a dangerous undertaking for persons trained only to the law to constitute themselves final judges of the worth of pictorial illustrations, outside of the narrowest and most obvious limits. At the one extreme some works of genius would be sure to miss appreciation. Their very novelty would make them repulsive until the public had learned the new language in which their author spoke. It may be more than doubted, for instance, whether the etchings of Goya or the paintings of Manet would have been sure of protection when seen for the first time. At the end, copyright would be denied to pictures which appealed to a public less educated than the judge. . . .

Notes and Questions

1. Justice Holmes' opinion in *Bleistein* is most noted for his warning that judges should not subject the determination of creative, original, and copyrightable works to a test based on a judge's individual taste or preference, except in "the narrowest and most obvious limits." What do the terms "narrowest and most obvious" limits mean? Is there any artistic or aesthetic component in the determination? Consider *Feist Pubs. v. Rural Tel Serv. Co.*, 499 U.S. at 345, 353, and *Diamond Direct, LLC v. Star Diamond Group, Inc.*, 116 F. Supp. 2d 525, 528 (S.D.N.Y. 2000).

2. *Bleistein* has come to be associated with the position that any work of art, created by any person with any level of artistic skill, should be eligible for copyright protection as long as the work is not a copy of

another work and subject to certain other limitations discussed in this chapter (regarding useful articles, derivative works, and others). Is this a good foundational principle for a copyright system that awards to the owner a long-term (life plus 70 years) monopoly on the copying and exploitation of the works?

3. What of the alternative public policy position—subjecting works to a certain standard of excellence based on the quality of the work, the nature of the media or the techniques used in its production, or the level of training or status of the author? What would artist clients prefer?

Current Case: Tribal Tattoos[50]

Are tattoos original? Certainly they can be. The recent dispute illustrated here[51] involved a tribal-style tattoo created by tattoo artist Victor Whitmill on the face of former boxing champion Mike Tyson, later duplicated on actor Ed Helms' face for the movie, *The Hangover Part II*. Was the tattoo copyrightable? The analysis would be:

Original?—Was the tattoo design original to the tattoo artist? Did he conceive of it himself, or was it a pre-existing design, a present or historical tribal mark, or one of a genre of tribal markings that the tattoo artist simply adopted and decided to put to use in a facial tattoo for his customer, Mike Tyson?

Creative?—We have every reason to believe that the tattoo artist created the tattoo on Tyson's face, but that is only half of the analysis. If he didn't conceive of the design as something original to himself, then he won't get a copyright for copying a pre-existing design.

---

50. This problem is based on the lawsuit between Victor Whitmill and Warner Brothers for the use without permission of Whitmill's copyrighted tattoo featured on the face of the boxer Mike Tyson, an alleged reproduction of which was later used on actor Ed Helms' face in *The Hangover Part II. See* Meredith Hatic, *Who Owns Your Body Art?: The Copyright and Constitutional Implications of Tattoos,* 23 FORDHAM INTELL. PROP. MEDIA & ENT. L.J. 396, 398 (2012); Yolanda M. King, *The Enforcement Challenges for Tattoo Copyrights,* 2014 J. INTELL. PROP. L. 22, 29. This lawsuit ultimately settled. Matthew Belloni, *"Hangover" Tattoo Lawsuit Settled,* REUTERS (June 20, 2011, 10:48 PM), *http://www.reuters.com/article/2011/06/21/us-hangover-idUSTRE75K0DF20110621.*

51. Michael D. Murray, Revised and resized thumbnail images of tribal-style tattoo created by tattoo artist Victor Whitmill on the face of former boxing champion Mike Tyson, and a similar tattoo on the face of actor Ed Helms, the subject of *Whitmill vs. Warner Bros., the Producers of the Motion Picture "The Hangover Part II"* (2014).

Act of Copying? — Again, it looks like the makeup artist for *The Hangover Part II* took great pains to copy Victor Whitmill's tattoo, so it appears that an act of copying took place. The *Hangover* tattoo probably would meet the strikingly similar test. Beyond that, Tyson's public figure status means that there are abundant opportunities for the *Hangover* people to know about his tattoo, satisfying the access issue. But we need not go further in the copyright infringement analysis, because the artist may not have a copyright over this tattoo design.

There are few limits to copyrightable subject matter beyond those discussed above — ideas, processes, procedures, concepts, methods, and the like. An author is able to copyright obscene and outrageous material such as pornography or obscenity.[52] An author can copyright false and fraudulent material.[53] Authors need only to be creative and original when they do it. Note, however, that the unclean hands doctrine may deny equitable (injunctive) relief if the copyright owner has misused its copyrights.[54]

G. Fixed and Tangible

Normally the "fixed in a tangible media" requirement is not an issue in the art world. The artist creates tangible, solid works with a high degree of permanence — paintings and sculptures and prints — and wants people to see and appreciate the work. But in some expressive endeavors, fixation requires a bit more.

Speeches, lectures, stage directions, or choreography directions that are not written down or recorded — copyrightable?

No. Oral expressions may be unique, creative and original to the author, but they are not fixed. The law provides that if a simultaneous recording is made, then the oral expressions and the recording become protected by copyright.[55] Choreography may be fixed in textual, pictorial, audio, or audio-visual records.[56]

An actual performance of a play or other live event or reenactment — copyrightable?

Not unless filmed, recorded or otherwise fixed in media.[57]

---

52. *See Mitchell Bros. Film Group v. Cinema Adult Theater*, 604 F.2d 852 (5th Cir. 1979) (the movie *Behind the Green Door* is copyrightable whether or not it is obscene).

53. *Belcher v. Tarbox*, 486 F.2d 1087 (9th Cir. 1973); *Jartech, Inc. v. Clancy*, 666 F.2d 403, 406 (9th Cir. 1982) (court cited *Belcher* with approval).

54. *See Alcatel USA, Inc. v. DGI Technologies, Inc.*, 166 F.3d 772, 792 (5th Cir. 1999).

55. *United States v. Martignon*, 492 F.3d 140, 142 (2d Cir. 2007); *Nat'l Basketball Ass'n v. Motorola, Inc.*, 105 F.3d 841, 847 (2d Cir. 1997).

56. *Martha Graham Sch. & Dance Found., Inc. v. Martha Graham Ctr. of Contemporary Dance, Inc.*, 380 F.3d 624, 632 (2d Cir. 2004) ("fixing" choreography by a written system of notation); *Horgan v. Macmillan, Inc.*, 789 F.2d 157, 161-62 and n.3 (2d Cir. 1986) (Ballanchine Nutcracker book could infringe choreography fixed by notations or by film and videotape).

57. *Martignon*, 492 F.3d at 142; *Nat'l Basketball Ass'n*, 105 F.3d at 847.

Improvised music or other improvised performance — copyrightable?

Not unless recorded or notated. Music typically receives several copyrights, one for the musical composition (the score, the notation, the sheet music), perhaps a separate one for the lyrics (as poetry and literature), and one for the musical recording. Improv is spontaneous, and supposedly unpredictable; the musician does not necessarily know where she is going with the music or where it will wind up. Most improv artists would resist the notion of planning and notating a performance; it simply is anathema to the genre. Nonetheless, a master of improvised music should get in the habit of writing a sketch of musical notations and verbal descriptions of what she created after it is performed in the improvised session, and at the very least, she should make a simultaneous recording of the performance even if it is just to fix the work in a tangible media. If the musician does not simultaneously record it, then anyone in the crowd who makes a recording will have created a fixed and tangible expression of the performance that would afford the taper in the crowd an opportunity to copyright the performance.

Current Issue: Wildflowers Installation

Kelley v. Chicago Park District (2011)[58]

Kelley v. Chicago Park District tells the tale of Chapman Kelley, an artist of landscapes (as opposed to a landscaper or floral designer) who created a large pictorial display of living wildflowers in Grant Park in downtown Chicago, titled *Wildflower Works*. Later, Chicago wanted to cut the whole thing down in size, changing and replanting the contents of the work.[59]

Kelley's Plan for *Wildflower Works*
http://www.rarin.org/index.php/File:Kelley ChicagoAerial.JPG

Wildflower Works *Installation*
http://clancco.com/wp/wp-content/uploads/2011/02/ CWFW1992.jpg

---

58. *Kelley v. Chicago Park Dist.*, 635 F.3d 290 (7th Cir. 2011).

59. Michael D. Murray, Cropped, revised, and resized thumbnail images derived from the image of Kelley's Plan for Wildflower Works, at http://www.rarin.org/index.php/File:KelleyChicagoAerial.JPG, and a photograph of the installation, the subject of *Kelley v. Chicago Park Dist.*, 635 F.3d 290 (7th Cir. 2011).

Kelley's primary claim was made pursuant to a section of the copyright code called the Visual Artists Rights Act, which might prevent the reshaping and reduction of the work *if* it were a copyrightable work to begin with, meaning original, creative, fixed in a tangible medium.[60] The Seventh Circuit Federal Court of Appeals found that the *Wildflowers Works* installation was original, but that it could not be copyrightable because of the nature of the living media, wildflowers, which were held to be not fixed in a tangible media, and it was not created (as in authored) by Kelley.[61]

Who authored the work? The Seventh Circuit apparently thought it was God or Mother Nature. The work is made up of plants; Kelley didn't create the plants (God did), so he is not the author of the plants. The plants make up the garden; Kelley is responsible for the garden being there, but he did not create the plants in the garden, so see the first answer here.

On fixation, the Seventh Circuit noted that plants sway in the breeze, they move, they grow, they wither, they die. Therefore, they are not fixed.

The Seventh Circuit is incorrect in a number of respects.[62] Fixation is not dependent on media. To assure that copyright law remained media neutral, Congress defined fixation of works to include "any tangible medium of expression, now known or later developed, from which they can be perceived, reproduced, or otherwise communicated, either directly or with the aid of a machine or device."[63] Congress further defined "fixed" to mean:

> A work is "fixed" in a tangible medium of expression when its embodiment in a copy . . . is sufficiently permanent or stable to permit it to be perceived, reproduced, or otherwise communicated for a period of more than transitory duration. A work consisting of sounds, images, or both, that are being transmitted, is "fixed" for purposes of this title if a fixation of the work is being made simultaneously with its transmission. . . .[64]

Contrary to the Seventh Circuit's highly restrictive notion of fixation, fixation is supposed to be a simple, open-ended, painfully easy to satisfy

---

60. Analogous cases such as *Cockburn v. SWS Industries, Inc.*, No. C10–1566RSL, 2011 WL 2295145 (W.D. Wash. Jun. 8, 2011), *Dimitrakopoulus v. Flowers by Demetrios*, 79 Civ. 6961 (RLC), 1983 WL 1135 (S.D.N.Y. July 7, 1983), and *Florabelle Flowers, Inc. v. Joseph Markovits, Inc.*, 296 F. Supp. 304 (S.D.N.Y. 1968), are somewhat useful in predicting the analysis of living media. The cases involved the creation of artificial flowers. The courts did not balk at copyright protection for these creations, they simply limited the copyright and the protectable elements according to the scènes à faire and merger doctrines.

61. *Kelley*, 635 F.3d at 303 ("The real impediment to copyright here is not that *Wildflower Works* fails the test for originality (understood as 'not copied' and 'possessing some creativity') but that a living garden lacks the kind of authorship and stable fixation normally required to support copyright. . . . ").

62. *See generally* Michael D. Murray, *Post-Myriad Genetics Copyright of Synthetic Biology and Living Media*, 10 Okla. J. L. & Tech. 71, 106-08 (2014).

63. 17 U.S.C. § 102(a); Deborah Tussey, *Technology Matters: The Courts, Media Neutrality, and New Technologies*, 12 J. Intell. Prop. L. 427, 429 (2005).

64. 17 U.S.C. § 101.

concept.[65] The ability to perceive the creation is all that matters, and even machines can be used to facilitate the perception.[66] If the creation is oral or fleeting or otherwise transitory in nature, you can record it with a longer-lasting media such as a visual, audio, or audio-visual recording that depicts or records the creation.[67]

Wildflower Works met each of the fixation criteria. It could be seen, felt, smelt, and tasted if you wanted to. It existed in drawings, photographs, and other depictions and descriptions. Its nature was known well enough to copy it or avoid copying it. The nature of the creation was no mystery to anyone.

The criticism that a work cannot be a painting because it consists of living items mistakes media for creation of expression. Every painting is made of something—its media. At some level of immediacy, the media is traceable to a natural organic or chemical substance that was formed or grown in or on the earth. The canvas is traced to cotton duck or linen, which is traced to the cotton plant, which grew out of the earth. The stretcher bars are made of wood which grew up as a tree. The paint medium might be a naturally occurring substance such as charcoal or raw umber, or a slightly more complicated composition of lapis lazuli and linseed oil making ultramarine, or a chemical composition of matter constituting Prussian blue, or one of the many synthetic hues that have become the normal media in artistic production. Sculpted media is similarly situated, substituting only a natural or manipulated media of clay, stone, metal, or a casting media that is plastic (i.e., malleable, able to be molded or shaped).[68]

The fact that creations of living media might move, change, grow, or wither, die and decompose again is not probative of copyright creativity. Consider that any work using wildflowers, or some other living, organic media, could be frozen in time by encasing it in Lucite or actually keeping it frozen at a sufficiently low temperature to keep it from decaying. Does that make the expression of the work different—regarding as we must that it is the expression of the work that causes us to think of copyright protection at all. Even absent that treatment, the comparison of the mobility of one form of work versus another simply is a matter of degree: all painting surfaces are susceptible to expansion and contraction from humidity levels and temperature; they just move at so small a rate that we would hardly trouble to measure it. Sculptures of stone may be less moveable from temperature than metal, but again, the movement in each case is hardly noticeable. The movement by wind and air current works a great effect on wildflowers and plants in the great outdoors, less so indoors, but not much less than the workings of air currents on paper mobiles and other delicate sculptures. All materials degrade over time, although with some care there are media that seem "permanent." All that this reflects is our comfort level with a semblance of permanence corresponding to our time of observation in the presence of the

65. *See* H.R. Rep. No. 94-1476, at 5665 (1976) (legislative history of 1976 Act that discusses the media-neutrality of fixation).

66. *See* 17 U.S.C. § 102(a).

67. *Id.*

68. *See* Murray, *Post-Myriad Genetics, supra,* at 107-09.

work. A highly fugitive dye placed in direct sunlight will give up its color faster than a wildflower. Neither is permanent, yet the chemical media will not draw the attention of a jurist in the manner that living media will.[69]

Last, the fact that some artistic installations might resemble something else — a garden — is not a question concerning copyrightability, it is one of aesthetics and philosophy. If the issue was 'is this art,' we might ponder for a time whether an expressive composition of living matter was sufficiently artistic to meet our standards when it was created by a self-proclaimed gardener as opposed to a self-proclaimed or externally-certified artist. We tend not to credit the work of first-time amateurs as high art, although on occasion the results are very intricate and beautiful. Nevertheless, the issue here is copyrightability, and the artistic merit of the work or the creator never has been a requirement for copyrightability.[70]

And what makes living media expressive? Color, shape, forms, textures — all of which are possessed by wildflowers and living media as well as, and often to a greater degree than other media such as paint in tubes, a blank canvas, or a mound of sculpting clay. The same attributes of color, shape, forms, and textures that provide the difference in the expression perceived from a blank white canvas compared to that of a highly-detailed landscape are provided by a palate of wildflowers combined and arranged on dark earth.[71]

Kelley is a peculiar case — not necessarily predictive of future cases, but for now it exists as a precedent in the law.

H. Limitations on Copyrightability: The Merger and Scènes à Faire Doctrines

The originality requirement and the idea-expression doctrine lead to two concepts of copyright law called scènes à faire and merger.[72] Both restrict the subject matter that may become subject to copyright. As noted above, only the artist's particularly original and creative expressions of the common attributes of a natural subject can achieve copyright protection.[73] No one can obtain a copyright on the actual appearance of Oscar Wilde or the realistic rendition of a tiger that features the animal with orangish fur and black slashing stripes because these are characteristics common to all tigers, and necessary to include so that the work can communicate the concept of a "tiger" to the viewer. Natural characteristics of objects and living things are examples of "scènes à faire" (translated from the French as "scenes that must be

---

69. *See id.* at 108-09.

70. *See id.* at 109.

71. *Id.*

72. *Oracle Am., Inc. v. Google Inc.*, 750 F.3d 1339, 1363 (Fed. Cir. 2014), *cert. denied*, 135 S. Ct. 2887 (2015); *Zalewski v. Cicero Builder Dev., Inc.*, 754 F.3d 95, 102 (2d Cir. 2014).

73. *Zalewski*, 754 F.3d at 102.

done").[74] Scènes à faire includes stock images (a building with a bell over the front door to mean a school; a building with a tower and cross over the front door to mean a church), standard depictions (a hammock, pitcher of lemonade, and sunglasses to mean summertime; a car with suitcases strapped to the roof to mean "on vacation"), the appearance of actual objects, and common themes and ideas associated with life that are not copyrightable and may be appropriated by any artist who wishes to depict the scene or the theme. The more realistic the depiction of a natural object or scene, the less of the work that can be protected under copyright.

Scènes à faire can be understood to reflect the fact that much art and literature builds on earlier works, and over time, certain themes, scenes, and ways of describing or depicting things have become standard.[75] Suspenseful stories start on dark and stormy nights; urban police dramas will have an old Irish cop or two on board; Westerns will involve a crime, a hunt down, a confrontation, and a resolution by violence. No one gains any credit or copyright protection from adopting these motifs, passages, or scenes — they simply must be done, as the term states — and they certainly are not created by, or original to, the artist.

The concept of merger in copyright parallels scènes à faire. Merger holds that if there are a limited number of ways to express a concept or idea, then copyright will not afford one author with a monopoly over those limited ways.[76] Copyright law states that in these circumstances the idea and the expression have merged, so that neither one will fall within one author's copyright, and both the idea and the expression will be free to all to use and exploit.[77]

There are a lot of simple examples of merger working in literature and other non-artistic contexts involving the written word.[78] With the limitations of language, there are often a limited number of ways of stating certain ideas and concepts.[79] If you want to talk about a dark and stormy night, you are going to have to use words such as dark, stormy, and night, so no author who wrote an earlier description of a dark and stormy night can sue to preclude you from writing your description.

Merger should have less impact in the visual arts, because intelligent jurists and lawyers should recognize that there are thousands of ways of depicting concepts and themes visually.[80] But merger does come up in the visual arts when a certain media and artistic technique produces a similar outward appearance in works. For example, certain glass blowing techniques will

---

74. *Oracle Am.*, 750 F.3d at 1363; *Zalewski*, 754 F.3d at 102.

75. *See Harney v. Sony Pictures Television, Inc.*, 704 F.3d 173, 181 (1st Cir. 2013).

76. *See id.*; *Oracle Am.*, 750 F.3d at 1359.

77. *See Nola Spice Designs, L.L.C. v. Haydel Enterprises, Inc.*, 783 F.3d 527, 549 (5th Cir. 2015); *Oracle Am.*, 750 F.3d at 1359; *Harney*, 704 F.3d at 181; *Satava v. Lowry*, 323 F.3d 805, 812 n. 5 (9th Cir. 2003).

78. *E.g.*, *Baker v. Selden*, 101 U.S. 99 (1879); *Kregos v. Associated Press*, 937 F.2d 700, 705 (2d Cir.1991); *Arica Inst., Inc. v. Palmer*, 970 F.2d 1067, 1076 (2d Cir. 1992).

79. *See, e.g.*, *Greene v. Ablon*, 794 F.3d 133, 160 (1st Cir. 2015); *Oracle Am.*, 750 F.3d at 1359; *Nola Spice Designs*, 783 F.3d at 549; *Zalewski*, 754 F.3d at 102.

80. *See* Murray, *Post-Myriad Genetics*, *supra*, at 107-09.

produce milky coloration, others will produce spirals and swirls. These techniques are generally not original to a single artist, and in any event, techniques and procedures are not copyrightable. If a similarity in appearance is attributed to the artists both using the same technique, it should not raise an issue of copyright infringement.[81]

Merger is sometimes described in the context of depicting scenes of a city that show its greatest landmark — the Eiffel Tower for Paris, the Leaning Tower for Pisa, the Gateway Arch for St. Louis — or common visual elements that are needed to tell the location, timing, season, or time period. For example, double-decker buses to indicate London; a shot of the moon and stars to show nighttime; orange leaves on trees to show autumn; clean-shaven soldiers carrying rifles with bayonets and wearing doughboy helmets and leggings to show World War I, as opposed to unshaven soldiers wearing rumpled jungle fatigues with helmets wrapped in mesh nets that hold packs of cigarettes and other small objects and carrying M-16 automatic rifles to indicate the Vietnam War. The idea of nightfall is merged with images that communicate dusk — dim lighting, fading sunset, silhouettes of trees, fireflies appearing, and the like. All of these are uncopyrightable imagery, free to be borrowed and exploited by all. In this manner, merger supplements scènes à faire with its "scenes that must be done" concept.

An artist who produces a work that has many uncopyrightable elements — either because the work is non-fictional and contains many facts, or is scientific and contains processes or procedures, or because the artist incorporated scènes à faire or merged elements that cannot be monopolized under copyright — is said to hold a "thin copyright" on the work.[82] Thin does not mean non-existent. However, it does mean that an alleged infringer will have to have taken a good chunk of the work in order to have copied enough *copyrightable* elements — in other words, with a thin copyright, virtually identical copying is required to bring an actionable case of infringement.[83]

Satava v. Lowry

323 F.3d 805 (9th Cir. 2003)*

GOULD, Circuit Judge.

In the Copyright Act, Congress sought to benefit the public by encouraging artists' creative expression. Congress carefully drew the contours of copyright

---

81. *See Nola Spice Designs*, 783 F.3d at 549; *Seng-Tiong Ho v. Taflove*, 648 F.3d 489, 497 (7th Cir. 2011); *Satava v. Lowry*, 323 F.3d 805, 812-13 (9th Cir. 2003); *Leigh v. Warner Bros.*, 212 F.3d 1210, 1215-16 (11th Cir. 2000); *Ets-Hokin v. Skyy Spirits, Inc.*, 323 F.3d 763, 765-66 (9th Cir. 2003).

82. *Zalewski*, 754 F.3d at 103; *Bldg. Graphics, Inc. v. Lennar Corp.*, 708 F.3d 573, 578 (4th Cir. 2013); *Mattel, Inc. v. MGA Entm't, Inc.*, 616 F.3d 904, 915 (9th Cir. 2010), *as amended on denial of reh'g* (Oct. 21, 2010).

83. E.g., *Mattel*, 616 F.3d at 915 (thin copyright only can protect against virtually identical copying); *Meshwerks, Inc. v. Toyota Motor Sales U.S.A., Inc.*, 528 F.3d 1258, 1265 (10th Cir. 2008) ("thin" copyright offers protection only from exact duplication by others).

* Citations and certain footnotes omitted.

protection to achieve this goal. It granted artists the exclusive right to the original expression in their works, thereby giving them a financial incentive to create works to enrich our culture.

 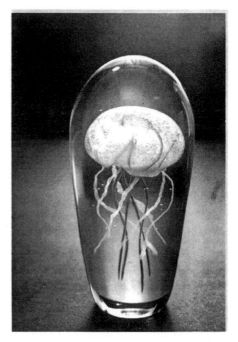

But it denied artists the exclusive right to ideas and standard elements in their works, thereby preventing them from monopolizing what rightfully belongs to the public. In this case, we must locate the faint line between unprotected idea and original expression in the context of realistic animal sculpture. We must decide whether an artist's lifelike glass-in-glass sculptures of jellyfish are protectable by copyright. [See photograph of Satava's sculpture, above at left, and photograph of Lowry's sculpture, above at right[84]]. . . .

Copyright protection is available for "original works of authorship fixed in any tangible medium of expression, now known or later developed, from which they can be perceived, reproduced, or otherwise communicated, either directly or with the aid of a machine or device." 17 U.S.C. § 102(a). Copyright protection does not, however, "extend to any idea, procedure, process, system, method of operation, concept, principle, or discovery. . . ." 17 U.S.C. § 102(b).

Any copyrighted expression must be "original." Although the amount of creative input by the author required to meet the originality standard is low, it is not negligible. There must be something more than a "merely trivial" variation, something recognizably the artist's own.

---

84. Michael D. Murray, Cropped, revised, and resized image of a Satava sculpture and a Lowey sculpture, derived from the exhibits to the Ninth Circuit's opinion in *Satava v. Lowry*, 323 F.3d 805 (9th Cir. 2003).

The originality requirement mandates that objective "facts" and ideas are not copyrightable. Similarly, expressions that are standard, stock, or common to a particular subject matter or medium are not protectable under copyright law.[2]

It follows from these principles that no copyright protection may be afforded to the idea of producing a glass-in-glass jellyfish sculpture or to elements of expression that naturally follow from the idea of such a sculpture. Satava may not prevent others from copying aspects of his sculptures resulting from either jellyfish physiology or from their depiction in the glass-in-glass medium. Satava may not prevent others from depicting jellyfish with tendril-like tentacles or rounded bells, because many jellyfish possess those body parts. He may not prevent others from depicting jellyfish in bright colors, because many jellyfish are brightly colored. He may not prevent others from depicting jellyfish swimming vertically, because jellyfish swim vertically in nature and often are depicted swimming vertically.[3]

Satava may not prevent others from depicting jellyfish within a clear outer layer of glass, because clear glass is the most appropriate setting for an aquatic animal. He may not prevent others from depicting jellyfish "almost filling the entire volume" of the outer glass shroud, because such proportion is standard in glass-in-glass sculpture. And he may not prevent others from tapering the shape of their shrouds, because that shape is standard in glass-in-glass sculpture.

Satava's glass-in-glass jellyfish sculptures, though beautiful, combine several unprotectable ideas and standard elements. These elements are part of the public domain. They are the common property of all, and Satava may not use copyright law to seize them for his exclusive use.

It is true, of course, that a combination of unprotectable elements may qualify for copyright protection. But it is not true that any combination of unprotectable elements automatically qualifies for copyright protection. Our case law suggests, and we hold today, that a combination of unprotectable elements is eligible for copyright protection only if those elements are numerous enough and their selection and arrangement original enough that their combination constitutes an original work of authorship.

The combination of unprotectable elements in Satava's sculpture falls short of this standard. The selection of the clear glass, oblong shroud, bright colors, proportion, vertical orientation, and stereotyped jellyfish form, considered together, lacks the quantum of originality needed to merit copyright protection. These elements are so commonplace in glass-in-glass sculpture and

---

2. Standard elements sometimes are called "scènes à faire," vaguely French for "scenes which 'must' be done." The Ninth Circuit treats scènes à faire as a defense to infringement rather than as a barrier to copyrightability.

3. Vertical orientation is a standard element partly because human beings prefer the world right-side-up.

so typical of jellyfish physiology that to recognize copyright protection in their combination effectively would give Satava a monopoly on lifelike glass-in-glass sculptures of single jellyfish with vertical tentacles. Because the quantum of originality Satava added in combining these standard and stereotyped elements must be considered "trivial" under our case law, Satava cannot prevent other artists from combining them. . . .

We do not mean to suggest that Satava has added nothing copyrightable to his jellyfish sculptures. He has made some copyrightable contributions: the distinctive curls of particular tendrils; the arrangement of certain hues; the unique shape of jellyfishes' bells. To the extent that these and other artistic choices were not governed by jellyfish physiology or the glass-in-glass medium, they are original elements that Satava theoretically may protect through copyright law. Satava's copyright on these original elements (or their combination) is "thin," however, comprising no more than his original contribution to ideas already in the public domain. Stated another way, Satava may prevent others from copying the original features he contributed, but he may not prevent others from copying elements of expression that nature displays for all observers, or that the glass-in-glass medium suggests to all sculptors. Satava possesses a thin copyright that protects against only virtually identical copying.

We do not hold that realistic depictions of live animals cannot be protected by copyright. In fact, we have held to the contrary. We recognize, however, that the scope of copyright protection in such works is narrow. Nature gives us ideas of animals in their natural surroundings: an eagle with talons extended to snatch a mouse; a grizzly bear clutching a salmon between its teeth; a butterfly emerging from its cocoon; a wolf howling at the full moon; a jellyfish swimming through tropical waters. These ideas, first expressed by nature, are the common heritage of humankind, and no artist may use copyright law to prevent others from depicting them.

An artist may, however, protect the original expression he or she contributes to these ideas. An artist may vary the pose, attitude, gesture, muscle structure, facial expression, coat, or texture of animal. An artist may vary the background, lighting, or perspective. Such variations, if original, may earn copyright protection. Because Satava's jellyfish sculptures contain few variations of this type, the scope of his copyright is narrow.

We do not mean to short-change the legitimate need of creative artists to protect their original works. After all, copyright law achieves its high purpose of enriching our culture by giving artists a financial incentive to create. But we must be careful in copyright cases not to cheat the public domain. Only by vigorously policing the line between idea and expression can we ensure both that artists receive due reward for their original creations and that proper latitude is granted other artists to make use of ideas that properly belong to us all.

REVERSED.

Mattel, Inc. v. Goldberger Doll Mfg. Co.

365 F.3d 133 (2d Cir. 2004)*

LEVAL, Circuit Judge.

Plaintiff Mattel, Inc., appeals from a grant of summary judgment by the United States District Court for the Southern District of New York (Rakoff, J.) in favor of the defendant Radio City Entertainment ("Radio City"). Mattel is the creator of, and owns copyrights in, the world famous "Barbie doll," whose current sales exceed $1 billion per year worldwide. Defendant Radio City operates the Radio City Music Hall theater in New York City, which features the widely renowned Rockettes chorus line. To celebrate the millennium, Radio City (together with its co-defendants) created a doll, which it named the "Rockettes 2000" doll. Mattel brought this suit alleging that in designing the Rockette doll, Radio City infringed its copyrights by copying facial features from two different Barbie dolls — "Neptune's Daughter Barbie," registered in 1992, and "CEO Barbie," registered in 1999. It is not reasonably subject to dispute that the Rockette doll is, in several respects including central features of the face, quite similar to the Barbie dolls. The district court granted the defendant's motion for summary judgment.

The court assumed for the purposes of the summary judgment motion that the defendant had copied the Rockette doll's eyes, nose, and mouth from Barbie. It concluded, however, "When it comes to something as common as a youthful, female doll, the unprotectible elements are legion, including, e.g., full faces; pert, upturned noses; bow lips; large, widely spaced eyes; and slim figures" (internal quotation marks omitted). Believing that copyright protection did not extend to Barbie's eyes, nose, and mouth, the court excluded similarity as to those features from the determination whether there was substantial similarity between plaintiff's and defendant's dolls. It concluded in comparing the other parts of the respective heads that there was no substantial similarity and therefore entered summary judgment for the defendant. *Mattel, Inc. v. Radio City Entm't*, 2002 WL 1300265, at *1 (S.D.N.Y. June 12, 2002), 2002 U.S. Dist. LEXIS 10517, at *3-*4. Mattel brought this appeal.

DISCUSSION

The court's conclusion that the eyes, nose, and mouth of the registered Barbie faces were not protected by copyright was erroneous.

In explanation of this conclusion, the court relied on our 1966 opinion in *Ideal Toy Corp. v. Fab-Lu Ltd.*, 360 F.2d 1021 (1966). In that case, the district court had denied a preliminary injunction to one doll manufacturer who accused another of copying. On appeal, we found that the district court had not abused its discretion in finding that the plaintiff had failed to show a likelihood of success on the merits, and therefore affirmed. Comparing the

---

* Footnotes omitted.

dolls at issue, we observed that "similarities exist as to standard doll features such as the full faces; pert, upturned noses; bow lips; large, widely spaced eyes; and slim figures." *Id.* at 1023. On the other hand we noted that there were "distinct differences" as to the neck, hair style, chin structure, overall craftsmanship, and head design, the last of which was "the gravamen of [the] infringement claim." *Id.* We thus concluded that the district court had not abused its discretion in its assessment that the plaintiff had not shown a likelihood of success on the "substantial similarity" prong of its claim.

Although in *Ideal Toy* we described the facial features of the dolls then before us as "standard," we did not say that those facial features were not protected by copyright. To the contrary, we included those features in our comparison of the dolls, noting both the similarity in those features and the differences in others. When the case returned to the district court for trial, following our affirmance of the denial of the preliminary injunction, the defendant, which had previously denied copying, now admitted it. *See Ideal Toy Corp. v. Fab-Lu, Ltd.*, 261 F. Supp. 238, 240 (S.D.N.Y. 1966). Judge Weinfeld then found infringement and imposed liability. *Id.* at 242. In describing the respects in which the defendant's dolls were substantially similar to those of the plaintiff, i.e. the similarities that sustained the judgment of liability, Judge Weinfeld specifically noted the similarity in the "large widely spaced eyes, . . . pert upturned noses, [and] bow lips." *Id.* Judge Weinfeld clearly did not understand our prior ruling as suggesting that the features we described as standard were unprotected.

The proposition that standard or common features are not protected is inconsistent with copyright law. To merit protection from copying, a work need not be particularly novel or unusual. It need only have been "independently created" by the author and possess "some minimal degree of creativity." *Feist Publ'ns, Inc. v. Rural Tel. Serv. Co.*, 499 U.S. 340, 345, 111 S. Ct. 1282, 113 L. Ed. 2d 358 (1991). As the Supreme Court has explained, the "requisite level of creativity is extremely low; even a slight amount will suffice. The vast majority of works make the grade quite easily, as they possess some creative spark, no matter how crude, humble or obvious it might be." *Id.* (internal quotation marks omitted). There are innumerable ways of making upturned noses, bow lips, and widely spaced eyes. Even if the record had shown that many dolls possess upturned noses, bow lips, and wide-spread eyes, it would not follow that each such doll — assuming it was independently created and not copied from others — would not enjoy protection from copying. We have often affirmed entitlement to copyright protection so long as the work was in fact created by its author, notwithstanding "lack of creativity," *Thomas Wilson & Co. v. Irving J. Dorfman Co.*, 433 F.2d 409, 411 (2d Cir. 1970) (lace design, although not a "work of art," possessed "more than the faint trace of originality required"), "lack of artistic merit," *Rushton v. Vitale*, 218 F.2d 434, 435-36 (2d Cir. 1955) (chimpanzee doll showed more than "merely trivial" originality), and absence of anything "strikingly unique or novel," *Alfred Bell &*

Co. v. Catalda Fine Arts, Inc., 191 F.2d 99, 102-03 (2d Cir. 1951) ("All that is needed . . . is that the author contributed something more than a merely trivial variation, something recognizably his own. Originality in this context means little more than a prohibition of actual copying. No matter how poor artistically the author's addition, it is enough if it be his own") (internal quotation marks omitted).

On Radio City's motion for summary judgment, we must view the evidence in the light most favorable to Mattel. Uncontradicted evidence shows the Barbie visage was independently created by Mattel. Nothing in the record gives reason to doubt that its creation involved whatever minimal creativity or originality is need to satisfy the requirement of authorship. The evidence Mattel submitted is sufficient to justify copyright protection for the central expressive features of Barbie's face.

The protection that flows from such a copyright is, of course, quite limited. The copyright does not protect ideas; it protects only the author's particularized expression of the idea. *See Attia v. Soc'y of the N.Y. Hosp.*, 201 F.3d 50, 55 (2d Cir. 1999) (architect's copyright was not infringed by copying of his "concepts and ideas"); *Peter Pan Fabrics, Inc. v. Martin Weiner Corp.*, 274 F.2d 487, 489 (2d Cir. 1960) (L. Hand, J.) ("[T]here can be no copyright in the 'ideas' disclosed but only in their 'expression.'"); *Nichols v. Universal Pictures Corp.*, 45 F.2d 119, 121 (2d Cir. 1930) (L. Hand, J.) (a playwright's copyright was not violated by a movie script on similar themes). Thus, Mattel's copyright in a doll visage with an upturned nose, bow lips, and widely spaced eyes will not prevent a competitor from making dolls with upturned noses, bow lips, and widely spaced eyes, even if the competitor has taken the idea from Mattel's example, so long as the competitor has not copied Mattel's particularized expression. An upturned nose, bow lips, and wide eyes are the "idea" of a certain type of doll face. That idea belongs not to Mattel but to the public domain. *See Mattel, Inc. v. Azrak-Hamway Int'l, Inc.*, 724 F.2d 357, 360 (2d Cir. 1983) (creator of a muscle-bound action doll has copyright in "particularized expression [such as] the decision to accentuate certain muscle groups relative to others" even though imitator is free to make dolls expressing the same general idea). But Mattel's copyright will protect its own particularized expression of that idea and bar a competitor from copying Mattel's realization of the Barbie features.

The distinction between the idea and the expression, although famously difficult to apply, is of great importance. One artist's version of a doll face with upturned nose, bow lips, and widely spaced eyes will be irresistible to an eight-year-old collector. Another artist's version, which to a grownup may look very like the first, will be a dud to the eight-year-old. The law of copyright guarantees to the designer of the successful version that, although its idea for a certain type of work is freely available to others who would imitate it, the designer cannot be deprived of the benefit of its successful design by others' copying it. We can surmise that in the highly competitive, billion-dollar doll industry, getting the doll's face and expression exactly right is crucial to success. Mattel's evidence showed that it frequently produces revisions and adjustments to the particular realization of the Barbie face in an effort to continue to appeal to its young customers, as their tastes change with time. It is entitled by its copyright not to have its design copied by competitors.

We express no view as to whether the Rockette doll was copied from Barbie. However, because the district court erred in concluding that the defendant could freely copy the central facial features of the Barbie dolls without infringing Mattel's copyright, we vacate the grant of summary judgment and remand for trial.

CONCLUSION

The judgment is vacated and the case remanded for further proceedings.

Total Concept, Look, and Feel of Doll Faces

The "total concept, look, and feel" test examines the entire composition of the first work as against the entire composition of the second work. If it finds similarities, then the court examines what compositional elements of the two works are similar. It may be that it is the total arrangement and composition of otherwise unoriginal, uncopyrightable parts that has been copied, and an original, creative compilation and arrangement can be copyrighted.

Take doll faces for example. Each is made up of some predictable elements — large, widely separated eyes with exaggerated eye lashes; a small, pert nose; small, bow-shaped lips; rosy, healthy looking cheeks.[85]

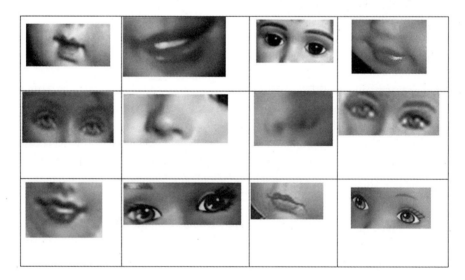

---

85. Michael D. Murray, Collage of cropped, revised, and resized thumbnail images derived from photographs of common features of doll faces, to illustrate the facts of *Mattel, Inc. v. Goldberger Doll Mfg. Co.*, 365 F.3d 133 (2d Cir. 2004).

If you add all of these together, you get your doll face — a unique compilation and arrangement.[86]

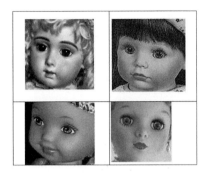

What you don't automatically get is Barbie's doll face. Look closely at the three doll heads here.[87] Two are real Barbies, one is an imposter bought on the streets of an Italian city. Which is the imposter?

If you said the doll in the middle without much hesitation, that is because Mattel has gone to great lengths to put together a unique combination of otherwise unprotectable features to make a Barbie face. Add standard bow lips, a pert nose, healthy cheeks to widely spaced, disproportionately large eyes, with just the right exaggeration of eye liner, brow, and lashes, and you have a Barbie — unmistakably so. Add too much eye liner and clumpy lashes, and you have a cheap counterfeit of Barbie. So, can Barbie win a copyright action? You bet, as long as the court uses the total concept, look, and feel test. This is what the court in *Mattel Inc. v. Goldberger Doll*[88] did, and found that Goldberger's Rocketts doll looked a whole lot like a Barbie, and infringed the doll.

---

86. Michael D. Murray, Collage of cropped, revised, and resized thumbnail images derived from photographs of doll faces, to illustrate the facts of *Mattel, Inc. v. Goldberger Doll Mfg. Co.*, 365 F.3d 133 (2d Cir. 2004).

87. Michael D. Murray, Cropped, revised, and resized photograph by Michael Murray (2007) depicting two actual Mattel Barbie dolls and one Italian counterfeit "Barbie" doll, to illustrate the facts of *Mattel, Inc. v. Goldberger Doll Mfg. Co.*, 365 F.3d 133 (2d Cir. 2004).

88. *Goldberger Doll*, 365 F.3d at 133.

> **Working within Scènes à faire and Merger**
>   How should an artist create works with the maximum number of copyrightable elements under the scènes à faire and merger doctrines?
>
>   ■ Be creative; arrange and compile uncopyrightable material in a very original way.
>   ■ Be impressionistic — not literal about depictions of things in the world.
>   ■ Think outside the box, and don't fall back on stock forms, scenes, images, and characters.

Notes and Questions

1. Did the plaintiff in *Satava* — the original creator of the glass-in-glass jellyfish works — get a raw deal? Should all of his hard work and years perfecting the art of making attractive jellyfish sculptures in glass count for nothing under the copyright law? Or did he just make a poor choice of subject matter for his efforts?

2. The plaintiff in *Satava* asked the court to evaluate the total concept and the look and feel of the two works to see if one copies off the other. This argument has not found favor in "thin copyright" cases in the Ninth Circuit. In *Apple Computer, Inc. v. Microsoft Corp.*, 35 F.3d 1435, 1446 (9th Cir. 1994), the court refused to look at the overall look and feel of Apple's desktop as compared with the look and feel of early versions of Microsoft's Windows' desktop, because many individual elements of the Apple product were unprotected and needed to be "filtered out" before the court would compare the total look and feel. In effect, the court applied a "sum of the protectable parts" approach rather than examining the total concept and look and feel of the two products.

3. In contrast to the Ninth Circuit's approach, the Second Circuit in *Mattel v. Goldberger Doll* found that the individual manifestations of common doll features (broad faces; large, widely set eyes; pert, upturned noses; bow lips) in Mattel's Barbie doll still were copyrightable because Mattel's particular configuration and realization of these features in its doll were original. *Compare JCW Investments, Inc. v. Novelty, Inc.*, 482 F.3d 910 (7th Cir. 2007), and *Winfield Collection, Ltd. v. Gemmy Industries, Corp.*, 147 Fed. Appx. 547 (6th Cir. 2005), and *Boisson v. Banian, Ltd.*, 273 F.3d 262, 272 (2d Cir. 2001) ("a court is not to dissect the works at issue into separate components and compare only the copyrightable elements," but rather to compare "the 'total concept and feel' of the contested works."), *with Corwin v. Walt Disney Co.*, 475 F.3d 1239 (11th Cir. 2007) (incidents, characters, or settings that are indispensable to or standard in a theme park with an international focus are not copyrightable; common ideas and themes could not

support a finding of striking similarity), *and Inkadinkado, Inc. v. Meyer,* 2003 WL 22282177, 2003 Copr. L. Dec. ¶26,681 (D. Mass. Sept. 16, 2003) (preliminary injunction denied for lack of showing of likelihood of success on merits of claim that combinations of public domain clip art were original and creative enough for copyright protection). *See also* Michael D. Murray, *Copyright, Originality, and the End of the Scènes à Faire and Merger Doctrines for Visual Works,* 58 BAYLOR L. REV. 779 (2006). Which is more fair — the Second Circuit's approach or the Ninth Circuit's? Would the outcome have been different in *Satava* if the case had been determined under the Second Circuit's approach? And would *Mattel v. Goldberger Doll* have had a different outcome if the Ninth Circuit's approach had been used?

4. The Ninth Circuit's "dissection and filtration" approach becomes tricky to manage once the case passes through the summary judgment phase and moves to a jury trial. In *Dream Games of Arizona, Inc. v. PC Onsite,* 561 F.3d 983 (9th Cir. 2009), the court held that it was appropriate for the jury in a copyright infringement action to see unprotected elements of a copyrighted electronic video bingo game, such as bingo cards and game function buttons, so that it could assess whether the combination of such elements warranted protection. The court instructed the jury that plaintiff had to show that accused screen displays were virtually identical to protected elements of corresponding screen displays of its game, and the court instructed that a combination of unprotectable elements could be entitled to some copyright protection if the two works are virtually identical. Under *Apple Computer,* the instructions must identify in detail those elements of the copyrighted work that are not protected, but the jury instructions were not required to identify one or more of the game's protectable elements singularly or describe the possible combinations of unprotected elements that could combine to produce a protectable whole.

5. The depiction of natural objects, such as wildlife, does present interesting issues in copyright cases. At what point does one visual work depicting a "fact" of reality become substantially similar to an earlier work depicting the same fact of reality so as to become actionable in an infringement suit? Visual art depicting wildlife presents this problem because one realistic depiction of a natural creature will necessarily resemble another depiction of the same type of creature regardless of the presence or absence of copying. Courts have wrestled with the problem, as in *Satava* above, with varying results. *Compare Dyer v. Napier,* No. CIV 04-0408-PHX-SMM, 2006 WL 2730747, 2006 COPR. L. Dec. P 29, 242, 81 U.S.P.Q.2d 1035, 71 FED. R. EVID. SERV. 413 (D. Ariz. Sept. 25, 2006) (similar depictions of a mountain lion with a cub in its mouth were not actionable because images of nature are public domain), *with Hart v. Dan Chase Taxidermy Supply Co.,* 86 F.3d 320 (2d Cir. 1996) (fish taxidermy mannequins were original and copyrightable; infringement found), *and Superior Form Builders, Inc. v. Dan*

Chase Taxidermy Supply Co., 74 F.3d 488 (4th Cir. 1996) (same — animal taxidermy mannequins), and *Yurman Studio, Inc. v. Castaneda*, 591 F. Supp. 2d 471 (S.D.N.Y. 2008) (jewelry reflecting original combinations of unprotected elements is copyrightable).

6. A functional item must be more than the sum of its uncopyrightable parts to qualify under the "originality" and "creativity" standards of § 102. In *Lamps Plus, Inc. v. Seattle Lighting Fixture Co.*, 345 F.3d 1140 (9th Cir. 2003), a manufacturer and retailer of lighting products combined a Tiffany lamp-shade assembly originally designed to be attached to a ceiling for use as an overhead light, with a table-lamp base to form its Victorian Tiffany table lamp. Each element combined in the lamp was a preexisting work purchased from vendors in China. The shade assembly consists of four discrete pieces: a finial, a cap, a glass light shade, and a metal filigree previously used to form a ceiling lamp. Lamps Plus mechanically modified these parts so that they could function as a table lamp. The Ninth Circuit refused to recognize that the combination of unprotectable parts could add up to a copyrightable design. The court also declared that the functional elements of the lamp were not separable from the decorative design elements, thus precluding copyright over the decorative elements. This concept will be discussed further in the section below.

7. *Incredible Technologies, Inc. v. Virtual Technologies, Inc.*, 400 F.3d 1007 (7th Cir. 2005), rejected the infringement claim of one golf simulation video game manufacturer against the manufacturer of a competing game. The court found that the text and instructional graphics for the accused game were sufficiently different from the largely functional text and graphics used in copyrighted video arcade golf games to avoid infringement. The court held it to be sufficiently different for the accused game to use different arrow designs and different graphics to illustrate shot-shaping possibilities. The layout of controls on video arcade golf games was held to be dictated by functional considerations, and thus not entitled to copyright protection. Golf-related images and standard video game menu screens contained in both golf games' video displays were scènes à faire, entitled to protection only from virtually identical copying. The copyrighted display of the first game used imaginary courses and generic players, while the accused display used real courses and golfers and added extra graphical features.

I. Limits on Copyrightability: Useful Articles and Functional Works

The useful articles doctrine withholds copyright protection from "useful articles" — namely, works that have utilitarian application. "A 'useful article' is an article having an intrinsic utilitarian function that is not merely to portray the appearance of the article or to convey information."[89] The doctrine is designed to prevent the long term of copyright to apply to useful articles and creations as opposed to purely ornamental works or purely expressive works such as literature, music, and the like.[90]

Patents for Utility, Copyrights for Expression

Patent law protects innovation and invention, but the term is far more limited (20 years) than copyright, and the requirements are high. Patent law requires a true invention, not anticipated by other works and not something easily and readily anticipated by others skilled in the art and science of the invention.

In copyright, works are supposed to be ornamental and expressive, not useful. If a form has both expressive characteristics and function, the functional aspects will not be tied up in a copyright monopoly for the life of the creator plus 70 years.

The useful articles doctrine seeks to preserve competition and progress in the production of useful articles.[91] By keeping useful, functional works out of copyright protection, the doctrine allows competitors in industry to make useful articles without fear that the first competitor to design a product will have right to exclude all others who want to make the same product. Where form follows or leads to function, copyright could tie up a certain form for a term of life plus 70 years. That is a long time for a monopoly on a useful object.

Utility issues come up most often with sculpture. Is the work functional, and if so, is there a way to separate the functional aspects from the non-functional, ornamental, or purely expressive aspects? The separation can be literal (you actually can pull the components apart), or conceptual (some of the creative, original expression is unrelated to the functioning of the item — e.g., decoration — that is easy to identify as a separate original creation).

---

89. *Varsity Brands, Inc. v. Star Athletica, LLC*, 799 F.3d 468, 481 (6th Cir. 2015).

90. *See, e.g.,* 17 U.S.C. § 101 (definition of pictorial and graphic works including two-dimensional works of applied art); *Varsity Brands*, 799 F.3d at 481; *Home Legend, LLC v. Mannington Mills, Inc.*, 784 F.3d 1404, 1412-13 (11th Cir.), *cert. denied*, 136 S. Ct. 232 (2015).

91. *See Pivot Point Int'l, Inc. v. Charlene Products, Inc.*, 372 F.3d 913, 919-30 (7th Cir. 2004).

Esquire, Inc. v. Ringer

591 F.2d 796 (D.C. Cir. 1978), cert. denied, 449 U.S. 908 (1979)*

BAZELON, Circuit Judge.

This case presents the question whether the overall shape of certain outdoor lighting fixtures is eligible for copyright as a "work of art."[92] ... Appellee, Esquire, Inc. (Esquire) submitted three applications to the Copyright Office for registration of what it described as "artistic design(s) for lighting fixture(s)." Photographs accompanying the applications showed stationary outdoor luminaries or floodlights, of contemporary design, with rounded or elliptically-shaped housings. The applications asserted that the designs were eligible for copyright protection as "works of art." 17 U.S.C. § 5(g).

The Register of Copyrights (Register) refused to register Esquire's claims to copyright. The principal reason given was that Copyright Office regulations, specifically 37 C.F.R. § 202.10(c) (1976), preclude registration of the design of a utilitarian article, such as lighting fixtures, "when all of the design elements . . . are directly related to the useful functions of the article. . . ." The fixtures, according to the Register's analysis, did not contain "elements, either alone or in combination, which are capable of independent existence as a copyrightable pictorial, graphic, or sculptural work apart from the utilitarian aspect." . . .

Section 5(g) of the Copyright Act of 1909, 17 U.S.C. § 5(g), indicates that "(w)orks of art; models or designs for works of art" are eligible for copyright. The terse language of the statute is more fully elaborated in regulations drafted by the Register pursuant to Congressional authorization. The provision at issue, 37 C.F.R. § 202.10(c), provides as follows:

> (c) If the sole intrinsic function of an article is its utility, the fact that the article is unique and attractively shaped will not qualify it as a work of art. However, if the shape of a utilitarian article incorporates features, such as artistic sculpture, carving, or pictorial representation, which can be identified separately and are capable of existing independently as a work of art, such features will be eligible for registration.

. . . The Register's interpretation of § 202.10(c) derives from the principle that industrial designs are not eligible for copyright. Congress has repeatedly

---

* Citations and footnotes omitted.

92. Michael D. Murray, Cropped, revised, and resized image of the Esquire Lamp whose design was litigated in *Esquire, Inc. v. Ringer*, 591 F.2d 796 (D.C. Cir. 1978), *cert. denied*, 449 U.S. 908 (1979).

rejected proposed legislation that would make copyright protection available for consumer or industrial products. Most recently, Congress deleted a proposed section from the Copyright Act of 1976 that would have "create(d) a new limited form of copyright protection for 'original' designs which are clearly a part of a useful article, regardless of whether such designs could stand by themselves, separate from the article itself." In rejecting proposed Title II, Congress noted the administration's concern that to make such designs eligible for copyright would be to create a "new monopoly" having obvious and significant anti-competitive effects. The issues raised by Title II were left for further consideration in "more complete hearings" to follow the enactment of the 1976 Act.

In the Register's view, registration of the overall shape or configuration of utilitarian articles would lead to widespread copyright protection for industrial designs. The Register reasons that aesthetic considerations enter into the design of most useful objects. Thus, if overall shape or configuration can qualify as a "work of art," "the whole realm of consumer products [such as] garments, toasters, refrigerators, furniture, bathtubs, automobiles, etc. and industrial products designed to have aesthetic appeal [such as] subway cars, computers, photocopying machines, typewriters, adding machines, etc. must also qualify as works of art." . . .

The regulation in question attempts to define the boundaries between copyrightable "works of art" and noncopyrightable industrial designs. This is an issue of long-standing concern to the Copyright Office, and is clearly a matter in which the Register has considerable expertise. . . .

The House Report indicates that the section of the 1976 Act governing "pictorial, graphic and sculptural works" was intended "to draw as clear a line as possible between copyrightable works of applied art and uncopyrighted works of industrial design." The Report illustrates the distinction in the following terms:

> . . . although the shape of an industrial product may be aesthetically satisfying and valuable, the Committee's intention is not to offer it copyright protection under the bill. Unless the shape of an automobile, airplane, ladies' dress, food processor, television set, or any other industrial product contains some element that, physically or conceptually, can be identified as separable from the utilitarian aspects of that article, the design would not be copyrighted under the bill. The test of separability and independence from "the utilitarian aspects of the article" does not depend upon the nature of the design that is, even if the appearance of an article is determined by esthetic (as opposed to functional) considerations, only elements, if any, which can be identified separately from the useful article as such are copyrightable. And even if the three dimensional design contains some such element (for example, a carving on the back of a chair or a floral relief design on silver flatware), copyright protection would extend only to that element, and would not cover the over-all configuration of the utilitarian article as such.

H. Rep. No. 1476, 94th Cong., 2d Sess. 55 (1976), U.S. CODE CONG. & ADMIN. NEWS 1976, p. 5668.

Current Cases: Conceptual and Physical Separability	
Varsity Brands, Inc. v. Star Athletica, LLC, 799 F.3d 468 (6th Cir. 2015)	In *Varsity Brands*, plaintiff Varsity alleged that defendant Star infringed Varsity's two-dimensional copyrights by manufacturing cheerleading uniforms incorporating the same two-dimensional designs. Defendant alleged that since the functional aspects of clothing (including uniforms) cannot be separated from the design elements that make each article useful, Varsity's designs[93] were not copyrightable. The district court held that a cheerleading uniform is not a cheerleading uniform without stripes, chevrons, etc., and that Varsity's copyrights were therefore invalid because the artistic elements were not physically or conceptually separable from the utilitarian aspects of the uniforms. However, the Sixth Circuit court reversed and remanded the case. The Sixth Circuit court used a hybrid approach to determining conceptual separability, asking (1) is the design a pictorial, graphic, or sculptural work, (2) if so, then is it a design of a useful article, (3) what are the utilitarian aspects of the useful article, (4) can the viewer of the design identify pictorial, graphic, or sculptural features separately from the utilitarian aspects of the useful article, and (5) can the pictorial, graphic, or sculptural features of the design of the useful article exist independently of the utilitarian aspects of the useful article, thereby combining the objectively-necessary approach with the design-process approach, as well as the Copyright-Office's approach in determining whether a work was copyrightable. 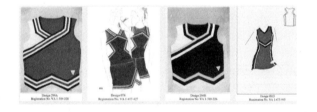
Home Legend, LLC v. Mannington Mills, Inc., 784 F.3d 1404 (11th Cir. 2015)	Both Plaintiff Home Legend and Defendant Mannington Mills sell laminated flooring products. Mannington claimed it owned a copyright for its "Glazed Maple" design, but Home Legend, maker of a similar "Distressed Maple Mendocino" design, argued that Mannington's copyright was invalid because Mannington could not obtain copyright protection for a useful article (among other claims). Mannington argued in turn that the décor paper layer of the flooring product was "for all intents and purposes, like putting a painting

---

93. Michael D. Murray, Cropped, revised, and resized thumbnail images derived from exhibits depicting Varsity Brand cheerleading uniform designs, at issue in *Varsity Brands, Inc. v. Star Athletica, LLC*, 799 F.3d 468 (6th Cir. 2015).

Current Cases: Conceptual and Physical Separability	
	on the floor," and was therefore copyrightable as a work of art. The district court held that even though Mannington had obtained a copyright for the 2-D artwork, the 2-D artwork element of the laminate flooring was not separable from the utilitarian aspect of the flooring since the laminate flooring was not marketable if its functional elements   Distressed Maple Mendocino Glazed Maple 94 were separated from the artistic elements, and conversely, the 2-D artwork would not be marketable if separated from the functional elements of the flooring. However, the circuit court disagreed, reasoning that the flooring and the décor paper were both physically separable (the décor paper was interchangeable and removable from the flooring) and conceptually separable (the pattern could reasonably be used as wallpaper, a picture frame, or just a piece of art). The court therefore concluded that the defendant's work was sufficiently original and conceptually separable from the utilitarian aspects of the flooring to qualify for copyright protection.
Inhale, Inc. v. Starbuzz Tobacco, Inc., 755 F.3d 1038 (9th Cir. 2014)	Plaintiff Inhale, Inc. claimed copyright protection for the shape of a hookah water container it registered with the U.S. Copyright Office in 2011. Plaintiff claimed that Defendant Starbuzz sold hookah water containers identical in shape to plaintiff's container.[95] Both plaintiff and defendant agreed that plaintiff's hookah water container is a "useful article," but differed on whether there is a sculptural feature that can be identified separately from, and is capable of existing independently of, the utilitarian aspects of the container. It is important to note that Inhale's container had the skull and cross-bones design on it, and Starbuzz's container did not; thus, the claim was not about the ornamental design on Inhale's container, but only the shape of the container.  Inhale, Inc. Starbuzz Tobacco

---

94. Michael D. Murray, Cropped, revised, and resized thumbnail images derived from exhibits depicting Home Legend's "Distressed Maple Mendocino" design and Mannington Mills' "Glazed Maple" design, at issue in *Home Legend, LLC v. Mannington Mills, Inc.*, 784 F.3d 1404 (11th Cir. 2015).

95. Michael D. Murray, Cropped, revised, and resized thumbnail images derived from exhibits depicting Inhale, Inc.'s and Starbuzz Tobacco's hookah water container designs, at issue in *Inhale, Inc. v. Starbuzz Tobacco, Inc.*, 755 F.3d 1038 (9th Cir. 2014).

Current Cases: Conceptual and Physical Separability	
	The Ninth Circuit relied on (1) *Ets-Hokin v Skyy Spirits, Inc.*, 745 F.2d 1239 (9th Cir. 1984) [discussed above in section H, "Limitations on Copyrightability: The Merger and Scènes à Faire Doctrines"], which held that the shape of a vodka bottle was not separable from its utilitarian features, and (2) the Copyright Office's reasoning that an item's distinctive shape does not affect separability, in its decision that the artistic element of the shape of Inhale's hookah water container was not conceptually separable from its utilitarian function and therefore was not copyrightable.
Klauber Bros., Inc. v. Target Corp., 2015 Copr. L. Dec. P 30, 795, 116 U.S.P.Q.2d 1165 (S.D.N.Y. Jul. 16, 2015)	

An in-house designer for Klauber created a lace design ("7725 Design").[96] Defendant Target chose the 7725 Design for undergarment waistbands in 2008; initially, its two manufacturers produced undergarments using Klauber's 7725 lace, but a Chinese lace company (Sei Hoi) "re-engineered" the 7725 lace. Target began selling panties featuring the Sei Hoi lace in 2010 or 2011. Defendants argued that the 7725 Design is not conceptually separable from the useful article of a waistband and is therefore unprotectable. Defendants argued the lace design was a functional part of a garment and that the lace design was not separable from the physical structure of the lace, and that certain aspects of the lace design were influenced by functional limitations relating to the inherent structure of lace. Plaintiffs countered with the argument that the 7725 Design is conceptually separable because the design could serve as something other than a waistband, such as a decorative trim or ornamental object. Plaintiff admitted that functional considerations affected parts of the 7725 Design but did not limit or dictate the designer's creativity. The court found that the 7725 Design was conceptually separable from the functional article of the waistband because it was "essentially a writing in the form of lace." |

96. Michael D. Murray, Cropped, revised, and resized thumbnail image derived from an exhibit depicting Klauber's lace design, at issue in *Klauber Bros., Inc. v. Target Corp.*, 2015 Copr. L. Dec. P 30, 795, 116 U.S.P.Q.2d 1165 (S.D.N.Y. 2015).

This excerpt is not entirely free from ambiguity. Esquire could arguably draw some support from the statement that a protectable element of a utilitarian article must be separable "physically or conceptually" from the utilitarian aspects of the design. But any possible ambiguity raised by this isolated reference disappears when the excerpt is considered in its entirety. The underscored passages indicate unequivocally that the overall design or configuration of a utilitarian object, even if it is determined by aesthetic as well as functional considerations, is not eligible for copyright. Thus the legislative history, taken as congressional understanding of existing law, reinforces the Register's position. . . .

For the aforesaid reasons, the decision of the district court is Reversed.

Notes and Questions

1. In the *Esquire Lamp* litigation, Judge Gesell of the district court took a different view from the Court of Appeals in his trial level opinion in *Esquire, Inc. v. Ringer*, 414 F. Supp. 939 (D.D.C. 1976), that was reversed by the Court of Appeals' opinion excerpted above:

   These outdoor lights serve both to decorate and to illuminate. Indeed, during the day they are exclusively decorative. They are a type of sculpture which is both original and aesthetically pleasing. Surely they would satisfy a Gropius or a Brancusi far more than would a Rembrandt portrait, and to many they are more artistic than some examples of sculpture found at such museums as the Corcoran or the Hirshhorn. Art through the ages has often served a utilitarian purpose. The Caryatids of the Acropolis or Cellini's exquisite saltcellar are two of many examples of traditional art serving such a purpose. There has always been a close link between art and science. The forms represented by Esquire's fixtures emphasize line and shape rather than the realistic or the ornate but it is not for the Register to reject them on artistic grounds, *Bleistein v. Donaldson Lithographing Co.*, supra, or because the form is accommodated to a utilitarian purpose, *Mazer v. Stein*, supra. There cannot be and there should not be any national standard of what constitutes art and the pleasing forms of the Esquire fixtures are entitled to the same recognition afforded more traditional sculpture.

2. In *Mazer v. Stein*, 347 U.S. 201 (1954), the Supreme Court found that statuettes used as lamp bases obviously were separable from the lamp

equipment, and thus could be independently copyrightable.[97] The fact that statuettes are a traditional form of artistic sculpture made it easier for the court to reach its decision. In *Esquire*, did the court of appeals simply fail to separate the artistic forms from "their mechanical or utilitarian aspects" or is something else going on here?

3. The Register's brief in the *Esquire* case illustrated the problems involved in allowing copyright of the shape of utilitarian articles:

> There are several economic considerations that Congress must weigh before deciding whether, for utilitarian articles, shape alone, no matter how aesthetically pleasing, is enough to warrant copyright protection. First, in the case of some utilitarian objects, like scissors or paper clips, shape is mandated by function. If one manufacturer were given the copyright to the design of such an article, it could completely prevent others from producing the same article. Second, consumer preference sometimes demands uniformity of shape for certain utilitarian articles, like stoves for instance. People simply expect and desire certain everyday useful articles to look the same particular way. Thus, to give one manufacturer the monopoly on such a shape would also be anticompetive [*sic*]. Third, insofar as geometric shapes are concerned, there are only a limited amount of basic shapes, such as circles, squares, rectangles and ellipses. These shapes are obviously in the public domain and accordingly it would be unfair to grant a monopoly on the use of any particular such shape, no matter how aesthetically well it was integrated into a utilitarian article.

Brief for Appellant at 18-19.

Is this argument persuasive, given that just about any form — modern or traditional, ornate or austere — can enclose the wiring and hold up the light socket and shade of a lamp? *Mazer* allowed statuette lamp bases to be copyrighted, so why not more modern sculptures?

---

97. Cropped, revised, and resized thumbnail images derived from photographs depicting statuettes used as lamp bases, derived from exhibits to the U.S. Supreme Court's opinion in *Mazer v. Stein*, 347 U.S. 201 (1954).

J. Duration of Copyright

The provisions of 17 U.S.C. § 302, 303, and 304, as amended by the Sonny Bono Copyright Term Extension Act of 1998, provide for the following terms:

Creation Date of Work	Initiation of Protection	Duration
After Jan. 1, 1978	When work is fixed in tangible medium of expression	Life + 70 years. [Jointly created works are measured by life of longest living coauthor]
		If work is of corporate authorship (including works for hire, anonymous, and pseudonymous works), duration is the shorter of 95 years from publication, or 120 years from creation
Before 1963	When published with notice [If no notice was given, the work has entered the public domain]	28 years, and it could have been renewed for 47 years and extended by law another 20 years for a total renewal of 67 years. [If not renewed, it is now in the public domain]
From 1964-1977	When published with notice [If no notice was given, the work has entered the public domain]	28 years, now automatically extended by law another renewal term of 67 years
Before Jan. 1, 1978 but not published	Jan. 1, 1978, the effective date of the 1976 Act which eliminated common law copyright	Life + 70 years or Dec. 31, 2002, whichever is greater
Before Jan. 1, 1978 but published between then and Dec. 31, 2002	Jan. 1, 1978, the effective date of the 1976 Act, which eliminated common law copyright	Life + 70 years or Dec. 31, 2047, whichever is greater
After Jan. 1, 1978 and before Mar. 1, 1989 (eff. date of Berne Convention Impl. Act)	When work is fixed in tangible medium of expression, but notice not given	Under § 405, registration must be made within five years of creation to retain copyright term of Life, + 70 years

The Constitution permits Congress to grant copyright protection only "for limited times." In general, the duration of a copyright in a work that is first fixed in a tangible medium of expression on or after January 1, 1978, is for the life of the author plus 70 years after the author's death. 17 U.S.C. § 302(a). Corporate owned works (including works for hire, anonymous, and pseudonymous works) enjoy a term of 95 years from first publication or for a term of 120 years from creation, whichever term expires first. 17 U.S.C. § 302(c). If the identity of one or more authors of such a work is revealed in a registration of the work or in a statement to the Copyright Office pursuant to § 302(c), providing the work is not a work made for hire, then the copyright shall extend for 70 years after the last author's death.

In *Eldred v. Ashcroft*,[98] the U.S. Supreme Court upheld the Copyright Term Extension Act (CTEA) — also known as the Sonny Bono Copyright Term Extension Act of 1998[99] — against a challenge that the Free Speech Clause, U.S. Const. amend. I, and the Copyright and Patent Clause, U.S. Const. art. I § 8, cl. 8, only allow Congress to extend the term of copyrights of future works, not the existing term of works already created or published. In rejecting the challenge, the Court noted that as in the case of prior extensions, principally in 1831, 1909, and 1976, in the Sonny Bono Copyright Term Extension Act, Congress provided for application of the enlarged terms to existing and future copyrights alike. The Court reasoned that copyright protection in general and extensions of copyright terms in particular do not impermissibly restrict free speech, for they grant the author an exclusive right only to the specific form of expression; they do not shield any idea or fact contained in the copyrighted work, and they allow for "fair use" even of the expression itself.

A majority of the court also rejected petitioners' Copyright Clause claim for interpretation of the "Limited Times" prescription with a view to the Clause's preambular statement of purpose: "To promote the Progress of Science." The Court found nothing in the constitutional text or history to suggest that a term of years for a copyright is not a "Limited Time" if it may later be extended for another "Limited Time." In rejecting petitioners' assertion that Congress could evade the limitation on its authority imposed by the Copyright Clause by stringing together an unlimited number of "Limited Times," the Court stated that such legislative misbehavior clearly was not before it. Rather, the Court emphasized, the CTEA matched the baseline term for United States copyrights with the European Union term in order to meet contemporary circumstances.

---

98. 537 U.S. 186 (2003).
99. Pub. L. 105-298, § 102(b) and (d), 112 Stat. 2827-28 (amending 17 U.S.C. §§ 302, 304).

K. International Protection

If international protection is desired, the copyright owner may have to supply additional text to the copyright notice. Under the Buenos Aires Convention (most Central and South American countries are signatories, as well as the United States), the statement "all rights reserved," in either Spanish or English, must be included in the notice. If there is any possibility that the work will be sold in Central or South America, it would be advisable to include this statement.

The Universal Copyright Convention (UCC) requires the use of the international copyright symbol, ©, accompanied by the name of the copyright owner and the year of first publication. If these requirements are met, any formalities required by the domestic law of a UCC signatory country are deemed to have been satisfied. The protection in the country where the work is sold will then be identical to the protection that country accords its own nationals. The United States and most European nations have signed the UCC, but UCC protection is available only for American works first published in the United States after the convention became effective, on September 16, 1955.

The United States became a party to the Berne Convention on October 31, 1988. The Berne Convention became effective with respect to the United States on March 1, 1989. Protection under the convention is available for works first published in the United States, although the Berne Convention's definition of publishable works is narrower than that found in the United States copyright law. *See* Berne Convention art. 3, subsection (3). Article 5 provides that authors of works subject to the convention shall receive the same protection in Berne signatory nations that the nation accords its own nationals.

Subsection (2) of article 5 of the convention prohibits signatory nations from requiring adherence to formalities as a condition of Berne protection. Congress, therefore, enacted the Berne Convention Implementation Act of 1988 ("BCIA"), which became effective on March 1, 1989. Section 2(2) of the BCIA provides that the "obligations of the United States under the Berne Convention may be performed only pursuant to appropriate domestic law." Thus, a copyright infringement action in the United States cannot be based on the Berne Convention itself, but must be based on the United States copyright statutes. BCIA § 2(3). The BCIA amendments do not apply to any cause of action arising before March 1, 1989. *See* BCIA § 13(b). Further, the BCIA does not provide protection for any work already in the public domain. BCIA § 12.

In order to comply with the United States' obligations under the Berne Convention, Congress eliminated or relaxed certain formalities. Most notable of these changes was the elimination of the notice requirement as a condition of copyright protection for works published after March 1, 1989. As earlier discussed, notice is no longer required on works published after March 1, 1989, although it may still be a good idea, as it may defeat the defense of innocent infringement. The BCIA also eliminated the requirement that transfers of a copyright be recorded as a precondition of a transferee filing an infringement suit. Additionally, for citizens of other Berne signatory countries, registration is no longer required as a condition of bringing an infringement suit. BCIA § 9. Registration is still required for U.S. citizens and citizens of countries that are not Berne signatories. As of August 2009, 164 countries have become Berne signatories. Deposit of copies is still required for all published works whether or not notice is used and regardless of country of origin.

Article 5 of the Berne Convention requires signatory nations to provide authors of works addressed by the convention the rights "specially granted" by the Berne Convention, as well as the rights the signatory nation accords its own nationals. These "specially granted" rights have been called "moral rights" because they are non-economic in nature. Article 6 of the convention states that, even after the transfer of an author's economic rights, "the author shall have the right to claim authorship of the work and to object to any distortion, mutilation, or other modification of, or other derogatory action in relation to, the said work, which would be prejudicial to his honor or reputation." As a copyright infringement action cannot be based on the Berne Convention itself, an action in the United States cannot be based on article 6 of the Berne Convention. *See Edison Bros. Stores v. Broadcast Music, Inc.*, 21 U.S.P.Q. 1440 (8th Cir. 1992) (the Eighth Circuit held that, in view of the unmistakably clear congressional directive that a copyright infringement action could not be based on the Berne Convention itself, a claim of right or interest by virtue of the adherence of the United States to article 11 of the Berne Convention could not be sustained). Further, § 3(b) of the BCIA states that the adherence of the United States to the Berne Convention shall not expand or reduce an author's moral rights whether claimed under federal, state, or the common law. Thus any protection of moral rights in the United States must be based on state or federal law.

Section 2(3) of the BCIA purports to satisfy the convention's requirement that signatories provide authors of Berne works the "specially granted" moral rights contained in article 6. Section 2(3) of the BCIA states that the obligations of the United States under the Berne Convention are satisfied by the BCIA and existing law. The Senate Report to the BCIA explains that "[t]his existing U.S. law includes various provisions of the Copyright Act and Lanham Act, various state statutes, and common law principles such as libel, defamation, misrepresentation, and unfair competition, which have been applied by the courts to redress authors' invocation of the right to claim authorship or the right to object to distortion." S. Rep. 100-352 at 9-10.

In 1990, Congress enacted the Visual Artists Rights Act (101 Pub. L. No. 650), providing moral rights for a very limited class of works of visual art. Was this an attempt by Congress to legitimatize its earlier statement that existing law adequately satisfies the United States' obligations to protect moral rights? For further discussion of the Visual Artists Rights Act, see Chapter 4, "Moral Rights and Economic Rights."

As of January 1, 1996, a provision of the General Agreement on Tariffs and Trade (GATT) automatically restores copyright protection to certain foreign works that were in the public domain. Congress enacted this provision to bring the United States into closer harmony with the Berne Convention. Referred to as the Uruguay Round Agreements Act (URAA), codified at 17 U.S.A. § 104A, the URAA restores United States copyright protection to certain works of foreign origin that had fallen into the public domain in the United States solely for reasons of non-compliance with statutory formalities of U.S. copyright law. Section 104A provides in pertinent part:

> (A) Copyright subsists, in accordance with this section, in restored works, and vests automatically on the date of restoration. . . .
> (6) The term "restored work" means an original work of authorship that —
> (B) is not in the public domain in its source country through expiration of term of protection;
> (C) is in the public domain in the United States due to —
>> (i) noncompliance with formalities imposed at any time by United States copyright law, including failure of renewal, lack of proper notice, or failure to comply with any manufacturing requirements; (ii) lack of subject matter protection in the case of sound recordings fixed before February 15, 1972; or (iii) lack of national eligibility; and
> (D) has at least one author or rightholder who was, at the time the work was created, a national or domiciliary of an eligible country, and if published was first published in an eligible country and not published in the United States during the 30-day period following publication in such eligible country.

Thus, to have its copyright restored pursuant to this provision, a work must:

(1) have a "source country" that is not the United States and that is a member of Berne or the World Trade Organization, or that is a country as to which the President has issued a proclamation;
(2) if the work is published, have been first published in a country that is not the United States and that is a member of Berne or the World Trade Organization or that is a country as to which the President has issued a proclamation and not have been published in the United States within 30 days of its first publication;
(3) still be protected by copyright in its source country; and
(4) be in the public domain in the United States for one of three designated reasons:
   (a) because the copyright owner failed to comply with formalities once imposed by U.S. copyright law, including a failure to renew, a lack of proper notice, or failure to comply with domestic manufacturing requirements;
   (b) because the work is a pre-February 15, 1972, sound recording; or
   (c) because the work was first published in a country with which the United States did not then have a copyright treaty or reciprocal proclamations.

A work's "source country" is the country of the author's or rightholder's nationality or domicile, and a "rightholder" is the person who first fixes a sound recording with authorization or who acquires the rights to a sound recording from such a person.

The duration of a copyright restored pursuant to this provision is the same as it would have been had the work never entered the public domain in the United States.[100] That is, the duration of restored copyrights will depend on whether the work in question was first published or registered before 1978.

Persons who copied or created derivative works of now-protected works which were previously in the public domain ("reliance parties") are granted some rights to continue to do so. The length of time depends on whether and when the copyright owner makes certain filings with the Copyright Office or serves certain notices on reliance parties.[101]

L. Works Made for Hire and Copyright Ownership

There are three kinds of copyright ownership: sole ownership, joint ownership, and works made for hire. As a general rule, the creator of a work owns the copyright. The author's exclusive rights begin when the work is fixed in a tangible medium and end with the expiration of the copyright's duration or with transfer or assignment of the rights.

Section 201(a) of the 1976 Act provides that the creators of a joint work are co-owners of the copyright in the work. A joint work is defined in § 101 as a work prepared by more than one person "with the intention that their contributions be merged into inseparable or interdependent parts of a unitary whole." Thus, whatever profit one creator makes from use of the work must be shared equally with the others unless they have a written agreement that states otherwise. If there is no intention to create a unitary, or indivisible, work, each creator may own the copyright to that creator's individual contribution. For example, one creator may own the rights to a manuscript and another the rights to the accompanying illustrations.

Work made for hire is a term for a work prepared by one person (the artist) but owned by another (the owner).[102] This separation of artist and owner has certain consequences in the law, the most obvious of which is that the artist does not control how the creation is going to be used, exploited, published, displayed, or what derivative works are going to be created from the original. If you are an artist reading this, be aware of the work for hire rules so that you will know when you might be in a position to lose control of your own work.

---

100. *See, e.g., Van Cleef & Arpels Logistics, S.A. v. Landau Jewelry*, 583 F. Supp. 2d 461 (S.D.N.Y. 2008).

101. *See* 17 U.S.C. § 104A; Sobel, *Back from the Public Domain*, 17 Ent. L. Rep. 3 (1995).

102. *See* 17 U.S.C. § 101 (definition of "Work Made for Hire").

17 U.S.C. § 101 states:

A "work made for hire" is —
(1) a work prepared by an employee within the scope of his or her employment; or
(2) a work specially ordered or commissioned for use as a contribution to a collective work, as a part of a motion picture or other audiovisual work, as a translation, as a supplementary work, as a compilation, as an instructional text, as a test, as answer material for a test, or as an atlas, if the parties expressly agree in a written instrument signed by them that the work shall be considered a work made for hire. For the purpose of the foregoing sentence, a "supplementary work" is a work prepared for publication as a secondary adjunct to a work by another author for the purpose of introducing, concluding, illustrating, explaining, revising, commenting upon, or assisting in the use of the other work, such as forewords, afterwords, pictorial illustrations, maps, charts, tables, editorial notes, musical arrangements, answer material for tests, bibliographies, appendixes, and indexes, and an "instructional text" is a literary, pictorial, or graphic work prepared for publication and with the purpose of use in systematic instructional activities.

The simple way to a work made for hire situation is as an employee who works for an employer in a creative capacity. The creative work must be done within the "scope of employment," which means:

■ The work is the kind of activity the employee is employed to perform;
■ The work occurs substantially within the authorized time and space limits; and
■ The work is actuated, at least in part, by a purpose to serve the master.[103]

In other words, the works of the employee artist belong to the employer if they are the kind of works the employee was hired to produce, and they were in fact produced while "on the job" in terms of time, space, and a motivation to produce work for the employer. The time, space, and motivation part might require some factual background on a case-by-case basis because some employees work from home at odd hours, and others do work for the employer while still maintaining a creative business on the side, which both the employer and the employee know about, and whose products are not the property of the employer.

---

103. *U.S. Auto Parts Network, Inc. v. Parts Geek, LLC*, 692 F.3d 1009, 1015 (9th Cir. 2012); *Shaul v. Cherry Valley–Springfield Cent. Sch. Dist.*, 363 F.3d 177, 186 (2d Cir. 2004); *Avtec Sys., Inc. v. Peiffer*, 21 F.3d 568, 571 (4th Cir. 1994). *See also* 4 MELVILLE B. NIMMER & DAVID NIMMER, NIMMER ON COPYRIGHT § 5.03[B][1][b][I] (2011).

Community for Creative Non-Violence (CCNV) v. Reid

490 U.S. 730 (1989)*

MARSHALL, Justice.

In this case, an artist and the organization that hired him to produce a sculpture contest the ownership of the copyright in that work. To resolve this dispute, we must construe the "work made for hire" provisions of the Copyright Act of 1976 (Act or 1976 Act), 17 U.S.C. §§ 101 and 201(b), and in particular, the provision in § 101, which defines as a "work made for hire" a "work prepared by an employee within the scope of his or her employment" (hereinafter § 101(1)).

Petitioners are the Community for Creative Non-Violence (CCNV), a nonprofit unincorporated association dedicated to eliminating homelessness in America, and Mitch Snyder, a member and trustee of CCNV. In the fall of 1985, CCNV decided to participate in the annual Christmastime Pageant of Peace in Washington, D.C., by sponsoring a display to dramatize the plight of the homeless. As the District Court recounted:

> "Snyder and fellow CCNV members conceived the idea for the nature of the display: a sculpture of a modern Nativity scene in which, in lieu of the traditional Holy Family, the two adult figures and the infant would appear as contemporary homeless people huddled on a streetside steam grate. The family was to be black (most of the homeless in Washington being black); the figures were to be life-sized, and the steam grate would be positioned atop a platform 'pedestal,' or base, within which special-effects equipment would be enclosed to emit simulated 'steam' through the grid to swirl about the figures. They also settled upon a title for the work — 'Third World America' — and a legend for the pedestal: 'and still there is no room at the inn.'" 652 F. Supp. 1453, 1454 (DC 1987).

Snyder made inquiries to locate an artist to produce the sculpture. He was referred to respondent James Earl Reid, a Baltimore, Maryland, sculptor. In the course of two telephone calls, Reid agreed to sculpt the three human figures.

CCNV agreed to make the steam grate and pedestal for the statue. Reid proposed that the work be cast in bronze, at a total cost of approximately $100,000 and taking six to eight months to complete. Snyder rejected that proposal because CCNV did not have sufficient funds, and because the statue had to be completed by December 12 to be included in the pageant. Reid then suggested, and Snyder agreed, that the sculpture would be made of a material known as "Design Cast 62," a synthetic substance that could meet CCNV's monetary and time constraints, could be tinted to resemble bronze, and could withstand the elements. The parties agreed that the project would cost no more than $15,000, not including Reid's services, which he offered to donate. The parties did not sign a written agreement. Neither party mentioned copyright.

---

* Footnotes and most citations omitted.

After Reid received an advance of $3,000, he made several sketches of figures in various poses. At Snyder's request, Reid sent CCNV a sketch of a proposed sculpture showing the family in a creche-like setting: the mother seated, cradling a baby in her lap; the father standing behind her, bending over her shoulder to touch the baby's foot. Reid testified that Snyder asked for the sketch to use in raising funds for the sculpture. Snyder testified that it was also for his approval. Reid sought a black family to serve as a model for the sculpture. Upon Snyder's suggestion, Reid visited a family living at CCNV's Washington shelter but decided that only their newly born child was a suitable model. While Reid was in Washington, Snyder took him to see homeless people living on the streets. Snyder pointed out that they tended to recline on steam grates, rather than sit or stand, in order to warm their bodies. From that time on, Reid's sketches contained only reclining figures.

Throughout November and the first two weeks of December 1985, Reid worked exclusively on the statue, assisted at various times by a dozen different people who were paid with funds provided in installments by CCNV. On a number of occasions, CCNV members visited Reid to check on his progress and to coordinate CCNV's construction of the base. CCNV rejected Reid's proposal to use suitcases or shopping bags to hold the family's personal belongings, insisting instead on a shopping cart. Reid and CCNV members did not discuss copyright ownership on any of these visits.

On December 24, 1985, 12 days after the agreed-upon date, Reid delivered the completed statue to Washington. There it was joined to the steam grate and pedestal prepared by CCNV and placed on display near the site of the pageant. Snyder paid Reid the final installment of the $15,000. The statue remained on display for a month. In late January 1986, CCNV members returned it to Reid's studio in Baltimore for minor repairs. Several weeks later, Snyder began making plans to take the statue on a tour of several cities to raise money for the homeless. Reid objected, contending that the Design Cast 62 material was not strong enough to withstand the ambitious itinerary. He urged CCNV to cast the statue in bronze at a cost of $35,000, or to create a master mold at a cost of $5,000. Snyder declined to spend more of CCNV's money on the project.

In March 1986, Snyder asked Reid to return the sculpture. Reid refused. He then filed a certificate of copyright registration for "Third World America" in his name and announced plans to take the sculpture on a more modest tour than the one CCNV had proposed. Snyder, acting in his capacity as CCNV's trustee, immediately filed a competing certificate of copyright registration.

Snyder and CCNV then commenced this action against Reid and his photographer, Ronald Purtee, seeking return of the sculpture and a determination of copyright ownership. The District Court granted a preliminary injunction, ordering the sculpture's return. After a 2-day bench trial, the District Court declared that "Third World America" was a "work made for hire" under § 101 of the Copyright Act and that Snyder, as trustee for CCNV, was the exclusive owner of the copyright in the sculpture. 652 F. Supp. at 1457. The court reasoned that Reid had been an "employee" of CCNV within the meaning of § 101(1) because CCNV was the motivating force in the statue's production. Snyder and other CCNV members, the court explained, "conceived the idea of a contemporary Nativity scene to contrast with the national celebration of the season," and "directed enough of [Reid's] effort to assure that, in the end, he had produced what they, not he, wanted." Id., at 1456.

The Court of Appeals for the District of Columbia Circuit reversed and remanded, holding that Reid owned the copyright because "Third World America" was not a work for hire. 270 U.S. App. D.C. 26, 35, 846 F.2d 1485, 1494 (1988). Adopting what it termed the "literal interpretation" of the Act as articulated by the Fifth Circuit in *Easter Seal Society for Crippled Children and Adults of Louisiana, Inc. v. Playboy Enterprises*, 815 F.2d 323, 329 (1987), cert. denied, 485 U.S. 981 (1988), the court read § 101 as creating "a simple dichotomy in fact between employees and independent contractors." 270 U.S. App. D.C., at 33, 846 F.2d, at 1492. Because, under agency law, Reid was an independent contractor, the court concluded that the work was not "prepared by an employee" under § 101(1). Id., at 35, 846 F.2d, at 1494. Nor was the sculpture a "work made for hire" under the second subsection of § 101 (hereinafter § 101(2)): sculpture is not one of the nine categories of works enumerated in that subsection, and the parties had not agreed in writing that the sculpture would be a work for hire. Ibid. The court suggested that the sculpture nevertheless may have been jointly authored by CCNV and Reid, id., at 36, 846 F.2d, at 1495, and remanded for a determination whether the sculpture is indeed a joint work under the Act, id., at 39-40, 846 F.2d, at 1498-1499.

We granted certiorari to resolve a conflict among the Courts of Appeals over the proper construction of the "work made for hire" provisions of the Act. 488 U.S. 940 (1988). We now affirm.

II

A

The Copyright Act of 1976 provides that copyright ownership "vests initially in the author or authors of the work." 17 U.S.C. § 201(a). As a general rule, the author is the party who actually creates the work, that is, the person who translates an idea into a fixed, tangible expression entitled to copyright protection. § 102. The Act carves out an important exception, however, for "works made for hire." If the work is for hire, "the employer or other person for whom the work was prepared is considered the author" and owns the copyright, unless there is a written agreement to the contrary. § 201(b). Classifying a work as "made for hire" determines not only the initial ownership of its copyright, but also the copyright's duration, § 302(c), and the owners' renewal rights, § 304(a), termination rights, § 203(a), and right to import certain goods bearing the copyright, § 601(b)(1). See 1 M. Nimmer & D. Nimmer, Nimmer on Copyright § 5.03 [A], pp. 5-10 (1988). The contours of the work for hire doctrine therefore carry profound significance for freelance creators — including artists, writers, photographers, designers, composers, and computer programmers — and for the publishing, advertising, music, and other industries which commission their works.

Section 101 of the 1976 Act provides that a work is "for hire" under two sets of circumstances:

(1) a work prepared by an employee within the scope of his or her employment; or

(2) a work specially ordered or commissioned for use as a contribution to a collective work, as a part of a motion picture or other audiovisual work, as a translation, as a supplementary work, as a compilation, as an instructional text, as a test, as answer material for a test, or as an atlas, if the parties expressly agree in a written instrument signed by them that the work shall be considered a work made for hire.

Petitioners do not claim that the statue satisfies the terms of § 101(2). Quite clearly, it does not. Sculpture does not fit within any of the nine categories of "specially ordered or commissioned" works enumerated in that subsection, and no written agreement between the parties establishes "Third World America" as a work for hire.

The dispositive inquiry in this case therefore is whether "Third World America" is "a work prepared by an employee within the scope of his or her employment" under § 101(1). The Act does not define these terms. In the absence of such guidance, four interpretations have emerged. The first holds that a work is prepared by an employee whenever the hiring party retains the right to control the product.

Petitioners take this view. A second, and closely related, view is that a work is prepared by an employee under § 101(1) when the hiring party has actually wielded control with respect to the creation of a particular work. . . . A third view is that the term "employee" within § 101(1) carries its common-law agency law meaning. . . . Finally, respondent and numerous amici curiae contend that the term "employee" only refers to "formal, salaried" employees. . . .

The starting point for our interpretation of a statute is always its language. The Act nowhere defines the terms "employee" or "scope of employment." It is, however, well established that "where Congress uses terms that have accumulated settled meaning under . . . the common law, a court must infer, unless the statute otherwise dictates, that Congress means to incorporate the established meaning of these terms." In the past, when Congress has used the term "employee" without defining it, we have concluded that Congress intended to describe the conventional master-servant relationship as understood by common-law agency doctrine. Nothing in the text of the work for hire provisions indicates that Congress used the words "employee" and "employment" to describe anything other than "the conventional relation of employer and employee." On the contrary, Congress' intent to incorporate the agency law definition is suggested by § 101(1)'s use of the term, "scope of employment," a widely used term of art in agency law. See Restatement (Second) of Agency § 228 (1958) (hereinafter Restatement).

In past cases of statutory interpretation, when we have concluded that Congress intended terms such as "employee," "employer," and "scope of employment" to be understood in light of agency law, we have relied on the general common law of agency, rather than on the law of any particular State, to give meaning to these terms. This practice reflects the fact that "federal statutes are generally intended to have uniform nationwide application." Establishment of a federal rule of agency, rather than reliance on state agency law, is particularly appropriate here given the Act's express objective of creating national, uniform copyright law by broadly pre-empting state statutory and common-law copyright regulation. See 17 U.S.C. § 301(a). We thus agree with the Court of Appeals that the term "employee" should be understood in light of the general common law of agency. . . .

The structure of § 101 indicates that a work for hire can arise through one of two mutually exclusive means, one for employees and one for independent contractors, and ordinary canons of statutory interpretation indicate that the classification of a particular hired party should be made with reference to agency law. . . .

In sum, we must reject petitioners' argument. Transforming a commissioned work into a work by an employee on the basis of the hiring party's right to control, or actual control of, the work is inconsistent with the language, structure, and legislative history of the work for hire provisions. To determine whether a work is for hire under the Act, a court first should ascertain, using principles of general common law of agency, whether the work was prepared by an employee or an independent contractor. After making this determination, the court can apply the appropriate subsection of § 101.

B.

We turn, finally, to an application of § 101 to Reid's production of "Third World America." In determining whether a hired party is an employee under the general common law of agency, we consider the hiring party's right to control the manner and means by which the product is accomplished. Among the other factors relevant to this inquiry are the skill required; the source of the instrumentalities and tools; the location of the work; the duration of the relationship between the parties; whether the hiring party has the right to assign additional projects to the hired party; the extent of the hired party's discretion over when and how long to work; the method of payment; the hired party's role in hiring and paying assistants; whether the work is part of the regular business of the hiring party; whether the hiring party is in business; the provision of employee benefits; and the tax treatment of the hired party. See Restatement § 220(2) (setting forth a nonexhaustive list of factors relevant to determining whether a hired party is an employee). No one of these factors is determinative.

Examining the circumstances of this case in light of these factors, we agree with the Court of Appeals that Reid was not an employee of CCNV but an independent contractor. True, CCNV members directed enough of Reid's work to ensure that he produced a sculpture that met their specifications. But the extent of control the hiring party exercises over the details of the product is not dispositive. Indeed, all the other circumstances weigh heavily against finding an employment relationship. Reid is a sculptor, a skilled occupation. Reid supplied his own tools. He worked in his own studio in Baltimore, making daily supervision of his activities from Washington practicably impossible. Reid was retained for less than two months, a relatively short period of time. During and after this time, CCNV had no right to assign additional projects to Reid. Apart from the deadline for completing the sculpture, Reid had absolute freedom to decide when and how long to work. CCNV paid Reid $15,000, a sum dependent on "completion of a specific job, a method by which independent contractors are often compensated." Reid had total discretion in hiring and paying assistants. "Creating sculptures was hardly 'regular business' for CCNV." Indeed, CCNV is not a business at all. Finally, CCNV did not pay payroll or Social Security taxes, provide any employee benefits, or contribute to unemployment insurance or workers' compensation funds.

Because Reid was an independent contractor, whether "Third World America" is a work for hire depends on whether it satisfies the terms of § 101(2). This petitioners concede it cannot do. Thus, CCNV is not the author of "Third World America" by virtue of the work for hire provisions of the Act. However, as the Court of Appeals made clear, CCNV nevertheless may be a joint author of the sculpture if, on remand, the District Court determines that CCNV and Reid prepared the work "with the intention that their contributions be merged into inseparable or interdependent parts of a unitary whole." 17 U.S.C. § 101. In that case, CCNV and Reid would be co-owners of the copyright in the work. See § 201(a).

For the aforestated reasons, we affirm the judgment of the Court of Appeals for the District of Columbia Circuit.

It is so ordered.

Case Study: Bratz Dolls

Mattel, Inc. v. MGA Entertainment, Inc.[104]

The scope of an employment agreement was very much at issue when Carter Bryant, one of Mattel's creators and designers of Mattel's hugely successful "Barbie" line, snuck off one day to consult with MGA Entertainment on the creation of a street-smart, multi-ethnic, "girl with an attitude" line of dolls known now as the "Bratz Dolls." Bryant and Mattel had a complicated employment arrangement that gave the court a lot to look at when it came to the determination of whether Bryant had created the designs for the Bratz collection as part of his employment with Mattel.

---

104. *Mattel, Inc. v. MGA Entm't, Inc.*, 616 F.3d 904, 907 (9th Cir. 2010), *as amended on denial of reh'g* (Oct. 21, 2010).

In his employment agreement, Bryant stated, "I agree to communicate to [Mattel] . . . all inventions (as defined below) conceived or reduced to practice by me (alone or jointly by others) at any time during my employment by the Company. I hereby assign to the Company . . . all my right, title and interest in such inventions, and all my right, title and interest in any patents, copyrights, patent applications or copyright applications based thereon."[105] The contract specifies that "the term 'inventions' includes, but is not limited to, all discoveries, improvements, processes, developments, designs, know-how, data computer programs and formulae, whether patentable or unpatentable."[106] The district court held that the agreement assigned Bryant's ideas to Mattel, even though ideas weren't included on that list or mentioned anywhere else in the contract.[107] It basically transferred all rights to the Bratz collection to Mattel in view of the work made for hire status of Bryant's designs.

The Ninth Circuit drew its own conclusions, and these conclusions did not serve Mattel's interests. It reversed the lower court's grant of summary judgment which relied on the lower court's finding that the employment agreement necessarily covered every "idea" that Bryant ever had while working at Mattel. It also reversed summary judgment on the question of whether it was possible that the employment agreement did not cover every waking minute of the day, but allowed for the possibility that Bryant created the Bratz designs on his own time and not within the scope of his employment with Mattel.[108] Mattel's coup of taking over the entire Bratz line largely on a work made for hire theory thus was thwarted.

The second path to work-made-for-hire status is a contract with an independent contractor that states in writing that the work is to be a work made for hire, and that is signed and entered into before the work is completed. However, this option is limited to a few key areas of creative activity. Section 101 of the Copyright Act states that this version of a work made for hire only applies to:

> a work specially ordered or commissioned for use as a contribution to a collective work, as a part of a motion picture or other audiovisual work, as a translation, as a supplementary work, as a compilation, as an instructional text, as a test, as answer material for a test, or as an atlas, . . . [or] as forewords, afterwords, pictorial illustrations, maps, charts, tables, editorial notes, musical arrangements, answer material for tests, bibliographies, appendixes, and indexes, and an "instructional text" is a literary, pictorial, or graphic work prepared for publication and with the purpose of use in systematic instructional activities.

---

105. *Id.* at 909.
106. *Id.*
107. *Id.*
108. *Id.* at 907-10, 912-13.

This limitation prevents the assertion of "work made for hire" status to every work produced under a contract. The categories listed represent several significant creative endeavors — all work created for inclusion in a motion picture, for example, may be governed by a work made for hire term of a contract — but the statute excludes large categories of the fine arts, such as painting, sculpting, and drawing.

Who is an employee?

In the absence of a specific employment agreement, such as the one possessed by Carter Bryant at Mattel, the law has a test for employees called the common law agency test. The goal is to differentiate **employees** from **independent contractors** who are not employees but are working for the employer on a piecemeal, special arrangement by agreement between both parties (i.e., by a contract). There are no hard and fast rules here, just criteria that cause the evaluation to lean toward one status or the other:

If the work situation is . . .	Then the situation leans toward a finding that the relationship is . . .
Employer has the right to control the manner and means of production — hours of work, time for completion, order and nature of work	Employer-Employee
Artist sets hours of work, time for completion, order and nature of work	Employer-Independent Contractor
Work must be done at employer's site	Employer-Employee
Work is done at artist's studio or home	Employer-Independent Contractor
Employer supplies tools, materials, equipment	Employer-Employee
Artist supplies tools, materials, equipment	Employer-Independent Contractor
Artist paid a salary	Employer-Employee
Artist paid a one-time fee	Employer-Independent Contractor
Artist paid on commission	Inconclusive. Could go either way
Employer has right to assign more work to artist	Employer-Employee (unless contract terms explain this another way)

If the work situation is . . .	Then the situation leans toward a finding that the relationship is . . .
Employer pays employee benefits or takes care of Social Security, FICA, and payroll tax withholding	Employer-Employee. This is a hugely important factor, the mother of all factors. If the employer is doing this, there is an excellent chance that the court will find an employer-employee relationship no matter what the other factors might argue for or against.[109]

There might be other factors to weigh in the determination, but remember to look for the 500 lb. gorilla factor: if the employer pays employee benefits or withholds Social Security, FICA, and payroll taxes, the artist is going to be determined to be an employee, and all works produced within the scope of the employment will belong to the employer. This works the other way, too — if the artist takes care of her own taxes and withholding, this is a huge factor in finding her a self-employed independent contractor who happens to have a project with the employer.

Work for Hire in Doubt? Just Buy the Copyright

If you want to own the copyright to the work of an independent contractor, and don't want to employ the person as an employee, there is a simple solution: Just buy the copyright. Contract with the independent contractor to purchase not only the works she produces but also the copyrights to the works. The two are separate — the work and the copyright to the work. You won't own the copyright unless the person is your employee *or* unless you buy the copyright. You can insert this provision in your original contract with the contractor or in a separate agreement. A purchase agreement will take the guesswork out of who owns the copyright to the work the contractor completes.

Current Cases: Work Made for Hire	
Gary Friedrich Enterprises, LLC v. Marvel Characters, Inc., 716 F.3d 302 (2d Cir. 2015)	Gary Friedrich was a part-time freelance comic book writer. He created the origin story and characters' appearances for Ghost Rider on his own initiative and at his own expense in 1971. Marvel agreed to publish the Ghost Rider comic book in *Spotlight 5*, and in return plaintiff agreed to assign his rights in the Ghost Rider characters to Marvel. Plaintiff and defendant never discussed renewal rights and did not execute a written agreement. Ghost Rider quickly became one of Marvel's most popular comic book heroes, and Marvel launched a separate

---

109. *See Aymes v. Bonelli,* 980 F.2d 857, 863 (2d Cir. 1992); *Carter v. Helmsley-Spear, Inc.,* 71 F.3d 77, 85-88 (2d Cir. 1995).

Current Cases: Work Made for Hire	
	Ghost Rider comic book series. Plaintiff wrote the story for several of the comics on a freelance basis and does not dispute that the stories written for the Ghost Rider comic books were works made for hire. Marvel filed registrations for the Ghost Rider comic books, but not for *Spotlight 5*. After the Copyright Act of 1976 was enacted, Marvel asked plaintiff to sign a work-made-for-hire agreement. Friedrich signed the Agreement but Marvel did not solicit any more freelance work from him. The initial copyright term for Ghost Rider expired at the end of 2000, and beginning in 2001 the renewal copyright would have vested in plaintiff by operation of law. However, Marvel continued to exploit the Ghost Rider character after 2000 by publishing reprints of Spotlight 5 and new issues of Ghost Rider comics, selling a Ghost Rider toy, filming the Ghost Rider movie, and releasing a Ghost Rider video game. Plaintiff alleged copyright infringement, while defendant asserted that Ghost Rider was a work-for-hire. The court first looked to the Agreement between plaintiff and defendant, but found that the Agreement's language was ambiguous as to whether it covered a work published six years before the Agreement was written to be dispositive. The court therefore looked to extrinsic evidence to determine the parties' intent at the time of the Agreement, and found that the record demonstrated that Friedrich was told the Agreement only covered future work. In addition, *Spotlight 5* had been published before the Agreement and by a different corporate entity, and had grown so popular that the court found it doubtful that the parties intended to convey rights in the Ghost Rider copyright without explicitly referencing it. Thus, the court held that Marvel was not entitled to summary judgment and remanded the case.
Lewis v. Activision Blizzard, Inc., No. 13–17391, 2015 WL 9258962 (9th Cir. Dec. 18, 2015)	Plaintiff worked for defendant Activision Blizzard as a "Game Master" for *World of Warcraft* (WoW), a multiplayer online role-playing game developed and owned by defendant. Plaintiff was employed in a customer-service position, but also responded to an internal email requesting voices for game creatures, and she provided her vocals for WoW creatures called baby murlocs. Plaintiff alleges that she was not employed by Blizzard to produce creative content and did not assign any rights in copyright to Blizzard. Blizzard contends that the baby murloc recordings are works made for hire since they were "work prepared by an employee within the scope of his or her employment." 17 U.S.C. § 101. The court found that the baby murloc recordings did indeed constitute works made for hire for three reasons: (1) the recordings were the kind of work that Lewis was employed to perform, since the Game Masters Training Manual stated that one of Lewis' duties was "assisting with the creation of content during the ever ongoing development of the game," (2) the recordings took place within the time and space limits of Lewis' employment, and (3) Lewis' work on the recordings was actuated by a purpose to serve Blizzard since she created the recordings at Blizzard's request.

Current Cases: Work Made for Hire	
Marvel Characters, Inc. v. Kirby, 726 F.3d 119 (2d Cir. 2013), *cert. dismissed*, Kirby v. Marvel Characters, Inc., 135 S. Ct. 42 (2014)	Defendants are the children of the late Jack Kirby, one of the most influential comic book artists of all time, and creator of Captain America, The Fantastic Four, The Incredible Hulk, The X–Men, and Spider–Man.[110] Between 1958 and 1963, Kirby was a freelancer and not a formal employee of Marvel Comics. He did not receive benefits, nor a fixed salary, and was not reimbursed for expenses in creating his drawings. However, despite the absence of a formal employment agreement, the record suggests that Kirby and Marvel were closely affiliated during that time. Since the works in question were produced before the 1976 Copyright Act, the district court used the "instance and expense" test to conclude that the works at issue were works made for hire, and therefore granted summary judgment in favor of Marvel. The circuit court affirmed the lower court's judgment on this point, citing the close and continuous relationship between Kirby and Marvel, Marvel's creative role in Kirby's works, and Marvel's payment of a flat rate for Kirby's pages as evidence that the works were made at Marvel's instance and expense and that the works were therefore made for hire. 
Lewin v. Richard Avedon Found., No. 11-CV-8767 (KMW) (FM), 2015 WL 3948824 (S.D.N.Y. Jun. 26, 2015)	Plaintiff Lewin worked for Richard Avedon, a world-renowned photographer and owner of Avedon Studio. After Avedon's death in 2004, Lewin claimed he owned the copyright to approximately 4,200 photographs Lewin took during his time working for Avedon as a photo assistant and studio manager because he took the photographs and did so as "personal snapshots" on his own time. Defendant Foundation argues it owns the copyright to the photographs because plaintiff took them as a part of his work responsibilities and that the photographs are therefore "works made for hire." The court decided that the photographs had to be evaluated categorically, if not individually, because even if Lewin's job did require him to take photographs at Avedon's request, this does not prove that every photograph Lewin took that concerns Avedon is

110. Michael D. Murray, Cropped, revised, and resized thumbnail image derived from an exhibit depicting Jack Kirby's most famous characters in Marvel Comics: Captain America, X-Men, Fantastic Four, Hulk, and Spiderman, at issue in *Marvel Characters, Inc. v Kirby*, 726 F.3d 119 (2d Cir. 2013).

Current Cases: Work Made for Hire	
	in some way owned by Avedon as a work made for hire. The court therefore granted summary judgment for a number of photographs where there was sufficient evidence that Lewin took photographs at Avedon's request; however, the court refused to grant summary judgment for the remainder of the photographs in which it was unclear whether the photographs were taken within the scope of employment or on personal time.
Foster v. Lee, 93 F. Supp. 3d 223 (S.D.N.Y. 2015)	Plaintiff photographer Foster was hired by Lashpia Corporation and Defendant Lee to produce a photograph of a model wearing JJ Eyelashes. According to Foster, she was told that the photographs would only be used on the physical premises of the JJ Eyelashes salons, a promotional calendar, on its website, and in a small-scale advertisement in *Allure* magazine. The photograph appeared in the March 2013 Manhattan subscriber edition of *Allure*, as well as on the PR Newswire digital billboard in Times Square. Foster reached out to Lashpia to express her concern. When Lashpia made it clear it would not pay her any additional fees for its use of the photograph, plaintiff registered a copyright in the photograph and filed an action for copyright infringement, but defendant argued that the photograph was a work made for hire. Court granted summary judgment in favor of plaintiff with regards to the defendant's work-for-hire argument, concluding that the photograph could not be a work for hire since there was no written work-for-hire agreement between plaintiff and defendant and plaintiff was not an employee of Lashpia.
Carol Wilson Fine Arts, Inc. v. Qian, 71 F. Supp. 3d 1151 (D. Or. 2014)	Plaintiff Carol Wilson Fine Arts designs, markets, and sells cards that incorporate original paintings and illustrations created by its in-house artists or independent contractors. Defendant was one such independent contractor. During the 21 years he was employed by plaintiff, defendant created numerous original artworks that were utilized in plaintiff's products. After his employment ceased, defendant began displaying some of the artworks created during his employment with plaintiff on his personal website. Plaintiff claims that the artworks were work made for hire under the Copyright Act and that defendant infringed on plaintiff's copyrights by displaying the artworks on his website. Defendant claims he owns copyrights of all such paintings because he did not have a written employment agreement and because plaintiff did not control or direct him in the making of the artworks in question. The court held that the artworks were indeed works made for hire because: (1) both the employment and severance agreement define plaintiff as the "Employer" and defendant as the "Employee," (2) defendant was paid an hourly wage to create original artwork for plaintiff's products, (3) defendant created the works within the time and space limits of his employment with plaintiff, and (4) defendant's creation of the artworks was actuated by a purpose to serve plaintiff's business of generating aesthetically-pleasing paper products featuring original artwork.

Notes and Questions

1. *CCNV v. Reid* could have been resolved ahead of time with a simple contract between the parties that covered who was going to own the sculpture and who was going to own the copyright. This case stands as a monument to the proposition that artists need contracts just as much as any other businessperson.

2. The Supreme Court's opinion in *Reid* applied common law agency requirements to the determination of employee versus independent contractor status for work for hire purposes. The court rejected the argument that simple control over the activities of the employee or the creative enterprise at issue in the suit would suffice for work for hire purposes. Is this the right outcome? What if the employer or commissioner supplied the artist with all the tools and materials needed for the job, and provided the artist with a workplace?

3. *Aymes v. Bonelli*, 980 F.2d 857 (2d Cir. 1992), applied the *Reid* factors to find that the defendant's failure to provide plaintiff computer programmer employment benefits or to pay his payroll taxes constituted a virtual admission of his status as independent contractor. Following *Aymes*, courts have continued to apply the agency factors laid out in *Reid*, giving heavy weight to the employee benefits and withholding factors. *E.g., Graham v. James*, 144 F.3d 229 (2d Cir. 1998); *Quintanilla v. Texas Television Inc.*, 139 F.3d 494 (5th Cir. 1998).

4. The work for hire doctrine has been used by a third party infringer as a defense to an infringement action. In order to bring an infringement action, the plaintiff must own a valid copyright in the infringed work. When plaintiff's claim of ownership of the copyright is based on the work for hire doctrine, a third party infringer can attack the validity of plaintiff's copyright by alleging that the creator of the work was an independent contractor rather than an employee of plaintiff. This tactic was successfully applied in *M.G.B. Homes, Inc. v. Ameron Homes*, 903 F.2d 1486 (11th Cir. 1990). The dispute in *Ameron* centered around an advertising flyer created by an incorporated drafting firm for plaintiff. The flyer contained a floor plan and an artist's rendition of the outside of the completed house. It was alleged that defendant used the floor plan to create architectural drawings necessary to build the house depicted in the flyer. Defendant argued, however, that the drafting firm that created the flyer was not plaintiff's employee, but rather an independent contractor. Applying common law agency principles as required by *Reid*, the *Ameron* court agreed with defendant that the drafting firm was an independent contractor, not an employee. *Id.* at 1492. As there was no evidence of a contract stating that the drawings would be considered a work for hire, the court concluded that plaintiff was not the author of the drawings under the work for hire doctrine. *Id.* The court also considered and rejected plaintiff's claim that plaintiff was the co-author of a joint work. *Id.* at 1493. The court, therefore, held that

defendant's actions were not an infringement because plaintiff did not have a valid copyright in the advertising flyer. *Id.*

5. Suppose an employee creates a work at home on his or her "own" time. Who owns the copyright? If the creation of the work would otherwise be within the scope of employment, should the employer own the copyright under the work for hire doctrine? Should the mere fact that a work is created during nonworking hours or outside the employer's business premises prevent a work from being a work for hire? Consider *Avtec Systems, Inc. v. Peiffer*, 21 F.3d 568, 571 (4th Cir. 1994); *Marshall v. Miles Laboratories, Inc.*, 647 F. Supp. 1326, 1330 (N.D. Ind. 1986).

6. Should the work for hire doctrine apply to scholarly articles written by professors at colleges and universities? *See generally* Sherri L. Burr, *A Critical Assessment of* Reid's *Work for Hire Framework and Its Potential Impact on the Marketplace for Scholarly Works*, 25 JOHN MARSHALL L. REV. 119 (Fall 1990). In *Hays v. Sony Corp.*, 847 F.2d 412, 416 (7th Cir. 1988), Circuit Judge Richard Posner stated, "Until 1976, the statutory term 'work made for hire' was not defined, and some courts had adopted a 'teacher exception' whereby academic writing was presumed not to be work made for hire." *Id.* [inner citation omitted]. Judge Posner went on to state in dictum:

> [t]he reasons for a presumption against finding academic writings to be work made for hire are as forceful today as they ever were. Nevertheless it is widely believed that the 1976 Act abolished the teacher exception. . . . But considering the havoc that such a conclusion would wreak in the settled practices of academic institutions . . . we might, if forced to decide the issue, conclude that the exception had survived the enactment of the 1976 Act. [*Id.* (citation omitted)]

In light of the *Reid* decision, however, which requires the application of common law agency principles to determine whether a work is "prepared by an employee within the scope of his or her employment," it seems unlikely that the so-called "teacher exception" survived the enactment of the 1976 Act. *Shaul v. Cherry Valley-Springfield Cent. School Dist.*, 218 F. Supp. 2d 266 (N.D.N.Y. 2002), held that quizzes and outlines prepared by elementary and secondary school teachers were work for hire prepared by employees of the school district, and *Vanderhurst v. Colorado Mountain College Dist.*, 16 F. Supp. 2d 1297 (D. Colo. 1998), held that a technical outline prepared by a college professor in the course of his teaching activities was work for hire of an employee and therefore owned by the college. *University of Colorado Foundation, Inc. v. American Cyanamid*, 880 F. Supp. 1387 (D. Colo. 1995), *aff'd in part, vacated in part on other grounds*, 196 F.3d 1366 (Fed. Cir. 1999), stated in dicta that a prima facie case of work for hire was established when two medical school professors registered a copyright for a scholarly article in the name of the regents of their university; the doctors were co-plaintiffs in the suit against American Cyanamid and were not challenging the work for hire designation in the suit.

7. The "moral rights" of attribution and integrity provided to authors of "works of visual arts" by § 106(A) of the 1976 Act do not extend to works for hire. The definition of "works of visual arts" in § 101 specifically excludes works for hire. For further discussion of this issue, see the next section of this chapter and Chapter 4, "Moral Rights and Economic Rights."

M. Transfer of Copyright

Copyrights can be transferred, which is referred to as a sale, assignment, and transfer. All three terms should be used in the agreement to sell or purchase a copyright. The owner or transferee may be a person, or a business, or a corporation. Note that copyright theory in the United States separates a work (the item) from its copyright (the right to copy or make derivative works from the original work). Thus, an artist can sell a work—a painting, for example—without selling, transferring, or assigning the copyright over the original creation embodied in the painting. The artist can retain the control over who, if anyone, gets to copy the painting or make derivative works from the painting. The purchaser of the painting does not have this right unless the artist or owner sells to the purchaser the copyright along with the painting.[111]

A major change brought about by the Copyright Revision Act of 1976 was the express rejection of the 1909 Act's doctrine of indivisibility.[112] Under § 201 of the 1976 law, a copyright owner may assign, transfer, license, or convey any one or more of the so-called "bundle of rights" contained in § 106 and retain the rest. The assignee, transferee, licensee, or owner of any one or more of the § 106 rights is expressly given the right to maintain any action to protect that right.[113]

Note, too, that 17 U.S.C. § 202 is a new innovation in United States copyright law since the passage of the 1976 Act. Before the effective date of the 1976 Act, under the 1909 Copyright Act, there was a presumption that copyright to works transferred to the purchasers of the works.[114] If you bought a painting, you also bought the copyright to the painting; or so went the presumption. This was amended under the laws of several states, including New York, and particularly with respect to transfers of works of

---

111. *See* 17 U.S.C. § 202.
112. *See* 17 U.S.C. § 201(d); H.R. 94-1476, supra, at 123.
113. *Id.* § 201. *See also* 17 U.S.C. § 205 (providing for the recordation of an interest in any one or more of the exclusive rights granted by § 106).
114. This is referred to as the *Pushman* Presumption, from *Pushman v. N.Y. Graphic Soc'y, Inc.*, 287 N.Y. 302 (1942).

fine arts.[115] You could rebut the presumption by agreement — inserting a clause in the sales agreement to the effect that, "In this sale of the painting, buyer will *not* receive the copyright to the painting" — but you had to do something affirmative to rebut the presumption. Since the passage of the 1976 Act, under 17 U.S.C. § 202, the opposite presumption is made, that the copyright to the work did *not* transfer to the purchaser of the work *unless* the two agreed to include the copyright in the sale.

N. Bundle of Rights Protected

The 1976 Act grants the copyright owner, in broad terms, five exclusive rights in 17 U.S.C. § 106. First is the right to reproduce a work by any means. The scope of this right can be hard to define, especially when it involves photocopying, microform, videotape, uploading of files to the Internet, and downloading of email attachments or files and graphics from websites. Under the 1976 Act, protected works may be reproduced without permission only if such reproduction involves either a fair or an exempted use as defined by the act, as explained later in this chapter. Posting of textual works to the Internet has been interpreted to be a right different from the right to publish in a hard copy,[116] but republication in a digital archive may be subsumed within the right to publish in print form.[117]

Second is the right to prepare derivative works based on the copyrighted work. A derivative work is one that transforms or adapts the subject matter of one or more preexisting works. Third is the right to distribute copies to the public for sale or lease. However, once a copyrighted work is sold or uncontrolled distribution is permitted, the right to control the further use of that work usually ends. Known as the "first sale" doctrine, it means that after the first sale of an item, the purchaser has the right to resell it or give it away or otherwise distribute it, as long as they do not copy it and try to sell the copies. The first sale doctrine does not apply if the work is merely in another's possession temporarily by virtue of a bailment, rental, lease, license, or loan. In these instances the copyright owner retains the right to control the further sale or other disposition of the work. Moreover, the first sale doctrine does not apply if the copyright owner has a contract with the purchaser restricting the purchaser's freedom to use the work. In such a case, if the purchaser exceeds

---

115. N.Y. Arts & Cult. Aff. Law § 14.01 (McKinney 2011). *See also* 1966 N.Y. Sess. Laws 2915 (McKinney) (memorandum of State Department of Law on N.Y. Arts & Cult. Aff. Law § 14.01).

116. *N.Y. Times Co. v. Tasini*, 533 U.S. 483 (2001) (newspaper could not post articles to Internet news page simply on the basis of a license to print the articles in hard copy newspaper format).

117. *Faulkner v. Nat'l Geographic Enters.*, 409 F.3d 26 (2d Cir. 2005) (digital archive was permissible "revision" of previously authorized print format of magazine); *Greenberg v. Nat'l Geographic Soc'y*, 533 F.3d 1244 (10th Cir. 2008) (publisher allowed to create searchable digitalized archive of complete issues of magazine under 17 U.S.C. § 201(c) without paying further compensation or obtaining license from freelance contributors to the magazine).

the restrictions, there may be liability. In this situation, the copyright owner's remedy will be governed by contract law rather than copyright law alone.

Fourth is the right to perform the work publicly, for example, to broadcast a film on television or show it in a lecture room or meeting room. Fifth is the right to display the work publicly. Once the copyright owner has sold a copy of the work, however, the artist no longer has an exclusive right of display. For a proposal that would change this and strengthen the artist's position.[118]

These five rights may be exercised by the copyright owner or the owner's authorized agent. They are cumulative and may overlap in some cases.[119] Sections 107 through 120 impose some limitations on these exclusive rights and must, therefore, be read in conjunction with the broad grant of § 106. Section 107, pertaining to fair use, will be discussed later. Other sections are beyond the scope of this text and will, therefore, not be analyzed here.[120]

O. Section 113 Rights in Visual Art

Because § 113 has particular relevance to the visual artist, it is important to understand the limitation contained therein. The section reads:

> § 113. Scope of exclusive rights in pictorial, graphic, and sculptural works.
>
> (a) Subject to the provisions of subsections (b) and (c) of this section, the exclusive right to reproduce a copyrighted pictorial, graphic, or sculptural work in copies under section 106 includes the right to reproduce the work in or on any kind of article, whether useful or otherwise.
>
> (b) This title does not afford, to the owner of copyright in a work that portrays a useful article as such, any greater or lesser rights with respect to the making, distribution, or display of the useful article so portrayed than those afforded to such works under the law, whether title 17 or the common law or statutes of a State, in effect on December 31, 1977, as held applicable and construed by a court in an action brought under this title.

---

118. *See* Goetzl & Sutton, *Copyright and the Visual Artist's Display Right: A New Doctrinal Analysis*, 9 COLUM.-VLA J.L. & ARTS 15 (1984).

119. *See* H.R. 94-1476, supra, at 61.

120. *See* § 108, reproduction by libraries; § 111, secondary transmissions; § 110, exemption of certain performances and displays; § 112, ephemeral recordings; § 114, exclusive rights in sound recordings; § 115, compulsory license for making and distributing phonorecords; § 116, public performances by means of coin-operated phonorecord players; § 117, use in conjunction with computers and similar information systems; § 118, use of certain works in connection with non-commercial broadcasting; § 119, limitations on exclusive rights, secondary transmissions of superstations; and § 120, scope of exclusive rights in architectural works. The reader who desires more information about these limitations should see generally H.R. 94-1476, supra; Congressional Record, Sept. 29, 1976, at H. 11739-50; L. DuBoff, *Book Publishers' Legal Guide* (1984).

(c) In the case of a work lawfully reproduced in useful articles that have been offered for sale or other distribution to the public, copyright does not include any right to prevent the making, distribution, or display of pictures or photographs of such articles in connection with advertisements or commentaries related to the distribution or display of such articles, or in connection with news reports.

This section is primarily designed to deal with limitations on copyright protection in applied arts. It is intended to reaffirm the holding in *Mazer v. Stein*, supra, that copyright protection is not affected by the fact that the copyrighted item is the design of a useful article or used in conjunction with a utilitarian object; however, the copyright would not necessarily grant the exclusive right to prevent another from reproducing the utilitarian object.[121] Thus, if an artist photographed, painted, or sculpted an automobile, others could not be prevented from manufacturing that car. The artist's copyright protection would extend only to the original design. H.R. 94-1476 points out that it is difficult to draw precise lines in this area and that § 113 is intended to carry forward the existing case law.[122]

P. Preemption of State Law Claims

In some instances, the common law right of publicity, and other torts created by state statute and common law, will be preempted by § 301 of the 1976 Act. 17 U.S.C. § 301 provides:

(a) On and after January 1, 1978, all legal or equitable rights that are equivalent to any of the exclusive rights within the general scope of copyright ... in works of authorship that are fixed in a tangible medium of expression and come within the subject matter of copyright ... whether created before or after that date and whether published or unpublished, are governed exclusively by this title. Thereafter, no person is entitled to any such right or equivalent right in any such work under the common law or statutes of any State.

(b) Nothing in this title annuls or limits any rights or remedies under the common law or statutes of any State with respect to —

(1) subject matter that does not come within the subject matter of copyright ... including works of authorship not fixed in any tangible medium or expression; or

---

121. *See Combustion Eng'g, Inc. v. Murray Tube Works, Inc.*, 222 U.S.P.Q. 239 (E.D. Tenn. 1984) (the court cited § 113(b) and held that the fabrication of a useful article depicted in a copyrighted engineering drawing was not protected).

122. H.R. 94-1476, supra, at 105.

(2) any cause of action arising from undertakings commenced before January 1, 1978; or

(3) activities violating legal or equitable rights that are not equivalent to any of the exclusive rights within the general scope of copyright. ...

Sturdza v. United Arab Emirates

281 F.3d 1287 (D.C. Cir. 2002)*

TATEL, Circuit Judge.

This case involves a dispute between two architects, one of whom, Elena Sturdza, accuses the other, Angelos Demetriou, of stealing her design for the United Arab Emirates' new embassy. In addition to suing Demetriou and the UAE for copyright infringement, Sturdza charges ... Demetriou with several torts: conspiracy to commit fraud, tortious interference with contract, and intentional infliction of emotional distress.

The district court dismissed Counts Five, Six, and Seven, which allege that Demetriou conspired to commit fraud, tortiously interfered with Sturdza's contract, and intentionally inflicted emotional distress, on the ground that all three claims are preempted under Section 301 of the Copyright Act. ... In broadly pre-empting state statutory and common-law copyright regulation, Congress sought to enhanc[e] predictability and certainty of copyright ownership by establishing a uniform method for protecting and enforcing certain rights in intellectual property. That said, "[n]othing in ... [the Copyright Act] annuls or limits any rights or remedies under the common laws or statutes of any State with respect to ... [a work] that does not come within the subject matter of copyright ... [or] activities violating legal or equitable rights that are not equivalent to any of the exclusive rights within the general scope of copyright." 17 U.S.C. §§ 301(b)(1), (3). In other words, preemption has both "subject matter" and "equivalency" requirements: the copyrighted work must be the type of work protected by copyright law and the state law right must be equivalent to a right protected by the Copyright Act.

Architectural designs unquestionably fall within the "subject matter" of copyright. Indeed, the Copyright Act expressly mentions "architectural works." See 17 U.S.C. § 102(a)(8). Preemption in this case thus turns on whether Counts Five, Six, and Seven assert state law rights "equivalent" to rights protected by the Copyright Act, namely, the exclusive rights of a copyright owner "to reproduce the copyrighted work[,] ... to prepare derivative works[,] ... to distribute copies ... of the copyrighted work to the public by sale or other [means,] ... to perform the copyrighted work publicly[,] ... [and] to display the copyrighted work publicly." 17 U.S.C. § 106. State law protects rights "equivalent" to an exclusive right within the general scope of copyright where the state law may be abridged by an act which,

---

* Citations and footnotes omitted.

in and of itself, would infringe one of those exclusive rights. Put another way, if an extra element is required instead of or in addition to the acts of reproduction, performance, distribution or display in order to constitute a state-created cause of action, there is no preemption, provided that the extra element changes the nature of the action so that it is qualitatively different from a copyright infringement claim. To determine whether a state law claim is qualitatively different from a copyright claim — that is, whether the state claim has an "extra element" — courts generally examine both the elements of the state law cause of action and the way the plaintiff has actually pled that cause of action. . . . With these standards in mind, we consider the three claims the district court found preempted by copyright law.

Count Six, the intentional interference with contract claim, alleges that Demetriou "had knowledge of the contract" between Sturdza and the UAE and "intentionally interfered" with that contract. Count Six incorporates by reference Count One, which in turn alleges that "[d]uring . . . [the UAE's] negotiations with [Sturdza] in connection with the performance of its agreement with . . . [her], . . . [the] UAE entered into an architectural services agreement with . . . Demetriou . . . without justification and without notice to plaintiff[,]" and that the UAE breached its agreement with Sturdza by among other things failing to execute a final contract and awarding the contract to Demetriou. Under D.C. law, tortious interference with contract has four elements: (1) existence of a contract, (2) knowledge of the contract, (3) intentional procurement of its breach by the defendant, and (4) damages resulting from the breach. . . .

The district court would have been entirely correct had Sturdza claimed only that Demetriou, by copying her design, intentionally procured the breach, that is, caused the UAE to cancel its contract with her. Such a claim would not differ qualitatively from a copyright claim because both would rest on Demetriou's unauthorized copying — an act which in and of itself would infringe on one of the exclusive rights protected by the Copyright Act. Although tortious interference with contract claims are typically found preempted for this very reason, a different result is warranted where the defendant interferes with the plaintiff's contractual rights through conduct other than reproduction . . . preparation . . . distribution . . . performance . . . or display" of the copyrighted work, 17 U.S.C. § 106. This is just such a case. As pled, the core of Sturdza's tortious interference with contract claim is her allegation that Demetriou, knowing the UAE had agreed to award the embassy contract to Sturdza, entered into his own contract with the UAE to build the embassy. True, Sturdza also alleges that the design Demetriou contracted to use infringes hers. But Count Six does not rise or fall on this allegation. Even if Demetriou's design were entirely his own, Sturdza could proceed on her tortious interference with contract claim based on her other allegations. Because Sturdza's claim differs qualitatively from her copyright infringement claim, it is not preempted.

Sturdza's intentional infliction of emotional distress claim, Count Seven, alleges that Demetriou's "acts as alleged herein were undertaken intentionally, beyond the bounds of all decency and with reckless disregard of the consequences, i.e., injury to plaintiff, especially since defendants knew how many years plaintiff had devoted to the Embassy project and how important this project was to her." Count Seven incorporates Sturdza's other allegations, including Count Six (tortious interference with contract) and Count One (breach of contract); the latter alleges that "[a]s a result of defendant UAE's breach of contract, plaintiff has suffered damages, including severe emotional distress." In the District of Columbia, intentional infliction of emotional distress has three elements: (1) extreme and outrageous conduct on the part of the defendant which (2) intentionally or recklessly (3) causes the plaintiff severe emotional distress. . . .

Had Sturdza alleged that Demetriou's "extreme and outrageous conduct" consisted solely of stealing her design, her claim would be preempted, for the core of such a claim would not differ qualitatively from a copyright infringe ment claim. But by incorporating Counts One and Six into Count Seven and expressly referencing infliction of emotional distress, the amended complaint premises Sturdza's emotional distress claim on the UAE's breach of contract and Demetriou's procurement of that breach through conduct other than the "reproduction[,] . . . preparation[,] . . . distribution[,] . . . performance[,] . . . or display," 17 U.S.C. § 106, of her design. Because Sturdza's intentional infliction of emotional distress claim is thus qualitatively different from her copyright claim, it is not preempted.

Count Five, the conspiracy to commit fraud claim, alleges that Demetriou "engaged in a concerted pattern of activity in furtherance of the scheme which was intended to and ultimately did defraud plaintiff" — a scheme whereby the UAE "intentionally and knowingly . . . misrepresent[ed][to Sturdza] . . . that it had entered into a contract with her for the construction of the Embassy." In the District of Columbia, a cause of action for civil conspiracy must allege the for mation and operation of the conspiracy, wrongful acts done in furtherance of the common scheme, and damages suffered as a result. It is not necessary to aver facts against an alleged conspirator that satisfy all of the elements of fraud.

Like Counts Six and Seven, Count Five rests on more than Demetriou's alleged unauthorized copying of Sturdza's design. Because Count Five defines the fraudulent scheme in terms of the UAE's misrepresentations regarding the status of its contract with Sturdza, and because it incorporates the complaint's other allegations, the count can be fairly read to allege that Demetriou "further[ed] . . . the [UAE's fraudulent] scheme" by entering into his own negotiations and contract with the UAE to design the embassy while knowing all along that the UAE had contracted with Sturdza to perform the very same work. Thus, Count Five is qualitatively different from Sturdza's copyright claim and not preempted.

Q. Steps of a Copyright Infringement Suit

This section will examine all of the steps of a copyright dispute. It will reinforce the rules and concepts that were examined above, and add to these some additional material that factors into the evaluation of whether the facts and circumstances of a dispute over similar works will sustain a copyright claim for infringement. The starting point for the discussion is a dispute over material that appears to have been copied. The two parties are the copyright owner and the copyist. To be fair, the proper name for the first party is "the alleged copyright owner" and the second party is "the alleged copyist." The owner may wind up in the analysis holding an empty bag instead of a copyright; the doctrines of originality, idea-expression, merger and scènes à faire, and functionality may strip the so-called work down to a nub of uncopyrightable nothingness. And the copyist is only thought to be a copyist at the initial stage. Later, after we establish that this party is a copyist, we might assign other terms to this party — infringer or fair user.

Although not listed as a "step" below, **registration** of the copyright with the Register of Copyrights in the Library of Congress is required before the suit can be filed. As discussed above, copyright suits only can be brought in federal court, and federal courts require the copyright to be registered. An artist can create a work and enjoy it right up to the point where the artist sees someone else copying it. Then the artist can register the work and go and file the lawsuit. Certain United States Courts of Appeals (the Fifth, Seventh, and Ninth Circuits) only require an **application for copyright registration** to be filed in order to be eligible to file suit in federal court,[123] while others (the Tenth and Eleventh Circuits) require the **completion of the registration process** before suit can be filed.[124] However, the advantage of registering earlier than that point is that the copyright owner can receive fairly generous statutorily-appointed damages for each act of infringement after federal registration, which saves the time and effort of proving actual damages in the lawsuit (which *is* a significant benefit). The steps below assume the copyright already is registered.

Step 1: Does the Owner Have a Copyright?

This text first looked at the basic requirements of copyrightable subject matter and alerted the reader to the possibility that the copyright owner in the dispute may well not own a viable copyright over the material that appears to have been

---

123. The Firth, Seventh, and Ninth Circuits, and certain other district courts, allow suit to be filed on the basis of an application for registration. *See Cosmetic Ideas, Inc. v. IAC/Interactivecorp.*, 606 F.3d 612, 614-615 (9th Cir. 2010); *Positive Black Talk Inc. v. Cash Money Records Inc.*, 394 F.3d 357 (5th Cir. 2004); *Chicago Bd. of Educ. v. Substance Inc.*, 354 F.3d 624, 631 (7th Cir. 2003); *Lakedreams v. Taylor*, 932 F.2d 1103 (5th Cir. 1991); *Apple Barrel Products Inc. v. Beard*, 730 F.2d 384 (5th Cir. 1984); *Iconbazaar L.L.C. v. America Online Inc.*, 308 F. Supp. 2d 630 (M.D.N.C. 2004); *Foraste v. Brown University*, 248 F. Supp. 2d 71 (D.R.I. 2003); *Well-Made Toy Manufacturing Corp. v. Goffa International Corp.*, 210 F. Supp. 2d 147 (E.D.N.Y. 2002), *aff'd on other grounds*, 354 F.3d 112 (2d Cir. 2003).

124. The Tenth and Eleventh Circuits, and certain district courts, require a completion of registration before suit may be filed. *La Resolana Architects PA v. Clay Realtors Angel Fire*, 416 F.3d 1195 (10th Cir. 2005); *M.G.B. Homes v. Ameron Homes Inc.*, 903 F.2d 1486 (11th Cir. 1990); *Mays & Associates v. Euler*, 470 F. Supp. 2d 362 (D. Md. 2005); *Capitol Records Inc. v. Wings Digital Corp.*, 218 F. Supp. 2d 280 (E.D.N.Y. 2002).

copied. A viable copyright has **protectable elements** that allegedly have been copied.

Copyrightable subject matter is the first stop in the determination of whether the copyright has protectable elements. The work needs to be **expressive** and **fixed in a tangible medium**. Expression is a broad concept — just about anything that is perceivable by the senses communicates something, even if it is a shallow and basic concept such as a color, shape, hardness, weight, or sound. (Additional criteria regarding originality and creativity will be discussed below). But the analysis would end here if the expression is not fixed. The expression might be ephemeral or fleeting, such as a conversation in an elevator, a speech delivered without a script, an impromptu session of choreography seen at a night club, or a jazz improv session performed without music, annotations, and without simultaneous recording. All of these fleeting expressions are uncopyrightable until they are fixed. Therefore, artists should be reminded to get out the camera, get out the tape recorder, get out the video camera and record that dance move, tape that improv session, and photograph that drawing in the sand before the tide washes it away forever.

Next, the **originality** and **creativity** of the owner's expression must be examined. Is the material in question copied, or is it original to the author? This is a loaded question, because the concept runs parallel to several other concepts and doctrines of this area. As noted in the question here, the basic idea of originality is that the work is original to the author, not copied. Scènes à faire in visual art refers to images we call stock images that the author copied or at least adapted for her own expressions. Merged ideas and expression are not original to one artist. Some arrangements and compilations of uncopyrightable material are held to be original, providing new expression that is attributable to the artist; others are held to be so unimaginative and predictable (alphabetical order of list items, numeric order of numbers, etc.) that they are held not to be material originating with the author.

Creativity is a separate requirement, made all the more troublesome because it sounds like a redundant synonym for originality. However, neither originality nor creativity require cleverness, innovation, freshness, or uniqueness. Instead, creativity is a requirement that demands that the work must first be conceived in the mind of the author, then executed into expression that is fixed in a tangible medium. This again is not as simple as it may seem — there are many instances where the problem concerns the use of pre-existing material that was taken and worked into the work, not conceived of and executed as the work. Things that are taken and not created are not part of the author's copyright. This side of creativity also drives the other doctrines we have mentioned: merger, scènes à faire, and a chunk of the idea-expression distinction.

The **idea-expression distinction** prevents the copyrighting of ideas. This is a simple concept to state, but it leads to the exclusion of all concepts, techniques, processes, procedures, methods, formulae, and recipes. It also circles back to provide the foundation for much of the merger and scènes à faire doctrines in the area of ideas merged with their expression, and images that are deemed to be essential to the communication of an idea. The actual outward appearance of things — animals, objects, people — fills in the remainder of the scènes à faire doctrine.

Last, there is a practical test to evaluate the effect of any **functionality** and **utility** of the owner's copyrighted material: if the work has utility, the court will look to see if there are creative, expressive parts that are physically separable (such as the statuette bases for the lamps in *Mazer*), or decoration or ornamentation that is conceptually separable from the functioning of the work (such as the ornamental stone carving around the top of a baptismal font). If the form and the function are not separable, the work is not copyrightable.

All of these tests — originality, idea-expression, merger, scènes à faire, and functionality-utility — are a stress on the plaintiff's copyright that might turn a properly thick copyright with a broad scope of protection against duplicates and unauthorized derivative works into a thin copyright. A **thin copyright** prevents little except near-exact duplicates. The court might find the plaintiff's copyright to be so thin that it cannot possibly preclude the defendant's work, and will dismiss the lawsuit.

Step 2: Have the Protected Elements of the Work Been Copied?

Copyright prevents copying, not independent creation, so copying is a requirement of the suit that the plaintiff must establish. One easy way is to catch the culprit in the act of copying. That is pretty rare. A second easy way is for the defendant to admit he copied. That might happen from time to time, especially where the defendant believes he has a strong fair use defense; it will sound more logical to admit the copying rather than deny it and then say "but I have an excuse." In all other cases, the plaintiff must prove access to the work, plus substantial similarity.

There are multiple ways to attempt to prove defendant's access to the work:

- Publication of the work in magazines that defendant subscribes to;
- Publication of the work on the internet, and proof that defendant had internet access;
- Showing of the work at a gallery exhibition, and proof that defendant attended that exhibition;
- Proof of distribution to the defendant, such as where defendant was a judge of an art fair or contest where the work was submitted for consideration, or the defendant was a professor or instructor and the work was submitted to the defendant as classwork.

Roundup on the Interaction of "Copying" Factors

Q. Do you need to prove access if you have evidence of actual copying?

A. No. Evidence of actual copying obviates need for traditional proof of access

Q. What if the two works are very similar — still need proof of access?

A. Extreme similarity (striking similarity, near identity, virtually identical) of two works may overcome scant evidence of access.

If evidence of actual access or probable access is fairly thin, there is one saving grace that might apply: **striking similarity**. If the two works in question look like near exact duplicates — with remarkable, extreme, striking, or breathtaking similarity — then the court may be persuaded that the defendant somehow must have had access to the work because it stretches the imagination to consider that random independent creation with that degree of similarity is possible.

Note, too, that this step is phrased as "Have the *protected elements* of the work been copied?" It matters not if unprotected elements of the work are copied — non-original material, scènes à faire material, processes or procedures, or functional parts of the first work can be copied without copyright implications. The proof of access typically attempts to establish access to the whole work, so the issue of whether protected elements have been copied really falls to Step 3 as to the elements of infringement.

Step 3: Have the Elements of Infringement Been Met?

The elements of the plaintiff's claim are:

- a copying
- of a "substantial and material" portion
- of protected elements of plaintiff's work
- producing a work that is substantially similar to plaintiff's work.

Substantial and Material vs. De Minimis

Plaintiff must establish that a "substantial and material portion" of the protected elements of plaintiff's work was copied. Substantial and material means more than trivial, more than a de minimis portion, but not necessarily the whole work.

Copying more modest amounts of plaintiff's work in and of itself is not a virtue or a defense to infringement. In other words, it is not a defense that the defendant could have copied a lot more of plaintiff's work, but didn't. As Learned Hand said, "no plagiarist can excuse the wrong by showing how much of his work he did not pirate."[125]

But the substantial and material standard means that the copied portion must be something *more than trivial*. There is a **de minimis** standard that applies to determine whether the copying is something so small, so trivial, that the court will not spend its time thinking about it — the actual legal phrase here is *de minimis non curat lex*, translated as "the law does not concern itself with trifles."

First, remember the potency of the derivative works right. Plaintiff, the copyright owner, has the right to authorize, control, or prevent any work based upon one or more of his preexisting works, such as a translation, musical arrangement, dramatization, art reproduction, *or any other form* in which the work may be recast, transformed, or adapted.

---

125. *Sheldon v. Metro-Goldwyn Pictures Corp.*, 81 F.2d 49, 56 (2d Cir. 1936).

Derivative works need not incorporate most of the original work or even the "heart" of the work — it potentially infringes the owner's rights if the second work incorporates a *portion* of the copyrighted work *in some form*.

How Big a Portion?

- ***Campbell v. Acuff Rose Music*** — 2 Live Crew took opening lines of Roy Orbison's "Oh, Pretty Woman" song and his bass riff and repeated the theme throughout the parody — it was substantial and material, not de minimis.[126]
- ***Harper & Row v. Nation Enters.*** — Took 300 words of verbatim quotes from Ford memoirs, considered by the Court to be the most interesting and important part of the memoirs — it was substantial and material, not de minimis.[127]
- ***Los Angeles News Service*** **"Beating of Reginald Denny" Tape Cases** — In actions against CBS, Reuters Television, and KCAL-TV, courts held that using a few seconds of a 4 minute 30 second videotape could be infringement — it was substantial and material, not de minimis.[128]
- ***Bridgeport Music*** **Cases** — Using just a few seconds of a sound recording and incorporating just a few notes or words into a new recording still can be infringement. The courts held that if the defendant thought it was worthwhile to take that little bit and copy it, loop it, or mash it, then that little bit must be substantial and material, not de minimis.[129]

Case Study: De Minimis Use

Ringgold v. Black Entertainment Television[130]

High Museum of Art

In *Ringgold*, the artist, Faith Ringgold, had created a story quilt that was part of the collection of the High Museum of Art in Atlanta, and the museum had issued and sold a poster of the quilt.[131] This poster wound up as set decoration on the Black Entertainment Television (BET) program *Roc*. In the episode discussed in the opinion, the poster of the story quilt was placed in a set that was used frequently for conversations between the major characters of the

126. *Campbell*, 510 U.S. at 579-83.
127. *Harper & Row*, 471 U.S. at 539.
128. *LA News Serv. v. CBS*, 305 F.3d at 929; *LA News Serv. v. Reuters*, 149 F.3d at 993; *LA News Serv. v. KCAL-TV*, 108 F.3d at 1120.
129. *Bridgeport Music, Inc. v. Dimension Films*, 383 F.3d 390, 399 (6th Cir.), *republished as modified on reh'g*, 401 F.3d 647 (6th Cir. 2004), *amended on reh'g*, 410 F.3d 792 (6th Cir. 2005); *Bridgeport Music, Inc. v. UMG Recordings, Inc.*, 585 F.3d 267 (6th Cir. 2009).
130. *Ringgold v. Black Entm't Television, Inc.*, 126 F.3d 70 (2d Cir. 1997).
131. Michael D. Murray, Cropped, revised, and resized thumbnail image derived from an exhibit depicting the High Museum of Art poster of the Ringgold story quilt at issue in *Ringgold v. Black Entm't Television, Inc.*, 126 F.3d 70 (2d Cir. 1997).

episode. The poster and the quilt depicted in the poster were seen several times in the episode, but only for a few seconds each time.

The court applied the following factors to determine if the use was de minimis:

- amount used
- time of exposure
- prominence — focus, lighting, camera angles.

The quilt poster was seen in its entirety, and was on air for a total of 27 seconds of air time — but again, each showing was a few seconds in length, and the poster never was featured as the subject of full screen shot. The camera did not dwell on the poster or use it in the promotion of the episode; it most often was seen in the background of the action, behind characters, in slant angles and partial shots.

The court also applied a fourth factor: whether the practice of the television industry was to license the kind of exposure and prominence that was at issue in the case. In this, the defendant BET ran into some bad luck, because plaintiff Ringgold proved that the Library of Congress charges PBS rates for uses of images in full screen, partial screen, or partial shots of the work, including use in the background of scenes. Thus, someone at copyright central (the Library of Congress) thought this kind of use was worth paying for, and the court of appeals did not disagree. The court found it was not a de minimis use, and therefore it infringed on Ringgold's copyright.

Actual De Minimis Uses

Ringgold tells a cautionary tale, and the court wrote a thorough opinion that is likely to be quoted and applied for years to come, but the case is not the only one to take up the issues of incidental appearance de minimis claims:

- ***Jackson v. Warner Bros.*** — Considered the use of two Jackson works in the *Made in America* movie. As in *Ringgold*, the works were hanging on the wall of one set in the movie, and got the most screen time in a scene in which the two main characters, played by Whoopie Goldberg and Ted Danson, had a fumbling, groping romantic embrace in which they actually bumped into one of the pictures and set it askew. Nevertheless, the court found the use to be de minimis.[132]
- ***Leicester v. Warner Bros.*** — Considered the use of a sculpture in the *Batman Forever* movie. The work was held to be part of the architectural features of an existing bank building, and the court declared that it is permissible to copy and use architectural features of buildings that are observable from the street. The images and footage of the sculpture later

---

132. *Jackson v. Warner Bros., Inc.*, 993 F. Supp. 585, 588-90 (E.D. Mich. 1997).

was adapted and transformed to become the International Bank of Gotham in the movie.[133]

Problem: Copying in a Different Medium

The derivative works standard fully embraces the concept of a copy that is rendered in a different medium than the original. Copying an artistic design into another medium is not a protected use. Going from drawing to a sculpture or from a photograph to a painting or sculpture is not allowed. In this way, 3-dimensional copies can infringe on 2-dimensional images, patterns, and designs, and vice versa, 2-dimensional pictures or photographs can violate the copyright of a 3-dimensional sculpture.

- **Jones Bros v. Underkoffler** — 3D gravesite memorial violated the copyright over a 2D design drawing of gravesite memorials.[134]
- **King Features Synd. v. Fleischer** — 3D toy based on 2D "Sparkplug" character from Barney Google cartoon violated the cartoon's copyright.[135]
- **Fleischer Studios v. Ralph A. Freundlich** — 3D "Betty Boop" doll violated the copyright over the 2D Betty Boop cartoon.[136]
- **Gaylord v. United States** — 2D photograph featured on a postage stamp violated the copyright over the 3D Korean War Memorial sculpture.[137]

Substantial Similarity in the Infringement Analysis

The substantial similarity analysis at the infringement stage is a little more complicated than the test of the same name at the "proof of access" stage. Most "proof of access" substantial similarity analyses can be done by the trial judge simply by examining the two works side-by-side. If it looks similar, it's similar. At the infringement stage, the law is more rigorous and requires more facts (more evidence and testimony), and often requires the input of experts.

For infringement claims, there are two tests for substantial similarity:

- **Extrinsic Similarity** — Asks the finder of fact to consider the general similarity of the protected elements of the two works. Do they have similar features? Do they look (sound, feel) the same?
- **Intrinsic Similarity** — Asks the finder of fact? Would an average viewer appreciate the value and expression of the two works the same? Would the average viewer weigh the desirable artistic merits of the two works as the same? Would this viewer assume that one work was based on the other?

Expert testimony is available on **extrinsic** features, but *not* on **intrinsic** similarity. In other words, an expert witness can instruct the jury to see and

---

133. *Leicester v. Warner Bros.*, 232 F.3d 1212, 1217-18 (9th Cir. 2000).
134. *Jones Bros. Co. v. Underkoffler*, 16 F. Supp. 729 (M.D. Pa. 1936).
135. *King Features Syndicate v. Fleischer*, 299 F. 533, 535-37 (2d Cir. 1924).
136. *Fleischer Studios v. Ralph A. Freundlich, Inc.*, 5 F. Supp. 808 (S.D.N.Y. 1934).
137. *Gaylord v. United States*, 595 F.3d 1364 (Fed. Cir. 2010).

hear things with a more educated eye or ear — for example, she could testify to the jury, "You may not notice this, but the brush strokes here are very similar ..." or "This passage repeats the passage of music from movement 1 of plaintiff's work. If you listen closely, the drumming pattern is the same ..." — but she cannot tell the jury how to appreciate the merits of the two works, nor whether one substitutes for the other or seems to be an extension of the other.

Step 4: Does the Defendant Have a Fair Use Defense?

We will discuss this topic next, in Section R below. At the end of the day, the plaintiff can fight the fight through all the steps of the action, all the way to proving infringement, and the defendant still can escape liability by proving a fair use defense. That is how the First Amendment protects expressive uses that benefit the public and balances them against the monopoly rights of copyright.

Step 5: Damages and Remedies

If successful, plaintiff will be entitled to prejudgment and post-judgment remedies under 17 U.S.C. § 501 et seq. Before trial, a copyright owner may obtain a preliminary court order against an infringer under 17 U.S.C. § 502(a). The copyright owner can petition the court to seize all copies of the alleged infringing work and the negatives or masters used to produce them. § 503(a). To do this, the copyright owner must file a sworn statement that the work is an infringement and provide a substantial bond approved by the court. After the seizure, the alleged infringer may object to the amount or form of the bond.

After trial, if the work is held to be an infringement, the court can order the destruction of all copies and enjoin future infringement. §§ 503(b), 502(a), 506(b). In addition, the copyright owner may be awarded damages. § 504. The copyright owner may request that the court award actual damages or statutory damages, a choice that can be made any time before the final judgment is recorded. §§ 504(a), (c)(1). Actual damages are either the amount of the financial injury sustained by the copyright owner or, as in most cases, the equivalent of the profits made by the infringer. § 504(b). In proving the infringer's profits, the copyright owner need only establish the gross revenues received for the illegal exploitation of the work. The infringer then must prove any deductible expenses. § 504(b). Courts are willing to entertain an actual damage theory based on the value lost by the rights owner or the value gained by the infringer if the latter better reflects the realities of defendant's use and still will serve to deter such infringement in the future.[138]

The second option is statutory damages. § 504(c). The amount of statutory damages is decided by the court, within specified limits: no less than $500 and

---

138. See, e.g., Broadcast Music, Inc. v. Star Amusements, 44 F.3d 485, 488 (7th Cir. 1995); Int'l Korwin Corp. v. Kowalczyk, 855 F.2d 375, 383 (7th Cir. 1988); Broadcast Music, Inc., v. Xanthas, Inc., 855 F.2d 233 (5th Cir. 1988); Chi-Boy Music v. Charlie Club, Inc., 930 F.2d 1224, 1227 (7th Cir. 1991); Broadcast Music, Inc. v. H.S.I., Inc., No. C2-06-482, 2007 WL 4207901 (S.D. Ohio 2007); Morley Music Co. v. Café Continental, Inc., 777 F. Supp. 1579 (S.D. Fla. 1991); Rilting Music v. Speakeasy Enters., Inc., 706 F. Supp. 550, 557-58 (S.D. Ohio 1988).

no more than $20,000. § 504(c)(2). The maximum possible recovery is increased to $100,000 if the copyright owner proves that the infringer knew it was an illegal act. § 504(c)(2). The minimum possible recovery is reduced to $200 if the infringer proves ignorance of the fact that the work was copyrighted. § 504(c)(2).

The court has the option to award the prevailing party its costs and attorneys' fees. § 505. A split in the circuits regarding whether defendants must prove that the suit was brought in bad faith in order to recover attorneys' fees from the plaintiff was resolved in 1994. *Fogerty v. Fantasy, Inc.*, 510 U.S. 517 (1994). The Supreme Court held that the so-called "dual approach" requiring defendants to prove bad faith was not in keeping with 17 U.S.C. § 505, and that the "evenhanded approach," in which plaintiffs and defendants are treated equally, must be used. The Court further determined that attorneys' fees are to be awarded only as a matter of the court's discretion, and not as a matter of course. As previously noted, statutory damages and attorneys' fees may not be awarded if the copyright was not registered prior to infringement, provided such infringement occurred more than three months after the work was published.

The U.S. Justice Department can prosecute a copyright infringer. If the prosecutor proves beyond a reasonable doubt that the infringement was committed willfully and for commercial gain, the infringer can be fined up to $25,000 and sentenced to jail for up to one year. § 506(a); 18 U.S.C. § 2319(b)(3). In certain cases involving sound recordings or motion pictures, the penalty for infringement is increased to a fine of up to $250,000 and imprisonment for up to five years. 18 U.S.C. § 2319. There is also a fine of up to $2,500 for fraudulently placing a false copyright notice on a work, for removing or obliterating a copyright notice, or for knowingly making a false statement in an application for a copyright. § § 506(c)–(e). A number of individuals have been imprisoned for large-scale copyright infringements.

Notes and Questions

1. Creative artistic products and ideas can come in many shapes and forms. In *Reader's Digest Ass'n v. Conservative Digest, Inc.*, 821 F.2d 800 (D.C. Cir. 1987), the court held that the distinctive arrangement and layout of lines, typeface, and colors of Reader's Digest were entitled to copyright protection.

2. Fictional characters from books, movies, and television can be protected by copyright if they are sufficiently developed to be distinguishable from stock character types such as a generic "Irish cop" or a "nagging housewife." Even an automobile can be a copyrightable character of a film if the author has imbued it with recognizable, identifiable traits. *E.g., Halicki Films, LLC v. Sanderson Sales and Marketing*, 547 F.3d 1213 (9th Cir. 2008).

3. "Idea submission" — whereby an artist submits artistic designs and ideas for a creative enterprise such as advertising — also can be

protected under an express or implied contract theory. *See, e.g., Wrench, LLC v. Taco Bell Corp.*, 256 F.3d 446 (6th Cir. 2001) (Taco Bell entertained creative ideas for ad campaign featuring plaintiffs' "Psycho Chihuahua" artwork, and after rejecting plaintiffs' proposal, later produced ad campaign featuring a Chihuahua "with attitude"); *Nadel v. Play-By-Play Toys & Novelties, Inc.*, 208 F.3d 368, 376 (2d Cir. 2000) (novelty to defendant of creative idea introduced by plaintiff to defendant is sufficient to support contract claim).

R. Fair Use

Fair use is the safety valve or escape hatch for copyright monopoly protection. A prohibition on copying is a prohibition on a certain form of expression, that of repeating and redistributing another person's expression. This is a form of censorship, a restraint on speech and expression. Now, copyright is a constitutionally mandated right — it is in the original constitution, Article I, Section 8, Clause 8: copyrights (and patents) are protected "[t]o promote the Progress of Science and useful Arts, by securing for limited Times to Authors and Inventors the exclusive Right to their respective Writings and Discoveries[.]" But the First Amendment also is a constitutionally recognized right, and although it is an amendment, it is the first of the amendments added in 1791 to secure civil rights to citizens, and it has significant clout. The First Amendment says, "Congress shall make no law . . . abridging the freedom of speech[.]"[139] In order to respect the two constitutional rights without one swallowing the other, the courts developed the idea-expression distinction and the concept of fair use.

Fair use has come a long way since its American origins in the early nineteenth century that followed on English traditions from the eighteenth century. Fair use now reflects the codification of the 1976 Copyright Act, § 107, which provides four criteria that are to be balanced in a case-by-case analysis of the facts and situation of the dispute. Balancing and case-by-case analysis are two of the reasons why lawyers are generally not going to be able to give you a definitive Yes-No answer on a fair use question.

Section 107 of the 1976 Act states:

[T]he fair use of a copyrighted work . . .

for purposes such as criticism, comment, news reporting, teaching (including multiple copies for classroom use), scholarship, or research, is not an infringement of copyright. In determining whether the use made of a work in any particular case is a fair use the factors to be considered shall include —

---

139. U.S. Const. amend. I.

(1) the purpose and character of the use, including whether such use is of a commercial nature or is for nonprofit educational purposes;

(2) the nature of the copyrighted work;

(3) the amount and substantiality of the portion used in relation to the copyrighted work as a whole; and

(4) the effect of the use upon the potential market for or value of the copyrighted work.

The fact that a work is unpublished shall not itself bar a finding of fair use if such finding is made upon consideration of all the above factors.[140]

The fair use provision allows expressions that involve the copying of existing, copyrighted works as long as they serve a public policy purpose that approaches the public policy purpose for which we granted a copyright in the first place. In other words, the use must benefit the public with something valuable — such as criticism, comment, news reporting, teaching, scholarship, or research. In some instances, the fair use evaluation is fairly straightforward:

- a newspaper can cover a news story and use copyrighted photos that are the subject of the news story;[141]
- an art critic can explain what she doesn't like about a painting, and show (i.e., copy) a portion of the painting to illustrate what she is talking about;[142]
- a teacher can make photocopies of two pages from a twenty page article and pass them out to her class for a lecture and class discussion (but it is a very good idea to collect them back when the discussion is finished);[143]
- a search engine can make thumbnail copies of visual works to illustrate the links to the actual visual works on the internet in the process of providing results to an image search query.[144]

In some cases, it is equally evident what can be predicted to be an *unfair* use:

- a teacher's copying of an entire book and passing it out to her students so she and they all can avoid the cost of purchasing the book;[145]

---

140. 17 U.S.C. § 107.

141. *See Nunez v. Caribbean Int'l News Corp.*, 235 F.3d 18, 24-25 (1st Cir. 2000) (earlier nude photos of pagent winner).

142. *See NXIVM Corp. v. Ross Inst.*, 364 F.3d 471, 482 (2d Cir. 2004); *Sundeman v. Seajay Soc'y, Inc.*, 142 F.3d 194, 202 (4th Cir. 1998).

143. *Agreement on Guidelines for Classroom Copying in Not-For-Profit Educational Institutions with Respect to Books and Periodicals*, (a/k/a Classroom Guidelines), *reprinted in* 1976 U.S.C.C.A.N. 5659, 5681. *See Cambridge Univ. Press v. Patton*, 769 F.3d 1232, 1245 (11th Cir. 2014).

144. *Perfect 10, Inc. v. Amazon.com, Inc.*, 508 F.3d 1146, 1165 (9th Cir. 2007).

145. "Agreement on Guidelines for Classroom Copying in Not-For-Profit Educational Institutions with Respect to Books and Periodicals," (a/k/a Classroom Guidelines), *reprinted in* 1976 U.S.C.C.A.N. 5659, 5681. *See Cambridge Univ. Press v. Patton*, 769 F.3d 1232, 1245 (11th Cir. 2014).

- a news magazine reprinting the most important part of an unpublished biography in an effort to scoop the competition;[146]
- downloading copyrighted MP3 music just because you do not want to pay for it;[147]
- copying just about any portion of a copyrighted sound recording and using it in another sound recording without permission;[148]
- any attempt at copying that primarily benefits the copyist by saving her time, effort, and money, as in saving her the drudgery of thinking up something new.[149]

Everything has its limits. You can see that educational uses are not categorically immune from infringement, nor is news reporting, and comment and criticism must be handled with care and attention to all of the factors, not just the purpose and character of the use.

Classic Fair Uses under Section 107

As mentioned above, fair use exceptions have been around for almost as long as copyright law. Over the years, the factors that tend to make uses fair or unfair were adopted and explained, and some uses were recognized over and over again as being fair. The process came to a head with the passage of Section 107 and the four factors used to evaluate fair uses that are quoted above: (1) purpose and character of the use, (2) nature of the original work, (3) amount taken, and (4) effect on the market for the original.

Campbell v. Acuff-Rose Music, Inc.

510 U.S. 569 (1994)*

SOUTER, Justice.

We are called upon to decide whether 2 Live Crew's commercial parody of Roy Orbison's song, "Oh, Pretty Woman," may be a fair use within the meaning of the Copyright Act of 1976, 17 U.S.C. § 107 (1988 ed. and Supp. IV). Although the District Court granted summary judgment for 2 Live Crew, the Court of Appeals reversed, holding the defense of fair use barred by the song's commercial character and excessive borrowing. Because we hold that a

---

146. *Harper & Row Publishers, Inc. v. Nation Enters.*, 471 U.S. 539, 566-67 (1985).

147. *A&M Records, Inc. v. Napster, Inc.*, 239 F.3d 1004, 1011 (9th Cir. 2001), *as amended* (Apr. 3, 2001), *aff'd sub nom. A&M Records, Inc. v. Napster, Inc.*, 284 F.3d 1091 (9th Cir. 2002), *and aff'd sub nom. A&M Records, Inc. v. Napster, Inc.*, 284 F.3d 1091 (9th Cir. 2002).

148. *Bridgeport Music, Inc. v. Dimension Films*, 383 F.3d 390, 399 (6th Cir.), *republished as modified on reh'g*, 401 F.3d 647 (6th Cir. 2004), *amended on reh'g*, 410 F.3d 792 (6th Cir. 2005).

149. *Murphy v. Millennium Radio Grp. LLC*, 650 F.3d 295, 307 (3d Cir. 2011). *See also Campbell v. Acuff-Rose Music, Inc.*, 510 U.S. 569, 579 (1994).

* Most footnotes and citations omitted.

parody's commercial character is only one element to be weighed in a fair use enquiry, and that insufficient consideration was given to the nature of parody in weighing the degree of copying, we reverse and remand. . . .

In 1964, Roy Orbison and William Dees wrote a rock ballad called "Oh, Pretty Woman" and assigned their rights in it to respondent Acuff-Rose Music, Inc. Acuff-Rose registered the song for copyright protection.

Petitioners Luther R. Campbell, Christopher Wongwon, Mark Ross, and David Hobbs are collectively known as 2 Live Crew, a popular rap music group. In 1989, Campbell wrote a song entitled "Pretty Woman," which he later described in an affidavit as intended, "through comical lyrics, to satirize the original work. . . ." On July 5, 1989, 2 Live Crew's manager informed Acuff-Rose that 2 Live Crew had written a parody of "Oh, Pretty Woman," that they would afford all credit for ownership and authorship of the original song to Acuff-Rose, Dees, and Orbison, and that they were willing to pay a fee for the use they wished to make of it. Enclosed with the letter were a copy of the lyrics and a recording of 2 Live Crew's song. Acuff-Rose's agent refused permission, stating that "I am aware of the success enjoyed by 'The 2 Live Crews', but I must inform you that we cannot permit the use of a parody of 'Oh, Pretty Woman.'" Nonetheless, in June or July 1989, 2 Live Crew released records, cassette tapes, and compact discs of "Pretty Woman" in a collection of songs entitled "As Clean As They Wanna Be." The albums and compact discs identify the authors of "Pretty Woman" as Orbison and Dees and its publisher as Acuff-Rose. . . .

[The lyrics of the two songs are provided in the appendices to the opinion. The audio of both songs is available at The Copyright Website, *http://www.benedict.com/Audio/Crew/Crew.aspx/*.]

Appendix A to Opinion of the Court
"Oh, Pretty Woman" by Roy Orbison and William Dees

Pretty Woman, walking down the street,
Pretty Woman, the kind I like to meet,
Pretty Woman, I don't believe you,
you're not the truth,
No one could look as good as you
Mercy
Pretty Woman, won't you pardon me,
Pretty Woman, I couldn't help but see,
Pretty Woman, that you look lovely as
can be
Are you lonely just like me?
Pretty Woman, stop a while,
Pretty Woman, talk a while,
Pretty Woman give your smile to me
Pretty Woman, yeah, yeah, yeah
Pretty Woman, look my way,

Pretty Woman, say you'll stay with me
'Cause I need you, I'll treat you right
Come to me baby, Be mine tonight
Pretty Woman, don't walk on by,
Pretty Woman, don't make me cry,
Pretty Woman, don't walk away,
Hey, O.K.
If that's the way it must be, O.K.
I guess I'll go on home, it's late
There'll be tomorrow night, but wait!
What do I see
Is she walking back to me?
Yeah, she's walking back to me!
Oh, Pretty Woman.

Appendix B to Opinion of the Court
"Pretty Woman" as recorded by 2 Live Crew

Pretty woman walkin' down the street
Pretty woman girl you look so sweet
Pretty woman you bring me down to that knee
Pretty woman you make me wanna beg please
Oh, pretty woman
Big hairy woman you need to shave that stuff
Big hairy woman you know I bet it's tough
Big hairy woman all that hair it ain't legit
'Cause you look like 'Cousin It'
Big hairy woman
Bald headed woman girl your hair won't grow
Bald headed woman you got a teeny weeny afro
Bald headed woman you know your hair could look nice
Bald headed woman first you got to roll it with rice

Bald headed woman here, let me get this hunk of biz for ya
Ya know what I'm saying you look better than rice a roni
Oh bald headed woman
Big hairy woman come on in
And don't forget your bald headed friend
Hey pretty woman let the boys jump in
Two timin' woman girl you know you ain't right
Two timin' woman you's out with my boy last night
Two timin' woman that takes a load off my mind
Two timin' woman now I know the baby ain't mine
Oh, two timin' woman
Oh pretty woman.

. . .

A

The first factor in a fair use enquiry is "the purpose and character of the use, including whether such use is of a commercial nature or is for nonprofit educational purposes." § 107(1). . . . The enquiry here may be guided by the examples given in the preamble to § 107, looking to whether the use is for criticism, or comment, or news reporting, and the like, see § 107. The central purpose of this investigation is to see . . . whether the new work merely "supersede[s] the objects" of the original creation, or instead adds something new, with a further purpose or different character, altering the first with new expression, meaning, or message; it asks, in other words, whether and to what extent the new work is "transformative." Although such transformative use is not absolutely necessary for a finding of fair use, the goal of copyright, to promote science and the arts, is generally furthered by the creation of transformative works. Such works thus lie at the heart of the fair use doctrine's guarantee of breathing space within the confines of copyright, and the more transformative the new work, the less will be the significance of other factors, like commercialism, that may weigh against a finding of fair use. . . .

Suffice it to say now that parody has an obvious claim to transformative value, as Acuff-Rose itself does not deny. Like less ostensibly humorous forms of criticism, it can provide social benefit, by shedding light on an earlier work, and, in the process, creating a new one. We thus line up with the courts that have held that parody, like other comment or criticism, may claim fair use under § 107.

The germ of parody lies in the definition of the Greek parodeia, . . . as "a song sung alongside another." Modern dictionaries accordingly describe a parody as a "literary or artistic work that imitates the characteristic style of an author or a work for comic effect or ridicule," or as a "composition in prose or verse in which the characteristic turns of thought and phrase in an author or class of authors are imitated in such a way as to make them appear ridiculous."

For the purposes of copyright law, the nub of the definitions, and the heart of any parodist's claim to quote from existing material, is the use of some elements of a prior author's composition to create a new one that, at least in part, comments on that author's works. If, on the contrary, the commentary has no critical bearing on the substance or style of the original composition, which the alleged infringer merely uses to get attention or to avoid the drudgery in working up something fresh, the claim to fairness in borrowing from another's work diminishes accordingly (if it does not vanish), and other factors, like the extent of its commerciality, loom larger.[4] Parody needs to mimic an original to make its point, and so has some claim to use the creation of its victim's (or collective victims') imagination, whereas satire can stand on its own two feet and so requires justification for the very act of borrowing.

The fact that parody can claim legitimacy for some appropriation does not, of course, tell either parodist or judge much about where to draw the line. Like a book review quoting the copyrighted material criticized, parody may or may not be fair use, and petitioners' suggestion that any parodic use is presumptively fair has no more justification in law or fact than the equally hopeful claim that any use for news reporting should be presumed fair. The Act has no hint of an evidentiary preference for parodists over their victims, and no workable presumption for parody could take account of the fact that parody often shades into satire when society is lampooned through its creative artifacts, or that a work may contain both parodic and nonparodic elements. Accordingly, parody, like any other use, has to work its way through the relevant factors, and be judged case by case, in light of the ends of the copyright law.

Here, the District Court held, and the Court of Appeals assumed, that 2 Live Crew's "Pretty Woman" contains parody, commenting on and criticizing the original work, whatever it may have to say about society at large. As the District Court remarked, the words of 2 Live Crew's song copy the original's

---

4. A parody that more loosely targets an original than the parody presented here may still be sufficiently aimed at an original work to come within our analysis of parody. If a parody whose wide dissemination in the market runs the risk of serving as a substitute for the original or licensed derivatives . . . it is more incumbent on one claiming fair use to establish the extent of transformation and the parody's critical relationship to the original. By contrast, when there is little or no risk of market substitution, whether because of the large extent of transformation of the earlier work, the new work's minimal distribution in the market, the small extent to which it borrows from an original, or other factors, taking parodic aim at an original is a less critical factor in the analysis, and looser forms of parody may be found to be fair use, as may satire with lesser justification for the borrowing than would otherwise be required.

first line, but then "quickly degenerat[e] into a play on words, substituting predictable lyrics with shocking ones . . . [that] derisively demonstrat[e] how bland and banal the Orbison song seems to them." 754 F. Supp., at 1155 (footnote omitted). Judge Nelson, dissenting below, came to the same conclusion, that the 2 Live Crew song "was clearly intended to ridicule the white-bread original" and "reminds us that sexual congress with nameless streetwalkers is not necessarily the stuff of romance and is not necessarily without its consequences. The singers (there are several) have the same thing on their minds as did the lonely man with the nasal voice, but here there is no hint of wine and roses." 972 F.2d, at 1442. Although the majority below had difficulty discerning any criticism of the original in 2 Live Crew's song, it assumed for purposes of its opinion that there was some. Id., at 1435-1436, and n.8.

We have less difficulty in finding that critical element in 2 Live Crew's song than the Court of Appeals did, although having found it we will not take the further step of evaluating its quality. The threshold question when fair use is raised in defense of parody is whether a parodic character may reasonably be perceived. Whether, going beyond that, parody is in good taste or bad does not and should not matter to fair use. As Justice Holmes explained, "[i]t would be a dangerous undertaking for persons trained only to the law to constitute themselves final judges of the worth of [a work], outside of the narrowest and most obvious limits. At the one extreme some works of genius would be sure to miss appreciation. Their very novelty would make them repulsive until the public had learned the new language in which their author spoke." *Bleistein v. Donaldson Lithographing Co.*, 188 U.S. 239, 251, 23 S. Ct. 298, 300, 47 L. Ed. 460 (1903) (circus posters have copyright protection); cf. *Yankee Publishing Inc. v. News America Publishing, Inc.*, 809 F. Supp. 267, 280 (S.D.N.Y. 1992) (Leval, J.) ("First Amendment protections do not apply only to those who speak clearly, whose jokes are funny, and whose parodies succeed") (trademark case).

While we might not assign a high rank to the parodic element here, we think it fair to say that 2 Live Crew's song reasonably could be perceived as commenting on the original or criticizing it, to some degree. 2 Live Crew juxtaposes the romantic musings of a man whose fantasy comes true, with degrading taunts, a bawdy demand for sex, and a sigh of relief from paternal responsibility. The later words can be taken as a comment on the naivete of the original of an earlier day, as a rejection of its sentiment that ignores the ugliness of street life and the debasement that it signifies. It is this joinder of reference and ridicule that marks off the author's choice of parody from the other types of comment and criticism that traditionally have had a claim to fair use protection as transformative works.

The Court of Appeals, however, immediately cut short the enquiry into 2 Live Crew's fair use claim by confining its treatment of the first factor essentially to one relevant fact, the commercial nature of the use. The court then inflated the significance of this fact by applying a presumption ostensibly culled from *Sony*, that "every commercial use of copyrighted material is presumptively . . . unfair. . . ." *Sony*, 464 U.S., at 451, 104 S. Ct., at 792.

In giving virtually dispositive weight to the commercial nature of the parody, the Court of Appeals erred.

The language of the statute makes clear that the commercial or nonprofit educational purpose of a work is only one element of the first factor enquiry into its purpose and character. Section 107(1) uses the term "including" to begin the dependent clause referring to commercial use, and the main clause speaks of a broader investigation into "purpose and character." . . . *Sony* itself called for no hard evidentiary presumption. There, we emphasized the need for a "sensitive balancing of interests," 464 U.S., at 455, n.40, 104 S. Ct., at 795, n.40, noted that Congress had "eschewed a rigid, bright-line approach to fair use," id., at 449, n.31, 104 S. Ct., at 792, n.31, and stated that the commercial or nonprofit educational character of a work is "not conclusive," id., at 448-449, 104 S. Ct., at 792, but rather a fact to be "weighed along with other[s] in fair use decisions," id., at 449, n.32, 104 S. Ct. at 792, n.32 (quoting House Report, p. 66), U.S. Code Cong. & Admin. News 1976, pp. 5659, 5679. The Court of Appeals's elevation of one sentence from *Sony* to a per se rule thus runs as much counter to *Sony* itself as to the long common-law tradition of fair use adjudication. Rather, as we explained in *Harper & Row*, *Sony* stands for the proposition that the "fact that a publication was commercial as opposed to nonprofit is a separate factor that tends to weigh against a finding of fair use." 471 U.S., at 562, 105 S. Ct., at 2231. But that is all, and the fact that even the force of that tendency will vary with the context is a further reason against elevating commerciality to hard presumptive significance. The use, for example, of a copyrighted work to advertise a product, even in a parody, will be entitled to less indulgence under the first factor of the fair use enquiry than the sale of a parody for its own sake, let alone one performed a single time by students in school.

B

The second statutory factor, "the nature of the copyrighted work,"§ 107(2), . . . calls for recognition that some works are closer to the core of intended copyright protection than others, with the consequence that fair use is more difficult to establish when the former works are copied. We agree with both the District Court and the Court of Appeals that the Orbison original's creative expression for public dissemination falls within the core of the copyright's protective purposes. This fact, however, is not much help in this case, or ever likely to help much in separating the fair use sheep from the infringing goats in a parody case, since parodies almost invariably copy publicly known, expressive works.

C

The third factor asks whether "the amount and substantiality of the portion used in relation to the copyrighted work as a whole,"§ 107(3) . . . are reasonable in relation to the purpose of the copying. Here, attention turns to the persuasiveness of a parodist's justification for the particular copying done, and the enquiry will harken back to the first of the statutory factors, for, as in prior cases, we recognize that the extent of permissible copying varies with the purpose and character of the use. The facts bearing on this factor will also tend to address the fourth, by revealing the degree to which the parody may serve as a market substitute for the original or potentially licensed derivatives.

The District Court considered the song's parodic purpose in finding that 2 Live Crew had not helped themselves overmuch. The Court of Appeals disagreed, stating that "[w]hile it may not be inappropriate to find that no more was taken than necessary, the copying was qualitatively substantial. . . . We conclude that taking the heart of the original and making it the heart of a new work was to purloin a substantial portion of the essence of the original."

The Court of Appeals is of course correct that this factor calls for thought not only about the quantity of the materials used, but about their quality and importance, too. In *Harper & Row*, for example, the Nation had taken only some 300 words out of President Ford's memoirs, but we signaled the significance of the quotations in finding them to amount to "the heart of the book," the part most likely to be newsworthy and important in licensing serialization. 471 U.S., at 564-566, 568, 105 S. Ct., at 2232-2234, 2234 (internal quotation marks omitted). We also agree with the Court of Appeals that whether "a substantial portion of the infringing work was copied verbatim" from the copyrighted work is a relevant question, see id., at 565, 105 S. Ct., at 2232, for it may reveal a dearth of transformative character or purpose under the first factor, or a greater likelihood of market harm under the fourth; a work composed primarily of an original, particularly its heart, with little added or changed, is more likely to be a merely superseding use, fulfilling demand for the original.

Where we part company with the court below is in applying these guides to parody, and in particular to parody in the song before us. Parody presents a difficult case. Parody's humor, or in any event its comment, necessarily springs from recognizable allusion to its object through distorted imitation. Its art lies in the tension between a known original and its parodic twin. When parody takes aim at a particular original work, the parody must be able to "conjure up" at least enough of that original to make the object of its critical wit recognizable. What makes for this recognition is quotation of the original's most distinctive or memorable features, which the parodist can be sure the audience will know. Once enough has been taken to assure identification, how much more is reasonable will depend, say, on the extent to which the song's overriding purpose and character is to parody the original or, in contrast, the likelihood that the parody may serve as a market substitute for the original. But using some characteristic features cannot be avoided.

We think the Court of Appeals was insufficiently appreciative of parody's need for the recognizable sight or sound when it ruled 2 Live Crew's use unreasonable as a matter of law. It is true, of course, that 2 Live Crew copied the characteristic opening bass riff (or musical phrase) of the original, and true that the words of the first line copy the Orbison lyrics. But if quotation of the opening riff and the first line may be said to go to the "heart" of the original, the heart is also what most readily conjures up the song for parody, and it is the heart at which parody takes aim. Copying does not become excessive in relation to parodic purpose merely because the portion taken was the original's heart. If 2 Live Crew had copied a significantly less memorable part of the original, it is difficult to see how its parodic character would have come through.

This is not, of course, to say that anyone who calls himself a parodist can skim the cream and get away scot free. In parody, as in news reporting, context is everything, and the question of fairness asks what else the parodist did besides go to the heart of the original. It is significant that 2 Live Crew not only copied the first line of the original, but thereafter departed markedly from the Orbison lyrics for its own ends. 2 Live Crew not only copied the bass riff and repeated it, but also produced otherwise distinctive sounds, interposing "scraper" noise, overlaying the music with solos in different keys, and altering the drum beat. This is not a case, then, where "a substantial portion" of the parody itself is composed of a "verbatim" copying of the original. It is not, that is, a case where the parody is so insubstantial, as compared to the copying, that the third factor must be resolved as a matter of law against the parodists. . . .

III

It was error for the Court of Appeals to conclude that the commercial nature of 2 Live Crew's parody of "Oh, Pretty Woman" rendered it presumptively unfair. No such evidentiary presumption is available to address either the first factor, the character and purpose of the use, or the fourth, market harm, in determining whether a transformative use, such as parody, is a fair one. The court also erred in holding that 2 Live Crew had necessarily copied excessively from the Orbison original, considering the parodic purpose of the use. We therefore reverse the judgment of the Court of Appeals and remand the case for further proceedings consistent with this opinion.

It is so ordered.

The Supreme Court case of *Campbell v. Acuff-Rose*[150] brought together a lot of the doctrine and interpretive principles of fair use that both predate and follow the § 107 factors. The Court said that the factors are to be balanced against each other. No single factor is the key factor anymore (note that commercial vs. non-commercial uses used to be the key factor; now it is just one of the factors). A bad score on one factor can be balanced by an extremely high score on another. And the evaluation is to be a case-by-case determination.[151]

Purpose and Character of the Use: Although *Campbell* said no factor is the key factor, the first factor — the purpose and character of the use — has more weight than the others. It achieves this by neutralizing some of the other

---

150. *Campbell v. Acuff-Rose Music, Inc.*, 510 U.S. 569 (1994).
151. *See generally id.*

factors or affecting how we will weigh other factors in the balance depending on the purpose and character of the copyist's use.

If the purpose and character of the use is commercial, money-grubbing or pecuniary in nature, this fact will hurt the score on all of the other factors. We don't pat people on the back who copy other people's works just to exploit them and make money. If you are making money, you probably can pay for the rights to the work, or so the logic goes. On the other hand, a non-commercial purpose tends to favor fair use, and will slightly help the weighing of other factors on fair use. Again, it is not a guarantee, but it will help to find fairness in the use.

Nature of the Copyrighted Work: This one has two main points. If the work is unpublished, keep your hands off of it. Publishing other people's works before they get a chance to is considered unfair. It will rarely qualify as a fair use. The other point is whether the copyrighted work is a purely expressive, wholly created work, such as a work of fiction or visual art that is completely original to the author or artist from start to finish. These are harder to copy on a fair use check. But if the work is non-fiction, or contains a significant amount of non-original material, non-copyrightable material, it can be copied fairly often, subject of course to the other factors.

Amount Taken: Less is more, but you have to know the media and context you are playing in, and you have to look at the purpose and character of the use before you can make any predictions on how much is too much. For example, one of the classic fair uses is parody — you copy elements of an earlier work so that you can spoof it and ridicule it. Parody is a form of comment and criticism, and comment and criticism is held to be good First Amendment speech that helps us maintain a robust constitutional democracy. In order to do a proper parody, you have to copy enough of the original work to reveal that which you are ridiculing — and sometimes that requires the copying of a lot of the original material. That is the origin of the word parody — a song sung at the same time as another — and in order to show two works at the same time, the original and the parody, you have do some significant copying. The law accepts these requirements, so if you prove that your purpose and character of use was that of a parody, you will be allowed to copy a lot of the original material. On the other hand, when the purpose is not parody, copying just a bit too much — more than is minimally needed for your purpose — will get you in the unfair use territory on this factor. For example, in educational uses, the amount taken matters a great deal, as does the character of how you use it:

- Simple copying of limited portions (10 percent or less of the contents) for display in class — **sounds fair**
- Copying of entire chapters for use in class — **starts to sound unfair**
- Copying of entire work (articles, books) — **sounds unfair from the get-go**
- Copying an entire work and displaying, publishing, distributing it further on the web, in course texts, or in college bookstore course packets — **unfair; hire a lawyer now**

Effect on the Market for the Original: This is a somewhat unusual factor. It almost always is affected by the purpose and character of the use. A parody or other form of harsh commentary and criticism is likely to have little impact on the market for the original. Fans of the original are unlikely to be interested in things that ridicule the original, and people who are disposed to dislike the original and thus will pay for the parody, are unlikely to decide to go out and buy the original. Other uses have a one-to-one, zero sum game with the market for the original. Even bona fide public interest-serving uses, such as news reporting and education, will deprive the owner of a sale if they reprint and give away a copy of the entire original work. In between, you have uses that tend to make the original more popular by bringing attention to the original — is that fair? Maybe the original owner didn't want that kind of publicity, or didn't want to be associated with the copyist and her activities. The market effect factor is the most complicated of the factors. It requires the input of economists and accountants to calculate the possible losses from a use. Unless you can slam dunk the fair use at the purpose and character of use stage, you may be in for a long, rough, expensive ride arguing for or against market effect from the use at hand.

Problem: News Reporting

Los Angeles News Service sends out news helicopters to capture video of news as it is occurring. During the riots in South Central Los Angeles on April 29, 1992, that followed the acquittal of the four white police officers tried for the beating of Rodney King, LA News Service captured some remarkable video of rioters pulling a truck driver, Reginald Denny, from his truck and beating him.[152]

LA Riot News Footage 1992 Pt.2

The video was 4 minutes and 30 seconds long. Many stations and news services wanted to show the video. Several of them decided not to pay for it, and showed a few key seconds without buying a license and paying a fee. **Question:** Did these news stations showing a few seconds of the video coverage enjoy a news reporting fair use? **Answer:** No.

Each court that considered the issue held this not to be a fair use in a series of lawsuits of Los Angeles News Service against Reuters Television, KCAL-TV, and CBS.[153] To put these rulings in perspective, it is important to note that

---

152. Michael D. Murray, Cropped, revised, and resized thumbnail image derived from a single frame of video of Los Angeles News Service coverage of South Central Los Angeles riots litigated in *Los Angeles News Serv. v. KCAL-TV Channel 9*, 108 F.3d 1119 (9th Cir. 1997).

153. *Los Angeles News Serv. v. CBS Broad., Inc.*, 305 F.3d 924, 929 (9th Cir.), *opinion amended and superseded*, 313 F.3d 1093 (9th Cir. 2002); *Los Angeles News Serv. v. Reuters Television Int'l, Ltd.*, 149 F.3d 987, 993 (9th Cir. 1998), *as amended on denial of reh'g and reh'g en banc* (Aug. 25, 1998); *Los Angeles News Serv. v. KCAL-TV Channel 9*, 108 F.3d 1119, 1120 (9th Cir. 1997).

freedom of the press is another constitutional freedom, believed to be the most important freedom for the preservation of a healthy constitutional democracy. This news footage was current, relevant, up-to-the second information about important events that were happening in South Central Los Angeles. But copyrighted images or footage are not fair game for sampling or other forms of duplication. Even taking very small amounts can be unfair.

You might be thinking, how can copyright put a clamp on this news story? It can't. Remember the idea-expression distinction. Anyone can report on the L.A. riots of April 1992, and on the beating of Reginald Denny. These are facts, ideas, open for anyone to use. You just can't report on the news by stealing L.A. News Service's footage. You can watch the footage, learn from it, write down what you see, and then make your own expression of what happened. All of that is basic research into the facts that you can harvest to make your own expression of the events. But you cannot copy someone else's creation of a record of what happened and rebroadcast and redistribute that expression without getting permission from the owner and paying for a license.

Current Case: On the Scene Photographs of Disaster

A more recent issue involved Daniel Morel, his Twitpic account, and the actions of Agence France Presse, *The Washington Post*, and Getty Images. Daniel Morel was staying in Haiti when it experienced a major earthquake in January 2010. Morel left his hotel and took photos on the aftermath of the disaster. He uploaded them to his Twitter–Twitpics under the account @photomorel. The photos were striking, and have gone on to win world press awards.[154]

Soon after he posted them, news agencies tried to get in touch with Morel to use some of the pictures, but failed. Then a random third party, Lisandro Suero, retweeted the photos claiming they were his own. Agence France Presse (AFP), during its current events coverage of the quake, grabbed photos from Suero's tweet, and uploaded them to its AFP site. Getty

---

154. Image 1: Michael D. Murray, Cropped, revised, and resized thumbnail image derived from Daniel Morel's Photograph of Haiti earthquake victim, at issue in the litigation of *Morel v. AFP, Getty Images, and the Washington Post* (2010). Image 2: Michael D. Murray, Collage of cropped, revised and resized thumbnail images derived from newspaper covers depicting Daniel Morel's Photograph of Haiti earthquake victim, at issue in the litigation of *Morel v. AFP, Getty Images, and the Washington Post* (2010).

obtained them from AFP, and further lent and licensed them to *The Washington Post*, and to many news outlets in the world. Morel's photo shown above became *the* cover photo used to illustrate the story of the quake.[155]

Do any of these news agencies and newspapers have a fair use right to use Morel's first hand, on the scene, irreplaceable image without authorization and payment? No, there is no news reporting fair use. The law does not weigh heavily the high value of the original to tell the story better than other alternatives — that is a factor that makes the copying *more unfair*, not more fair. If the photo is so stupendous and irreplaceable, pay for it. As with the *LA News Service* footage, you can look at this photo and others, and learn from it, and make your own expression of what happened, even of what you saw in the photograph. What the photo depicts are facts, and you can report the facts — a girl was partially covered in rubble, caked in plaster dust, and reaches out for help minutes after the quake occurred. What you cannot do (for free) is republish and redistribute Morel's expression of those facts that he created through his authorship with a camera.

The Zapruder Film

One of the most important works of news and historical footage is the short film taken by Abraham Zapruder of the assassination of President John F. Kennedy on November 22, 1963. Yet *Life Magazine*, who purchased the rights to the film for $150,000 at the time of the events, resisted anyone's unauthorized use of the film for any purpose, news, education, or commentary. Many years later, the U.S. government declared the work to be an assassination record, and took over the copyright to the work. Later still, the rights were donated to the 6th Floor Museum in Dallas at the site of the assassination.

We will discuss one more example that follows nicely on the others.

Example: Fair Use for Political Commentary?

We have previously mentioned the power of political speech under the First Amendment. It is the highest, most cherished form of speech, described by the founding fathers as being essential for the health and welfare of a constitutional democracy. The electorate must be informed about its rulers and their governance. Open and robust commentary and criticism of government must be

---

155. Michael D. Murray, Cropped, revised, and resized thumbnail image derived from frame 312 of the film taken by Abraham Zapruder of the assassination of President John F. Kennedy on November 22, 1963.

preserved. Government must have an extraordinarily compelling reason before it can censor political speech. Add to that the explanation that comment and criticism alone is a classic fair use purpose, recognized in § 107 of the code. Use of limited portions of copyrighted materials for illustration of points of comment or criticism is a classic fair use situation. But that is where the free ride ends. The comment and criticism fair use, even in a political speech context, is not a license to reprint the highlights of the work.

Harper & Row v. Nation Enterprises (1985)[156] brought this point home for us. In the case, retired President Gerald Ford had contracted with Harper & Row to publish his autobiography, *A Time to Heal,* and Harper & Row made a deal with *Time Magazine* to print an authorized excerpt of the work in its magazine. Nation Enterprises received a purloined copy of the unpublished manuscript and proceeded to scoop *Time* and Harper & Row by reprinting verbatim some 300 words of the memoir in *The Nation* magazine.[157] The words were not about Ford's football career at Michigan, or his stellar career in the House of Representatives, nor his take on the several deranged people who tried unsuccessfully to assassinate him. No, the topic of the excerpt was Ford's take on his pardon of disgraced President Nixon, a controversial topic at the time of the pardon, and not much less controversial at the time of the memoirs' excerpted publication in 1979. The excerpt was printed in a magazine known for its political commentary, although the publisher had held off writing commentary about the excerpt itself in its effort to beat the other publishers to press. The excerpt was only a small part of the original memoir which contained tens of thousands of words. But the Supreme Court didn't like the fair use claim for two reasons: reproducing the heart of the work to comment on the work is not fair use. And scooping another publisher by publishing an unpublished excerpt is not an appropriate purpose for a fair use. The fact that it was done in the context of political speech did not change the Court's mind.

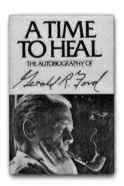 

156. *Harper & Row Publishers, Inc. v. Nation Enters.,* 471 U.S. 539 (1985).

157. Michael D. Murray, Cropped, revised, and resized thumbnail images derived from exhibits depicting the cover of Gerald Ford's biography, "A Time to Heal," and the cover of Nation Magazine's article excerpting Gerald Ford's biography, "A Time to Heal," the subject of *Harper & Row Publishers, Inc. v. Nation Enters.,* 471 U.S. 539 (1985).

Parody – the Granddaddy of Fair Use Exceptions

Parody is an excellent fair use, one of most potent of the classic fair uses. When you have a parody, you are well on your way to a successful fair use analysis. The key is having a **parodic purpose**. A parodic purpose is one to criticize the original work or its author. It will not suffice to criticize society or some other aspect of modern culture — an effort to do this may come in under another exception, but not parody. For a parody, you must show that your purpose is to ridicule the original work or its author. And you must show it in the work itself — it will not suffice for you to write an explanation or give an interview trying to explain that you meant to criticize the work. No, it must be obvious from the contents of the work itself that there are two songs being sung, the original and your spoof of the original.

If you achieve a purpose and character of parody, the other factors fall neatly into line:

- it allows commercial uses of the original material (factor 1);
- you can use famous, extremely valuable, copyrighted works, and produce your parody in the same medium as the original — e.g., a sound recording parody of another sound recording; a motion picture parody of another motion picture (factor 2);
- you get to take vast amounts of the work in order to "conjure up" the original — meaning, identify the target of your criticism (factor 3); and
- you've got a fair chance to convince the court that your parody will not dilute or undercut the market for the original because people who like and pay for the original are unlikely to want to pay for a spoof of the original (factor 4).

You must convince the court that one of your purposes for creating the work is to make fun of, spoof, or criticize the original work; after that, it will not hurt you that you also wanted to accomplish other objectives with your work. Parody does not have to be the sole purpose or even the primary purpose, as long as *one* purpose for the work is parody.

Parody Example 1

Elsmere Music v. NBC[158]

Elsmere Music owned the rights to the New York State tourism song, "I love New York," that played incessantly over all broadcast media in the down times of New York City's financial crisis of 1976-77. This did not escape *Saturday Night Live*'s notice, and the show on NBC staged a spoof comedy sketch featuring a mock Chamber of Commerce meeting for the Biblical city of Sodom that ending with a parodic arrangement of the New York tourism song as "I Love Sodom." Prior to the singing of the jingle, the sketch made a series of jokes and innuendo regarding the Biblical town's reputation for gambling, gluttony, idol worship,

---

158. *Elsmere Music, Inc. v. National Broadcasting Co.*, 482 F. Supp. 741, 747 (S.D.N.Y. 1980).

and, of course, sodomy. The jingle that closed the sketch was the only thing that directly connected New York's tourism song to Sodom.[159]

"I love Sodom" on Saturday Night Live

The trial court wasted little time finding a good, old fashioned parody and satire fair use, following the path paved by *Berlin v. E.C. Publications, Inc.*,[160] which had exonerated certain parody lyrics to Irving Berlin songs printed in Mad Magazine. The court briefly mentioned the 1976 Copyright Act which had just gone into effect at the time of the parody broadcast in May 1977. It held that both "parody and satire are deserving of substantial freedom," and because the "defendants had taken no more of the original song than was necessary to 'recall' or 'conjure up' the object of its satire," and as the parody had "neither the intent nor the effect of fulfilling the demand for the original," no infringement had taken place. Thus, the *Elsmere* court equated parody and satire and found that each provided a ground for copyright fair use. The Court of Appeals affirmed the trial court on the basis of the lower court's rationale.

Parody Example 2

Leibovitz v. Paramount Pictures[161]

Leibovitz cover	Naked Gun 33 1/3 Poster

162

---

159. Michael D. Murray, Cropped, revised, and resized thumbnail image derived from a single frame from NBC's 1977 Saturday Night Live television skit, "I Love Sodom," the subject of *Elsmere Music, Inc. v. National Broadcasting Co.*, 482 F. Supp. 741, 747 (S.D.N.Y. 1980).

160. *Berlin v. E.C. Publications, Inc.*, 329 F.2d 541, 543 (2d Cir. 1964).

161. *Leibovitz v. Paramount Pictures Corp.*, 137 F.3d 109, 110 (2d Cir. 1998).

162. Michael D. Murray, Cropped, revised, and resized thumbnail images derived from exhibits depicting the Vanity Fair cover with Annie Leibovitz's photograph of Demi Moore, and the Naked Gun 33 1/3 Movie Poster depicting Leslie Neilson in a pose reminiscent of Demi Moore on Vanity Fair, both of which are the subject of *Leibovitz v. Paramount Pictures Corp.*, 137 F.3d 109, 110 (2d Cir. 1998).

The *Leibovitz v. Paramount Pictures* case featured celebrity photographer Annie Leibovitz and her celebrated cover photo of a hugely pregnant and quite naked Demi Moore on the cover of *Vanity Fair* magazine. Paramount was in the process of promoting its latest sequel in the *Naked Gun* line of comedic films, and took the image of Moore from the *Vanity Fair* cover, recreated the shot, and place *Naked Gun* star Leslie Neilson's head on the pregnant female body. Why? Apparently to criticize Annie Leibovitz and the way she created the Moore cover photo — or so the attorneys for Paramount argued. Apparently, you can tell all this just by looking at the two works. In any event, the court agreed with this theory and found a parody fair use. Leibovitz's artistic approach was deemed to be pretentious, using a classical "Modest Venus" pose from Botticelli's *Venus,* and approaching the work with a serious artistic flair, even though Moore was a more of a pop film star than glamour icon, and her pregnancy was less of an artistic event and more suited for check-out line tabloid material than mythology. Paramount was allowed to take a large portion of the work in order to turn it on its head.

Modern Transformative Fair Uses

The list of public purposes for fair use is not exclusive, and in the area of visual arts, it has been expanded in recent years by the overarching, non-codified, but massively important concept of **transformation**. Transformation is now the X-factor, the factor not listed in § 107, the one that can make or break certain expressive uses of works. Highly transformed works are fair; non-transformed works must find some other justification for their fairness (such as a classic fair use for education or comment and criticism).

The formula that led the Supreme Court to adopt the overarching fair use concept of transformation[163] is deceptively simple: transformation of existing material creates new material or expressions that communicate new ideas and new meaning through new content or a new context. The promotion of new expression to benefit the public was the reason we have copyright protection in the first place.

The transformative test looks to whether a fair use merely supersedes the objects and intentions of the original work; meaning, does it simply take the whole or part of the original and repeat it for its original expressive purpose, or does the new work add something new — creating new content, meaning and expression, because of some transformative treatment of the original material.[164] The transformation can be by adding an overwhelming amount of new content, so that the original work no longer shines through in the final work.[165] It can also be by "recontextualizing" the original work, placing it in a

---

163. *Campbell,* 510 U.S. at 579.
164. *Id.*
165. *Seltzer v. Green Day, Inc.,* 725 F.3d 1170, 1176 (9th Cir. 2013).

new context so that it no longer serves the same function and purpose for which it originally was created.[166] The new function and purpose should be something beneficial to the public (although it usually benefits the new user, as well).

The problem is that transformation (and its companion words, transform, transformative, and transformativeness) are a family of concepts that are difficult to define and even more difficult to use to predict whether certain uses are transformative or not.

Case Study: Transformation without Parody — a Successful Satire

Blanch v. Koons[167]

One section of the *Campbell* case compared parodies to satires.[168] Parody uses another person's material to make fun of that material or the other person who created it. Satire just uses another person's material, sometimes in a general spoof of modern life, or as a vehicle to criticize something or someone specific. Satire does not make an obvious attempt to criticize the earlier material it borrows; more often it chooses the material because it is useful in making the satirist's point without any criticism of the original material or its author. The Supreme Court endorsed parodies as a transformative fair use, but stated that satires needed additional justification for their use of someone else's work.[169]

This treatment held back the satire world for quite some time, at least in terms of cases that made their way through the courts. The *Dr. Seuss Enterprises v. Penguin Books*[170] case was a casualty of this thinking. The case involved an O.J. Simpson murder trial satire entitled *The Cat Not in the Hat*, and although the new work made drastic alterations to the content of the Dr. Seuss book *The Cat in the Hat*, and used it for a completely new function and purpose, the court wound up categorizing the work as a satire, not a parody, because the new work did not appear to criticize anything about Dr. Seuss himself or *The Cat in the Hat* book itself. Since parodies were fair, and satires were unfair, the court denied the defendants' fair use defense.[171]

Eventually, a famous artist named Jeffrey Koons took a case all the way to the United States Court of Appeals for the Second Circuit, and argued that his satire of fashion and society's tastes should count as a transformative fair use.

Koons took the work of a fashion photographer named Blanch. Blanch's work, *Silk Sandals*, was standard fare fashion photography — a shapely set of

166. *A.V. ex rel. Vanderhye v. iParadigms, LLC*, 562 F.3d 630, 639 (4th Cir. 2009); *Perfect 10*, 508 F.3d at 1165; *Blanch v. Koons*, 467 F.3d 244, 252 (2d Cir. 2006); *Bill Graham Archives v. Dorling Kindersley Ltd.*, 448 F.3d 605, 608-09 (2d Cir. 2006).
167. *Blanch*, 467 F.3d at 252.
168. *Campbell*, 510 U.S. at 579-83.
169. *Id.*
170. *Dr. Seuss Enterprises v. Penguin Books USA, Inc.*, 109 F.3d 1394, 1401 (9th Cir. 1997).
171. *Id.*

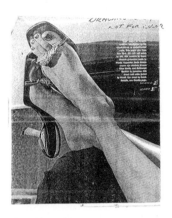

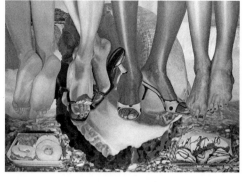

Koons' *Niagara*

Blanch's *Silk Sandals*

sandals on a shapely woman's feet. The Koons work, *Niagara*, recontextualized the image into a splashy scene of four women's legs and feet hanging down somewhat like Niagara Falls (which itself appears in the background), in the context of fatty and sugary foods. Koons asserted that the work commented on society's tastes and motivations regarding food and women's fashions. It was clear that the work was not a criticism of Blanch or her photography. He used her work solely because it was one indicative example of how women are photographed in fashion advertising. Koons dressed up the basic fashion photography through painting.[172]

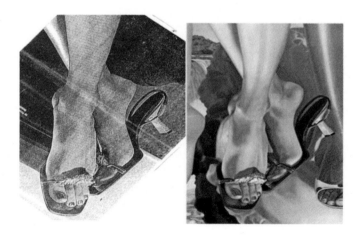

---

172. Michael D. Murray, Collage of cropped, revised, and resized thumbnail images derived from exhibits, including excerpt of Blanch's "Silk Sandals" photograph, excerpt from Koon's "Niagara" painting, and grayscale comparison of Blanch's feet to Koon's treatment of the feet, all of which are the subject of *Blanch v. Koons*, 467 F.3d 244 (2d Cir. 2006).

Nevertheless, the court liked it. The court thought Koons had a genuine creative rationale for borrowing Blanch's image, rather than using it merely to get attention or avoid the drudgery in working up something fresh. In other words, the predominant purpose for his use of the work was creative and expressive, not commercial and exploitive, and the recontextualization and massive alteration in content created a new work with new content, meaning, and expression that was very different in purpose and function from Blanch's original work. All of this added up to a transformative fair use, albeit a satire, not a parody.

Case Study: Applying Your Own Bold Style as Transformation

Cariou v. Prince[173]

Richard Prince is an unabashed, unapologetic appropriationist artist. In 2007 and 2008, Prince appropriated photographs of Rastafarians in their native environment that had been taken by photographer Patrick Cariou, and compiled in Cariou's book, *Yes Rasta*. As described in the appellate opinion,

> Prince had a show at the Eden Rock hotel in St. Barth's that included a collage, titled *Canal Zone* (2007), comprising 35 photographs torn out of *Yes Rasta* and pinned to a piece of plywood. Prince altered those photographs significantly, by among other things painting "lozenges" over their subjects' facial features and using only portions of some of the images. In June 2008, Prince purchased three additional copies of *Yes Rasta*. He went on to create thirty additional artworks in the Canal Zone series, twenty-nine of which incorporated partial or whole images from *Yes Rasta*. The portions of *Yes Rasta* photographs used, and the amount of each artwork that they constitute, vary significantly from piece to piece.[174]

A sampling of the Canal Zone images are shown on the next page:

The trial court granted summary judgment in favor of Cariou, finding that Prince's images were not transformative and Prince had not established a fair use defense regarding the images.[175] The Second Circuit reversed, in part because it believed the District Court had interpreted and applied the transformative test incorrectly, relying too much on the concept that a transformative work must "comment on, relate to the historical context of, or critically refer back to the original works."[176] The Second Circuit interpreted the law differently:

> The law imposes no requirement that a work comment on the original or its author in order to be considered transformative, and a secondary work may constitute a fair use even if it serves some purpose other than those (criticism, comment, news reporting, teaching, scholarship, and research) identified in

---

173. *Cariou v. Prince*, 714 F.3d 694 (2d Cir.), *cert. denied*, 134 S. Ct. 618 (2013).
174. *Id.* at 699-700 (inner footnote omitted).
175. *Cariou v. Prince*, 784 F. Supp. 2d 337, 349-50 (S.D.N.Y. 2011).
176. *Cariou*, 714 F.3d at 706 (referring to *Cariou*, 784 F. Supp. 2d at 348).

177

the preamble to the statute. [Campbell, 510 U.S.] at 577, 114 S. Ct. 1164; Harper & Row, 471 U.S. at 561, 105 S. Ct. 2218. Instead, as the Supreme Court as well as decisions from our court have emphasized, to qualify as a fair use, a new work generally must alter the original with "new expression, meaning, or message." Campbell, 510 U.S. at 579, 114 S. Ct. 1164; see also Blanch, 467 F.3d at 253 (original must be employed "in the creation of new information, new aesthetics, new insights and understandings" (quotation marks omitted)); Castle Rock, 150 F.3d at 142.

The court was impressed with the additions Prince made to Cariou's *Yes Rasta* works, the lozenges imposed over facial features and childlike line drawings on the photos, and found that Prince had scored highly on the first fair use factor, "the purpose and character of the use," by his transformative treatments, and also on the fourth fair use factor, "the effect on the market for the original," because his works served a completely different, "high end" art market that did not usurp Cariou's own market.[178] Prince also scored well enough on the second and third factors to preserve his fair use defense.[179] The Second Circuit reversed the District Court's ruling and ordered summary judgment in favor of Prince on all but five of his thirty works in the *Canal Zone* show, choosing to remand these five to the District Court for further

---

177. Michael D. Murray, Collage of cropped, revised, and resized thumbnail images derived from exhibits depicting Richard Prince's "Canal Zone" work incorporating in part the photographs of Patrick Cariou from his book, "Yes Rasta," which are the subject of *Cariou v. Prince*, 714 F.3d 694 (2d Cir.), *cert. denied*, 134 S. Ct. 618 (2013).

178. *Id.* at 708-10.

179. *Id.*

consideration.[180] These five had fewer and more minimal alterations than the other works from the Canal Zone show. Two of the five works are shown here — Cariou's photograph appears on the left of each grouping, Prince's work on the right[181]:

After remand, the lawsuit settled.[182]

Case Study: A Green Light for Transformation

Seltzer v. Green Day[183]

Street artist, Dereck Seltzer, is the creator of a street artwork entitled, *Scream Icon* (shown below). Seltzer sued the alternative/punk rock group Green Day and Roger Staub, an artist who created the backgrounds for Green Day videos, because Staub used a modified version (i.e., an unauthorized derivative work) of *Scream Icon* as a prominent part of a backdrop of graffiti art that served as the background design for the music video and concert staging of a specific song, East Jesus Nowhere, *http://www.youtube.com/watch?v=iPu18Wt8e7Y*. The modifications to *Scream Icon* were a large red cross and several markings and scratches superimposed on the face of the image. As revealed in the video, much of which contains concert footage, the modified *Scream Icon* image was placed roughly at center stage behind the rock group, and it was larger than the other images placed on either side of it.

180. *Id.* at 710.

181. Michael D. Murray, Collage of cropped, revised, and resized thumbnail images derived from exhibits depicting Richard Prince's "Canal Zone" images next to the original photographs of Patrick Cariou from his book "Yes Rasta," which reflect two of the Prince images remanded by the court in *Cariou v. Prince*, 714 F.3d 694 (2d Cir.), *cert. denied*, 134 S. Ct. 618 (2013), for further consideration of their "transformative" nature.

182. David McAfee, *Artist Prince, Photographer Cariou Settle Fair Use Feud* (March 18, 2014, 9:27 PM ET), *http://www.law360.com/articles/519819/artist-prince-photographer-cariou-settle-fair-use-feud* .

183. *Seltzer v. Green Day, Inc.*, 725 F.3d 1170, 1175-79 (9th Cir. 2013).

Scream Icon[184]

*Modified Scream Icon as Displayed
in the Concert Footage and Music
Video of Green Day's East Jesus Nowhere.*[185]

The District Court and the Ninth Circuit both found the *Scream Icon* work had been transformed both by the artistic overlay of the red cross and other markings, and by the recontextualization of the work with other works in the concert presentation of a specific song whose theme is "the hypocrisy of some religious people who preach one thing but act otherwise . . . [and] the violence that is done in the name of religion."[186] The Ninth Circuit went back to basics, quoting the grandfather of the transformative test, Pierre Laval:

> The use must be productive and must employ the quoted matter in a different manner or for a different purpose from the original. A quotation of copyrighted material that merely repackages or republishes the original is unlikely to pass the test; in Justice Story's words, it would merely "supersede the objects" of the original. If, on the other hand, the secondary use adds value to the original — if the quoted matter is used as raw material, transformed in the creation of new information, new aesthetics, new insights and understandings — this is the very type of activity that the fair use doctrine intends to protect for the enrichment of society.[187]

The court found the band and its artistic designer prevailed on each factor of the fair use test in 17 U.S.C. § 107.[188] This is a noteworthy holding, because the context of the use of the *Scream Icon* was a commercial, for-profit enterprise, and in particular, a music video intended to advertise and promote the music sales and concert ticket sales of the rock band, yet the physical changes and recontextualization of the *Scream Icon* work from street art to concert stage-dress was deemed to be a transformative fair use.

184. Michael D. Murray, Cropped, revised, and resized thumbnail image derived from Dereck Seltzer's "Scream Icon" (2003), the subject of *Seltzer v. Green Day, Inc.*, 725 F.3d 1170 (9th Cir. 2013).
185. Michael D. Murray, Cropped, revised, and resized thumbnail image derived from a single frame of concert footage from the music video of Green Day's "East Jesus Nowhere," *http://www.youtube.com/watch?v=iPu18Wt8e7Y* (2009), featuring "Scream Icon," the subject of *Seltzer v. Green Day, Inc.*, 725 F.3d 1170 (9th Cir. 2013).
186. *Seltzer*, 725 F.3d at 1174.
187. *Id.* at 1176 (quoting Leval, *Toward a Fair Use Standard*, 103 HARV. L. REV. at 1111).
188. *Id.* at 1175-79.

Current Cases: Transformative Fair Use	
The Authors Guild v. Google, Inc., 804 F.3d 202 (2d Cir. 2015)	Google made digital copies of tens of millions of books, including plaintiffs', which were submitted to Google for that purpose by major libraries. Google scanned the digital copies and established a publicly available search function, such that any Internet user can search without charge to determine whether the book contains a specific word and see snippets of text containing the searched-for terms. Plaintiffs contended that Google infringed their copyrights; however, both the district and circuit court held that Google's making of a digital copy to provide a search function constituted a transformative use that augments public knowledge without providing the public with a substantial substitute for plaintiffs' protected matter.
Katz v. Google Inc., 802 F.3d 1178 (11th Cir. 2015)	Plaintiff businessman Katz brought action against defendant blogger Irina Chevaldina for copyright infringement in use of a candid photograph of himself on defendant's blog. Defendant created a blog devoted to criticizing plaintiff and his business practices, publishing 25 blog posts reproducing the photo in three ways: (1) copied in its unaltered, original state, (2) accompanied by sharply worded captions, or (3) cropped and pasted into mocking cartoons. Court affirmed lower court's decision to grant summary judgment in favor of defendant, reasoning that defendant's use of the photo was transformative because, in the context of the blog post's surrounding commentary, she used plaintiff's "ugly" and "compromising" appearance to ridicule and satirize his character. Citing *Suntrust Bank v Houghton Mifflin Co.*, 268 F.3d 1257, 1270 (11th Cir. 2001), the court noted that a work may be transformative where it is "principally and purposefully a critical statement."
Neri v. Monroe, No. 11–CV–429–SLC, 2014 Copr. L. Dec. P 30, 571, 110 U.S.P.Q.2d 1506 (W.D. Wis. 2014)	Plaintiff Neri is a glass-blowing artist who worked with a fellow artist to create a composition of about 60 individual blown glass pieces that were installed onto the remodeled ceiling of an entryway designed and modeled by defendant Monroe. As per industry practice, defendant took "before," "during," and "after" photographs of the remodeling project, which included two photographs of the entryway and ceiling containing the glass pieces created by plaintiff. Plaintiff claimed defendant's photographs had infringed on the copyright she had registered for her glass installation. However, the court granted summary judgment in favor of defendant, finding defendant's photographs to be highly transformative of plaintiff's work. The court reasoned that plaintiff's sculpture was a "three-dimensional, impressionistic composition of multiple colored pieces of translucent glass designed intentionally to cast spiral-shaped shadows

Current Cases: Transformative Fair Use	
	on the vaulted ceiling, providing an aquatic quality to the entire space," while defendant's photographs are two-dimensional, realistic photographs of an interior space with a commercial aesthetic.
Morris v. Young, 925 F. Supp. 2d 1078 (C.D. Cal. 2013)	Plaintiff photographer Dennis Morris holds copyrights to a photograph of the Sex Pistols performing on stage.[189] Defendant artist found the photograph on the Internet without a copyright notice and therefore believed it was in the public domain. Defendant cropped the photograph and altered the colors, shades, and contrast between the black and white portions of the image. In his deposition, defendant stated he did not recall why he decided to use  plaintiff's photograph and did not recall if he was trying to make any sort of statement or criticism through his use of the image. Citing *Wall Data Inc. v Los Angeles Cty. Sheriff's Dep't*, 447 F.3d 769, 778 (9th Cir. 2006), as the basis for its analysis that a use is "considered transformative only where a defendant changes . . . or uses the plaintiff's copyrighted work in a different context such that the plaintiff's work is transformed into a new creation," the court held that defendant's work did not pass the transformative test since the works "appear to be little more than reproductions of the Subject Photograph with minor alterations . . . add[ing] only marginal artistic innovation to the Subject Photograph."
Morris v. Guetta, No. LA CV12-00684 JAK, 2013 WL 440127 (C.D. Cal. Feb. 4, 2013)	Plaintiff photographer Dennis Morris holds the copyright to a photograph of Sid Vicious of the Sex Pistols. Defendant Thierry Guetta (also known as Mr. Brainwash) is an appropriationist artist who used plaintiff's photograph in seven artworks. Some of  Sid Vicious by Dennis Morris / Sid Vicious by Tierry Guetta-Mr. Brainwash [190] defendant's works added elements such as splashes of brightly colored paint. One work features Sid Vicious wearing sunglasses and is printed on a backdrop with

189. Michael D. Murray, Cropped, revised, and resized thumbnail image derived from Dennis Morris's photograph of the Sex Pistols performing on stage, the subject of *Morris v. Young*, 925 F. Supp. 2d 1078 (C.D. Cal. 2013).

190. Michael D. Murray, Cropped, revised, and resized thumbnail images derived from exhibits depicting Dennis Morris's Photograph of Sid Vicious juxtaposed with Thierry Guetta's work featuring the Morris Photograph of Sid Vicious, at issue in the case *Morris v. Guetta*, No. LA CV12-00684 JAK, 2013 WL 440127 (C.D. Cal. Feb. 4, 2013).

Current Cases: Transformative Fair Use	
	the character Snoopy and palm trees. One is a mural. One is made out of broken vinyl records. Two works add a mole on the image of the face of Sid Vicious and an overlay of blonde hair. Defendant argued that his use of the photograph constituted fair use, but the court did not find defendant's works to be sufficiently transformative, reasoning that although the works add certain new elements to plaintiff's photograph of Sid Vicious making a distinctive facial expression, the overall effect of the defendant's changes were not transformative and remained at their core pictures of Sid Vicious making a distinctive facial expression.
North Jersey Media Group Inc. v. Pirro and Fox News Network, LLC, 74 F. Supp. 3d 605 (S.D.N.Y. 2015)	Plaintiff North Jersey Media Group ("NJMG") alleged that defendants infringed on plaintiff's copyright in its now iconic photograph of three firefighters raising the American flag at the ruins of the World Trade Center site on September 11, 2001 ("Photo"). Defendant network posted a photograph that juxtaposed the Photo with the classic World War II photograph of four U.S. Marines raising the American flag on Iwo Jima ("Combined Image") on a Facebook page associated with one of defendant's television programs.[191] Defendants alleged that their posting of the Combined Image was protected fair use under the Copyright Act. Defendants argued that the connection drawn between the events of September 11, 2001 and Iwo Jima can be "comfortably categorized as 'comment'"; however, plaintiff argued that Fox News did not create any new content, use existing content for a materially different purpose, or disseminate existing content to a new audience that might not have seen it otherwise. Court conceded that defendant did not simply copy the Photo wholesale since the Photo was cropped, of a lower resolution, and smaller scale than the original photograph, and included the tag #neverforget; however, the court could not conclude as a matter of law that the Combined Image sufficiently transformed the Photo to merit fair use protection. The court found defendant's use of the Combined Image to be a much closer call than the situations presented in *Cariou v Prince*, 714 F.3d 694 (2d Cir. 2013), and *Blanch v. Koons*, 467 F.3d 244 (2d Cir. 2006), and so refused to grant summary judgment.

---

191. Michael D. Murray, Cropped, revised, and resized thumbnail images derived from exhibits depicting Joe Rosenthal/Associated Press's photograph of marines raising the American flag on Iwo Jima (1945), juxtaposed with Thomas E. Franklin/North Jersey Media's photograph of fireman raising the flag over the World Trade Center Ground Zero Site (2001), at issue in *North Jersey Media Group Inc. v. Pirro and Fox News Network, LLC,* 74 F. Supp. 3d 605 (S.D.N.Y. 2015).

Lessons on How to Be "Transformative"

The lessons to be learned from the precedents are the following: "transformation" is best achieved with a change in the purpose and character of the original work. It is evident from the record of cases above that the courts take the "purpose" part of that rule very seriously, for all of the approved fair uses in the appellate cases involved a change in the predominant purpose for the use of the work rather than simply a change in the character (the form, the contents) of the work. Even if the works were not changed in form, function, or genre, the fair use works were transformed in predominant purpose either through alteration of the contents, or recontextualization of the copied material, or by the addition of significant creative expression so that the predominant purpose of the new work was significantly different from the original work. Non-alteration of the contents and expression of artistic and literary works still can be justified as fair use, but the function and purpose of the original works must be changed in the second works in a manner that fulfills fair use objectives that promote the progress of the arts and the creation of new, original expression that benefits the public.

The strongest transformative fair uses are those that modify the contents, function, and purpose in a significant and obvious manner, turning the meaning of the original work on its head, or openly criticizing the original work. Uses that do not modify the contents, function, or purpose of the original works in a significant and obvious manner fail the transformative test and are found not to be fair.

The most troubling fair use cases for secondary users of artistic or literary works are those such as *Salinger*,[192] *Gaylord*,[193] and *Dr. Seuss*,[194] that appear to have greatly altered significant aspects of the original works, but were not found to be fair uses. These seemingly incongruous outcomes may be explained by looking to the common underpinning and public policy objectives pursued by the courts in these opinions: even significant alteration of the form, genre, theme, tone, or even the overall meaning of the works will not be found to be fair use if some of the creative, artistic, and expressive virtues of the original works are not replaced or overwhelmed by the expression in the second work. If the creative, artistic, and expressive virtues of the original works still are discernible in the second work and still add value to the

---

192. *Salinger v. Colting*, 607 F.3d 68 (2d Cir. 2010).
193. *Gaylord v. United States*, 595 F.3d 1364 (Fed. Cir. 2010).
194. *Dr. Seuss Enterprises*, 109 F.3d at 1394.

secondary work, the use of the original work will be deemed unfair (e.g., *Salinger*[195]; *Gaylord*[196]; *Bridgeport Music-UMG*[197]; *Castle Rock*[198]; Dr. Seuss[199]).

Current Case: A Post-Transformative Circuit?

Kienitz v. Sconnie National LLC[200]

From time to time, the United States Court of Appeals for the Seventh Circuit seems intent to write its own circuit-specific copyright law, rather than following nationally recognized law.[201] One instance of this phenomenon is the recent case of *Kienitz v. Sconnie National LLC.*[202]

In *Kienitz*, Plaintiff photographer Kienitz brought an action against Defendant Sconnie National who had developed and sold t-shirts featuring Kienitz's photograph of Madison, Wisconsin Mayor Paul Soglin. Plaintiff's photograph of Soglin was posterized, the background removed, and Soglin's face turned lime green and surrounded by multi-colored writing, and placed on a t-shirt.[203] The image and shirts were used to comment on and criticize the mayor, who had attended the inaugural event of a popular street festival in Madison while a student at the University of Wisconsin, but decades later, and after becoming the mayor, now was trying to shut the street festival down.

---

195. *Salinger*, 607 F.3d at 68.

196. *Gaylord*, 595 F.3d at 1364.

197. *Bridgeport Music, Inc. v. UMG Recordings, Inc.*, 585 F.3d 267 (6th Cir. 2009).

198. *Castle Rock Entertainment, Inc. v. Carol Publishing Group*, 150 F.3d 132 (2nd Cir. 1998).

199. *Dr. Seuss Enterprises*, 109 F.3d at 1394.

200. *Kienitz v. Sconnie National LLC*, 766 F.3d 756 (7th Cir. 2014).

201. *See Ty, Inc. v. Publications Int'l Ltd.*, 292 F.3d 512 (7th Cir. 2002).

202. *Kienitz*, 766 F.3d at 756.

203. Michael D. Murray, Cropped, revised, and resized thumbnail images derived from exhibits depicting Michael Kienitz's photograph of Paul Soglin (2011), juxtaposed with Sconnie Nation's revised image of Paul Soglin (2012), excerpted from the court exhibits in *Kienitz v. Sconnie Nation LLC*, 766 F.3d 756 (7th Cir. 2014).

The district court debated whether the t-shirts were a transformative use of the photo, holding that the "robust transformative nature" of the defendant's t-shirts made the use of the photograph fair. The circuit court, however, rejected the use of the transformative test. The Seventh Circuit made the remarkable statement that the Supreme Court in *Campbell* had merely "mentioned the transformative test,"[204] which ignores over two decades of copyright case law that has recognized that the Supreme Court *adopted* the test as part of the analysis of the "purpose and character of the use" requirement in factor one of the 17 U.S.C. § 107 fair use factors. The Seventh Circuit observed that the transformative test was not found in § 107 (true enough), and that it had trouble reconciling the application of the test in cases such as *Cariou*,[205] discussed above, with the right to prevent the creation of derivative works under 17 U.S.C. § 106(2).[206]

Attorneys should note this argument for future reference: if other courts follow the Seventh Circuit's lead, copyright holders might have additional grounds to challenge a purported transformative use because it attempts to refute the holder's right to control and produce derivative works, given that most transformative works are, in fact, derivative of the original. Most fair uses are derivative of the original in some manner — they use all or part of the original to create a different work, sometimes with additional content, meaning, and expression, and sometimes for a different function or purpose from the original. If they didn't use some part of the original, they would not come under attack in a copyright infringement suit. But the message of the Seventh Circuit is that: (1) the transformative test should not apply in these circumstances, and (2) the very nature of many allegedly transformative works involves the creation of the exact type of work that should be precluded by the 17 U.S.C. § 106(2) derivative works right.

Although the Seventh Circuit ultimately reached the same conclusion as the district court, instead of using the transformative test, it reasoned that the company's alterations to the photograph were so drastic that "by the time the defendants were done, almost none of the copyrighted work remained," and thereby decided to affirm the award of summary judgment in favor of defendant.[207]

The transformative test has changed copyright law, and (aside from the Seventh Circuit) it has become the defining standard for fair use. Copyright law seeks first to promote new, original expression in the arts and literature, and second to allow other public interest activities such as education, research, archiving, news reporting, and comment and criticism of existing works. Transformation requires the copyist to fulfill these objectives.

204. *Kienitz*, 766 F.3d at 758 (citing *Campbell*, 510 U.S. at 579).
205. *Cariou*, 714 F.3d at 699-700.
206. *Kienitz*, 766 F.3d at 758.
207. *Id.* at 759-60.

The duplication of works just to show off their same creative, artistic, or literary virtues in a new time, a new place, a new mode or medium of communication or for a new audience does not fulfill the goals of copyright. No new and original expression results from simple replication of the same communication and expression found in the original. The derivative works doctrine gives those rights to the original author or artist, not to the public at large.

The lessons of the transformative test for those engaged in creative, artistic, or literary pursuits may be summed up in the following way: if an artist is going to copy an original work, she should use it for a different purpose than the purpose for which the original work was created. She should modify the contents, function, and meaning of the original work through alteration of the original expression or the addition of significant new expression. Otherwise, the artist is making an unauthorized exploitation of the creative expression of the work for exactly the same reasons and purposes that the original author or artist created the work, and she will be depriving the original author or artist of the derivative work rights guaranteed by copyright.

Notes and Questions

1. *Campbell* is significant for reducing the detrimental effect of commercial profit seeking in fair use cases. Prior to *Campbell*, an unabashedly commercial exploitation of a copyrighted work was virtually the kiss of death to any fair use defense, *e.g., Harper & Row Publishers, Inc. v. Nation Enters.*, 471 U.S. 539, 562, 566 (1985); but after *Campbell*, commercial motive is back to being one of several fair use factors, and it is treated simply as one more factor, no more and no less important than the others. The *Leibovitz* case involved actual commercial speech — an advertisement of a movie — which traditionally has been afforded less protection under the first amendment and copyright fair use cases; but the court nonetheless found Paramount's use of Leibovitz's photograph to be fair. By comparison, in the pre-*Campbell* world, the case *Steinberg v. Columbia Pictures Industries, Inc.*, 663 F. Supp. 706 (S.D.N.Y. 1987), also involved a movie advertisement (for *Moscow on the Hudson*) that incorporated some original art by cartoonist Steinberg in a satirical manner, but the defense of fair use failed.

2. There is something to be said about choosing the subject matter that you are going to copy and arguably parody. Paramount chose to make fun of Annie Leibovitz's solemn, dignified, even "pretentious" posing of Demi Moore while nude and pregnant, and were successful in their parody defense. Penguin Books was not successful in copying large portions of the character, layout, rhyming structure, and general look and feel of Dr. Seuss' popular *Cat in the Hat* book in order to produce an alleged parodic book that was an ironic commentary on the O.J.

Simpson murder trial proceedings, called *The Cat Not in the Hat. Dr. Seuss Enters. v. Penguin Books*, 109 F.3d 1394 (9th Cir. 1997).[208]

Miramax Films was not successful in borrowing many elements of a poster advertising the Columbia Pictures *Men in Black* movie and attempting to make a humorous, allegedly parodic statement for a poster advertising the Michael Moore spoof documentary, *The Big One. Columbia Pictures v. Miramax Films*, 11 F. Supp. 2d 1179 (C.D. Cal. 1998). This case teaches us that commercial exploitation of another entity's creative design dressed up in the guise of parody still will rarely succeed.

3. But how does a court decide whether a particular use is fair? Fair use is an equitable rule of reason incapable of being defined; thus, each case must be decided on the basis of all the surrounding facts and circumstances examined in light of the relevant factors. Congress has listed the four most important factors for consideration in § 107, but this list was not meant to be exclusive. *Id.* Other factors that the courts have examined include "bad faith by the user of copyrighted material that suggests unfairness" and "prejudice suffered by the alleged infringer as the result of the copyright holder's unreasonable and inexcusable delay in bringing the action." *New Era Publications v. Carol Publishing Group*, 904 F.2d 152, 160 (2d Cir. 1990). Thus, a court will look at the facts and determine which factors weigh in favor and which factors weigh against a finding of fair use. Depending on the circumstances, some factors may weigh more heavily than others.

In *Bill Graham Archives v. Dorling Kindersley Ltd.*, 448 F.3d 605 (2d Cir. 2006), the defendant published an illustrated biography of The Grateful Dead musical group. The court found that the defendant publisher used the plaintiff copyright holder's images of posters and tickets from The Grateful Dead's performances as historical artifacts that could document concert events and provide a visual context for the accompanying text. The court found that the publishers' use of the images as historical artifacts of the musical group's performances was

---

208. Michael D. Murray, Cropped, revised, and resized thumbnail image derived from exhibits depicting characters from "The Cat Not in the Hat," juxtaposed with original Dr. Seuss "Cat in the Hat" characters, as displayed in the exhibits to the court opinion in *Dr. Seuss Enters. v. Penguin Books*, 109 F.3d 1394 (9th Cir. 1997).

transformatively different from the original expressive purpose of the images and thus were a fair use of the copyrighted materials. *Accord, Calkins v. Playboy Enterprises Int'l, Inc.*, 561 F. Supp. 2d 1136 (E.D. Cal. 2008) (magazine's use of copyrighted high school yearbook photo as part of bio on model appearing in magazine was proper informative, historical use).

4. Jeffrey Koons may feel vindicated after his "appropriation art" finally survived judicial scrutiny as a fair use commentary on the media and depiction of women and fashion in society. After losing a string of lawsuits, *Rogers v. Koons*, 960 F.2d 301 (2d Cir.), *cert. denied*, 506 U.S. 934, 113 S. Ct. 365, 121 L. Ed. 2d 278 (1992); *Campbell v. Koons*, No. 91 Civ. 6055, 1993 WL 97381, 1993 U.S. Dist. LEXIS 3957 (S.D.N.Y. Apr. 1, 1993); *United Feature Syndicate v. Koons*, 817 F. Supp. 370 (S.D.N.Y. 1993), Koons finally won one. In *Blanch v. Koons*, 467 F.3d 244 (2d Cir. 2006), the Second Circuit emphasized the transformative nature of Koons's use of Blanch's photo and found that Koons's use as an artistic comment on media and society was fair use. Koons's use, however lucrative, was far removed from the original use of the work as fashion photography with "erotic" sensibilities created by Blanch, and even Blanch admitted she did not think that Koons's use had any impact on her commercial exploitation of the original photo.

   Blanch v. Koons might be the harbinger for a greater reliance on transformation as a defining element for fair uses under 17 U.S.C. §107, rather than an approach that relies heavily on tried and true categories of fair uses such as news reporting and parody, and rejects other categories, such as satire and other less-favored forms of commentary. *See, e.g., Zomba Enterprises, Inc. v. Panorama Records, Inc.*, 491 F.3d 574 (6th Cir. 2007) (in a claim of copyright infringement, the more transformative the new work, the less will be the significance of other factors, like commercialism, that may weigh against a finding of fair use).

5. As with many other areas of law, the Internet and World Wide Web and the growing popularity of weblogs (blogs), Twitter, social networking sites such as Facebook and MySpace, and user-generated content sites such as YouTube have complicated the analyses of fair use of copyrighted works. *See, e.g.,* Jonathan Purow, *The Copyright Implications of YouTube*, 18 N.Y.S.B.A. Ent. Arts & Sports L.J. 58 (2007). Issues of fair use are raised by efforts of news outlets and bloggers to comment on current events by excerpting and quoting from the copyrighted publication of others — the most basic question being 'How much is too much?' when it comes to quoting and excerpting. *See, e.g.,* Brian Stelter, *Copyright Challenge for Sites that Excerpt*, N.Y. Times, Mar. 2, 2009, at *www.nytimes.com/2009/03/02/business/media/*.

6. The "creative commons" concept where content providers have forfeited much of their authors' rights to common usage has introduced

new problems when these content providers still seek to retain and enforce limited rights such as a requirement that all future users (adaptors and creators of derivative works) give attribution to the original creator of the work and a requirement that all future adaptors and creators of derivative works also agree to donate their works to the public domain creative commons. Courts are willing to enforce these requirements as license terms under copyright law as opposed to treating them as running covenants under contract law. *See Jacobsen v. Katzer*, 535 F.3d 1373 (Fed. Cir. 2008).

ASSESSMENT

  1. Are these works[209] original enough for copyright purposes?

  (A) Yes, because they are "original" (not copied), and "creative" (conceived of as a work of the mind)
  (B) No, because the photographer simply rendered a photograph of another sculptural work
  (C) No, because they are not "creative," meaning the author did not create the scene depicted in the photographs
  (D) Yes, because photographs are copyrightable

  2. Dale Chihuly is one of the most successful modern day artists. Supporters describe him as "the most inventive glass sculptor in the history of the medium." Chihuly is suing a former employee, Rudy Brian, alleging that Brian — using techniques he learned while working for Chihuly — reviewed picture books of Chihuly's works and made unauthorized copies. Brian responded by asserting that Chihuly is attempting to keep him and other glass artists from making similar shapes inspired by similar natural forms and using basic glass blowing techniques that have been around for centuries. According to Brian, Chihuly uses ancient techniques to create biomorphic shapes found in nature or inspired by nature. Brian contends that Chihuly is trying to copyright these techniques, as well as the natural shapes, and in so doing, Chihuly is preventing Brian from pursuing his livelihood as a glass blower. According to Brian, the "biomorphic form of asymmetrical glass and other features such as colors, arrangements and presentation" are not

209. Michael D. Murray, Cropped and resized images derived from two Michael Murray photographs of Sacré-Coeur Basilica in Paris, France (2007).

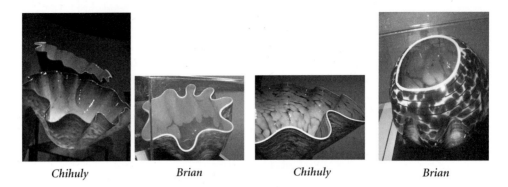

| Chihuly | Brian | Chihuly | Brian |

copyrightable in and of themselves, and Brian did not infringe Chihuly's copyright by creating biomorphic forms using standard glass blowing techniques.[210] Who has the better of this dispute?

(A) Chihuly has the better of the dispute, because Brian is copying his techniques

(B) Brian has the better of the dispute, because both artists are doing free flowing biomorphic glass sculptures inspired by natural creatures, and some of the resemblance comes from the sculpted glass media itself

(C) Chihuly has the better of this dispute, because Brian's works are works made for hire

(D) Brian has the better of the dispute, because his works are not exact duplicates of Chihuly's

3. Sara paints portraits for Sargent Whistler LLC (SW), a commercial studio that takes commissions for painted portraits and assigns them to a stable of artists who have agreed to work 20-30 hours a week for SW. Sara receives 20 percent of the commission fees for each portrait she paints for SW. SW routinely withholds income taxes, FICA, and state payroll taxes from her payments. SW provides no health insurance, retirement plan, or any other employee benefit to Sara and the other artists working for SW. SW has a large studio where many of the artists work, but Sara prefers the lighting and work space at her own home, and so she routinely performs her work at home with the knowledge and consent of SW. SW supplies paint, thinners, painting media, and canvases to its artists but not their palates, brushes, knives, or other painting tools and cleaning supplies. In any event, Sara prefers to select her own paints and so she rarely uses the paint supplied by SW, again with the knowledge and consent of SW. Sara, instead, takes a tax

210. Michael D. Murray, Cropped, revised, and resized thumbnail images derived from four Michael Murray photographs of Dale Chihuly "Macchia" glass sculptures displayed at the Missouri Botanical Gardens, St. Louis, MO (2006).

write-off for the supplies she expends in her work with SW in the years she earns enough to owe income tax. Sara also accepts her own commissions for portrait work and performs work on those projects in the same place as she does her work for SW; given that the portraits are in oil with its prolonged drying time, Sara often has two or three works in progress for SW sitting in her home studio alongside two or three projects for her own private commissions. Sara has never signed any contract or agreement mentioning ownership of the copyright for works she creates for SW's customers. Who owns the copyright over works Sara has created for SW's customers?

(A) Sara owns the copyrights, because she works from home
(B) Sara owns the copyrights, because she uses her own supplies and materials
(C) SW owns the copyrights, because SW provided Sara with a workplace, supplies, and clients
(D) SW owns the copyrights, because SW routinely withholds income taxes, FICA, and state payroll taxes from Sara's payments

4. Pop singing sensation Normandy Javelin grabbed media attention by shaving her head. Your client mocked up newspaper cover pages using the actual mastheads and portions of the *New Tropolis Newsworld* and the *New Tropolis Post Messenger* newspapers' copyrighted cover page material, combined with photographs that were published by the newspapers, to make it appear that the newspapers had put the star's head shaving incident on the cover of the newspapers along with outrageously worded headlines (e.g., "Newsworld is Nuts Over Normandy's New Noggin"). In fact, the newspapers had not carried the story on their front pages but rather made a brief mention of it without outrageous headlines in the entertainment section of the papers. Your client posted his mocked up newspaper covers on his internet blog, *Media Stormtrooper*. Is this a proper copyright fair use of the newspapers' masthead and cover page materials and their photographs of the singing star? (Later, in Chapter 5 ("Right of Publicity"), you may consider whether this was a proper parody fair use of the name, image, and likeness of Normandy Javelin depicted in the mock newspaper covers.)

(A) This is a fair use, because Javelin is newsworthy
(B) This is not a fair use, because the blog used too much of the photos of Javelin
(C) This is a fair use, if the court finds that blog was making fun of the newspapers and the way that the newspapers cover and photograph celebrities
(D) This is not a fair use, because the works do not transform the original works

5. Advocates of Alternative Marriage (AAM) started fund-raising efforts to support reformation of state laws regarding gay marriage and civil

unions. Some of the materials developed in this effort were posters in which AAM used several copyrighted images owned by the tabloid magazine *Zip Mag* ("*Zip*"). The images related to Normandy Javelin's 55-hour marriage to Joshua Philips that started and finished in Las Vegas, and to movie and singing star Juanita Perez's 2-week marriage to the singer, Matt Tony. AAM did not ask permission to use the images. AAM modified the Javelin-Philips marriage license image by adding a faint image of Normandy Javelin as a background, and by adding text at the bottom reading: "*Good for 55 hours only." AAM modified the Javelin-Philips wedding photograph by superimposing the heads of Matt Tony and Juanita Perez onto the bodies of the unnamed couple appearing next to Javelin and Philips in the photograph, and by adding captioned names for each person: "Matt," "J-Pez," "Normandy," and "Josh," and also by adding text at the bottom reading "Ending Soon." AAM also superimposed the heading, "Little White Wedding Chapel, Las Vegas," over the heads of the celebrities in the wedding photograph. The rest of the poster had large, bold letters stating, "By all means, let us preserve the sacred institution of marriage." AAM used portions of *Zip*'s copyrighted images for each of the modifications described above. *Zip* sued AAM for copyright infringement. Evaluate whether AAM may assert a fair use defense in copyright law. (Later, in Chapter 5, you may consider whether this was a proper parody fair use of the name, image, and likeness of the celebrities featured in the posters).

(A) This is a fair use, because AAM created a satire, not a parody

(B) This is not a fair use, because AAM is commenting on marriage equality, not on the celebrities

(C) This is not a fair use, unless the court finds that AAM has created new, transformed works with a different function and purpose from the originals, and the new purpose in part was to comment on or criticize *Zip Magazine*

(D) This is a fair use, because the works make fun of the celebrities' short marriages

ASSESSMENT ANSWERS

1. Are these works original enough for copyright purposes ?

(A) Yes, because they are "original" (not copied), and "creative" (conceived of as a work of the mind

(B) No, because the photographer simply rendered a photograph of another sculptural work

(C) No, because they are not "creative," meaning the author did not create the scene depicted in the photographs

(D) Yes, because photographs are copyrightable

ANSWER: The answer is choice (A). Digital photography is just another media, another form of expression. These photographs are "authored"—they are created by an author (a photographer), and thus may qualify as "original" (not copied), and "creative" (conceived of as a work of the mind, and rendered into expressive existence through the tools of digital photography) works. Because of this, (B) and (C) are incorrect. Choice (D) does not say enough—all photographs are potentially copyrightable, but they must be original and creative.

2. Dale Chihuly is one of the most successful modern day artists. Supporters describe him as "the most inventive glass sculptor in the history of the medium." Chihuly is suing a former employee, Rudy Brian, alleging that Brian—using techniques he learned while working for Chihuly—reviewed picture books of Chihuly's works and made unauthorized copies. Brian responded by asserting that Chihuly is attempting to keep him and other glass artists from making similar shapes inspired by similar natural forms and using basic glass blowing techniques that have been around for centuries. According to Brian, Chihuly uses ancient techniques to create biomorphic shapes found in nature or inspired by nature. Brian contends that Chihuly is trying to copyright these techniques, as well as the natural shapes, and in so doing, Chihuly is preventing Brian from pursuing his livelihood as a glass blower. According to Brian, the "biomorphic form of asymmetrical glass and other features such as colors, arrangements and presentation" are not copyrightable in and of themselves, and Brian did not infringe Chihuly's copyright by creating biomorphic forms using standard glass blowing techniques. Who has the better of this dispute?

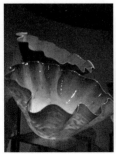  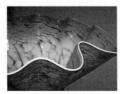 

Chihuly *Brian* *Chihuly* *Brian*

(A) Chihuly has the better of the dispute, because Brian is copying his techniques
(B) Brian has the better of the dispute, because both artists are doing free flowing biomorphic glass sculptures inspired by natural creatures, and some of the resemblance comes from the sculpted glass media itself
(C) Chihuly has the better of this dispute, because Brian's works are works made for hire
(D) Brian has the better of the dispute, because his works are not exact duplicates of Chihuly's

ANSWER: The answer is choice (B). The dispute revolves around the application of the scènes à faire and merger doctrines to the creation of polymorphous or natural-appearing shapes molded in glass. It also requires attention to the overarching originality and creativity question that gives rise to the merger and scènes à faire doctrines: did the authors, Chihuly on the one hand, and Brian on the other, create the appearance of the works, or is the appearance dictated by the media? (Note that the appearance is not dictated by the actual outward appearance of the subject matter, because neither Chihuly nor Brian is rendering images of actual objects, sea plants, or sea creatures. Their works simply are "inspired" by such things.) It will matter if all glass sculptors working with glass in a free-flowing format produce works that, at some level, resemble each other. Or, on the contrary, is it the case that the sculptor has full control over the outcome and final appearance of the works, such that any resemblance between works is dictated by the sculptor. If the media dictates a portion of the appearance, this should prevent the exercise of copyright protection over the portion of the appearance dictated by the media (*see Satava v. Lowry,*[211] supra, where the court held that certain aspects of glass-in-glass sculptures simply are dictated by the media itself). But if artistic, creative choices were made (conceived of in the mind, and rendered into existence by the sculptor), then these choices and the expression produced could and should enjoy copyright protection. Thus, (B) is the best choice. (A) is incorrect — you can copy techniques, they are uncopyrightable. (C) is incorrect — nothing indicates these are works made for hire, and (D) is incorrect, because exact duplication is not the only form of copying that is prevented under copyright.

3. Sara paints portraits for Sargent Whistler LLC (SW), a commercial studio that takes commissions for painted portraits and assigns them to a stable of artists who have agreed to work 20-30 hours a week for SW. Sara receives 20 percent of the commission fees for each portrait she paints for SW. SW routinely withholds income taxes, FICA, and state payroll taxes from her payments. SW provides no health insurance,

---

211. *Satava v. Lowry,* 323 F.3d 805 (9th Cir. 2003).

retirement plan, or any other employee benefit to Sara and the other artists working for SW. SW has a large studio where many of the artists work, but Sara prefers the lighting and work space at her own home, and so she routinely performs her work at home with the knowledge and consent of SW. SW supplies paint, thinners and painting media, and canvases to its artists but not their palates, brushes, knives, or other painting tools and cleaning supplies. In any event, Sara prefers to select her own paints and so she rarely uses the paint supplied by SW, again with the knowledge and consent of SW. Sara, instead, takes a tax write-off for the supplies she expends in her work with SW in the years she earns enough to owe income tax. Sara also accepts her own commissions for portrait work and performs work on those projects in the same place as she does her work for SW; given that the portraits are in oil with its prolonged drying time, Sara often has two or three works in progress for SW sitting in her home studio alongside two or three projects for her own private commissions. Sara has never signed any contract or agreement mentioning ownership of the copyright for works she creates for SW's customers. Who owns the copyright over works Sara has created for SW's customers?

(A) Sara owns the copyrights, because she works from home
(B) Sara owns the copyrights, because she uses her own supplies and materials
(C) SW owns the copyrights, because SW provided Sara with a work-place, supplies, and clients
(D) SW owns the copyrights, because SW routinely withholds income taxes, FICA, and state payroll taxes from Sara's payments

ANSWER: The answer is choice (D). This problem concerning Sara and Sargent Whistler (SW) places the question of whether Sara is an employee or an independent contract or right in the middle of the common law agency test. Choices (A), (B), and (C) give us facts that can be balanced, but no clear prediction can be made about how these factors would tip the scale. Sara has control over many aspects of her work — the time and place of her work, the materials, the tools — but still works regularly for SW, takes orders from SW, expects and receives a regular stream of new work, and performs her tasks according to SW's schedule. The most important factor is, however, that: "SW routinely withholds income taxes, FICA, and state payroll taxes from her payments." This alone should make the analysis come out in favor of a finding that Sara is an "employee" for work made for hire purposes with regard to the works created at the direction of and for the benefit of SW. Therefore, (D) provides the most definitive answer to this question.

4. Pop singing sensation Normandy Javelin grabbed media attention by shaving her head. Your client mocked up newspaper cover pages using the actual mastheads and portions of the *New Tropolis Newsworld* and the *New Tropolis Post Messenger* newspapers' copyrighted cover page

material, combined with photographs that were published by the newspapers, to make it appear that the newspapers had put the star's head shaving incident on the cover of the newspapers along with outrageously worded headlines (e.g., "Newsworld is Nuts Over Normandy's New Noggin"). In fact, the newspapers had not carried the story on their front pages but rather made a brief mention of it without outrageous headlines in the entertainment section of the papers. Your client posted his mocked up newspaper covers on his internet blog, *Media Stormtrooper*. Is this a proper copyright fair use of the newspapers' masthead and cover page materials and their photographs of the singing star? [Later, in Chapter 5 ("Right of Publicity"), you may consider whether this was a proper parody fair use of the name, image, and likeness of Normandy Javelin depicted in the mock newspaper covers.]

(A) This is a fair use, because Javelin is newsworthy
(B) This is not a fair use, because the blog used too much of the photos of Javelin
(C) This is a fair use, if the court finds that blog was making fun of the newspapers and the way that the newspapers cover and photograph celebrities
(D) This is not a fair use, because the works do not transform the original works

ANSWER: The answer is choice (C). The use of the two newspapers' copyrighted expression implicates the fair use factors in the following way: the purpose and character of the use appears at first blush to be a parody, but of what? Is it making fun of the newspapers and how they cover celebrities? Is it ridiculing the photography put forth by the newspapers? These are important questions, because a true parody makes fun of the artist or her artwork (*see Leibovitz v. Paramount Pictures*, supra), while a satire makes fun of a different target by using the work of the artist (*e.g., Blanch v. Koons*). In this scenario, the work seems to be ridiculing Normandy Javelin, not the newspapers that covered her haircut incident. A satire still can make it through the factors as a fair use (*e.g., Blanch v. Koons*), but it is not as powerful on the fair use factors as a true parody. Perhaps the title of the client's blog, *Media Stormtrooper*, gives some evidence that the main focus of the blog is the media, and that the client regularly criticizes and comments on newspapers and other media, and how they cover celebrities, which would go a long way toward establishing a commentary and criticism purpose and character of the use, and thereby go a long way toward establishing a fair use defense. The client's use on his blog arguably is beneficial to the client, which trends toward a commercial rather than non-commercial rating, but the client did not sell, market, or further distribute the work, which weighs slightly in favor of fair use. On factors two and three, the newspapers' works were published (a plus for fair use), and part of their works, the photography, was used in the context of non-fictional reports of "news" and current events of some public interest, which is beneficial to a fair use. (The use of the masthead and cover page material suggests other areas of intellectual property law, mainly trademark, which is discussed in Chapter 3 of this text). But the actual photographs were purely expressive, creative works, sold and licensed by the owner, which ultimately tips factor two against fair use. Factor three, amount taken, relies heavily on the purpose and character of the use under factor one, and in this case, finding that the use either was a parody or a satire most likely will justify the amount of the originals that was taken. The effect on the market for the original (factor four) will tend to work against fair use, because newspapers and photographers for news media do license and resell photographs as a routine part of their business, so taking for free what is otherwise sold or licensed means that the second use here does cut into the owners' market. Only choice (C) provides a true reason to find a fair use here.

5. Advocates of Alternative Marriage (AAM) started fund-raising efforts to support reformation of state laws regarding gay marriage and civil unions. One of the materials developed in this effort was posters in which AAM used several copyrighted images owned by the tabloid magazine *Zip Mag* ("*Zip*"). The images related to Normandy Javelin's 55-hour marriage to Joshua Philips that started and finished in Las Vegas, and to movie and singing star Juanita Perez's 2-week marriage to the singer, Matt Tony. AAM did not ask permission to use the images. AAM modified the Javelin-Philips marriage license image by adding a faint image of Normandy Javelin as a background, and by adding text at the bottom reading: "*Good for 55 hours only." AAM modified the Javelin-Philips wedding photograph by superimposing the heads of Matt Tony and Juanita Perez onto the bodies of the unnamed couple appearing next to Javelin and Philips in the photograph, and by adding captioned names for each person: "Matt," "J-Pez," "Normandy," and "Josh," and also by adding text at the bottom reading "Ending Soon." AAM also superimposed the heading, "Little White Wedding Chapel, Las Vegas," over the heads of the celebrities in the wedding photograph. The rest of the poster had large, bold letters stating, "By all means, let us preserve the sacred institution of marriage." AAM used portions of *Zip's* copyrighted images for each of the modifications described above. *Zip* sued AAM for copyright infringement. Evaluate whether AAM may assert a fair use defense in copyright law? [Later, in Chapter 5, you may consider whether this was a proper parody fair use of the name, image, and likeness of the celebrities featured in the posters].

(A) This is a fair use, because AAM created a satire, not a parody
(B) This is not a fair use, because AAM is commenting on marriage equality, not on the celebrities
(C) This is not a fair use, unless the court finds that AAM has created new, transformed works with a different function and purpose

from the originals, and the new purpose in part was to commenting on or criticize *Zip Magazine*

(D) This is a fair use, because the works make fun of the celebrities' short marriages

ANSWER: The answer is choice (C). Like question 4, question 5 suggests a parody, but again, the question should be asked, "What is the parody making fun of?" Is the AAM organization making fun of *Zip Mag* and its photography? The way *Zip Mag* covers celebrities? The authorities who issued the marriage license? Most likely, the work will be evaluated as satire, not a parody, which makes it a little less powerful on the fair use factors because the purpose and character of a satire under factor one is less forgiving (or less influential) on the other factors compared to a true parody. As with question 4 above, the newspapers' works were published (a plus for fair use), and the photography was used in the context of non-fictional reports of "news" and public interest events, which is beneficial to a fair use. But the actual photographs were purely expressive, creative works, sold and licensed by the owner, which ultimately tips factor two against fair use. Factor three, amount taken, relies heavily on the purpose and character of the use under factor one, and, as in question 4, a finding that the use either was a parody or a satire most likely will justify the amount of the originals that was taken. The effect on the market for the original (factor four) will tend to work against fair use, because newspapers and photographers for news media do license and resell photographs as a routine part of their business, so taking for free what is otherwise sold or licensed means that the second use here does cut into the owners' market. Only choice (C) provides a reason that there might be a fair use here: if the court finds that AAM has created new, transformed works with a different function and purpose from the originals, and the new purpose in part was to comment on or criticize *Zip Magazine*, then the use may be evaluated as fair.

3 | TRADEMARK RIGHTS

In addition to copyright protection, discussed in the preceding chapter, another form of intellectual property important to the art community is trademark.[1] On the federal level, the Lanham Act of 1946 and Trademark Revision Act of 1988 govern the regulation of trade and service marks and provide for their registration with the U.S. Patent and Trademark Office (PTO).

The legal context of trademark law is found in trade, commerce, and consumer protection — which are regulated by equitable considerations of fairness and unjust enrichment, as well as the parallel and sometimes overlapping law regulating fraud and unfair business practices.

A. Background Principles of Trademark Law

1. The Fundamental Goals of Trademark Law

Although traditionally included in any list of intellectual property rights, trademark is the least intellectual of the intellectual property topics. Trademark does not require an invention and innovation with practical application, which patent law requires. Nor does it require original creative expression, as copyright law does. It is also not about protecting valuable knowledge and information through secrecy, confidentiality agreements, and covenants not to compete,

---

1. Image on this page: Michael D. Murray, Collage of Revised and Resized Thumbnail Images of 18 Trademark Logos (2016), derived from *Fabrily Campaigns: Trademark vs. Copyright*, https://fabrily.wordpress.com/2014/06/26/fabrily-campaigns-trademark-vs-copyright/ (2014).

which are encompassed within trade secret law; although both trademark and trade secret law are supported by equitable principle regarding good faith and fair dealing as well as the avoidance of unjust enrichment. Trademarks are about commerce, and more specifically, the proper identification of goods in commerce to avoid consumer confusion about the origin and source of the goods.

Property and Intellectual Property

As a reminder from Chapter 2, **property** in law is the right to control and exclude others from something that is owned. With **intellectual property**, the *something* generally is a right associated with a work or creation that is a product of the intellect, a work of the mind of the author or artist. Trademark law stretches this definition because it does not require much intellect or effort to come up with a mark, although it is difficult to maintain a going concern in business that is worthy of the support of trademarks. Trademarks were brought under intellectual property law because they are intangible rights, and they are protected and enforced under a similar system of infringement damages and injunctive relief as other intellectual property rights.

The rationale for trademark law is not to protect intellectual property *per se,* but to protect consumers. Trademark law is not trying to directly or indirectly reward or encourage those who come up with good trademarks, and it is not set up to reward people for achievements in commerce, trademark design, or the arts and sciences. The only function of trademark law is to prevent consumer confusion regarding the origin and source of the goods in the marketplace. There is no such thing as a mark that has no use or association with selling and producing goods, or offering services. All valid marks have to be an identifier of something — goods, services, a brand of goods, a company, an organization, or a group.

Commerce is the key in trademark law, but "commerce," when used in trademark law, does not carry its usual day-to-day meaning: "use in commerce" just means that the parties (the owner and the alleged infringer) participate in the world, offering and exchanging goods or services. It does not require both parties to be engaged in trying to make money — all non-profits can qualify for trademarks, and you can maintain your trademarks even if you never make a dime with your good or services. The same is said about those who use other people's marks intentionally or unintentionally: they do not have to be competitors of the original owner, and do not have to be engaged in some serious commercial activity. All that is needed is that they be engaged in the world and would gain some advantage from the use or display of the mark.

2. Duration of Trademarks, and Incontestable Marks

A trademark can last forever if you keep using and renewing the mark. *See* 15 U.S.C. §§ 1058, 1059. There is no term limit for trademarks. In fact, the law admires and more highly protects marks that are old and long lasting.

After five years of federal registration and uncontested use, the mark can become incontestable, and if the mark is used long enough to obtain some notoriety, it can become what the law calls a "famous mark," which will be protected under an additional set of laws that prevent trademark dilution.

> **What is the Statute of Repose? Can it Allow Marks to Become Incontestable?**
> The trademark statute of repose is a five-year statute under which marks can become incontestable if registered and used continuously for five years without challenge. Incontestable does not mean permanent or that the mark can never be challenged, but it does limit the kinds of challenges and defenses others can raise against your mark. *See* 15 U.S.C. § 1065.

3. Sources of Trademark Law

There are federal trademark laws that apply across the entire United States, coast to coast, and there are state trademark laws that apply within a single state, such as Indiana. The federal law is enacted by Congress, and is called the United States Trademark Law, which is found in the United States Code at 15 U.S.C. § 1051 et seq. The federal law codifies:

- The Lanham Act of 1946
- The Trademark Law Revision Act of 1988
- The Federal Trademark Dilution Act of 1995
- The Anticybersquatting Consumer Protection Act (1999)
- The Madrid Protocol Implementation Act (2002)[2]
- The Trademark Dilution Revision Act of 2006

There also is such a thing as "Common Law trademark," which is based on the law derived from judicial determinations of trademark disputes over time and which has developed principles that predate and currently parallel the federal and state trademark laws.

B. Requirements of Marks

Two Pesos, Inc. v. Taco Cabana, Inc.

505 U.S. 763 (1992)[3]

Justice WHITE delivered the opinion of the Court.

Respondent Taco Cabana, Inc., operates a chain of fast-food restaurants in Texas. The restaurants serve Mexican food. . . . In December 1985, a Two

---

2. Codified in United States law as 15 U.S.C. §§ 1141-41n.
3. Inner citations omitted.

Pesos, Inc., restaurant was opened in Houston. Two Pesos adopted a motif very similar to . . . Taco Cabana's trade dress.

. . .

II

The Lanham Act was intended to make "actionable the deceptive and misleading use of marks" and "to protect persons engaged in . . . commerce against unfair competition." . . .

A trademark is defined in 15 U.S.C. § 1127 as including "any word, name, symbol, or device or any combination thereof" used by any person "to identify and distinguish his or her goods, including a unique product, from those manufactured or sold by others and to indicate the source of the goods, even if that source is unknown." In order to be registered, a mark must be capable of distinguishing the applicant's goods from those of others. Marks are often classified in categories of generally increasing distinctiveness; following the classic formulation set out by Judge Friendly, they may be (1) generic; (2) descriptive; (3) suggestive; (4) arbitrary; or (5) fanciful. . . . The latter three categories of marks, because their intrinsic nature serves to identify a particular source of a product, are deemed inherently distinctive and are entitled to protection. In contrast, generic marks — those that "refe[r] to the genus of which the particular product is a species" — are not registrable as trademarks.

Marks which are merely descriptive of a product are not inherently distinctive. When used to describe a product, they do not inherently identify a particular source, and hence cannot be protected. However, descriptive marks may acquire the distinctiveness which will allow them to be protected under the Act. Section 2 of the Lanham Act provides that a descriptive mark that otherwise could not be registered under the Act may be registered if it "has become distinctive of the applicant's goods in commerce." This acquired distinctiveness is generally called "secondary meaning." . . .

The general rule regarding distinctiveness is clear: An identifying mark is distinctive and capable of being protected if it either (1) is inherently distinctive or (2) has acquired distinctiveness through secondary meaning. It is also clear that eligibility for protection under § 43(a) depends on nonfunctionality. It is, of course, also undisputed that liability under § 43(a) requires proof of the likelihood of confusion. . . .

The Court of Appeals determined that . . . Taco Cabana's trade dress was not descriptive but rather inherently distinctive, and that it was not functional. . . . [W]e agree with [the] resolution by the Court of Appeals. There is no persuasive reason to apply to trade dress a general requirement of secondary meaning which is at odds with the principles generally applicable to infringement suits under § 43(a). . . . We agree with the Court of Appeals that proof of secondary meaning is not required to prevail on a claim under

§43(a) of the Lanham Act where the trade dress at issue is inherently distinctive, and accordingly the judgment of that court is affirmed.[4]

---

1. Trademarks and Service Marks

The basic requirement of any mark is that it is used in commerce as an identifier of specific goods from a specific manufacturer. Trademark law protects distinctive words, text, letters, symbols, slogans, designs, and packaging that are used as an identifier of goods and services in commerce.[5] The term "trademark" is used for goods (products, items, art works, and other objects) sold in commerce, and is used to indicate the origin of these goods and to *distinguish* them from goods of another source. The term "service mark" is used for service providers to distinguish their services from other providers' services.

A mark is used by consumers to differentiate goods of a certain manufacturer and which possess a certain level of quality and value, from goods of a different manufacturer which potentially might possess a different level of quality and value. The quality and value do not have to be high in each case. Wal-Mart is known for selling items of cheap cost but acceptable value. That is what the Wal-Mart mark stands for, and it is what the consumers who shop at Wal-Mart want and what they go looking for when they look for Wal-Mart branded goods. Macy's wants you to know that the Macy's mark stands for better quality goods than the Wal-Marts and K-Marts of the world will provide, but Macy's goods still will be affordable. The higher end stores stand for exclusivity — their goods are more expensive, but they will allow you to have uniquely desirable items with greater style and fashion sense than all lower-classed stores. Some years ago, Target stores moved from a "cheap goods with value" model to a "fashionable goods at reasonable prices" model.

All of this indicates that marks are a commerce-based heuristic (a cognitive shorthand) for consumer decisions. In other words, a consumer might think, "If I want the best, I should shop at X, but if all I want is the cheapest I should go to Y, and if I really want a low price but good quality, Z is the place." It is easier to remember the shorthand "X for the best, Y for the cheapest, and Z for low price and good quality" than it would be to go out on each shopping excursion and carefully examine all of the options for goods one after the other before making a decision. Hence the use of the term "heuristic" — a cognitive shorthand for decision making. Trademarks provide that shorthand for on-the-spot consumer decisions.

The same applies to individual products. Throughout its existence, Anheuser Busch came out with a succession of beers all targeted to different consumer

---

4. The U.S. Supreme Court later modified this holding when it held that unregistered product design trade dress cannot be inherently distinctive, and thus it requires proof of secondary association. *Wal-Mart Stores, Inc. v. Samara Bros.*, 529 U.S. 205 (2000) (design trade dress for children's clothing).

5. *See* 15 U.S.C. §1127 (definition of "trademark").

expectations: Busch beer for the "bargain basement beer" crowd; Budweiser for the "good, solid, American beer" crowd; Michelob for the discriminating palate; Bud Light for the calorie conscious; and so on. With micro-brewers and small batch brewers, and small volume lines from large volume brewers, the world of beer becomes a confusing place for consumers. Trademark helps to sort the situation out by allowing manufacturers to label their line with a useful identifier in the form of words, visual imagery, or a combination of the two, so that consumers can pick that manufacturer's goods out of the crowd. It stands to reason that this function will not work if other manufacturers are allowed to use the same or a confusingly similar mark to identify their goods — consumers will be confused and possibly will be tricked into buying the wrong goods. So, the enforcement of a trademark means exercising the right to exclude others from the same and all confusingly similar marks in areas of commerce where the use of a confusingly similar mark might trick consumers into buying the wrong goods. When is it legal and proper to exclude other marks from the market? That is the subject of the remaining topics of this chapter.

2. Functionality vs. Distinctive Appearance

Trademarks must be distinctive, but they cannot be functional. What this means is that trademark law cannot tie up a certain design element that actually improves the functioning of the product and call it a "trademark" of the product in question. Yes, a distinctive design can help consumers identify a product and learn to associate that product with a certain manufacturer. But trademark protection will not apply if the distinctive design is functional.

The functionality must actually help the product function *as the product*; it is not enough that some element of the design does something. All things have functionality — letters communicate language, words have meaning, colors function as coloration — but for the limitation to apply, the design must help the product be better, more useful, more functional as the type of product that it is. Thus, a Coca-Cola bottle design will be trademark-worthy if it is purely decorative and not functional, but a design that helps you grip the bottle better or makes the bottle stack on the shelf a certain way may not be protectable.

The trademark rejection of functional design elements parallels the same rejection of functional designs in copyright law. The reasons also are similar:

- ■ Patent law (not trademark or copyright law) is supposed to protect useful, functional designs. Patent law has its own requirements and limitations that make sure that proper inventors of innovative designs get the protection, and not everyone with a supposedly good design.
- ■ Patent protection lasts 20 years. Copyright protection lasts for the lifetime of the creator plus 70 more years. Trademark protection can last forever. *Compare* 35 U.S.C. §§ 154, 173, *with* 15 U.S.C. §§ 1058, 1059, *and* 17 U.S.C. § 302.
- ■ Public policy holds that it does not benefit the public for one manufacturer to have monopoly power over useful, functional designs for terms

exceeding patent law's 20 year term. Useful, helpful designs should be made free for all to manufacture and sell after a relatively short protection period.

Thus, functional elements will not be protected under trademark law either as logos, marks, trade dress, or under the consumer confusion claim of false designation of origin.

C. Strength of Marks

Marks vary in strength. The term, "strength," refers to the ability of the owner of the mark to exclude another mark from existing in the same or similar lines of goods and services, and the potential range of fair uses and copying of the mark that will be precluded. A strong mark will preclude a full range of marks that look like, sound like, or simply suggest the original mark, and will support injunctive relief to keep similar marks out of a wide range of similar, competing lines of goods or services. A weaker mark will not be enforced so robustly, and it may not be enforced at all.

Marks must be distinctive, and there are ways to categorize the potential distinction of marks based on their wording or visual components. Consider the following marks:

- Exxon, Kodak, Colgate Toothpaste, Budweiser Beer, Michelob Beer, Coca Cola
- Hidden Valley Ranch, Red Baron Pizza, Starkist Tuna, Octagon Soap, Dutch Boy Paint
- Pepsi, Snap-On Tools, Velveeta Cheese, Viagra, Cheerios, Windex, Turtle Wax
- Baby Oil, Puppy Chow
- safari hats, aspirin, thermos bottle, cellophane, cola

From the top of the list to the bottom, the marks descend from the strongest marks to the weakest, because the top marks are "fanciful," the second group marks are "arbitrary," the third group marks are "suggestive," the fourth group marks are "descriptive" (but with secondary association), and the last group of marks (actually, non-marks) are "generic."

1. Fanciful Marks

- Exxon, Kodak, Colgate Toothpaste, Budweiser Beer, Michelob Beer, Coca Cola.

The above marks are fanciful — the highest, strongest category of marks. These marks are called "fanciful" because they stand for nothing in the real world; they only have literal real world meaning as trademarks.

Fanciful marks are strong marks because they only can function as an identifier of goods. A Budweiser means nothing to an American consumer except a certain brand of beer. Any manufacturer thinking of using the term Budweiser may be presumed to be using it solely to grab the attention of consumers who look for Budweiser products in the marketplace. The use of the term for another beer or other products that might be associated with beer drinking would work to confuse the consumers, and trademark law will shut the effort down.

2. Arbitrary Marks

> ■ Hidden Valley Ranch, Red Baron Pizza, Starkist Tuna, Octagon Soap, Dutch Boy Paint, Apple Computers

The above marks are arbitrary marks. Arbitrary marks are strong marks. Together with fanciful marks, they typically meet the requirements of the law for distinctiveness.[6]

Arbitrary marks are called "arbitrary" because, although these words have a definite meaning in the world, this meaning has no connection at all to the products to which the marks have been assigned. In other words, the assignment of the name, "Red Baron" to pizza is a random, fortuitous assignment. The historical World War I flying ace, known as the "Red Baron" because of his red-colored triplane, has nothing to do with pizza, baking, or Italian food (the Baron was German). Hidden valleys might be a nice place to visit, but they are not associated with wonderful salads.

To be suggestive or not to be?
Suggestive marks present a dilemma for business people. On the one hand, a mark that suggests a positive attribute of your product is good marketing; on the other hand, it may make your mark less distinctive and less able to exclude other, similar marks from your area of commerce.

The fact that the assignment is arbitrary and capricious helps the strength of the mark because there is no logic and motivation for a competitor to want to use the mark or a similar mark, except to confuse consumers into heading for their goods when the consumers are really looking for the original mark's goods. That kind of trickery is exactly what the trademark laws want to prevent.

3. Suggestive Marks

> ■ Pepsi, Snap-On Tools, Velveeta Cheese, Viagra, Cheerios, Windex, Turtle Wax

---

6. *See id.*; *Two Pesos*, 505 U.S. at 768; *Grubbs v. Sheakley Grp., Inc.*, 807 F.3d 785, 794–95 (6th Cir. 2015); *Juice Generation, Inc. v. GS Enterprises LLC*, 794 F.3d 1334, 1339 (Fed. Cir. 2015).

These marks are suggestive, which still can be a mark of distinction sufficient to obtain trademark protection, but are not as strong as the fanciful or arbitrary marks because the mark itself suggests desirable attributes of the product.[7] A mark is suggestive if it connotes, without describing, some quality, ingredient, or characteristic of the product." Pepsi gives you pep; Snap-On tools snap right on to get the job done; Velveeta melts smoothly, as smooth as velvet; Viagra makes you more viable (in one particular activity, at least); Windex is for windows; and so on. The fact that product descriptions will be used by others to tout their own productions, and that similar kinds of suggestive descriptions might be used and might become associated with two or more products, means that suggestive marks invite a certain amount of similar sounding or similar meaning marks in the marketplace. And that reduces their distinctive power as an identifier of one particular product.

4. Descriptive Marks and Secondary Association

■ Baby Oil, Puppy Chow

A descriptive mark describes the product itself. Oil for babies is baby oil. Food for puppies is puppy chow. A helpful rule of thumb to distinguish suggestive marks from descriptive marks is that if the mark imparts information about the attributes of the product directly, it is descriptive, but if the mark stands for an idea which requires some operation of the imagination to connect it with the qualities of the goods, it is suggestive.[8] Using a description of your product as a trademark is dangerous because other people would have just as much incentive to use the same exact descriptions for their products of the same species as you are using for your mark. Thus, descriptive marks by themselves are not distinctive.

Descriptive terms become marks through the development of "**secondary meaning**" or "**secondary association.**" If an owner proves that her mark has achieved a secondary meaning, aside from the simple descriptive terms used in the mark, and the secondary meaning is a fixed association of the products produced under the mark with a single manufacturer, then the marks can be enforced to exclude others from using these exact descriptive terms in their exact grouping and configuring to describe the second user's products. For example, people don't hear "puppy chow" and think it is just another name for dog food that anybody could have produced. Instead, people have come to understand that it refers to one kind of dog food, that of Ralston

---

7. *See Two Pesos,* 505 U.S. at 768; *Multi Time Mach., Inc. v. Amazon.com, Inc.,* 804 F.3d 930, 944 (9th Cir. 2015), *cert. denied,* 136 S. Ct. 1231, 194 L. Ed. 2d 185 (2016); *Sorensen v. WD-40 Co.,* 792 F.3d 712, 731 (7th Cir. 2015), *cert. denied,* 136 S. Ct. 801, 193 L. Ed. 2d 712 (2016); *Grubbs,* 807 F.3d at 795; *Juice Generation,* 794 F.3d at 1339.

8. *Retail Servs., Inc. v. Freebies Publ'g,* 364 F.3d 535, 539 (4th Cir. 2004); *Union Carbide Corp. v. Ever-Ready, Inc.,* 531 F.2d 366, 379 (7th Cir. 1976).

Purina. They have a secondary association of the words "puppy" and "chow" with the dog food of Ralston Purina, and only Ralston Purina.

To prove secondary association, the owner must assemble evidence through surveys, polling, study groups, and other means to demonstrate that consumers (hopefully, a statistically significant number of consumers) connect the mark with the product. Once the owner achieves secondary association, the mark can be used and enforced like other marks, and a strong secondary association will bring these descriptive marks up to an enforceability level that approaches fanciful or arbitrary marks.

5. Generic Words

■ safari hats, aspirin, thermos bottle, cellophane, cola, escalator

Note that the heading of this section does not call generic words "marks." Generic words are not trademarks — or at least they are not trademarks anymore. Generic former marks have suffered the fate of "genericization" — the words no longer refer to one manufacturer's product but instead refer to the product itself, no matter who makes and sells it. Genericization, ironically, is one possible consequence of an innovator whose products become so popular and ubiquitous that consumers simply start asking for them by tradename, not by product type plus tradename. In other words, we love those Bayer "Aspirin" brand acetylsalicylic acid tablets so much that we start asking for "aspirin" wherever we go, and at some point that kind of pill simply *is* an aspirin. *See Bayer Co. v. United Drug Co.*, 272 F. 505 (S.D.N.Y. 1921). The word aspirin becomes a noun (an aspirin), not an adjective describing a noun (i.e., Aspirin brand acetylsalicylic acid pills). This process was applied to the Otis Company, when the Otis "Escalator" brand elevating staircase became known only as an escalator. *See Haughton Elevator Company v. Seeberger (Otis Elevator Company Substituted)*, 85 U.S.P.Q. (BNA) 80, 1950 WL 4178 (Comm'r Pat. & Trademarks 1950). Generic words are public domain — they refer to the product itself, and anyone who has the right to make the product itself can and will use that term for the product.

To recap the requirements of distinction:

Level of Distinctiveness	Name of Category	Description
HIGH	*Fanciful Marks*	Have no meaning or connotation that relates to the products and their qualities.
	Arbitrary Marks	Have an independent meaning but one that is unrelated to the products' qualities.

Level of Distinctiveness	Name of Category	Description
MODERATE	*Suggestive Marks*	Suggest attributes of the products; this opens the door for other producers to try to use similar marks.
LOW	*Descriptive Marks*	Simply describe the product itself, but they can be enforced if consumers have formed a secondary association of the descriptive words with one manufacturer's products.
NONE	*Generic Words*	**Not a mark.** They are generic descriptions with no secondary association. The words *are* the product no matter who makes it. They no longer refer to one manufacturer's version of the product.

D. Protectable Attributes of Trademarks

A mark is intended to be distinctive so that it can do its job as a reliable identifier of goods in the marketplace. Whether the mark has strength because of its fanciful or arbitrary status, or has strong secondary association, the protection comes by excluding other marks from the same general area of commerce.[9]

Note that the types of products and the geographic area of commerce matter to the potential coexistence of two marks. One theoretically can have two identical marks as long as the two marks are for products and services that are different and unrelated, or which are sold in geographic areas that are separate and unconnected to each other.[10] The separation must be enough that no possible consumer confusion is anticipated.

Marks can be infringing for sounding alike, looking alike, or having the same meaning in English or a foreign language,[11] particularly if the trademarks

---

9. *See generally Two Pesos*, 505 U.S. at 768; *Park 'N Fly, Inc. v. Dollar Park & Fly, Inc.*, 469 U.S. 189, 194 (1985); *Grubbs*, 807 F.3d at 795.

10. *Compare Brookfield Comm'ns, Inc. v. W. Coast Entm't Corp.*, 174 F.3d 1036, 1054 (9th Cir. 1999) (denying coexistence of two internet services with same name, *moviebuff.com*, in the same geographic region), *with Weiner King, Inc. v. Wiener King Corp.*, 615 F.2d 512, 520 (C.C.P.A. 1980) (allowing exact same name, "Weiner King," for two food-related businesses in different geographic areas), *and Pinocchio's Pizza Inc.*, 11 U.S.P.Q. 2d 1227 (P.T.O. Apr. 25, 1989) (allowing registration of "Pinocchio's Pizza" in states other than Maryland where competitor had been using the exact same mark).

11. *In re Spirits Int'l, N.V.*, 563 F.3d 1347, 1351 (Fed. Cir. 2009) (translation purporting to be geographic origin designation); *Enrique Bernat F., S.A. v. Guadalajara, Inc.*, 210 F.3d 439, 443 (5th Cir. 2000) (translation); *Dreamwerks Prod. Grp., Inc. v. SKG Studio*, 142 F.3d 1127, 1131 (9th Cir. 1998) (analyzing sound-alikes, "Dreamwerks" and "DreamWorks"). *Cf. In re Bayer Aktiengesellschaft*, 488 F.3d at 963 (affirming denial of registration for "aspirina" as simply being a Spanish translation of the generic term, aspirin).

are affixed to similar products or if the products are marketed throughout similar channels of commerce.[12] "Gallo" cheese and "Gallo" wine, for example, were held to be confusingly similar because cheese and wine are often served together.[13] If, on the other hand, two products bearing similar trademarks are unrelated or marketed in different areas, there may be no infringement. For instance, "Gold Circle" department stores and "Gold Circle" insurance were held not to be confusingly similar.[14]

Trademarks	Infringing?	Discussion
Jello brand gelatin and **Gel-O** brand hair styling gel	Maybe	Sound-alikes are actionable. But here, the two areas of commerce are distant from each other. If one is looking for something to eat, one usually does not go into the hair care products aisle. It is true that you'll find both products at the average grocery store, drugstore, or discount store. But the food vs. hair care separation, and the difference in spelling, might be enough to allow coexistence. Each mark is suggestive (of gelatin), so that level of distinctiveness is not going to help resolve this dispute.
Sticky brand gummed post-able note sheets and **Sticky** brand maple syrup	Maybe	Another case of two types of products that are pretty far apart, and yet, you'll find both products at the average grocery store, drugstore, or discount store. Here we have the exact word repeated in the same geographic area—that's a bad thing in most cases.[15] A separation in type of product or geographic region of commerce could allow both to coexist. In addition, both marks are descriptive, the postable notes being even more tied to a descriptive term than the syrup. That could hold back the postable notes from excluding the syrup.
Johnson's **Baby Oil** and Jean's **Huile de Bébé**	Most likely	If Johnson has proven a secondary association with the mark, Baby Oil, and the manufacturer, Johnson, then it could exclude the French translation of baby oil shown here.

---

12. *See Tillamook Country Smoker, Inc. v. Tillamook County Creamery Ass'n*, 465 F.3d 1102 (9th Cir. 2006).

13. *See E. & J. Gallo Winery v. Gallo Cattle Co.*, 967 F.2d 1280, 1291 (9th Cir. 1992).

14. *See Federated Dep't Stores, Inc. v. Gold Circle Ins. Co.*, 226 U.S.P.Q. 262 (1985).

15. *Brookfield Communications*, 174 F.3d at 1054 (denying coexistence of two internet services with same name, *moviebuff.com*); *Weiner King, Inc.*, 615 F.2d at 520 (allowing exact same name, "Weiner King," for two food-related businesses in different geographic areas); *Pinocchio's Pizza Inc.*, 11 U.S.P.Q. 2d 1227 (allowing registration of "Pinocchio's Pizza" in states other than Maryland where competitor had been using the exact same mark).

Trademarks	Infringing?	Discussion
Exxon brand petroleum products and **X-on** brand exam grading software	Unlikely	Petroleum products such as oil and gasoline simply seem too far removed from exam grading software to cause this one to be infringing. It helps that the second mark is only a sound-alike but looks quite different than the original mark. Exxon is particularly keen on stopping others from using the connected double-XX in marks,[16] and the X-on mark avoids this. Exxon almost certainly is a famous mark by this point in time, so it could have a separate complaint against X-on for trademark dilution, but that is a topic for the trademark dilution section (section K) of this chapter.

1. Personal Names

A person generally can use their own name as a mark. One's name can be distinctive from the start, but even if the name is somewhat common and not inherently distinctive, it can acquire a secondary association with a product so as to be fully protected as a mark. Thus, we have Bob Evans Restaurants serving Jimmy Dean Sausage and Paul Newman Salad Dressing with Ben and Jerry's Ice Cream for dessert. However, no one is guaranteed the right to use their own name in commerce if it would cause consumer confusion with an older trademark.

If a person strongly desires to use a personal name on goods, the person could try to negotiate with the senior mark owner—agree to keep out of certain areas of commerce and agree to use a disclaimer ("XY products have no affiliation with XYZ Industries, Inc.")—or go ahead and try to get a license. Alternatively, many problems can be overcome with a disclaimer or the addition of first names, initials, or other words—using "John L. McDonald's Sprinkler Company" as opposed to going with "McDonald's Co.," or using "Janice Coors Printing Co." instead of just "Coors Printing."

> **Same Name**
> The author, Michael Murray, cannot start selling bicycles or lawnmowers under the name "Murray" tomorrow. There already is an established manufacturer of bicycles and lawn mowers with the name of Murray. The author's use of his own name in these areas of commerce would certainly be confusing.

---

16. *E.g., Exxon Corp. v. Oxxford Clothes, Inc.,* 109 F.3d 1070, 1072-73 (5th Cir. 1997) (identical interlocking "XX" designs).

Michael Murray   Murray mower   Murray bicycle[17]

However, if Michael Murray had his heart set on using his name, he probably would be fine selling certain products under the full name, "Michael Murray." But probably not bicycles and lawn mowers, because the risk for confusion would still be present when consumers frequently cut off or shorten marks and might start calling Michael Murray Bicycles, "Murray bikes."

Even a mark with extra words and initials added may not avoid a dispute, as in this day and age, well established marks will resist any similar marks intruding into their sphere of influence. The authors would predict that John Deere would not sit still if another company tried to use the name "John Deere" for anything, even a fast-food restaurant, and even if it is owned by a Mr. John Deere, so protective would they be with their mark. In general, a mark owner cannot use another person's name or persona as a mark — "Tiger Woods" Golf Balls, "Elvis" Brand Jumpsuits, for example — for reasons discussed in section H of this chapter, "False Endorsement and False Designation of Origin," and in Chapter 5 of this text on "Right of Publicity."

2. Flags, Seals, Emblems, and other Public Symbols

What is wrong with these purported marks?[18]

In God We Trust

---

17. Images at the top of this page: Michael D. Murray, Collage of three cropped, revised, resized thumbnail images of Michael Murray, a Murray lawnmower, and a Murray bicycle (2014).

18. Michael D. Murray, Collage of cropped, revised, and resized thumbnail images derived from images depicting non-trademarkable seals, flags, symbols, coats of arms, and slogans (2015).

A trademark owner cannot use a symbol or slogan as a trademark if the mark would fail to be a distinctive identifier of goods of a particular source. This is the case with ubiquitous symbols and icons, including flags, seals, the bald eagle, religious symbols, and coats of arms. You also cannot use a trademark that suggests connections with organizations, institutions, or religions other than the owner's own business or enterprise if the use presents a risk that consumers will perceive a false or misleading association of the religion or organization with your product. There are several reasons for this: it would be unfair for a small number of enterprises to tie up a religious or national symbol in a mark. Assuming, for example, that a business received a trademark in the Roman cross, no other business, institution, or organization (including Christian religious organizations) could display the cross in the course of their operations without running afoul of the first business's mark. As a result, a Christian organization or congregation can display the cross, and use it on their signage and letterhead, but they cannot hope to protect it as a mark. The same goes for the use of the American flag in a mark or trade dress — the flag element will not be protected as a mark because it would be a poor identifier of goods of a certain source and certain quality because of the ubiquity of the use of the symbol.[19]

15 U.S.C. § 1052(a) currently precludes the use of scandalous or obscene marks.[20] This is a standard imposed by the legislature as a bit of morality, saving the delicate consumer from the scandal of marks that might be an affront to her sensibilities. Curse words, and marks with obscene images or sexually-charged content traditionally have had a difficult time being registered as a mark, and might be rejected.[21] However, section 1052(a) recently has come under attack as a content-based and viewpoint-based regulation on speech, and the "disparagement" language of section 1052(a) has been declared unconstitutional in *In re Tam*, 808 F.3d 1321 (Fed. Cir. 2015), *cert. granted sub nom Lee v. Tam*, No. 15-1293, 2016 WL 1587871 (U.S. Sept. 29, 2016).[22] Therefore, as of the date of submission of this manuscript, October 1, 2016, ethnic and racial slurs, such as the

---

19. A flag might be incorporated with other elements into a protectable mark if the combination is a distinctive identifier of the source of the goods. *See* 15 U.S.C. § 1052(a, b, e, f); *Two Pesos*, 505 U.S. at 768-69.

20. 15 U.S.C. § 1052(a). *See, e.g., In re Boulevard Entm't, Inc.*, 334 F.3d 1336, 1342 (Fed. Cir. 2003) (rejecting the registration of "jack-off" as a mark); *In Re Love Bottling Co.*, SERIAL 78171270, 2005 WL 1787238, at *9 (June 22, 2005) (application for "WIFEBEATER" as to tank top shirt design was rejected). These cases arguably are abrogated or at least called into question by *In re Tam*, 808 F.3d 1321 (Fed. Cir. 2015), *cert. granted sub nom., Lee v. Tam*, No. 15-1293, 2016 WL 1587871 (U.S. Sept. 29, 2016).

21. Historically, marks were rejected in cases such as *In re McGinley*, 660 F.2d 481 (Cust. & Pat. App. 1981), where the court affirmed the trademark examiner's rejection of a trademark consisting of a photograph of a nude man and woman kissing and embracing in a manner appearing to expose the male genitalia, on the grounds that such a mark was scandalous. *See also In re Boulevard Entertainment, Inc.*, 334 F.3d 1336 (Fed. Cir. 2003) (rejecting vulgar, profane words in trademark registration).

22. As indicated in the citation, certiorari was granted in the case on September 29, 2016.

term "The Slants" at issue in *Tam*, will not be precluded on the basis of their disparaging nature, and any other rejection of a registration on the basis that the content or viewpoint of the mark is objectionable will be subject to a strict scrutiny challenge.

E. Federal, State, and Common Law Protection of Marks

Trademarks exist and are protected at three levels of law: common law, state registered and regulated marks, and federal registered and regulated marks. Naturally, the three have many overlapping features — more in common than not — but the differences are worth knowing and understanding.

1. Common Law Protection

There are two basic requirements for common law protection as a mark:

■ Adoption as a mark
■ Use in Commerce

"Adoption" means coming up with or choosing a mark, and "use in commerce" means that the mark is placed on products, packaging, displays, tags or labels, and in advertising, so that the mark will come to be associated with the product at the point of sale.

Once a mark owner embarks on the use of a trademark, it will be best to use it constantly. Using it in only half of the owner's advertising or only on some of the owner's products might be questioned later as not having truly adopted the mark as an identifier of goods. Using more than one mark is acceptable as long as both are used constantly and consistently. The superscripted ^{TM} symbol (or ^{SM} symbol for service marks) next to a mark is an indication that the owner claims rights in the mark. (The ® symbol may not be used unless the mark is federally registered.)

A common law mark will be enforced as broadly as it seems reasonable to enforce. If the mark is used constantly and consistently over a wide area, it may receive full protection in that area. But the area will be limited to the geography in which the mark actually is used — it will not necessarily be tied to a unit of territory, such as a county or an entire state. Remember that use includes advertising, so if the advertising runs over several states, the owner could receive protection in all of those states. However, if the owner files an action to enforce the mark in a state court, that court most likely will only be able to adjudicate claims about infringement occurring in that state, so a second suit may have to be filed to prosecute claims for infringements in the other state.

The protection received for a common law mark is the prevention of other similar marks in similar lines of commerce. Common law trademark disputes generally are litigated in state court (there is a small exception if the owner and the opponent are citizens of different states and the amount claimed in damages exceeds $75,000 — at that point the suit could be brought in federal court under diversity jurisdiction, but the owner still could chose to file in state court). Injunctive relief and damages are possible.

Suing to protect a common law trademark opens the owner up to any and all challenges that a defendant can assert against a rights-holder — namely, that defendant started using or actually registered the same or a similar mark before the litigant did, that the litigant's mark is not distinctive, that the litigant committed fraud or misrepresentation concerning the source of the goods in conjunction with the use of the mark, that the litigant has not used the mark consistently or properly in commerce, that the mark has fallen prey to one of the trademark limiting doctrines (abandonment, laches, unclean hands, genericization — described below), that the use of the mark violates the antitrust laws, that the defendant's mark is not confusingly similar, or that the defendant is making a fair use of the mark.

2. State Registration and Protection

A state may have a statewide registration system for marks used within that state. Most state systems will resemble the system described below for federal registration and protection. A state registration will provide statewide protection over the mark. As with common law marks, you may use the superscript ^{TM} symbol or ^{SM} symbol next to your state-registered mark as an indication that you claim rights in the mark, but you may not use the ® symbol that stands for federal registration.

All of the same types of defenses and challenges that apply with common law marks will apply in lawsuits over state-registered marks. A statewide register will assist those who will perform trademark rights-clearing searches and who wish to identify all marks registered for use within the state.

3. Federal Registration: The Principal Register and Protection[23]

Federal registration on the Principal Register increases the power of a common law or state-registered mark. Federal registration on the Principal Register does not create a new mark — that is done by adopting the mark and using it in commerce — but it bolsters the power of the existing mark in the following ways:

- Enables nationwide protection and priority in use of the mark; the Patent and Trademark Office will not register any marks that are confusingly similar to the mark

---

23. This part of the chapter summarizes the provisions of 15 U.S.C. §§ 1051-96.

- Makes the mark eligible for "incontestability" after five years of continuous, unchallenged use of the mark[24]
- The mark owner automatically is eligible to sue to protect the mark in federal court
- The mark owner is spared the time and expense of "proving" the validity of the mark in the litigation — the federal registration is the prima facie proof of validity
- The mark owner is eligible to receive triple damages and attorneys' fees from the opponent if the opponent is found guilty of an especially egregious infringement of the mark
- The owner can use the ® symbol, which prevents opponents from asserting a defense of "innocent infringement"
- The owner can call upon the U.S. Customs Service to help police imports that may infringe the mark
- The Principal Register gives notice to all of the existence of the mark when people do a trademark search in the U.S. Patent and Trademark Office online database
- The mark owner can take advantage of international trademark treaties to gain United States priority of use status

Nationwide protection is probably the single most important benefit of federal registration. It would be difficult and, quite often, prohibitively expensive to roll out a trademarked product coast to coast, registering separately in every state. With federal registration, as long as the owner (1) has adopted the mark, (2) uses it on the product and with the advertising, packaging, displays, and promotional material of the product at the point of purchase, and (3) is doing all of this in interstate commerce (which generally means trading in commerce between at least two states), then the owner is eligible to seek a federal registration.

Incontestability does not mean that the mark is permanent and untouchable; it is still subject to attack for many of the same defects that were listed above — namely, that defendant started using or actually registered the same or a similar mark before the owner did, that the owner committed fraud or misrepresentation concerning the source of the goods in conjunction with the use of the mark, that the mark has fallen prey to one of the trademark limiting doctrines (abandonment, laches, unclean hands, genericization — described below), that the use of the mark violates the antitrust laws, or that the defendant is making a fair use of the mark. Thus, the protection is that it precludes claims that the mark is not distinctive, that it is confusingly similar to another mark, that it is functional, that it lacks secondary meaning, or that the mark has not been used consistently or properly in interstate commerce — in other words, what is incontestable is that the owner has a good, valid mark that can be protected under federal law.

---

24. 15 U.S.C. § 1065.

To obtain incontestable status, a filing under 15 U.S.C. § 1065(c) of the Lanham Act is required. The marks owner must assert that:

- The mark has been registered on the federal principal register for five consecutive years
- No final legal decision has been issued against the mark
- No challenge to the mark is pending
- A declaration describing the mark's continuous use in interstate commerce was filed on a timely basis
- The mark is not and has not become generic[25]

The eligibility to sue in federal court is a benefit — many litigators appreciate the procedures and speed of disposition of federal courts over most state courts. The additional benefit of being eligible to receive triple damages and attorneys' fees from the opponent if the opponent is found guilty of an especially egregious infringement of the mark is another perk of federal registration.

4. Supplemental Register

Common law marks claimed by marks owners that are not inherently distinctive (in most cases, this means they are descriptive marks) still can obtain a federal registration on the Supplemental Register. Trademarks that are registrable on the Supplemental Register include:

- Descriptive marks that are capable of acquiring distinctiveness;
- Surnames;
- Marks consisting of geographic terms; and
- Nondistinctive, but nonfunctional trade dress.

Like a registration on the Principal Register, a registration on the Supplemental Register: (1) entitles the owner to use a notice of federal trademark registration, such as the ® symbol; (2) gives the owner the right to bring a trademark infringement suit in federal court, along with a claim of unfair competition; and (3) can be cited by a United States Patent and Trademark Office examining attorney against a later-filed application to register a confusingly similar mark for related goods/services, even on the Principal Register.[26]

A registration on the Supplemental Register does not provide all the protection of a registration on the Principal Register. For example, a supplemental registration does not convey the presumptions of validity, ownership and exclusive rights to use the mark that arise with a registration on the Principal Register. In addition, a supplemental registration cannot be used to prevent the importation of infringing or counterfeit products. Finally, a supplemental registration can never become incontestable.

---

25. *Id.* § 1065(c).
26. *See* 15 U.S.C. §§ 1091, 1094.

A mark registered on the Supplemental Register can attempt to move up in registration to the Principal Register by filing a new application for registration that is supported by a showing of acquired distinctiveness through secondary association. Secondary meaning arises when a nondistinctive mark becomes known to consumers as an indication of source for particular products or services as a result of the mark's long-term and extensive use. The exact amount of time for the mark to be in use in order to demonstrate that a mark has achieved secondary meaning varies depending on the mark's level of descriptiveness and proof of consumer recognition of the mark. However, a presumption of secondary meaning may arise after five years of substantially continuous and exclusive use of a mark in commerce.

5. Classifications

When a mark is federally registered, it will be listed in the registry in one or more classifications for the areas of commerce and trade in which it is used.[27] There are numerous classifications for goods and services — all marks must be classified in at least one. The classifications are only a matter of administrative convenience to sort out the hundreds of thousands of marks that are registered. Classification does not extend or add to a mark-holder's rights. Classification provides some reference for those doing trademark searches to try to figure out if a certain mark has been registered — a search can be made within certain classifications of commerce. Theoretically, the same or similar marks could coexist if used for very dissimilar classes of goods or services, but the onus is on the second user of the mark to try to register and convince the Patent and Trademark Office that no confusion is possible. Classification is not evidence (prima facie or otherwise) that two marks in the same or related classes are not confusingly similar.

F. Assignments, Assignments in Gross, and Naked Licensing

Trademarks are not sold per se; they are "assigned." And when a trademark is assigned, it must be assigned to a person or entity that already has or receives in the same transaction the means to produce the same goods at the same level of quality that have previously been produced in association with the assigned mark. In many cases, that requires the transfer of the production equipment, designs, molds, patterns, and the corporate "good will" associated with the products as a "going concern" in order for the trademark on the products to be continued at full strength and effectiveness. If an owner attempts to assign the trademark to a person or entity that lacks the capacity to produce the goods at the same quality level, and does not transfer the means and good will in the

---

27. *See* 15 U.S.C. § 1112.

same transaction, this is referred to as an "assignment in gross" of trademark. The potential confusion caused by an assignment in gross ("these products have the same name as the XYZ brand products I have come to know and love, but they sure aren't the same as they used to be") lessens the strength of the mark, and puts the entire mark in jeopardy. In proper cases, the trademark may be cancelled (declared to be abandoned) as a result of an assignment in gross.

In similar fashion, an owner should not willy-nilly license (i.e., issue naked licenses of) a trademark for any and every product and service that asks for such a license. A mark has one function: to be a distinctive identifier of goods of a certain quality in the market, so that the consumer can pick out the right kind and quality of goods without confusion. If a mark owner allows her mark to be used on high-end goods and then on a separate line of bargain basement goods, the owner is running the risk of confusing consumers. The same is true if the owner licenses the mark for every kind of product in sight. An owner must exercise control over the nature and quality of goods or services for which the mark is used, or consumers will (correctly) come to realize that the mark stands for nothing. At that point, the owner will be deemed to have "abandoned" the mark as a distinctive identifier of goods of a certain quality from a certain source.

The name "Picasso," for example, has been held to be a protectable trademark and was afforded protection under § 43(a). Pablo Picasso and his heirs licensed various goods, such as carpeting, eyewear, clocks, art reproductions, posters, and scarves, which were distributed throughout the United States. The Picasso heirs, as the owner of the Picasso mark, exercised control over the nature and quality of the goods or services for which the mark was used. In the Picasso case, the licensees were subject to periodic inspection and the licensors' prior approval of the goods was required before any merchandise could be sold. For these reasons, the court in *Visual Arts & Galleries Association v. Various John Does,* 80 Civ. 4487 (S.D.N.Y. 1980), recognized that the name "Picasso" and the famous signature had acquired secondary meaning, and that Picasso's heirs had a continuing right to advertise and profit from the use of the painter's name and reputation. The court also enjoined the unauthorized use of a facsimile of Picasso's signature on t-shirts.

G. Requirements of an Infringement Claim

Rock and Roll Hall of Fame and Museum, Inc.
v. Gentile Productions

134 F.3d 749 (6th Cir. 1998)*

RYAN, Circuit Judge.

The Rock and Roll Hall of Fame and Museum, Inc., and The Rock and Roll Hall of Fame Foundation, Inc., filed suit against Charles Gentile and Gentile

---

* Footnotes and most citations omitted.

Productions, alleging various trademark and unfair-competition claims under state and federal law. . . .

In 1988, The Rock and Roll Hall of Fame Foundation registered the words, "THE ROCK AND ROLL HALL OF FAME," as its service mark, on the principal register at the United States Patent and Trademark Office. In 1991, the Foundation commissioned I.M. Pei, a world famous architect, to design a facility for The Rock and Roll Hall of Fame and Museum in Cleveland, Ohio. Pei's design was brought to life on the edge of Lake Erie, in the form of The Rock and Roll Hall of Fame and Museum which opened in September 1995. In their briefs to this court, The Rock and Roll Hall of Fame and Museum and The Rock and Roll Hall of Fame Foundation have referred to themselves collectively as "the Museum." Throughout the remainder of this opinion, we will do the same.

The Museum states that its building design is "a unique and inherently distinctive symbol of the freedom, youthful energy, rebellion and movement of rock and roll music." Whatever its symbolism, there can be no doubt that the Museum's design is unique and distinctive. The front of the Museum is dominated by a large, reclining, triangular facade of steel and glass, while the rear of the building, which extends out over Lake Erie, is a striking combination of interconnected and unusually shaped white buildings. On May 3, 1996, the State of Ohio approved the registration of the Museum's building design for trademark and service-mark purposes. The Museum has similar applications pending with the United States Patent and Trademark Office.

Charles Gentile is a professional photographer whose work is marketed and distributed through Gentile Productions. In the spring of 1996, Gentile began to sell, for $40 to $50, a poster featuring a photograph of the Museum against a colorful sunset. The photograph is framed by a black border. In gold lettering in the border underneath the photograph, the words, "ROCK N' ROLL HALL OF FAME," appear above the smaller, but elongated word, "CLEVELAND." Gentile's signature appears in small blue print beneath the picture of the building. Along the right-hand side of the photograph, in very fine print, is the following explanation: "Copr. 1996 Gentile Productions . . . Photographed by: Charles M. Gentile[;] Design: Division Street Design [;] Paper: Mead Signature Gloss Cover 80#[;] Printing: Custom Graphics Inc. [;] Finishing: Northern Ohio Finishing, Inc."

In reaction to Gentile's poster, the Museum filed a five-count complaint against Gentile in the district court. The Museum's complaint contends that the Museum has used both its registered service mark, "THE ROCK AND ROLL HALL OF FAME," and its building design as trademarks, and that Gentile's poster infringes upon, dilutes, and unfairly competes with these marks. The Museum's somewhat unusual claims regarding its building design, then, are quite unlike a claim to a service-mark right in a building design that might be asserted to prevent the construction of a confusingly similar building. Specifically, count one of the Museum's complaint alleges trademark infringement, in violation of 15 U.S.C. §1114(1). Count two alleges unfair competition, false or misleading representations, and false designation of origin, in violation of 15 U.S.C. § 1125(a). Count three alleges dilution of trademarks, in violation of 15 U.S.C. § 1125(c) and Ohio common law. Counts four and five allege unfair competition and trademark infringement under Ohio law.

The Museum sought a preliminary injunction and the district court held a hearing on the motion. It is clear from a review of the Museum's motion and the hearing transcript that, whatever the scope of the Museum's complaint, the Museum's request for a preliminary injunction was based on the theory: (1) that the Museum has used both its building design and its service mark, "THE ROCK AND ROLL HALL OF FAME," as trademarks; and (2) that both the photograph of the Museum and the words identifying the Museum in Gentile's poster are uses of the Museum's trademarks that should be enjoined because they are likely to lead consumers to believe that Gentile's poster is produced or sponsored by the Museum. Thus, in its motion, the Museum argued that, because Gentile is "using the Museum's trademarks on posters in a manner which reflects a deliberate attempt to confuse, mislead and deceive the public into believing that the posters are affiliated with the Museum, . . . [t]he Museum has an extremely strong probability of success on the merits of its claims for trademark infringement and unfair competition." Similarly, at the hearing, the Museum stated only that its motion was "about trademark infringement, [section] 43(a), violations of the Lanham Act in passing off," although its complaint was broader. Accordingly, the district court explained to Gentile that he needed to respond only to the Museum's arguments in support of its motion, not its entire complaint.

. . .

Robert Bosak, the controller of the Museum, averred that "the Museum has used versions of the building shape trademark on T-shirts and a wide variety of products, including posters, since as early as June, 1993." According to his review of sales reports from the Museum's store, merchandise "featur[ing] the building shape have been among [the Museum's store's] top selling items." Rachel Schmelzer, an employee in the Museum's licensing and sponsorship department, averred that she informed Gentile, on more than one occasion before Gentile began selling his poster, that the Museum considered Gentile's poster to be an infringing trademark use of the Museum's building design.

On May 30, 1996, the district court concluded that the Museum had "shown a likelihood of success in proving its federal and state claims," and it granted the Museum's motion for a preliminary injunction. Rock and Roll Hall of Fame and Museum, Inc. v. Gentile Prods., 934 F. Supp. 868, 872–73 (N.D. Ohio 1996). The district court explained, inter alia, that [a]s a result of the extensive advertising and promotional activities involving the [Museum's] "ROCK AND ROLL HALL OF FAME" and building design trademarks, the public has come to recognize these trademarks as being connected with or sold by the Museum, its official licensees and/or official sponsors.

The district court found that the Museum's building design was a fanciful mark, and that Gentile's use of the Museum's building design and the words, "ROCK N' ROLL HALL OF FAME," was likely to cause confusion. It then determined that the balance of equities favored granting the injunction, and it ordered Gentile to refrain from further infringements of the Museum's trademarks and to "deliver . . . for destruction all copies of defendants' poster in their possession."

II.

. . .

A trademark is a designation, "any word, name, symbol, or device, or any combination thereof," which serves "to identify and distinguish [the] goods [of the mark's owner] . . . from those manufactured or sold by others and to indicate the source of the goods, even if that source is unknown." 15 U.S.C. § 1127. Although some marks are classified as inherently distinctive and therefore capable of protection, it is not the case that all inherently distinctive symbols or words on a product function as trademarks. Rather, in order to be protected as a valid trademark, a designation must create "a separate and distinct commercial impression, which . . . performs the trademark function of identifying the source of the merchandise to the customers."

It is well established that "[t]here is no such thing as property in a trademark except as a right appurtenant to an established business or trade in connection with which the mark is employed." Thus, whether alleging infringement of a registered trademark, pursuant to 15 U.S.C. § 1114(1), or infringement of an unregistered trademark, pursuant to 15 U.S.C. § 1125(a)(1), it is clear that a plaintiff must show that it has actually used the designation at issue as a trademark, and that the defendant has also used the same or a similar designation as a trademark. In other words, the plaintiff must establish a likelihood that the defendant's designation will be confused with the plaintiff's trademark, such that consumers are mistakenly led to believe that the defendant's goods are produced or sponsored by the plaintiff. Although the parties have not discussed the Museum's state-law claims, we note that trademark claims under Ohio law follow the same analysis.

. . .

[W]hen we view the photograph in Gentile's poster, we do not readily recognize the design of the Museum's building as an indicator of source or sponsorship. What we see, rather, is a photograph of an accessible, well-known, public landmark. Stated somewhat differently, in Gentile's poster, the Museum's building strikes us not as a separate and distinct mark on the good, but, rather, as the good itself. . . .

[A]fter reviewing the record before us with this possibility in mind, we are not persuaded that the Museum uses its building design as a trademark. Thus, we are not dissuaded from our initial impression that the photograph in Gentile's poster does not function as a trademark.

The district court found that the Museum's building design is fanciful, that the Museum has used its building design as a trademark, and that "the public has come to recognize [the Museum's building design] trademark[] as being connected with or sold by the Muscum." There are several problems with these critical findings. First, we find absolutely no evidence in the record which documents or demonstrates public recognition of the Museum's building design as a trademark. Such evidence might be pivotal in this case, but it is lacking. Indeed, we are at a loss to understand the district court's basis for this significant finding of fact.

Second, although no one could doubt that the Museum's building design is fanciful, it is less clear that a picture or a drawing of the Museum is fanciful in a trademark sense. Fanciful marks are usually understood as "totally new and unique combination[s] of letters or symbols" that are "invented or selected for the sole purpose of functioning as a trademark." Although the plaintiffs "invented" the Museum, the Museum's existence as a landmark in downtown Cleveland undermines its "fancifulness" as a trademark. A picture or a drawing of the Museum is not fanciful in the same way that a word like Exxon is when it is coined as a service mark. Such a word is distinctive as a mark because it readily appears to a consumer to have no other purpose. In contrast, a picture of the Museum on a product might be more readily perceived as ornamentation than as an identifier of source.

We recognize, of course, that a designation may serve both ornamental and source-identifying purposes, and this brings us to our principal difficulty with the Museum's argument and the district court's judgment. As we described supra, although the Museum has used drawings or pictures of its building design on various goods, it has not done so with any consistency. As Bosak stated in his affidavit, "the Museum has used versions of the building shape trademark on . . . a wide variety of products." Several items marketed by the Museum display only the rear of the Museum's building, which looks dramatically different from the front. Drawings of the front of the Museum on the two T-shirts in the record are similar, but they are quite different from the photograph featured in the Museum's poster. And, although the photograph from the poster is also used on a postcard, another postcard displays various close-up photographs of the Museum which, individually and perhaps even collectively, are not even immediately recognizable as photographs of the Museum.

. . .

In reviewing the Museum's disparate uses of several different perspectives of its building design, we cannot conclude that they create a consistent and distinct commercial impression as an indicator of a single source of origin or sponsorship. To be more specific, we cannot conclude on this record that it is likely that the Museum has established a valid trademark in every photograph which, like Gentile's, prominently displays the front of the Museum's building, "no matter how dissimilar." Even if we accept that consumers recognize the various drawings and pictures of the Museum's building design as being drawings and pictures of the Museum, the Museum's argument would still fall short. Such recognition is not the equivalent of the recognition that these various drawings or photographs indicate a single source of the goods on which they appear. Consistent and repetitive use of a designation as an indicator of source is the hallmark of a trademark. Although the record before us supports the conclusion that the Museum has used its composite mark in this manner, it will not support the conclusion that the Museum has made such use of its building design.

In the end, then, we believe that the district court abused its discretion by treating the "Museum's building design" as a single entity, and by concomitantly failing to consider whether and to what extent the Museum's use of its building design served the source-identifying function that is the essence of a trademark. . . .

Notes and Questions

1. *Rock and Roll Hall of Fame* presented a trademark issue that is shared by another 6th Circuit case involving Tiger Woods, *ETW Corp. v. Jireh Publishing*, 332 F.3d 915 (6th Cir. 2003) (excerpted *infra* in Chapter 5, "Right of Publicity"). In both cases, the failure of the plaintiff to adopt and use a single image of their asset (Rock and Roll Hall of Fame's museum building; Tiger Wood's likeness) as a trademark, and consistently to use that image as an identifier of goods and services, doomed their respective trademark claims. *Compare Nova Wines, Inc. v. Adler Fels Winery LLC*, 467 F. Supp. 2d 965 (N.D. Cal. 2006) (winery's unique, long-standing practice of placing various images of Marilyn Monroe on its wines created inherently distinctive trade dress specifically limited to sale of wine). In spite of the similar outcomes in *Rock and Roll Hall of Fame* and *ETW Corp.*, can you think of ways to distinguish these two situations? Should any of these differences change the outcome of one or both of these cases?

2. The Rock and Roll Hall of Fame has since limited itself to a small number of line drawing logos that are based on the outside structure of their unique building and has adopted these as trademarks to be used in identifying goods sold or licensed by the Rock and Roll Hall of Fame. See illustrations at *http://www.rockhall.com*. Tiger Woods could do the same thing, but are there any drawbacks to this approach that would fail to meet Tiger's particular needs? Are the drawbacks fair given the purposes of trademark law as compared to other intellectual property rights of action?

3. Technological advances do not rid us of our problems and complications in using and protecting trademarks, but instead create new areas for complication and concern. *E.g., Monotype Imaging v. Bitstream, Inc.*,

376 F. Supp. 2d 877 (N.D. Ill. 2005). The Internet has created a new arena for fighting over the use of trademark and service mark language. In general, the Internet has allowed people to register and "own" a top-level domain name (e.g., thisismycompanyname.com) or second-level domain name (e.g., webhostname.com/second_level_domain_name/) simply by being the first to pay the registration fee and register the name. Is it good public policy to allow people to grab the exclusive right to use a top-level domain name of a manifestly well-known and successful company just by meeting the "first come, first served" requirements? On the other hand, what if the early bird has a bona fide reason to use the name — for instance, if co-author Michael Murray had had the foresight to register "murray.com" in the early 1990s and used it in his websites and marketing materials — should Murray, Inc. of bicycle and lawn mower manufacturing fame have the right to kick him off this top-level domain name? Consider *Panavision Int'l, L.P. v. Toeppen*, 141 F.3d 1316 (9th Cir.1998), and cases interpreting the Anti-Cybersquatting Consumer Protection Act of 1999, 15 U.S.C. § 1125(d). *E.g., Southern Co. v. Dauben Inc.*, 324 Fed. Appx. 309 (5th Cir. 2009).

4. In *Leigh v. Warner Bros., Inc.*, 212 F.3d 1210 (11th Cir. 2000), Leigh took a picture of the "Bird Girl" statue in Savannah, which was used on the cover of the book, *Midnight in the Garden of Good and Evil*. Defendant made a movie based on the book, bearing the same title as the book, and used pictures of the "Bird Girl" statue in promotional clips, parts of the movie, promotional photographs, the film's website and Internet icon, movie posters, newspaper advertisements, and the cover for the soundtrack. Leigh sued for infringement of his trademark rights in his Bird Girl photo. The court found that Leigh's Bird Girl photo was never used as a trademark by Leigh and thus he had no trademark rights in the photo prior to the release of the movie. The court held that the Bird Girl image "strikes us not as a separate and distinct mark on the good, but, rather, as the good itself."

H. False Endorsement and False Designation of Origin

The most important source of federal trademark law is the Lanham Act, and within the Act is Section 43(a), codified at 15 U.S.C. § 1125(a), that protects against "false description of origin, or any false or misleading representation" regarding goods in commerce. This prohibition includes false endorsement — which is a false expression or implied representation that a particular person has authorized or approved use of a product.

False Endorsement Hypothetical

Does this hypothetical advertisement pose a potential trademark law problem?[28] Yes, it does. Tiger Woods is (was) paid a great deal of money by Nike to endorse Nike Brand golf balls, and he endorses his own line of Tiger Woods brand golf equipment. He is not supposed to be endorsing ProStaff brand golf balls. The problem with using this image of Tiger with this image of a ProStaff golf ball in an advertisement is that it easily gives the viewer the impression that Tiger Woods approves of, uses, endorses, or is in some way connected with ProStaff golf balls, and that (mistaken) association is very valuable to ProStaff. Protection under the Lanham Act includes protection from false endorsements.

False endorsement can be cleverly executed, as in the hypothetical above. ProStaff told no lies in this imaginary ad, it was not engaging in outright fraud or misrepresentation to get you to stop and look. Nowhere did it say, "Tiger Woods loves ProStaff golf balls" or "Tiger Woods suggests ProStaff for your next golf ball purchase." But all it takes is the confusing association suggested by the placement of an image of Tiger Woods next to a golf-related item to trigger the operation of the law. A mere suggestion of approval and

---

28. Michael D. Murray, Composite diagram with cropped, revised, and resized thumbnail images derived from images of Tiger Woods wearing Nike and TW brand golf attire and using a Nike golf club, shown next to a ProStaff golf ball. This advertisement and the images therein all were created by Michael D. Murray as a hypothetical illustration of the principles of false endorsement.

therefore endorsement is sufficient. And because Tiger Woods has endorsed many other products — Buick automobiles, Gillette razors and shaving products, EA Sports video games, Rolex watches, and more — it would not be safe to place Tiger's image in *any* commercial advertisement for any product without his permission.

False Designation of Origin

False designation of origin seeks to protect false or misleading identifications of goods. There are three basic kinds of false designation of origin:

Passing Off   Which refers to a junior user making it appear that his goods are the goods of a more senior producer. Typically, this is done because the senior user's goods are more valuable and desirable, so the junior user reaps a benefit by selling more of his own goods to consumers who are confused into thinking that they actually are buying goods from the senior producer. Most cases of product "knock-offs" and counterfeit goods are cases of the "passing off" variety.

Product Knock-Offs or Counterfeits[29]

Reverse Passing Off   Which refers to a junior user selling the actual goods of a senior user but under the name and mark of the junior user. This may sound incongruous — it will cost the junior user something to be able to obtain the actual goods of a senior user, so why would a company sell more expensive goods under its own mark when its own goods cost less? The answer is that this strategy builds up the mark and strengthens the association of the mark with valuable and desirable goods. Eventually, this will raise the perception of quality and value of all goods that are branded with the mark. That works to the junior user's advantage, but at the cost of tricking the consumer. In this case, it is not that the consumers received less than they thought they were bargaining for — the company didn't pass off shoddy goods as valuable goods — but the consumer was confused into thinking they were buying one thing when they were buying another. The confusion may

---

29. Images: Michael D. Murray, Collage of cropped, revised, and resized thumbnail images derived from images of product knockoffs or counterfeits for J Crew, Nike (Nkie), M & Ms (S & Ms) (2015).

continue — the next time the consumer goes shopping she may look for the junior company's brand thinking that the brand stands for something good and desirable, when in fact the company created that false impression by the reverse passing off of another's goods as its own.

Misbranding or Mislabeling The last kind is a more straightforward kind of fraud or misrepresentation: the goods may be fine, but the designation on the label is not. It may not confuse the goods of a senior user with those of a junior user, but somehow the label is misbranded or mislabeled to confuse the origin or contents of the goods, perhaps to confuse or obfuscate their geographic origin, and a consumer will not be getting what they intended when they selected the item. Labels like "Organic" or "Green" or "Fat Free" often become so popular as designators that an organization or regulatory body, such as the United States Food and Drug Administration, must step in to define and regulate what products get to be called "organic" or "fat free," so as to prevent cheaters from adopting a label falsely just to gain the popularity factor. With many goods, geographic indications are a valuable identifier — for example, they separate true champagne produced in the Champagne region of France from other sparkling wines from other regions across the world. A California Champagne is a misnomer, and a faked geographic indication would certainly cause confusion in the marketplace.[30]

Café de Colombia

Dastar Corp. v. Twentieth Century Fox Film Corp.

539 U.S. 23 (2003)*

Justice SCALIA delivered the opinion of the Court.

In this case, we are asked to decide whether § 43(a) of the Lanham Act, 15 U.S.C. § 1125(a), prevents the unaccredited copying of a work, and if so, whether a court may double a profit award under § 1117(a), in order to deter future infringing conduct.

---

30. Images: Michael D. Murray, Collage of revised and resized thumbnail images derived from geographic indication logos (2015).
* Footnotes and most citations omitted.

I

In 1948, three and a half years after the German surrender at Reims, General Dwight D. Eisenhower completed Crusade in Europe, his written account of the allied campaign in Europe during World War II. Doubleday published the book, registered it with the Copyright Office in 1948, and granted exclusive television rights to an affiliate of respondent Twentieth Century Fox Film Corporation (Fox). Fox, in turn, arranged for Time, Inc., to produce a television series, also called Crusade in Europe, based on the book, and Time assigned its copyright in the series to Fox. The television series, consisting of 26 episodes, was first broadcast in 1949. It combined a soundtrack based on a narration of the book with film footage from the United States Army, Navy, and Coast Guard, the British Ministry of Information and War Office, the National Film Board of Canada, and unidentified "Newsreel Pool Cameramen." In 1975, Doubleday renewed the copyright on the book as the "'proprietor of copyright in a work made for hire.'" Fox, however, did not renew the copyright on the Crusade television series, which expired in 1977, leaving the television series in the public domain.

In 1988, Fox reacquired the television rights in General Eisenhower's book, including the exclusive right to distribute the Crusade television series on video and to sub-license others to do so. Respondents SFM Entertainment and New Line Home Video, Inc., in turn, acquired from Fox the exclusive rights to distribute Crusade on video. SFM obtained the negatives of the original television series, restored them, and repackaged the series on videotape; New Line distributed the videotapes.

Enter petitioner Dastar. In 1995, Dastar decided to expand its product line from music compact discs to videos. Anticipating renewed interest in World War II on the 50th anniversary of the war's end, Dastar released a video set entitled World War II Campaigns in Europe. To make Campaigns, Dastar purchased eight beta cam tapes of the original version of the Crusade television series, which is in the public domain, copied them, and then edited the series. Dastar's Campaigns series is slightly more than half as long as the original Crusade television series. Dastar substituted a new opening sequence, credit page, and final closing for those of the Crusade television series; inserted new chapter-title sequences and narrated chapter introductions; moved the "recap" in the Crusade television series to the beginning and retitled it as a "preview"; and removed references to and images of the book. Dastar created new packaging for its Campaigns series and (as already noted) a new title.

Dastar manufactured and sold the Campaigns video set as its own product. The advertising states: "Produced and Distributed by: Entertainment Distributing" (which is owned by Dastar), and makes no reference to the Crusade television series. Similarly, the screen credits state "DASTAR CORP presents" and "an ENTERTAINMENT DISTRIBUTING Production," and list as executive producer, producer, and associate producer, employees of Dastar. The Campaigns videos themselves also make no reference to the Crusade television series, New Line's Crusade videotapes, or the book. Dastar sells its

Campaigns videos to Sam's Club, Costco, Best Buy, and other retailers and mail-order companies for $25 per set, substantially less than New Line's video set.

In 1998, respondents Fox, SFM, and New Line brought this action alleging that Dastar's sale of its Campaigns video set infringes Doubleday's copyright in General Eisenhower's book and, thus, their exclusive television rights in the book. Respondents later amended their complaint to add claims that Dastar's sale of Campaigns "without proper credit" to the Crusade television series constitutes "reverse passing off" in violation of § 43(a) of the Lanham Act, 15 U.S.C. § 1125(a), and in violation of state unfair-competition law. On cross-motions for summary judgment, the District Court found for respondents on all three counts, treating its resolution of the Lanham Act claim as controlling on the state-law unfair-competition claim because "the ultimate test under both is whether the public is likely to be deceived or confused[.]" The court awarded Dastar's profits to respondents and doubled them pursuant to § 35 of the Lanham Act, 15 U.S.C. § 1117(a), to deter future infringing conduct by petitioner.

The Court of Appeals for the Ninth Circuit affirmed the judgment for respondents on the Lanham Act claim, . . . reason[ing] that "Dastar copied substantially the entire Crusade in Europe series created by Twentieth Century Fox, labeled the resulting product with a different name and marketed it without attribution to Fox[, and] therefore committed a 'bodily appropriation' of Fox's series." It concluded that "Dastar's 'bodily appropriation' of Fox's original [television] series is sufficient to establish the reverse passing off." The court also affirmed the District Court's award under the Lanham Act of twice Dastar's profits. We granted certiorari.

II

The Lanham Act was intended to make "actionable the deceptive and misleading use of marks," and "to protect persons engaged in . . . commerce against unfair competition." 15 U.S.C. § 1127. While much of the Lanham Act addresses the registration, use, and infringement of trademarks and related marks, § 43(a), 15 U.S.C. § 1125(a) is one of the few provisions that goes beyond trademark protection. As originally enacted, § 43(a) created a federal remedy against a person who used in commerce either "a false designation of origin, or any false description or representation" in connection with "any goods or services." 60 Stat. 441. As . . . remains true after the 1988 revision — § 43(a) "does not have boundless application as a remedy for unfair trade practices[.]" "[B]ecause of its inherently limited wording, § 43(a) can never be a federal 'codification' of the overall law of 'unfair competition,'" but can apply only to certain unfair trade practices prohibited by its text.

. . .

The Trademark Law Revision Act of 1988 made clear that § 43(a) covers origin of production as well as geographic origin. Its language is amply inclusive, moreover, of reverse passing off — if indeed it does not implicitly adopt the unanimous court-of-appeals jurisprudence on that subject.

Thus, as it comes to us, the gravamen of respondents' claim is that, in marketing and selling Campaigns as its own product without acknowledging its nearly wholesale reliance on the Crusade television series, Dastar has made a "false designation of origin, false or misleading description of fact, or false or misleading representation of fact, which . . . is likely to cause confusion . . . as to the origin . . . of his or her goods." That claim would undoubtedly be sustained if Dastar had bought some of New Line's Crusade videotapes and merely repackaged them as its own. Dastar's alleged wrongdoing, however, is vastly different: it took a creative work in the public domain — the Crusade television series — copied it, made modifications (arguably minor), and produced its very own series of videotapes. If "origin" refers only to the manufacturer or producer of the physical "goods" that are made available to the public (in this case the videotapes), Dastar was the origin. If, however, "origin" includes the creator of the underlying work that Dastar copied, then someone else (perhaps Fox) was the origin of Dastar's product. At bottom, we must decide what § 43(a)(1)(A) of the Lanham Act means by the "origin" of "goods."

III

The dictionary definition of "origin" is "[t]he fact or process of coming into being from a source," and "[t]hat from which anything primarily proceeds; source." Webster's New International Dictionary 1720-21 (2d ed. 1949). And the dictionary definition of "goods" (as relevant here) is "[w]ares; merchandise." Id., at 1079. We think the most natural understanding of the "origin" of "goods" — the source of wares — is the producer of the tangible product sold in the marketplace, in this case the physical Campaigns videotape sold by Dastar. The concept might be stretched (as it was under the original version of § 43(a)) to include not only the actual producer, but also the trademark owner who commissioned or assumed responsibility for ("stood behind") production of the physical product. But as used in the Lanham Act, the phrase "origin of goods" is in our view incapable of connoting the person or entity that originated the ideas or communications that "goods" embody or contain. Such an extension would not only stretch the text, but it would be out of accord with the history and purpose of the Lanham Act and inconsistent with precedent.

Section 43(a) of the Lanham Act prohibits actions like trademark infringement that deceive consumers and impair a producer's goodwill. It forbids, for example, the Coca-Cola Company's passing off its product as Pepsi-Cola or reverse passing off Pepsi-Cola as its product. But the brand-loyal consumer who prefers the drink that the Coca-Cola Company or PepsiCo sells, while he believes that that company produced (or at least stands behind the production of) that product, surely does not necessarily believe that that company was the "origin" of the drink in the sense that it was the very first to devise the formula. The consumer who buys a branded product does not automatically assume that the brand-name company is the same entity that came up with the idea for the product, or designed the product — and typically does not care whether it is. The words of the Lanham Act should not be stretched to cover matters that are typically of no consequence to purchasers.

It could be argued, perhaps, that the reality of purchaser concern is different for what might be called a communicative product — one that is valued not primarily for its physical qualities, such as a hammer, but for the intellectual content that it conveys, such as a book or, as here, a video. The purchaser of a novel is interested not merely, if at all, in the identity of the producer of the physical tome (the publisher), but also, and indeed primarily, in the identity of the creator of the story it conveys (the author). And the author, of course, has at least as much interest in avoiding passing-off (or reverse passing-off) of his creation as does the publisher. For such a communicative product (the argument goes) "origin of goods" in § 43(a) must be deemed to include not merely the producer of the physical item (the publishing house Farrar, Straus and Giroux, or the video producer Dastar) but also the creator of the content that the physical item conveys (the author Tom Wolfe, or — assertedly — respondents).

The problem with this argument according special treatment to communicative products is that it causes the Lanham Act to conflict with the law of copyright, which addresses that subject specifically. The right to copy, and to copy without attribution, once a copyright has expired, like "the right to make [an article whose patent has expired] — including the right to make it in precisely the shape it carried when patented — passes to the public." "In general, unless an intellectual property right such as a patent or copyright protects an item, it will be subject to copying." The rights of a patentee or copyright holder are part of a "carefully crafted bargain," under which, once the patent or copyright monopoly has expired, the public may use the invention or work at will and without attribution. Thus, in construing the Lanham Act, we have been "careful to caution against misuse or over-extension" of trademark and related protections into areas traditionally occupied by patent or copyright. "The Lanham Act," we have said, "does not exist to reward manufacturers for their innovation in creating a particular device; that is the purpose of the patent law and its period of exclusivity." Federal trademark law "has no necessary relation to invention or discovery," but rather, by preventing competitors from copying "a source-identifying mark," "reduce[s] the customer's costs of shopping and making purchasing decisions," and "helps assure a producer that it (and not an imitating competitor) will reap the financial, reputation-related rewards associated with a desirable product[.]" Assuming for the sake of argument that Dastar's representation of itself as the "Producer" of its videos amounted to a representation that it originated the creative work conveyed by the videos, allowing a cause of action under § 43(a) for that representation would create a species of mutant copyright law that limits the public's "federal right to 'copy and to use,'" expired copyrights.

When Congress has wished to create such an addition to the law of copyright, it has done so with much more specificity than the Lanham Act's ambiguous use of "origin." The Visual Artists Rights Act of 1990, § 603(a), 104 Stat. 5128, provides that the author of an artistic work "shall have the right . . . to claim authorship of that work." 17 U.S.C. § 106A(a)(1)(A). That express right of attribution is carefully limited and focused: It attaches only to specified "work[s] of visual art," § 101, is personal to the artist, § 106A(b) and (e), and endures only for "the life of the author," at § 106A(d)(1). Recognizing in § 43(a) a cause of action for misrepresentation of authorship of noncopyrighted works (visual or otherwise) would render these limitations superfluous. A statutory interpretation that renders another statute superfluous is of course to be avoided.

Reading "origin" in § 43(a) to require attribution of uncopyrighted materials would pose serious practical problems. Without a copyrighted work as the basepoint, the word "origin" has no discernable limits. A video of the MGM film Carmen Jones, after its copyright has expired, would presumably require attribution not just to MGM, but to Oscar Hammerstein II (who wrote the musical on which the film was based), to Georges Bizet (who wrote the opera on which the musical was based), and to Prosper Merimee (who wrote the novel on which the opera was based). In many cases, figuring out who is in the line of "origin" would be no simple task. Indeed, in the present case it is far from clear that respondents have that status. Neither SFM nor New Line had anything to do with the production of the Crusade television series — they merely were licensed to distribute the video version. While Fox might have a claim to being in the line of origin, its involvement with the creation of the television series was limited at best. Time, Inc., was the principal if not the exclusive creator, albeit under arrangement with Fox. And of course it was neither Fox nor Time, Inc., that shot the film used in the Crusade television series. Rather, that footage came from the United States Army, Navy, and Coast Guard, the British Ministry of Information and War Office, the National Film Board of Canada, and unidentified "Newsreel Pool Cameramen." If anyone has a claim to being the original creator of the material used in both the Crusade television series and the Campaigns videotapes, it would be those groups, rather than Fox. We do not think the Lanham Act requires this search for the source of the Nile and all its tributaries.

Another practical difficulty of adopting a special definition of "origin" for communicative products is that it places the manufacturers of those products in a difficult position. On the one hand, they would face Lanham Act liability for failing to credit the creator of a work on which their lawful copies are based; and on the other hand they could face Lanham Act liability for crediting the creator if that should be regarded as implying the creator's "sponsorship or approval" of the copy, 15 U.S.C. § 1125(a)(1)(A). In this case, for example, if Dastar had simply "copied [the television series] as Crusade in Europe and sold it as Crusade in Europe," without changing the title or packaging (including the original credits to Fox), it is hard to have confidence in respondents' assurance that they "would not be here on a Lanham Act cause of action."

. . .

In sum, reading the phrase "origin of goods" in the Lanham Act in accordance with the Act's common-law foundations (which were not designed to protect originality or creativity), and in light of the copyright and patent laws (which were), we conclude that the phrase refers to the producer of the tangible goods that are offered for sale, and not to the author of any idea, concept, or communication embodied in those goods. Cf. 17 U.S.C. § 202 (distinguishing between a copyrighted work and "any material object in which the work is embodied"). To hold otherwise would be akin to finding that § 43(a) created a species of perpetual patent and copyright, which Congress may not do.

. . .

Because we conclude that Dastar was the "origin" of the products it sold as its own, respondents cannot prevail on their Lanham Act claim. . . . The judgment of the Court of Appeals for the Ninth Circuit is reversed, and the case is remanded for further proceedings consistent with this opinion.

It is so ordered.

Notes and Questions

1. The Supreme Court necessarily is vigilant to regulate the well-defined intellectual property rights and limitations of copyright law and patent law, and to prevent any end runs around these limits that may be exploited if trademark and trade dress law were to be extended beyond their proper limits. Copyright and patent law is based on a direct grant of rights to authors and inventors in the U.S. Constitution, art. I § 8, while trademark is justified under the more general grant of power to Congress to regulate interstate commerce. Also, copyright and patent law are tied to originality and invention, and to some extent, creativity, while trademark law is not. Thus, it does not behoove the courts to imply a savings of lapsed copyright and patent rights from trademark law, as this might create a kind of perpetual copyright or patent grant that violates the Constitution's grant of authors' and inventors' rights for "limited" periods of time.

2. In *Bretford Mfg., Inc. v. Smith Sys. Mfg. Corp.*, 419 F.3d 576 (7th Cir. 2005), the Seventh Circuit held that a competitor had the right (so far as the Lanham Act was concerned) to incorporate parts manufactured by others, provided that it manufactured the finished product and did not mislead anyone about who should be held responsible for shortcomings. The Lanham Act focused on the consumer rather than the trade dress owner. Because, as far as the school district was concerned, the "origin" of the tables it was buying was the competitor, there was no false designation of origin.

3. Similarly, in *Boston Int'l Music, Inc. v. Austin*, 2003 Copr. L. Dec. 28,719 (D. Mass. 2003), plaintiffs sued defendants for copying a distinctive part of plaintiff's song and using it in a song that defendants created. The court dismissed plaintiff's claim for false designation of origin in violation of § 43 of the Lanham Act, stating, "Plaintiff's claims are sufficiently covered by the law of copyright, and I decline to construe § 43 of

the Lanham Act to require attribution to plaintiff Johnson for "I Like It," where the defendants here are the "origin" of the product they recorded, produced, and sold on their own, and there is therefore no false designation of origin within the meaning of the Lanham Act." The court quoted *Dastar*, stating that the origin of goods "refers to the producer of the tangible goods that are offered for sale, and not to the author of any idea, concept, or communication embodied in those goods."

4. In *Bonito Boats v. Thunder Craft Boats*, 489 U.S. 141 (1989), the Court rejected a Lanham Act "passing off" claim against defendants who had used molds to duplicate the plaintiff's unpatented boat hulls, apparently without crediting the plaintiff. And in *TrafFix Devices v. Marketing Displays*, 532 U.S. 23 (2001), the Court held that the plaintiff, whose patents on flexible road signs had expired, could not prevail on a trade-dress claim under §43(a) of the Lanham Act because the formerly protected features of the signs (i.e., flexibility) were functional. *See also Fuji Kogyo Co., Ltd. v. Pac. Bay Int'l, Inc.*, 461 F.3d 675 (6th Cir. 2006). Justice Scalia in *Dastar* further emphasized that the plaintiff in *TrafFix Devices* did not have a "passing off" claim for unattributed copying of his design.

5. Although the theory espoused in *Dastar* makes good sense in relation to functional items such as a boat hulls and traffic signs, the theory seems a little ridiculous when you consider that it may mean that anyone can reproduce a public domain work and pass it off as their own. Jane Doe's play, *Romeo and Juliet*, and John Doe's paintings, "Sunflowers" and "Waterlilies," would be permitted. Is this good public policy? Did Justice Scalia go a bit far in finding that consumers have little or no interest in knowing who actually created the goods that they buy?

6. Early in the opinion, Justice Scalia opined in dicta that respondent New Line's claim against Dastar "would undoubtedly be sustained if Dastar had bought some of New Line's Crusade videotapes and merely repackaged them as its own." Assuming that statement still is true after the *Dastar* holding, why would New Line have a Lanham Act claim in these circumstances but not in the circumstances of the *Dastar* case?

I. Trademark Infringement

1. Elements of Infringement

Trademark infringement actions follow the logic of the creation of the marks. The marks are supposed to identify goods and prevent or mitigate consumer confusion. Therefore, the three main elements of infringement are:

- Likelihood of confusion
- by a reasonably prudent buyer
- concerning goods identified by two similar marks.

All of these initial requirements are case-specific. There is no baseline where a certain mark always is going to induce confusion when used in the market with another mark. The class of goods may affect the standard for confusion. High class, expensive goods may call for a test of the likelihood that a "reasonably discriminating buyer" will be confused by the presence of two marks in the same channel of commerce. This reasonably discriminating buyer is going to stop, think, do some careful comparison of the choices, and then make a decision, meaning she is less likely to make a mistake based on the same color of packaging or a slightly similar sounding name. Goods that are marketed and sold to professional buyers may call for a test of the likelihood of confusion of a reasonably prudent expert. An expert is the least likely to be fooled by packaging or jingles or clever-sounding names. An expert is going to spend some time and brain power picking the exact right product for an application.

With a standard of likelihood of confusion, proof of actual confusion among consumers is not required and, in fact, is not conclusive on the issue of likelihood of confusion, but it does go a long way by demonstrating that some confusion among some consumers did occur. How do you prove actual confusion? With surveys, polling, or questionnaires that demonstrate that people actually thought they were getting product Y when they bought product X. Remember that the confusion can occur in several directions — confusion over buying junior user's goods thinking they were senior user's goods (passing off claim), confusion over buying senior user's goods thinking they were junior user's (reverse passing off claim), or some other form of confusion as to the source or sponsorship of the good.

Likelihood of confusion does not depend on the marks being exactly similar; just similar enough in some way to present the potential for confusion. Of course, exact similitude would be a helpful fact for the plaintiff, all things considered.

There are several additional factors that courts will look at when assessing the likelihood of confusion:

- Strength of the plaintiff's mark
- Relatedness of goods and services — e.g., wine and cheese, vs. wine and motor oil
- Degree of similarity between the designation and the trademark in: (1) appearance, (2) pronunciation of the words used, (3) verbal translations of the pictures or designs involved, (4) suggestion
- Proof of actual confusion
- Marketing channels — how the goods are marketed, where they are marketed and sold, the kinds of consumers to whom the goods are marketed
- Intent of the actor in adopting the designation
- Degree of care likely to be exercised by purchasers — average consumer, discriminating consumer, or expert consumer

- The reasonableness and likelihood of plaintiff's expansion into the product lines used by the defendant.

For a likelihood of confusion analysis, bonus facts (facts not required to be proved in order to prevail, but which would be very helpful) are:

- Proof of fraud—lying, cheating, misrepresenting one's use of the competing mark, or other proof of outright, intentional deception. It is not required, but it would be helpful to have actual proof that the defendant tried to intentionally defraud and cheat consumers.
- Exact or close similarity of the two marks. This tends to negate the argument of innocence or accidental similarity.
- Proof of pretender's knowledge of owner's mark. This is another fact that tends to negate claims of innocence or accidental similarity.
- Proof of defendant's direct copying of plaintiff's mark—e.g., proof that shows that defendant used plaintiff's own trademark "clip art" and exemplars to produce the identical marks on defendant's goods.

As mentioned above, the consideration of who might be confused varies from situation to situation, and from the nature and type of goods involved in the dispute. Trademark law's definition of a reasonably prudent buyer is less rigorous than one might expect. Not to put too fine a point on it, but some obviously stupid consumers might still qualify as "reasonably prudent." As one example, there once was a trademark dispute involving Mutual of Omaha Insurance Company in which the defendant, a young person named Novak, tried to have some fun with the Mutual of Omaha "Native American in headdress" logo. Novak created a "Mutant of Omaha—Nuclear Holocaust Insurance" logo with a mutated head under a battered version of the headdress[31]:

---

31. Image: Michael D. Murray, Cropped, revised, and resized images derived from excerpts of exhibits depicting the Mutual of Omaha logo and the Novak "Mutant of Omaha" logo, the subject of *Mutual of Omaha Ins. Co. v. Novak*, 836 F. 2d 397 (8th Cir. 1987).

Mutual of Omaha did not like the joke, and they sued Novak. Mutual of Omaha was able to introduce evidence of actual consumer confusion — in other words, some living, breathing persons, with the ability to navigate out of their homes to the place where Mutual of Omaha's legal team was conducting the survey, and who looked at Nolan's "Mutant of Omaha" design and thought that it was an actual product offered by Mutual of Omaha. These must have been "reasonably undiscerning buyers" indeed.

But that is not the only example. In a case involving Anheuser Busch Brewing Company, makers (at the time) of a beer brand called "Michelob Dry," against a man named Balducci, publisher of a humor magazine in which Balducci ran a fake ad for "Michelob Oily." Michelob Dry's trademarked tagline was, "One taste and you'll drink it dry." Balducci changed the tagline to, "One taste and you'll drink it oily," and showed a can of Michelob Oily pouring black crude oil out. Other Anheuser Busch and Michelob brand marks were besmirched — including the famous "A and Eagle" mark of Anheuser Busch, shown in the fake ad drenched in oil, and with a shell at the top replacing a star, most likely to conjure the idea of Shell Oil Company.[32]

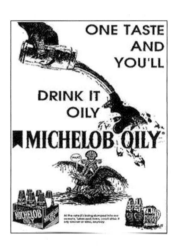

All in good fun, right? Not to Anheuser Busch, who sued Balducci. In the course of the suit, Anheuser Busch introduced evidence of actual consumer confusion from polling conducted at a shopping mall in St. Louis (the hometown of Anheuser Busch), and the evidence was that 6 percent of poll takers thought Michelob Oily was a real Anheuser Busch product, and that Anheuser Busch had sponsored the Michelob Oily ad! So, do not overestimate the discerning capabilities of the reasonably prudent consumer.

---

32. Image: Michael D. Murray, Revised and resized images derived from excerpts of exhibits depicting Anheuser Busch Michelob Dry and A & Eagle logos, and the Balducci "Michelob Oily" spoof ad, the subject of *Anheuser-Busch, Inc. v. Balducci Publications*, 28 F.3d 769 (8th Cir. 1994).

2. Remedies

A trademark proprietor may sue an infringing party for monetary damages or an injunction prohibiting the infringing use, or both, and in proper cases, attorneys' fees and punitive damages may be awarded. Monetary recovery for trademark infringement and unfair competition is measured variously by defendant's profits, plaintiff's actual business damages and losses caused by the wrong, or plaintiff's loss of profits caused by the wrong.

The court has great latitude in formulating injunctive relief. It may grant an injunction merely limiting the use of the mark by the infringer, such as requiring some change in format or the addition of prefixes, suffixes, or disclaimers; or it may allow defendant to continue using the contested mark, but only in connection with its own distinctive mark or logo. An injunction may also require affirmative steps to avoid confusion, such as corrective advertising, or product recall.

Section 35 of the Lanham Act provides for monetary damages in the case of infringement, subject to the principles of equity. Monetary relief is denied where an injunction will satisfy the equities of the case and where there has been no showing of fraud or palming off. The courts have discretion to increase the damages to treble damages, or decrease the damages if an award of profits is excessive.

In certain exceptional circumstances where defendant's conduct is willful and flagrant, plaintiff might also be entitled to punitive damages and attorneys' fees. Proper use of symbols such as ®, ^{TM}, and ^{SM} in conjunction with the proprietor's uses of the mark can aid the proprietor in establishing that infringement was willful.

J. Affirmative Defenses and Avoidances

Trademark law polices the activities of each trademark owner to make sure the owner itself is not getting sloppy with its mark in ways that could, in and of themselves, cause consumer confusion. There are five significant affirmative defenses or avoidances that can defeat the claims of the trademark owner by defeating its trademark rights:

Abandonment
Genericization
Laches
Acquiescence
Unclean hands

These defenses are generally called "affirmative defenses" because a defendant has to affirmatively assert them as a defense to a trademark infringement suit, and affirmatively bring forth evidence sufficient to establish the defense. Thus, the owner could have long abandoned the mark, but no one will be the wiser unless the defendant raises and proves the defense of abandonment. These defenses are sometimes called "avoidances" because they work to allow the defendant to avoid liability for a potential infringement. Not listed above is the separate category of "fair use" of trademarks, which is a category of affirmative defenses, too, but one which we will consider in, section M below.

Abandonment

In order to maintain the rights and power of your mark, you have to keep using it. Using it means using it in commerce, on and in association with the marketing, advertising, packaging, and displays concerning your product at the point of purchase and beyond. If you don't use it, you lose it. And we call that "abandonment."

In other areas of law, the concept of abandonment with property means an intentional relinquishment of a known right. In trademark law, it is a little different. Abandonment requires:

- Discontinuation of use of the mark
- with intent not to resume . . . but
- Intent not resume can be inferred from three consecutive years of nonuse.

The reason for this defense is prevention of consumer confusion and fairness to competitors in the marketplace. Remember: the basic public policy reason for trademark law is to prevent consumer confusion. If you stop making your goods and stop using the mark, perhaps all is well on your end; you have intentionally abandoned the product line and the mark. But sometimes you have just taken a break — you aren't making and selling the goods or providing the services, but you might want to resume the work someday. In the meantime, you don't have anything on which or with which to use the trademark — no advertising, no packaging, no goods. That might cause confusion with consumers — where did Company X's products go? Where are my favorite Brand X goods? Worse (from a consumer standpoint) is simply ceasing to use the mark but continuing to manufacture and sell the same line of products. Now consumers really can get confused — Is Company X still making these products? Who is making these products now? Where are the Brand X products I used to buy? Are these new products as good as the old ones I used to buy? This is the kind of confusion that can be caused by stopping the use of a mark in commerce, and trademark law seeks to stamp it out.

The other reason for the abandonment defense is simple fairness to competitors in the marketplace. It is conceivable that one company could establish a whole wide range of desirable trademarks in the marketplace, tying up the channels of commerce with dozens or scores of marks. This would make it a little more difficult for others to compete in the same channels of commerce. It is not that competitors will be unable to come up with a different mark — that statement simply defies logic and the capacities for human imagination — but the channel of commerce might become clogged with all sorts of marks chasing the same kinds of products. Some channels are clogged because there are so many products being offered in the channel — beer, toothpaste, soft drinks, jeans, athletic shoes, and many more channels of commerce have a plethora of product offerings, each of which may have a distinguishing mark to identify them. But if some of these marks are not actually being used with actual products, then competitors are fighting paper tigers to try to out-distinguish their competition and get some attention (and hopefully sales) for their products. A mark must be an identifier of an actual product that actually exists, currently, in the channel of commerce. Otherwise, the mark may be held to be abandoned.

Intent to abandon and not resume use is inferred in the following way: if a mark is not used in commerce for three consecutive years, the presumption is that it was intentionally abandoned with no plan to resume it. That legal language — "presumption" — should trigger the expectation that one could fight the presumption and attempt to rebut the presumption. This could be as simple as providing evidence that the challenger is wrong, that in fact the mark was used during that three year period. Otherwise, in the event that the challenger is right and the mark owner stopped using the mark for three consecutive years, the original owner will need to bring forth substantial, reliable evidence to explain and justify why it hasn't been using the mark. It will not suffice for the original owner to promise that it will start using the mark again very soon because that doesn't justify the absence of use for the three year period, and now, because of the presence of the challenger who almost certainly has a competing mark it wants to use, the challenger will have a leg up (priority in time) even if the original owner starts to try to use the same mark in commerce. In essence, the old mark fell into the public domain, and competitors all can use the old mark or a close facsimile of the old mark in a quest to connect the mark as an identifier of the competitors' goods of a certain quality. If the original owner starts up again with the old mark, it potentially will infringe one of the newer but now more senior users of the same or a similar mark.

Genericization

We examined generic marks and genericization in section C on the strength of marks. Genericization refers to an owner that "allows" its mark to become a generic description for goods — a genus, of which its own and other competitors' goods become species. A mark is supposed to be an adjective — a descriptor and identifier of one type of a thing. Generic descriptions are nouns — the thing itself. The difference is reflected in asking for the installation of an "Escalator brand moving staircase" and asking for the installation of an "escalator." The latter is the generic effect.

Genericization happens when the owner uses or allows others to use the mark name as a noun or verb, instead of an adjective modifying a noun. How to stop it? Search for and write nasty letters to everyone who uses the trademark like a noun; make sure they correct it, write a redaction, and stop doing it in the future. If the product lends itself to being made into a noun, the owner may be fighting a difficult fight to stave off genericization, but if it doesn't fight hard enough, the rights will disappear. Aspirin, yo-yo, cellophane, thermos bottles, escalators, safari hats, shredded wheat, lanolin — all went generic, and ceased to represent a trademark descriptor for a certain type of thing and became the name of the thing itself. Thus, the original user of the name had no more trademark rights in the name — anyone could produce cellulose-based wrapping sheets and call it "cellophane."

There are two types of surveys commonly used to prove or disprove that a mark is generic. The first type is the "Thermos" survey, which included questions such as: "What do you call these containers?" "Do you know the names of any manufacturers who make these containers that keep liquids hot or cold?" "Can you name any trademarks or brand names that are used on these containers?" This survey found that 75 percent of adults in the United States called such a container a "thermos," and only about 12 percent knew that "thermos" had trademark significance. In contrast, the "Teflon" survey asked whether each of eight names ("STP," "Thermos," "Margarine," "Teflon," "Jello," "Refrigerator," "Aspirin" and "Coke") was a brand name or common name. Sixty-eight percent of the respondents said they thought "Teflon" was a brand name.

Laches

Laches in trademark law means a delay that prejudices or inconveniences someone else. In most cases, the someone else is the potential defendant, and the delay is a delay in enforcing one's rights over a mark. In other words, plaintiff could have sued to enforce its rights concerning a mark earlier, but didn't, and defendant went on in blissful ignorance using the mark. Now, at the later time, plaintiff sues defendant, and defendant has been injured by the delay — for example, defendant may have spent a lot of time or money using the competing mark while plaintiff sat on its hands.

Laches has three elements: (1) a delay in asserting one's trademark rights, (2) lack of excuse for the delay, and (3) undue prejudice to the alleged infringer caused by the delay. The delay must be measured from the period at which the trademark owner knew or should have known of an infringing use. If the injury to defendant from the delay is significant, and plaintiff does not have any excuse for the delay, the court may cut off plaintiff's action. Like other equitable defenses, even if the elements of the defense are met, the defendant's own unclean hands may act to bar laches relief.

Laches is not granted very often. Typically, defendants have reason to know that they are treading on someone else's mark, and typically, plaintiffs do act promptly once they figure out that someone is trespassing on their mark. Even then, it takes time to get the litigation prepared and ready for filing; every enforcement action takes time to set up. Therefore, it is very easy for a defendant to argue, "You could have moved faster, you could have sued me yesterday, or last week, or last month." But the reality is the defense will not work if the delay has an explanation, and it will not work unless the prejudice to defendant is unusual and significant. So, this defense is easy to allege but hard to prevail upon.

Acquiescence

Acquiescence as a defense is a reflection on the trademark owner's lack of diligence in protecting and enforcing its trademark rights. The defense requires proof that the owner demonstrated an intent not to enforce its rights. Acquiescence is related to laches, but acquiescence has a separate requirement that the mark owner give assurances explicitly or implicitly that it intends not to enforce its rights against the potential defendant. The defendant then relies on the explicit or implicit assurance in some manner that causes undue prejudice to the defendant. With laches, the owner's inaction in enforcing its rights over the mark is determined to be an unexcused delay that causes undue prejudice to the alleged infringer; with acquiescence, the owner's actions or statements cause the alleged infringer to believe that the owner is not going to enforce its marks, and that belief causes the alleged infringer's undue prejudice.

Mark Owner Inaction as Proof of Laches or Acquiescence

One element of the proof in a laches or acquiescence affirmative defense can be that the mark owner failed to be active and even proactive in searching for potential infringers, writing "cease and desist" and "takedown" letters to them, threatening litigation, and most importantly, by failing to follow through by actually suing everyone who persists in infringing on its marks. A trademark owner who neither searches for nor pursues infringers and instead acts passively or not at all in the face of infringement will lose its trademark rights. The policy here once again follows the purpose of the trademark laws: to prevent or mitigate consumer confusion. If you allow your mark to be misused directly (by competitors) or indirectly (by the press or other media), your mark loses its distinctive power as an identifier of goods of a certain quality from a certain manufacturer. Consumers will see the mark or similar marks being used for all manner of goods, and won't be able to identify your goods any more. If you don't search for these people, get in their face and demand that they stop, and follow up by actually suing them, you may lose your trademark rights.

The risk of acquiescence leads to the cottage industry of trademark lawyers reading every trade publication and scanning all media for misuse of their clients' marks. Every website, blog post, tweet, and news article that misuses the mark should receive a letter, and those who defy the letter must be dealt with further.

Unclean Hands

Trademark law affords the owner with equitable remedies—primarily, injunctions—and so the owner has to pay service to the requirements of equity, one of which is the avoidance of unclean hands. The saying goes that "All who seek equity must do equity." This means you cannot seek for a court to grant you a special remedy such as a restraining order or injunction if you have been abusing and treating others unfairly. If you play hardball in enforcing your rights, harassing and threatening those who hardly touch your mark, you may have your own relief cut off because you came to a court seeking equity but your hands were dirty from your own misdeeds.

The inequitable conduct must relate directly (i.e., have a direct connection) to the very transactions, activities, and occurrences that give rise to the mark owner's claim for equitable relief on the particular mark at issue in the suit. It will not suffice simply to show that the plaintiff has done bad deeds at some time and in some place, if the allegations do not relate to the exercise of rights regarding the very trademark sought to be enforced in the present action. The defendant need not be the target of the offensive, inequitable conduct, as long as the defendant proves that other parties were abused by the plaintiff in the exercise of this trademark, or that the public in general was abused, as by proving that the plaintiff engaged in fraud or spread misleading information concerning the trademark at issue.

K. Trademark Dilution

Trademark dilution is an extension of regular trademark law. The concept is to give broader protection for actions that do not directly infringe on a trademark, but which blur its ability to identify specific goods, or tarnish the mark so that its positive associations of quality and good value become confused with negative ideas. Dilution rights are reserved for the most important and successful trademarks of manufacturers. Dilution is balanced a little more toward rewarding good manufacturers and service providers as opposed to being tied to the overall prevention of consumer confusion.

1. State Anti-Dilution Laws

The states led the way with anti-dilution laws. States wanted to protect their best industries and employers, and wrote these laws as a way to give companies a way to keep their marks strong. The extended protection is that dilution laws do not require proof of consumer confusion—which is the hardest, most expensive, and most time-consuming element to prove in an infringement lawsuit. The laws look instead to the nature of the mark (is it a truly "famous" mark, long-lasting, well-established), and the nature of the activity questioned (is the activity of the opponent one that might "tarnish" the famous mark, or is it one that blurs some of the mark's distinctiveness and singularity as an identifier of goods and services). Tarnishing activities are ones that associate the mark with scandal or degrading activities in an unfair manner—for example, tying the mark to sex, drugs, rock n' roll, or something anathema to the mark or the company that stands behind the mark. Note that it must be an unfair association. Many companies use sex-appeal in their own advertising, and many others use rock n' roll, and it would not amount to a dilution action for tarnishment for someone to feature those marks together with sex and rock.

Dilution also does not prevent direct comment on and criticism of a mark or the company behind the mark. This kind of speech might actually cause others to think less of the mark and the company that owns it, but this is not what the law means by tarnishment. The First Amendment protects these expressive activities as fair uses of famous marks. Nevertheless, you must study the general concept of fair use in trademark and dilution law because it might not match up with your own expectations of what is fair comment, and we will do so in section M of this chapter, on "Fair Use."

Blurring refers to uses of the mark or of closely similar words, phrases, or images that suggest the mark in a manner that reduces the distinctive qualities of the famous mark as a singular identifier of goods of a certain quality from a certain manufacturer. If this sounds a lot like the standard trademark infringement claim, it is, but the difference is dilution laws go beyond consumer confusion as a driving force and simply look to the nature of the mark and the nature of the uses. If a use or activity potentially will interfere with the distinctive and singular nature of the famous mark, particularly a repeated, widespread use of a similar looking image or similar sounding phrase, then this use may be challenged with a blurring dilution claim.

Dilution looks to uses or references affecting a famous mark in a commercial setting, although the opponent need not be using the famous mark or something similar to it as a trademark. Once again, the concept of "commercial" is not as business and profit driven a concept in trademark dilution law as the average lay person might think. Excessive uses of a mark in settings that appear to be largely non-commercial but that tarnish the mark or blur the mark's uniqueness and singularity may be actionable.

2. Federal Trademark Dilution Act

Eventually, the concept of trademark dilution made its way from the states to the federal government, and Congress enacted a federal, nationwide anti-dilution act, which is found in the United States Code at 15 U.S.C. § 1125(c).

The concepts of dilution — famous marks, dilution by blurring or tarnishing, and no need to prove consumer confusion — all were imported from the states to the national act. The elements of a federal trademark dilution claim are:

- commercial use;
- of a famous mark or trade name;
- that is likely to dilute the distinctive quality of the mark, regardless of the presence or absence of actual or likely confusion, of competition, or of actual economic injury.

"Famous" marks under the federal law are supposed to be nationally famous marks. The courts have wrestled with this concept, and the statute adopted the following set of criteria for the analysis:

- degree of inherent or acquired distinctiveness of the mark;
- duration and extent of owner's use of the mark;
- duration and extent of advertising and publicity of the mark;
- geographical extent of the trading area in which the mark is used;
- channels of trade for the goods or services with which the mark is used;
- degree of recognition of the mark in the trading areas and channels of trade;
- nature and extent of use of the same or similar marks by third parties; and
- whether the mark was registered under earlier (pre-1943) trademark statutes of 1881, 1905, or the Principal Register.

Dilution under the federal act is very similar to the states' concept: lessening of the capacity of a famous mark to identify and distinguish goods or services, regardless of the presence of competition between the parties or likelihood of confusion, mistake, or deception of consumers. Federal courts will consider concepts of tarnishing, degrading, or diluting marks borrowed from state law.

The federal act has built in some exceptions to the coverage of the act. These statutory exceptions are:

- Fair use of a famous mark by another person in comparative commercial advertising or promotion where the goods or services of the owner of the famous mark are compared with the goods or services of the competing company (in other words, you need not compare your goods to "Brand X," you can actually say, "OxyClean" is better than "Chlorox")
- Noncommercial use of a mark (generally this refers to expressive uses in some form of media)
- All forms of news reporting and news commentary
- Parody and other forms of comment and criticism.

The original incarnation of the federal act left a question unanswered: do you need to show actual harm (actual damages) from the defendant's activities vis-à-vis your mark? The Supreme Court tried to answer it in the case of *Moseley v. V Secret Catalogue.*[33] In *Moseley*, a store dealing in women's lingerie called Victor's Little Secret was sued by the better known dealer of women's lingerie called Victoria's Secret. The Supreme Court resolved a dispute between the lower federal courts and held that proof of actual dilution (actual harm, actual damages) was required for a federal dilution act claim. This was an unwelcome result for many established manufacturers and retailers whose marks might be thought of as famous, because actual dilution can be very

---

33. *Moseley v. V Secret Catalogue, Inc.,* 537 U.S. 418 (2003).

hard to prove. Surveys and polling will not necessarily suffice, because these prove consumer confusion, while dilution requires economic damage — a downturn in sales or some other concrete evidence of damage from the activities of the defendant. Victoria's Secret didn't have that kind of evidence, and lost the lawsuit. Other manufacturers and retailers expected their chances of proving such harm and prevailing in a dilution suit would be difficult, too. So, they did what good corporate citizens oppressed by the law do: they lobbied Congress to change the law and reverse the effect of the Supreme Court's ruling. And Congress did exactly that.

Congress passed the Trademark Dilution Revision Act of 2006, which retained the basic concept of dilution but added new language to rebut the Supreme Court's opinion: ". . . [use] in commerce that is likely to cause dilution by blurring or dilution by tarnishment of the famous mark regardless of the presence or absence of actual or likely confusion, of competition, or of actual economic injury."

The remedies for a federal dilution action are injunctive relief only (you force the defendant to stop their activities that affect the mark), unless plaintiff proves willful intent to trade on the owner's reputation or to cause dilution of the famous mark; then the owner of the famous mark will also be entitled to trademark infringement remedies.

L. Trade Dress

Trade dress is a subset of trademark law designed to protect a distinctive look and feel designed and adopted for product packaging, labeling, or marketing materials (advertising, displays, etc.), or for the products themselves. The basic requirements are:

- adoption;
- of inherently distinctive trade dress;
- use in commerce;
- the look and feel of your trade dress is not functional; and
- the competitor's trade dress is confusingly similar.

Trade dress can be protected and even registered if it meets federal register criteria of use in interstate commerce. The difference may be that the federal registration will put your trade dress to the test of the United States Patent and Trademark Office (PTO), who will determine whether the trade dress really is inherently distinctive. Alternatively, you can try to prove to the PTO that your trade dress has acquired secondary meaning and association with a certain product of a certain manufacturer.

Sooner or later, you might have to face the question of secondary meaning, because in any action to prove a claim of infringement of unregistered trade dress, you must prove secondary meaning (secondary association) of your trade dress with your products and your business. This was the ruling in *Wal-Mart v. Samara Bros.*, that considered the following children's clothing:[34]

Samara   Wal-Mart

Whomever Wal-Mart hired to copy the Samara dress did a bang-up job. But the court let Wal-Mart off the hook because Samara did not or could not prove secondary association of its dress design with "Samara" in the marketplace.

With registered trade dress, you need only prove:

■ your trade dress is inherently distinctive;
■ the look and feel of your trade dress is not functional; and
■ the competitor's trade dress is confusingly similar.

Functionality shows up a great deal with product design in trademark cases because manufacturers want their products to be cool, slick, and attractive in appearance. That is a good thing under trade dress law, until the design itself helps the product function better as the type of product it is. A lamp shade that has an eye-catching shape but one that also disperses the light differently would most likely be called functional. A woman's body-suit that is made of a distinctive, shiny-looking material might be called a good candidate for trade dress protection, until you discover that the material makes the suit water-resistant or fire-resistant.

Some designs are obviously decorative and not functional. The "DG" logo and decoration on Dolce & Gabbana works adds nothing to the capacity of belt buckles to clasp, or sunglass cases to stay closed, or bracelets to stay on your arm.

---

34. Images: Michael D. Murray, Cropped, revised, and resized images derived from excerpts of exhibits depicting Samara's children's clothing compared to Wal-Mart's children's clothing, the subject of *Wal-Mart Stores, Inc. v. Samara Brothers, Inc.*, 529 U.S. 205 (2000).

35

Chanel's distinctive dress designs do not make the dress function better *as a dress*; they only help the consumer find the Chanel items in the dress department.[36]

Although colors generally are regarded as functional and available for use as public domain items, it is possible to obtain trade dress protection over a color. Two important cases have made this law.

Case Study: Strategic Placement of Color

Louboutin v. Yves Saint Laurent[37]

In a celebrated dust-up between designer Christian Louboutin and established mega-giant Yves Saint Laurent over bright red used on the out-soles of women's shoes, Louboutin prevailed at the Court of Appeals. The court held that the red color used by Louboutin as a contrasting color on the soles had been used in commerce as a designator of Louboutin shoes, and that it now enjoyed secondary association with the manufacturer.

---

35. Images: Michael D. Murray, Collage of cropped, revised, and resized thumbnail images derived from images of Dolce & Gabbana products to show the non-functionality of the DG logo (2015).

36. Images: Michael D. Murray, Collage of cropped, revised, and resized thumbnail images derived from images of Chanel clothing to show the non-functionality of the Chanel designs (2015).

37. *Christian Louboutin S.A. v. Yves Saint Laurent America Holdings, Inc.,* 696 F.3d 206 (2d Cir. 2012).

LOUBOUTIN   YSL   38

The court was not prepared to find that red soles on red shoes had that same distinctive quality, and would not allow monochromatic red shoes in which the soles matched the color of the rest of the shoe to be included in Louboutin's protected trade dress.

Case Study: Secondary Association with a Specific Shade of Color

Qualitex Co. v. Jacobson Products Co., Inc.[39]

The United States Supreme Court had paved the way for designers such as Louboutin to protect specific shades of color in the *Qualitex* case. The case involved a certain "green-gold" color used on dry-cleaning pads sold by Qualitex. Qualitex had used this shade to differentiate its dry-cleaning pads from those of its competitors — trying to communicate, in other words, "That's not just any pad, that's a Qualitex cover pad."[40]

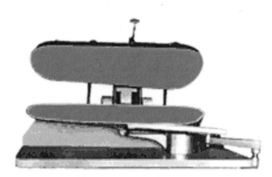

The Court allowed the green-gold color of Qualitex to be protected as trade dress because Qualitex proved secondary association in the marketplace of this color and its products. This is a more limited holding than at first it might appear. The Court's holding should not be interpreted to mean that Qualitex

38. Images: Michael D. Murray, Collage of cropped, revised, and resized thumbnail images derived from photographs of Christian Louboutin shoes compared to Yves Saint Laurent shoes (2015), the subject of *Christian Louboutin S.A. v. Yves Saint Laurent America Holdings, Inc.*, 696 F.3d 206 (2d Cir. 2012).

39. *Qualitex Co. v. Jacobson Products Co., Inc.*, 514 U.S. 159 (1995).

40. Image: Michael D. Murray, Cropped, revised, and resized thumbnail excerpt of an exhibit depicting Qualitex's dry cleaning pad (2015), the subject of *Qualitex Co. v. Jacobson Products Co., Inc.*, 514 U.S. 159 (1995).

now has a monopoly on this shade of green-gold, period. Instead, it has a trademark monopoly on this particular shade of green-gold when used on dry-cleaning products. Could you make a car in this shade of green-gold (if you wanted to)? Almost assuredly, yes. Could you make a dress or a handbag in this shade of green-gold? Again, almost assuredly, yes. But if you wanted to sell dry cleaning pads in this color, or associated items (e.g., dry cleaning chemicals or spray starch) in packaging bearing the green-gold color, you most likely would run afoul of Qualitex's trade dress protection.

Diamond Direct, LLC v. Star Diamond Group, Inc.

116 F. Supp. 2d 525 (S.D.N.Y. 2000)*

KAPLAN, District Judge.

This is an action for alleged [trade dress] infringement of plaintiff's . . . diamond ring designs . . . under the Lanham Act. . . .

The allegedly infringed ring styles "utilize[] a base or 'skirt' consisting of tapered baguettes set upon rows of narrow vertical prongs and therefore . . . fall stylistically within the broad category of rings referred to as 'ballerina' style rings."

. . .

Plaintiff claims . . . that the designs of its rings are protectable trade dress and that defendant is infringing its rights in violation of Section 43(a) of the Lanham Act. Defendant responds that plaintiff has failed to raise a genuine issue of material fact as to the alleged secondary meaning of its designs and that the action therefore should be dismissed.

. . . [U]nregistered product design trade dress cannot be inherently distinctive and therefore . . . product design, or configuration, is protected under Section 43(a) only upon a showing that it has acquired a secondary meaning—in other words, that "in the minds of the public, the primary significance of a product feature . . . is to identify the source of the product rather than the product itself." The Court reasoned that (1) product design almost invariably serves purposes other than source identification, and (2) "[c]onsumers should not be deprived of the benefits of competition with regard to the utilitarian and esthetic purposes that product design ordinarily serves by a rule of law that facilitates plausible threats of suit against new entrants based upon alleged inherent distinctiveness." Thus, the success of plaintiff's product configuration trade dress claim depends in the first instance on a showing of secondary meaning.

. . .

The question whether a product design serves principally to identify the source of the product often is determined inferentially. Relevant factors include (1) plaintiff's advertising expenditures; (2) consumer surveys linking the trade dress to a particular source; (3) sales success; (4) unsolicited media coverage; (5) attempts to plagiarize the trade dress; and (6) the length and exclusivity of

---

* Citations and footnotes omitted.

the use. Moreover, the degree to which plaintiff's product design differs from others in the marketplace obviously is relevant in a design case like this.

Here, the variations between plaintiff's designs and others in the marketplace are very modest, so much so that the relevant audiences would be exceptionally unlikely to associate them with a particular source. Plaintiff has not met the "vigorous evidentiary requirements" required to show secondary meaning. Plaintiff offers no survey evidence, a point of special note. And while evidence of advertising, promotion, and sales success can be significant in permitting an inference of secondary meaning, plaintiff's evidence here is much too sparse. The only concrete evidence of advertising was the expenditure of $7,000 on cooperative advertising for No. R8070, $10,000 for No. R8158 and $135,000 for No. R8431, hardly overwhelming sums. There is no evidence of promotion except for exhibition of these designs as part of plaintiff's line at a number of trade shows. And the evidence of sales also is limited: plaintiff has sold 225 units of No. R8070, 145 units of No. R8158 and 2,624 units of No. R8431. While these figures may be important to the plaintiff, they are weak support indeed for the proposition for which they are offered. In the last analysis, the Court holds that no reasonable trier of fact could infer that the primary significance of plaintiff's product designs is to identify their source. Accordingly, defendant is entitled to summary judgment dismissing the Lanham Act claim on the ground that there is no genuine issue of material fact on the issue of secondary meaning.

Hartford House, Ltd. v. Hallmark Cards, Inc.

846 F.2d 1268 (10th Cir. 1988)*

McKay, Circuit Judge.

I.

Plaintiffs, Susan Polis Schutz, Stephen Schutz, and Hartford House, Ltd., d/b/a Blue Mountain Arts (hereinafter collectively referred to as "Blue Mountain"), are in the greeting card business. Presently, Blue Mountain's two major lines of cards are entitled "AireBrush Feelings" and "WaterColor Feelings."

. . .

Blue Mountain claimed that Hallmark's "Personal Touch" cards infringed the protected trade dress of Blue Mountain's "AireBrush Feelings" and "WaterColor Feelings" lines. . . .

The district court . . . found that the "AireBrush Feelings" and "WaterColor Feelings" cards have an inherently distinctive and highly uniform overall appearance that is recognizable and attributable to Blue Mountain. According to the district court, some or all of the following features comprise that overall look:

1. A two-fold card containing poetry on the first and third pages.
2. Unprinted surfaces on the inside three panels.
3. A deckle edge on the right side of the first page.

---

* Footnotes and most citations omitted.

4. A rough-edge stripe of color, or wide stripe, on the outside of the deckle edge of the first page.
5. A high-quality, uncoated, and textured art paper for the cards.
6. Fluorescent ink for some of the colors printed on the cards.
7. Lengthy poetry, written in free verse, typically with a personal message.
8. Appearance of hand-lettered calligraphy on the first and third pages with the first letter of the words often enlarged.
9. An illustration that wraps around the card and is spread over three pages, including the back of the card.
10. The look of the cards primarily characterized by backgrounds of soft colors done with air brush blends or light watercolor strokes, usually depicting simple contrasting foreground scenes superimposed in the background.

. . .

"Although historically trade dress infringement consisted of copying a product's packaging, . . . 'trade dress' in its more modern sense [may] refer to the appearance of the [product] itself. . . ." Trade dress is a complex composite of features. One may be size, another may be color or color combinations, another may be texture, another may be graphics and arrangement and so on. Trade dress is a term reflecting the overall general impact, usually visual, but sometimes also tactile, of all these features taken together. The district court described Blue Mountain's trade dress as a combination of some or all of ten features listed above, which produces an overall uniform look and distinctive appearance of Blue Mountain's "AireBrush Feelings" and "WaterColor Feelings" lines of cards.

A product's trade dress is eligible for protection under section 43(a) if it is so distinctive as to become, in effect, an unregistered trademark. For a plaintiff to establish unprivileged imitation, prevail on a trade dress infringement claim, and thus prevent copying of the appearance of a product, (1) the trade dress, whether a single feature or a combination of features, must be nonfunctional; (2) the trade dress must have acquired a secondary meaning; and (3) there must be a likelihood of confusion among consumers as to the source of the competing products.

. . .

On this appeal Hallmark does not challenge the district court's preliminary determinations pertaining to secondary meaning and likelihood of confusion. Rather, Hallmark challenges the district court's determination that Blue Mountain's trade dress is nonfunctional. Consequently, our decision is limited to the resolution of the functionality issue.

. . .

"Whether the feature is functional should turn on 'whether the protection of the [feature] would hinder competition or impinge upon the rights of others to compete effectively in the sale of goods.'"

. . .

[A] trade dress may be a composite of several features in a certain arrangement or combination which produces an overall distinctive appearance. In this context, the question is whether the combination of features comprising the trade dress is functional. As the district court correctly stated, "[t]he creation and arrangement of individual product features into a particular overall design may itself constitute a non-functional product feature." A combination of features may be nonfunctional and thus protectable, even though the combination includes functional features. "Indeed, virtually every product is a combination of functional and non-functional features and a rule denying protection to any combination of features including a functional one would emasculate the law of trade dress infringement." Contrary to Hallmark's contention, the appropriate inquiry is not whether each individual feature of the trade dress is functional but whether the whole collection of features, taken together, is functional.

. . .

[T]he availability of alternative appealing designs is a key factor in determining that a trade dress is nonfunctional. In this respect, the district court correctly stated that "[s]ince the effect upon competition 'is really the crux of the matter,' it is of course significant that there are other alternatives available."

The district court focused on the design features of emotionally expressive non-occasion greeting cards and determined that alternative designs could be developed by Hallmark. In this regard, the district court stated:

> Further evidence that the features developed by [Blue Mountain] are non-functional are the infinite alternative designs available to [Hallmark]. Introduced into evidence were cards of the "highly emotional non-occasion" genre, manufactured by Hallmark and [Blue Mountain's] other competitors, with varying features quite different from [Blue Mountain's] trade dress. This is not a case where there are a limited number of designs available, thus mandating a finding of functionality.

> Indeed, the evidence satisfied the district court that "it would not be difficult for Hallmark to devise distinguishing features for its ['Personal Touch'] line. Hallmark tested five different potential 'looks' for the ['Personal Touch'] line."

Hallmark, however, chose "a look so similar to Blue Mountain's that it [was] nearly impossible to differentiate between the respective card lines." Additionally, a competitor of both Hallmark and Blue Mountain, whose testimony the district court found to be "quite credible," indicated that "there is room for innovation and profit in the emotional non-occasion greeting card market without duplicating or copying another's products." The district court concluded, therefore, that "many design alternatives are available. There is no necessity to simulate Blue Mountain's trade dress." Indeed, "[a]n emotional non-occasion greeting card can be folded, colored, shaped, cut, edged, and designed in infinite ways and still function to send its message." In light of the available alternatives, the district court further concluded that allowing Blue

Mountain to exclude others from using its trade dress "will not hinder competition nor will it interfere with the rights of others to compete." Consequently, the district court found that the overall appearance, i.e., trade dress, of Blue Mountain's cards was nonfunctional. In the district court's words: "Paper, verse and ink are functional features of a greeting card. The design and amalgamation of those features in a uniform fashion with other features, however, has produced the non-functional Blue Mountain 'look.'"

Based on the record as it now stands, we are convinced that the district court was not clearly erroneous in finding that it is feasible for Hallmark to avoid the potential for confusion and compete effectively without having to slavishly copy or imitate the distinctive combination of features comprising Blue Mountain's trade dress. Consequently, the district court's finding that Blue Mountain's trade dress is nonfunctional... is also not clearly erroneous. ...

Case Study: Trade Dress and Artistic Style?

Romm Art Creations Ltd. v. Simcha Int'l Arts, Inc.[41]

Trade dress has, to the best of the authors' knowledge, only been used once to try to protect an artist's distinctive style of painting. This dispute involved the artists Itzchak Tarkay and Patricia Govezensky, reported as *Romm Art Creations Ltd. v. Simcha Int'l Arts, Inc.*[42]

Tarkay.[43]

Govezensky

41. *Romm Art Creations Ltd. v. Simcha Int'l, Inc.,* 786 F. Supp. 1126 (E.D.N.Y. 1992).
42. *Id.*
43. Images: Michael D. Murray, Collage of cropped, revised, and resized thumbnail images of exhibits depicting Itzchak Tarkay "Women in Cafes" paintings, and Patricia Govezensky paintings (2009), the subject of *Romm Art Creations Ltd. v. Simcha Int'l, Inc.,* 786 F. Supp. 1126 (E.D.N.Y. 1992).

Tarkay

Govezensky

The case raised the question of how far Govezensky can go in "emulating" the style and subject matter and even the exact scene and composition of some of Tarkay's works. As you can see from the prints in the first two sets above, Govezensky appears to copy the setting, the theme, the composition, the framing, the pose, the hair, the style of clothing, and the pastel coloration of Tarkay's works. Although Govezensky's works are brighter, more vivid, and more saturated in the hues she has used (some might say more "gaudy") compared to Tarkay, she appears to be trying to capture the overall look and feel of the Tarkay "Women in Cafes" series. Romm Art, the printer and distributer of the Tarkay works, complained when Simcha, Govezensky's printer or distributer, added the same band at the edge of the art prints and posters, saying "Patricia" instead of "Tarkay," but in a very similar layout and somewhat similar font, so that the actual "trade dress" of the prints was similar in addition to the artistic style being similar.

The court (a federal trial court) held that an artist's style of painting could be protected as trade dress. The trade dress style only need create the "same overall impression" to be sufficiently similar to infringe.[44] This is an unusual case, one that has not been repeated. It is potentially damaging to traditional notions of art training, progress and development of artistic style, and the concept of "schools of art." If artists cannot learn from each other, and be inspired to experiment along the lines of an innovator in the arts, the traditional progress of the arts might be sidetracked or even halted in some areas.

---

44. *Romm Art Creations*, 786 F. Supp. at 1138-40.

Notes and Questions

1. *Romm Art Creations Ltd. v. Simcha Int'l, Inc.* is remarkable for attempting to set up a barrier between two artists who are painting in the same developing genre, movement, or artistic school. If carried out to its farthest logical extent, this case might have prevented George Braque from following up on Pablo Picasso and Picasso from following up on Braque in developing Cubism. It might have stood to prevent Monet, Renoir, and Sisley from studying each other's works and developing the Impressionistic style of painting, and it might have stopped Cezanne and Matisse from producing confusingly similar paintings of nude bathers.

2. The art market of an earlier day gave incentives for artistic schools to develop an avant garde of several artists who would stand a better chance of attracting attention than one eccentric stand out, and all the participants of the school or movement can benefit from the publicity attained by one or more members whose recognition and success arrives earlier than the others. Does this advantage carry over to the present? At what point should the law intervene and prevent some of the lesser stars from copying off the distinctive style and overall appearance of the more successful members? What factors would the courts look at to determine if an artist's general style and the look and feel of her works can be protected?

3. Since design is an important factor in marketing products, the protection of product design creates a new substantive area of protection, similar to copyright, which encourages sellers to design creatively. Unlike copyright, however, trade dress can protect the overall design and look and feel of useful products, such as clothing, outdoor lighting, and automobiles as long as the design elements are not in and of themselves "functional" — i.e., necessitated by the object's function. What requirements separate a copyright claim from a trade dress infringement claim?

4. At some point, trade dress must give way to copyright under 17 U.S.C. § 301 when the subject of the claim involves rights obviously protected under the copyright laws. In *Galerie Furstenberg v. Coffaro*, 697 F. Supp. 1282 (S.D.N.Y. 1988), Galerie Furstenberg, which held the exclusive rights to certain etchings and drawings by Salvador Dali, sued defendants for, inter alia, trademark infringement for reproduction of those etchings and drawings. Plaintiff argued that it held a trademark in the works, based on Dali's unique style and interpretation of his subjects as expressed on paper. The court, however, concluded that such a claim was properly brought only under the copyright laws.

5. As mentioned above, trade dress itself cannot be "functional," meaning if the proper functioning of a product cannot be accomplished without designing the product in a certain shape or with a certain overall appearance, trade dress cannot be claimed or the first creator would hold a trade dress monopoly over all others who wished to enter the market

and produce that type of item. Would this mean that two artists employing a pointillist style — creating a painting from tiny dots of paint — would be free from trade dress claims against each other, as there is no other way to build a painting from dots without the two works having a similar look and feel owing to the functioning of dots of paint on canvas? Would the same go to the idea of brashly laying color on with impasto techniques (visibly three-dimensional streaks of paint), even though the end result may necessarily resemble the style of later works of Van Gogh and other famous artists?

M. Fair Use

The last topic of trademarks is fair use. As with other intellectual property protections, the courts (and sometimes the legislatures) have provided exceptions to the normal coverage of the laws for valuable, expressive uses of marks that also benefit the general public. Trademark parallels the course of copyright fair use — many labels for fair uses in copyright also appear in trademark law — but the extent of protection for the two sets of fair uses do not overlap. Trademark law is stingier than copyright law in accepting certain activities as fair uses or in recognizing the scope of these fair uses. The situation has only gotten worse since the adoption of the trademark dilution laws[45] — now persons and entities that are in no way competing with a trademark owner on any level, and do not present even a hint of anticipated consumer confusion, can find themselves in trouble with the trademark owner because their activities allegedly blur or tarnish the owner's famous mark. Add to this the fact that trademark owners are never to sit idly by while their marks are being "used" in some manner (or they risk allowing acquiescence or laches defenses to brew), and one can begin to see that using someone's trademark, even in a manifestly expressive, communicative manner, is fraught with peril.

Not every use is perilous. A good faith, non-trademark (non-commercial) use of a mark, the use of a similar descriptive term to describe one's own products, or geographic term that happens to be all or part of someone's trademark will not be actionable. Thus, you can say in your advertising, "our jackets kept these climbers warm and dry on the north face of K2" without necessarily violating the mark of North Face® outerwear products. However, coming out with marks for "The South Butt" and "The Butt Face" will invite a lawsuit from North Face.[46] A manufacturer producing permanent

---

45. *See* Section J, *supra.*
46. *See The North Face Apparel Corp. v. Williams Pharmacy,* No. 4:09-CV-02029-RWS (E.D. Mo. Aug. 3, 2012), *available at http://www.techdirt.com/articles/20120809/10470219979/north-face-wants-court-to-spank-butt-face.shtml.*

makeup used for cosmetic coverage of scars sued for the right to use the term "micro color" not as a mark but simply as a description of the characteristics of its product. The Supreme Court allowed this kind of use.[47]

1. Nominative and Comparative Uses and News Reporting

Nominative uses of marks in media generally are permitted. Thus, a newspaper or news broadcast, or even a blog, can say "The intruder wrapped the camera in Reynolds Wrap aluminum foil before fleeing the home," or "Tom Arnold parked next to a Ford Focus," without running afoul of these marks. However, even with a nominative fair use, it pays to acknowledge the registered ® or trademarked ™ status of the mark you are referring to and its owner to avoid the owner going after you — i.e., drop a note at the end of your news story or blog post that says "'Reynolds Wrap®' is a registered trademark of Reynolds Consumer Products Company."

Comparative use of marks by competitors in advertising or promotional material tends to be fair. Thus, it should be okay for an ad to say "OxyClean gets clothes as white as Chlorox and is safer for the environment." It is important that you tell the truth about the product because, while you may not have a trademark problem on your hands if you tell lies about a competitor or its product, you may have other legal problems for product defamation, disparagement, unfair business competition, fraud, or other forms of misrepresentation. So, if in test after test, OxyClean really does *not* get clothes as white as Chlorox, you should not run the ad in the form described here.

As with other nominative uses, news outlets are permitted to discuss news about brands and trademarks and the companies who own them without fear of trademark law problems, although even news media outlets will do well to make plain the registered trademark status of the marks discussed in news stories.

2. Parodies and Other Forms of Comment and Criticism

Comment and criticism is a recognized fair use in trademark law. If all you are doing is writing a critique of a brand or its owner, you should not expect adverse action from the trademark owner. The predominant purpose of your message must be comment and criticism — anyone can say they prominently featured someone's trademark in their art, or music video, or other message because they wanted to comment on it, but in order to prevail on this defense, the comment and criticism must be substantive and it should be obvious that comment and criticism is the primary purpose for the communication. You also should be aware that the comment must be fair and tell the

---

47. *See KP Permanent Make-Up, Inc. v. Lasting Impression I, Inc.*, 543 U.S. 111, 113 (2004).

truth about the competitors' products, even if the "truth" simply is that you don't like the products for one or more reasons. If you lie about the quality or nature of the products, you will risk adverse legal problems not relating to trademark.

If you are promoting a new product but prominently displaying the mark of another manufacturer, a court may consider this to be an unfair use that attempts to sponge off the popularity of the other mark. Your "commentary," if any, may be drowned out by the risk of consumer confusion over the use of the competing mark in a commercial context. Commentary, if it is going to be safe, should be at least partly critical of its subject.

And then there are parodies — or it might be more appropriate to call this category "attempted parodies" in trademark law, because so many of them fail. Parodies are a big risk in trademark. Yes, the law has recognized that is it *possible* to successfully create a parody of a mark and get away with it under fair use. But the parodist of a trademark has chosen a path that almost always will draw adverse attention from the trademark owner, often a lawsuit, with little to show for it other than that you or your friends had a good laugh (until you are sued).

Why is parody so difficult in trademark law compared to copyright law? Three reasons: one, we can make a prediction about trademark parody that is like no other prediction in this treatise — it is that manufacturers and service providers will have absolutely no sense of humor whatsoever about their products and services when they are spoofed. No manufacturer or service provider will simply laugh off your parody and call it a day. Second, the law encourages trademark owners to have no sense of humor and to track down and write a nasty letter and threaten a lawsuit and then follow through and sue into oblivion anyone with the audacity to attempt a parody of one of the owners' marks. Trademark owners face the defenses of acquiescence, laches, and abandonment, and if a trademark owner does not pursue the near misses as well as the near hits on its mark, it may lose its rights. Third, the law simply favors trademark owners on fair use issues because of trademark dilution laws. An attempted parody often states a prima facie case for trademark dilution by tarnishment, or if the parody is fairly weak, then for dilution by blurring. In short, all of these factors working against the success of a parody lead to the statement that trademark parody is like shooting at the king: whether you hit your mark or miss, there will be serious consequences.

Artistically, in a trademark parody, you will want to use enough of the mark to conjure up the original mark, but be transformative (outrageous, ridiculous, etc.) enough so that you do not suggest that the original owner sponsored your use. A non-commercial usage will be helpful if not critical to your success because if you start using your parody as a way to make money and compete with others in the marketplace, you are losing the public policy support for your expressive commentary that justified the exemption for the trademark use.

Targeting the original and what it stands for is the clearest form of parody. Simply borrowing a trademark to make a generalized point of comment or satire of society is risky—*See Anheuser Busch v. Balducci, supra.* The "Michelob Oily" spoof wasn't directed so much at the beer or the beer maker but at the problems of environmental pollution from spilled crude oil.

Ridiculous parodies of "serious" companies is the safest path to follow. Hormel, the meat company and producer of "Spam," a chopped pork and ham product, sued Jim Henson, the famous "muppeteer" showman, for creating a muppet called "Spa'am" who was a feral island pig whose flesh matched the color of the Spam product.[48] The use was called a parody and a fair use of the Spam mark.[49]

Trademark parody cases are all over the board—that is the main reason why it is so risky to attempt a trademark parody. It is difficult to find one unifying principle to explain these results. In any event, be aware that even if your client produces a great parody, it most likely will be sued anyway. The client might prevail, but at great expense of time, effort, and attorneys' fees and costs. And it might lose, and be on the hook for the opponent's damages and, in some cases, for its attorneys' fees and costs.

ASSESSMENT

1. The problem with the *Rock and Roll Hall of Fame*'s trademark claim was:

    (A) The Rock Hall had not used a singular image of the hall as a designator of goods in commerce

    (B) Rock and roll music is a newsworthy topic of public interest

    (C) The Rock Hall had waived its trademark rights in its contract with architect and designer I.M. Pei

---

48. Images: Michael D. Murray, Cropped, revised, and resized thumbnail images derived from exhibits depicting Hormel Foods Corp.'s Spam product and the Spa'am Muppet Character (2016), at issue in *Hormel Foods Corp. v. Jim Henson Prods., Inc.*, 73 F.3d 497 (2d Cir. 1996).

49. *Hormel Foods Corp. v. Jim Henson Prods., Inc.*, 73 F.3d 497, 502-05 (2d Cir. 1996).

(D) The Rock Hall building can be photographed from the street or from the air

2. A trademark owner's failure to challenge improper, unauthorized uses of its trademark may result in the infringer successfully raising a defense of:

I.   Acquiescence
II. Laches
III. Genericization
IV. Bad faith

(A) I only
(B) I and II only
(C) I and IV only
(D) I, II, III, and IV

3. How might a descriptive mark like "Puppy Chow" become a strong, enforceable trademark?

(A) By uses in commerce as an identifier of goods
(B) By uses in commercial advertising of goods
(C) By uses in commerce that build secondary association
(D) By uses in commerce on and with high quality products

ASSESSMENT ANSWERS

1. The problem with the *Rock and Roll Hall of Fame*'s trademark claim was:

(A) The Rock Hall had not used a singular image of the hall as a designator of goods in commerce
(B) Rock and roll music is a newsworthy topic of public interest
(C) The Rock Hall had waived its trademark rights in its contract with architect and designer I.M. Pei
(D) The Rock Hall building can be photographed from the street or from the air

ANSWER: Choice (A) is the correct answer. If a business or person wants to have an image be a mark, it must pick one image and use it on products or services at the point of sale and in advertising. Choice (B), newsworthiness, might have played a role if the case was a fair use case, but it was not. (C) was a fiction — nothing in the case suggested that the Rock Hall had waived its trademark rights in its contract with architect and designer I.M. Pei. Choice (D) would have been important in a copyright fair use case: if the Rock Hall building, as a work of architecture, can be photographed from the street or from the air, then it can be freely copied and reproduced in this manner under copyright law.

2. A trademark owner's failure to challenge improper, unauthorized uses of its trademark may result in the infringer successfully raising a defense of:

   I. Acquiescence
  II. Laches
 III. Genericization
 IV. Bad faith

    (A) I only
    (B) I and II only
    (C) I and IV only
    (D) I, II, III, and IV

ANSWER: Choice (B), I and II only, is the correct answer. Both Acquiescence and Laches involve a trademark owner's failure to challenge improper, unauthorized uses of its trademark. Genericization involves a mark, that should function as an adjective, becoming so popular that it begins to be used as a noun — it becomes the name for the thing itself, not a descriptor of the thing. Bad faith involves actions that misuse a mark — oppressive licensing or bullying of distributors and licensees, or other conduct that is not in the public interest.

3. How might a descriptive mark like "Puppy Chow" become a strong, enforceable trademark?

    (A) By uses in commerce as an identifier of goods
    (B) By uses in commercial advertising of goods
    (C) By uses in commerce that build secondary association
    (D) By uses in commerce on and with high quality products

ANSWER: Choice (C), by uses in commerce that build secondary association, is the correct answer. Secondary association, if proven, can turn a descriptive mark into a distinctive mark that has strength and can exclude other similar marks from the marketplace. Choice (A), uses in commerce as an identifier of goods, simply is the procedure to obtain a mark of any kind or any strength. (B), uses in commercial advertising of goods, is further evidence of a use in commerce, but it has no direct relationship to the strength of the mark. (D), uses in commerce on and with high quality products, may make the product line and the manufacturer's business stronger, but not the mark per se.

4 MORAL RIGHTS AND ECONOMIC RIGHTS

Art is a form of property requiring unique consideration. Nations have an interest in protecting art as part of their cultural heritage. In addition, art has its own special economic significance. Copyright law recognizes the relationship between an artist and a product and provides the creator with the means for participation in the economic exploitation of his or her art. This relationship exists because part of the artist's personality is projected into each work. The intimate bond thus created produces a need for certain non-pecuniary rights in the artist that do not arise in connection with other forms of property. The artist has a personal interest in seeing that a creation retains the form it was given and in ensuring that the artist is credited with its creation. While these rights might indirectly affect an economic interest, they more fundamentally affect the personality and reputation of the artist and are, therefore, generally referred to as "moral rights" or, as known on the European continent, *les droits moraux* (shortened to *le droit moral*).[1]

This chapter analyzes the civil law doctrine of droit moral and compares it with the protection afforded artists' moral rights in the United States. It will become apparent that artists in the United States have had limited success in attempting to duplicate moral rights protection under traditional common law theories. Recent legislation by Congress and a number of states will be examined as a partial step toward full and explicit recognition of moral rights. This chapter also considers the continental doctrine of *droit de suite* (economic right), a companion right to droit moral that is, likewise, the subject of increasing debate in the United States and has been implemented in California since 1976. *See* Cal. Civ. Code § 986 (West 1982, Supp. 2000), discussed later in this chapter.

---

1. *See generally* Susan P. Liemer, *Understanding Artists' Moral Rights: A Primer*, 7 B.U. PUB. INT. L.J. 41 (1998).

PROBLEM 4-1

> Art is unique and uniquely valuable. People ready to pay good money for a work of art on a contract or commission are anxious to get their hands on the art. Creditors or dealers working with the artist would like to get their hands on completed works. Who should decide when the art is finished, or at least finished enough to take it? The client? The dealer? The creditor? A court or tribunal of some kind? Or just the artist?
>
> What if the artist starts to work, but the client cancels the order? Too bad for the artist, or does the artist get to finish and be paid and have the work displayed or installed as originally agreed?
>
> What if the artist starts to work and then loses her inspiration, or never gets started, or for some other reason the artist refuses to finish? What is the remedy, if any, for the client or commissioner in these circumstances? Can she demand that the artist finish the job or at least turn over the work even if it is not completed?

A. Droit Moral

"Everyone has a right to the protection of the moral and material interests resulting from any scientific, literary, or artistic production of which he is the author." Art. 27(2), Universal Declaration of Human Rights, 6 UN Bull. 6, 8 (Jan. 1, 1949).

Artists' moral rights have been codified in the Berne Copyright Convention, Rome, 1928, found in 2 Copyright Laws of the World, Item E-1. Berne is the oldest and most comprehensive international treaty giving authors rights outside their home countries. One hundred sixty-four countries, including the United States, are signatories to Berne. *See http://www.wipo.int/treaties/ en/documents/pdf/berne.pdf; http://www.wipo.int/treaties/en/ShowResults.jsp? treaty_id=15.*

The relationship between the artist and his or her creation and the legal expression given it have been most extensively studied and implemented in France. Prior to actual codification in 1957, in the nineteenth and twentieth centuries, French courts recognized various moral rights of artists and authors. Note that, under a civil law system such as France's, judges are not expected to create law, nor does the doctrine of stare decisis operate to bind courts to follow prior court decisions. Nevertheless, droit moral was a judicially created right recognized and enforced in France prior to 1957. In 1957, moral rights received statutory recognition in France in the codification of literary and artistic rights. *See* The Law of March 11, 1957, # 57-296, J.O. 2723, B.L.D. 197; Sarraute, La loi du 11 Mars 1957 et le droit moral des artistes sur leurs oeuvres, [1959] GAZ. PAL. 2 DOCTR. 2, codifying — without major change — prior law. Although a number of other countries have codified moral rights, French law — by virtue of its longevity — has generated more litigation than many other nations' laws. Many rights are included within the doctrine of droit moral. Each will be considered in this section.

1. The Right to Create

The right to create, or to refrain from creating, is a function of the right to individual liberty. The right of the artist to be the sole judge of whether a work is worthy and ready to be placed before the public can be described as the protection of the right to create. This would seem axiomatic, but conflicts do arise, for instance, when the artist has agreed under contract to produce a specific product or when a creditor wishes to collect a debt by attaching the artist's work.

French courts have long held that completion of a creation cannot be judicially mandated. In *Eden c. Whistler*, [1898] Recueil Periodique et Critique, II.4.65 (Civ. Trib. Seine) [1900] S.II.201 (Cour d'Appel, Paris), [1900] Recueil Periodique Sirey [hereinafter S. Jur.] I.490 (Cass. Civ.), the artist contracted to paint a portrait of Eden's wife. After an exhibition of the painting, Whistler, the artist, refused to deliver it. It was found that Eden had contracted to pay the artist between 100 and 150 guineas for the portrait of Lady Eden. Eden sent the artist a check for 100 guineas, which Whistler cashed, although he felt the payment was insufficient.

Attempted restoration of Whistler's overpainted portrait of Lady Eden[2]

Whistler thereupon over-painted the portrait. The lower court ordered the artist to restore the painting to its original condition and deliver it to Eden. As an alternative, Whistler would be allowed to return the fee plus 5 percent interest and pay 1,000 francs damages. The Paris Court of Appeals modified the judgment by providing only for monetary damages, noting:

> Whereas the agreement by which a painter engaged himself to execute a portrait for a pre-determined price constitutes a contract of a special nature, by virtue of which ownership of the painting is not definitely acquired by the

---

2. Michael D. Murray, Cropped, revised, and resized thumbnail excerpt of an exhibit depicting the attempted restoration of James Abbott McNeill Whistler's overpainted portrait of Lady Eden (2014), the subject of *Eden c. Whistler*, [1898] Recueil Periodique et Critique, II.4.65 (Civ. Trib. Seine) [1900] S.II.201 (Cour d'Appel, Paris), [1900] Recueil Periodique Sirey [hereinafter S. Jur.] I.490 (Cass. Civ.).

party which commissioned it until the artist has put the painting at the party's disposal and the party has accepted it;

Until that moment, the painter remains master of his work, without, however, it being permissible for him to retain it for himself or to assign it to a third party in the state of a portrait, since the right to reproduce the model's features has been ceded to him only conditionally, for the purpose of fulfilling a contract; and if the artist fails to perform his contract, he is liable for damages.

For a similar case holding that an artist need not deliver a bust not completely satisfactory to the artist, *see Bouillot-Rebef c. Davoine*, [1949] Droit d' Auteur [hereinafter D.A.] 1950, 83 (Civ. Trib. Charolles).

Under French law, lack of inspiration is a normal risk in a contract for creation that is reasonably foreseen by both parties, and no damages may be had for non-performance of the contract on this ground. *Plaisant, Juris-Casseur Civil v. Prop. Lit. et Art*, fasc. 8, no. 22 — Desbois, D.A., no. 540, al. 1. In addition, an artist may not be required to produce a specified quantity of paintings under a requirements-type contract specifying a rhythm of production. *Leroux c. Damiano*, [1966] Recueil Dalloz-Surez [D.S. Jur.] 166 (Cour d'Appel, Aix eu Provence) (note by Savatier). On the other hand, a dissatisfied patron cannot obtain an injunction forbidding the creation. *See* Martin A. Roeder, *The Doctrine of Moral Rights: A Study in the Law of Artists, Authors and Creators*, 53 Harv. L. Rev. 554, 559 (1940) [hereinafter Roeder].

Case Study on the Right to Create

Dubuffet and Renault Corp. (Fr. Cass. 1983)

In France, when the commissioner of a work of art changes its mind regarding completion of that work, the artist may be able to mandate its completion. This is true even where the parties have included a liquidated damages clause in their contract.

In 1973, Jean-Philippe Dubuffet, the modern art sculptor, entered into an agreement with Renault Corporation to create and install a sculpture in the French car maker's headquarters.

Before completion, Renault's board of directors changed its mind and ordered a halt to the project. The artist's hands-on work had only progressed to the stage of a completed model for the work (seen in the images below), although Renault had gone further by excavating and creating a foundation for the sculpture. Dubuffet sued for completion, and the case made its way through the court system all the way to France's High Court. The Cour de Cassation ruled that, as creator of the model, Dubuffet did have a moral right in the full-scale sculpture. Renault was ordered to allow Dubuffet to have specific performance in the form of completion of the work in spite of the fact that the commission between the parties had a liquidated damages provision. Renault could refrain from completing the work only if circumstances beyond its control (force majeure) prevented completion. Absent such circumstances, Renault was required not only to complete the work but

3

(implicitly) to preserve its long-term integrity as well. Artists, therefore, were held to have a right to compel completion of the work, but contractors and commissioners have no corresponding right to call off the work. Nor do the contractors or commissioners have any right to compel the completion of the work as discussed above under the right of respect to determine completeness.[4]

A more recent case is that of *Mlle Hong Yon Park et Spadem c. Association des Amis de la Chapelle de la Salpêtrière*, Cour d'appel de Paris, 10 Apr. 1995, 166 Revue Internationale du Droit D'auteur ("RIDA") Oct. 1995. Hong Yon Park had an agreement with the Society of Friends of the Chapel of Saint-Louis of the Saltpetre ("Chapel"), which was a popular contemporary arts venue. Park's exhibition was installed but the Chapel took it down immediately after the opening. The Chapel claimed that it had accepted Park's exhibition on the basis of photographs taken from an earlier show; it claimed the works in that show were of a style and message that was compatible with the overall purpose and religious mission of the Chapel. On the other hand, the exhibition Park had installed in the Chapel consisted of several rows of toilet bowls put together with sanitary napkins arranged to look like coffins. The Chapel did not believe the contents and message of this exhibit were as compatible with the church and its operations. Park complained that her moral right of integrity had been infringed in addition to a breach of the agreement wherein the Chapel had contractually obliged themselves to show Park's work. (Although phrased as a right of respect or integrity, discussed *infra*, Park's claim related

---

3. Images: Michael D. Murray, Cropped, revised, and resized thumbnail images derived from two photographs depicting Jean Dubuffet and his model for an installation at Renault Headquarters (2015), the subject of *Dubuffet v. Régie Nationales des Usines Renault*, Judgment of Jan. 8, 1980, Cass. civ. Ire, R.I.D.A. April 1980, at 154, A. Francon obs./ Judgment of March 16, 1983, Cass. civ. Ire, R.I.D.A. July 1983, at 80.

4. For additional discussion of this problem and other disputes over completion or non-completion of commissions, *see* Andre Francon & Jane C. Ginsburg, *Authors' Rights in France: The Moral Right of the Creator of a Commissioned Work to Compel the Commissioning Party to Complete the Work*, 9 Colum.-VLA J.L. & Arts 281 (1985).

directly to the right to have one's work shown — the right of divulgation.) When it took the show down, the Chapel was found to have 'prevented the artist from showing her works in public.' The Court of Appeals of Paris found that if the Chapel did not want to stage the show in its main sanctuary, an alternative venue should have been provided. The Chapel was ordered to pay the nominal sum of 1 franc for damages as well as Park's costs of 10,000 francs.

American authorities traditionally did not show this kind of respect to artists. The case below discusses Salvador Dali's cancellation of a charitable promotion. The court handled the issues solely as questions of contract law.

National Historic Shrines Foundation, Inc. v. Dali

N.Y.L.J. Mar. 16, 1967, at 15
4 U.C.C. Rep. Serv. 71 (Sup. Ct. N.Y. 1967)

Geller, Justice.

Defendant, Dali, an artist, moves for an order granting summary judgment dismissing the complaint or, in the alternative, determining that the plaintiff's maximum damages recoverable are its out-of-pocket expenses of $264.91.

In this action plaintiff, a non-profit corporation, sues Dali for breach of an oral agreement whereby, allegedly, Dali agreed to appear on a television program designed to raise funds for plaintiff. As part of the program Dali was to paint before the cameras a picture of the Statue of Liberty (the location of a museum to be completed by the National Park Service of the United States Department of the Interior with funds to be raised by plaintiff) and present the completed painting at the end of the program to plaintiff, to be sold for its charitable purposes. The value of such a painting, estimated by Dali, according to plaintiff, would have been $25,000. Dali is alleged to have at the last moment refused to go through with the planned arrangements, and the program was not held.

The facts claimed by plaintiff to support its theory that a binding oral contract was entered into are vigorously disputed by Dali. Accordingly, a trial would appear to be necessary to resolve the factual issues. But Dali urges that no cognizable or enforceable cause of action is asserted against him on the basis of any credible evidence presented by plaintiff at an inquest for a pleading default subsequently opened or which could be adduced by plaintiff.

Plaintiff's theory is that under the special circumstances of this case a contract supported by consideration was made with Dali for his appearance and rendition of services on a television program, time for which, plaintiff claims, had been given for a certain date by a named station. Plaintiff claims to have received definite promises as the result of conversations with Dali and a person referred to as his agent, allegedly confirmed in part by correspondence. The consideration to Dali is claimed to be his own stated acceptance of plaintiff's offer on the ground of his obtaining appropriate publicity out of the idea.

This publicity aspect was actually carried out in a preliminary public wreath-laying ceremony by Dali at the foot of the Washington statue in Wall Street and at a party in a hotel, sponsored with expenses of $264.91 paid by plaintiff; Dali then announcing to the press that he intended to participate in plaintiff's television program in the manner outlined.

It will be noted that the nature of the understanding and arrangements, as here claimed by plaintiff, may conceivably spell out a contractual obligation, as distinguished from the usual practice whereby celebrities and performers voluntarily and without any contractual obligation contribute their talents and names to various public and charitable functions.

On this motion Dali urges that the agreement, as alleged, is too indefinite to be binding; founded upon insufficient consideration; void for lack of mutuality; and unenforceable under the statute of frauds.

With respect to the contention of indefiniteness, there is sufficiently shown in the testimony offered by plaintiff on the inquest and in the present supporting papers, if believed, to indicate a binding commitment to the extent that plaintiff relied thereon in making its arrangements. As to consideration, that is sufficiently shown, for the purpose of entitling plaintiff to a trial of the issues, by plaintiff's testimony, if believed, regarding Dali's acceptance on the ground of the publicity inuring to him and by the two preliminary promotional events. Concerning lack of mutuality, there appears to be no reason under these particular circumstances why Dali could not have recovered damages had he in reliance upon plaintiff's final and definite arrangements suffered actual damages if plaintiff had thereafter unjustifiably canceled the program.

Regarding the statute of frauds, Dali's argument is that this is an alleged agreement for the sale of goods, consisting of the painting he was to make, of the value of $500 or more, which must be writing signed by the party against whom enforcement is sought (Uniform Commercial Code, § 2-201). Plaintiff's theory and offer of proof on this submission shows, however, an alleged agreement for rendition of services by Dali during an appearance before the cameras with resultant contribution of the painting then made and subsequent hope of sale thereof by plaintiff to the public. This is not viewed as a sale of goods within the terms of the statute of frauds.

Defendant's motion for summary judgment is denied. While plaintiff's theory of a binding oral contract may be difficult to establish in the context of this type of transaction, the special circumstances here shown entitle it to a trial at which it may present proof of its alleged cause of action. . . .

Notes and Questions

1. There doesn't seem to be anything shocking about the *Dali* case, except perhaps in comparison with the drastically different approach taken in the French cases discussed above. What possible public policies are furthered by the two contrasting approaches — American and French?

2. What dangers are presented by the generous French accommodation of the artist's right to create and not to create? Is there any way to differentiate between the bona fide needs of conscientious artists and the whims and quirks of those who simply wish to shirk their responsibilities?

3. Can the moral right protection of the right to create or not to create be handled by contract? Is it likely or unlikely that the same protections could be achieved through contract terms?

4. The artist's right not to create is protected in the United States through the well-established principle that contracts for personal service are not specifically enforceable. 5A Corbin on Contracts § 1204 (1964). But even artists must bow to the law of contracts, and a breaching party may be liable for damages. Corbin on Contracts § 1184 (Supp. 1990). In addition, an aggrieved party may be able to obtain an order enjoining the artist from breaching an express or implied negative covenant. This injunction may have the same effect as a grant of specific enforcement. Courts will enforce negative covenants in written contracts where the service to be performed is unique. *Shubert Theatrical Co. v. Rath*, 271 F. 827 (2d Cir. 1921); *Nazarro v. Washington*, 81 N.Y.S. 2d 769 (1948) (performers with unique talents can be enjoined from breaching any part of the employment contract). Courts have implied negative covenants not to create for others when the artist breaches or threatens to breach. *Paramount Pictures Corp. v. Davis*, 228 Cal. App. 2d 827 (1964) (Bette Davis was required to complete production of *Hush Hush Sweet Charlotte* before fulfilling a subsequent contract). The promise to perform in the original contract can be seen as a promise not to do anything that impairs the required performance. *See* 4 Witkin, Summary of California Law 2816 (9th ed. 1987).

2. The Right to Disclose and to Determine Completeness

The right to decide whether to disclose a work also allows an artist to enjoin another from publishing that which the artist has discarded. In *Carco c. Camoin*, [1931] D.P.II. 88, CA Paris, note Nast, the artist, Camoin, had cut up and discarded a number of painted canvases. Carco found the pieces, reconstructed the works, and sold them at auction. Camoin had the paintings seized and asked for their destruction. The Paris Court of Appeals declared:

> Whereas literary and artistic rights comprise a right which is in no way pecuniary in nature but which, attached to the very person of the author or of the artist, permits him during his lifetime to surrender his work to the public only in such a manner and under such conditions as he sees fit, the gesture of the painter who lacerates a painting and throws away the pieces because he is dissatisfied with his composition does not impair this right; and although whoever gathers up the pieces becomes the indisputable owner of

them through possession, this ownership is limited to the physical quality of the fragments, and does not deprive the painter of the moral right which he always retains over his work. If the artist continues to believe that his paintings should not be put into circulation, he is within his rights to oppose any restoring of the canvas and to demand, if necessary, that it be destroyed.

The order to destroy has been criticized as interfering with the right of a finder of abandoned property. Critics argue that the artist is not injured where the work is not attributed to him or her. *See* Raymond Sarraute, *Current Theory on the Moral Right of Authors and Artists Under French Law*, 16 Am. J. Comp. L. 465, 479 (1968) [hereinafter Sarraute]. However, the difficulty in rendering anonymous the work of a unique stylist, plus the problems of policing the use of a reconstructed work, may make destruction the only practical remedy for protecting the artist.

The right to destroy may not extend to fakes. In *Vlaminck*, [1961] Gaz. Pal. II.218, CA Paris, a painting was submitted to its purported creator for authentication. After concluding that the work was a forgery, the angry artist removed his name from the canvas. The court held that the painter had no right to alter the property without the owner's permission and, of course, no moral rights could be claimed in the work of another. *See* Sarraute, *supra*, at 477.

The case of *Anatole France c. Lemerre*, [1911] Pataille 1912.1.98, considered whether an artist might rescind a contract for the publication of a work after it has been delivered. In 1882, Anatole France sold to Lemerre a history of France. Lemerre delayed publication for 25 years, by which time much of the content of the book was outdated and inaccurate. Anatole France was allowed to rescind the contract and return the money in exchange for the manuscript. Subsequent cases do not allow rescission of a contract when the publisher is not at fault. Performance is not specifically enforced, but the contract is considered breached and damages are allowed. Sarraute, *supra*, at 477.

What constitutes wrongful delay in publication probably depends upon the content of the work, as well as the amount and rapidity of change in that field. *See Wormser c. Biardot*, 2 Olangier, D.A. 32 (1934), Com. Trib. Seine (holding that three years was excessive); *but see Raynal c. Bloch*, [1939] S. Jur. II.17, CA Paris (four years delay was not excessive).

Another difficulty arises when the artist's legal relationships change or the artist dies. There may be a question of whether to destroy a work or release it in its present state. Who is to decide which works have been completed? What criteria may be used?

In *Rouault c. Consorts Vollard*, [1947] S. Jur. II.3 (note by Desbois), Le Semaine Juridigue [J.C.P.] II, No. 3405 (Tribunal Civil de la Seine) (note by Plaisant), the artist Rouault was under contract to turn over his entire production to the dealer Vollard. Rouault stored many unfinished canvases in a room in Vollard's gallery, where he occasionally worked on them. When Vollard died, his heirs claimed ownership of the canvases. Rouault argued that, because they were unfinished and could not be considered delivered before completion, they were still his property. The court agreed with Rouault, and ordered the paintings returned to the artist:

Whereas, one who negotiates with an artist for an uncompleted work which the author retains in his possession, reserving the right to finish it, contracts for future goods whose ownership can be only transferred by delivery without reservation after completion, and is not like the buyer who purchases an artistic production in any state which the painter intends definitively to part with even though it is in the form of a sketch;

Therefore, until final delivery the painter remains master of his work, and may perfect it, modify it, or even leave it unfinished if he loses all hope of making it worthy of himself;

This inalienable right, an attribute of the artist's moral right, persists notwithstanding any agreement to the contrary; and the breach of any such agreement exposes the author, who changes his mind, only to damages.

The problem was further explored in the community property case of *Bowers c. Bonnard*, [1952] D. Jur. 390, note Desbois, [1951] Gaz. Pal. II. 290, Tribunal Civil de la Seine, REVUE INTERNATIONALE DU DROIT D'AUTEUR 1959 p. 179, note Vaunois, RIDA 1959 p. 67, note Havert. The artist claimed that only the canvases existing and considered by him as complete before his wife's death could be subject to division between himself and his wife's heirs. (A difficulty not dealt with in *Rouault* is that, unless extremely generous, the artist in such a situation is likely to consider himself master of few finished canvases.) The case was heard five times before the final appeal. Decisions ranged from holding that all the work had market value and was thus partitionable, to holding that the court would judge which works were complete, each obviously violating the well-settled right of the artist to determine the completeness of a work. The latter decision placed the court in the position of evaluating the aesthetic quality of a work of art. It requires no great imagination to envision the inherent dangers in such a position. The final solution, based on the 1957 codification of artist's rights (not binding on the court, as it was enacted after commencement of the litigation), reinstated the artist's traditional right to full control over a work not communicated to the public. The court held that works not yet published by the artist could not be subject to partition. Experts were appointed to decide not which works were finished at the time of the wife's death, but which works had, in some way, been publicly shown by the artist as of that date. On this point, *see also Martinez-Picabia c. Dome Mahler-Picabia*, [1970] J.C.P.IV.154, 63 RIDA p. 191, CA Paris, [1971] J.C.P. II.17164, Cass. Civ.

In some cases, the deceased artist's express intentions, no matter how inspecific, may prevail over the objections of the artist's heirs. In *Malaussena c. Editions Gallimard*, CA Paris, Dec. 19, 1997, D. 1999 somm. 67, obs. Colombet, RIDA Apr. 1998 p. 433, the court held that a person holding a post-mortem right of disclosure must exercise the right consistently with the author's wishes as they were expressed while the author was living. The post-mortem right of disclosure is not discretionary or absolute. Antonin Artaud gave the rights to publish (in French, in all formats, under any current or future laws) all of his works to Gallimard. Artaud's nephew Malaussena and niece Gaulier inherited Artaud's moral rights. Malaussena opposed the publication of a volume of Artaud's works based on the right of disclosure. Gallimard argued that Malaussena's was abusing the post-mortem right of disclosure. Artaud contracted with Gallimard for the publication of his complete works. Gallimard denied any violation of the integrity of the work. The Paris Cour d'Appel held that a post-mortem rightsholder did not have discretion over the use of the right. The court agreed that Malaussena did have a post-mortem right of disclosure but said that he abused that right in refusing to disclose the work.

The Cour de Cassation affirmed the appellate court's decision. Cass. 1e Civ., Oct. 24, 2000, D. 2001, 918, note Caron. The court held that moral rights protect the author. Malaussena's opposition to publication was abusive. Artaud had a desire to communicate with the public. The court stated that only a violation of the integrity of the work could allow an heir to object to publication.

French law provides that the post-mortem moral rights of integrity and attribution pass to the artist's legal heirs (spouse and children), but the moral right of disclosure of authors passes to a literary executor. In *Mr. Lionel and Stephane X v. Luxury Goods France, Gucci SPA, et Mantero Seta SPA*, No. 03-12159, Cour de Cassation 1e Civ. Feb. 15, 2005, Bull. Civ. I, No. 84, p. 74, two of the four nephews of an artist (who had died in 1986) filed suit against Luxury Goods France/Gucci SPA to defend their moral rights. Gucci used their uncle's colored flower pot design on their scarves, without attributing the painter. The design was taken from a painting series that had been on display in the Musée d'Art Moderne in Paris in 1983. In 1991, the gallery owners assigned the property rights to Gucci. The court found for the nephews and instructed Gucci to pay costs. The lower court had found that when there are several heirs, the droit moral can only be dubfacts in this case; each heir is an owner of the work, and whether acting as a group or not, can exercise the property rights of the artist. There was a question raised regarding whether the heirs had renounced the inheritance from their father (who died in 1995 and was the artist's original heir), but the court found that it had not been established that the two heirs had refused their father's interests.

In *Société Benoit Jacob c. Lemee*, CA Paris, Sep. 13, 1999, RIDA Apr. 2000 p. 284, note Kéréver, Société Benoit Jacob published a book, *La cuisine de Marguerite*, a book of recipes and photographs, after the death of Marguerite Duras. Société Benoit Jacob was owned by Duras' son and legal heir, Jean Mascolo. Lemee was Duras' literary executor. Lemee opposed the publication of the book and asserted his moral rights to block the book from continued exploitation. The Court said that the right of disclosure could be exercised by the executor under Art L. 121-2 CPI. Thus, the literary executor had the right of disclosure. The rights of attribution and integrity went to Duras' heirs on her death, so her son had those moral rights. Lemee could not assert the rights of integrity or attribution. The Court considered whether blocking the book would be an abuse of the right of disclosure. The Court said that the book was a compilation of photographs and writings which Duras never intended for publication. Lemee did not abuse the right of disclosure in refusing to disclose the material. The Court ordered Société Benoit Jacob to stop publication of the book. The Court reversed the lower court on its award of damages for moral rights violation to Lemee because Lemee could not assert those rights.

Another problem arises where there is a collaboration. The right of one artist to refuse to disclose a creation may interfere with the right of another to have the work disclosed, delaying completion indefinitely. The French resolved this dilemma by prohibiting the exercise of moral rights in a collaborated effort until the work is finished.

The right to determine completeness has a temporal limit. The Cour de Cassation in *Société PLON et Francois Ceresa c. Pierre Hugo, Société des Gens des Lettres de France,* Cour de Cassation, 1ere Chambre Civile, 30 Janvier 2007, RIDA 212 RIDA, Avril 2007, p. 249, *rev'g* CA Paris, 31 Mars 2004, RIDA 202 RIDA, Octobre 2004, p. 292, rejected the claim of the heir of Victor Hugo who sought to prevent publication of new works by Société PLON that were billed as sequels to Victor Hugo's work, *Les Miserables.* The high court found that the moral rights associated with preventing such derivatives of the original work expired at the time that the exploitation monopoly over the work ended, and that the concept of "creative freedom" allowed subsequent authors such as PLON to pursue this project.

The moral right of disclosure may allow an artist to prevent the disclosure of a reproduction of a draft instead of the original work. In *Mr. Le X v. Mr. Y,* No. 01-17034, Cour de Cassation, 1e Civ. Nov. 29, 2005, Bull. Civ. I, No. 457, p. 383, a painter, who had designed the set of the ballet *Gisèle* for the L'Opéra de Paris in 1991 filed suit for violation of his moral right of disclosure. In 1998, an auctioneer reproduced a draft the artist had made of the set at the time of the performance for the cover of a catalogue, the sale of which the artist objected to. The auctioneer went ahead with the sale, prompting the suit. The court found that the auctioneer, in selling a reproduction of the draft over the protests of the artist, violated the artist's moral rights. The court ordered the auctioneer to pay the artist $2,000.

The right of disclosure does not extend to the disclosure of ideas, only creative works. In *Ms. X v. Marie Claire Album SA,* No. 04-12721, Cour de Cassation, 1e Civ. Nov. 29, 2005, Bull. Civ. I, No. 458, p. 384, a former editor of the beauty column of Marie-Claire filed suit alleging violation of her property rights and moral right of disclosure. Just prior to leaving the magazine, the editor developed the concept of the "beauty product of the year." The editor came up with a system to determine the winners and came up with the various classifications of the award. The court held that the law does not protect ideas or concepts, but only the original form in which they are expressed, and does not provide a moral right for disclosure of ideas. It affirmed the dismissal of her case.

In the United States, the creator of a work of art may withhold a masterpiece from the public indefinitely. Only upon publication is this right limited.

Common law copyright establishes a cause of action for an artist against anyone publishing a work without permission. *See Wheaton v. Peters*, 33 U.S. (8 Pet.) 591 (1834).

Chamberlain v. Feldman, 89 N.E. 2d 863 (N.Y. 1949), held that an artist's heirs may indefinitely withhold the disclosure of an unpublished work, even when the physical property (as opposed to the copyright) is owned by a stranger. In that case, the manuscript of a short story written by Mark Twain was purchased at an auction long after the author's death. The heirs enjoined the owner from publishing the work even though Twain had once submitted it to a publisher. This result would seem to extend the author's rights even further than that of the comparable French law. In addition, under the doctrine of limited publication, certain exhibitions and performances are not considered publications, and the artist thereby retains his or her control over the works.

The right of disclosure is well-recognized in the United States. However, an artist may waive the right to prevent disclosure by accepting an employment contract to create. American law has, relatively speaking, a callous disregard for the paternity rights of creative persons. Section 26 of the Copyright Act provides that "the word 'author' shall include an employer in the case of works made for hire." Under a "work for hire" arrangement, the person whose mind generates the creative process can be regarded as a mere employee and his employer, perhaps a corporation, can be regarded as the "author." The "work for hire" arrangement severs completely the relation between the creator and ownership of his work. James M. Treece, *American Law Analogues of the Author's "Moral Right,"* 16 Am. J. Comp. L. 487, 494 (1968) [hereinafter Treece].

In *Stella v. Mazoh*, No. 07585-82 (N.Y. Sup. Ct. Apr. 1, 1982), artist Frank Stella claimed the right to control disclosure of discarded works when two rain-damaged canvases left on the landing outside his loft-studio disappeared and then reappeared several years later for sale in a New York gallery. Stella sued to enjoin their sale and prevent them from being represented as his work. He stated in his affidavit:

> I verily believe that as an artist and as a creator, I am entitled to pick and choose and select those items which are to be sold, distributed and more important, to be known to the general public and the world as a painting or work of Frank Stella. . . . I respectfully submit that no one is entitled to cause another to have his reputation demeaned, diminished or tarnished by taking his rejected paintings from within or without his premises and then offer them to the public and to the world as the artist's works and representative of his abilities, talents, and creativity.

Affidavit of Frank Stella at 6-7 (emphasis in original). The court granted a temporary restraining order and the parties settled. *See* Sarah Ann Smith, *Note, The New York Artists' Authorship Rights Act: Increased Protection and Enhanced Status for Visual Artists*, 70 Cornell L. Rev. 158, 166 (1984).

The concept of common law copyright under New York law as a form of right to control distribution and disclosure was discussed in *Capitol Records, Inc. v. Naxos of America, Inc.*, 830 N.E. 2d 250 (N.Y. 2005). Capitol's parent company had recorded classical music performances in the 1930s and granted Capitol exclusive rights to distribute the performances. Naxos obtained copies of the original recordings and began selling remastered copies. Capitol brought suit against Naxos in Federal District Court, and on appeal on a grant of summary judgment for Naxos, the Second Circuit requested that the New York court determine if common law copyright protection existed for the recordings in New York. The New York Court of Appeals determined that for sound recordings under New York law, common law copyright protections do not cease to exist at the time of public sale.

The right to determine completeness has had a rocky road to follow when artists attempt to assert the right as a component of the right of attribution or integrity under the Visual Artists Rights Act (VARA) (discussed below in section B). In *Massachusetts Museum of Contemporary Art Foundation, Inc. v. Büchel*, 565 F. Supp. 2d 245 (D. Mass. 2008), an artist, Büchel, and an art museum, Massachusetts Museum of Contemporary Art, had arranged for the artist to create an art installation at the museum. Their relationship soured, and the artist stopped working on the installation before completion. The art museum brought an action against Büchel seeking a declaratory judgment that it was entitled to present to the public the materials and partial constructions assembled in connection with the exhibit. Büchel counter-claimed, seeking, inter alia, a declaratory judgment holding that any public display of the incomplete installation would violate his "right of integrity to determine the completeness and display-readiness of his creations" and a permanent injunction barring any such public display. In effect, Büchel sought to combine the concept of a right of respect to determine complete-ness with the right of integrity provided under VARA. The parties filed cross motions for summary judgment. The District Court held that the museum's display of the artist's unfinished installation would not violate the artist's right of attribution or his right of integrity. The court reasoned that, assuming even that VARA applied to the artist's unfinished installation at the art museum, the museum's display of the unfinished installation would not have violated the artist's right of integrity because there was no completed work of art that ever existed for the museum to distort, mutilate, or modify. Thus, the court would not imply that the right of integrity under VARA assumed a right of respect to determine completeness. Further, the court determined that there was no violation of VARA's right of attribution because the museum stated that it had no intention of labeling the unfinished installation as the work of the artist unless the artist requested it. The U.S. Court of Appeals for the First Circuit reversed the district court, and found that VARA indeed applied to the partial installation and could encompass the claims made by Büchel. This opinion is excerpted in section B.6, *infra* p. 219.

PROBLEM 4-2

> When, if ever, should art be removed from display, hidden from view, or even destroyed? — When it becomes old-fashioned and tiresome? When it starts to look dated compared to newer work by the same artist? When it is damaged or deteriorated from age? When it becomes dangerous to passersby?
>
> Who decides when art should be removed or destroyed? The property owner where the art is located? Local government? Local citizens who have to live or work around the art? Or just the artist herself?

3. The Right to Withdraw

Related to the right to decide whether to communicate a work to the public is the right to withdraw it after publication. This right is not as old as the right to disclose, being first formally recognized in France upon the 1957 codification of artistic and literary rights. It applies, however, only to publishing contracts, and (a) requires the author to pay for all sold copies of the work withdrawn, and (b) allows damages to the publisher. Thus, even in France, its utility is questionable, as it may be too expensive for the artist. The right to withdraw after publication is a companion to the right of rescission before publication. It is thought that, when circumstances have changed so drastically that the artist believes his or her reputation will be damaged by the published work, the work should be allowed to be withdrawn. Sarraute, *supra*, at 476. *See also Vlaminck*, [1961] Gaz. Pal. II.218 (CA Paris), in which the right was denied to an artist in the case of a forgery.

What of honestly described look-alikes that do not rise to the level of a copyright violation and are described honestly as being "not the work of X?" The right to seize and withdraw works that resembled works of Maurice Utrillo and produced with a signature that also looked like Utrillo's was denied in *Fabris c. Barthélémy*, Cass. 1e Civ., Jul. 18, 2000, JCP 2002, II, 10041, note Lefranc; D. 2001, somm. 2080, obs. Caron; D. 2001, 541, note Dreyer. The appellate court correctly found that the painting was not an illegal reproduction of a work by Maurice Utrillo. The sellers of the painting disclosed the inauthenticity of the signature before sale. It was not a copy or an imitation of any work by Utrillo. The sale of the painting was not a violation of Utrillo's moral rights but of his right of publicity. Fabris could not assert moral rights because the work was not by Utrillo and was not a copy of a work by Utrillo, and the right of publicity in France does not descend to the celebrity's heirs. Although the subject matter of the work was the same as Utrillo, the judges determined that the painting was not an imitation. The court found that the perspective and style were different. Fabris also argued that although the buyer of the painting would know the signature was false, there was nothing to prevent that buyer from selling the painting to a third person as an original. The Court refused to find liability for a future or hypothetical harm. The Court determined that the seizure was illegal.

The right to withdraw is not recognized in the United States. *See, e.g., Autry v. Republic Prods., Inc.*, 213 F.2d 667 (9th Cir. 1954) (actor may not withdraw films of his work even though they injured his present reputation due to their inferior quality; this was a risk assumed by the artist as inherent in the performer's art). The artist may, however, sue the displayer for damage to the artist's reputation occasioned by the publication.

Notes and Questions

1. An artist's right to withdraw from society's view and appreciation works that the artist no longer thinks are a credit to her reputation may have a negative impact on society's interest in recording and maintaining the history and progress of its artists and their styles. Rights protecting the physical integrity and appearance of the art work itself and attribution of authorship to the artist fulfill the public policy goals of preventing distortion and misrepresentation of the history of the artist's work and art history in general. This argument is supported by statutes such as California's Art Preservation Act, which cite this public interest in addition to the artist's personal interests as a justification for the rights of attribution and integrity provided by the legislation. The right to withdraw may go against these interests as it allows works to be removed from the public record simply because the artist has changed her mind about whether the works are a credit to the artist or not, regardless of their importance to the record of the artist's work and art history in general.

2. Pop musician Ringo Starr sought to prevent the publication of recordings he made while suffering from alcoholism. In his opinion, the recordings did not fairly represent the true quality of his work and would be harmful to his reputation. The record company argued that Starr merely wanted to prevent the release of any record that might detract attention or sales from a collection of live recordings the performer was planning to release. Nevertheless, the Superior Court of Atlanta granted a temporary restraining order. *See Record Rubs Ringo Wrong*, NAT'L L.J., Aug. 7, 1989, at 59.

3. A limited right of withdrawal after a work is damaged or misused might satisfy both the artist's and society's goals. It occasionally happens that a particular work is damaged or deteriorates in some way after it is sold, or that it is used or displayed in some fashion completely antagonistic to

the artist's conception. Both of these situations may be harmful to the artist's reputation. Under a limited right to withdraw, the artist could either retrieve the work temporarily in order to restore it to its original form, or withdraw it completely when it is misused.

4. The right to withdraw a work in order to restore it has not traditionally been recognized. Consider the case of Alexander Calder, who created one of his famous oversized mobiles for Allegheny County in Pennsylvania, only to find out later that county officials had locked the suspension device of the mobile to keep it still, then repainted the piece in the bright colors of Allegheny County, and relocated it in the Pittsburgh airport. *See* Rose, *Calder's "Pittsburgh": A Violated and Immobile Mobile*, ARTnews, Jan. 1978, at 39. Calder's efforts to withdraw and restore the work were frustrated.

Calder Mobile[5]

5. The Visual Artists Rights Act of 1990 (VARA), discussed below in section B, provides a limited right of integrity that would allow an artist access to works of visual art (which are carefully defined in the statute) to repair or restore them or prevent their destruction. However, the right to prevent destruction only may be asserted to works of recognized status, which has proven to be a significant stumbling block for artists in the United States. *See, e.g., Pollara v. Seymour*, 344 F.3d 265 (2d Cir. 2003); *Scott v. Dixon*, 309 F. Supp. 2d 395 (E.D.N.Y. 2004).

---

5. Michael D. Murray, Cropped, revised, and resized thumbnail image derived from Michael Murray's photograph (2014) of a Calder Mobile on display at the National Gallery, Washington D.C.

PROBLEM 4-3

> The desire of an artist to be recognized for and associated with her work is understandable, but what of works made for hire? What of collaborative works such as motion pictures? What if the artist no longer wants to be associated with the work?

4. The Right of Attribution (Paternity)

After an artist makes a decision to communicate a creation to the public, the artist obviously has an interest in seeing that it is attributed correctly. This is true whether the work is popularly considered trivial or acknowledged as a masterpiece. The right of paternity is not intended to protect reputation so much as to protect the creative act itself. In France, the right to create includes the right to be acclaimed the creator. It applies to the artist's choice of a nom de plume as well as the artist's real name. Thus, a third person may not substitute his or her name for that of the creator. *Fontin c. Prevast-Blondel*, [1890] D.P. II.243 (Cour de Paris).

Under French law, a contract negating this right may be declared void. The Paris Court of Appeals considered a contract in which an artist was to sign a certain pseudonym to some of his work and to place no signature on the rest. This violated the artist's right to have his name respected and his authorship recognized. The court held that the 10-year contract was designed to injure the artist's reputation. *Guille c. Colmant*, [1967] Gaz. Pal. I.17 (Cour d'Appel, Paris) (criticized as failing to recognize that the right is basically protective of the creative act regardless of reputation).

Paternity was again considered in *Guino c. Consorts, Renoir*, [1971] J.C.P. II. No. 16697, Gaz. Pal. I.235, digested in [1971] D.S. Jur. 1974 (Tribunal de la Grande Instance de Paris), English translation reprinted in Feldman & Weil, *Art Works: Law, Policy, Practice* (1974). There, the sculptor, Guino, successfully claimed co-authorship of works he had executed under minimal direction from Renoir. After hearing the opinions of many experts, the Tribunal held that Guino had sufficiently imprinted on the work his own personality such that the work was no longer solely and completely that of Renoir. The court also upheld the protection against false imputation of paternity by refusing to allow Guino to disclose works that Renoir might not have authorized as "publishable." This aspect of the right is closely related to the right of the artist not to have his or her name attached to a work that the artist does not acknowledge as the artist's own. The right to paternity has long been held in France to apply to collaborative efforts. Collaborations are distinguished, however, from compilations, which do not lend themselves to imputations of paternity. The right of multiple authors to have their names appear was upheld in *Fleg c. Gaumont*,

[1922] Gaz. Trib. II.282 (Civ. Trib. Seine), and *Marquet c. Lehmann*, [1923] Gaz. Trib. II.271 (Civ. Trib. Seine).

American courts resisted the recognition of any right of attribution beyond what is provided in the contractual agreement between the parties. Thus, if the artist did not retain such a right when he transferred the copyright to his work to another, no right was inserted as an implied term of the contract and no right was found under the Lanham Act regarding false or misleading attribution of origin.

Vargas v. Esquire, Inc.

164 F.2d 522 (7th Cir. 1947)*

MAJOR, Circuit Judge.

This appeal is from an order, entered December 17, 1946, dismissing plaintiff's complaint and supplemental complaint for failure to state a cause of action. Plaintiff, an artist, sued to enjoin the reproduction of certain pictures made by him and delivered to defendant, a publisher, upon the ground that the same were wrongfully used in that they were published without the signature of plaintiff and without being accredited to him. Plaintiff also sued for damages on account of such publication alleged to violate his contract and his property right in the pictures and unfairly to represent them as the work of others. Defendant moved to dismiss on the ground that the plaintiff at the time of publication had no property right in the pictures and no right to control or to direct their disposition.

Details of Images of Varga Girls[6]

The facts alleged by the complaint enter about and relate largely to two contracts of which the plaintiff and defendant were parties. ... [P]laintiff made and delivered certain pictures, one of which was reproduced each month, beginning October 1, 1940, in the magazine Esquire, published by defendant. Plaintiff also made and delivered twelve pictures each year, beginning in the fall of 1940, for a calendar published and sold the following year by defendant.

At first the pictures furnished bore plaintiff's name or signature, "Vargas," and they were reproduced

---

* Footnotes omitted.

6. Michael D. Murray, Collage of cropped, revised, and resized thumbnail images of exhibits depicting details of paintings by Alberto Vargas (2014), the subject of *Vargas v. Esquire, Inc.*, 164 F.2d 522 (7th Cir. 1947).

and published with his name thereon. Later, by agreement of the parties, the name "Vargas" was changed to "Varga." Thereafter, the pictures made by plaintiff and published by defendant were called "Varga Girls," and the name of the plaintiff appearing thereon was "A. Varga." The name was used only in connection with pictures made by plaintiff and was thus used by the defendant until March 1, 1946. No name was on the pictures when they were furnished by plaintiff to the defendant. . . .

[O]n March 1, 1946, the defendant published its magazine, Esquire, which contained a two-page reproduction of a picture made by the plaintiff. At the top thereof, instead of the words, "The Varga Girl," appeared the words, "The Esquire Girl." The reproduction did not bear plaintiff's signature, "A. Varga," or any other signature. . . . [O]n October 1, 1946, defendant published a certain calendar enclosed in an outside envelope on which appeared the words and figures, "The 1947 Esquire Calendar 35 cents Copyright Esquire, Inc. 1946 Printed in U.S.A." On the envelope was a reproduction of a picture painted for defendant by plaintiff. The calendar contained in said envelope was composed of the reproduction of twelve pictures of plaintiff made and intended to be used for the Varga Esquire 1947 calendar. Each of the said pictures bore the words, "The Esquire Girl Calendar." None of such pictures carried plaintiff's name or any name, word or legend indicating them to be the work of plaintiff or any other person. . . .

The [parties'] contract, after expressing the desire of the parties to enter into an agreement defining their mutual rights and obligations, contains a paragraph around which this controversy revolves and which we think is determinative of the issues involved. It provides:

> "Vargas agrees for a period of ten years and six months, beginning January 1, 1944, as an independent contractor, to supply Esquire with not less than twenty-six (26) drawings during each six-months' period. . . . The drawings so furnished, and also the name 'Varga', 'Varga Girl,' 'Varga, Esq.,' and any and all other names, designs or material used in connection therewith, shall forever belong exclusively to Esquire, and Esquire shall have all rights with respect thereto, including (without limiting the generality of the foregoing) the right to use, lease, sell or otherwise dispose of the same as it shall see fit, and all radio, motion picture and reprint rights. Esquire shall also have the right to copyright any of said drawings, names, designs or material or take any other action it shall deem advisable for the purpose of protecting its rights therein." . . .

Plaintiff's principal contention is that the publication of the reproductions of paintings produced by him, without his name appearing thereon, without credit to him and without any name appearing thereon, violated an implied agreement that the defendant would not do so. Plaintiff concedes that the contract defines defendant's rights in the pictures, but in his brief argues "that despite its broad generality, despite the fact that the defendant took all rights in the pictures, it is bound by the implied agreement not to publish them in the manner complained of." Plaintiff cites and relies upon a number of cases in support of this alleged implied agreement. *Uproar Co. v. National Broadcasting Co.*, 1 Cir., 81 F.2d 373; Kirke La Shelle Co. v. Armstrong Co., 263 N.Y. 79, 188 N.E. 163; *Manners v. Morosco*, 252 U.S. 317, 40 S. Ct. 335, 64 L. Ed. 590. We have read these cases, and without attempting to discuss them in detail, we think they are inapplicable to the instant situation. In each of them an author signed a contract or license which conferred on the other party certain limited rights in a literary reproduction and reserved for the author the balance of the rights therein. The holding in each of these cases is to the effect that where certain of the rights to a literary composition were conferred and other rights retained, it would be implied that the author could not use the rights retained in such a way as to destroy or materially injure the rights conferred. Such a contractual situation is in marked contrast to that of the instant case where the plaintiff by plain and unambiguous language completely divested himself of every vestige of title and ownership of the pictures, as well as the right to their possession, control and use. The language by which the extent of the grant is to be measured, "shall forever belong exclusively to Esquire, and Esquire shall have all rights with respect thereto, including (without limiting the generality of the foregoing) the right to use, lease, sell or otherwise dispose of the same as it shall see fit," would appear to leave no room for a contention that any right, claim or interest in the pictures remained in the plaintiff after he had sold and delivered them to the defendant. Not only did plaintiff by the contract divest himself of all title, claim, and interest in such drawings and designs, but also in the names "Varga," "Varga Girl," "Varga Esquire," when used in connection therewith.

Of the many cases where it has been sought to engraft an implied condition upon the terms of a written document, we like the rule announced in *Domeyer v. O'Connell*, 364 Ill. 467, at page 470, 4 N.E. 2d 830, 832, 108 A.L.R. 476, where the language used is pertinent to the instant situation. The court stated:

> "The rules concerning the construction of contracts are so well established as to require but brief attention. The object of construction is to ascertain the intention of the parties. . . . That intention is to be determined from the language used in the instrument and not from any surmises that the parties intended certain conditions which they failed to express. Where there is no ambiguity in the language used, from that, and that alone, may the intention of the parties be gathered. . . . An implied intention is one necessarily arising from language used or a situation created by such language. If such intention does not necessarily arise, it cannot be implied. On the other hand, absence of a provision from a contract is evidence of an intention to exclude such provision."

As already shown, we think there is no ambiguity in the granting language of the contract, nor can there be an implied intention from the language thus employed of an intention of the parties of any reservation of rights in the grantor. The parties had been dealing with each other for a number of years, and the fact that no reservation was contained in the contract strongly indicates that it was intentionally omitted. Such a reservation will not be presumed; it must be expressed and clearly imposed. Grant v. Kellogg Co., D.C., 58 F. Supp. 48, 51, affirmed 2 Cir., 154 F.2d 59.

Plaintiff advances another theory which needs little discussion. It is predicated upon the contention that there is a distinction between the economic rights of an author capable of assignment and what are called "moral rights" of the author, said to be those necessary for the protection of his honor and integrity. These so-called "moral rights," so we are informed, are recognized by the civil law of certain foreign countries. In support of this phase of his argument, plaintiff relied upon a work by Stephen P. Ladas entitled "The International Protection of Literary and Artistic Property" (page 575, et seq.). It appears, however, that the author's discussion relied upon by plaintiff relates to the law of foreign countries. As to the United States, Ladas in the same work states (page 802): "The conception of 'moral rights' of authors so fully recognized and developed in the civil law countries has not yet received acceptance in the law of the United States. No such right is referred to by legislation, court decision, or writers." What plaintiff in reality seeks is a change in the law of this country to conform to that of certain other countries. We need not stop to inquire whether such a change, if desirable, is a matter for the legislative or judicial branch of the government; in any event, we are not disposed to make any new law in this respect.

Plaintiff's third and last contention is that the manner of reproduction by defendant of plaintiff's work was such as to constitute a misrepresentation and was unfair competition. The concurring opinion of Mr. Justice Holmes in *International New Service v. Associated Press*, 248 U.S. 215, 246, 247, 39 S. Ct. 68, 63 L. Ed. 211, 2 A.L.R. 293; and *Fisher v. Star Co.*, 231 N.Y. 414, 433, 132 N.E. 133, 136, 19 A.L.R. 937, are the only cases cited and relied upon as supporting this contention. We think that neither case affords any support for such theory. In both, the holding as to unfair competition rested on the premise that the defendants, without the consent or approval of the plaintiffs, had taken and used to their own advantage something in which the plaintiffs had a property right—more specifically, that the defendants had pirated or stolen plaintiff's property and used it in their business in competition with that of the plaintiffs. It is difficult to discern how there could be any pirating or unlawful taking of property in the instant case in view of the rights (heretofore discussed) which the plaintiff by contract conferred upon the defendant.

Plaintiff argues that the use of "Esquire Girl" as a title for the pictures was a representation that the author was someone other than the plaintiff. We do not agree with this contention. The title used was the name of the well-known and widely circulated magazine in which they were published, and we think the public would readily recognize the word "Esquire" referred to such magazine and not to the name of an artist.

More than that, as already shown, it was provided in the contract that both the pictures and the name "shall forever belong exclusively to Esquire, and

Esquire shall have all rights with respect thereto, including . . . the right to use . . . or otherwise dispose of the same as it shall see fit." This was the basis both upon which plaintiff was paid for his pictures and upon which Esquire acquired their possession and ownership. Under these circumstances, we are of the view that there was no unfair competition by the defendant in the manner of their use.

The order appealed from is affirmed.

Notes and Questions

1. In *Vargas*, Esquire Magazine decided to print some of Vargas's drawings without attribution to Vargas. The court denied the implication of a right of attribution from common law contractual principles or from the Lanham Act's false or misleading designation of origin provision. The Lanham Act holding was reaffirmed in *Dastar Corp. v. Twentieth Century Fox Film Corp.*, 539 U.S. 23 (2003), wherein the court found that a film series created by Twentieth Century Fox that had slipped into the public domain through a failure to renew its copyright could be copied and adapted into a new film and sold without any attribution credit for the original creators of the film. The Court held that trademark law could not be used to create perpetual rights of authorship, such as attribution, that are not provided in the copyright act.

2. *Dastar* expressly construed copyright and trademark law to preclude the implication of a right of attribution. *See Harbour v. Farquhar*, 245 Fed. Appx. 582 (9th Cir. 2007) (no separate attribution rights under Lanham Act for creators of music incorporated into television and video programming where producers accurately described their role as creators and producers of the programming itself). As it stands, unless the right of attribution is possessed under a copyright or trademark license or otherwise bargained for by contract, the right of attribution will not be implied. *See Zyla v. Wadsworth*, 360 F.3d 243 (1st Cir. 2004) (no right to attribution where plaintiff's work was included in three editions of a textbook, and defendant owned copyright to books, and defendants included earlier works of plaintiff in fourth edition without attribution and without her permission); *Williams v. UMG Recordings, Inc.*, 281 F. Supp. 2d 1177 (C.D. Cal. 2003) (no requirement beyond contract and copyright law to identify individual contributors to film script); *Keane v. Fox TV Stations, Inc.*, 297 F. Supp. 2d 921 (S.D. Tex. 2004), *aff'd*, 129 Fed. Appx. 874 (5th Cir.), *cert. denied*, 546 U.S. 938 (2005) (no requirement beyond contract and copyright law to identify person who came up with title of popular television show).

PROBLEM 4-4

> Silvia Berne painted a mural inside an early eighteenth-century church. She is the most famous and only female member of the "Extraordinaries School" of painting that had a short-lived existence from 1703-1722. Her mural is one of the last surviving public works created by her or any other artist of the Extraordinaries School. The church is falling apart and would require massive restoration at a cost of $900,000 in order to become functional again. The local township and parish and diocese have nowhere near that amount of money for the restoration; aside from the mural, the building has very few other redeeming features, and the town and diocese want to tear the building down and replace it with a smaller, modern structure. Art preservation and restoration experts from the National Technological University have a method that can lift the paint from the surface of the church's wall and remount it on canvas so that the mural can be removed and restored to a satisfactory viewable condition; however, given the size and scope of the project, it would cost $1.3 million to remove and restore the Berne mural. Berne's descendants are alive and well and do not consent to the destruction of the mural. What should the town and diocese do — leave the mural and the church alone, attempt to remove and restore the mural, or tear the church down, mural and all, as it is not practicable in a monetary sense to save the mural? Analyze the issue under the national laws discussed below.

5. The Right of Integrity

A work may lose its essential meaning when it is altered in size, discolored, or reconstructed, and it may no longer represent the intentions of the artist. Attributing such a work to a particular artist may damage the artist's honor and reputation.

The right of integrity of artistic creations is unquestioned in France. When a work of art is communicated to the public and is acknowledged to be the work of a particular artist, the artist has an interest in seeing that it retains its original form. In *Buffet c. Fersig*, CA Paris, [1962] Recueil Dalloz (D. Jur.) 570, note by Desbois, *aff'd*, [1965] Gaz. Pal. II.126, the artist painted the exterior of a refrigerator as an "indivisible artistic unit." Some time later, the refrigerator was disassembled, but the artist was able to enjoin the sale of the separated individual panels. *See* John Henry Merryman, *The Refrigerator of Bernard Buffet (pt. 2)*, 27 HASTINGS L.J. 1023 (1976). *See also Vasarely c. Régie nationale des usines Renault*, CA Versailles, Jan. 28, 1999, D. 1999 inf. rap. 89, RIDA Apr. 2000 p. 276, note Kéréver (artist recovered damages when Renault remodeled its dining room and split up the 31 panels that made up artist's work, putting some in storage while others were lost).

A conflict arises when the artist allows a work to be created in a different medium. How may an artist's right to the integrity of a work be balanced against the adapter's right of creative freedom? The question most often arises under a contract.

A contract permitting the adaptation of an original work does not waive the author's right of integrity but it does allow the adapter some freedom. Adaptations are permitted as long as they are true to the spirit of the work and maintain the major characters of the work. *See Societe PLON et Francois Ceresa c. Pierre Hugo, Société des Gens des Lettres de France*, Cour de Cassation, 1ere Chambre Civile, 30 Janvier 2007, 212 RIDA, Avril 2007, p. 249; *Kapagama et Société Kosinus c. Poulet*, Cour de Cassation, 1ere Chambre Civile, 13 Juin 2006, 210 RIDA Octobre 2006, p. 338; *Frank c. Société Sofracima*, Cour d'Appel de Paris, 29 Apr. 1982, 114 RIDA Oct. 1982, p. 172. In *Consorts de Giraud d'Agay c. Société Alpha Film*, Cass. 1e Civ., Jun. 12, 2001, RIDA Jan. 2002 p. 266, Giraud d'Agay was the successor in title to Antoine de Saint-Exupéry. Giraud d'Agay claimed a violation of the author's right of integrity when Alpha Film created an animated film based on Saint-Exupéry's book *Le petit prince*. The Cour de Cassation said that an adaptation of a work must respect the spirit and substance of the original work. Thus, an adapter cannot add new characters to the story. In this case, as the Cour d'Appel determined, the adapter respected the spirit of the work by adhering to the original plot and having a consistent main character. The court affirmed the Cour d'Appel's decision that there was no moral rights violation.

An artist may prevent the affixing of his or her name to a disfigured work. *Merson c. Banque de France*, [1936] Recueil Hebdomadaire de Jurisprudence Dalloz [D.H.] II.246 (Civ. Trib. Seine). The right to prohibit distortions of the work was recognized quite early. *Sorel c. Fayard Freres*, [1900] D.P. II.152 (Civ. Trib. Seine). No criminal action has yet been allowed against those who deface a work of art based on moral rights, although property rights may give rise to a civil action. *See Clesinger et Laneuville c. Gauvain*, [1850] D.P. III.14 (Trib. Corr. de Lyon), reversed [1852] D.P. II.159 (Cour de Paris) (criminal action not allowed, but court hinted that a civil case could be filed).

The alteration of old motion pictures through the computer-enabled process of "colorization" has sparked vigorous protests by film makers. Ordinarily, the contributions of directors or screenwriters to a film are performed under a contract for creative services and are, thus, governed by the work-for-hire doctrine. *See* Chapter 2. Under this doctrine, the copyright in a film, including the right to produce derivative works made possible through technological advances, belongs to the producer of a film who hired the artistic contributors. France, however, has recognized colorization as an alteration of film that can be prevented by an artist who otherwise holds no copyright in the film.

In the first case to arise in France from the development of colorization, heirs of the late director John Huston sought and received an injunction

against the television broadcast of *The Asphalt Jungle*,[7] a film co-written and directed by Huston for MGM in 1950. Turner Entertainment Company acquired the rights to the film from MGM and produced the colorized version in 1988. Broadcast of the altered version in France was ultimately enjoined as a matter of public policy in favor of the author's moral rights.

Ultimately, the French Supreme Court held that, while the law of the country of origin normally governs the question of who has standing to assert rights in a work (i.e., Turner, in this case, as the owner of the American copyrights), the Universal Copyright Convention does not preclude the law of the country from which protection is sought from enjoining an alteration when broadcast in that country. *See* Boyer, *"The Asphalt Jungle"—in France—Entitlement to Moral Rights*, 2 ENT. L. REV. E-55 (1991); David R. Toraya, *Federal Jurisdiction over Foreign Copyright Infringement Actions—An Unsolicited Reply to Professor Nimmer*, 70 CORNELL L. REV. 1165 (1985). Another example of the difference between holdings in the United States and France arising out of a single set of facts is seen in *Shostakovich v. Twentieth Century-Fox Film Corp.*, 80 N.Y.S. 2d 575 (Sup. Ct. 1948), *aff'd*, 87 N.Y.S. 2d 430 (App. Div. 1949).

Colorization still irks artists and their heirs in France and other nations. *See Zinnemann v. TeleMontecarlo*, Rome Civ. Ct., Italy, Nov. 2006 (airing of colorized version of Zinnemann's B/W classic film, *The Seventh Cross*, violated his moral rights of integrity in Italy); *Société Le Nouvel Observateur du Monde c. Mirkine*, CA Paris, Jan. 23, 2001; RIDA Jul. 2001 p. 372 (partially colorizing, reversing, and recentering a photograph of actress Jeanne Moreau to commemorate the fiftieth anniversary of the Cannes Film Festival violated the artist's moral rights). It appears that colorization is to visual arts what karaoke has become for the recording arts. *See Ferrat c. Société Petraco Distribution*, Cass. 1e Civ., Nov. 13, 2003, RIDA Apr. 2004 p. 282; *Vangarde c. Société Petraco Distribution*, T.G.I. Paris, Nov. 26, 1997, RIDA Apr. 1998 p. 457.

While French law is typical of the continental attitude toward droit moral, other European members of the Berne Convention vary somewhat in their protection of certain rights. *See, e.g.,* [Italy] Law of Apr. 22, 1941, no. 633, *Gazetta Ufficiale della Republica Italiana* [Gaz. Uff.], *as amended by* Law of Aug. 23, 1946, no. 92 and Law of Jan. 8, 1979, no. 19; [Germany] Law of Sept. 13, 1965, Bundesgesetzblatt [BGB] 1273. *See also* UNESCO, Copyright Laws and Treaties of the World (1980).

---

7. Image: Michael D. Murray, Cropped, revised, and resized thumbnail image derived from the movie poster for the *Asphalt Jungle* (2014), the subject of *Turner Entertainment Co. v. Huston*, Judgment of December 19, 1994, CA Versailles, Civ. ch.

Dishonor and disrespect of the author caused by an action taken with the artist's work remains a principle that the French courts will evaluate in moral right of integrity claims. In *Warner Chappell Music France c. Pierre Perret*, Cour de Cassation, 1ere Chambre Civile, 7 Novembre 2006, 211 RIDA Janvier 2007, p. 320, the Cour de Cassation found that a recording artist's moral right was not infringed when the record company holding the license to the exploitation rights to his song recording included the song in a compilation without seeking approval from the artist. The court found that the exploitation of a work in a compilation piece does not require the author's consent unless the new work in some way impairs the work or discredits the author. Since the song was presented in the classic manner and was not impaired in any way, Perret's moral right was not infringed upon. Similarly, in *Barbelivien, Montagne et SNAC c. Universal Music Pub.*, Cour de Cassation, 1ere Chambre Civile, 5 Decembre 2006, 211 RIDA Janvier 2007, p. 358, authors of the song "On va s'aimer" filed suit against Universal on the grounds that the changing of the words of the song to "on va fluncher" and the use of the song to promote the Flunch chain of restaurants[8] infringed their right to respect for the song. The authors had assigned their right of exploitation of the song to Universal under a contract of 1983, in which the authors agreed that the song could be used as a theme in television, radio, or advertising and the words could also be altered. The court found that since the authors had agreed that the song could be used for advertising purposes, the onus was on them to show that the use of the song was detrimental to their reputation and infringed their moral right, despite the fact that public policy precludes an author from abandoning moral rights generally and in advance to the assignee the exclusive power to determine what use, adaptations, or changes to a work may be made. But in *Kapagama et Société Kosinus c. Poulet*, Cour de Cassation, 1ere Chambre Civile, 13 Juin 2006, 210 RIDA Octobre 2006, p. 338, the Cour de Cassation found that a clause in an audiovisual adaptation contract violated the Intellectual Property Code by allowing the publisher to permit adaptation of the work without first seeking the original author's consent. This clause was held to have violated the principle of inalienability of the author's moral right in the work. The Court found that the author should be informed and could object if the adaptation did not keep in line with the original work's purpose.

Integrity claims may arise from the arrangement, packaging, or trade dress associated with the publication of a work. *Mussotte c. Nestlé Waters France*, Cour de Cassation, 1ere Chambre Civile, 12 Juillet 2006, 210 RIDA Octobre 2006, p. 366 (even though artist transferred all rights of exploitation and

---

8. Image: Michael D. Murray, Cropped, revised, and resized thumbnail excerpt of a photograph depicting a "Flunch" restaurant (2014), the subject of *Barbelivien, Montagne et SNAC c. Universal Music Pub.*, Judgment of December 5, 2006, Cour de Cassation, 1ere Chambre Civile, 211 RIDA Janvier 2007, p. 358.

reproduction of a photograph without limitation, the Cour de Cassation found that the author's moral right of integrity in his work was violated by Nestlé's alterations of the photograph used on water bottle label without the author's consent). In *Chambelland c. Paseyro*, Cour d'Appel de Paris, 1 Feb. 1993, D.1993.158, aff'g in part the judgment of the TGI de Paris, 30 May 1991, the Paris Court of Appeal affirmed that an author has moral rights arising from the design of a book. The publisher of a collection of Chambelland's poems printed the book without the final approval of the poet. The court agreed that the book had been assembled in a negligent and inconsistent manner that was detrimental to the character and reputation of the poet as well as having a detrimental effect on the poet's ability to promote and market the book. The court noted that readers of collections of poems look for and expect an aesthetically attractive presentation of the work. The poet was awarded damages and interest of 20,000 francs.

Fabris c. Loudmer, Cour d'Appel de Versailles, 20 Nov. 1991, dealt with the related problem of permissible reproduction for artistic citation versus violations of integrity rights from negligent cropping of works. Defendant Loudmer, an art dealer, had published a catalog in 1986 containing illustrations of paintings for sale. Among the represented works were two paintings by Maurice Utrillo in which Jean Farbis, the plaintiff, owned the copyright. Farbis complained that Loudmer had infringed his author's right of reproduction. The court ruled in favor of the defendant finding that he had merely exercised his right of artistic citation ("citation artistic"). Although the works had been reproduced in their entirety, they were in a much reduced, small-format size in the catalog, and the court found that there would be no risk of confusion or competition between actual reproductions and these citations. Furthermore, the Court noted, had Loudmer decided to show cropped reproductions of the works, he might well have made himself guilty of "dénaturation" — infringement of the integrity of the works through derogatory cropping that changes the scene, perspective, composition, or meaning of the works. *But see Société 1633 c. Société de Conception de Presse et D'edition (SCPE)*, Cour de Cassation, 1ere Chambre Civile, 7 Novembre 2006, 211 RIDA Janvier 2007, p. 312 (use of an original work in full cannot ever constitute a "short quotation" under the Intellectual Property Code).

A dénaturation problem that is conceptually similar to cropping might arise with literary editing. In *Soc. Éditions des Femmes c. Farny*, Cour de Paris, 8 Dec. 1988, D.1990.53(SC), appeal from TGI de Paris, 27 Nov. 1986, Farny had been commissioned to translate a work by the publisher Soc. Éditions des Femmes. Without informing the translator, the publisher allowed an editor to revise her translation but still published the translation with her name on it. The Court of Paris found this to be an infringement of the translator's moral right — in particular, the "droit de ne pas signer cette traduction et de ne pas apparaître comme responsable du texte modifié" — the right not to be associated with a modified work that had been amended without the approval of the author.

Unapproved editing also presented a moral rights problem in *S.A. Librairie Larousse c. Hodeir*, Cour d'Appel de Paris (4e chambre), 6 Nov. 1986, 136 RIDA 149. In 1976, Larousse, a publishing house, prepared to publish an encyclopedia of music, *Larousse de la Musique*, in which articles on jazz written by André Hodeir were to be included. When the first volume of the work came out in 1982, Hodeir found that several of his articles had been omitted and offensive edits and erroneous additions had been made to his remaining work. The first court hearing the action acknowledged that *Larousse de la Musique* was an "œuvre de collaboration," suggesting that the editor retained a right to edit the work in order to preserve a unity of style and tone. This right also was a condition in the contract between the parties. However, the Court noted that the editor's primary goal appeared to have been to spice up or popularize the text ("vulgariser" was the term used by the court), and in this pursuit, the editor had made many changes to Hodeir's contributions. The first Court granted Hodeir damages, finding that the modifications had infringed his moral rights. On appeal, however, the Court of Appeal was not convinced that the edits had exceeded what was allowed by the contract. The Court of Appeal attempted to evaluate whether Hodeir's reputation had suffered as a result of the alterations. The evidence indicated that it had not, and, in fact, Larousse's encyclopedia had been very well received and had been given numerous favorable reviews. Therefore, the Court of Appeal concluded, "les fautes commises par Larousse n'ont pas gravement porté atteinte à la réputation et au prestige de Hodeir" — the misdeeds of Larousse were not severe enough to affect Hodeir's reputation. But the story did not end there: a separate detail caused the Court of Appeal to find that Hodeir's right of integrity had been infringed. In the preface to the first volume of the encyclopedia, the editor declared that "il va de soi qu'une totale liberté dans l'interprétation historique et critique a été laissée à chacun des spécialistes dont les initiales figurent en fin d'article" — each contributor had had unfettered freedom to present his own historical and critical interpretations, and each of the contributed views of the authors were completely their own as indicated by the author's initials that followed each submission. This direct misrepresentation of the contents was unacceptable to the court, and it found that the active, false representation that the text in its entirety was the approved work of Hodeir prejudiced the moral right of integrity of the author: "en attribuant à Hodeir des articles qu'il n'avait pas rédigés et en affirmant dans la préface de l'ouvrage qu'il avait joui d'une totale liberté, la Librairie Larousse a commis des fautes généatrices d'un préjudice moral pour André Hodeir." Hodeir was awarded damages of 50,000 francs.

In like manner, and in the more publicized case of *Frank c. Société Sofracima*, Cour d'Appel de Paris, 29 Apr. 1982, 114 RIDA Oct. 1982, p. 172, the Paris Court of Appeal ruled that a scriptwriter, Christopher Frank, had violated the right of integrity of the original author of the work that had served as the source for the adapted screenplay. Sofracima, a film company, held the adaptation and exploitation rights in the literary work, *La plus longue course d'Abraham Coles, chauffeur de taxi* by Claude Brami. In February 1978, Frank was commissioned by Sofracima to write a screenplay based on the book. After Frank completed the project, Sofracima informed Frank that in their opinion his adaptation constituted a corruption of Brami's work. They alleged that Frank had turned a cerebral examination of the psychology of the main character, Abraham Coles, into an action piece with scenes of violence. Sofracima passed on a letter of Brami, the original author, in which he stated: "A la lecture de ce début d'adaptation, j'ai été stupéfait de voir qu'elle était sans rapport avec mon roman dont elle trahissait gravement l'esprit, les personages et les événements. J'atteste formellement que si un film devait voir le jour sur la base de ce que j'ai pu lire, je considérais le dit film comme une atteinte à mon droit moral d'auteur" — "I was shocked to read the adapted work. It did not conform to the ideas, characters, and events of the original work and the adaptation and seriously betrayed those aspects of the original work. If a film were made from this script, I would consider it to be an infringement of my moral rights as an author." Frank's position was that he had fairly adapted the work to make it viable for the new media of film, which necessitated changes of a technical and stylistic nature. He asserted that he was well within his rights as an author of a film adaptation to make these changes. Yet, it appeared from Brami's letter that if a film were to be made on the basis of the script, Brami would consider it an infringement of his moral rights as an author. Brami's letter impressed the Court sufficiently to resist the recent trend in French court opinions which had allowed an extensive editorial freedom when transforming a book to a film. Accordingly, the initial court hearing the case nullified the contract between the parties, finding Frank at fault for having produced a defective work. The Paris Court of Appeal affirmed the decision, and Frank was ordered to pay damages of 30,000 francs.

There are several sides to the question of destruction in moral rights law. There can be destruction of a work out of spite or indifference to the reputation of the artist and the value of the artwork. Or, there can be destruction to preserve the reputation of the artist by removing from display a work that has deteriorated or simply gone out of style in a way detrimental to the artist's reputation. Finally, there can be destruction to negate the effects of the art on health, public safety, or structural integrity of the location of the installation.

The case of *Roger Bezombes, A.D.A.G.P. c. M. L'Huillier*, Cour d'Appel de Paris, 25 Nov. 1980, 108 RIDA Apr. 1981, p. 162, illustrates the first kind of destruction. The case involved a sculpture by Roger Bezombes entitled *La condition humaine* which had been exhibited in a church. Members of the church community declared it to be blasphemous and destroyed it. The Paris Court of Appeal did not allow the alleged provocative nature of the work to serve as a justification or mitigation of the destruction, nor did it allow the defendants' assertion that they acted in good faith regarding the destruction to be a defense of their actions. The Court ruled that the artist's right of integrity had been infringed. Bezombes was awarded damages and was granted the right to have the judgment published in two newspapers of his own choosing.

Destruction of the third variety (to preserve health, public safety, or the usability and structural integrity of the location of the art) was at issue in *Scrive c. S.C.I. Centre commercial Rennes-Alma*, Cour d'Appel de Paris, 10 July 1975, D.1977.342; 91 RIDA Jan. 1977, p. 114. Scrive had designed and installed a fountain in the Alma shopping center in Rennes. Soon after installation, the fountain experienced several technical problems that caused it to leak. Repairs were undertaken, but the leaking persisted, causing the floor around the fountain to be slippery, but also exposing passersby to the risk of electrocution from the wiring of the lighting and water pumps of the fountain. In light of this risk to the public, the directors of the Alma shopping center decided to have the fountain removed, but Scrive complained that this was an infringement of his right of integrity. The Court of Appeal set out to balance the need to preserve a work of creative genius against the legitimate rights of property owners. The court construed the parties' agreement to contemplate that the work would be displayed in a public, commercial center and not just held for the pleasure and private enjoyment of the commissioner, and it was reasonable for Scrive to believe that the fountain would be maintained by its owner. In light of the totality of these circumstances, the Court found that the directors of Alma were guilty of neglect of their obligations towards the artist. The Court ruled that Scrive's right of integrity had been violated and Scrive was awarded damages. However, the Court did not order the fountain to be reconstructed.

In contrast to the *Scrive* case, the Court in *Zobda c. Farrugia*, Cour d'Appel de Basse-Terre, 30 Sept. 1996, D.1998.58, allowed the owner of frescoes decorating the inside of a church to destroy them after it was discovered that the frescoes had been damaged by dampness. The Court of Appeal considered this to be a valid reason for the destruction and obliteration of the works, particularly because the artist should not expect the works to be displayed in perpetuity in a damaged and deteriorating condition.

Great Britain has amended its law to comply with Berne in the Copyright, Designs and Patents Act (1988), ch. 48. Chapter IV of the act provides the following rights: to be identified as author of a copyrighted literary, dramatic, musical, or artistic work or, as the case may be, as the director of a copyrighted film (§ 77); the right of an author or director not to have a work subjected to derogatory treatment (integrity) if the treatment "amounts to distortion or mutilation of the work or is otherwise prejudicial to the honour or reputation of the author or director" (§ 80); the right in certain circumstances of a person not to have a literary, dramatic, musical, or artistic work or film (whether or not a copyrighted work) falsely attributed to him or her as author or director (§ 84); the right of a person in certain circumstances who, for private and domestic purposes, commissions the taking of a copyrighted photograph or the making of a copyrighted film not to have copies of those works issued to the public or exhibited or shown in public or broadcast or included in a cable program service (§ 85). *See* Glass, *"Moral Rights" and the New Copyright Law*, 134 S.J. 6-7 (Jan. 5, 1990).

In Germany, *von Gerkan v. Deutsche Bahn*, 16th Berlin Superior Court of Justice, AZ 16 O 240/05 (2006), tells the successful tale of an architect who

Berlin Hauptbahnhof

would not let his railway station plans be derailed. In late November 2006, architect Meinhard von Gerkan sued the German railway company Deutsche Bahn over unauthorized changes to his competition-winning design for the renovation of the main Berlin railway station, the Hauptbahnhof station.[9] In 2001, Deutsche Bahn had ordered the upper platform hall of the station shortened by a third, and von Gerkan reluctantly complied. Later, Deutsche Bahn replaced the architect's airily vaulted arches design with a flat-paneling ceiling design by a rival firm without von Gerkan's knowledge. Berlin's regional court upheld the architect's claim that Deutsche Bahn violated his intellectual-property rights by building a "considerably defaced" version of his original design. The court ruled that Deutsche Bahn must pay to rebuild the lower-level platform ceilings with von Gerkan's original airily vaulted arches design at an estimated cost of $25.9-$51.7 million.

In Spain, the case *Waits v. Volkswagen-Audi*, Barcelona Court of Appeals (Nov. 17, 2005) (*see* N.Y. TIMES, Jan. 20, 2006), reports singer Tom Waits' landmark legal victory establishing his moral rights in a case brought against car manufacturer Volkswagen-Audi (VAESA) and Tandem Company Guasch, a Spanish production company, for adapting one of Waits' songs and impersonating his gravelly voice in a television commercial. This is the first time that a Spanish court has recognized a moral rights claim that replicates the typical privacy or publicity claim to prevent commercial appropriation of a famous singer's voice. Spain has long protected the privacy, personality, and reputation of writers, authors, and other celebrities, but this case purportedly recognizes an artist's voice as his creative work. The judgment of the Appellate Court of Barcelona also recognized that VW/Audi and Tandem Company Guasch had infringed the intellectual property rights of both Waits and Hans Kusters Music, Waits' music publisher in Spain. The commercial for Audi cars was originally screened in Spain in 2000. The soundtrack replicated Tom Waits' song "Innocent When You Dream," and featured a Tom Waits' vocal impersonation. At the time of making the commercial Tandem Campany Guasch had sought permission to use Waits' original version of "Innocent When You Dream," a request he rejected in conformity never to allow his work to be used in commercials. Waits commented on the victory, stating, "Now they understand the words to the song better. It wasn't 'Innocent When You Scheme' it was 'Innocent When You Dream.'" The Court awarded damages of

---

9. Images: Michael D. Murray, Two cropped, revised, and resized thumbnail excerpts of exhibits depicting the Berlin Hauptbahnhof (2014), the subject of *von Gerkan v. Deutsche Bahn*, 16th Berlin Superior Court of Justice, AZ 16 O 240/05 (2006).

36,000 euros for copyright infringement and 30,000 euros for the violation of Waits's moral rights.

The Monty Python group asserted the right of integrity in the Southern District of New York and the Second Circuit under the guise of two American causes of action: copyright law protection from unauthorized derivative works and contractual limitations on a licensee's right to allow a sub-licensee to alter the licensed work.

Gilliam v. American Broadcasting Companies

538 F.2d 14 (2d Cir. 1976)*

LUMBARD, Circuit Judge.

Plaintiffs, a group of British writers and performers known as "Monty Python," appeal from a denial by Judge Lasker in the Southern District of a preliminary injunction to restrain the American Broadcasting Company (ABC) from broadcasting edited versions of three separate programs originally written and performed by Monty Python for broadcast by the British Broadcasting Corporation (BBC). We agree with Judge Lasker that the appellants have demonstrated that the excising done for ABC impairs the integrity of the original work. We further find that the countervailing injuries that Judge Lasker found might have accrued to ABC as a result of an injunction at a prior date no longer exist. We therefore direct the issuance of a preliminary injunction by the district court.

The principal Monty Python writers and players in 1976; Gilliam at far right[10]

Since its formation in 1969, the Monty Python group has gained popularity primarily through its thirty-minute television programs created for BBC as part of a comedy series entitled "Monty Python's Flying Circus." In accordance with an agreement between Monty Python and BBC, the group writes and delivers to BBC scripts for use in the television series. This scriptwriters' agreement recites in great detail the procedure to be followed

---

* Footnotes and most citations omitted.

10. Michael D. Murray, Cropped, revised, and resized thumbnail image (2007) derived from a photograph of the principal Monty Python writers and players in 1976, the litigants in *Gilliam v. American Broadcasting Companies*, 538 F.2d 14 (2d Cir. 1976).

when any alterations are to be made in the script prior to recording of the program. The essence of this section of the agreement is that, while BBC retains final authority to make changes, appellants or their representatives exercise optimum control over the scripts consistent with BBC's authority and only minor changes may be made without prior consultation with the writers. Nothing in the scriptwriters' agreement entitles BBC to alter a program once it has been recorded. The agreement further provides that, subject to the terms therein, the group retains all rights in the script. . . .

Under the agreement, BBC may license the transmission of recordings of the television programs in any overseas territory. The series has been broadcast in this country primarily on non-commercial public broadcasting television stations, although several of the programs have been broadcast on commercial stations in Texas and Nevada. In each instance, the thirty-minute programs have been broadcast as originally recorded and broadcast in England in their entirety and without commercial interruption.

In October 1973, Time-Life Films acquired the right to distribute in the United States certain BBC television programs, including the Monty Python series. Time-Life was permitted to edit the programs only "for insertion of commercials, applicable censorship or governmental . . . rules and regulations, and National Association of Broadcasters and time segment requirements." No similar clause was included in the scriptwriters' agreement between appellants and BBC. Prior to this time, ABC had sought to acquire the right to broadcast excerpts from various Monty Python programs in the spring of 1975, but the group rejected the proposal for such a disjoined format. Thereafter, in July 1975, ABC agreed with Time-Life to broadcast two ninety-minute specials each comprising three thirty-minute Monty Python programs that had not previously been shown in this country.

Correspondence between representatives of BBC and Monty Python reveals that these parties assumed that ABC would broadcast each of the Monty Python programs "in its entirety." On September 5, 1975, however, the group's British representative inquired of BBC how ABC planned to show the programs in their entirety if approximately 24 minutes of each 90 minute program were to be devoted to commercials. BBC replied on September 12, "we can only reassure you that ABC have decided to run the programmes 'back to back,' and that there is a firm undertaking not to segment them."

ABC broadcast the first of the specials on October 3, 1975. Appellants did not see a tape of the program until late November and were allegedly "appalled" at the discontinuity and "mutilation" that had resulted from the editing done by Time-Life for ABC. Twenty-four minutes of the original 90 minutes of recording had been omitted. Some of the editing had been done in order to make time for commercials; other material had been edited, according to ABC, because the original programs contained offensive or obscene matter. . . .

There is nothing clearly erroneous in Judge Lasker's conclusion that any injury suffered by appellants as a result of the broadcast of edited versions of their programs was irreparable by its nature. ABC presented the appellants with their first opportunity for broadcast to a nationwide network audience in this country. If ABC adversely misrepresented the quality of Monty Python's work, it is likely that many members of the audience, many of whom, by defendant's admission, were previously unfamiliar with appellants, would not become loyal followers of Monty Python productions. The subsequent injury to appellants' theatrical reputation would imperil their ability to attract the large audience necessary to the success of their venture. Such an injury to professional reputation cannot be measured in monetary terms or recompensed by other relief.

***

We then reach the question whether there is a likelihood that appellants will succeed on the merits. In concluding that there is a likelihood of infringement here, we rely especially on the fact that the editing was substantial, i.e., approximately 27 per cent of the original program was omitted, and the editing contravened contractual provisions that limited the right to edit Monty Python material. It should be emphasized that our discussion of these matters refers only to such facts as have been developed upon the hearing for a preliminary injunction. Modified or contrary findings may become appropriate after a plenary trial.

Judge Lasker denied the preliminary injunction in part because he was unsure of the ownership of the copyright in the recorded program. Appellants first contend that the question of ownership is irrelevant because the recorded program was merely a derivative work taken from the script in which they hold the uncontested copyright. Thus, even if BBC owned the copyright in the recorded program, its use of that work would be limited by the license granted to BBC by Monty Python for use of the underlying script. We agree.

Section 7 of the Copyright Law, 17 U.S.C. § 7, provides in part that "adaptations, arrangements, dramatizations . . . or other versions of . . . copyrighted works when produced with the consent of the proprietor of the copyright in such works . . . shall be regarded as new works subject to copyright. . . ." Manifestly, the recorded program falls into this category as a dramatization of the script, and thus the program was itself entitled to copyright protection. However, section 7 limits the copyright protection of the derivative work, as works adapted from previously existing scripts have become known, to the novel additions made to the underlying work, and the derivative work does not affect the "force or validity" of the copyright in the matter from which it is derived. Thus, any ownership by BBC of the copyright in the recorded program would not affect the scope or ownership of the copyright in the underlying script. . . .

Since the copyright in the underlying script survives intact despite the incorporation of that work into a derivative work, one who uses the script, even with the permission of the proprietor of the derivative work, may infringe the underlying copyright. If the proprietor of the derivative work is licensed by the proprietor of the copyright in the underlying work to vend or distribute the derivative work to third parties, those parties will, of course, suffer no liability for their use of the underlying work consistent with the license to the proprietor of the derivative work. Obviously, it was just this type of arrangement that was contemplated in this instance. The scriptwriters' agreement between Monty Python and BBC specifically permitted the latter to license the transmission of the recordings made by BBC to distributors such as Time-Life for broadcast in overseas territories.

One who obtains permission to use a copyrighted script in the production of a derivative work, however, may not exceed the specific purpose for which permission was granted. . . . Appellants herein do not claim that the broadcast by ABC violated media or time restrictions contained in the license of the script to BBC. Rather, they claim that revisions in the script, and ultimately in the program, could be made only after consultation with Monty Python, and that ABC's broadcast of a program edited after recording and without consultation with Monty Python exceeded the scope of any license that BBC was entitled to grant.

The rationale for finding infringement when a licensee exceeds time or media restrictions on his license and the need to allow the proprietor of the underlying copyright to control the method in which his work is presented to the public applies equally to the situation in which a licensee makes an unauthorized use of the underlying work by publishing it in a truncated version. Whether intended to allow greater economic exploitation of the work, as in the media and time cases, or to ensure that the copyright proprietor retains a veto power over revisions desired for the derivative work, the ability of the copyright holder to control his work remains paramount in our copyright law. We find, therefore, that unauthorized editing of the underlying work, if proven, would constitute an infringement of the copyright in that work similar to any other use of a work that exceeded the license granted by the proprietor of the copyright.

If the broadcast of an edited version of the Monty Python program infringed the group's copyright in the script, ABC may obtain no solace from the fact that editing was permitted in the agreements between BBC and Time-Life or Time-Life and ABC. BBC was not entitled to make unilateral changes in the script and was not specifically empowered to alter the recordings once made; Monty Python, moreover, had reserved to itself any rights not granted to BBC. Since a grantor may not convey greater rights than it owns, BBC's permission to allow Time-Life, and hence ABC, to edit appears to have been a nullity. . . .

Our resolution of these technical arguments serves to reinforce our initial inclination that the copyright law should be used to recognize the important role of the artist in our society and the need to encourage production and dissemination of artistic works by providing adequate legal protection for one who submits his work to the public. We therefore conclude that there is a substantial likelihood that, after a full trial, appellants will succeed in proving infringement of their copyright by ABC's broadcast of edited versions of Monty Python programs. In reaching this conclusion, however, we need not accept appellants' assertion that any editing whatsoever would constitute infringement. Courts have recognized that licensees are entitled to some small degree of latitude in arranging the licensed work for presentation to the public in a manner consistent with the licensee's style or standards. That privilege, however, does not extend to the degree of editing that occurred here especially in light of contractual provisions that limited the right to edit Monty Python material.

II

It also seems likely that appellants will succeed on the theory that, regardless of the right ABC had to broadcast an edited program, the cuts made constituted an actionable mutilation of Monty Python's work. This cause of action, which seeks redress for deformation of an artist's work, finds its roots in the continental concept of droit moral, or moral right, which may generally be summarized as including the right of the artist to have his work attributed to him in the form in which he created it.

American copyright law, as presently written, does not recognize moral rights or provide a cause of action for their violation, since the law seeks to vindicate the economic, rather than the personal, rights of authors. Nevertheless, the economic incentive for artistic and intellectual creation that serves as the foundation for American copyright law cannot be reconciled with the inability of artists to obtain relief for mutilation or misrepresentation of their work to the public on which the artists are financially dependent. Thus courts have long granted relief for misrepresentation of an artist's work by relying on theories outside the statutory law of copyright, such as contract law, *Granz v. Harris*, 198 F.2d 585 (2d Cir. 1952) (substantial cutting of original work constitutes misrepresentation), or the tort of unfair competition, *Prouty v. National Broadcasting Co.*, 26 F. Supp. 265 (D. Mass. 1939). See Strauss, The Moral Right of the Author 128-38, in *Studies on Copyright* (1963). Although such decisions are clothed in terms of proprietary right in one's creation, they also properly vindicate the author's personal right to prevent the presentation of his work to the public in a distorted form. *See Gardella v. Log Cabin Products Co.*, 89 F.2d 891, 895-96 (2d Cir. 1937); Roeder, The Doctrine of Moral Right, 53 HARV. L. REV. 554, 568 (1940).

Here, the appellants claim that the editing done for ABC mutilated the original work and that consequently the broadcast of those programs as the creation of Monty Python violated the Lanham Act §43(a), 15 U.S.C. s1125(a).

These cases cannot be distinguished from the situation in which a television network broadcasts a program properly designated as having been written and performed by a group, but which has been edited, without the writer's consent, into a form that departs substantially from the original work. "To deform his work is to present him to the public as the creator of a work not his own, and thus makes him subject to criticism for work he has not done." In such a case, it is the writer or performer, rather than the network, who suffers the consequences of the mutilation, for the public will have only the final product by which to evaluate the work. Thus, an allegation that a defendant has presented to the public a "garbled," distorted version of plaintiff's work seeks to redress the very rights sought to be protected by the Lanham Act, 15 U.S.C. § 1125(a), and should be recognized as stating a cause of action under that statute. *See Autry v. Republic Productions, Inc.*, 213 F.2d 667 (9th Cir. 1954); *Jaeger v. American Int'l Pictures, Inc.*, 330 F. Supp. 274 (S.D.N.Y.1971), which suggest the violation of such a right if mutilation could be proven.

This result is not changed by the fact that the network, as here, takes public responsibility for editing. During the hearing on the preliminary injunction, Judge Lasker viewed the edited version of the Monty Python program broadcast on December 26 and the original, unedited version. After hearing argument of this appeal, this panel also viewed and compared the two versions. We find that the truncated version at times omitted the climax of the skits to which appellants' rare brand of humor was leading and at other times deleted essential elements in the schematic development of a story line. We therefore agree with Judge Lasker's conclusion that the edited version broadcast by ABC impaired the integrity of appellants' work and represented to the public as the product of appellants what was actually a mere caricature of their talents. We believe that a valid cause of action for such distortion exists and that therefore a preliminary injunction may issue to prevent repetition of the broadcast prior to final determination of the issues. . . .

For these reasons we direct that the district court issue the preliminary injunction sought by the appellants.

Notes and Questions

1. *Gilliam v. ABC*—the Monty Python case—showed two American alternatives to a French moral right of integrity claim: the first was that the licensee exceeded its rights under the original license when it in turn licensed the work to an overseas party (ABC) without controlling or specifying how the work was to be rebroadcast; thus the second licensee did not obtain the rights it needed to show the work in edited form. What should future art lawyers learn from this about artists and licenses of their works?

2. A third claim, touched on but not pursued in the case, was that rebroadcast of the works in distorted, edited form, but with attribution to the Monty Python gang as the authors, was a false and misleading designation of origin under § 43 of the Lanham Act. Would the Lanham Act cause of action mentioned in *Gilliam* survive the *Dastar* opinion, 539 U.S. 23 (2003)? In *Dastar*, the Supreme Court held that a film series that had slipped into the public domain could be copied and adapted into a new film and sold without any attribution credit for the original creators of the film. The trademark law cause of action of "false designation of origin" could not be used to create perpetual rights of

authorship, such as attribution, that are not provided in the Copyright Act. The "origin" of the new film was held to be the new filmmakers, Dastar, who compiled the new film from the public domain source; thus, there was nothing fraudulent about Dastar's putting its own name on the new film without acknowledging the creators of the public domain source material. In contrast, are there ways in which the designation of origin of the Monty Python episodes at issue in the *Gilliam* case is false even under the *Dastar* standards?

Detail of David Wojnarowicz, Water *(1987)*[11]

3. In *Wojnarowicz v. American Family Ass'n,* 745 F. Supp. 130 (S.D.N.Y. 1990), plaintiff prevailed under the New York Artists' Authorship Rights Act, N.Y. Cultural Affairs Law Section 14.03 (McKinney's Supp. 1990), when defendant, a "family values" organization, cropped and rearranged portions of plaintiff's art work in an attempt to reveal that plaintiff produced obscene sexual and homoerotic material. Plaintiff's right of integrity under the statute was violated when defendant sampled and selected small bits of the artist's work that contained the suspect images without displaying the work as a whole, which denied the images their proper context and revealed a significantly different artistic meaning for the work.

The *Wojnarowicz* case rejected plaintiff's Lanham Act claim because defendant was not engaged in commercial activity — the sale or promotion of goods — but instead was advocating a political and moral position as an exercise of its freedom of expression. If another artist altered and displayed fragments of Wojnarowicz's work to reveal what she felt was the genius of Wojnarowicz's work and to explain the type of art that she and Wojnarowicz produce, would this be commercial activity or an exercise of free expression? What if the artist incorporated fragments of Wojnarowicz's work into her own political protest art complaining of the lack of resources and attention devoted to AIDS among the artistic community — commercial or not?

The *Wojnarowicz* court granted the plaintiff relief under the New York Artists' Authorship Rights statute but denied the claim that defendants had violated the copyright laws by making unauthorized derivative works of Wojnarowicz's paintings because it found that defendants had made a fair use of the material. Evaluate the potential

---

11. Image: Michael D. Murray, Cropped, revised, and resized image derived from a grayscale image of David Wojnarowicz, "Water" (1987), the subject of *Wojnarowicz v. American Family Ass'n,* 745 F. Supp. 130 (S.D.N.Y. 1990).

"fair use" defenses in the two scenarios described here — the two fellow artists who use fragments of Wojnarowicz's works, one to champion the work and the genre of art to which it belongs, and the other to create political protest art?

B. American States' Art Preservation Acts

The need for legislation granting moral rights beyond the rights provided in the 1976 Copyright Act and beyond what the average artist can obtain through contract negotiation was highlighted by the passage of moral rights legislation in 11 states after enactment of the 1976 Copyright Act. *See* Visual Artists Rights Act (1989), Hearings on S. 1198 Before the Subcomm. on Patents, Copyrights and Trademarks of the Senate Comm. on the Judiciary, 101st Cong., 1st Sess. 146, 149 (1989) (statement of Ralph Oman, categorizing each of the 10 statutes as following one of three models: (1) the preservation model, protecting attribution and integrity, including destruction of works, (2) the moral rights model, protecting attribution and integrity but not protecting against destruction, (3) the public works model, protecting works of particular value to the state as an exercise of keeping the peace).

California acted first, in 1979, when it enacted the California Art Preservation Act, Cal. Civ. Code § § 987 et seq. (West 1982 & Supp. 1995). This was followed in 1983 by New York's enactment of the Artist's Authorship Rights Act (AARA), N.Y. Arts & Cult. Aff. Law § 14.03 (McKinney Supp. 1995). The New York statute was discussed at length in the *Wojnarowicz* case cited above. Massachusetts passed its Art Preservation Act (MAPA), G.L. c. 231, § 85S, in 1985. Other states have followed the models set out in California and New York.

Most art preservation laws protect artists' rights of integrity and attribution. Under the Visual Artists Rights Act of 1990 (VARA) (discussed in section B below), it is expected that many provisions of these state laws will be preempted by the federal rights of integrity and attribution provided in VARA. VARA was codified as part of the U.S. copyright law in Title 17 of the U.S. Code, 17 U.S.C. § 106A, and it enjoys the same federal copyright law preemptive power over state law. 17 U.S.C. § 301; *see, e.g., R.W. Beck, Inc. v. E3 Consulting, LLC,* 577 F.3d 1133 (10th Cir. 2009). For example, *Board of Managers of Soho Int'l Arts Condominium v. City of New York,* No. 01 Civ. 1226 DAB, 2003 WL 21403333 (S.D.N.Y. June 17, 2003), found that VARA preempted the New York State art preservation statute (AARA) because VARA's protections against destruction of works of art duplicated and exceeded the protections of New York's law. *Grauer v. Deutsch,* 64 U.S.P.Q. 2d 1636, 2002 WL 31288937 (S.D.N.Y. Oct. 11, 2002), also declared that VARA preempts the New York AARA law.

In *Lubner v. City of Los Angeles*, 53 Cal. Rptr. 2d 24 (Ct. App. 2d Dist. 1996), the court found that a California Art Preservation Act claim was preempted by VARA. VARA prohibits the intentional or grossly negligent destruction of a work of art. Simple negligence is not enough to state a claim under VARA. The California Act was held to require the same elements and level of culpability as VARA, and thus was preempted.

Although VARA may preempt many state preservation acts that duplicate the rights of integrity and attribution defined in VARA, state legislatures may be able to provide additional moral rights protections beyond those provided in VARA. To the extent that state laws provide additional protections beyond those provided in VARA, there is a strong argument that the state laws should survive preemption. For example, Massachusetts and New Mexico, in their moral rights statutes, additionally provide the right to pseudonymity. Mass. Gen. Laws Ann. ch. 231, § 85S(d) (West Supp. 1992); N.M. Stat. Ann. § 13-4b-3B (1991). Certain laws (e.g., Massachusetts' preservation act) also provide a right of "nonattribution," meaning that for a just and valid reason, an artist also may disclaim authorship of works. Several state laws have a broader coverage than VARA. For example, there are more expansive definitions of protected works, including film and video, in Massachusetts and New Mexico (*see* Mass. Gen. Laws Ann. ch. 231, § 85S(b) (West Supp. 1999); N.M. Stat. Ann. § 13-4b-2B (1991)), and California has extended rights of action to artists' unions or organizations and made provisions for punitive remedies payable to charitable and educational arts organizations (*see* Cal. Civ. Code § 987(d) (West Supp. 1992)). Several states have more stringent standards of care, and, as seen in *Wojnarowicz*, New York's right of integrity has been extended to reproductions.

PROBLEM 4-5

The artist known as Tanto created and installed a sculpture in the center of a plaza in the capital city of the nation. The work was designed to bisect the radial lines of the plaza in such a way that, as explained by the artist, "it creates the artistic and aesthetic display of a rift in the lines of the plaza's structure that simulates a rift in the space-time continuum." Soon after the installation, persons living and working near the plaza began to complain about the appearance of the huge sculpture in the plaza. The outcries against the sculpture only increased in intensity when the Cor-Ten steel of the sculpture began to rust in a hugely obvious way, and when the local pigeon population made the sculpture a frequent stopping point for their bathroom breaks. Eventually, the owners of the plaza sought to move the sculpture to a new site in the middle of a field in a public park in the countryside 15 miles outside the capital city. There was no evidence

> that the sculpture would be physically harmed or changed in any way by the removal and reinstallation. Nevertheless, Tanto firmly resisted the move, claiming that the sculpture specifically was designed for the plaza and any move from the plaza would render the work meaningless. Analyze this dispute under the French moral rights laws discussed above and the U.S. states' laws and VARA discussed below.

Site-specific art, particularly in outdoor settings, continues to be a major source of disputes under state preservation acts. *See, e.g.,* Anna Belle Wilder Norton, *Site-Specific Art Gets a Bum Wrap: Illustrating the Limitations of the Visual Artists Rights Act of 1990 Through a Study of Christo and Jeanne-Claude's Unique Art,* 39 Cumb. L. Rev. 749 (2009). As quoted in *Moakley v. Eastwick,* 666 N.E. 2d 505 (Mass. 1996), the Massachusetts Art Preservation Act (MAPA) protects a "work of fine art," defined as an "original work of visual or graphic art of any media." The artistic community and art experts determine what constitutes "fine art."

Serra's Tilted Arc and Site-Specific Art

Richard Serra, a well-known sculptor, enjoyed a period of popularity for his massive outdoor sculptural installations. Several of his large scale works of unadorned corten steel were installed in public places, including on government property. The corten steel was intended by the artist to rust naturally in the open air and elements — it would, over time, acquire an orange-red patina (also known as rust) over most of the work, lovely to some, but to many others with an untrained eye, the sight was a big, ugly wall of rusting metal.

One such installation was *Tilted Arc,* acquired by the General Services Administration for installation at the plaza in front of the United States Court of International Trade in downtown New York City. The work was a large, long wall of corten steel, slightly curved to form an arc, which cut across the longitudinal lines of the plaza.

All was fine until some federal employees and other users of the plaza and the court said that this work was an eyesore. The corten steel does not rust uniformly, nor quickly enough for some observers, who complained that the partially rusted wall of steel simply looked like a mess (not to mention the fact that the local bird population adorned it with other non-decorative elements, too). The employees and visitors said they could not enjoy eating their lunch out in the plaza anymore or even passing by the work on their way into and out of the court building.

The GSA apparently was sympathetic to these complaints, and endeavored to remove the work. Richard Serra sued the GSA to prevent the

12

removal.[13] The removal itself was claimed to be a destruction of the integrity of the work. The GSA promised it could yank it out of the plaza without hurting the sculpture, but Serra pointed out that the conception and design of the work was the important thing that was going to be destroyed. It was a sculpture specifically designed to be installed in a specific location where the arc of the sculpture intersected with the longitudinal lines of the plaza. It was not meant to be a portable work able to be shown here, there, or anywhere. The sculpture would be rendered meaningless if removed from this plaza, and such dishonor to the work would have a tremendously negative effect on Serra's reputation. The GSA said, in effect, "Nuts."

The court in *Serra v. Gen. Services Admin.*[14] agreed with the GSA, and rejected all of Serra's claims and theories about how the work was going to be destroyed by moving it. Serra did not own the work, and he didn't even maintain the copyright to the work. The court read the contract between the GSA and Serra, and found nothing that suggested the work was to be permanently installed in one location. In fact, it found the contrary — that the GSA owned the object and therefore, could do with it what it wanted. It wanted to move it out of the plaza, and there was nothing to stop it from doing so.

Even to this day, after the passage of the United States Visual Artists Rights Act in 1990, which provides a right of integrity, the courts still have trouble understanding or caring about the integrity of site-specific works.[15] In *Phillips v. Pembroke Real Estate, Inc.*, 288 F. Supp. 2d 89 (D. Mass. 2003),

---

12. Images: Michael D. Murray, Collage of three cropped, revised, and resized thumbnail images derived from photographs depicting Richard Serra's "Tilted Arc" sculpture in Foley Square, New York City (2014), the subject of *Serra v. United States Gen. Servs. Admin.*, 847 F.2d 1045 (2d Cir. 1988).

13. *Serra v. United States Gen. Servs. Admin.*, 847 F.2d 1045 (2d Cir. 1988). *See also* Richard Serra, *The Tilted Arc Controversy, Address at the Symposium Art and the Law: Suppression and Liberty*, 19 Cardozo Arts & Ent. L.J. 39 (2001).

14. *Serra*, 847 F.2d at 1045.

15. Francesca Garson, *Before That Artist Came Along, It Was Just A Bridge: The Visual Artists Rights Act and the Removal of Site-Specific Artwork*, 11 Cornell J.L. & Pub. Pol'y 203, 211 (2001); Justin Hughes, *The Line Between Work and Framework, Text and Context*, 19 Cardozo Arts & Ent. L.J. 19 (2001).

aff'd, 459 F.3d 128 (1st Cir. 2006), Phillips claimed that the real estate defendant could not move certain site-specific sculptures designed and installed in an outdoor park.[16] The district court found that the sculpture park as a whole would not meet the definition of a work of "fine art" protected by MAPA, but certain sculptures and other design elements created by the artist and installed along an axis of the park could be considered a single work of fine art. The artist incorporated the landscape as a medium for these works of art. But on review of a certified question of law, the Supreme Judicial Court of Massachusetts held that MAPA protects against physical alteration only, not conceptual alteration (destruction of the meaning of the work). *Phillips v. Pembroke Real Estate, Inc.*, 819 N.E. 2d 579 (Mass. 2004). The First Circuit agreed and found that VARA, too, simply does not afford any protection for site-specific art from conceptual alteration or destruction by removal from its site as long as the physical work itself is not damaged or altered. Phillips' argument that the sculpture installation would lose its meaning if disassembled and removed from its site-specific location was found not to be actionable under either MAPA or VARA. The Court found that the sculptures and design elements could be moved under MAPA and VARA as long they would not suffer physical alteration by removal.

Kelley v. Chicago Park District[17]

In the case of Chapman Kelley against the Chicago Park District, Kelley had installed a conceptual work of art that constituted specifically designed, shaped, and planted installations of wildflowers. The design and planting was intended to produce swathes of color that would change over time as one group of wildflowers bloomed, while others wilted and faded. The installation was completed in 1985.

The work required maintenance, and Kelley had recruited crews of volunteers to weed and care for the installation, but the process was not perfect, and from time to time the installation looked a little weedy and chewed up. Eventually, after several decades, the Park District wanted to cut back on the installation to make room for newer fixtures in the Millennium Park area. Chapman was not consulted; the Park District simply reshaped the beds into a rectangle, planted hedges around each rectangle, replanted some flowers

---

16. Image: Michael D. Murray, Cropped, revised, and resized image derived from a photograph of David Phillips' Eastport Park installation, the subject of *Phillips v. Pembroke Real Estate, Inc.*, 288 F. Supp. 2d 89 (D. Mass. 2003), *aff'd*, 459 F.3d 128 (1st Cir. 2006)

17. *Kelley v. Chicago Park Dist.*, 635 F.3d 290 (7th Cir. 2011).

18

(not according to Kelley's design and intentions), and cut the size down by a third. The new rectangles of flowers are seen here:[19]

Kelley sued the Park District. The district court and the court of appeals denied Kelley's claims under VARA.[20] Kelley never even got close to the terms and requirements of VARA — his lawsuit ship hit an iceberg called the copyright-ability requirements.

The court in each case referred to Kelley's work as a garden. This was a bad start to the narrative of the case. As a garden, it didn't sound much like a work of art — a painting or sculpture — let alone a specific work of visual art. But this observation came second to the court's conception of what Kelley had actually *done* when he produced *Wildflower Works* in the park. The two courts both failed to see how Kelley had created anything because God created plants and flowers, God made them bloom and grow, and let them wither and die, not

---

18. Images: Michael D. Murray, Collage of three cropped, revised, and resized thumbnail images derived from photographs of Chapman Kelley's "Wildflower Works" art installation in Chicago (2014), the subject of *Kelley v. Chicago Park Dist.*, 635 F.3d 290 (7th Cir. 2011).

19. Images: Michael D. Murray, Collage of three cropped, revised, and resized thumbnail images derived from photographs depicting the changes to Chapman Kelley's "Wildflower Works" art installation in Chicago (2014), the subject of *Kelley v. Chicago Park Dist.*, 635 F.3d 290 (7th Cir. 2011).

20. *Kelley v. Chicago Park Dist.*, 635 F.3d 290, 296-306 (7th Cir. 2011).

Kelley. The courts also didn't understand how the work was fixed in a tangible medium of expression; no matter that the work had been extensively designed and described, drawn up in sketches and drawings, and, once planted, was able to be seen, heard, touched, smelt, and felt. This very section of the text has photographs of the work in its conception stage and as installed, and the photos are as real and tangible as the photographic record of any other of the works shown in this book. Nevertheless, plants move, plants grow, and they do a lot of that in spite of Kelley's actions vis-à-vis the plants. So, the work was not fixed, as required for copyright protection, and not created, also as required for copyright protection. Therefore, the work was held to be not copyrightable, and because it is not copyrightable, it was held not to be subject to protection under VARA.[21]

Notes and Questions

1. Do you think moral rights protection encourages the growth of a successful and diverse art market or simply protects artists from exploitation (or both)?

2. Does the protection of moral rights create transaction costs for any patron who wishes to do business with artists? Would the problem be alleviated if moral rights were protected as the default rule, but the rights could be bargained away by express contract terms supported by consideration? Or does this arrangement provide too little protection for all but the most successful, established artists?

3. Although VARA (discussed in the section below) may preempt many state preservation acts that duplicate the rights of integrity and attribution defined in VARA, state legislatures may be able to provide additional moral rights protections beyond those provided in VARA. What are the advantages and disadvantages of having local state protections of certain rights and federal (national) protection of other rights? What if the state-granted rights cannot be waived by contract?

C. Visual Artists Rights Act of 1990

Moral rights principles developed in civil law jurisdictions have long been considered antagonistic to the firmly entrenched property rights of owners in common law jurisdictions. Copyright law in the United States was formulated to guarantee the artist's exploitation rights in a work and steered as far as possible away from intangible rights of personality stemming directly from the

---

21. *Id.*

act of creation. Legal theories such as defamation, unfair competition, and invasion of privacy, in conjunction with contract law and copyrights, can sometimes approximate and even duplicate explicit moral rights protection. *See* Comment, *Toward Artistic Integrity: Implementing Moral Rights Through Extension of Existing American Legal Doctrines*, 60 GEO. L.J. 1539 (1972). Significant gaps in protection, nevertheless, exist at the expense of the artistic community.

Protection of certain minimal moral rights became mandatory when the United States became a signatory to the Berne Convention in 1988. Prior to that time, the United States had been a signatory to the Universal Copyright Convention (UCC), promulgated by the United States in 1952 as a compromise to joining Berne. *See* Chapter 2, "Copyrights." As was seen in the *Huston* case (concerning the colorized version of *The Asphalt Jungle*), the UCC requires that a country protect works of aliens in the same way residents' works are protected, although protection is afforded only on the basis of national copyright laws.[22]

The Copyright Revision Act of 1976 opened the door to U.S. Berne membership. Ratification finally occurred in 1988 as a result of extensive lobbying, although it appears that much of the lobbying was on behalf of exporters of copyrighted material rather than artists' rights advocates. *See* Ossola, *Law for Art's Sake*, LEGAL TIMES, Dec. 10, 1990, at 27. As the Berne treaty is not self-executing, Congress was required to pass enabling legislation which needed to encompass artist protection commensurate with the treaty's terms.

In 1990, Congress finally passed VARA in a scarcely-noticed amendment to the Judicial Improvement Act. Pub. L. No. 101-650 (codified at 17 U.S.C. §§ 101, 106A, and 113).[23] VARA amends the Copyright Revision Act by providing to "authors" of certain types of singular or limited edition artwork the rights of attribution and integrity. These rights may be enforced by any applicable remedy, other than criminal penalties, available for infringement under the Copyright Act. Consistent with their European models, but unlike many of the other rights guaranteed by the Copyright Act, the rights provided under VARA belong solely to the artist and are not transferable. Assignment of the copyright or any part thereof in works covered by VARA does not deprive the artist of VARA protection, and an assignee of the copyright or any part thereof does not thereby obtain standing under VARA. Similarly, joint authors of works covered by VARA are co-owners of these rights.

The following sections will examine the effect that VARA is expected to have on recurring and novel problems facing artists.

---

22. *See* Note, *Protection for Creators in the United States and Abroad*, 24 U. PITT. L. REV. 817 (1963).

23. Pub. L. 101-650, Title VI, § 603(a), Dec. 1, 1990, 104 Stat. 5128 (as mentioned in Part 1 above, VARA was a rider to a Judicial Improvements Bill). One of the co-authors of this book, Leonard D. DuBoff, was involved in drafting this law at the request of the late Ted Kennedy, senator of Massachusetts. DuBoff also testified in Congress in support of VARA's adoption. Interestingly enough, his former colleague from Stanford Law School and another lawyer in this field, John Henry Merryman, testified against the adoption of VARA.

1. Visual Art under VARA

The Visual Artists Rights Act offers protection to a more limited class of works than does the Copyright Act, applying only to a "work of visual art" that is defined as "a painting, drawing, print, or sculpture, existing in a single copy, in a limited edition of 200 copies or fewer that are signed and consecutively numbered by the author, or, in the case of a sculpture, in multiple cast, carved, or fabricated sculptures of 200 or fewer that are consecutively numbered by the author and bear the signature or other identifying mark of the author...." 17 U.S.C. § 101.

Coverage also extends to a photographic image produced for exhibition purposes only as a signed single copy or signed, numbered limited edition of 200 or fewer. *Id.* The Act's protection does not extend to any "poster, map, globe, chart, technical drawing, diagram, model, applied art, motion picture, or other audio-visual work, book, magazine, newspaper, periodical, data base, electronic information service, electronic publication, or similar publication; nor any merchandising item or advertising, promotional, descriptive, covering, or packaging material or container"; nor to any work for hire; nor any work not subject to copyright protection under the Copyright Act. *Id.*

Notes and Questions

1. *Silberman v. Innovation Luggage, Inc.*, 2003 Copr. L. Dec. ¶28,600, 67 U.S.P.Q. 2d 1489 (S.D.N.Y. Apr. 3, 2003), points out an immediate problem with VARA's limited definition of "visual art": second generation copies are not protected. Thus, artists whose work is produced and shown in series or otherwise intended for reproduction beyond the narrow limits in the Act lose the protections of VARA except as to the original prints or paintings, which may not be intended to be exposed to the public. What could be the rationale for these distinctions?
2. Computer artists may never obtain the protections of VARA because their "original" works most likely are digitalized files on the artist's own hard drive, and any manifestation of the work that can be seen and enjoyed by the public — whether uploaded to a website or downloaded to a viewer's computer or transferred to a client by hard media or electronic transmission — is going to be a copy of the original work. Should an exception be made for computer art, or not?

2. Right of Attribution

The Visual Artists Rights Act allows an artist to claim authorship of a work he or she created. § 603(a). The author also has the right "to prevent the use of his or her name as the author of any work of visual art which he or she did not create." In addition, the author may "prevent the use of his or her name as author of the work of visual art in the event of a distortion, mutilation, or other modification of the work which would be prejudicial to his or her honor or reputation." *Id.*

The rights guaranteed under VARA may be waived if the author expressly agrees to such waiver in a written instrument that is signed by the author and which applies to specifically identified works and uses of those works. 17 U.S.C. § 106A(e). Transfer of copyright in a work does not itself, however, constitute waiver.

Given the waiver allowance under VARA, it would appear, in light of *Vargas v. Esquire, supra,* that Congress did not go far enough toward that end. The waiver provision was a contentious element of the final version of VARA, given its obvious potential to effectively nullify the Act's moral rights protection. Earlier versions of the bill excluded the provision, which reads:

> [T]hose rights may be waived if the author expressly agrees to such waiver in a written instrument signed by the author. Such instrument shall specifically identify the work, and uses of that work, to which the waiver applies, and the waiver shall apply only to the work and uses so identified. In the case of a joint work prepared by two or more authors, a waiver of rights under this paragraph made by one such author waives such rights for all such authors.

17 U.S.C. § 106A(e)(1).

By way of compromise, the Register of Copyrights was instructed to conduct a study on the extent to which such waivers take place and report to Congress. Note that, under VARA, the right to paternity for works within its purview is presumed, absent waiver, which is the opposite of prior law. *See Granz v. Harris,* 198 F.2d 585 (2d Cir. 1952); *Lake v. Universal Pictures Co.,* 95 F. Supp. 768 (S.D. Cal. 1950) (holding that the right of paternity, recognizing authorship, must be spelled out in a contract); *but see Harms, Inc. v. Tops Music Enters., Inc.,* 160 F. Supp. 77 (S.D. Cal. 1958) (courts will protect against "the omission of the author's name, unless by contract, the right is given to the publisher to do so").

VARA excludes from coverage any book, magazine, newspaper, or periodical. 17 U.S.C. § 101. The act provides that joint authors are co-owners of their rights, including the right of attribution. 17 U.S.C. § 106A(b).

The converse of the artist's right of paternity, as provided by VARA, is "to prevent the use of his or her name as the author of any work . . . which he or she did not create." 17 U.S.C. § 106A(a)(1)(B). The act does not expressly grant the right to use pseudonyms.

3. The Right of Integrity

The right to integrity is the moral right that is most dependent upon a clear and explicit recognition of the intimate relationship between the artist and the artist's creation. The Visual Artists Rights Act accords artists the right "to prevent any intentional distortion, mutilation, or other modification of that work which would be prejudicial to his or her honor or reputation." 17 U.S.C. § 106(a)(3). The act further states "any intentional distortion, mutilation or modification of that work is a violation of that right." *Id.*

VARA provides the artist the right to "prevent any destruction of a work of recognized stature," adding that "any intentional or grossly negligent destruction of that work is a violation of that right." 17 U.S.C. § 106A(a)(3)(B). The Act limits the integrity protection to guard against intentional acts by persons other than the artist. Drafters of VARA were careful to exclude from prohibition any "modification resulting from passage of time or the inherent nature of the materials, [and any] modification which is the result of conservation, or of the public presentation, including lighting and placement of the work is not a destruction, distortion or other modification unless caused by gross negligence." 17 U.S.C. § 106A(c)(1), (2).

Carter v. Helmsley-Spear, Inc.

71 F.3d 77 (2d Cir. 1995)*

CARDAMONE, Circuit Judge.

Defendants 474431 Associates and Helmsley-Spear, Inc. (defendants or appellants), as the owner and managing agent respectively, of a commercial building in Queens, New York, appeal from an order of the United States District Court for the Southern District of New York (Edelstein, J.), entered on September 6, 1994 following a bench trial. The order granted plaintiffs, who are three artists, a permanent injunction that enjoined defendants from removing, modifying or destroying a work of visual art that had been installed in defendants' building by plaintiffs-artists commissioned by a former tenant to install the work. . . .

On this appeal we deal with an Act of Congress that protects the rights of artists to preserve their works. One of America's most insightful thinkers observed that a country is not truly civilized "where the arts, such as they have, are all imported, having no indigenous life." 7 Works of Ralph Waldo Emerson, Society and Solitude, Chap. II Civilization 34 (AMS ed. 1968). From such reflection it follows that American artists are to be encouraged by laws that protect their works. Although Congress in the statute before us did just that, it did not mandate the preservation of art at all costs and without due regard for the rights of others.

For the reasons that follow, we reverse and vacate the grant of injunctive relief to plaintiffs. . . .

BACKGROUND

Defendant 474431 Associates (Associates) is the owner of a mixed use commercial building located at 47-44 31st Street, Queens, New York, which

---

* Footnotes and some citations omitted.

it has owned since 1978. Associates is a New York general partnership. The general partners are Alvin Schwartz and Supervisory Management Corp., a wholly-owned subsidiary of Helmsley Enterprises, Inc. Defendant Helmsley-Spear, Inc. is the current managing agent of the property for Associates.

On February 1, 1990 Associates entered into a 48-year net lease, leasing the building to 47-44 31st Street Associates, L.P. (Limited Partnership), a Delaware limited partnership. From February 1, 1990 until June 1993, Irwin Cohen or an entity under his control was the general partner of the Limited Partnership, and managed the property through Cohen's SIG Management Company (SIG). Corporate Life Insurance Company (Corporate Life) was a limited partner in the Limited Partnership. In June 1993 SIG ceased its involvement with the property and Corporate Life, through an entity controlled by it, became the general partner of the Limited Partnership. The property was then managed by the Limited Partnership, through Theodore Nering, a Corporate Life representative. *See* 861 F. Supp. at 312. There is no relationship, other than the lease, between Associates, the lessor, and the Limited Partnership, the lessee. . . .

Plaintiffs John Carter, John Swing and John Veronis (artists or plaintiffs) are professional sculptors who work together and are known collectively as the "Three-J's" or "Jx3." On December 16, 1991 SIG entered into a one-year agreement with the plaintiffs "engag[ing] and hir[ing] the Artists . . . to design, create and install sculpture and other permanent installations" in the building, primarily the lobby. Under the agreement plaintiffs had "full authority in design, color and style," and SIG retained authority to direct the location and installation of the artwork within the building. The artists were to retain copyrights to their work and SIG was to receive 50 percent of any proceeds from its exploitation. On January 20, 1993 SIG and the artists signed an agreement extending the duration of their commission for an additional year. When Corporate Life became a general partner of the Limited Partnership, the Limited Partnership assumed the agreement with plaintiffs and in December 1993 again extended the agreement.

The artwork that is the subject of this litigation is a very large "walk-through sculpture" occupying most, but not all, of the building's lobby. The artwork consists of a variety of sculptural elements constructed from recycled materials, much of it metal, affixed to the walls and ceiling, and a vast mosaic made from pieces of recycled glass embedded in the floor and walls. Elements of the work include a giant hand fashioned from an old school bus, a face made of automobile parts, and a number of interactive components. These assorted elements make up a theme relating to environmental concerns and the significance of recycling.

The Limited Partnership's lease on the building was terminated on March 31, 1994. It filed for bankruptcy one week later. The property was surrendered to defendant Associates on April 6, 1994 and defendant Helmsley-Spear, Inc. took over management of the property. Representatives of defendants informed the artists that they could no longer continue to install artwork at the property, and instead had to vacate the building. These representatives also made statements indicating that defendants intended to remove the artwork already in place in the building's lobby.

As a result of defendants' actions, artists commenced this litigation. On April 26, 1994 the district court issued a temporary restraining order enjoining defendants from taking any action to alter, deface, modify or mutilate the artwork installed in the building. In May 1994 a hearing was held on whether a preliminary injunction should issue. The district court subsequently granted a preliminary injunction enjoining defendants from removing the artwork pending the resolution of the instant litigation. A bench trial was subsequently held in June and July 1994, at the conclusion of which the trial court granted the artists the permanent injunction prohibiting defendants from distorting, mutilating, modifying, destroying and removing plaintiffs' artwork. The injunction is to remain in effect for the lifetimes of the three plaintiffs. . . .

DISCUSSION

II. Work of Visual Art

. . . The district court determined that the work of art installed in the lobby of Associates' building was a work of visual art as defined by VARA; that distortion, mutilation, or modification of the work would prejudice plaintiffs' honor and reputations; that the work was of recognized stature, thus protecting it from destruction (including removal that would result in destruction); and that Associates consented to or ratified the installation of the work in its building. The result was that defendants were enjoined from removing or otherwise altering the work during the lifetimes of the three artists. . . .

B. The Statutory Definition

A "work of visual art" is defined by the Act in terms both positive (what it is) and negative (what it is not). In relevant part VARA defines a work of visual art as "a painting, drawing, print, or sculpture, existing in a single copy" or in a limited edition of 200 copies or fewer. 17 U.S.C. § 101. Although defendants aver that elements of the work are not visual art, their contention is foreclosed by the factual finding that the work is a single, indivisible whole. Concededly, considered as a whole, the work is a sculpture and exists only in a single copy. Therefore, the work satisfies the Act's positive definition of a work of visual art. We next turn to the second part of the statutory definition — what is not a work of visual art.

The definition of visual art excludes "any poster, map, globe, chart, technical drawing, diagram, model, applied art, motion picture or other audio-visual work." 17 U.S.C. § 101. Congress meant to distinguish works of visual art from other media, such as audio-visual works and motion pictures, due to the different circumstances surrounding how works of each genre are created and disseminated. See H.R. Rep. No. 514 at 9. Although this concern led to a narrow definition of works of visual art,

[t]he courts should use common sense and generally accepted standards of the artistic community in determining whether a particular work falls within the scope of the definition. Artists may work in a variety of media, and use any number of materials in creating their works. Therefore, whether a particular work falls within the definition should not depend on the medium or materials used.

Id. at 11.

"Applied art" describes "two- and three-dimensional ornamentation or decoration that is affixed to otherwise utilitarian objects." *Carter,* 861 F. Supp. at 315, citing *Kieselstein-Cord v. Accessories By Pearl, Inc.,* 632 F.2d 989, 997 (2d Cir. 1980). Defendants' assertion that at least parts of the work are applied art appears to rest on the fact that some of the sculptural elements are affixed to the lobby's floor, walls, and ceiling—all utilitarian objects. Interpreting applied art to include such works would render meaningless VARA's protection for works of visual art installed in buildings. A court should not read one part of a statute so as to deprive another part of meaning.

Appellants do not suggest the entire work is applied art. The district court correctly stated that even if components of the work standing alone were applied art, "nothing in VARA proscribes protection of works of visual art that incorporate elements of, rather than constitute, applied art." 861 F. Supp. at 315. VARA's legislative history leaves no doubt that "a new and independent work created from snippets of [excluded] materials, such as a collage, is of course not excluded" from the definition of a work of visual art. H.R. Rep. No. 514 at 14. The trial judge correctly ruled the work is not applied art precluded from protection under the Act.

III. Work Made for Hire

Also excluded from the definition of a work of visual art is any work made for hire. 17 U.S.C. § 101(2)(B). A "work made for hire" is defined in the Copyright Act, in relevant part, as "a work prepared by an employee within the scope of his or her employment." *Id.* § 101(1). Appellants maintain the work was made for hire and therefore is not a work of visual art under VARA. The district court held otherwise, finding that the plaintiffs were hired as independent contractors. . . .

The district court properly noted that *Aymes*[*v. Bonelli,* 980 F.2d 857 (2d Cir. 1992),] established five factors which would be relevant in nearly all cases: the right to control the manner and means of production; requisite skill; provision of employee benefits; tax treatment of the hired party; whether the hired party may be assigned additional projects. *See* 980 F.2d at 861. Analysis begins with a discussion of these factors.

First, plaintiffs had complete artistic freedom with respect to every aspect of the sculpture's creation. Although the artists heeded advice or accepted suggestions from building engineers, architects, and others, such actions were not a relinquishment of their artistic freedom. The evidence strongly supports the finding that plaintiffs controlled the work's "manner and means." This fact, in turn, lent credence to their contention that they were independent contractors. While artistic freedom remains a central factor in our inquiry, the Supreme Court has cautioned that "the extent of control the hiring party exercises over the details of the product is not dispositive." *Reid*, 490 U.S. at 752, 109 S. Ct. at 2179. Hence, resolving the question of whether plaintiffs had artistic freedom does not end the analysis.

The district court also correctly found the artists' conception and execution of the work required great skill in execution. Appellants' contention that the plaintiffs' reliance on assistants in some way mitigates the skill required for this work is meritless, particularly because each of the plaintiffs is a professional sculptor and the parties stipulated that professional sculpting is a highly skilled occupation. The right to control the manner and means and the requisite skill needed for execution of this project were both properly found by the district court to weigh against "work for hire" status.

The trial court erred, however, when it ruled that the defendants could not assign the artists additional projects. First, the employment agreement between SIG Management Company and the artists clearly states that the artists agreed not only to install the sculpture but also to "render such other related services and duties as may be assigned to [them] from time to time by the Company." By the very terms of the contract the defendants and their predecessors in interest had the right to assign other related projects to the artists. The district court incorrectly decided that this language supported the artists' claim to be independent contractors. While the artists' obligations were limited to related services and duties, the defendants nonetheless did have the right to assign to plaintiffs work other than the principal sculpture.

Further, the defendants did, in fact, assign such other projects. The district court concedes as much, explaining that "plaintiffs did create art work on the property other than that in the Lobby." *Carter*, 861 F. Supp. at 319. The record shows the artists performed projects on the sixth floor of the building, on the eighth floor, and in the boiler room. Thus, on at least three different occasions the plaintiffs were assigned additional projects, which they completed without further compensation. The trial court suggests this fact "does not undermine plaintiffs' contention that they were hired solely to install art work on the Property." *Id.* We disagree. If the artists were hired to perform work other than the sculpture (as both their employment agreement and their actual practice suggests) then they were not hired solely to install the sculpture. It makes no difference that all work performed by the plaintiffs was artistic in nature. The point is that the performance of other assigned work not of the artists' choosing supports a conclusion that the artists were not independent contractors but employees.

We must also consider factors the district court correctly found to favor finding the sculpture to be work for hire. Specifically, the provision of employee benefits and the tax treatment of the plaintiffs weigh strongly in favor of employee status. The defendants paid payroll and social security taxes, provided employee benefits such as life, health, and liability insurance and paid vacations, and contributed to unemployment insurance and workers' compensation funds on plaintiffs' behalf. Moreover, two of the three artists filed for unemployment benefits after their positions were terminated, listing the building's management company as their former employer. Other formal indicia of an employment relationship existed. For instance, each plaintiff was paid a weekly salary. The artists also agreed in their written contract that they would work principally for the defendants for the duration of their agreement on a 40-hour per week basis and they would only do other work to the extent that it would not "interfere with services to be provided" to the defendants. All of these facts strongly suggest the artists were employees.

Some of the other *Reid* factors bolster this view. The artists were provided with many (if not most) of the supplies used to create the sculpture. This factor was not, as the district court found, "inconclusive." The court also wrongly ruled that plaintiffs were hired for a "finite term of engagement." In fact, they were employed for a substantial period of time, their work continuing for over two years with no set date of termination (other than the sculpture's completion). Nor was the fact that the artists could not hire paid assistants without the defendants' approval "inconclusive" as the trial court erroneously found. Instead, this and the other just enumerated factors point towards an employer-employee relationship between the parties.

In reaching its conclusion, the district court also relied partly on the artists' copyright ownership of the sculpture, viewing such ownership as a "plus factor." We are not certain whether this element is a "plus factor," and therefore put off for another day deciding whether copyright ownership is probative of independent contractor status. Even were it to be weighed as a "plus factor," it would not change the outcome in this case....

These factors, properly considered and weighed with the employee benefits granted plaintiffs and the tax treatment accorded them, are more than sufficient to demonstrate that the artists were employees, and the sculpture is therefore a work made for hire as a matter of law....

Finally, since we have determined that the work is one made for hire and therefore outside the scope of VARA's protection, we need not discuss that Act's broad protection of visual art and the protection it affords works of art incorporated into a building. Also, as plaintiffs' sculpture was not protected from removal because the artists were employees and not independent contractors, we need not reach the defendants' Fifth Amendment takings argument. Moreover, because the sculpture is not protected by VARA from removal resulting in its destruction or alteration, we do not address plaintiffs' contentions that VARA entitles them to complete the "unfinished" portion of the work, that they are entitled to reasonable costs and attorney's fees, and that appellants tortiously interfered with the artists' contract with SIG and the Limited Partnership....

Accordingly, the district court's order insofar as it held the work was one not made for hire is reversed and the injunction vacated.

Mural, Mural . . . on the Wall

An entire mini-course could be taught just on the topic of murals and moral rights. Building owners ask for the murals, commission the murals, or just allow the work of an artist to remain on their walls. All is fine, until the owner's interest wanes, the art fades or starts to peel off, or the owner simply decides he wants something else on his wall.

24

Enter the moral rights question: does the building owner simply get to paint over the work or is this a violation of the right of integrity? Even in the United States, the artist may have a claim, but it will depend on whether the mural is removable or not. If it is not removable, it is held to be part of the owner's property, and the artist has no integrity rights in the mural. But if it is removable, the owner must notify the artist and give her a chance to remove the work, and if the owner simply paints over the work, the owner may be liable to the artist for damages to the artist's reputation.

The Right of Integrity and Murals

Murals have their own required analysis in 17 U.S.C. § 113, which applies to murals installed before VARA, or murals installed by written agreement with the property owner after the passage of VARA:

> Point 1: If the mural was installed with the artist and the building owner knowing that the art cannot be removed without damage affecting the integrity of the work, then no VARA protection applies.

This may sound incongruous — removal would hurt the art, so VARA does not protect the art at all — but it has a practical aspect. In these scenarios, the art has become part of the building, so the building owner has the paramount right to control the property. The artist is presumed to know that this situation means that she is donating her work to become part of the building. She should understand that this act constitutes a waiver of VARA rights over the mural, and by going through with the project, the artist is treated as having consented to the de facto waiver of VARA protection.

> Point 2: If the mural can be removed without destruction or damage affecting the integrity of the work, then the building owner must give notice to the artist or

---

24. Michael D. Murray, Two cropped, revised, and resized thumbnail images derived from photographs depicting Shepard Fairey's "Duality of Humanity 4 Pike Street" mural in Cincinnati, and a man painting over that same mural (2016).

make a diligent attempt to locate the artist so as to be able to notify them of the intention to remove the art. If the artist receives the notice, the artist has 90 days to remove or pay for removal of the art. If the artist received notice and does nothing for 90 days, or if the artist cannot be located after diligent attempts, then the owner may proceed to remove or obliterate the art as he sees fit.

This provision may have become a little more troublesome for building owners, because modern art restoration and preservation technology now allows technicians the opportunity to remove and preserve intact almost any mural painted on a surface. Murals can be lifted off of the surface with special adhesives that attach the paint to a new mount (the "transport mount"), which allows the whole mural or large pieces of it to be moved to a new surface, and the transported paint is then attached to the new surface with a different set of special adhesives, and lastly, the paint is loosened from the transport mount by special solvents that free the paint from the transport mount without harming the paint and without loosening it from its new installation surface. This technique works on many painted surfaces, but not all. What is excluded is the kind of installation where the paint soaks in or otherwise becomes part of the surface of the wall. For example, the creation of frescos — a centuries-old technique whereby paint pigments are spread on wet plaster that is left to dry with the plaster retaining the coloration of the paint — produces a single colored mass of plaster, rather than a skin of paint sitting on the surface of the wall. Applications such as these are not susceptible to removal by the adhesion-transfer method described above, and would fall under the "not removable" terms excluding them from VARA protection. But for many other applications, the murals are removable without destroying the painting, putting the onus on building owners to find and give notice to the artist. (Note that VARA itself provides a registration system for murals considered to be removable, which registers the name and address of the artist, and it is considered duly diligent to send the notice to the artist at that last known, registered address). Even when notice is given, however, the artist may not want to pay the expense and expend the effort to remove the art. If notice is given, and there is no action by the artist for 90 days, the mural may be painted over or otherwise removed by the building owner.

Case Study: Ruscha Mural

Kent Twitchell's mural of artist, Ed Ruscha, located on a building in Los Angeles, was painted in 1978. VARA still applies to works installed before its effective date in 1991, as long as the artist still owns the copyright to the work and has not waived his moral rights in a subsequent contract. In 2006, the mural was completely painted over. Does VARA apply?

- It was a painting — so, it was a work of visual art.
- It was original, created by the artist, and fixed in a tangible medium — so, it was copyrightable.

Was it a work of recognized stature?

- Apparently yes, the artist and the work were fairly well renowned in the Los Angeles area.

25

Under 17 U.S.C. § 113, was it removable?

■ Maybe not at the time of painting, but certainly today. This one would require some research and thought.

Was notice given to the artist?

■ No, and the artist would have wanted to try to do something other than just paint over the work.

Was there damage to the artist's reputation?

■ Very likely. The work was large and proudly displayed, so its complete obliteration would be a large reputational slap in the face to the artist.

The building owners responsible for painting over the work must have felt guilty — i.e., they anticipated that they had some measure of exposure to liability — because they settled with the artist for $1.1 million.

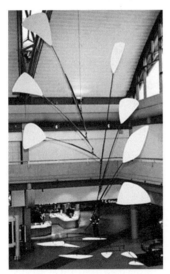

Calder's Pittsburgh mobile, restored to its original colors and mobility

Notes and Questions

1. VARA was designed to curb the kind of notorious abuses against artists that received a great deal of negative publicity, such as the painting over and immobilizing of Calder's mobile by Allegheny County, Pennsylvania officials, *see* Rose, *Calder's "Pittsburgh": A Violated and Immobile Mobile*, ARTnews, Jan. 1978, at 39.[26] The violation of Calder's work also prompted the passage of the Pennsylvania Fine Arts Preservation Act (Pa. Stat. Ann. tit. 73, §§ 2101-10). In 1946, a mural by Alfred Crimi that had been incorporated into a church interior was painted over in order to cover up more of Christ's chest than was originally

---

25. Michael D. Murray, Cropped, revised, and resized thumbnail image derived from a photograph of Kent Twitchell's mural, "Portrait of artist, Ed Ruscha" (1978), located on a building in Los Angeles (2014).

26. Image: Michael D. Murray, Cropped, revised, and resized thumbnail image derived from a photograph of Alexander Calder's Pittsburgh mobile, restored to its original colors and mobility, the subject of Calder's dispute with Allegheny County, PA (2014).

displayed in the painting. *See Crimi v. Rutgers Presbyterian Church,* 89 N.Y.S. 2d 813 (1949). Crimi was one of the most powerful and effective voices to testify before the Senate subcommittee that was considering the VARA bill and is regarded as having played a large role in helping the bill become law.

2. In spite of the limitations of VARA noted above, the Act does have teeth and can successfully be used to vindicate artists' moral rights. Jan Martin, an artist who had created a large outdoor sculpture on property later acquired by the City of Indianapolis, brought suit after the city demolished the sculpture. The sculpture was installed well before VARA's effective date in 1991, but the court found that VARA recognizes continuing rights of artists in their works installed prior to enactment. The court found that the city had failed to make any attempt to give Martin notice and afford him a chance to remove the work, and therefore had violated Martin's rights under VARA, and awarded him $20,000 in statutory damages plus $131,253 in attorneys' fees and costs. *Martin v. City of Indianapolis,* 982 F. Supp. 625 (S.D. Ind. 1997), *aff'd,* 192 F.3d 608 (7th Cir. 1999), and 4 F. Supp. 2d 808, *aff'd,* 192 F.3d 608 (7th Cir. 1999).

3. In *Pollara v. Seymour,* 344 F.3d 265 (2d Cir. 2003), Pollara claimed that defendants, Seymour and Casey, unlawfully damaged and destroyed a work of art created by her. The work in question was a large painted banner created for a nonprofit group's information table. Upon learning of the display of the banner one evening, Casey removed it, tearing it in the process. In describing its role in determining whether a work is a work of art, the court stated: "We steer clear of an interpretation of VARA that would require courts to assess either the worth of a purported work of visual art, or the worth of the purpose for which the work was created. Congress chose to protect in VARA only a narrow subset of the many different forms and types of what can be called art, and expressly left unprotected works created for the primary purpose of promoting or advertising. Having concluded that the banner is such a work, our task is done." *Id.* at 271.

4. VARA excludes protection for motion pictures or other audio visual works, thus avoiding some of the trickier disputes over editing (*Gilliam, supra*) and colorization (*Huston, supra*) of films and television programs that troubled both the moral rights regime in France and the non-moral rights regime in the United States. Issues regarding aftermarket editing of motion pictures to remove violent, scatological, and other adult content present a thorny issue under the non-VARA copyright and trademark principles discussed in *Gilliam* and *Dastar. See* Michael P. Glasser, *"To Clean or not to Clean:" An Analysis of the Copyright and Trademark Issues Surrounding the Legal Battles Between Third Party Film Editors and the Film Industry,* 22 Cardozo Arts & Ent. L.J. 129 (2004).

5. For work that may be protected from copying or alteration by protective devices, in particular, works that can exist in a digital media, the Digital

Millennium Copyright Act (DMCA), 17 U.S.C. §§ 1201 et seq., might protect copyrights better than moral rights. Many copyright owners use technological measures to protect their works from alteration. The DMCA makes it illegal to distribute devices or services to circumvent the technological measures. If a person does circumvent the measures and alter the work, it would be copyright infringement. *See* Jane C. Ginsburg, *Suppression and Liberty: Have Moral Rights Come of (Digital) Age in the United States?*, 19 Cardozo Arts & Ent. L.J. 9, 13 (2001).

6. In *Lilley v. Stout*, 384 F. Supp. 2d 83 (D.D.C. 2005), plaintiff brought a cause of action under VARA stating that defendant violated the plaintiff's right of attribution and integrity. Defendant created photographs from the negatives of photos taken of the plaintiff and used the actual photos in the artwork rather than use the photos as a model for artwork (as per the parties' agreement). The court found the photographs produced from a negative to be still photographic images of art that were visual. Nevertheless, the suit was dismissed for failure to state a claim because the "plaintiff's own assertions demonstrate that the discrete photographs at issue were not produced solely for exhibition purposes" as required by 17 U.S.C. § 101's definition of photographic visual art for VARA purposes. Accordingly, the photographic prints were found not to be "work[s] of visual art" and did not trigger VARA's protection. *See also Nogueras v. Home Depot*, 330 F. Supp. 2d 48 (D.P.R. 2004) (VARA does not apply to use on advertising material).

7. *English v. CFC&R East 11th Street LLC*, No. 97 Civ. 7446(HB), 1997 WL 746444 (S.D.N.Y. Dec. 3, 1997), *aff'd sub nom English v. BFC Partners*, 198 F.3d 233 (2nd Cir. 1999) (TABLE), held that VARA does not apply to artwork that is illegally placed on the property of others without their consent. Plaintiffs claimed a protectable interest in an outdoor garden project, claiming it was a single unified work of art, but the court rejected the claim, deciding that whether or not it was a single work of art, it could not enjoy VARA integrity protection because it was illegally placed on city property and could not be removed as a whole.

4. Works of Recognized Stature

VARA's protection against destruction only extends to works of "recognized stature." The French moral rights law makes no such "recognized stature" distinction and, as a result, judges in that country may avoid the spectacle of "putting the victim on trial" or otherwise engaging in case-by-case aesthetic evaluations. Congress has instructed the courts to use common sense in deciding what is "art" for purposes of the Act. H. Rep. No. 101-514 (1990).

Carter v. Helmsley Spear, supra, created a test for determining works of recognized stature. The test formulated by the district court required:

(1) that the visual art in question has "stature," i.e. is viewed as merito-rious, and

(2) that this stature is "recognized" by art experts, other members of the artistic community, or by some cross-section of society.

In making this showing, plaintiffs generally, but not inevitably, will need to call expert witnesses to testify before the trier of fact. *Carter*, 861 F. Supp. at 325.

Martin v. City of Indianapolis, 192 F.3d 612-13, adopted the stature test laid out in *Carter*. Plaintiff Martin's evidence of "stature" consisted of certain newspaper and magazine articles, and various letters, including a letter from an art gallery director and a letter to the editor of The Indianapolis News, all in support of the sculpture. The court accepted this proof that this work had reached recognized stature over defendant's hearsay objections and ruled that plaintiff had met his burden on the "stature" element. *Id.* at 612-13. The court did not require expert testimony as to the value of the work, which would have presented enormous problems for the plaintiff because defendant had destroyed the work in question before experts had any chance to examine the work in connection with the suit. *Id.*

Later cases have adopted a more conservative approach in defining a work of "recognized stature" under VARA. For example, in *Scott v. Dixon*, 309 F. Supp. 2d 395 (E.D.N.Y. 2004), Scott created a swan sculpture for Dixon's backyard. Scott is best known for creating the sculpture, "Stargazer Deer," located in the same county as the swan sculpture. When Dixon sold the property he removed the swan sculpture. Dixon paid a construction company to remove the sculpture and put it in storage. Due to improper storage, the sculpture became rusted and bent. Scott sued under VARA. In evaluating whether the work was a "work of recognized stature," the court affirmed that "The stature of a work of art is generally established through expert testimony." Scott only had local notoriety, which did not extend to each one of her sculptures. The swan sculpture was not viewed by the public or critics. Scott did not submit any evidence about the notoriety of the swan sculpture. Therefore, the court found that Scott failed to establish this element of the cause of action, and dismissed Scott's claim.

In *Pollara v. Seymour*, 206 F. Supp. 2d 333 (N.D.N.Y. 2002), the court found that while plaintiff's works in general were unquestionably meritorious, and this merit was recognized by her experts, the work at issue in the case (a mural painted upon a banner) was intended solely as a display piece for a one-time event. The court stated, "It defies the underlying purposes of VARA to assume that the statute was intended to protect works of artistic merit without regard to whether such works were ever intended as 'art' or whether they were intended to be displayed as art or were otherwise intended to be preserved for posterity as works of artistic merit. This is particularly true where, as here, there was never any intent by the artist to preserve her work for future display." *Id.* at 336. The court found that the mural at issue in the case would have been used solely to publicize a one-time event and would not have been preserved as a work of stature—recognized or otherwise. *Id.* at 337. Accordingly, the court held that plaintiff had failed to meet her burden of demonstrating that her mural was a "work of recognized stature," and her VARA claim was dismissed as a matter of law.

Notes and Questions

1. What should be the standard for a work of "recognized stature" under VARA? What is the public policy purpose served by requiring such a determination? As noted above, Congress has instructed the courts to use common sense in deciding what is "art" for purposes of the Act. H. Rep. No. 101-514 (1990). The question of what constitutes a "work of recognized stature" for purposes of the prohibition of destruction is to be determined by the expert testimony of scholars, curators, and, presumably, collectors. Does this system provide appropriate protection for new and not-yet-established artists whose works nonetheless may contribute a great deal to the culture and art scene of a university, a town, or a region?

2. Should an artist be forced to prove actual damage to his honor and reputation? The French law contains no requirement for a showing of damage to honor or reputation. The Visual Artists Rights Act is drafted to presume such damage, but the requirement is nevertheless bound to focus attention on an issue unrelated to rights that, in theory, stem from the personality of the artist. The act's orientation toward the artist's reputation is, perhaps, a justification for its unprecedented use of the federal commerce power in this instance. It would seem that such a limitation on traditional property rights for an indefinite number of years beyond the sale of a work is uniquely within the state's police power to protect the public welfare. By emphasizing potential damage to an artist's reputation, Congress retained the posture of commercial regulation in its protection of artists' moral rights. In any event, the reputation requirement is likely to be of little consequence. In applying the requirement, the legislative history admonishes the courts to "focus on the artistic or professional honor or reputation of the individual as embodied in the work that is protected." H. Rep. No. 101-514 (1990).

5. Duration

Signatories to the Berne Convention typically protect covered work for a period of the life of the author plus 50 to 70 years. Although copyright protection for works created by individuals runs for the same term under the Copyright Revision Act, the protection offered by VARA runs only for the life of the author or, in the case of joint authors, for the life of the last surviving author. 17 U.S.C. § 106A(d)(1), (3). Coverage is prospective, protecting works created and sold after June 1, 1991. Oddly, works created but not sold before the effective date are covered for the same term as works covered under the other sections of the Copyright Act, rather than for the limited period specified in VARA. 17 U.S.C. § 106A(d)(2). Thus, works created after January 1, 1978, but not sold until after June 1, 1991, are protected for a period of life plus 70 years.

6. Unfinished Works

Massachusetts Museum of Contemporary Art Foundation v. Büchel

593 F.3d 38 (1st Cir. 2010)*

LIPEZ, Circuit Judge.

As one observer has noted, this case, which raises important and unsettled legal issues under the Visual Artists Rights Act ("VARA"), may well serve as "the ultimate how-not-to guide in the complicated world of installation art." Geoff Edgers, Dismantled, The Boston Globe, Oct. 21, 2007. Artist Christoph Büchel conceived of an ambitious, football-field-sized art installation entitled "Training Ground for Democracy," which was to be exhibited at the Massachusetts Museum of Contemporary Art ("MASS MoCA," or "the Museum"). Unfortunately, the parties never memorialized the terms of their relationship or their understanding of the intellectual property issues involved in the installation in a written agreement. Even more unfortunately, the project was never completed. Numerous conflicts and a steadily deteriorating relationship between the artist and the Museum prevented the completion of "Training Ground for Democracy" in its final form.

In the wake of this failed endeavor, the Museum went to federal court seeking a declaration that it was "entitled to present to the public the materials and partial constructions" it had collected for "Training Ground for Democracy." Büchel responded with several counterclaims under VARA and the Copyright Act, seeking an injunction that would prevent MASS MoCA from displaying the unfinished installation and damages for the Museum's alleged violations of his rights under both VARA and the general Copyright Act.

On cross-motions for summary judgment, the district court assumed that VARA applies to unfinished works of art, but it nonetheless ruled for the Museum in all respects because, even granting VARA's applicability, it found no genuine issues of material fact. *Massachusetts Museum of Contemporary Art Found., Inc. v. Büchel*, 565 F. Supp. 2d 245 (D. Mass. 2008). Büchel appeals. Because we find that, if VARA applies, genuine issues of material fact would foreclose summary judgment on one of Büchel's

---

* Footnotes omitted.

VARA claims — that MASS MoCA violated his right of artistic integrity by modifying the installation — we cannot assume that VARA applies to unfinished works but instead must decide its applicability. We conclude that the statute does apply to such works. . . .

I.

[The facts of the case are both lengthy and regrettable. MASS MoCA and Büchel orally agreed in principle to a large-scale installation, "Training Ground for Democracy." Büchel conceived of the exhibit as "essentially a village, . . . contain[ing] several major architectural and structural elements integrated into a whole, through which a visitor could walk (and climb)." Büchel drafted a model, and the museum was to acquire the objects and materials for the structures and implement the installation. Once underway, friction between the artist and the museum arose over the museum's performance of the installation — the museum complained that Büchel's instructions were too vague, and Büchel complained that the museum was ignoring his instructions and cutting corners. Eventually, unresolved issues over the budget for the project and the artist's willingness to see the project through to completion forced the museum to cancel the completion of the installation, but large parts of the project were installed or partially installed and were visible to museum goers. Büchel resisted any display of the unfinished works, with or without attribution to Büchel, and he further objected when the museum attempted to cover over part of the installation with tarps — the tarps did not cover all of the installation and curious museum goers could peek around or under the tarps to see what was partially installed. The litigation ensued to resolve issues relating to the applicability of VARA to the dispute and the extent of Büchel's rights of attribution and integrity concerning the partial installation.]

. . .

C. Procedural Background

The Museum sued Büchel on May 21, 2007, in the United States District Court for the District of Massachusetts. The complaint asserted a single claim for declaratory relief under VARA. The Museum sought a declaration that it was "entitled to present to the public the materials and partial constructions assembled in connection with an exhibit planned with the Swiss artist Büchel." Büchel responded by asserting five counterclaims against the Museum. The first sought a declaratory judgment and an injunction under VARA prohibiting the Museum from publicly displaying "the unfinished Work of Art or any of its component elements." The second sought damages for MASS MoCA's alleged violations of Büchel's VARA rights by "intentionally distort[ing] and modif[ying] the Work of Art" and allowing members of the public to "see and pass through" the unfinished work, both with and without the yellow tarpaulins. The third, fourth and fifth counterclaims sought damages and injunctive relief under the Copyright Act based on alleged violations of Büchel's right to publicly display and create derivative works from his work.

On MASS MoCA's motion, the court ordered an expedited discovery schedule that included a private viewing by the district court of Building 5 and the unfinished installation. After the close of discovery, both sides filed cross-motions seeking summary judgment on the complaint and all counter-claims. On September 21, 2007, the court held oral argument on the cross-motions and ruled from the bench. That decision addressed only the Museum's original complaint seeking declaratory relief to allow public display of the partially completed project and Büchel's corresponding counterclaim seeking to prevent the Museum from showing the then-existing work. The court ruled in favor of the Museum, noting that nothing in VARA prevented MASS MoCA from showing the incomplete project. Therefore, MASS MoCA was "entitled to present" the unfinished installation to the public as long as it posted a disclaimer that would "inform anyone viewing the exhibit that the materials assembled in Building 5 constitute an unfinished project that [did] not carry out the installation's original intent." The court correspondingly denied the artist's request for injunctive relief barring public display of the unfinished installation, ruling that he had failed to prove a likelihood of success on the merits of his VARA claim. The court stated that it would "in the coming weeks" issue a detailed memorandum explaining its oral rulings and addressing the remaining claims.

However, several days after obtaining the ruling in its favor, MASS MoCA changed course. The Museum posted an announcement on its website stating that it had "begun removing materials gathered for Training Ground for Democracy and [would] not permit the public to enter the planned installation." MASS MoCA Blog, "We'll Remove Training Ground," *http://blog.massmoca.org/2007/09/28/well-remove-training-ground/* (Sept. 28, 2007) (last visited Jan. 13, 2010).

On July 11, 2008, the district court issued its written opinion, recognizing that some of the issues presented in the case were now moot, but nevertheless wishing to explain its holding and to address the VARA and Copyright Act claims remaining in the case. The court summarized its holding this way:

> When an artist makes a decision to begin work on a piece of art and handles the process of creation long-distance via e-mail, using someone else's property, someone else's materials, someone else's money, someone else's staff, and, to a significant extent, someone else's suggestions regarding the details of fabrication—with no enforceable written or oral contract defining the parties' relationship—and that artist becomes unhappy part-way through the project and abandons it, then nothing in the Visual Artists Rights Act or elsewhere in the Copyright Act gives that artist the right to dictate what that "someone else" does with what he has left behind, so long as the remnant is not explicitly labeled as the artist's work. No right of artistic "attribution" or "integrity," as those terms are conceived by VARA, is implicated, let alone violated in these circumstances. Similarly, the Copyright Act provides no mechanism for relief, legal or equitable, to an artist such as Defendant Büchel

here, based on the decision of an exhibitor such as Plaintiff MASS MoCA to allow patrons to walk past covered components of an unfinished installation.

565 F. Supp. 2d at 248-29. The court therefore granted MASS MoCA's motion for summary judgment and denied Büchel's, entering judgment for the Museum on its claim for declaratory relief as well as on all five of Büchel's counterclaims. Büchel appeals.

II.

Passed in 1990, the Visual Artists Rights Act, 17 U.S.C. § 106A, was an amendment to the Copyright Act that protects the "moral rights" of certain visual artists in the works they create, consistent with Article 6 bis of the Berne Convention. Phillips v. Pembroke Real Estate, Inc., 459 F.3d 128, 133 (1st Cir. 2006); Carter v. Helmsley-Spear, Inc., 71 F.3d 77, 83 (2d Cir. 1995) (citing H.R. Rep. No. 101-514, at 5 (1990) ("House Report"), as reprinted in 1990 U.S.C.C.A.N. 6915, 6917). The "rubric of moral rights encompasses many varieties of rights," but the two most widely recognized are attribution and integrity. Id. at 81 (citing Ralph E. Lerner & Judith Bresler, Art Law 417, 420 (1989)). We will discuss both of these in detail below, but note briefly now that the right of attribution protects the author's right to be identified as the author of his work and also protects against the use of his name in connection with works created by others. Id. The right of integrity "allows the author to prevent any deforming or mutilating changes to his work." Id. Although these moral rights "exist independent[ly] of the economic rights" granted to all authors under the Copyright Act, 5 William F. Patry, Patry on Copyright § 16:1 (2009), they are part of the same statutory framework.

. . .

B. VARA

Beyond the Copyright Act's protections of certain economic rights, VARA provides additional and independent protections to authors of works of visual art. See Carter, 71 F.3d at 81-83. A work of visual art is defined to include "a painting, drawing, print, or sculpture, existing in a single copy" or in a limited edition. 17 U.S.C. § 101. The definition specifically excludes a number of works that are otherwise copyrightable, including motion pictures and other audiovisual works, books, posters, periodicals, works made for hire, and merchandising, advertising, promotional, or packaging materials. Id.

VARA provides that, in addition to the exclusive rights provided by section 106 of the Copyright Act, but subject to certain limitations, the author of a work of visual art

(1) shall have the right—

(A) to claim authorship of that work, and
(B) to prevent the use of his or her name as the author of any work of visual art which he or she did not create;

(2) shall have the right to prevent the use of his or her name as the author of the work of visual art in the event of a distortion, mutilation, or other modification of the work which would be prejudicial to his or her honor or reputation; and

(3) subject to the limitations set forth in section 113(d), shall have the right —

(A) to prevent any intentional distortion, mutilation, or other modification of that work which would be prejudicial to his or her honor or reputation, and any intentional distortion, mutilation, or modification of that work is a violation of that right, and

(B) to prevent any destruction of a work of recognized stature, and any intentional or grossly negligent destruction of that work is a violation of that right.

17 U.S.C. § 106A(a).

VARA's passage reflected Congress's belief that the art covered by the Act "meet[s] a special societal need, and [its] protection and preservation serve an important public interest." House Report at 5-6, as reprinted in 1990 U.S.C.C.A.N. at 6915-16. To encourage the creation of such art, VARA protects the "moral rights" of its creators. These are "rights of a spiritual, non-economic and personal nature" that exist "independently of an artist's copyright in his or her work" and "spring from a belief that an artist in the process of creation injects his spirit into the work and that the artist's personality, as well as the integrity of the work, should therefore be protected and preserved." *Carter*, 71 F.3d at 81. The recognition of moral rights fosters a "'climate of artistic worth and honor that encourages the author in the arduous act of creation.'" *Id.* at 83 (quoting House Report at 6, as reprinted in 1990 U.S.C.C.A.N. at 6915). Although an artist may not transfer his VARA rights (as they are considered an extension of his personality), he may waive those rights by "expressly agree[ing] to such waiver in a written instrument." 17 U.S.C. § 106A(e)(1). Also, "[a]ll remedies available under copyright law, other than criminal remedies, are available in an action for infringement of moral rights." *Carter*, 71 F.3d at 83 (citing 17 U.S.C. § 506); *see also* 17 U.S.C. § 501(a).

More specifically, by guaranteeing the moral rights of "attribution" and "integrity," VARA "'protects both the reputations of certain visual artists and the works of art they create.'" *Carter*, 71 F.3d at 83 (quoting House Report at 6, as reprinted in 1990 U.S.C.C.A.N. at 6915). Before discussing the precise contours of these rights, we consider whether, as a threshold matter, the indisputably unfinished "Training Ground for Democracy" was a "work of visual art" within the meaning of VARA.

C. Does VARA Apply to Unfinished Works of Art?

Büchel argues that the district court erred by failing to recognize that VARA applies with equal force to incomplete artistic endeavors that would otherwise be subject to VARA protection. He asserts that the Act's plain language compels such a conclusion, which he claims is confirmed by the legislative history and sparse case law interpreting the statute. The Museum, for its part, does not argue that unfinished works are excluded from VARA's scope. Instead, it interprets the district court's opinion as "expressly assum-[ing]" that VARA applied to "Training Ground for Democracy" in its incomplete state, and then concluding that Büchel had failed to put forth sufficient evidence to raise a triable issue regarding the violation of his rights under the statute.

We do not read the district court's ruling to conclude categorically that VARA does not apply to unfinished works. Rather, the court held that, if the statute applied, "display of th[e] unfinished installation would have violated neither Büchel's right of attribution nor his right of integrity." 565 F. Supp. 2d at 259. Nonetheless, the court repeatedly expressed skepticism about Büchel's claim that the incomplete "Training Ground" fell within VARA's scope, observing at one point in its opinion that "unfinished art may not be covered by VARA at all." *Id.* at 258; *see also id.* at 259 ("[I]t is doubtful that VARA even covered the assembled materials that constituted this unfinished installation"). Moreover, the court qualified the statute's application to unfinished works: "To the extent that an artist seeks protection for an uncompleted work, a violation of one of VARA's two explicitly recognized rights must be demonstrated with special clarity." *Id.* at 258.

Our review of the district court's interpretation of VARA is de novo. *Phillips,* 459 F.3d at 139. "'As in all statutory construction cases, we begin with the language of the statute,'" *id.* (quoting *Barnhart v. Sigmon Coal Co.,* 534 U.S. 438, 450, 122 S. Ct. 941, 151 L. ED. 2d 908 (2002)), and "[i]f the meaning of the text is unambiguous our task ends there as well," *United States v. Godin,* 534 F.3d 51, 56 (1st Cir. 2008). "If the statute's language is plain, the sole function of the courts — at least where the disposition required by the text is not absurd — is to enforce it according to its terms." *In re Rudler,* 576 F.3d 37, 44 (1st Cir. 2009) (quotation marks and citations omitted).

The definition of a "work of visual art" for VARA purposes is stated "in terms both positive (what it is) and negative (what it is not)." *Carter,* 71 F.3d at 84. An unfinished sculptural installation such as "Training Ground for Democracy" is not one of the items specifically excluded from VARA protection, and MASS MoCA wisely does not attempt to argue otherwise. Instead, we must determine whether the "positive" aspect of the definition of "work of visual art" includes an unfinished version of a "sculpture[] existing in a single copy." 17 U.S.C. § 101.

The text of VARA itself does not state when an artistic project becomes a work of visual art subject to its protections. However, VARA is part of the Copyright Act, and that Act's definition section, which defines "work of visual art," specifies that its definitions, unless otherwise provided, control throughout Title 17. *See* 17 U.S.C. § 101. That general definitional section of the Copyright Act states that a work is "created" when it "is fixed in a copy . . . for the first time." Further, "where a work is prepared over a period of time, the portion of it that has been fixed at any particular time constitutes the work as of that time." 17 U.S.C. § 101. A work is "fixed" when it has been formed, "by or under the authority of the author," in a way that is "sufficiently permanent or stable to permit it to be perceived, reproduced, or otherwise communicated for a period of more than transitory duration." *Id.*

Not surprisingly, based on section 101's general definitions, courts have held that the Copyright Act's protections extend to unfinished works. *See, e.g., Dumas v. Gommerman,* 865 F.2d 1093, 1097 (9th Cir. 1989), rejected on other grounds by *Community for Creative Non-Violence v. Reid,* 490 U.S. 730, 739, 742 n.8, 109 S. Ct. 2166, 104 L. ED. 2d 811 (1989); *Zyware, Inc. v. Middlegate, Inc.,* No. 96 Civ. 2348(SHS), 1997 WL 685336, at *4 (S.D.N.Y. Nov. 4, 1997) (noting that there is "no requirement that a work be complete before it is protected by the Copyright Act"); *Playboy Enters. Inc. v. Dumas,* 831 F. Supp. 295, 314 (S.D.N.Y. 1993) ("[T]he [Copyright] Act protects works in progress"), modified on other grounds by 840 F. Supp. 256 (S.D.N.Y. 1993), aff'd in part, rev'd in part by 53 F.3d 549 (2d Cir. 1995).

Reading VARA in accordance with the definitions in section 101, it too must be read to protect unfinished, but "fixed," works of art that, if completed, would qualify for protection under the statute. To conclude otherwise would be "contrary to the rule that provisions of a single act should be construed in as harmonious a fashion as possible." *United States v. Maravilla,* 907 F.2d 216, 231 (1st Cir. 1990) (citation omitted). At least one circuit has previously assumed VARA's applicability to unfinished works. *See Carter,* 71 F.3d at 83-88 (discussing VARA claims stemming from an unfinished, walk-through sculpture being installed in the lobby of a building).

We thus hold that VARA protects the moral rights of artists who have "created" works of art within the meaning of the Copyright Act even if those works are not yet complete.

III.

Given Büchel's right to protection under VARA for his artistic investment in a partially completed artwork, we must now assess the district court's ruling that Büchel failed to raise a genuine issue of material fact with respect to any of his claims. We review the district court's grant of summary judgment de novo. *Insituform Techs., Inc. v. Am. Home Assur. Co.,* 566 F.3d 274, 276 (1st Cir. 2009). . . . We first consider Büchel's claims asserting violations of his attribution and integrity rights under VARA and then address his claims under other provisions of the Copyright Act, which assert violations of his rights to control the display of the installation and to create derivative works based on it.

A. The Scope of VARA's Integrity and Attribution Rights

1. The Right of Integrity

VARA's right of integrity, codified at 17 U.S.C. § 106A(a)(3)(A), provides that an artist shall have the right "to prevent any intentional distortion, mutilation, or other modification of [his or her] work which would be prejudicial to his or her honor or reputation, and [that] any intentional distortion, mutilation, or modification of that work is a violation of that right." It thus allows artists to protect their works against intentional modifications that would be prejudicial to their honor or reputations. House Report at 6, as reprinted in 1990 U.S.C.C.A.N. at 6915.

There is arguably some uncertainty about the plaintiff's burden of proof in a case such as this because the second part of section (a)(3)(A) — stating that "any intentional distortion, mutilation, or modification of th[e] work is a violation" of the right of integrity — does not explicitly require a showing of prejudice when the alteration already has occurred and damages, rather than injunctive relief, would be the appropriate remedy. *See* 5 Patry, *supra*, § 16:22 (noting the ambiguity). Because those VARA cases that make it to court are "generally . . . decided on threshold questions such as whether the artist's work is a work of visual art within the scope of the Act," *Pa & Robinson*, *supra*, at 26, courts have had little occasion to give content to the rights that VARA guarantees. *See* Wu, *supra*, at 159 ("[C]ourts avoid construing the extent of VARA protection by finding that works do not meet the threshold requirements for 'visual art' protected by VARA"). Unsurprisingly, therefore, we have found no case law discussing a possible difference in the showing required for injunctive relief and damages for right-of-integrity claims.

Some courts, however, have assumed without analysis that the prejudice showing is necessary for both injunctive relief and damages. *See, e.g., Hanrahan v. Ramirez*, No. 2:97-CV-7470, 1998 WL 34369997, at *3 (C.D. Cal. June 3, 1998) (citing 17 U.S.C. § 106A(a)(3)); *Carter v. Helmsley-Spear, Inc.*, 861 F. Supp. 303, 329-30 (S.D.N.Y. 1994), aff'd in part, vacated in part, and rev'd in part by Carter, 71 F.3d at 77. At least one commentator likewise accepts, without discussion, that the damages remedy requires a showing of prejudice. *See* Melville B. Nimmer, 3-8D Nimmer on Copyright § 8D.06[C][1] (noting that "an intentional and prejudicial mutilation is an integrity violation, remediable through not only an injunction, but damages as well"). Interestingly, Nimmer raises, and dismisses, a different imprecision in section (a)(3)(A):

> The statutory language — "distortion, mutilation, or other modification of the work which would be prejudicial to his or her honor or reputation" — is susceptible of a reading whereby the requisite prejudice applies only to "modification," not to the antecedents of "distortion" or "mutilation." Though not without ambiguity, the better view under the Berne Convention, from which this language is drawn, is that prejudice applies in all three instances.

Id. We agree with Nimmer's view of the provision, including the application of the prejudice requirement to a claim for damages, and consider that construction soundly grounded in VARA's legislative history. Under the heading "Purpose of the Legislation," the House Report notes that the right of integrity "allows artists to protect their works against modifications and destructions that are prejudicial to their honor or reputations." House Report at 6, as reprinted in 1990 U.S.C.C.A.N. at 6915. The Report also notes that the rights provided by VARA are "analogous to those protected by Article 6bis of the

Berne Convention," *id.*, which in turn describes the right of integrity as applicable to "certain modifications and other derogatory actions" that would be prejudicial to the artist's honor or reputation. Given the stated purpose of the legislation and the similar depiction of the integrity right in the Berne Convention, we conclude that Congress intended the prejudice requirement to apply to the right of integrity whether the remedy sought is injunctive relief or damages.

Although VARA does not define the terms "prejudicial," "honor," or "reputation," the House Report recommended that the prejudice inquiry "focus on the artistic or professional honor or reputation of the individual as embodied in the work that is protected," and "examine the way in which a work has been modified and the professional reputation of the author of the work." House Report at 15, as reprinted in 1990 U.S.C.C.A.N. at 6925-26 (footnotes omitted). Relying on dictionary definitions of prejudice, honor, and reputation, the district court in Carter concluded that it should "consider whether [the proposed] alteration would cause injury or damage to plaintiffs' good name, public esteem, or reputation in the artistic community." 861 F. Supp. at 323. We think this a useful approach, but emphasize that the focus is on the artist's reputation in relation to the altered work of art; the artist need not have public stature beyond the context of the creation at issue. *See* House Report at 15, as reprinted in 1990 U.S.C.C.A.N. at 6925 ("[A]n author need not prove a pre-existing standing in the artistic community").

2. The Right of Attribution

VARA's right of attribution grants the author of a work of visual art the right, in part, (1) "to claim authorship of that work"; (2) "to prevent the use of his or her name as the author of any work of visual art which he or she did not create"; and (3) "to prevent the use of his or her name as the author of the work of visual art in the event of a distortion, mutilation, or other modification of the work which would be prejudicial to his or her honor or reputation." 17 U.S.C. § 106A(a)(1), (2). The right "ensures that artists are correctly identified with the works of art they create, and that they are not identified with works created by others." House Report at 6, as reprinted in 1990 U.S.C.C.A.N. at 6915. In addition, if a work of visual art has been distorted or modified (and, unlike the integrity right, the original distortion or modification need not be intentional), associating the author's name with the distorted work against his wishes would violate his right of attribution.

The right of attribution under VARA thus gives an artist a claim for injunctive relief to, inter alia, assert or disclaim authorship of a work. Whether VARA entitles an artist to damages for violation of the right of attribution is a separate question. We find the answer in the difference between the statutory language on the right of integrity and the language on the right of attribution. Subsection (a)(3) of section 106A, which codifies the right of integrity, is further divided into two subsections: (A) confers the right to protect the work against intentional alterations that would be prejudicial to honor or reputation, and (B) confers the right to protect a work of "recognized stature" from destruction. Although both subsections are framed as rights "to prevent" certain conduct, they both also contain an additional clause stating that the occurrence of that conduct is, at least in certain circumstances, "a violation of th[e] right" to prevent the conduct from happening. *See* 17 U.S.C. § 106A(a)(3)(A) ("any intentional distortion, mutilation, or modification of that work is a violation of that right"); *id.* at § 106(a)(3)(B) ("any intentional or grossly negligent destruction of that work is a violation of that right").

No such "violation" clause is included in the sections codifying the right of attribution. *See* Nimmer, supra, at § 8D.06[B][1] ("The statute does not make any provision to redress violation of any of the foregoing three attribution rights."). The legislative history sheds no light on this difference, but Nimmer speculates as follows:

> Perhaps the implication is that whereas an integrity violation could give rise to a monetary recovery, failure to attribute is remediable solely through injunction. If that conclusion were intended, Congress certainly could have expressed its intent less obliquely.

Id. We agree with Nimmer's surmise that VARA does not provide a damages remedy for an attribution violation. Where the statutory language is framed as a right "to prevent" conduct, it does not necessarily follow that a plaintiff is entitled to damages once the conduct occurs. The question is whether "doing" the act the artist has a right to prevent also triggers a damages remedy, and the statutory language indicates that Congress answered that question for the attribution right differently from the integrity right.

It is also noteworthy that Congress crafted a damages remedy for the destruction of a work of recognized stature that is narrower than the right to prevent destruction of such works. While an artist may "prevent any destruction of a work of recognized stature," only an "intentional or grossly negligent destruction of that work is a violation of that right." 17 U.S.C. § 106A(a)(3)(B) (emphasis added). This narrowing further indicates that Congress did not intend a damages remedy to arise automatically from the right to prevent conduct. In failing to provide a damages remedy for any type of violation of the moral right of attribution, Congress may have concluded that artists could obtain adequate relief for the harms of false attribution by resorting to the Copyright Act and other traditional claims.

B. Büchel's VARA Claims

With this legal framework in mind, we turn to the record before the district court. By dismantling "Training Ground," the Museum prevented the further use of Büchel's name in connection with the work, eliminating any basis for injunctive relief, and we therefore do not address the attribution claim in our VARA analysis. We thus consider the evidence in the light most favorable to Büchel in determining whether there are genuine issues of material fact regarding the alleged violations of his right of integrity.

As noted above, the district court concluded that Büchel's right of integrity was not implicated by MASS MoCA's conduct. The court found that "nothing in MASS MoCA's planned display of the unfinished installation would have violated Büchel's right of integrity, for the simple reason that no completed work of art ever existed on these facts for the museum to distort, mutilate or modify." 56 F. Supp. 2d at 260. Although the court stated that it would assume that VARA applied to unfinished works, its analysis appears to be influenced by a more limited view of the statute's scope. The court stated that "[t]o suggest that the display of an unfinished and abandoned work somehow constitutes a distortion, mutilation, or modification of that non-existent work is simply inconsistent with the ordinary usage of those terms." *Id.* Having concluded that VARA applies with full force to unfinished works, however, we cannot accept the district court's reliance on the unfinished state of "Training Ground" to minimize the rights of its creator.

It cannot be disputed that, at least by the time Büchel left North Adams in December 2006, "Training Ground" was "fixed" within the meaning of the Copyright Act — i.e., materials had been placed in Building 5 "by or under the authority of the author" in a "sufficiently permanent or stable" manner to allow the work to be "communicated for a period of more than transitory duration." 17 U.S.C. § 101. The elements of the installation had been chosen by Büchel, and his assistants and the Museum workers had put numerous components of the project in place under his direct supervision. Although far from complete, the work by the end of 2006 included parts of the "Saddam Compound" and the cinema, and Büchel and his assistants had begun detailing several of the containers intended to house elements such as a jail, museum, and voting booths. With this substantial work in place, the sculpture had an established presence in Building 5. Büchel thus had rights in the work that were protected under VARA, notwithstanding its unfinished state.

Büchel alleges that MASS MoCA violated his right to integrity in three distinct ways: first, by continuing to work on the installation without his authorization, particularly in early 2007, and by then exhibiting the distorted artwork to the public; second, by using tarpaulins to "partially cover []" — and thus modify and distort — the installation, and allowing Museum visitors to see it in that condition; and third, merely by showing Büchel's work in its unfinished state, which he claims was a distortion. Büchel asserts that these actions caused prejudice to his honor or reputation.

As we shall explain, we conclude that summary judgment was improperly granted to MASS MoCA because material disputes of fact exist concerning the first of Büchel's integrity claims — i.e., that MASS MoCA modified "Training Ground" over his objections, to his detriment. We further conclude that the record contains sufficient evidence to allow a jury to find that MASS MoCA's actions caused prejudice to Büchel's honor or reputation. The other integrity claims, however, are unavailing.

1. Continuing Work on "Training Ground"

Büchel asserts that, in the months following his departure from North Adams in December 2006, the Museum encroached on his artistic vision by making modifications to the installation that in some instances were directly contrary to his instructions. In rejecting Büchel's VARA claims, the district court described the Museum's actions as perhaps "occasionally misguided" attempts "to implement Büchel's long-distance instructions." 565 F. Supp. 2d at 260. The court found that these "[f]umbled efforts to assist in creating, or failing to create, a work of art are not equivalent to distortion, modification, or mutilation of the art." *Id.* at 260-61.

Although a jury might agree with the court's assessment, the evidence viewed in the light most favorable to Büchel would allow a finding that at least some of the Museum's actions violated VARA. The record permits the inference that, even during his time as an artist-in-residence at MASS MoCA, Museum staff members were disregarding his instructions and intentionally modifying "Training Ground" in a manner that he did not approve. For example, on December 14, 2006, just before he left for the holidays, Büchel complained to Thompson that in "many cases people just do stuff without checking back if its ok to do s[omething], when they think by themselves the plan has to be changed." Büchel expressed further concerns in an email to Thompson later that month: "I don't [k]now if this is really a great opportunity when you get an invitation to do a show, where you have to make constantly tons of compromises, where you have to fight constantly against stubborn[n]ess as well [as] against the institution and work with people that think they know my art better than I do as well [as] try to sabotage the project. . . ."

In early 2007, when he was no longer on-site, Büchel again accused the Museum of "sabotage acts" and, in a January 16 letter, issued an ultimatum: he would return to North Adams to complete "Training Ground" only if the Museum assented to a number of specific conditions. Aside from certain budgetary concerns irrelevant here, Büchel included the following among his list of demands:

> There is NO negotiation about the scope of the project.
>
> There are no elements to be eliminated as you propose and I don't accept any orders and any more pressure or compromises how things have to be done, neither from you or your crew. . . .
>
> I will not give you any permission to show an unfinished project nor will I show nor let you show any work in progress, as you proposed already earlier.
>
> I will not accept without consequences any additional sabotage acts, as done to artworks of mine and as well done to the installation in progress[.]

The letter also identified several points of disagreement with the Museum concerning the content of the project, including Büchel's insistence that there be "no transport street through the exhibition" and that he did not "need to be told if an airplane fuselage section fits in the show or not. I don't negotiate constantly my art with you or Nato. . . ." Accusing the

Museum director of showing "little respect towards [his] plans," he told Thompson "please don't tell me all the time how I have to do my project regarding its scope and it's [sic] methods that needs [sic] to be applied."

Unsatisfied with the Museum's response to his list of demands, Büchel wrote to Thompson again on January 27, 2007. He warned that, based on the information he had been provided, "there [was] a lot of stuff not being done according to my instructions." Again, he noted several elements of the work that had been installed against his wishes. Thompson and Büchel traded emails during the first few days of February, with Büchel stating that he would "not negotiate further this matter . . . because almost any of the main conditions are simply not fulfilled" and Thompson writing that he believed the Museum had "responded to [Büchel's] main issues."

After that, direct communication between Büchel and the Museum became sparse. It was during this time, Büchel alleges, that the Museum developed a "Plan B" to be implemented in the event — which was looking increasingly likely — that he did not return to finish the exhibit. Plan B, which involved publicly exhibiting the unfinished installation without the artist's permission, called for completing various elements of the installation in a way the Museum knew might differ from Büchel's artistic concept. Büchel cites an email chain on February 14 that included Joseph Thompson and Dante Birch, in which Thompson, stating that the Museum "seem[ed] to be getting closer and closer to Plan B," gave specific instructions on various elements of the installation. Thompson suggested that Museum staff do "[a]nything else Dante and Nato feel is known with 80% certainty."

At least some Museum staff members recognized that continuing to work on the installation without Büchel's input might be problematic. Later in the February 14 email chain, Dante Birch noted that he was "interested in protecting the museum from intellectual property issues." Pointing out that the show was advertised as a Büchel in the Museum's schedule, he stated that when reviewers came, "the question will be 'what is it?' . . . and if it's reviewed as a Buchel we're in deep shit." Thompson's plans also raised concern among other MASS MoCA employees, including curator Susan Cross, who cautioned Thompson in a January 31 email that "we tend to forget that whether we're doing the welding or not, there is an 'author' — an artist for whom we shouldn't make decisions. . . . At what point, if at all, does an artist lose his right to owning the idea and his/her 'intellectual property?' . . . I think it is still art and still belongs to Buchel."

Both in his deposition and in his affidavit, Büchel described ways in which he felt the Museum had knowingly disregarded his specific instructions. For example, MASS MoCA's decision to build a cinderblock wall through the Cape Cod-style house in the installation, despite Büchel's expressed desire that the construction await his return, resulted in what Büchel considered a "big distortion of the meaning of that element." The record is replete with similar allegations concerning other components of the installation, including the cinema, the bomb carousel, the Saddam spiderhole, the police car and the mobile home. Indeed, even the Museum, in its August 31, 2007 memorandum of law in support of its motion for summary judgment, admitted that the installation "[m]aterials as they now stand reflect significant aesthetic and design choices by MASS MoCA personnel, including with respect to the layout of the [m]aterials, and with respect to the selection and procurement of pre-existing buildings and vehicles that have been modified and incorporated into the [m]aterials."

MASS MoCA argues that the evidence, taken in its entirety, does not add up to a triable issue with respect to a violation of Büchel's right of integrity, but shows only that Museum personnel were attempting to carry out Büchel's vision based on his instructions. Indeed, the Museum notes that the work slowed as Büchel's instructions became unavailable. MASS MoCA specifically disputes Büchel's reading of the February 14 email chain as demonstrating the Museum's disregard of his creative rights over the installation, asserting that the discussion among its staff members in fact reflects a conscious effort to determine how far the Museum could appropriately go in light of the remaining instructions left by the artist. In one email, for example, Thompson noted that "we are putting the correct objects in the spaces cb indicated. . . . That's not 'doing a buechel [sic]' that's prepping for buechel [sic] assuming, as we still are, that there is some chance we'll see him here again." Other communications in the record also could be interpreted as showing the Museum doing its best to carry out Büchel's concept for the art work.

As we have noted, a jury may well accept the Museum's depiction of its intention and its actions. At this juncture, however, the record must be viewed in the light most favorable to Büchel. The evidence we have described would permit a jury to find that the Museum forged ahead with the installation in the first half of 2007 knowing that the continuing construction in Büchel's absence would frustrate — and likely contradict — Büchel's artistic vision. We thus conclude that a jury issue exists as to whether these actions effected an intentional distortion or other modification of "Training Ground" that subjected MASS MoCA to liability under VARA.

The record also contains evidence from which a jury could conclude that the Museum's alterations had a detrimental impact on Büchel's honor or reputation. An article in the Boston Globe reported that, in February, Museum officials had shown the unfinished project to a group of Museum directors and curators who were attending an arts conference in the area. *See* Geoff Edgers, Behind Doors, a World Unseen: Dispute Cloaks Massive Installation at MASS MoCA, Boston Globe (March 28, 2007), available at www.boston.com/ae/theater_arts/articles/2007/03/28/behind_doors_a_world_unseen/ ("Behind doors, a world unseen"). Another journalist reported on observing the unfinished (and still untarped) work. *See* The Show Will Go On, supra.

Although the commentary generated by these visits is not all negative, there was sufficient evidence for a jury to find that the changes to "Training Ground" caused prejudice to Büchel. The New York Times noted that the exhibition would "certainly give people unfamiliar with his obsessive, history-driven aesthetic an inaccurate sense of his art, and this is indeed a form of damage." Is It Art Yet?, supra. A critic for the Boston Globe similarly observed that "many people are going to judge [Büchel] and his work on the basis of this experience." Ken Johnson, No Admittance: MASS MoCA Has Mishandled Disputed Art Installation, Boston Globe, July 1, 2007, at 1N. One viewer, writing in Commentary magazine, observed that "I am not sure that it suffers from being enveiled." Michael J. Lewis, The Cost of Transgression, http://www.commentarymagazine.com/blogs/index.php/lewis/499 (June 4, 2007). A review published in Berkshire Fine Arts — subtitled "Crap Under Wrap" — concluded that it would be a "huge mistake" to uncover the installation, which offered "virtually nothing of substance or interest." Crap Under Wrap, supra.

The record thus shows that some viewers of the installation reacted unfavorably to the work in its allegedly modified and distorted form. A factfinder might conclude, of course, that it was Büchel's underlying concept (notwithstanding its unfinished state) rather than MASS MoCA's actions that elicited the negative reactions. However, a jury could also reasonably infer that the negative impressions resulted from the Museum's unauthorized modifications to "Training Ground," diminishing the quality of the work and thereby harming Büchel's professional honor or reputation as a visual artist.

In concluding that Büchel has adduced sufficient evidence to support a right-of-integrity claim, we reject the Museum's assertion that to find a violation of Büchel's right of integrity in these circumstances would make it impossible for parties to collaborate on large-scale artistic works. The Museum warns that, under Büchel's interpretation, "no one other than the artist himself . . . may ever perform any work in fabricating visual art unless that specific task has been authorized by the artist." We disagree. Although the artist's vision must govern, that principle does not prevent collaboration at the implementation level so long as the artist's vision guides that implementation. Here, Büchel alleges a campaign of intentional distortion and modification to his work in which Museum personnel repeatedly ignored his express wishes. Our holding that the summary judgment record precludes an affirmance of the district court on this claim may serve as a cautionary tale to museums contemplating similar installations in the future — guiding them to document the terms of their relationship and obtain VARA waivers where necessary — but it does not prevent museums or other collaborators from working cooperatively with artists on such non-traditional artworks.

2. Showing "Training Ground" Covered with Tarpaulins

Büchel also claims that MASS MoCA improperly modified and distorted "Training Ground" when it partially covered it with the yellow tarpaulins and displayed it in that condition. He asserts that the record shows beyond dispute that visitors looked behind the tarps, that the tarp-adorned installation was "judged by others to be Büchel's work, and that his honor and reputation were harmed by it." In response, the Museum argues that the yellow tarpaulins were merely functional — a way of keeping people "out" of the installation — rather than an aesthetic modification of the artwork that gave MASS MoCA patrons a distorted view of it.

Although the tarpaulins did prevent visitors to the Museum from seeing the entire unfinished installation, the record shows that a number of people were able to form an impression of "Training Ground" despite the partial covering. For example, according to one observer,

> [the tarps] don't reach the floor, and they rise only about two feet above eye level, so they don't cover much. You can easily crouch down to slip your head underneath or peek through the slits between the vinyl sheets. Beyond the passageway formed by the tarps, the monumental elements of the installation rise all around you, plain as day — the cinderblock walls, the two-story house, the guard tower, the trailers, the carnival ride, all compacted together in a claustrophobic, politically surreal borough of hell, George Orwell by way of David Lynch.

Thomas Micchelli, Christoph Büchel Training Ground for Democracy, The Brooklyn Rail (September 2007), available at http://www.brooklynrail .org/2007/09/artseen/buchel. Another critic noted that the installation "under all the tarps is really kind of a conceptual peep show. It doesn't take much effort or imagination to see most of the work. . . . Mass MoCA is hiding an elephant behind a napkin," and called it a "wink, wink, wrap show." Crap Under Wrap, supra. Photographs in the record confirm that the covers did not obscure the general path and layout of the installation. Indeed, given the location of "Training Ground," visitors to "Made at MASS MoCA" could not avoid seeing the unfinished "Training Ground" bedecked in tarpaulins.

Nonetheless, although the installation unquestionably looked different with the tarpaulins partially covering it, we agree with the district court that the mere covering of the artwork by the Museum, its host, cannot reasonably be deemed an intentional act of distortion or modification of Büchel's creation. To conclude otherwise would be to say that, even if all had gone well, the Museum would have been subject to a right-of-integrity claim if it had partially covered the work before its formal opening to prevent visitors from seeing it prematurely.

This is not to say that MASS MoCA was necessarily acting with pure intentions when it created "Made at MASS MoCA" in close proximity to the tarped "Training Ground." It might be a fair inference that the Museum was deliberately communicating its anger with Büchel by juxtaposing his unfinished work with the successful artistic collaborations depicted in its new exhibition. The partial covering of "Training Ground" may have been intended to highlight, rather than hide, the failed collaboration. The right of integrity under VARA, however, protects the artist from distortions of his work, not from disparaging commentary about his behavior. In our view, a finding that the Museum's covering of the installation constituted an intentional act of distortion or modification of Büchel's artistic creation would stretch VARA beyond sensible boundaries.

3. Exhibiting "Training Ground" in Its Unfinished State

Büchel maintains that, even aside from the alleged modifications to "Training Ground," merely exhibiting the work of art in its unfinished state, without the artist's consent, constitutes a distortion. We reject this claim. A separate moral right of disclosure (also known as the right of divulgation) protects an author's authority to "prevent third parties from disclosing [his or her] work to the public without the author's consent," and is not covered by VARA. *See* Cyrill P. Rigamonti, *Deconstructing Moral Rights*, 47 HARV. INT'L L.J. 353, 373, 405 (2006) "([T]he VARA ignores the rights of disclosure and withdrawal and instead focuses on the rights of attribution and integrity...").

Although Büchel proffered an expert who opined that showing an unfinished work without the artist's permission is inherently a distortion, we decline to interpret VARA to include such a claim where a separate moral right of disclosure is widely recognized in other jurisdictions and Congress explicitly limited the statute's coverage to the rights of attribution and integrity. *See* Amy M. Adler, *Against Moral Rights*, 97 CAL. L. REV. 263, 268 (2009) (noting that most European countries "recognize a right of divulgation, giving the artist the right to decide when (and whether) the work is complete and can be shown"); Rigamonti, supra, at 356 ("The standard set of moral rights recognized in the literature consists of the author's right to claim authorship (right of attribution), the right to object to modifications of the work (right of integrity), the right to decide when and how the work in question will be published (right of disclosure), and the right to withdraw a work after publication (right of withdrawal)." (footnotes omitted)); 5 Patry on Copyright § 16:23 (noting that VARA does not give the artist "a right to prohibit display of mutilated versions of his or her work, only the right to prohibit the mutilation itself"). Any right Büchel possesses to withhold display of his artwork must be found outside VARA. . . .

4. Summary of VARA Claims

After careful review of the record, we are persuaded that a reasonable jury could find that Büchel is entitled to relief under VARA based on the Museum's continuing work on "Training Ground" over his objections. Genuine disputes of material fact foreclose summary judgment for either Büchel or MASS MoCA on that claim. We find no merit, however, in Büchel's claim that MASS MoCA intentionally modified or distorted "Training Ground" by covering it with tarpaulins, and we reject as outside the scope of the statute Büchel's claim that the Museum violated VARA by displaying the installation over his objections. We affirm the district court's grant of summary judgment for the Museum on Büchel's right-of-attribution claim, which became moot when MASS MoCA dismantled the installation in 2007. . . .

We thus remand the case for further proceedings on Büchel's remaining right-of-integrity claim under VARA and his public display claim under section 106 of the Copyright Act.

Affirmed in part, vacated in part, and remanded for further proceedings consistent with this decision. Each party is to bear its own costs.

Current VARA Cases

The Destruction of 5Poinz – *Cohen v. G & M Realty L.P.*, 988 F. Supp. 2d 212 (E.D.N.Y. 2013):[27] The case of *Cohen v. G & M Realty* chronicles the beginning of the end for the 5Poinz graffiti mecca in Long Island City, N.Y. The aerosol artists who brought the claim, led by Jonathan Cohen (known as Meres One in the art world), claimed that VARA should protect their artistic creations. The court struggled mightily with the application of VARA to the examples of graffiti art brought forward by the plaintiffs. The opinion indicates that the court considered a variety of "expert" opinions on both sides of the issue of whether the works at issue at 5Poinz were of "recognized stature." Ultimately, the court bypassed ruling on that particular issue by virtue of the fact that the motion before him was a preliminary injunction motion, and the court believed that the ultimate issue of "recognized stature" could be left to further development of the evidence toward resolution on the merits. The court denied the motion on the basis of lack of sufficient proof of likelihood of success on the merits and the element of irreparable harm, because of the impermanent nature of many of the works. The court believed the artists had manufactured a great deal of their own harm by continuing to add works to the 5Poinz site without any tangible guaranty that the works would be permanent fixtures at the site. The owners wasted no time in reacting to this preliminary ruling. They whitewashed over the graffiti, and subsequently in 2015, they demolished the structure at 5Poinz thus ending the saga.[28]

27. Images: Michael D. Murray, Collage of three cropped, revised, and resized thumbnail images derived from photographs relating to the destruction of 5Poinz (2016), the subject *of Cohen v. G & M Realty L.P.*, 988 F. Supp. 2d 212 (E.D.N.Y. 2013).

28. *Demolition Work Begins at 5 Pointz*, CIRCA (Mar. 9, 2015, 9:37 AM), *http://cir.ca/news/5-pointz-demolition*; Christian Murray, *5 Pointz Demolished: 'It is like an Old Friend That Has Gone,' Wolkoff Says*, LIC POST (Feb. 2, 2015), *http://licpost.com/2015/02/02/5-pointz-has-beendemolished-six-months-of-digging-is-next/*.

Current VARA Cases

Paul Jackson's *Tiger Spot*: Missouri artist Paul Jackson, installed a work at a prominent location on the campus of his alma mater, the University of Missouri.[29] Unfortunately, the work had a rough start and mistreatment afterwards. When the work was initially laid in, the concrete bed needed time to cure and was covered by a protective tarp to keep off the rain. The University took the tarp off too early, the concrete got wet, and it never set properly. Some vandals rode motorcycles over the work, causing more damage. As shown in the picture, people liked to walk on the surface of the image, causing still more damage. The situation raises many questions under VARA: Does the University have to allow Jackson the right to come in and per-form restoration? Does the University have to pay for the restoration? Can the University move it somewhere else?

Jackson sued the UM System Board of Curators for violating his rights under VARA.

Tiger Spot is a sculptural installation, and if not that, it would be a painting, so it is a work of visual art. Although the copyright over the work would be limited because of the depiction of a natural, living thing — a tiger's face — there is nothing to suggest that the work is not otherwise original, created by the artist, fixed in a tangible medium, and thus copyrightable. Paul Jackson enjoys a healthy rep-utation within Missouri and the surrounding region, and he is well known for his "tiger" images, so the work would have a good chance of being declared a work of recognized stature. That brings us to the VARA issues: It would seem that the unfortunate events that brought physical damage and deface-ment to the work do present a risk of harm to the artist's reputation. Certainly, this is a very prominent place for Jackson's art to be installed when com-pared to works that are hanging in a museum, or in a private home, or even on some building somewhere. Jackson is known as a proud son of Missouri, and a proud alum of the University of Mis-souri. He is a proud *Missouri Tiger*. And the deface-ment and damage to the work could easily be interpreted by the casual observer as reflecting flaws in the way the work was executed and installed. "Poor Paul Jackson, he doesn't know how to lay in an image in concrete; look at how

29. Images: Michael D. Murray, Cropped, revised, and resized thumbnail images derived from photographs depicting the newly unveiled "Tiger Spot" sculpture at the University of Missouri (2001), and a photograph depicting a dejected Paul Jackson inspecting his damaged "Tiger Spot" sculpture (2006).

Current VARA Cases

	his work is breaking up and looking like crap," the passers-by might think. All of this would present a significant risk to the artist's reputation. The University owned the work, and was at least a little culpable for allowing the work to be damaged. The University in fact believed the work would never be right if left out in the rain and snow where people would walk on it and potentially keep on damaging it. It wanted to move the work indoors, to an installation on the floor of a lobby in a campus building, where it could be cordoned off to prevent people from walking on it. But Jackson resisted this move because removal would destroy the integrity of the work. The new location would not have been as prominent as the original location, and would cost him reputational credit for the work. Ultimately, the university and Jackson reached an agreement to pay Jackson $125,000 "to dismiss the litigation, resolve all claims, relinquish his artist's rights to the mosaic, and give the university the right to permanently remove the mosaic." In accordance with this agreement, the installation was permanently removed and not relocated.[30]
	David Ascalon's Holocaust Memorial Artist David Ascalon constructed a Holocaust memorial in 1994. The work was metallic, with a tarnished, blackened exterior structure that resembled barbed wire, which represented Nazi and other oppressive forces, over a shiny core structure, representing the resilient nature of the Jewish people that still shined through the oppression. After twelve years, the owners of the sculpture decided it needed a little sprucing up. They had the whole work cleaned and polished so each piece was made shiny and sparkling—both the "Jews" and the "Nazis." The restorer was so proud of his work that he chiseled and sanded off Ascalon's name from the sculpture and replaced it with his own name and the new date of restoration in 2006.

---

30. Hannah Spaar, *Update: Tiger Spot mosaic removed from Lowry Mall, Missourian* (May 15, 2012), *http://www.columbiamissourian.com/news/update-tiger-spot-mosaic-removed-from-lowry-mall/article_89bc9f10-4062-5ebc-9a22-dbdd7e755667.html.*

Current VARA Cases

31

The Ascalon problem is a good capstone for the discussions of this chapter. Everything we have discussed is at issue in this problem. The work is a sculpture, so it meets the requirement of a work of visual art. It appears to be original, created by the artist, fixed in a tangible medium, and thus copyrightable. Ascalon received the commission for the sculpture in a juried contest, so this particular work was chosen for its merit over other competitors, and has since received many positive reviews, so it should easily meet the requirement of a work of recognized stature. The VARA claim for attribution is a no-brainer: the restorer removed the artist's name from the sculpture, added his own name, and added a new date for the sculpture. Nothing could constitute a clearer violation of attribution rights. The integrity claim is almost as obvious—yes, the work is now completely shiny and bright, but that defeats the entire artistic design of the original work. The Nazi symbolic element was supposed to be tarnished, corroded, and blackened, and it was supposed to look different, in stark contrast to the Jewish symbolic element of the work. By making the Nazis shiny and bright, the restorer destroyed the intentions of Ascalon for the work, and it would present a clear and present threat to his artistic reputation for people to miss or mistake his original design and intentions for the work, in addition to the dishonor and disrespect of having his name sanded off the work.

31. Images: Michael D. Murray, Four cropped, revised, and resized thumbnail images derived from "before and after" photographs depicting the alterations to David Ascalon's Holocaust Memorial (2014).

D. Droit de Suite

While the doctrine of moral rights has not yet been universally adopted, most nations, recognizing the need to protect the economic rights of authors, have enacted some form of copyright legislation. The creator is, thereby, provided with the means to participate in the exploitation of the first sale of the creator's work. (*See* Chapter 2.) But what of the person whose creation is not intended for reproduction, duplication, or merchandising? Unique and singular works often are resold for profit several times after the initial sale in which the artist was compensated, and much of the increase in value of these unique and singular works may be attributed to the growing fame and "value" of the artist and her body of works as a whole in the art market; but traditionally, the artist did not receive a penny from these resales. Much of the work produced by visual artists falls into this category of unique and singular works not intended for reproduction, duplication, or merchandising. A growing body of law, referred to here as droit de suite laws, protecting the economic right of continuation in the resale of art works, is emerging in many nations in the world. This section will consider the economic rights artists have in their works under civil law nations and in the United States.

1. The French Concept of Droit de Suite

Droit de suite, or the right of continuation, as conceived in France, gave the artist a pecuniary right greater than that afforded the author through copyright by allowing the artist to collect 3 percent of the total sale price of a work each time it was sold at public auction. The right was inalienable and inured to the artist for his or her life plus 50 years. *Leudet et Lefebvre c. Turquin*, [1937] Gaz. Pal. (Civ. Trib. Seine), cited in Hauser, *The French Droit de Suite: The Problem of Protection for the Underprivileged Artist Under the Copyright Law*, 6 BULL. CR. SOC. 94 (1959) [hereinafter Hauser]. Under Article 24 of the 1957 act, only the surviving spouse and heirs can claim its benefit; legatees and assignees are barred.

The act requires registration of the work by the artist before he or she can claim the right. It was hoped that this registration would also serve to authenticate the work. The data required for registration includes name, address, artistic signature, and legal signature by the artist or his or her agent. The Société de la Propriété Artistique et des Dessins et Modeles (SPADEM) was formed to aid members in collecting royalties in France and other nations in the same way as ASCAP, BMI, and Fox collect and distribute royalties to performing artists in the United States. SPADEM was a private organization acting as a buffer between the creator and the ultimate purchaser. SPADEM was dissolved in 1996 due to financial and management problems. *Adieu, SPADEM*, ARTnews, Sept. 1996, at 60.

While the reaction to droit de suite in France was generally favorable, it did have its critics. Art dealers were the most vociferous in their objections, and perhaps as a result, the 1920 act applied only to sales at public auction. Even so, it was feared that the public auction might disappear in France, with sellers taking their art abroad to avoid the loss of profit. This was not the case. In fact, the doctrine of droit de suite seems to have had no adverse effect on the sale of art in France, which encouraged Parliament to include "sales through the intermediary of a merchant," including dealers and agents, in the 1957 revision of droit de suite legislation. *See* Diane B. Schulder, *Art Proceeds Act: A Study of the Droit de Suite and a Proposed Enactment for the United States*, 61 Nw. U. L. Rev. 19 (1966) [hereinafter Schulder].

It would appear, however, that the revised law was not vigorously enforced by SPADEM against dealers until recently, resulting in a controversy based not only on pecuniary impact, but on the necessity of galleries divulging prices and the identities of buyers. *See French Laws for Artists' Rights — Under Fire from Auctioneers*, J. of Art, Nov. 1991, at 87 (discussing, in addition to the droit de suite controversy, a dispute concerning reproduction rights as applied to auction catalogs). The concern over eliminating the confidential nature of private sales raises a persistent dilemma in the application of droit de suite and is a major roadblock to implementation in the United States.

2. Other Continental Approaches to Droit de Suite

The French theory is based on the premise that an artist has a right to participate in any exploitive use of his or her creation. The German right is justified on the basis of "intrinsic value." This is a slightly different presumption, namely that any increase in the value of a work is due to the artist's earlier labors. That value is intrinsic in the work in latent form and the artist, therefore, has a right to participate in the economic benefit realized when the public becomes aware of this latent value. While the difference in theories may seem a matter of semantics, the result in practical operation is real. German artists are allowed one fourth of the difference between the present and prior selling price. *See* Hauser, *The French Droit de Suite: The Problem of Protection for the Underprivileged Artist Under the Copyright Law*, 18 ASCAP Cr. L. Symp. 1, 17 (1962).

The Italian system is quite complex, with a sliding scale allowing the artist a larger percent of the profit when the profit is greatly in excess of the original sale price. Private sales are included only if the resale price quadruples the original purchase price. The complexity of this system makes it unduly burdensome and almost unworkable. For a description of the various adaptations of the droit de suite doctrine, *see* Schulder, *supra*, at 30-32.

A German appellate court ruled that Germany's droit de suite laws do not apply to transactions taking place outside the country's borders. Painter Gotthard Graubner sold three Beuys objects at Christie's London auction house, netting $868,000 and hoping to avoid the 5 percent artist's royalty. *See* Phillips, *Court Fight Over Beuys Resale Royalties*, Art in Am., July 1992, at 29.

In all, 36 countries have adopted some form of droit de suite. Marilyn J. Kretsinger, *Droit de Suite: The Artist's Right to a Resale Royalty*, 15 HASTINGS COMM. & ENT. L.J. 967, 968 (1993) [hereinafter Kretsinger].

There has been some controversy as to whether droit de suite is an artist's moral right aligned with the concept of moral rights, or an author's economic right aligned with the concept of copyright. France did not incorporate the doctrine into its copyright law until 1957, in spite of the fact that one of the strongest arguments in favor of adoption of droit de suite in 1920 was that the right was parallel to that accorded authors and composers under copyright law. This controversy kept droit de suite from being incorporated into the Berne Convention for some time. However, in 1948, the concept of droit de suite was included in article 4 of the convention. Most nations agreed that it was an author's right, with only The Netherlands specifically stating that it was not within the scope of copyright law.

It has been suggested that American artists may be protected by droit de suite in the exploitation of works in France. Note, *Protection for Creators in the United States and Abroad*, 13 Copyright L. Symp. 1,10 (1963), also published as an unauthored article in 24 U. PITT. L. REV. 817 (1963). This idea, however, is specifically refuted by the limitation of remedy to foreigners whose states provide material reciprocity. *See* Hauser, *supra* (quoting Documents of the Berne Convention 5 to 26 (June 1948) (Berne Bureau of International Union for the Protection of Literary and Artistic works, 1951)); Rothenberg, *The New French Copyright Act: Article 35*, 5 Bull. Copyright Soc'y 12 (1957) (stating that this protection is denied under article 14 of the Berne Convention (Brussels Revision), at least where a sale has also been consummated in the United States). The matter is still unclear in light of the *Huston* decision, as that case elevated the author's moral right of integrity to the status of national public policy but presented no opportunity to consider the corresponding economic right. *Huston c. La Cinq*, Court of Appeals, July 6, 1989.

France has allowed certain foreigners to claim droit de suite even when their country does not reciprocate, but only those individuals with five years' residence in France and a claim to participation in France's art world.

3. The European Union Directive on the Resale Right of 2001

In 2001, the European Parliament issued a directive requiring a resale right in EU counties. The Commission of the European Parliament investigating this matter noted that its purpose was to resolve disparities in resale rights in the EU. The Commission said that the unequal rights resulted in disproportionate sales in some countries.

The Commission presented the proposal for resale rights in 1996 which was reviewed by the European Parliament in 1997 and revised by the Commission in 1998. The European Council at the urging of Britain (and its thriving art auction businesses in London) added a ten-year transitional period. However, the Council and the Parliament agreed on a directive on July 3, 2001.

The resale right applies to subsequent sales of original works of graphical or plastic art. The works must be made by the artist himself in limited numbers or under the artist's authority. The right is inalienable and cannot be waived. The right applies to sales involving sellers, buyers, or intermediary art professionals. The resale right does not apply to sales between private persons or entities without an intermediary art professional, or to sales occurring less than three years after the first purchase from the artist when the resale price is less than €10,000. The seller of the art work is responsible for paying the royalty.

The resale royalty is a percentage of the sale price. The percentage is higher for works sold at lower prices. The total amount of resale royalty cannot exceed €12,500. This cap in effect exempts works selling at higher prices from the resale royalty. The directive will also result in a decrease in the set royalty rates in countries such as France, Spain, Belgium, Germany, Denmark, Greece, Finland, and Sweden, which provide higher resale royalties for the works with higher sale prices than the EU directive.

The minimum sale price for resale royalties is €3,000. This price is higher than the minimum prices in France, Germany, Greece, Portugal, Sweden, Finland, Belgium, Denmark, and Spain. Many of those countries do not even have a minimum sale price and the resale royalty applies to all sale prices. The Council arrived at the €3,000 minimum based on the determination that sales under €4,000 are almost always domestic sales.

The beneficiaries of the resale right are the artist or, after the artist's death, the artist's heirs. The member state's laws of succession determine the artist's heirs. The resale right applies only to artists who are citizens of EU countries or citizens of countries which grant the same protection. The resale right endures for the life of the artist plus 70 years.

Member states are responsible for ensuring that royalties are collected and distributed to the artists. Member states should adopt collective management societies for resale royalties. Although not required by the directive, collective societies can better protect the artists' interests because it is difficult for the individual artist to monitor all the sales of the artist's work and difficult for individual sellers to locate the artist to pay the royalty.

The directive was enacted on October 13, 2001. The directive permitted member states until January 1, 2006, to incorporate the provisions into their national laws. Member states that did not previously have a resale right (Austria, Ireland, The Netherlands, The United Kingdom) were permitted until January 1, 2010 to add the provisions. The UK did the most foot-dragging and requested a two-year extension. Thus, the directive did not take full effect in the EU until January 1, 2012. *See* Birgit Brenner, *The Resale Right Directive*, BILD-KUNST (2016), *http://www.bildkunst.de/en/copyright/resale-right/resale-right-in-the-european-union.html. See also* Wladimir Duchemin, *The Community Directive on the Resale Right*, RIDA Jan 2002 p. 3; Jennifer B. Pfeffer, *The Costs and Legal Impracticalities Facing Implementation of the European Union's* Droit de Suite *Directive in the United Kingdom*, 24 Nw. J. Int'l L. & Bus. 533 (2004).

The United Kingdom finally moved into compliance with the directive with the enactment of the Artist's Resale Rights Regulations 2006, U.K. Artist's Resale Right Regulations 2006 (S.I. 2006/346), which came into force on February 14, 2007. The UK provision allows the right for the same duration as copyright (life plus 70 years), and affords the right to public sales at auction or between dealers where the sale price is over 1,000 pounds. In addition, if the work in question was acquired from the artist within three years of the resale, the sale must exceed 10,000 pounds. The UK regulation mandates a sliding scale of royalty rates applied to the sale based on the sale price with a cap on the maximum royalty payable of 12,500 pounds. It is too early to tell whether the UK's vote to withdraw from the EU on June 23, 2016, will end its participation in the European resale royalty regime.

E. Economic Rights in the United States

Early versions of VARA contained a resale royalty provision that would have paid artists 7 percent of the appreciated value of a resold work as measured by its preceding purchase price. The proposed royalty would have been available only if the work had appreciated at least 150 percent and the resale price was at least $1,000. This provision of VARA would have run for a term of the life of the author plus 50 years. Congress instead directed the Register of Copyrights, in consultation with the Chair of the National Endowment for the Arts, to "study the feasibility of implementing" the proposed or a similar measure. The Copyright Office submitted its final report to Congress on December 1, 1992. This report suggested guidelines for incorporation of a resale royalty right, including the following: managing droit de suite through a private authors' rights-collecting society; initially applying droit de suite only to public auction sales; basing the royalty on the total resale price of the work; providing for a 3 to 5 percent royalty; providing that the term for droit de suite be the same as the copyright term; and applying droit de suite to foreign artists on the basis of reciprocity. *See* Kretsinger, *supra*, at 988.

1. Arguments Against Adoption of a U.S.A. Resale Royalty Statute

Jeffrey C. Wu, Art Resale Rights and the Art Resale Market: A Follow-Up Study

46 J. COPR. SOC. 531 (Summer 1999)*

Tom R. Camp, in the only investigation of its kind, studied Sotheby Parke Bernet auction results between 1973 and 1977 to establish the size and distribution of the secondary art market. Camp found that, indeed, very few

---

* Footnotes and citations omitted.

American artists have a significant secondary market, and that those artists tend to be the established ones.

This study is an update of Camp's 1980 study. In the twenty years since Camp's original project, auction results have become more easily available, allowing the compilation of a data set more representative of the overall secondary market. As well, changes in the world of contemporary art may have changed the size and distribution of this secondary market. This study aims to discover:

- How many artists have a significant resale market in the U.S.?
- How skewed would the distribution of resale proceeds be among U.S. artists? Among young and old artists? Among living artists and those recently dead? Among foreign artists?

II. THE STUDY

A. Objectives of the Study

The study set out to reproduce Camp's original 1980 investigation. Specifically, the study tried to answer six sets of questions:

- How many artists have a significant U.S. resale market?
- How skewed would the distribution of resale royalties be?
- Is there a young, starving artist?
- Does art appreciate after the artist's death?
- How many foreign artists would benefit from U.S. resale proceeds?
- How robust are the results?

C. Results of the Study

1) How many artists have a significant U.S. resale market?

Of the 233,000 U.S. citizens who classified themselves as "painters, sculptors, craft-artists, and artist printmakers," 357 (0.15 percent) have an art resale market of greater than $1,000 over the latest fifty-one month period. The mean total value in resales was $751,000, and the median $34,000 (translating into an average monthly resale income of $736, and a median monthly resale income of under $34). On average, each artist had twenty-one works resell (though the median artist only had five works resell over the fifty-one months — assuming, of course, that all works sold through public auction through these two-hundred U.S. auction houses represent resales).

Although the average value of works resold seems reasonably high, it should be noted that there is a remarkable skew in the results. In fact, only 118 artists had a fifty-one month resale market of greater than $102,000 — corresponding to a resale income of $100 per month, assuming a five percent resale royalty.

2) How Skewed Would the Distribution of Resale Royalties Be?

A handful of artists, notably de Kooning, Johns, Lichtenstein, Stella, and Rauschenberg, accounted for a disproportionate share of the resales by number and dollar value. . . .

Thus, the highest earning twenty percent of the artists (i.e., the highest earning seventy-two U.S. artists) would have received a median monthly resale royalty income of $1,084, and would have earned almost ninety-five percent of the total resale royalties accorded the top 357 U.S. artists, while artists ranked 73-144 would have earned only $125 per month, on average.

Even within the top quintile, there exists a skewed distribution. The five top artists would have earned more than fifty-five percent of the total resale rights. . . .

Comparing data between the Camp and the Wu study, it appears that over the last twenty years, the skewed concentration of resale value among artists has significantly increased.

3) Is There a Young, Starving Artist?

In his original study, Camp found that generally, the works that were resold were works of middle-aged artists. The average age of the artist at time of resale, he found, was fifty-four. To explain this seeming violation of the "romantic" notion of the young, starving artist, he argued that artists tend to improve as they mature, and that it is only at the end of the artist's career that we can look back and realize which works were truly great, and which works were merely signposts along the way.

Similarly, the 1994-1997 data indicate that the average age of the artist when her work was resold was fifty-six — slightly higher. But if one weights the artists' ages by the number of works resold or the value of works resold (thus giving greater weight to the more important pieces — the ones about which, presumably, we would be most outraged to hear a story of a "young, starving artist"), the average age of the artist at the time of sale increases first to sixty-three, then to an elderly seventy-one! This study strongly accords with Camp's tenuous conclusion that "[T]he idea of starving young artists selling works for a pittance which resell at fabulous prices in the future is not a particularly common problem."

4) Does Art Appreciate After the Artist's Death?

Camp tried to study the impact of the death of the artist upon the value of the artworks sold, since resale rights generally extend past the death of the artist, and are vested in the heirs of the artist — sometimes for as long as fifty years. Although he had little data on this point — his findings were statistically insignificant — Camp found little reason to believe that prices appreciate after death.

Similarly, the current study found only three U.S. artists with a significant number of works of art that sold both before and after their death during the period studied. This study also found no reason to believe that the price of artists' work increases after death. . . .

5) How many foreign artists would benefit from U.S. resale proceeds?

[I]t appears that over the last twenty years, the trend in the foreign contemporary art market has been the reverse of the trend in the domestic market — the concentration of resale value among foreign artists has dramatically fallen. However, the most likely explanation of this phenomenon lies not in any secular shift in the market, but in Camp's small data set: Camp's foreign artist analysis is skewed because that part of his study used data from only one year. In any particular year, if one work by an artist fetched an outstanding price, it would bring in an inordinately large share of the total dollar resale value. The benefits of the more robust sample, then, are most apparent here, where Camp's study was the thinnest.

It appears, then, that a larger data set confirms that resale concentrations among foreign artists reselling work in the United States is very similar to concentrations among U.S artists with a significant resale market (though perhaps slightly less concentrated, as signaled by the difference in percentage of the value captured by the top quintile of foreign artists (81.9%) as compared to domestic artists (94.7%)). . . .

III. CONCLUSION

In the debate over the droit de suite, both sides have been guilty of making arguments before fully examining the evidence. This investigation, a follow-up to a twenty-year-old study that remains the only major empirical one of its kind, demonstrates that at least some of that evidence is readily attainable, and that some of the assumptions currently being made are inaccurate. This investigation has come to five broad conclusions.

First, that the secondary market for contemporary art in the United States is very small. Only a tiny proportion of contemporary artists will ever see one of their works resold.

Second, that the secondary market for contemporary art that does exist is highly skewed towards a few established artists. A resale right, then, especially one with a high minimum resale floor, will not benefit any but the most successful contemporary artists. Conversely, a resale right with a low minimum resale floor is likely to affect a larger number (but still insignificant proportion) of artists, but will have a negligible impact on them.

Third, that cases like the Rauschenberg-Scull incident, in which art bought just a few years earlier while an artist is relatively unknown appreciates wildly, rarely occur. Most art that is resold — especially art that is resold at high prices — is sold towards the end of an artist's career, while he is relatively established.

Fourth, that the secondary market for foreign artists in the U.S. is distributed similarly to the market for U.S. artists.

And fifth, that the results obtained by using data generated from the upper end of the secondary market are likely to hold generally for the entire secondary market.

2. The California Resale Royalty Statute

In 1975, Representative Sieroty introduced a bill into the California legislature (AB 1391). Unfortunately, the bill failed to pass but was resubmitted in

1976 and was passed and signed into law on September 22, 1976. California thus became the first American state to recognize and adopt the European concept of droit de suite. *See* Cal. Civ. Code § 986.[32] This law represented a step forward in economic rights of artists, although it does have many problems still to be judicially resolved. Section 986(a) provides:

> Whenever a work of fine art is sold and the seller resides in California or the sale takes place in California, the seller or the seller's agent shall pay to the artist of such work of fine art; or to such artist's agent; 5 percent of the amount of such sale. The right of the artist to receive an amount equal to 5 percent of the amount of such sale may be waived only by a contract in writing providing for an amount in excess of 5 percent of the amount of such sale. An artist may assign the right to collect the royalty payment provided by this section to another individual or entity. However, the assignment shall not have the effect of creating a waiver prohibited by this subdivision.

Subsection (a)(1) of California's statute provides: "When a work of fine art is sold at an auction or by a gallery, dealer, broker, museum, or other person acting as the agent for the seller the agent shall withhold 5 percent of the amount of the sale, locate that artist and pay the artist." The extraterritorial problems discussed above are underscored when it is noted that the duty would be imposed on the nonresident agent specified in this subsection. Thus, if Sotheby Parke-Bernet in New York sold a painting owned by a Californian, it would be required to withhold the artist's royalty from the auction price and attempt to locate the artist in order to transmit such amount. Note that "artist" is defined as "the person who creates a work of fine art and who, at the time of resale, is a citizen of the United States, or a resident of the state who has resided in the state for a minimum of two years." § 986(c)(1). A gallery, for example, apparently would be required to search the entire country and if, after 90 days, it is unsuccessful in locating the artist, pay the proceeds to the California Arts Council. § 986(a)(2). No provision is made for deducting the cost of this search from the amount due the artist. Subsection (a)(3) gives the artist three years from the date of sale or one year from the date of the discovery of the sale, whichever is longer, within which to commence an action against the seller or seller's agent if the royalty is not paid. Amendments added to this section during the 1982-83 legislative session provide for attorneys' fees to the prevailing party as determined by the court. § 986(a)(3).

The mechanics for administering the proceeds paid into the "Arts Council" are addressed in §§ 986(a)(4) and (5). The monies held by a seller or seller's agent for the artist under this statute are beyond the reach of seller's or agent's creditors. § 986(a)(6). Apparently the droit de suite proceeds are to be treated as trust funds for the artist when the money is held by the seller or seller's agent. Monies held by the council and not claimed by the artist within

---

32. Leonard D. DuBoff, a co-author of this book, helped draft the California Resale Royalty Act.

seven years are to be spent by the council on California's "Art in Public Buildings" program. § 986(a)(5).

Subsection (b) of § 986 provides that the droit de suite statute does not apply:

> (1) To the initial sale of a work of fine art where legal title to such work at the time of such initial sale is vested in the artist thereof; (2) To the resale of a work of fine art for a gross sales price of less than one thousand dollars ($1,000); (3) Except as provided in paragraph (7) of subdivision (a), to a resale after the death of such artist; (4) To the resale of the work of fine art for a gross sales price less than the purchase price paid by the seller; (5) To a transfer of a work of fine art which is exchanged for one or more works of fine art or for a combination of cash, other property, and one or more works of fine art where the fair market value of the property exchanged is less than one thousand dollars ($1,000); (6) To the resale of a work of fine art by an art dealer to a purchaser within 10 years of the initial sale of the work of fine art by the artist to an art dealer, provided all intervening resales are between art dealers; (7) To a sale of a work of stained glass artistry where the work has been permanently attached to real property and is sold as part of the sale of the real property to which it is attached.

Amendments in 1982 modified subsection (3), which now allows heirs, legatees, or personal representatives of the artist to claim the royalty for a period of 20 years after the death of the artist. The amendment applies to any artist who dies after January 1, 1983. § 986(a)(7). This amendment, in addition to enhancing the benefits ultimately accruing to the artist, lessens the practical problem of determining whether an artist is still alive when a work is being sold. If, for example, the artist is Picasso, the media probably will have carried the story of his death, although the demise of a less famous artist is not likely to be accorded the same publicity.

The exemption for pieces resold for a gross sales price that is less than the purchase price paid by the seller implies that a droit de suite royalty is payable when the gross resale price and the original price are equal. This means that a seller who was forced to pay a sales commission when he or she only received the exact amount originally paid for the piece will be losing money. A seller will have to resell for a price exceeding the artist's royalty before the seller can break even, regardless of the inflation factor.

Perhaps the most difficult constitutional problem with the California statute is the fact that it appears to apply to works created before it became effective, meaning that sellers would have their property taken without receiving just compensation, as they currently own their art without any droit de suite restrictions. It is well established under the 14th Amendment to the U.S. Constitution that a state may not constitutionally take an individual's property without paying just compensation. *See Chicago, Burlington & Quincy R.R. v. Chicago*, 166 U.S. 226 (1897).

The legislature may have foreseen some of these difficulties because both § 986(e) and § 2 of the statute are designed to preserve the droit de suite wherever possible in the event that some portion of the law is struck down or amended. Section 986(e) states that

[i]f any provision of this section or the application thereof to any person or circumstance is held invalid for any reason, such invalidity shall not affect any other provisions or applications of this section which can be effected, without the invalid provision or application, and to this end the provisions of this section are severable.

Section 2 reads as follows:

The rights of an artist of a work of fine art to receive payment of an amount equal to 5 percent of the amount of a sale of fine art within the provisions of Section 986 shall be vested at the time of such sale; except that an artist shall have no rights to any payment pursuant to this act, if any provision therein is subsequently repealed so as to remove the provisions for such payment, as to any sale which occurs subsequent to such repeal; and except that, in the event any provision in this act is otherwise subsequently amended or changed, an artist shall have only those rights to payment provided for by such subsequent amendment or change and shall have no rights to any payment pursuant to this act, as to any sale which occurs subsequent to such amendment or change.

California's droit de suite legislation has withstood at least one judicial challenge based on federal copyright preemption. In *Morseburg v. Balyon,* 621 F.2d 972 (9th Cir.), *cert. denied,* 449 U.S. 983 (1980), the Ninth Circuit Court of Appeals held that the 1909 Copyright Act did not preempt the state resale royalty right. The case involved a gallery owner who challenged the constitutionality of the California statute, basing his claim on §§ 1 and 27 of the 1909 Copyright Act. (The concepts contained in these sections were carried forward in the new Copyright Revision Act of 1976, and codified at § 106 and § 109, respectively.) Section 1 stated that anyone complying with the provisions of the copyright law had the exclusive right to "vend" the copyrighted work. Section 27 stated that nothing in the law would be deemed to prohibit the transfer of a lawfully obtained copy of a copyrighted work. The gallery owner alleged that California violated the two sections of the 1909 Act because the Resale Royalties Act impaired an artist's ability to sell works and restricted the subsequent transfer of works to the purchaser.

The Court of Appeals held that the right to "vend" a work, as provided by § 1 of the 1909 Act, did not give one the right to transfer the work at all times and all places free of all claims of others. Rather, the right to sell gave the artist an exclusive right to transfer title for consideration to others or the right of first sale. According to the court, the California statute did not impair this right but created an additional right in personam against a subsequent seller of a work of fine art. Furthermore, the act did not violate § 27, because the fact that a resale may create a liability to the creator artist does not in any way restrict the transfer of artwork. For these reasons, the court ruled that the 1909 Act did not preempt the California statute and indicated that the result would be the same under the Copyright Revision Act of 1976.

One of the statute's more vocal critics also has been a recipient of royalty payments. Artist Bruce Beasley, after receiving approximately $600 in resale royalties, complained that the law was inequitable as it only benefited top artists, ignoring "younger artists at the bottom of the pyramid." It was his position that the statute would deter galleries from helping newcomers. *See* Collector/Investor, Aug. 1981, at 5.

ASSESSMENT

1. If a court closely followed the holding of the Monty Python case, *Gilliam v. ABC*, what activity would the court be most likely to punish or prohibit?

    (A) Significant cropping of a photograph by a magazine that obtained the rights to reproduce the photograph from the photographer's licensee

    (B) Destruction of a mural by the owner of the property on which the mural was painted

    (C) A sub-licensee's failure to deliver a miniaturized version of a sculpture after the client saw and approved of the sculpture

    (D) Both (A) and (C) above

2. Assuming an artist did not contract her rights away and assuming she maintained ownership of the copyright to the work, would the artist be able to prevail on a VARA right of integrity claim to prevent the destruction of or allow the artist to remove her mural painted in the lobby of a federal courthouse?

    (A) Yes, if the work is of "recognized stature" and removal would be prejudicial to the artist's reputation

    (B) Yes, if the work can be removed without affecting the integrity of the building, then the owner should give her notice and allow her to remove it

    (C) Yes, U.S. courts consistently recognize a special "site specific" claim under VARA

    (D) Both (A) and (B) above

3. Which of the following is not a feature or provision of the California Right of Continuation Statute?

    (A) It only applies to art whose sale price exceeds $1,000

    (B) If an effort to track down the artist fails, the money is paid to the California Arts Commission in trust for the artist; if unclaimed after 7 years, it is used for public art

    (C) Receipt of the money can be waived by contract

    (D) All of the above are features or provisions of the statute

4. What was special about Bernard Buffet's refrigerator?

    (A) A French moral rights claim prevented the work from being sold in six separate pieces

(B) A French droit de suite claim brought a great deal of money to Buffet when the work was sold at auction to a taxi cab mogul

(C) A French moral rights claim assured Buffet of the right to complete the installation of the work in the headquarters of Renault Corporation

(D) A French right of respect claim allowed Buffet to determine whether or not the work was complete for purposes of division of community property upon his divorce from his wife

ASSESSMENT ANSWERS

1. If a court closely followed the holding of the Monty Python case, *Gilliam v. ABC*, what activity would the court be most likely to punish or prohibit?

   (A) Significant cropping of a photograph by a magazine that obtained the rights to reproduce the photograph from the photographer's licensee

   (B) Destruction of a mural by the owner of the property on which the mural was painted

   (C) A sub-licensee's failure to deliver a miniaturized version of a sculpture after the client saw and approved of the sculpture

   (D) Both (A) and (C) above

   ANSWER: The answer is (A), significant cropping of a photograph by a magazine that obtained the rights to reproduce the photograph from the photographer's licensee. This answer represents the parallel situation of one whose license to republish a work did not include the rights to alter the work or to create derivative works in copyright law. Choice (B), destruction of a mural by the owner of the property on which the mural was painted, is incorrect — the issue in *Gilliam* was not about destruction of the work. Choice (C), a sub-licensee's failure to deliver a miniaturized version of a sculpture after the client saw and approved of the sculpture, is far removed from the facts and issues of *Gilliam*. Therefore, (D), "Both (A) and (C) above," cannot be correct.

2. Assuming an artist did not contract her rights away and assuming she maintained ownership of the copyright to the work, would the artist be able to prevail on a VARA right of integrity claim to prevent the destruction of or allow the artist to remove her mural painted in the lobby of a federal courthouse?

   (A) Yes, if the work is of "recognized stature" and removal would be prejudicial to the artist's reputation

   (B) Yes, if the work can be removed without affecting the integrity of the building, then the owner should give her notice and allow her to remove it

(C) Yes, U.S. courts consistently recognize a special "site specific" claim under VARA

(D) Both (A) and (B) above

ANSWER: The answer is (D), "Both (A) and (B) above." VARA requires a finding that a work is "of recognized stature" in order to be protected under the right of integrity, and requires proof of reputational injury to sustain a claim, making Choice (A) correct. VARA also provides that if a work can be removed without affecting the integrity of the building, then the owner should give the artist notice and allow her to remove it, making Choice (B) correct. Choice (C), on the other hand, is incorrect because U.S. courts continue to resist the full recognition of the meaning and value of conceptual art, including site-specific art, leading to less protection of site-specific art.

3. Which of the following is not a feature or provision of the California Right of Continuation Statute?

(A) It only applies to art whose sale price exceeds $1,000

(B) If an effort to track down the artist fails, the money is paid to the California Arts Commission in trust for the artist; if unclaimed after 7 years, it is used for public art

(C) Receipt of the money can be waived by contract

(D) All of the above are features or provisions of the statute

ANSWER: The answer is (C), receipt of the money can be waived by contract. Waiver of receipt of resale royalties is not permitted under the California statute. The parties can contract for a different rate of resale royalty, but it cannot be lower than the statutory rate. The other choices, (A) and (B), are part of the statute.

4. What was special about Bernard Buffet's refrigerator?

(A) A French moral rights claim prevented the work from being sold in six separate pieces

(B) A French droit de suite claim brought a great deal of money to Buffet when the work was sold at auction to a taxi cab mogul

(C) A French moral rights claim assured Buffet of the right to complete the installation of the work in the headquarters of Renault Corporation

(D) A French right of respect claim allowed Buffet to determine whether or not the work was complete for purposes of division of community property upon his divorce from his wife

ANSWER: The answer is (A), a French moral rights claim prevented the work from being sold in six separate pieces. Bernard Buffet's case drew attention for its strict adherence to the French right of integrity formula, even in a case where the art was painted on a household appliance whose panels were separable from the whole. Choice (B) suggests the incident where Robert Rauschenberg lashed out at taxi mogul Robert Scull after Scull sold Rauschenberg's *Thaw* for $85,000, having paid $900 for the piece 15 years earlier, and Rauschenberg, disappointed at the lack of an American droit de suite right, is said to have told Scull, "I've been working my ass off for you to make that profit!" Choice (C) recalls the Dubuffet dispute with Renault Corporation where Renault was compelled to allow Dubuffet to finish the art he had planned for Renault headquarters. Choice (D) recalls the dispute of Pierre Bonnard, who faced an issue over "completed" vs. incomplete paintings in a community property settlement with the heirs of his deceased wife.

5 | RIGHT OF PUBLICITY

The right of publicity protects a person's name, image, likeness, persona, and often their voice or other distinctive characteristics, from unauthorized commercial exploitation by others. The general idea is that persons have the right to control the exploitation of their name and other features of their personality, and a wrong is done when someone usurps that right without permission. In the United States, these personality rights travel under two names with two widely different theoretical justifications: the right of privacy and the right of publicity. Some state laws, such as New York Civil Rights Law §§ 50, 51, still include both concepts of the rights, privacy and publicity, to be protected within the same law. Federal law does not supersede the field of publicity law, although Section 43(a)(1) of the Lanham Act, 15 U.S.C. § 1125(a)(1), creates a federal remedy for false representations or false designations of origin used in connection with the sale of a product that sometimes is used to attempt to vindicate an unauthorized use of a celebrity's name or likeness in commerce or trade.

Publicity and privacy laws attempt to regulate and prevent: (1) privacy torts such as invasion of privacy, or publication of private facts in a false light, or the wrongful appropriation of a private person's likeness or persona for commercial purposes, and (more importantly to our discussion here) (2) the property offense of wrongful appropriation of a famous person's valuable name, likeness, or persona. America is one of the first, if not the first, nations to identify personality rights (specifically, privacy rights), which are traced to an 1890 law review article by Louis Brandeis and Samuel Warren.[1] American legislatures and courts developed the law in fits and starts in the first half of the twentieth century, but did not separate the tort claims of privacy law from the entirely property-driven claims of the right of publicity until the mid-1950s.[2]

---

1. Samuel Warren & Louis D. Brandeis, *The Right to Privacy*, 4 HARV. L. REV. 193 (1890) (hereinafter, "Warren & Brandeis").

2. In *Haelan Laboratories, Inc. v. Topps Chewing Gum, Inc.*, 202 F.2d 866 (2d Cir. 1953), to be exact.

There is no single theoretical justification for the protection of personality rights in the United States. Like trademark rights, personality rights have little or no intellectual requirements as compared to other intellectual property rights such as patents and copyrights. In blunt terms, nothing requires you to be original or clever to become a famous celebrity or the victim of an invasion of privacy. Nonetheless, several of the theoretical justifications for the protection of personality rights parallel the justifications for the protection of intellectual property: (1) to encourage the development of skills and the amassing of accomplishments that coincidentally lead to valuable celebrity-status and fame so as to benefit society and culture (the intellectual property theory of the United States); (2) to protect property rights earned through effort and labor, honing one's skills or perfecting one's art (the "labor" theory of intellectual property rights); (3) to prevent unjust enrichment at the expense of others, taking for free what others pay for (a nearly universal concept of fairness and equity); and (4) to compensate for a wrong inflicted on the claimant under a simple tort theory of duty and breach and harm (another nearly universal concept of tort law).

No single justification fits every claimant and every legal situation: the overnight celebrity has expended little labor and has not necessarily achieved a high level of skill in any useful endeavor, but still has valuable rights to protect. The private person whose name or image is used in association with a disreputable product causing shame and hurt to the person has no fame or valuable image to protect, nor has the person necessarily expended labor to become or remain "private"; this claimant merely seeks restitution or compensation for injuries suffered to her person. Add to this the issue that personality rights may or may not descend to a person's heirs — a popular outcome if you take a strictly property-driven view of the matter, but an unlikely outcome if your theory is based on tort law and personal injuries — and you begin to see the scope of the problems in this rapidly developing area of the law.

Why are personality rights discussed in an art law course text? The answer is that artists are as likely as anyone to become entangled in a dispute over the use of another person's name, likeness, or persona. Artists often communicate through symbolic speech (images or names and the meanings connoted by the images or names), and celebrities have an instrumental purpose of "standing for something." If symbols are a shortcut from mind to mind,[3] celebrities and sports figures can be a shorthand expression for bravery, hubris, debauchery, sophistication, or many other aspects of the human condition. A few fine arts artists achieve celebrity-status of their own and will seek to protect it, but most artists will face the law from the perspective of an alleged infringer of personality rights.

---

3. *West Virginia Board of Education v. Barnette*, 319 U.S. 624, 632 (1943).

A. The Right of Publicity as a Property Interest

PROBLEM 5-1

 David Beckham is an internationally known football (soccer) star. In 2009, shortly after Beckham left his team, the Los Angeles Galaxy, in order to play for Italian super-team AC Milan, Toro Sports International Ltd. starting giving out small, hand-squeezable stress relievers shaped like footballs (soccer balls) at international trade shows and to buyers and sales persons at major sports retailers worldwide.[4] The stress relievers had the image of Beckham on one side and the distinctive "T" logo and Toro Sports Int'l Ltd. mark on the other side. Each stress reliever also bore the following message that circled the image of Beckham: "I'll retire in England Spain Los Angeles? Italy? Wherever they pay me the mo$t!" There were versions of the ball created with the text in English, Chinese, French, German, Italian, Japanese, Portuguese, and Spanish. Beckham did not authorize this use of his image, and he seeks advice on how to combat this blatant theft of his image and persona.

Zacchini v. Scripps-Howard Broadcasting Company

433 U.S. 562 (1977)*

Mr. Justice WHITE delivered the opinion of the Court.

Petitioner, Hugo Zacchini, is an entertainer. He performs a "human cannonball" act in which he is shot from a cannon into a net some 200 feet away. Each performance occupies some 15 seconds. In August and September 1972, petitioner was engaged to perform his act on a regular basis at the Geauga County Fair in Burton, Ohio. He performed in a fenced area, surrounded by grandstands, at the fair grounds. Members of the public attending the fair were not charged a separate admission fee to observe his act.

---

4. Michael D. Murray, Composite image of soccer ball bearing a cropped, revised, and resized thumbnail image of soccer player, David Beckham, surrounded by ironic words (2009).

* Some footnotes eliminated.

On August 30, a freelance reporter for Scripps-Howard Broadcasting Co., the operator of a television broadcasting station and respondent in this case, attended the fair. He carried a small movie camera. Petitioner noticed the reporter and asked him not to film the performance. The reporter did not do so on that day; but on the instructions of the producer of respondent's daily newscast, he returned the following day and videotaped the entire act. This film clip, approximately 15 seconds in length, was shown on the 11 o'clock news program that night, together with favorable commentary.*

Petitioner then brought this action for damages, alleging that he is "engaged in the entertainment business," that the act he performs is one "invented by his father and . . . performed only by his family for the last fifty years," that respondent "showed and commercialized the film of his act without his consent," and that such conduct was an "unlawful appropriation of plaintiff's professional property." Respondent answered and moved for summary judgment, which was granted by the trial court.

The Court of Appeals of Ohio reversed. The majority held that petitioner's complaint stated a cause of action for conversion and for infringement of a common-law copyright, and one judge concurred in the judgment on the ground that the complaint stated a cause of action for appropriation of petitioner's "right of publicity" in the film of his act. All three judges agreed that the First Amendment did not privilege the press to show the entire performance on a news program without compensating petitioner for any financial injury he could prove at trial.

Like the concurring judge in the Court of Appeals, the Supreme Court of Ohio rested petitioner's cause of action under state law on his "right to the

---

5. Michael D. Murray, Collage of three cropped, revised, and resized thumbnail images derived from photographs depicting Human Cannonball Hugo Zacchini (2014), the claimant in *Zacchini v. Scripps-Howard Broadcasting Co.*, 433 U.S. 562 (1977).

* The script of the commentary accompanying the film clip read as follows:

This . . . now . . . is the story of a true spectator sport . . . the sport of human cannonballing . . . in fact, the great Zacchini is about the only human cannonball around, these days . . . just happens that, where he is, is the Great Geauga County Fair, in Burton . . . and believe me, although it's not a long act, it's a thriller . . . and you really need to see it in person . . . to appreciate it. . . . App. 12.

publicity value of his performance." 47 Ohio St. 2d 224, 351 N.E. 2d 454, 455 (1976). The opinion syllabus, to which we are to look for the rule of law used to decide the case, declared first that one may not use for his own benefit the name or likeness of another, whether or not the use or benefit is a commercial one, and second that respondent would be liable for the appropriation over petitioner's objection and in the absence of license or privilege, of petitioner's right to the publicity value of his performance. *Ibid.* The court nevertheless gave judgment for respondent because, in the words of the syllabus:

> A TV station has a privilege to report in its newscasts matters of legitimate public interest which would otherwise be protected by an individual's right of publicity, unless the actual intent of the TV station was to appropriate the benefit of the publicity for some non-privileged private use, or unless the actual intent was to injure the individual. *Ibid.*

We granted certiorari, 429 U.S. 1037, 97 S. Ct. 730, 50 L. Ed. 2d 74 (1977), to consider an issue unresolved by this Court: whether the First and Fourteenth Amendments immunized respondent from damages for its alleged infringement of petitioner's state law "right of publicity." Insofar as the Ohio Supreme Court held that the First and Fourteenth Amendments of the United States Constitution required judgment for respondent, we reverse the judgment of that court. . . .

The Ohio Supreme Court held that respondent is constitutionally privileged to include in its newscasts matters of public interest that would otherwise be protected by the right of publicity, absent an intent to injure or to appropriate for some nonprivileged purpose. If under this standard respondent had merely reported that petitioner was performing at the fair and described or commented on his act, with or without showing his picture on television, we would have a very different case. But petitioner is not contending that his appearance at the fair and his performance could not be reported by the press as newsworthy items. His complaint is that respondent filmed his entire act and displayed that film on television for the public to see and enjoy. This, he claimed, was an appropriation of his professional property. The Ohio Supreme Court agreed that petitioner had "a right of publicity" that gave him "personal control over commercial display and exploitation of his personality and the exercise of his talents." This right of "exclusive control over the publicity given to his performances" was said to be such a "valuable part of the benefit which may be attained by his talents and efforts" that it was entitled to legal protection. It was also observed, or at least expressly assumed, that petitioner had not abandoned his rights by performing under the circumstances present at the Geauga County Fair Grounds.

The Ohio Supreme Court nevertheless held that the challenged invasion was privileged, saying that the press "must be accorded broad latitude in its choice of how much it presents of each story or incident, and of the emphasis to be given to such presentation. No fixed standard which would bar the press from reporting or depicting either an entire occurrence or an entire discrete part of a public performance can be formulated which would not unduly restrict the 'breathing room' in reporting which freedom of the press requires."

47 Ohio St. 2d, at 235, 351 N.E. 2d, at 461. Under this view, respondent was thus constitutionally free to film and display petitioner's entire act. The Ohio Supreme Court relied heavily on *Time, Inc. v. Hill*, 385 U.S. 374, 87 S. Ct. 534, 17 L. Ed. 2d 456 (1967), but that case does not mandate a media privilege to televise a performer's entire act without his consent. . . .

Time, Inc. v. Hill, which was hotly contested and decided by a divided Court, involved an entirely different tort from the "right of publicity" recognized by the Ohio Supreme Court. As the opinion reveals in *Time, Inc. v. Hill*, the Court was steeped in the literature of privacy law and was aware of the developing distinctions and nuances in this branch of the law. The Court, for example, cited W. Prosser, Law of Torts 831-832 (3d ed. 1964), and the same author's well-known article, *Privacy*, 48 CALIF. L. REV. 383 (1960), both of which divided privacy into four distinct branches. The Court was aware that it was adjudicating a "false light" privacy case involving a matter of public interest, not a case involving "intrusion," 385 U.S., at 384-385, n. 9, 87 S. Ct., at 540, "appropriation" of a name or likeness for the purposes of trade, *id.*, at 381, 87 S. Ct., at 538, or "private details" about a non-newsworthy person or event, *id.*, at 383 n. 7, 87 S. Ct., at 539. It is also abundantly clear that *Time, Inc. v. Hill* did not involve a performer, a person with a name having commercial value, or any claim to a "right of publicity." This discrete kind of "appropriation" case was plainly identified in the literature cited by the Court.

The differences between these two torts are important. First, the State's interests in providing a cause of action in each instance are different. "The interest protected" in permitting recovery for placing the plaintiff in a false light "is clearly that of reputation, with the same overtones of mental distress as in defamation." Prosser, *supra*, 48 CALIF. L. REV., at 400. By contrast, the State's interest in permitting a 'right of publicity' is in protecting the proprietary interest of the individual in his act in part to encourage such entertainment. As we later note, the State's interest is closely analogous to the goals of patent and copyright law, focusing on the right of the individual to reap the reward of his endeavors and having little to do with protecting feelings or reputation. Second, the two torts differ in the degree to which they intrude on dissemination of information to the public. In "false light" cases the only way to protect the interests involved is to attempt to minimize publication of the damaging matter, while in "right of publicity" cases the only question is who gets to do the publishing. An entertainer such as petitioner usually has no objection to the widespread publication of his act as long as he gets the commercial benefit of such publication. Indeed, in the present case petitioner did not seek to enjoin the broadcast of his act; he simply sought compensation for the broadcast in the form of damages. . . .

The broadcast of a film of petitioner's entire act poses a substantial threat to the economic value of that performance. As the Ohio court recognized, this act is the product of petitioner's own talents and energy, the end result of much time, effort, and expense. Much of its economic value lies in the "right of exclusive control over the publicity given to his performance"; if the public can see the act free on television, it will be less willing to pay to see it at the fair.

The effect of a public broadcast of the performance is similar to preventing petitioner from charging an admission fee. "The rationale for (protecting the right of publicity) is the straightforward one of preventing unjust enrichment by the theft of good will. No social purpose is served by having the defendant get free some aspect of the plaintiff that would have market value and for which he would normally pay." Kalven, *Privacy in Tort Law: Were Warren and Brandeis Wrong?*, 31 Law & Contemp. Probs. 326, 331 (1966). Moreover, the broadcast of petitioner's entire performance, unlike the unauthorized use of another's name for purposes of trade or the incidental use of a name or picture by the press, goes to the heart of petitioner's ability to earn a living as an entertainer. Thus, in this case, Ohio has recognized what may be the strongest case for a "right of publicity" involving, not the appropriation of an entertainer's reputation to enhance the attractiveness of a commercial product, but the appropriation of the very activity by which the entertainer acquired his reputation in the first place.

Of course, Ohio's decision to protect petitioner's right of publicity here rests on more than a desire to compensate the performer for the time and effort invested in his act; the protection provides an economic incentive for him to make the investment required to produce a performance of interest to the public. This same consideration underlies the patent and copyright laws long enforced by this Court. As the Court stated in *Mazer v. Stein*, 347 U.S. 201, 219, 74 S. Ct. 460, 471, 98 L. Ed. 630 (1954):

> 376. The economic philosophy behind the clause empowering Congress to grant patents and copyrights is the conviction that encouragement of individual effort by personal gain is the best way to advance public welfare through the talents of authors and inventors in "Science and useful Arts." Sacrificial days devoted to such creative activities deserve rewards commensurate with the services rendered.

. . . There is no doubt that entertainment, as well as news, enjoys First Amendment protection. It is also true that entertainment itself can be important news. *Time, Inc. v. Hill.* But it is important to note that neither the public nor respondent will be deprived of the benefit of petitioner's performance as long as his commercial stake in his act is appropriately recognized. Petitioner does not seek to enjoin the broadcast of his performance; he simply wants to be paid for it. Nor do we think that a state-law damages remedy against respondent would represent a species of liability without fault contrary to the letter or spirit of *Gertz v. Robert Welch, Inc.*, 418 U.S. 323, 94 S. Ct. 2997, 41 L. Ed. 2d 789 (1974). Respondent knew that petitioner objected to televising his act, but nevertheless displayed the entire film.

We conclude that although the State of Ohio may as a matter of its own law privilege the press in the circumstances of this case, the First and Fourteenth Amendments do not require it to do so.

Reversed.

Notes and Questions

1. *Zacchini* justified the right of publicity on three grounds: (1) don't take for free what everyone else pays for; (2) the need to reward the sweat of the brow of entertainers and celebrities who spend years perfecting their craft; (3) the need to encourage people to invest effort in creative endeavors that lead to celebrity because that will enrich society as a whole.

2. *Carson v. Here's Johnny Portable Toilets,* 698 F.2d 831 (6th Cir. 1983), shows the breadth of the right of publicity. Johnny Carson was allowed to protect a catch phrase, "Here's Johnny!," that he doesn't even utter but which is firmly and undeniably associated with him. *See also Facenda v. N.F.L. Films, Inc.,* 543 F.3d 1007 (3d Cir. 2008) (appropriation of distinctive NFL announcer's voice); *Doe v. TCI Cablevision,* 110 S.W. 3d 363 (Mo. 2003) (appropriation of hockey player Tony Twist's name and his role and hockey-playing public reputation as an "enforcer"), *cert. denied sub nom McFarlane v. Twist,* 540 U.S. 1106 (2004), *appeal after new trial, Doe v. McFarlane,* 207 S.W. 3d 52 (Mo. Ct. App. E. Dist. 2006); *Prima v. Darden Restaurants, Inc.,* 78 F. Supp. 2d 337 (D.N.J. 2000) (appropriation of singer's voice); *Henley v. Dillard Dep't Stores,* 46 F. Supp. 2d 587 (N.D. Tex. 1999) (appropriation of singer's name); *Elvis Presley Enters. v. Capece,* 141 F.3d 188 (5th Cir. 1998) (appropriation of celebrity's name and aspects of his life and reputation); *Newcombe v. Adolf Coors Co.,* 157 F.3d 686 (9th Cir. 1998) (appropriation of likeness of baseball pitcher; drawing depicted his player number and his unique stance on the pitcher's mound); *Abdul-Jabbar v. General Motors Corp.,* 85 F.3d 407 (9th Cir. 1996) (use of film clips of basketball player in NCAA tournament when player went by the name Lew Alcindor; celebrity did not waive or abandon claims regarding his image and persona when he changed his name); *Ali v. Playgirl, Inc.,* 447 F. Supp. 723 (S.D.N.Y. 1978) (appropriation of silhouette of boxer Muhammad Ali in context of his famous moniker, "The Greatest," was actionable). The breadth of the publicity law is, of course, dependent on the local courts' interpretation of the law; New York, for example, has given a fairly narrow interpretation to its right of privacy and publicity law requiring the use of plaintiff's "portrait or picture." *E.g., Burck v. Mars, Inc.,* 571 F. Supp. 2d 446 (S.D.N.Y. 2008) (M&M candy figure dressed in the costume of plaintiff street performer Burck, a/k/a "The Naked Cowboy," was not a use in trade of Burck's "portrait or picture," and was not actionable under the N.Y. Civ. Rights Law § 51).

3. Public figures may have an additional problem when their adversaries are the news media — newspapers and other media outlets have a First Amendment freedom of press to publish information and images of newsworthy people and events. *See, e.g., Hoffman v. Capital Cities/*

ABC, Inc., 255 F.3d 1180 (9th Cir. 2001) (photo-spread of current fashions was proper subject of public interest allowing defendant to include allusion to plaintiff's "Tootsie" character in the photo-spread).

4. The right of publicity is one of the four torts born out of the right of privacy, wherein a person who appropriates the name or likeness of another for his benefit may be liable for invasion of the other's privacy. Restatement (Second) of Torts § 652C (Am. Law Inst. 1965). As of the middle of the twentieth century, the right of publicity frequently was recognized as a cause of action distinct from the right of privacy. *See, e.g., Haelan Laboratories, Inc. v. Topps Chewing Gum, Inc.*, 202 F.2d 866 (2d Cir. 1953); *State ex. rel. Elvis Presley v. Crowell*, 733 S.W. 2d 89, 97 (Tenn. Ct. App. 1987); *Martin Luther King, Jr. Center for Social Change, Inc. v. American Heritage Products Inc.*, 250 Ga. 135, 296 S.E. 2d 697, 703 (1982); *Lugosi v. Universal Pictures*, 25 Cal. 3d 813, 160 Cal. Rptr. 323, 329, 603 P.2d 425, 431 (1979).

5. The right of publicity allows a person to recover damages only for pecuniary gain from misappropriation of their likeness. *Haelan*, 202 F.2d at 867-68. It protects a person from losing the benefit of their work in creating a publicly recognizable persona. *Id.* In contrast to the right of privacy, the right of publicity is not intended to protect the person's feelings but provides a cause of action where a defendant has been unjustly enriched by misappropriation of the person's valuable public persona or image. *Id.* It may also be necessary to have publicity to protect. In some jurisdictions, establishing the fame or value of one's image or likeness is a necessary element for the cause of action. *See, e.g., Ji v. Bose Corp.*, 538 F. Supp. 2d 349 (D. Mass. 2008) (plaintiff model did not establish that she has a recognizable and valueable image and likeness to protect).

6. Not all uses of another's name or likeness are tortious. A cause of action for common law misappropriation of a plaintiff's name or likeness may be pled by alleging: (a) the defendant's use of the plaintiff's identity; (b) the appropriation of plaintiff's name or likeness to defendant's advantage, commercially or otherwise; (c) lack of consent; and (d) resulting injury. *See Jackson v. MPI Home Video*, 694 F. Supp. 483, 492 (N.D. Ill. 1988); *Haelan*, 202 F.2d at 867-68.

7. Although all people have the right to be free from the unauthorized exploitation of their likeness, not every publication of someone's likeness gives rise to an appropriation action. *Compare Downing v. Abercrombie & Fitch*, 265 F.3d 994 (9th Cir. 2001) (use of photographs of famous surfer in defendant's catalog violated surfer's right of publicity because catalog was commercial speech), *and Toney v. L'Oreal USA, Inc.*, 406 F.3d 905 (7th Cir. 2005) (unauthorized use of photo on hair product trade dress), *and Christoff v. Nestle USA, Inc.*, 62 Cal. Rptr. 3d 122 (Ct. App.) (unauthorized use of image on coffee label), *rev. granted and op. superseded*, 69 P.3d 888 (Cal. 2007), *with Tyne v. Time Warner Entertainment Co.*, L.P., 901 So. 2d 802 (Fla. 2005) (the term

"commercial purpose" as used in Fla. Rt. of Publicity statute does not apply to publications, including motion pictures, which do not directly promote a product or service), *and Nichols v. Moore*, 334 F. Supp. 2d 944 (E.D. Mich. 2004) (same), *and Dora v. Frontline Video, Inc.*, 18 Cal. Rptr. 2d 790 (Ct. App. 2d Dist. 1993) (use of images of famous surfer in documentary was protected, as documentary reported newsworthy topics and was not commercial speech), *and Gionfriddo v. Major League Baseball*, 114 Cal. Rptr. 2d 307 (Ct. App. 2d Dist. 2001) (use of players' names, statistics, and images in videos commemorating All-Star and World Series events was protected reporting of newsworthy information and matters of public interest), *and C.B.C. Distribution and Marketing, Inc. v. Major League Baseball Advanced Media, L.P.*, 443 F. Supp. 2d 1077 (E.D. Mo. 2006), *aff'd*, 505 F.3d 818 (8th Cir. 2007) (publication of lists and statistics about baseball players has First Amendment current affairs value that preempts players' right of publicity in their identity). Right of publicity claims will be preempted if the claim attempts to adjudicate rights that are covered by copyright. *Compare Laws v. Sony Music Entertainment, Inc.*, 448 F.3d 1134 (9th Cir. 2006) (claim for appropriation of voice preempted by defendants' copyright license to the contents of the recording used), *with Facenda v. N.F.L. Films, Inc.*, 542 F.3d 1007 (3d Cir. 2008) (NFL owned copyrights to NFL films featuring distinctive voice-over of plaintiff Facenda, but this did not automatically allow NFL to license use of these distinctive voice recordings for voice-over in documentary program on the making of Madden NFL football simulation computer game).

8. The use of a celebrity's image in connection with the attempt to report news still must be fair and not misleading. In *Solano v. Playgirl, Inc.*, 292 F.3d 1078 (9th Cir. 2002), *Playgirl* used plaintiff's image taken from his appearance on Baywatch television show on the cover of their magazine and included a short biography of plaintiff in the issue. The use was held to be actionable and not related to a newsworthy event or matter of public interest because *Playgirl* suggested that nude photographs of plaintiff would be found in the issue when they were not.

9. In *Booth v. Curtis Publishing Company*, 15 A.D. 2d 343, 334 N.Y.S. 2d 737, 738-739 (1st Dep't 1962), Shirley Booth, a well-known actress, brought an action against the publisher for the unauthorized use of her image in a magazine and subsequently in another medium as an advertisement for the first publication. The pictures were taken by a photographer of a travel magazine while the actress was on vacation in Jamaica. The photos were later published in the travel magazine and then used as a part of an advertisement for the magazine. The New York court held that the use of the actress's image in this instance was protected by the First Amendment of the U.S. Constitution. Addressing the original photograph, published by a travel

magazine, the court held that the reproduction was for news purposes; therefore, it was not a violation of privacy. *Id.* at 344. Furthermore, the court held that the republication of the photograph as advertisement of the magazine was also permissible. *Id.* at 349. The court held that the reproduction of the photos was allowable as long as it was incidental advertising of the news medium. *Id.* The court explained that a publication can best prove its worth through an extraction from past editions. *Id.* at 347.

10. In *Namath v. Sports Illustrated*, 371 N.Y.S. 2d 10 (Ct. App. 1975), *Sports Illustrated* used a picture of Joe Namath, with his consent, in an issue of the magazine. Namath sued when, later, *Sports Illustrated* republished the picture as an advertisement of the magazine. The court held, where use of professional athlete's photograph was merely incidental to advertising of publisher's magazine in which athlete had earlier been properly and fairly depicted, and language of advertisement did not indicate athlete's endorsement of the magazine, there was no invasion of athlete's right to privacy in violation of N.Y. Civil Rights Law. *Id.* at 12.

11. The Ninth Circuit Court of Appeals followed similar reasoning in *Cher v. Forum International, Ltd.*, 692 F.2d 634 (9th Cir. 1982). In this case, Cher, a well-known actress and singer, sued a freelance writer who conducted an interview with her for *Us Magazine*. Later, Cher and *Us* agreed that the article would not run in *Us Magazine*. The freelance writer then sold the article or portions of the article to *Star* magazine and *Forum*. Cher sued for exploitation of her celebrity value to sell magazines without her consent by implied endorsement. The court stated that constitutional protection extends to the truthful use of a public figure's name and likeness in advertising which is merely an adjunct of the protected publication and promotes only the protected publication. *Id.* at 638. Furthermore, the court emphasized that advertising to promote a news medium is not actionable under an appropriation of publicity theory so long as the advertising does not falsely claim that the public figure endorses the news medium. *Id.*

12. The court in *Montana v. San Jose Mercury News, Inc.*, 34 Cal. App. 4th 790, 794-797, 40 Cal. Rptr. 2d 639 (6th Dist. 1995), stated that the "First Amendment protects [defendant's 49ers Super Bowl victory] posters . . . because the posters themselves report newsworthy items of public interest." The newspaper printed a front-page story on the San Francisco 49ers' multiple Super Bowl victories and in conjunction with that news story, printed a picture featuring the 49ers' quarterback, Joe Montana. Both the news story itself and Mr. Montana's involvement in it were considered to be newsworthy. The posters merely reprinted the front page of the newspaper's reporting of this newsworthy story. The newspaper did not simply create a poster solely to exploit the image of Joe Montana.

13. Approval to use an image for one purpose does not automatically imply that the image can later be used for unrelated purposes, such as commercial speech. In *Robinson v. Snapple Bev. Corp.*, No. 99 Civ. 344 (LMM), 2000 U.S. Dist. LEXIS 8534 (S.D.N.Y. Jun. 15, 2000), the Sugar Hill Gang agreed to appear to promote a charity benefit sponsored by defendant and were filmed. Defendant later used the footage for a commercial advertisement for its soft drink products. The second use was not protected by the first use as the second use was a bare advertisement for commercial merchandise that did not relate back to the reporting of any newsworthy event.

14. The press has a privilege to report matters of legitimate public interest even though such reports might intrude on matters otherwise private. *New York Times Co. v. Sullivan*, 376 U.S. 254 (1964). Images of private citizens who are involved must be used in a manner directly related to the reporting of the newsworthy event, and not exploited for commercial speech. In *Shulman v. Group W Prods., Inc.*, 955 P.2d 469 (Cal. 1998), a car accident victim was filmed in the hands of an EMT crew. The court held, "The contents of the publication or broadcast are protected only if they have 'some substantial relevance to a matter of legitimate public interest.' Thus, recent decisions have generally tested newsworthiness with regard to such individuals by assessing the logical relationship or nexus, or the lack thereof, between the events or activities that brought the person into the public eye and the particular facts disclosed." *Id.* at 484-85. *See also D'Andrea v. Rafla-Demetrious*, 972 F. Supp. 154 (S.D.N.Y. 1997) (resident at hospital photographed for promotional brochure; use of image held incidental to purpose of brochure, and thus non-actionable).

15. Death is normally not a bar to successful exploitation of publicity rights, as the heirs and owners of the rights of exploitation of Elvis and Jerry Garcia certainly could attest to, but it appears from recent authority that the rights must have been recognized by a court or legislature of the applicable jurisdiction while the celebrity was alive. The heirs of Marilyn Monroe learned this the hard way in *Shaw Family Archives Ltd. v. CMG Worldwide, Inc.*, 486 F. Supp. 2d 309 (S.D.N.Y. 2007). At the time of her death in 1962, Marilyn Monroe had no descendible postmortem publicity rights under the law of either New York or California, her only possible domiciles at the time of her death, and thus the court found she lacked testamentary capacity to devise such rights, despite claim that her will should have been construed as devising postmortem publicity rights that were later conferred on her by an Indiana or California statute. The court declared that only property she actually owned at the time of her death could be devised by will.

PROBLEM 5-2

 Abraham Baum was walking along the street of a major city when, without his knowledge or consent, he was photographed by Tomas Garcia Vega. Unknown to Baum at the time, his picture was to become a part of a collection of photographs taken by Vega, a professional photographer who surreptitiously took the pictures of a random group of private citizens as they walked the public streets of this major city. Vega waited to take the photograph until the unsuspecting subjects walked across the spot on the sidewalk to which he had pointed his hidden camera and artificially illuminated with small strobe lights. Once Vega had enough of the photos, he selected and edited some 17 of the pictures, one of which was "Head No. 13," the photograph of Baum, and published them at the world-famous Gallery of IMAGEinternational in a collection entitled "HEADS." In addition to taking, producing, and exhibiting these photos, Vega published and distributed a catalogue, which included "Head No. 13," advertising the "HEADS" collection. The photos in the exhibition were 5 feet tall and 4 feet wide. Vega has defended his actions by explaining that, "the artistic expression and commentary [he is] making is how wonderful and telling each common, human face is when revealed by large format photography and special lighting. Each face speaks volumes about the human condition, existence, isolation, or the interconnection of all people, even when they are just walking down the street, woolgathering in the most private manner." Vega eventually sold for a price of between $20,000 and $30,000 all ten of the copies of "Head No. 13" which he produced. The commercial objective and profitable use of the "HEADS" collection is not disputed. At no time did Vega seek or obtain the permission from any of his subjects to take or use these photos of them. Upon learning of these activities, Baum immediately contacted Vega regarding the use of his photo and at which time Vega informed him that he intended to continue exhibiting "Head No. 13."

Baum is an Orthodox Hasidic Jew and a member of the Klausenberg sect, a group who suffered particular persecution in Nazi-held Europe during World War II. His offense at Vega's use of his photograph in this manner is a product of his deeply held personal and religious convictions that such a public or commercial use of his image violates the Biblical prohibition against worship of graven images. Having been informed that Vega would not withdraw "Head No. 13" from exhibition or sale in deference to his request, Baum sought to protect his right to privacy through legal means, instituting the instant action under the local law of the jurisdiction. Evaluate plaintiff Baum's likelihood of success in this action.

B. Defining the Boundaries of Publicity Rights and Artistic Expression

Simeonov v. Tiegs

602 N.Y.S. 2d 1014 (N.Y. City Civ. Ct. 1993)*

BRAUN, Justice.

Plaintiff Mihail Simeonov is an internationally known sculptor. Defendant Cheryl Tiegs ("Tiegs") is a leading model. Defendant 829 Park Avenue Corp. ("829") was the landlord of the building in which Defendant Tiegs resided in Manhattan. Defendant Albert B. Ashforth, Inc. ("Ashforth") was the managing agent of the building.

In 1979, Defendant Tiegs and her husband were trustees of a wildlife preservation organization, Cast the Sleeping Elephant Trust, one of whose goals was to have Plaintiff make a sculpture of an elephant by tranquilizing the elephant and then making an impression of the sleeping elephant with alginate, a quick drying substance. Some people involved with the Trust proposal expressed the fear that the alginate process might harm the elephant. Defendant Tiegs was so confident that the process would not do so that she volunteered to have her face covered with the alginate in order to demonstrate that it was harmless. Defendant Tiegs posed for Plaintiff in three sittings, during which time he applied alginate to her face, throat and a small part of her chest. As she was not injured, the project was subsequently completed by using the alginate to make a casting of an elephant. The casting was to be installed at the United Nations building in Manhattan.

Over the course of the next two years, Plaintiff modified the alginate impression of Defendant Tiegs to make a plaster casting of her head in deep repose upon a pillow (at oral argument of the motion, this Court viewed photographs of the plaster casting). Plaintiff never obtained the written consent of Defendant Tiegs to do so.[6]

Tiegs

Simeonov bust

---

* Some citations omitted.

6. Michael D. Murray, Two cropped, revised, and resized thumbnail images derived from photographs of Cheryl Tiegs and a Mihail Simeonov bust (2009), the subject of *Simeonov v. Tiegs*, 602 N.Y.S. 2d 1014 (N.Y. City Civ. Ct. 1993).

In November 1981, the plaster cast was taken to Defendant Tiegs' apartment, and remained there for approximately two months. Plaintiff contends that the plaster cast was taken to the apartment at the request of Defendant Tiegs' husband so that she could view it. Defendants contend that Plaintiff in no way had the permission of Defendant Tiegs to reproduce her likeness or sell reproductions from it. On or about January 27, 1982, building maintenance workers employed by Defendants Ashforth and/or 829 came to the apartment in order to install a television set in a cabinet at the request of Defendant Tiegs. While doing so, the workers broke the plaster sculpture beyond repair. Besides exhibiting the sculpture, Plaintiff had intended to make a limited edition of ten bronze copies thereof. The price of each copy was to be $20,000.00. The sculpture was to be called "Sleeping Beauty." The amount sought in these actions is $200,000.00. Defendants assert a challenge under Civil Rights Law sections 50 and 51 to Plaintiff's introducing evidence at trial as to his claim to recover damages for the ten castings.

Civil Rights Law section 50 is a criminal law. Section 51 provides for equitable relief, and compensatory and punitive damages. Although generally the statutes are utilized to obtain affirmative relief, the concept that underlies them can be used defensively, as Defendants do here. Civil Rights Law section 50 provides:

> A person, firm or corporation that uses for advertising purposes, or for the purposes of trade, the name, portrait, or picture of any living person without having first obtained the written consent of such person, or if a minor of his or her parent or guardian, is guilty of a misdemeanor.

Civil Rights Law section 51 provides in part:

> Any person whose name, portrait, or picture is used within this state for advertising purposes or for the purposes of trade without the written consent first obtained as above provided [in Civil Rights Law section 50] may maintain an equitable action in the supreme court of this state against the person, firm or corporation so using his name, portrait or picture, to prevent and restrain the use thereof; and may also sue and recover damages for any injuries sustained by reason of such use and if the defendant shall have knowingly used such person's name, portrait or picture in such manner as is forbidden or declared to be unlawful by section fifty of this article, the jury, in its discretion, may award exemplary damages.

Defendants contend that, because Plaintiff made the plaster casting without the written consent of Defendant Tiegs, and because his intention was to sell copies thereof, his actual and intended actions together would have constituted trade under the aforesaid statutes, for which Defendant Tiegs could have obtained injunctive relief and damages, and thus that Defendants cannot be held liable to Plaintiff for damages due to his inability to have been able to sell copies of the plaster casting. . . .

If Civil Rights Law section 50 were applicable to the circumstances here, as a penal provision it would have to be strictly construed. However, because it is such a provision, it does not apply to the civil act here, and thus it is only section 51 upon which Defendants may rely.

It has long been the law of this State that there is no common law right of privacy. (*Howell v. New York Post Co., Inc.* ("*Howell*"), 81 N.Y. 2d 115, 123, 596 N.Y.S. 2d 350, 612 N.E. 2d 699 [1993]; *Roberson v. Rochester Folding Box Co.* ("*Roberson*"), 171 N.Y. 538, 556, 64 N.E. 442 [1902]). The Legislature enacted a limited statutory right of privacy in Civil Rights Law sections 50 and 51 in response to *Roberson*. (*Howell, supra*, at 123, 596 N.Y.S. 2d 350, 612 N.E. 2d 699). This statutory right of privacy is at times in tension with the right of a person to express himself or herself freely, as exemplified by the instant case.

One distinctive manner of human expression is through creation of works of art. The importance of this was recognized by the Appellate Division, First Department, in overturning an injunction against a book and a movie which was granted pursuant to Civil Rights Law section 51, and stating that to do otherwise "would outlaw large areas heretofore deemed permissible subject matter for literature and the arts." (*Univ. of Notre Dame Du Lac v. Twentieth Century-Fox Film Corp.*, 22 A.D. 2d 452, 457, 256 N.Y.S. 2d 301 [1965]). However, the Court of Appeals has indicated in dictum that Civil Rights Law sections 50 and 51 presumably were intended by the Legislature to apply to an artistically created portrait. (*Cohen v. Herbal Concepts, Inc.* ("*Cohen*"), 63 N.Y. 2d 379, 384, 482 N.Y.S. 2d 457, 472 N.E. 2d 307 [1984]). Later that year, the Court of Appeals re-affirmed that the statute must be more narrowly construed where the Federal and State constitutional rights of free speech are concerned. (*Stephano v. News Group Publs., Inc.* ("*Stephano*"), 64 N.Y. 2d 174, 184, 485 N.Y.S. 2d 220, 474 N.E. 2d 580 [1984]; accord, *Brinkley v. Casablancas* ("*Brinkley*"), 80 A.D. 2d 428, 432, 438 N.Y.S. 2d 1004 [1st Dept 1981]). Non-verbal expression can be protected by the First Amendment. (*Ward v. Rock Against Racism*, 491 U.S. 781, 790, 109 S. Ct. 2746, 2753, 105 L. Ed. 2d 661 [1989][music]; *Zacchini v. Scripps-Howard Broadcasting Co.*, 433 U.S. 562, 578, 97 S. Ct. 2849, 2859, 53 L. Ed. 2d 965 [1977][entertainment]). Non-verbal expression includes works of art like a sculpture. Courts have held that at least some works of art are protected by the First Amendment. (*See, Serra v. United States Gen. Servs. Admin.*, 847 F. 2d 1045, 1048 [2d Cir. 1988][sculpture]; *Contemporary Arts Ctr. v. Ney*, 735 F. Supp. 743, 744 [S.D. Ohio 1990][photographs]; *Sefick v. City of Chicago*, 485 F. Supp. 644, 648 [N.D. Ill. 1979][sculptures]). . . .

Plaintiff is an artist who created a work of art out of the alginate impression of Defendant Tiegs. The sculpture was Plaintiff's creative expression which grew out of that impression. Just because he incidentally intended to sell a limited number of copies of his creation, that does not mean that he was acting "for the purposes of trade." Part of the protection of free speech under the United States and New York State Constitutions is the right to disseminate the "speech," and that includes selling it, at least under certain circumstances. In construing Civil Rights Law sections 50 and 51, the United States Supreme Court reaffirmed its earlier statement: "'That books, newspapers, and magazines are published and sold for profit does not prevent them from being a form of expression whose liberty is safeguarded by the First Amendment.'" (citations omitted). (*Time, Inc. v. Hill*, 385 U.S. 374, 397, 87 S. Ct. 534, 546, 17 L. Ed. 2d 456 [1967]). Whether the sale of the castings of the sculpture for profit would bring it under Civil Rights Law sections 50 and 51 does not depend on the motivation of Plaintiff in selling them. The dissemination for profit is not the sole determinant of what constitutes trade under these statutes. It is the content that counts.

Without people having the freedom to disseminate ideas, a society is not free. Works of art, including sculptures, convey ideas, just as do literature, movies or theater. Although a person's right of privacy as protected by Civil Rights Law sections 50 and 51 is also a very significant right, it must fall to the constitutionally protected right of freedom of speech. It is a maxim of constitutional law that, if a Court can avoid declaring a provision of law unconstitutional, it must do so. Here, this Court need not rule at this time on the constitutionality of the statutes as applied to the facts here because the facts before the Court lead to the conclusion, for the purpose of this motion, that Civil Rights Law sections 50 and 51 do not apply to Plaintiff's actual and intended acts. An artist may make a work of art that includes a recognizable likeness of a person without her or his written consent and sell at least a limited number of copies thereof without violating Civil Rights Law sections 50 and 51. . . .

Therefore, the motion is denied.

Comedy III Productions, Inc. v. Gary Saderup, Inc.

21 P.3d 797 (Cal. 2001)*

Mosk, Justice.

. . . Plaintiff Comedy III Productions, Inc. (hereafter Comedy III), brought this action against defendants Gary Saderup and Gary Saderup, Inc. (hereafter collectively Saderup), seeking damages and injunctive relief for violation of section 990 and related business torts. The parties waived the right to jury trial and the right to put on evidence, and submitted the case for decision on the following stipulated facts:

> Comedy III is the registered owner of all rights to the former comedy act known as The Three Stooges, who are deceased personalities within the meaning of the statute.
>
> Saderup is an artist with over 25 years' experience in making charcoal drawings of celebrities. These drawings are used to create lithographic and silkscreen masters, which in turn are used to produce multiple reproductions in the form, respectively, of lithographic prints and silkscreened images on T-shirts. Saderup creates the original drawings and is actively involved in the ensuing lithographic and silkscreening processes.

---

* Footnotes omitted.

Without securing Comedy III's consent, Saderup sold lithographs and T-shirts bearing a likeness of The Three Stooges reproduced from a charcoal drawing he had made. [*See* Appendix image of Saderup's portrait, reproduced below.] These lithographs and T-shirts did not constitute an advertisement, endorsement, or sponsorship of any product. . . .

B. THE CONSTITUTIONAL ISSUE

Saderup next contends that enforcement of the judgment against him violates his right of free speech and expression under the First Amendment. He raises a difficult issue, which we address below. . . .

The Three Stooges—You Nazty Spy[7]

Gary Saderup's charcoal drawing of the Three Stooges[8]

It is admittedly not a simple matter to develop a test that will unerringly distinguish between forms of artistic expression protected by the First Amendment and those that must give way to the right of publicity. Certainly, any such test must incorporate the principle that the right of publicity cannot, consistent with the First Amendment, be a right to control the celebrity's image by

---

7. Michael D. Murray, Cropped, revised, and resized image of the Three Stooges (2016) that was derived from a still from the motion picture, *You Natzy Spy,* that was used a reference for Gary Saderup's work at issue in *Comedy III Productions, Inc. v. Gary Saderup, Inc.,* 21 P.3d 797 (Cal. 2001).

8. Michael D. Murray, Revised and resized image of Gary Saderup's charcoal drawing of the Three Stooges (2007) from the Appendix to the court's opinion in *Comedy III Productions, Inc. v. Gary Saderup, Inc.,* 21 P.3d 797 (Cal. 2001).

censoring disagreeable portrayals. Once the celebrity thrusts himself or herself forward into the limelight, the First Amendment dictates that the right to comment on, parody, lampoon, and make other expressive uses of the celebrity image must be given broad scope. The necessary implication of this observation is that the right of publicity is essentially an economic right. What the right of publicity holder possesses is not a right of censorship, but a right to prevent others from misappropriating the economic value generated by the celebrity's fame through the merchandising of the "name, voice, signature, photograph, or likeness" of the celebrity. (§ 990.)

Beyond this precept, how may courts distinguish between protected and unprotected expression? Some commentators have proposed importing the fair use defense from copyright law (17 U.S.C. § 107), which has the advantage of employing an established doctrine developed from a related area of the law. (*See* Barnett, *First Amendment Limits on the Right of Publicity* (1995) 30 TORT & INS. L.J. 635, 650-657; Coyne, *Toward a Modified Fair Use Defense in Right of Publicity Cases* (1988) 29 WM. & MARY L. REV. 781, 812-820.) Others disagree, pointing to the murkiness of the fair use doctrine and arguing that the idea/expression dichotomy, rather than fair use, is the principal means of reconciling copyright protection and First Amendment rights. (2 McCarthy, *supra*, § 8.38, pp. 8-358 to 8-360; *see also* Kwall, *The Right of Publicity vs. The First Amendment: A Property and Liability Rule Analysis* (1994) 70 IND. L.J. 47, 58, fn. 54.)

We conclude that a wholesale importation of the fair use doctrine into right of publicity law would not be advisable. At least two of the factors employed in the fair use test, "the nature of the copyrighted work" and "the amount and substantiality of the portion used" (17 U.S.C. § 107(2), (3)), seem particularly designed to be applied to the partial copying of works of authorship "fixed in [a] tangible medium of expression" (17 U.S.C. § 102); it is difficult to understand why these factors would be especially useful for determining whether the depiction of a celebrity likeness is protected by the First Amendment.

Nonetheless, the first fair use factor — "the purpose and character of the use" (17 U.S.C. § 107(1)) — does seem particularly pertinent to the task of reconciling the rights of free expression and publicity. As the Supreme Court has stated, the central purpose of the inquiry into this fair use factor "is to see, in Justice Story's words, whether the new work merely 'supersede[s] the objects' of the original creation [citations], or instead adds something new, with a further purpose or different character, altering the first with new expression, meaning, or message; it asks, in other words, whether and to what extent the new work is 'transformative.'[Citation.] Although such transformative use is not absolutely necessary for a finding of fair use, [citation] the goal of copyright, to promote science and the arts, is generally furthered by the creation of transformative works." (*Campbell v. Acuff-Rose Music, Inc.* (1994) 510 U.S. 569, 579, 114 S. Ct. 1164, 127 L. Ed. 2d 500, fn. omitted.)

This inquiry into whether a work is "transformative" appears to us to be necessarily at the heart of any judicial attempt to square the right of publicity with the First Amendment. As the above quotation suggests, both the First Amendment and copyright law have a common goal of encouragement of free expression and creativity, the former by protecting such expression from government interference, the latter by protecting the creative fruits of intellectual and artistic labor. (*See* 1 Nimmer on Copyright (2000 ed.) § 1.10, pp. 1-66.43 to 1-66.44 (Nimmer).) The right of publicity, at least theoretically, shares this goal with copyright law. (1 McCarthy, *supra*, § 2.6, pp. 2-14 to 2-19.) When artistic expression takes the form of a literal depiction or imitation of a celebrity for commercial gain, directly trespassing on the right of publicity without adding significant expression beyond that trespass, the state law interest in protecting the fruits of artistic labor outweighs the expressive interests of the imitative artist. (*See Zacchini, supra*, 433 U.S. at pp. 575-576, 97 S. Ct. 2849.)

On the other hand, when a work contains significant transformative elements, it is not only especially worthy of First Amendment protection, but it is also less likely to interfere with the economic interest protected by the right of publicity. As has been observed, works of parody or other distortions of the celebrity figure are not, from the celebrity fan's viewpoint, good substitutes for conventional depictions of the celebrity and therefore do not generally threaten markets for celebrity memorabilia that the right of publicity is designed to protect. (*See Cardtoons, L.C. v. Major League Baseball Players Association* (10th Cir. 1996) 95 F.3d 959, 974 (*Cardtoons*).) Accordingly, First Amendment protection of such works outweighs whatever interest the state may have in enforcing the right of publicity. The right-of-publicity holder continues to enforce the right to monopolize the production of conventional, more or less fungible, images of the celebrity. . . .

We emphasize that the transformative elements or creative contributions that require First Amendment protection are not confined to parody and can take many forms, from factual reporting (*see, e.g., Rosemont Enterprises, Inc. v. Random House, Inc.* (N.Y. Sup. Ct. 1968) 58 Misc. 2d 1, 294 N.Y.S. 2d 122, 129, affd. mem. (1969) 32 A.D. 2d 892, 301 N.Y.S. 2d 948) to fictionalized portrayal (*Guglielmi, supra*, 25 Cal. 3d at pp. 871-872, 160 Cal. Rptr. 352, 603 P.2d 454; see also *Parks v. LaFace Records* (E.D. Mich. 1999) 76 F. Supp. 2d 775, 779-782 [use of civil rights figure Rosa Parks in song title is protected expression]), from heavy-handed lampooning (see *Hustler Magazine v. Falwell* (1988) 485 U.S. 46, 108 S. Ct. 876, 99 L. Ed. 2d 41) to subtle social criticism (see Coplans et al., Andy Warhol (1970) pp. 50-52 [explaining Warhol's celebrity portraits as a critique of the celebrity phenomenon]).

Another way of stating the inquiry is whether the celebrity likeness is one of the "raw materials" from which an original work is synthesized, or whether the depiction or imitation of the celebrity is the very sum and substance of the work in question. We ask, in other words, whether a product containing a celebrity's likeness is so transformed that it has become primarily the defendant's own expression rather than the celebrity's likeness. And when we use the word "expression," we mean expression of something other than the likeness of the celebrity. We further emphasize that in determining whether the work is transformative, courts are not to be concerned with the quality of the artistic contribution — vulgar forms of expression fully qualify for First Amendment protection. (*See, e.g., Hustler Magazine v. Falwell, supra,* 485 U.S. 46, 108 S. Ct. 876, 99 L. Ed. 2d 41; *see also Campbell v. Acuff — Rose Music, Inc., supra,* 510 U.S. at p. 582, 114 S. Ct. 1164.) On the other hand, a literal depiction of a celebrity, even if accomplished with great skill, may still be subject to a right of publicity challenge. The inquiry is in a sense more quantitative than qualitative, asking whether the literal and imitative or the creative elements predominate in the work.

Furthermore, in determining whether a work is sufficiently transformative, courts may find useful a subsidiary inquiry, particularly in close cases: does the marketability and economic value of the challenged work derive primarily from the fame of the celebrity depicted? If this question is answered in the negative, then there would generally be no actionable right of publicity. When the value of the work comes principally from some source other than the fame of the celebrity — from the creativity, skill, and reputation of the artist — it may be presumed that sufficient transformative elements are present to warrant First Amendment protection. If the question is answered in the affirmative, however, it does not necessarily follow that the work is without First Amendment protection — it may still be a transformative work.

In sum, when an artist is faced with a right of publicity challenge to his or her work, he or she may raise as affirmative defense that the work is protected by the First Amendment inasmuch as it contains significant transformative elements or that the value of the work does not derive primarily from the celebrity's fame. Turning to the present case, we note that the trial court, in ruling against Saderup, stated that "the commercial enterprise conducted by [Saderup] involves the sale of lithographs and T-shirts which are not original single works of art, and which are not protected by the First Amendment; the enterprise conducted by [Saderup] was a commercial enterprise designed to generate profits solely from the use of the likeness of The Three Stooges which is the right of publicity . . . protected by section 990." Although not entirely clear, the trial court seemed to be holding that reproductions of celebrity images are categorically outside First Amendment protection. The Court of Appeal was more explicit in adopting this rationale: "Simply put, although the First Amendment protects speech that is sold [citation], reproductions of an image, made to be sold for profit do not per se constitute speech." But this position has no basis in logic or authority. No one would claim that a published book, because it is one of many copies, receives less First Amendment protection than the original manuscript. It is true that the statute at issue here makes a distinction between a single and original work of fine art and a reproduction. (§ 990, subd. (n)(3).) Because the statute evidently aims at preventing the illicit merchandising of celebrity images, and because single original works of fine art are not forms of merchandising, the state has little if any interest in preventing the exhibition and sale of such works, and the First Amendment rights of the artist should therefore prevail. But the inverse — that a reproduction receives no First Amendment protection — is patently false: a reproduction of a celebrity image that, as explained above, contains significant creative elements is entitled to as much First Amendment protection as an original work of art. The trial court and the Court of Appeal therefore erred in this respect.

Rather, the inquiry is into whether Saderup's work is sufficiently transformative. Correctly anticipating this inquiry, he argues that all portraiture involves creative decisions, that therefore no portrait portrays a mere literal likeness, and that accordingly all portraiture, including reproductions, is protected by the First Amendment. We reject any such categorical position. Without denying that all portraiture involves the making of artistic choices, we find it equally undeniable, under the test formulated above, that when an artist's skill and talent is manifestly subordinated to the overall goal of creating a conventional portrait of a celebrity so as to commercially exploit his or her fame, then the artist's right of free expression is outweighed by the right of publicity. As is the case with fair use in the area of copyright law, an artist depicting a celebrity must contribute something more than a "merely trivial" variation, [but must create] something recognizably "his own" (*L. Batlin & Son, Inc. v. Snyder* (2d Cir. 1976) 536 F. 2d 486, 490), in order to qualify for legal protection.

On the other hand, we do not hold that all reproductions of celebrity portraits are unprotected by the First Amendment. The silkscreens of Andy Warhol, for example, have as their subjects the images of such celebrities as Marilyn Monroe, Elizabeth Taylor, and Elvis Presley. Through distortion and the careful manipulation of context, Warhol was able to convey a message that went beyond the commercial exploitation of celebrity images and became a form of ironic social comment on the dehumanization of celebrity itself. (*See* Coplans et al., *supra*, at p. 52.) Such expression may well be entitled to First Amendment protection. Although the distinction between protected and unprotected expression will sometimes be subtle, it is no more so than other distinctions triers of fact are called on to make in First Amendment jurisprudence. (*See, e.g., Miller v. California* (1973) 413 U.S. 15, 24, 93 S. Ct. 2607, 37 L. Ed. 2d 419 [requiring determination, in the context of work alleged to be obscene, of "whether the work, taken as a whole, lacks serious literary, artistic, political, or scientific value"].)

Turning to Saderup's work, we can discern no significant transformative or creative contribution. His undeniable skill is manifestly subordinated to the overall goal of creating literal, conventional depictions of The Three Stooges so as to exploit their fame. Indeed, were we to decide that Saderup's depictions were protected by the First Amendment, we cannot perceive how the right of publicity would remain a viable right other than in cases of falsified celebrity endorsements.

Moreover, the marketability and economic value of Saderup's work derives primarily from the fame of the celebrities depicted. While that fact alone does not necessarily mean the work receives no First Amendment protection, we can perceive no transformative elements in Saderup's works that would require such protection. Saderup argues that it would be incongruous and unjust to protect parodies and other distortions of celebrity figures but not wholesome, reverential portraits of such celebrities. The test we articulate today, however, does not express a value judgment or preference for one type of depiction over another. Rather, it reflects a recognition that the Legislature has granted to the heirs and assigns of celebrities the property right to exploit the celebrities' images, and that certain forms of expressive activity protected by the First Amendment fall outside the boundaries of that right. Stated another way, we are concerned not with whether conventional celebrity images should be produced but with who produces them and, more pertinently, who appropriates the value from their production. Thus, under section 990, if Saderup wishes to continue to depict The Three Stooges as he has done, he may do so only with the consent of the right of publicity holder.

IV. DISPOSITION

The judgment of the Court of Appeal is affirmed.

Hoepker v. Kruger

200 F. Supp. 2d 340 (S.D.N.Y. 2002)*

HELLERSTEIN, District Judge.

This right of privacy case is before the Court on defendants' motion to dismiss the Amended Complaint, on the ground that plaintiff Dabney has failed to state a claim upon which relief can be granted. . . . For the reasons discussed below, I grant defendants' motion dismissing the Amended Complaint, and deny their motion for costs and fees.

FACTUAL BACKGROUND

Plaintiff Thomas Hoepker is a well-known German photographer. In 1960, during the early days of his career, Hoepker created a photographic image of plaintiff Charlotte Dabney. The image, "Charlotte As Seen By Thomas," pictures Dabney from the waist up, holding a large magnifying glass over her right eye. Dabney's eye fills the lens of the magnifying glass, and the lens covers a large portion of Dabney's face. The image was published once in the German photography magazine FOTO PRISMA in 1960.

9   Defendant Barbara Kruger also is a well-known artist, specializing in collage works combining photographs and text. In 1990, Kruger created an untitled work incorporating

---

* Footnotes and some citations omitted.

9. Image: Michael D. Murray, Cropped, revised, and resized image (2016) derived from a photograph of Barbara Kruger's work, "It's a Small World But Not if You Have to clean It," the subject of *Hoepker v. Kruger*, 200 F. Supp. 2d 340 (S.D.N.Y. 2002).

Hoepker's "Charlotte As Seen By Thomas." To create her work (the "Kruger Composite"), Kruger cropped and enlarged Hoepker's photographic image, transferred it to silkscreen and, in her characteristic style, superimposed three large red blocks containing words that can be read together as, "It's a small world but not if you have to clean it."

In April of 1990, Kruger sold the Kruger Composite to defendant Museum of Contemporary Art L.A. ("MOCA"). . . . From October 17, 1999 to February 13, 2000, MOCA displayed the Kruger Composite as one of sixty-four works of art in an exhibit dedicated to Kruger (the "Kruger Exhibit"). In conjunction with the exhibition, MOCA sold gift items in its museum shop featuring the Kruger Composite in the form of postcards, note cubes, magnets and t-shirts. MOCA also sold a book respecting Kruger's works and ideas entitled "Barbara Kruger" (the "Kruger Catalog") that was published jointly with defendant M.I.T. Press. The Kruger Catalog contains three depictions of the Kruger Composite among the hundreds of pictures in the 200-plus page book. . . .

After closing in Los Angeles, the Kruger Exhibit traveled to New York and was presented at defendant Whitney Museum of American Art (the "Whitney") from July 13 through October 22, 2000. The Whitney advertised the Kruger Exhibit in various ways, including newsletters and brochures that incorporated the Kruger Composite. The Whitney also purchased from MOCA an inventory of the Kruger Catalog and various gift items to sell at its museum shop in conjunction with the exhibition. . . .

Around the time the Whitney presented the Kruger Exhibit, reproductions of the Kruger Composite appeared as five-story-high "billboard art" at one or more locations in Manhattan. The Amended Complaint alleges that these billboard installments were commissioned by the Whitney to advertise the Kruger exhibition. The Whitney denies that it paid for the billboards or that the billboards were used to advertise its exhibit, but admits (at least it is evidenced from the Whitney's submissions) that the "Barbara Kruger: Big Picture" billboards were an art project "co-produc[ed]" by "the Public Art Fund and the Whitney Museum of American Art, with additional support from MegaArt," and that the Whitney's name, along with Kruger's and the other sponsors' names, appeared at the bottom of the billboards in comparatively small font. Presumably, by denying that the billboards were advertisements, the Whitney contends they were instead art.

DISCUSSION

II. Violation of Dabney's Right to Privacy

Plaintiff Dabney has alleged violation of her right of privacy based on defendants' various activities. . . . The right of privacy in New York is derived solely from statute. *Groden v. Random House, Inc.*, 61 F.3d 1045, 1048-49 (2d Cir. 1995). The two relevant statutes are Sections 50 and 51 of New York Civil Rights Law. To succeed on right of privacy claim, a plaintiff must prove (1) use of plaintiff's name, portrait, picture, or voice (2) "for advertising purposes or for the purposes of trade" (3) without consent and (4) within the state of New York. *Titan Sports, Inc. v. Comics World Corp.*, 870 F. 2d 85, 87 (2d Cir. 1989). There is no debate that at least some of the defendants used plaintiff's picture (as incorporated in the Kruger Composite) without her consent in the state of New York. The only question is whether the defendants' various uses of Dabney's picture were "for advertising purposes or for purposes of trade," as those terms are limited by New York and constitutional case law.

The advertising and trade limitation in New York's privacy statutes was crafted with the First Amendment in mind. Through Sections 50 and 51, the New York legislature sought to protect a person's right to be free from unwarranted intrusions into his or her privacy, while at the same time protecting the quintessential American right to freedom of expression. *See Waters v. Moore*, 70 Misc. 2d 372, 334 N.Y.S. 2d 428, 434 (N.Y. Sup. Ct. 1972); *Rubino v. Slaughter*, 136 N.Y.S. 2d 873, 874 (N.Y. Sup. Ct. 1954). While First Amendment concerns do come into play, "the rights guaranteed by the First Amendment do not require total abrogation of the right to privacy," *Briscoe v. Reader's Digest Ass'n, Inc.*, 4 Cal. 3d 529, 93 Cal. Rptr. 866, 483 P. 2d 34, 42 (1971), and a careful weighing of interests, on a case by case basis, is therefore necessary. The balance struck in the privacy laws and in their application is consistent with First Amendment jurisprudence, for government may encumber or restrict commercial speech more readily than "pure" First Amendment expression such as political discourse. *See Central Hudson Gas & Electric Corp. v. Public Serv. Comm'n of N.Y.*, 447 U.S. 557, 100 S. Ct. 2343, 65 L. Ed. 2d 341 (1980).

In the end, free speech rights clearly transcend privacy rights when the speech concerns "newsworthy events or matters of public interest." *Stephano v. News Group Publications, Inc.*, 64 N.Y. 2d 174, 485 N.Y.S. 2d 220, 224-25, 474 N.E. 2d 580 (1984) (use of plaintiff's photograph in connection with an article of public interest held not to be the kind of use prohibited by the statute and held to fall within the statute's First Amendment "exception [that] reflects Federal and State constitutional concerns for free dissemination of news and other matters of interest to the public"); *see also Arrington v. New York Times Co.*, 55 N.Y. 2d 433, 440, 449 N.Y.S. 2d 941, 434 N.E. 2d 1319 (1982). When other types of speech are at issue, most notably when the speech is in the form of art, the application of the First Amendment exception to the right of privacy statute is less clear cut.

New York courts have taken the position in the right of privacy context that art is speech, and, accordingly, that art is entitled to First Amendment protection vis-à-vis the right of privacy. In *Simeonov v. Tiegs*, 159 Misc. 2d 54, 602 N.Y.S. 2d 1014 (N.Y. City Civ. Ct. 1993), for example, . . . [t]he court held that "[a]n artist may make a work of art that includes a recognizable likeness of a person without her or his written consent and sell at least a limited number of copies thereof without violating [sections 50-51]. . . . Although a person's right of privacy as protected by Civil Rights Law sections 50 and 51 is also a very significant right, it must fall to the constitutionally protected right of freedom of speech." 602 N.Y.S. 2d at 1018.

The California courts recently took a slightly different position on the issue in *Comedy III Productions, Inc. v. Gary Saderup, Inc.*, 25 Cal. 4th 387, 106 Cal. Rptr. 2d 126, 21 P.3d 797 (2001), cert. denied, _____ U.S. _____, 122 S. Ct. 806, 151 L. Ed. 2d 692 (2002), determining that only sufficiently "transformative" art was entitled to First Amendment protection against right of publicity claims. . . . The test in *Comedy III* seems to be whether it is the art, or the celebrity, that is being sold or displayed. *See* 106 Cal. Rptr. 2d 126, 21 P.3d at 809 (stating that the central inquiry for determining if a work is "transformative" is "whether the celebrity likeness is one of the 'raw materials' from which an original work is synthesized, or whether the depiction or imitation of the celebrity is the very sum and substance of the work in question").

Regardless whether I use the New York standard as applied in cases like *Simeonov*, or adopt the "transformative" requirement from the California courts, the Kruger Composite should be shielded from Dabney's right of privacy claim by the First Amendment. The Kruger Composite itself is pure First Amendment speech in the form of artistic expression (with sufficiently transformative elements to satisfy *Comedy III*) and deserves full protection, even against Dabney's statutorily-protected privacy interests. *See Bery v. City of New York*, 97 F.3d 689, 695 (2d Cir. 1996) ("Visual art is as wide ranging in its depiction of ideas, concepts and emotions as any book, treatise, pamphlet or other writing, and is similarly entitled to a full First Amendment protection"). Therefore, the Whitney's display of the Kruger Composite and EBS's display of a digital reproduction of the Kruger Composite in its virtual gallery fall within the scope of the First Amendment and outside the range of Sections 50 and 51. *See Simeonov, supra*; cf. *Costanza v. Seinfeld*, 279 A.D. 2d 255, 719 N.Y.S. 2d 29, 30 (1st Dep't 2001) (use of plaintiff's name in work of fiction was not use for trade or advertising purposes within meaning of statute).

Similarly, the reproduction of the Kruger Composite in the Exhibit Catalog is pure speech, made to further discussion and commentary on Kruger and her body of work. . . .

Certain other uses complained of by plaintiff are also clearly exempt from Dabney's right of privacy action under the "ancillary use" exception created by New York courts. While the privacy laws prohibit nonconsensual use of a person's image for advertising purposes, advertising that is undertaken in connection with a use protected by the First Amendment falls outside the statute's reach. The ancillary use exception gives news agencies, magazine publishers, etc. the ability to publicize their newsworthy articles without violating the right of privacy statutes. *Stern v. Delphi Internet Services Corp.*, 165 Misc. 2d 21, 626 N.Y.S. 2d 694, 700 (N.Y. Sup. Ct. 1995). For example, the exception protects the use of a person's name and picture in a newspaper advertisement announcing an article about that person. *See Sidis v. F-R Pub. Corp.*, 113 F.2d 806 (2d Cir. 1940); *see also Groden*, 61 F.3d 1045 (defendant did not violate plaintiff's right of privacy by using plaintiff's name and picture in advertisements for book in which plaintiff's work is discussed); *Namath v.*

Sports Illustrated, 48 A.D. 2d 487, 371 N.Y.S. 2d 10, 11-12 (1st Dep't 1975) (publisher could use plaintiff's picture to solicit subscriptions where photograph indicated content of defendant's magazine); *Friedan v. Friedan*, 414 F. Supp. 77 (D.C.N.Y. 1976) (use of plaintiff's photograph on television commercials advertising magazine issue featuring article on plaintiff was not actionable).

Although the ancillary use exception was first developed in the context of advertisements for books and periodicals, it applies equally well here to advertising undertaken by the Whitney to promote the Kruger Exhibit. As discussed above, the Kruger Exhibit is pure First Amendment speech outside the proscription of Sections 50 and 51. While the brochures and newsletter distributed by the Whitney to promote the Kruger Exhibit may have been used for advertising purposes — specifically, to increase patronage of the museum and the exhibit — that use was related to the protected exhibition of the Kruger Composite itself. The brochures, newsletters and other advertisements merely "'prove[d] the worth and illustrate[d][the] content'" of the Kruger Exhibit and the Whitney itself, *Groden*, 61 F.3d at 1049 (quoting *Booth v. Curtis Publ'g Co.*, 15 A.D. 2d 343, 223 N.Y.S. 2d 737, 743 (1st Dep't), aff'd, 11 N.Y. 2d 907, 228 N.Y.S. 2d 468, 182 N.E. 2d 812 (1962)), and are therefore immune from Dabney's right of privacy claim. The billboard art reproduction of the Kruger Composite is also protected against Dabney's right of privacy claim. Whether the billboard art reproduction is "pure" First Amendment speech as the Whitney claims, or an advertisement of the Kruger Exhibit as Dabney claims, it falls outside the sphere of activity prohibited by New York's privacy statutes for the reasons discussed above.

Whether the remaining uses complained of — the use of Dabney's image on the museum gift shop items sold by the Whitney and MOCA — fall with the privacy statute's ambit is a more complicated question. The museums argue that the gift merchandise is protected First Amendment expression as clearly as the Kruger Composite itself, in that the gift items are merely reproductions of the Kruger Composite in a medium better able to "disseminat[e][the] protected visual expression for public enjoyment," carrying the message of the original artwork to a broader class of people than could afford to own the original artwork and to a larger number of people than would otherwise have a chance to view the Kruger Composite itself. Dabney, on the other hand, argues that the museums' First Amendment arguments are merely subterfuge, that Dabney's image was emblazoned on gift trinkets solely to promote sales of those trinkets. *See Lane v. F.W. Woolworth Co.*, 171 Misc. 66, 11 N.Y.S. 2d 199 (N.Y. Sup.) (use of actress's picture in locket to make lockets more attractive to potential consumers was for purposes of trade), aff'd, 256 A.D. 1065, 12 N.Y.S. 2d 352 (1st Dep't 1939); cf. *Zacchini v. Scripps-Howard Broadcasting Co.*, 433 U.S. 562, 581, 97 S. Ct. 2849, 53 L. Ed. 2d 965 (1977) (Powell, J., dissenting) (First Amendment does not protect "a subterfuge or cover for private or commercial exploitation").

Case law makes clear that the sale for profit of an item bearing a person's name or likeness does not entirely determine whether use of that person's name or likeness is for trade or advertising purposes within the meaning of the statute. *See Simeonov*, 602 N.Y.S. 2d at 1018 ("Part of the protection of free speech . . . is the right to disseminate the 'speech,' and that includes selling it") (quoting *Time, Inc. v. Hill*, 385 U.S. 374, 397, 87 S. Ct. 534, 17 L. Ed. 2d 456 (1967)); *see also Guglielmi v. Spelling-Goldberg Productions*, 25 Cal. 3d 860, 160 Cal. Rptr. 352, 603 P.2d 454, 459-60 (1979) ("The First Amendment is not limited to those who publish without charge"); cf. *Riley v. National Federation of Blind of North Carolina*, 487 U.S. 781, 801, 108 S. Ct. 2667, 101 L. Ed. 2d 669 (1988) ("It is well settled that a speaker's rights are not lost merely because compensation is received; a speaker is no less a speaker because he or she is paid to speak"); *Bery v. New York City*, 97 F.3d 689 (2d Cir. 1996) ("The sale of protected materials [under the First Amendment] is also protected").

Rather than focusing on the motive of the person creating the work at issue, New York state courts deciding Section 51 cases have focused on the underlying nature of the work itself. *See, e.g., Simeonov*, 602 N.Y.S. 2d at 1018; *Stephano*, 485 N.Y.S. 2d at 225, 474 N.E.2d 580 ("It is the content of the article and not the defendant's motive or primary motive to increase circulation which determines whether it is a newsworthy item, as opposed to a trade usage, under [Section 51]"). But using such a test invites judges to decide what constitutes art or expression — and what does not — thus asking them to make or draw potentially artificial lines. For example, *Simeonov* held that a bronze bust did not violate the model's right to privacy, but suggested that a mere mannequin might. *See Simeonov*, 602 N.Y.S. 2d at 1017, distinguishing and approving *Young v. Greneker Studios, Inc.*, 175 Misc. 1027, 26 N.Y.S. 2d 357 (N.Y. City Sup. Ct. 1941). And a dissenting judge in the California Supreme Court suggested that "the sale of such objects as plastic toy pencil sharpeners, soap products, target games, candy dispensers and beverage stirring rods [emblazoned with Lugosi-as-Dracula likenesses] . . . hardly implicates the First Amendment." *Lugosi v. Universal Pictures*, 25 Cal. 3d 813, 851, 160 Cal. Rptr. 323, 603 P.2d 425 (1979) (Byrd, C.J., dissenting).

Yet, mannequins and pencil sharpeners and other such products can also qualify as art, and museums sometimes collect and display them as such. And case law makes clear that "First Amendment doctrine does not disfavor non-traditional media of expression." *Comedy III Productions*, 106 Cal. Rptr. 2d 126, 21 P.3d at 804; *see also Cardtoons, L.C. v. Major League Baseball Players Association*, 95 F.3d 959 (10th Cir. 1996) (trading cards containing caricatures of baseball players provided social commentary, and therefore were entitled to First Amendment protection); cf. *Ayres v. City of Chicago*, 125 F.3d 1010, 1017 (7th Cir. 1997) (defendant's t-shirts, which advocated the legalization of marijuana, "are to [the seller] what the New York Times is to the Sulzbergers and the Ochses — the vehicle of her ideas and opinions"). Courts should not be asked to draw arbitrary lines between what may be art and what may be prosaic as the touchstone of First Amendment protection. . . .

Here, Dabney's image was affixed to various gift items not to flaunt her visage, but because the gift items reproduced the Kruger Composite, a work of art displayed by the Whitney in its museum galleries. Borrowing language from the California Supreme Court, "[Dabney's] likeness appeared in the [gift merchandise] for precisely the same reason [it] appeared on the original [Kruger Composite]," *Montana v. San Jose Mercury News, Inc.*, 34 Cal. App. 4th 790, 794, 40 Cal. Rptr. 2d 639 (1995) (emphasis in original). Viewed in this light, it is easy to distinguish this case from the facts presented in *Titan Sports.* Here, the museums are selling art, albeit on t-shirts and refrigerator magnets, whereas the *Titan Sports* defendants were selling nothing more than the wrestlers' images. My holding, in the context of a museum store selling items reflecting art displayed in its galleries, should not be interpreted as conflating "the right to speak" into "the right to manufacture in bulk." *See* Jane Graines, *Contested Culture: The Image, the Voice and the Law* (1991) (quoted in Jane C. Ginsburg, *Exploiting the Artist's Commercial Identity: The Merchandizing of Art Images*, 19 COLUM.-VLA J.L. & ARTS 1 (1994/1995)). Museum gift shops sell merchandise that, in general, replicates the art displayed in the museum, thus enabling the museum to distribute art in a common and ordinary form that can be appreciated in everyday life. That the art is reproduced in formats and in quantities sold for modest sums makes the art popular, but does not change the essential nature of the artistic expression that is entitled to First Amendment protection.

In sum, none of the uses of Dabney's image, as incorporated in the Kruger Composite, complained of by plaintiff are actionable under New York's right of privacy statute. Plaintiff has failed to state a legally sufficient claim for right of privacy violation and the Amended Complaint must therefore be dismissed. . . .

CONCLUSION

For the reasons stated above, defendants' motion to dismiss the Amended Complaint is hereby granted, . . . SO ORDERED.

ETW Corp. v. Jireh Publ'g, Inc.

332 F.3d 915 (6th Cir. 2003)*

GRAHAM, District Judge [sitting by designation].

Plaintiff-Appellant ETW Corporation ("ETW") is the licensing agent of Eldrick "Tiger" Woods ("Woods"), one of the world's most famous professional golfers. Woods, chairman of the board of ETW, has assigned to it the exclusive right to exploit his name, image, likeness, and signature, and all other publicity rights. ETW owns a United States trademark registration for the mark "TIGER WOODS" (Registration No. 2,194,381) for use in connection with "art prints, calendars, mounted photographs, notebooks, pencils, pens, posters, trading cards, and unmounted photographs."

---

* Some footnotes omitted.

Defendant-Appellee Jireh Publishing, Inc. ("Jireh") of Tuscaloosa, Alabama, is the publisher of artwork created by Rick Rush ("Rush"). Rush, who refers to himself as "America's sports artist," has created paintings of famous figures in sports and famous sports events. A few examples include Michael Jordan, Mark McGuire, Coach Paul "Bear" Bryant, the Pebble Beach Golf Tournament, and the America's Cup Yacht Race. Jireh has produced and successfully marketed limited edition art prints made from Rush's paintings.

In 1998, Rush created a painting entitled The Masters of Augusta, which commemorates Woods's victory at the Masters Tournament in Augusta, Georgia, in 1997.[10] At that event, Woods became the youngest player ever to win the Masters Tournament, while setting a 72-hole record for the tournament and a record 12-stroke margin of victory. In the foreground of Rush's painting are three views of Woods in different poses. In the center, he is completing the swing of a golf club, and on each side he is crouching, lining up and/or observing the progress of a putt. To the left of Woods is his caddy, Mike "Fluff" Cowan, and to his right is his final round partner's caddy. Behind these figures is the Augusta National Clubhouse. In a blue background behind the clubhouse are likenesses of famous golfers of the past looking down on Woods. These include Arnold Palmer, Sam Snead, Ben Hogan, Walter Hagen, Bobby Jones, and Jack Nicklaus. Behind them is the Masters leader board.

The limited edition prints distributed by Jireh consist of an image of Rush's painting which includes Rush's signature at the bottom right hand corner. Beneath the image of the painting, in block letters, is its title, "The Masters Of Augusta." Beneath the title, in block letters of equal height, is the artist's name, "Rick Rush," and beneath the artist's name, in smaller upper and lower case letters, is the legend "Painting America Through Sports." ...

ETW filed suit against Jireh on June 26, 1998, in the United States District Court for the Northern District of Ohio, alleging trademark infringement in violation of the Lanham Act, 15 U.S.C. § 1114; dilution of the mark under the Lanham Act, 15 U.S.C. § 1125(c); unfair competition and false advertising under the Lanham Act, 15 U.S.C. § 1125(a); unfair competition and deceptive trade practices under Ohio Revised Code § 4165.01; unfair competition and

---

10. Michael D. Murray, Cropped, revised and resized image (2007) derived from a photograph of Rick Rush's *The Masters of Augusta*, the subject of *ETW Corp. v. Jireh Publ'g, Inc.*, 332 F.3d 915 (6th Cir. 2003).

trademark infringement under Ohio common law; and violation of Woods's right of publicity under Ohio common law. Jireh counterclaimed, seeking a declaratory judgment that Rush's art prints are protected by the First Amendment and do not violate the Lanham Act. Both parties moved for summary judgment.

The district court granted Jireh's motion for summary judgment and dismissed the case. *See ETW Corp. v. Jireh Pub., Inc.*, 99 F. Supp. 2d 829 (N.D. Ohio 2000). ETW timely perfected an appeal to this court. . . .

IV. LANHAM ACT UNFAIR COMPETITION AND FALSE ENDORSEMENT CLAIMS, OHIO RIGHT TO PRIVACY CLAIMS, AND THE FIRST AMENDMENT DEFENSE

A. Introduction

ETW's claims under §43(a) of the Lanham Act, 15 U.S.C. §1125(a), include claims of unfair competition and false advertising in the nature of false endorsement. ETW has also asserted a claim for infringement of the right of publicity under Ohio law. The elements of a Lanham Act false endorsement claim are similar to the elements of a right of publicity claim under Ohio law. In fact, one legal scholar has said that a Lanham Act false endorsement claim is the federal equivalent of the right of publicity. *See* Bruce P. Keller, *The Right Of Publicity: Past, Present, and Future*, 1207 PLI CORP. LAW and PRAC. HANDBOOK, 159, 170 (October 2000). Therefore, cases which address both these types of claims should be instructive in determining whether Jireh is entitled to summary judgment on those claims.

In addition, Jireh has raised the First Amendment as a defense to all of ETW's claims, arguing that Rush's use of Woods's image in his painting is protected expression. Cases involving Lanham Act false endorsement claims and state law claims of the right of publicity have considered the impact of the First Amendment on those types of claims. . . .

B. First Amendment Defense

The protection of the First Amendment is not limited to written or spoken words, but includes other mediums of expression, including music, pictures, films, photographs, paintings, drawings, engravings, prints, and sculptures. *See Hurley v. Irish-American Gay, Lesbian and Bisexual Group of Boston*, 515 U.S. 557, 569, 115 S. Ct. 2338, 132 L. Ed. 2d 487 (1995) ("[T]he Constitution looks beyond written or spoken words as mediums of expression"); *Ward v. Rock Against Racism*, 491 U.S. 781, 790, 109 S. Ct. 2746, 105 L. Ed. 2d 661 (1989) ("Music, as a form of expression and communication, is protected under the First Amendment"); *Zacchini v. Scripps-Howard Broadcasting Co.*, 433 U.S. 562, 578, 97 S. Ct. 2849, 53 L. Ed. 2d 965 (1977) ("There is no doubt that entertainment, as well as news, enjoys First Amendment protection"); *Kaplan v. California*, 413 U.S. 115, 119-120, 93 S. Ct. 2680, 37 L. Ed. 2d 492 (1973) ("[P]ictures, films, paintings, drawings, and engravings . . . have

First Amendment protection"); *Bery v. City of New York*, 97 F.3d 689, 695 (2d Cir. 1996) ("[V]isual art is as wide ranging in its depiction of ideas, concepts and emotions as any book, treatise, pamphlet or other writing, and is similarly entitled to full First Amendment protection").

Speech is protected even though it is carried in a form that is sold for profit. *See Smith v. California*, 361 U.S. 147, 150, 80 S. Ct. 215, 4 L. Ed. 2d 205 (1959) ("It is of course no matter that the dissemination [of books and other forms of the printed word] takes place under commercial auspices"); *see also Buckley v. Valeo*, 424 U.S. 1, 96 S. Ct. 612, 46 L. Ed. 2d 659 (1976) (paid advertisement); *Time, Inc. v. Hill*, 385 U.S. 374, 397, 87 S. Ct. 534, 17 L. Ed. 2d 456 (1967) ("'That books, newspapers, and magazines are published and sold for profit does not prevent them from being a form of expression whose liberty is safe-guarded by the First Amendment'")(quoting *Joseph Burstyn, Inc. v. Wilson*, 343 U.S. 495, 501-502, 72 S. Ct. 777, 96 L. Ed. 1098) (1952); *New York Times Co. v. Sullivan*, 376 U.S. 254, 84 S. Ct. 710, 11 L. Ed. 2d 686 (1964) (solicitation to pay or contribute money). The fact that expressive materials are sold does not diminish the degree of protection to which they are entitled under the First Amendment. *City of Lakewood v. Plain Dealer Publ'g Co.*, 486 U.S. 750, 756 n.5, 108 S. Ct. 2138, 100 L. Ed. 2d 771 (1988).

Publishers disseminating the work of others who create expressive mate-rials also come wholly within the protective shield of the First Amendment. *See, e.g., Simon & Schuster, Inc. v. Members of New York State Crime Victims Bd.*, 502 U.S. 105, 116, 112 S. Ct. 501, 116 L. Ed. 2d 476 (1991) (both the author and the publishing house are "speakers" for purposes of the First Amendment); *Sullivan*, 376 U.S. at 286-88, 84 S. Ct. 710 (finding New York Times fully protected by the First Amendment for publishing a paid editorial advertise-ment). *See also First Nat'l Bank of Boston v. Bellotti*, 435 U.S. 765, 782, 98 S. Ct. 1407, 55 L. Ed. 2d 707 (1978).[11]

Even pure commercial speech is entitled to significant First Amendment protection. *See City of Cincinnati v. Discovery Network, Inc.*, 507 U.S. 410, 423, 113 S. Ct. 1505, 123 L. Ed. 2d 99 (1993); *Bd. of Trustees of the State University of New York v. Fox*, 492 U.S. 469, 473-74, 109 S. Ct. 3028, 106 L. Ed. 2d 388 (1989); *Central Hudson Gas and Electric Corp. v. Pub. Serv. Comm'n of New York*, 447 U.S. 557, 100 S. Ct. 2343, 65 L. Ed. 2d 341 (1980); *Virginia State Bd. Of Pharmacy v. Virginia Citizens Consumer Council, Inc.*, 425 U.S. 748, 96 S. Ct. 1817, 48 L. Ed. 2d 346 (1976). Commercial speech is "speech which does 'no more than propose a commercial transaction[.]'" *Virginia State Bd. of Pharmacy*, 425 U.S. at 762, 96 S. Ct. 1817 (quoting *Pittsburgh Press Co. v. Pittsburgh Comm'n on Human Relations*, 413 U.S. 376, 385, 93 S. Ct. 2553, 37 L. Ed. 2d 669 (1973)); *see also Central Hudson Gas and Electric Corp.*,

---

11. ETW's argument that only the original work and not its copies are protected would lead to absurd results. For example, the original manuscript of an unauthorized biography would be pro-tected, but not the published copies. The original script of a play or a movie would be protected, but not live performances or films produced from it.

447 U.S. at 566, 100 S. Ct. 2343 (articulating a four part test to bring commercial speech within the protection of the First Amendment).

Rush's prints are not commercial speech. They do not propose a commercial transaction. Accordingly, they are entitled to the full protection of the First Amendment. Thus, we are called upon to decide whether Woods's intellectual property rights must yield to Rush's First Amendment rights. . . .

D. Right of Publicity Claim

ETW claims that Jireh's publication and marketing of prints of Rush's painting violates Woods's right of publicity. The right of publicity is an intellectual property right of recent origin which has been defined as the inherent right of every human being to control the commercial use of his or her identity. *See* McCarthy on Publicity and Privacy, § 1:3. The right of publicity is a creature of state law and its violation gives rise to a cause of action for the commercial tort of unfair competition. *Id.* . . .

There is an inherent tension between the right of publicity and the right of freedom of expression under the First Amendment. This tension becomes particularly acute when the person seeking to enforce the right is a famous actor, athlete, politician, or otherwise famous person whose exploits, activities, accomplishments, and personal life are subject to constant scrutiny and comment in the public media. . . .

We conclude that in deciding whether the sale of Rush's prints violate Woods's right of publicity, we will look to the Ohio case law and the Restatement (Third) of Unfair Competition. In deciding where the line should be drawn between Woods's intellectual property rights and the First Amendment, we find ourselves in agreement with the dissenting judges in *White*, the Tenth Circuit's decision in *Cardtoons*, and the Ninth Circuit's decision in *Hoffman*, and we will follow them in determining whether Rush's work is protected by the First Amendment. Finally, we believe that the transformative elements test adopted by the Supreme Court of California in *Comedy III Productions*, will assist us in determining where the proper balance lies between the First Amendment and Woods's intellectual property rights. We turn now to a further examination of Rush's work and its subject.

E. Application of the Law to the Evidence in this Case

The evidence in the record reveals that Rush's work consists of much more than a mere literal likeness of Woods. It is a panorama of Woods's victory at the 1997 Masters Tournament, with all of the trappings of that tournament in full view, including the Augusta clubhouse, the leader board, images of Woods's caddy, and his final round partner's caddy. These elements in themselves are sufficient to bring Rush's work within the protection of the First Amendment. The Masters Tournament is probably the world's most famous golf tournament and Woods's victory in the 1997 tournament was a historic event in the world of sports. A piece of art that portrays a historic sporting event communicates and celebrates the value our culture attaches to such events. It would be ironic indeed if the presence of the image of the victorious athlete would deny the work First Amendment protection. Furthermore, Rush's work includes not only images of Woods and the two caddies, but also carefully crafted likenesses of six past winners of the Masters Tournament: Arnold Palmer, Sam Snead, Ben Hogan, Walter Hagen, Bobby Jones, and Jack Nicklaus, a veritable pantheon of golf's greats. Rush's work conveys the message that Woods himself will someday join that revered group.

Turning first to ETW's Lanham Act false endorsement claim, we agree with the courts that hold that the Lanham Act should be applied to artistic works only where the public interest in avoiding confusion outweighs the public interest in free expression. The *Rogers* test is helpful in striking that balance in the instant case. We find that the presence of Woods's image in Rush's painting The Masters Of Augusta does have artistic relevance to the underlying work and that it does not explicitly mislead as to the source of the work.[12]

We believe that the principles followed in *Cardtoons, Hoffman* and *Comedy III* are also relevant in determining whether the Lanham Act applies to Rush's work, and we find that it does not.

We find, like the court in *Rogers,* that plaintiff's survey evidence, even if its validity is assumed, indicates at most that some members of the public would draw the incorrect inference that Woods had some connection with Rush's print.[13]

The risk of misunderstanding, not engendered by any explicit indication on the face of the print, is so outweighed by the interest in artistic expression as to preclude application of the Act. We disagree with the dissent's suggestion that a jury must decide where the balance should be struck and where the boundaries should be drawn between the rights conferred by the Lanham Act and the protections of the First Amendment.

In regard to the Ohio law right of publicity claim, we conclude that Ohio would construe its right of publicity as suggested in the restatement (Third) Of Unfair Competition, Chapter 4, Section 47, Comment d., which articulates a rule analogous to the rule of fair use in copyright law. Under this rule, the substantiality and market effect of the use of the celebrity's image is analyzed in

---

12. Unlike *Parks,* here there is no genuine issue of material fact about the artistic relevance of the image of Woods in Rush's print. *See Ruffin-Steinback v. dePasse,* 82 F. Supp. 2d 723 (E.D. Mich. 2000), aff'd, 267 F.3d 457 (6th Cir. 2001) (likeness of members of Motown group "Temptations" used to promote televised mini-series and video cassette based on partly fictionalized story about group); *Seale v. Gramercy Pictures,* 949 F. Supp. 331 (E.D. Pa. 1996) (use of plaintiff's name and likeness on cover of pictorial history book and home video clearly related to content of book and film).

13. Respondents in the survey were handed a copy of Rush's print and were asked the question: "Do you believe that Tiger Woods has an affiliation or connection with this print or that he has given his approval or has sponsored it?" Sixty-two percent answered "Yes"; eleven percent said "No"; and twenty-seven percent said "Don't Know." The terms "affiliated with" and "connected with" were not defined. Some respondents may have thought that Woods's mere presence in the print was itself an affiliation or connection. No control questions were asked to clarify this. Furthermore, the respondents were not given the packaging in which Jireh distributed the prints which prominently features Rush and contains no suggestion that Woods sponsored or approved the print.

light of the informational and creative content of the defendant's use. Applying this rule, we conclude that Rush's work has substantial informational and creative content which outweighs any adverse effect on ETW's market and that Rush's work does not violate Woods's right of publicity.

We further find that Rush's work is expression which is entitled to the full protection of the First Amendment and not the more limited protection afforded to commercial speech. When we balance the magnitude of the speech restriction against the interest in protecting Woods's intellectual property right, we encounter precisely the same considerations weighed by the Tenth Circuit in *Cardtoons*. These include consideration of the fact that through their pervasive presence in the media, sports and entertainment celebrities have come to symbolize certain ideas and values in our society and have become a valuable means of expression in our culture. As the Tenth Circuit observed "[c]elebrities . . . are an important element of the shared communicative resources of our cultural domain." *Cardtoons*, 95 F.3d at 972.

In balancing these interests against Woods's right of publicity, we note that Woods, like most sports and entertainment celebrities with commercially valuable identities, engages in an activity, professional golf, that in itself generates a significant amount of income which is unrelated to his right of publicity. Even in the absence of his right of publicity, he would still be able to reap substantial financial rewards from authorized appearances and endorsements. It is not at all clear that the appearance of Woods's likeness in artwork prints which display one of his major achievements will reduce the commercial value of his likeness.

While the right of publicity allows celebrities like Woods to enjoy the fruits of their labors, here Rush has added a significant creative component of his own to Woods's identity. Permitting Woods's right of publicity to trump Rush's right of freedom of expression would extinguish Rush's right to profit from his creative enterprise. After balancing the societal and personal interests embodied in the First Amendment against Woods's property rights, we conclude that the effect of limiting Woods's right of publicity in this case is negligible and significantly outweighed by society's interest in freedom of artistic expression.

Finally, applying the transformative effects test adopted by the Supreme Court of California in *Comedy III*, we find that Rush's work does contain significant transformative elements which make it especially worthy of First Amendment protection and also less likely to interfere with the economic interest protected by Woods' right of publicity. Unlike the unadorned, nearly photographic reproduction of the faces of The Three Stooges in *Comedy III*, Rush's work does not capitalize solely on a literal depiction of Woods. Rather, Rush's work consists of a collage of images in addition to Woods's image which are combined to describe, in artistic form, a historic event in sports history and to convey a message about the significance of Woods's achievement in that event. Because Rush's work has substantial transformative elements, it is entitled to the full protection of the First Amendment. In this case, we find that Woods's right of publicity must yield to the First Amendment.

V. CONCLUSION

In accordance with the foregoing, the judgment of the District Court granting summary judgment to Jireh Publishing is affirmed.

Notes and Questions

1. The *Rogers v. Grimaldi* test and the "transformative" test of *Comedy III v. Saderup* have grown to be the most popular tests affording protection to both publicity interests and First Amendment artistic expression concerns. (*See* section D, Fair Use of Celebrity Names, Images, and Likenesses, *infra*). The *Rogers v. Grimaldi* test requires: (1) artistic relevance of the use of the name or image in the work, and (2) the work does not "explicitly mislead as to the source or the content of the work." *Comedy III*, borrowing language from copyright fair uses cases, requires a use to be "transformative": the artist must add new value to the work either by dint of artistic embellishments to the original (quantity of alteration being regarded as more important than quality), or by bringing to the table the artist's own fame and the market value of the artist's name. In either case, the end result must not supersede the objects of the original.

2. The *Comedy III* court held out Andy Warhol as a prime example of an artist whose use of famous celebrity images was transformative. There appears to be a "genius standard" at work in this test — that artists whose personal fame allows them to sell works for their own artistic value even though they borrow other celebrities' images will be allowed to make use of the images, but lesser known artists, such as Gary Saderup, must produce something truly unique and creative in order to escape a right of publicity claim.

3. Aside from news reporting, parody remains as the most appropriate, non-actionable use of famous celebrities' names and images. *See Winter v. DC Comics*, 30 Cal. 4th 881, 69 P.3d 473, 134 Cal. Rptr. 2d 634 (2003) (discussed below in section D on Fair Use) (anthropomorphic portrayal of singers as bastard, half-worm beings was parody and non-actionable under *Comedy III* test); *World Wrestling Fed. Entm't, Inc. v. Big Dog Holdings, Inc.*, 280 F. Supp. 2d 413 (W.D. Pa. 2003) (anthropomorphic portrayal of WWF wrestling stars as dogs was parody and non-actionable).

4. Artists and their counsel should be wary of using images of unsuspecting persons taken on a city street. The results of disputes over such acquisitions of images is varied. *Compare Nieves v. Home Box Office, Inc.*, 817 N.Y.S. 2d 227 (App. Div. 1st Dep't 2006) (complaint of person filmed on street and used in bounty hunter reality TV show stated a claim), *and Mendonsa v. Time Inc.*, 678 F. Supp. 967 (D.R.I. 1988) (male subject of famous Eisenstadt photograph on V-J Day of a sailor kissing a

nurse in New York City's Times Square stated claim for misappropriation of his image), *with Nussenzweig v. diCorcia*, 832 N.Y.S. 2d 510 (App. Div. 1st Dep't 2007) (summary judgment awarded to street photographer who used close-up image of head of man taken on city street).

C. Current Trends in Right of Publicity Law

Current Cases: Virtual College Football Players

Hart v. Electronic Arts,[14] and *In re NCAA Student-Athlete Name & Likeness Licensing Litigation*[15]

In the first listed case above, former Rutgers quarterback Ryan Hart, on behalf of a class of NCAA athletes, sued Electronic Arts (EA Sports) for unauthorized uses of images, likenesses, and statistics — but not the names — of college athletes. In the second named case, a proposed class of NCAA student athletes also sued EA Sports for use of their names and likenesses in sports simulation games. The centerpiece of both suits was an EA Sports computer simulation game called *NCAA Football.*[16]

EA Sports had a copyright and trademark license for the college team's uniforms, logos, team names, mascots, fight songs, and university affiliations. It did not have a separate publicity license with the players. EA Sports attempted to avoid any complications by not using the players' names — instead of saying "Hart back to pass," in the course of a simulated game, it said "No. 13 back to pass." In the *Hart* case, Hart argued that this did not avoid the issue, because his uniform number was used at the position he played, quarterback, for his particular team, and the vital statistics for this "Quarterback, No. 13" were his own — his height, weight, throwing arm, hometown, and the like.

In *Hart,* the District Court for the District of New Jersey noted that NCAA student athletes were not permitted to license and profit from their actual identities as players under strictly enforced NCAA rules. The student

---

14. *Hart v. Elec. Arts, Inc.*, 717 F.3d 141, 165-70 (3d Cir. 2013).

15. *In re NCAA Student-Athlete Name & Likeness Licensing Litig.*, 724 F.3d 1268 (9th Cir. 2013), *aff'g, Keller v. Elecs. Arts, Inc.*, No. C 09-1967 CW, 2010 WL 530108, at *1 (N.D. Cal. Feb. 8, 2010).

16. Image: Michael D. Murray, Thumbnail-Sized-Sized Excerpt of a Portion of the Cover Art of EA Sport's NCAA Football 2006 Video Game (2015), the subject of *Hart v. Elec. Arts, Inc.*, 717 F.3d 141, 165-70 (3d Cir. 2013), and *In re NCAA Student-Athlete Name & Likeness Licensing Litig.*, 724 F.3d 1268 (9th Cir. 2013), *aff'g, Keller v. Elecs. Arts, Inc.*, No. C 09-1967 CW, 2010 WL 530108, at *1 (N.D. Cal. Feb. 8, 2010).

athletes could not sell their own jerseys or sell autographs or engage in other commercial activities relating to their athletic endeavors. This undercut the logic of the suit severely; it seemed that even if the rest of their complaint stated a cause of action for violations of publicity rights, there were no functional damages. The game maker also successfully alleged fair uses in defense of the suit, the most important of which was that the game was transformative.[17] Hart's suit was dismissed, and the *Hart* case went up on appeal.

On appeal, the United States Court of Appeals for the Third Circuit carefully examined whether EA Sports was entitled to the First Amendment defense recognized by the District Court. The Third Circuit reviewed three of the prevailing fair use tests (*see* section D, "Fair Use of Celebrity Names, Images, and Likenesses," below): the predominant purpose test,[18] the relatedness test (or *Rogers* test),[19] and the transformative test,[20] and determined that the transformative test from California state law was the most apt for the situation of Hart's case.[21]

The Third Circuit painstakingly broke down the issue of the high First Amendment protection for expressive media such as video games,[22] and the meaning and application of the transformative test.[23] In spite of the completely different meaning, purpose, context, and message, and the transformation from a real life player in actual football games to a completely fanciful, visual recreation in a digital virtual reality of a computerized football *simulation* game, the Court made the remarkable observation that there was no real difference between a depiction of Hart the actual football player in actual football games, and the avatar appearance of Quarterback No. 13 for Rutgers in the football simulation computer game.[24] EA Sports has not made sufficient change in "context, meaning, and expression" from the actual Hart's appearance to the avatar in the video game to justify the label of transformation and the fair use protection that goes with the label.

The issue in *In re NCAA Student-Athletes Name & Likeness Licensing Litigation* was framed differently, because the court had to respond to a motion by EA Sports that the entire lawsuit was a "Strategic lawsuit against public participation" (SLAPP) under California's anti-SLAPP statute — meaning that the only reason for the suit was to put pressure on EA Sports to cease exercising

---

17. Applying the transformative test from *Comedy III Prods., Inc. v. Gary Saderup, Inc.*, 21 P.3d 797, 804–08 (Cal. 2001).

18. The predominant purpose test was developed in *Doe v. TCI Cablevision*, 110 S.W. 3d 363 (Mo. 2003). *See Hart*, 717 F.3d at 153-54.

19. The relatedness test was created by *Rogers v. Grimaldi*, 875 F.2d 994 (2d Cir.1989). *See Hart*, 717 F.3d at 154-58.

20. The transformative test originated in copyright fair use law, *see Campbell v. Acuff–Rose Music, Inc.*, 510 U.S. 569, 579 (1994), and was adopted for use in California law in right of publicity cases in *Comedy III Prods., Inc. v. Gary Saderup, Inc.*, 21 P.3d 797, 804–08 (Cal. 2001).

21. *See Hart*, 717 F.3d at 158-63.

22. *Id.* at 149-50 (citing, inter alia, *Brown v. Entm't Merchants Ass'n*, 131 S. Ct. 2729, 2733 (2011); *Whitney v. California*, 274 U.S. 357, 376 (1927) (Brandeis, J., concurring)).

23. *Id.* at 158-63.

24. *Id.* at 160-70.

its free expression rights, which it typically exercised by making and selling video games. The District Court denied the motion for the somewhat unusual reason that the motion was improper because EA Sports did not have First Amendment rights and protections in the video game that would need to be protected in the anti-SLAPP motion. What the court meant was that the lawsuit of the athletes had merit — therefore, it was not just a bullying technique to "quiet" the video game maker's speech. And the reason was that EA Sports did not enjoy a transformative fair use over the images of the athletes.[25] The Ninth Circuit agreed, and affirmed the case on appeal.[26]

In essence the Ninth Circuit opinion followed *Hart*: it agreed that the transformative test was the superior test (it considered the relatedness test of *Rogers*, too[27]), and it found that the treatments of the athletes' images was not transformative.[28] The lawsuit only represents a disposition on the anti-SLAPP motion to dismiss, but the ruling indicates that the athletes' claims have merit and are likely to succeed, so it telegraphs to the parties that EA Sports is not going to sail through the case on the strength of its First Amendment defenses.

Case Study: I "Doubt" that's Nirvana

No Doubt v. Activision,[29] and *Love v. Activision*[30]

Guitar Hero and *Band Hero* are two rock music simulation games produced by another video game maker, Activision.[31] In the game, you can cause an avatar of your favorite singers and musicians to rock out to their hits. At advanced levels of the game, after "unlocking" certain avatars, you can cause avatars of famous musicians or bands to virtually perform other bands' music.

You can, in fact, unlock the Kurt Cobain or *No Doubt* avatars and have Kurt Cobain or Gwen Stefani rock out to *Air Supply* or *The Rolling Stones'* songs. This may sound like a fun evening to a gamer, but it is dreadful sacrilege to some persons near and dear to the original groups, including Courtney Love, the surviving heir of Cobain, and the *No Doubt* band members, who,

25. *Keller v. Elecs. Arts, Inc.*, No. C 09-1967 CW, 2010 WL 530108, at *5 (N.D. Cal. Feb. 8, 2010).

26. *In re NCAA Student-Athlete Name & Likeness Licensing Litig.*, 724 F.3d 1268, 1284 (9th Cir. 2013).

27. *Id.* at 1279-84.

28. *Id.* at 1273-79.

29. *No Doubt v. Activision Publishing, Inc.*, 122 Cal. Rptr. 3d 397, 400 (App. Ct. 2011)

30. G. Yang, *Courtney Love's Lawyer Issues Statement on Guitar Hero Dispute*, Prefixmag (Sep. 11, 2009, 1:46 p.m.), *http://www.prefixmag.com/news/courtney-loves-lawyer-issues-statement-on-guitar-h/32587/*.

31. Image: Michael D. Murray, Cropped, revised and resized thumbnail image of Activision's Band Hero video game cover art (2015), the subject of *No Doubt v. Activision Publishing, Inc.*, 122 Cal. Rptr. 3d 397, 400 (App. Ct. 2011).

Stefani   *Stefani avatar*   *Cobain*   *Cobain avatar* [32]

respectively, have strong objections to even the virtual, simulated use of Cobain or members of *No Doubt* playing and singing other bands' songs.[33]

Is this an actionable right of publicity claim? The claims were undercut by licenses given to Activision for the use of the musicians' images, likenesses, names, sounds of their singing voices, and attributes of their performances. Love and *No Doubt* had signed off on the contracts that licensed all of these things to Activision. The claims raised about the "unlocked" avatars were more akin to "moral rights" claims — that the unlocking and allowing of the avatars to perform other bands' music created a new performance (albeit, usually a very private one, in one's own home) that could be detrimental to the performers' reputations. It was a right to artistic integrity and legacy, threatened by these new performances with completely different music. *No Doubt* survived a motion to dismiss the suit,[34] and Activision subsequently settled with *No Doubt* (the terms, as usual, were not disclosed),[35] while Courtney Love never actually sued, and apparently backed down after she reportedly lost control over Kurt Cobain's publicity rights to Cobain's daughter.[36]

1. The Effect of Copyright and Licensing

If the rights asserted by a celebrity are the same rights that were licensed under copyright law to a media company or other publisher, the copyright license

---

32. Images: Michael D. Murray, Cropped, revised and resized thumbnail images of Gwen Stefani and Kurt Cobain, and the avatars of Stefani and Cobain (2015), as appearing the Activision video game Band Hero, the subject of *No Doubt v. Activision Publishing, Inc.*, 122 Cal. Rptr. 3d 397, 400 (App. Ct. 2011).

33. *No Doubt*, 122 Cal. Rptr. 3d at 398-400; Mark Milian, *Courtney Love and Nirvana members unhappy with Kurt Cobain in Guitar Hero*, Pop & Hiss, L.A. Times Music Blog (Sep. 10, 2009, 7:57 pm).

34. *No Doubt*, 122 Cal. Rptr. 3d at 400.

35. Eriq Gardner, *No Doubt, Activision Settle Lawsuit Over Avatars in 'Band Hero'*, The Hollywood Reporter (Oct. 30, 2012, 3:38pm PST), *http://www.hollywoodreporter.com/thr-esq/ no-doubt-activision-lawsuit-band-hero-376217*.

36. Courtney Garcia, *Courtney Love's interest in Kurt Cobain fades as she reportedly loses control of his image rights*, NBC News, Entertainment (May 3, 2012, 8:11 AM), *http://entertainment.nbcnews. com/_news/2012/05/03/11520786-courtney-loves-interest-in-kurt-cobain-fades-as-she-reportedly-loses-control-of-his-image-rights*.

trumps the right of publicity claim.[37] The theory is that the exercise of the copyrights over the items protected by copyright (works fixed in a tangible medium of expression) is sufficient to preclude any publicity rights of performers whose performances also are fixed within that work.[38] Implicitly, by agreeing to allow one's voice, appearance, or performance to be fixed within a work that will be protected by copyright, the performer has consented to the licensing and further use of that fixed recording under the exercise of the copyrights to the recording.

If publicity rights duplicate the rights that are covered by copyright law — such as the situation of a rebroadcast or republication of a taped event, sports contest, or publication — then copyright law might preempt the publicity claim.[39] Preemption means that the rights asserted under a right of publicity claim are the same in every way to the rights protected under copyright law, and potentially controlled by a copyright license,[40] and so copyright law is given priority to control how the publicity rights are recognized and enforced. An example of this is when major league baseball players wanted to be compensated for the airing of their baseball games. The Major League Baseball Players Association owned the copyright to the broadcast. This was held to be the entire right to the public "performances" of the athletes — there were no additional rights concerning the individual players' appearances and the broadcasting of their names, images, and likenesses.[41]

Right of publicity claims are not preempted if the claim attempts to adjudicate rights that are different from those covered by copyright, such as the claim to the quality and sound of a voice, as opposed to a copyright over a sound recording.[42]

---

37. *Laws v. Sony Music Entm't, Inc.*, 448 F.3d 1134, 1143-44 (9th Cir. 2006) (exercise of rights to copyrighted sound recording cannot violate publicity rights of singer whose voice is heard in that very recording); *Fleet v. CBS, Inc.*, 58 Cal. Rptr. 2d 645 (Ct. App. 1996) (copyrights to video recording preempt publicity claim of actor appearing in the recording).

38. *Laws*, 448 F.3d at 1141-44; *Fleet*, 58 Cal. Rptr. 2d at 645.

39. *E.g., Baltimore Orioles, Inc. v. Major League Baseball Players Ass'n*, 805 F.2d 663, 674-79 (7th Cir. 1986).

40. *Jules Jordan Video, Inc. v. 144942 Canada Inc.*, 617 F.3d 1146, 1153-54 (9th Cir. 2010); *Laws*, 448 F.3d at 1141-44.

41. *Baltimore Orioles, Inc.*, 805 F.2d at 674-79.

42. *Compare Laws*, 448 F.3d at 1143-44 (claim for appropriation of voice preempted by defendants' copyright license to the contents of the recording used), *with Facenda v. N.F.L. Films, Inc.*, 542 F.3d 1007, 1028 (3d Cir. 2008) (NFL owned copyrights to NFL films featuring the distinctive voice-over narration of plaintiff Facenda, but this did not automatically allow NFL to license the distinctive sound of the announcer's voice that the NFL attempted to replicate so as to make new voice-over narration for a documentary program on the making of Electronic Arts' Madden NFL Football simulation computer game), *and Midler v. Ford Motor Co.*, 849 F.2d 460, 462 (9th Cir. 1988) (copyright to lyrics and music does not preempt publicity rights against making a new recording with a soundalike mimicking the sound of original singer's voice), *and Waits v. Frito–Lay, Inc.*, 978 F.2d 1093 (9th Cir. 1992) (same), *and Toney v. L'Oreal USA, Inc.*, 406 F.3d 905 (7th Cir. 2005) (rights to use photograph for a limited time did not extend to preempt right of publicity of the person in the photograph to sue for uses after the limited time).

2. Statistics, Facts, and Public Interest Information

The publication of statistics and facts of matters that are within the general public interest, including facts and statistics of sports figures and celebrities, is not subject to protection under the right of publicity. This has been litigated several times, and each time the cases have resulted in a ruling that the publication of information concerning sports figures' names, statistics, and records of achievements is not actionable under the right of publicity.[43]

Although all people have the right to be free from the unauthorized exploitation of their likeness, not every publication of someone's likeness gives rise to an appropriation action.[44] The use of a celebrity's image in connection with the attempt to report news still must be fair and not misleading. In *Solano v. Playgirl, Inc.*,[45] *Playgirl* used plaintiff's image taken from his appearance on the *Baywatch* television show on the cover of their magazine and included a short biography of plaintiff in the issue. The use was held to be actionable and not related to a newsworthy event or matter of public interest because *Playgirl* suggested that nude photographs of plaintiff would be found in the issue when they were not.[46]

D. Fair Use of Celebrity Names, Images, and Likenesses

There are no less than *five* separate and distinct fair use tests that have been applied by courts in right of publicity cases. All of them speak to the same issue:

---

43. *See Gionfriddo v. Major League Baseball*, 114 Cal. Rptr. 2d 307, 310 (Ct. App. 2001) (use of players' names, statistics and images in videos commemorating All-Star and World Series events was protected reporting of newsworthy information and matters of public interest that was not subject to right of publicity protection); *C.B.C. Distribution & Mktg., Inc. v. Major League Baseball Advanced Media, L.P.*, 505 F.3d 818, 820 (8th Cir. 2007) (publication of lists, thumbnail images, and statistics about baseball players has First Amendment current affairs value that preempts players' right of publicity in their identity, even though the publication was used in for-profit fantasy baseball information service).

44. *Compare Downing v. Abercrombie & Fitch*, 265 F.3d 994, 1004 (9th Cir. 2001) (use of photographs of famous surfer in defendant's catalog violated surfer's right of publicity because catalog was commercial advertising of products, it was not a news or public interest publication), *and Toney*, 406 F.3d at 905 (unauthorized, untimely use of model's photo on packaging of hair product was a use to help sell the product, not a news or public information use), *and Christoff v. Nestle USA, Inc.*, 213 P.3d 132, 136 (Cal. 2009) (unauthorized use of image on coffee label was a use to help sell the product), *with Tyne v. Time Warner Entm't Co.*, 901 So. 2d 802 (Fla. 2005) (the term "commercial purpose" as used in Fla. Rt. of Publicity statute does not apply to publications, including motion pictures, which do not directly promote a product or service), *and Nichols v. Moore*, 396 F. Supp. 2d 783, 787 (E.D. Mich. 2005), *aff'd*, 477 F.3d 396 (6th Cir. 2007) (same), *and Dora v. Frontline Video, Inc.*, 18 Cal. Rptr. 2d 790, 792 (Ct. App. 1993) (use of images of famous surfer in documentary was protected, as documentary reported newsworthy topics and was not commercial advertising).

45. *Solano v. Playgirl, Inc.*, 292 F.3d 1078 (9th Cir. 2002).

46. *Id.* at 1082.

the proper balance of First Amendment expression and other public policy benefits weighed against the protection of publicity rights.

Cardtoons — Balancing test	10th Cir.	Court to balance the value of expression under 1st Amendment against the value of celebrity name-image-likeness used. *Cardtoons, L.C. v. Major League Baseball Players Ass'n*, 95 F.3d 959, 968-76 (10th Cir. 1996)
Rogers — Relatedness test	2d Cir.	Court to determine if the use of the celebrity name-image-likeness is directly related to the content of the expression or if instead it is a disguised advertisement and exploitation. *Rogers v. Grimaldi*, 875 F.2d 994, 999-1005 (2d Cir. 1989)
Comedy III — Transformative test	Cal. S. Ct.	Court to determine if the artist adds value to the depiction beyond the value of the celebrity image either through artistic additions or because of the status of the artist (e.g., Warhol). Ask if people would buy it for the art/artist or for the celebrity image. *Comedy III Prods., Inc. v. Gary Saderup, Inc.*, 21 P.3d 797, 804–08 (Cal. 2001)
Simeonov — NY Artistic Expression test	N.Y. Civil Ct.	Court ruled that any artist can make a representation of a celebrity if done in "limited numbers." *Simeonov v. Tiegs*, 602 N.Y.S. 2d 1014, 1018 (Civ. Ct. N.Y. Cty. 1993)
CBC, Doe — Predominant Purpose test	8th Cir., Mo. S. Ct.	Court to determine if the predominant purpose of the activity is expressive, artistic, for the news, or is to unfairly exploit the celebrity name-image-likeness. *C.B.C. Distribution & Mktg., Inc. v. Major League Baseball Advanced Media, L.P.*, 505 F.3d 818, 820 (8th Cir. 2007); *Doe v. TCI Cablevision*, 110 S.W.3d 363 (Mo. 2003)

Balancing Test

Cardtoons LC v. Major League Baseball Players Assoc.[47]

Balancing tests are popular in the law, and no less so in the right of publicity area. The criteria to be balanced — defined here as the expressive value of the

---

47. *Cardtoons, L.C. v. Major League Baseball Players Ass'n*, 95 F.3d 959 (10th Cir. 1996).

use compared to the property value of the celebrity name-image-likeness used — leads to a case-by-case determination. Therefore, lawyers and law professors have to carefully compile the record of cases applying the test to see patterns in successful narratives as well as patterns of unsuccessful narratives.

The *Cardtoons* case involved a manufacturer of comic baseball cards that emphasized the more outrageous egos and behaviors of the game's biggest stars.[48] Instead of statistics of batting average, slugging percentage, earned run average, and walks plus hits per inning pitched, the cards talked about lifestyle, personality, and the general inflated arrogance and inflated salaries of many stars. For example, Barry Bonds was identified as "Treasury Bonds" and the Cardtoons card made ironic statements about his salary and his worth through several banking and monetary system puns. The team names and logos were altered, too, to try to match the commentary. In the above example, the San Francisco Giants appear as the "Gents" with a fancy top hat as their new logo, although the Giants' orange and black color scheme was maintained in the player picture:[49]

 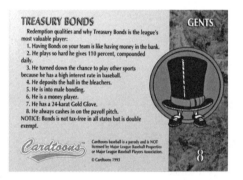

The cards presented a form of humorous commentary on the players. The Cardtoons people printed a disclaimer on the back of the cards that is shown at right above: "Cardtoons baseball is a parody and is NOT licensed by Major League Baseball Properties or Major League Baseball Players Association." A disclaimer in the law is not a guarantee that people will leave you alone, or that no one will confuse your work with genuine authorized works of the people whose endorsement you are disclaiming. But in this case, the disclaimer most likely helped the courts to determine that this was a parody, and that it was a bona fide comment on and criticism of the players.

So begins the balancing. In the one scale is the value of the publicity rights and how they are used or displayed in the context of the use. In this case, the publicity rights involved were expensive. Cardtoons had chosen a high value

---

48. *Id.* at 963-65.

49. Images: Michael D. Murray, Cropped, revised, and resized thumbnail excerpts of exhibits depicting the front and back of Cardtoon's card depicting a caricature of Barry Bonds, at issue in the case, *Cardtoons, L.C. v. Major League Baseball Players Ass'n*, 95 F.3d 959 (10th Cir. 1996).

target — professional baseball players — whose publicity values are very high on the food chain for celebrities in general, and for marketing and promotion in particular. And Cardtoons took the best, most famous of the players for their cards. The use was commercial — the cards were being sold — but the use of the images wasn't blatantly commercial in the sense of commercial advertising. The only thing being promoted was the cards themselves. In the other scale is the value of the public policies being served by the use. Here, there are two very important, high value public policies: freedom of speech, and the right to criticize public figures. This was tempered by a very practical consideration — that celebrities will never authorize the use of their names, images, or likenesses in a use that criticizes them. It is both contrary to human nature and against the celebrity's business interests to give the green light to someone who wants to take you down a peg. And if the outcome of the case was that a parody spoof of baseball players was not fair, and was a violation of the baseball players' rights of publicity, then this would shut down almost all critical commentary on athletes in particular, and public entertainment figures in general. The loss of criticism of public figures would be viewed as a tremendous loss in our First Amendment jurisprudence, so the scales were tipped in favor of allowing the parody as a fair use. And that is how the case came out.

Cardtoons is a narrative of success as to how the balancing should work out in situations, such as *Cardtoons,* where there is strong First Amendment critical speech involving celebrities and moderate commercial exploitation of the celebrities' persona.

Parodies of celebrities
with low to moderate commercial exploitation –
Very high chance of success as fair use

Specific criticism of celebrities but not parody
with low to moderate commercial exploitation –
High chance of success as fair use

General criticism of celebrities
with low to moderate commercial exploitation –
Good chance of success as fair use

As the situation moves away from classic commentary, and toward more general levels of criticism, the odds of proving a fair use go down. The factors are in play, meaning that if the commercial exploitation appears to be great, as in the case of a product or publication that prominently uses a celebrity name or likeness on its face with little substantive critical commentary, then the balance would tip away from fair use.

Cardtoons is one case; predictions are improved if we have multiple cases to work with. Fortunately, many of the other cases used *Cardtoons'* balancing test as one of their tests of fair use, so we have several other examples of success or failure narratives to look at.

Relatedness Test

Rogers v. Grimaldi[50]

Frederico Fellini, the famous Italian film director, and Alberto Grimaldi, a film producer, made a movie, *Ginger & Fred* (*Ginger e Fred* in Italian), about Argentinian ballroom dancers known in the movie as the "Fred and Ginger of Argentina." Other than the occupation of the aging ballroom dancers, the movie has nothing else in common with the careers of the real "Ginger" and "Fred" — Ginger Rogers and Fred Astaire, the dancing duo of many American 1930s and 40s movie offerings.[51] In Fellini's film, there is no other image or dialogue included about Ginger Rogers, and her picture or likeness was not used in any promotional material for the film. Nevertheless, Ginger Rogers wanted to protect her persona from exploitation, and believed that her first name in the title of any movie involving ballroom dancing was exploitation enough. She sued Fellini, the director, and Grimaldi, the producer of the film.

The court ruled for Grimaldi and Fellini on the basis of fair use. The court applied a new test (new to the context of right of publicity claims that overlap with the concept of false endorsement trademark claims, at least) referred to as the relatedness test:

- In cases involving speech or artistic expression,
- if the use of a celebrity name or image is directly related to the underlying content and meaning of the expression, the use is fair,

50. *Rogers v. Grimaldi*, 875 F.2d 994 (2d Cir. 1989).
51. Images: Michael D. Murray, Cropped, revised, and resized thumbnail excerpts of exhibits depicting Ginger Rogers and Fred Astaire dancing, and an image of Fellini's *Ginger e Fred* motion picture promotion, at issue in *Rogers v. Grimaldi*, 875 F.2d 994 (2d Cir. 1989).

■ but if the use is not related to the content of the speech, and it appears that the use might be a disguised advertisement and thus, exploitation, then the use is not fair.[52]

Rogers' relatedness test evaluates the "artistic relevance of the image or name used to the work" and polices whether the use, if not directly related, is therefore "explicitly misleading" as to the source or the content of the work and suggests sponsorship or endorsement of the work by the celebrity.[53] Although not phrased in exactly this manner, the court is looking for outward exploitation of the image, especially in a manner that looks like commercial advertising or trade dress (trade dress being the packaging or display of products at the point of sale), as opposed to speech or artistic expression that logically discusses or features the celebrity name or image.

In *Rogers*, the court found that Grimaldi and Fellini had a bona fide reason for including the name "Ginger" in the content of the work and in the title of the work — their narrative was about aging ballroom dancers, and it was logical for the fictional pair to have been given a nickname such as Ginger and Fred. Also, the adoption of the nickname alone for the title appeared to be related to the expression, and not simply used as a marketing ploy to exploit the good name and reputation of Ginger Rogers.[54]

Rogers and *Cardtoons* have been used many times since in right of publicity cases, and often they are used in the same case. The same goes for the next two tests, the "transformative" test and the "artistic expression" test.[55]

Transformative Test

Comedy III Productions v. Gary Saderup, Inc.[56]

From time to time, courts struggling with the concept of fair use in right of publicity law have looked for guidance in other areas of the law that have analogous subject matter and public policy underpinnings as publicity law. Copyright law was an obvious place to look: both publicity law and copyright law are property-law based actions. The two areas of law have, at least in part, the same public policy of encouraging the development of talent and expertise for the betterment and enrichment of the public at large, and indirectly, for the support of artists and entertainers. Both deal with First Amendment expressive fair uses. So, the California Supreme Court case of *Comedy III Productions v. Gary Saderup, Inc.* excerpted above looked like it had a great idea when it

---

52. *Rogers*, 875 F.2d at 999-1005.
53. *Id.*
54. *Id.* at 1004-05.
55. *E.g., In re NCAA Student-Athlete Name & Likeness Licensing Litig.*, 724 F.3d at 1268, and *Hart*, 717 F.3d at 165-70 (discussed *supra*), both considered and rejected several tests — *Rogers'* relatedness test, *Doe* and *C.B.C. Distribution*'s predominant purpose test, and *Cardtoons'* balancing test — before settling on *Comedy III*'s transformative test.
56. *Comedy III Prods., Inc. v. Gary Saderup, Inc.*, 21 P.3d 797 (Cal. 2001).

borrowed the transformative test from copyright fair use law.[57] However, although the court adopted an interesting and potentially useful test, it applied it in a manner that may set back artists for years in California.

The transformative test is not as simple and straightforward as the balancing test and the relatedness test. It requires an examination of the use of the name and image of the celebrity, and whether the new work transforms the content and appearance of the celebrity or her persona or aspects of her performance in such a way that the use no longer looks like exploitation, and appears to be more like new expression. Consider the manner in which the transformative test works in copyright law:

> In copyright law, the transformative test is used for the evaluation of copyright fair uses, and the test works out to mean that if a person copies a portion or the whole of another artist's or author's creation, then the second user must transform the original work in one of several ways: (a) add new content to the old expression, so that it has new meaning; (b) put the old work into a new context — this is known as "recontextualization," and the new context should be one that changes the overall function, purpose, and meaning of the old work; (c) put the old expression to work for an entirely new function and purpose; or (d) best of all, do two or three of (a), (b), and (c) together, to really upend the original work's content, meaning, function, *and* purpose. The idea is not to replicate the original work and show it again for its original expressive purpose and value. If the original shines through in the second work, then the transformation is incomplete and the fair use fails.[58]

There is a basic problem with importing the transformative test from copyright law into right of publicity law: copyright deals with works — paintings, books, films, and other expressive works. Publicity law deals with people. There is not a ready metaphor for *transforming* people and their persona the way that there is for physical, expressive works. We all know of paintings, songs, films, and books that have been altered or adapted. We have less to go on with transformations of celebrity names, images, and likenesses. (We assume the law does not require the kind of transformations that some celebrities engage in, such as with Lady Gaga, Madonna, or David Bowie, who went through many phases in their public personae).

As a replacement for the concept of adaptation, alteration, or recontextualization, *Comedy III* offered the following criteria for what is transformative of a celebrity persona when it appears in another expressive work:

> Primary inquiry: Is the work merely a depiction of the celebrity, no matter how skillfully executed, or did the artist add new creative expression that has value beyond that of star's image?
> Subsidiary inquiry: Would an average member of the public buy the work for the art or the artist, or for the celebrity's image?[59]

---

57. *Id.* at 804-08.
58. *See* Michael D. Murray, *What Is Transformative? An Explanatory Synthesis of the Convergence of Transformation and Predominant Purpose in Copyright Fair Use Law,* 11 Chi.-Kent J. Intell. Prop. 260, 264 (2012).
59. *Comedy III,* 21 P.3d at 809, 810.

Comedy III made "supplementation" and "augmentation" actions of transformation when it comes to depictions involving a celebrity image. The artist must add new creative expression beyond simply applying artistic techniques to render a depiction of the celebrity.[60]

The subsidiary inquiry stated above sets up a potentially difficult standard for new and up-and-coming artists to meet — if a buyer is more likely to pick their item because it depicts a certain celebrity than because it is by a particular artist or because of its artistic techniques, then the work fails the transformative test and is not a fair use of the celebrity image.

The test might still sound very workable, especially for well-known artists, but the sour note in the story here is that the California Supreme Court declared that the defendant, an artist by the name of Gary Saderup, had done a skillful, artistic rendering in charcoal of images of the Three Stooges comedy team, and that there was no denying that the work reflected superior artistic skill and technique[61]:

The Three Stooges in You Nazty Spy

Saderup's rendering of the Three Stooges

---

60. *Id.* at 809-11 (finding that the skillful artistic rendering of Saderup's depiction of the Three Stooges in fact did not meet the court's standards of transformation of the appearance of the celebrities).

61. Images: Michael D. Murray, Thumbnail-Sized-Sized Excerpts of the Source Material Depiction of the Three Stooges in a Motion Picture Promotional Image for *You Nazty Spy*, Compared to Gary Saderup's Depiction of the Three Stooges in the Work at issue in *Comedy III Prods., Inc. v. Gary Saderup, Inc.*, 21 P.3d 797 (Cal. 2001).

The court then proceeded to declare that the work was not transformative, and therefore not a fair use.[62] On the subsidiary inquiry, the court found that the work would obviously be purchased by Three Stooges enthusiasts because it depicted the celebrities' images and not by any association of the work with Saderup.[63]

Note that Saderup had a small scale business tied up in charcoal, black-and-white renditions of celebrities. His output included original works and art prints. He was not a purveyor of memorabilia or kitsch merchandise of the t-shirt, towel, apron, and coffee mug varieties. Yet, his skillfully rendered art or burgeoning reputation were not enough to get him over the transformative test, as interpreted by the California Supreme Court.

The *Comedy III* court held out Andy Warhol as a prime example of an artist whose uses of famous celebrity images were transformative:[64]

Warhol Celebrity Portraits

The example of Warhol suggests that there is a "genius standard" at work in this test — that artists gain the protection of a fair use if the artist's personal fame allows them to sell works for their own artistic value even though they borrow other celebrities' images, but lesser known artists, such as Gary Saderup, must produce something truly unique and creative in order to escape a right of publicity claim.

Transformative Mockery

Winter v. D.C. Comics[65]

Just when the transformative test might have appeared to be hopelessly limited by a genius and superstar standard in California, the California Supreme Court

---

62. *Comedy III*, 21 P.2d at 810-11.

63. *Id.* at 811.

64. Images: Michael D. Murray, Cropped, revised, and resized thumbnail excerpts of exhibits depicting Andy Warhol's Portraits of Jackie O, Marilyn Monroe, and Ingrid Bergman, as discussed in the case, *Comedy III Prods., Inc. v. Gary Saderup, Inc.*, 21 P.3d 797 (Cal. 2001).

65. *Winter v. DC Comics*, 69 P.3d 473 (Cal. 2003).

took another case with artistic expression and the claims of celebrities for violation of the right of publicity. The claim was brought by Johnny and Edgar Winter, who were country singers and brothers known for their very white blonde hair caused by their albinism.[66]

Autumn Brothers on the cover of Jonah Hex comic   *Johnny and Edgar, the Winter Brothers*

The D.C. Comic *Jonah Hex* spoofed the two singers by having them appear in the comic as large albino worms, with characteristically white hair, named "the Autumn brothers" in the comic. They were featured on at least one cover of the comic (shown above).

The Winter brothers sued. They lost. The California Supreme Court recognized that the purpose of the work was a parody, and in the course of spoofing the singing duo, the artists and author of the comics engaged in a significant alteration of their appearance.[67] There was a significant amount of recontextualization, too, with the change from twentieth century country performers to supernatural, gun-slinging, "Wild West" era worms. The parody purpose and altered appearance and context were enough to find that the work was transformative and a fair use.

Artistic Expression Alone

Simeonov v. Tiegs[68]

Simeonov v. Tiegs [excerpted above] has given us one of the most artist-friendly tests for fair use in a right of publicity context: the **artistic expression**

---

66. Images: Michael D. Murray, Composite of two cropped, revised, and resized thumbnail excerpts of exhibits depicting Jonah Hex comic book cover depicting Autumn Brothers, and an actual photograph depicting the two Winter Brothers, the subjects of the case, *Winter v. DC Comics*, 69 P.3d 473 (Cal. 2003).

67. *Winter*, 69 P.3d at 480.

68. *Simeonov*, 602 N.Y.S.2d at 1018.

test. The case takes us back to New York, and N.Y. Civil Rights Law §§ 50 and 51.

Tiegs

Simeonov bust

The New York Civil Court looked to the First Amendment and the right of free expression, including artistic expression, and sided with the artist, Simeonov. Far from declaring a genius standard, the New York Civil Court (a trial court with limited jurisdiction in New York County) declared that: "any artist can make a recognizable likeness of a celebrity and make a limited number of copies without violating New York's right of publicity statute."[69] Simeonov had made twenty copies of the sculpture, so presumably twenty is an appropriate limited number.

The *Simeonov* case was issued by the Civil Court of New York City, a limited jurisdiction trial level court in New York, thus it is not precedential (i.e., not controlling authority for other courts in New York), and it is of somewhat limited persuasive power for other jurisdictions to follow. But the case has been followed by several New York courts, including federal courts in New York applying New York law,[70] and thus may be interpreted as accurately stating the law in New York regarding the artistic expression defense to N.Y. Civil Rights Law § 51 right of privacy and publicity claims. Nevertheless, the simplicity of the test has not sold it to other states. It remains on the books, and is available to use to make one more argument if you are arguing for an artistic fair use.

---

69. *Id.*

70. The following cases all follow *Simeonov*: *Foster v. Svenson*, 7 N.Y.S. 3d 96, 101 (App. Div. 1st Dep't 2015); *Nussenzweig v. diCorcia*, 11 Misc. 3d 1051(A), (N.Y. Cty. 2006), *aff'd*, 38 A.D. 3d 339 (1st Dep't), *certified question answered, order aff'd*, 9 N.Y. 3d 184 (2007); *Lohan v. Perez*, 924 F. Supp. 2d 447 (E.D.N.Y. 2013) (Lindsay Lohan suing Pitbull); *Hoepker v. Kruger*, 200 F. Supp. 2d 340, 349 (S.D.N.Y. 2002).

Predominant Purpose Test

Doe v. TCI Cablevision,[71] and *C.B.C. Distrib. and Mktg., Inc. v. Major League Baseball Advanced Media*[72]

Missouri is responsible for making some law on the question of the right of publicity fair use analysis. The earlier case identified above is the cryptically named *Doe v. TCI Cablevision* in the Missouri Supreme Court. It actually is the suit of hockey player Tony Twist, then of the St. Louis Blues, against comic artist and entrepreneur Todd McFarlane, creator of the *Spawn* comic. McFarlane is a hockey fan, and St. Louis Blues fan, and decided to link his passions by creating a character in *Spawn* called Antonio Twistelli, who goes by nickname, "Tony Twist" (now you see the lawsuit issue). Another connection was that hockey's Tony Twist was known as a tough guy, an "enforcer" in hockey parlance, who goes out and levels "hits" on people who intentionally bump the star scorers of the team. So, too, was "Tony Twist" in *Spawn*: he was a gangster tough guy, also referred to as an "enforcer" in the comic. McFarlane went farther and included references to Tony Twist the hockey player in promotional activities for the comic, including a reference on a subscription solicitation page. This added to the commercialization allegations against McFarlane's use of Tony Twist's name and attributes of his persona.

Hockey's Tony Twist, in
St. Louis Blues uniform[73]

Spawn's Tony Twist, created by
Todd McFarlane[74]

---

71. *Doe v. TCI Cablevision*, 110 S.W. 3d 363 (Mo. 2003).

72. *C.B.C. Distribution & Mktg., Inc. v. Major League Baseball Advanced Media, L.P.*, 505 F.3d 818, 820 (8th Cir. 2007).

73. Image: Michael D. Murray, Cropped, revised, and resized thumbnail excerpts of exhibit depicting hockey player Tony Twist, at issue in *Doe v. TCI Cablevision*, 110 S.W. 3d 363 (Mo. 2003).

74. Image: Michael D. Murray, Cropped, revised, and resized thumbnail excerpts of exhibit depicting cover art of the *Spawn* Comic, featuring the character, Tony Twist, at issue in *Doe v. TCI Cablevision*, 110 S.W. 3d 363 (Mo. 2003).

Twist sued, under a John Doe name, and named one of McFarlane's businesses as the first-named defendant. (Perhaps he didn't want McFarlane the person to get publicity value from being sued by a famous—or infamous—hockey player?) The court had to determine if the creative artistic expression of the comic and the nominal convergence of the two Tony Twist names was permitted under the Missouri right of publicity law (which was a court-developed, common law right in Missouri), as balanced by the First Amendment right of free speech and artistic expression. The court had its choice of the fair use tests used in *Cardtoons*, *Rogers*, *Comedy III*, *Simeonov*, and a few other, lesser-known cases. It decided to invent one of its own: the predominant purpose test.[75]

The predominant purpose test looks at the nature of the expression, its content, its depth, and, to some extent, its value, and compares that to the nature of the use of the celebrity name, image, or likeness, and the commercialized advertising, merchandising, or other aspects of exploitation of the image or name, and makes a determination as to whether the use is *more expressive* or *more exploitative*.[76]

We cannot explain exactly how this test differs from the *Cardtoons'* balancing test, but the court in *Doe* considered *Cardtoons* and still determined to write its test this way. The test is cognizant of the First Amendment public policies at work in this area, but also cognizant of the fact that some uses (such as McFarlane's) may start out as heavy artistic expression, and thus fair, but are dragged into commercialization and greater and greater exploitation, making them seem decidedly unfair. Yes, it is a sliding scale, and yes, it has all the unpredictability of a balancing test, but for the Missouri Supreme Court, it supplies the right analysis of the competing policies of this issue.

Missouri had a follow-up case that wound up being litigated in the federal courts associated with Missouri, namely the Eastern District of Missouri trial level court, and the Eighth Circuit United States Court of Appeals. The case was *C.B.C. Distribution and Marketing, Inc. v. Major League Baseball Advanced Media, L.P.*[77] The CBC case is about fantasy baseball, but instead of a league run by a group of friends who gather around a ping pong table in someone's basement, CBC is a for-profit service that supplies a lot of value for your fantasy team experience. The Major League Baseball Advanced Media people took note of it, and complained that the CBC package included small thumbnail images, names, and especially vital and professional statistics of major league baseball players that are vital to planning, managing, drafting,

75. *Doe*, 110 S.W.3d at 374 (quoting Mark S. Lee, *Agents of Chaos: Judicial Confusion in Defining the Right of Publicity–Free Speech Interface*, 23 Loy. L.A. Ent. L. Rev. 471, 500 (2003)).

76. *Id.*

77. *C.B.C. Distribution & Mktg., Inc. v. Major League Baseball Advanced Media, L.P.*, 505 F.3d 818 (8th Cir. 2007).

and trading your players on your fantasy teams. The court of appeals looked to Missouri law and found the *Doe* case and its predominant purpose test. The court of appeals had the benefit of other cases on baseball and the right of publicity,[78] and found that the publication of baseball news and statistics generally has been protected as a public-interest kind of news and speech. Baseball is the national pastime, sayeth the courts, so the distribution of information about players and what they do is an important First Amendment protected activity. The details of identifying players by name and thumbnail image was regarded as incidental to the overall public interest in baseball activities. The for-profit nature of the enterprise did not doom it. The court balanced the factors on both sides, and found that the predominant purpose was expressive and communicative of important public interest information, and was not predominantly exploitative of the players and their personae.[79]

Picking and Choosing: Application of Fair Use Tests in Publicity Cases

Rogers' relatedness test and *Comedy III's* transformative test have grown to be the most popular tests affording protection to both publicity interests and First Amendment artistic expression concerns. *Cardtoons* continues to be cited and discussed, but it has not been followed in making the ultimate determination of whether a use is fair or not in many years.[80] *Simeonov* gets mentioned in cases that involve fine arts, but it rarely has been used out of New York State, and never as the sole test of fair use. *Doe* and *CBC* are used less often than the tests from *Rogers* and *Comedy III*, but they are cited from time to time.[81] The important take-away from this discussion is that courts, no matter where they are located, rarely pick one test and run with it. Instead, courts treat the tests as a buffet where they can have a little of one test, run a little analysis through a different test, and ultimately finish up with a run through of a third test.[82] The state of the law is as disjointed as it ever has been, and things are not likely to get much better in a "predictability of outcome" sense until one test becomes the norm in right of publicity situations.

---

78. *E.g., Gionfriddo*, 114 Cal. Rptr. 2d at 310.

79. *C.B.C.*, 505 F.3d at 824.

80. *ETW Corp.*, 332 F.3d at 915, worked through the analysis under the *Cardtoons'* test, but also applied the *Rogers'* relatedness test and *Comedy III's* transformative Test. *C.B.C.*, 505 F.3d at 822-24, also cited and discussed the *Cardtoons'* test, but ultimately applied the predominant purpose Test from *Doe*, 110 S.W.3d at 374.

81. *Hart*, 717 F.3d at 151, cited and discussed the predominant purpose test from *Doe*, 110 S.W.3d at 374, but ultimately settled on the transformative test.

82. *Hart*, 717 F.3d at 151-54.

Parks v. LaFace Records[83]

Rosa Parks, the civil rights pioneer, was not pleased when the hip hop band, *OutKast*, used her name as a song title.[84] The band, whose works are distributed by the first named defendant, LaFace Records, had written a song whose lyrics instructed upstart, newbie rappers and hip hop artists to "go to the back of the bus," which apparently, in *OutKast's* eyes, called for the application of Ms. Parks' name as being someone famously associated with a request to move to the back of a bus.

The court sympathized with Parks, not *OutKast*, but faced a dilemma of how to make the case come out in her favor. The court decided to apply two tests — *Cardtoons* and *Rogers*. Under *Cardtoons*,[85] the court found little value to the lyrics of the song, especially as they were (un)connected to Ms. Parks. The song was not about civil rights, or Birmingham, Alabama, or busing, or Ms. Parks at all. Thus, it had a hard time balancing out the exploitation potential of a prominent use of her famous name. The hip hop artists did not add new value to the work either by dint of artistic embellishments to the original (quantity of alteration being regarded as more important than quality). The court failed to note that the group brought to the table *OutKast's*, the band's, own fame and the market value of the band's name; surely, to their buying and listening public, *OutKast* is a worthy name, at least equal in importance to a civil rights figure from the 1950s. In either case, the end result was that the name's publicity value was not overwhelmed by the new context of appearing on a hip hop album as a song title.

The court last considered the *Rogers v. Grimaldi* test,[86] and the court thought that this test was the most apt for the circumstances. It considered: (1) artistic relevance of the use of the name "Rosa Parks" in the context of the work, and (2) whether it appeared that the use of the name might "explicitly mislead" viewers or listeners as to the source or the content of the work. This test, and the way the court framed the application of the two criteria, did not favor *OutKast*. As mentioned above, the song itself had nothing to do with Rosa Parks or the events and history that she represented. The song title and prominent placement on the covers of the single release of the song placed the *OutKast* release on shelves of record stores alongside other albums of civil rights era music that Parks actually endorsed, thus giving the band a lot of "stop and look at our album" value, as well as giving a competitive edge on

83. *Parks v. LaFace Records*, 329 F.3d 437 (6th Cir. 2003).
84. Image: Michael D. Murray, Cropped, revised, and resized thumbnail excerpt of exhibit depicting *OutKast's* "Rosa Parks" single release, the subject of *Parks v. LaFace Records*, 329 F.3d 437 (6th Cir. 2003).
85. *Id.* at 446, 448, 449, 459-60.
86. *Id.* at 448-59, 460-61.

albums that Parks herself endorsed. This worked out to be a case of disguised advertisement and exploitation, as opposed to be protected expression.[87]

ETW Corp. v. Jireh Pub.[88]

ETW v. Jireh, the Tiger Woods case[89] first discussed in section B above, and earlier in Chapter 3, was decided by the same court in the same week as *Parks*.

The court applied many of the same tests to determine fair use. This time, the court was pleased with the expression evident in Rick Rush's art work.[90] The court found that Rush had provided worthwhile commentary on the sports and historical interest value of the Tiger Woods Masters tournament victory, thus giving him strong weights to throw into the scale on *Cardtoons* balancing. Rush prevailed on the balancing test. The court found that his entire effort to depict and describe the historical events revolved around the name, image, and likeness of Tiger, so the relatedness test of *Rogers* was satisfied in Rush's favor. The court also applied the *Comedy III* transformative test, and found that Rush's artistic treatment, additions, and embellishments (the multiple images, the backdrop, the addition of Butler Cabin, the addition of ghostly images of past champions, the addition of the famous leader board) all combined to sufficiently transform the image of Tiger in a manner that allowed Rush to prevail on that test, too. The result: fair use victory for Rick Rush.[91]

Hoepker v. Kruger[92]

Artist Barbara Kruger got into a bit of a tussle when she used a work by German photographer, Thomas Hoepker, titled *Charlotte, as seen by Thomas*. The work was supposed to be in the public domain, but it had been restored to copyright status by changes in U.S. law to accommodate our international obligations.[93]

---

87. *Id.* at 460-61.

88. *ETW Corp. v. Jireh Pub., Inc.*, 332 F.3d 915 (6th Cir. 2003).

89. Image: Michael D. Murray, Cropped, revised and resized image derived from a photograph of Rick Rush's "Masters of Augusta," the subject of *ETW Corp. v. Jireh Publ'g, Inc.*, 332 F.3d 915 (6th Cir. 2003).

90. *ETW*, 332 F.3d at 922-23.

91. *Id.*

92. *Hoepker v. Kruger*, 200 F. Supp. 2d 340 (S.D.N.Y. 2002).

93. *See* 17 U.S.C. § 104A; *Hoepker*, 200 F. Supp. 2d at 345.

The publicity issue came not from Hoepker, but from Charlotte — as in Charlotte Dabney — the model who appears in the work. She objected to appearing in a Barbara Kruger work known as, *It's a Small World But Not if You Have to Clean It.*[94]

Kruger asserted a fair use defense to Dabney's right of publicity claims. As per usual in right of publicity cases, the court applied more than one test. *Simeonov* was a no-brainer under New York law — Kruger created an artistic rendition of a celebrity's image. That adds up to fair use.[95] *Cardtoons* balanced in Kruger's favor, her strong artistic expression over-balancing an incidental exploitation of a photograph of a model showing her appearance thirty years ago. The court also applied the *Comedy III* transformative test, and found that Kruger's creative additions transformed the original image of the celebrity, and also, on the subsidiary inquiry, that Kruger is well known for these artistic constructions of older photographs with new, ironic wording, so it would be very likely that people would collect the piece because it was a Kruger, not because someone named Charlotte Dabney was seen in it.[96] All of these tests added up to a fair use victory for Kruger.

Kirby v. Sega of America, Inc[97]

In *Kirby v. Sega of America, Inc.*, the California Court of Appeals evaluated the alleged use of a singer's image in a video game. Kierin Kirby, better known as Lady Miss Kier, the lead singer of the band *Deee-Lite*, brought a Lanham Act claim, right of publicity claim, misappropriation of likeness claim, and unfair competition claim against Sega for using her likeness. Kirby alleged that her look, which combines "retro and futuristic" styles, was unique. A character in Sega's video game *Space Channel 5* allegedly was based on her likeness.[98] The character, Ulala, had a name that apparently mimicked the lyrics of

Kirby (left) and Ulala (right)

---

94. Image: Michael D. Murray, Cropped, revised, and reduced-size excerpt of Barbara Kruger's *It's a Small World But Not if You Have to Clean It*, the painting at issue in the case, *Hoepker v. Kruger*, 200 F. Supp. 2d 340 (S.D.N.Y. 2002).

95. *Hoepker*, 200 F. Supp. 2d at 349, 351, 352.

96. *Hoepker*, 200 F. Supp. 2d at 349-51.

97. *Kirby v. Sega of Am., Inc.*, 50 Cal. Rptr. 3d 607 (Ct. App. 2006).

98. Images: Michael D. Murray, Cropped, revised, and resized thumbnail excerpts of exhibits depicting Kierin Kirby, better known as Lady Miss Kier, and the Sega video game character Ulala, the subjects of the case *Kirby v. Sega of Am., Inc.*, 50 Cal. Rptr. 3d 607 (Ct. App. 2006).

Groove is in the Heart, which generally is recognized as *Deee-Lite*'s most famous song, and that has an "Oo-la-la" lyric that is sung by Kirby.

Sega looked as if it were up to something, because the entertainment and toy company had approached Kirby in 2000 to see if she was interested in her hit single being used on their European version of the game, but Kirby refused. The court held that the video game use of the celebrity likeness was transformative and therefore merited First Amendment protection.[99] The case was remanded to determine attorney's fees for Sega, as California law requires the prevailing party in such a claim receive fees and costs.

Romantics v. Activision Pub., Inc.[100]

Activision's *Guitar Hero* and *Band Hero* franchises attracted another lawsuit in 2008, which had a similar outcome as *Kirby*. In *Romantics v. Activision*, the music group *The Romantics* complained under the Michigan right of publicity law regarding the use of the band's name, which popped up at the bottom of the screen in association with the use of one of the band's songs, "That's What I Like About You," in the popular rock-and-roll simulation game *Guitar Hero*. The game's creator, Activision, licensed the use of the song but did not license any of the band's or band members' publicity rights. But Activision did *not* display in the game the images, likenesses, or voices of the band members. Only the band's name showed up when the song was selected.

The band claimed Activision was exploiting their image and popularity because the group was so intimately associated with this song. The band alleged, in effect, that this was their "trademark" and signature song, and thus they claimed exploitation when their name was displayed in the game in the phrase, "as made famous by The Romantics," that was displayed when the song was selected. The court found there was no right of publicity claim surviving beyond the copyrights to the lyrics and music which had been licensed to Activision. Further, even if a right of publicity claim survived, the court found that the First Amendment would allow the use of the name *The Romantics* to be associated with Activision' use of the song because the use in a video game was creative, expressive, and artistic, and the display of the band's name related directly to the content of the work.[101]

E. The Future of the Right of Publicity

In the future, the following scenario may occur more and more frequently in right of publicity disputes: how will the right of publicity control the situation

---

99. *Kirby*, 50 Cal. Rptr. 3d at 613-18.
100. *Romantics v. Activision Pub., Inc.*, 574 F. Supp. 2d 758 (E.D. Mich. 2008).
101. *Id.* at 763-66.

if you create new performances with the persona of a deceased artist? Modern digitalization and 3D animation techniques allow artists and technicians to create new performances using the image of deceased artists. (They could do it with living artists, too, but living people tend to complain louder). With the development of advanced artificial intelligence, these images may become spontaneous and interactive, moving far beyond any gimmickry that places cherished stars in advertisements for products whose producers would like to associate with the beloved former stars.

Tupac Shakur, who was killed in 1996, was "revived" in a virtual sort of way for a performance at Coachella in 2012.[102] The discussion began (or at least was "revived") about creations of new performances of deceased artists. Assuming you have the right footage or actual 3D digitalized files on hand, could you create new virtual performances without the consent of the heirs of the performers? Is the new work transformative under *Comedy III*? What if you own the copyrights to recordings of the earlier performances?

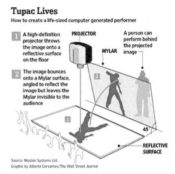

The technology for this kind of recreated performance exists. The actual performance of Tupac at Coachella used a modernized version of technology from the nineteenth century called Pepper's Ghost, which used reflective on-stage screens, and below the stage, mirrors on which images were projected to produce the appearance of a "live on-stage" performance.[103]

Does this recreated performance potentially violate the right of publicity of the deceased artist?

First, know that some states do not protect a right of publicity after death.[104] If the estate of the artist is located in one of those states, the question is moot. Rights for the deceased vary among the states that do recognize them:

> "Tennessee recognizes the right for 10 years after death (but the right can continue in perpetuity contingent on use), Virginia for 20 years. Florida for

---

102. Image: Michael D. Murray, Cropped, revised, and resized thumbnail excerpt of exhibit (2015) depicting a single frame taken from the video recording by westfesttv, "Tupac Hologram Snoop Dogg and Dr. Dre Perform Coachella Live 2012," https://www.youtube.com/watch?v=TGbrFmPBV0Y (Apr. 17, 2012).

103. Image: Michael D. Murray, Cropped, revised, and resized thumbnail excerpt of exhibit (2015) depicting the modern version of the old "Pepper's Ghost" illusion used at the Coachella 2012 concert to allow the virtual performance of the deceased Tupac Shakur; Original Source: Musion Systems Ltd; Original Graphic by Alberto Cervantes for the Wall Street Journal (2012).

104. Famously, New York does not. N.Y. Civ. Rts. Law § § 50, 51 only apply to living persons.

40 years, Kentucky, Nevada, and Texas for 50 years, California for 70 years, and Washington for 75 years. Indiana provides recognition for the Right of Publicity for 100 years after the death of the personality, and endeavors to reach backward for the full extent of those 100 years. Oklahoma, while providing a similar 100 year term of recognition as Indiana, limits the reach-back provision to 50 years."[105]

Second, there is the issue of whether the right of publicity is implicated by a recreated performance of a deceased celebrity. This seems to have an easy answer, too: yes, the posthumous right of publicity, if it exists in the state of the deceased's estate, is implicated by this blatant use of the artist's performance style and persona. The technology recreates almost 100 percent of the desirable qualities of the experience of the artist's performance, much more than the mere sound of the singing voice in *Midler*,[106] the sound of the speaking voice in *Facenda*,[107] and the single tag-line in *Carson*.[108] Note that the technology allows the creation of new performances; it is not just a new and fun way to reshow recorded performances. Therefore, seeking the consent of the heirs or others who control the estate of the deceased artist is a very good idea. (This occurred with Tupac — his mother, the administrator of his estate, approved of the Coachella virtual performance.)

What if you don't seek consent and approval?

As a fair use, the creation of new, virtual performances that replicate almost 100% of the creative, valuable, desirable attributes of the artist's persona when living is a technological achievement, but it is difficult to make a prediction as to whether it would be evaluated as transformative. On the one hand, the whole idea is to reproduce as much of the creative, valuable, desirable attributes of the artist's performances when living as you can. Success means that the viewer is fooled into believing that the artist himself, in full persona, is really there, performing, just the way he used to, in front of their very eyes. That is near exact duplication, not transformation. It is not a new rapper compiled by manipulation of samples of several other rappers in a new composite. No, it is the one and only Tupac Shakur — or as close to the real Tupac as the technicians can get.

On the other hand, digital reanimation is nothing like any other depiction or reproduction of the image or likeness of a celebrity that we have ever seen before. Digital reanimation creates an entirely new context with a completely new expression of the celebrity. Under a copyright law transformative test

105. *See* Jonathan Faber, *Brief History of the Right of Publicity*, http://rightofpublicity.com/brief-history-of-rop. Adapted from Res Gestae, March 2000, Vol. 43, No. 9, and last updated July 31, 2015.
106. *Midler v. Ford Motor Co.*, 849 F.2d 460 (9th Cir. 1988).
107. *Facenda v. N.F.L. Films, Inc.*, 543 F.3d 1007 (3d Cir. 2008).
108. *Carson v. Here's Johnny Portable Toilets*, 698 F.2d 831 (6th Cir. 1983).

analysis, the recontextualization and addition of completely new content, meaning, and expression, which potentially could be employed for a completely new function and purpose, all would add up to a finding that the new works were transformative and a fair use. But right of publicity is different from copyright, and the new work still shows the celebrity for all of what the celebrity was famous for.

All of the rest of the potential commercial exploitation of the celebrity's name, image, and persona exists, too — the concert promotions, the new recordings, the new music videos, the potential tie-in to other product promotions — all of which would affect the relatedness-balancing-predominant purpose tests of *Rogers*, *Cardtoons*, and *Doe* in a non-fair use direction. Potentially, all of our deceased film stars and other performers could virtually appear in new films. Remember that the technology does not just recontextualize old Tupac footage into a 2012 concert with Snoop Dogg and others. It is a new experience of Tupac's persona.

Would it matter if the person doing the creation of new, virtual performances owned the copyrights to the records of the performer's appearances and performances that were used to create the new, virtual performances?

This is a hard question. Yes, it would certainly be a good idea to own or have a license to use these recorded appearances, sounds, and performances that are used as the source material to make the new digitalized, animated appearances and performances. If you didn't, then you would probably violate the copyrights of the old recordings by creating unauthorized derivative works.

But is copyright alone enough to answer the right of publicity questions?

We think not. The meaning and power of the new technology is in the creation of new, virtual appearances and performances that go far beyond the existing recordings. The idea is to give the audience the experience that that performer really is live before them, doing something new. Strutting, dancing, singing, sweating — giving them a live exposure to his persona, albeit by virtual means. That seems to go beyond the rights that copyright protects in *fixed*, tangible, existing works. *Facenda* sued and prevailed when the NFL wanted to make new voiceover "performances" using the sound of his voice as collected and recorded in existing copyrighted recordings of NFL Films. This was only one aspect of the John Facenda experience. With Tupac, the audience was treated to a much broader experience — a virtual performance of the man himself — that is not tied to one or even a dozen recorded and copyrighted performances. The whole persona of a performer is not easily captured in copyrightable recordings, and for that reason, we do not believe the law would allow copyright to preempt the assertion of separate rights of publicity of the estate of deceased artists and performers.

ASSESSMENT

1. Which of the following speech activities will most likely violate the publicity rights of the author, artist, or celebrity involved in the problem?

   (A) An unauthorized and unlicensed book review in a magazine that comments on the published autobiography by the international socialite and reality TV star Paris Hilton

   (B) A political "Get Out the Vote, Democrats!" flyer with an unauthorized and unlicensed cartoon portraying former California Governor Arnold Schwarzenegger as a gun-wielding maniac robot

   (C) A subscription page advertisement for a paid-subscription-based newsletter, *Financial Tips*, that uses an unauthorized and unlicensed photo of investment superstar Warren Buffet, and states in large print: "Just like Warren — we are right 95% of the time"

   (D) A subscription page advertisement for a recording industry magazine that reproduces an image of the cover of the same magazine that features an unauthorized and unlicensed photograph of the famous singer, Taylor Swift

2. Which of the following uses of an image or likeness most likely will *not* be considered a fair use of the image or likeness under right of publicity law?

   (A) A scandalous unauthorized and unlicensed image of two married celebrities swimming together at a beach in France (and not with their respective spouses) featured in a supermarket tabloid newspaper without the celebrities' permission

   (B) An unauthorized and unlicensed image of a pro-golfer playing in the Masters tournament featured on the cover of a golf magazine without the pro-golfer's permission

   (C) An unauthorized and unlicensed image of a pro-golfer playing in the Masters tournament featured in an ad for Big Drive golf balls without the pro-golfer's permission

   (D) All of the above are likely to be fair uses of the image or likeness

3. If Barbara Kruger's work *It's a Small World But Not if You Have to Clean It* was to satisfy the *Comedy III v. Gary Saderup* test from California, it would do so because:

   (A) Kruger's work added valuable new content meaning and expression to the existing image of the claimant

   (B) The use of the image of the claimant was directly related to the content of Kruger's message

   (C) The dominant theme of Kruger's work was artistic, not commercial

(D) On balance, Kruger's artistic, expressive message outweighed any impact on the ability of the claimant to exploit her image and persona

4. If Barbara Kruger's work *It's a Small World But Not if You Have to Clean It* was to satisfy the *Parks v. LaFace Records* test from the U.S. Court of Appeals for the 6th Circuit and the *Rogers v. Grimaldi* test from the 2nd Circuit, it would do so because:

(A) Kruger's work added valuable new content, meaning, and expression to the existing image of the claimant

(B) The use of the image of the claimant was directly related to the content of Kruger's message

(C) The dominant theme of Kruger's work was artistic, not commercial

(D) On balance, the artistic, expressive message outweighed any impact on the ability of the claimant to exploit her image and persona

5. *Zacchini*, the U.S. Supreme Court's only foray into right of publicity law, is a troublesome precedent because:

I. The facts of the case are atypical and unique, because a news broadcast was able to capture and air the entire life's work of a performer in a 15 second segment

II. The Court applied several public policy theories for the right of publicity — unjust enrichment, intellectual property, etc. — without reconciling these theories

III. The Court held that news reporting would never be a fair use in right of publicity law

IV. The Court recognized that the claim had evolved from a privacy tort claim to a property publicity claim

(A) I, II, III, and IV

(B) I, II, and IV only

(C) I, III, and IV only

(D) I and II only

ASSESSMENT ANSWERS

1. Which of the following speech activities will most likely violate the publicity rights of the author, artist, or celebrity involved in the problem:

(A) An unauthorized and unlicensed book review in a magazine that comments on the published autobiography by the international socialite and reality TV star Paris Hilton

(B) A political "Get Out the Vote, Democrats!" flyer with an unauthorized and unlicensed cartoon portraying former California Governor Arnold Schwarzenegger as a gun-wielding maniac robot

(C) A subscription page advertisement for a paid-subscription-based newsletter, *Financial Tips,* that uses an unauthorized and unlicensed photo of investment superstar, Warren Buffet, and states in large print: "Just like Warren — we are right 95% of the time"

(D) A subscription page advertisement for a recording industry magazine that reproduces an image of the cover of the same magazine that features an unauthorized and unlicensed photograph of the famous singer, Taylor Swift

ANSWER: The correct answer is Choice (C). A subscription page advertisement for a paid-subscription-based newsletter, *Financial Tips,* that uses an unauthorized and unlicensed photo of investment superstar, Warren Buffet, and states in large print: "Just like Warren — we are right 95% of the time." Choice (C) fully exploits the name and image of Warren Buffet for commercial gain. It is not making some form of commentary or criticism about Buffet; it only is using the name to attract attention and to gain some reflected glory from Buffet's reputation as a stock-picker. Choice (A) is not likely to violate Paris Hilton's publicity rights because an unauthorized biography itself generally is framed by the author as a form of commentary on the entire life to date of a celebrity, and most often functions as a form of commentary and criticism, both of which are fair uses in publicity law. Choice (A) further framed the publication at issue as a commentary and criticism of the biography itself, so it would be triply protected. The political context of Choice (B) most likely will insulate the speech involved; it also would most likely be viewed as commentary and criticism. Choice (D) reflects a recognized fair use in publicity law — that a public interest publication can reproduce covers and contents of its own publication when those covers and contents reflect the good and valuable speech that the publication has engaged in in the past.

2. Which of the following uses of an image or likeness most likely will <u>not</u> be considered a fair use of the image or likeness under right of publicity law?

(A) A scandalous unauthorized and unlicensed image of two married celebrities swimming together at a beach in France (and not with their respective spouses) featured in a supermarket tabloid newspaper without the celebrities' permission

(B) An unauthorized and unlicensed image of a pro-golfer playing in the Masters tournament featured on the cover of a golf magazine without the pro-golfer's permission

(C) An unauthorized and unlicensed image of a pro-golfer playing in the Masters tournament featured in an ad for Big Drive golf balls without the pro-golfer's permission

(D) All of the above are likely to be fair uses of the image or likeness

ANSWER: The correct answer is (C). Similar to question 1, this answer aims to find the activity that would not be a fair use of publicity rights. Choice (C) is a pure "false endorsement"-type right of publicity claim where a celebrity's image is used to attract attention to a product in hopes of forming some positive connection in the buyer's mind with the celebrity. There is no commentary or criticism of the celebrity suggested by the scenario. Choices (A) and (B), on the other hand, represented the typical coverage of and commentary on newsworthy people who have public affairs and public interest value. This form of attention is accepted and does not violate the celebrity's publicity rights.

3. If Barbara Kruger's work, *It's a Small World But Not if You Have to Clean It*, was to satisfy the *Comedy III v. Gary Saderup* test from California, it would do so because:

(A) Kruger's work added valuable new content meaning and expression to the existing image of the claimant

(B) The use of the image of the claimant was directly related to the content of Kruger's message

(C) The dominant theme of Kruger's work was artistic, not commercial

(D) On balance, Kruger's artistic, expressive message outweighed any impact on the ability of the claimant to exploit her image and persona

ANSWER: The correct answer is (A). *Comedy III* is all about the value of the artist or her contributions to the art in a transformative sense, compared to the value of the celebrity image that remains visible in the work. Choice (B) is the *Rogers* relatedness test, Choice (C) is the *Doe* and *CBC* predominant purpose test, and Choice (D) is the *Cardtoons* balancing test.

4. If Barbara Kruger's work, *It's a Small World But Not if You Have to Clean It*, was to satisfy the *Parks v. LaFace Records* test from the U.S. Court of Appeals for the 6th Circuit and the *Rogers v. Grimaldi* test from the 2nd Circuit, it would do so because:

(A) Kruger's work added valuable new content meaning and expression to the existing image of the claimant

(B) The use of the image of the claimant was directly related to the content of Kruger's message

(C) The dominant theme of Kruger's work was artistic, not commercial

(D) On balance, the artistic, expressive message outweighed any impact on the ability of the claimant to exploit her image and persona

ANSWER: The correct answer is (B). *Parks* and *Rogers'* test examines the relationship of the celebrity image to the overall expressive content of the work; if there is a direct relationship, then the use will be permitted, but if there is not, the use of the image will be suspect as a form of deceptive advertising or false endorsement. Choice (A) is the *Comedy III* transformative test, Choice (C) is the *Doe* and *CBC* predominant purpose test, and Choice (D) is the *Cardtoons* balancing test.

5. *Zacchini*, the U.S. Supreme Court's only foray into right of publicity law, is a troublesome precedent because
    I.   The facts of the case are atypical and unique, because a news broadcast was able to capture and air the entire life's work of a performer in a 15 second segment
    II. The Court applied several public policy theories for the right of publicity–unjust enrichment, intellectual property, etc.–without reconciling these theories
    III. The Court held that news reporting would never be a fair use in right of publicity law
    IV. The Court recognized that the claim had evolved from a privacy tort claim to a property publicity claim

    (A) I, II, III, and IV
    (B) I, II, and IV only
    (C) I, III, and IV only
    (D) I and II only

ANSWER: The correct answer is (B). Item I is correct because *Zacchini* had fairly unique facts and subject matter: a celebrity whose entire valuable persona and money-earning potential is tied up in 15 second performances, and a freelance news reporter who captured the whole value in one recording of a 15 second performance that was shown for free on a late news broadcast. Item II is correct — the *Zacchini* court did introduce a whole menu of public policy points to support the protection of publicity rights without making distinctions or attempting to reconcile the differing values or policies. Item IV is true because the Court did note that the old tort of privacy in the first half of the twentieth century had given way to the modern cause of action of publicity rights in the second half of the twentieth century. Item III is not correct. The Court did not rule out news reporting as a fair use; it merely found that the particular and unusual facts of the case did not support a news reporting fair use in those circumstances.

6 FIRST AMENDMENT RIGHTS

An artist is a citizen with free expression rights guaranteed by the First Amendment of the United States Constitution. There is no debate that artistic expression is a powerful medium in society. The artistic expression of artists may be moving, enthralling, provocative, or controversial all at once.

The First Amendment of the United States Constitution ensures individuals the right of freedom of speech and freedom of the press. The Amendment appears to be broad and all-encompassing — "Congress shall make no law . . . abridging the freedom of speech" — yet it was held early on that the language did not protect all forms of expression. Perhaps the framers believed that the realm of free speech should be flexible enough to evolve as society changed and, therefore, left the task of defining the boundary between protected and unprotected expression to the Supreme Court in its role as ultimate interpreter of the Constitution.

While the atmosphere in which an artist creates should ideally be free of external constraints, numerous limitations are imposed on free expression. Artists are restrained by the rather vague concepts of obscenity and pornography that the Supreme Court has devised in its attempts to interpret the First Amendment. Even where First Amendment doctrine and interpretation have made it difficult for government to regulate the content of speech, government and private entities engage in various forms of indirect censorship which often are just as effective in squelching the speech as a direct ban on the content of the speech.

The human form has repeatedly been portrayed in art, from early cave paintings to Michelangelo's "David" to Andrew Wyeth's nudes. Although praised by critics and treasured by historians, such expressions may offend some individuals' concepts of contemporary morality. In this chapter, we consider the extent to which an artist's free expression may be restrained.

Fig-leafing to censor art in Florence, Italy

A. Censorship of Symbolic Expression

This chapters begins with censorship of symbolic expression because that is the form of expression that artists predominantly use to communicate. Symbols communicate ideas as effectively as text or oral communication. In fact, some symbols, such as the United States flag, are so powerful that people would be willing to cut a swath out of the First Amendment or amend the Constitution itself to protect the dignity and sanctity of them. As the Supreme Court has noted, symbols are both primitive and effective.[2] They exist as a shortcut from mind to mind.[3]

> **Artistic Expression and Symbolic Speech**
>
> Artistic expression communicates through symbolic speech, and therefore falls directly within a difficult area of First Amendment jurisprudence. Symbolic expression is sometimes regarded as possessing all the qualities and character-istics of pure speech, and is protected at that high level of strict scrutiny. But on other occasions, when art is regarded as being a form of expressive conduct, like

---

1. Image: Michael D. Murray, Cropped, revised, resized photograph by Michael D. Murray of the Satyr "Anapauomenos" Sculpture, Palazzo Medici Riccardi, Florence (2009).

2. *West Virginia Bd. of Ed. v. Barnette*, 319 U.S. 624, 632 (1943).

3. *Id.*

other forms of conduct, it is regulated with lower level intermediate scrutiny. If the regulation of artistic activity can be achieved through a content-neutral time, place, or manner regulation, then it will be easier for government to control the activity and the art associated with the activity.

Painters, sculptors, illustrators, and other practitioners of the visual arts know this well. A work of art can be stunning, awe inspiring, arresting, rendering the viewer speechless, and it can evoke hatred, fear, and disgust, provoking anger and violence, all without uttering a single word. The power of symbolism is the power wielded by artists which can communicate with the illiterate, the uneducated, and the uninformed viewer, as well as with the literate, the educated, and the well informed viewer.

Nevertheless, the constitutional protection available for symbolic speech and visual art is less than that afforded to written or oral communication. The perceptible distinction between symbolic speech and visual art on the one hand and so called "pure speech" on the other has been used to justify limited protection for the former. As mentioned above, public debate with a particularized political message is held to be the highest form of speech under the First Amendment. Although symbolic speech and conduct and visual art are designed to communicate ideas and would, thus, appear to be entitled to similar constitutional treatment, they often lack a particularized message, and sometimes the judiciary misses the point; often, in more than one way. For example, in the cases excerpted below, the display of a red flag in *Stromberg*, the act of refraining from saluting the flag in *Barnette*, the wearing of a black armband to protest the Vietnam War in *Tinker*, and the burning of a flag in *Eichman* all were held to be the functional equivalent of "pure speech," and thus protected at the highest level of scrutiny, while burning a draft card in protest of the Vietnam War and the selective service in *O'Brien* (excerpted in Topic 3, Part 1, below), was held to be expressive conduct, not pure speech, and protected only under what has come to be called "intermediate level scrutiny."[4]

The cases excerpted in this section discuss the origin of the First Amendment doctrine on symbolic speech. The differing standards for school children in school settings will be examined. Finally, this section will examine the particular power of the flag as a protest vehicle and the cases that, so far, have left the flag open to manipulation, destruction, and desecration in the pursuance of a message of protest against the United States.

Stromberg v. California

283 U.S. 359 (1931)

Stromberg is an interesting case because of the times (1931 — over a decade after the First World War, and a decade before the U.S.A. would become involved in the Second World War), and the fact that the case involved the

---

4. E.g., *Rumsfeld v. Forum for Academic and Institutional Rights, Inc.*, 547 U.S. 47, 67 (2006).

actions of a true, card-carrying member of the Communist Party, who lived and operated a day camp for children in California. Stromberg's day camp tried to indoctrinate children in the theories and policies of communism, socialism, and the international labor movement.

One daily activity of the camp brought it under the scrutiny of the government: the camp leaders and the students raised a red flag—meaning a communist red flag—every morning as they sang the *Internationale* anthem. This action violated the "no display of a red flag" part of California law, which was a companion to California's criminal syndicalism statute that had been considered and approved of in *Whitney v. California*, 274 U.S. 357 (1927).

The Supreme Court took on this important matter of the flag display. The topic, of course, was more meaningful than just whether people who raised a red flag could be prosecuted. The case weighed the government's ability to regulate the symbolic expression inherent in the choice to display a red flag for a particular purpose. Here, the symbolic expression related to the camp director's desire to express her allegiance to the communist international labor movement. Another person might decide to raise a red flag to celebrate the achievements of the St. Louis Cardinals or the Nebraska football team.

The Court struck down the "no display of a red flag" on a facial challenge. The law was found to be overbroad, because it swept so many innocent flag-displaying activities within its coverage. The Court found that the simple display of a red flag presented no clear and present danger of imminent unlawful action; really, it presented no danger of harm at all. The court was not endorsing the view that actual acts of insurrection should go unpunished. Rather, it endorsed the practice of peaceful and orderly opposition to government. The Court recounted that the First Amendment was designed to allow fair and free political discussion and criticism of government, so that the government can be responsive to the will of the people, and that changes may be made by lawful means. The opinion was a bit vague, however, about how "fair" the opportunity for such criticism must be.

West Virginia State Board of Education v. Barnette

319 U.S. 624 (1943)

Barnette takes symbolic speech to new heights with its eloquent defense of the meaning and value of symbolic communication. The case is one of the friendliest authorities that artistic expression could ever hope for.

Barnette has the same back story as *Chaplinsky v. New Hampshire*, 315 U.S. 568 (1942) (establishing the fighting words doctrine): following the decision by the U.S. Supreme Court on June 3, 1940, in *Minersville School District v. Gobitis*,[5] the West Virginia legislature amended its statutes to require all schools therein to conduct courses of instruction in history, civics, and in the Constitutions of the United States and of the State "for the purpose of

---

5. 310 U.S. 586.

teaching, fostering and perpetuating the ideals, principles and spirit of Americanism, and increasing the knowledge of the organization and machinery of the government." The appellant Board of Education in *Barnette* was directed, with advice of the State Superintendent of Schools, to "prescribe the courses of study covering these subjects" for public schools. The Act made it the duty of private, parochial and denominational schools to prescribe courses of study "similar to those required for the public schools."

The Board of Education on January 9, 1942, adopted a resolution containing recitals taken largely from the Court's *Gobitis* opinion and ordering that the salute to the flag become "a regular part of the program of activities in the public schools," that all teachers and pupils "shall be required to participate in the salute honoring the Nation represented by the Flag; provided, however, that refusal to salute the Flag be regarded as an Act of insubordination, and shall be dealt with accordingly."

The resolution originally required the "commonly accepted salute to the Flag" which it defined. Objections to the salute as "being too much like Hitler's" were raised by the Parent and Teachers Association, the Boy and Girl Scouts, the Red Cross, and the Federation of Women's Clubs. (Footnote 3 of the opinion states: "The National Headquarters of the United States Flag Association takes the position that the extension of the right arm in this salute to the flag is not the Nazi-Fascist salute, 'although quite similar to it. In the Pledge to the Flag the right arm is extended and raised, palm Upward, whereas the Nazis extend the arm practically straight to the front (the finger tips being about even with the eyes), palm Downward, and the Fascists do the same except they raise the arm slightly higher.' James A. Moss, *The Flag of the United States: Its History and Symbolism* (1914) 108.")

Barnette and the other appellees brought suit for themselves and others similarly situated asking the court to enjoin the enforcement of the West Virginia flag salute laws and regulations against Jehovah's Witnesses. The Witnesses are an unincorporated body teaching that the obligation imposed by law of God is superior to that of laws enacted by temporal government. Their religious beliefs include a literal version of Exodus, Chapter 20, verses 4 and 5, which says: "Thou shalt not make unto thee any graven image, or any likeness of anything that is in heaven above, or that is in the earth beneath, or that is in the water under the earth; thou shalt not bow down thyself to them nor serve them." They consider that the flag is an "image" within this command. For this reason they refuse to salute it.

The Court's opinion is telling on the topic of symbolic communication:

> There is no doubt that, in connection with the pledges, the flag salute is a form of utterance. Symbolism is a primitive but effective way of communicating ideas. The use of an emblem or flag to symbolize some system, idea,

institution, or personality, is a short cut from mind to mind. Causes and nations, political parties, lodges, and ecclesiastical groups seek to knit the loyalty of their followings to a flag or banner, a color or design. The State announces rank, function, and authority through crowns and maces, uniforms and black robes; the church speaks through the Cross, the Crucifix, the altar and shrine, and clerical raiment. Symbols of State often convey political ideas just as religious symbols come to convey theological ones. Associated with many of these symbols are appropriate gestures of acceptance or respect: a salute, a bowed or bared head, a bended knee. A person gets from a symbol the meaning he puts into it, and what is one man's comfort and inspiration is another's jest and scorn.

. . .

It is also to be noted that the compulsory flag salute and pledge requires affirmation of a belief and an attitude of mind. It is not clear whether the regulation contemplates that pupils forego any contrary convictions of their own and become unwilling converts to the prescribed ceremony or whether it will be acceptable if they simulate assent by words without belief and by a gesture barren of meaning. It is now a commonplace that censorship or suppression of expression of opinion is tolerated by our Constitution only when the expression presents a clear and present danger of action of a kind the State is empowered to prevent and punish. It would seem that involuntary affirmation could be commanded only on even more immediate and urgent grounds than silence. But here the power of compulsion is invoked without any allegation that remaining passive during a flag salute ritual creates a clear and present danger that would justify an effort even to muffle expression. To sustain the compulsory flag salute we are required to say that a Bill of Rights which guards the individual's right to speak his own mind, left it open to public authorities to compel him to utter what is not in his mind.

. . .

The very purpose of a Bill of Rights was to withdraw certain subjects from the vicissitudes of political controversy, to place them beyond the reach of majorities and officials and to establish them as legal principles to be applied by the courts. One's right to life, liberty, and property, to free speech, a free press, freedom of worship and assembly, and other fundamental rights may not be submitted to vote; they depend on the outcome of no elections.

. . .

It seems trite but necessary to say that the First Amendment to our Constitution was designed to avoid these ends by avoiding these beginnings. There is no mysticism in the American concept of the State or of the nature or origin of its authority. We set up government by consent of the governed, and the Bill of Rights denies those in power any legal opportunity to coerce that consent. Authority here is to be controlled by public opinion, not public opinion by authority.

. . .

If there is any fixed star in our constitutional constellation, it is that no official, high or petty, can prescribe what shall be orthodox in politics, nationalism, religion, or other matters of opinion or force citizens to confess by word or act their faith therein. If there are any circumstances which permit an exception, they do not now occur to us.

We think the action of the local authorities in compelling the flag salute and pledge transcends constitutional limitations on their power and invades the sphere of intellect and spirit which it is the purpose of the First Amendment to our Constitution to reserve from all official control.

The decision of this Court in *Minersville School District v. Gobitis* and the holdings of those few per curiam decisions which preceded and foreshadowed it are overruled, and the judgment enjoining enforcement of the West Virginia Regulation is affirmed.

Barnette's majority opinion was written by Justice Robert Jackson, whose eloquence in expressing American ideals was soon employed in the Nuremburg Trials against Nazi war criminals.

The law on symbolic speech can be fast-forwarded a bit to the Vietnam War era, when peaceful symbolic protests became a more common feature of the nation's expressions for and against the war.

Tinker v. Des Moines Independent Community School Dist.

393 U.S. 503 (1969)

The *Tinker* case involved a peaceful, silent, and symbolic protest of the Vietnam War. On December 16 and 17, 1965, Mary Beth Tinker, her brother,

and three other students wore black armbands to their schools. (Mary Beth Tinker and her armband are depicted at left)[6] The students were all sent home and suspended from school until they would come back without their armbands. They did not return to school until after the planned period for wearing armbands had expired — that is, until after New Year's Day.

The Court recognized that the wearing of an armband for the purpose of expressing certain views is the type of symbolic act that is within the Free Speech Clause of the First Amendment. The wearing of armbands in the circumstances of the case was held to be entirely divorced from any actually or potentially disruptive conduct by those participating in the silent protest. It was closely akin to 'pure speech' which the Court had previously held on several occasions was entitled to comprehensive protection under the First Amendment.[7]

In a well-known portion of the case, the Court affirmed that schoolchildren maintain their First Amendment rights while attending classes — the

---

6. Images: Michael D. Murray, Composite of two cropped, revised, and resized thumbnail excerpts of photographs depicting Mary Beth Tinker, the named litigant in the case, *Tinker v. Des Moines Independent Community School Dist.*, 393 U.S. 503 (1969).

7. *Cox v. Louisiana*, 379 U.S. 536, 555 (1965); *Adderley v. Florida*, 385 U.S. 39 (1966).

exact quote being that neither "students or teachers shed their constitutional rights to freedom of speech or expression at the schoolhouse gate."[8]

The Court concluded that the action of the school authorities was not reasonable because it was based upon their undifferentiated fear or apprehension of disturbance, which was held not to be enough to overcome the right to freedom of expression. Instead of undifferentiated fear of disruption, in order for school officials to justify prohibition of a particular expression of opinion, it must be able to show that its action was caused by something more than a mere desire to avoid the discomfort and unpleasantness that always accompany an unpopular viewpoint. Where there is no finding and no showing that engaging in the forbidden conduct would "materially and substantially interfere with the requirements of appropriate discipline in the operation of the school," the prohibition cannot be sustained.

Flag Burning as Symbolic Communication

Texas v. Johnson, 491 U.S. 397 (1989), and
United States v. Eichman, 496 U.S. 310 (1990)

The Supreme Court's two flag-burning cases neatly set out the law on conduct that is both saturated with meaningful symbolic expression, and capable of invoking intense emotions. In *Johnson*, the Court held that a Texas statute criminalizing the desecration of venerated objects, including the United States flag, was unconstitutional as applied to an individual who had set such a flag on fire during a political demonstration. The Texas statute provided that "[a] person commits an offense if he intentionally or knowingly desecrates . . . [a] national flag," where "desecrate" meant to "deface, damage, or otherwise physically mistreat in a way that the actor knows will seriously offend one or more persons likely to observe or discover his action."[9] The Court found that Johnson's flag-burning was "conduct 'sufficiently imbued with elements of communication' to implicate the First Amendment" and that the State's concern with protecting the flag's symbolic meaning is implicated "only when a person's treatment of the flag communicates some message." Thus, the Court subjected the statute to "'the most exacting scrutiny,'" and concluded that the State's asserted interests could not justify the infringement on the demonstrator's First Amendment rights.

After the decision in *Johnson*, Congress passed the Flag Protection Act of 1989. The Act provides in relevant part:

> (a)(1) Whoever knowingly mutilates, defaces, physically defiles, burns, maintains on the floor or ground, or tramples upon any flag of the United States shall be fined under this title or imprisoned for not more than one year, or both. (2) This subsection does not prohibit any conduct consisting of the disposal of a flag when it has become worn or soiled.

---

8. *Tinker*, 393 U.S. at 506.
9. Tex. Penal Code Ann. § 42.09 (1989).

> (b) As used in this section, the term 'flag of the United States' means any flag of the United States, or any part thereof, made of any substance, of any size, in a form that is commonly displayed.[10]

Johnson showed up to protest the new law with Eichman and other protestors, and they all determined to burn more flags in a challenge of the law; Eichman got his flag lit, but for some reason Johnson was unable to ignite his flag on the day of their demonstration. Therefore, Eichman became the named respondent in the second flag-burning case.

In the second go-round, the United States government asserted that flag-burning was an unprotected mode of expression, like obscenity or "fighting words," and therefore, it should not enjoy the full protection of the First Amendment. The Court said no. The government then contended that the new Flag Protection Act was constitutional because, unlike the statute addressed in *Johnson*, the Act did not target expressive conduct on the basis of the content of its message. The Government asserted an interest in "protect[ing] the physical integrity of the flag under all circumstances" in order to safeguard the flag's identity "'as the unique and unalloyed symbol of the Nation.'"[11] The Act proscribes conduct (other than disposal) that damages or mistreats a flag, without regard to the actor's motive, his intended message, or the likely effects of his conduct on onlookers. By contrast, the Texas statute expressly prohibited only those acts of physical flag desecration "that the actor knows will seriously offend" onlookers, and the former federal statute prohibited only those acts of desecration that "cas[t] contempt upon" the flag. The Court considered this new argument, but rejected it particularly because, in spite of the newly professed agnosticism about a flag-burner's motives, it was nevertheless clear that the Government's asserted interest is "related 'to the suppression of free expression,'" Government may create national symbols, promote them, and encourage their respectful treatment. But the Flag Protection Act goes well beyond this by criminally proscribing expressive conduct because of its likely communicative impact.

The Court concluded, stating, "We are aware that desecration of the flag is deeply offensive to many. But the same might be said, for example, of virulent ethnic and religious epithets, vulgar repudiations of the draft, and scurrilous caricatures. If there is a bedrock principle underlying the First Amendment, it is that the Government may not prohibit the expression of an idea simply because society finds the idea itself offensive or disagreeable. Punishing desecration of the flag dilutes the very freedom that makes this emblem so revered, and worth revering."[12]

---

10. 18 U.S.C. §700 (Supp. 1990).
11. Brief for United States 28, 29, in *Eichman*, 496 U.S. at 320.
12. *Eichman*, 496 U.S. at 320.

Morse v. Frederick

551 U.S. 393 (2007)

Morse v. Frederick takes us back to school to evaluate the actions of some rambunctious teens who thought it would be funny to display a "Bong Hits 4 Jesus" banner[13] at the Olympic torch run that was going on in their Alaska town. The students were on a school-sanctioned and school-supervised event (the torch relay), when their high school principal saw them unfurl a large banner conveying the aforementioned message. The principal read into the banner a message not of Christianity but one promoting illegal drug use. The principal directed the students to take down the banner. One student among those who had brought the banner to the event, Frederick, refused to do so. The principal confiscated the banner and later suspended Frederick.

The Court did not forget that students do not "shed their constitutional rights to freedom of speech or expression at the schoolhouse gate," but it also remembered that the rights of students "must be 'applied in light of the special characteristics of the school environment.'"[14] Consistent with these principles, the Court held that schools may take steps to safeguard those entrusted to their care from speech that can reasonably be regarded as encouraging illegal drug use. Although the speech took place out of school and off of the school grounds, the Court pointed to the fact that the torch-watching event was school-sponsored and school-sanctioned, and the banner was displayed openly to all of the students in attendance. The Court reversed the Ninth Circuit's opinion in favor of Frederick, the banner-displayer.

This initial section on symbolic expression serves as a prologue to all that follows in this chapter. Speech in the United States is highly protected, but not perfectly and uniformly exempt from regulation. Some words and images are regarded as non-speech — fighting words, obscenity, and child pornography

---

13. Image: Michael D. Murray, Cropped, revised, and resized thumbnail excerpt of an exhibit depicting the "Bong Hits 4 Jesus" banner that was the subject of *Morse v. Frederick*, 551 U.S. 393 (2007).

14. *Hazelwood School Dist. v. Kuhlmeier*, 484 U.S. 260, 266 (1988); *Tinker*, 393 U.S. at 506.

being three prominent examples (discussed in sections B, C, and D, below). On the other end of the spectrum, political speech in words and expressive conduct generally is subject to the highest protection. It is noteworthy that the Supreme Court twice found (in *Eichman* and *Johnson*) that laws directed to burning of the flag were content-based regulations of expression, subjecting them to the highest level of First Amendment scrutiny and protection. But in certain instances, expressive political conduct is regulated as conduct first, and speech second, and subjected to a lesser level of scrutiny. In *United States v. O'Brien*[15] (discussed in section E, below), the Supreme Court found that a law prohibiting the burning of draft cards was a content-neutral regulation of expressive conduct, and the Court defined and created a lower level of scrutiny — intermediate scrutiny — specifically for First Amendment issues involving content-neutral regulations of speech and expressive conduct. The content-neutral standard was applied even though the law under scrutiny was applied in the context of a protest of the Vietnam War and the draft. It was true that the *O'Brien* statute was phrased as a simple prohibition on destruction of government property (the Selective Service cards at issue being government property), and not as a prohibition on degrading or defacing the cards for a particular expressive purpose. However, most likely, it was not the government property nature of the draft card that made the message powerful; destroying a government-owned mail box or breaking the windows of a federal building would not have carried the same message. Instead, it was what the draft card stood for — the draft itself during the Vietnam War — that caused O'Brien to want to burn it in a public display. The message seemed equally plain and unambiguous, as close to "pure speech" as you can get, in both the flag burning situation and the draft card burning situation, yet the latter received a lower level of scrutiny.

The law of content-based restrictions and of content-neutral, conduct-based restrictions produces unusual outcomes (discussed in section E, below).[16] Artists in particular express their ideas in symbolic speech and conduct, and so must be cognizant of the fine line drawn between regulations suppressing expressive speech for its content, as in *Eichman* above, and content-neutral regulations of expressive conduct, as in *O'Brien*. The courts are willing to find that a great deal of conduct has expressive content, and thus carries First Amendment protection. In *Hurley v. Irish American Gay, Lesbian, and Bisexual Group*,[17] the Supreme Court found that marching in a parade was expressive and worthy of First Amendment protection. In *Bery v. City of New York*,[18] the Second Circuit found that selling art on sidewalks and public

---

15. *United States v. O'Brien*, 391 U.S. 367 (1968).

16. *See generally* Wilson R. Huhn, *Assessing the Constitutionality of Laws That Are Both Content-Based and Content-Neutral: The Emerging Constitutional Calculus*, 79 IND. L.J. 801, 840-42 (2004); Heidi Kitrosser, *From Marshall McLuhan to Anthropomorphic Cows: Communicative Manner and the First Amendment*, 96 NW. U. L. REV. 1339, 1353-54 (2002); Nicole B. Cásarez, *Public Forums, Selective Subsidies, and Shifting Standards of Viewpoint Discrimination*, 64 ALB. L. REV. 501, 511 (2000).

17. *Hurley v. Irish American Gay, Lesbian, and Bisexual Group*, 515 U.S. 557, 569 (1995).

18. *Bery v. City of New York*, 97 F.3d 689 (2d Cir. 1996), *cert. denied*, 520 U.S. 1251 (1997).

places was conduct linked to expressive content and thus protected by the First Amendment.[19] Commentators have argued that courts should accept and rely on background cultural knowledge in interpreting symbolic gestures because this context allows the interpretation of some gestures and symbols that so obviously carry expressive meaning they should be treated as pure speech.[20]

Although the First Amendment does not stop at the schoolhouse door,[21] school children in general enjoy less freedom of speech because their First Amendment rights may be limited for legitimate academic reasons relating to the work of the school.[22] Even off-campus activities may be curtailed if they have an impact on the operation of the school.[23] The *Morse* case drives home the point that "school" property extends to areas where sponsored school events are going on. Frederick, the defendant in *Morse*, stood across the street from his school in attendance of a parade, but the Court found it significant that Morse, the principal of the school, had authorized students' attendance of the torch run as an officially sanctioned school outing, and thus the same constitutional limitations on students' speech activities applied outside the school property. Other courts have extended this to actions taken off site that had a substantial adverse impact on the academic operations of the school.[24]

---

19. *See also Weinberg v. City of Chicago*, 310 F.3d 1029 (7th Cir. 2002) (same). *But see Mastrovincenzo v. City of New York*, 435 F.3d 78 (2nd Cir. 2006) (although selling hand-painted clothing was found to be expressive conduct, city's licensing regime to limit selling clothing was held to be valid content-neutral regulation of speech).

20. *See* Timothy Zick, *Cross Burning, Cockfighting, and Symbolic Meaning: Toward a First Amendment Ethnography*, 45 Wm. & Mary L. Rev. 2261, 2336-38, 2274-75 (2004).

21. *See, e.g., Tinker*, 393 U.S. at 503.

22. *See Morse, supra; Axson-Flynn v. Johnson*, 356 F.3d 1277 (10th Cir. 2004); *J.S. ex rel. H.S. v. Bethlehem Area Sch. Dist.*, 807 A.2d 847 (Pa. 2002).

23. *J.S.*, 807 A.2d 847. *See* Clay Calvert, *Off-Campus Speech, On-Campus Punishment: Censorship of the Emerging Internet Underground*, 7 B.U. J. Sci. & Tech. L. 243, 270-71 (2001) (discussing limits of school authority to regulate student-created websites).

24. *Compare Wisniewski v. Board of Educ. of Weedsport Cent. School Dist.*, 494 F.3d 34 (2nd Cir. 2007) (middle-school student's sending of instant messages over Internet to classmates displaying drawing of pistol firing bullet at teacher's head, above which were dots representing splattered blood, and beneath which appeared word "kill" posed reasonably foreseeable risk drawing would come to attention of school authorities and would materially and substantially disrupt work and discipline of school, and thus, school officials did not violate student's First Amendment free speech rights by suspending him; although student created and transmitted drawing off school property, drawing's potentially threatening content and its distribution to 15 recipients, including classmates, during three-week period, made it reasonably foreseeable it would come to school authorities' attention), *and Layshock v. Hermitage School Dist.*, 496 F. Supp. 2d 587 (W.D. Pa. 2007) (MySpace page created offsite using non-school computer still presented potential for disruption of school environment; student eventually prevailed in suit), *and J.S. v. Bethlehem Area School District*, 807 A.2d 847 (Pa. 2002) (action against student-created website about school staff), *with Killion v. Franklin Regional School Dist.*, 136 F. Supp. 2d 446 (W.D. Pa. 2001) (school could not punish student for list disparaging athletic director), *and Flaherty v. Keystone Oaks School Dist.*, 247 F. Supp. 2d 698 (W.D. Pa. 2003) (school could not punish student for "trash talk" about volleyball game), *and Latour v. Riverside Beaver School Dist.*, No. 05-1076, 2005 WL 2106562 (W.D. Pa. Aug. 24, 2005) (enjoining school from punishing student for rap song lyrics), *and Guiles ex rel. Guiles v. Marineau*, 461 F.3d 320 (2nd Cir. 2006), *cert. denied sub nom Marineau v. Guiles*, 551 U.S. 1162 (2007) (school could not

B. Censorship of Obscenity

The human form has been a staple subject of art for as long there has been art. In certain times and certain cultures, the naked human form and aspects of the human condition, including human sexuality, have been welcomed and accepted as a subject for art. In other times and in other cultures, questions of decency, propriety, and morality have clouded the appreciation of art involving human bodies and human sexuality. Over the centuries, standards have changed from more to less restrictive and back again concerning the nature, meaning, and treatment of the depiction of human forms and human sexuality. This section explores the experience of the United States, whose law was heavily influenced by the British Victorian era legal standards represented in the case *Regina v. Hicklin* (excerpted below), and later by less restrictive but much more legally complicated standards as seen in the *Roth* and *Miller* opinions.

PROBLEM 6-1

> Zeli is distributing videos with graphic sexual content from an internet website. Each video is completely computer generated—no humans were involved as actors or models. In fact, the only person involved in any way in the production of the videos is Zeli himself, the programmer. Zeli uses an advanced animation technique that makes the videos appear to be slightly grainy super-8 video footage of actual persons and events. Should the work be censored? Would the analysis change if the virtual persons depicted in the videos were virtual children, obviously presented as underage, teenage and pre-teenage subjects engaged in graphic sexual acts with adults and with each other?

---

punish student for wearing t-shirt bearing images of cocaine and a martini glass along with text criticizing George W. Bush).

Student speech activities involving the fine arts were also involved in *Ponce v. Socorro Independent School Dist.*, 432 F. Supp. 2d 682 (W.D. Tex. 2006) (suspension of student for writing in student's own diary a fictional story of student, as leader of Nazi group, planning for takeover of school violated student's rights under First, Fourth, and Fourteenth Amendments); *Behymer-Smith ex rel. Behymer v. Coral Academy of Science*, 427 F. Supp. 2d 969 (D. Nev. 2006) (defendant school district violated student's First Amendment rights when they prohibited him from reciting a poem that contained the words "hell" and "damn" at a poetry competition).

Regina v. Hicklin

(1867-68) L.R. 3 Q.B. 360 (April 29, 1868)

COCKBURN, Chief Judge.

... We have considered this matter, and we are of opinion that the judgment of the learned recorder must be reversed, and the decision of the magistrates affirmed. This was a proceeding under 20 & 21 Vict. c.83, s.1, whereby it is provided that, in respect of obscene books, &c., kept to be sold or distributed, magistrates may order the seizure and condemnation of such works, in case they are of opinion that the publication of them would have been the subject-matter of an indictment at law, and that such a prosecution ought to have been instituted. Now, it is found here as a fact that the work which is the subject-matter of the present proceeding was, to a considerable extent, an obscene publication, and, by reason of the obscene matter in it, calculated to produce a pernicious effect in depraving and debauching the minds of the persons into whose hands it might come. . . .

It is quite clear that the publishing an obscene book is an offence against the law of the land. It is perfectly true, as has been pointed out by Mr. Kydd, that there are a great many publications of high repute in the literary productions of this country the tendency of which is immodest, and, if you please, immoral, and possibly there might have been subject-matter for indictment in many of the works which have been referred to. But it is not to be said, because there are in many standard and established works objectionable passages, that therefore the law is not as alleged on the part of this prosecution, namely, that obscene works are the subject-matter of indictment; and I think the test of obscenity is this, whether the tendency of the matter charged as obscenity is to deprave and corrupt those whose minds are open to such immoral influences, and into whose hands a publication of this sort may fall.

Now, with regard to this work, it is quite certain that it would suggest to the minds of the young of either sex, or even to persons of more advanced years, thoughts of a most impure and libidinous character. The very reason why this work is put forward to expose the practices of the Roman Catholic confessional is the tendency of questions, involving practices and propensities of a certain description, to do mischief to the minds of those to whom such questions are addressed, by suggesting thoughts and desires which otherwise would not have occurred to their minds. If that be the case as between the priest and the person confessing, it manifestly must equally be so when the whole is put into the shape of a series of paragraphs, one following upon another, each involving some impure practices, some of them of the most filthy and disgusting and unnatural description it is possible to imagine. I take it therefore, that, apart from the ulterior object which the publisher of this work had in view, the work itself is, in every sense of the term, an obscene publication, and that, consequently, as the law of England does not allow of any obscene publication, such publication is indictable. We have it, therefore, that the publication itself is a breach of the law. . . . This work, I am told, is sold at the corners of streets, and in all directions, and of course it falls into the hands of persons of all classes, young and old, and the minds of those hitherto pure are exposed to the danger of contamination and pollution from the impurity it contains. . . .

I think, therefore, that the recorder's judgment must be reversed, and the order must stand.

Notes

1. The pamphlet in *Hicklin* was called, "The Confessional Unmasked, shewing the depravity of the Romish priesthood, the iniquity of the Confessional, and the questions put to females in confession." The British Queen's Bench opinion in *Hicklin* provided a reference for American courts in the second half of the nineteenth century and early twentieth century. The standard here is particularly onerous for artists and authors: if the work may fall into the hands of particularly susceptible persons and has a tendency to corrupt those minds toward "impure and libidinous" thoughts, "depraving and debauching the minds," then it may be suppressed as obscene. Works inappropriate for children thus are encompassed by this standard. If artists and authors are required to depict or discuss the human condition and human sexuality at a level appropriate for children, is this a significant limitation on the artists' and authors' ability to express themselves?

2. It is of little help to know that obscenity and pornography may be prohibited unless we also know what they are. Unfortunately, there is probably no area of First Amendment law that is more unclear. The Supreme Court has never managed to give a concise definition of obscenity, although it has made many attempts to identify the problem.

Roth v. United States

354 U.S. 476 (1957)*

BRENNAN, Justice.

The constitutionality of a criminal statute is the question in each of these cases. In *Roth*, the primary constitutional question is whether the federal obscenity statute ["Every obscene, lewd, lascivious, or filthy book, pamphlet, picture, paper, letter, writing, print, or other publication of an indecent character; . . . [i]s declared to be nonmailable matter and shall not be conveyed in the mails or delivered from any post office or by any letter carrier." 18 U.S.C. § 1461] violates the provision of the First Amendment that "Congress shall make no law . . . abridging the freedom of speech, or of the press. . . ." In *Alberts*, the primary constitutional question is whether the obscenity provisions of the California Penal Code ["Every person who wilfully and lewdly, either: . . . Writes, composes, stereotypes, prints, publishes, sells, distributes,

---

* Footnotes and most citations omitted.

keeps for sale, or exhibits any obscene or indecent writing, paper, or book; or designs, copies, draws, engraves, paints, or otherwise prepares any obscene or indecent picture or print; or molds, cuts, casts, or otherwise makes any obscene or indecent figure; . . . is guilty of a misdemeanor." West's Cal. Penal Code Ann., 1955, § 311] invade the freedoms of speech and press as they may be incorporated in the liberty protected from state action by the Due Process Clause of the Fourteenth Amendment.

Roth conducted a business in New York in the publication and sale of books, photographs and magazines. . . . He was convicted by a jury in the District Court for the Southern District of New York upon 4 counts of a 26-count indictment charging him with mailing obscene circulars and advertising, and an obscene book, in violation of the federal obscenity statute. His conviction was affirmed by the Court of Appeals for the Second Circuit. . . .

Alberts conducted a mail-order business from Los Angeles. He was convicted by the Judge of the Municipal Court of the Beverly Hills Judicial District (having waived a jury trial) under a misdemeanor complaint which charged him with lewdly keeping for sale obscene and indecent books, and with writing, composing, and publishing an obscene advertisement of them, in violation of the California Penal Code. The conviction was affirmed by the Appellate Department of the Superior Court of the State of California in and for the County of Los Angeles. . . .

The dispositive question is whether obscenity is utterance within the area of protected speech and press. Although this is the first time the question has been squarely presented to this Court, either under the First Amendment or under the Fourteenth Amendment, expressions found in numerous opinions indicate that this Court has always assumed that obscenity is not protected by the freedoms of speech and press. . . .

All ideas having even the slightest redeeming social importance — unorthodox ideas, controversial ideas, even ideas hateful to the prevailing climate of opinion — have the full protection of the guarantees, unless excludable because they encroach upon the limited area of more important interests. But implicit in the history of the First Amendment is the rejection of obscenity as utterly without redeeming social importance. This rejection for that reason is mirrored in the universal judgment that obscenity should be restrained, reflected in the international agreement of over 50 nations, in the obscenity laws of all of the 48 States, and in the 20 obscenity laws enacted by the Congress from 1842 to 1956. This is the same judgment expressed by this Court in *Chaplinsky v. New Hampshire*, 315 U.S. 568, 571-72, 62 S. Ct. 766, 769, 86 L. Ed. 1031:

> . . . There are certain well-defined and narrowly limited classes of speech, the prevention and punishment of which have never been thought to raise any Constitutional problem. These include the lewd and obscene. . . . It has been well observed that such utterances are no essential part of any exposition of ideas, and are of such slight social value as a step to truth that any benefit that may be derived from them is clearly outweighed by the social interest in order and morality. . . .

We hold that obscenity is not within the area of constitutionally protected speech or press.

It is strenuously urged that these obscenity statutes offend the constitutional guarantees because they punish incitation to impure sexual thoughts, not shown to be related to any overt antisocial conduct which is or may be incited in the persons stimulated to such thoughts. In *Roth*, the trial judge instructed the jury: "The words 'obscene, lewd and lascivious' as used in the law, signify that form of immorality which has relation to sexual impurity and has a tendency to excite lustful thoughts." In *Alberts*, the trial judge applied the test laid down in *People v. Wepplo*, 78 Cal. App. 2d Supp. 959, 178 P.2d 853, 855, namely, whether the material has "a substantial tendency to deprave or corrupt its readers by inciting lascivious thoughts or arousing lustful desires." It is insisted that the constitutional guarantees are violated because convictions may be had without proof either that obscene material will perceptibly create a clear and present danger of antisocial conduct, or will probably induce its recipients to such conduct. But, in light of our holding that obscenity is not protected speech, the complete answer to this argument is in the holding of this Court in *Beauharnais v. People of State of Illinois*, supra, 343 U.S. at page 266, 72 S. Ct. at page 735:

> Libelous utterances not being within the area of constitutionally protected speech, it is unnecessary, either for us or for the State courts, to consider the issues behind the phrase "clear and present danger." Certainly no one would contend that obscene speech, for example, may be punished only upon a showing of such circumstances. Libel, as we have seen, is in the same class.

However, sex and obscenity are not synonymous. Obscene material is material which deals with sex in a manner appealing to prurient interest. The portrayal of sex, e.g., in art, literature, and scientific works, is not itself sufficient reason to deny material the constitutional protection of freedom of speech and press. Sex, a great and mysterious motive force in human life, has indisputably been a subject of absorbing interest to mankind through the ages; it is one of the vital problems of human interest and public concern. As to all such problems, this Court said in *Thornhill v. State of Alabama*, 310 U.S. 88, 101-102, 60 S. Ct. 736, 744, 84 L. Ed. 1093:

> The freedom of speech and of the press guaranteed by the Constitution embraces at the least the liberty to discuss publicly and truthfully all matters of public concern without previous restraint or fear of subsequent punishment. The exigencies of the colonial period and the efforts to secure freedom from oppressive administration developed a broadened conception of these liberties as adequate to supply the public need for information and education with respect to the significant issues of the times. . . . Freedom of discussion, if it would fulfill its historic function in this nation, must embrace all issues about which information is needed or appropriate to enable the members of society to cope with the exigencies of their period.

The fundamental freedom of speech and press have contributed greatly to the development and well-being of our free society and are indispensable to its continued growth. Ceaseless vigilance is the watchword to prevent their erosion by Congress or by the States. The door barring federal and state intrusion into this area cannot be left ajar; it must be kept tightly closed and opened only the slightest crack necessary to prevent encroachment upon more important interests. It is therefore vital that the standards for judging obscenity safeguard the protection of freedom of speech and press for material which does not treat sex in a manner appealing to prurient interest.

The early leading standard of obscenity allowed material to be judged merely by the effect of an isolated excerpt upon particularly susceptible persons. *Regina v. Hicklin*, (1868) L.R. 3 Q.B. 360. Some American courts adopted this standard but later decisions have rejected it and substituted this test: whether to the average person, applying contemporary community standards, the dominant theme of the material taken as a whole appeals to prurient interest. The *Hicklin* test, judging obscenity by the effect of isolated passages upon the most susceptible persons, might well encompass material legitimately treating with sex, and so it must be rejected as unconstitutionally restrictive of the freedoms of speech and press. On the other hand, the substituted standard provides safeguards adequate to withstand the charge of constitutional infirmity.

Both trial courts below sufficiently followed the proper standard. Both courts used the proper definition of obscenity. In addition, in the *Alberts* case, in ruling on a motion to dismiss, the trial judge indicated that, as the trier of facts, he was judging each item as a whole as it would affect the normal person, and in *Roth*, the trial judge instructed the jury as follows:

> ... The test is not whether it would arouse sexual desires or sexual impure thoughts in those comprising a particular segment of the community, the young, the immature or the highly prudish or would leave another segment, the scientific or highly educated or the so-called worldly-wise and sophisticated indifferent and unmoved. ... The test in each case is the effect of the book, picture or publication considered as a whole, not upon any particular class, but upon all those whom it is likely to reach. In other words, you determine its impact upon the average person in the community. The books, pictures and circulars must be judged as a whole, in their entire context, and you are not to consider detached or separate portions in reaching a conclusion. You judge the circulars, pictures and publications which have been put in evidence by present-day standards of the community. You may ask yourselves does it offend the common conscience of the community by present-day standards.
>
> In this case, ladies and gentlemen of the jury, you and you alone are the exclusive judges of what the common conscience of the community is, and in determining that conscience you are to consider the community as a whole, young and old, educated and uneducated, the religious and the irreligious — men, women and children.

... In summary, then, we hold that these statutes, applied according to the proper standard for judging obscenity, do not offend constitutional safeguards against convictions based upon protected material, or fail to give men in acting adequate notice of what is prohibited. ...

The judgments are affirmed.

Note and Questions

1. Roth rejected the test of *Regina v. Hicklin*, which had been to judge material according to its effect upon persons particularly susceptible to being scandalized or corrupted by exposure to the material — especially children. Does *Hicklin*'s "most susceptible audience" standard sound hopelessly outdated in this day and age? Consider Congress's efforts to regulate Internet content on the basis that children may be exposed to the material — is this a return to *Hicklin*'s standard or does it make more sense to focus on children when regulating the Internet?

2. In *Jacobellis v. Ohio*, 378 U.S. 184 (1964), the Court reversed a conviction under an Ohio statute that prohibited the possession and exhibition of obscene film. The Court, not convinced that the film, a French import entitled *Les Amants* ("The Lovers"),[25] really was obscene, rejected the state's argument that the "community standards" referred to in *Roth* were local community standards rather than national standards. It was thought that allowing local standards to govern would have the  undesirable consequence of denying some sections of the country access to material (material that was acceptable by those communities' standards but unacceptable elsewhere) because publishers and distributors would be reluctant to risk prosecution under the vagaries of different local laws. What are the pros and cons of allowing a hypothetical national standard of what is obscene to regulate material as opposed to the standards of a small, local community? Whose standards should carry the day on a national scale — the most prudish (Smallville, USA) or the most lax (Las Vegas or New York City)?

When the Attorney General of Massachusetts moved to have John Cleland's book *Fanny Hill: Memoirs of a Woman of Pleasure*,[26] declared obscene, the Massachusetts courts ruled in his favor. On appeal, the Supreme Court reversed, holding that the mere risk that a work might be exploited by panderers because of its pervasive treatment of sexual matters is not sufficient to make it obscene. *Memoirs v. Massachusetts*, 383 U.S. 413, 418 (1966). Instead, the Court held, the state must prove each of the following three elements: (a) the dominant theme of the material

---

25. Image: Michael D. Murray, Cropped, revised, and resized thumbnail excerpt of an exhibit depicting the poster art for "Les Amants," the subject of *Jacobellis v. Ohio*, 378 U.S. 184 (1964).

26. Image: Michael D. Murray, Cropped, revised, and resized thumbnail excerpt of an exhibit depicting the cover of the Wordsworth Classics edition of John Cleland's book, *Fanny Hill: Memoirs of a Woman of Pleasure*, the subject of *Memoirs v. Massachusetts*, 383 U.S. 413, 418 (1966).

taken as a whole appeals to a prurient interest in sex; (b) the material is patently offensive because it affronts contemporary community standards relating to the description or representation of sexual matters; and (c) the material is utterly without redeeming social value. Why does the standard call for us to evaluate "the dominant theme of the material taken as a whole" — what if one small but significant section is particularly obscene and offensive? What does "utterly without redeeming social value" even mean as a regulation? Does it keep anything out? Doesn't the most graphic "hardcore" pornography have some minimal value in the study of human anatomy or sexual education?

Miller v. California

413 U.S. 15 (1973)*

BURGER, Chief Justice.

This is one of a group of "obscenity-pornography" cases being reviewed by the Court in a re-examination of standards enunciated in earlier cases involving what Mr. Justice HARLAN called "the intractable obscenity problem." *Interstate Circuit, Inc. v. Dallas*, 390 U.S. 676, 704, 88 S. Ct. 1298, 1313, 20 L. Ed. 2d 225 (1968) (concurring and dissenting). Appellant conducted a mass mailing campaign to advertise the sale of illustrated books, euphemistically called "adult" material. After a jury trial, he was convicted of violating California Penal Code § 311.2(a), a misdemeanor, by knowingly distributing obscene matter, and the Appellate Department, Superior Court of California, County of Orange, summarily affirmed the judgment without opinion. Appellant's conviction was specifically based on his conduct in causing five unsolicited advertising brochures to be sent through the mail in an envelope addressed to a restaurant in Newport Beach, California. The envelope was opened by the manager of the restaurant and his mother. They had not requested the brochures; they complained to the police. . . .

The brochures advertise four books entitled "Intercourse," "Man-Woman," "Sex Orgies Illustrated," and "An Illustrated History of Pornography," and a film entitled "Marital Intercourse." While the brochures contain some descriptive printed material, primarily they consist of pictures and drawings very explicitly depicting men and women in groups of two or more engaging in a variety of sexual activities, with genitals often prominently displayed.

I

This case involves the application of a State's criminal obscenity statute to a situation in which sexually explicit materials have been thrust by aggressive sales action upon unwilling recipients who had in no way indicated any desire to receive such materials. This Court has recognized that the States have a legitimate interest in prohibiting dissemination or exhibition of obscene

* Footnotes and some citations omitted.

material when the mode of dissemination carries with it a significant danger of offending the sensibilities of unwilling recipients or of exposure to juveniles. . . .

II

This much has been categorically settled by the Court, that obscene material is unprotected by the First Amendment. . . . As a result, we now confine the permissible scope of such regulation to works which depict or describe sexual conduct. That conduct must be specifically defined by the applicable state law, as written or authoritatively construed. A state offense must also be limited to works which, taken as a whole, appeal to the prurient interest in sex, which portray sexual conduct in a patently offensive way, and which, taken as a whole, do not have serious literary, artistic, political, or scientific value. . . .

The basic guidelines for the trier of fact must be: (a) whether "the average person, applying contemporary community standards" would find that the work, taken as a whole, appeals to the prurient interest; (b) whether the work depicts or describes, in a patently offensive way, sexual conduct specifically defined by the applicable state law; and (c) whether the work, taken as a whole, lacks serious literary, artistic, political, or scientific value.

We do not adopt as a constitutional standard the "utterly without redeeming social value" test of *Memoirs v. Massachusetts*, 383 U.S., at 419, 86 S. Ct., at 977; that concept has never commanded the adherence of more than three Justices at one time. . . .

We emphasize that it is not our function to propose regulatory schemes for the States. That must await their concrete legislative efforts. It is possible, however, to give a few plain examples of what a state statute could define for regulation under part (b) of the standard announced in this opinion, supra:

> (a) Patently offensive representations or descriptions of ultimate sexual acts, normal or perverted, actual or simulated.
> (b) Patently offensive representation or descriptions of masturbation, excretory functions, and lewd exhibition of the genitals.

Sex and nudity may not be exploited without limit by films or pictures exhibited or sold in places of public accommodation any more than live sex and nudity can be exhibited or sold without limit in such public places. At a minimum, prurient, patently offensive depiction or description of sexual conduct must have serious literary, artistic, political, or scientific value to merit First Amendment protection. For example, medical books for the education of physicians and related personnel necessarily use graphic illustrations and descriptions of human anatomy. In resolving the inevitably sensitive questions of fact and law, we must continue to rely on the jury system, accompanied by the safeguards that judges, rules of evidence, presumption of innocence, and other protective features provide, as we do with rape, murder, and a host of other offenses against society and its individual members. . . .

Under the holdings announced today, no one will be subject to prosecution for the sale or exposure of obscene materials unless these materials depict or describe patently offensive 'hard core' sexual conduct specifically defined by the regulating state law, as written or construed. We are satisfied that these specific prerequisites will provide fair notice to a dealer in such materials that his public and commercial activities may bring prosecution. If the inability to define regulated materials with ultimate, god-like precision altogether removes the power of the States or the Congress to regulate, then "hard core" pornography may be exposed without limit to the juvenile, the passerby, and the consenting adult alike, as, indeed, Mr. Justice DOUGLAS contends. . . .

III

Under a National Constitution, fundamental First Amendment limitations on the powers of the States do not vary from community to community, but this does not mean that there are, or should or can be, fixed, uniform national standards of precisely what appeals to the "prurient interest" or is "patently offensive." These are essentially questions of fact, and our Nation is simply too big and too diverse for this Court to reasonably expect that such standards could be articulated for all 50 States in a single formulation, even assuming the prerequisite consensus exists. When triers of fact are asked to decide whether "the average person, applying contemporary community standards" would consider certain materials "prurient," it would be unrealistic to require that the answer be based on some abstract formulation. The adversary system, with lay jurors as the usual ultimate factfinders in criminal prosecutions, has historically permitted triers of fact to draw on the standards of their community, guided always by limiting instructions on the law. To require a State to structure obscenity proceedings around evidence of a national 'community standard' would be an exercise in futility.

As noted before, this case was tried on the theory that the California obscenity statute sought to incorporate the tripartite test of *Memoirs*. This, a "national" standard of First Amendment protection enumerated by a plurality of this Court, was correctly regarded at the time of trial as limiting state prosecution under the controlling case law. The jury, however, was explicitly instructed that, in determining whether the "dominant theme of the material as a whole . . . appeals to the prurient interest" and in determining whether the material "goes substantially beyond customary limits of candor and affronts contemporary community standards of decency," it was to apply "contemporary community standards of the State of California."

During the trial, both the prosecution and the defense assumed that the relevant "community standards" in making the factual determination of obscenity were those of the State of California, not some hypothetical standard of the entire United States of America. Defense counsel at trial never objected to the testimony of the State's expert on community standards or to the instructions of the trial judge on "statewide" standards. On appeal to the Appellate Department, Superior Court of California, County of Orange, appellant for the first time contended that application of state, rather than national, standards violated the First and Fourteenth Amendments.

We conclude that neither the State's alleged failure to offer evidence of "national standards," nor the trial court's charge that the jury consider state community standards, were constitutional errors. Nothing in the First Amendment requires that a jury must consider hypothetical and unascertainable "national standards" when attempting to determine whether certain materials are obscene as a matter of fact. Mr. Chief Justice WARREN pointedly commented in his dissent in *Jacobellis v. Ohio*, supra, at 200, 84 S. Ct., at 1685:

> It is my belief that when the Court said in *Roth* that obscenity is to be defined by reference to "community standards," it meant community standards — not a national standard, as is sometimes argued. I believe that there is no provable "national standard." . . . At all events, this Court has not been able to enunciate one, and it would be unreasonable to expect local courts to divine one.

It is neither realistic nor constitutionally sound to read the First Amendment as requiring that the people of Maine or Mississippi accept public depictions of conduct found tolerable in Las Vegas, or New York City. People in different States vary in their tastes and attitudes, and this diversity is not to be strangled by the absolutism of imposed uniformity. As the Court made clear in *Mishkin v. New York*, 383 U.S., at 508-09, 86 S. Ct., at 963, the primary concern with requiring a jury to apply the standard of "the average person, applying contemporary community standards" is to be certain that, so far as material is not aimed at a deviant group, it will be judged by its impact on an average person, rather than a particularly susceptible or sensitive person — or indeed a totally insensitive one. *See Roth v. United States*, supra, 354 U.S., at 489, 77 S. Ct., at 1311. Cf. the now discredited test in *Regina v. Hicklin*, (1868) L.R. 3 Q.B. 360. We hold that the requirement that the jury evaluate the materials with reference to "contemporary standards of the State of California" serves this protective purpose and is constitutionally adequate.

IV

The dissenting Justices sound the alarm of repression. But, in our view, to equate the free and robust exchange of ideas and political debate with commercial exploitation of obscene material demeans the grand conception of the First Amendment and its high purposes in the historic struggle for freedom. It is a "misuse of the great guarantees of free speech and free press. . . ." *Breard v. Alexandria*, 341 U.S., at 645, 71 S. Ct., at 934. The First Amendment protects works which, taken as a whole, have serious literary, artistic, political, or scientific value, regardless of whether the government or a majority of the people approve of the ideas these works represent. "The protection given speech and press was fashioned to assure unfettered interchange of ideas for the bringing about of political and social changes desired by the people," *Roth v. United States*, supra, 354 U.S., at 484, 77 S.

Ct., at 1308 (emphasis added). *See Kois v. Wisconsin*, 408 U.S., at 230-32, 92 S. Ct., at 2246-47; *Thornhill v. Alabama*, 310 U.S., at 101-02, 60 S. Ct., at 743-44. But the public portrayal of hard-core sexual conduct for its own sake, and for the ensuing commercial gain, is a different matter. . . .

In sum, we (a) reaffirm the *Roth* holding that obscene material is not protected by the First Amendment; (b) hold that such material can be regulated by the States, subject to the specific safeguards enunciated above, without a showing that the material is "utterly without redeeming social value"; and (c) hold that obscenity is to be determined by applying "contemporary community standards," *see Kois v. Wisconsin*, supra, 408 U.S., at 230, 92 S. Ct., at 2246, and *Roth v. United States, supra*, 354 U.S., at 489, 77 S. Ct., at 1311, not "national standards." The judgment of the Appellate Department of the Superior Court, Orange County, California, is vacated and the case remanded to that court for further proceedings not inconsistent with the First Amendment standards established by this opinion.

Vacated and remanded.

Amy Adler, What's Left?: Hate Speech, Pornography, and the Problem for Artistic Expression

84 Cal. L. Rev. 1499 (Dec. 1996)*

Some portion of the political left in the United States has called for the restriction of pornography and hate speech. Those who advocate such censorship do so on the ground that pornography and hate speech cause harm to disadvantaged "outsider" groups in society. For this reason, the leftist censorship advocates do not accept traditional First Amendment doctrines that protect much pornography and hate speech. In calling for censorship, the author argues, leftists endanger a great deal of activist speech, particularly in the form of artwork, that in fact seeks to undermine the very pornography and hate speech the censorship advocates target. Because much postmodern art appropriates the language and images of hate speech and pornography in order to deconstruct or otherwise subvert them, leftist attempts at censorship carry a grave danger of silencing leftist activists. Furthermore, the author maintains, leftist advocates of censorship have not, and ultimately cannot, develop theories of interpretation capable of protecting activist expression while still restricting or banning pornography and hate speech. Because of the indeterminacy of language, censorship advocates must choose whether to sacrifice vital voices of protest and criticism from within the left or whether to suppress pornography and hate speech. . . .

---

* Footnotes omitted.

IV. HOW TO DISTINGUISH BETWEEN THE SUBVERSIVE
AND THE OPPRESSIVE

The word "queer" shouted at a gay man on a dark street in the dead of night by a gang wielding weapons is different from the word "queer" spoken with pride at a "Queer Nation" gay rights rally. Traditional First Amendment standards, such as the fighting words doctrine, might offer some rudimentary, albeit flawed, method to distinguish between these two uses of speech. Many anti-hate speech scholars, however, reject these traditional First Amendment standards, just as anti-pornography feminists reject the law of obscenity. Members of both new censorship schools regard accepted First Amendment doctrines as insufficient to protect victims and society from the harms of speech. Indeed, they offer compelling arguments that such standards are themselves racist and sexist. For example, scholars argue that the fighting words doctrine, which hinges on whether words might "incite an immediate breach of the peace," evidences a white male point of view. Because only an already empowered person would "fight" when faced with an insult, the doctrine assumes that the victim has power equal to the perpetrator's. A black woman who sees Klansmen burning a cross on her lawn would be unlikely to fight back when faced with such a threat. In a similar vein, leftist anti-pornography censors view the law of obscenity as inherently sexist. In their view, obscenity law is concerned with "the male point of view, meaning the standpoint of male dominance," and is therefore inadequate to protect women against the harms of pornography.

Many leftist censors wish to go much further than existing First Amendment standards would allow. But once they leave these standards behind, how would they prevent banning activist uses of racist or sexist images? Is there a way to limit the proliferation of images of cross-burning, such as those produced by the Klan for propaganda, while saving images of cross-burning used by anti-Klan activists? Is there a way to silence homophobic graffiti writers who scrawl messages like "Fight AIDS Kill a Queer" on public walls while guaranteeing a voice for the David Wojnarowiczes of the world? Is there a way to ban Hustler and protect Karen Finley? In short, can we distinguish the activist from the oppressor?

In this Section, I will examine . . . criteria that may bear on the inquiry. . . .

A. Artistic Status

Is it possible to preserve activist speech while banning sexist or oppressive hate speech by making a blanket exception in a censorship theory for speech that may be classified as "art"? At first, this possibility may appear promising. Because I have drawn most of my examples of threatened activist speech from the realm of political art, an exception for "art" might solve many of the problems I have raised. Furthermore, such an approach could draw on the already existing doctrine that has grown up around the definition of obscenity under *Miller v. California*, which protects works of "serious . . . artistic . . . value."

The problems with this approach, however, are manifold. First, a great deal of contemporary political art challenges its own categorization as "art." For example, should we characterize activist artist Gregg Bordowitz's "safe sex porn" videos, displayed in x-rated movie theaters and in art and academic settings, as "art"? What about AIDS activist posters that grace the sides of buses, but are also displayed in museums? What about Karen Finley, who performs in both nightclubs and galleries? Works such as these challenge traditional notions of the definition of art. Introducing the complex philosophical question "What is art?" into the definition of hate speech or pornography would complicate rather than clarify the debate. Moreover, an exception for art would fail to save subversive work that didn't come in the form of art; it would therefore protect only a narrow and, some would say, rarefied sector of political speech.

Most importantly, distinguishing works on this basis would serve none of the goals that motivate leftist censors in the first place. Whether speech is "art" is irrelevant to leftist censors, who care not about the value of a work, but instead question why any such value should override the harm that speech does to real victims. As Catherine MacKinnon has stated, "Existing standards of literature [and] art . . . are, in feminist light, remarkably consonant with pornography's mode, meaning, and message." Just because a work is art does not guarantee its political purity; a work of art can be as racist and sexist as non-art. Thus, even though many of the examples of activist speech we have examined have been deemed art, their status as art is irrelevant to whether they should merit protection under a system of political censorship.

A blanket exception for art therefore proves to be both underinclusive and overinclusive. It is underinclusive because it would omit from the definition of "art" the kind of activist work leftists might wish to save, and overinclusive because it would protect work that leftist censors would wish to ban. . . .

Note and Questions

1. Artists face censorship threats from all sides, as eloquently pointed out by Professor Adler in her article. What is the most important message here for legislators and judges concerning writing laws and regulations on obscenity, hate speech, and pornography? How can Professor Adler's advice best be employed in the *Miller* test?

2. Professor Adler points out the ironic fact that so called left-wing censorship is the same animal as so called right-wing censorship; both seek to quash speech for what they believe are moral reasons, and similarly, each side thinks the goals and morals asserted by the other side are insufficient to justify curtailing free speech. Does this point to the wisdom of the First Amendment itself — simply stating that Congress shall make no law abridging the freedom of expression without attempting to itemize goals and morals that might justify a little abridgment?

C. Evidentiary Issues for Censorship of Obscenity under *Miller*

PROBLEM 6-2

When you say "community" standards, how big is your community? Just the town or village in which the material appears? Just the neighborhood? The entire county? The entire state? Which standard is fair to artists?

1. Community Standards

A greater number of appellate decisions under *Miller* have focused on the method of determining community standards than on any of the other *Miller* standards. While there is no rigid rule, a brief examination of the cases provides some guidance.

The fact that the conduct complained of takes place in a state or locality without a statutory proscription against the distribution of obscene material is not a significant benefit to the accused. In *Smith v. United States*, 431 U.S. 291 (1977), defendant was convicted for mailing obscene magazines within the State of Iowa. At the time Smith mailed his publications, Iowa had no law regulating the distribution of obscene materials to adults, as the state Supreme Court had invalidated, at least by implication, Iowa's obscenity statute. Although the legislature did enact a new law prohibiting the distribution of obscene materials to minors, it did not pass a parallel law addressing the dissemination of obscene matter to adults. Smith argued that this legislative action, or lack thereof, conclusively determined the community standard. The United States Supreme Court, however, in an opinion by Justice Blackmun, held that the state statutory policy was merely a factor for the jury to consider in determining community standards.

In *People v. Hart*, 101 Ill. App. 3d 343, 427 N.E. 2d 1352 (1981), the court held that the prosecution need not present any proof, lay or expert, of the applicable standard. The prosecution apparently met its burden simply by offering the subject materials into evidence. It has also been held that the prosecution need not present expert testimony concerning the lack of serious literary, artistic, political or scientific value in the allegedly obscene matter. *Commonwealth v. Kocinski*, 11 Mass. App. Ct. 120, 414 N.E. 2d 378 (1981). It is, however, an error to instruct the jury that the state need not have produced the expert testimony because the instruction increases the likelihood that the jurors may impermissibly apply a personal, rather than statewide, community standard. *Hart*, 101 Ill. App. 3d at 350, 427 N.E. 2d at 1358.

While the defense may present expert testimony concerning the community's acceptance of the materials at issue, it may be barred from attempting to demonstrate the general availability of comparable materials. As the court said in *Long v. 130 Market St. Gift & Novelty*, 294 Pa. Super. 383, 440 A.2d 517 (1982):

> The fact that one can walk into an 'adult bookstore' in some of the towns and cities of the Commonwealth and purchase a film or publication devoted, on the whole, to bestiality, sado-masochism, or any of a number of other often-questioned sexual predilections, by no means implies the average Pennsylvanian would not find the subject matter appealing to the prurient interests.

440 A.2d at 522; *but see Berg v. State*, 599 S.W.2d 802 (Tex. Crim. App. 1980) (in which the court admitted into evidence magazines and films purchased in the same area and at the same time as the materials at issue to help the jury divine the contemporary community standard). It seems that, at least to some courts, the availability of comparable materials is circumstantial evidence of their acceptability.

Many courts appear to prefer statistical evidence that shows a community's acceptance of certain materials. For example, in *People v. Nelson*, 88 Ill. App. 3d 196, 410 N.E. 2d 476 (1980), it was held that the trial court erred in refusing to admit the expert testimony of an opinion pollster, stating that there was no consensus in Illinois as to whether it was acceptable to make sexually explicit materials available to adults. Similarly, in *Keller v. State*, 606 S.W. 2d 931 (Tex. Crim. App. 1980), it was found that the trial court had erroneously excluded a theater operator's statistical evidence of community patronage of *Deep Throat* (a film comparable to that shown by the defendant) offered as circumstantial evidence of contemporary community standards.

Ultimately, however, trial court judges retain a great deal of discretion as to the relevance of proffered evidence. In *United States v. Battista*, 646 F.2d 237 (6th Cir.), *cert. denied*, 454 U.S. 1046 (1981), defendants contended that slides used in Memphis area sex education programs (portraying activity comparable to scenes depicted in *Deep Throat*) should have been admitted to determine the community standard. The trial court excluded the evidence because both the manner of presentation and the audience for whom the slides were intended differentiated the slides from the movie to such an extent as to be of no probative value on the issue of community standards. On appeal, it was held that the exclusion was proper.

Because a jury must determine community standards relating to the depiction of sex and nudity, the composition of the jury may make more of a difference in the outcome of an obscenity case than in criminal cases, such as arson for example, in which only factual events are at issue.

The nature of the questions that can be posed to a prospective juror is within the trial court's discretion. In one case, defendant's attorney sought to inquire into each juror's knowledge and understanding of contemporary community standards. The Supreme Court, however, refused to sanction this line of voir dire because the information elicited would be of little help to a court in determining the qualifications of a juror. *Smith v. United States*, 431 U.S. 291,

308 (1977). On the other hand, some trial judges have given defense counsel great leeway to explore possible juror prejudice, at times refusing only the defendant's request to conduct a separate, private voir dire of each prospective juror. This approach has been affirmed by the appellate courts. *See, e.g., Morrison v. State*, 619 P.2d 203 (Okla. Crim. App. 1980).

Knowledge of a juror's background can aid in the planning of a defendant's case. Courts may be more willing to allow a defendant to introduce expert testimony about the relevant community standards, such as an opinion poll, if counsel elicits on voir dire that jurors are not long-time residents of the community and are not well-read. In that situation, the jurors would have little practical experience upon which to base their opinion of what community standards might be. *See People v. Nelson*, 88 Ill. App. 3d 196, 410 N.E. 2d 476 (1980). For an interesting report on the jury selection proceedings in the Mapplethorpe case, *see* Merkel, *Report from Cincinnati: Art on Trial*, ART in AM., Dec. 1990, at 41.

A varying community standard for obscenity may be impossible for a federal agency to apply. *See Bella Lewitsky Dance Found. v. Frohnmayer*, 754 F. Supp. 774 (C.D. Cal. 1991). The National Endowment for the Arts (NEA) agreed that it would follow the test for obscenity set forth in *Miller* when it announced a prerequisite to the receipt of federal funding, namely, that applicants pledge not to use NEA funds to produce "obscene" works. The district court in *Bella Lewitsky* held that the anti-obscenity pledge was unconstitutionally vague because: (1) the agency remained free to change from the *Miller* standard to any other it chose, and (2) the agency was incapable of applying a varying community standard of obscenity. Finally, the NEA pledge would, to the court, have an impermissible, chilling effect on speech and creative expression.

While community standards differ across the country, it is interesting to note how drastically different community standards can be abroad. The Beijing Art Gallery displayed 120 works in an exhibition of art nudes. Record-breaking crowds showed up to view what is rare in Chinese art — the nude figure. In China, the human figure is traditionally portrayed as austere and subordinate to nature, and during the Cultural Revolution of 1966–76, the nude figure disappeared from public exhibition. It was reported that some of the women who posed for the artists (an act considered scandalous) went insane after being recognized. *See* Staggs, *The Naked and the Damned*, ART-news, Apr. 1989, at 24. *See also Prehistoric Pornography Found in China*, J. OF ART, May 1991, at 69. Canadian courts, on the other hand, have concluded that the community standards test is a national standard. Providing further certainty in obscenity prosecutions, Canada's obscenity law is federal in nature. Nevertheless, critics contend that the Canadian law lacks a rule of prior restraint, as well as provisions requiring the option of a jury trial for obscenity prosecutions, the inclusion of evidence at trial regarding community standards, and a check on the censor power of film review boards. *See Canadian Obscenity Laws as Nasty as the U.S.*, ENT. & SPORTS LAW, Fall 1991, at 5-7. Commentators have noted the difficulty of implementing a local "community standard" when the allegedly obscene material is offered over the Internet. The ability of the Internet to disseminate materials internationally has caused some commentators to call for the implementation of a national standard. *See Cybersex and Community Standards*, 75 B.U. L. REV. 865 (1995).

2. Taken as a Whole

PROBLEM 6-3

Is every page of an "adult" magazine obscene? Are there any redeeming features in a literary, artistic, educational, or cultural sense in adult works? Does this matter? Should we make sure we throw out the baby with all of the bath water, or can we salvage parts of works? Should we leave the whole work alone if it has enough redeeming features even though it has some obscene parts?

Cincinnati v. Contemporary Arts Center

566 N.E. 2d 214 (Ohio Mun. 1990)*

ALBANESE, Judge.

For purposes of these decisions the court has consolidated the motion in limine filed by the state of Ohio and the motion to dismiss the second count of the indictment filed by the defendants, the Contemporary Arts Center ("CAC") and Dennis Barrie ("Barrie"). The court will first address itself to the issue raised by the defendants that Count Two of the indictment should be dismissed because the defendants have not violated R.C. 2907.32 ["No person . . . shall do any of the following: . . . Promote, . . . display, [or] exhibit . . . any obscene material"] as a matter of constitutional law.

There is no question that *Miller v. California* (1973), 413 U.S. 15, 93 S. Ct. 2607, 37 L. Ed. 2d 419, sets out the standard for determining whether material is obscene. The three-pronged *Miller* test is as follows:

a. Whether the average person applying contemporary community standards would find that the work, taken as a whole, appeals to the prurient interest;

b. Whether the work depicts or describes, in a patently offensive way, sexual conduct specifically defined by the applicable state law; and

c. Whether the work, taken as a whole, lacks serious literary, artistic, political, or scientific value.

Id. at 24, 93 S. Ct. at 2614.

---

* Footnotes omitted.

All of these requirements are issues of fact for the jury to determine, not the court's by intervention as a matter of constitutional law. *See Pope v. Illinois* (1987), 481 U.S. 497, 107 S. Ct. 1918, 95 L. Ed. 2d 439. . . .

In dealing with photographs displayed in an art gallery, this court must follow general guidelines on the issue of the meaning of the phrase "taken as a whole" because neither the Supreme Court of Ohio nor the Supreme Court of the United States has decided this issue. For example, the United States Supreme Court in *Kois v. Wisconsin* (1972), 408 U.S. 229, 231, 92 S. Ct. 2245, 2246, 33 L. Ed. 2d 312, said that the reviewing court must ". . . look at the context of the material, as well as its content." But *Kois* dealt with the issues of "sex poems" as published in an underground newspaper; pictures were not involved at all in that case. Attempting to apply the "content" and "context" rule to pictures is questionable; the pictures speak for themselves. The content of a picture may be the context itself. The picture itself can be out of context if it is blurred or cut or discolored, thereby distorting the substance and arrangement of its content. The context of an exhibit is illusive as it changes by design.

The court is not unmindful of the fact that "ratiocination has little to do with esthetics, the fabled 'reasonable man' is of little help in the inquiry, and would have to be replaced with, perhaps, the 'man of tolerably good taste' — a description that betrays the lack of an ascertainable standard. . . ." But we, as a civilized nation, do have principles and guidelines.

The court has carefully heard all the testimony of the witnesses in the evidentiary hearing, and has reviewed the exhibits, arguments and briefs of counsel; an effort is made, then, to decide whether all the pictures, taken as a whole, and displayed in an art gallery, must be judged as one indivisible unit, or if each individual photograph must be judged separately.

IV

The defendants adroitly formulate the contention that the Robert Mapplethorpe "Perfect Moment" exhibition is necessarily non-obscene; the grand jury chose only to indict the defendants with pandering five photographs as obscene. Therefore, since the exhibition — the whole — is non-obscene, it is undeniable, the defendants urge, that the five photographs are parts of the whole, and also have to be non-obscene.

This presumption, however, is rebuttable since the defendants failed to appreciate the liability inherent within the four corners of each photograph. The defendants have anticipated and inferred that the legal focus of the phrase "taken as a whole" is the comparison of each photograph to all of the photographs in the exhibit. This theory could result in a finding that the entire exhibit would be obscene if the evidence shows that the "five S & M" photos are, indeed, obscene.

This court finds that each photograph has a separate identity; each photograph has a visual and unique image permanently recorded. The click of the shutter has frozen the dots, colors, shapes, and whatever finishing chemicals necessary, into a manmade instant of time. Never can that "moment" be legitimately changed.

But the defendants press for the rationalization that an exhibition curator is a professional and has the ability and credentials to present a retrospective show of an artist's work. The claim is that there is an absolute right to present any work by any artist. The defendants are outraged that the quality and historical significance of the photographs are distinguished in the indictments. The claim is that all the photographs are inseparable and should be "taken as a whole" to determine the basis for artistic quality and scrutiny. The state is concerned about pictorial manipulation — the use of discretion without guidelines.

The court finds that the photographs have been individually collected from private owners and public institutions; each photograph exists as a single presentation or work. A retrospective exhibition is the accumulation of important impressions of an artist's work over the years to demonstrate a productive lifespan by showing breadth, diversity, expression, sequence, quality, and perfection. However, the court finds the exhibition itself to be a vehicle for displaying the "five S & M" pictures. It is unnecessary to pretend that the "five S & M" pictures have appeared anywhere else by themselves, individually, in any other art gallery; this exhibition is the first.

In deciding this matter, therefore, the court will systematically attempt to do so without succumbing to the subjective tests so often criticized.

First, the "five S & M" pictures are "coat-tailed" with one hundred sixty-eight non-obscene pictures in the exhibition, but the "five S & M" pictures are displayed in separate arrangements.

Second, the curator explained that even without the "five S & M" pictures, the exhibition probably would have been arranged retrospectively for viewing to the public. The "whole" would be reduced by five and, therefore, would result in a change from the original exhibition.

Third, the accompanying catalogue containing a checklist of the contents of the exhibition was prepared by the same curator; the catalogue and the exhibition purported to be the same with one exception — the "five S & M" pictures are absent from the catalogue. The indispensable "five S & M" pictures to be included in "the whole" were deleted from the catalogue book because of "budget restraints and esthetic design composition." This is a change by design.

Fourth, continuing the objectivity test, the court cannot help but notice that the nude pictures of the two minor children are necessarily isolated because of legal precedent. The Supreme Court has doggedly insisted that government has a legitimate interest in the protection of minors. The tests for obscenity in cases involving minors are different. *See New York v. Ferber* (1982), 458 U.S. 747, 102 S. Ct. 3348, 73 L. Ed. 2d 1113. In other words, the pictures in the exhibition to be "taken as a whole" do not include the pictures of the nude children. This reduces the total number of pictures in the original exhibit by two; therefore, making it not entirely retrospective.

In conclusion, when finding that each photograph is a whole image, the focus will be each picture "taken as a whole." Arranging photographs within an exhibition to claim a privilege of acceptability is not the test; the "whole" is a single picture, and no amount of manipulation can change its identity. To argue that possible obscene photographs as displayed are nevertheless non-obscene because they are part of an otherwise acceptable exhibit is rejected.

To rule otherwise would allow displays of such incongruity that imagination would be the only guideline for the arranging of a flagrant display resulting in a cultural calamity. It matters not whether there is a commercial market or an audience at the art gallery. In this court's judgment, independent evaluation of the "five S & M" photographs is required. To paraphrase the concurring opinion of Judge Clark in *Penthouse Internatl., Ltd. v. McAuliffe* (C.A. 5, 1980), 610 F.2d 1353, 1373, it becomes apparent that the state should not be required to deal with such an "overboard interpretation" of the phrase "taken as a whole" that it would render the standards for prosecution in obscenity cases unworkable.

This case is set for trial on both counts of the indictments against both defendants on September 24, 1990. The "five S & M" photographs will be individually "taken as a whole," each measured against the *Miller* obscenity standards by the trier of the facts. The state's motion in limine is granted and a temporary protective order is issued.

So ordered.

Note and Questions

1. Near the end of his career and after his death, Robert Mapplethorpe's work frequently was targeted for censorship. As discussed in the *Finley* case, excerpted in section D.3 below, the partial funding of certain Mapplethorpe displays, such as the Cincinnati display, was one of the main examples that caused several conservative senators to lash out at the National Endowment for the Arts in the late 1980s and in 1990 and to take measures to restrict and reduce its funding.

2. Although it is easy to suspect the motives of the court in *Cincinnati v. Contemporary Arts Center*, the case is fairly even-handed. Note that the ruling clearly suggests that the Mapplethorpe retrospective will continue with 188 works on display. Would it not have been worse if the court had found that the five controversial photographs had infected the entire exhibition, and so, when "taken as a whole," the entire exhibition was found to be obscene?

3. Pandering and Prurient Interest

The requirement that material "appeal to a prurient interest" in sex is as slippery a legal standard to apply as any other of the *Miller* standards. The basic concept is that obscene materials are materials that are designed to appeal to a lewd, leering, perverted interest in sex, not simply to a person's normal, natural, healthy interest in sex and sexuality. That said, the primary problem in applying this legal standard is that law enforcement personnel, judges, and jurors most often are normal people with normal, healthy interests (or non-interests) in sex and sexuality. Few would happily adopt the title of "pervert" to step forward and declare that certain material is obscene because "I'm a pervert and it appeals to me." Yet, somehow each player in the legal process must make a determination as to which materials are designed to appeal to a prurient interest without the aid, counsel, and advice of actual perverts.

Obscene material need not arouse a sexual interest in the average person in order to be found to "appeal to a prurient interest." *See, e.g., Ripplinger v. Collins*, 868 F.2d 1043 (9th Cir. 1989). This turns out to be a useful and practical distinction, because the most deviant, hard-core pornography most often would be a huge turn-off to the average judge or juror, but would fit the *Miller* definition in all other respects. Statutory standards and jury instructions on "prurient interest" must not allow a jury to find material obscene if it appeals to normal sexual responses, and the jury must not judge material by its own personal standards, but rather by community standards. *Id. United States v. Guglielmi*, 819 F.2d 451, 454 (4th Cir. 1987), *cert. denied*, 484 U.S. 1019 (1988), quoted in *Ripplinger*, held that the "average person comes into the test not as the object of the appeal but as its judge."

Note and Questions

1. Explain the distinction when the "average person comes into the test not as the object of the appeal but as its judge."
2. The "appeals to a prurient interest" test is the lynchpin of the obscenity standard, yet it is the most difficult to conceptualize. How is an artist to make decisions about the art that she creates on the basis of whether it has a tendency to arouse a prurient interest in the average member of a hypothetical community? Are focus groups necessary? Who would you put in your focus group? Is it practical to think that an artist would be able to adapt her work according to the input of a focus group?
3. Although the holding in *Ripplinger*—that jurors are not to make decisions based on their own personal standards—appears to respect the intentions of the Supreme Court in *Miller*, how is a juror supposed to make a decision on this basis? Is this method perfectly analogous to the reasonable person standard applied in tort law and many other areas of the law? Is a legal fiction that a juror can understand and apply the standards of an average member of her community, whether or not they are different from her own, a good standard to apply in a sensitive area such as First Amendment rights?

D. Censorship of Child Pornography

Osborne v. Ohio

495 U.S. 103, *reh'g denied*, 496 U.S. 913 (1990)*

WHITE, Justice.

In order to combat child pornography, Ohio enacted Rev. Code Ann. § 2907.323(A)(3) (Supp. 1989), which provides in pertinent part: "(A) No person shall do any of the following: ... (3) Possess or view any material or performance that shows a minor who is not the person's child or ward in a state of nudity. ..."

... Petitioner, Clyde Osborne, was convicted of violating this statute and sentenced to six months in prison, after the Columbus, Ohio, police, pursuant to a valid search, found four photographs in Osborne's home. Each photograph depicts a nude male adolescent posed in a sexually explicit position. ...

Relying on one of its earlier decisions, the Court first rejected Osborne's contention that the First Amendment prohibits the States from proscribing the private possession of child pornography. Next, the Court found that § 2907.323(A)(3) is not unconstitutionally over-broad. In so doing, the Court, relying on the statutory exceptions, read § 2907.323(A)(3) as only applying to depictions of nudity involving a lewd exhibition or graphic focus on a minor's genitals. The Court also found that scienter is an essential element of a § 2907.323(A)(3) offense. ...

I

The threshold question in this case is whether Ohio may constitutionally proscribe the possession and viewing of child pornography or whether, as Osborne argues, our decision in *Stanley v. Georgia*, 394 U.S. 557, 89 S. Ct. 1243, 22 L. Ed. 2d 542 (1969), compels the contrary result. In Stanley, we struck down a Georgia law outlawing the private possession of obscene material. We recognized that the statute impinged upon Stanley's right to receive information in the privacy of his home, and we found Georgia's justifications for its law inadequate. *Id.*, at 564-68, 89 S. Ct., at 1247-50.

Stanley should not be read too broadly. We have previously noted that Stanley was a narrow holding, *see United States v. 12 200-ft. Reels of Film*, 413 U.S. 123, 127, 93 S. Ct. 2665, 2668, 37 L. Ed. 2d 500 (1973), and, since the decision in that case, the value of permitting child pornography has been characterized as "exceedingly modest, if not de minimis." *New York v. Ferber*, 458 U.S. 747, 762, 102 S. Ct. 3348, 3357, 73 L. Ed. 2d 1113 (1982). But assuming, for the sake of argument, that Osborne has a First Amendment interest in viewing and possessing child pornography, we nonetheless find this case

---

* Footnotes omitted.

distinct from *Stanley* because the interests underlying child pornography prohibitions far exceed the interests justifying the Georgia law at issue in *Stanley.* Every court to address the issue has so concluded. *See, e.g., People v. Geever,* 122 Ill. 2d 313, 327-28, 119 Ill. Dec. 341, 347-48, 522 N.E.2d 1200, 1206-07 (1988); *Felton v. State,* 526 So. 2d 635, 637 (Ala. Ct. Crim. App.), aff'd sub nom. *Ex parte Felton,* 526 So. 2d 638, 641 (Ala. 1988); *State v. Davis,* 53 Wash. App. 502, 505, 768 P.2d 499, 501 (1989); *Savery v. Texas,* 767 S.W. 2d 242, 245 (Tex. App. 1989); *United States v. Boffardi,* 684 F. Supp. 1263, 1267 (S.D.N.Y. 1988).

In *Stanley,* Georgia primarily sought to proscribe the private possession of obscenity because it was concerned that obscenity would poison the minds of its viewers. 394 U.S., at 565, 89 S. Ct., at 1248. We responded that "[w]hatever the power of the state to control public dissemination of ideas inimical to the public morality, it cannot constitutionally premise legislation on the desirability of controlling a person's private thoughts." *Id.,* at 566, 89 S. Ct., at 1248. The difference here is obvious: the State does not rely on a paternalistic interest in regulating Osborne's mind. Rather, Ohio has enacted § 2907.323(A)(3) in order to protect the victims of child pornography; it hopes to destroy a market for the exploitative use of children.

"It is evident beyond the need for elaboration that a State's interest in "safeguarding the physical and psychological well-being of a minor" is "compelling." ... The legislative judgment, as well as the judgment found in relevant literature, is that the use of children as subjects of pornographic materials is harmful to the physiological, emotional, and mental health of the child. That judgment, we think, easily passes muster under the First Amendment." *Ferber,* 458 U.S., at 756-58, 102 S. Ct., at 3354-55 (citations omitted). It is also surely reasonable for the State to conclude that it will decrease the production of child pornography if it penalizes those who possess and view the product, thereby decreasing demand. In *Ferber,* where we upheld a New York statute outlawing the distribution of child pornography, we found a similar argument persuasive: "[t]he advertising and selling of child pornography provide an economic motive for and are thus an integral part of the production of such materials, an activity illegal throughout the Nation. 'It rarely has been suggested that the constitutional freedom for speech and press extends its immunity to speech or writing used as an integral part of conduct in violation of a valid criminal statute.'" *Id.,* at 761-62, 102 S. Ct., at 3356-57 quoting *Giboney v. Empire Storage & Ice Co.,* 336 U.S. 490, 498, 69 S. Ct. 684, 688, 93 L. Ed. 834 (1949).

Osborne contends that the State should use other measures, besides penalizing possession, to dry up the child pornography market. Osborne points out that in *Stanley* we rejected Georgia's argument that its prohibition on obscenity possession was a necessary incident to its proscription on obscenity distribution. 394 U.S., at 567-68, 89 S. Ct., at 1249-50. This holding, however, must be viewed in light of the weak interests asserted by the State in that case. *Stanley* itself emphasized that we did not "mean to express any opinion on statutes making criminal possession of other types of printed, filmed, or recorded materials. . . . In such cases, compelling reasons may exist for overriding the right of the individual to possess those materials." *Id.*, at 4568, n.11, 89 S. Ct., at 1249, n.11.

Given the importance of the State's interest in protecting the victims of child pornography, we cannot fault Ohio for attempting to stamp out this vice at all levels in the distribution chain. According to the State, since the time of our decision in *Ferber*, much of the child pornography market has been driven underground; as a result, it is now difficult, if not impossible, to solve the child pornography problem by only attacking production and distribution. Indeed, 19 States have found it necessary to proscribe the possession of this material.

Other interests also support the Ohio law. First, as *Ferber* recognized, the materials produced by child pornographers permanently record the victim's abuse. The pornography's continued existence causes the child victims continuing harm by haunting the children in years to come. 458 U.S., at 759, 102 S. Ct., at 3355. The State's ban on possession and viewing encourages the possessors of these materials to destroy them. Second, encouraging the destruction of these materials is also desirable because evidence suggests that pedophiles use child pornography to seduce other children into sexual activity.

Given the gravity of the State's interests in this context, we find that Ohio may constitutionally proscribe the possession and viewing of child pornography. . . .

The Ohio statute, on its face, purports to prohibit the possession of "nude" photographs of minors. We have stated that depictions of nudity, without more, constitute protected expression. *See Ferber*, supra, at 765, n.8, 102 S. Ct., at 3359, n.18. Relying on this observation, Osborne argues that the statute as written is substantially over-broad. We are skeptical of this claim because, in light of the statute's exemptions and "proper purposes" provisions, the statute may not be substantially over-broad under our cases. However that may be, Osborne's overbreadth challenge, in any event, fails because the statute, as construed by the Ohio Supreme Court on Osborne's direct appeal, plainly survives overbreadth scrutiny. Under the Ohio Supreme Court reading, the statute prohibits "the possession or viewing of material or performance of a minor who is in a state of nudity, where such nudity constitutes a lewd exhibition or involves a graphic focus on the genitals, and where the person depicted is neither the child nor the ward of the person charged." 37 Ohio St. 3d, at 252, 525 N.E. 2d, at 1368. By limiting the statute's operation in this manner, the Ohio Supreme Court avoided penalizing persons for viewing or possessing innocuous photographs of naked children. We have upheld similar language against overbreadth challenges in the past. In *Ferber*, we affirmed a conviction under a New York statute that made it a crime to promote the "'lewd exhibition of [a child's] genitals.'" 458 U.S., at 751, 102 S. Ct., at 3351. We noted that "[t]he term 'lewd exhibition of the genitals' is not unknown in this area and, indeed, was given in *Miller v. California*, 413 U.S. 15, 93 S. Ct. 2607, 37 L. Ed. 2d 419 (1973)] as an example of a permissible regulation." *Id.*, at 765, 102 S. Ct., at 3359.

The Ohio Supreme Court also concluded that the State had to establish scienter in order to prove a violation of § 2907.323(A)(3) based on the Ohio default statute specifying that recklessness applies when another statutory provision lacks an intent specification. The statute on its face lacks a mens rea requirement, but that omission brings into play and is cured by another law that plainly satisfies the requirement laid down in *Ferber* that prohibitions on child pornography include some element of scienter. 458 U.S., at 765, 102 S. Ct., at 3359. . . .

To conclude, although we find Osborne's First Amendment arguments unpersuasive, we reverse his conviction and remand for a new trial in order to ensure that Osborne's conviction stemmed from a finding that the State had proved each of the elements of § 29007.323(A)(3).

So ordered.

Note and Questions

1. Child pornography is different from pornography featuring adults. Very few people would attempt to argue that child porn has any redeeming value of a scientific, educational, or artistic nature. It is far from a victimless crime. It is out of this context that the Court in *Osborne* finds that mere possession of child pornography in the total privacy of one's home still is actionable. Do you agree with the public policies used and the way they are marshaled in support of the outcome in *Osborne*?

2. *Osborne* states that a mens rea or scienter requirement must be met for conviction under child pornography statutes. What nature of guilty mind should be sufficient to meet the requirement — a desire to create child pornography, to distribute material, to support and actively participate in the market by paying for pornographic material, to be found using the material, or simply to knowingly possess the material?

Amy Adler, Inverting the First Amendment

149 U. Penn. L. Rev. 921 (Apr. 2001)*

The sexual abuse of a child to create pornography is a repulsive crime. That is something we can agree on. It is no wonder then that we as a society have "declared war" on child pornography and that Congress, prosecutors, and the courts have rushed into the battle. In fact, it seems at times as if they have been striving to outdo one another in being tough on child pornography, as if the interplay between legislatures, prosecutors, and courts were a contest in moral outrage.

---

* Footnotes omitted.

This contest has revealed a strangely acquiescent Supreme Court. Typically, in First Amendment decisions, when the Court eliminates a category of expression from constitutional protection, it carefully defines the speech that can be banned; the definition then serves as a limit on legislative enactments. This method recurs throughout free speech jurisprudence. It is, for example, the approach taken by the Court in the subversive advocacy cases, which evolved into the current *Brandenburg* "incitement to imminent lawless action" standard. It is also the approach that the Court used in its obscenity jurisprudence, in which it struggled for years, beginning with *Roth v. United States*, to create a precise constitutional definition of the "obscene."

In defining "child pornography," however, the Court has adopted a peculiarly passive pose: since it first declared in the 1982 case of *New York v. Ferber* that child pornography was a category of speech unprotected by the First Amendment, the Court has never attempted to define "child pornography" itself. Rather, it has merely upheld the statutory definitions it has confronted.

One explanation for the Court's passive pose in defining child pornography could be that it has so far only upheld child pornography statutes, whereas in *Brandenburg*, for example, it invalidated a statute and then devised a test for dividing protected and unprotected speech. It is arguable that striking down a statute requires an explanation of constitutional limits in a way that upholding a statute might not. But this was not the case in *Roth*, the Court's first obscenity case. Even though the Court upheld both the statute and Roth's conviction under it, the Court nonetheless created a constitutional definition of obscenity, one that it would revisit and reshape in later cases. The Court's approach to child pornography jurisprudence has been remarkably different. Aside from declaring the requirement of a few standard protective features (such as the requisite scienter or the need for a statute to specifically define the prohibited material), the Court has primarily accepted legislative enactments and then sought to justify them within the First Amendment. With Congress and states pushing further and further for limits on child pornography and with prosecutors pressing the confines of the law, this lack of a clear boundary — and the suggestion of some Justices that they would entertain even broader definitions of child pornography than current ones — has made the Court's work seem like an invitation to statutory expansion and prosecutorial enterprise.

A. THE LAW'S ELUSIVE TARGET

Although the Supreme Court in *Ferber* announced five reasons supporting the exclusion of child pornography from First Amendment protection, the primary thrust of these rationales was that child pornography must be prohibited because of the harm done to children in its production. This notion — that the production of child pornography requires an act of child abuse — was the key to the Court's reasoning. This urgent rationale — to protect children from abuse — explains why the Court's child pornography jurisprudence departs so dramatically from the contours of obscenity law: obscenity law is based on the worthlessness of certain expression, whereas child pornography law excludes speech because of the grievous crime from which it stems.

Thus, unlike obscenity law, child pornography law makes no exception for works of "serious literary, artistic, political or scientific value." As the Court explained, a work may possess serious value, but that "bears no connection to the issue of whether or not a child has been physically or psychologically harmed in the production of the work." Unlike obscenity law, child pornography law does not require the trier of fact to judge a work as a whole, but allows a work to be evaluated in isolated passages and out of context. Unlike obscenity law, child pornography law allows for the prosecution of mere home possession, as opposed to distribution or production, of a suspect picture. If the State finds one photograph in a drawer in a defendant's home, that is enough to convict. As the Court explained, the underlying crime of child sexual abuse entitles the states to "greater leeway in the regulation" of child pornography than of obscenity. This compelling rationale justifies the extreme measures that child pornography law permits.

But a strange thing has happened. As the crisis of child sexual abuse has escalated, the definition of what constitutes "child pornography" also has expanded dramatically, in a direction that makes it increasingly unrelated to the harm that the law was designed to combat. In fact, the direction of the law's expansion has rendered it more constitutionally problematic from two different perspectives. First, it presents obvious problems of vagueness and overbreadth, thereby threatening a wide array of pictures of children that ought to be protected. Second, as the definition has grown, it has become so capacious that it allows for the prosecution of pictures in which there was no underlying act of child molestation. Thus, the definition of child pornography has evolved in a way that has less and less to do with the atrocious danger that justified the law's novel and unyielding ways. Its expansion has therefore rendered child pornography law internally disjointed and constitutionally flawed.

To illustrate the problem, imagine two different photographs. The first is horrible: it depicts a naked ten-year-old girl being fondled by an adult. The child had been kidnapped, imprisoned by an underworld child sex ring, and used to make pornography. The pornographers sell the picture to pedophiles around the world.

Now imagine a second photograph: it is taken while a ten-year-old girl wearing a bikini plays on the beach with her mother. Unbeknownst to either the girl or her mother, a man far away on the beach has a camera with a telephoto lens. He takes a picture of the little girl, zooming in on her genitals, which are covered only by her bathing suit. The girl and her mother never see the man; they never know the photo has been taken. The photographer, who finds the resulting picture sexually stimulating, keeps the photograph to himself, in his secret stash of "child pornography." He never shows it to anyone else.

This first photograph I described is precisely the kind of picture that child pornography law was intended to combat: made under horrifying conditions, the photograph is the result, and indeed the goal, of a crime of child sexual abuse. It is the product of what the Supreme Court labeled the "low-profile, clandestine" child pornography industry. The content of the picture — a child being molested — exemplifies the definition of "child pornography" as set out in the Supreme Court's child pornography jurisprudence.

But what about the second picture? The girl playing on the beach with her mother was never attacked or abused. There is no underlying harmful act to prevent. The girl in the first photograph was held in sexual slavery and molested. The girl on the beach never even knows of her violation. Far from being imprisoned in a "low-profile, clandestine industry" of the sort the Court hoped to combat through child pornography law, the girl was happily playing with her mother, unaware that she entered the mind, let alone the lens frame, of the photographer. We may not like that this picture has been taken of the girl. And we may not like the way the photographer thinks of the photo, nor the way he thinks of the little girl. These are troubling concerns. But would it be correct to say that the picture is "child pornography" and to bring all the attendant severity of child pornography law to bear on its possessor?

The developments in the law of child pornography that I will analyze below indicate that the answer is yes. These developments have allowed for the prosecution of possessors of pictures such as the second one described above, pictures taken with no underlying act of abuse.

Why has the law expanded in this direction? The answer has to do with the peculiar nature of pedophilic desire. The problem is that pedophiles like a far wider range of pictures than the explicit pornography that must be produced through acts of abuse. Pedophiles also like pictures of children just being children — doing gymnastics and twirling batons, playing in swimming pools and on playgrounds, or even pictures of children bundled up in heavy winter coats.

In fact, the pictures that pedophiles enjoy and find sexually stimulating are often the very pictures of children that society extols and values. Thus the Arizona Court of Appeals considered a child pornography case in 1994 involving pictures of children in "normal situations and poses," such as store advertisements and pictures of girls in "ballet costumes and in dance class." The defendant had admitted to sexually fantasizing about the images. One recent target of a child pornography investigation was a photographer who supposedly found sexual stimulation from pictures he took of "boys walking to school and riding their bikes." As a medical researcher explained, some pedophiles "look at the children's underwear section of a Sears catalogue and become aroused." An assistant state attorney in Florida commented, "'[t]o most of us, a picture of a small boy in a bathtub is OK. . . . But . . . what is not pornographic to most of us, is pornographic to [a pedophile].'"

In fact, the mundane innocence of pictures is often their draw. Pedophiles may prefer "innocent" pictures. For example, one distributor of child pornography advertised his wares, such as a videotape of little girls wearing their panties and bathing suits, as "so revealing it's almost like seeing them naked (some say even better)." According to certain theorists, the stimulation derived from a picture can be inversely proportional to its overtly sexualized nature. It is often the very innocence — the sexual naivete — of the child subject that is sexually stimulating. As a child pornography investigator explained, "Seldom do photo labs — or investigators — find pictures that are blatantly pornographic." The Chief Postal Inspector testified before Congress in 1995: "Often, we conduct searches in our investigations and we find photographs of children who are not involved in sexual activity." Yet the Inspector went on to describe these nonsexual pictures as "photographs taken by pedophiles for their own gratification." In fact, government investigators admit that they have investigated pictures that "clearly have no sexual content."

In 1986 the Attorney General's Commission on Pornography noted these problems in a footnote to its Report on Pornography:

> There is also evidence that commercially produced pictures of children in erotic settings, or in non-erotic settings that are perceived by some adults as erotic, are collected and used by pedophiles. . . . [F]or example, advertisements for underwear might be used for vastly different purposes than those intended by the photographer or publisher. . . .

Yet the Attorney General's Report also indicated that although it was important to identify this kind of material, "[t]here is little that can be done about" it. As we shall see, legislatures did not agree. The push to criminalize this sector of "child pornography" was already underway. Thus, the law presses inexorably in the direction of prohibiting more and more of this speech that is susceptible to alternate interpretations. And it chases a criterion — appeal to pedophiles — that is a poor proxy for whether children were abused in the production of the material.

The problem we confront in child pornography law is therefore not the familiar free speech puzzle: that it is difficult to draw the line between bad speech and good, that they exist on a hazy continuum. Instead, the problem is that bad speech and good may often be one and the same thing: the cute pictures of our children playing on playgrounds or riding their bikes may be precisely the same pictures that most appeal to the pedophile. In fact, the peculiar quality of pedophilic desire may make the governance of child pornography an impossible task. In the following Part, I explore how the law has stretched to capture this elusive target of pedophilic desire, and how, in doing so, it has come to threaten pictures of children that ought to be protected.

B. THE EXPANDING DEFINITION OF "CHILD PORNOGRAPHY"

1. Doctrinal Growth

The problem began in *Ferber* when the Supreme Court approved the statutory definition of child "sexual conduct" that included not only obvious sexual acts, such as "'intercourse, sexual bestiality [or] sadomasochistic abuse,'" but also "'lewd exhibition of the genitals.'" It would seem to be a relatively straightforward task to determine, for example, whether a photograph depicts a child engaged in intercourse, and it would also seem obvious that a child pictured in such a sexual act is the victim of abuse. But what does "lewd exhibition of the genitals" mean? How does it differ from an "innocuous" photograph of a naked child—a family photograph of a child taking a bath, or an artistic masterpiece portraying a nude child model? As I will explain below, it is at this margin of child pornography law, where its prohibitions threaten "innocent" speech, that the law poses the most significant danger of overbreadth and its resultant chill. It is also where the law bears the least connection to its foundational rationale. And yet, it is in this haziest realm that the definition of "child pornography" has grown.

The Supreme Court and lower federal courts since *Ferber* have tolerated statutes that define this margin of child "sexual conduct" in increasingly broad and subjective terms. Each subtle reiteration of the definition of "lewd" or "lascivious exhibition of the genitals" since *Ferber* has expanded it. If we pushed the case law to the extreme, it seems to threaten all pictures of unclothed children, whether "lewd" or not, and even pictures of clothed children, if they meet the increasingly hazy definition of "lascivious" or "lewd." . . .

Recent developments in art, as well as recent prosecutions, suggest that the Court seriously underestimated the threat posed to artistic expression. Over the last decade, just as the law has expanded, child sexuality has emerged as a major subject in artistic culture. From the best-selling high-art photographer Sally Mann, who takes nudes of her prepubescent children in poses that many people consider erotic, to the soaring craze for artist Henry Darger, the "'Poussin of pedophilia,'" child sexuality has become central to contemporary art.

The threat to artistic expression is more urgent because of another facet of child pornography law: the Court's refusal to make an exception in the definition of "child pornography" for works of "serious literary, artistic, political, or scientific value." It has long been a principle of adult obscenity law that no matter how shocking or how offensive a sexually explicit work might otherwise be, it should be protected speech if it demonstrates serious artistic value. Although the defense of serious value has not yet been raised before the Court in a child pornography case, the Court has noted in dicta that the whole notion of whether a work is art—a central consideration when dealing with adult obscenity—is extraneous to the problem of child pornography. The *Ferber* Court observed: "It is irrelevant to the child [who has been abused] whether or not the material . . . has . . . artistic value." Justice White remarked that a work which has serious value "may nevertheless embody the hardest core of child pornography." In a separate opinion, Justice O'Connor argued the point further. She wrote: "The audience's appreciation of the depiction is simply irrelevant to [the] interest in protecting children. . . ."

Coupled with the expanding definition of child pornography as chronicled above, this rejection of an exception for works of serious value means that many contemporary artworks have no protection under the First Amendment. Consider, for example, photographer Sally Mann's nudes of her children. Although Mann has so far escaped prosecution, her work would appear to fit squarely within the definition of child pornography as courts have developed it. For example, a photograph of Mann's daughter entitled Venus After School pictures the naked child languorously spread on a divan in the precise position of Manet's famous portrait of a prostitute. In Mann's portrait of her son Jesse, entitled Popsicle Drips, the artist focuses on the young boy's naked torso. The boy's genitals are the centerpiece of the picture, which is cropped at the knees and at the shoulders. Certainly these works seem to fit easily within recent, expansive interpretations by courts of the definition of "child pornography."

Though these photographs may be disturbing, they are also rich with artistic resonance. Popsicle Drips alludes to a famous work by acclaimed photographer Edward Weston of his son Neil's nude body. Both Mann's and Weston's pictures recall classical sculptures of kouroi, youthful naked figures. Even Mann's photograph Venus After School, with its provocative title, has rich artistic allusions. The photograph's composition makes direct reference to the Manet portrait, as well as to Titian's great masterpiece, the Venus of Urbino. If Mann or other artists like her were prosecuted for child pornography violations, it seems that there would be no protection for such work under existing child pornography law. Only an exception for value could save them, an exception the Court has so far refused to draw.

Other artists have already been arrested. For instance, art photographer Alice Sims was arrested and her two small children were seized when a lab developed some of her pictures. Recent child pornography prosecutions against mainstream targets suggest just how far the law has drifted: both Alabama and Tennessee prosecuted the bookstore chain Barnes & Noble for selling photography books by artists Jock Sturges, whose work hangs in the Metropolitan Museum of Art, and David Hamilton. The FBI raided and ransacked Sturges's studio in 1993, but a grand jury refused to indict him for child pornography violations. In 1997, Oklahoma brought child pornography charges against a video store that rented the Academy Award-winning film The Tin Drum, based on a novel by Gunter Grass. Hollywood studios reportedly shunned the remake of the film Lolita based on fears of criminal prosecution; despite the filmmakers' careful use of body doubles for all controversial scenes, it took a year, as well as significant cutting, to find a studio willing to release the film.

Perhaps there should be no exception for value in child pornography law. Perhaps harm to child participants should render any resulting artistic value irrelevant to legal analysis. But to understand the true costs of the decision not to except works of value, we must assess this stance in light of the evolving definition of "child pornography" and the growing artistic interest in depicting children's bodies. Taken together, these developments mean that even case-by-case analysis, a method the Court thought certain to cure "whatever overbreadth may exist," will not protect valuable artistic speech that depicts child nudity. A far more significant amount of artistic speech than the Court has acknowledged is vulnerable under child pornography law. . . .

Although child pornography law still claims to be aimed at protecting children from abuse in the production of the material, the category no longer does what it says it does. So I ask: what does it actually do? What is the rationale for banning pictures of children who were not harmed in the production? Why do we regulate images that appeal to the lascivious interests of pedophile viewers, but do not stem from acts of abuse? Implicit in our regulation of such material is the view that there is another harm to these pictures.

Child pornography has become a thought crime. Quite simply, we do not like the way people think about certain pictures of children. This is evident in the ever-expanding definition of "lascivious exhibition of the genitals" and the attempt of courts and legislatures, as I demonstrated in Part II, to police pictures that appeal to the sexual fantasies of pedophiles, regardless of how those pictures were produced.

The law demands that we examine pictures to determine how a pedophile would see them; we then criminalize these pictures, or not, depending on that viewpoint. As amici argued before the Supreme Court in *Knox*, the question becomes, does the picture "invite pedophiles to fantasize"? Indeed, the law acknowledges that pictures may be susceptible to multiple interpretations. It may not be obvious whether pictures are child pornography. Therefore, we must "study" them and conjecture the possible response of the pedophile voyeur. But once our interpretation depends on the pedophile's imagined response to the picture, we have begun to police thoughts and fantasy, not actions. The harm of the pictures no longer turns on what happened to the child. It now occurs in the possibility of seeing a picture in a certain way, in how someone might perceive the child. The determination of whether a picture is child pornography has grown increasingly bound up in our projections of whether these pictures will permit pedophiles to fantasize about them. Thus, child pornography law has begun to police speech based on how people may respond to it. This is in direct contravention of traditional First Amendment tenets. . . .

The desire to erase the distinction between speech and conduct is at the core of many censorship movements. When it comes to pornography or hate speech or violence in the media, we repeatedly hear this argument: speech is so powerful that it will conjure up what it depicts, as if a picture carried within it the thing it represented, or operated as an imperative to repeat the act it portrayed.

This view has deep cultural roots. Despite our strong free tradition to the contrary, there is an equally strong cultural tradition from which these new developments in child pornography law have sprung. The tendency to equate speech with what it represents is an ancient instinct. It is evident, for example, in the widespread belief among native peoples that a picture captures your soul. It is also evident in the longstanding worship of images as religious icons or the belief that certain pictures have talismanic properties. Such uses depend on a fusion between speech and its subject or its effects.

The law of free speech has long struggled against this view of representation. For a while, in the early subversive advocacy cases, the Court succumbed to it. Political anxieties of the day led the Court to compromise the First Amendment. But later decisions rejected this view of representation. By insisting on the division between speech and what it represents or causes, modern First Amendment law marked a triumph of rationality over religious, magical, or superstitious views of speech.

At times of great cultural anxiety, however, this other view of speech reasserts itself. Such is the case with the crisis of child pornography and the law that has grown up to combat it. A fear of speech, an urge to fuse representation with reality, lurks as a dark undercurrent in our rationalistic free speech jurisprudence.

Ashcroft v. Free Speech Coalition

535 U.S. 234 (2002)*

Kennedy, Justice.

We consider in this case whether the Child Pornography Prevention Act of 1996 (CPPA), 18 U.S.C. § 2251 et seq., abridges the freedom of speech. The CPPA extends the federal prohibition against child pornography to sexually explicit images that appear to depict minors but were produced without using any real children. The statute prohibits, in specific circumstances, possessing or distributing these images, which may be created by using adults who look like minors or by using computer imaging. The new technology, according to Congress, makes it possible to create realistic images of children who do not exist. *See* Congressional Findings, notes following 18 U.S.C. § 2251.

By prohibiting child pornography that does not depict an actual child, the statute goes beyond *New York v. Ferber*, 458 U.S. 747, 102 S. Ct. 3348, 73 L. Ed. 2d 1113 (1982), which distinguished child pornography from other sexually explicit speech because of the State's interest in protecting the children exploited by the production process. *See id.*, at 758, 102 S. Ct. 3348. As a general rule, pornography can be banned only if obscene, but under *Ferber*, pornography showing minors can be proscribed whether or not the images are obscene under the definition set forth in *Miller v. California*, 413 U.S. 15, 93 S. Ct. 2607, 37 L. Ed. 2d 419 (1973). *Ferber* recognized that "[t]he *Miller* standard, like all general definitions of what may be banned as obscene, does not reflect the State's particular and more compelling interest in prosecuting those who promote the sexual exploitation of children." 458 U.S., at 761, 102 S. Ct. 3348.

While we have not had occasion to consider the question, we may assume that the apparent age of persons engaged in sexual conduct is relevant to whether a depiction offends community standards. Pictures of young children engaged in certain acts might be obscene where similar depictions of adults, or perhaps even older adolescents, would not. The CPPA, however, is not directed at speech that is obscene; Congress has proscribed those materials through a

---

* Footnotes and some citations omitted.

separate statute. 18 U.S.C. §§ 1460-66. Like the law in *Ferber*, the CPPA seeks to reach beyond obscenity, and it makes no attempt to conform to the *Miller* standard. For instance, the statute would reach visual depictions, such as movies, even if they have redeeming social value.

The principal question to be resolved, then, is whether the CPPA is constitutional where it proscribes a significant universe of speech that is neither obscene under *Miller* nor child pornography under *Ferber*.

I

Before 1996, Congress defined child pornography as the type of depictions at issue in *Ferber*, images made using actual minors. 18 U.S.C. § 2252 (1994 ed.). The CPPA retains that prohibition at 18 U.S.C. § 2256(8)(A) and adds three other prohibited categories of speech, of which the first, § 2256(8)(B), and the third, § 2256(8)(D), are at issue in this case. Section 2256(8)(B) prohibits "any visual depiction, including any photograph, film, video, picture, or computer or computer-generated image or picture" that "is, or appears to be, of a minor engaging in sexually explicit conduct." The prohibition on "any visual depiction" does not depend at all on how the image is produced. The section captures a range of depictions, sometimes called "virtual child pornography," which include computer-generated images, as well as images produced by more traditional means. For instance, the literal terms of the statute embrace a Renaissance painting depicting a scene from classical mythology, a "picture" that "appears to be, of a minor engaging in sexually explicit conduct." The statute also prohibits Hollywood movies, filmed without any child actors, if a jury believes an actor "appears to be" a minor engaging in "actual or simulated . . . sexual intercourse." § 2256(2).

These images do not involve, let alone harm, any children in the production process; but Congress decided the materials threaten children in other, less direct, ways. Pedophiles might use the materials to encourage children to participate in sexual activity. "[A] child who is reluctant to engage in sexual activity with an adult, or to pose for sexually explicit photographs, can sometimes be convinced by viewing depictions of other children 'having fun' participating in such activity." Congressional Finding note (3), notes following § 2251. Furthermore, pedophiles might "whet their own sexual appetites" with the pornographic images, "thereby increasing the creation and distribution of child pornography and the sexual abuse and exploitation of actual children." *Id.*, Findings (4), (10)(B). Under these rationales, harm flows from the content of the images, not from the means of their production. In addition, Congress identified another problem created by computer-generated images: their existence can make it harder to prosecute pornographers who do use real minors. *See id.*, Finding (6)(A). As imaging technology improves, Congress found, it becomes more difficult to prove that a particular picture was produced using actual children. To ensure that defendants possessing child pornography using real minors cannot evade prosecution, Congress extended the ban to virtual child pornography.

Section 2256(8)(C) prohibits a more common and lower tech means of creating virtual images, known as computer morphing. Rather than creating original images, pornographers can alter innocent pictures of real children so that the children appear to be engaged in sexual activity. Although morphed images may fall within the definition of virtual child pornography, they implicate the interests of real children and are in that sense closer to the images in *Ferber*. Respondents do not challenge this provision, and we do not consider it.

Respondents do challenge § 2256(8)(D). Like the text of the "appears to be" provision, the sweep of this provision is quite broad. Section 2256(8)(D) defines child pornography to include any sexually explicit image that was "advertised, promoted, presented, described, or distributed in such a manner that conveys the impression" it depicts "a minor engaging in sexually explicit conduct." One Committee Report identified the provision as directed at sexually explicit images pandered as child pornography. *See* S. Rep. No. 104-358, p. 22 (1996) ("This provision prevents child pornographers and pedophiles from exploiting prurient interests in child sexuality and sexual activity through the production or distribution of pornographic material which is intentionally pandered as child pornography"). The statute is not so limited in its reach, however, as it punishes even those possessors who took no part in pandering. Once a work has been described as child pornography, the taint remains on the speech in the hands of subsequent possessors, making possession unlawful even though the content otherwise would not be objectionable.

Fearing that the CPPA threatened the activities of its members, respondent Free Speech Coalition and others challenged the statute in the United States District Court for the Northern District of California. The Coalition, a California trade association for the adult-entertainment industry, alleged that its members did not use minors in their sexually explicit works, but they believed some of these materials might fall within the CPPA's expanded definition of child pornography. The other respondents are Bold Type, Inc., the publisher of a book advocating the nudist lifestyle; Jim Gingerich, a painter of nudes; and Ron Raffaelli, a photographer specializing in erotic images. Respondents alleged that the "appears to be" and "conveys the impression" provisions are overbroad and vague, chilling them from producing works protected by the First Amendment. The District Court disagreed and granted summary judgment to the Government. The court dismissed the overbreadth claim because it was "highly unlikely" that any "adaptations of sexual works like 'Romeo and Juliet,' . . . will be treated as 'criminal contraband.'" App. to Pet. for Cert. 62a-63a.

The Court of Appeals for the Ninth Circuit reversed. *See* 198 F.3d 1083 (1999). The court reasoned that the Government could not prohibit speech because of its tendency to persuade viewers to commit illegal acts. The court held the CPPA to be substantially overbroad because it bans materials that are neither obscene nor produced by the exploitation of real children as in *New York v. Ferber*, 458 U.S. 747, 102 S. Ct. 3348, 73 L. Ed. 2d 1113 (1982). Judge Ferguson dissented on the ground that virtual images, like obscenity and real child pornography, should be treated as a category of speech unprotected by the First Amendment. 198 F.3d, at 1097. The Court of Appeals voted to deny the petition for rehearing en banc, over the dissent of three judges. *See* 220 F.3d 1113 (2000).

While the Ninth Circuit found the CPPA invalid on its face, four other Courts of Appeals have sustained it. *See United States v. Fox,* 248 F.3d 394 (C.A. 5 2001); *United States v. Mento,* 231 F.3d 912 (C.A. 4 2000); *United States v. Acheson,* 195 F.3d 645 (C.A. 11 1999); *United States v. Hilton,* 167 F.3d 61(C.A. 1), cert. denied, 528 U.S. 844, 120 S. Ct. 115, 145 L. Ed. 2d 98 (1999). We granted certiorari. 531 U.S. 1124, 121 S. Ct. 876, 148 L. Ed. 2d 788 (2001).

II

The First Amendment commands, "Congress shall make no law ... abridging the freedom of speech." The government may violate this mandate in many ways, e.g., *Rosenberger v. Rector and Visitors of Univ. of Va.,* 515 U.S. 819, 115 S. Ct. 2510, 132 L. Ed. 2d 700 (1995); *Keller v. State Bar of Cal.,* 496 U.S. 1, 110 S. Ct. 2228, 110 L. Ed. 2d 1 (1990), but a law imposing criminal penalties on protected speech is a stark example of speech suppression. The CPPA's penalties are indeed severe. A first offender may be imprisoned for 15 years. § 2252A(b)(1). A repeat offender faces a prison sentence of not less than 5 years and not more than 30 years in prison. *Ibid.* While even minor punishments can chill protected speech, *see Wooley v. Maynard,* 430 U.S. 705, 97 S. Ct. 1428, 51 L. Ed. 2d 752 (1977), this case provides a textbook example of why we permit facial challenges to statutes that burden expression. With these severe penalties in force, few legitimate movie producers or book publishers, or few other speakers in any capacity, would risk distributing images in or near the uncertain reach of this law. The Constitution gives significant protection from overbroad laws that chill speech within the First Amendment's vast and privileged sphere. Under this principle, the CPPA is unconstitutional on its face if it prohibits a substantial amount of protected expression. *See Broadrick v. Oklahoma,* 413 U.S. 601, 612, 93 S. Ct. 2908, 37 L. Ed. 2d 830 (1973).

The sexual abuse of a child is a most serious crime and an act repugnant to the moral instincts of a decent people. In its legislative findings, Congress recognized that there are subcultures of persons who harbor illicit desires for children and commit criminal acts to gratify the impulses. *See* Congressional Findings, notes following § 2251; *see also* U.S. Dept. of Health and Human Services, Administration on Children, Youth and Families, Child Maltreatment 1999 (estimating that 93,000 children were victims of sexual abuse in 1999). Congress also found that surrounding the serious offenders are those who flirt with these impulses and trade pictures and written accounts of sexual activity with young children.

Congress may pass valid laws to protect children from abuse, and it has. *E.g.,* 18 U.S.C. §§ 2241, 2251. The prospect of crime, however, by itself does not justify laws suppressing protected speech. *See Kingsley Int'l Pictures Corp. v. Regents of Univ. of N.Y.,* 360 U.S. 684, 689, 79 S. Ct. 1362, 3 L. Ed. 2d

1512 (1959) ("Among free men, the deterrents ordinarily to be applied to prevent crime are education and punishment for violations of the law, not abridgment of the rights of free speech" (internal quotation marks and citation omitted)). It is also well established that speech may not be prohibited because it concerns subjects offending our sensibilities. *See FCC v. Pacifica Foundation*, 438 U.S. 726, 745, 98 S. Ct. 3026, 57 L. Ed. 2d 1073 (1978) ("[T]he fact that society may find speech offensive is not a sufficient reason for suppressing it"); *see also Reno v. American Civil Liberties Union*, 521 U.S. 844, 874, 117 S. Ct. 2329, 138 L. Ed. 2d 874 (1997) ("In evaluating the free speech rights of adults, we have made it perfectly clear that '[s]exual expression which is indecent but not obscene is protected by the First Amendment'") (quoting *Sable Communications of Cal., Inc. v. FCC*, 492 U.S. 115, 126, 109 S. Ct. 2829, 106 L. Ed. 2d 93 (1989)); *Carey v. Population Services Int'l*, 431 U.S. 678, 701, 97 S. Ct. 2010, 52 L. Ed. 2d 675 (1977) ("[T]he fact that protected speech may be offensive to some does not justify its suppression").

As a general principle, the First Amendment bars the government from dictating what we see or read or speak or hear. The freedom of speech has its limits; it does not embrace certain categories of speech, including defamation, incitement, obscenity, and pornography produced with real children. *See Simon & Schuster, Inc. v. Members of N.Y. State Crime Victims Bd.*, 502 U.S. 105, 127, 112 S. Ct. 501, 116 L. Ed. 2d 476 (1991) (Kennedy, J., concurring). While these categories may be prohibited without violating the First Amendment, none of them includes the speech prohibited by the CPPA. In his dissent from the opinion of the Court of Appeals, Judge Ferguson recognized this to be the law and proposed that virtual child pornography should be regarded as an additional category of unprotected speech. *See* 198 F.3d, at 1101. It would be necessary for us to take this step to uphold the statute.

As we have noted, the CPPA is much more than a supplement to the existing federal prohibition on obscenity. Under *Miller v. California*, 413 U.S. 15, 93 S. Ct. 2607, 37 L. Ed. 2d 419 (1973), the Government must prove that the work, taken as a whole, appeals to the prurient interest, is patently offensive in light of community standards, and lacks serious literary, artistic, political, or scientific value. *Id.*, at 24, 93 S. Ct. 2607. The CPPA, however, extends to images that appear to depict a minor engaging in sexually explicit activity without regard to the *Miller* requirements. The materials need not appeal to the prurient interest. Any depiction of sexually explicit activity, no matter how it is presented, is proscribed. The CPPA applies to a picture in a psychology manual, as well as a movie depicting the horrors of sexual abuse. It is not necessary, moreover, that the image be patently offensive. Pictures of what appear to be 17-year-olds engaging in sexually explicit activity do not in every case contravene community standards.

The CPPA prohibits speech despite its serious literary, artistic, political, or scientific value. The statute proscribes the visual depiction of an idea — that of teenagers engaging in sexual activity — that is a fact of modern society and has been a theme in art and literature throughout the ages. Under the CPPA, images are prohibited so long as the persons appear to be under 18 years of age. 18 U.S.C. § 2256(1). This is higher than the legal age for marriage in many States, as well as the age at which persons may consent to sexual relations. *See* § 2243(a) (age of consent in the federal maritime and territorial jurisdiction is 16); U.S. National Survey of State Laws 384–88 (R. Leiter ed., 3d ed. 1999) (48 States permit 16-year-olds to marry with parental consent); W. Eskridge & N. Hunter, *Sexuality, Gender, and the Law* 1021-1022 (1997) (in 39 States and the District of Columbia, the age of consent is 16 or younger). It is, of course, undeniable that some youths engage in sexual activity before the legal age, either on their own inclination or because they are victims of sexual abuse.

Both themes — teenage sexual activity and the sexual abuse of children — have inspired countless literary works. William Shakespeare created the most famous pair of teenage lovers, one of whom is just 13 years of age. *See* Romeo and Juliet, act I, sc. 2, l. 9 ("She hath not seen the change of fourteen years"). In the drama, Shakespeare portrays the relationship as something splendid and innocent, but not juvenile. The work has inspired no less than 40 motion pictures, some of which suggest that the teenagers consummated their relationship. *E.g.*, Romeo and Juliet (B. Luhrmann director, 1996). Shakespeare may not have written sexually explicit scenes for the Elizabethan audience, but were modern directors to adopt a less conventional approach, that fact alone would not compel the conclusion that the work was obscene.

Contemporary movies pursue similar themes. Last year's Academy Awards featured the movie *Traffic*, which was nominated for Best Picture. *See* "Predictable and Less So, the Academy Award Contenders," *N.Y. Times*, Feb. 14, 2001, p. E11. The film portrays a teenager, identified as a 16-year-old, who becomes addicted to drugs. The viewer sees the degradation of her addiction, which in the end leads her to a filthy room to trade sex for drugs. The year before, American Beauty won the Academy Award for Best Picture. *See* "'American Beauty' Tops the Oscars," *N.Y. Times*, Mar. 27, 2000, p. E1. In the course of the movie, a teenage girl engages in sexual relations with her teenage boyfriend, and another yields herself to the gratification of a middle-aged man. The film also contains a scene where, although the movie audience understands the act is not taking place, one character believes he is watching a teenage boy performing a sexual act on an older man. . . .

Ferber upheld a prohibition on the distribution and sale of child pornography, as well as its production, because these acts were "intrinsically related" to the sexual abuse of children in two ways. *Id.*, at 759, 102 S. Ct. 3348. First, as a permanent record of a child's abuse, the continued circulation itself would harm the child who had participated. Like a defamatory statement, each new publication of the speech would cause new injury to the child's reputation and emotional well-being. *See id.*, at 759, and n.10, 102 S. Ct. 3348. Second, because the traffic in child pornography was an economic motive for its production, the State had an interest in closing the distribution network. "The most expeditious if not the only practical method of law enforcement may be to dry up the market for this material by imposing severe criminal penalties on persons selling, advertising, or otherwise promoting the product." *Id.*, at 760, 102 S. Ct. 3348. Under either rationale, the speech had what the Court in effect held was a proximate link to the crime from which it came.

Later, in *Osborne v. Ohio*, 495 U.S. 103, 110 S. Ct. 1691, 109 L. Ed. 2d 98 (1990), the Court ruled that these same interests justified a ban on the possession of pornography produced by using children. "Given the importance of the State's interest in protecting the victims of child pornography," the State was justified in "attempting to stamp out this vice at all levels in the distribution chain." *Id.*, at 110. Osborne also noted the State's interest in preventing child pornography from being used as an aid in the solicitation of minors. *Id.*, at 111, 110 S. Ct. 1691. The Court, however, anchored its holding in the concern for the participants, those whom it called the "victims of child pornography." *Id.*, at 110, 110 S. Ct. 1691. It did not suggest that, absent this concern, other governmental interests would suffice. *See infra*, at 1402-03.

In contrast to the speech in Ferber, speech that itself is the record of sexual abuse, the CPPA prohibits speech that records no crime and creates no victims by its production. Virtual child pornography is not "intrinsically related" to the sexual abuse of children, as were the materials in *Ferber.* 458 U.S., at 759, 102 S. Ct. 3348. While the Government asserts that the images can lead to actual instances of child abuse, *see infra*, at 1402-04, the causal link is contingent and indirect. The harm does not necessarily follow from the speech, but depends upon some unquantified potential for subsequent criminal acts.

The Government says these indirect harms are sufficient because, as *Ferber* acknowledged, child pornography rarely can be valuable speech. *See* 458 U.S., at 762, 102 S. Ct. 3348 ("The value of permitting live performances and photographic reproductions of children engaged in lewd sexual conduct is exceedingly modest, if not de minimis"). This argument, however, suffers from two flaws. First, *Ferber*'s judgment about child pornography was based upon how it was made, not on what it communicated. The case reaffirmed that where the speech is neither obscene nor the product of sexual abuse, it does not fall outside the protection of the First Amendment. *See id.*, at 764-65, 102 S. Ct. 3348 ("[T]he distribution of descriptions or other depictions of sexual conduct, not otherwise obscene, which do not involve live performance or photographic or other visual reproduction of live performances, retains First Amendment protection").

The second flaw in the Government's position is that Ferber did not hold that child pornography is by definition without value. On the contrary, the Court recognized some works in this category might have significant value, *see id.*, at 761, 102 S. Ct. 3348, but relied on virtual images — the very images prohibited by the CPPA — as an alternative and permissible means of expression: "[I]f it were necessary for literary or artistic value, a person over the statutory age who perhaps looked younger could be utilized. Simulation outside of the prohibition of the statute could provide another alternative." *Id.*, at 763, 102 S. Ct. 3348. *Ferber*, then, not only referred to the distinction between actual and virtual child pornography, it relied on it as a reason supporting its holding. *Ferber* provides no support for a statute that eliminates the distinction and makes the alternative mode criminal as well.

III

The CPPA, for reasons we have explored, is inconsistent with *Miller* and finds no support in *Ferber*. The Government seeks to justify its prohibitions in other ways. It argues that the CPPA is necessary because pedophiles may use virtual child pornography to seduce children. There are many things innocent in themselves, however, such as cartoons, video games, and candy, that might be used for immoral purposes, yet we would not expect those to be prohibited because they can be misused. The Government, of course, may punish adults who provide unsuitable materials to children, *see Ginsberg v. New York,* 390 U.S. 629, 88 S. Ct. 1274, 20 L. Ed. 2d 195 (1968), and it may enforce criminal penalties for unlawful solicitation. The precedents establish, however, that speech within the rights of adults to hear may not be silenced completely in an attempt to shield children from it. *See Sable Communications of Cal., Inc. v. FCC,* 492 U.S. 115, 109 S. Ct. 2829, 106 L. Ed. 2d 93 (1989). In *Butler v. Michigan,* 352 U.S. 380, 381, 77 S. Ct. 524, 1 L. Ed. 2d 412 (1957), the Court invalidated a statute prohibiting distribution of an indecent publication because of its tendency to "'incite minors to violent or depraved or immoral acts.'" A unanimous Court agreed upon the important First Amendment principle that the State could not "reduce the adult population . . . to reading only what is fit for children." *Id.,* at 383, 77 S. Ct. 524. We have reaffirmed this holding. *See United States v. Playboy Entertainment Group, Inc.,* 529 U.S. 803, 814, 120 S. Ct. 1878, 146 L. Ed. 2d 865 (2000) ("[T]he objective of shielding children does not suffice to support a blanket ban if the protection can be accomplished by a less restrictive alternative"); *Reno v. American Civil Liberties Union,* 521 U.S., at 875, 117 S. Ct. 2329 (The "governmental interest in protecting children from harmful materials . . . does not justify an unnecessarily broad suppression of speech addressed to adults"); *Sable Communications v. FCC, supra,* at 130-31, 109 S. Ct. 2829 (striking down a ban on "dial-a-porn" messages that had "the invalid effect of limiting the content of adult telephone conversations to that which is suitable for children to hear").

Here, the Government wants to keep speech from children not to protect them from its content but to protect them from those who would commit other crimes. The principle, however, remains the same: the Government cannot ban speech fit for adults simply because it may fall into the hands of children. The evil in question depends upon the actor's unlawful conduct, conduct defined as criminal quite apart from any link to the speech in question. This establishes that the speech ban is not narrowly drawn. The objective is to prohibit illegal conduct, but this restriction goes well beyond that interest by restricting the speech available to law-abiding adults. The Government submits further that virtual child pornography whets the appetites of pedophiles and encourages them to engage in illegal conduct. This rationale cannot sustain the provision in question. The mere tendency of speech to encourage unlawful acts is not a sufficient reason for banning it. The government "cannot constitutionally premise legislation on the desirability of controlling a person's private thoughts." *Stanley v. Georgia*, 394 U.S. 557, 566, 89 S. Ct. 1243, 22 L. Ed. 2d 542 (1969). First Amendment freedoms are most in danger when the government seeks to control thought or to justify its laws for that impermissible end. The right to think is the beginning of freedom, and speech must be protected from the government because speech is the beginning of thought.

To preserve these freedoms, and to protect speech for its own sake, the Court's First Amendment cases draw vital distinctions between words and deeds, between ideas and conduct. *See Kingsley Int'l Pictures Corp.*, 360 U.S., at 689, 79 S. Ct. 1362; *see also Bartnicki v. Vopper*, 532 U.S. 514, 529, 121 S. Ct. 1753, 149 L. Ed. 2d 787 (2001) ("The normal method of deterring unlawful conduct is to impose an appropriate punishment on the person who engages in it"). The government may not prohibit speech because it increases the chance an unlawful act will be committed "at some indefinite future time." *Hess v. Indiana*, 414 U.S. 105, 108, 94 S. Ct. 326, 38 L. Ed. 2d 303 (1973) (per curiam). The government may suppress speech for advocating the use of force or a violation of law only if "such advocacy is directed to inciting or producing imminent lawless action and is likely to incite or produce such action." *Brandenburg v. Ohio*, 395 U.S. 444, 447, 89 S. Ct. 1827, 23 L. Ed. 2d 430 (1969) (per curiam). There is here no attempt, incitement, solicitation, or conspiracy. The Government has shown no more than a remote connection between speech that might encourage thoughts or impulses and any resulting child abuse. Without a significantly stronger, more direct connection, the Government may not prohibit speech on the ground that it may encourage pedophiles to engage in illegal conduct.

The Government next argues that its objective of eliminating the market for pornography produced using real children necessitates a prohibition on virtual images as well. Virtual images, the Government contends, are indistinguishable from real ones; they are part of the same market and are often exchanged. In this way, it is said, virtual images promote the trafficking in works produced through the exploitation of real children. The hypothesis is somewhat implausible. If virtual images were identical to illegal child pornography, the illegal images would be driven from the market by the indistinguishable substitutes. Few pornographers would risk prosecution by abusing real children if fictional, computerized images would suffice. . . .

Finally, the Government says that the possibility of producing images by using computer imaging makes it very difficult for it to prosecute those who produce pornography by using real children. Experts, we are told, may have difficulty in saying whether the pictures were made by using real children or by using computer imaging. The necessary solution, the argument runs, is to prohibit both kinds of images. The argument, in essence, is that protected speech may be banned as a means to ban unprotected speech. This analysis turns the First Amendment upside down.

The Government may not suppress lawful speech as the means to suppress unlawful speech. Protected speech does not become unprotected merely because it resembles the latter. The Constitution requires the reverse. "[T]he possible harm to society in permitting some unprotected speech to go unpunished is outweighed by the possibility that protected speech of others may be muted. . . ." *Broadrick v. Oklahoma*, 413 U.S., at 612, 93 S. Ct. 2908. The overbreadth doctrine prohibits the Government from banning unprotected speech if a substantial amount of protected speech is prohibited or chilled in the process. . . .

In sum, § 2256(8)(B) covers materials beyond the categories recognized in *Ferber* and *Miller*, and the reasons the Government offers in support of limiting the freedom of speech have no justification in our precedents or in the law of the First Amendment. The provision abridges the freedom to engage in a substantial amount of lawful speech. For this reason, it is overbroad and unconstitutional. . . .

V

For the reasons we have set forth, the prohibitions of §§ 2256(8)(B) and 2256(8)(D) are overbroad and unconstitutional. Having reached this conclusion, we need not address respondents' further contention that the provisions are unconstitutional because of vague statutory language.

The judgment of the Court of Appeals is affirmed.

It is so ordered.

Note and Questions

1. *Ashcroft v. Free Speech Coalition* avoided driving the car off one of the cliffs described by Professor Adler in her article on the expansion of the definition of child pornography: the Court refused to allow prosecution for virtual child pornography, created using computers with no actual models or child victims or human beings used at all in the production. Thus, part of the rationale that *Osborne* used for eliminating child porn — that it subjects children to unspeakable abuse and stands as a testament to that abuse, haunting the children forever — is absent. But did the Court give enough attention to the public policy argument that allowing distribution of any kind of child pornography feeds the market and encourages the creation and distribution of child pornography in general, perpetuating the industry and the process of victimization of children?

2. The Court returned its attention to the problem of the market and distribution chain for child pornography in *United States v. Williams*, 553 U.S. 285 (2008), which upheld the Prosecutorial Remedies and Other Tools to end the Exploitation of Children Today (PROTECT) Act section prohibiting "pandering" and "solicitation" of child

pornography. Under the Act, offers to provide and requests to obtain child pornography do not require the actual existence of child pornography backing up these offers. Rather than targeting the underlying material, the Act was construed to ban collateral speech that introduces such material into the child-pornography distribution network. Thus, an internet user who solicits child pornography from an undercover agent violates the statute even if the officer possesses no child pornography, and likewise, a person who is selling virtual child pornography but who advertises it as depicting actual children also falls within the reach of the statute, 18 U.S.C. § 2252A(a)(3)(B).

3. So called "innocent" or "artistic" nude photographs of young children are swept within the scope of the most aggressively defined prohibitions on child pornography. "Sexting," the practice of underage youths who send pictures of their own or other youths' nude genitalia for fun or flirting or for other purposes, has been prosecuted from time to time as a violation of laws prohibiting the distribution, receipt, or possession of child pornography. Are these prosecutions taking the definition of child pornography too far?

4. Even though depiction of children in arguably erotic poses may be artistically valuable for the posing, composition, and conception of the works, and may conjure up historical references to famous paintings, should artists be allowed to subject even their own children to this kind of display? Might this be a quiet form of child abuse?

Current Issues: Extreme Violence (as in Video games) as Obscene Speech?

Brown v. Entertainment Merchants Association[27]

In 2005, California passed a statute regulating the content of violent video games.[28] The statute prohibited the sale or rental of "violent video games" to minors, and required their packaging to be labeled "18." The Act covered games "in which the range of options available to a player includes killing, maiming, dismembering, or sexually assaulting an image of a human being, if those acts are depicted" in a manner that "[a] reasonable person, considering the game as a whole, would find appeals to a deviant or morbid interest of minors," that is "patently offensive to prevailing standards in the community as to what is suitable for minors," and that "causes the game, as a whole, to lack serious literary, artistic, political, or scientific value for minors." Violation of the Act was to be punishable by a civil fine of up to $1,000.

Violence has never been considered a category of non-speech, and the Court reminded us that new categories of non-speech are not going to be

27. *Brown v. Entertainment Merchants Association*, 564 U.S. 786 (2011).
28. California Assembly Bill 1179 (2005), Cal. Civ. Code Ann. §§ 1746–1746.5 (West 2009).

created by legislative action.[29] California attempted to bring forth evidence — social science, child development, psychological and behavioral science — to establish secondary effects of violent video games that might justify a content-based or content-neutral regulation with an aim to curb those secondary effects. Unfortunately, the evidence was neither conclusive nor compelling.[30] The court, under the authorship of the late Justice Antonin Scalia, would only accept that the statute was a content-based restriction on speech, and it failed strict scrutiny and was struck down.[31]

E. Content-Neutral Regulation and Censorship of Art

PROBLEM 6-4

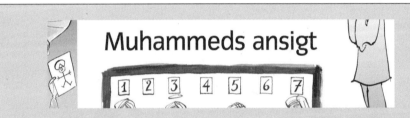

A series of cartoons depicting the Prophet Muhammad were published in a newspaper.[32] The cartoonist who created them did so in reaction to an article which detailed an author's struggle to find an artist willing to help him illustrate a book entitled *The Qur'an and the life of the Prophet Muhammad*. The cartoons are particularly offensive to Muslims because there is a strict prohibition on the creation or display of any depiction of the Prophet Muhammad under Islamic law and tradition, and protests against the newspaper publishing the cartoons, journalists of the country, and many other government and media-related institutions have grown violent, causing the death of three persons and the injuring of dozens more. Should the symbolic speech represented in the cartoons be censored by the government?

---

29. *United States v. Stevens*, 130 S. Ct. 1577, 1584 (2010). *See also Brown*, 564 U.S. at 791-92.
30. *Brown*, 564 U.S. at 799-804.
31. *Brown*, 564 U.S. at 804-05.
32. Image: Michael D. Murray, Cropped, revised, and resized thumbnail excerpt of an exhibit depicting a portion of the Danish newspaper, *Morgenavisen Jyllands-Posten*, KulturWeekend section (Sep. 30, 2005), featuring "Muhammeds Ansigt" cartoons.

1. Origin of Content-Neutral Time-Place-Manner Restrictions on Expression

United States v. O'Brien

391 U.S. 367 (1968)*

Mr. Chief Justice WARREN delivered the opinion of the Court.

On the morning of March 31, 1966, David Paul O'Brien and three companions burned their Selective Service registration certificates on the steps of the South Boston Courthouse. A sizable crowd, including several agents of the Federal Bureau of Investigation, witnessed the event. Immediately after the burning, members of the crowd began attacking O'Brien and his companions. An FBI agent ushered O'Brien to safety inside the courthouse. After he was advised of his right to counsel and to silence, O'Brien stated to FBI agents that he had burned his registration certificate because of his beliefs, knowing that he was violating federal law. He produced the charred remains of the certificate, which, with his consent, were photographed.[33]

---

* Footnotes and some inner citations omitted.

33. Cropped, revised, and resized thumbnail excerpts from the Government's trial exhibits depicting O'Brien and others burning their draft cards, and the burnt remains of O'Brien's draft card, at issue in *United States v. O'Brien*, 391 U.S. 367 (1968).

For this act, O'Brien was indicted, tried, convicted, and sentenced in the United States District Court for the District of Massachusetts. [He was sentenced under the Youth Corrections Act, 18 U.S.C. § 5010(b), to the custody of the Attorney General for a maximum period of six years for supervision and treatment.] He did not contest the fact that he had burned the certificate. He stated in argument to the jury that he burned the certificate publicly to influence others to adopt his antiwar beliefs, as he put it, "so that other people would reevaluate their positions with Selective Service, with the armed forces, and reevaluate their place in the culture of today, to hopefully consider my position."

The indictment upon which he was tried charged that he "willfully and knowingly did mutilate, destroy, and change by burning . . . (his) Registration Certificate (Selective Service System Form No. 2); in violation of Title 50, App., United States Code, Section 462(b)." Section 462(b) is part of the Universal Military Training and Service Act of 1948. Section 462(b)(3), one of six numbered subdivisions of § 462(b), was amended by Congress in 1965, 79 Stat. 586 . . . , so that at the time O'Brien burned his certificate an offense was committed by any person, "who forges, alters, knowingly destroys, knowingly mutilates, or in any manner changes any such certificate. . . ."

In the District Court, O'Brien argued that the 1965 Amendment prohibiting the knowing destruction or mutilation of certificates was unconstitutional because it was enacted to abridge free speech, and because it served no legitimate legislative purpose. The District Court rejected these arguments, holding that the statute on its face did not abridge First Amendment rights, that the court was not competent to inquire into the motives of Congress in enacting the 1965 Amendment, and that the Amendment was a reasonable exercise of the power of Congress to raise armies. [The Court of Appeals reversed]. . . .

. . . We granted the Government's petition to resolve the conflict in the circuits, and we also granted O'Brien's cross-petition. We hold that the 1965 Amendment is constitutional both as enacted and as applied. We therefore vacate the judgment of the Court of Appeals and reinstate the judgment and sentence of the District Court without reaching the issue raised by O'Brien in No. 233.

I

... By the 1965 Amendment, Congress added to § 12(b)(3) of the 1948 Act the provision here at issue, subjecting to criminal liability not only one who "forges, alters, or in any manner changes" but also one who "knowingly destroys (or) knowingly mutilates" a certificate. We note at the outset that the 1965 Amendment plainly does not abridge free speech on its face, and we do not understand O'Brien to argue otherwise. Amended § 12(b)(3) on its face deals with conduct having no connection with speech. It prohibits the knowing destruction of certificates issued by the Selective Service System, and there is nothing necessarily expressive about such conduct. The Amendment does not distinguish between public and private destruction, and it does not punish only destruction engaged in for the purpose of expressing views. *Compare Stromberg v. People of State of California,* 283 U.S. 359, 51 S. Ct. 532, 75 L. Ed. 1117 (1931). A law prohibiting destruction of Selective Service certificates no more abridges free speech on its face than a motor vehicle law prohibiting the destruction of drivers' licenses, or a tax law prohibiting the destruction of books and records.

O'Brien nonetheless argues that the 1965 Amendment is unconstitutional in its application to him, and is unconstitutional as enacted because what he calls the "purpose" of Congress was "to suppress freedom of speech." We consider these arguments separately.

II

O'Brien first argues that the 1965 Amendment is unconstitutional as applied to him because his act of burning his registration certificate was protected "symbolic speech" within the First Amendment. His argument is that the freedom of expression which the First Amendment guarantees includes all modes of "communication of ideas by conduct," and that his conduct is within this definition because he did it in "demonstration against the war and against the draft."

We cannot accept the view that an apparently limitless variety of conduct can be labeled "speech" whenever the person engaging in the conduct intends thereby to express an idea. However, even on the assumption that the alleged communicative element in O'Brien's conduct is sufficient to bring into play the First Amendment, it does not necessarily follow that the destruction of a registration certificate is constitutionally protected activity.

This Court has held that when "speech" and "nonspeech" elements are combined in the same course of conduct, a sufficiently important governmental interest in regulating the nonspeech element can justify incidental limitations on First Amendment freedoms. To characterize the quality of the governmental interest which must appear, the Court has employed a variety of descriptive terms: compelling; substantial; subordinating; paramount; cogent; strong.

Whatever imprecision inheres in these terms, we think it clear that a government regulation is sufficiently justified if it is within the constitutional power of the Government; if it furthers an important or substantial governmental interest; if the governmental interest is unrelated to the suppression of free expression; and if the incidental restriction on alleged First Amendment freedoms is no greater than is essential to the furtherance of that interest.

We find that the 1965 Amendment to § 12(b)(3) of the Universal Military Training and Service Act meets all of these requirements, and consequently that O'Brien can be constitutionally convicted for violating it.

The constitutional power of Congress to raise and support armies and to make all laws necessary and proper to that end is broad and sweeping. *Lichter v. United States*, 334 U.S. 742, 755-758, 68 S. Ct. 1294, 1301-1303, 92 L. Ed. 1694 (1948); *Selective Draft Law Cases*, 245 U.S. 366, 38 S. Ct. 159, 62 L. Ed. 349 (1918); *see also Ex parte Quirin*, 317 U.S. 1, 25-26, 63 S. Ct. 1, 9-10, 87 L. Ed. 3 (1942). The power of Congress to classify and conscript manpower for military service is "beyond question." . . . Pursuant to this power, Congress may establish a system of registration for individuals liable for training and service, and may require such individuals within reason to cooperate in the registration system. The issuance of certificates indicating the registration and eligibility classification of individuals is a legitimate and substantial administrative aid in the functioning of this system. And legislation to insure the continuing availability of issued certificates serves a legitimate and substantial purpose in the system's administration. . . .

The many functions performed by Selective Service certificates establish beyond doubt that Congress has a legitimate and substantial interest in preventing their wanton and unrestrained destruction and assuring their continuing availability by punishing people who knowingly and wilfully destroy or mutilate them. And we are unpersuaded that the pre-existence of the nonpossession regulations in any way negates this interest. . . .

We think it apparent that the continuing availability to each registrant of his Selective Service certificates substantially furthers the smooth and proper functioning of the system that Congress has established to raise armies. We think it also apparent that the Nation has a vital interest in having a system for raising armies that functions with maximum efficiency and is capable of easily and quickly responding to continually changing circumstances. For these reasons, the Government has a substantial interest in assuring the continuing availability of issued Selective Service certificates.

It is equally clear that the 1965 Amendment specifically protects this substantial governmental interest. We perceive no alternative means that would more precisely and narrowly assure the continuing availability of issued Selective Service certificates than a law which prohibits their willful mutilation or destruction. . . .

The 1965 Amendment prohibits such conduct and does nothing more. In other words, both the governmental interest and the operation of the 1965 Amendment are limited to the noncommunicative aspect of O'Brien's conduct. The governmental interest and the scope of the 1965 Amendment are limited to preventing harm to the smooth and efficient functioning of the Selective Service System. When O'Brien deliberately rendered unavailable his registration certificate, he willfully frustrated this governmental interest. For this noncommunicative impact of his conduct, and for nothing else, he was convicted.

The case at bar is therefore unlike one where the alleged governmental interest in regulating conduct arises in some measure because the communication allegedly integral to the conduct is itself thought to be harmful. In *Stromberg v. People of State of California*, 283 U.S. 359, 51 S. Ct. 532, 75 L. Ed. 1117 (1931), for example, this Court struck down a statutory phrase which punished people who expressed their "opposition to organized government" by displaying "any flag, badge, banner, or device." Since the statute there was aimed at suppressing communication it could not be sustained as a regulation of noncommunicative conduct. . . .

In conclusion, we find that because of the Government's substantial interest in assuring the continuing availability of issued Selective Service certificates, because amended § 462(b) is an appropriately narrow means of protecting this interest and condemns only the independent noncommunicative impact of conduct within its reach, and because the noncommunicative impact of O'Brien's act of burning his registration certificate frustrated the Government's interest, a sufficient governmental interest has been shown to justify O'Brien's conviction. . . .

It is so ordered.

2. Regulation and Censorship of Art on Government Property

a. Installations in and on Government Property

Serra v. U.S. General Services Admin.

847 F.2d 1045 (2d Cir. 1988)*

NEWMAN, Circuit Judge.

This appeal presents the question whether the removal of a government-owned artwork from federal property violates the free expression and due process rights of the artist. Richard Serra, a prominent American sculptor, brought the action seeking to bar the United States General Services Administration (GSA) from removing his controversial sculpture "Tilted Arc" from Federal Plaza in lower Manhattan. The District Court for the Southern District of New York (Milton Pollack, Judge) granted summary judgment against Serra on his constitutional claims. For the reasons that follow, we affirm the judgment of the District Court.

---

* Footnotes and some citations omitted.

BACKGROUND

. . . In 1979, GSA selected Serra to create an outdoor sculpture to be installed on the plaza adjacent to the federal office complex at 26 Federal Plaza in lower Manhattan (the "Plaza" or "Federal Plaza"). The sculpture was commissioned under GSA's art-in-architecture program pursuant to which one half of one percent of the construction cost of federal buildings is reserved for the funding of artworks by living American artists. Serra is an internationally renowned sculptor, known primarily for his "site-specific" work. According to Serra, a site-specific sculpture "is one which is conceived and created in relation to the particular conditions of a specific site." Site-specific sculpture is meaningful only when displayed in the particular location for which it is created; such works are not intended to be displayed in more than one place. Serra's site-specific works consist primarily of steel plates or "forgings" that are welded together to form large abstract forms. Serra's sculptures have been displayed in many prominent locations throughout the world, including the Tuilleries Gardens in Paris.

In September 1979, Serra signed a contract with GSA setting forth the terms of his commission. The contract provided that Serra would receive a fee of $175,000 for building a sculpture on Federal Plaza. The contract further provided that "all designs, sketches, models, and the work produced under this Agreement . . . shall be the property of [the United States]." The contract contained no provisions restricting the Government's use of the sculpture after it was purchased.

"Tilted Arc" was completed and installed at Federal Plaza in 1981.[34] The work is an arc of steel 120 feet long, 12 feet tall, and several inches thick. It is fabricated out of Cor-Ten steel, a material designed to oxidize naturally over time. Consequently, the work is now coated with what the artist refers to as "a golden amber patina" and what the sculpture's critics refer to as

---

34. Images: Michael D. Murray, Cropped, revised, and resized thumbnail excerpts of exhibits depicting Richard Serra's "Tilted Arc" sculpture in Manhattan, the subject of *Serra v. U.S. General Services Admin.*, 847 F.2d 1045 (2d Cir. 1988)

"rust." The sculpture bisects Federal Plaza. According to Serra, "Tilted Arc" is site-specific: it was designed for the Federal Plaza and is artistically inseparable from its location. Serra maintains that removing "Tilted Arc" to another site will destroy it.

The pigeons had barely begun to roost on "Tilted Arc" before the sculpture became the object of intense public criticism. GSA received hundreds of letters from community residents and federal employees complaining about the sculpture's appearance and its obstruction of Federal Plaza's previously open space. Initially, GSA took the position that critics should give the work time to gain public acceptance. However, when hostility to the work had not abated after several years, GSA agreed to hold a hearing on the possible relocation of the sculpture.

A public hearing was held in March 1985, presided over by William A. Diamond, GSA Regional Administrator. More than 150 persons spoke at the hearing, representing a wide range of constituencies including artists, civic leaders, employees at the Federal Plaza complex, and community residents. In addition, Serra was given the opportunity to state his views on the site-specific nature of "Tilted Arc" and the need to keep it at Federal Plaza. Those urging removal tended to be federal employees and area residents who complained primarily of the obstruction of Federal Plaza and the sculpture's unappealing aesthetic qualities. Those against removal tended to be artists and others from the art world who pointed to the work's significance in 20th Century sculpture and the importance of protecting the artist's freedom of expression.

Following the hearing, Diamond prepared a report in which he recommended to Dwight Ink, Acting Administrator of GSA, that "Tilted Arc" be relocated. Diamond urged primarily that the sculpture obstructed Federal Plaza, preventing the public from using the space for recreation and community events. Additionally, he noted concerns expressed at the hearing regarding potential safety hazards caused by the sculpture and its vulnerability to graffiti. Though Diamond included in the report his opinion that the atmosphere of the Plaza had been "turned into affrontery," he also stated that "my consideration of the issue of whether to relocate the sculpture would not be in any way based upon the arguments of its beauty, its ugliness, or its place in art history."

Diamond's report and the entire administrative record were reviewed by Ink. Ink also met with Serra and his attorney so that Serra could personally articulate his concern about site-specificity. In a written decision issued in May 1985, Ink decided that "Tilted Arc" should be relocated. He relied largely on the views of federal employees and community residents that the sculpture interfered with their use of Federal Plaza. Like Diamond, Ink expressly avoided linking his decision to his personal evaluation of the work's artistic merit; he stated that he "made no judgment whatsoever concerning the aesthetic value of the Tilted Arc."

Serra initiated this lawsuit in December 1986. His complaint named as defendants GSA and administrators Diamond and Ink in their individual capacities. He alleged that GSA's decision to remove "Tilted Arc" violated his rights under the Free Speech Clause of the First Amendment, the Due

Process Clause of the Fifth Amendment, federal trademark and copyright laws, and state law. Serra sought a declaratory judgment that his rights had been violated, an injunction against removal of the sculpture, and damages from the individual defendants in excess of $30,000,000.

. . . On appeal from the judgment dismissing his suit, Serra challenges only the rejection of his free expression and due process claims.

DISCUSSION

A. Free Expression

The District Court assumed, without deciding the issue, that "Tilted Arc" is expression protected to some extent by the First Amendment. The Court reasoned that "ideas need not necessarily be spoken or written to qualify for First Amendment protection." 667 F. Supp. at 1055. While we agree that artwork, like other non-verbal forms of expression, may under some circumstances constitute speech for First Amendment purposes, *see, e.g., Doran v. Salem Inn, Inc.,* 422 U.S. 922, 932, 95 S. Ct. 2561, 2568, 45 L. Ed. 2d 648 (1975) (topless dancing); *Piarowski v. Illinois Community College,* 759 F.2d 625, 628 (7th Cir.), cert. denied, 474 U.S. 1007, 106 S. Ct. 528, 88 L. Ed. 2d 460 (1985) (art), we believe that the First Amendment has only limited application in a case like the present one where the artistic expression belongs to the Government rather than a private individual.

"The purpose of the First Amendment is to protect private expression and nothing in the guarantee precludes the government from controlling its own expression or that of its agents." Consequently, the Government may advance or restrict its own speech in a manner that would clearly be forbidden were it regulating the speech of a private citizen.

In this case, the speaker is the United States Government. "Tilted Arc" is entirely owned by the Government and is displayed on Government property. Serra relinquished his own speech rights in the sculpture when he voluntarily sold it to GSA; if he wished to retain some degree of control as to the duration and location of the display of his work, he had the opportunity to bargain for such rights in making the contract for sale of his work. Nothing GSA has done limits the right of any private citizen to say what he pleases, nor has Serra been prevented from making any sculpture or displaying those that he has not sold. Rather, the Government's action in this case is limited to an exercise of discretion with respect to the display of its own property. Though there are conceivably situations in which the Government's exercise of its discretion in this regard could violate the First Amendment rights of the public, nothing GSA has done here encroaches in any way on Serra's or any other individual's right to communicate.

Even assuming that Serra retains some First Amendment interest in the continued display of "Tilted Arc," we agree with the District Court that removal of the sculpture is a permissible time, place, and manner restriction. Such restrictions are valid "provided that they are justified without reference to the content of the regulated speech, that they are narrowly tailored to serve a significant governmental interest, and that they leave open ample alternative channels for communication of the information." *Clark v. Community for Creative Non-Violence*, 468 U.S. 288, 293, 104 S. Ct. 3065, 3069, 82 L. Ed. 2d 221 (1984); *see City Council of Los Angeles v. Taxpayers for Vincent*, 466 U.S. 789, 804-05, 104 S. Ct. 2118, 2128, 80 L. Ed. 2d 772 (1984); *United States v. O'Brien*, 391 U.S. 367, 377, 88 S. Ct. 1673, 1679, 20 L. Ed. 2d 673 (1968). Relocation of "Tilted Arc" conforms with these requirements.

GSA has a significant interest in keeping the Plaza unobstructed, an interest that may be furthered only by removing the sculpture. This interest stems from GSA's clearly established authority to maintain, operate, and alter federal buildings, including their "grounds, approaches, and appurtenances," 40 U.S.C. §§ 490, 603(a), 612(1) (1982), which in turn derives from Congress' power under the Constitution "to dispose of and make all needful Rules and Regulations respecting the ... Property belonging to the United States." Art. IV, § 3, cl. 2.

Nor does relocation of "Tilted Arc" preclude Serra from communicating his ideas in other ways. First, Serra has already had six years to convey his message through the sculpture's presence in the Plaza. Since the First Amendment protects the freedom to express one's views, not the freedom to continue speaking forever, the relocation of the sculpture after a lengthy period of initial display does not significantly impair Serra's right to free speech. Second, Serra has not shown that removal of the sculpture creates "any barrier to delivering to the media, or to the public by other means," whatever message he intended to convey with "Tilted Arc." Notwithstanding that the sculpture is site-specific and may lose its artistic value if relocated, Serra is free to express his artistic and political views through the press and through other means that do not entail obstructing the Plaza.

Finally, the decision to remove "Tilted Arc" was not impermissibly content-based. According to the reports of GSA administrators Diamond and Ink, the primary reason for removal was the fact that the sculpture interfered with the public's use of Federal Plaza. Additionally, GSA was concerned about public safety and graffiti. Both Diamond and Ink expressly represented that they had not based their decisions on the work's artistic merit or its message. . . .

Serra is unable to identify any particular message conveyed by "Tilted Arc" that he believes may have led to its removal. In view of the uncertainty as to the meaning of "Tilted Arc" and in the face of the overwhelming evidence that it was removed solely because of its obstructive effect on the Plaza, Serra has failed to present any facts to support a claim that Government officials acted in a "narrowly partisan or political manner."

To the extent that GSA's decision may have been motivated by the sculpture's lack of aesthetic appeal, the decision was entirely permissible. . . . GSA, which is charged with providing office space for federal employees, may remove from its buildings artworks that it decides are aesthetically unsuitable for particular locations. Moreover, the Supreme Court has consistently recognized that consideration of aesthetics is a legitimate government function that does not render a decision to restrict expression impermissibly content-based. *See, e.g., City Council v. Taxpayers For Vincent, supra,* 466 U.S. at 805-07, 104 S. Ct. at 2128-30; *Metromedia, Inc. v. City of San Diego,* 453 U.S. 490, 507-08,

101 S. Ct. 2882, 2892-93, 69 L. Ed. 2d 800 (1981); *Kovacs v. Cooper*, 336 U.S. 77, 69 S. Ct. 448, 93 L. Ed. 513 (1949). Finally, several courts have held that the state may regulate the display and location of art based on its aesthetic qualities and suitability for the viewing public without running afoul of First Amendment concerns. *See Piarowski v. Illinois Community College, supra*, 759 F.2d at 630-32; *Close v. Lederle*, 424 F.2d 988 (1st Cir.), cert. denied, 400 U.S. 903, 91 S. Ct. 141, 27 L. Ed. 2d 140 (1970).

We recognize that courts considering First Amendment challenges by artists to governmental decisions to remove purchased works of art must proceed with some caution, lest a removal ostensibly based on unsuitable physical characteristics of the work or an unfavorable assessment of its aesthetic appeal camouflage an impermissible condemnation of political viewpoint. At the same time, artists must recognize that overly intrusive judicial restraints upon the prerogatives of government to decide when, where, and whether to display works of art that it has purchased would pose a serious threat to the vigor of such commendable ventures as GSA's art-in-architecture program. Government can be a significant patron of the arts. Its incentive to fulfill that role must not be dampened by unwarranted restrictions on its freedom to decide what to do with art it has purchased. If Serra had presented any facts to create a genuine issue as to whether GSA was removing "Tilted Arc" to condemn a political point of view or otherwise to trench upon First Amendment rights, we would require a trial, just as we did in *Pico. Pico v. Board of Education*, 638 F.2d 404 (2d Cir. 1980), aff'd, 457 U.S. 853, 102 S. Ct. 2799, 73 L. Ed. 2d 435 (1982). But he has not done so. In the absence of such facts, his lawsuit is really an invitation to the courts to announce a new rule, without any basis in First Amendment law, that an artist retains a constitutional right to have permanently displayed at the intended site a work of art that he has sold to a government agency. Neither the values of the First Amendment nor the cause of public art would be served by accepting that invitation.

B. Due Process

Serra claims that he was denied due process because GSA administrator Diamond "prejudged" the issue of whether "Tilted Arc" should be removed. Serra claims that Diamond had decided that he was opposed to the sculpture even before the public hearing had begun. . . . Serra argues that Diamond's conduct violated his right to a fair and impartial hearing on the removal issue.

Accepting Serra's factual allegations as true for purposes of this appeal, we conclude that his due process claim fails as a matter of law. First, Serra has no protected property interest in the continued display of "Tilted Arc" at Federal Plaza. Pursuant to Serra's contract, the sculpture is the property of GSA, not the artist. Moreover, though Serra might suffer injury to his reputation as a result of relocation of the sculpture, such an injury without an accompanying loss of government employment would not constitute a constitutionally cognizable deprivation of property or liberty. And without a protected property or liberty interest, Serra was not constitutionally entitled to a hearing before the sculpture could be removed. . . .

The judgment of the District Court is affirmed.

Note and Questions

1. It is important to note that Serra's case arose prior to the enactment of the Visual Artists Rights Act of 1990 (VARA) (discussed in Chapter 4, "Moral Rights and Economic Rights"). Under VARA, Serra arguably would have a claim against removal and potential destruction of the installation under the right of integrity provision in VARA, as long as these rights were not construed to have been waived in his contract with the GSA. His work was "of recognized stature" as required by the integrity provision, and does not appear to have been permanently attached to a building. Since Serra had no federal moral rights protection, he attempted to assert his broader First Amendment and due process rights, but these failed.

2. Couldn't the Court have found that an implied term of the contract was that the work, once installed, would not be removed in as short a time as six years? Isn't it logical to assume that part of Serra's expected returns on the contract was the satisfaction, increased visibility and notoriety, and expected increase in the value of all of his works, by having a work installed and displayed in so prominent a place as Federal Plaza in downtown Manhattan? What lesson can we learn from this in drafting contracts for artist clients?

3. On the other hand, isn't it a bit silly to say that moving the work from the initial site of its installation "destroys" the work as Serra asserted, even though the work could be moved without affecting its physical integrity? What substance is there to this "site specific" argument? Is it just artists being elitist, irrational "artists"?

4. What if the sculpture presented a health and safety hazard because it contained arsenic or lead, or because parts of it were about to fall apart from poor design or simple wear and tear? Would these be more acceptable reasons to remove the sculpture than simple aesthetics?

Claudio v. United States

836 F. Supp. 1230 (E.D.N.C. 1993)*

Fox, Chief Judge.

BACKGROUND FACTS

In March, 1992, plaintiff Claudio, a California resident, telephoned defendant Grant seeking permission to mount an art exhibit in the Raleigh

---

* Footnotes and some citations omitted.

Federal Building pursuant to the Public Buildings Cooperative Use Act, 40 U.S.C. §§ 490, 601a, 606, 611, 612, which permits federal building space to be available to the public for cultural purposes. Claudio had never been to the Raleigh Federal Building but advised Grant that he would need wall space capable of accommodating a large painting. Based on Grant's descriptions of the various available spaces, Claudio wrote to request permission "to use the wall (10 ft. × 20 ft.) in the main lobby space" for "an art exhibit." At no time was Claudio asked to describe the subject of his "art exhibit." Claudio subsequently received a revocable license permitting the display of an "art exhibit" from May 4-29, 1992. Before traveling from his home in California cross-country to North Carolina to hang his work, Claudio contacted Jim Shields, who apparently was at the time the Executive Director of the American Civil Liberties Union/North Carolina Civil Liberties Union Legal Foundation. Upon his arrival in North Carolina, Claudio met with Mr. Shields and Ms. Ross, one of his attorneys in the instant litigation. The press was notified of the upcoming unveiling and dispatched photographers to the Federal Building lobby on May 4th. Shields, Ross, members of the press, courthouse employees including Court Security Officers, and visitors to the Federal Building were present as Claudio mounted the painting, which remained covered until mounted. When Claudio unveiled his work, observers were assaulted by a visual horror entitled, "Sex, Laws, and Coathangers,"[depicted below] which defendants accurately have described as follows:

> The work's main elements are larger-than-life depictions of a nude woman, a coathanger, and a fetus. The main nude is depicted frontally, from her knees to the top of her head; this depiction is seven feet, eight inches tall. She is painted, with alkyd paint, in such a way as to create the illusion of three dimensions. The woman's right breast, which faces the observer in the center of the work, measures approximately eight inches across. The woman wears only a gold-colored crucifix, which hangs from her neck. . . .

35

---

35. Image: Michael D. Murray, Cropped, revised, and resized thumbnail excerpt of an exhibit depicting Claudio's "Sex, Laws, and Coathangers" work, the subject of *Claudio v. United States*, 836 F. Supp. 1230 (E.D.N.C. 1993).

To the left of the main nude is a black coathanger. It is a constructed representation made of polyethylene tubing, and measures approximately three and one-half feet across. Its two ends are unwound, and the end that would normally take a corkscrew shape is straightened. That end is pointed vertically at the word "laws" in the title. More of the silver metallic pigment appears in and around the coathanger.

The fetus is attached to the right of the main nude and the torso. It is thirteen and one-half inches long, and its umbilical cord and placenta are intact. The fetus, cord, and placenta are in the form of a bas relief, so that they protrude somewhat from the surface of the painting. They are tinged with red, and a dark-red streak with a liquid appearance extends upward from the fetus for several inches, then to the right toward the main nude. Several dark-red streaks or blotches also appear to the right of the fetus. The background on which the fetus rests is dark-red. . . .

Memorandum in Support of Defendants' Motion for Summary Judgment at 6–9 (citations and footnotes omitted). The painting itself is in the form of a crucifix.

Almost immediately upon the unveiling, defendant Grant, General Services Administration ("GSA") Field Office Manager, informed Claudio that his revocable license was revoked. Grant left the lobby area, accompanied by Claudio, and prepared a written revocation. Grant's notice stated in part that:

> Although your display may be in the form of art it is more properly described as a political expression concerning the highly controversial issue of abortion.
>
> Since your work is considered to be political in nature it is not permitted on federal property and your license is hereby revoked.

Chief Deputy United States Marshal Dwight Rich and court security officer ("CSO") James C. Ball were responsible for courthouse security while the painting was on the wall. The lobby of the Federal Building is quite small—approximately 27.8 feet by 18.8 feet and most of it is occupied by security devices and equipment—an X-ray machine, a magnetometer, security partitions and small items of furniture. The lobby is devoted primarily to maintaining the security of the building. Any member of the public entering the Federal Building must place all personal items on the x-ray machine to be examined for security purposes. In doing so, the person must face the wall upon which Claudio chose to display his painting, before walking through the magnetometer.

According to depositions of Steve Grant and CSO Ball, and the declaration of Donald P. Connelly, Jr. (Law Enforcement Coordination Specialist in the Office of the United States Attorney, Raleigh, North Carolina), the size and nature of the lobby will not accommodate a crowd of any size without impeding the flow of traffic and endangering building security and Government property. This court already has concluded, based on the undisputed physical evidence in the case as well as personal experience, that the lobby is "entirely unsuitable for any expressive activity which would attract a crowd, generate noise, or incite disruptive behavior." February 2, 1993, Order at 14.

According to Deputy Rich and CSO Ball, the display of Claudio's work caused a crowd of people to gather in the lobby in front of the security post, the magnetometer and the x-ray machine. This "congestion" obstructed those who attempted to enter and exit the building; they were forced to walk through a "maze" of bystanders. The crowd and resulting "chaos" interfered with CSO Ball's efforts to screen people entering the building and to assure that all who entered passed through the magnetometer. . . .

Claudio, through counsel, appealed the revocation of the revocable license, and defendant David H. Jameson, Director of the Real Property Management and Safety Division in GSA's Region 4, decided the appeal. Jameson affirmed the revocation both because "the U.S. Courts in the building are part of the judicial system now hearing cases specifically on [the] subject [of abortion]" and because "the exhibition interfered with security in the building and could cause disruption and damage to Government property." Jameson Declaration, Exhibit J to Defendant's Memorandum in Support of Motion for Summary Judgment.

As the basis for his administrative appeal, as well as for this civil action, Claudio alleges violation of his constitutional rights (primarily his First Amendment rights) and revocation of his license to display the painting in violation of the Administrative Procedures Act. Specifically, plaintiff's Complaint, as amended, asserts four claims: (i) that the revocation violated the First Amendment; (ii) that the revocation violated the equal protection clause; (iii) that basing the affirmance of the revocation partly on security concerns violated the due process clause, on the theory that the revocation itself was not based on such concerns; and (iv) that the revocation violated the Administrative Procedures Act and the Public Buildings Cooperative Use Act, on the theory that none of the regulations' grounds for revoking a license existed in this case. Plaintiff seeks damages, a declaration that his rights were violated, and injunctions undoing the cancellation of his permit, giving him a new permit, and forbidding interference with the display of his work under the new permit.

ANALYSIS

Stripped to the bone and devoid of all extraneous legalese, plaintiff's position is as follows: any person is entitled by the United States Constitution to exhibit in any manner designated by anyone as "art," any rendition of any subject, idea, or issue in or on any federal building. It would not stretch plaintiff's interpretation of the First Amendment to extend constitutional protection to the product of a citizen's decision to paint a mural realistically depicting the crimes of murder and rape along the outer facade of the Supreme Court Building in Washington, D.C., or to display a "living sculpture" enacting a suicide by violent means in the lobby of the U.S. Courthouse, housing the Fourth Circuit Court of Appeals in Richmond.

Claudio's perception of First Amendment protection of his right to express himself in a public forum is this: there can be absolutely no governmental "censorship" of the subject or content of his work. It is plain that plaintiff believes any limitation the Government may put on the subject matter of artwork sought to be displayed in or on its property amounts to an attempt to quash viewpoint expression. In other words, there is no place in his Constitutional analysis for taste, decorum, sensitivity, or respect.

During the arduous process of contemplating the basic questions raised by this litigation, the court has struggled to apply the many pronouncements and "tests" promulgated by the Supreme Court over the years in its own efforts to define the parameters of free speech and expression. The case, conceptually, most like this one at bar is *Cohen v. California*, 403 U.S. 15, 91 S. Ct. 1780, 29 L. Ed. 2d 284 (1971), in which the Court decided that the Government could not prohibit a young man from wearing a jacket with the message, "Fuck the Draft," inside a courthouse. The Court suggested that anyone offended by the message could merely "avert their eyes." Plaintiff herein proclaims that, "If Cohen can wear his jacket in a courthouse, Claudio can display his painting in the Federal Building."

At first blush, it seems that *Cohen* indeed dictates such a result. Upon closer examination, however, there are critical distinctions. The most important distinction is that no one who was forced to see the jacket possibly could have attributed the message to the Government; it plainly was an expression conveyed and/or an opinion held, by the wearer. Its appearance in a courthouse (rather than in a department store or church) carried no enhanced meaning. In the instant case, the offensive expression literally was physically attached to the courthouse itself, and it was so large and situated in such a location that anyone entering the Federal Building had to look at it.

There also is an element of compulsion here that was not present in *Cohen*. Claudio's huge painting, "Sex, Laws, and Coathangers" was displayed in the direct line of vision of everyone who entered the Federal Courthouse. Many of those persons were in the courthouse involuntarily — as prospective jurors, witnesses under subpoena, probationers reporting under court order, and so forth. All of these persons are further required by Court Security Officers to place their personal items on the x-ray machine conveyor belt, and, in complying, they must face the wall upon which the painting was displayed.

Equally as precious as is our right to express ourselves is our right to be left alone. The court is unaware of any Constitutional requirement that we involuntarily endure the expression of someone else's "artwork," regardless of its subject matter. This court is unwilling to find that GSA is compelled to display a vulgar, shocking, and tasteless painting in the lobby of the Federal Building. The fact that a property owner is the Government cannot deprive it of the right afforded everyone else to prohibit others from defacing its property. Claudio may be refused the opportunity to display "Sex, Laws, and Coathangers" in the Raleigh Federal Building lobby for the same reason he may be refused the opportunity to express himself by painting that building pink polka-dotted. These forms of expression are incompatible with the image and sense of decorum which the Federal Government, like any other property owner, is entitled to project. . . .

With regard to First Amendment constraints, the court concludes that Claudio's complaints are unavailing. The Government may, consistent with the Constitution, limit the exercise of First Amendment rights on public property. "[T]he First Amendment does not guarantee access to property simply because it is owned or controlled by the government." *United States Postal Service v. Council of Greenburgh Civic Ass'ns*, 453 U.S. 114, 129, 101 S. Ct. 2676, 2685, 69 L. Ed. 2d 517 (1981). Indeed, governmental actions are subject to a lower level of First Amendment scrutiny when the activity in question is not regulation or lawmaking, but the management of governmental properties, as proprietor. *United States v. Kokinda*, 497 U.S. 720, 725, 110 S. Ct. 3115, 3118, 111 L. Ed. 2d 571 (1990) (plurality opinion).

The degree to which the Government may restrict First Amendment activity on public property varies depending on the "character" and "purpose" of the property involved. *Perry Educ. Ass'n v. Perry Local Educators' Ass'n*, 460 U.S. 37, 44-45, 103 S. Ct. 948, 954, 74 L. Ed. 2d 794 (1983); *Kokinda*, 497 U.S. at 732, 110 S. Ct. at 3122. Generally the Supreme Court classifies Government-owned property into three categories for this purpose: "the traditional public forum, the public forum created by government designation, and the nonpublic forum." *Cornelius v. NAACP Legal Defense & Educ. Fund, Inc.*, 473 U.S. 788, 802, 105 S. Ct. 3439, 3449, 87 L. Ed. 2d 567 (1985). First Amendment activity may be more freely restricted in non-public forums than in traditional or designated public forums. *See Perry*, 460 U.S. at 45, 103 S. Ct. at 954.

The law of this case is that the lobby of the Raleigh Federal Building is a nonpublic forum. Therefore, restrictions on First Amendment activity in that forum must only be "reasonable and not an effort to suppress expression merely because public officials oppose the speaker's view." *Kokinda*, 497 U.S. at 730, 110 S. Ct. at 3121 (emphasis added). "Control over access to a nonpublic forum can be based on subject matter and speaker identity so long as the distinctions drawn are reasonable in light of the purpose served by the forum and are viewpoint neutral." *Cornelius*, 473 U.S. at 806, 105 S. Ct. at 3451. Mere "common sense" is sufficient to uphold agency action under the reasonableness standard. *Kokinda*, 497 U.S. at 734-35, 110 S. Ct. at 3123-24. . . .

This court already has concluded that the revocation of Claudio's revocable permit was not motivated by a desire to suppress viewpoint. It is impossible to perceive the artist's viewpoint regarding abortion by looking at the painting; the painting is ambiguous in its position on abortion and likely was designed that way. In light of the size of the forum — the tiny Federal Building lobby — the purpose to which the lobby has been dedicated — building security — and the manner in which Claudio chose to express himself — painting a much-larger-than-life frontal female nude, accompanied by a realistic depiction of a disembodied human fetus, umbilical cord and placenta and a huge coathanger dripping with blood, the court concludes that revocation of Claudio's revocable license was consistent with First Amendment law and policy in that it was reasonable, was not motivated by a desire to suppress viewpoint, and was effected in the Government's permissible role as proprietor to maintain the dignity and aesthetic quality of a building dedicated to administration of justice and public service. Defendants' Motion for Summary Judgment is ALLOWED and this matter is DISMISSED in its entirety. SO ORDERED.

Note and Questions

1. Certainly one of the most popular law school cases, *Cohen v. California,* 403 U.S. 15 (1971), established that an expletive on the back of a jacket incorporated into a political statement could not be suppressed, in part because viewers did not have to stare at it but could avert their eyes. Did the court in *Claudio* adequately distinguish the case?

2. Is it somewhat surprising for the district court in *Claudio* to declare that the lobby of a federal courthouse is not a public forum when it is a government building, open to the public during regular business hours, and a place where grave matters of public concern are debated and resolved?

3. Did the government create a limited public forum when it accepted the display of art of any kind, given that all art has expressive qualities?

b. The Public Forum Doctrine Meets the Government Speech Doctrine

Case Study: Kara Walker and the Newark Public Library

Kara Walker's work, *The Moral Arc of History,*[36] was on loan at Newark Public Library. The work, in part, depicts a nude, female African slave in a

subjugated position who appears to be performing a sex act on a white male. The nature of the depiction drew complaints starting with employees of the library, who were later joined by some patrons who objected to the graphic nature of the depiction. The painting was then "draped"—it remained on the wall, but was covered from view.

---

36. Image: Michael D. Murray, Cropped, revised, and resized thumbnail excerpt of an exhibit depicting Kara Walker's work, *The Moral Arc of History,* the subject of censorship by the Newark Public Library.

Speakers' Corner — the Northeast corner of Hyde Park in London

Newark Public Library is a government-funded institution, intended to be open and accessible to the public for their education, self-improvement, and general informational benefit, but the courts do not consider public libraries to be a public forum.

The importance of this holding is that libraries are not part of the public forum doctrine, which holds that certain public areas — typically understood to be public parks and public spaces (sometimes, public sidewalks), particularly those in areas where groups frequently congregate — are held to be areas where the speech should be particularly free and unhindered.

The paradigm for this concept was the "Speakers' Corner"[37] (the northeast corner) of Hyde Park in London, England, where speakers routinely appeared to hold forth on various topics, often bringing their own "soap box" or other platform to stand on,[38] and drawing whatever crowd of listeners happened to show up to listen. In a public forum, the government must meet an extra burden in any attempt to quash speech for its content and quiet the speaker, and this burden extends even to content-neutral regulation of expressive conduct regulated for its effects, but to a proportionately lesser degree. It does not turn a content-neutral regulation of the speech into a content-based restriction on speech. But libraries, although government-funded public places, are not held to be public forums. People traditionally do not congregate in libraries to give speeches, and therefore, it is not held to be a state action of censorship when a library acts to control a message featured and sponsored by the public institution.

A second doctrine implicated by Kara Walker's display is the government speech doctrine, which holds that government has the right to control speech when the speech occurs in a government-sponsored venue, created and sponsored by government, in which the speech may reasonably be construed to be sponsored, supported, or promoted by the government. This is a twist on the public forum doctrine, where "limited public forums" are supposed to be operated in a content-neutral, come one, come all manner, and not engage in viewpoint discrimination or censorship of speakers or content of the speech. The twist is the situation where the forum appears to the public to be a forum where government itself is speaking, and in that context, the government can choose what is featured as "its speech" by limiting the content of certain speakers in that forum. The courts make distinctions between public forums used for speaking and transitory communication, and the placement of more permanent expressive structures and monuments than are more readily associated with the government planting its message in the forum. The sponsorship and display of a painting on the wall of a public library was held to be government speech that fits under the doctrine.

---

37. Image: Michael D. Murray, Cropped, revised, and resized thumbnail excerpt of public domain photograph of Speaker's Corner at Hyde Park in London.

38. Hence the phrase, "I'll get off my soap box now and stop talking about this issue."

Pleasant Grove City, Utah v. Summum[39]

The United States Supreme Court case of *Pleasant Grove City, Utah v. Summum* is the source of the Government Speech doctrine. In this case, a

public park in Utah was held to be a forum where government had sponsored certain speech through the installation of monuments. One such monument accepted by the government was a monument to the "Ten Commandments" of the Judeo-Christian religion.[40] But the Utah city excluded the Summum religious group, a less-than-mainstream religion, from placing a monument to the "Seven Aphorisms of Summum" in the park alongside the other

fifteen approved monuments, a few of which were religious-oriented, but most were secular in nature. The Supreme Court backed up the government's decision under the newly-coined "government speech" doctrine that limits the public forum doctrine. In contexts such as the Pleasant Grove City park, where permanent markers and structures lend the appearance that government is speaking in the forum, or at least sponsors, supports, and approves of the speech installed in the park, government can be choosy and act in a discriminatory manner as to who gets to place their speech more permanently in the forum so as to avoid the appearance that government espouses, supports, or approves of certain speakers, topics, or viewpoints of which the government in fact does not approve.

Government Speech and Place and Manner Restrictions: Newton v. LePage[41]

The Maine Department of Labor Mural Panels 7-9

"The 1937 Strike"   "Francis Perkins"   "Rosie the Riveter"

Artist Judy Taylor won a contest and was commissioned to paint a large mural to celebrate Maine's labor history. An eleven-panel, seven-foot high mural was created in the main waiting room of the Maine Department of Labor (MDOL).[42] Some time later, a new Republican governor, Paul LePage, took office, and began an extended campaign to limit the power of unions in the state. One side action of this campaign was that LePage

39. *Pleasant Grove City, Utah v. Summum*, 555 U.S. 460 (2009).

40. Image: Michael D. Murray, Cropped, revised, and resized thumbnail excerpt of an exhibit depicting the Ten Commandments monument in a Pleasant Grove City Park (2014), the subject matter of *Pleasant Grove City, Utah v. Summum*, 555 U.S. 460 (2009).

41. *Newton v. LePage*, 700 F.3d 595 (1st Cir. 2012).

42. Images: Michael D. Murray, Cropped, revised, and resized thumbnail excerpt of an exhibit (2015) depicting three panels of Judy Taylor's "Mural of the History of Maine's Labor Movement," at issue in *Newton v. LePage*, 700 F.3d 595 (1st Cir. 2012).

declared that Taylor's mural was too one-sided in favor of organized labor, and ordered that the mural should be removed and relocated.

A lawsuit was brought by five Maine residents who were artists and who had viewed the mural and planned to view it again at the MDOL offices.[43] (Taylor was not one of the plaintiff artists). The suit challenged the removal of the mural on First Amendment grounds.[44]

The suit[45] was a spectacular failure. The U.S. Court of Appeals for the First Circuit was not receptive to the plaintiffs' claims because of the prior holdings of cases that the interiors of government buildings are not a public forum (*see* Kara Walker's scenario above), and because of the government speech doctrine in *Summum*[46] (also discussed immediately above). The court determined that any visitor to the Maine Department of Labor waiting room could reasonably perceive that the mural represented speech that was officially endorsed by the government of Maine. The Labor Department officials who had commented on the mural expressed the view that the message of the mural communicated that the Department of Labor was more receptive to the views of organized labor than it was to employer concerns, and this negatively affected their mission to serve both constituencies.

The Court did not determine the issue raised by the plaintiffs that the movement of the art must be evaluated as a place-and-manner regulation that must meet intermediate scrutiny standards. It would seem to most reasonable observers that the government action was not content-neutral, and in fact was viewpoint-based, because the record was clear that Governor LePage did not want the mural to remain in place because of its pro-labor meaning and message. The Court simply ignored the issue, and determined to follow *Serra*,[47] *supra*, in holding that the movement and prospective relocation of artwork that was owned by the government does not raise a question of censorship subject to any level of scrutiny.

The ending of the story is a happy one: Governor LePage proved to be good to his word that the work would be relocated, and in 2013, all eleven panels of Taylor's *Maine Labor History Mural* were officially relocated to hang in the atrium of the Cultural Building that houses the Maine State Museum.

3. Censorship of Art through Licenses, Regulations on Selling, and Permit Schemes

The government does not have to attack artistic expression head on. There are many indirect and insidious ways to regulate speech. Artists sometimes must take

---

43. *Newton,* 700 F.3d at 600.
44. Note that the suit did not allege claims under the Visual Artists Rights Act (discussed in Chapter 4, *supra*), most likely because the artist, Taylor, was not a plaintiff in the action.
45. *Newton v. LePage,* 700 F.3d 595 (1st Cir. 2012).
46. *Pleasant Grove City, Utah v. Summum,* 555 U.S. 460 (2009).
47. *Serra v. U.S. General Services Admin.,* 847 F.2d 1045 (2d Cir. 1988).

to the streets and sidewalks to display and sell their art. Cities and towns and other government entities, in turn, have attempted to require licenses, permits, leases, and impose other regulatory schemes to put limits on the artists. Artists, in turn, have claimed First Amendment protection for the display of their works as a necessary outlet for their artistic expression. Thus, artists have argued that they should be exempt from licensing schemes and other general restraints on open sales of art, and these arguments have proved on more than one occasion to be successful. *Bery v. City of New York*, 97 F.3d 689 (2d Cir. 1996), *cert. denied*, 520 U.S. 1251 (1997) (selling art on sidewalks and public places was conduct linked to expressive content and thus protected by the First Amendment); *Weinberg v. City of Chicago*, 310 F.3d 1029 (7th Cir. 2002) (same), *cert. denied sub nom., City of Chicago v. Weinberg*, 540 U.S. 817 (2003); *Lederman v. Rosado*, 70 Fed. Appx. 39 (2d Cir. 2003) (same — art vendors); *Celli v. City of St. Augustine*, 214 F. Supp. 2d 1255 (M.D. Fla. 2000) (same); *Wexler v. City of New Orleans*, 267 F. Supp. 2d 559 (E.D. La. 2003) (same — booksellers).

Artists do not always prevail; sometimes the licensing or permit scheme is upheld. *See Second City Music, Inc. v. City of Chicago*, 333 F.3d 846 (7th Cir. 2003) (music reseller subject to vending license requirements); *One World One Family Now v. City and County of Honolulu*, 76 F.3d 1009 (9th Cir. 1996) (ordinance regulating sale of t-shirts bearing message was upheld as content-neutral time-place-manner restriction); *State v. Chepilko*, 965 A.2d 190 (N.J. Super. A.D. 2009) (hawker snapping pictures of passersby with his camera in order to solicit sale of the snapshots to the passersby was not engaged in First Amendment expressive activity); *Baker v. City of New York*, 01 Civ. 48888 (NRB), 2002 U.S. Dist. LEXIS 18100 (S.D.N.Y. Sept. 26, 2002) (street photographer regulated from obstructing pedestrian and vehicular traffic; valid time-place-manner restriction); *Turley v. Giuliani*, 86 F. Supp. 2d 291 (S.D.N.Y. 2000) (street musicians may be subjected to clearly defined decibel volume restrictions that take into account ambient noise conditions); *People v. Saul*, 3 Misc. 3d 260, 776 N.Y.S. 2d 189 (Crim. Ct. City of New York Feb. 19, 2004) (selling Iraqi picture cards on street subject to vending laws because cards were collectible merchandise, not art); *see* John Nivala, *The Landscape Art of Daniel Urban Kiley*, 29 Wm. & Mary Envt'l L. & Pol'y Rev. 267 (2005). The debate is ongoing, and government regulation of public exhibition and performance of artistic expression is a very current issue in First Amendment jurisprudence.

In *Berger v. City of Seattle*, 569 F.3d 1029 (9th Cir. 2009), a street performer brought an action against Seattle alleging that rules concerning the use of public parks violated the First Amendment by restricting his speech activity. The United States District Court for the Western District of Washington granted summary judgment in favor of the performer. The city appealed, and a panel of the Ninth Circuit reversed and remanded. 512 F.3d 582. The Ninth Circuit granted a rehearing en banc, and held that:

> (1) the rule requiring performers to obtain permits before performing was not sufficiently narrowly tailored to meet the standards for a valid time, place, and manner regulation of speech;

(2) genuine issue of material fact exists as to whether the rule limiting performers to designated locations left open ample alternative channels for communication, which precluded summary judgment on the claim that this rule violated the First Amendment;

(3) the rule allowing performers to passively, but not actively, solicit donations was content-based;

(4) the rule governing solicitation was not the least restrictive means by which city could have discouraged aggressive solicitation;

(5) public park-goers were not a protectable captive audience; and

(6) even if the city had a substantial interest in protecting certain park-goers from communications by others, the rule prohibiting all speech activities within 30 feet of any captive audience was not narrowly tailored to meet that interest.

The district court's opinion was affirmed in part and the case was remanded. 569 F.3d 1029.

Bery is not the end of the story on the display and sale of art as protected First Amendment expression even in the Second Circuit. The Second Circuit returned to the issue in *Mastrovincenzo v. City of New York*, 435 F.3d 78 (2d Cir. 2006), *vacating* 313 F. Supp. 2d 280 (S.D.N.Y. 2004). Here, unlicensed street vendors of painted clothing challenged the application of an ordinance which required sidewalk sellers of non-food goods to be licensed. Vendors argued that their painted clothes fell within the visual art First Amendment protection outlined by the court in *Bery*. The appellate court found that the vendors' painted clothing might not be within the meaning of visual arts, such as paintings, intended by the court in creating the "*Bery* injunction." The court applied a predominant purpose test and ultimately found that the purpose of the clothing was more commercial than artistic and expressive, but in the balance, the ordinance's application to the vendors did not work an impermissible restraint on the vendors' free expression rights because New York City's licensing requirement is a content-neutral restriction on speech that is narrowly tailored to achieve the objective of reducing urban congestion. *See also State v. Chepilko*, 965 A.2d 190 (N.J. Super. A.D. 2009) (following *Mastrovincenzo* and *One World One Family Now*, the court found that a hawker snapping pictures of passersby with his camera in order to solicit sale of the snapshots to the passersby was not engaged in First Amendment expressive activity); *Hobbs v. County of Westchester*, 397 F.3d 133 (2d Cir. 2005) (plaintiff was a street performer who brought an action against the county for precluding him from performing his busking act in public forum areas of a city park. The court held that the county did not act contrary to the protections of the First Amendment when it prohibited plaintiff from obtaining a permit for performance on county property because he had a conviction for sexual offenses against minors and such a performance might encourage the gathering of minors around the plaintiff).

Current Case: Street Sales and Street Performances

Chase v. Ocean City, MD[48]

Mark Chase does not simply sell art on the boardwalk at Ocean City, Maryland — he performs it. Chase spray paints art right in front of his

potential customers.[49] His performance, the creation of the art on the spot, right in front of his potential clientele, is most definitely part of Chase's appeal, and it creates the market for sales. But Ocean City tried to shut down his shtick. A new ordinance banned these performances and the sale of art on the boardwalk. In fact, the ordinance went so far as to ban every commercial activity on the boardwalk,

and specifically, every street performance. The law also required registration for any solicitation of money. Chase challenged the law.

The District of Maryland evaluated the law as a content-neutral time-place-manner restriction. Under this intermediate scrutiny, the ordinance failed because its standards and regulations were too vague, and its coverage was far too overbroad for its arguable purposes of protecting the safety, accessibility, and health of patrons on the boardwalk, and fighting crime.

Current Controversy: The Off-Again Ban on L.A. Murals

For ten years from 2003 to 2013, Los Angeles enforced a ban on all murals and large outdoor signage, because it determined that this flat ban was the proper way to eliminate the evil of billboard advertising for aesthetic and property value concerns, and it was willing to throw out the murals with the bathwater. The Supreme Court case, [50] *City Council of Los Angeles v. Taxpayers for Vincent,*[51] had guided this decision

by approving a complete ban on all large billboards and signage in the early 1980's. Although Los Angeles had garnered the nickname of the "City of

---

48. *Chase v. Town of Ocean City, Maryland*, 825 F. Supp. 2d 599 (D. Md. 2011).

49. Image: Michael D. Murray, Cropped, revised, and resized thumbnail excerpt of an exhibit depicting Mark Chase performing art on the Ocean City Boardwalk (2014), the subject matter of *Chase v. Town of Ocean City, Maryland*, 825 F. Supp. 2d 599 (D. Md. 2011).

50. Image: Michael D. Murray, Cropped, revised, and resized thumbnail excerpts of exhibits depicting two of Mike McNeilly's censorship protest murals regarding the ban on murals in Los Angeles (2014).

51. *Members of City Council of City of Los Angeles v. Taxpayers for Vincent*, 466 U.S. 789, 810 (1984).

Murals," the ban caused many muralists to chaff at the restriction. In particular, large-scale muralist Mike McNeilly had a series of post-9/11 "Liberty" murals cancelled, which caused him to protest by putting up illegal murals on the issue of censorship.

On August 28, 2013, the City Council of Los Angeles voted to lift the ban with regard to murals on businesses and privately owned structures, but left the restriction on murals on single-family dwellings in place.

Public Official Helps Ban Private Art Show

The government-private sector divide sometimes becomes blurred when a public outcry against art turns into a private campaign by a government official to shut down the entity housing the art. This story starts when Rensselaer

Polytechnic Institute (RPI) in Troy, NY, invited the artist Wafaa Bilal (a professor at the School of the Art Institute of Chicago) to display his *Virtual Jihadi* video game[52] in March 2008. Bilal, an American citizen who escaped Iraq, had hacked an Al Qaeda-created online video game in which a terrorist hunts down President George W. Bush, entitled *The Night of Bush Capturing*. Wafaa Bilal changed the Al Qaeda version of the game to put his own more nuanced spin on this epic conflict.

The work was meant to bring attention to the vulnerability of Iraqi civilians in the Iraq War, and to criticize racist generalizations and stereotypes as exhibited in American video games, such as *Quest for*

Saddam, which had inspired Al Qaeda to create *The Night of Bush Capturing*. Bilal's game commented on the increased abilities of Al Qaeda to recruit Iraqis because of the United States' failed strategy in securing Iraq. The work also aimed to shed light on groups that traffic in crass and hateful stereotypes of Arab culture with games like *Quest for Saddam*, and was intended to commu-

nicate a distinctly anti-war and anti-violence narrative. But protesters thought any "game" where a user would appear to be playing a terrorist is bad.

The government hook inserted itself when the Head of Public Works in Rensselaer County began to lead the protests against the display.[53] RPI caved in to public pressure and canceled the show, but the sponsors found a replacement site, the Sanctuary for Independent Media. The public works department

---

52. Image: Michael D. Murray, Cropped, revised, and resized thumbnail excerpts of an exhibit depicting the Avatar of Wafaa Bilal's character in the "Virtual Jihadi" video game that was censored in 2008 in Troy, NY (2008).

53. Michael D. Murray, Cropped, revised, and resized thumbnail excerpt of an exhibit depicting the Head of Public Works in Rensselaer County, NY, who took steps to censor Wafaa Bilal's "Virtual Jihadi" video game (2008).

acted once again, and shut down the Sanctuary for purported code violations. This caused the ACLU to bring a federal civil rights lawsuit, which later settled, but, of course, after the time the art show was to have run its course at the replacement site.

Gang Injunction to Clean Up Taggers

Taggers known as MTA (Metro Transit Assassins) made a big, splashy graffiti installation in the Los Angeles River (i.e., drainage canal), a huge pro-ject that was very expensive to clean up.[54] As a result, the Los Angeles County prosecutors brought a "gang injunction" against MTA and individual artists believed to be associated with MTA. Normally, gang injunctions have been used to curb and restrict the activities of members of violent gangs, but like the adaptation of the Racketeer Influenced and Corrupt Organizations Act (RICO) to go beyond organized crime so as to reach securities fraud conspiracies and Medicare/Medicaid fraud violators, so the gang injunction started to look like a useful hammer to drive down some nails.

The injunction of MTA and the individual artists imposed the following conditions: (1) do not associate with other MTA members; (2) create no graffiti; (3) do not possess graffiti tools (i.e., spray paint, paint, brushes, etc.); (4) no trespassing; (5) obey curfews; (6) stay away from certain locations; (7) do not possess firearms, ammunition, dangerous or illegal weapons; (8) do not obstruct, resist, or delay any peace officer; (9) do not profit from unlawful acts; (10) obey all laws.

This prior restraint and somewhat permanent restriction of future activities was problematic because it worked out to be an injunction on the "life and livelihood" of several of the artists. One of the former members of MTA was a street artist known as "Smear," known outside the art world as Cristian Gheorghiu,[55] who had begun to have success in the art world in selling and promoting his works. Gheorghiu had been swept up into the injunction unfairly because of his higher profile and because his name was better-known to the authorities than the other, actual MTA taggers. True, Gheorghiu had been in scrapes with the law for

54. Image: Michael D. Murray, Cropped, revised, and resized thumbnail excerpt from an exhibit depicting the massive L.A. River street art display of MTA, which provoked the imposition of a gang injunction against all MTA Members (2014).

55. Image: Michael D. Murray, Cropped, revised, and resized thumbnail excerpt of an exhibit depicting the likeness of Cristian Gheorghiu, aka "Smear," a street artist alleged to have been involved in the massive L.A. River street art display of MTA, which provoked the imposition of a gang injunction against all MTA Members (2014).

trespassing and other actions relating to his street art, but until the prosecution of MTA was sorted out, the injunction, for all practical purposes, shut down Gheorghiu's livelihood because he could not possess paint and could not profit from his art. The creation of his art was now, according to the injunction, regarded as an unlawful act. As noted, the prosecution came to terms with the defendants enjoined in the suit; for his part, Gheorghiu performed community service (not involving the clean-up of the L.A. River installation, however), and was allowed to continue his art career.

Flying Dog Brewery is Not Shot Down by Licensing Agency

Flying Dog Brewery v. Michigan Liquor Control Commission[56]

Flying Dog Brewery, a craft brewer in Frederick, Maryland, has adorned its bottles with artwork celebrating the "Gonzo Art" style of artist Ralph Stead-

man, a friend of Hunter S. Thompson and of the brewery's owner. The beers themselves were given eye-catching and edgy names, such as "Raging Bitch Belgian-Style India Pale Ale."[57]

Flying Dog filed an application to sell Raging Bitch beer in Michigan, but the application was denied under Michigan Administrative Code Rule 436.1611(1)(d), a regulation that authorized rejection of any beer label submitted for registration that was "deemed to promote violence, racism, sexism, intemperance or intoxication or to be detrimental to the health, safety or welfare of the general public."

Flying Dog sued the Commission and its members for First Amendment violations. The District Court ruled in favor of the Liquor Control Commission, finding that the commissioners had both quasi-judicial immunity and qualified immunity from suit. After the U.S. Court of Appeals for the Sixth Circuit reversed the rulings on both quasi-judicial immunity and qualified immunity, the court opined that in light of other persuasive authorities, there was a distinct possibility that the Commission's rule and the application of the rule to the brewery violated the First Amendment. The rule on its face had vague and overbroad standards. The standards did not appear to have been established and justified by concrete evidence of harmful conditions caused by the effects of the speech appearing on the labels. In short, no evidence had been generated that the beer label restriction was tailored to correct any particular effects of the speech that needed to be controlled by regulation. In the

---

56. *Flying Dog Brewery, LLLP v. Mich. Liquor Control Comm'n*, 870 F. Supp. 2d 477 (W.D. Mich. 2012), *rev'd*, 597 Fed. Appx. 342, 344 (6th Cir. 2015).

57. Image: Michael D. Murray, Cropped, revised, and resized thumbnail excerpt of an exhibit depicting Flying Dog Brewery's "Raging Bitch Belgian-Style India Pale Ale" label that helped provoke the lawsuit, *Flying Dog Brewery, LLLP v. Mich. Liquor Control Comm'n*, 870 F. Supp. 2d 477 (W.D. Mich. 2012), *rev'd*, 597 Fed. Appx. 342, 344 (6th Cir. 2015).

application of the rule, there was insufficient procedural due process (hearing, evidence, review) provided to the brewery, and there was no specific explanation of how "raging" or "bitch" on a beer label presented a danger of the sort that should be regulated by the rule. In short, the case was remanded with a direct implication that the rule might be unconstitutional facially or as applied.[58] Several months after remand, the Commission reversed its original decision, allowing "Raging Bitch" to finally be sold in the state of Michigan.

Tattoo Parlor Denied a Business Permit

Coleman v. City of Mesa[59]

Tattoos are copyrightable art (*see* Chapter 1, *supra*), but the parlors where the art is created are not necessarily a welcome addition to a community. Ryan and

Lactitia Coleman[60] applied for a business permit to operate a tattoo parlor in Mesa, Arizona. The City denied the application based largely on a concern that the parlor would be "inappropriate" for the neighborhood where it was to be located. The Colemans sued the City, alleging that its denial of their permit violated the Colemans' rights to free speech, due process, and equal protection under the United States and Arizona Constitutions. In the trial court, the City successfully moved to dismiss the complaint for failure to state a claim upon which relief can be granted, but the Arizona Court of Appeals reversed the trial court's dismissal of the Colemans' suit.

On review, the Arizona Supreme Court held that tattoos, as well as the process and business of tattooing, is purely expressive activity entitled to First Amendment protection. This expressive activity, and the actual artistic expression produced in the activity, can be regulated only through generally applicable laws imposing reasonable time, place, and manner restrictions that are subject to review under intermediate scrutiny. The Court noted that "[a] tattoo involves expressive elements beyond those present in a 'pen-and-ink' drawing, inasmuch as a tattoo reflects not only the work of the tattoo artist but also the self-expression of the person displaying the tattoo's relatively permanent image." Under this definition, the Colemans stated a claim under the First Amendment because they alleged the City's denial of their permit was not a reasonable time, place, and manner regulation of their speech; it was a ban on operation of a business conducting an expressive speech activity

---

58. *Flying Dog Brewery, LLLP v. Michigan Liquor Control Commn.*, 597 Fed. Appx. 342, 356 (6th Cir. 2015).

59. *Coleman v. City of Mesa*, 284 P.3d 863 (Ariz. 2012).

60. Image: Michael D. Murray, Cropped, revised, and resized thumbnail excerpt of an exhibit depicting Ryan and Laetitia Coleman (2015), the plaintiffs in *Coleman v. City of Mesa*, 284 P.3d 863 (Ariz. 2012)

that relied on the vague criteria that this speech activity was "inappropriate."[61] Government has to have reasons to restrict the speech, and must develop concrete evidence and data to back up those reasons. The alleged defects served by the tattoo parlor restriction were vague or non-existent; there were no specific data of crime, safety, health, or property value problems to support the general development plan that was used as an excuse to justify the permit scheme that kept out this business; there was no evidence there were ample alternative locations for the business in the community; and the enforcement of the permit standards, to the extent there were standards, appeared to be arbitrary. The Court also approved the Colemans' claims for violations of due process and equal protection because, under intermediate scrutiny, the City "acted arbitrarily in denying them a permit[,] and that the action did not further any legitimate government purpose." Having recognized the Colemans' claims as legally cognizable, the Court remanded the case to the Superior Court for further proceedings.

4. Indirect Censorship of Art through Government Funding Restrictions

Regulations and licensing schemes may slow down some artists, but government often can obtain better results by attacking artists' funding for expression. Limiting or cutting off funding can be an indirect but highly successful way for government to accomplish censorship of ideas that are held to be distasteful and unpopular.

National Endowment for the Arts v. Finley

524 U.S. 569 (1998)*

O'CONNOR, Justice.

The National Foundation on the Arts and the Humanities Act of 1965, as amended in 1990, 104 Stat. 1963, requires the Chairperson of the National Endowment for the Arts (NEA) to ensure that "artistic excellence and artistic merit are the criteria by which [grant] applications are judged, taking into consideration general standards of decency and respect for the diverse beliefs and values of the American public." 20 U.S.C. § 954(d)(1). In this case, we review the Court of Appeals' determination that § 954(d)(1), on its face, impermissibly discriminates on the basis of viewpoint and is void for vagueness under the First and Fifth Amendments. We conclude that § 954(d)(1) is

---

61. *See also Anderson v. City of Hermosa Beach*, 621 F.3d 1051 (9th Cir. 2010) (Ninth Circuit struck down a municipal ban on tattooing because tattooing was held to be expressive conduct, the tattoos themselves were speech, and the ordinance imposing a complete ban on this activity was held not to be a reasonable time, place, or manner restriction on free expression).

* Some footnotes and citations omitted.

facially valid, as it neither inherently interferes with First Amendment rights nor violates constitutional vagueness principles.

I

A

With the establishment of the NEA in 1965, Congress embarked on a "broadly conceived national policy of support for the . . . arts in the United States," *see* § 953(b), pledging federal funds to "help create and sustain not only a climate encouraging freedom of thought, imagination, and inquiry but also the material conditions facilitating the release of . . . creative talent." § 951(7). The enabling statute vests the NEA with substantial discretion to award grants; it identifies only the broadest funding priorities, including "artistic and cultural significance, giving emphasis to American creativity ʾand cultural diversity," "professional excellence," and the encouragement of "public knowledge, education, understanding, and appreciation of the arts." *See* §§ 954(c)(1)–(10).

Applications for NEA funding are initially reviewed by advisory panels composed of experts in the relevant field of the arts. Under the 1990 amendments to the enabling statute, those panels must reflect "diverse artistic and cultural points of view" and include "wide geographic, ethnic, and minority representation," as well as "lay individuals who are knowledgeable about the arts." §§ 959(c)(1)–(2). The panels report to the 26-member National Council on the Arts (Council), which, in turn, advises the NEA Chairperson. The Chairperson has the ultimate authority to award grants but may not approve an application as to which the Council has made a negative recommendation. § 955(f).

Since 1965, the NEA has distributed over $3 billion in grants to individuals and organizations, funding that has served as a catalyst for increased state, corporate, and foundation support for the arts. Congress has recently restricted the availability of federal funding for individual artists, confining grants primarily to qualifying organizations and state arts agencies, and constraining subgranting. *See* Department of the Interior and Related Agencies Appropriations Act, 1998, § 329, 111 Stat. 1600. By far the largest portion of the grants distributed in fiscal year 1998 were awarded directly to state arts agencies. In the remaining categories, the most substantial grants were allocated to symphony orchestras, fine arts museums, dance theater foundations, and opera associations. *See* National Endowment for the Arts, FY 1998 Grants, Creation & Presentation 5–8, 20, 21, 27.

Throughout the NEA's history, only a handful of the agency's roughly 100,000 awards have generated formal complaints about misapplied funds or abuse of the public's trust. Two provocative works, however, prompted public controversy in 1989 and led to congressional revaluation of the NEA's funding priorities and efforts to increase oversight of its grant-making procedures. The Institute of Contemporary Art at the University of Pennsylvania had used $30,000 of a visual arts grant it received from the NEA to fund a 1989 retrospective of photographer Robert Mapplethorpe's work. The exhibit, entitled *The Perfect Moment*, included homoerotic photographs that several Members of Congress condemned as pornographic. *See, e.g.,* 135 Cong. Rec. 22372 (1989). Members also denounced artist Andres Serrano's work *Piss Christ*, a photograph of a crucifix immersed in urine. *See, e.g., id.,* at 9789. Serrano had been awarded a $15,000 grant from the Southeast Center for Contemporary Art, an organization that received NEA support.

When considering the NEA's appropriations for fiscal year 1990, Congress reacted to the controversy surrounding the Mapplethorpe and Serrano photographs by eliminating $45,000 from the agency's budget, the precise amount contributed to the two exhibits by NEA grant recipients. Congress also enacted an amendment providing that no NEA funds "may be used to promote, disseminate, or produce materials which in the judgment of [the NEA] may be considered obscene, including but not limited to, depictions of sadomasochism, homoeroticism, the sexual exploitation of children, or individuals engaged in sex acts and which, when taken as a whole, do not have serious literary, artistic, political, or scientific value." Department of the Interior and Related Agencies Appropriations Act, 1990, 103 Stat. 738-42. The NEA implemented Congress' mandate by instituting a requirement that all grantees certify in writing that they would not utilize federal funding to engage in projects inconsistent with the criteria in the 1990 appropriations bill. That certification requirement was subsequently invalidated as unconstitutionally vague by a Federal District Court, *see Bella Lewitzky Dance Foundation v. Frohnmayer,* 754 F. Supp. 774 (C.D. Cal. 1991), and the NEA did not appeal the decision.

In the 1990 appropriations bill, Congress also agreed to create an Independent Commission of constitutional law scholars to review the NEA's grant-making procedures and assess the possibility of more focused standards for public arts funding. The Commission's report, issued in September 1990, concluded that there is no constitutional obligation to provide arts funding, but also recommended that the NEA rescind the certification requirement and cautioned against legislation setting forth any content restrictions. Instead, the Commission suggested procedural changes to enhance the role of advisory panels and a statutory reaffirmation of "the high place the nation accords to the fostering of mutual respect for the disparate beliefs and values among us." *See* Independent Commission, Report to Congress on the National Endowment for the Arts 83-91 (Sept. 1990), 3 Record, Doc. No. 51, Exh. K (hereinafter Report to Congress).

Informed by the Commission's recommendations, and cognizant of pending judicial challenges to the funding limitations in the 1990 appropriations bill, Congress debated several proposals to reform the NEA's grant-making process when it considered the agency's reauthorization in the fall of 1990. The House rejected the Crane Amendment, which would have virtually eliminated the NEA, *see* 136 Cong. Rec. 28656-57 (1990), and the Rohrabacher Amendment, which would have introduced a prohibition on awarding any grants that could be used to "promote, distribute, disseminate, or produce matter that has the purpose or effect of denigrating the beliefs, tenets, or objects of a particular religion" or "of denigrating an individual, or group of individuals, on the basis of race, sex, handicap, or national origin," *id.*, at 28657-64. Ultimately, Congress adopted the Williams/Coleman Amendment, a bipartisan compromise between Members opposing any funding restrictions and those favoring some guidance to the agency. In relevant part, the Amendment became § 954(d)(1), which directs the Chairperson, in establishing procedures to judge the artistic merit of grant applications, to "tak[e] into consideration general standards of decency and respect for the diverse beliefs and values of the American public."*

B

The four individual respondents in this case, Karen Finley, John Fleck, Holly Hughes, and Tim Miller, are performance artists who applied for NEA grants before § 954(d)(1) was enacted. An advisory panel recommended approval of respondents' projects, both initially and after receiving Frohnmayer's request to reconsider three of the applications. A majority of the Council subsequently recommended disapproval, and in June 1990, the NEA informed respondents that they had been denied funding. Respondents filed suit, alleging that the NEA had violated their First Amendment rights by rejecting the applications on political grounds, had failed to follow statutory procedures by basing the denial on criteria other than those set forth in the NEA's enabling statute. . . . Respondents sought restoration of the recommended grants or reconsideration of their applications. . . . When Congress enacted § 954(d)(1), respondents, now joined by the National Association of Artists' Organizations (NAAO), amended their complaint to challenge the provision as void for vagueness and impermissibly viewpoint based. . . .

The District Court then granted summary judgment in favor of respondents on their facial constitutional challenge to § 954(d)(1) and enjoined enforcement of the provision. *See* 795 F. Supp., at 1476. . . . A divided panel of the Court of Appeals affirmed the District Court's ruling. 100 F.3d 671 (C.A.9 1996). . . . We granted certiorari, 522 U.S. 991, 118 S. Ct. 554, 139 L. Ed. 2d 396 (1997), and now reverse the judgment of the Court of Appeals.

---

* Title 20 U.S.C. § 954(d) provides in full that:

"No payment shall be made under this section except upon application therefor which is submitted to the National Endowment for the Arts in accordance with regulations issued and procedures established by the Chairperson. In establishing such regulations and procedures, the Chairperson shall ensure that —

"(1) artistic excellence and artistic merit are the criteria by which applications are judged, taking into consideration general standards of decency and respect for the diverse beliefs and values of the American public; and

"(2) applications are consistent with the purposes of this section. Such regulations and procedures shall clearly indicate that obscenity is without artistic merit, is not protected speech, and shall not be funded."

II

A

Respondents raise a facial constitutional challenge to §954(d)(1), and consequently they confront "a heavy burden" in advancing their claim. . . . To prevail, respondents must demonstrate a substantial risk that application of the provision will lead to the suppression of speech.

Respondents argue that the provision is a paradigmatic example of view-point discrimination because it rejects any artistic speech that either fails to respect mainstream values or offends standards of decency. The premise of respondents' claim is that §954(d)(1) constrains the agency's ability to fund certain categories of artistic expression. The NEA, however, reads the provision as merely hortatory, and contends that it stops well short of an absolute restriction. Section 954(d)(1) adds "considerations" to the grant-making process; it does not preclude awards to projects that might be deemed "indecent" or "disrespectful," nor place conditions on grants, or even specify that those factors must be given any particular weight in reviewing an application. Indeed, the agency asserts that it has adequately implemented §954(d)(1) merely by ensuring the representation of various backgrounds and points of view on the advisory panels that analyze grant applications. . . .

That §954(d)(1) admonishes the NEA merely to take "decency and respect" into consideration and that the legislation was aimed at reforming procedures rather than precluding speech undercut respondents' argument that the provision inevitably will be utilized as a tool for invidious viewpoint discrimination. In cases where we have struck down legislation as facially unconstitutional, the dangers were both more evident and more substantial. In *R.A.V. v. St. Paul*, 505 U.S. 377, 112 S. Ct. 2538, 120 L. Ed. 2d 305 (1992), for example, we invalidated on its face a municipal ordinance that defined as a criminal offense the placement of a symbol on public or private property "'which one knows or has reasonable grounds to know arouses anger, alarm or resentment in others on the basis of race, color, creed, religion or gender.'" *See id.*, at 380, 112 S. Ct., at 2541. That provision set forth a clear penalty, proscribed views on particular "disfavored subjects," *id.*, at 391, 112 S. Ct., at 2547-48, and suppressed "distinctive idea[s], conveyed by a distinctive message," *id.*, at 393, 112 S. Ct., at 2548.

In contrast, the "decency and respect" criteria do not silence speakers by expressly "threaten[ing] censorship of ideas." *See ibid.* Thus, we do not per-ceive a realistic danger that §954(d)(1) will compromise First Amendment values. As respondents' own arguments demonstrate, the considerations that the provision introduces, by their nature, do not engender the kind of directed viewpoint discrimination that would prompt this Court to invalidate a statute on its face. Respondents assert, for example, that "[o]ne would be hard-pressed to find two people in the United States who could agree on what the 'diverse beliefs and values of the American public' are, much less on whether a particular work of art 'respects' them"; and they claim that "'[d]ecency' is likely to mean something very different to a septuagenarian in Tuscaloosa and a teenager in Las Vegas." . . . Accordingly, the provision does not introduce considerations that, in practice, would effectively preclude or punish the expression of particular views. Indeed, one could hardly anticipate how "decency" or "respect" would bear on grant applications in categories such as funding for symphony orchestras.

Respondents' claim that the provision is facially unconstitutional may be reduced to the argument that the criteria in §954(d)(1) are sufficiently subjective that the agency could utilize them to engage in viewpoint discrimination. Given the varied interpretations of the criteria and the vague exhortation to "take them into consideration," it seems unlikely that this provision will introduce any greater element of selectivity than the determination of "artistic excellence" itself. And we are reluctant, in any event, to invalidate legislation "on the basis of its hypothetical application to situations not before the Court." *FCC v. Pacifica Foundation*, 438 U.S. 726, 743, 98 S. Ct. 3026, 3037, 57 L. Ed. 2d 1073 (1978). . . .

We recognize, of course, that reference to these permissible applications would not alone be sufficient to sustain the statute against respondents' First Amendment challenge. But neither are we persuaded that, in other applications, the language of §954(d)(1) itself will give rise to the suppression of protected expression. Any content-based considerations that may be taken into account in the grant-making process are a consequence of the nature of arts funding. The NEA has limited resources, and it must deny the majority of the grant applications that it receives, including many that propose "artistically excellent" projects. The agency may decide to fund particular projects for a wide variety of reasons, "such as the technical proficiency of the artist, the creativity of the work, the anticipated public interest in or appreciation of the work, the work's contemporary relevance, its educational value, its suitability for or appeal to special audiences (such as children or the disabled), its service to a rural or isolated community, or even simply that the work could increase public knowledge of an art form." Brief for Petitioners 32. As the dissent below noted, it would be "impossible to have a highly selective grant program without denying money to a large amount of constitutionally protected expression." 100 F.3d, at 685 (opinion of Kleinfeld, J.). The "very assumption" of the NEA is that grants will be awarded according to the "artistic worth of competing applicants," and absolute neutrality is simply "inconceivable." *Advocates for the Arts v. Thomson*, 532 F.2d 792, 795-96 (C.A.1), cert. denied, 429 U.S. 894, 97 S. Ct. 254, 50 L. Ed. 2d 177 (1976). . . .

Respondents do not allege discrimination in any particular funding decision. . . . Thus, we have no occasion here to address an as-applied challenge in a situation where the denial of a grant may be shown to be the product of invidious viewpoint discrimination. If the NEA were to leverage its power to award subsidies on the basis of subjective criteria into a penalty on disfavored viewpoints, then we would confront a different case. We have stated that, even in the provision of subsidies, the Government may not "ai[m] at the suppression of dangerous ideas," *Regan v. Taxation With Representation of Wash.*, 461 U.S. 540, 550, 103 S. Ct. 1997, 2003, 76 L. Ed. 2d 129 (1983) (internal quotation marks omitted), and if a subsidy were "manipulated" to have a "coercive effect," then relief could be appropriate. In addition, as the NEA itself concedes, a more pressing constitutional question would arise if Government funding resulted in the imposition of a disproportionate burden calculated to drive "certain ideas or viewpoints from the marketplace." Unless § 954(d)(1) is applied in a manner that raises concern about the suppression of disfavored viewpoints, however, we uphold the constitutionality of the provision.

B

Finally, although the First Amendment certainly has application in the subsidy context, we note that the Government may allocate competitive funding according to criteria that would be impermissible were direct regulation of speech or a criminal penalty at stake. So long as legislation does not infringe on other constitutionally protected rights, Congress has wide latitude to set spending priorities. *See Regan,* supra, at 549, 103 S. Ct., at 2002-03. In the 1990 amendments that incorporated § 954(d)(1), Congress modified the declaration of purpose in the NEA's enabling Act to provide that arts funding should "contribute to public support and confidence in the use of taxpayer funds," and that "[p]ublic funds . . . must ultimately serve public purposes the Congress defines." § 951(5). And as we held in *Rust,* Congress may "selectively fund a program to encourage certain activities it believes to be in the public interest, without at the same time funding an alternative program which seeks to deal with the problem in another way." 500 U.S., at 193, 111 S. Ct., at 1772. In doing so, "the Government has not discriminated on the basis of viewpoint; it has merely chosen to fund one activity to the exclusion of the other." *Ibid.; see also Maher v. Roe,* 432 U.S. 464, 475, 97 S. Ct. 2376, 2383, 53 L. Ed. 2d 484 (1977) ("There is a basic difference between direct state interference with a protected activity and state encouragement of an alternative activity consonant with legislative policy").

III

The lower courts also erred in invalidating § 954(d)(1) as unconstitutionally vague. Under the First and Fifth Amendments, speakers are protected from arbitrary and discriminatory enforcement of vague standards. The terms of the provision are undeniably opaque, and if they appeared in a criminal statute or regulatory scheme, they could raise substantial vagueness concerns. It is unlikely, however, that speakers will be compelled to steer too far clear of any "forbidden area" in the context of grants of this nature. We recognize, as a practical matter, that artists may conform their speech to what they believe to be the decisionmaking criteria in order to acquire funding. But when the Government is acting as patron rather than as sovereign, the consequences of imprecision are not constitutionally severe.

In the context of selective subsidies, it is not always feasible for Congress to legislate with clarity. Indeed, if this statute is unconstitutionally vague, then so too are all Government programs awarding scholarships and grants on the basis of subjective criteria such as "excellence." To accept respondents' vagueness argument would be to call into question the constitutionality of these valuable Government programs and countless others like them.

Section 954(d)(1) merely adds some imprecise considerations to an already subjective selection process. It does not, on its face, impermissibly infringe on First or Fifth Amendment rights. Accordingly, the judgment of the Court of Appeals is reversed, and the case is remanded for further proceedings consistent with this opinion.

It is so ordered.

Note and Questions

1. Given the history of Congress's hostility to "obscene" and "indecent" art recounted in the *Finley* case, should the Court have been so ready to turn a blind eye to ulterior motives and simply decide that the distribution of limited funds according to vague and imprecise criteria (*e.g.*, decency) has no impact on artists' First Amendment rights? Would it be hard for an NEA administrator to trace the history and come to the conclusion that if he or she funds questionable projects, the NEA's funds are going to be cut or eliminated altogether?

2. Given the reality that the NEA will never have enough money to fund every grant request it receives, what alternatives to the "decency and diverse views" criteria might be employed? Should the grants be awarded simply by lottery? Or on a first-come, first-served basis until the money runs out?

Brooklyn Institute of Arts and Sciences v. City of New York

64 F. Supp. 2d 184 (E.D.N.Y. 1999)*

GERSHON, District Judge.

III. The Controversy over the Sensation Exhibit

The Sensation Exhibit was first shown in 1997 at the Royal Academy of Art in London, where it drew record crowds for a contemporary art exhibit and generated controversy and some protest demonstrations. The Brooklyn Museum's Director, Arnold Lehman, viewed the Exhibit in London and decided to attempt to bring it to New York after its scheduled showing at a museum in Berlin. The Exhibit includes approximately ninety works of some forty contemporary British artists, a number of whom have received recognition by the artistic community. Chris Ofili, Damien Hirst, and Rachel Whiteread, for example, have received the Turner Award from the Tate Gallery. After being shown in Brooklyn, the Exhibit is scheduled to be shown at the National Gallery of Australia, and the Toyota City Museum outside of Tokyo.

---

* Footnotes omitted.

Mr. Lehman's efforts to bring the Exhibit to Brooklyn continued through 1998, and plans were finalized in April 1999. Mr. Lehman, starting in 1998, kept the Museum's Board of Trustees informed of his efforts, and of the Exhibit's controversial nature. The Mayor of the City is an ex officio member of the Board, but his representative did not attend certain meetings at which the Exhibit was discussed, although minutes of the meetings were sent to him. The Commissioner of the City's Department of Cultural Affairs, Schuyler Chapin, also is an ex officio member of the Board of Trustees. His designated representative did attend meetings regularly and receive minutes of Board meetings. On or about March 10, 1999, Mr. Lehman gave Commissioner Chapin a copy of the catalog for the Exhibit and discussed its content. The catalog includes photographs and descriptions of virtually all of the works in the Exhibit, including every work that the City now finds objectionable. For example, it contains a full page color photograph of "The Holy Virgin Mary" and a description of the materials of which it is made, including elephant dung. On or about April 6, 1999, Mr. Lehman sent letters to members of the Board of Trustees, including Commissioner Chapin and other public officials, stating that the Exhibit was controversial, and he set forth the Museum's plans to charge an admission fee for the Exhibit and to require that all children be accompanied by an adult. The letters specifically described the work of the artist Damien Hirst, recognized "for his sections of various animals (sharks, lambs, etc.) individually preserved and presented in sealed, formaldehyde-filled glass containers." The Museum issued a similar press release on about the same date. A New York Times article on April 8, 1999, entitled "British Outrage Heads for Brooklyn," described reactions of shock and condemnation, together with protests, that the Exhibit had generated in London, as well as accusations by detractors that the Exhibit promoted the commercial interests of Charles Saatchi, owner of all of the works in the Exhibit. The article described some of the controversial works in the Exhibit, including that of Hirst.

Detail of Chris Ofili, Holy Virgin Mary *(1996)*

Detail of Damien Hirst, Some Comfort Gained from the Acceptance
of the Inherent Lies in Everything *(1996)*

Commissioner Chapin, in a letter dated April 14, thanked Mr. Lehman for his "fascinating letter" about the Exhibit, which, he wrote, seemed designed to "shake up New York's art world." Commissioner Chapin voiced no objection to the Museum's planned admission policies and promised to convey "any thoughts about funding he might have." There is no evidence that the Mayor himself was personally aware of the specific contents of the Exhibit.

The Exhibit was scheduled to open to the public at the Museum on October 2, 1999. City officials first began raising objections to the Exhibit on September 22. On that date, Commissioner Chapin, stating that he was acting on behalf of the Mayor, advised Mr. Lehman by telephone that the City would terminate all funding to the Museum unless it canceled the Exhibit. Commissioner Chapin specifically referred to the fact that the Mayor found objectionable "The Holy Virgin Mary" by Chris Ofili. (All of the five Ofili works in the Exhibit use elephant dung together with other materials. In addition, on the painting entitled "The Holy Virgin Mary," there are small photographs of buttocks and female genitalia scattered on the background.) The Mayor explained his position publicly that day, taking particular exception to "The Holy Virgin Mary." The Mayor stated that this work "offends me" and "is sick," and he explained his decision to terminate City funding as follows:

> You don't have a right to a government subsidy to desecrate someone else's religion. And therefore we will do everything that we can to remove funding from the [Museum] until the director comes to his senses. And realizes that if you are a government subsidized enterprise then you can't do things that desecrate the most personal and deeply held views of the people in society.

The Mayor also referred to a Hirst work of two pigs in formaldehyde as "sick stuff" to be exhibited in an art museum.

The following day, the Mayor accused the Museum of violating the Lease by mounting an exhibit which was inaccessible to schoolchildren and by failing to obtain his permission to restrict access to the Exhibit, which he made clear he would not give because of his view that taxpayer-funded property should not be used to "desecrate religion" or "do things that are disgusting with regard to animals." In a letter from New York City Corporation Counsel Michael D. Hess to Mr. Lehman, dated September 23, 1999, Mr. Hess stated that "[t]he Mayor will not approve a modification of the Contract to allow [the Museum] to restrict admission to the museum. In light of the fact that [the Museum] has already determined that it would be inappropriate for those under 17 years of age to be admitted to the exhibit without adult supervision (a determination with which the City does not disagree), [the Museum] cannot proceed with the exhibit as planned."

The Mayor and other senior City officials continued, and escalated, their attacks on the Exhibit and their threats to the Museum, vowing to cut off all funding, including construction funding, to seek to replace the Board of Trustees, to cancel the Lease, and to assume possession of the Museum building, unless the Exhibit were canceled. The Mayor asserted on September 24 that he would not "have any compunction about trying to put them out of business, meaning the board." On September 28, the Mayor publicly stated that taxpayer dollars should not "be used to support the desecration of important national or religious symbol, of any religion." A City press release that day denounced "an exhibit which besmirches religion and is an insult to the community." The press release announced that, in response to the Museum Board's formal decision that day to proceed with the Exhibit, the City would end its funding of the Museum immediately. In his deposition, Deputy Mayor Joseph Lhota acknowledged that he had earlier told the Chairman of the Museum's Board of Trustees, Robert Rubin, that all City funding to the Museum would be canceled unless the Museum agreed to remove "The Holy Virgin Mary" from the Exhibit.

In response to the City's threats, including explicit statements by senior officials that the City would withhold its monthly payment of $497,554 due on October 1, 1999, the Museum commenced this action against the City and the Mayor on September 28, 1999, pursuant to 42 U.S.C. § 1983, seeking declaratory and injunctive relief, to prevent the defendants from punishing or retaliating against the Museum for displaying the Exhibit, in violation of the Museum's rights under the First and Fourteenth Amendments, including cutting off funding, terminating the lease, seizing the building or attempting to fire the Board of Trustees. The City has in fact withheld the scheduled October payment to the Museum. Plaintiff filed an amended complaint on October 1, 1999, adding claims for damages against the defendants, and claims of violation of the Equal Protection Clause and state and local law.

Meanwhile, on September 30, 1999, shortly before a conference scheduled by this court began, the City filed an action for ejectment against the Museum in New York State Supreme Court, Kings County. On the basis of that suit, the City invoked the abstention principles of *Younger v. Harris*, 401 U.S. 37, 91 S. Ct. 746, 27 L. Ed. 2d 669 (1971), and asked this court to dismiss plaintiff's claims for injunctive and declaratory relief. . . .

The City's state court ejectment action alleges that the Museum forfeited its right to occupy the premises by violating the Lease, the Contract, and the Museum's enabling legislation, in the following respects: (1) imposing a $9.75 admission charge for the Exhibit, without the Mayor's approval; (2) violating the Museum's obligation to "educate and enlighten school children and the public" and to serve a public purpose, in that the Museum intended to proceed with the Exhibit, which the City contends contains inappropriate, "sensational" matter that is "offensive to significant segments of the public"; and (3) improperly furthering "the commercial interests of private parties," rather than public purposes, because the works in the Exhibit come from the private collection of Charles Saatchi, who is a client of Christie's, the auction house, which also gave financial support to the Exhibit.

As described above, City officials had also claimed that the Museum's decision to restrict admission of children to the Exhibit violated the terms of the Lease, which, they claimed, requires open and equal access to the Museum by schoolchildren. Two days before the City initiated its ejectment action, the Museum's Board responded to this complaint by rescinding the requirement that children under seventeen be accompanied by adults, and instead posted warning notices.

At oral argument on October 8, the City announced that it was abandoning two of the three grounds for its ejectment action. The abandoned grounds are that the City is entitled to eject the Museum based upon the admission charge, and upon a perceived impropriety in the relationship among Mr. Saatchi, Christie's and the Museum. The City also abandoned any claim based upon the initial restriction on the admission of minors. The City now claims a right to eject the Museum based solely on its perception of the content of works in the Sensation Exhibit. The defendants' supplemental memorandum, filed after oral argument, asserts that the First Amendment does not prohibit the City from refusing to subsidize displays of art that are offensive and foster religious intolerance; it does not rely upon either of the grounds abandoned in the ejectment action. . . .

THE FIRST AMENDMENT CLAIM: THE MUSEUM'S MOTION FOR A PRELIMINARY INJUNCTION

I. Standard for Issuing a Preliminary Injunction

A party seeking a preliminary injunction must ordinarily demonstrate (a) irreparable harm and (b) either (1) likelihood of success on the merits or (2) sufficiently serious questions going to the merits to make them a fair ground of litigation and a balance of hardships tipping decidedly in its favor. *Time Warner Cable of New York City v. Bloomberg L.P.*, 118 F.3d 917, 923 (2d Cir. 1997). The defendants argue that the second, lesser standard is inapplicable to them as governmental actors, but the kind of governmental conduct entitled to a "higher degree of deference" and therefore requiring a showing of a likelihood of success on the merits, *see Able v. United States*, 44 F.3d 128, 131 (2d Cir. 1995) (per curiam), is not involved in this case, where defendants

essentially rely on the Lease, which restates the purposes of the enabling legislation, and the Contract. In any event, as will be seen, the Museum easily
establishes a likelihood of success on the merits.

II. Irreparable Harm

The Museum is suffering and will continue to suffer irreparable harm if an
injunction is not granted. "The loss of First Amendment freedoms, for even
minimal periods of time, unquestionably constitutes irreparable injury."
Elrod v. Burns, 427 U.S. 347, 373, 96 S. Ct. 2673, 49 L. Ed. 2d 547 (1976)
(plurality opinion); *Bery v. City of New York*, 97 F.3d 689, 693 (2d Cir.
1996), cert. denied 520 U.S. 1251, 117 S. Ct. 2408, 138 L. Ed. 2d
174 (1997). Because of this, it is sometimes said that "when an injunction is
sought to protect First Amendment rights, likelihood of success on the merits
and irreparable harm merge into a single threshold requirement." *801 Conklin
St. Ltd. v. Town of Babylon*, 38 F. Supp. 2d 228, 235 (E.D.N.Y. 1999) (citations
omitted); *Blum v. Schlegel*, 830 F. Supp. 712, 723 (W.D.N.Y. 1993), aff'd,
18 F.3d 1005 (2d Cir. 1994) (citations omitted). *See also Beal v. Stern*,
184 F.3d 117, 123-24 (2d Cir. 1999).

The City and the Mayor argue that there is no irreparable injury because
the Museum has not shown that the withholding of funding prevented it from
showing the Sensation Exhibit or that the loss of its operating and maintenance
subsidy will force the imminent closing of the Museum. Counsel for defendants further stated at oral argument that the City's own ejectment suit cannot
be a sound basis for a preliminary injunction motion because the suit has just
begun and, "in the event that that particular action gets to a critical stage," the
motion can be renewed. These arguments ignore the very reason that interference with First Amendment rights constitutes irreparable injury.

This is not a case involving the mere assertion of an incidental infringement of First Amendment rights insufficient to establish irreparable harm. *See,
e.g.*, *Hohe v. Casey*, 868 F.2d 69, 72-73 (3d Cir.), cert. denied 493 U.S. 848,
110 S. Ct. 144, 107 L. Ed. 2d 102 (1989). Nor does the Museum rely on remote
or speculative fears of future retaliation. *See, e.g.*, *Latino Officers Association v.
Safir*, 170 F.3d 167, 171 (2d Cir. 1999); *Alvarez v. City of New York*,
2 F. Supp. 2d 509, 513 (S.D.N.Y. 1998). The Museum has already suffered
direct and purposeful penalization by the City in response to its exercise of
First Amendment rights. First, the City has cut off appropriated funding.
Second, the City has sued in state court to evict the Museum from the property
which it has occupied for over one hundred years and in which it houses its
enormous collections of ancient and modern art. In its abstention motion, the
City asks the court to treat its ejectment suit as brought in good faith, that is, as
brought with the goal of ejecting the Museum. It cannot on the one hand seek
so serious a penalty (it could, after all, have brought only a declaratory judgment action) and on the other hand claim that no harm is imminent. For a
museum of the magnitude of the Brooklyn Museum, planning for a move of
one and a half million art objects would obviously be a monumental task.

Given the finding of a likelihood of success on the merits of the Museum's claim of a First Amendment violation, the Museum should not have to wait until a City sheriff is at the door to seek equitable relief.

In addition, the facts establish an ongoing effort by the Mayor and the City to coerce the Museum into relinquishing its First Amendment rights. On September 24, the Mayor stated that "since they [the Museum Board members] seem to have no compunction about putting their hands in the taxpayers' pockets . . . and throwing dung on important religious symbols, I'm not going to have any compunction about trying to put them out of business, meaning the board." Then, on September 28, the Mayor went on to state that "[t]he Corporation Counsel told them what we're going to do, the lease tells us what we're required to do, which is to evict them and to stop dealing with them as a board. We'll do that over a period of time. We'll hold back their funds because they are not a properly constituted board at this point and then over a period of time there will be a substitute board put in place."

That the Museum has so far stood up to these efforts does not deprive it of the right to injunctive relief. The prospect of money damages does not cure the irreparable injury of an already existing, purposeful penalization for the exercise of First Amendment rights. Nor must the Museum endure ongoing efforts to coerce the relinquishment of those rights, including the continuing threat of ejectment, because money damages are available at the conclusion of the suit. Irreparable injury has been established.

III. The Museum's Likelihood of Success on its First Amendment Claim

"If there is any fixed star in our constitutional constellation, it is that no official, high or petty, can prescribe what shall be orthodox in politics, nationalism, religion, or other matters of opinion. . . ." *West Virginia State Bd. of Educ. v. Barnette*, 319 U.S. 624, 642, 63 S. Ct. 1178, 87 L. Ed. 1628 (1943). In keeping with that principle, the First Amendment bars government officials from censoring works said to be "offensive," *Texas v. Johnson*, 491 U.S. 397, 414, 109 S. Ct. 2533, 105 L. Ed. 2d 342 (1989), "sacrilegious," *Joseph Burstyn, Inc. v. Wilson*, 343 U.S. 495, 531, 72 S. Ct. 777, 96 L. Ed. 1098 (1952), "morally improper," *Hannegan v. Esquire*, 327 U.S. 146, 149, 66 S. Ct. 456, 90 L. Ed. 586 (1946), or even "dangerous," *Regan v. Taxation with Representation of Washington*, 461 U.S. 540, 548, 103 S. Ct. 1997, 76 L. Ed. 2d 129 (1983). "If there is a bedrock principle underlying the First Amendment, it is that the government may not prohibit the expression of an idea simply because society finds the idea itself offensive or disagreeable." *Texas v. Johnson*, 491 U.S. at 414, 109 S. Ct. 2533. . . .

The City and the Mayor acknowledge that the art being shown at the Museum and the ideas which they find that art to express are within the protections of the First and Fourteenth Amendments. Contrary to their assertions, however, although they did not physically remove the art objects from the Museum, they are not insulated from a claim that they are violating the overwhelming body of First Amendment law establishing that government cannot suppress ideas indirectly any more than it can do so directly.

Governmental efforts to suppress expression can take many forms, and the courts have not hesitated to invalidate those efforts, no matter how indirect the form. In *Speiser v. Randall*, 357 U.S. 513, 78 S. Ct. 1332, 2 L. Ed. 2d 1460 (1958), for example, the Supreme Court noted that "[t]o deny an exemption to claimants [of property tax exemptions] who engage in certain forms of speech is in effect to penalize them for such speech. Its deterrent effect is the same as if the State were to fine them for this speech." 357 U.S. at 518, 78 S. Ct. 1332. In *Hannegan*, the Court recognized that "[t]he second-class [mail] privilege is a form of subsidy," 327 U.S. at 151, 66 S. Ct. 456 (footnote omitted), and found that the denial of the privilege based on the immorality of a publication amounted to illegal censorship. *Id.* at 157, 66 S. Ct. 456.

In yet another line of cases illustrating that freedom of speech cannot be subjected to indirect violations, the Supreme Court has held that the First Amendment protects government employees and those who have independent contracts with the government from termination based solely on speech found offensive to the government. *See, e.g., Bd. of County Commissioners, Wabaunsee County, Kansas v. Umbehr*, 518 U.S. 668, 116 S. Ct. 2342, 135 L. Ed. 2d 843 (1996); *Perry v. Sindermann*, 408 U.S. 593, 92 S. Ct. 2694, 33 L. Ed. 2d 570 (1972). For example, in *Perry*, the Supreme Court held that a professor at a State college who lacked any contractual or tenure right to re-employment could not be denied renewal of his contract on the ground that he had publicly criticized the policies of the college administration. The Court stated:

> For at least a quarter-century, this Court has made clear that even though a person has no "right" to a valuable governmental benefit and even though the government may deny him the benefit for any number of reasons, there are some reasons upon which the government may not rely. It may not deny a benefit to a person on a basis that infringes his constitutionally protected interests — especially, his interest in freedom of speech. For if the government could deny a benefit to a person because of his constitutionally protected speech or associations, his exercise of those freedoms would in effect be penalized and inhibited. This would allow the government to "produce a result which (it) could not command directly." Such interference with constitutional rights is impermissible.

408 U.S. at 597, 92 S. Ct. 2694 (citation omitted).

In many different contexts, then, the Supreme Court has made clear that, although the government is under no obligation to provide various kinds of benefits, it may not deny them if the reason for the denial would require a choice between exercising First Amendment rights and obtaining the benefit. That is, it may not "discriminate invidiously in its subsidies in such a way as to 'aim[] at the suppression of dangerous ideas.'" *Regan*, 461 U.S. at 548, 103 S. Ct. 1997 (citation omitted).

The decision to withhold an already appropriated general operating subsidy from an institution which has been supported by the City for over one hundred years, and to eject it from its City-owned building, because of the Mayor's objection to certain works in a current exhibit, is, in its own way, to "discriminate invidiously in its subsidies in such a way as to 'aim[] at the suppression of dangerous ideas.'" *Id.* "The Government's purpose is the controlling consideration" in determining whether a restriction on speech is viewpoint discriminatory. *Ward v. Rock Against Racism,* 491 U.S. 781, 791, 109 S. Ct. 2746, 105 L. Ed. 2d 661 (1989). By its own words, the City here threatened to withhold funding if the Museum continued with its plans to show the Exhibit. When the Museum resisted, the City withheld its funding and filed a suit for ejectment. While initially the City engaged in various claims of a violation of its Lease and Contract, unrelated to the content of the Exhibit, the City has now admitted the obvious; it has acknowledged that its purpose is directly related, not just to the content of the Exhibit, but to the particular viewpoints expressed. There can be no greater showing of a First Amendment violation.

In a case remarkably similar to this one, *Cuban Museum of Arts and Culture, Inc. v. City of Miami,* 766 F. Supp. 1121 (S.D. Fla. 1991), the City of Miami was enjoined from refusing to renew an expired lease with the Cuban Museum because the Court held that the City had violated the museum's First Amendment rights, in that the refusal to renew was motivated by the City's opposition to the museum's exhibition of works of Cuban artists who were either living in Cuba or who had not denounced Fidel Castro. These works were highly offensive to a large segment of the Cuban population of Miami. The Court found that the exhibition was fully protected by the First Amendment, that the absence of a "right" to renewal did not defeat the First Amendment claim, and that the claimed lease violations were pretextual. *See Cuban Museum,* 766 F. Supp. at 1126-27 ("the Conduct of the City Commission with respect to the asserted grounds for the denial of continued possession reveals that the reasons asserted were either minor concerns or a pretextual basis upon which to remove the Cuban Museum and its present directors"). It found that the "City would not have acted to deny the plaintiffs' continued use and possession of the premises but for the plaintiffs' controversial exercise of their First Amendment rights." *Id.* at 1129. The same is true here.

The cases establishing the principle that the government cannot avoid the reach of the First Amendment by acting indirectly rather than directly also illustrate the fallacy in the claim of the Mayor and the City that, while the Exhibit can be shown privately, "the taxpayers don't have to pay for it." Federal taxpayers in effect pay for the mailing of periodicals that many of them find objectionable; and they subsidize all manner of views with which they do not agree, indeed, which they may abhor, through tax exemptions and deductions given to other taxpayers. State taxpayers pay the salary for the professor whom the State wants to fire for speaking out against the State college. In sum, where the denial of a benefit, subsidy or contract is motivated by a desire to suppress speech in violation of the First Amendment, that denial will be enjoined. That is all that is involved here. . . .

Clarifying what the case at bar is not about will further illustrate the distinction between requiring the taxpayer to support a particular point of view, which is not involved here, and barring government officials from invidiously discriminating against ideas they find offensive, either to themselves or to members of the community.

First, there is no issue presented here about the City's right to itself take positions, even controversial ones. The Museum does not challenge the principle that government may choose, through its funding, to espouse a viewpoint on a matter of public concern without, as a result, being required to give equal time to an opposing view. *See Rust v. Sullivan*, 500 U.S. 173, 111 S. Ct. 1759, 114 L. Ed. 2d 233 (1991). Thus, the doctrine of *Rust*, upon which defendants rely, has no relevance here. That is, the Mayor and the City are permitted to foster the values that they claim to be seeking to foster, such as respect for the most dearly held beliefs of others and lack of vulgarity in art. As the Court stated in *Barnette*, 319 U.S. at 640, 63 S. Ct. 1178, however, "[n]ational unity as an end which officials may foster by persuasion and example is not in question. The problem is whether under our Constitution compulsion as here employed is a permissible means for its achievement." Indeed, the notion that government officials can stifle expression in order to protect the public good reverses our most basic principles. As Justice Jackson so compellingly described in *Barnette*, in striking a compulsory flag salute and pledge of allegiance statute:

> Government of limited power need not be anemic government. Assurance that rights are secure tends to diminish fear and jealousy of strong government, and by making us feel safe to live under it makes for its better support. Without promise of a limiting Bill of Rights it is doubtful if our Constitution could have mustered enough strength to enable its ratification. To enforce those rights today is not to choose weak government over strong government. It is only to adhere as a means of strength to individual freedom of mind in preference to officially disciplined uniformity for which history indicates a disappointing and disastrous end.

Id. at 636-37, 63 S. Ct. 1178.

Second, the City and the Mayor argue that, if they are not allowed to cut off all financial support to the Museum as a result of its display of the Sensation Exhibit, there will be no limit on what the public is required to support in the name of the First Amendment. This is incorrect. The Museum makes no claim in this case that government has an obligation to fund particular forums of expression such as museums. *See generally Regan*, 461 U.S. at 540, 103 S. Ct. 1997 (citations omitted). Nor is there an issue in this case as to whether the City could be required to provide funding to support the Sensation Exhibit or any other particular exhibit, if the Museum had sought funding on an exhibit-by-exhibit basis. The City has not in fact provided the funding — some $2 million — to cover the various expenses involved in presenting the Sensation Exhibit. Thus, the issue is not whether the City could have been required to provide funding for the Sensation Exhibit, but whether the Museum, having been allocated a general operating subsidy, can now be penalized with the loss of that subsidy, and ejectment from a City-owned building, because of the perceived viewpoint of the works in the Exhibit. The answer to that question is no.

The reliance of the City and the Mayor on *National Endowment for the Arts v. Finley*, 524 U.S. 569, 118 S. Ct. 2168, 141 L. Ed. 2d 500 (1998), as support for their claim that viewpoint discrimination in arts funding is permissible, is misplaced. In *Finley*, the Supreme Court rejected a facial challenge to a provision adding "general standards of decency and respect for the diverse beliefs and values of the American public" to the "considerations" to be applied by the NEA in the awarding of grants to individual artists and arts organizations. The Court described the provision's legislative history, including Congress's rejection of language that would have prohibited awards of grants that would have the purpose or effect of denigrating particular religions, or of denigrating people on the basis of race, sex, handicap, or national origin. 118 S. Ct. at 2173. It noted that, ultimately, "[t]he legislation was a bipartisan proposal introduced as a counterweight to amendments aimed at eliminating the NEA's funding or substantially constraining its grant-making authority." *Id.* at 2176. The Court also noted that "Congress declined to disallow any particular viewpoints," *id.*, and it went on to hold the challenged provision facially constitutional upon finding that it "[did] not preclude awards to projects that might be deemed 'indecent' or 'disrespectful' nor place conditions on grants ..." and, further, because the Court did "not perceive a realistic danger" that it will be used "to effectively preclude or punish the expression of particular views." *Id.* at 2175-77. Thus, even in *Finley*, where the issue was the "considerations" that could apply in the awarding of grants, unlike here, where funding has already been appropriated for general operating expenses, the Supreme Court upheld the "decency" and "respect" considerations only by reading them, on their face, as not permitting viewpoint discrimination.

When questioned on oral argument whether the City could direct a publicly supported library to remove particular books on pain of a loss of financial support, counsel for defendants responded that the visual art in the Exhibit has a greater impact than do books. Counsel for the Museum, in reply, noted that books like *Mein Kampf* have done enormous harm, but are still protected by the First Amendment. The relative power of books and visual art is of course immaterial. The communicative power of visual art is not a basis for restricting it but rather the very reason it is protected by the First Amendment. As recently stated by the Court of Appeals for the Second Circuit, "[v]isual art is as wide ranging in its depiction of ideas, concepts and emotions as any book, treatise, pamphlet or other writing, and is similarly entitled to full First Amendment protection." *Bery*, 97 F.3d at 695. *See also Ward*, 491 U.S. at 790, 109 S. Ct. 2746 (citations omitted), where the Supreme Court, speaking of music, said:

> From Plato's discourse in the Republic to the totalitarian state in our own times, rulers have known its capacity to appeal to the intellect and to the emotions, and have censored musical compositions to serve the needs of the state. .... The Constitution prohibits any like attempts in our own legal order.

In their supplemental memorandum, the Mayor and the City argue that libraries are different from art museums because they are less selective; unlike the works in museums, they say, the inclusion of a book in a library carries "no connotation of worthiness or endorsement of its content." On the contrary, public libraries are, of physical and fiscal necessity, selective; they do not contain every book published. And there is no basis in the record for concluding that the Brooklyn Museum, with its one and a half million art objects, any more than a public library, endorses the perceived content of every work it makes available to the public. Whether or not the City and the Mayor agree with the Museum's judgment that a particular exhibit is worthy of showing is no different, in constitutional terms, from whether or not they agree that particular books are worthy of being made available to the public in a public library.

The City and the Mayor argue that they can avoid an injunction based upon the First Amendment because the showing of the Sensation Exhibit violates the Museum's statutory purposes and the terms of its Lease and Contract with the City. According to defendants, the withholding of financial support does not reflect a violation of the First Amendment but only an effort to vindicate the City's contractual rights. As in the *Cuban Museum* case, this claim is pretextual. *See supra* at 200-01. In addition, it is without evidentiary basis. The language of the statutes, the Lease and the Contract, and the undisputed evidence as to how the City itself has viewed these documents, shows a high likelihood that the Museum will defeat any claims that it is acting in violation of its statutory and contractual purposes as an art museum providing the public with enjoyment and education about art.

Whether the art shown is perceived as offensive or respectful, vulgar or banal, "good" art or "bad" art, the Mayor and the City offer no basis for the court to conclude that the Exhibit falls outside the broad parameters of the enabling legislation. Nor is there any basis for the City's accusation that the Museum has failed in its duty to educate. As for the defendants' emphasis on the unsuitability of the Sensation Exhibit for children, they acknowledge that there is nothing in the Lease or Contract which requires that every exhibit be suitable for schoolchildren of all ages. Nor is there anything which prevents the Museum from imposing reasonable restrictions on the access of schoolchildren to certain exhibits, in order to accommodate the Museum's undisputed right to display what Deputy Mayor Lhota called "mature" works of art.

There is also no language in the Lease or Contract that gives the Mayor or the City the right to veto works chosen for exhibition by the Museum. The Contract provides for the City to make maintenance payments to the Museum, without stating any conditions regarding the content of the Museum's artworks. The inability of the City and the Mayor to identify any standard for what constitutes a Lease or Contract violation, other than the Mayor and Deputy Mayor's personal views, reinforces the conclusion that it has never been contemplated that the City or the Mayor would have veto power over the Museum's decisions as to what to display. Deputy Mayor Lhota testified that there are no rules, regulations or procedures or even an ad hoc method for determining whether the City would view a particular work as inappropriate. The City's Procedures Manual confirms this.

That the advertising for the Exhibit cautions viewers that "the contents of the exhibition may cause shock, vomiting, confusion, panic, euphoria and anxiety" is not, as the City urges, an admission by the Museum that the Exhibit violates the Lease and Contract. Taking the advertising at face value (although the City has also argued that it is a crude effort to attract attention to the Exhibit), the City fails to show that art that is considered shocking, provocative, or disturbing gives rise to a violation of the Lease or the Contract.

The City and the Mayor argue that, if the court enjoins the withholding of its subsidy, the Museum will be free, under the protection of the First Amendment, to do anything at all, even transform itself into, for example, a museum of pornography. That, of course, is absurd. The Museum has been publicly supported for over one hundred years as a broad-based art museum. If it now sold its collections and became a pornography museum, the withholding of operating subsidies and the claims of a lease or contract violation would arise under vastly different facts from those presented here. The City and the Mayor have not shown that the funding provided has not been spent for the purpose authorized.

Finally, the City and the Mayor argue that they have a "duty" to withdraw support for the Museum because it showed paintings that are offensive and that desecrate religion in a public building. Given the Mayor's emphasis on the anti-Catholic sentiment he finds in the Ofili work, and despite the defendants' explicit disavowal of reliance on the Establishment Clause on oral argument, it is important to note the requirement that government remain neutral with regard to religious expression, whether "it manifest a religious view, an anti-religious view, or neither." *Rosenberger v. Rector and Visitors of University of Virginia*, 515 U.S. 819, 841, 115 S. Ct. 2510, 132 L. Ed. 2d 700 (1995). In *Rosenberger*, the Supreme Court held unconstitutional a state university's denial of funding to a student journal solely because the journal espoused a Christian viewpoint. *See generally Joseph Burstyn, Inc.*, 343 U.S. 495, 72 S. Ct. 777, 96 L. Ed. 1098. It is undisputed that the Museum's permanent collections contain many reverential depictions of the Madonna as well as other religious paintings and ritual objects. Just as there is no suggestion that the Museum is violating the Establishment Clause and endorsing religion by showing these works, *see, e.g., Agostini v. Felton*, 521 U.S. 203, 117 S. Ct. 1997, 138 L. Ed. 2d 391 (1997) and *Lemon v. Kurtzman*, 403 U.S. 602, 91 S. Ct. 2105, 29 L. Ed. 2d 745 (1971), there can equally be no suggestion that the Museum is violating the Establishment Clause by showing Mr. Ofili's work. The question of endorsement is evaluated from the perspective of the "objective observer." *See Wallace v. Jaffree*, 472 U.S. 38, 76, 105 S. Ct. 2479, 86 L. Ed. 2d 29 (1985) (O'Connor, J., concurring). The Brooklyn Museum contains art from all over world, from many traditions and many centuries. No objective observer could conclude that the Museum's showing of the work of an individual artist which is viewed by some as sacrilegious constitutes endorsement of anti-religious views by the City or the Mayor, or for that matter, by the Museum, any more than that the Museum's showing of religiously reverential works constitutes an endorsement by them of religion. The suggestion that the

Mayor and the City have an obligation to punish the Museum for showing the Ofili work turns well-established principles developed under the Establishment Clause on their head. If anything, it is the Mayor and the City who by their actions have threatened the neutrality required of government in the sphere of religion.

CONCLUSION

The City's motion to dismiss is denied. As the Museum has established irreparable harm and a likelihood of success on its First Amendment claim, its motion for a preliminary injunction is granted. An injunction, in the following form, will issue:

> The court having granted plaintiff's motion for a preliminary injunction pursuant to Federal Rule of Civil Procedure 65 by opinion and order dated November 1, 1999:
>
>> Defendants the City of New York and Rudolph W. Giuliani, individually and in his official capacity as Mayor of the City of New York, and all those acting in concert with them are hereby enjoined, during the pendency of this action, from inflicting, or taking any steps to inflict, any punishment, retaliation, discrimination, or sanction of any kind against the Brooklyn Institute of Arts and Sciences, doing business as the Brooklyn Museum of Art as well as against any of the Brooklyn Museum of Art's directors, officers or representatives, as a result of the Brooklyn Museum of Art's displaying the Exhibit "SENSATION: Young British Artists from the Saatchi Collection" (the Exhibit), including but not limited to:
>>
>>> 1) withholding or otherwise failing to provide the Brooklyn Museum of Art any sums of money appropriated, allocated, promised or otherwise payable to the Brooklyn Museum of Art;
>>>
>>> 2) denying, delaying, or otherwise discriminatorily treating pending or future funding requests of any type as the result of the Exhibit;
>>>
>>> 3) evicting or seeking to evict the Brooklyn Museum of Art from its premises at 200 Eastern Parkway, Brooklyn, or otherwise directly or indirectly interfering with the Brooklyn Museum of Art's occupancy and use of those premises, including prosecuting against the Brooklyn Museum of Art the action styled *The City of New York v. The Brooklyn Institute of Arts and Sciences*, filed September 30, 1999 in the Supreme Court of the State of New York, Kings County, Index No. 35376/99;
>>>
>>> 4) interfering in any manner, directly or indirectly, with the composition of the Board of Trustees of the Brooklyn Museum of Art, other than those members of the Board of Trustees who are the designees of the defendants, or interfering with the Board of Trustees' exercise of its authority.

The parties are directed to confer and to submit their positions, in writing, on the giving of security pursuant to Rule 65(c), by the close of business today.
SO ORDERED.

Note and Questions

1. *Brooklyn Institute* is a high water mark in museums' First Amendment rights jurisprudence. The case discusses another victory for the arts in *Cuban Museum of Arts and Culture, Inc. v. City of Miami*, 766 F. Supp. 1121 (S.D. Fla. 1991), in which a museum displaying works by Cuban artists who lived in Cuba or who arguably were pro-Castro (or at least not anti-Castro enough for a large segment of the Miami Cuban community) was targeted by Miami with non-renewal of its lease. The Southern District of Florida enjoined the attempt to punish the museum, making the point that:

   > It is ironic that the curtailment and punishment of expression in this case is the result of actions taken by those who claim to so loathe the governmental intolerance existing in a communist Cuba. Rather than foster peace and understanding, such conduct seeks the type of intolerant governmental behavior that the opponents of the Cuban Museum so rightly oppose in the first instance. It is truly unfortunate when citizens put government in a position where it must choose between the wishes of the majority and the expression of those who are in the minority. Nonetheless, First Amendment freedom of expression must prevail.

   Id. at 1130.

2. Although *Brooklyn Institute* and *Cuban Museum* thrust into stark focus the issue of the government's right to fund the kind of arts and education that it finds acceptable balanced against artists' and art institutions' rights to create and display whatever they feel like, the issue does not always arise in such clear terms of action and reaction over a compressed time frame. What would have happened if the cities had just gotten mad but did not take drastic and immediate steps to "get even," preferring instead to reduce their contribution to the operating budget of the museums each year until the museums found themselves in a fiscal disaster? What if the cities reduced the contributions to the disfavored institutions and began to fund other institutions that the cities believed were carrying out their duties more responsibly?

3. The courts in *Brooklyn Institute* and *Cuban Museum* were offended by what they saw as an obvious pretextual justification for the actions taken by the museum when the context revealed a different intent and motivation. Why was intent and pretext not given more consideration in the *Finley* case?

4. After the court's ruling in *Brooklyn Institute*, Mayor Giuliani and the museum settled their differences, and the exhibition ran its course, bolstered in attendance by the massive publicity created by Giuliani's fuss over the exhibition. As alluded to in the opinion, the big winner of all of this exposure was Charles Saatchi, the owner of the works in the Sensation show. It is opined that Mr. Saatchi collected the works of these young British artists at relatively reasonable prices and (perhaps in

conjunction with Christie's and other art dealers) came up with a plan to show the works together in a series of massive, controversial exhibitions starting in England at the Royal Academy, and later in Germany, Brooklyn, Australia, and Tokyo. If this was the intent, the strategy certainly paid off in spades, for the publicity received in England and America alone virtually guarantees that the works in this collection will increase in value. Should the court have looked into this further, or is this just a happy coincidence for Mr. Saatchi with no real legal impact on the issues of the case?

5. In 2000, the Whitney Museum's American Arts Biennial generated controversy with its exhibition of "Sanitation," an installation by Hans Haacke. This work included quotations from Rudolph Giuliani, Jesse Helms, Pat Robertson, and Patrick Buchanan regarding funding of art, especially the Sensation exhibit. The quotes were written in the Fraktur script favored by the Third Reich, and an audio of marching troops is played. *Signs Point to New 'Sensation' at the Whitney*, N.Y. Times, Mar. 9, 2000, at 1. The comparison of such art funding issues to Nazi cultural policies was criticized by the Anti-Defamation League and many others. *Whitney's Sanitation Troubles*, Art News, Apr. 2000, at 68.

6. In November 1999, "Art Until Now," an exhibit of controversial art at the Detroit Institute of Art, was closed when museum director Graham Beal padlocked the doors to the exhibit. Mr. Beal closed off access to the exhibit because he feared that some of the works featured, namely the ones with religious and racial overtones, would be found offensive by members of the community. *See All About Art: The Good, the Bad, and the Ugly*, available at *http://www.ncac.org/cn76detroitinstitute.html*.

United States v. American Library Association, Inc.

539 U.S. 194 (2003)*

REHNQUIST, Chief Justice.

To address the problems associated with the availability of Internet pornography in public libraries, Congress enacted the Children's Internet Protection Act (CIPA), 114 Stat. 2763A-335. Under CIPA, a public library may not receive federal assistance to provide Internet access unless it installs software to block images that constitute obscenity or child pornography, and to prevent minors from obtaining access to material that is harmful to them. The District Court held these provisions facially invalid on the ground that they induce public libraries to violate patrons' First Amendment rights. We now reverse.

To help public libraries provide their patrons with Internet access, Congress offers two forms of federal assistance. First, the E-rate program established by the Telecommunications Act of 1996 entitles qualifying libraries to buy Internet access at a discount. 110 Stat. 71, 47 U.S.C. § 254(h)(1)(B). In the

---

* Footnotes omitted.

year ending June 30, 2002, libraries received $58.5 million in such discounts. Redacted Joint Trial Stipulations of All Parties in Nos. 01-CV-1303, etc. (ED Pa.), ¶128, p. 16 (hereinafter Jt. Tr. Stip.). Second, pursuant to the Library Services and Technology Act (LSTA), 110 Stat. 3009-295, as amended, 20 U.S.C. §9101 et seq., the Institute of Museum and Library Services makes grants to state library administrative agencies to "electronically lin[k] libraries with educational, social, or information services," "assis[t] libraries in accessing information through electronic networks," and "pa[y] costs for libraries to acquire or share computer systems and telecommunications technologies." §§9141(a)(1)(B), (C), (E). In fiscal year 2002, Congress appropriated more than $149 million in LSTA grants. Jt. Tr. Stip. ¶185, p. 26. These programs have succeeded greatly in bringing Internet access to public libraries: by 2000, 95% of the Nation's libraries provided public Internet access. J. Bertot & C. McClure, "Public Libraries and the Internet 2000: Summary Findings and Data Tables," p. 3 (Sept. 7, 2000), *http://www.nclis.gov/statsuru/2000plo.pdf* (all Internet materials as visited Mar. 25, 2003, and available in Clerk of Court's case file).

By connecting to the Internet, public libraries provide patrons with a vast amount of valuable information. But there is also an enormous amount of pornography on the Internet, much of which is easily obtained. 201 F. Supp. 2d 401, 419 (E.D. Pa. 2002). The accessibility of this material has created serious problems for libraries, which have found that patrons of all ages, including minors, regularly search for online pornography. *Id.*, at 406. Some patrons also expose others to pornographic images by leaving them displayed on Internet terminals or printed at library printers. *Id.*, at 423.

Upon discovering these problems, Congress became concerned that the E-rate and LSTA programs were facilitating access to illegal and harmful pornography. S. Rep. No. 105-226, p. 5 (1998). Congress learned that adults "us[e] library computers to access pornography that is then exposed to staff, passersby, and children," and that "minors acces[s] child and adult pornography in libraries."

But Congress also learned that filtering software that blocks access to pornographic Web sites could provide a reasonably effective way to prevent such uses of library resources. *Id.*, at 20-26. By 2000, before Congress enacted CIPA, almost 17% of public libraries used such software on at least some of their Internet terminals, and 7% had filters on all of them. Library Research Center of U. Ill., Survey of Internet Access Management in Public Libraries 8, *http://alexia.lis.uiuc.edu/gslis/research/internet.pdf.* A library can set such software to block categories of material, such as "Pornography" or "Violence." 201 F. Supp. 2d, at 428. When a patron tries to view a site that falls within such a category, a screen appears indicating that the site is blocked. *Id.*, at 429. But a filter set to block pornography may sometimes block other sites that present neither obscene nor pornographic material, but that nevertheless trigger the filter. To minimize this problem, a library can set its software to prevent the blocking of material that falls into categories like "Education," "History," and "Medical." *Id.*, at 428-429. A library may also add or delete specific sites from a blocking category, *Id.*, at 429, and anyone can ask companies that furnish filtering software to unblock particular sites, *Id.*, at 430.

Responding to this information, Congress enacted CIPA. It provides that a library may not receive E-rate or LSTA assistance unless it has "a policy of Internet safety for minors that includes the operation of a technology protection measure . . . that protects against access" by all persons to "visual depictions" that constitute "obscen[ity]" or "child pornography," and that protects against access by minors to "visual depictions" that are "harmful to minors." 20 U.S.C. §§ 9134(f)(1)(A)(i) and (B)(i); 47 U.S.C. §§ 254(h)(6)(B)(i) and (C)(i). The statute defines a "[t]echnology protection measure" as "a specific technology that blocks or filters Internet access to material covered by" CIPA. § 254(h)(7)(I). CIPA also permits the library to "disable" the filter "to enable access for bona fide research or other lawful purposes." 20 U.S.C. § 9134(f)(3); 47 U.S.C. § 254(h)(6)(D). Under the E-rate program, disabling is permitted "during use by an adult." § 254(h)(6)(D). Under the LSTA program, disabling is permitted during use by any person. 20 U.S.C. § 9134(f)(3).

Appellees are a group of libraries, library associations, library patrons, and Web site publishers, including the American Library Association (ALA) and the Multnomah County Public Library in Portland, Oregon (Multnomah). They sued the United States and the Government agencies and officials responsible for administering the E-rate and LSTA programs in District Court, challenging the constitutionality of CIPA's filtering provisions. A three-judge District Court convened pursuant to § 1741(a) of CIPA, 114 Stat. 2763A-351, note following 20 U.S.C. § 7001.

After a trial, the District Court ruled that CIPA was facially unconstitutional and enjoined the relevant agencies and officials from withholding federal assistance for failure to comply with CIPA. The District Court held that Congress had exceeded its authority under the Spending Clause, U.S. Const., Art. I, § 8, cl. 1, because, in the court's view, "any public library that complies with CIPA's conditions will necessarily violate the First Amendment." 201 F. Supp. 2d, at 453. The court acknowledged that "generally the First Amendment subjects libraries' content-based decisions about which print materials to acquire for their collections to only rational [basis] review." *Id.*, at 462. But it distinguished libraries' decisions to make certain Internet material inaccessible. "The central difference," the court stated, "is that by providing patrons with even filtered Internet access, the library permits patrons to receive speech on a virtually unlimited number of topics, from a virtually unlimited number of speakers, without attempting to restrict patrons' access to speech that the library, in the exercise of its professional judgment, determines to be particularly valuable." *Id.* Reasoning that "the provision of Internet access within a public library . . . is for use by the public . . . for expressive activity," the court analyzed such access as a "designated public forum." *Id.*, at 457 (citation and internal quotation marks omitted). The District Court also likened Internet access in libraries to "traditional public fora . . . such as sidewalks and parks" because it "promotes First Amendment values in an analogous manner." *Id.*, at 466.

Based on both of these grounds, the court held that the filtering software contemplated by CIPA was a content-based restriction on access to a public forum, and was therefore subject to strict scrutiny. *Id.* Applying this standard, the District Court held that, although the Government has a compelling interest "in preventing the dissemination of obscenity, child pornography, or, in the case of minors, material harmful to minors," *Id.*, at 471, the use of software filters is not narrowly tailored to further those interests, *Id.*, at 479. We noted probable jurisdiction, 537 U.S. 1017, 123 S. Ct. 551, 154 L. Ed. 2d 424 (2002), and now reverse.

Congress has wide latitude to attach conditions to the receipt of federal assistance in order to further its policy objectives. *South Dakota v. Dole,* 483 U.S. 203, 206, 107 S. Ct. 2793, 97 L. Ed. 2d 171 (1987). But Congress may not "induce" the recipient "to engage in activities that would themselves be unconstitutional." *Id.*, at 210, 107 S. Ct. 2793. To determine whether libraries would violate the First Amendment by employing the filtering software that CIPA requires, we must first examine the role of libraries in our society.

Public libraries pursue the worthy missions of facilitating learning and cultural enrichment. Appellee ALA's Library Bill of Rights states that libraries should provide "[b]ooks and other . . . resources . . . for the interest, information, and enlightenment of all people of the community the library serves." 201 F. Supp. 2d, at 420 (internal quotation marks omitted). To fulfill their traditional missions, public libraries must have broad discretion to decide what material to provide to their patrons. Although they seek to provide a wide array of information, their goal has never been to provide "universal coverage." *Id.*, at 421. Instead, public libraries seek to provide materials "that would be of the greatest direct benefit or interest to the community." *Id.* To this end, libraries collect only those materials deemed to have "requisite and appropriate quality." *Id. See* W. Katz, *Collection Development: The Selection of Materials for Libraries* 6 (1980) ("The librarian's responsibility . . . is to separate out the gold from the garbage, not to preserve everything"); F. Drury, *Book Selection* xi (1930) ("[I]t is the aim of the selector to give the public, not everything it wants, but the best that it will read or use to advantage"); App. 636 (Rebuttal Expert Report of Donald G. Davis, Jr.) ("A hypothetical collection of everything that has been produced is not only of dubious value, but actually detrimental to users trying to find what they want to find and really need"). . . .

The public forum principles on which the District Court relied, 201 F. Supp.2 d, at 457-470, are out of place in the context of this case. Internet access in public libraries is neither a "traditional" nor a "designated" public forum. *See Cornelius v. NAACP Legal Defense & Ed. Fund, Inc.,* 473 U.S. 788, 802, 105 S. Ct. 3439, 87 L. Ed. 2d 567 (1985) (describing types of forums). First, this resource — which did not exist until quite recently — has not "immemorially been held in trust for the use of the public and, time out of mind, . . . been used for purposes of assembly, communication of thoughts between citizens, and discussing public questions." *International Soc. for Krishna Consciousness, Inc. v. Lee,* 505 U.S. 672, 679, 112 S. Ct. 2701, 120 L. Ed. 2d 541 (1992) (internal quotation marks omitted). We have "rejected the view that traditional public forum status extends beyond its historic confines." *Forbes, supra*, at 678, 118 S. Ct. 1633. The doctrines surrounding traditional public forums may not be extended to situations where such history is lacking.

Nor does Internet access in a public library satisfy our definition of a "designated public forum." To create such a forum, the government must make an affirmative choice to open up its property for use as a public forum. *Cornelius, supra*, at 802-803, 105 S. Ct. 3439; *Perry Ed. Assn. v. Perry Local Educators' Assn.*, 460 U.S. 37, 45, 103 S. Ct. 948, 74 L. Ed. 2d 794 (1983). "The government does not create a public forum by inaction or by permitting limited discourse, but only by intentionally opening a non-traditional forum for public discourse." *Cornelius, supra*, at 802, 105 S. Ct. 3439. The District Court likened public libraries' Internet terminals to the forum at issue in *Rosenberger v. Rector and Visitors of Univ. of Va.*, 515 U.S. 819, 115 S. Ct. 2510, 132 L. Ed. 2d 700 (1995). 201 F. Supp. 2d, at 465. In *Rosenberger*, we considered the "Student Activity Fund" established by the University of Virginia that subsidized all manner of student publications except those based on religion. We held that the fund had created a limited public forum by giving public money to student groups who wished to publish, and therefore could not discriminate on the basis of viewpoint.

The situation here is very different. A public library does not acquire Internet terminals in order to create a public forum for Web publishers to express themselves, any more than it collects books in order to provide a public forum for the authors of books to speak. It provides Internet access, not to "encourage a diversity of views from private speakers," *Rosenberger, supra*, at 834, 115 S. Ct. 2510, but for the same reasons it offers other library resources: to facilitate research, learning, and recreational pursuits by furnishing materials of requisite and appropriate quality. *See Cornelius, supra*, at 805, 105 S. Ct. 3439 (noting, in upholding limits on participation in the Combined Federal Campaign (CFC), that "[t]he Government did not create the CFC for purposes of providing a forum for expressive activity"). As Congress recognized, "[t]he Internet is simply another method for making information available in a school or library." S. Rep. No. 106-141, p. 7 (1999). It is "no more than a technological extension of the book stack." *Id.* . . .

Appellees urge us to affirm the District Court's judgment on the alternative ground that CIPA imposes an unconstitutional condition on the receipt of federal assistance. Under this doctrine, "the government 'may not deny a benefit to a person on a basis that infringes his constitutionally protected . . . freedom of speech' even if he has no entitlement to that benefit." *Board of Comm'rs, Wabaunsee Cty. v. Umbehr*, 518 U.S. 668, 674, 116 S. Ct. 2342, 135 L. Ed. 2d 843 (1996) (quoting *Perry v. Sindermann*, 408 U.S. 593, 597, 92 S. Ct. 2694, 33 L. Ed. 2d 570 (1972)). Appellees argue that CIPA imposes an unconstitutional condition on libraries that receive E-rate and LSTA subsidies by requiring them, as a condition on their receipt of federal funds, to surrender their First Amendment right to provide the public with access to constitutionally protected speech. The Government counters that this claim fails because Government entities do not have First Amendment rights. *See Columbia*

Broadcasting System, Inc. v. Democratic National Committee, 412 U.S. 94, 139, 93 S. Ct. 2080, 36 L. Ed. 2d 772 (1973) (Stewart, J., concurring) ("The First Amendment protects the press from governmental interference; it confers no analogous protection on the government"); *Id.*, at 139, n. 7, 93 S. Ct. 2080 ("'The purpose of the First Amendment is to protect private expression'" (quoting T. Emerson, *The System of Freedom of Expression* 700 (1970))). *See also Warner Cable Communications, Inc., v. Niceville*, 911 F.2d 634, 638 (C.A. 11 1990); *Student Govt. Assn. v. Board of Trustees of the Univ. of Mass.*, 868 F.2d 473, 481 (C.A. 1 1989); *Estiverne v. Louisiana State Bar Assn.*, 863 F.2d 371, 379 (C.A. 5 1989).

We need not decide this question because, even assuming that appellees may assert an "unconstitutional conditions" claim, this claim would fail on the merits. Within broad limits, "when the Government appropriates public funds to establish a program it is entitled to define the limits of that program." *Rust v. Sullivan*, 500 U.S. 173, 194, 111 S. Ct. 1759, 114 L. Ed. 2d 233 (1991). In *Rust*, Congress had appropriated federal funding for family planning services and forbidden the use of such funds in programs that provided abortion counseling. *Id.*, at 178, 111 S. Ct. 1759. Recipients of these funds challenged this restriction, arguing that it impermissibly conditioned the receipt of a benefit on the relinquishment of their constitutional right to engage in abortion counseling. *Id.*, at 196, 111 S. Ct. 1759. We rejected that claim, recognizing that "the Government [was] not denying a benefit to anyone, but [was] instead simply insisting that public funds be spent for the purposes for which they were authorized." *Id.*

The same is true here. The E-rate and LSTA programs were intended to help public libraries fulfill their traditional role of obtaining material of requisite and appropriate quality for educational and informational purposes. Congress may certainly insist that these "public funds be spent for the purposes for which they were authorized." *Id.* Especially because public libraries have traditionally excluded pornographic material from their other collections, Congress could reasonably impose a parallel limitation on its Internet assistance programs. As the use of filtering software helps to carry out these programs, it is a permissible condition under *Rust*. . . .

Because public libraries' use of Internet filtering software does not violate their patrons' First Amendment rights, CIPA does not induce libraries to violate the Constitution, and is a valid exercise of Congress' spending power. Nor does CIPA impose an unconstitutional condition on public libraries. Therefore, the judgment of the District Court for the Eastern District of Pennsylvania is

Reversed.

Note and Questions

1. The plurality opinion in *American Libraries Association* points out that Congress had broad powers to limit what it has chosen to fund. Thus, recipients of funds may be limited in the kind of art or other material they

get to provide or display. This is very close to a content-based restriction on libraries' speech and conduct. Congress is clearly saying, "Thou shall not display pornography," and libraries face a Hobson's choice of taking the government's funding and imposing content-based restrictions themselves or refusing the funding and not offering Internet access to patrons due to lack of funding. *See* Amitai Etzioni, *On Protecting Children from Speech*, 79 CHI.-KENT L. REV. 3, 16-21 (2004) (criticizing opinion and Children's Internet Protection Act of 2000); William Galston, *When Well-Being Trumps Liberty: Political Theory, Jurisprudence, and Children's Rights*, 79 CHI.-KENT L. REV. 279, 297-98 (2004) (endorsing opinion); Wilson R. Huhn, *Assessing the Constitutionality of Laws That Are Both Content-Based and Content-Neutral: The Emerging Constitutional Calculus*, 79 IND. L.J. 801, 840-42 (2004) (analyzing recent "dual-effect" cases).

2. The Court emphasized that it did not view the government's promotion of Internet access in public libraries as the creation of a designated public forum for speech. The results of the creation of such a forum would be to allow much less government restriction on the kind of speech that is to occur in the forum. For example, in *Hopper v. City of Pasco*, 241 F.3d 1067 (9th Cir. 2001), defendant city opened a gallery within city hall for display of work by local artists. Plaintiff artists, having been invited to display their work at the gallery, were summarily uninvited when their submissions provoked controversy. The artists sued under 42 U.S.C. § 1983 for violation of their First Amendment rights. Evidence showed that prior to exclusion of the artists' works, art submissions had never been pre-screened or otherwise rejected for display. The parties agreed that the artists' works were neither obscene nor pornographic. The city received summary judgment at the district court level, but on appeal, the Ninth Circuit held that the city had violated the artists' First Amendment rights by creating a designated public forum and then excluding the artists' artwork without a compelling governmental interest. In a "designated" public forum (i.e., a nontraditional forum intentionally opened up for public discourse), restrictions on expressive activity are subject to the same strict scrutiny standard that governs a traditional public forum; in a nonpublic forum, a more lenient "reasonableness" standard governs. The city's alleged policy not to accept "controversial" works for display was insufficient to prevent city hall from becoming a designated public forum, given the lack of definite standards for distinguishing "controversial" from "noncontroversial" art and the city's haphazard enforcement of its policy. The mere fact that the artwork caused controversy was not a compelling reason for the artwork's exclusion from a designated public forum. The city was not required to open its property for display of artwork. Nor was the city required to leave that property open for such display indefinitely. However, the city could not, absent a compelling government interest, open a designated public forum to some and close it to others solely in order to suppress content of protected expression.

3. In contrast to *Hopper* above, *see People for the Ethical Treatment of Animals, Inc. v. Gittens*, 414 F.3d 23 (D.C. Cir. 2005). Here, the D.C. Circuit evaluated the District of Columbia's sponsorship of an outdoor art exhibit, pursuant to which, for a $5,000 donation, individuals or organizations could choose an artist to decorate a preformed donkey or elephant sculpture for display in a "prime public location" during the exhibition. The court held that this sponsorship did not create a designated public forum protected from viewpoint discrimination by the First Amendment. The District was not regulating private speech but, instead, was engaging in government speech, and the District was permitted to make esthetic judgments in its role as arts patron. While the payment of a $5,000 fee gave entrants greater privileges than those who engaged in the exhibit's general competition, and potentially a claim for breach of contract if the District failed to abide by any of its commitments, it did not transform the program into a limited public forum. The District of Columbia engaged in government speech when it decided which entrants' designs to accept and which to reject, and, as a speaker, the court held that the District's decisions were not limited by the First Amendment.

5. Private, Non-Governmental Censorship

Indirect censorship by the government imposed by limiting funding or making collateral attacks against leases or other benefits is an insidious problem that may allow the government to put a check on artistic expression if the action undertaken by the government is not obviously linked in time or by definition to the suppression of a particular example or form of expression. Yet, government's response to outrageous or edgy art still is secondary to the reaction of lay people. Far from exercising their right to avert their eyes and vote with their feet, the vocalized opinions of a vociferous group of people, no matter how small a minority of the local population they may be, can exercise a tremendous force toward the censorship (most often self-censorship) of institutions that rely on support and patronage of the general public for their existence. It is risky to take a stand on the principle that arts are free and should not be suppressed when a vocal group of concerned citizens are questioning your morality, judgment, and common sense, and your public

62

*Detail of Alma Lopez,
Our Lady (1999)*

---

62. Image: Michael D. Murray, Cropped, revised, and resized thumbnail excerpt (2007) of an exhibit depicting Alma Lopez, "Our Lady" (1999), the subject of a private censorship campaign by residents of Santa Fe, NM.

reputation will determine the continued existence of your institution. Patrons of the arts also may feel the heat, and not want to be associated with scandal. Although some acts of private citizen censorship receive a great deal of publicity, as in the case described below, many other decisions of self-censorship are made quietly, in trustee and board meetings, without fanfare and press releases, but nonetheless result in the suppression of artistic expression.

What constitutes a scandalous display certainly is in the eye of the beholder. Residents of Santa Fe created an uproar concerning a fairly modest work by Alma Lopez depicting Our Lady of Guadalupe in an unconventional manner of posing and conception; she was depicted wearing something akin to a floral bikini and was attended by a bare-breasted angel. *See* Ann Constable, *Catholics Protest Our Lady's Depiction*, Santa Fe New Mexican (Mar. 24, 2001), available at *http://www.almalopez.net/news/010324sfnm.html/*.

Nelson v. Streeter

16 F.3d 145 (7th Cir. 1994)*

Posner, Chief Judge.

Detail of David Nelson, Mirth and Girth (1988)

Harold Washington, Chicago's first black mayor, died suddenly of a heart attack in November 1987, shortly after being reelected. He had become a revered figure to the black community of Chicago — so much so that shortly after his death a poster went on sale in which a smiling Harold Washington is shown in the company of Jesus Christ floating above the Chicago skyline; the poster is captioned "Worry Ye Not." David Nelson, a student at the School of the Art Institute of Chicago, did not think Washington deserving of deification, and so for his entry in the school's annual fellowship competition Nelson submitted a painting intended (he claims) to portray Washington in a more human light. The painting, entitled "Mirth and Girth"[63] and based on a rumor that doctors at the hospital to which Washington had been brought when he suffered his fatal heart attack had discovered that underneath his suit he was wearing female underwear, is a full-length frontal portrait of a portly, grim-faced Harold Washington clad in a white bra and G-string, garter belt, and stockings.

Nelson's painting, together with the submissions of the other students, was placed on exhibition on May 11, 1988. The exhibition was open to students,

---

* Footnotes and some citations omitted.

63. Image: Michael D. Murray, Cropped, revised, and resized thumbnail excerpt (2007) of an exhibit depicting David Nelson, "Mirth and Girth" (1988), the subject of *Nelson v. Streeter*, 16 F.3d 145 (7th Cir. 1994).

faculty, and invited guests, but not to the public at large. The students' works were to be judged by four experts. The winners would receive cash prizes, and their winning works would be exhibited at a public exhibition. "Mirth and Girth," however, was destined not to be judged — not in the expected fashion, at any rate. As soon as the exhibition of student work opened and visitors saw Nelson's painting, it became the focus of outraged attention. A security guard was quickly posted in front of it to protect it from an angry crowd of students. The school began receiving enraged phone calls. School officials asked Nelson to remove the painting. He refused.

Word of the painting came to the Chicago City Council, which was in session. Alderman Bobby Rush prepared a resolution, which was signed by, among others, Aldermen Allan Streeter and Dorothy Tillman, threatening to cut off the City's contribution to the Art Institute unless the Institute apologized for displaying "Mirth and Girth." The resolution passed, together with another resolution, which requested the Art Institute to remove the painting immediately.

The aldermen (one of whom has since become a Congressman) whom we have named are three of the defendants in this suit, and are the appellants in this appeal. But they were not the first aldermen to arrive at the scene. Aldermen Henry and Jones arrived first. Henry brandished a gun, and Jones removed the painting from the wall and placed it on the floor, facing the wall. They left, and a student rehung the painting. Then the defendants arrived. They took the painting down and tried to carry it out of the school, but were stopped by a school official, then diverted (carrying the painting) to the office of the pres-ident of the School of the Art Institute, Anthony Jones. When the painting arrived in Jones's office, it had a one-foot gash, but it is not known precisely when, or by whom, the gash had been inflicted. The aldermen told Jones that they were there to carry out the City Council's resolution to remove the painting from the Art Institute. The aldermen wrapped the painting in brown paper to prevent anyone from seeing it. According to one witness, Alderman Tillman threatened to burn the painting right there in President Jones's office but was dissuaded by a police lieutenant who was present, Raymond Patterson. Another alderman (not one of the defendants) called Chicago Police Superintendent Leroy Martin, a defendant but not an appellant. Martin telephoned Patterson in President Jones's office and ordered him to take the painting into police custody. A police sergeant, accom-panied by the three defendant aldermen, carried the wrapped painting to a police car [see photograph above[64]]. The scene was televised, and broadcast widely,

---

64. Image: Michael D. Murray, Cropped, revised, and resized thumbnail excerpt (2007) of an exhibit depicting Chicago aldermen carrying David Nelson's painting, "Mirth and Girth" (1988) away from the Art Institute of Chicago, the subject of *Nelson v. Streeter*, 16 F.3d 145 (7th Cir. 1994).

confirming, if confirmation was needed, that Chicago had replaced Boston as the censorship capital of the United States.

Mirth and Girth was kept in custody until the evening of the following day, when it was released (we assume on its own recognizance) to David Nelson. The painting has not been repaired, exhibited, or sold. It is an exhibit in this suit, and Nelson's counsel has physical custody of it. During the set-to in the president's office Jones had signed a statement promising that if the painting was returned it would not be "displayed or shown in any way without a meeting and resolution of the Board of Trustees and members of the City Council." Later the president of the Art Institute's board, Marshall Field, issued a public apology in which he promised that the painting would not be returned to public display.

Nelson filed this civil rights damages suit in 1988, shortly after the incident. The suit, based on 42 U.S.C. § 1983, charges that the defendants, acting under color of state law, deprived Nelson of rights secured to him by the First and Fourth Amendments, made applicable to state and local government by interpretation of the Fourteenth Amendment. Although the bizarre facts and the prominence of the defendants have attracted public attention to the case, it is straightforward from a legal standpoint and we are distressed by its protraction. We are being asked to resolve the threshold issue of immunity in a case that is five years old.

The appeals are from the district judge's rejection of the defense of official immunity. . . . So we must ask whether in 1988 the law was clear that local government officials may not go onto private property without invitation (the aldermen had not been invited to the exhibition of student work), seize a painting that they do not like because it vilifies a public official with whom they had been associated, and wrap it in brown paper and remove it so that no one can see it. To ask the question is pretty much to answer it. As Chief Justice Warren said in another case involving an effort to suppress public criticism of a mayor of Chicago, "This is a simple case." *Gregory v. City of Chicago, supra,* 394 U.S., at 111, 89 S. Ct., at 946.

If the City owned the Art Institute, it would have some power — how much we need not decide — to regulate offensive displays. *Piarowski v. Illinois Community College Dist. 515,* 759 F.2d 625 (7th Cir. 1985); *Close v. Lederle,* 424 F.2d 988 (1st Cir. 1970). The City does not own the Art Institute, and its officials have no more right to enter it uninvited and take the art off its walls than they would have to enter a private home and take "offensive" art off its walls. Cf. *Spence v. Washington,* 418 U.S. 405, 94 S. Ct. 2727, 41 L. Ed. 2d 842 (1974) (per curiam). It has been clear since long before 1988 that government officials are not permitted to burn books that offend them, and we do not see any difference between burning an offensive book and burning an offensive painting. Since *Hogarth,* and indeed since long before, the visual arts have been a medium of political and social commentary. David Nelson had as much right to paint Mayor Washington in women's underwear as Thomas Nast had to caricature Boss Tweed. *Hustler Magazine, Inc. v. Falwell,* 485 U.S. 46, 108 S. Ct.

876, 99 L. Ed. 2d 41 (1988), eliminates any possible doubt on that score, and it was decided two and a half months before the seizure of Nelson's painting.

We do not understand the aldermen's counsel to disagree. They do not argue that a city with a black mayor and a large black population is entitled to a dispensation from the restraints that constitutional and civil rights law places on public officials, merely because blacks are a minority of the national population and have long been victims of racial discrimination. Even the most extreme advocates of "hate speech" codes, designed to shield groups perceived as vulnerable from offensive, hurtful, and wounding speech, do not argue that a public official should be immune from offensive, hurtful, and wounding criticism merely because he is a member of a minority group. "Transvestite" is not a racial epithet. While Alderman Rush testified that Nelson's painting was one more effort to depict the black male as "impotent," many is the white official who has been vilified for his sexual activities or preferences, real or conjectured. The appellants' counsel make two different points. The first is that when they took down the painting the aldermen were acting as private citizens — as personal friends and admirers of the late Mayor Washington — rather than as government officials, much as President Truman was acting as a private citizen rather than as President of the United States when he lashed out at critics of his daughter Margaret's singing. . . .

The aldermen's second argument is that they took down the painting in order to save it from destruction at the hands of a mob, or alternatively to spare Chicago the devastating riots that the continued exhibition of the painting might have sparked, and that it was unclear in 1988 and it is unclear today that the temporary removal of a painting, so motivated, deprives the artist of his constitutional rights. This argument is germane to the aldermen's defense of immunity, but it is based on an interpretation of the facts that we are not authorized to accept at this stage in the litigation. An official is entitled to immunity only if the uncontested or uncontestable facts reveal that his acts did not invade the plaintiff's clearly established constitutional rights. . . .

The aldermen's version of the facts is not only contestable and contested, but unsupported. This is clearest with respect to the first branch of the "angry mob" defense, the branch in which the aldermen cast themselves as First Amendment Good Samaritans. Alderman Tillman testified at her deposition that she did not want the painting hung in any public place and that if it were rehung she would attempt once again to remove it. She wanted to burn the painting, not to protect it from an angry mob. And there was no mob. There were angry people at the Art Institute — not least the aldermen, who should have been setting an example of cool self-restraint rather than threatening to seize and destroy private property. But the police, though there were only a handful of them, had the situation well in hand.

The second branch of the argument — that but for the aldermen's timely intervention, "Mirth and Girth" might have sparked a riot to match that touched off by the assassination of Dr. Martin Luther King, Jr. in 1968 — also depends on contested facts. . . . And the aldermen cannot be permitted to defend their actions by reference to such unrest within the black community as their own lawless, provocative, and publicity-mongering actions may have stirred up. . . . The First Amendment does not protect a speaker who eggs his audience on to commit a violent act, whether against himself or against others, *Brandenburg v. Ohio*, 395 U.S. 444, 447, 89 S. Ct. 1827, 1829, 23 L. Ed. 2d 430 (1969) (per curiam); *Feiner v. New York*, 340 U.S. 315, 320-21, 71 S. Ct. 303, 306-07, 95 L. Ed. 295 (1951); *Chaplinsky v. New Hampshire*, 315 U.S. 568, 572, 62 S. Ct. 766, 769, 86 L. Ed. 1031 (1942), though even in that case, provided the speech or other work has some expressive content, proof may be required that the danger of violence was more than theoretical, was, in Holmes's famous formula, "clear and present." *Brandenburg v. Ohio, supra*, 395 U.S., at 447, 89 S. Ct., at 1829 (1969); *Feiner v. New York, supra*, 340 U.S., at 320, 71 S. Ct., at 306. There is no evidence that in creating and exhibiting "Mirth and Girth" as his entry in an art students' competition Nelson intended to provoke a riot or that the danger of a riot was great.

In the second situation, the artist's intentions are innocent, at least innocent of any desire to cause a riot, but his work so inflames the community as to cause a riot in which people are killed and injured. First Amendment rights are not subject to the heckler's veto. *Cox v. Louisiana, supra*, 379 U.S., at 551, 85 S. Ct., at 462-63. The rioters are the culpable parties, not the artist whose work unintentionally provoked them to violence. Even if *DeShaney v. Winnebago County Dept. of Social Services*, 489 U.S. 189, 109 S. Ct. 998, 103 L. Ed. 2d 249 (1989), which holds that the Constitution does not create a right to be protected against private violence, might be thought to imply that the police do not have a constitutionally enforceable duty to protect an artist and the populace from a mob, there is nothing in that decision to suggest that police and other public officials can seek to protect the populace at the expense of the artist, by "arresting" the offensive painting rather than the violent rioters. . . .

The purpose of the doctrine of official immunity is to protect officials from legal surprises. The defendants could not have been surprised to learn that they were not free to take down paintings from the walls of the Art Institute.

. . .

AFFIRMED.

Note and Questions

1. Nelson's § 1983 action succeeded in vindicating his artistic vision and netted him a sizeable judgment, yet the painting was not restored to the Art Institute of Chicago for this or (as far as we know) any other exhibition of art. Assuming that Nelson was serious in his intentions to make a career as an artist, was this case a pyrrhic victory?

2. If the aldermen and others had simply complained loudly, and the Art Institute had simply capitulated by taking down the painting, would Nelson have had a viable claim for violation of his civil rights by the Art Institute? Regardless of his legal position, would it have been practical and worthwhile for an art student to sue his school in this manner?

ASSESSMENT

1. What is the best way to distinguish *U.S. v. O'Brien* (draft card burning) from *U.S. v. Eichman* (flag burning)?

   (A) The flag has more expression in it than a draft card; a burning flag has more expression than a burning draft card

   (B) The law violated in *O'Brien* related to being without a draft card — it said nothing about speech, whereas the law violated in *Eichman* was about the content of the negative expression inherent in flag burning

   (C) The draft card in *O'Brien* was government property whereas the flags in *Eichman* were private property

   (D) The government regulation in *O'Brien* left open ample alternative channels for the communication of the message, whereas the government regulation in *Eichman* did not

2. Why did the U.S. Supreme Court in *Brown v. Enter. Merchants Ass'n* (2011) strike down California's violent video games statute?

   I. The court rejected the statutes' time-place-manner restrictions on speech because they failed to allow ample alternative channels for the communication

   II. The court rejected the statute's attempt to balance the harms of the speech against the benefits of the speech

   III. The court held that the evidence of the dangers presented by violent video games did not provide a compelling government interest sufficient to meet strict scrutiny requirements

   IV. The court refused to create a new category of "non-speech" for violent video games

   (A) I, II, and III only

   (B) II, III, and IV only

   (C) I, II, III, and IV

   (D) II and III only

3. Under the *Miller* test, how must the court or finder of fact assess the "taken as a whole" requirement regarding a publication?

   (A) By counting the number of arguably obscene pages compared to the number of non-obscene pages

   (B) By counting and adjudging the number and quality of "serious" articles in the publication

   (C) By considering the dominant theme of the publication and whether or not the obscene material predominates

   (D) All of the above are acceptable means

4. Which of the following statements is true about *Tinker* (Vietnam War black armbands) and *Morse* ("Bong Hits 4 Jesus" case)?

    I.   The court found the black armbands in *Tinker* not to be disruptive of the educational functioning of the school

    II.   The speech activity in both cases, *Tinker* and *Morse*, took place on school grounds

    III.   The court found the "Bong Hits 4 Jesus" banner in *Morse* to be disruptive of the educational functioning of the school

    IV.   *Morse* reversed *Tinker*'s holding that schoolchildren maintain First Amendment civil rights while engaged in school activities

  (A) I and II only

  (B) I, II, and III only

  (C) I and III only

  (D) I, II, III, and IV

5. Which of the following are true of the U.S. Supreme Court *Roth* opinion in obscenity law?

    I.   It held that works should be taken as a whole

    II.   It held that obscenity is not speech

    III.   It upheld the *Regina v. Hicklin* standard

    IV.   It upheld the application of contemporary community standards

  (A) I and II only

  (B) II, III, and IV only

  (C) I, II, and IV only

  (D) I, II, III, and IV

6. Can you be prosecuted for mere possession of pornography in your own home?

  (A) Yes, if it is child pornography

  (B) Yes, if it is obscene under *Miller*

  (C) Yes, if it is child pornography or obscene material under *Miller* and it traveled in interstate commerce

  (D) All of the above

7. The best way to distinguish *NEA v. Finley* from the *Brooklyn Museum* and the *Cuban Museum of Miami* cases is:

  (A) Finley had not received her NEA grant yet, but the Brooklyn and Cuban Museums had received their money and it was then taken away in response to their speech

  (B) *Finley* is a case of the government acting as a patron of the arts making an allocation of limited funds, while Brooklyn and Cuban museums encountered the government as a policeman of expression ending a long funding relationship

(C) *Finley* engaged in actual obscene speech, while Brooklyn and Cuban Museums merely engaged in unpopular speech

(D) *Finley* was a time-place-manner restriction on speech while *Brooklyn* and *Cuban* were censorship cases involving the leases and licenses of the museums

ASSESSMENT ANSWERS

1. What is the best way to distinguish *U.S. v. O'Brien* (draft card burning) from *U.S. v. Eichman* (flag burning)?

   (A) The flag has more expression in it than a draft card; a burning flag has more expression than a burning draft card

   (B) The law violated in *O'Brien* related to being without a draft card–it said nothing about speech, whereas the law violated in *Eichman* was about the content of the negative expression inherent in flag burning

   (C) The draft card in *O'Brien* was government property whereas the flags in *Eichman* were private property

   (D) The government regulation in *O'Brien* left open ample alternative channels for the communication of the message, whereas the government regulation in *Eichman* did not

   ANSWER: The answer is Choice (B). In *O'Brien*, the Court held that the government's action (the law at issue in the case) did not relate to suppression of speech. The law only involved the possession and maintenance of a draft card for the orderly administration of the Selective Service Administration. It did not seek to suppress any speech or viewpoint about speech. In *Eichman*, the law was deemed to be a direct attempt to suppress a certain kind of viewpoint about the flag and the United States by preventing a potent form of expressive conduct, namely the burning of a U.S. flag. These decisions did not turn on one object having more expressive potential than the other Choice (A), or the flags in *Eichman* being private property Choice (C), or about leaving open other avenues for communication Choice (D).

2. Why did the U.S. Supreme Court in *Brown v. Enter. Merchants Ass'n* (2011) strike down California's violent video games statute?

   I. The court rejected the statutes' time-place-manner restrictions on speech because they failed to allow ample alternative channels for the communication

   II. The court rejected the statute's attempt to balance the harms of the speech against the benefits of the speech

III. The court held that the evidence of the dangers presented by violent video games did not provide a compelling government interest sufficient to meet strict scrutiny requirements

IV. The court refused to create a new category of "non-speech" for violent video games

(A) I, II, and III only

(B) II, III, and IV only

(C) I, II, III, and IV

(D) II and III only

ANSWER: Choice (B) is the answer. Item I is incorrect because *Brown* did not involve a time-place-manner restriction on speech. Items II, II, and IV all are correct. The Court would not engage in a balancing of the potential harms vs. the potential benefits of the speech. The Court was not persuaded that the government's social science evidence had proved a link between violent video games and violence and delinquency among juveniles. And the Court rejected the possibility of creating a new category of "non-speech" for violent video games.

3. Under the *Miller* test, how must the court or finder of fact assess the "taken as a whole" requirement regarding a publication?

(A) By counting the number of arguably obscene pages compared to the number of non-obscene pages

(B) By counting and adjudging the number and quality of "serious" articles in the publication

(C) By considering the dominant theme of the publication and whether or not the obscene material predominates

(D) All of the above are acceptable means

ANSWER: Choice (D) is the answer. All of the means listed are acceptable means of attempting to assess the "taken as a whole factor" of the *Miller* test.

4. Which of the following statements is true about *Tinker* (Vietnam War black armbands) and *Morse* ("Bong Hits 4 Jesus" case)?

I. The court found the black armbands in *Tinker* not to be disruptive of the educational functioning of the school

II. The speech activity in both cases, *Tinker* and *Morse*, took place on school grounds

III. The court found the "Bong Hits 4 Jesus" banner in *Morse* to be disruptive of the educational functioning of the school

IV. *Morse* reversed *Tinker*'s holding that schoolchildren maintain First Amendment civil rights while engaged in school activities

(A) I and II only

(B) I, II, and III only

(C) I and III only

(D) I, II, III, and IV

ANSWER: Choice (C) is the answer. Only Items I and III are correct — the Court in *Tinker* found that the cloth armbands would not pose a threat to the educational functioning of the school, but the Court in *Morse* found that the banner display, off of school grounds but during a school-sponsored event, would disrupt the educational functioning of the school. Item II is incorrect — *Morse's* activity took place off of school grounds, and Item IV is incorrect, because *Morse* did not reverse *Tinker's* holding; it affirmed that students maintain First Amendment rights, but the Court didn't protect the speech in that case's circumstances.

5. Which of the following are true of the U.S. Supreme Court *Roth* opinion in obscenity law?

   I. It held that works should be taken as a whole

  II. It held that obscenity is not speech

 III. It upheld the *Regina v. Hicklin* standard

 IV. It upheld the application of contemporary community standards

(A) I and II only

(B) II, III, and IV only

(C) I, II, and IV only

(D) I, II, III, and IV

ANSWER: The answer is Choice (C). Items I, II, and IV are correct — *Roth* held that works should be taken as a whole; it held that obscenity is not speech; and it upheld the application of the contemporary community standards test. However, *Roth* reversed the prior cases that relied on *Regina v. Hicklin* and rejected the *Hicklin* standard.

6. Can you be prosecuted for mere possession of pornography in your own home?

(A) Yes, if it is child pornography

(B) Yes, if it is obscene under *Miller*

(C) Yes, if it is child pornography or obscene material under *Miller* and it traveled in interstate commerce

(D) All of the above

ANSWER: The answer is Choice (A). You can be prosecuted for mere possession of child pornography, even if you only possessed it in the privacy of your own home. This is not true of other obscene materials whether or not they traveled in interstate commerce, making (B), (C), and (D) false.

7. The best way to distinguish *NEA v. Finley* from the *Brooklyn Museum* and the *Cuban Museum of Miami* cases is

   (A) Finley had not received her NEA grant yet, but the Brooklyn and Cuban Museums had received their money and it was then taken away in response to their speech

   (B) *Finley* is a case of the government acting as a patron of the arts making an allocation of limited funds, while Brooklyn and Cuban museums encountered the government as a policeman of expression ending a long funding relationship

   (C) Finley engaged in actual obscene speech, while Brooklyn and Cuban Museums merely engaged in unpopular speech

   (D) *Finley* was a time-place-manner restriction on speech while *Brooklyn* and *Cuban* were censorship cases involving the leases and licenses of the museums

   ANSWER: The answer is Choice (B). The difference between *Finley* on the one hand and *Brooklyn Museum* and *Cuban Museum* on the other is that *Finley* is a patronage case involving an allocation of limited funds, but the two museum cases involved a course of funding by the government over time, that was ended precipitously by a government reaction to a speech activity. Choice (A) is incorrect because the cases did not turn specifically on timing — it is true that Finley had not received the grant when the decision was made to deny it, but in the museum cases, the museums merely had an expectation of continued funding from the budgetary decisions that had been made over the course of time; they hadn't already received the money. Choice (C) is incorrect — neither *Finley* nor the museum cases involved speech that was deemed obscene under the Miller test. Choice (D) is incorrect because *Finley* was a grant-award decision, not a time-place-manner restriction on speech.

7 | ART GALLERIES, DEALERS, AND CLIENTS

Art is a business like many others, and yet, not like many others in several respects. Artists produce items to sell, and the artists sell these items themselves or through intermediaries and middlemen. Unlike other businesses, art is a product and trade with its own culture and expectations. A work of art can be uniquely valuable both as a collectible item and as an artifact that might have tremendous value to the culture and education of a society. As a result, clients and customers often make tremendous demands on artists. Galleries and deal-

Michelangelo, Self-Portrait as Nicodemus in The Florence Pietà *or* The Deposition of Christ, *Florence, Italy (1547-1555)*

ers, the intermediaries of the art trade, often are institutions and entities with enormous bargaining powers compared to the average artist.

Historically, artists, regardless of their abilities, have found themselves victimized by the economics of society and the business world. Even Michelangelo,[1] when dealing with the Pope, found his skill and reputation no shield from exploitation. *See Unit Perspective: The Artist,* from The Letters of Michelangelo 26 (Park Ramsder ed. 1963). Today, artists must avail themselves of every legal and economic provision designed for their benefit and seek professional counsel when required if they are to pursue success on a level playing field.

This chapter spotlights the artist's practical problems in dealing with galleries, dealers, and customers, and presents

---

1. Image: Michael D. Murray, Cropped, revised, and resized thumbnail excerpt of a Michael D. Murray photograph (2007) of the public domain sculpture by Michelangelo, "Self-Portrait as Nicodemus in The Florence Pietà" or "The Deposition of Christ," Florence, Italy (1547-1555).

suggestions for their resolution. An artist's legal situation may be uniquely complicated and challenging, making it essential for attorneys to study various fields of law to best protect their artist clients.

A. Artists Selling Art

All artists face the obstacle of finding an outlet for their work. The depressing experience of having a portfolio rejected by one gallery after another has caused some artists to postpone gallery contact until they have had their work acknowledged in contests or juried shows. Even more ego-deflating can be the attempt to sell one's own wares at fairs or craft exhibits, where lack of sales often is equated with personal rejection.

Some artists have resorted to showing their work on the sidewalks of urban areas. Artists, in displaying their artwork on city sidewalks, have claimed First Amendment protection for the display of their works as a necessary outlet for their artistic expression. Thus, artists have argued that they should be exempt from vending licensing schemes and other general restraints on open sales of art, and these arguments have proved on more than one occasion to be successful.[2] Nevertheless, not every artist prevails and sometimes the license or permit regime is upheld.[3] The debate is ongoing, and government regulation of public exhibition and performance of artistic expression is a very current issue in First Amendment jurisprudence.

An important and growing means of exposure to critics and potential buyers for emerging artists are so-called "alternative spaces."[4] Alternative spaces are typically former public buildings or warehouses renovated to provide studio and display space to unknown artists at minimal cost. Renovators seek to provide unaffiliated artists with exposure while increasing community awareness of new trends in the arts. Often, their most important function is to

---

2. See *Bery v. City of New York*, 97 F.3d 689 (2d Cir. 1996), *cert. denied*, 520 U.S. 1251 (1997) (selling art on sidewalks and in public places was conduct linked to expressive content and thus protected by the First Amendment).

3. See *Second City Music, Inc. v. City of Chicago*, 333 F.3d 846 (7th Cir. 2003) (music reseller subject to vending license requirements); *One World One Family Now v. City and County of Honolulu*, 76 F.3d 1009 (9th Cir. 1996) (ordinance regulating sale of t-shirts bearing message was upheld as content-neutral time-place-manner restriction); *State v. Chepilko*, 965 A.2d 190 (N.J. Super. A.D. 2009) (hawker snapping pictures of passersby with his camera in order to solicit sale of the snapshots to the passersby was not engaged in First Amendment expressive activity); *Baker v. City of New York*, 01 Civ. 48888 (NRB), 2002 U.S. Dist. LEXIS 18100 (S.D.N.Y. Sept. 26, 2002) (street photographer regulated from obstructing pedestrian and vehicular traffic; valid time-place-manner restriction); *Turley v. Giuliani*, 86 F. Supp. 2d 291 (S.D.N.Y. 2000) (street musicians may be subjected to clearly defined decibel volume restrictions that take into account ambient noise conditions); *People v. Saul*, 3 Misc. 3d 260, 776 N.Y.S.2d 189 (Crim. Ct. City of New York Feb. 19, 2004) (selling Iraqi picture cards on street subject to vending laws because cards were collectible merchandise, not art); *see* John Nivala, *The Landscape Art of Daniel Urban Kiley*, 29 Wm. & Mary Envt'l L. & Pol'y Rev. 267 (2005).

4. *See, e.g.*, Phil Patton, *Other Voices, Other Rooms: The Rise of the Alternative Space*, Art Am., July/Aug. 1977, at 80.

serve as conduits for state and federal arts funding, provided they are structured as non-profit organizations. Leading alternative spaces are indexed each year along with conventional commercial outlets for art works in the publication *Art in America*.[5]

Some art proponents have left behind the realm of alternative spaces for that of cyberspace. Franklin Furnace was an early adopter of a web presence as a means of spreading the avant-garde experience to a wider audience. Founded in 1976 as a mode by which artists could "democratically" voice their ideas, Franklin Furnace uses its website as a way for artists to express their First Amendment freedom of expression. One aspect of the website is a chance for viewers to watch a live performance and to discuss the art in an online chat session. Other features include options to click on a particular artist and view their prior and present work.[6]

Many artists have their own websites. Some use these sites merely for publicity purposes and refer individuals interested in purchasing their works to the dealers by which they are represented. Others actually sell their works through their own sites. If an artist is represented by a dealer, care must be taken not to compete with that dealer.

Another way for artists to break into the commercial art market is through the formation of cooperative galleries, in which artists pool works and rotate sales responsibility. This form of marketing has met with mixed success, however, as artists' temperament and lack of business acumen often interfere with effective merchandising techniques.[7] In addition, cooperative galleries usually provide for equal apportionment of earnings among the members. The better artists, once recognized, often resent supporting their less fortunate colleagues and move on. A few cooperative galleries have survived by devoting some attention to the inevitable internal conflicts and resolving them at the outset.[8]

Some art galleries have attempted to function as tax-exempt entities in an effort to reduce overhead costs. In order to qualify as a tax-exempt organization under the Internal Revenue Code (IRC), an organization must be created and operated exclusively for charitable, educational, or scientific purposes.[9] Tax regulations such as Treas. Reg. § 1.501(c)(3) state that museums and similar organizations are examples of exempt educational organizations. In Rev. Rul. 71-395, 1971-2 C.B. 228, the IRS took the position that a cooperative gallery that did not charge admission but sold the works of its members and remitted a portion of the proceeds of sale to the artist who created the work was not entitled to tax-exempt status, citing

---

5. *See* Art in Am. (Annual Guide to Museums, Galleries, and Artists edition), Aug. 1990, at 215.

6. *See, e.g.,* http://www.franklinfurnace.org; *Alternative Space in Cyberspace*, ARTnews, Mar. 1997, at 40.

7. *Cf.* Calvin J. Goodman, *Are You a Professional Artist?*, Am. Artist, Jan. 1974, at 19.

8. *See* Melinda Popham, *Portrait of the Artist as Collective*, Ms., Jan. 1974, at 40; Betty Chamberlain, *Up the Organization* (Professional Page section), Am. Artist, June 1973, at 11 (discussing some less formal, but successful, arrangements).

9. *See generally* John D. Colombo, *In Search of Private Benefit*, 58 FLA. L. REV. 1063 (2006).

§ 1.501(c)(3) of the regulations. The IRS apparently viewed the economic benefit to the artist members as sufficient to deprive the organization of its exempt status.

Many galleries deal exclusively in contemporary crafts rather than so-called fine arts. The distinction between the two types of creations is not clear.[10] Nor is it justified. For example, the federal government confiscated an artist's interpretation of currency appearing in the form of bow ties, boxer shorts, and sponges under the impression that "the items are not art, but counterfeit money and therefore not protected by the First Amendment."[11] The artist argued that the items were actually performance art and that the government had violated his right to free expression by taking the items in question. *See id.* Such a debate is indicative of the age-old question of "what is art?" Some state statutes ignore the distinction between crafts and fine arts (as is more fully discussed in Chapter 1). Nevertheless, labeling a work of art as a craft, some argue, reduces consumer interest.[12] It also deprives the craft artist of some forms of legal protection. Conversely, the vast nationwide network of crafts wholesalers and festivals is a testimonial to the success of the "crafts movement," and has opened a potentially enormous market to the enterprising craftsperson.[13] Nevertheless, even after the artist's work has been acknowledged and a degree of financial independence has been achieved, other issues remain to be considered.

State of New York v. Wright Hepburn Webster Gallery, Limited

64 Misc. 2d 423, 314 N.Y.S.2d 661 (Sup. Ct. N.Y. County 1970)

FEIN, Justice.

This is an application by the Attorney General for an order granting the appointment of a receiver pendente lite of approximately sixty-eight paintings made by one David Stein, and the proceeds of any sale thereof, which are in the possession of defendant Wright Hepburn Webster Gallery, Ltd. ("Gallery").

Pending the determination of this motion, the order to show cause dated September 14, 1970, (1) temporarily restrained defendant, Gallery, from physically transferring any of Stein's paintings and the proceeds derived from the sale of said paintings; (2) permitted sale of such paintings only "subject to cancellation"; and (3) impressed a trust on the proceeds of any sale of said paintings.

This novel application by the Attorney General is based on the bizarre career of defendant, David Stein, who has not been served with process. In 1967, Stein, a former art dealer, was convicted in this county, on his plea of guilty, of six counts

---

10. Leonard D. DuBoff, *What Is Art? Toward a Legal Definition*, 12 HASTINGS COMM. & ENT. L.J. 303, 336-37 (1990).

11. *See* Robin Campbell, *Illegal Tender*, ARTnews, Oct. 1999, at 66.

12. Lisa Hammel, *Craftsmen Losing Major Showcase*, N.Y. Times, Oct. 15, 1975, at 51.

13. *See, e.g.,* Crabtree, *Memphis Craftsmen Break into National Catalogue Sales*, Memphis Bus. J., Nov. 13, 1989, § 1, at 3.

David Stein and one of his forgeries[14]

of counterfeiting art work and grand larceny. He had mastered the styles of such great artists as Chagall, Picasso, Matisse, Braque, Klee, Miro, Cocteau, and Roualt, to such an extent that he was able to and did sell as the original works of such artists watercolors, gouaches and other paintings which he himself had created.

After serving his jail sentence, Stein was deported to France where he was arrested and subsequently convicted for selling art forgeries in that country. Stein is now in jail in Paris where he has apparently been permitted by the French authorities to produce paintings "in the style of" such renowned artists as Chagall, Matisse, Picasso, Braque and others, subject to the proviso that they bear his own signature, "Stein, D.," rather than the simulated signatures of these masters as had been his prior practice.

In April, 1969, Gallery's affiliate in London exhibited and sold a number of such paintings made by Stein during his confinement. Gallery is now exhibiting in its New York showroom approximately 68 such paintings made by defendant Stein. Gallery has placed a sign in its windows advertising: "Forgeries by Stein." However, each painting bears the signature of Stein. Attached as exhibits to the moving papers are a circular and press release issued by Gallery announcing the date for an "official" exhibition of "Master Forger David Stein" paintings. Both promotion pieces clearly indicate that the paintings are by Stein and are offered to the public as being "in the style of" "Chagall, Picasso, Matisse, etc." The circular states: "Master Forger David Stein Presents Braque, Klee, Miro, Chagall, Matisse, Picasso." The underlying action on behalf of the State of New York demands that the court (1) declare these paintings a public nuisance to be abated; (2) enjoin their sale or transfer; (3) appoint a permanent receiver over them with appropriate instructions to turn them over to a museum or similar institution for use in research, identification and education in the detection of art forgeries and not to be disposed of in such a manner as to circulate in the art market and not to eradicate Stein's signature.

The Attorney General contends that Stein's name can easily be removed from these paintings and that they will eventually find their way into the art market as original works of Chagall, Picasso, etc. The Attorney General argues

---

14. Image: Michael D. Murray, Cropped, revised, and resized thumbnail excerpt of an exhibit depicting forger David Stein and one of his forgeries, the subject of *State of New York v. Wright Hepburn Webster Gallery, Limited*, 64 Misc. 2d 423, 314 N.Y.S.2d 661 (Sup. Ct. N.Y. County 1970).

that because of the ability of Stein to simulate the works of the aforementioned great painters, Stein paintings constitute a continuing, potential threat and hazard to the cultural welfare of that segment of the public which buys, sells, and collects art and to art lovers and the cultural institutions which exhibit the works of the artists that Stein is simulating.

The issues presented by this application involve a case of first impression. The court is asked to find that the possible harm to the public from the sale of paintings made by a convicted forger "in the style of" acknowledged great painters warrants preventing this man from earning a livelihood by utilizing his peculiar and unusual artistic talents. It cannot be disputed that whatever Stein's motives, he is an artist, both in terms of dictionary definitions and as a matter of practical application. His work in perfecting the style of the masters may properly be ascribed to that special talent with which true artists are uniquely endowed. Otherwise it cannot be argued seriously that harm could result from the sale of his works.

No claim is made by the Attorney General that Stein is guilty of some criminal behavior by offering the subject paintings for sale to the public. However fraudulent or criminal his past transgressions have been, they cannot militate against Stein's right as an artist to sell his own works, acknowledged as such. Although Stein's prior deceptive practices cannot be completely over-looked in weighing the allegations that the same result will occur if his works are permitted to be sold commercially, at this juncture the court is merely presented with the possibility of the future commission of a crime, by Stein or some purchaser of his works. A court of equity will not enjoin the commission of a crime as such, much less a possible crime, although a nuisance may be enjoined, albeit the activity enjoined is also criminal. Not one iota of proof has been submitted that anyone is now engaged or about to engage in the removal of Stein's name for the purpose of passing off his work as an original work of one of the masters. It is difficult to perceive how these paintings constitute a public nuisance on the basis of the possibility or suspicion that this may occur. . . .

Section 1530 of the old Penal Law, in force until September 1, 1967, defined a public nuisance as:

> . . . a crime against the order and economy of the state, . . . in unlawfully doing an act, or omitting to perform a duty, which act or omission:
>
> 1. Annoys, injures or endangers the comfort, repose, health or safety of any considerable number of persons; or
> 2. offends public decency; or . . .
> 4. in any way renders a considerable number of persons insecure in life or the use of property.

The current Penal Law does not specifically define the term "public nuisance." Instead, Section 240.45 simply provides:

> A person is guilty of criminal nuisance when: (1) By conduct either unlawful in itself or unreasonable under all the circumstances, he knowingly or

recklessly creates or maintains a condition which endangers the safety or health of a considerable number of persons; or (2) He knowingly conducts or maintains any premises, place or resort where persons gather for the purposes of engaging in unlawful conduct.

It is manifest that Stein cannot be charged with the crime of nuisance. Prosecutions for the crime of nuisance as a practical matter generally fall into two categories: the maintenance of manufacturing plants, entertainment resorts and the like which by virtue of excessive noise, noxious gases, odors, etc. annoy or offend large areas of the community, or the conduct of resorts where persons gather for illegal or immoral purposes. (*See* Practice Commentary by Richard Denzer and Peter McQuillan; *McKinney's Consolidated Laws of New York*, Book 39, § 240.45, page 177.) These statutory definitions of a public nuisance codify the distinction drawn at common law between public and private nuisances (*see People v. Rubenfeld*, 254 N.Y. 245, 172 N.E. 485). The teachings of the statutes and the cases are that a public nuisance is an offense to the public of a neighborhood or community in the enjoyment of its common rights, as distinguished from activity which results merely in injury even to a large number of persons in the enjoyment of private rights not shared by the members of the community or neighborhood at large. (*Laman*, supra; *Rubenfeld*, supra; *N.Y. Trap Rock Corp. v. Clarkstown*, 299 N.Y. 77, 85 N.E.2d 873; *see* 42 N.Y. Jur., Nuisances § 5, p. 449). Moreover, to establish a public nuisance it is essential to prove the injury as an accomplished fact. (*People on Complaint of Green v. Willis*, 173 Misc. 442, 17 N.Y.S.2d 784). Consequently, the conduct of a lawful business may not be deemed to constitute a public nuisance unless something is done in the operation thereof which is unlawful or its maintenance is negligent or improper in such degree or respect as to work an unreasonable obstruction or injury to the public. No such showing is made here.

The relief sought here is novel and drastic. It should not be granted in the absence of a clear showing that defendants have committed some public wrong amounting to a nuisance.

It may well be that Stein's paintings "in the style of" the masters are an attempt to appropriate ideas not his own and that the law should not permit one to profit who "is endeavoring to reap where (he) has not sown; . . ." (*International News Service v. Associated Press*, 248 U.S. 215, 239, 39 S. Ct. 68, 72, 63 L. Ed. 211). However, such conduct does not constitute a public wrong. Stein's work may, under the circumstances, run afoul of some appropriate copyright law, or may even constitute a violation of General Business Law, Art. 12-E, Section 224, limiting the right to reproduce works of fine art. If so, the rights violated are private and do not form a basis for action by the Attorney-General.

In this context, perhaps consideration should be given to Goethe's query:

"People are always talking about mean? As soon as we are born the world begins to work upon us, and keeps on to the end. What can we call ours, except energy, strength, will? If I could give an account of what I owe to great predecessors and contemporaries, there would be but a small remainder." (Eckermann, *Conversations with Goethe in the Last Years of His Life*, p. 147).

So it must seriously be doubted whether the court, at the insistance of the State, should prevent conscious appropriation of knowledge where no deception of the public is proven. In essence this is acknowledged by the Attorney-General. He concedes that the case does not fall within any of the sections of the Penal Law. The "criminal simulation" section 170.45(1) and (2) of the Penal Law requires a showing of intent to defraud, not shown here. Paintings such as these are not included among the items declared in Penal Law Section 400.05 to be a nuisance subject to abatement. As has been noted, the criminal nuisance section 240.45 is limited to acts endangering the public health or safety. The Attorney-General argues that the acts here complained of should be enjoined because they endanger the public welfare, citing the State's concern with the "moral, intellectual and spiritual needs" of the citizen. (*Barrett v. State of New York*, 220 N.Y. 423, 428, 116 N.E. 99, 101). But that case merely sustained the right of the State to preserve the dwindling beaver population, a conservation measure, without being liable in damages to a landowner whose trees were damaged or destroyed by the protected beaver. The proper state concern to protect the beaver in the interest of the public welfare hardly provides a basis for state action to suppress paintings. . . .

There remains only to consider the significance of defendant's window sign and other publicity describing the exhibit as being "Forgeries By Stein." Both sides concede these paintings are not forgeries, as well they must. The essence of forgery, as recognized by Penal Law, Article 170, the forgery article in its various sections, is the utilization as a "means of defrauding another" of that which "purports to be in all respects an authentic creation of" or "fully authorized by its ostensible maker." The signature of Stein on these paintings establishes there is no forgery even if a painting could be considered as within the condemnation of the article.

On this count, the advertising by defendant "Forgeries By Stein" is false, although when read in context this "tag line" is manifestly only an exaggerated form of "puffing," a sales "gimmick," like all too much advertising. This does not appear to violate the Penal Law or any other statute. Nor does the Attorney-General make any such claim. Neither this advertising nor the possibility or suspicion that in the future someone may remove Stein's name and substitute the name or signature of one of the masters is a sufficient basis for finding that the exhibition and sale of these paintings is a public nuisance. Although defendant submitted no papers and no brief in opposition, it did move to dismiss on the oral argument. No useful purpose would be served by requiring an answer or by a trial.

Accordingly, plaintiff's application is denied, the temporary restraining order is vacated, and the complaint is dismissed. Settle order.

Notes and Questions

1. Stein died in 1999. It is a recognized practice of art education to send students off to practice copying great works of art so as to hone their artistic skills and techniques. It is a mark of achievement to produce a copy that can be mistaken for the original. From time to time, artists probably are tempted to sell these "forgeries" as replicas or reproductions "in the style of" a famous artist.

2. New York's Attorney General made a somewhat cumbersome attempt to prohibit this practice under the nuisance laws. What other criminal law or private, civil legal theories might be employed to curb this practice? What advice to artist clients should you give to avoid liability under these legal theories?

B. Artists and Dealers

While many artists are loath to view their profession as a business, most must sell their work in order to survive and, before long, they may seek to sell their art through a dealer. Art schools are only now beginning to prepare their students for the rigors of the marketplace through business and marketing training. But even if the artist knows the market forces involved and how to exploit them, most are not aware of the legal basis for this relationship and the rights they can insist upon. The lawyer must understand the peculiar needs of both the dealer and the artist in order to effectively advise each client. This section considers many of the legal problems peculiar to the artist-dealer relationship. For a code of fair practice between artists and purchasers, *see* The Joint Ethics Committee, Code of Fair Practice, 1989.

1. Defining Responsibilities

Nakian v. DiLaurenti

673 F. Supp. 699 (S.D.N.Y. 1987)

SWEET, District Judge.

Plaintiff Paul Nakian ("Nakian") moved by notice of motion of September 21, 1987, for a preliminary injunction seeking certain works of art created by his father, Reuben Nakian, now in the possession of defendant Marco DiLaurenti, President of DiLaurenti Galleries, Ltd. and agent for Reuben Nakian. The motion was heard on affidavits and argument on November 6, 1987. On the facts and conclusions set forth below, a preliminary injunction will issue.

PRIOR PROCEEDINGS

This diversity action was commenced on March 27, 1987, seeking rescission of the agency agreement between Reuben Nakian, Nakian's decedent and

DiLaurenti dated March 13, 1985, recovery of pieces of art, and monetary damages. Some discovery has been undertaken and the instant motion was brought on by motion dated September 21, 1987, and was heard on affidavits on November 6, 1987.

FACTS

Reuben Nakian is a well known sculptor of substantial works who died at the age of 89 on December 4, 1986. His son, Paul Nakian, is executor of his estate. DiLaurenti is President of DiLaurenti Galleries Ltd. ("Galleries") and Petit Palais Ltd. Galleries is a subsidiary of Petit Palais Ltd. and is located at 383 West Broadway in New York City.

Reuben Nakian, Paul Nakian and Galleries entered into the Agreement on March 13, 1985 which provided that Galleries would act as the exclusive agent for Reuben Nakian and use its best efforts to promote the sale of the artist's works. The agreement has a five year term and among other things provides:

> 6. The Agent shall have the right to select and retain possession of the Artist's works for exhibition, display and consignment to various galleries, art dealers, museums, and exhibitions. . . .
> 8. . . . . The Agent shall be given possession of those of the Artist's works which he reasonably requires to carry out the terms, intent, and purposes of this Agreement.

By November 1986, the parties to the Agreement were in substantial disagreement as to whether or not Galleries had breached the Agreement.

At issue then as now are questions of accounting under the Agreement, the extent of Galleries' best efforts, the adequacy of Galleries' insurance, and the possession of works by the artist by Galleries. By correspondence, meetings, and conferences between counsel, efforts were made, unsuccessfully or not depending on the point of view, to resolve these disputes. While the affidavits submitted delineate without question a factual dispute as to the alleged breach by Galleries of the Agreement, there are certain facts established by the affidavits in support of the motion without contravention by those in opposition.

Galleries is in possession of some 300 pieces of Nakian art work, including 32 pieces belonging to the Nakian family, not offered for resale. There is an exhibition planned at the Fundacao Calouste Gulbenkian Museum in Lisbon, Portugal for September, 1988. The Museum has requested a commitment for the use of 65 works commencing June 1, 1988, and access to all works for cataloging, photography, documentation, and insurance. The plans for the Lisbon exhibition have been in progress over the past four years.

Galleries has not indicated any plans for future exhibitions or displays other than the permanent exhibition at the gallery of 12 bronze sculptures which are rotated each month. No facts are set forth to indicate a basis for requirement of the Nakian pieces by Galleries for the purposes of exhibition other than what is set forth above.

What appears to be most hotly controverted are the provisions relating to casting of additional works from molds in possession of Nakian. It may well be that this issue is the main spring which drives this litigation. In any case, there are factual disputes galore with respect to Nakian's right to rescission.

CONCLUSIONS

The test for issuance of preliminary injunctive relief in this Circuit is well known. A plaintiff can succeed upon showing: "(a) irreparable harm and (b) either (1) likelihood of success on the merits or (2) sufficiently serious questions going to the merits to make them a fair ground for litigation and a balance of hardships tipping decidedly toward the party requesting the preliminary relief." *Jackson Dairy, Inc. v. H.P. Hood & Sons*, 596 F.2d 70, 72 (2d Cir. 1979).

The facts with respect to this Lisbon exhibition demonstrate both the need for immediate relief and irreparable injury. There is no showing to contradict Nakian's allegations that the interests of Nakian's estate would be damaged in an incalculable fashion were the long planned exhibition not to go forward.

Serious issues as to the good faith efforts of Galleries, its accountings and insurance coverage have been raised, both on the law and the facts. There has been no showing that Galleries would suffer a hardship if required to return the pieces owned by the family, to designate and make available the 65 pieces for the Lisbon exhibition, and to provide the necessary cooperation to prepare for the exhibition.

Assuming that 72 pieces will be required to maintain the schedule of exhibition at the gallery, for the next six months in the absence of any further showing of requirement by Galleries it would appear that another 100 pieces should be returned.

Obviously, this order will be subject to further modification upon an appropriate showing. Discovery will be completed by February 10 and the pretrial order filed February 17, 1988, on which date a final pretrial conference will be held and the action will be placed upon the trial calendar.

IT IS SO ORDERED.

Notes and Questions

1. Who is responsible for the cost of art exhibitions? Which party should insure the work? How long may the gallery keep the art? What about the cost of returning unsold pieces? And what is to be the gallery's commission? All of these issues should have been of great concern to the artists and the gallery, yet neither side appeared to have considered them.

2. Article 2 of the Uniform Commercial Code (UCC) may be applicable to some of these issues. For example, § 2-509, Risk of Loss in Absence of Breach, states that the risk of loss is generally on the party possessing the goods. *See also* § 2-309 (providing for a reasonable time); § 2-501(1) (requiring that tender be made at a reasonable hour); § 2-308 (providing that, normally, the place of seller's business is the place for delivery); § 2-305 (indicating that if the price is not settled, it

shall be a reasonable price). For additional gap-fillers and an analysis of the UCC's open term provisions, *see* James J. White & Robert S. Summers, *Handbook of the Law under the Uniform Commercial Code* 82 (1972). The minimum requirements under UCC § 2-204 are contractual intent and a reasonably certain basis upon which relief can be granted. However, the code provisions may not be what the parties actually desire and many of its sections have been given strained interpretations. *See, e.g.,* Lobell, *Representing Artists, Collectors and Dealers: Business Relationships,* 297 PLI/Pat (Practicing Law Institute) 425 (1990).

3. The Court in *Sonnabend Gallery, Inc. v. Peter Halley,* Index No. 12723/92 (Sup. Ct. N.Y. County June 18, 1992) (*see* Laurie Ziegler, *Power Shifts in the Art World: The Importance of the Artist-Dealer Contract,* 10 ENT. & SPORTS L. 19 (1992), denied Sonnabend's request for a preliminary injunction prohibiting Halley from showing his works at another gallery. Sonnabend based its request on an alleged oral agreement whereby Halley agreed to exhibit his works biannually at Sonnabend. Halley argued that there was no agreement as to the term of this arrangement with Sonnabend. The court found that no enforceable contract existed, because there was no agreement as to its duration, the method of terminating it, and how and when amounts paid the artist should be reviewed.

4. *O'Keeffe v. Bry,* 456 F. Supp. 822 (S.D.N.Y. 1978), also illustrated the importance of reducing all contract terms to writing. When O'Keeffe terminated Bry as her exclusive sales agent, Bry sued the artist for breaching her employment agreement. However, the agreement on which Bry based her claim to an exclusive lifetime agency was an agreement between O'Keeffe and Harvard University in which the artist was to leave a gift of her works to the University. The Harvard agreement merely expressed O'Keeffe's wish that the University use Bry to dispose of the donated works after O'Keeffe died. As such, the enforcement of Bry's alleged employment contract was barred by the statute of frauds. Even if the statute of frauds defense was unavailable, it is doubtful whether the precatory language in the Harvard agreement would be sufficient to bind O'Keeffe.

5. There is implied in every contract a duty that the parties will use their best efforts to fulfill it. UCC § 2-306 specifically provides that a buyer (dealer) with an exclusive sales agreement must use best efforts to promote sales, while the seller (artist) must use best efforts to supply the goods. When the subject matter is a work of art, it is a good idea to define the extent of the duty as courts are reluctant to imply strict requirements. *See, e.g., Liedloff v. Greneker Corp.,* 137 N.Y.S.2d 238 (Sup. Ct. 1954) (defendant's subsequent alteration of mannequins created by artist was held not to interfere with the creator's rights, notwithstanding the fact that none of the modified mannequins was ever sold).

6. An artist should carefully read, understand, and be willing to abide by all the terms of a contract before signing it. If this is not done, the artist

may subsequently find the agreement intolerable and a breach can be costly. *See* Johnston, *Notes on People*, N.Y. Times, Feb. 6, 1975, at 29 (Sarah Churchill, daughter of the late Sir Winston Churchill, was sued for breach of contract when she refused to allow her paintings to be converted into lithographs).

7. A disagreement once sparked the interest of the artistic community within the artist/dealer context when the late artist Robert Rauschenberg had 15 works seized by law enforcement officials in 1998 during an exhibition in Texas, the artist's home state. The seizure was based upon a disagreement over commissions to a Rauschenberg dealer. *See, e.g.*, Jeffrey Kastner, *Sins of Commission*, ARTnews, Apr. 1998, at 51-52; Shaila Dewan, *Culture Clash*, Hous. Press, Feb. 26, 1998. The dealer involved, Alfred Kren, claimed to have earned $335,000 in commissions from sales of Rauschenberg's work during the years 1993-96. *See* Dewan, *id.* Kren met Rauschenberg in the mid-'80s and started selling the artist's work to German museums and other parties in the U.S. *Id.* Rauschenberg and Kren's relationship was stormy as Rauschenberg felt that Kren's promotional efforts had become "an embarrassment and a disgrace." *Id.* While Kren had secured a $5.5 million judgment against Rauschenberg, the two "amicably settled the unfortunate disagreement" in 1998. *See News in Brief*, ARTnews, May 1998, at 62.

8. Another dispute arose between artist and dealer in Mexico when painter Roger Von Gunten accused his art dealer of reneging on contracts promising to (1) promote the artist's work internationally, and (2) include his work in a permanent collection. Von Gunten then stopped painting and, consequently, the dealer sued. When an appeals court ordered the artist to pay back the dealer a certain amount in art, Von Gunten made approximately 19 paintings, stating in various colors that the dealer was greedy and a liar. The dealer refused to accept the paintings as payment, alleging that they were not art, yet supporters of Von Gunten staged an exhibition of the paintings, juxtaposing them beside works by famous Mexican artists. *See Art is Long, Litigation Longer*, ARTnews, May 1996, at 28.

9. In *Zucker v. Hirschl & Adler Galleries, Inc.*, 648 N.Y.S.2d 521 (Sup. Ct. N.Y. County 1996), an artist and a gallery found themselves involved in a complicated litigation because the two sides never had committed the finer points of their relationship to writing, nor had they documented in writing the nature of the monies extended from the gallery to the artist. Instead, oral agreements and handshakes stood in for proper contracts and written loan agreements. The artist and the gallery disputed the amount of the commissions owed and the nature of the moneys extended to the artist by the gallery (loans versus advances against commissions), and it was difficult to resolve the dispute because written records were lacking. The gallery attempted to protect itself by imposing a lien on the artist's works in the possession of the gallery, but the court found that under the plain terms of New York

Arts and Cultural Affairs Law § 12.01(1)(a)(v), the gallery was prohibited from taking a security interest in the artist's work at the gallery to cover unpaid debts of the artist owed to the gallery.

10. Informal arrangements and "hand-shake agreements" work just fine when business is good, everyone is happy, and everyone is getting along. Business relationships based on undocumented agreements break down when one of these three circumstances goes the other direction. Cases like *Zucker* in note 9 above would have been a great deal simpler to resolve if the gallery simply had reduced these agreements on "loans" or "advances" to writing laying out the terms of repayment.

11. New York Art & Cultural Affairs Law § 12.01(1)(a)(v), cited in *Zucker*, still has not been amended to provide for security interests of the consignee against the consignor. As noted in the case, the consignment laws of the majority of states enacting such laws protect the artist's works from attachment and execution by creditors of the consignee — the artist's dealer or gallery. In states where such laws do not exist, the artist can protect her works from seizure by recording a UCC-1 financing statement for security consignment that gives notice that the artist has perfected a security interest in the work deposited with the gallery or dealer on consignment, and will retain a superior security interest in the work until its sale. *See* U.C.C., Article 9, § 9-319 and Article 2, § 2-326. To avoid further confusion and litigation expense, the artist should request that the dealer or gallery mark the works subject to consignment with signage indicating that they are goods under consignment that are to be separated from the dealer's or gallery's other inventory. *See generally* Hilary Jay, *Picture Imperfect: The Rights of Art Consignor-Collectors when their Art Gallery Files for Bankruptcy*, 58 Duke L.J. 1859-93 (2009).

12. Another ambiguity in the terms of the Sales Agreement between the parties was whether the gallery's exclusive representation of the artist and right to receive commissions on sales of his works extended to so-called "private sales" by the artist to his friends, or was limited to "consigned works" that were "offered for sale to the public." Once again, a proper written agreement between the parties that covered the effect of private sales by the artist would have gone a long way toward avoiding this dispute.

2. Types of Arrangements

There are two basic types of legal arrangements between an artist and a dealer or a gallery. The first is an outright purchase agreement, where the dealer or gallery purchases the work from the artist and resells it. The dealer or gallery is under no contractual obligation to the artist beyond payment of the purchase price. The agreement may apply to the artist's entire output or only a portion of it. It may consist wholly or in part of an artist's duty to offer his or her work to the dealer or gallery first, and the dealer's or gallery's option to buy. Called the right of first refusal, such an agreement might read:

> The artist agrees to give the dealer a continuing first choice of all of the artist's new works, available for the dealer's inspection and selection at least once every three months for the dealer's account at a price shown on the attached schedule. Works not selected by the dealer within 30 days of inspection may then be sold by the artist, but in no event for less than the price shown on the attached schedule, unless sold by the artist no less than three years after being offered to the dealer.

Such an agreement may, likewise, provide for resale royalty rights and other reserved rights on behalf of the artist. *See* Chapter 4, "Moral Rights and Economic Rights." An artist would find it very difficult to have an outright purchase arrangement with more than one dealer or gallery because of complex bookkeeping requirements and the potential for conflicts if each of the dealers or galleries contracting with the artist wound up selecting the same work for acquisition.

The outright purchase agreement is more typical in Europe and with craft artists, while the second legal arrangement — consignment — is the norm in the United States for so-called "fine artists". In fact, 29 states and the District of Columbia have passed legislation creating automatic consignments upon delivery of artwork by an artist to a dealer. A consignment arrangement creates an agency in which the gallery or dealer (the consignee) acts as selling agent for the artist (the consignor).[15]

Although, there may also be variations on these most common agreements, the fiduciary relationship requires the dealer to act only in the interest of the artist and to forego all personal advantage aside from just compensation. The dealer is also under a duty to respect the confidential nature of the arrangement.[16]

PROBLEM 7-1

First, draft a short agreement between an artist (your client) and a dealer or gallery that will carry your client's work. Decide whether the arrangement will be exclusive, and write up other terms, duties, and responsibilities as defined in this chapter.

Second, redraft the agreement as if your client was the dealer or a gallery. What terms, duties, and responsibilities would you change to better protect your gallery or dealer client?

---

15. *See generally* Hilary Jay, *Picture Imperfect: The Rights of Art Consignor-Collectors when their Art Gallery Files for Bankruptcy*, 58 DUKE L.J. 1859-93 (2009).

16. *See* 1 Floyd R. Mechem, Treatise on the Law of Agency § 1188 (1914); Restatement (Second) of Agency §§ 13, 379, 381 (1956).

Matter of Friedman

64 A.D.2d 70; 407 N.Y.S.2d 999 (2d Dep't 1978)*

MARGETT, Judge.

Arnold Friedman was an important American artist who derived his style from Impressionism, but who expanded and transcended that idiom with his own unique personal style. Friedman's biography reads like the classic (some might say stereotyped) tale of a struggling artist whose work was never appreciated in financial terms until well after his death. Born in 1874, Friedman grew up on the east side of Manhattan. His father — who had emigrated from Hungary with his wife — died in 1878, leaving his mother with three other small children to support. In his early teens Friedman became a wage earner, working at the Produce Exchange. At the age of 17 he was virtually the sole support of his family and began to work for the New York Post Office.

At age 32, while still employed by the Post Office, Friedman began to study art at the Art Students League in New York. In 1908, after three years of evenings at the League, he took a leave of absence from his job and traveled to Paris, where he lived for six months. While there he met his wife. Upon his return to New York, he continued to work six days a week, as many as 10 hours a day, at the New York Post Office. Two or three years after his marriage, with $25 coming in every week, he purchased a house in then rural Corona, Queens, complete with an attic studio. He worked there as time permitted. His daily routine of travel to and from the New York Post Office went on until his retirement on a meager pension in the 1930's.

In terms of quantity, his production was limited by his job and by his responsibilities to his wife and four children. Friedman was 42 years old before he participated in his first group show and 52 before he had his first one-man show. Although a number of his paintings were sold to collectors and museums during his lifetime, his only assets when he died intestate in 1946 consisted of his work. Today, Friedman's legacy of over 300 works of art is worth approximately a half-million dollars.

This appeal involves a dispute over the ownership of that legacy. The dispute is between Elizabeth Becque, Friedman's daughter and the administratrix of his widow's estate, and Charles Egan, an art dealer. The origin of this controversy is an agreement entered into in May, 1963 between the artist's widow, Renee (Wilhelmina) Friedman, and Charles Egan, "d/b/a EGAN GALLERY." The agreement recites that Renee's children have "duly assigned to . . . [her] all of their right, title and interest in and to the estate of their late father Arnold Friedman"; that Renee "is now the sole owner of the unsold works of the late Arnold Friedman"; that "Egan, who is conducting an art gallery at 313 E. 79th Street, New York, N.Y. was a friend and admirer of the late Arnold Friedman"; and that "Renee wishes to have her late husband's works properly distributed in the art world." It is then agreed that "Renee . . .

---

* Footnotes omitted. Emphasis shown as in original.

sells, transferrs [sic] and assigns over to Charles Egan all of the works of the late Arnold Friedman now in her possession ... absolutely and forever." The parties further agreed to make an inventory of the collection. The consideration for this "sale, transfer and assignment" is as follows: "Egan agrees to accept the said works and properly prepare them for sale and exhibition, to put forth his best efforts to sell said works at prices which will be consonant with the merit of said works, and to pay to Renee, from time to time as said works are sold and payment therefor received, one half of the total received by him in the sale of any and all of the said works, it being understood that Renee's share of the proceeds of such sale is not to be diminished in any manner by expenses or charges of any kind." However, the agreement further provided that Renee "shall have no voice in determining the manner of sale or exhibition ... or the prices at which ... [the paintings] will be sold." It is recited that "having parted with title to said works, Renee's interest is limited to the receipt of one half of the proceeds from the sale thereof." This "agreement" was prepared by Egan's lawyer.

Mrs. Friedman could not afford her own lawyer. She was about 75 years of age at the time. Although she had been employed since the 1950's doing light housework in exchange for room and board, she received no monetary compensation. Mrs. Friedman had been "completely devoted" during her entire life to giving her late "husband an opportunity to paint and she believed very much in the quality of his paintings." She wanted to see her husband's work exhibited and sold, but the bulk of the collection had been in the basement of a gallery which was closed or in the process of closing. In late 1961 or early 1962, Mrs. Friedman approached Egan, an experienced art dealer who had known her husband since 1939 or 1940. According to Egan, Mrs. Friedman wanted to "give ... [him] the work with the idea that ... [he] would take care of it." Egan did in fact take possession of the collection and he sold a small oil painting — a still-life — in 1962 for $300. He remitted $150 to Mrs. Friedman, since they "were on a fifty-fifty basis."

The following year, Mrs. Friedman and Egan went to the office of Egan's attorney, Samuel Duker, to see about having a written agreement drafted. At that meeting, it "came out" that Arnold Friedman had died intestate and Mr. Duker suggested to Mrs. Friedman that she have an attorney draw up assignments of her children's interests in the paintings. Duker testified that Mrs. Friedman told him she could not afford a lawyer and that he thereupon drafted such assignments for her. He gave these documents to Mrs. Friedman and told both her and Egan that they should notify him when the assignments were signed; he would then draft the "agreement" that they sought.

Duker was subsequently notified by Egan that the assignments had been executed and he proceeded to draft the contract. When Mrs. Friedman and Egan arrived at his office for the execution of the contract, Duker "went over the agreement, word for word, and ... [he] explained [it] to her and ... [he] cleared up some misconceptions that she had about it." Duker testified that "at the end of the session ... [he] said" to Mrs. Friedman: "Look, I'm Charlie's lawyer and, of course, he will pay me but I would like to have a picture and, in view of the fact that I drew this agreement — this assignment — and I had to go through this agreement and explain it to you word by word, would you mind if I picked out a small picture?" Mrs. Friedman gave Duker two paintings as a fee for his services.

For the next 14 years, Egan maintained exclusive custody of the Friedman collection. During that period he held only one Arnold Friedman exhibition — in 1969. No sales resulted from that exhibition. According to petitioner, Elizabeth Becque, Egan failed to maintain any contact with Mrs. Friedman during the year immediately following the exhibition. Mrs. Becque testified that in 1970, in her mother's presence, she telephoned Mr. Egan to inquire as to his efforts to promote the paintings. Mrs. Becque stated that she mentioned her mother's need for money at the time. Mr. Egan allegedly told her that he was negotiating with a museum and that she should be patient. Mrs. Becque testified that Egan then said: "Look. You can have the paintings and see what you can do." Before she could respond, Egan added: "But, look, let's wait for the first of the year and we'll have an exhibition and see what happens then."

No exhibition was held in 1971, or thereafter. On the contrary, Egan closed his gallery in 1971 and began operating out of his apartment as a private dealer. Those Friedman works which were not in storage were hung on his apartment walls or stacked in a small room used as an office.

According to Elizabeth Becque, nothing was heard from Egan after her 1970 call, and she phoned him again in 1971 to ask about his promotional efforts. He allegedly repeated that he was still negotiating with museums and that if Mrs. Becque "thought . . . [she] could do better" she should "[take] the paintings and see what you can do."

In 1974 Mr. Egan did sell one painting to a noted collector for $1,000. Mrs. Friedman received a remittance of $500 on this sale. The sale price of $1,000 was considerably lower than the $3,000 to $15,000 range of prices at the 1969 exhibition. Mr. Egan explained at the trial that he wanted the collector "to buy a whole lot of . . . [Friedman's work] and wanted to make a very low price for him . . . but he . . . liked [only] one painting."

In 1974 or 1975 Mrs. Friedman entered a nursing home; she died there on March 31, 1976. Shortly after her death, her estate demanded that Egan return the Arnold Friedman paintings (and memorabilia consisting of letters, etc.) in his possession. When Egan refused, the instant proceeding, pursuant to SCPA 2103, was commenced. . . .

In an opinion dated August 1, 1977, Surrogate Laurino reasoned that although the "subject contract speaks in terms of an absolute conveyance of title . . . [Egan's] duties thereunder were fiduciary in nature with complete accountability for proceeds of sale to the decedent." (Matter of Friedman, 91 Misc. 2d 201, 204.) This "patent inconsistency" could only be resolved by resort to the acts of the parties and by the application of custom and usage. In reviewing the evidence adduced with respect to those standards, the Surrogate concluded (p. 205) that the contract was "a consignment arrangement."

The Surrogate noted that Egan has consistently acted, by his own testimony, as the "agent" for the decedent, collecting "sales commissions" on the two works of art that he did sell. Furthermore, the Surrogate credited petitioner's testimony that Egan had told her (p. 204), "'Look. You can have the paintings back and see what you can do.'" The court concluded that these were not the words of a man who has full title and interest in the paintings.

On the issue of custom and usage, the Surrogate credited the expert testimony to the effect that "with the rare exception of an outright sale for a sum certain . . . the common practice in the trade is consignment of art works from artist to dealer for a specified period of time, normally 2 to 5 years." (91 Misc. 2d 205.) The court also took note of subdivision 1 of section 219-a of the General Business Law (enacted as section 220 in 1966 [L 1966, ch 984]), which provides that "whenever an artist delivers . . . a work of fine art of his own creation to an art dealer for the purpose of exhibition and/or sale on a commission, fee or other basis of compensation, the delivery to and acceptance thereof by the art dealer is deemed to be 'on consignment,' and (i) such art dealer shall thereafter . . . be deemed to be the agent of such artist." While recognizing that this statute had been enacted subsequent to the date of the contract at issue, the court took note (p. 205) of authority for the proposition that the statute had been enacted "'to clarify the inherently fiduciary character of the "consignment arrangement" in the artist-art dealer relationship' which had existed through custom and usage prior to the enactment of . . . [the] statute" (citing Memorandum of the State Department of Law, 2 *McKinney's Session Laws of NY*, 1969, pp. 2412-13).

Accordingly, the Surrogate held (p. 205) that the 1963 contract was "a consignment agreement which terminated on the date of death of decedent principal." He directed, inter alia, that "all the art works of the late Arnold Friedman presently in the possession of [Egan] . . . be turned over to petitioner." The resulting decree, dated August 16, 1977, is appealed by Egan. We affirm. . . .

On the basis of the evidence received, the Surrogate's characterization of this contract as a consignment was the correct one. There was overwhelming evidence, uncontradicted by appellant, that consignments of art — not sales — are the prevalent business arrangement between artists, or their estates, and art dealers. This evidence is, of course, buttressed by the 1966 enactment of legislation which "[deems]" an artist's delivery of fine art to a dealer "to be 'on consignment'" (General Business Law, § 219-a). As noted by the Surrogate, that legislation was intended "to clarify the inherently fiduciary character of the 'consignment arrangement' in the artist-art dealer relationship" (*see* Memorandum of the State Department of Law, 2 *McKinney's Session Laws of NY*, 1969, p. 2413). The expert testimony at the hearing further established that when an outright sale from an artist to an art dealer occurs, the consideration paid is customarily an absolute sum of money. In addition, appellant's statements to petitioner, in 1970 and 1971, to the effect that she should take the paintings if she thought she could do a better job of selling them, are consistent with an understanding that he had the paintings on consignment. Those words would not be spoken by one who owned the paintings.

Well-established tenets of contract construction also support the Surrogate's conclusion. "[Parties] to an agreement are presumed to act sensibly . . . and an interpretation that produces an absurdly harsh result is to be avoided" (*River View Assoc. v. Sheraton Corp. of Amer.*, 33 A.D.2d 187, 190). Since there exists, in every contract, an implied covenant of good faith and fair dealing, the courts may take into consideration the fact that one construction would make the contract unreasonable. Thus, courts "will endeavor to give the construction most equitable to both parties instead of one which will give one of the parties an unfair or unreasonable advantage over the other" (*Rush v. Rush*, 19 A.D.2d 846). Furthermore, it is a "basic principle of contract law that a written document is to be construed against the party who prepared it where there are ambiguous or contradictory provisions" (*Gillette v. Heinrich Motors*, 55 A.D.2d 841).

These standards uniformly point toward the interpretation of this "agreement" as a consignment. . . .

At bar, the contract of the parties qua "sale" is grossly unconscionable in the substantive sense. In return for the stated conveyance of more than 300 works of art, Mrs. Friedman received neither the payment of a purchase price at the time of the "agreement" nor the right to receive a fixed price within a definite time in the future. Instead, she obtained only the uncertainty of payment to be made if and when sales were effected. Complete control over the timing of these "future sales" was placed in the hands of the dealer.

The "consideration" given by the dealer actually resulted in a situation where his interests were potentially adverse to the widow's. By holding out for a price far in excess of the fair market for the art works, the dealer could deny Mrs. Friedman any payment whatsoever. The dealer would, however, still retain title to the paintings. The incentive for the dealer to make any sales was therefore questionable. If he made no sales, he owned the collection outright. If he made sales, he would have to part with 50% of the purchase price.

This conflict of interest is reflected by the actual course of events over the last 15 years. From the date the contract was signed until Mrs. Friedman's death, Egan held only one exhibition of the Friedman paintings and made only one sale. Although the expert testimony established that dealers ordinarily seek to promote an artist's reputation through exhibits, catalogs, and other efforts, Egan's own testimony was that he "protected," "watched," and "nursed" the paintings (at least during the period 1963-1969). It was certainly in his own self-interest to do that — and nothing more.

Viewed as a sale, the contract gave Egan similar latitude in the opposite direction. He could "dump" the paintings at a minimal price in order to raise immediate cash. While there is no indication that he did so, the opportunity for such abuse was present.

In sum, the "consideration" given for this "sale" was so contingent and so dependent upon the discretion of one who had a "built-in" conflict of interest as to be grossly inadequate. This patent inadequacy so permeates the "agreement" as to render it unconscionable. As Virginia Zabriskie put it at the hearing, "[there] is nothing in it for the artist."

Furthermore, although the substantive unconscionability here present predominates, there are elements of procedural unconscionability attendant upon the execution of this contract which negate the possibility of any salvation for this "agreement." At the time the "agreement" was entered into, Mrs. Friedman was about 75 years of age. Her only formal education had been at a convent in France. There was testimony at the hearing to the effect that she had no real business experience and that she displayed "an unworldly attitude" towards business matters. She did not have her own lawyer and professed that she could not afford one.

In contrast, when the agreement was executed, Charles Egan had been in business nearly 30 years and had spent 18 years as the owner of his own gallery. He was represented by his own attorney who had participated in previous transactions between Egan and other artists. His attorney drafted the agreement and "explained" it to the widow.

It strains credulity to believe that Mrs. Friedman was told the full ramifications of the document she was signing. Was she told, for instance, that the "consideration" given by Egan was subject to an inherent conflict of interest? True it is that there exists in every contract an implied covenant of good faith and that Egan promised to use his "best efforts" to promote the paintings. But the phrase "best efforts" is a slippery one in the absence of any checks on the promisor, and the potential for abuse here was so great, that it is difficult to conceive of any truly informed person entering into such an "agreement."

After 15 years of exile, Arnold Friedman's legacy should be returned to his family.

Matter of Rothko's Estate

43 N.Y.2d 305, 372 N.E.2d 291 (1977)*

COOKE, Judge.

Mark Rothko, an abstract expressionist painter whose works through the years gained for him an international reputation of greatness, died testate on February 25, 1970. The principal asset of his estate consisted of 798 paintings of tremendous value, and the dispute underlying this appeal involves the conduct of his three executors in their disposition of these works of art. In sum, that conduct as portrayed in the record and sketched in the opinions was manifestly wrongful and indeed shocking.

Rothkos' will was admitted to probate on April 27, 1970, and letters testamentary were issued to Bernard J. Reis, Theodoros Stamos, and Morton Levine. Hastily and within a period of only about three weeks and by virtue of two contracts each dated May 21, 1970, the executors dealt with all 798 paintings.

By a contract of sale, the estate executors agreed to sell to Marlborough A.G., a Liechtenstein corporation (hereinafter MAG), 100 Rothko paintings as

---

* Footnotes omitted.

listed for $1,800,000, $200,000 to be paid on execution of the agreement and the balance of $1,600,000 in 12 equal interest-free installments over a 12-year period. Under the second agreement, the executors consigned to Marlborough Gallery, Inc., a domestic corporation (hereinafter MNY), "approximately 700 paintings listed on a Schedule to be prepared," the consignee to be responsible for costs covering items such as insurance, storage restoration, and promotion. By its provisos, MNY could sell up to 35 paintings a year from each of two groups, pre-1947 and post-1947, for 12 years at the best price obtainable but not less than the appraised estate value, and it would receive a 50% commission on each painting sold, except for a commission of 40% on those sold to or through other dealers.

Petitioner Kate Rothko, decedent's daughter and a person entitled to share in his estate by virtue of an election under EPTL 5-3.3, instituted this proceeding to remove the executors, to enjoin MNY and MAG from disposing of the paintings, to rescind the aforesaid agreements between the executors and said corporations, for a return of the paintings still in possession of those corporations, and for damages. She was joined by the guardian of her brother Christopher Rothko, likewise interested in the estate, who answered by adopting the allegations of his sister's petition and by demanding the same relief. The Attorney-General of the State, as the representative of the ultimate beneficiaries of the Mark Rothko Foundation, Inc., a charitable corporation and the residuary legatee under decedent's will, joined in requesting relief substantially similar to that prayed for by petitioner. On June 26, 1972, the Surrogate issued a temporary restraining order and on September 26, 1972, a preliminary injunction enjoining MAG, MNY, and the three executors from selling or otherwise disposing of the paintings referred to in the agreements dated May 21, 1970, except for sales or dispositions made with court permission. The Appellate Division modified the preliminary injunction order by increasing the amount of the bond and otherwise affirmed. By a 1974 petition, the Attorney-General, on behalf of the ultimate charitable beneficiaries of the Mark Rothko Foundation, sought the punishment of MNY, MAG, Lloyd, and Reis for contempt and other relief. . . .

The Surrogate [found] that MNY, MAG and Lloyd were guilty of contempt in shipping, disposing of, and selling 57 paintings in violation of the temporary restraining order dated June 26, 1972 and of the injunction dated September 26, 1972; that the contracts for sale and consignment of paintings between the executors and MNY and MAG provided inadequate value to the estate, amounting to a lack of mutuality and fairness resulting from conflicts on the part of Reis and Stamos and improvidence on the part of all executors; that said contracts were voidable and were set aside by reason of violation of the duty of loyalty and improvidence of the executors, knowingly participated in and induced by MNY and MAG; that the fact that these agreements were voidable did not revive the 1969 inter vivos agreements since the parties by their conduct evinced an intent to abandon and abrogate these compacts. The Surrogate held that the present value at the time of trial of the paintings sold is the proper measure of damages as to MNY, MAG, Lloyd, Reis, and

Stamos. He imposed a civil fine of $3,332,000 upon MNY, MAG, and Lloyd, same being the appreciated value at the time of trial of the 57 paintings sold in violation of the temporary restraining order and injunction. . . .

In seeking a reversal, it is urged that an improper legal standard was applied in voiding the estate contracts of May, 1970, that the "no further inquiry" rule applies only to self-dealing and that in case of a conflict of interest, absent self-dealing, a challenged transaction must be shown to be unfair. The subject of fairness of the contracts is intertwined with the issue of whether Reis and Stamos were guilty of conflicts of interest. Scott is quoted to the effect that "(a) trustee does not necessarily incur liability merely because he has an individual interest in the transaction. . . . In *Bullivant v. First Nat. Bank* (246 Mass. 324, 141 N.E. 41) it was held that . . . the fact that the bank was also a creditor of the corporation did not make its assent invalid, if it acted in good faith and the plan was fair" (2 Scott, Trusts, § 170.24, p. 1384 (emphasis added)), and our attention has been called to the statement in *Phelan v. Middle States Oil Corp.*, 220 F.2d 593, 603, 2 Cir., *cert. den. sub nom. Cohen v. Glass*, 349 U.S. 929, 75 S. Ct. 772, 99 L. Ed. 1260 that Judge Learned Hand found "no decisions that have applied (the no further inquiry rule) inflexibly to every occasion in which the fiduciary has been shown to have had a personal interest that might in fact have conflicted with his loyalty."

These contentions should be rejected. First, a review of the opinions of the Surrogate and the Appellate Division manifests that they did not rely solely on a "no further inquiry rule," and secondly, there is more than an adequate basis to conclude that the agreements between the Marlborough corporations and the estate were neither fair nor in the best interests of the estate. This is demonstrated, for example, by the comments of the Surrogate concerning the commissions on the consignment of the 698 paintings (*see* 84 Misc. 2d 830, 852-53, 379 N.Y.S.2d 923, 947-48) and those of the Appellate Division concerning the sale of the 100 paintings (*see* 56 A.D.2d, at pp. 501-02, 392 N.Y.S.2d, at pp. 872-73). The opinions under review demonstrate that neither the Surrogate nor the Appellate Division set aside the contracts by merely applying the no further inquiry rule without regard to fairness. Rather they determined, quite properly indeed, that these agreements were neither fair nor in the best interests of the estate.

To be sure, the assertions that there were no conflicts of interest on the part of Reis or Stamos indulge in sheer fantasy. Besides being a director and officer of MNY, for which there was financial remuneration, however slight, Reis, as noted by the Surrogate, had different inducements to favor the Marlborough interests, including his own aggrandizement of status and financial advantage through sales of almost one million dollars for items from his own and his family's extensive private art collection by the Marlborough interests (*see* 84 Misc. 2d, at pp. 843-44, 379 N.Y.S.2d at pp. 939-40). Similarly, Stamos benefitted as an artist under contract with Marlborough and, interestingly, Marlborough purchased a Stamos painting from a third party for $4,000 during the week in May, 1970 when the estate contract negotiations were pending (*see* 84 Misc. 2d, at p. 845, 379 N.Y.S.2d at p. 941). The conflicts are manifest. Further, as noted in Bogert, *Trusts and Trustees* (2d ed.), "The duty of loyalty imposed on the fiduciary prevents him from accepting employment from a third party who is entering into a business transaction with the trust" (§ 543, subd. (S), p. 573). "While he (a trustee) is administering the trust he must refrain from placing himself in a position where his personal interest or that of a third person does or may conflict with the interest of the beneficiaries" (Bogert, *Trusts* (Hornbook Series 5th ed.), p. 343). Here, Reis was employed and Stamos benefited in a manner contemplated by Bogert (*see also Meinhard v. Salmon*, 249 N.Y. 458, 464, 466-67, 164 N.E. 545, 547-48; *Schmidt v. Chambers*, 265 Md. 9, 33-38, 288 A.2d 356). In short, one must strain the law rather than follow it to reach the result suggested on behalf of Reis and Stamos.

Levine contends that, having acted prudently and upon the advice of counsel, a complete defense was established. Suffice it to say, an executor who knows that his coexecutor is committing breaches of trust and not only fails to exert efforts directed towards prevention but accedes to them is legally accountable even though he was acting on the advice of counsel (*Matter of Westerfield*, 32 App. Div. 324, 344, 53 N.Y.S. 25, 39; 3 Scott, Trusts (3d ed.), § 201, p. 1657). When confronted with the question of whether to enter into the Marlborough contracts, Levine was acting in a business capacity, not a legal one, in which he was required as an executor primarily to employ such diligence and prudence to the care and management of the estate assets and affairs as would prudent persons of discretion and intelligence (*King v. Talbot*, 40 N.Y. 76, 85-86), accented by "(n)ot honesty alone, but the punctilio of an honor the most sensitive" (*Meinhard v. Salmon*, 249 N.Y. 458, 464, 164 N.E. 545, 546, *supra*). Alleged good faith on the part of a fiduciary forgetful of his duty is not enough (*Wendt v. Fischer*, 243 N.Y. 439, 443, 154 N.E. 303, 304). He could not close his eyes, remain passive or move with unconcern in the face of the obvious loss to be visited upon the estate by participation in those business arrangements and then shelter himself behind the claimed counsel of an attorney (*see Matter of Niles*, 113 N.Y. 547, 558, 21 N.E. 687, 689; *Matter of Huntley*, 13 Misc. 375, 380, 35 N.Y.S. 113, 116; 3 Warren's *Heaton, Surrogates' Courts* (6th ed.), § 217, subd. 3, par. (b)).

Further, there is no merit to the argument that MNY and MAG lacked notice of the breach of trust. The record amply supports the determination that they are chargeable with notice of the executors' breach of duty. . . .

We have considered the other alleged errors urged by the parties, and find those arguments to be without merit. In short, we find no basis for disturbing the result reached below. Accordingly, the order of the Appellate Division should be affirmed, with costs to the prevailing parties against appellants, and the question certified answered in the affirmative.

Notes and Questions

1. Mark Rothko committed suicide on February 25, 1970, after a prolonged state of depression. The entire history of the disposition of

the Mark Rothko estate makes interesting, if not chilling and gut-wrenching, reading for anyone choosing fiduciaries for their art and other assets. *See Estate of Rothko*, 379 N.Y.S.2d 923 (1975), *modified and aff'd*, 56 A.D.2d 499, 392 N.Y.S.2d. 870, *aff'd*, 43 N.Y.2d 305, 401 N.Y.S.2d 499 (1977), *on remand*, 95 Misc. 2d 492, 407 N.Y.S.2d 954 (1978). *See also* Gustave Harrow, *Reflections on Estate of Rothko: The Role of the Legal Advisor in Relation to the Artist*, 26 Clev. St. L. Rev. 573 (1978); Gustave Harrow, *The Final Work in the Rothko Case: Salient Legal Holdings of the Court of Appeals*, 4 Art & L. 33 (1978); Barry L. Zins, *Trustee Liability for Breach of the Duty of Loyalty: Good Faith Inquiry and Appreciation Damages*, 49 Fordham L. Rev. 1012, 1030-34; Hon. Millard L. Midonick, *Trial Tactics*, 16 Real Prop. Prob. & Tr. J. 725 (1991).

2. The claims of the plaintiffs in the *Rothko* cases were based not only on the obvious conflicting interests of the executors but also on a shocking series of transactions conducted by them before and immediately after Rothko's death. The executors first sold 100 works to Marlborough's Leichtenstein affiliate for $1,800,000 payable over 12 years without interest. Within a few months, the Marlborough Gallery, by selling only 12 paintings at six to ten times the amount paid for them, had realized proceeds sufficient to cover the down payment plus almost half the amount owing on the 100 works.

3. The remaining 698 paintings were consigned by the executors to Marlborough's New York branch under a 12-year irrevocable contract with a commission set at 50 percent for every painting sold by the gallery. Rothko works sold prior to his death had earned Marlborough a commission closer to 10 percent. Furthermore, the contract negotiated by the executors did not specify minimum resale prices, and no accounting on the inventory was sought nor received by the executors during the period leading up to the suit. (The court noted that the contract Stamos negotiated for his own dealings with Marlborough was more favorable in every respect than the one just completed on behalf of the estate.) Finally, many of the paintings sold pursuant to the consignment contract were to the Leichtenstein affiliate in "bulk transactions," which resulted in extremely low prices.

4. The *Rothko* case carries many important lessons for the attorney representing the artist or collector. Although the estate ultimately received the relief it sought, including recovery of substantial damages, the initial trial lasted 89 days and generated 15,000 pages of transcripts. Its final disposition on appeal culminated six years of litigation, although the artist's desires concerning the disposition of his works can never be completely effectuated due to the loss of certain key paintings.

3. The Contract's Contents

Sherri L. Burr, Introducing Art Law

37 *Copyright World* 22 (1994)*

A. SELLING ART THROUGH COMMERCIAL ART DEALERS

Most artists sell their works to dealers, patrons, or other purchasers through oral and written contracts. An art dealer is often defined as "a person primarily engaged in the business of selling works of art." Lerner and Bresler write that the term "dealer" covers the commercial spectrum of business from an individual proprietor dealing in a small stock, to a one-branch commercial gallery, to a numerous-branch gallery, to a conglomerate.

Historically, most U.S. contracts between art dealers and artists have been oral contracts, cemented by a handshake. This is common throughout the country when the contract can be completed within one year. If the contract is to last for longer than a year, then it must be written to avoid invalidation under the Statute of Frauds. Artists and dealers typically prefer oral contracts because they see their relationship as one based on friendship and trust that does not need to be formalized in writing. For the most part, these oral contracts work well as long as the parties are able to resolve their disputes through amicable discussion and negotiation. If there is a dispute that cannot be resolved amicably, the terms of the agreement become of critical importance.

The value of written contracts is that they specify the agreement between the parties in clear terms if well drafted. Some states, such as Oregon, require written contracts between artists and dealers if the work is consigned. In the U.S., unlike in Japan, for example, the dealer's lawyers either draft contracts from a number of available forms or they review contracts that have been written by the dealer and the artist. In the typical written contract, the dealer becomes an agent for the artist and is responsible for the care of the art work, for dealing fairly with the artist, for accounting periodically to the artist for the work, and for disclosing any relevant information that the artist may need. The most important responsibility of the artist is to deliver sufficient art work and in sufficient quality so that the dealer can remain in the business of selling that particular artist's work.

Several model contracts are available. Author Leonard DuBoff published five such agreements in *The Deskbook of Art Law* . . . which contains an entire section on artist/dealer agreements. Lerner and Bresler published a Model Artist-Gallery Agreement in their 1989 *Art Law: The Guide for Collectors, Investors, Dealers, and Artists.*[17] All of these model contracts have a number

---

* Footnotes omitted.

17. Since this article was first published, additional agreements have become available in the appendix to *The Law (in Plain English)*® *for Crafts* (6th Edition) and in the Second Edition to the Lerner and Bresler two volume guide.

of critical terms that should be carefully drafted. Twelve of these are discussed below:

1. Nature of the Agreement

The contract should specify whether it is a consignment or an outright sale agreement. In a consignment agreement, the dealer acts as the artist's agent. The artist does not get paid until the work has been sold, and the dealer keeps a commission on the sale. In an outright sale agreement, the dealer buys the work from the artist and resells it, keeping as a profit the difference in price.

The general preference of most dealers is for the consignment agreement because it requires them to commit fewer of their resources in advance. The form contracts of the Artists Equity Association, of the Bay Area Lawyers for the Arts (which has subsequently merged with a Los Angeles art law group and renamed itself the California Lawyers for the Arts), and of Lerner and Bresler are all consignment agreements. Many states have artist/dealer consignment laws that govern the relationship and some of these states require written agreements.

2. Exclusivity of the Contract

The contract should indicate whether the relationship between the artist and the dealer will be exclusive or non-exclusive. In an exclusive-agency relationship, the dealer becomes the artist's exclusive agent and is the only dealer who can sell the artist's work.

In an exclusive power-to-sell relationship, the dealer is the only person, including even the artist, who can sell the artist's work. In a non-exclusive agency relationship, the artist may designate several dealers as his or her agent, frequently designating a city or state, or a portion of a city or state, as the dealer's exclusive territory. In New York City, for example, an artist could designate separate dealers in the Soho district, midtown Manhattan, and Greenwich Village. In the form contracts, a blank space is available for the parties to fill in the territory.

3. Duration of the Contract

The parties should stipulate the duration of their contract. The parties may agree to any length of time, usually with provisions for automatic renewal for the same amount of time, unless either party provides notice of intent to terminate the agreement.

4. Scope of the Artist's Work

This term specifies the type of work that the artist will provide to the dealer and that the dealer will agree to sell. In the Bay Area Lawyers for the Arts' agreement, for example, clause #2 requires the parties to indicate the medium of the art works to be provided, to indicate that the gallery has a right of first selection from all new works, and to indicate how many new works will be produced in the year.

5. Sales Price

The consignment contract should provide the initial selling price, or a range of initial selling prices, for the art work, and should include a term for periodic updates of the artist's price in accordance with the increasing or diminishing reputation of the artist. The Bay Area Lawyers for the Arts' agreement grants the gallery "discretion to vary the agreed price by _____ % in the case of discount sales." This is an important term because the author believes that pricing a work can be an art form in itself: an artist's work might sell for $750,000, but not sell for $75,000, due to differences in market placement.

6. Payment

The consignment contract should specify whether the artist is to be paid after each sale or on a monthly, quarterly, or semiannual basis. Artist/dealer consignment statutes in some jurisdictions impose requirements on the timing of payment.

7. Allocating Cost

The consignment contract should specify particular costs — crating, shipping, storage, promotion, etc. — and designate which party has the responsibility to pay.

8. Insurance and Liability for Loss or Damage

The consignment contract should specify whether the dealer or the artist is to insure the artist's work. If the dealer, which is usual, is to insure the work, the contract should specify an amount of insurance or connect the insurance to a range of the selling price, usually 40 to 70 percent.

The contract should also address liability in the event that the artist's work is lost or damaged, or when the buyer was a bad credit risk. The parties should indicate whether the artist or the dealer will bear such risks of loss.

9. Copyright Notice

The contract should specify where the copyright notice will be placed and indicate whether the copyright will be transferred with the physical object. Commonly, copyright notice is placed on the back of the work, as with a painting, or the bottom of a work, as with sculpture. Copyright notice may also be placed on a separate piece of paper, which [should] be "permanently affixed" to the back of the work to satisfy the requirement. The purpose of notice should be to alert purchasers that they are purchasing only the art work and not the copyright. The artist should also seek to avoid purchaser shock if he plans further merchandising of the work, turning a painting, for example, into lithographs, prints, or even greeting cards.

10. Prohibition of Assignment of the Contract

Because of the personal nature of the artist/dealer relationship, the contract will usually prohibit assignment of contract by either party. Even without this prohibition, the dealer could not be forced to accept another artist's work that is not comparable to the original contract artist, nor could the artist be forced to sell his work through a dealer not noted for selling his type of work because of the personal nature of the agreement. With this clause, neither the artist, nor the dealer can be forced to deal with someone who does not meet with his or her approval.

11. Arbitration and Mediation Clauses

The contract might specify that in the event of a dispute, the parties agree to try mediation, or, if mediation does not work, to require binding arbitration. The purpose is to avoid lawsuits. The contracts of the Bay Area Lawyers for the Arts, for example, provides for binding arbitration in the event of a dispute.

12. Governing Law

The contract should specify which law will govern the contract. This is a particularly important term when the artist and dealer's places of business are in different states. If the contract term does not specify governing law and there is a dispute, then the contract will be governed by applicable conflicts of law principles.

In summary, there are, of course, many other terms that could be included in a consignment agreement, but these twelve are essential. . . .

***

The following agreement is used by the Dartmouth Street Gallery (DSG) in Albuquerque, New Mexico, to sign artists to a co-op arrangement. The DSG, whose website is available at *www.dsg-art.com*, is divided into two sides. On the core artists side, which consists of six to twelve artists who sell upwards of $20,000 a year, the artists share the commission 50-50 with the gallery and do not pay additional fees. On the co-op side, the artists pay a fee to join, a monthly rental fee, and then split the commission 75-25 when the work is sold. This agreement is reprinted with permission from the owner of the DSG, John Cacciatore.

DSG ART GROUP Agreement

Date _____
Artist Info:
Name _____
Address _____
City _____ State _____ ZIP _____
Phone _____ E-mail _____

The purpose of this agreement is to exhibit and sell works of art.

This agreement is for 30 days and will automatically renew every 30 days with rent payment, until terminated in writing by either party for any reason or no reason.

The Artist hereby provides to DSG Art Group, and DSG Art Group accepts, those Artworks listed on the attached Inventory Sheet which is a part of this Agreement. Additional Inventory Sheets may be incorporated into this Agreement at such time as both parties agree to the inventory of other works of art or return works to the artist. All Inventory Sheets shall be signed by Artist and DSG Art Group.

Packing and shipping charges, insurance costs, other handling expenses, and risk of loss or damage incurred in the delivery of Artworks from the Artist to the DSG Art Group, and in their return of the Artist, shall be the responsibility of the Artist.

DSG Art Group shall exercise reasonable care for the safekeeping of all Artworks while they are in its custody. However, it is understood that there may be normal wear and tear in the handling of Artworks. The Artist is liable for any insurance protection for any loss that may happen to the Artworks while at the gallery.

COMMISSION: Artist will receive 75% of the retail price of Artworks sold. DSG Art Group will receive 25% sales commission, 5% of which will go into a promotional fund to be spent semi-annually with comments and feedback on how it is spent by all the artists in DSG Art Group. Artists who are in DSG Group for 6 consecutive months are eligible for the promotion.

DSG Art Group will pay Artist their proceeds of all sales within 30 days of proceeds collected.

FEES: Upon acceptance of Artist by DSG Art Group, Artist will remit to DSG Art Group a $300 initiation fee which is non-refundable.

Artist will remit to DSG Art Group $200 per month rent for exhibition space, which will be approximately 6′ to 10′ of lineal wall space, at the discretion of DSG Art Group director.

In the event that Artist is more than 30 days late with rental fee, and prior arrangement has not been made, this agreement will immediately terminate and Artist agrees to immediately remove all Artworks from the gallery.

DSG will encourage interaction between artists and clients. Any sales that result from these interactions are bound by this agreement.

Agreed by:

_____   _____

For Dartmouth Street Gallery, Inc.   Artist
d/b/a DSG Art Group

Notes and Questions

1. What are the advantages and disadvantages for artists who enter into cooperative agreements such as the one presented above? When the artist signs this agreement, he or she is obtaining sufficient space to

hang approximately four pieces of art. The artist and the gallery may negotiate on the prices of the art. While the artist gains the benefit of the gallery's foot traffic and website, which broadcasts artwork on the Internet, can you think of other benefits to the artist? Should artists seek out galleries who are already showing their style of work?

2. Notice that artists who sign this agreement are responsible for their own insurance costs. John Cacciatore, the DSG owner, says that his gallery is only insured for a major disaster, like a catastrophic fire. He says that insurance companies have become reluctant to insure small businesses like his and so he is forced to carry a large deductible to make insurance affordable. Are there advantages for artists to being required to carry their own insurance? As you read the following case, observe what happens to the insurance proceeds.

Pelletier v. Eisenberg

177 Cal. App. 3d 558, 223 Cal. Rptr. 84 (4th Dist. 1986)

WORK, Justice.

A. John Pelletier sued Jerome M. Eisenberg, Betty Eisenberg and The Galleries at La Jolla (owned by the Eisenbergs) (hereafter referred to collectively as Eisenbergs) for conversion, breach of trust, and damage to and destruction of fine art. (Civ. Code, § 1738 et seq.) The jury returned a verdict in favor of Pelletier. The Eisenbergs were granted a new trial limited to the measure of damages for the loss of the paintings and the damages assessed for Pelletier's pursuit of converted insurance proceeds. After the court granted the Eisenbergs a new trial, Pelletier moved for a new trial. His motion was denied as untimely. Pelletier appeals the trial court's grant of the Eisenbergs' motion for new trial and denial of his own motion. We affirm the denial of Pelletier's motion, and affirm in part and reverse in part the grant of the Eisenbergs' motion.

FACTS

Pelletier, an artist, consigned 10 paintings to the Eisenbergs' art gallery. Nine paintings were destroyed or damaged in a fire. A bifurcated trial produced two special jury verdicts. The first verdict separately assessed the fair market value of each painting; found the paintings entrusted to the Eisenbergs; and separately assessed the losses, in addition to fair market value, Pelletier would suffer from future income or benefits from each painting. The second verdict found the Eisenbergs had converted the insurance proceeds from the paintings; assessed the damages for time and money expended in pursuit of the property ($42,500); and found the Eisenbergs were not guilty of oppression, fraud or malice. The trial court entered a judgment on the verdict for $55,603, plus interest on a portion of the amount.

The trial court granted the Eisenbergs' motion for new trial . . . only on the issues of (1) whether Pelletier was entitled to the fair market value of the paintings without reduction for the 40 percent commission due the Eisenbergs if the paintings were sold under the consignment contract; and (2) the amount to which Pelletier was entitled for time and money spent pursuing the converted insurance proceeds.

Regarding the first issue, the trial court stated it was a legal issue for the judge at the new trial to determine the proper method for computing the damages and then compute them, using the fair market value already assessed by the jury. Regarding the second issue, the trial court stated it could not substantiate the $42,500 with the evidence received on the amount spent to recover the converted insurance proceeds. The trial court noted it would be more equitable to grant a new trial on both the issues of damages for pursuit and punitive damages, because the jury may have erroneously believed they could award the extra damages as compensatory damages. However, the trial court concluded it had no authority to include the issue of punitive damages in the new trial order since no motion was made on that ground. On June 25, 1984, Pelletier filed and served a notice of intention to move for new trial on the issue of punitive damages. This motion was denied as untimely. . . .

III. The Trial Court Erred in Granting a New Trial to Determine Damages for the Loss of the Paintings

On the issue of the damages for the loss of the paintings, the jury instructions included the following: "An art gallery consignee is not entitled to a commission if the artwork consigned is destroyed and not sold. The artist is entitled to recover 100% of the fair market value, whether that is less or more than any consignment contract, in the event of the art's destruction or loss. A commission agreed upon for the sale of artwork is not binding if the item is destroyed as compared to being sold."

In granting the Eisenbergs' motion for a limited new trial, the trial court concluded it was error to award Pelletier the fair market value rather than the wholesale value (i.e., 60 percent of the selling price) he would have received had the paintings been sold. We find the trial court correctly instructed the jury, and erroneously granted the motion for new trial. The Civil Code provisions governing the legal relationship between artists and art dealers state: "[the] consignee shall be responsible for the loss of, or damages to, the work of fine art" (Civ. Code, § 1738.6, subd. (c)) and "[any] provision of a contract or agreement whereby the consignor waives any provision of this title is void" (Civ. Code, § 1738.8).

This is an action for damages arising from liability imposed by statute. Civil Code section 3333 states: "For the breach of an obligation not arising from contract, the measure of damages, except where otherwise expressly provided by this Code, is the amount which will compensate for all the detriment proximately caused thereby, whether it could have been anticipated or not." It is well established that under section 3333, the measure of damages for the loss or destruction of personal property is generally determined by the value of the property at the time of such loss or destruction. (*Lane v. Spurgeon* (1950) 100 Cal. App. 2d 460, 463 [223 P.2d 889]; 4 Witkin, *Summary of*

California Law (8th ed. 1974) Torts, § 911, p. 3198; *see also Heninger v. Dunn* (1980) 101 Cal. App. 3d 858, 861-62 [162 Cal. Rptr. 104].)

We see no reason to depart from the standard fair market value measure of damages for the destruction of Pelletier's paintings. . . . The parties agreed to a commission if the paintings were sold, not if they were destroyed, and thus the Eisenbergs have not earned their commission. Since the paintings cannot be sold, Pelletier has lost all benefits emanating from a potential sale (i.e., enhancement of his reputation). Even payment of the full fair market value cannot compensate Pelletier for the intangible aspects of a work of art which are forever lost when the property is destroyed. . . . Indeed, the peculiar value which can be maintained only if the art work continues in existence is recognized in Civil Code section 987, which states: "The Legislature hereby finds and declares that the physical alteration or destruction of fine art, which is an expression of the artist's personality, is detrimental to the artist's reputation, and artists therefore have an interest in protecting their works of fine art against such alteration or destruction; and that there is also a public interest in preserving the integrity of cultural and artistic creations." . . . Pelletier would not be compensated for his losses if he had to pay for something which he never acquired (i.e., benefits from the sale of his paintings), and which the Eisenbergs never earned (i.e., the commission for the sale of the paintings). We conclude that the fair market value of the paintings is the most accurate measure of damages to compensate Pelletier for his losses.

We note that under Civil Code section 3358, "Except as expressly provided by statute, no person can recover a greater amount in damages for the breach of an obligation, than he could have gained by the full performance thereof on both sides." This case falls within the exception in the first clause of Civil Code section 3358; that is, it is expressly provided by Civil Code section 1738, subdivision (c) that an art consignee is responsible for the loss of fine art. The absolute liability imposed under Civil Code section 1738, subdivision (c), regardless of the terms of the consignment contract, recognizes that the destruction of fine art results in peculiar losses to the artist apart from the "benefit of the bargain" losses normally arising from a failure to perform other types of obligations.

The order of the trial court granting a limited new trial is reversed to the extent inconsistent with this opinion, and affirmed in all other respects. A new trial is ordered to determine the compensatory damages resulting from the pursuit of the converted property, and the punitive damages, if any, for the conversion of the property.

Basquiat v. Baghoomian

1992 Copyright. L. Dec. P 26,824 (S.D.N.Y Nov. 19, 1991)*

FREEH, District Judge.

In this action, plaintiff Gerard Basquiat ("Basquiat"), administrator of the estate and father of the late Jean-Michel Basquiat ("Jean-Michel"), alleges that

* Citations to the record removed.

defendant Vrej Baghoomian ("Baghoomian"), individually and through his company, Vrej Baghoomian, Inc., infringed the estate's copyright in numerous works of art created by Jean-Michel. More specifically, Basquiat claims that Baghoomian published a book containing photographs of sixty-nine (69) of Jean-Michel's paintings, prints, and drawings without obtaining permission from or paying any royalties to the estate. Baghoomian does not deny publishing the book, but claims it was produced as a "catalogue" in conjunction with an exhibition of the works depicted. Basquiat has moved for partial summary judgment on the issue of copyright infringement. Baghoomian opposes that motion on the grounds that the publication at issue constitutes "fair use" and thus, that no liability should be imposed. For the reasons stated below, Basquiat's motion for partial summary judgment is denied.

FACTS

The artist Jean-Michel Basquiat died intestate on August 12, 1988. His father, Gerard Basquiat, was named administrator of Jean-Michel's estate. During his lifetime, Jean-Michel created numerous works of art, including the sixty-nine paintings, prints and drawings at issue in this case. Pursuant to 17 U.S.C. § 410(a), in 1990 the estate registered those sixty-nine paintings and prints with the United States Copyright Office. Following Jean-Michel's death, the Vrej Baghoomian Gallery, allegedly the "exclusive representative and dealer exhibiting and selling all of the works of Jean-Michel Basquiat," planned and conducted an exhibition as a "tribute" to Jean-Michel. In conjunction with that exhibition, Baghoomian and his staff prepared a one hundred fifty-four page, hardcover book containing photographs of all the works displayed at the exhibition, as well as two essays commissioned specifically for that purpose (the "Basquiat book"). In 1989, Baghoomian purported to copyright the book in the name of his gallery and corporation, Vrej Baghoomian, Inc. (*Id.*).

According to Baghoomian, only 4000 copies of the Basquiat book were ever published. Baghoomian has also stated that while the Basquiat book cost $116,000 to produce, to date the gallery has received only $58,812 from its sales.

DISCUSSION

Under Fed. R. Civ. P. 56, summary judgment is only appropriate where "there is no genuine issue as to any material fact and . . . the moving party is entitled to a judgment as a matter of law." Because questions of fact remain in dispute here, Basquiat's motion for partial summary judgment must be denied.

In his complaint, Basquiat claims that Baghoomian is "currently exhibiting, selling, reproducing, and publishing" Jean-Michel's art in violation of the estate's exclusive right under the Copyright Act to reproduce the copyrighted works, to prepare derivative works based on the copyrighted works, and to distribute copies of the copyrighted works. 17 U.S.C. § 106. In their papers before this Court, the parties have focused exclusively on the publication of the

Basquiat book as the allegedly infringing activity. Accordingly, the Court cannot address Basquiat's other claim, that Baghoomian is also exhibiting and selling Jean-Michel's work without authorization.

Baghoomian does not deny that he prepared and sold a hardcover book containing photographs of sixty-nine of Jean-Michel's paintings, drawings and prints. Baghoomian defends against the claim of infringement, however, on the grounds that the "catalogue" he prepared constitutes "fair use." Section 107 of the Copyright Act specifically states that "the fair use of a copyrighted work, including such use by reproduction in copies ... or by any other means ... for purposes such as criticism, comment, news reporting, reaching..., scholarship, or research, is not an infringement of copyright." 17 U.S.C. § 107. In determining whether the use made of a particular copyrighted work constitutes fair use within the meaning of Section 107, courts must consider four factors:

> (1) the purpose and character of the use, including whether such use is of a commercial nature or is for nonprofit educational purposes;
> (2) the nature of the copyrighted work;
> (3) the amount and substantiality of the portion used in relation to the copyrighted work as a whole; and
> (4) the effect of the use upon the potential market for or value of the copyrighted work.

17 U.S.C. § 107.

The question of fair use is a mixed question of fact and law. *Harper & Row Publishers v. Nation Enterprises*, 471 U.S. 539, 560, 105 S. Ct. 2218, 2230 (1985). If sufficient facts are established for each of the four statutory factors, a court may determine as a matter of law whether the allegedly infringing conduct constitutes fair use. *Id.* However, where, as here, numerous issues of material fact remain in dispute, summary judgment would be inappropriate on the infringement issue.

It is undisputed that Baghoomian prepared the Basquiat book for commercial purposes. It is also undisputed that the Basquiat book contained reproductions of all sixty-nine of the works in their entirety. However, on the "single most important element of fair use"—the effect of the use on the potential market for or value of the copyrighted work, *Harper & Row*, 471 U.S. at 566, 105 S. Ct. at 2233—a number of factual questions remain. Neither party has presented evidence of the number of Basquiat books sold. Basquiat contends that such sales are currently continuing, while Baghoomian claims that he is not actively promoting or encouraging sales of the Basquiat book at this time. Although it appears that Baghoomian has not profited from sales of the Basquiat book, that net loss is irrelevant to the potential impact the existence of such a book may have on the estate's ability to prepare a similar book of its own. Moreover, while there is little evidence that the publication of the Basquiat book had a negative financial impact on the value of the copyrighted works, or the potential market for another book on Jean-Michel's work, Basquiat has testified that he terminated plans for his own book on Jean-Michel's work when he learned of the Basquiat book.

Given the uncertain state of the evidence, the Court cannot find that the Basquiat book constitutes fair use as a matter of law. Until the fair use issue is developed and resolved, the Court also cannot determine the question of infringement. Accordingly, Basquiat's motion for partial summary judgment must be denied.

SO ORDERED.

Notes and Questions

1. Traditionally, artists have not executed written agreements with their dealers. This is unfortunate, as the act of reducing an agreement to writing can have the effect of clarifying the parties' needs and expectations and, thereby, avoid potential misunderstandings. Betty Chamberlain, the Director of Art Information Center, Inc. (New York City), and a columnist for the *American Artist* magazine, believes that the artist should at least give the dealer a copy of a letter outlining what the artist understands to be the agreement.

2. The unique and elite nature of art as perceived by artists and their corresponding disdain for commercial formality are surely the main causes for artists' reluctance to enter into formal contracts. The lesser-known artist's traditional lack of bargaining power with dealers compounds this problem. But even some highly successful artists forego formal contractual arrangements. Their reason seems to be that, given the special nature of the art world, an artist-dealer relationship is more akin to a marriage; it is a relationship based on friendship and trust, which can easily be attained by emphasis on binding legal responsibilities rather than on written agreements. *See* Lee Rosenbaum, *Scenes from a Marriage* (Issues and Commentary section), Art. in Am., July/Aug. 1977, at 10.

3. Another concern is the lack of flexibility that may result from the rigid application of a comprehensive contract, even though formality is desired in some artist-gallery relationships. For instance, an artist dealing with a gallery for the first time may want the freedom to continue informally selling to friends and relatives with the gallery's approval. Both parties may agree in principle but may be dissuaded by the daunting task of reducing every conceivable variation of such activity to writing.

4. Exclusivity arrangements are often a bone of contention with artists who become dissatisfied with a dealer's efforts to promote sales. Nevertheless, such arrangements are intertwined with gallery commissions as the quid pro quo of the dealer's marketing efforts. If a dealer devotes time and gallery space to promote an up-and-coming artist, it is reasonable that the dealer obtain assurances that the artist will not run to the first dealer offering better terms once the artist becomes popular. *See* Ivan S. Karp, *A Curious Relationship*, Art. in Am., Mar. 1989, at 51. The artist should attempt to negotiate exclusivity agreements of modest

duration in order to avoid being locked into unfavorable sales relationships.

5. Attorney Richard Weiner, a member of the New York Attorney General's Fine Arts Committee, represents numerous artists. He suggests that the following three areas should be addressed in an artist/dealer contract, in addition to what was discussed earlier:

   a. Commission Clause
   [The usual commission charged by galleries is 40-50% of the gross sales price. The Artists Equity contract provides that different percentages be paid to the gallery depending on its degree of participation. The concept is good, but lack of bargaining power will often prevent the artist from imposing this condition.]

   b. Advances Clause
   Only the largest and most successful galleries make advances. Even if the gallery will advance the money, they may charge "interest" by increasing their commission on the works sold. This often costs the artist a great deal more than the legal rate of interest on borrowed money.

   c. Death Clause
   A clause might be included to provide that the artist's work, any monies owed to him, and an accounting should immediately be sent to him in case of the death of the gallery owner. In effect, if the agreement contains a clause covering this contingency, the agreement is terminated on the death of the gallery owner.
      If the artist wishes to provide for the contingency of his own death, this is the clause in which to do it. He may wish the gallery to sell his work on hand and to pay the proceeds to his estate. Other artists may prefer that the agreement terminate on their deaths. It is wise, especially for the artist, to execute a valid will that includes clear directions as to what happens to his work after his death.

   Richard Weiner, *The Artist and his Gallery: Legal Agreements that Work*, Am. Artist, Jan. 1974, at 22.

6. Note that a gallery may have its own agreement with another agent relative to that artist's work, which may result in the creator losing some control over his or her art, as the second agent is not necessarily bound by provisions of the original artist-gallery contract. The gallery's arrangement also could subvert an artist's desire to have work sold in a particular locale or by a prestigious dealer.

4. Contracts with Public Entities

Another source of revenue for artists is to enter into competitions to supply public art. In this section, you will find an article about artist Betty Sabo, who has created public art and been involved with public art fiascos. Following the

Betty Sabo interview are excerpts from the New Mexico County of Bernalillo Professional Services Agreement.

Sherri L. Burr,
Creating Public Art, Evoking Emotional Responses

Author Interview with Betty Sabo*

Betty Sabo has been painting the winter landscapes of New Mexico in oils for over 40 years. A white-haired lady with twinkling blue eyes and a serene disposition, Sabo commenced sculpting bronzes in the early 1990s and received an immediate commission with Sun Healthcare Group, an international company headquartered in Albuquerque. In her lengthy career, she has sold works to private individuals, corporations, cities, museums, and universities. Her elaborate bronze sculptures are displayed in public.

After she began drawing as a child, Sabo majored in art at the University of New Mexico. Sabo was a younger contemporary of Georgia O'Keeffe, whom she calls "very quiet, withdrawn, very much into her art." "It was all she lived for," says Sabo.

Sabo loves painting New Mexico "because of the quality of the light, the glow that comes just after the sun goes down." She continues, "Sometimes the snow is almost navy blue, whereas back East, the shadow in the snow is gray. It reflects the sky. Generally speaking, even after the worst New Mexico snow, the next day the sky is blue."

Sabo says that experienced artists "can almost sit and take apart the color in something." She adds, "I don't think people realize just how complicated doing a painting is. It takes a long time to develop your skill to the point where you don't spend two months on each painting."

She encourages young artists to "learn to draw." "I recommend that, even if they want to do contemporary work," she says. "It trains your hands and eyes to work together. Today, it's anything goes, but artists need formal training. I recommend a good drawing course about every semester for the rest of an artist's life."

Sabo finds modern art to be "more mechanical, or geometric." She says, "There's no place to do the flows and curves and lines that I like to do."

"Older people are fun to paint. I've done a few portraits, but not many," says Sabo. She finds that older people's faces show "what life has stamped on them." When people get face lifts, Sabo says "Their character is gone. It's an awful thing to do, although I've toyed with the idea."

"I've painted everything in New Mexico," says Sabo. "I've found as I grow older that sculpturing is the more serene thing to do. It isn't as exciting in a way and, in a way, it's more exciting. With a painting, the process is transitional, as you can change it. But with a sculpture, once it's in a mold I have little opportunity to make corrections. Then they do a wax, and that's it. However, with paintings, you can make corrections all the way through."

As a sculptor, Sabo has experienced her share of public art successes and fiascos. When art is placed in the public venue, she says, "If they love it, I tell them that there's one in the next block down that they'll hate. And if they say they hate it, I say, get in your car, drive down the street, you'll find one you love. That's how it is with public art."

She was chairman of the Albuquerque Arts Board in 1991 when it installed "Cruising San Mateo," a public art sculpture whose nickname became "Chevy on a Stick" because it encompassed a decorated turquoise Chevrolet automobile suspended on a pole. Sabo says, "I stood by the artist when people were screaming at her out of their cars. She went through a great deal. It was tough."

Detail of Barbara Grygutis, Cruising San Mateo, *Albuquerque, New Mexico (1991)*[18]

"Even now, I can be grocery shopping and some old bag will come up to me and say, 'I hate that thing.' That's when I tell her to 'just go down the street and you'll find one you love.'" With its nickname, "Chevy on a Stick" eventually became one of Albuquerque's most recognized symbols.

Sabo believes that the goal of art is to elicit an emotional reaction. "The words 'Isn't that nice' are the kiss of death. I'd rather have them say, 'God, I hate that.' If they say, 'Isn't that nice,' I know I need to start all over again on something else. Whatever it is that can evoke emotion of any kind is a good thing in art."

In 1997, the Albuquerque Arts Board voted to commission a $10,000 bust of Juan de Onate, the Spanish conquistador who explored New Mexico in the 1500s. By 2002, the project had mushroomed into a $5 million project because of the controversy surrounding Onate, who had ordered the feet of Acoma Pueblo men cut off. Says Sabo, who ultimately became a part of a larger project to include Anglo and Native American contributions to early New Mexico, "The city council voted 7-2 to do the project. I'm glad to be doing it. I may not live through it. I've had my windows in my car broken out. People have left horrible notes in my mailbox."

---

18. Image: Michael D. Murray, Cropped, revised, and resized thumbnail excerpt of an exhibit depicting Barbara Grygutis, "Cruising San Mateo" (1991), the subject of vocal community disapproval in Albuquerque, New Mexico.

Sabo also believes that artists who do public art need to be responsible in formulating their projects. She recalls her tenure on the Arts Board, "We had given a commission to an artist and it had a specific feeling to it. When we went to check on the work, the feeling had changed. We stopped him, and he redid it."

She believes that it's almost illegal for an artist to change the work after receiving approval. "The artist should go back to the board and tell them what he's going to do. Then sometimes they'll accept it. The arrogance of changing it after they've been selected is questionable to me. I know there are artists who would disagree, but I think that once you've made a contract, you're just like any other business person. We are artists, but we're also business people. You can't sell one thing and then give another."

When questioned about business rivalries, Sabo says, "The competition is good for you." Sabo acknowledges that "there are different strata of artists. The ones that put their hearts into it, and it becomes their life's work, are the ones who rise to the top. It almost has to be an obsession. I raised five kids and I painted in the closet, but I still painted. Nothing ever stopped me."

Note and Questions

1. As you review the following contract, compare it to the issues that Betty Sabo raises. Has the public entity protected itself from potential artist changes? Further, observe how the artist benefits from entering into such a contract. Are there any disadvantages to legal arrangements with public entities?

County of Bernalillo, New Mexico Arts Professional Services Contract
This contract is made and entered into by Bernalillo County, a political sub-division in the State of New Mexico, hereinafter referred to as "County," and Artist's Name, hereinafter referred to as "Artist," and located at: P.O. Box XXXXX, Albuquerque, New Mexico, 87184, phone: (505) XXX-XXXX, is made in Albuquerque, New Mexico, and is entered into as of the date of final execution of this Contract.

Section 1. DEFINITIONS
As used in this Contract:

A. "Work of Art" means the artwork designed and created by the Artist, as selected by the Bernalillo County Arts Board and accepted by the Bernalillo County Commission. It consists of (a complete description of the artwork here). A copy of the preliminary design and a copy of the Artist's Letter of Intent are attached as Exhibit A (1), Exhibit A (2), and Exhibit A (3).
B. "Work Base" means the entity upon which the Work of Art is mounted.
C. "Work Location" means the building, area, and community in which the Work of Art will be located.

D. "Work Site" means the specific public area within, upon, or around the Work Location in which the Work of Art is to be located. ...

Section 2. SCOPE OF SERVICES

A. Artist's Duties. The Artist shall perform the following services in a satisfactory and proper manner as determined by the County, and is responsible for and shall pay for:

1. All services, supplies, materials and equipment necessary for the design and execution of the Work of Art and the Work Base. Services shall be performed in an artistic and professional manner and in strict compliance with all the terms and conditions of this Contract. The Work of Art shall be of materials mutually acceptable to the County and to the Artist. The Work of Art shall be permanently installed at the Work Site. Any changes to the design by the Artist must be presented to and approved in writing by the Bernalillo County Arts Board before the Artist can proceed.
2. The Artist shall provide to the County a written description of the manner in which the Work of Art shall be installed and incorporated into the Work Site, including details addressing any preparatory work which must be performed to ready the Work Site where the Work of Art is to be located.
3. Delivery of the Work of Art to the Work Site. Delivery means the transport to and the arrival at the Work Site of the Work of Art. The Artist shall consult with the County regarding the date and time for delivery.
4. The Artist shall properly and timely install the Work of Art at the Work Site to the satisfaction of the County. Installation costs, including but not limited to related transportation, labor costs, and materials, shall be the responsibility of the Artist.
5. Provide a project identification plaque for the Art Work, which shall state the title of the Work of Art, the Artist's name, the year the Work of Art was created and the fact that purchase of the Work of Art was funded through the 1% for Public Art Program of Bernalillo County. ...

Section 3. COUNTY'S RESPONSIBILITY

The County shall be responsible for and shall pay for:

A. Any necessary preparation of the Work Site before installation of the Work Base or the Work of Art. Installation at the work site shall not begin until such preparation of the Work Site is completed.

Section 4. COMPENSATION

A. Bernalillo County shall pay to the Artist for services rendered a sum not to exceed Fifty Thousand Dollars ($50,000.00). This amount includes applicable gross receipts tax, which must be paid by the Artist, if the Artist is not exempt from the payment of gross receipts tax. This amount shall constitute full and complete compensation for the Artist's services under this Contract. The Artist shall be solely responsible for all expenses necessary, for the performance of this Contract except as set forth in Section 3 of this Contract. Cost overruns shall be the sole responsibility of the Artist. ...

Section 7. GUARANTEE

For a period of one year from the date of acceptance by the County as established by the Notice of Acceptance issued pursuant to Section 9 of this Contract, the Artist warrants and guarantees all workmanship on and materials used in the Work of Art, and, if provided by the Artist, all workmanship on and materials used in the Work Site, to be of good quality and free of defects, to be suitable for the particular purposes intended, to meet or exceed specifications, representations, or requirements contained in the proposal submitted by the Artist upon which the Artist was selected, or contained in other documents, or made orally by the Artist. The Artist agrees to make necessary repairs or replacements in the event that any of the warranties or guarantees of this section are breached. . . .

Section 10. OWNERSHIP

Ownership of the Work of Art shall be transferred from the Artist to the County upon issuance by the County of the Notice of Acceptance. The Artist hereby sells and transfers to the County the Artist's rights, except those limited by this Contract, title, and interest in and to the Work of Art. The Artist represents to the County that the Artist currently owns the Work of Art, that no lien or encumbrance exists against the Work of Art and that following the County's purchase of the Work of Art no individual or entity will have any right or interest in the Work of Art which is prior or superior to the County's right and interest. . . .

Section 12. ADDITIONAL WARRANTIES AND RELEASE

The Artist warrants that the Artist is sole creator of the Work of Art, that the Artist has the full power and authority to make this Contract, and that the Work of Art does not infringe any copyright or violate any property right or other rights. The Artist agrees to defend, indemnify, and hold harmless the County, their officials, agents, and employees from and against any and all claims, actions, suits, or proceeding of any kind brought against said parties for or on account of any matter arising from or out of the Services and other obligations performed by the Artist under this Contract. Unless otherwise provided, the Artist acknowledges that until the ownership of the Work of Art is transferred to the County pursuant to Section 10 of this Contract any injury to property or persons caused by the Work of Art or any damage to, theft of, vandalism to, or acts of God affecting Work of Art are the sole responsibility of the Artist, including, but not limited to, any loss occurring during the creation, storage, transportation, delivery, or installation of the Work of Art, regardless of where such loss occurs.

Section 13. INDEMNITY

The Artist agrees to defend, indemnify, and hold harmless the County and their officials, agents, and employees from and against any and all claims, actions, suits, or proceedings of any kind brought against said parties for or on account of any matter arising from the services performed by the Artist under this Contract. The indemnity required herein shall not be limited because of the specification of any particular insurance coverage in the Contract.

Section 14. INSURANCE COVERAGE

The Contracting Agency (Bernalillo County) shall not provide the Artist with any insurance coverage against any loss or risks included but not limited to those identified in Section 11 of this Contract. . . .

Section 20. COPYRIGHT AND REPRODUCTION RIGHTS

A. The Artist expressly reserves every right available to the Artist under the Federal Copyright Act to control the making or dissemination of copies or reproductions of the Work of Art, except the rights which are limited by this Contract.
B. The Artist certifies that the Work of Art created pursuant to this Contract is a unique work of art and has not been and will not be substantially duplicated by the Artist without the prior written permission of the County, unless the Work of Art is one in a series of editions, which shall be stated in this Contract. Should the Artist decide to reproduce the Work of Art in an edition or reproduce the Work of Art in any other way, the Artist shall first obtain the written permission of the County to do so.
C. The County retains the right to publish and distribute photographs, drawings or other forms of reproductions of the Work of Art as installed and formally accepted by the County, for reference, promotional, educational, and scholarly purposes. The County agrees to make no commercial use of the Work of Art without the Artist's written consent. If written permission is obtained from the Artist, all reproductions of the Work of Art by the County shall contain a credit to the Artist in the following form: "Artist's name, year of creation, and commissioning agency."
D. The Artist agrees to include on or in any form of reproduction of the Work of Art, initiated or authorized by the Artist, a credit to the County in the following form: "Collection of the Bernalillo County 1% for Public Art Program, Albuquerque, NM."

Section 21. NON-DESTRUCTION/ALTERATION/MODIFICATION

To the extent required by the Visual Artist's Rights Act of 1990, Title 17, United States Code (the "Act"), as amended, or other applicable laws and regulations, during the Artist's lifetime, the County will not intentionally destroy or alter the Work of Art in any way whatsoever during the Artist's lifetime without first making a reasonable effort to locate and to inform the Artist, and to obtain the Artist's written permission, if possible. However, the Act allows the Artist to waive some or all of the Artist's rights described in this section by signing a written instrument identifying the Work and the right waived. As provided in the Act, the Modifications shall not include modifications caused by the passage of time, the inherent nature of the materials, or the result of conservation, lighting, or placement in connection with public presentation. If any significant alteration occurs to the Work of Art after it is formally accepted by the County, whether such change is intentional, unintentional, or malicious, and if the Artist makes a written request to the County that the Work of Art no longer be represented as the work of the Artist.

Note

1. Public art adorns buildings, roads, and parks throughout the United States and the world. Some of the art has been well received, whereas other work has been questioned and disparaged. For an interesting article reviewing the public reaction to public art, *see* Roberta Smith, *Public Art, Eyesore to Eye Candy*, N.Y. Times, Aug. 24, 2008.

PROBLEM 7-2

> A collector of Andy Warhol self-portraits wants a Pittsburgh art gallery to be its agent in locating and purchasing these self-portraits. Draft a short agreement between the buyer and the gallery-agent. Define duties and responsibilities as described in this chapter.

C. The Commission

Occasionally, an artist is commissioned to create a specific piece. Because a work of art exists in the mind of the creator until it is actually completed, it is difficult, if not impossible, for a collector to know what a prospective art object will look like. How much artistic license will be allowed? Can the collector be forced to accept the final product?

Wolff v. Smith

25 N.E.2d 399 (Ill. App. Ct. 1940)*

[Plaintiff/artist agreed to paint a portrait of defendant's deceased father for $500. The picture, which was to hang in defendant's office, was accepted and plaintiff was paid. Subsequently, defendant requested that the artist paint a second portrait. This arrangement was confirmed by a letter which read in part:

---

* Footnotes omitted.

My dear Mr. Smith: . . . Please be assured that I will do all in my power to make the second portrait of your dear father as outstanding and exact a likeness as the first one and to your entire satisfaction. And herewith beg to reiterate my statement to you last evening that I am very pleased to paint this second portrait on my own initiative and request no obligation at no time [sic].

When this portrait was delivered, defendant was dissatisfied and refused to pay for it, although the picture remained in his house for some time. After some futile attempts to correct the portrait and some correspondence, plaintiff instituted this action to recover for breach of contract. A judgment was rendered in favor of plaintiff and defendant appealed.]

... In 13 C.J. page 675 it is said: "Contracts in which one party agrees to perform to the satisfaction of the other are ordinarily divided into two classes: (1) where fancy, taste, sensibility or judgment are involved; and (2) where the question is merely one of operative fitness or mechanical utility. In contracts involving matters of fancy, taste, or judgment, when one party agrees to perform to the satisfaction of the other, he renders the other party the sole judge of his satisfaction without regard to the justice or reasonableness of his decision, and a court or jury can not say that such party should have been satisfied where he asserts that he is not." In a note, cases illustrating and supporting the text are cited and the statement is made that contracts have been held to fall within the first class and support the rule stated in the text where they have related to portraits, a portrait bust, a legal, literary, or scientific article for an encyclopedia, a play to be written by an author for an actor. . . .

In *Pennington v. Howland*, 41 A. 891 (R.I. 1898), the plaintiff was employed to paint a pastel portrait of the defendant's wife. The court stated that an instruction to the effect that an artist, if he agreed to paint a picture to one's satisfaction, has no cause of action for the price unless the buyer is satisfied, however good the picture may be, would state the law correctly and in the course of its opinion said: "When the subject of the contract is one which involves personal taste or feeling, an agreement that it shall be satisfactory to the buyer necessarily makes him the sole judge whether it answers that condition. He cannot be required to take it because other people might be satisfied with it; for that is not what he agreed to do. Personal tastes differ widely, and if one has agreed to submit his work to such a test, he must abide by the result. A large number of witnesses might be brought to testify that the work was satisfactory to them, that they considered it perfect, and that they could see no reasonable ground for objecting to it. But that would not be the test of the contract, nor should a jury be allowed to say in such a case that a defendant must pay because, by the preponderance of evidence, he ought to have been satisfied with the work, or, in other words, that it was 'reasonably satisfactory.' Upon this principle numerous cases have been decided."

Zaleski v. Clark, 1876 WL 1785 (Conn. 1876) was an action by a sculptor to recover the contract price of a bust of the defendant's deceased husband which he had modeled. In its opinion the court said: "Courts of law must allow parties to make their own contracts, and can enforce only such as they actually make. Whether the contract is wise or unwise, reasonable or unreasonable, is ordinarily an immaterial inquiry. The simple inquiry is, what is the contract? and has the plaintiff performed his part of it? In this case the plaintiff undertook to make a bust which should be satisfactory to the defendant. The case shows that she was not satisfied with it. The plaintiff has not yet then fulfilled his contract. . . .

A contract to produce a bust perfect in every respect, and one with which the defendant ought to be satisfied, is one thing; an undertaking to make one with which she will be satisfied is quite another thing. The former can only be determined by experts, or those whose education and habits of life qualify them to judge of such matters. The latter can only be determined by the defendant herself. It may have been unwise in the plaintiff to make such a contract, but having made it, he is bound by it."

Gibson v. Cranage, 1878 WL 7022 (Mich. 1878), was a suit to recover the contract price for making a portrait of the deceased daughter of the defendant. After the picture was finished it was shown the defendant, who was dissatisfied with it and refused to accept it. In sustaining a judgment for the defendant, the court said: ". . . an agreement which violates no rule of public policy, and which is free from all taint of fraud or mistake, there is no hardship whatever in holding them bound by it. Artists or third parties might consider a portrait an excellent one, and yet it prove very unsatisfactory to the person who had ordered it and who might be unable to point out with clearness or certainty the defects or objections. And if the person giving the order stipulates that the portrait when finished must be satisfactory to him or else he will not accept or pay for it, and this is agreed to, he may insist upon his right as given him by the contract."

In his letter . . . from Toledo on August 3rd, 1937, appellee wrote that he would do all in his power to make this second portrait as outstanding and exact a likeness of appellant's father as the first one, that he was pleased to paint it on his own initiative without obligation on the part of appellant and added "and to your entire satisfaction." Under the foregoing and many other authorities, under this arrangement appellant must be held to be the sole judge whether he would accept the portrait and the trial court erred in not so instructing the jury. . . .

[The case was remanded to determine whether there had been an acceptance notwithstanding the defendant's apparent dissatisfaction.]

Notes and Questions

1. The "satisfaction guaranteed" contract has resulted in much litigation, especially in the area of art law. As early as 1887, personal dissatisfaction with commissioned artwork was held a sufficient reason to reject tendered performance under an acknowledged contract. *See Moore v. Goodwin*, 43 Hun. 534 (N.Y. 1887); *Clausen v. Vonnoh*, 55 Misc. 220,

105 N.Y.S. 102, appeal denied, 122 App. Div. 917, 107 N.Y.S. 1147 (1907); *Bowan v. Buckner* 183 S.W. 704 (Mo. App. 1916).

2. In the classic portrait controversy, the artist and purchaser disagree on what the subject looks like. For example, in *McCrady v. Roy*, 85 So. 2d 527 (La. App. 1956), the artist did not give a personal guarantee, but insisted that "likenesses are interpretations" and that the portrait was his interpretation of the appearance of the defendant's wife. The court implied a provision of personal satisfaction and established a "reasonable likeness" standard:

> In the course of oral argument the portrait was unveiled and defendant's wife was seated beside it in order to facilitate our evaluation of the likeness of the portrait to Mrs. Roy. Our reaction to the absence of "likeness" was both spontaneous and instantaneous. It is now our considered opinion that the portrait fails to depict a reasonableness likeness of Mrs. Roy. She is an attractive woman of refined and relatively youthful appearance, possessed of fine regular features, good coloring and of a slight trim figure, whereas the portrait reveals a buxom, unattractive middle aged woman, lacking in refinement of appearance and possessed of coarse features.

85 So. 2d at 528.

The dissenting judge felt that the portrait, while not pleasing, was a fairly good likeness. Apparently, not trusting his own eyes, however, he wanted an expert's opinion on it.

3. In *McCrady*, the artist apparently mistook his function. Customers (and judges) may think that a portrait calls for a slightly flattering, accurate likeness, rather than an interpretive creation. The problem, therefore, can be avoided by communication between the artist and the customer. Preliminary sketches and color studies of the final work may be submitted for the customer's comments and approval. If the artist discusses his or her ideas concerning what the picture should portray, it is possible that the person commissioning it could be convinced that the creation should portray the inner soul, rather than the outer covering. Caveat — if the inner soul is dowdy, better not use a "satisfaction guaranteed" clause.

4. Another important factor raised by *Wolff* is the proper period of inspection after receipt. In *Hayes v. Kluge*, 92 A. 358 (N.J. 1914), the court considered the reasonableness of the time between rejection and receipt. As the issue was a question of fact under the Sales Act then in force, the jury's decision in favor of the purchaser was affirmed. It was determined that 55 days was not too long to hold a portrait without rejecting it, particularly where the artist had failed to keep appointments made to discuss the painting and the individual who commissioned the work was frequently out of the country.

5. In *Berke v. Sherman*, 213 N.Y.S.2d 210 (Sup. Ct. 1961), the court enforced a contract that required defendant to pay "$100 per design

accepted, regardless of whether said design was ever manufactured, imported or marketed." This logic could be extended to embrace a contractual provision requiring the commissioner of a portrait to pay for materials and labor, whether or not the work was ultimately accepted.

6. When the performance of one party requires cooperation from the other, the formation of a contract necessarily implies a willingness to supply this cooperation. *See* Calamari & Perillo on Contracts § 165 (1970). This proposition is very important to the portrait painter as it is obviously necessary to have the subject's cooperation. In *Brockhurst v. Ryan*, 146 N.Y.S.2d 386 (Sup. Ct. 1955), plaintiff/artist contracted to paint five separate portraits of defendant and each of the members of his family. Two pictures were completed and paid for. The remainder of the commission was not fulfilled because defendant refrained from arranging for any further sittings. The artist sued for breach of contract and was allowed to recover the contract price of $11,000 less the $24 cost of completing the portraits.

7. Artists often employ agents to obtain commissions. If this representative acts beyond the scope of his or her actual authority, the principal may, nevertheless, be bound under the doctrine of apparent authority. *See Zaleski v. Clark*, 1876 WL 1785 (Conn. 1876). *See generally* Mecham on Agency (2d ed. 1914) for the steps that may be taken by a principal to protect himself or herself from the unauthorized acts of an agent.

8. For a form contract to use in the commissioning of an artist to paint a portrait, *see Contract to Paint Portrait*, 13B Am. Jur. Legal Forms 2d § 190:39 (rev. 1996).

PROBLEM 7-3

Prepare a form contract for an artist who seeks commissions to paint portraits. Include appropriate terms and protections for the artist as described in this chapter.

D. Intra-Gallery Disputes

As a business, galleries can incur a multitude of disputes. In the following case, one gallery charged that another gallery and its owner disparaged it with false claims.

Gmurzynska v. Hutton

355 F.3d 206 (2d Cir. 2004)*

Before Oakes, Meskill and B.D. Parker, Circuit Judges.
Per Curiam.

Plaintiff-appellant Galerie Gmurzynska ("Galerie"), an art gallery in Germany, sued defendant-appellees Leonard Hutton Galleries, Inc., a competing New York gallery, and its owner, Ingrid Hutton (collectively, "Hutton Galleries"), as well as three art experts, Magdalena Dabrowski, Eugena Ordonez, and Alexandra Shatskikh. The complaint alleged that Hutton Galleries promoted itself and disparaged Galerie in the Russian avant-garde art world by conspiring with the art experts to have them falsely question the authenticity of Galerie's artwork in their expert opinions. The complaint asserted a claim under section 43(a)(1)(B) of the Lanham Act, 15 U.S.C. § 1125(a)(1)(B), and state law claims for tortious interference with business expectancy and defamation. It also sought declaratory judgment that the works of art Galerie sold were genuine.

The United States District Court for the Southern District of New York, Richard M. Berman, Judge, dismissed the complaint as to all defendants, finding that the Lanham Act claims against the art experts failed because there was no allegation the experts were in commercial competition with Galerie, and that the claims against Hutton Galleries failed because there was no allegation that Hutton Galleries made any false or misleading representations. The court held that the conclusory allegations of conspiracy failed to salvage plaintiff's Lanham Act claims. With no justiciable controversy remaining, the court also dismissed the declaratory judgment claim and declined to exercise jurisdiction over the pendent state law claims.

Galerie now appeals, claiming that the district court improperly applied a heightened pleading standard contrary to the liberal pleading standards of the Federal Rules of Civil Procedure recently reaffirmed in *Swierkiewicz v. Sorema N.A.*, 534 U.S. 506, 122 S. Ct. 992, 152 L. Ed. 2d 1 (2002). Under the federal rules, "a complaint must include only 'a short and plain statement of the claim showing that the pleader is entitled to relief.'" *Swierkiewicz*, 534 U.S. at 513, 122 S. Ct. 992 (quoting Fed. R. Civ. P. 8(a)(2)). A short and plain statement "must simply 'give the defendant fair notice of what the plaintiff's claim is and the grounds upon which it rests.'" *Id.* (quoting *Conley v. Gibson*, 355 U.S. 41, 47, 78 S. Ct. 99, 2 L. Ed. 2d 80 (1957)). We find that even under this liberal pleading standard, the complaint does not state a claim for violation of the Lanham Act. Accordingly, we affirm its dismissal.

BACKGROUND

The 33-page complaint describes a long-simmering hostility between the two competing art galleries. In the allegations relevant to this decision, the complaint distills two schemes as the basis for its claims.

---

* All footnotes have been removed.

In one scheme, Ms. Dabrowski, an art historian and a former senior curator at the Museum of Modern Art ("MOMA"), allegedly disparaged Galerie in three private consultations with Mr. Norbert du Carrois, an art collector, on April 20, October 25 and November 28, 2000. In each of these meetings, du Carrois inquired about certain works that Galerie had shown or was offering for sale. In response to these inquiries, Dabrowski said in the first meeting that one work was "not what you want for your collection," and that du Carrois should go to the Hutton Gallery because there, "you will find what you are looking for." In the second meeting, Dabrowski told du Carrois that a drawing offered for sale by Galerie was worthless, that Krystyna Gmurzynska "has no knowledge of Russian art," and that she was "only working for the money." Furthermore, she said Galerie was selling fake works by a non-existent artist. In the third meeting, du Carrois showed Dabrowski a drawing from Galerie he was considering purchasing, and "she immediately replied, 'it's nothing,'" and told du Carrois she had advised another customer that certain works were "not worth to be acquired." She also said that a painting owned by Galerie was "so bad" and made by the artist's pupils. When du Carrois mentioned an expert who had supported the authenticity of works in a particular collection, she said the works in that collection were "doubtful" and that the said expert was not credible. She then criticized other drawings as "'ridiculous,' 'fakes,' 'caricatures,' and 'like a child's drawing.'" She went on to say that all the works that Ernst Schwitters, a collector, bought from Galerie were fakes, that the Sprengel Museum in Hanover, Germany, had asked a restorer to check up on them, and that all were made after 1940.

In a second scheme, the Sprengel Museum allegedly solicited and relied upon expert opinions by Ordonez, an art historian and assistant conservator for MOMA, and Shatskikh, an expert in Russian art, to support statements the museum had already published in its exhibition catalogue challenging the authenticity of eight works that had been purchased from Galerie. As part of this museum scheme, the experts influenced a reporter for the journal ARTnews to write a negative article about the ensuing controversy between Galerie and the museum. Although the article was not published, the journal had advertised that it would be publishing an article concerning Galerie's dispute with the museum.

Galerie's complaint refers to the defendants as conspirators throughout, and alleges that their conduct in the two schemes was "part of a larger illicit compact pursuant to which Dabrowski, Ordonez, and Shatskikh . . . do Hutton's bidding," and that the defendants agreed to deliver the opinions Hutton wanted. The complaint states this conspiracy created a prospective customer for Hutton Galleries each time defendants persuaded a customer not to deal with Galerie.

DISCUSSION

We review de novo the Rule 12(b)(6) dismissal of plaintiff's complaint. *Chambers v. Time Warner, Inc.*, 282 F.3d 147, 152 (2d Cir. 2002). A complaint "should not be dismissed for failure to state a claim unless it appears beyond doubt that the plaintiff can prove no set of facts in support of his claim which would entitle him to relief." *Conley v. Gibson*, 355 U.S. at 45-46, 78 S. Ct. 99. An appellate court is "free to affirm a district court decision on any grounds for which there is a record sufficient to permit conclusions of law, even grounds not relied upon by the district court." *Alfaro Motors, Inc. v. Ward*, 814 F.2d 883, 887 (2d Cir. 1987).

Galerie claims a violation of the Lanham Act, which provides, in relevant part:

> (a) Civil action
>
>   (1) Any person who, on or in connection with any goods or services, . . . uses in commerce any . . . false or misleading description of fact, or false or misleading representation of fact, which—
>
>   (A) [. . .], or
>
>   (B) (in commercial advertising or promotion, misrepresents the nature, characteristics, qualities, or geographic origin of his or her or another person's goods, services, or commercial activities, shall be liable in a civil action by any person who believes that he or she is or is likely to be damaged by such act.)

15 U.S.C. § 1125(a)(1)(B)(2003).

In this circuit, to constitute "commercial advertising or promotion" under the Lanham Act, a statement must be: (1) "commercial speech," (2) made "for the purpose of influencing consumers to buy defendant's goods or services," and (3) "although representations less formal than those made as part of a classic advertising campaign may suffice, they must be disseminated sufficiently to the relevant purchasing public." *See Fashion Boutique of Short Hills, Inc. v. Fendi USA, Inc.*, 314 F.3d 48, 56, 57-58 (2d Cir. 2002). . . . Commercial speech is "'speech which does no more than propose a commercial transaction.'" *City of Cincinnati v. Discovery Network, Inc.*, 507 U.S. 410, 422, 113 S. Ct. 1505, 123 L. Ed. 2d 99. . . .

Galerie has not pleaded a violation of the Lanham Act because it has not alleged any false statements "in commercial advertising or promotion." The art experts' opinions and assertions, solicited by either the art collector or by the museum, are not commercial advertising or commercial promotion for Hutton Galleries. The museum exhibition catalogue is not commercial advertising or promotion for Hutton Galleries. Furthermore, Hutton Galleries did not make any of the alleged misrepresentations, and the complaint specifically alleges that the museum, and not the expert defendants, made the alleged misrepresentations in the museum catalogue, both before and after the defendants offered their support.

The allegation that defendants caused a journalist to write an article about the controversy with the museum is similarly inadequate under the Lanham Act. The journalist's article is not commercial advertising, commercial promotion, or commercial speech. Rather, it is speech that is traditionally granted full protection under the First Amendment. "As always with the public expression of opinion, 'we have been careful not to permit overextension of the Lanham Act to intrude on First Amendment values.'" *Boule v. Hutton*, 328 F.3d 84, 91-92 (2d Cir. 2003) (quoting *Groden v. Random House, Inc.*, 61 F.3d 1045, 1052 (2d Cir. 1995)). In *Boule*, this court decided with little hesitation that, as a matter of law, a similar ARTnews article about fraud in the art market and the defendants' statements quoted in it were not commercial speech. *Id.* at 91. Furthermore, Galerie's complaint does not allege that the announcement of the forthcoming article, which was never published, made a factual assertion about Galerie's goods or services. Rather, the complaint alleges that the article included a statement about the existence of a dispute between the museum and Galerie — a statement which is true by the complaint's own admissions.

The acts of the individual defendants do not constitute violations of the Lanham Act and Galerie's allegations of conspiracy cannot transform them into such. . . . Because Galerie has not adequately pled any actionable underlying federal claim, its allegations of conspiracy are without legal import.

In sum, we find that, even when considered under the Rules' liberal pleading standards, Galerie's allegations are insufficient to withstand a motion to dismiss. We therefore affirm the decision of the district court dismissing the complaint.

CONCLUSION

For the foregoing reasons, the judgment of the district court is affirmed.

The following case addresses issues concerning the dissolution of a gallery partnership and the failure of the parties to adhere to the settlement agreement.

Campbell v. Lopez

2009 WL 1878701 (Cal. App. 1st Dist., June 30, 2009)

SIGGINS, J.

Steven Lopez appeals from a judgment entered pursuant to a motion to enforce a settlement brought under Code of Civil Procedure section 664.6. He contends the judgment materially departs from the terms of the settlement and from findings made by the court when it ruled on the motion to enforce the settlement. Respondents Charles and Glenna Campbell assert the judgment accurately reflects the parties' settlement and is supported by substantial evidence. We agree, and therefore affirm the judgment.

BACKGROUND

This case arises from the dissolution of a partnership formed to operate a San Francisco art gallery. Charles Campbell founded the Charles Campbell Gallery in or around 1971 and operated it continuously until he retired in 2006. The gallery was housed in a building on Chestnut Street owned by the Campbells through the Charles and Glenna Campbell Revocable Trust.

Campbell hired Lopez to help manage the gallery in 2002, when Campbell was 87 years old. In 2004, he and Lopez formed a general partnership, Campbell Gallery Partners, for the purpose of owning and operating the gallery.

In 2006, at the age of 91 and suffering from macular degeneration, Campbell notified Lopez he intended to disassociate from the partnership and sell the Chestnut Street building. The complaint alleges that around this time Campbell discovered that Lopez had fraudulently caused a provision to be added to the lease to allow him to rent the gallery premises for $1,000 per month in perpetuity. The Campbells sued Lopez for dissolution of the partnership, an accounting, fraud, elder abuse, and declaratory relief. Lopez and his domestic partner, Eric Koehler, cross-complained against the Campbells for breach of contact, fraud, negligence, conversion, defamation, breach of fiduciary duty, and various other causes of action.

The parties settled at a court-supervised settlement conference after six months of litigation. The terms of the settlement were reported to the court by the Campbells' counsel as follows: [Mr. and Mrs. Campbell will pay to Lopez and Koehler $50,000 by check. All parties will waive any claims they have to recover costs or attorney's fees from the other side. The complaint and the cross-complaint will be dismissed with prejudice. The defendant and cross-complainants will have the right to continue a gallery business at a location other than the one at which it is operated now, and they agree to vacate the current premises by April 22, and turn over the keys. The defendant and cross-complainants will be able to take consigned art with them to their new location, and they will not owe Mr. Campbell any of the proceeds of the sale of consigned art. All of the art that's in the current premises that is personally owned by Mr. or Mrs. Campbell will be left behind and will remain the property of Mr. and Mrs. Campbell. The defendants/cross-complainants will keep revenues received from the sale of consigned art since November of 2006 as their property, and do not have to pay any of the money to Mr. or Mrs. Campbell. The defendants and cross-complainants will not have the right to use the name Charles Campbell Gallery for their new gallery, but they will be permitted to say that they are the successors to the Charles Campbell Gallery. The defendants and cross complainants can take all moveable gallery furniture that is not built-in except Mr. Campbell's desk, a Chinese chest, the file cabinet containing Mr. Campbell's files, and all of Mr. Campbell and Mrs. Campbell's personal property.]

Other stated terms concerned future consignment sales of art owned by the Campbells, Lopez's retention of the gallery's computer equipment, website, phone numbers, and URL, and the division of books, catalogs, and posters. The court confirmed that all parties and their counsel agreed to the terms of settlement as stated on the open record. Counsel also stipulated the settlement was immediately enforceable under Code of Civil Procedure section 664.6.

Three months later, the Campbells moved to enforce the settlement. They asserted the parties could not agree on a division of the library; that Lopez threatened to remove from the gallery some 80 to 100 pieces of art and other personal property owned by the Campbells; and that he was refusing to vacate the gallery premises until the ownership of the artwork and the library were resolved. In opposition, Lopez asserted the settlement did not allocate ownership over a category of works he referred to as "gallery inventory" artwork, which, he maintained, were neither being held for sale on consignment nor personally owned by the Campbells.

Following an evidentiary hearing held April 25, 2008, the court granted the Campbells' motion to enforce the settlement and entered its judgment. The court found that there was no category of "gallery inventory" art that was owned by the gallery and unaccounted for in the settlement. Accordingly, all non-consigned art (with the exception of one painting the parties agreed Lopez would keep) was to remain with the Campbells. The court also found the Campbells had paid Lopez $50,000 pursuant to the settlement; that, per the parties' stipulation, Lopez would vacate the gallery by April 30, 2008; and that at the April 25, 2008, hearing, the parties agreed to a specific division of the books and other items.

The judgment provides, inter alia, that: "Steven Lopez and Eric Koehler may remove from the premises only the art that is there 'on consignment' and the painting by James Weeks known as 'Piano and Man.' Steven Lopez and Eric Koehler will not have to pay Charles or Glenna Campbell any of the proceeds that they receive from sales of the consigned art that they are hereby authorized to take with them. Steven Lopez and Eric Koehler shall leave behind at the premises all other art, which is found by the Court to be the personal property of Charles Campbell or Glenna Campbell or both of them. . . ." The judgment also assigned 20 of 30 books and catalogs identified on a document introduced as Exhibit 3 to Lopez and Koehler, and directed that they leave at the gallery premises "(1) All books and catalogs listed on said Exhibit 3 that are not identified in the preceding paragraph; and (2) All of the books and catalogs that, prior to the hearing on April 25, 2008, neither Charles nor Glenna Campbell had authorized them to remove, which are found by the Court to be the personal property of Charles Campbell or Glenna Campbell or both of them."

On July 25, 2008, the Campbells filed an ex parte application for a temporary restraining order to prohibit Lopez and Koehler from selling several works of non-consigned art in violation of the judgment. The court granted the application and issued an order that prohibited defendants "from selling any art work that was not consigned to them for sale, or that is not owned by either or both of them." Lopez filed a timely appeal from the judgment.

DISCUSSION

1. The Artwork

Lopez's primary contention is that the settlement did not resolve the ownership of the "gallery inventory" category of art, i.e., art that was neither on consignment nor owned by the Campbells, but which Lopez claims was owned by the partnership. Lopez asserts the judgment is inconsistent with the terms of the settlement because it identifies as belonging to the Campbells all nonconsignment art at the gallery. The Campbells maintain that the court appropriately found the settlement divided all of the art in the gallery into only two categories: between consignment works and art owned by the Campbells. They are correct. . . .

Here, the trial court determined the settlement agreement did not create a "gallery inventory" category of art, but, rather, divided all artwork between consigned art and art personally owned by the Campbells. Its determination is supported by substantial evidence. In reaching its decision, the court considered the transcript of the hearing convened to memorialize the terms of the settlement and testimony by Lopez and his attorney. The transcript confirms that neither Lopez nor his counsel mentioned any third category of art at the hearing, even after the Campbells' attorney stated the terms of the proposed settlement and the court specifically inquired of all parties whether there were any additional terms. At the April 25, 2008, hearing on the motion to enforce the settlement, the court asked Lopez's attorney whether he had intended at the settlement conference to reserve from the settlement a third category of art. Counsel responded when the case was settled, he "believed that there was art on consignment and art owned by the Campbells, and I cannot recall, to be honest with you, whether or not I knew of any additional art that may have been there." Moreover, he testified that at that time he believed the settlement resolved all issues in the litigation "subject to what was to be defined afterwards with the art and the art catalogs, the posters, and the personal property and that type of thing." He also agreed that a draft settlement agreement prepared by the Campbells' attorney that he had edited after the settlement hearing divided all of the art in the gallery between consigned art and art belonging to the Campbells. Campbell submitted a declaration that confirmed there were only two categories of art in the gallery: consignment art, and "all other art, which is personally owned by me or Mrs. Campbell." When Lopez testified, he was unable to identify any works of art sold to or whose title was held by the partnership, rather than the Campbells. There is ample evidence to support the trial court's determination that under the settlement all art other than consigned works was the personal property of the Campbells, and that there was no third category of "gallery inventory." There is no inconsistency between that determination and the settlement or judgment. Accordingly, we reject Lopez's claim of error. . . .

DISPOSITION

The judgment is deemed amended to include in paragraph seven the book by Christiansen, Kanter, and Strehlke entitled *Painting in Renaissance Sienna 1420-1500*. In all other respects, the judgment and order granting the application for a temporary restraining order are affirmed.

We concur: McGUINESS, P.J., and JENKINS, J.

Notes

1. By 2009, art galleries began experiencing the effects of the national and global economic downturn. Over two dozen galleries folded in New York City and many began slashing prices, offering deep discounts, laying off employees, and dropping artists with poor sales records. *See* Dorothy Spears, *This Summer, Some Galleries are Sweating*, N.Y. Times, June 21, 2009.

2. A gallery owner in Albuquerque, New Mexico, lost a lawsuit in August 2009. The jury awarded a former client $15,000 for a pair of William Herbet Dunton oil paintings that she sold to Peter Eller for $4,500 and he immediately resold for $35,000. In less than two years, the paintings sold for more than $600,000. *See* Scott Sandlin, *Jury Awards $15K in Art Sale Dispute*, Albuquerque J., Aug. 26, 2009.

ASSESSMENT

1. Which of the following was not associated with the *In re Rothko Estate* litigation?
   (A) The dumping of paintings — selling them all at once, which places a negative pressure on the price of all Rothko works
   (B) Negligence and self-dealing among the executors of the estate
   (C) Estate planning documents and trusts that spelled out duties, terms and conditions, review and approval by heirs/beneficiaries, and dispute resolution
   (D) All of the above were associated with the *In re Rothko Estate* litigation

2. An "output" agreement between an artist and dealer may involve which of the following:
   (A) Purchase or consignment of the artist's works
   (B) Exclusive or nonexclusive relationship
   (C) Total output, partial/percentage output, or right of first refusal as to outputs
   (D) All of the above

3. In the absence of contract terms, UCC will not imply stop-gap terms as to:
   (A) Price
   (B) Time of delivery, payment
   (C) Quantity
   (D) All of the above

ASSESSMENT ANSWERS

1. Which of the following was not associated with the *In re Rothko Estate* litigation?

(A) The dumping of paintings — selling them all at once which cases a negative pressure on the price of all Rothko works
(B) Negligence and self-dealing among the executors of the estate
(C) Estate planning documents and trusts that spelled out duties, terms and conditions, review and approval by heirs/beneficiaries, and dispute resolution
(D) All of the above were associated with the *In re Rothko Estate* litigation

ANSWER: The correct answer is (C). Most if not all of the problems of the estate were caused by inadequate estate contracts, trusts, and estate planning documents that failed to spell out duties, terms and conditions, review and approval by heirs/beneficiaries, and provide for dispute resolution.

2. An "output" agreement between an artist and dealer may involve which of the following:
   (A) Purchase or consignment of the artist's works
   (B) Exclusive or nonexclusive relationship
   (C) Total output, partial/percentage output, or right of first refusal as to outputs
   (D) All of the above

ANSWER: The correct answer is (D). Artist-Dealer arrangements are very flexible, and can involve any of the terms listed in (A), (B), or (C).

3. In the absence of contract terms, UCC will not imply stop-gap terms as to:
   (A) Price
   (B) Time of delivery, payment
   (C) Quantity
   (D) All of the above

ANSWER: The correct answer is (C). The UCC, and the lawyers or judges interpreting it, have no means to answer how many of a certain item were contemplated by the parties to a contract, so quantity will not be implied. Price and time of delivery or payment may be calculated based on the market price, history of transactions between the parties, industry practices, or what is reasonable in the circumstances.

8 | AUCTIONS

This chapter analyzes auctions as mechanisms for buying and selling art. Auctions are one of the most popular art markets, accounting for an estimated 50 percent of the value of art sold annually in the United States. Ninety-five percent of the multibillion dollar art auction market worldwide is controlled by Sotheby's, based in New York, and Christie's, with headquarters in London. In 2015, for example, Sotheby's net auction sales totaled $6.72 billion, whereas Christie's global auction and private sales totaled $7.4 billion. Cases and materials involving these and other auction venues can be found throughout this chapter.

Customarily, well-informed art dealers and professionals were the principal auction purchasers and comprised 90 percent of those attending auctions. Starting in the late 1980s, however, non-professional collectors became more than half of all auction attendees. Sajbel, *Hammering it Down: A Record-setting Auctioneer Looks to the Novice Collector*, Chi. Tribune, Nov. 12, 1989, § Home, at 8. One consequence of the growth of public interest in collecting art as an investment is the increase in efforts to regulate the auction industry.

Technology has transformed conventional auction markets from live to virtual experiences. On October 6, 2009, eBay, the most popular electronic auction market, had 346,110 art items for sale, ranging from an oil painting of "Two Noble Cats" on canvas (opening bid price $0.01) to "Riggs Art Abstract Expressionism" (opening bid price $21 million). According to one commentator, "[o]n any given day, eBay adds approximately one million new goods or services to its data base, servicing approximately 42.4 million customers on a global scale." Lori Jones, *The Online Copyright Auction: How High Will Bidding Go?*, 2 J. HIGH. TECH. L. 45, 46 (2003).

Sotheby's partnered temporarily with Amazon.com to launch its own Internet art business. However, in the first nine months of 2001, for example, online auctions at *Sothebys.com* cost the company $18.7 million, considerably more than corresponding revenues. *See http://www2.artnet.com/Magazine/*

news/artnetnews/artnetnews12-6-01.asp. Sotheby's closed its online auction house, but kept select sales open for bids via the Internet in 2009. *See http:// www.sothebys.com/about/corporate/as_corphistory.html/.*

Because auctions may be one of the least understood methods for conducting sales, this chapter first discusses selling methods, and then presents a brief historical sketch of the auction's development. Later, it analyzes the various types of auctions, the roles of the auctioneer and the auction house, the warranties available, and concludes by exploring some important tactics and antitrust problems.

Perhaps the best advice that can be given to a newcomer to the auction world is to be alert and exercise extreme caution in this unique market.

A. Introduction

Sherri L. Burr, Introducing Art Law

37 Copyright World 22, 28-29 (1994)*

In light of the prominence of auction houses in establishing the value of art, it is important to recognize that at the core of the auction system are the legal relationships between the consignor and the auctioneer, between the auctioneer and the purchaser, and between the purchaser and the consignor.

In the relationship between the consignor and the auctioneer, both endeavor to obtain the highest prices for the art work, with the auctioneer attempting to create "auction fever" to induce excitement in purchasers. The contractual relationship consists of a consignment agreement in which the auctioneer becomes the consignor's agent and undertakes fiduciary responsibility towards the consignor.

The typical Sotheby's and Christie's consignment agreements, for example, establish the consignor's commissions and other charges, such as for insurance, shipping, and illustration costs. To limit the consignor's risk, the agreement may also specify that reserves will be set, which will establish a confidential minimum price below which the art work will not be sold. Perhaps one of the most important provisions is that of the seller's representations and warranties, whereby the seller will represent and warrant that (i) the seller has the title to the art work; (ii) the art work is free and clear of all liens, claims, and encumbrances; (iii) upon sale, good title and right to possession will pass to the purchaser free of such liens, claims, and encumbrances; and (iv) that there are no limits on the copyright of the item that will prohibit its public display and/or illustration in advertising publications.

In the relationship between the purchaser and the auctioneer, the purchaser is concerned about whether the consignor has clear ownership (title) of the work, whether the work is authentic, and whether the auction process is

---

* Footnotes omitted.

fair and has not been subjected to illegal manipulation by the auctioneer in order to obtain higher prices. The auctioneer and the consignor will also be concerned that purchasers have not engaged in any illegal schemes to limit prices.

As the number of forgeries, frauds, thefts, and other modifications detrimental to the value of art work have risen over the last twenty years, perhaps in direct proportion to increase in values of art, purchasers have an increased obligation to determine, to the best of their ability, that the seller has good title. The representations that the consignor must make to the auctioneer will probably reassure most purchasers.

As for authenticity, the purchaser may feel comfortable accepting the seller's or auctioneer's warranties. In its "Catalogue for Old Master Paintings," dated October 14, 1992, Sotheby's utilizes seven terms to indicate the authorship, period, culture, source, or origin as qualified statements. For example, if Sotheby's declares "attributed to Giovanni Bellini," it indicates that in their best opinion it is "probably a work by the artist;" more certainty is expressed when Sotheby's simply writes the name "Giovanni Bellini."[Sotheby's. Old Master Paintings, 14th Oct. 1992.] These terms alert the purchaser that there are levels of the auctioneer's representations as to authenticity.

For older works, for works of significant value, or for works by artists such as Salvador Dali, whose names have been associated with fraudulent schemes, the purchaser may wish to consider consulting an independent investigator of authenticity. Experts verify authenticity of art work through one or several methods available. Lerner and Bresler identify three methods: by stylistic inquiry, in which the expert examines the work to determine if it is in the style of the artist; by documentation, in which the expert examines the documents to see if they indicate each stage of ownership; and by scientific verification, in which the expert uses various types of technology to determine that the work is by the artist. [Lerner & Brelser, *Art Law: The Guide for Collectors, Investors, Dealers and Artists* (1989), at 56-57.] DuBoff divides the various methods into objective (scientific) authentication and subjective (expert) authentication. [Leonard D. DuBoff, *The Deskbook of Art Law*, Ch. XI (2d ed. . . . 1993).][1]

In summary, auctions are an important method of acquiring art, but they are not without risk. Through careful attention to issues such as authenticity and title, purchasers can increase the likelihood that their acquisitions are genuine.

Foxley v. Sotheby's Inc.

893 F. Supp. 1224 (S.D.N.Y. 1995)*

SCHEINDLIN, Judge.

William Foxley ("Foxley") has filed a Proposed Second Amended Complaint ("SAC") alleging seventeen causes of action against Sotheby's, Inc.

---

1. *See also* DuBoff, King & Murray, *The Deskbook of Art Law, Booklet K—Authentication* (Oxford Univ. Press 2012).

* Footnotes and most citations omitted.

("Sotheby's"), a leading auction house for fine art. Foxley seeks damages in connection with his purchase at auction of a painting subsequently regarded as inauthentic. Defendant moves to dismiss all counts.

I. FACTS

Foxley brought this action approximately seven years after his December 3, 1987 purchase at auction of a painting entitled "Lydia Reclining on a Divan." . . . The piece was represented to be the work of Mary Cassatt. . . . Based on this representation, plaintiff bid and paid $ 632,500, which included a 10% auction house premium. . . .

Sotheby's auction catalog stated that the painting would be accompanied by a copy of a letter "discussing" the work from Adelyn Dohme Breeskin ("Breeskin letter"), who, at one time was considered an authority on Cassatt. . . . Auction Catalog, December 3, 1987. The catalog guaranteed the authenticity of the painting for five years from the date of the sale. . . . Foxley asserts that in 1992 he realized he did not have a copy of the Breeskin letter in his files. After notifying Sotheby's, Foxley received a letter stating that Sotheby's did not have the letter in its "immediate possession" at that time. . . . Foxley asserts that he did not receive a copy of the Breeskin letter until 1993, when he learned for the first time that Breeskin's comments were predicated upon her review of a color transparency of the painting rather than the original. . . . Plaintiff alleges he would not have bid on the painting if he had prior knowledge of this fact or the fact that, as Sotheby's allegedly knew, Breeskin had alerted the art world to massive Cassatt forgeries. . . .

Nearly six years after his purchase, in August 1993, plaintiff consigned the painting to Sotheby's for auction to be held on December 2, 1993. . . . Prior to the auction, on November 30, 1993, Sotheby's advised Foxley that the Cassatt Committee determined the painting might be inauthentic and advised that he remove it from the auction. . . . Foxley alleges this is when he first received actual notice of inauthenticity. . . . Foxley removed the painting from the auction block. However, he agreed to refrain from causing "damage" to the auction and Sotheby's by withdrawing the remainder of his consignment in consideration for defendant's alleged promise to refund Foxley's purchase price. . . . As a result of Sotheby's refusal to refund Foxley's purchase price, this action was commenced on September 28, 1994. . . .

II. DISCUSSION

A. Fraud

Foxley's first cause of action alleges fraud. Sotheby's seeks dismissal based on the failure to state a claim and the statute of limitations.

1. Failure to State a Claim

Under New York law, the elements of common law fraud are: (1) false representation(s) of (2) material fact with (3) intent to defraud thereby [scienter] and (4) reasonable reliance on the representation (5) causing damage to plaintiff. *Turtur v. Rothschild Registry Int., Inc.*, 26 F.3d 304, 310 (2d Cir. 1994). Plaintiff alleges several bases for his fraud claim.

a. Sotheby's Failure to Provide the Breeskin Letter

First, despite defendant's statement that the Breeskin letter would accompany the painting, Foxley claims "upon information and belief" that Sotheby's did not have a copy of the Breeskin letter at the time of the auction. . . . The complaint fails to provide a factual basis for this allegation. As an allegation of fraud, therefore, it is not plead with sufficient specificity. The Second Circuit has spoken clearly on this issue.

> Allegations may be based on information and belief when facts are peculiarly within the opposing party's knowledge. This exception to the general rule must not be mistaken for license to base claims of fraud on speculation and conclusory allegations. Where pleading is permitted on information and belief, a complaint must adduce specific facts supporting a strong inference of fraud or it will not satisfy even a relaxed pleading standard. *Wexner v. First Manhattan Co.*, 902 F.2d 169, 172 (2d Cir. 1990); *see also IUE AFL-CIO v. Herrmann*, 9 F.3d 1049, 1057 (2d Cir. 1993).

Further, even if Sotheby's did not have a copy of the letter at the time of the auction, fraud cannot be established on these facts. Rather, since fraud requires false representation(s) and intent, the claim could stand only if defendant knowingly misrepresented that the letter would accompany the painting. The critical allegation that is absent from the complaint is that Sotheby's falsely represented that it would deliver a copy of the Breeskin letter together with the painting.

b. Sotheby's Failure to Disclose That Breeskin Relied on a Photograph

Second, Foxley alleges that if Sotheby's did have a copy of the letter, it "intentionally hid" the fact that Breeskin had relied on a photograph to authenticate the painting. . . . This allegation cannot serve as a basis for fraud. Sotheby's made only one representation with respect to the Breeskin Letter in its Auction Catalog: "A copy of a letter from Adelyn Dohme Breeskin discussing the painting will accompany the lot." The letter does just that; it discusses the painting. Despite plaintiff's assertions to the contrary, the Auction Catalog never represents that the Breeskin letter authenticates the painting. More importantly, Foxley never alleges how Sotheby's made a false misrepresentation and therefore has failed to state a claim based on this set of facts.

Further, this allegation fails to establish that Foxley justifiably relied upon Sotheby's representation that the painting would be accompanied by a letter. Foxley bought the painting in 1987 but allegedly did not receive the Breeskin letter until 1993. . . . There was more than enough time during this period to either attempt to obtain the letter or to realize that Sotheby's had failed to comply with its representation in the Auction Catalog.

Only two factual scenarios are possible; plaintiff either received the letter or he did not. Had Foxley obtained the letter, he would have discovered that Breeskin's discussion of the painting had been based on a transparency. Therefore, he could not have justifiably relied upon the letter as authentication for the painting. Alternatively if, as Foxley alleges, he did not acquire the letter for close to six years following his purchase, he could not justifiably rely on a letter he had not read.

Finally, the failure to receive the Breeskin letter does not establish fraud because it is an alleged omission of fact to which Foxley had access. "The principle that access bars claims of justifiable reliance is well settled. . . ." *Congress Fin. Corp. v. John Morrell & Co.*, 790 F. Supp. 459, 470-71 (S.D.N.Y. 1992). The New York Court of Appeals established in *Danann Realty Corp. v. Harris*, 5 N.Y.2d 317, 320, 184 N.Y.S.2d 599, 157 N.E.2d 597 (1959) that where: facts represented are not matters peculiarly within the party's knowledge, and the other party has the means available to him of knowing, by the exercise of ordinary intelligence . . . he must make use of those means, or he will not be heard to complain that he was induced to enter into the transaction by misrepresentation. *See also Grumman Allied Indus., Inc. v. Rohr Indus., Inc.*, 748 F.2d 729, 737 (2d Cir. 1984) ("where sophisticated businessmen engaged in major transactions enjoy access to critical information but fail to take advantage of the access, New York courts are particularly disinclined to entertain claims of justifiable reliance"); *Aaron Ferer & Sons, Ltd. v. Chase Manhattan Bank, N.A.*, 731 F.2d 112, 123 (2d Cir. 1984).

While plaintiff does allege lack of sophistication and familiarity with respect to American Impressionism, Cassatt's specialty, Foxley was a sophisticated purchaser of art at auction. He certainly knew how to demand a letter described in an auction catalog, something he successfully accomplished in 1993. . . .

In *Aaron*, justifiable reliance was rejected because "all of the information [claimed to be concealed] was either public record, not pursued by plaintiffs or disclosed [by defendant], at least in part." *Id.* at 123. In Foxley's case, a reasonable response should have led him either to obtain the letter (and thereby inform himself that Breeskin relied upon a photograph) or to deduce that Sotheby's conduct was suspect and take appropriate action. Therefore, the fact that Breeskin relied on a color transparency was readily available, in the public domain, and plaintiff did not reasonably rely on or ascertain the existence and content of the letter. This allegation cannot serve as the basis for a fraud cause of action.

c. Sotheby's Failure to Disclose Breeskin's Unreliability

Foxley's third set of factual allegations asserts that Sotheby's "failed to disclose that in the late 1970's it was common knowledge in the French/American Impressionist art community to which Sotheby's belongs, that Breeskin's authentications had become suspect, 'unreliable' and 'doubtful.'" . . . For the reasons set forth above regarding inability to base fraud on an omission when the undisclosed information is in the public domain, this allegation fails as a basis for Foxley's fraud claim. . . .

d. False Provenance

Foxley's fourth factual allegation is based on the provenance of the painting. Foxley claims Sotheby's falsely listed the "last owner of record or consignor [as]'Private Collection, Paris'" when in fact the most recent owner, the consignor, was a Mr. Michael Altman. . . . Foxley alleges that it is widely known that Mr. Altman is not a trustworthy dealer, and that Sotheby's knowingly omitted his name to avoid placing a cloud over the painting. Plaintiff claims he relied on defendant's misrepresentation as he would not have purchased the painting if he had known of Altman's place in the provenance.

In its reply brief, Sotheby's sought to convert its Motion to Dismiss into a Motion for Partial Summary Judgment on the provenance issue. The Court granted the request to convert, and plaintiff received notice to this effect. Foxley argues that summary judgment should be denied because of "numerous factual issues" and failure to comply with Local Rule 3(g) and Chambers Rule 2(f).

Nonetheless, because defendant is clearly entitled to summary judgment on this issue, there has been no prejudice to Foxley. As is manifest from the affidavits and from oral argument, Foxley's allegation regarding the way Sotheby's lists ownership in its auction catalog is simply wrong. Foxley incorrectly assumed the line of ownership was listed in reverse chronological order. . . . By referring the Court to other provenance listings, Sotheby's irrefutably established that provenance is always listed in chronological order. . . .

Moreover, Foxley knew that an auction house — and in particular, Sotheby's — frequently does not disclose the name of the consignor of a painting. In fact, Foxley, himself, had consigned paintings to Sotheby's and had his name withheld. . . . Foxley's argument that one's name should be disclosed when a consignor also happens to be an art dealer is not persuasive as no authority exists for that novel proposition.

Alternatively, even if provenance were misrepresented, a fraud claim is precluded because the auction catalog stated that Sotheby's made no representations or warranties of provenance:

> The authenticity of the Authorship of property listed in the catalogue is guaranteed as stated in the Terms of Guarantee . . . neither we nor the Consignor make any warranties or representations of the correctness of the catalogue or other description [including] . . . provenance . . . and no statement anywhere, whether written or oral, shall be deemed such a warranty or representation. . . .

Accordingly, Foxley fails to state a claim for fraud. . . .

2. Statute of Limitations

A fraud claim is timely filed six years from its commission, two years from plaintiff's discovery or two years from when plaintiff could have discovered the fraud "with reasonable diligence. . . ." N.Y. Civ. Prac. L. & R. §§ 213(8), 203(g) (McKinney 1994). Neither party disputes that six years from the commission of the alleged fraud had lapsed when plaintiff filed his first complaint. Whether or not the claim is timely, therefore, turns solely on when plaintiff discovered or should have discovered the alleged fraud. Further, "the test as to when fraud should with reasonable diligence have been discovered is an objective one." *Armstrong v. McAlpin*, 699 F.2d 79, 88 (2d Cir. 1983). Once plaintiff has notice of the fraud, "[he] is charged with whatever knowledge an inquiry would have revealed." *Stone v. Williams*, 970 F.2d 1043 (2d Cir. 1992).

The Second Circuit recently held that the time at which plaintiff was placed on inquiry notice could be appropriately determined as a matter of law:

> Where, as here, the facts needed for determination of when a reasonable investor of ordinary intelligence would have been aware of the existence of fraud can be gleaned from the complaint and papers such as the prospectuses and disclosure forms that are integral to the complaint, resolution of the issue on a motion to dismiss is appropriate. *Dodds v. Cigna Securities, Inc.*, 12 F.3d 346, 352 n.3 (2d Cir. 1993), *cert. denied*, 128 L. Ed. 2d 74, 114 S. Ct. 1401 (1994).

As in *Dodds, supra*, "the facts needed for determination of when a reasonable [buyer] of ordinary intelligence would have been aware of the existence of fraud can be gleaned from the complaint." *Id.* at 352. Here, plaintiff failed to act upon his alleged failure to receive the Breeskin letter. Regardless of what Sotheby's knew, plaintiff failed to obtain the letter from Sotheby's or to learn the widely known fact that Breeskin's reliability for authentication of Cassatts was in question. Foxley's fraud claim is barred by the statute of limitations. . . .

G. Breach of Separate/Modified Contract

As noted above, after Foxley consigned the Cassatt to Sotheby's for the 1993 auction, he was notified of questions as to the painting's authenticity. Sotheby's advised him to withdraw the piece from the auction block. Foxley alleges that he, in turn, stated that he would withdraw all his works from the auction which would effectively ruin the event and harm the reputation and goodwill of Sotheby's. . . . Foxley alleges that Sotheby's, in consideration for his refraining from withdrawing his goods, promised to "make good on the painting [and hold him] harmless." . . . Foxley argues that Sotheby's thereby created a new or modified contract, which it subsequently breached.

Sotheby's first contends that the allegations cannot form the basis for a separate contract because the alleged conversation relates to issues explicitly raised in the Consignment Agreement. The Court disagrees. According to the complaint, an independent, express oral agreement with consideration was reached between the parties. . . . It was capable of being performed within one year as required by the Statute of Frauds. N.Y. Gen. Oblig. § 5-701(a)(1) (McKinney 1989). Further, if the parties did enter into a new contract, plaintiff has sufficiently alleged defendant's breach of that agreement.

Sotheby's also contends that ¶15 of the Consignment Agreement expressly prohibits oral modifications. Plaintiff responds that the modification became enforceable because it was partially performed by his leaving his other paintings with Sotheby's after being advised to withdraw the Cassatt. Defendant argues that the doctrine of partial performance is not available to a party unless the performance is "unequivocally referable" to the modification. The doctrine is available to plaintiff only if:

> [his] actions can be characterized as "unequivocally referable" to the agreement alleged. It is not sufficient . . . that the oral agreement gives significance to plaintiff's actions. Rather, the actions alone must be "unintelligible or at least extraordinary," explainable only with reference to the oral agreement. Plaintiff's actions, viewed alone, are not "unequivocally referable" to an agreement to convey a one-half interest in defendant's corporation. While the agreement alleged provides a possible motivation for plaintiff's actions, the performance is equivocal, for it is as reasonably explained by the possibility of other expectations. . . . *Anostario v. Vicinanzo*, 59 N.Y.2d 662, 663, 463 N.Y.S.2d 409, 410, 450 N.E.2d 215 (1983); *see also Towers Charter & Marine Corp. v. Cadillac Ins. Co.*, 894 F.2d 516, 522 (2d Cir. 1990).

Sotheby's argues that Foxley partially performed not simply so that Sotheby's would fulfill its alleged agreement to "make good" on the Cassatt, but to avoid incurring withdrawal fees pursuant to paragraph 8 of the Consignment Agreement. Foxley denied this claim. . . . Construing the allegations of the complaint as true, as required, Foxley's claim of breach of an oral contract modification and/or a separate contract survives defendant's motion to dismiss.

H. Remaining Claims Withdrawn or Dismissed at Oral Argument

At oral argument, plaintiff withdrew his claims for (i) "damage to business representation and emotional distress," (ii) promissory estoppel, (iii) deceptive trade practices, and (iv) professional malpractice. Also at oral argument, the Court dismissed five other claims. . . .

The four remaining claims were premised upon subsequent appraisals of the painting. Plaintiff alleged that Sotheby's was negligent in performing two appraisals in 1989 and 1993, and also breached its contract with Foxley. Defendant correctly argued that appraisals are for the purpose of estimating fair market value and, unlike authentications, do not purport to confirm provenance or authorship. Clearly demonstrating this fact, the appraisal agreements set forth a disclaimer: "our appraisal . . . is not to be deemed a representation or warranty with respect to the authenticity of authorship . . . genuineness . . . [or] attribution." Appraisal Agreements at p. 1.

The appraisal agreements also include an exculpatory clause, which releases Sotheby's from liability stemming from appraisals. It states: "in consideration of our furnishing the appraisal, you hereby release Sotheby's . . . from any liability or damages whatsoever arising out of or related to the appraisal . . . unless . . . due to Sotheby's gross negligence or bad faith."

Generally, exculpatory clauses which are explicit in a contract foreclose damage claims alleging reliance on the subject matter disclaimed. *See, e.g., Manufacturer's Hanover Trust Co. v. Yanakas*, 7 F.3d 310 (2d Cir. 1993). . . .

Foxley, however, alleges that the 1993 appraisal suggests bad faith. . . .

The Court has reconsidered its oral ruling. Sufficient facts exist to support the two claims that the 1989 and 1993 appraisals of the painting were negligently performed. Defendant twice re-appraised the Cassatt at $650,000 when, in fact, it might have been worthless. . . . Accordingly, the claims for negligent appraisal survive the motion to dismiss. . . .

III. CONCLUSION

For the foregoing reasons, all causes of action are dismissed except the negligent appraisal claims and those relating to the 1993 oral contract. Attorneys' fees are denied.

Notes

1. Do you think that consumers would be less likely to encounter the level of fraud with which Foxley charged Sotheby's using an online auction service? In his 2003 article, *Stopping Another Phantom Menace: Using the Commerce Clause to Force States to Police Online Auction Shill Bidding or Face Congressional Mandates*, Shawn Haynes argues that

   > EBay has been in business for approximately eight years, however during that time, eBay has established only minimal, reactive controls to seriously deter users who shill bid" on their own goods. . . . Shill bidding is accomplished by (a) a single user with many e-mail accounts who uses those accounts to register to bid under numerous identities, or (b) a consortium of users who agree on a plan to bid-up/feel-out the maximum price that legitimate and honest users are willing to pay. . . . Other types of online fraud, such as the purported sale of fake or nonexistent goods, or goods that are never delivered, are probably more easily regulated by the free market than shill bidding. . . . The difficulty with regulating and preventing shill bidding derives from the fact that no unique personal identification system exists (or is trusted, for privacy reasons, by consumers).

   Shawn Haynes, *Stopping Another Phantom Menace: Using the Commerce Clause to Force States to Police Online Auction Shill Bidding or Face Congressional Mandates*, 5 U. Pa. J. Const. L. 763, 764 (2003) (footnote omitted).

2. In *Art Finance Partners, LLC v. Christie's Inc.*, 58 A.D.3d 469, 870 N.Y.S.2d 331 (N.Y. Sup. Ct., App. Div. 2009), it was the auction house that charged the bidder committed fraud. This case arises from an alleged attempt to manipulate an art auction at Christie's by the Rose Entities and the art dealers at Berry-Hill Galleries, the owner of the

artwork. Andrew Rose consigned the artwork to Christie's for auction, claiming he was acting for an unnamed divorcing couple, and then bid on the artwork himself. Christie's standard consignment agreement prohibits a consignor (both principal and agent) from bidding on the consigned property at the auction. When Christie's discovered that Coram Capital LLC, a special-purpose entity formed by the owners of Berry-Hill, was the true owner of the artwork and that Berry-Hill knew in advance of the auction that Andrew Rose had misrepresented the ownership, Christie's canceled all sales of the artwork, offered rescission to purchasers of artwork from the consignment that also had been bid on by Andrew Rose or Berry-Hill, and withheld proceeds to mitigate its anticipated damages. Eventually, Berry-Hill settled with Christie's, permitting the auction house to retain claims for $3 million for the canceled sale of a particular painting and for $1 million for actual damages related to the auction.

B. How Auctions Work

At live auctions, property for sale is presented to auctioneers for bidding. Not all bidders need be physically present at the site of the auction. Major auction houses accept written order bids and telephone bids as discussed herein. Bids are accepted and the property is sold for the offer most favorable to the seller. At the same time, all auctions involve competition among individuals trying to acquire specified items for the best price possible, and many different methods have been employed to inspire this competition. This section discusses some of the more popular forms of auction, and reviews several different techniques of bidding.

In the online auction world, someone registers to become a member of a website. The individual accepts the company's user agreement and privacy policy. On eBay.com, for example, sellers agree not to violate any laws, fail to deliver items purchased, not manipulate the price, not post false and misleading information, and so forth. The eBay user agreement is available at *http://pages.ebay.com/help/policies/user-agreement.html.*

1. Types of Auctions

Although auctioning techniques vary, three types appear to be most common. Named for the countries that popularized them, they are the ascending or progressive bid (English method), the descending bid (Dutch method), and the simultaneous bid (Japanese method).

According to the English method, the auctioneer first solicits a bid. If no prospective buyer offers a bid in response, the auctioneer will suggest an opening bid that is lowered until adopted. Once a bid is made, the auctioneer may either allow free bidding or guide the bidding by calling out the next acceptable bid. Either way, the bidding is paced by the auctioneer recognizing a bidder at each plateau and by announcing that bid, thus encouraging or exciting higher bidding.

The Dutch auction has its derivation in the traditional method used for the sale of flowers in the Netherlands. The auctioneer starts the auction at a high price, lowering that figure at graduated intervals until a bidder accepts the bid. Unlike the English method, the first and only bidder, as opposed to the last bidder, successfully captures the item. The competition must, therefore, accurately be evaluated, as a single utterance precludes further bidding. The auction rules may require that bids be entered only at specific time intervals. To avoid dispute, time-stamping clocks are sometimes used to record the exact moment the first bid is entered. Today, merchants occasionally use this technique as a sales device.

According to the Japanese system of bidding, the traditional auction is customarily a closed, invitation-only affair run by dealers, for dealers. A Japanese law that requires anyone holding a public auction to submit a list of potential bidders and items to be auctioned to local authorities at least ten days before the auction deters impulse attendance and, consequently, impulse buying. Items that go on the block are not consigned through an independent, privately owned company, such as Sotheby's or Christie's, but through the Tokyo Art Dealers Association. Like many other areas of Japanese business, dealers band together in order to control the art market. As a result, dealers' rings are common at closed auctions.[4]

All bids are entered at the same time either by use of hand signs designating a specified amount or by sealed bids handed to the auctioneer. It is the auctioneer's duty to determine who offered the highest bid during the short time period permitted for bid entry. The seller may either accept the highest bid or withdraw the piece while stating the reasons for doing so. Some simultaneous auctions are closer to the English method, in that bids are called out. Unlike the other two auction methods, however, neither catalogs nor prices are published and pieces are rarely displayed before sale. Instead, the owner of each piece displays and describes it. While many Western auction houses charge both the seller and the buyer a premium or commission, in Japan only the seller pays a premium.[5]

Although Japan's old-line dealers are well established and, generally, united, Western-style auctions are more frequently being conducted in Japan for collectors as well as dealers.[6]

---

4. *Buying by the Go*, ARTnews, Oct. 1986, at 19.

5. *Id.*

6. *See, e.g.*, Malone, *A Japanese Buying Spree*, Newsweek, May 28, 1990, at 75; Miller, *Japan Becomes the Land of the Falling Gavel*, Bus. Week, Feb. 25, 1991, at 68; Nunn, *Land of the Rising Bids*, Autoweek, May 20, 1991, at 20.

At online auctions, buyers can submit a bid at any time during the auction period. If the buyer wins an auction on eBay.com, the person becomes obligated to complete the transaction.

2. Bidding Methods

The means of entering bids at an auction also vary. The major auction houses require bidders to register in advance and bidders unfamiliar to the house may be required to provide some financial reference.[7] The oral bid is used most frequently, although a raised card or paddle is a common method to communicate a bid. These procedures openly reveal the potential buyer. A number of techniques can be used to conceal this information and prevent exposing the bidder. For instance, a bidder may secretly convey his offer by a writing, a handshake, or a whisper. The auctioneer then compares bids without disclosing them.

Secret signals between the house and established collectors and dealers have always been used at auctions, but are becoming more popular for average buyers. A prearranged signal may be used to notify an auctioneer that the individual is in the bidding until another prearranged signal indicates withdrawal. Typical signals include removing a handkerchief from the pocket, taking off or putting on glasses, fingering a tie, and placing an umbrella on the floor.

John Marion, the former chairman and chief auctioneer of Sotheby's North America, relates the elaborate bidding instructions given to a London auctioneer by avid collector Norton Simon. "When Mr. Simon is sitting down, he is bidding. If he bids openly, he is also bidding. If he sits down again, he is not bidding unless he raises his finger. Having raised his finger, he is bidding until he stands up again."[8]

Auction house officials agree that concealed bidding takes place frequently. As a consequence, the name of the successful bidder may not be called out when the gavel falls. In addition, there is usually no announcement if a lot does not sell. In either case, the auctioneer may or may not say "sold," may or may not name a buyer, and may use a real name or a pseudonym. Auction goers may find it nearly impossible to discover the results of bidding. Sometimes experienced collectors and dealers are uncertain, even after the gavel falls, whether a work has been sold.[9] Today, most auction houses publish after-auction reports stating the hammer price for the works sold in the auction, and identifying those works which either did not meet the reserve or were withdrawn for other reasons.

---

7. Reif, *How to Bid at an Auction*, N.Y. Times, July 26, 1985, §C, at 23.

8. Gardner, *Auction Signals: How to Bid Like an Insider*, ARTnews, Feb. 1987, at 101, 103.

9. For a discussion of the difficulty in knowing whether a work has been sold, *see* Reif, *Auctions*, N.Y. Times, July 12, 1985, §C, at 22 [hereinafter Reif].

The sealed-bid device has several undesirable features. It requires more time than other bidding techniques, as the submission period must be long enough to afford all interested parties the opportunity to participate. One variation frequently used to overcome this problem is to open bid on several lots simultaneously. When more than one item is offered concurrently to hasten the process, however, potential buyers may be precluded from bidding on all items. Thus, a bidder will not know whether he or she has been successful on any or all of the items until the bidding is closed and the results are announced. If a buyer has bid on several lots simultaneously, it may be that he or she has acquired more merchandise than desired or can be afforded.

Another disadvantage is that each bidder has only one chance to bid. In the open English auction, a bidder will learn the valuations of other bidders. In a sealed-bid auction, the bidder can only guess what competitors will submit. Once committed, there is no ability to negotiate or change a bid. One variation avoids this situation by permitting submission of several bids on each item. The individual's lowest bid that exceeds all competitors' bids is accepted.

An auctioneer may simultaneously use both disclosed and sealed bidding. For example, order bids may be submitted in advance by those who cannot attend the auction. The auctioneer is thus authorized to bid up to the designated price. In addition to the sealed absentee bids, auction houses may accommodate those unable to attend by using telephone hookups to allow participation in the bidding. In *Parke Bernet v. Franklyn*,[10] an auction house allowed a bidder in California to participate by long-distance telephone in a New York auction. This subjected the bidder to New York court jurisdiction.

Both auctioneers and auction participants have been known to engage in questionable practices. Unethical auctioneers may accept "phantom bids" in order to drive up prices. This practice, known as "chandelier bidding" because the auctioneers had traditionally pointed to the chandelier when calling out a bid, is unlawful but often hard to detect. For this reason, experienced bidders like to sit in a corner in the last possible row of the auction house so that they can see the competition.

Dealers may band together and form a "ring" agreeing not to bid against each other on a desired piece. This practice is also unlawful, though it frequently occurs. One of the dealers is customarily appointed to bid for the group. Once the piece is "knocked down" to the ring's representative, the real "knock out" auction occurs in a private location among the ring members. All amounts bid at the "knock out" auction in excess of the price the ring paid for the work in question are equally divided among the members, and if the work sells to a ring member for less, each member is assessed enough to make up the loss. This so-called "ring" and "knock out" has been expressly declared illegal in England and likely violates the anti-trust laws in the United States as well.

---

10. *Parke Bernet v. Franklyn*, 26 N.Y.2d 13, 308 N.Y.S.2d 337, 256 N.E.2d 506 (1970).

William J. Jenack Estate Appraisers & Auctioneers, Inc. v. Rabizadeh

22 N.Y.3d 470, 5 N.E. 3d 976, 982 N.Y.S.2d 813 (2013)*

RIVERA, J.:

William J. Jenack Estate Appraisers and Auctioneers, Inc. ("Jenack") appeals from an order of the Appellate Division granting defendant Albert Rabizadeh ("Rabizadeh") summary judgment, and dismissing the complaint in its entirety. We reverse because the Appellate Division erred in concluding that Jenack failed to comply with the statutory requirement of a writing in support of its breach of contract claim.

Jenack sells fine art and antiques at public auctions. The underlying dispute arises from Jenack's claim for damages resulting from Rabizadeh's failure to pay for an item offered at a Jenack public auction. The central issue in contention between the parties is whether the sale of the auction item to Rabizadeh is memorialized in a writing that satisfies the Statute of Frauds.

As is common practice in public auction houses, Jenack permits bidding online and by telephone, or "absentee bidding," in addition to traditional in-person bidding, for items numbered and described on its website and in its published auction catalogue. At all times relevant to this appeal, Jenack's website set forth information about the auction process, as well as terms of sales for absentee bidders. The website stated, under the subsection titled "Bid Forms," that "If you are unable to attend the auction in person, and wish to place absentee bids we will be happy to bid on your behalf, according to the Terms & Conditions of sale." It further stated that "Your credit card guarantees the good will of your bidding!" It informed any and all prospective bidders of payment obligation by stating "if your bid is successful you are legally responsible to make payment according to the terms set forth here."

To facilitate absentee bidding, and in order for Jenack to serve on behalf of an absentee customer, Jenack required the prospective bidder to submit in advance an "Absentee Bid Form" posted on the website. At the top of the form, Jenack notified bidders that payment was due within five days of a successful bid. Directly above the signature line, the form included a pre-printed notification that "Bids will not be executed without signature. Signature denotes that you agree to our terms."

Several days prior to a September 21, 2008 auction, Rabizadeh submitted a signed, absentee bidder form wherein he provided, as required by Jenack, his name, e-mail address, telephone numbers, fax number, address, credit card number, and a list of items that Rabizadeh intended to bid on by telephone. Rabizadeh's list included the item at issue in this case, designated by Jenack as "Item 193," and described in the online and printed catalogue as a "Fine Russian silver/enamel covered box with gilt interior, signed I.P. Khlebnikov, 19th Century Height 1 1/2 top 1/2 x $3\frac{5}{8}$ (Estimate \$4000-\$6000)." Upon receipt

---

* Footnotes omitted.

of this form, Jenack assigned bidder number 305 to Rabizadeh, and included this number on the top of the form.

At the September auction, Rabizadeh submitted a $400,000 bid on item 193, and successfully outbid a competing bidder. At the close of the bidding for this item, the chief clerk recorded the winning bid on Jenack's "clerking sheet." This clerking sheet sets forth in a preprinted tabulated column format, a running list of the items presented at the public auction, with a separate line for each item that includes the item's lot number, catalogue description, and the number assigned by Jenack to the consignor. At the top of the clerking sheet Jenack's name and title are set forth as "William J. Jenack Appraisers/ Auctioneers." On the line for item 193, the chief clerk filled in Rabizadeh's previously assigned bidding number to reflect him as the buyer, and the amount of his winning bid, $400,00.

Shortly after the auction, Jenack, who was in possession of item 193, sent Rabizadeh an invoice for $497,398, which reflected the bidding price, the 15% "buyer's premium" and applicable taxes. When Rabizadeh failed to pay, Jenack commenced this action for breach of contract, seeking damages, including the bid price and buyer's premium.

Rabizadeh moved for summary judgment claiming, as relevant here, that he was not liable for any monies to Jenack related to the auction because there was no writing memorializing any contract between Jenack and Rabizadeh, as required by the Statute of Frauds. Jenack responded by cross moving for summary judgment, asserting that the clerking sheet and related bidding documents complied with General Obligations Law ("GOL") § 5-701(a)(6). Supreme Court denied Rabizadeh's motion and granted Jenack summary judgment on liability. After a non-jury trial on the issue of damages, Supreme Court entered judgment in favor of Jenack for the principal sum of $402,398.

Rabizadeh appealed. The Appellate Division, Second Department, reversed, concluding that Rabizadeh demonstrated prima facie that Jenack failed to comply with GOL § 5-701(a)(6) because the clerking sheet did not include "the name of the person on whose account the sale is made," as required by the statute, and Jenack failed to raise a triable issue as to this matter (99 A.D.3d 271, 278). This Court granted Jenack leave to appeal.

On appeal, Jenack contends that there was a bid agreement between the parties, pursuant to that agreement Rabizadeh submitted the winning bid at the September auction and that the documents related to Rabizadeh's $400,000 bid satisfy the Statute of Frauds. Jenack and Rabizadeh dispute whether the clerking sheet constitutes the writing required by GOL § 5-701(a)(6), and whether any other document commemorates an agreement between them to purchase item 193.

This appeal comes to us in the posture of a summary judgment motion, thus we must consider whether Rabizadeh has met his burden to establish "a prima facie showing of entitlement to judgment as a matter of law, tendering sufficient evidence to demonstrate the absence of any material issues of fact" (*Alvarez v Prospect Hosp.*, 68 N.Y.2d 320, 324 [1986]; *see also* CPLR 3212[b]). This burden is a heavy one and on a motion for summary judgment, facts must be viewed in the light most favorable to the non-moving party (*Vega v. Restani Const. Corp.*, 18 N.Y.3d 499, 503 [2012][citations and quotations omitted). Where the moving party fails to meet this burden, summary judgment cannot be granted, and the non-moving party bears no burden to otherwise persuade the Court against summary judgment (*id.*). Indeed, the moving party's failure to make a prima facie showing of entitlement to summary judgment requires a denial of the motion, regardless of the sufficiency of the opposing papers (*id.* [citations and quotations omitted]).

To successfully establish his entitlement to summary judgment based on his claim that there is no writing reflecting the sale agreement for item 193, Rabizadeh must show that the record is bereft of documentation establishing such agreement, as provided for under the law. Based on the record in this case, we conclude that Rabizadeh has not met his burden because there exists sufficient documentation of a statutorily adequate writing.

The Statute of Frauds is designed to protect the parties and preserve the integrity of contractual agreements. It is meant "to guard against the peril of perjury; to prevent the enforcement of unfounded fraudulent claims" (*Morris Cohon & Co. v. Russell*, 23 N.Y.2d 569, 574 [1969]). The Statute "decrease[s] uncertainties, litigation, and opportunities for fraud and perjury", and primarily "discourage[s] false claims" (73 Am. Jur. 2d Statute of Frauds § 403). "In short, the purpose of the Statute of Frauds is simply to prevent a party from being held responsible, by oral, and perhaps false, testimony, for a contract that the party claims never to have made" (*id.*).

Only certain types of agreements must comply with the Statue of Frauds. In general, a contract for the sale of goods at a price of $500 or more must comply with the signed writing requirement of UCC 2-201(1). As relevant to this case, the GOL sets forth a special provision for the auctioning of such goods:

> § 5-701. Agreements required to be in writing
>   a. Every agreement, promise or undertaking is void, unless it or some note or memorandum thereof be in writing, and subscribed by the party to be charged therewith, or by his lawful agent. . . .
>   6. Notwithstanding section 2-201 of the uniform commercial code, if the goods be sold at public auction, and the auctioneer at the time of the sale, enters in a sale book, a memorandum specifying the nature and price of the property sold, the terms of the sale, the name of the purchaser, and the name of the person on whose account the sale was made, such memorandum is equivalent in effect to a note of the contract or sale, subscribed by the party to be charged therewith.

Thus, in the case of a public auction, a bid may satisfy the Statute of Frauds where there exists an appropriate writing "signed by the party against whom enforcement is sought to be charged" (*see* UCC 2-201), or a memorandum in satisfaction of GOL § 5-701(a)(6). Here, the dispute is centered on whether there is compliance with the latter.

It is well established that the statutorily required writing need not be contained in one single document, but rather may be furnished by "piecing together other, related writings" (*Henry L. Fox Co., Inc. v. William Kaufman Org., Ltd.*, 74 N.Y.2d 136, 140 [1989][citing *Crabtree v. Elizabeth Arden Sales Corp.*, 305 N.Y. 48 [1953]). Therefore, in determining whether there is compliance with the GOL § 5-701(a)(6), a court may look to documents relevant to the bidding and the auction.

The Appellate Division properly concluded that the clerking sheet, on its face and in isolation, does not satisfy the requirements of GOL § 5-701(a)(6), because this provision requires the disclosure of the name of the buyer and the name of "the person on whose account the sale was made." We are unpersuaded by Jenack's arguments that this requirement can be satisfied by Jenack's insertion of numbers in place of those names.

We construe the terms of a statute that are clear and unambiguous, "so as to give effect to the plain meaning of the words used" (*Matter of Auerbach v. Board of Educ.*, 86 N.Y.2d 198, 204 [1995] [citations and quotations omitted]; accord McKinney's Cons. Laws of N.Y., Book 1, Statutes § 94, at 194 [1971 ed.]). The GOL states clearly that the memorandum must include names. It makes no provision for an alternative to a name, including some other mode of identification designed by an auction house to facilitate the auction process, such as, in this case, numeric identifiers. To allow for numbers, rather than names, would also undermine the purpose of the Statute by increasing the possibility of fraud. Thus, the numbers assigned by Jenack to represent the buyer and seller/consignor on the clerking sheet do not satisfy GOL § 5-701(a)(6).

Our analysis does not end with our conclusion that the clerking sheet in this case by itself fails to satisfy the requirements of the GOL because we must consider whether there are "related writings" that supply the required names, and which may be read, along with the clerking sheet, to provide the information necessary to constitute a memorandum in accordance with GOL § 5-701(a)(6). We agree with the Appellate Division that the absentee bidder form, along with the clerking sheet, provide the necessary information to establish the name of Rabizadeh as the buyer. This conclusion is inescapable given that each of the documents contained information pertaining to the terms of the sale as required by the Statute. Both contain the item number, the bidder number, the auctioneer, and a detailed description of the item.

In addition to the buyer's name, the GOL requires disclosure of "the name of the person on whose account the sale was made." Jenack urges a reading of the statute that would not require disclosure of the seller's identity, and that would permit it to continue to honor a seller's request to remain anonymous throughout the consignment and bidding process. Jenack and amici argue that the auction business is important to New York State and that it is a time honored and necessary custom and practice of auction houses to maintain the confidentiality of the seller. It is their contention that a requirement that the seller's identify be divulged would undermine the industry. However, the GOL does not reference the "seller," making it clear that the seller's name need not be provided in order to satisfy the requirement of "the name of thperson on whose account the sale was made."

More than a century and a half ago, the New York Supreme Court of Judicature, then the highest common law court in the State, held "[t]he entry in the sale book of the name of an agent, factor, consignee, or of any person having legal authority to sell, is a compliance with the requirement of the statute that 'the name of the person on whose account the sale is made' shall be entered" (*Hicks v. Whitmore*, 12 Wend 548 [Sup Ct 1834]). It is well settled that an auctioneer serves as a consignor's agent (*City of New York v. Union News Co.*, 169 A.D. 278, 281 [1st Dept 1915] affd, 222 N.Y. 263 [1918]; *see also Christallina S.A. v. Christie, Manson & Woods Intern., Inc.*, 117 A.D.2d 284, 292 [1st Dept 1986]; *Mentz v. Newwitter*, 122 N.Y. 491, 494 [1890]; 10 Williston on Contracts § 29:40 [4th ed.]). Obviously, requiring the name of an agent in cases where the seller wishes to remain anonymous in no way undermines the industry practice, because the seller need not be divulged without the seller's consent.

Here, the clerking sheet lists Jenack as the auctioneer, and as such it served as the agent of the seller. The clerking sheet, therefore, provides "the name of the person on whose account the sale was made" and satisfies GOL § 5-701(a)(6) [fn.2]. Nothing in the record suggests that Jenack served as anything other than the seller's agent. Thus, Jenack established an enforceable agreement and Supreme Court properly granted summary judgment on liability.

It bears repeating in such a case as this that:

> The Statute of Frauds was not enacted to afford persons a means of evading just obligations; nor was it intended to supply a cloak of immunity to hedging litigants lacking integrity; nor was it adopted to enable defendants to interpose the Statute as a bar to a contract fairly, and admittedly, made

(*Morris Cohon & Co. v. Russell*, 23 N.Y.2d 569, 574 [1969][citing 4 Williston on Contracts § 567A [3d ed.]). Using the Statute of Frauds as a "means of evading" a "just obligation" is precisely what Rabizadeh attempts to do here, but the law and the facts foreclose him from doing so. Rabizadeh took affirmative steps to participate in Jenack's auction, including executing an absentee bidder form with the required personal information. He then successfully won the bidding for item 193, closing out other interested bidders, with his $400,000 bid. He cannot seek to avoid the consequences of his actions by ignoring the existence of a documentary trail leading to him.

Accordingly, the order of the Appellate Division should be reversed, with costs, and judgment of the Supreme Court reinstated.

Notes and Questions

1. Besides telephone bidding, what are some other forms of undisclosed bidding? The secretive handshake, said to have originated in China and used in Pakistan, is far more mysterious. Pressing a certain number of fingers in the auctioneer's hand indicates a bid. Multiple squeezing indicates progressively higher bids. The bidder may bluff by appearing to bid,

only to cancel immediately by scratching the auctioneer's palm with a particular finger. This technique is obviously time-consuming and lends itself to manipulation and arbitrariness on the part of the auctioneer.

2. In *Robert C. Eldred Co. v. Acevedo,* 21 Mass. App. Ct. 945, 486 N.E.2d 777 (1985), Acevedo's telephone bids on two pictures he had seen advertised in a magazine were the highest and successful bids at auction. He properly submitted a check for payment due no later than 30 days after the sale, but stopped payment when he learned the pictures were being held pending bank clearance of his check. Upon receiving Acevedo's complaint of the delayed shipment, Eldred shipped the pictures without waiting for the check to clear, but Acevedo refused to accept delivery. Acevedo asserted a defense that the withholding of shipment was a breach of contract by Eldred. He further claimed that he had detrimentally relied on misrepresentations by Eldred in a phone conversation concerning the value and condition of the pictures. However, the court held that the auctioneer's alleged statements of the expected price of the pictures at auction could not be fairly taken as a distinct representation of value, particularly when Acevedo refused delivery without even taking a look at the pictures. The court affirmed judgment for the auctioneer, stating, "Having been hoist by his own egoism or vanity, Acevedo out of desperation presents a defense which does not deserve to succeed."

3. For a popular look at the auction business, consider reading Nicholas Sparks' *The Longest Ride,* or watching the film by the same name.

3. The Reserve Concept and Withdrawing Goods or Bids

One factor complicating the identification issue is whether the items being auctioned have a reserve price. In other words, is there a minimum price set by the seller and the auction house below which the item will not be sold? If there is no reserve price, will any bid by a potential buyer be an acceptance of the auctioneer's offer of the goods? At an auction with reserve, however, this theory is no longer applicable, for an auctioneer cannot affect a contract of sale if the highest bid falls below the reserve price. According to the Uniform Commercial Code § 2-328(3), auctions are "with reserve" unless the goods are in explicit terms put up without reserve.[11]

New York City regulations, City of New York Admin. Code. Title 6, ch. 2, subch. M, § 2-122 (f), require auction houses to identify those items in their auction catalogs that have a reserve, although they are not required to state the amount of the reserve:

(1) If the consignor has fixed a price below which an article will not be sold, the "reserve price," the fact that the lot is being sold subject to reserve must be

---

11. *See also* Leonard DuBoff, *Going, Going, Gone,* 26 Clev. St. L. Rev. 499 (1977).

disclosed in connection with the description of any lot so affected in the catalogue or any other printed material published or distributed in relation to the sale. The existence of a reserve price may be denoted by a symbol or letter which will refer the reader to an explanation of reserve price. . . .

(2) When a lot is not subject to a reserve price, the auctioneer shall not indicate in any manner that the lot is subject to a reserve price.

During auctions, the house typically bids on the object until the reserve has been met, but drops out of the competition at that point. If the bidding does not reach the reserve, the auction house has the last bid, and the property is "bought in," an auction term meaning the item was not sold. The item may then be returned to the seller, sold privately, or offered again at a later date.

Auction catalogs typically present low to high range estimates of the auction houses' predictions of sales prices as a guide to buyers. Reserves at the major auction houses are generally lower than the low estimates.[12]

Critics of the reserve claim it is misleading, because it is often not clear after an item is knocked down by the auctioneer whether the item has been sold or bought in. The auction houses say the secret reserve is necessary, however, to ensure a reasonable sale price for the seller and to prevent collusive bidding practices by auction buyers, usually dealers.[13]

Another important question is whether the seller may legally withdraw the goods or the buyer withdraw the bid before the goods are sold or knocked down. If the sale is announced to be "without reserve," the sale must be made to the highest bidder. UCC § 2-328(3) states that "[i]n an auction without reserve, after the auctioneer calls for bids on an article or lot, that article or lot cannot be withdrawn unless no bid is made within a reasonable time."

In the following case, sellers sued the auction house and its auctioneer for a failed auction, contending that the auctioneer's selection of paintings did not have auction appeal, that the auctioneer negligently failed to provide the seller with material information concerning the auction value of the paintings, that Christie's presale estimates provided the public with contradictory advice, and that the auctioneer violated auction house policy by recommending reserves higher than the highest presale estimate.

Cristallina S.A. v. Christie, Manson, & Woods

117 A.D.2d 284, 502 N.Y.S.2d 165 (1986)*

SULLIVAN, Judge.

At issue is the responsibility, if any, of an auction house to the consignor of works of art for sale at public auction. Cristallina S.A., a Panamanian corporation engaged solely in the purchase and sale of works of art, consigned for

---

12. Decker, *Going, Going . . .* ; *N.Y. Investigators Not Sold on Art Auction Practices*, Chi. Trib., Aug. 18, 1985, § Arts, at 13 [hereinafter Decker].

13. McGill, *Sweeping Reassessment in the Auction Trade*, N.Y. Times, July 31, 1985, § A, at 1 [hereinafter McGill].

* Some footnotes and citations omitted.

sale eight Impressionist paintings to Christie, Manson, and Woods International, Inc., the international auction house. The auction was a conceded failure, and as a result Cristallina brought this action against Christie's and its former president, David Bathurst, for monetary redress, including punitive damages. Cristallina claims, inter alia, that Christie's and Bathurst intentionally or negligently misrepresented the sum the paintings would bring at auction and failed to advise it of the risks inherent in such a sale. The matter is before us on appeal from a grant of summary judgment dismissing the complaint.

In January 1981, Cristallina, anxious to raise $10,000,000 to purchase additional paintings, contacted Christie's about the possibility of selling several Impressionist paintings that it owned, and a meeting with Bathurst, an expert on Impressionist art, was arranged.

At a February 10, 1981 meeting in Switzerland with Cristallina's representative, Dimitry Jodidio, Bathurst inspected a group of eleven paintings, tentatively appraising the value of each and eventually recommending that eight of them be put up for sale at a public auction. To demonstrate the advantage of a public auction, Bathurst prepared a memorandum showing what the paintings would obtain at auction as opposed to private sale. According to Jodidio, Bathurst played down the lowest anticipated private sale figure of $7,850,000, as well as the lowest auction estimate $8,500,000, to focus on the high auction gross figure of $12,600,000. On the strength of Bathurst's advice, Jodidio agreed to a public auction and, after subsequent negotiations, Cristallina consigned the eight selected paintings to Christie's for sale in New York City on May 19, 1981. Christie's commission was set at 4%. In the event, however, the total sales did not exceed $9,400,000, Christie's was to forego its commission entirely and accept, instead, a buyer's premium, which would amount to much less. Since it was also agreed that the seller's identity was not to be disclosed, Bathurst was instructed to use code words in referring to Cristallina and Jodidio. . . .

Christie's proceeded to advertise and generate curiosity and interest in the sale, designated as "Eight Important Paintings from a Private Collector." It is undisputed that it placed advertisements, solicited and supplied information for articles, directly contacted collectors and compiled a color catalog of the paintings. It also released sale estimates of possible selling price ranges to the media and the public.

After returning to New York, Bathurst undertook to reach agreement with Jodidio on the reserves which would be set for each of the paintings. Besides monitoring the art market and speaking to other auctioneers, dealers, and collectors, Bathurst, in contemplating the reserve prices, also consulted Christopher Burge, the head of Christie's Impressionist painting department. In his first conversation with Jodidio on the subject on February 23, 1981, Bathurst recommended a reserve totaling $9,300,000, and prepared a memorandum to that effect listing the reserve assigned to each painting. The next day Christie's picked up the eight paintings in Switzerland and shipped them to New York for research and cataloguing. In arranging for insurance, Christie's assigned a specific value to each of the paintings based on Bathurst's appraisals. Jodidio also wrote Bathurst on that day and set forth his understanding of the agreement reached on reserves. Jodidio's reserves matched the insurance values Christie's assigned to the paintings, and exceeded the total of the reserves recommended by Bathurst on February 23rd by $700,000.

Noting the discrepancies in their respective views as to the reserves, Bathurst contacted Jodidio and they agreed that since the auction was still several months away the final setting of reserves would be deferred until just before the auction. As of March, Bathurst still believed that the reserves contained in his February 23rd memorandum were appropriate, but the parties understood that his view of the appropriateness of the reserves was subject to change in the event Christie's concluded that market conditions had changed.

When the paintings arrived in New York in early March, Burge, who had "broadly concurred" with the values placed on them by Bathurst, began his research and cataloguing of them. Although he did not change his view as to their value, he disagreed with Bathurst as to the auction appeal of the selected paintings. Many of the paintings, he believed, irrespective of their true value, would be "difficult" to sell at auction since "a prettier picture will be easier to sell than a tough picture, even though the tough picture is important." For example, Burge considered the Cezanne to be "a tough picture" while Bathurst predicted possible proceeds as high as $3,200,000, a figure which Burge dismissed as "unobtainable." Burge had even less faith in the Morisot and the Van Gogh "rats," which he dismissed as being "pretty horrible." Burge's concerns were never reported to Jodidio. At the time, the paintings had not been catalogued or a public announcement of the sale made, and thus the sale could have been cancelled without the harm to their value which apparently would result if they were withdrawn from sale after they had been catalogued and placed on the public market.

Among Burge's assignments with respect to the auction was the responsibility for advising potential purchasers of the high and low presale estimates for each of the paintings. These estimates reflected Christie's belief as to the range within which the paintings would sell. Christie's quoted presale estimates on May 4, 1981 for seven of the paintings reveal a substantial difference in amounts from the figures quoted to Jodidio by Bathurst on February 10th. On May 4th, just weeks before the auction, the total of the high estimates for the seven paintings (excluding the Monet) was $8,550,000.... In contrast, on February 10th, Bathurst had stated that with respect to the same paintings, the high estimates totaled $10,800,000. Moreover, for the same seven paintings, Bathurst had in February recommended reserves totaling $8,500,000 — a figure which was barely under the high estimates ($8,550,000) quoted on May 4th.

In giving the low and high presale estimates, Christie's apparently violated its long-standing policy, stated in every catalogue which it published, not to set reserves higher than the announced high presale estimates. For example, in February the Van Gogh "Houses" reserve was initially set at $2,200,000. At

Bathurst's recommendation, that reserve was raised on May 18th to $2,300,000. Yet, the high estimate for that painting was only $2,000,000. In other cases, in violation of normal practice, the high estimates and the reserves coincided exactly. As Burge noted: "Ideally, reserves should be around 80 percent of our published estimates." No discussion was had with Jodidio about the high and low presale estimates being quoted to the public, nor did Jodidio ever approve any specific high or low presale estimate.

As the May 19th auction date approached, Burge and Bathurst continued to discuss the Cristallina paintings. Burge told Bathurst in early May that the Monet and Cezanne estimates were high. Indeed, according to Burge, he and Bathurst agreed that the $3,200,000 Cezanne estimate quoted to Jodidio "was unobtainable." On May 12, 1981, Christie's public relations officer, who received her information from Burge, wrote to CBS in connection with her promotional activities for the upcoming auction, stating that Christie's expected to receive between $5,000,000 and $9,000,000 for the paintings. Thus, eight days after its May 4th quote setting forth the high and low estimates and only one week before the auction, Christie's was advising the media that the paintings were worth even less than the estimates quoted on May 4th.

Apparently, sometime during the month of May, rumors began to circulate with regard to Jodidio's supposed ownership of the eight paintings. In fact, on May 15, 1981, Jodidio was named in a New York Times article as the owner.[14] According to Cristallina, the emergence of Jodidio's name may have given rise to questions about the ownership of the paintings and title thereto. An International Herald Tribune article which appeared shortly after the auction stated that the Cristallina sale "appears to have been the object of a hostile rumor campaign reportedly started by one of the world's leading dealers in old and modern masters." While Christie's denies having had any knowledge of these rumors, its denial is at least subject to challenge on the basis of a May 11, 1981 telex from its Geneva office indicating that, on the basis of information obtained from two different clients, Bathurst had notice of the "mystery and the doubts" concerning Cristallina. In any event, Cristallina was never aware of the rumors.

During the period between May 4th and May 18th, according to Bathurst, the public's reaction to the paintings "was quite favorable." Burge confirmed this by testifying that initially "there was considerable interest in a number of the [paintings]." While, ordinarily, this positive public reaction would cause him to revise the reserves upwards, Bathurst wanted to lower the reserves based on a negative "feeling" he had developed about the outcome of the auction. At his final meeting with Jodidio the day before the auction, Bathurst recommended reserves totaling $9,250,000, which was only $50,000 less than the reserves recommended by him in the February 23rd memorandum. This gross reserve figure was, of course, inconsistent with Christie's prior advice

---

14. In pertinent part the article stated: "Several sources in the art trade had reported that the owner of the 'mystery collection' is Dimitry Jodidio. . . ."

to the media that the paintings would earn between $5,000,000 and $9,000,000 and the fact that the bidding public had already been given, as high presale estimates, figures which were lower than the reserves Bathurst was recommending.

A comparison of the February reserves with the May reserves shows that Bathurst had increased the reserve on both the Gauguin and the Van Gogh "Houses" by $100,000 each. When this was noted at his deposition, he sought to justify the increase on the ground that those two paintings were the ones he "thought would do best."[15] In discussing the reserves at the May 18th meeting, Bathurst did not advise Jodidio that Christie's had publicly announced that the paintings would sell for between $5,000,000 and $9,000,000 or that the recommended reserves, in violation of Christie's own policy, were greater than the high estimates. Not having this information available to him, Jodidio alleges that he agreed to the reserves recommended by Bathurst.

According to Bathurst, he was also given the unilateral right to add to the total reserve of $9,250,000 an additional $150,000 (the "floating reserve"), which he could use to increase the reserves on whichever paintings he felt was appropriate. Jodidio has denied that any agreement was ever reached with respect to the $150,000 floating reserve. The addition of the $150,000 floating reserve not only increased the reserves beyond what they had been in February, but was at odds with Bathurst's stated position that the reserves as of May should be lowered, not increased. When asked why he suggested that there be a floating reserve, Bathurst stated that he "was trying to meet Mr. Jodidio's insistence to obtaining this, as near to this $10,000,000 figure as possible." As even Bathurst conceded, however, an auctioneer does not increase his chances of obtaining better sale results by raising reserves. In his deposition Bathurst testified, "By raising reserves on a specific painting, that increases the chances of the item being bought in."

As matters turned out, Bathurst decided, several hours before the auction, to add the $150,000 floating reserve to two of the paintings. Without advising Cristallina, he increased the reserve on the Gauguin from $1,300,000 to $1,350,000 and the Van Gogh "Houses" from $2,300,000 to $2,400,000.

The sale was held during a week of intensive activity at Christie's and Sotheby's. According to pre-auction publicity, sale proceeds were expected to equal or surpass the large sums collected in previous sales of this magnitude. Despite extensive publicity, media coverage and a sell-out crowd, the sale went badly. Seven of the eight paintings were not sold. The one painting which was sold, the Degas, fetched a record $2,200,000. The Gauguin was hammered down at $1,300,000, which was the reserve price agreed to by Christie's and Cristallina. Christie's, however, has refused to acknowledge the sale, claiming that because Bathurst had decided to add $50,000 to the reserve, the $1,300,000 bid was below the reserve.

---

15. The February reserve on the Van Gogh "Houses" exceeded the high presale estimate given for that painting by $200,000. As a result of the reserve agreed to in May it exceeded the high pre-sale estimate by $300,000.

Immediately upon the completion of the auction, Bathurst advised Christie's press office that three paintings had been sold, the Degas, the Gauguin for $1,300,000, and the Van Gogh "Houses" for $2,100,000. Two weeks later, on June 1, 1981, Christie's issued a formal press release, approved by both Bathurst and Burge confirming these sales. No other press release on the subject has ever been released. Bathurst's explanation for this deception is that it was for "the benefit of [Cristallina] and the art market."

Apparently, changes in the art market were not a factor in the auction's failure. Indeed, as reported in a New York Times article dated June 7, 1981, Christie's main competitor, Sotheby's, enjoyed record sales within days of the May 19, 1981 auction and the auction market for that month was as strong as ever.

Cristallina commenced this action in May 1982, asserting eight causes of action grounded in, inter alia, fraudulent misrepresentation, negligence, breach of contract, and breach of fiduciary duty. In essence, Cristallina claims that the auction's failure was due to Bathurst's selection of paintings lacking in auction appeal,[16] the failure to bring vital information to its attention, Christie's advice to the public and the media that the value of the paintings was substantially less than the values given to Jodidio, and the recommendation of reserves in violation of Christie's public policy of not setting reserves higher than the high estimates. In sum, Cristallina contends, Christie's and Bathurst, by their own actions, created an environment which could only lead to failure. Almost one year after the case had been placed on the trial calendar, Christie's and Bathurst moved for summary judgment, which Special Term granted. Since we believe that factual issues exist which bar the grant of summary judgment, we reinstate the complaint except for the fifth and seventh causes of action which are based on a failure to remit the sale proceeds from the sale of two of the paintings and the violation of General Business Law § 25, respectively.

Christie's concedes, as it must, that an auction house acts as an agent on behalf of its consignors. The auctioneer is the agent of the consignor. . . . As an agent, Christie's had a fiduciary duty to act in the utmost good faith and in the interest of Cristallina, its principal, throughout their relationship. . . . When a breach of that duty occurs, the agent is liable for damages caused to the principal, whether the cause of action is based on contract. . . .

Cristallina argues that Christie's and Bathurst withheld information which materially affected its interests. They cite the failure to disclose that Burge strongly disagreed with Bathurst's assessment of the auction appeal of the consigned paintings. Although Burge was of the opinion that they had a value of $10,000,000, he also believed that the paintings would be difficult

_____

16. According to Bathurst, the three "highest quality paintings" were the Cezanne, Gauguin and the Van Gogh "Houses." Not one of them, however, was sold.

to sell at auction.[17] Had this information been conveyed to Cristallina, it could have avoided any potential damage by, inter alia, withdrawing the paintings from auction prior to their being catalogued. "[A]n agent is subject to a duty to use reasonable efforts to give his principal information which is relevant to affairs entrusted to him and which, as the agent has notice, the principal would desire to have and which can be communicated without violating a superior duty to a third person." (Restatement of Agency 2nd, § 381, p. 182; *see also, Dickinson v. Tysen*, 209 N.Y. 395, 400, 103 N.E. 703. . . .)

Cristallina also argues that Christie's and Bathurst failed to inform it of the information Christie's released in May 1981 to members of the public and the media shortly before the time Bathurst and Jodidio met to set the final reserves. Christie's, a self-avowed expert, inexplicably advised the public and the media that the values of the paintings were less than what it knew the reserves to be. Besides prejudicing Cristallina, those actions also violated a policy set by Christie's that reserves were not to exceed the high estimates. Based on the public and media disclosures, Christie's and Bathurst knew or should have known that it would be virtually impossible to sell the paintings unless the reserves were lowered. Yet, at his May 18th meeting with Jodidio, Bathurst failed to recommend that the reserves be substantially lowered below those recommended in February. Instead, he recommended that certain of the reserves be increased, which was done, with the result, Cristallina claims, that the paintings were bought in and their value thereby adversely affected.

Moreover, where, as here, an agent is selected because of its special fitness for the performance of the duties to be undertaken, the principal is entitled to rely on the agent's judgment and integrity. An agent has an "implied good faith obligation [to] . . . use his best efforts to promote the principal's product" (*Griffin & Evans Cosmetic Marketing v. Madeleine Mono, Ltd., supra,* 73 A.D.2d 957, 424 N.Y.S.2d 269, citing *Van Valkenburgh, Nooger & Neville v. Hayden Pub. Co.,* 30 N.Y.2d 34, 330 N.Y.S.2d 329, 281 N.E.2d 142). While an auctioneer, acting as the agent of an art seller, is not required to guarantee the results of a sale or, for that matter, even predict the price that a particular item will bring, he is nonetheless held to a standard of care commensurate with the special skill which is the norm in the locality for that kind of work. Thus, the breach of contract, negligence, and breach of fiduciary duty causes of action should not have been dismissed since sufficient cause has been shown to present a factual question as to whether Christie's and Bathurst acted in a manner commensurate with their skill and expertise.

In support of its cause of action for misrepresentation Cristallina claims that Bathurst, by placing a value on each of the paintings that he knew was not and could not be true, improperly induced it to agree to a sale of the paintings at public auction. Moreover, Cristallina alleges, Bathurst failed to disclose the

---

17. In this regard, Christie's may also have violated its duty not to attempt the impossible or impracticable, which section 384 of the Restatement of Agency 2d, at p. 189, defines as a duty "not to continue to render service which subjects the principal to risk of expense if it reasonably appears to him to be impossible or impracticable for him to accomplish the objects of the principal. . . ."

risks attendant to such an auction. Had it been made aware of these risks and the paintings' lack of auction appeal it would never have agreed to a public auction. Christie's and Bathurst argue that the representations as to the estimated value of the eight paintings were mere expressions of opinion and not representations of existing fact.

Even assuming that Bathurst, in advising Cristallina as to the value of the paintings and setting reserves, was merely expressing an opinion, which is not actionable . . . , rather than a representation as to an existing fact, which is . . . , he had an obligation to render such opinion truthfully. Thus, his selection of eight paintings, many of which, according to Burge, would be difficult, if not impossible, to sell and the dissemination of estimates at variance with the reserves and his earlier predictions, raise serious questions as to whether Bathurst misrepresented the prices which could be obtained at public auction. Statements of value can, in certain circumstances, be regarded as a representation of existing fact. . . . An expression or prediction as to some future event, known by the author to be false or made despite the anticipation that the event will not occur, "is deemed a statement of a material existing fact, sufficient [evidence] to support a fraud action." (*Channel Master Corp. v. Aluminum Ltd. Sales*, 4 N.Y.2d 403, 407, 176 N.Y.S.2d 259, 151 N.E.2d 833; *Chase Manhattan Bank, N.A. v. Perla*, 65 A.D.2d 207, 210, 411 N.Y.S.2d 66.)

As further justification for its dismissal of the complaint, Special Term, citing the failure to present any expert affidavit as to the paintings' present value, found that Cristallina's claim for damages was speculative. The paintings' pre-auction value may, of course, be established by estimates, including Bathurst's, and the value Christie's placed on them for insurance purposes. The measure of damages is the difference between the paintings' pre-auction value and their value after the auction. . . . Appraisals and bona fide sales are indicative of value and may serve as the basis of a damage award. . . . As the record discloses, four of the paintings have been sold since the auction, three in September 1982 and another, the Gauguin, in 1984, at significantly less than Bathurst's pre-auction appraisal figures. In each case Cristallina advised Christie's of the offer and afforded it the opportunity to match or better it. In any event, "the difficulty of ascertaining damages does not excuse their determination." (*Tobin v. Union News Co.*, 18 A.D.2d 243, 245, 239 N.Y.S.2d 22, aff'd, 13 N.Y.2d 1155, 247 N.Y.S.2d 385, 196 N.E.2d 735.) While damages may not be determined by mere speculation or guess, evidence that, "as a matter of just and reasonable inference," shows their existence and the extent thereof will suffice, even though the result is only an approximation. (*Story Parchment Co. v. Paterson Parch. Paper Co.*, 282 U.S. 555, 563, 51 S. Ct. 248, 250-51, 75 L. Ed. 544.)

Cristallina's claim for punitive damages, stated not as a separate cause of action but as part of the ad damnum clause, also should stand at this stage of the litigation. The complaint pleads the requisite allegations of recklessness and conscious disregard of Cristallina's rights. . . . Whether the alleged misconduct warrants the imposition of a punitive damage award should, in the circumstances, be left for the trier of the facts . . . Cristallina argues that punitive damages are particularly appropriate in this case since "the business of an auctioneer . . . has always been affected with a public interest. . . ." In further support of the punitive damage claim, Cristallina cites the entry of a consent judgment between the New York City Consumer Affairs Department and Christie's in connection with the issuance of the false press release for violations of Administrative Code § B32-149.0. . . . Christie's was fined $80,000 and Burge's and Bathurst's auction licenses were suspended.

We agree with Special Term's determination that the fifth and seventh causes of action, which we are not reinstating, are fatally defective. In the fifth cause of action Cristallina claims entitlement to $3,610,000, the purported purchase price of the two paintings falsely listed as sold in Christie's press release. Cristallina has no claim, legal or equitable, to the proceeds of these spurious sales. The two paintings were returned to it and eventually sold. Thus, it cannot show that the paintings were rendered worthless as a result of the false representation. As already indicated, its damages are limited to the loss in value allegedly incurred as a result of Christie's and Bathurst's wrongdoing, if any, and that damage claim is preserved in the other causes of action.

The seventh cause of action, claiming a violation of section 25 of the General Business Law, which sets forth the type of records required to be maintained by an auctioneer, is based on Christie's failure to record the two false sales in its records as actual sales. Aside from its obvious lack of merit and even assuming, arguendo, that section 25 created a private right of action for damages, an issue we need not reach, it is clear to us that any such violation as might have occurred here did not cause Cristallina to suffer any damages.

Accordingly, the order of the Supreme Court, New York County (Eugene R. Wolin, J.), entered July 15, 1985, granting defendants' motion for summary judgment dismissing the complaint should be modified, on the law, to deny the motion as to the first, second, third, fourth, sixth and eighth causes of action, and, except as thus modified, affirmed, without costs or disbursements.

Notes and Questions

1. Cristallina appealed the appellate court's decision and the case was tried in the New York State Supreme Court. One week into the trial the parties reached an out-of-court settlement. In exchange for a cash payment of an undisclosed amount, Cristallina agreed to drop all charges against the auction house, including that the Christie's $12.6 million estimate before the auction was fraudulent. Cristallina also dropped a similar fraud charge brought against David Bathurst, former president of Christie's, who had made the estimates. McGill, *An Out-of-Court Settlement Reached in Christie's Case*, N.Y. Times, Jan. 22, 1987, § C, at 20. Following the undisclosed financial settlement in the principal case, jurors indicated that had the case not been settled, Cristallina would have prevailed against Christie's. *See* Galen, *Sizzle Fizzles*, NAT'L L.J., Feb. 2, 1987.

2. In a post-auction statement to the press, Bathurst falsely reported that three of Cristallina's paintings had been sold at the auction. His statement was confirmed by Christie's formal press release announcing that three of the paintings had been sold, a Degas, that sold for a record price of $2,000,000, and two Impressionist paintings that sold for more than $1 million. However, in an affidavit made public after the suit was dismissed, Mr. Bathurst admitted that of the eight paintings only one, the Degas, was actually purchased. Reif, *supra.* Bathurst said he lied "to maintain stability in the art market" and to protect the value of the paintings, which are said to be "burned," or devalued, after a buy-in. At least one art dealer said he used one of the falsely reported prices to support a price for a similar painting he sold privately shortly after the Christie's sale. McGuigan, *For a Few Dollars More,* Newsweek, July 29, 1985, at 59.

3. Following the *Cristallina* allegations, the New York City Department of Consumer Affairs, which enforces and monitors auction house practices, conducted an exhaustive investigation of possible auction industry irregularities. The only material change to its regulations resulting from the department's two-year study, however, was the requirement that auctioneers announce whether a work remained unsold. *See* City of New York Admin. Code, tit. 20, ch. 2, subch. 13; Gregory, *Auction Trade Faces Regulation,* J. of Art, Apr. 1991, at 74. The auction houses themselves have established a convention which should prevent the abuse that was the subject of the *Cristallina* case. Today the vast majority of auction houses, including Christie's and Sotheby's, publish an after-auction report disclosing the price at which the items in the auction have sold and whether any of the items were withdrawn or the reserve not met. Many online auctions follow this convention as well.

4. UCC § 2-328(3) also provides that the high bidder "may retract his bid until the auctioneer's announcement of completion of the sale," and that the retraction does not revive any previous bids which have lapsed during the making of a higher bid.

UCC § 2-328(3) further states that all sales are subject to reserve prices unless the goods are in explicit terms put up without reserve. Comment 2 of that section points out that "with reserve" is the normal procedure. This means that goods may be withdrawn from sale even after being placed on the block or offered for sale, if the minimum dollar amount set by the seller is not bid. The buyer must assume the risk that the property may be withdrawn before being sold. The apparent reason for giving the seller this advantage is that it is the function of an auction to generate competition.

5. The vast majority of auctions are held "with reserve," although the actual reserve price is rarely disclosed. This secrecy has stimulated considerable controversy. Proponents argue that the system was instituted as a protection for sellers against the effects of bad weather, boycotts, and collusive bidding practices, while opponents argue that use of the reserve creates an artificial auction until the reserve is reached. *See* R. Lerner & J. Bresler, *Art Law: The Guide for Collectors, Investors, Dealers, and Artists* 156 (1st ed. 1989) and (2d ed. 1998) [hereinafter Lerner & Bresler]; McGill, *supra.*

6. Does the regulation of auction houses vary by country? In her article, *The International Art Auction Industry: Has Competition Tarnished Its Finish*, Brenna Adler argues that

> While the United States (New York) has attempted to emphasize the fiduciary duty of auctioneers (as evidenced in the *Cristallina* case as well as the City of New York Rules), the civil law countries of the Netherlands and France tend to have a tighter stronghold on their auctioneers due in large part to those states' interest and participation in the auction industry. The relatively ineffective domestic regulation, in conjunction with paltry international regulations, allows for controversial activities by auction houses, including keeping secret reserves and giving guarantees. . . . Ultimately, it is the lack of domestic and international regulation that creates an opening for the auction houses to commit illegal behavior. In addition, the glamour and prestige of the art world allow auctioneers to continue to attract customers.

Brenna Adler, *The International Art Auction Industry: Has Competition Tarnished Its Finish*, 23 Nw. J. Int'l L. & Bus. 433 (2003).

C. The Auctioneer's Role

Obviously, a key figure in all auctions is the auctioneer. He or she serves multiple functions, as an agent of the seller, the buyer, and, possibly, of the auction house. In these roles, the auctioneer has a number of responsibilities, including obtaining a license to do business in the locale, using strategic efforts to exact maximum prices for the items, being informed of the nature and market price of the goods, knocking down the goods to the highest bidder, assuming responsibility for any unauthorized express warranty, following the principal's instructions, accepting payment, and insuring delivery to the successful bidder.

The auctioneer acts as agent of the seller by whom the auctioneer is chosen and paid until a sale is contracted. *See* Restatement (Second) of Agency § 1, comment e (1957). Upon formation of an enforceable contract, the auctioneer assumes a dual agency. This dual role is limited, however, to the drawing and signing (contemporaneously with the sale) of whatever writing is required by the statute of frauds. The auctioneer is authorized to make and sign this memorandum, which is then binding on both parties. The buyer's bid is seen as an agreement to allow the auctioneer to enter the buyer's signature on a contract for that amount. This power of attorney may be revoked at any time if not exercised; once exercised, however, it binds the principals. Restatement of Contracts § 212(2) (1932). Failure to comply with the statute of frauds may render the auctioneer liable for negligence.

Where the goods involved in the transaction are stolen, most states hold that an auctioneer is personally liable to the true owner for conversion, even where the auctioneer acted in good faith and without knowledge, actual or constructive, of the true owner's title.[18] Similarly, a majority of jurisdictions, including the federal courts, impose liability for conversion regardless of the fact that the auctioneer acted in good faith and with actual or constructive knowledge of a security interest.[19]

Even where actual or constructive knowledge is required to establish conversion, courts have held that the existence of a perfected security interest is constructive knowledge.[20] However, where a secured party knows what is occurring and would be expected to speak in order to protect the secured party's interests, acquiescence indicates tacit consent.

If goods were obtained by fraud, the auctioneer who sells without notice of the defect is not liable for conversion.[21] But if the auctioneer had actual knowledge or the circumstances were such that a prudent person would inquire further, the auctioneer is liable to the true owner of the property.[22] Such holdings tend to discourage theft and require that the auctioneer verify the vendor's title, while absolving the auctioneer of liability for defects beyond his or her control.

Many auctioneers act as independent contractors and their services can be procured for either a fixed price or a percentage of the amount of auction sales. They will conduct the auction at the seller's residence, place of business, or quarters procured for the event. The services of these individuals are commonly sought for estate sales and business liquidations. The auctioneer is customarily entitled to all commissions, even if the contract of sale is rescinded or abandoned.

Unless the auctioneer's contract specifies otherwise, the commission is earned, not by the consummated sales contract, but by the auctioneer's procurement of a bona fide bid acceptable to the owner. In *Childs v. Ragonese*,[23] the court's decision was based on a finding that the auctioneer had expressly agreed that he would not be entitled to a designated percent of the sale if the

---

18. *See, e.g., Hagan v. Brzozowski*, 336 S.W.2d 213 (Tex. Civ. App. 1960); *Allred v. Hinkley*, 8 Utah 2d 73, 328 P.2d 726 (1959); *Jones v. Ballard*, 573 So. 2d 783 (Miss. 1990).

19. *See, e.g, United States v. Matthews*, 244 F.2d 626 (9th Cir. 1957) (notwithstanding state law, an auctioneer is strictly liable in conversion against the government, even though he acted in good faith).

20. *Top Line Equip. Co. v. Nat'l Auction Serv.*, 35 Wash. App. 685, 649 P.2d 165 (1982).

21. *See, e.g., Jessup v. Cattle Center, Inc.*, 259 Cal. App. 2d 434, 66 Cal. Rptr. 361 (1968).

22. *See., e.g., Morrow Shoe Mg. Co. v. New England Shoe Co.*, 57 F. 685, *mod. as to costs*, 60 F. 342 (7th Cir. 1894).

23. *Childs v. Ragonese*, 51 Md. App. 428, 443 A.2d 665 (1982), *rev'd*, 296 Md. 130, 460 A.2d 1031 (1983).

purchaser failed to carry out the contract of sale. Similarly, when the owner of goods enters into an irrevocable agreement to provide certain goods for a scheduled auction but fails to do so, the auctioneer is entitled to recover as damages reasonable profits lost by the owner's breach.[24]

Callimanopulos v. Christie's Inc.

621 F. Supp. 2d 127 (S.D.N.Y. 2009)*

William H. PAULEY III, District Judge:

Plaintiff Gregory Callimanopulos ("Callimanopulos") brings this action against Defendant Christie's Inc. ("Christie's") seeking a declaratory judgment that he entered into a binding contract with Christie's for the purchase of the painting "Grey" by Sam Francis (the "Work") and that he holds title to the Work, subject to his payment to Christie's of $3 million and any applicable fees or charges. Callimanopulos also brings a claim for breach of contract and seeks performance of the contract by transfer of title and possession of the Work.

On May 15, 2009, this Court granted a temporary restraining order enjoining Christie's from (1) disposing, altering, or changing any audio and/or video recordings of Christie's May 13, 2009 Post-War and Contemporary Art Evening Sale Auction (the "Auction"); and (2) completing the sale of the Work or transfer of title to any putative purchaser. On May 27, 2009, this Court granted a request by the putative purchaser, Eli Broad, to intervene in this action. Callimanopulos now moves for a preliminary injunction. For the following reasons, the motion is denied.

BACKGROUND

Callimanopulos participated in the Auction by telephone. Valentina Casacchia ("Casacchia"), curator of Callimanopulos's collection, and Heidi Waumboldt ("Waumboldt"), Callimanopulos's assistant, attended the Auction in person. Callimanopulos was connected by telephone to April Richon Jacobs ("Jacobs"), Christie's Co-Head of Evening Sale, who conveyed his bids to the auctioneer, Christopher Burge ("Burge"). Burge, who has been an auctioneer for over 34 years and has conducted more than 1,000 auctions, is Honorary Chairman of Christie's. Joanne Heyler ("Heyler"), the Director/Chief Curator of the Broad Art Foundation, attended the Auction as Eli Broad's representative. (Both Broad and Callimanopulos had determined prior to the Auction to bid on the Work.)

At the auction, Heyler was seated in the front row, to the right of Burge. Heyler raised concerns about being seated in the front row because it can be a blind spot for the auctioneer. As a result, two Christie's employees — Brett Gorvey and Laura Paulson — paid attention to Heyler during the auction. Jacobs was seated at a bank of telephones located along the side wall, many

---

24. *Thorp Sales Corp. v. Gyuro Grading Co.*, 111 Wisc. 2d 431, 331 N.W.2d 342 (1983).
* Citations to the record deleted.

rows back and to the left of Burge. Jacobs did not have a clear view of the first row of bidders. Gorvey and Paulson were standing on a raised platform facing the first row of seats to the right of Burge. Casacchia and Waumboldt sat in the front row.

Bidding on the Work commenced at $1.3 million and, through Jacobs, Callimanopulos entered at $2.9 million. After Callimanopulos bid $3 million, Burge surveyed the room for other bids, before stating: "Sold to the phone for three million dollars" and dropping the hammer. Jacobs told Callimanopulos that they had secured the Work. However, seconds later, Jacobs informed Callimanopulos that Burge had re-opened the bidding and accepted a bid for $3.1 million. That bidder was Heyler.

Callimanopulos protested the re-opening through Jacobs. After Burge rejected his challenge, Callimanopulos bid $3.15 million, with the intention of disputing the additional $150,000 later. However, after Heyler bid $3.2 million, Callimanopulos refused to bid further and Burge called the sale to Heyler.

According to Burge, at the same time that he called the sale to Callimanopulos, Christie's employees, including Gorvey, signaled to him that Heyler had raised her paddle prior to the fall of the hammer. Burge states that the use of spotters to signal to the auctioneer is common practice at auctions. Burge admits that he did not see Heyler's bid. Upon re-opening the bidding, Burge stated: "You all saw it, except for me." He also stated: "3,100,000 in time, with the hammer." Gorvey and Paulson confirm that Heyler had raised her paddle to bid prior to the fall of the hammer. The morning after the Auction, Jacobs conveyed to Callimanopulos that she believed he was the final bidder. However, she admits that from her vantage point she could not see whether or when Heyler placed her bid.

This Court has reviewed a video of the relevant portion of the Auction. In the video, a woman seated in the front row can be seen raising her paddle to chest-height as Burge calls "fair warning" and then raising it above her head as Burge is bringing down the hammer. Burge recognizes the woman's bid a few seconds after striking the hammer. The video also confirms that it would have been difficult for Jacobs to see bidding from the front row.

Christie's Conditions of Sale, included in the catalog for the Auction, provide that:

> The auctioneer has the right at his absolute and sole discretion . . . in the case of error or dispute, and whether during or after the sale, to determine the successful bidder, to continue the bidding, to cancel the sale or to reoffer and resell the item in dispute. If any dispute arises after the sale, our sale record is conclusive.

. . . Auction catalog Conditions of Sale ¶3(i). The terms "error" and "dispute" are not defined in the Conditions of Sale. The Conditions of Sale also provide that "[s]ubject to the auctioneer's discretion, the highest bidder accepted by the auctioneer will be the buyer and the striking of his hammer marks the acceptance of the highest bid and the conclusion of a contract for sale between the seller and the buyer." (. . . Auction Catalog Conditions of Sale ¶3(j).)

DISCUSSION

A party seeking a preliminary injunction must establish: (1) either (a) a likelihood of success on the merits of its case or (b) sufficiently serious questions going to the merits to make them a fair ground for litigation and a balance of hardships tipping decidedly in its favor, and (2) a likelihood of irreparable harm if the requested relief is denied. *Time Warner Cable, Inc. v. DIRECTV Inc.*, 497 F.3d 144, 153 (2d Cir. 2007).

The Uniform Commercial Code (U.C.C.) which the parties agree governs this action, provides that:

> A sale by auction is complete when the auctioneer so announces by the fall of the hammer or in other customary manner. Where a bid is made while the hammer is falling in acceptance of a prior bid the auctioneer may in his discretion reopen the bidding or declare the goods sold under the bid on which the hammer was falling.

N.Y. U.C.C. § 2-328. Thus, under the U.C.C. it is clear that while the fall of the hammer concludes a sale, where a bid is made while the hammer is falling, the auctioneer has the discretion to recognize that bid even after the hammer has fallen. Christie's Conditions of Sale is consistent with the U.C.C.

Here, Burge exercised his discretion and re-opened the bidding, seconds after striking the hammer. The videotape and two Christie's employees confirm that Heyler raised her paddle as Burge said "fair warning" and then raised it even higher as he brought down the hammer. While Plaintiff argues that Burge could not exercise his discretion because he did not see Heyler's bid himself, nothing in the plain language of the U.C.C. or Christie's Conditions of Sale prevents an auctioneer from relying on Christie's employees in the exercise of his discretion. Moreover, as a highly experienced auctioneer, Burge represents that it is the custom of auctioneers to rely on spotters. Callimanopulos presents no evidence that this is not the custom. Accordingly, no contract was formed between Callimanopulos and Christie's. Because Callimanopulos fails to raise sufficiently serious questions going to the merits to make them a fair ground for litigation, let alone a likelihood of success, Callimanopulos's motion for a preliminary injunction is denied.

CONCLUSION

For the foregoing reasons, Plaintiff Gregory Callimanopulos's motion for a preliminary injunction is denied.

Notes and Questions

1. The New York City Department of Consumer Affairs fined Christie's $80,000 and temporarily suspended the auctioneer's license of Christopher Burge, Christie's New York president, who the department said was aware of the false information. The department suspended the

license of David Bathurst, the sale auctioneer, for two years. Bathurst resigned from his positions as chairman of Christie's New York board of directors and as president of Christie's in London. Decker, *supra*.

2. Is eBay an auctioneer or auction house? This issue is discussed in the case of *Ewart v. Ebay*, excerpted immediately below.

Ewert v. eBay, Inc.

2008 WL 906162 (N.D. Cal. Mar. 31, 2008)*

Ronald M. WHYTE, District Judge.

Defendant eBay, Inc. ("eBay") moves to dismiss the first through third causes of action set forth in plaintiff Michael Ewert's first amended complaint ("FAC"). The court grants the motion.

Plaintiff Michael Ewert purchased "auction" services from eBay on January 6 and January 14, 2007. Ewert utilized eBay's "Online Auction Format," which utilizes a form that purports to allow an eBay user to select a fixed duration for the auction of 1, 3, 5, 7, or 10 days and to permit the user to have the auction begin when the form is submitted. Ewert selected 5 days for both of his January 2007 auctions and specified that they were to begin when submitted. According to Ewert, neither auction began when submitted nor did either auction last for the 5 days specified. He claims that his experience is not unique among eBay users.

Ewert filed a proposed class action complaint on April 20, 2007 and subsequently filed his FAC on July 18, 2007. His FAC asserts that eBay's practices violate (1) the California Auction Act ("Auction Act"), Cal. Civ. Code § 1812.601 et seq.; (2) California's Unfair Competition Law ("UCL"), Cal. Bus. & Prof. Code § 17200 et seq.; (3) the California Consumers Legal Remedies Act ("CLRA"), Cal. Civ. Code § 1750 et seq.; and (4) Cal. Civ. Code §§ 1709, 1710 and 1572. Ewert's FAC also sets forth a claim for unjust enrichment and a common law claim for money had and received. eBay asserts by its current motion that the first through third claims alleging violations of the Auction Act fail to state a claim. eBay also objects to the use of the alleged violations as predicate acts for liability under the UCL.

eBay was previously sued in this district in an essentially identical suit, *Butler v. eBay Inc.*, action no. 06-02704 JW. There, the court granted a motion to dismiss and held that the Auction Act does not apply to eBay's conduct as a matter of law. The *Butler* court's rationale was that eBay is neither an "auctioneer" nor an "auction company" as defined by the Auction Act. This court agrees.

Plaintiff's attempt to place eBay's conduct within the scope of the Auction Act is like trying to put a round peg in a square hole. The Auction Act was enacted before Internet "auctions" like eBay's and other similar business

---

* Footnotes and citations to the record omitted.

platforms were in vogue. A review of the Auction Act reveals a number of reasons why it does not apply here:

(1) the history of the Auction Act suggests it was designed to protect customers of auction houses from unscrupulous auctioneers absconding with goods entrusted to them and to protect bidders from misrepresentations of the value of goods being auctioned. Under the eBay business model, eBay never takes possession of goods being sold and never makes representations as to value;

(2) eBay is not an "auctioneer" as defined by the Act as it is not an "individual";

(3) eBay does not conduct "auctions" within the meaning of the Auction Act because the sale does not culminate by acceptance by the auctioneer of the highest offer but rather at the expiration of the fixed period designated by the seller;

(4) eBay does not conduct "auctions" within the meaning of the Auction Act because there is no auctioneer who makes a series of invitations for offers;

(5) eBay is not an "Auction Company" because it does not make "auction sales"; and

(6) provisions of the Auction Act negate any suggestion that it applies to eBay because application of those provisions would be nonsensical (*e.g.*, requirement of the posting of an 18 x 24 inch sign at the entrance to the auction).

Plaintiff pleads in the alternative that even assuming that eBay is not itself an auctioneer or an auction company pursuant to the definitions set forth in the Auction Act, it nevertheless aids and abets eBay customers in conducting auctions and is therefore liable under § 1812.608(b) of the Auction Act. This section provides that it is a violation of the Auction Act "for any person to ... (b) Aid or abet the activity of any other person that violates any provision of this title. A violation of this subdivision is a misdemeanor subject to a fine of one thousand dollars ($1,000)."

To violate the Auction Act, an eBay customer would have to be engaging in or involved with an auction as defined by the Act. The complaint alleges that eBay serves as the platform through which auctions are conducted. As alleged, an eBay customer does not accept the final offer to purchase, rather the eBay system stops the bidding at the time designated by the eBay customer (or stops the bidding before the designated time as alleged by the plaintiff). As set forth in § 1812.601(b), an auction "must culminate in the acceptance by the auctioneer of the highest or most favorable offer made by a member of the participating audience," thus because eBay's system effectively stops the exchanges and the court has determined that eBay is not an auctioneer, an eBay customer's use of the eBay site to list goods for sale is not an auction under the Auction Act. . . .

For the foregoing reasons, the court grants eBay's motion to dismiss plaintiff's first through third claims with prejudice.

PROBLEM 8-1

Can auction houses be held secondarily liable for copyright infringement?

Consider *Hendrickson v. eBay, Inc.*, 165 F. Supp. 2d 1082 (C.D. Cal. 2001). Robert Hendrickson advised eBay that he was the copyright owner of the documentary "Manson" and that pirated DVD copies of Manson were being offered for sale on eBay. eBay encouraged Hendrickson to join its Verified Rights Owner program, by submitting eBay's Notice of Infringement form. He refused and filed suit. The court granted summary judgment on behalf of eBay. *Id.*

Does your answer to the above question change when you also consider the article *The Online Copyright Auction: How High Will Bidding Go?*, in which Lori Jones argued that the result of this case "illustrates a move away from providing copyright protection on the Internet and a move towards protecting e-commerce"? 2 J. HIGH. TECH. L. 45 (2003).

D. Auction Houses

This section explores several auction house problems, including the extent of the successful bidder's duty to pay, and the buyer's rights when the item is paid for by another. The art market has grown from a local enterprise to a global industry. Auction houses have been significantly affected by this growth. The major auction houses, or galleries — those having several auctioneers and conducting sales on a relatively fixed schedule — are located throughout the world. For example, Christie's maintains 77 offices in 26 countries on five continents and employs 1,200 persons. Even in the midst of the worst recession since the Great Depression, auction houses continued to sell art for prices that exceeded their high estimate. For example, on November 6, 2007, Christie's sold Matisse's 1937 *L'Odalisque, Harmonie Bleue* for $33.6 million, approximately 50 percent more than its pre-sale estimate of $15 million to $20 million. 2013 was regarded as the best art auction year ever, with $12 billion in worldwide sales.[25]

Auction houses have the discretion to cancel a sale and to return the property to the seller if the buyer does not pay. Christie's consignment agreement further reserves the right to enforce payment by the buyer or take any other action permitted by law; however, the agreement states that it shall not, under any circumstances, be liable for any incidental or consequential damages

25. *The Art Market in 2013*, http://imgpublic.artprice.com/pdf/trends2013_en_fr_de_es_online.pdf.

resulting to the seller from a breach or failure by the buyer. Sotheby's contract specifically provides that it has no obligation to enforce payment by any purchaser. In its discretion and with the seller's authorization, it may impose upon the purchaser and retain for Sotheby's account a late charge if payment is not made in accordance with the conditions of sale.[26]

Where an auction house financed the buyer's purchase of two paintings from a dealer, the court held that the buyer failed to assert a valid defense to non-payment of a promissory note. In *Sotheby's, Inc. v. Dumba*,[27] Dumba had purchased two paintings on separate occasions, fully financed through Sotheby's. The second purchase followed Sotheby's representation that the work was in good condition as well as an explicit statement that the auction house made no representations or warranties concerning the painting. When Dumba was unable to sell the paintings for a profit, he executed a promissory note with Sotheby's Financial Services but subsequently defaulted on the obligation. In his defense, Dumba asserted that Sotheby's note was invalid because of unilateral mistake, fraud, and duress. His counterclaim alleged that Sotheby's misrepresentation of the second painting's condition and value induced him to purchase the work. The court held that the release executed at the time of the note specifically precluded such a claim.

Notes

1. Sotheby's withdrew a Roman Jewish liturgical manuscript from auction after the auction house received documentation asserting that the consigned manuscript was stolen. *Stein v. Annenberg Research Inst.*, No. 90 Civ. 5224, 1991 U.S. Dist. Lexis 9964 (S.D.N.Y. July 19, 1991) (rejecting an attempt to assert jurisdiction over an out-of-state defendant who had sent an allegedly tortious letter into New York).
2. After the Peruvian embassy in Washington learned of pre-Columbian gold and turquoise jewelry offered for sale by Sotheby's, Peru requested that Sotheby's withdraw the items from sale. Sotheby's declined to do so and a seizure warrant was served on Sotheby's pursuant to the Cultural Property Implementation Act. *See* Chapter 11 for a discussion of this law. *Jewelry Repatriated*, Archaeology, Sept./Oct. 1996, at 30.

E. Warranties

In auctions, as in other methods of sale, one of the most frequently litigated contractual provisions is the warranty. Sellers occasionally disclaim all

---

26. Lerner & Bresler, *supra*, at 198-205.
27. *Sotheby's, Inc. v. Dumba*, 1992 U.S. Dist. Lexis 965 (S.D.N.Y. Jan. 28, 1992).

warranties; however, according to UCC § 2-313(1), an affirmation of fact relating to goods that becomes the basis of the bargain is an express warranty. In addition, the UCC provides for several implied warranties. Art warranties generally involve issues of either authenticity or seller's title. *See Menzel v. List,* discussed in Chapter 10.

The court in *Jendwine v. Slade*[28] established the traditional approach to a breach of the warranty given by a seller to a purchaser. *Jendwine* examined whether the appearance of the artist's name in a catalog constituted a warranty or whether it was merely the seller's description and opinion on which the buyer was not intended to rely. The court held that the catalog did not form a warranty because the period of the artist's work was so far removed that it was not possible to determine whether the paintings were originals. The catalog could, therefore, only indicate the seller's opinion that the paintings were originals, and "if the seller only represents what he himself believes, he can be guilty of no fraud."[29] However, after the completed sale in *Powers v. Barham,*[30] the seller gave the buyer a written receipt specifying the artist of the work, and this was held to be a warranty given at the time of sale, and not merely a description or statement of opinion. Thus, under common law the purchaser who seeks to recover must prove that the seller's statement was an express warranty, not merely an expression of opinion, and that, at the time of the sale, the seller knew the statement was false.

Weisz v. Parke-Bernet Galleries, Inc.

67 Misc. 2d 1077, 325 N.Y.S.2d 576 (Civ. Ct. 1971)

SANDLER, Judge.

On May 16, 1962, Dr. Arthur Weisz attended an auction conducted by the Parke-Bernet Galleries, Inc., where he ultimately bought for the sum of $3,347.50 a painting listed in the auction catalogue as the work of Raoul Dufy. Some two years later, on May 13, 1964, David and Irene Schwartz bought for $9,360.00 at a Parke-Bernet auction a painting also listed in the catalogue as the work of Raoul Dufy.

Several years after the second auction, as a result of an investigation conducted by the New York County District Attorney's office, the plaintiffs received information that the paintings were in fact forgeries. When this was called to Parke-Bernet's attention, Parke-Bernet denied any legal responsibility, asserting among other things that the conditions of sale for both auctions included a disclaimer of warranty as to genuineness, authorship and the like. . . .

As to the actions against Parke-Bernet, I find that the following facts were quite clearly established by the evidence.

---

28. *Jendwine v. Slade,* 170 Eng. Rep. 459 (1797).
29. *Id.* at 460.
30. *Powers v. Barham,* 111 Eng. Rep. 865 (1836).

(1) Each of the plaintiffs bought the paintings in question in the belief that they were painted by Raoul Dufy, had formed this conclusion because Parke-Bernet so stated in the respective catalogues, and would not have bought the paintings if they were not believed to be genuine.

(2) At the time of the auctions Parke-Bernet also believed the paintings ascribed to Dufy in the catalogues were his work.

(3) Neither of the paintings was in fact painted by Dufy. Both are forgeries with negligible commercial value.

The most substantial of the defenses interposed by Parke-Bernet is that the conditions of sale of the auctions, appearing on a preliminary page of each catalogue, included a disclaimer of any warranty and that the plaintiffs are bound by its terms.

This issue embraces two separate questions, each of which merits careful examination.

First, did the plaintiffs in fact know of the disclaimer, and, if they did not, are they legally chargeable with such knowledge.

Second, if the answer to either part of the first question is yes, was the disclaimer effective, under all the circumstances of the auctions, to immunize Parke-Bernet from the legal consequences that would normally follow where a sale results from a representation of genuiness that is thereafter disclosed to be completely inaccurate.

Although the auctions were separated in time by two years, the catalogues were quite similar in all legally significant respects, and the basic auction procedure was the same.

The catalogues open with several introductory pages of no direct relevance to the lawsuits. There then follows a page headed "Conditions of Sale," in large black print, under which some 15 numbered paragraphs appear, covering the side of one page and most of a second side. These provisions are in clear black print, somewhat smaller than the print used in the greater part of the catalogue.

Paragraph 2, on which Parke-Bernet relies, provides as follows:

The Galleries has endeavored to catalogue and describe the property correctly, but all property is sold "as is" and neither the Galleries nor its consignor warrants or represents, and they shall in no event be responsible for, the correctness of description, genuineness, authorship, provenience, or condition of the property, and no statement contained in the catalogue or made orally at the sale or elsewhere shall be deemed to be such a warranty or representation, or an assumption of liability.

The next page in each catalogue is headed "List of Artists," and contains in alphabetical order, one under the other, a list of the artists with a catalogue number or numbers appearing on the same line with the named artist. The implicit affirmation that the listed artists are represented in the auction and that the catalogue numbers appearing after their names represent their work could scarcely be clearer.

The name of Raoul Dufy is listed in each catalogue, together with several catalogue numbers.

After the pages on which the artists are listed, over 80 pages follow in each catalogue on which the catalogue numbers appear in numerical order with descriptive material about the artist and the work.

Turning in each catalogue to the catalogue numbers for the paintings involved in the lawsuits, there appears on the top of the page a conventional black-and-white catalogue reproduction of the painting, directly under it the catalogue number in brackets, and the name RAOUL DUFY in large black print, followed in smaller print by the words "French 1880-1953."

On the next line the catalogue number is repeated together with the name of the painting, a description of it, and the words, "Signed at lower right RAOUL DUFY." Finally, there appears a note that a certificate, by M. Andre Pacitti, will be given to the purchaser.

The procedure followed at both auctions was to announce at the beginning of the auction that it was subject to the conditions of sale, without repeating the announcement, and at no point alluding directly to the disclaimer.

As to the first auction, I am satisfied that Dr. Weisz did not in fact know of the Conditions of Sale and may not properly be charged with knowledge of its contents. I accept as entirely accurate his testimony that on his prior appearances at Parke-Bernet auctions he had not made any bids, and that on the occasion of his purchase he did not observe the conditions of sale and was not aware of its existence.

The test proposed for this kind of issue by Williston, quite consistent with the decided cases, is whether "the person ... should as a reasonable man understand that it contains terms of the contract which he must read at his peril." 1 Williston, *Contracts*, § 90D (1937); *see Linn v. Radio Center Delicatessen*, 169 Misc. 879, 9 N.Y.S.2d 110 (Mun. Ct. 1939); *Moore v. Schlossman's Inc.*, 5 Misc. 2d 693, 161 N.Y.S.2d 213 (Mun. Ct., 1957); *Wilson v. Manhasset Ford, Inc.*, 27 Misc. 2d 154, 209 N.Y.S.2d 210 (Dist. Ct. Nassau, 1960); 1 *Corbin On Contracts*, § 33 (1963); "Necessity of Buyer's Actual Knowledge of Disclaimer of Warranty of Personal Property," 160 A.L.R. 357 (1946).

The most obvious characteristic of the two Parke-Bernet auctions is that they attracted people on the basis of their interest in owning works of art, not on the basis of their legal experience or business sophistication. Surely it is unrealistic to assume that people who bid at such auctions will ordinarily understand that a gallery catalogue overwhelmingly devoted to descriptions of works of art also includes on its preliminary pages conditions of sale. Even less reasonable does it seem to me to expect a bidder at such an auction to appreciate the possibility that the conditions of sale would include a disclaimer of liability for the accuracy of the basic information presented throughout the catalogue in unqualified form with every appearance of certainty and reliability.

For someone in Dr. Weisz' position to be bound by conditions of sale, of which he in fact knew nothing, considerably more was required of Parke-Bernet to call those Conditions of Sale to his attention than occurred here.

The cases relied upon by Parke-Bernet where buyers were held to be bound by conditions of sale in auction catalogues are not at all apposite. For one thing, in only one of the cases does the opinion recite that the buyer flatly denied knowledge of the provision. *See Henry v. Salisbury*, 14 App. Div. 526, 43 N.Y.S. 851 (2d Dept., 1897). And in that case the buyer, a frequent bidder at the auction in question, acknowledged that he knew there were conditions of sale but had not undertaken to become familiar with them. More importantly, these auction cases for the most part concern business auctions, in which sellers and buyers were part of a business grouping in which a general knowledge of the governing rules and usages was reasonably to be anticipated. *See, e.g., Lewitus v. Brown & Seccomb*, 228 App. Div. 146, 239 N.Y.S. 261 (1st Dept., 1930); *Navarette v. Travis-Ziegler Co.*, 194 N.Y.S. 832 (Mun. Ct., 1922); *Alexander v. Sola*, 185 N.Y.S. 869 (A.T. 1st Dept., 1921).

As to the Schwartz case, I am satisfied from the evidence that Mrs. Schwartz knew of the Conditions of Sale, and that both Schwartz plaintiffs are chargeable with that knowledge since they both participated in the purchase.

This factual conclusion leads to consideration of the extremely interesting question whether the language of disclaimer relied upon as a bar to the actions should be deemed effective for that purpose. No case has come to my attention that squarely presents the issue raised by the underlying realities of this case.

What is immediately apparent from any review of the evidence is that, notwithstanding the language of disclaimer, Parke-Bernet expected that bidders at its auctions would rely upon the accuracy of its descriptions, and intended that they should. Parke-Bernet, as the evidence confirms, is an exceedingly well-known gallery, linked in the minds of people with the handling, exhibition and sale of valuable artistic works and invested with an aura of expertness and reliability. The very fact that Parke-Bernet was offering a work of art for sale would inspire confidence that it was genuine and that the listed artist in fact was the creator of the work.

The wording of the catalogue was clearly designed to emphasize the genuineness of the works to be offered. The list of artists followed by catalogue numbers, the black-and-white reproductions of the more important works, the simple listing of the name of the artist with the years of his birth and death, could not have failed to impress upon the buyer that these facts could be relied on and that one could safely part with large sums of money in the confident knowledge that a genuine artistic work was being acquired.

Where one party in a contractual relationship occupies a position of superior knowledge and experience, and where that superior knowledge is relied upon and intended to be relied upon by the other, surely more is required for an effective disclaimer than appears here.

After reassuring the reader that Parke-Bernet endeavored to catalogue the works of art correctly, there follow highly technical and legalistic words of disclaimer in a situation in which plain and emphatic words are required. And this provision, in light of the critical importance to the buyer of a warning that he may not rely on the fact that a work attributed to an artist was in fact his creation, is in no way given the special prominence that it clearly requires.

The language used, the understated manner of its presentation, the failure to refer to it explicitly in the preliminary oral announcement at the auction, all lead to the conclusion that Parke-Bernet did not expect the bidders to take the disclaimer too seriously or to be too concerned about it. I am convinced that the average reader of this provision would view it as some kind of technicality that should in no way derogate from the certainty that he was buying genuine artistic works, and that this was precisely the impression intended to be conveyed.

In denying legal effect to the disclaimer I am acting consistently with a whole body of law that reflects an increasing sensitivity to the requirements of fair dealing where there is a relationship between parties in which there is a basic inequality of knowledge, expertness or economic power. *Cf. Klar v. H & M Parcel Room*, 270 App. Div. 538, 61 N.Y.S.2d 285 (1st Dept., 1946); *Lachs v. Fidelity & Casualty Co. of New York*, 306 N.Y. 357, 118 N.E. 555 (1954); *Abel v. Paterno*, 245 App. Div. 285, 281 N.Y.S. 58 (1st Dept., 1935).

Another defense of some interest is the claim that the actions are barred by paragraph 14 of the Conditions of Sale, which provides that "any and all claims of a purchaser shall be deemed to be waived and shall be without validity unless made in writing to the Galleries within ten days after the sale."

This provision is of course inapplicable to Weisz in view of my earlier finding that he is not chargeable with knowledge of the Conditions of Sale.

Assuming arguendo that this provision is properly construed to apply to claims not known to the purchaser within the prescribed period, it clearly cannot stand. The rule was well established under the former Sales Act (and continues to be followed under the Uniform Commercial Code) that a limitation which applied to a claim that could not realistically be known before the end of the limitation was unreasonable and invalid. *Jessel v. Lockwood Textile Corp.*, 276 App. Div. 378, 95 N.Y.S.2d 77 (1st Dept., 1950).

The instant facts — where a buyer justifiably relied on a representation that a named artist created a work of art, was intended to rely on it, and no reason was presented for questioning the accuracy of the representation during the 10-day period — clearly come within that rule.

In any event, I believe that the provision in question is most reasonably and fairly construed as applying only to claims which were known or should have been known to the buyer during the 10-day period. Parke-Bernet's related argument that the purchaser did not act within the reasonable time required by subdivision 3 of Sec. 150 of the former Personal Property Law seems to me unsound for similar factual reasons.

Judgment may be entered for the plaintiff Weisz against Parke-Bernet in the sum of $3,347.50, and for the plaintiffs David and Irene Schwartz in the sum of $9,360.00, both judgments of course with appropriate interest and costs.

Notes and Questions

1. In a brief *per curiam* opinion, the New York Supreme Court, Appellate Division, 1st Department, reversed the decision in *Weisz*, stating that:

One of the factors necessarily entering into the competition among bidders at the public auction was the variable value of the paintings depending upon the degree of certainty with which they could be authenticated and established as the works of the ascribed artist. (*See* Backus v. MacLaury, 278 App. Div. 504, 507, 106 N.Y.S.2d 401, 403). Since no element of a willful intent to deceive is remotely suggested in the circumstances here present the purchasers assumed the risk that in judging the paintings as readily-identifiable, original works of the named artist, and scaling their bids accordingly, they might be mistaken. [Restatement of Contracts, sec. 504, comment f., P.964 (1932).] They will not now be heard to complain that, in failing to act with the auction of one in circumstances abound with signals of *caveat emptor*, they made a bad bargain.

Weisz v. Parke-Bernet Galleries, Inc., 77 Misc. 2d 80, 80-81, 351 N.Y.S.2d 911, 912 (Sup. Ct. 1974).

2. In *Weisz*, apparently both the auction house and the buyers were innocent parties. It is, therefore, necessary to determine which of them should bear the loss. The trial court and the appellate division differed on the ultimate decision in *Weisz*. It can be argued in support of the trial court's decision that the auction house is in a better position to spread this loss among those who participate in an auction. In addition, Parke-Bernet was in a better position to protect against this type of injury and could reasonably expect some pieces to be forgeries. Perhaps an insurance requirement could be imposed on all auctioneers selling fine art, thus providing protection for the consumer.

3. Conditions of sale are frequently long, detailed, and written in language most familiar to a lawyer; nevertheless, the buyer must become acquainted with these conditions. You can often find the terms on an auction house's website.

4. In *Nataros v. Fine Arts Gallery of Scottsdale*, 126 Ariz. 44, 612 P.2d 500 (1980), the gallery conducting an auction ran an advertisement that might have reasonably led purchasers to believe that all items offered were part of the estate of Walker McCune, although the gallery sold other items as well. However, plaintiffs could not show that they had actually been damaged when they purchased items that were not from the McCune estate. The court held that there was no evidence to show that had the items purchased by plaintiffs been from the McCune estate, they would have had a greater value. Moreover, plaintiffs could not show that they had been damaged by their reliance on the gallery salesman's representations of the value of the items sold. Plaintiffs purchased the items through competitive bidding, in which more than one bid was received and in which the plaintiffs made more than one bid on each item. There was no evidence that the auction was rigged or that the other bidders were not bona fide prospective purchasers. Thus, the price plaintiffs paid was fair market value, indicating that the salesman's appraisal was accurate.

PROBLEM 8-2

> Can inducing an individual to bid at an auction be considered fraud or misrepresentation? Would the alleged inducement entitle the aggrieved purchaser to rescind the contract?
>
> See *Pasternack v. Esskay Art Galleries*, 90 F. Supp. 849 (W.D. Ark. 1950). There, an auction house representative advised plaintiff that jewelry was worth approximately $46,000 and urged the plaintiff to bid on it. In addition, it was agreed that the jewelry would be resold at a subsequent auction and the profit split between the two parties. In fact, the jewelry was worth approximately $11,000 and plaintiff's $14,000 contract for its purchase was rescinded.

F. Antitrust Problems

We began this chapter with a discussion of Christie's and Sotheby's and their substantial share of the market for auctioning art. Apparently for the leaders of these companies, A. Alfred Taubman of Sotheby's and Sir Anthony Tennant of Christie's, controlling 95 percent of the $4 billion art market (of the early 1990's) was not enough. Federal prosecutors initiated an antitrust investigation and uncovered evidence of a scheme to limit competition by establishing identical commission charges for buyers in 1992 and sellers in 1995. In 1992, at a time when the art market was in the doldrums, Sotheby's announced an increase in the commissions paid by buyers at auction. Seven weeks later, Christie's followed with an identical commission structure. In 1995, Christie's announced it was changing the fee charged to sellers, and Sotheby's followed suit within weeks. The houses also exchanged confidential lists of top-drawer customers who were not to be charged a commission.[31] The two leaders discussed the arrangement in person and then instructed their chief executives, Christopher Davidge and Diana D. (Dede) Brooks, to meet to carry out the scheme.[32]

Mr. Taubman had earned a fortune developing shopping malls in the United States before purchasing a majority stake in Sotheby's in 1983, and has been credited with revamping the auction house by transforming it into a retail enterprise with vastly expanded services. Mr. Davidge acknowledged to prosecutors that he and Ms. Brooks met secretly many times over three years in

---

31. *See* Frantz et al., *Ex-Leaders of Two Auction Giants Are Said to Initiate Price-Fixing*, N.Y. Times, Apr. 7, 2000, at A1.
32. *Id.*

New York and London to work out the details of the collusion and exchange information.[33]

Davidge resigned from Christie's on Christmas Eve, 1999, and Brooks stepped down at Sotheby's on February 21, 2000, the same day Taubman resigned as Sotheby's chairman of the board, although he remained Sotheby's majority shareholder. Brooks approached prosecutors in January 2000 with an offer to cooperate in exchange for leniency, but was told by prosecutors that Christie's had already reached an agreement, according to people involved in the case. "She missed out by a week," said one of those involved in the case. "They beat her to the door."[34]

Mr. Davidge and Christie's were granted conditional amnesty from prosecution by the government for turning over evidence first. Under antitrust law, the first participant in a cartel to agree to cooperate with the government can receive leniency, including reduced fines and the likelihood that no criminal charges will be filed.[35] Sir Anthony, who served as chairman of Christie's from 1993 to 1996, was indicted for price-fixing, along with Taubman, but lives in England and cannot be extradited on antitrust charges.

Sotheby's and Brooks engaged in a high-stakes battle to win leniency from prosecutors. *Id.* Brooks, a graduate of Miss Porter's School in Connecticut, (whose graduates include Jacqueline Kennedy Onassis), and Yale University, pled guilty to price-fixing. Brooks was sentenced on April 29, 2002, to three years of probation, including six months of house arrest. She was fined $350,000, and required to perform 1,000 hours of community service.

Taubman was convicted of price-fixing in December 2001, sentenced on April 22, 2002 to a year and a day in prison, and assessed a $7.5 million fine. In the following case, he sought a new trial.

United States v. Taubman

2002 WL 54873 (S.D.N.Y. Apr. 11, 2002), *aff'd*, 297 F.3d 161 (2d Cir. 2002)*

DANIELS, District J.

Defendant A. Alfred Taubman moves for a new trial, pursuant to Federal Rule of Criminal Procedure 33, arguing that two rulings by the Court during trial were error requiring a new trial. Defendant contends that those two rulings in combination substantially limited his ability to respond to the Government's arguments regarding twelve meetings between himself and codefendant Sir Anthony Tennant, . . . and created an unacceptable risk that the jury would impermissibly conclude that the mere fact of these meetings was itself sufficient proof of Taubman's guilt.

. . . From the very beginning of the trial and throughout, there was no dispute that a conspiracy existed to fix seller's commission rates charged to

---

33. *Id.*
34. *Id.*
35. *Id.*
* Footnotes and most citations deleted.

customers of Sotheby's and Christie's. By its very nature, the members joined that conspiracy with the intent to unreasonably restrain competition between the two auction houses. Sotheby's CEO Diana (Dede) Brooks and Christie's CEO Christopher Davidge admitted and chronicled a series of meetings between them, over a period of years, in which they negotiated and executed the details of that illegal conspiracy.

The only disputed element of the charged offense was whether the defendant A. Alfred Taubman knowingly and intentionally became a member of that conspiracy. The direct evidence presented by the Government was the testimony of both Brooks and Davidge that Taubman and Tennant, the chairmen of Sotheby's and Christie's respectively, met with one another on several occasions and agreed to eliminate competition on a number of levels, including fixing sellers commission prices. Both Brooks and Davidge unequivocally testified that they were directed by their respective chairmen to work out the specifics of the illegal agreement.

To corroborate this direct testimonial evidence, the Government presented testimony and records concerning meetings between Taubman and Tennant, as well as notes reflecting some of the topics discussed at some of these meetings. Both Brooks and Davidge testified that during the course of these meetings, there were discussions formulating, and in furtherance of, the charged conspiracy. The Government introduced a number of calendars and itineraries which established that Taubman and Tennant met on twelve occasions on the following dates: February 3rd, April 1st, April 30th, and September 7th of 1993; January 12th, March 9th, June 23rd and November 28th of 1994; June 19th and October 19th of 1995; and April 11th and October 31st of 1996. . . .

The defendant requested that the jury be specifically instructed that "[e]vidence of meetings . . . between Mr. Taubman and Anthony Tennant and between Mr. Taubman and Diana Brooks does not by itself prove that Mr. Taubman was a participant in a conspiracy or that he had the required knowledge and intent." The defense claims that the requested charge was necessary in light of the Government's focus on the fact that these twelve meetings took place between defendant Taubman and Tennant. Defendant further argues that the Government sought to create the impression that there was no permissible reason for Tennant and Taubman to be communicating. According to the defendant, the risk that the jury might make the impermissible leap from the mere fact of the meetings to Taubman's guilt was exponentially increased when the Government decided to quote Adam Smith in its summation. Therefore, he contends that the proposed charge was necessary to prevent the jury from impermissibly concluding that defendant was guilty solely because he met with Tennant on several occasions. Absent the instruction, the defendant claims that the jury was "left to its own devices in considering either (1) whether the Tennant/Taubman meetings were permissible in the first instance, or (2) whether they constituted sufficient circumstantial evidence of Taubman's knowing and intentional participation in the alleged conspiracy." . . .

At trial, Christopher Davidge testified that in 1993, Tennant informed him that soon after Tennant's appointment as chairman of Christie's in September of 1992, Taubman contacted Tennant to congratulate him. . . . Taubman told Tennant that he did not believe that Tennant's predecessor was focused on the bottom line. . . . Taubman extended a number of invitations to Tennant to meet with him. . . . Tennant told Davidge that the two chairmen had met, but Davidge did not know the dates of these initial meetings. . . . Tennant told Davidge that at one of the meetings, Taubman gave Tennant Government exhibit 94, a document detailing certain of Christie's sales to demonstrate that Christie's was not making sensible and profitable deals. . . .

Taubman and Tennant met on the morning of April 30, 1993. . . . Tennant and Davidge met that very same afternoon. . . . Tennant informed Davidge that Taubman and Tennant had a "very good meeting." . . . Tennant provided Davidge with a written three page summary of the two chairmen's conversations. . . .

Davidge understood the quoted portion reflected certain topics that Taubman and Tennant had specifically agreed to: no more disparaging comments; cease making market share claims; no straight guarantees; no advances on single lots; no loans below LIBOR; trade vendors would not get a commission rate better than five percent, and pay their own insurance; no offers of more than 90 days credit to trade buyers; introductory commissions to third parties would not exceed one percent of the premium where there was no vendor's commission; no offers to vendors already contracted; cooperating on heritage issues, credit control, and introductory commissions to intermediaries; and cease making charitable donations. . . .

Davidge testified that the portion of Tennant's April 30th meeting summary which read, "A schedule exists. We should get back to it. 15% downward on a sliding scale." refers to the companies' published scale of fees for the seller's commission. . . . He further explained that the sentence which reads, "They are considering publishing a scale as with the buyer's premium," meant that Tennant and Taubman had discussed the possibility of producing a scale which would be the same as the buyer's premium which would be not negotiable." . . . The summary goes on to state, "If anyone wants to bargain on their new scale they will tell them to go elsewhere." . . .

Tennant told Davidge that there was an agreement to achieve a non-negotiable seller's commission. . . . Davidge was instructed to "work on a program on the basis of a fixed vendor's commission basis which [Tennant] would like adopted before the end of '93, and that it would be Christie's turn to go next on making an announcement about the change in the commission structures." . . . Davidge understood that "The core of the April 30th agreement was maximizing vendor's commissions." . . . He was instructed by Tennant to work out the details of all agreements with Brooks. Tennant indicated that "the major issue to work on was the issue of non-negotiable vendors' commissions." Davidge was told that Brooks would contact him directly on behalf of Sotheby's. At the chairmen's April 30th meeting, Tennant had given

Taubman the telephone number to Davidge's London flat so that Taubman could pass it on to Brooks.

Tennant had also instructed Davidge that "obviously this is a sensitive matter and that it would be wise to keep it to the four of us." . . . Tennant indicated to Davidge "that it was in everyone's best interests if only he and [Davidge] knew about this and he felt that was the way it should be at Sotheby's, that only Mr. Taubman and Ms. Brooks should know about it."

[Davidge further testified that he received a phone call from Brooks. They met initially in a London hotel and subsequently at Brooks's London apartment. One of their eight to ten meetings took place at Brooks's automobile parked at Kennedy Airport.] A few weeks after Christie's formal announcement, Sotheby's made its announcement about a change in the seller's commissions, which Davidge found to be substantially in accordance with his discussions with Brooks. . . . In May of 1995, Christie's made another announcement concerning the seller's commission rates, which set forth certain changes in some of the scales so as to fit more in line with the Sotheby's announcement. . . . Therefore, by September of 1995, as agreed to in conversations between Taubman, Tennant, Brooks, and Davidge, Christie's and Sotheby's were essentially charging the same seller's commissions rates and those rates were non-negotiable. . . .

[Brooks testified that Taubman summoned her to his office on April 30, 1993, to inform her of his "good meeting" with Taubman. He showed her a note that included topics such as "guarantees, interest free or single lot advances, no disparaging remarks, the quoting of market share, no poaching of the other's staff, introductory commissions, and charitable contributions." Taubman instructed Brooks not to tell anyone about the agreements. The parties then implemented the agreement over the course of two years. On May 30, 1995, Christie's issued a press release making changes to its seller's commission rates to become effective on September 1, 1995. These changes were similar to the ones Sotheby's had announced on April 13, 1995.]

TAUBMAN'S DEFENSE

It is important to note at the outset that two significant concessions were made by the defense at trial: (1) the undisputed existence of a conspiracy to fix auction commission rates charged to sellers at Sotheby's and Christies; and (2) Taubman met with Tennant on a number of occasions at his New York and London apartments at the times claimed by the prosecution. Taubman's defense was that the conspiracy was committed by Brooks and Davidge, without his knowledge or participation, even if the evidence indicated the involvement of Christie's chairman Tennant. As a result, the defendant essentially narrowed the jury's focus to the only disputed element of the crime, whether he knowingly and intentionally was a member of the charged conspiracy. In this regard, attacking the credibility of Davidge, and, more importantly, Brooks was the cornerstone of that defense. The testimony of these two admitted co-conspirators constituted the direct evidence that Taubman and

Tennant met to discuss fixing prices, agreed to fix prices, and ordered their respective CEO's to carry out and execute that illegal scheme. . . .

THE COURT'S JURY INSTRUCTIONS

The Court instructed the jury that the that there are three elements that the Government must prove beyond a reasonable doubt, namely: (1) that the conspiracy to fix auction commission rates charged to sellers existed at or about the time stated in the indictment; (2) that the defendant knowingly and intentionally became a member of that conspiracy; and (3) that the defendant joined that conspiracy with the intent to unreasonably restrain trade. . . . With respect to the second element, which was the only element in dispute, the jury was specifically charged that the "government must prove that the defendant knowingly joined the conspiracy to fix auction commission rates charged to sellers with the intent to aid or advance the purpose of the conspiracy and not because of a mistake, accident or some other innocent reason." . . . The Court's charge further instructed that ". . . a person who has no knowledge of a conspiracy but who happens to act in a way which furthers some purpose of the conspiracy does not thereby become a member of the conspiracy."

The defense conceded the existence of a price fixing conspiracy to the jury. The jury did not require an instruction that one cannot infer the existence of a conspiracy solely because of meetings or contacts between competitors. The Government did not use the mere existence of meetings between Taubman and Tennant to imply the existence of the conspiracy. Therefore, there was no risk that the jury would improperly infer, simply from the mere fact that Taubman and Tennant met, the existence of a price fixing conspiracy. . . .

Defendant contends that absent the proposed instruction, the jury was left to speculate as to the purpose of the meetings. However, given the direct evidence of defendant's involvement in the conspiracy, the jury was never in a position to simply speculate that because Taubman and Tennant met, one could infer that they must have necessarily conspired to fix seller's commission rates. Both the Government and defense offered detailed evidence of specific topics discussed, which were both a part of and outside of the charged conspiratorial agreement. The jury was never asked to speculate regarding the criminal nature of the meetings between Taubman and Tennant. Brooks and Davidge's testimony, and notes of those meetings, were the evidence in the record directly reflecting the purpose and nature of the meetings.

Defendant's contention that the Government presented "no evidence whatsoever about the substance of the Tennant/Taubman meetings" is belied by the record. . . . There was substantial evidence indicating that there were continuous discussions and agreements on numerous competitive issues, including pricing. It is of no consequence that the evidence does not reflect the substance of every conversation that took place between defendant and Tennant, or for that matter, between any of the four conspirators. The jury only had to find that part of those discussions concerned fixing the seller's commission rates, and that defendant and Tennant agreed to do so. The testimony of Brooks and Davidge clearly indicated that such an illegal conversation and agreement between defendant and Tennant occurred. . . .

The defense even argued that the two "were social friends" who met "when Mr. Taubman was in London for a board meeting.". . . In addition, the defense argued that since "other people from Christie's and Sotheby's were meeting and talking about issues affecting the auction industry," the jury could infer that "these same issues were raised between Mr. Tennant and Mr. Taubman."

It was impossible for the jury to find the defendant guilty solely because he met with Tennant to discuss only uncharged agreements reflected in the April 30th summary, or any other non-conspiratorial topic. At the request of the defense, the Court gave the following instruction to ensure that the defendant would not be convicted based upon evidence of any legal or illegal agreement other than a knowing and intentional conspiracy to fix seller's commission rates:

> Both the government and defense have elicited testimony concerning other allegedagreements on such topics as interest free advances, charitable contributions, introductory commissions, guarantees, insurance charges and the buyer's premium. I want to caution you that the indictment does not charge the defendant with any crime with respect to these subjects. The sole charge in this case is that the defendant participated in a conspiracy to fix auction commission rates charged to sellers. Accordingly, you may consider evidence of other alleged agreements only to the extent you believe it bears on that charge.

The jury was thereby specifically instructed that much of the discussions between Taubman and Tennant did not constitute criminal activity charged in this case. The question for the jury was not whether Taubman and Tennant had "legitimate and lawful reasons to have contact with each other" . . . , but whether the witnesses were credible when they testified that those meetings included an agreement to fix prices. Had the jury found that the subject matters of the meetings only concerned topics other than fixing seller's commission rates, the Court's instructions precluded a finding that those other discussions could impose criminal liability upon the defendant. Instead, the Court focused the jury on the specific criminal conduct that formed the basis of the charged indictment. . . .

Defendant's arguments in support of his application for a new trial are based upon a simplistic mischaracterization of the jury's verdict. It ignores the jury's thorough analysis of the totality of the evidence during their deliberations. Once the issue of the credibility of the main witnesses was resolved against the defendant, that evidence overwhelmingly established the defendant's guilt of the crime charged beyond a reasonable doubt. In fact, the evidence revealed that defendant was not merely a member of the conspiracy, but rather, the initiating and driving force behind it. The jury's verdict was supported by competent, satisfactory and sufficient evidence, and does not constitute a miscarriage of justice. *United States v. Ferguson*, 246 F.3d 129, 134 (2d Cir. 2001); *United States v. Landau*, 155 F.3d 93, 104 (2d Cir. 1998); *United States v. Sanchez*, 969 F.2d 1049, 1414 (2d Cir. 1992); Fed. R. Crim. P. 33.

Accordingly, the defendant's motion for a new trial is denied.

Notes and Questions

1. After serving his sentence, Taubman was released from prison on June 13, 2003. Given the hundreds of millions of dollars that he and his co-conspirators bilked out of customers, do you consider Taubman's and Brooks's sentences too lenient? Consider that a bank robber, who retrieves $1,000 on an average heist, faces ten years in prison. *See* Sherri L. Burr, *When the Rich Scam the Rich, Punishment Goes Begging*, Albuquerque Trib., May 23, 2002, at C1. When asked "How honest is the art game?" by Louis Rukeyser in a 1997 *Wall Street Week* interview, Brooks replied, "I am confident that we are really setting a new level of standards in the business, because, after all, our integrity is all we have." *Id.*

2. Between the two of them, Christie's and Sotheby's control 95 percent of the multi-billion dollar art auction market. Dominick Dunne said in his February 2002 *Vanity Fair* column their intrigue amounted to "rich people cheating other rich people, most of whom were so rich they didn't know they were being cheated." Do you consider Christie's and Sotheby's efforts to fix prices so that buyers and sellers could not negotiate an example of greed personified? Is this case another example of the maxim *buyer beware*?

3. After the disclosure that Christie's was cooperating with the federal investigation, former auction buyers and sellers initiated numerous civil suits. Sotheby's shareholders also sued because the value of their stock declined once the investigation was launched. Christie's is privately held. *See* Frantz et al, *Ex-Leaders of Two Auction Giants are Said to Initiate Price-Fixing*, N.Y. Times, Apr. 7, 2000, at A1. Sotheby's and Christie's eventually agreed to pay $256 million each to settle a class-action lawsuit brought by angry clients. Taubman paid $156 million of Sotheby's share himself. Goldman, *Toppling Off the Auction Block*, L.A. Times, Jan. 10, 2001, at E1. Sotheby's also pled guilty to criminal charges and agreed to pay a $45 million criminal fine.

4. At trial, Davidge testified that Tennant told him "it would be wise to keep it to the four of us." Do the results of what happened recall the old adage, "A secret is only a secret as long as one of the two parties to it is dead?" Do four parties to a conspiracy guarantee that it will one day be revealed?

5. Taubman appealed his conviction and the denial of a motion for a new trial. The Court of Appeals in *U.S. v. Taubman*, 293 F.3d 161 (2002),

affirmed the judgment of the district court, finding no abuse of discretion and that any errors were harmless.

6. By 2004, the auction market had rebounded from its antitrust problems as customers began to return. On May 5, 2004, Sotheby's sold Picasso's *Boy with a Pipe (The Young Apprentice)*, a 1905 work from Picasso's Rose Period, for $104.2 million. On November 9, 2015, Amedeo Modigliani's *Reclining Nude* sold for $170.4 million.

7. Sotheby's and Christie's auction houses are not the only auction sellers who have faced claims of antitrust violations. eBay was charged with violating the Sherman Antitrust Act in *Mazur v. eBay Inc.*, 257 F.R.D. 563 (N.D. Cal. 2009). In a proposed class action, the plaintiffs accused defendants of engaging in fake or "shill" bidding and eBay of acquiescing to the illegal activity. The judge denied the motion to certify the class, holding that: (1) the proposed class definition was imprecise, overbroad, and unascertainable; (2) named plaintiff's claims did not satisfy typicality requirement for class certification; and (3) common questions of law or fact did not predominate over individual questions.

ASSESSMENT

1. Barry Buyer was an avid art collector who loved attending auctions. Although he lived in Alaska, Barry often attended auctions throughout the United States. One spring, a large Florida art auction was announced in an art magazine. Barry immediately booked his flight out there, excited to acquire some new pieces for his collection. Unfortunately, on his way to the airport, Barry's Uber driver decided not to listen to his cellphone directions, which resulted in Barry missing his flight.

    Desperate to get his hands on several of the paintings at the auction, Barry resorted to begging his cousin in Florida, Stanley Standin, to attend the auction in his place. Stan agreed, as long as Barry would guide him through the process by texting him instructions during the auction. Which of the following is the most accurate statement?

    (A) Barry Buyer will not be able to keep the works of art he successfully bids on because Stanley Standin did all of the work at the auction house and made the deals happen, so he deserves to own the paintings

    (B) If anything goes wrong at the auction, Barry Buyer will still be subject to Florida jurisdiction because he acted through an agent who was physically present in the Florida auction room

    (C) Stanley Standin will not be allowed into the auction house because he was not invited by invitation, which is required to get into these types of events

    (D) None of the above

    (E) Both (B) and (C)

2. Betty Bidder attended an auction after receiving a fancy invitation to the event. She had never been to an auction, but was excited to participate. As the auction began, an art seller went up to the front and displayed his art while providing a detailed description of the piece. It was a beautiful vase and Betty was anxious to buy it. She wrote down her bid of $10,000, sealed it and handed it to the auctioneer. Betty was convinced she would have the highest bid. However, to Betty's disappointment and shock, the seller withdrew his sale of the vase. He later stated that he decided he could not part with the piece. Although Betty was sad to not have acquired the base, she was happy with the experience. What type of auction was Betty Bidder most likely attending?

(A) The Japanese system
(B) The English, and most common, auction system
(C) A virtual online bidding system
(D) The Dutch auction system
(E) None of the above

3. According to Brenna Adler's article, why did she believe auction houses are allowed to get away with controversial and possibly illegal activities?

(A) Customers enjoy the secretive nature of the art auction world, so they never bring complaints against auction houses
(B) Lack of domestic and international regulation
(C) A continuing stream of customers due to the art world's glamour and prestige
(D) Both (B) and (C)
(E) None of the above

4. In *Callimanopulous*, the court was faced with the question of whether a valid contract was formed between a bidder and the auction house when the bidder entered a bid before the auctioneer struck the hammer. The court ultimately held that no valid contract was formed. Which of the following reason(s) did the court give to support its reasoning?

(A) The auction houses are allowed to do whatever they want because they are private entities
(B) The auctioneer is not prevented from relying on employees working as spotters
(C) The auctioneer can do whatever he wants with his hammer
(D) An auctioneer has the power to exercise discretion to reopen bidding within a reasonable time of striking the hammer
(E) Both (B) and (D)

5. In New York, Art Buyer's Delight (ABD), a famous auction house, began preparing for its spring auction. ABD was very excited because

the owner of a Picasso, Sally Seller, was planning to be involved in the auction. Sally was not sure how much the Picasso was worth so she did not want to set a reserve price on the item, which was put into explicit terms in her contract with ABD. The Picasso was put in the ABD spring catalog and was not identified as having a reserve.

On the day of the auction, Sally was present and waited eagerly to see how much money she could get for the piece. After showing the piece to the awaiting buyers, the auctioneer called for the bidding to begin. After a few bids went up, Sally realized that no one at the auction house had enough money to buy the Picasso for the price she wanted to sell it for, so she withdrew the painting.

Was Sally Seller's withdrawal of her Picasso painting valid?

(A) Sally Seller's withdrawal is invalid because the auctioneer had already called for bids
(B) The withdrawal of Sally Seller's Picasso is valid because she owns the painting and can therefore do whatever she wants with it
(C) The withdrawal was invalid because a bid was made within a reasonable time after the auctioneer called for bids
(D) (A) and (C) only
(E) (A) and (B) only

ASSESSMENT ANSWERS

1. Barry Buyer was an avid art collector who loved attending auctions. Although he lived in Alaska, Barry often attended auctions throughout the United States. One spring, a large Florida art auction was announced in an art magazine. Barry immediately booked his flight out there, excited to acquire some new pieces for his collection. Unfortunately, on his way to the airport, Barry's Uber driver decided not to listen to his cellphone directions, which resulted in Barry missing his flight.

Desperate to get his hands on several of the paintings at the auction, Barry resorted to begging his cousin in Florida, Stanley Standin, to attend the auction in his place. Stan agreed, as long as Barry would guide him through the process by texting him instructions during the auction. Which of the following is the most accurate statement?

(A) Barry Buyer will not be able to keep the works of art he successfully bids on because Stanley Standin did all of the work at the auction house and made the deals happen, so he deserves to own the paintings
(B) If anything goes wrong at the auction, Barry Buyer will still be subject to Florida jurisdiction because he acted through an agent who was physically present in the Florida auction room

(C) Stanley Standin will not be allowed into the auction house because he was not invited by invitation, which is required to get into these types of events

(D) None of the above

(E) Both (B) and (C)

ANSWER: The answer is (B). The case law makes clear that participating in a telephone bid subjects the buyer to the jurisdiction where the auction took place.

2. Betty Bidder attended an auction after receiving a fancy invitation to the event. She had never been to an auction, but was excited to participate. As the auction began, an art seller went up to the front and displayed his art while providing a detailed description of the piece. It was a beautiful vase and Betty was anxious to buy it. She wrote down her bid of $10,000, sealed it and handed it to the auctioneer. Betty was convinced she would have the highest bid. However, to Betty's disappointment and shock, the seller withdrew his sale of the vase. He later stated that he decided he could not part with the piece. Although Betty was sad to not have acquired the base, she was happy with the experience. What type of auction was Betty Bidder most likely attending?

(A) The Japanese system

(B) The English, and most common, auction system

(C) A virtual online bidding system

(D) The Dutch auction system

(E) None of the above

ANSWER: The answer is (A). These facts present the Japanese system of auctioning where the auctioneer can accept a sealed bid.

3. According to Brenna Adler's article, why did she believe auction houses are allowed to get away with controversial and possibly illegal activities?

(A) Customers enjoy the secretive nature of the art auction world so they never bring complaints against auction houses

(B) Lack of domestic and international regulation

(C) A continuing stream of customers due to the art world's glamour and prestige

(D) Both (B) and (C)

(E) None of the above

ANSWER: The Answer is (C). Adler's article argues that auction houses may get away with controversial and possibly illegal activities because of both a lack of domestic and international regulation and a continuing stream of customers due to the art world's glamour and prestige.

4. In *Callimanopulous*, the court was faced with the question of whether a valid contract was formed between a bidder and the auction house,

when the bidder entered a bid before the auctioneer struck the hammer. The court ultimately held that no valid contract was formed. Which of the following reason(s) did the court give to support its reasoning?

(A) The auction houses are allowed to do whatever they want because they are private entities
(B) The auctioneer is not prevented from relying on employees working as spotters
(C) The auctioneer can do whatever he wants with his hammer
(D) An auctioneer has the power to exercise discretion to reopen bidding within a reasonable time of striking the hammer
(E) Both (B) and (D)

ANSWER: The Answer is (E). An auctioneer can rely on employees to work as spotters and the auctioneer can reopen bidding within a reasonable time of striking the hammer.

5. In New York, Art Buyer's Delight (ABD), a famous auction house, began preparing for its spring auction. ABD was very excited because the owner of a Picasso, Sally Seller, was planning to be involved in the auction. Sally was not sure how much the Picasso was worth so she did not want to set a reserve price on the item, which was put into explicit terms in her contract with ABD. The Picasso was put in the ABD spring catalog and was not identified as having a reserve.

On the day of the auction, Sally was present and waited eagerly to see how much money she could get for the piece. After showing the piece to the awaiting buyers, the auctioneer called for the bidding to begin. After a few bids went up, Sally realized that no one at the auction house had enough money to buy the Picasso for the price she wanted to sell it for, so she withdrew the painting.

Was Sally Seller's withdrawal of her Picasso painting valid?

(A) Sally Seller's withdrawal is invalid because the auctioneer had already called for bids
(B) The withdrawal of Sally Seller's Picasso is valid because she owns the painting and can therefore do whatever she wants with it
(C) The withdrawal was invalid because a bid was made within a reasonable time after the auctioneer called for bids
(D) (A) and (C) only
(E) (A) and (B) only

ANSWER: The answer is (D). The withdrawal was invalid because the auctioneer had already called for bids and the bid was made within a reasonable time after the auctioneer called for bids.

9 | MUSEUMS

Museums have been established to showcase art, like the Musée du Louvre in Paris, or to preserve culture, like Egyptian Museum in Cairo. Sometimes museums, like the Georgia O'Keeffe in Santa Fe, New Mexico, capture a segment of a person's life. Others, like the Tenniseum Roland Garros, showcase a particular sport. During May 2009, for example, the Tenniseum featured a photography exhibit showcasing tennis star Venus Williams in a variety of poses:

Venus *par (by) Koto Bolofo, Tenniseum, Roland Garros, France*[1]

Some museums, like those for children, provide sensory experiences, permitting their visitors to touch and feel art objects. Others focus on items for adults. China's Museum of Sex in Shanghai features 3,500 Chinese sex artifacts dating back 5,000 years, including a fourteenth-century chair specially designed to enhance lovemaking. The BMW Museum in Munich displays an array of cars and posters addressing its role in Germany during World War II. As a manufacturer of planes for the Third Reich, the main BMW factory was bombed, which led the company to move completely away from defense contracting and toward private commerce. In 2015, consumer activist Ralph Nader opened a Museum of Tort Law in his home town of Winstead, Connecticut, to increase understanding of the law of wrongful injury.

---

1. Image: Sherri Burr, Cropped, revised, and resized thumbnail excerpt of a Sherri Burr photograph of "Venus" by Koto Bolofo, Tenniseum, Roland Garros, France (2009).

As the largest group of art collectors and the most visible participants in the art market, museums occupy a unique position in the art world. This chapter analyzes the legal structures of museums, their management liability, their role in society, and how they acquire and manage property. The reader may encounter these situations involving museums as counsel or on behalf of a donor or artist.

A. The Legal Entity

This section considers organizational structures used to govern museums and analyzes the roles of key personnel, pointing out potential pitfalls that may result in the imposition of liability. In addition to the formidable task of gathering objects for display, institutions purchase items, lease or acquire buildings, and, in general, fulfill public purposes.

1. The Trust Form

A museum may be either a public or charitable trust or a charitable corporation. The Restatement (Third) of Trusts § 27 (2003) states "a trust may be created for charitable purposes . . . or for private purposes, or for a combination of charitable and private purposes." G. Bogert, *Law of Trusts* § 54 (6th ed., 1987) [hereinafter Bogert], states that "[a] charitable trust is a trust the performance of which will, in the opinion of the court of chancery, accomplish a substantial amount of social benefit to the public or some reasonably large class thereof."

A charitable or public trust must be created in compliance with the law of trusts. Generally, this requires an owner of property (referred to as the settlor) to manifest an intent to create the trust. The settlor must transfer the property's legal title to trustees, who administer it for the benefit of the public. The public or charitable trust is usually created by a written instrument, which may be either *inter vivos* or testamentary. The document will generally set forth the trustees' names or criteria for their selection, a description of the trust property (referred to as the corpus of the trust), any limitations or restrictions imposed by the settlor, and the trust's purpose. In the event the trust's objective cannot be fulfilled or its purpose is unclear, a court may use the *cy pres* doctrine to apply the corpus to a similar purpose. Before doing so, however, the court must be satisfied that the settlor had a general charitable purpose in mind when the trust was created. Note the concerns in the following case.

Georgia O'Keeffe Foundation (Museum) v. Fisk University

2009 WL 2047376 (Tenn. Ct. App. July 14, 2009)

Frank G. CLEMENT, Jr., Judge.

At issue in this appeal are the respective rights of three parties concerning charitable gifts of 101 pieces of art given, subject to conditions, to Fisk

University in the late 1940s and early 1950s. The collection has an estimated present value in excess of $60 million. Four of the pieces, including the painting *Radiator Building-Night, New York*, were the property of Georgia O'Keeffe and given to the University by Ms. O'Keeffe. The other ninety-seven pieces were part of a much larger collection formerly owned by Alfred Stieglitz, Georgia O'Keeffe's late husband. The ninety-seven pieces were gifted to the University by Ms. O'Keeffe as executrix of the estate and/or as the owner of a life estate in the ninety-seven pieces. All 101 pieces were charitable, conditional gifts that were subject to several restrictions, two of which are at issue here; the pieces could not be sold and the various pieces of art were to be displayed at Fisk University as one collection.

These proceedings began when Fisk University filed an *ex parte* declaratory judgment action seeking permission to sell two valuable pieces of the collection because it could no longer afford to maintain the collection pursuant to the conditions imposed 50 years earlier. Thereafter, the Georgia O'Keeffe Museum intervened, followed by the Tennessee Attorney General. The O'Keeffe Museum contended that any sale of the collection violated the conditions of the gifts and should result in the entire collection reverting to the Museum as the successor in interest to Ms. O'Keeffe's estate. Later on, an offer by the Crystal Bridges Museum of Benton, Arkansas, was presented to the court pursuant to which the Crystal Bridges Museum would pay Fisk University $30 million to acquire a one-half interest in the entire collection and the right to exhibit the collection six months each year.

The trial court determined that the Georgia O'Keeffe Museum had standing to contest the sale of the pieces gifted by Georgia O'Keeffe and the Stieglitz estate; that the doctrine of *cy pres* was not an available remedy to Fisk University because the gifts were the result of a specific charitable intent, not a general charitable intent, and the petition to sell the collection was denied and dismissed. On appeal, we have determined the Georgia O'Keeffe Museum lacks standing to participate in this action and therefore dismiss its intervening petition and relief sought. Further, we have determined that the trial court erred in finding that Ms. O'Keeffe lacked general charitable intent. Accordingly, we reinstate the University's *cy pres* petition and remand for the trial court to determine whether *cy pres* relief is available and, if so, to fashion the appropriate relief. . . .

THE UNIVERSITY'S PRAYER FOR *CY PRES* RELIEF
FROM THE CONDITIONS

In its Amended Petition, the University sought relief, pursuant to the *cy pres* doctrine, from certain conditions imposed on the University when the Collection was gifted. The reasons for the requested relief are the University's bleak financial circumstance, which the University contends jeopardize its viability and make it "impractical to comply with the literal terms" of the gifts, along with other material changes in circumstances that have occurred in the more than fifty years since the conditional gifts were made.

The University's petition for *cy pres* relief was dismissed upon the finding that the University could not prove some of the essential elements necessary to be entitled to *cy pres* relief. For reasons we explain in detail below, we have determined the trial court erred in concluding that the University could not establish that it was entitled to *cy pres* relief based upon the court's finding that Ms. O'Keeffe's charitable intent was specific, not general. Whether *cy pres* relief is available, and if so, in what fashion and to what extent, will have to be decided by the trial court on remand. . . .

THE *CY PRES* DOCTRINE

New York law, which the parties agree applies to this issue, requires that a donee of a charitable gift with conditions must obtain court approval of changes in conditions placed on charitable gifts if the donor is no longer living. This type of relief is known as *cy pres* relief. The phrase "*cy pres*" is Anglo-French in origin and literally means "as near as possible." . . . *In re Catholic Child Care Soc'y of Diocese of Brooklyn*, No. 3522/1968, 2009 WL 1194970, at *1 (N.Y. Sur. Ct. Apr. 30, 2009). "The doctrine proceeds upon the principle that it is the duty of the court to give effect to the general charitable intention of the testator as nearly as possible, when the subsidiary intent that a gift take effect in a particular manner is impossible to implement." *Id.* . . .

A donee's request for *cy pres* relief is a two-step process. First, the donee must establish that *cy pres* relief is available. New York courts have developed a three-pronged test for determining whether *cy pres* relief is available. *In re Hummel*, 805 N.Y. S.2d 236, 248-49 (N.Y. Sup. Ct. 2005). One, the gift must have been charitable in nature. *Id.* Two, the donor must have demonstrated a general, rather than a specific, charitable intent. *Id.* Three, the circumstances have changed subsequent to the gift that render literal compliance with the restriction impossible or impracticable. *Id.* If the donee proves each prong of the three-pronged test stated above, then *cy pres* relief is available; however, that determination does not satisfy the last requirement of the *cy pres* doctrine, which is that the proposed modification most closely approximates the donor's charitable intent. . . . Accordingly, we need not consider whether the proposed agreement with the Crystal Bridges Museum is or is not as near as possible to the intent expressed by Georgia O'Keeffe until it is determined that the University has successfully proven all three prongs under the New York *cy pres* test. . . .

In this case, it is undisputed that the gifts to the University were charitable in nature, thus satisfying the first essential element of the *cy pres* analysis. We will, therefore, proceed to the second prong of the *cy pres* analysis to determine whether Ms. O'Keeffe demonstrated a general, rather than a specific, charitable intent when the Collection, including her four pieces, [was] given to the University.

MS. O'KEEFFE'S CHARITABLE INTENT — SPECIFIC OR GENERAL?

The University must establish, *inter alia*, that Alfred Stieglitz and/or Ms. O'Keeffe were motivated by a general charitable intent when the Collection was given to the University in the 1950s. . . . The courts generally favor a finding of general charitable intent, *see In re Kraetzer's Will*, 462 N.Y.S.2d 1009, 1013 (N.Y. Sur. Ct. 1983) . . . , and "absent an express divesting condition, *cy pres* is almost invariably applied." *In re Kraetzer's Will*, 462 N.Y.S.2d at 1013. . . .

A donor's charitable intent may be evidenced in several ways. First, a donor's general charitable intent may be evidenced by other charitable gifts and the provisions of the gift. *In re Catholic Child Care Soc'y of Diocese of Brooklyn*, 2009 WL 1194970, at *1. . . . Similarly, the fact that a donor made similar charitable gifts to several different charities also demonstrates "a general charitable intent." *In re Estate of Othmer*, 815 N.Y.S.2d 444, 447 (N.Y. Sur. Ct. 2006). . . . Finally, the absence of a divesting clause in the event of the conditions being breached is indicative of a general charitable intent. *In re Estate of Othmer*, 815 N.Y.S.2d at 447. . . .

It is apparent from Alfred Stieglitz's will, the 1948 Petition Georgia O'Keeffe filed in the surrogate's court, and Ms. O'Keeffe's letters to [then Fisk University] President Johnson that followed, that the charitable intent motivating the gifts of the Stieglitz Collection and Ms. O'Keeffe's four pieces to the University was to make the Collection available to the public in Nashville and the South for the benefit of those who did not have access to comparable collections to promote the general study of art. The express language used in Alfred Stieglitz's will reveals that he desired his collection be donated to institutions to promote the study of art. The record in this case also reveals that Georgia O'Keeffe not only affirmed his expressed intent when making the gifts from his vast collection to the University and other institutions, but she also adopted her husband's charitable intent when she donated four pieces from her personal collection to the University.

In her correspondence to President Johnson, before and after the completion of the gifts from her collection, Ms. O'Keeffe expressed her intent that the Collection, inter alia, be identified as the Stieglitz Collection (including her four pieces) and preserved, intact, for its educational study and historical value to the public. Considering the facts in the record, we have concluded that the clear intent for giving the Collection to the University was to enable the public — in Nashville and the South — to have the opportunity to study the Collection in order to promote the general study of art.

We acknowledge the fact that Ms. O'Keeffe had a specific purpose in mind and that she imposed specific conditions on the gifts, but a specific purpose and the imposition of specific conditions does not mean that the gifts were motivated by a specific intent, as that term is applied in a *cy pres* analysis. See, *e.g., In re Estate of Othmer*, 815 N.Y. S.2d at 447. Thus, the fact that Ms. O'Keeffe had a specific purpose and imposed specific conditions does not alter the fact that the motivation for the gifts to the University was to promote the study of art in Nashville and the South.

We also find it significant that Ms. O'Keeffe made similar charitable gifts to several different charities at the same time the gifts were made to the

University. This is significant, as New York law instructs, because it demonstrates "a general charitable intent." *In re Estate of Othmer*, 815 N.Y.S.2d at 447. . . .

It is also significant that an "express divesting condition" cannot be found in the record. This is significant because the donee of a charitable conditional gift is "almost invariably" eligible for *cy pres* relief, assuming the other conditions are met, if there is no express divesting condition associated with the charitable gift. *In re Kraetzer's Will*, 462 N.Y.S.2d at 1013 (emphasis added). There is no express divesting clause in any of the correspondence between Ms. O'Keeffe and President Johnson prior to or at the completion of the respective gifts to the University.[13] For that matter, there is no express divesting provision in any of the relevant correspondence or court documents after the completion of the gifts. After the gifting of the Stieglitz Collection was completed and while Ms. O'Keeffe's four pieces were still on "permanent loan," Ms. O'Keeffe corresponded with President Johnson expressing "requests" and "recommendations" for the return of the Collection if the conditions of the gift could not be met; however, none of her requests or recommendations constitute a declaration of a "legal right" arising out of a divesting provision. Ms. O'Keeffe's correspondence merely constituted expressions of disappointment and frustration with the manner in which the University was maintaining, or not appropriately maintaining, the Collection.[14] Moreover, the subsequent correspondence could not alter the terms or conditions of the gift of the Alfred Stieglitz collection. . . . The disappointment expressed in Ms. O'Keeffe's correspondence with President Johnson in 1951 provided more than reasonable justification for Ms. O'Keeffe to include an express divesting clause in the subsequent gifts of her four pieces to the University; but she did not include an express divesting clause as a condition of her separate gifts and the absence of such a clause indicates that Ms. O'Keeffe did not intend for her gifts to revert to her or her estate in the event of a material breach. Based upon these facts, we find no factual basis upon which to conclude that the conditional, charitable gifts contained an express divesting clause. Accordingly, we have concluded there is no basis for a reversion of any of the gifts in the event of a material breach by the University.

---

13. To be binding, conditions on a charitable gift must have been imposed prior to or at the time of the completion of the gift; not thereafter. *See Phillippsen v. Emigrant Indus. Sav. Bank*, 86 N.Y.S.2d 133, 136-37 (N.Y. Sup. Ct. 1948) (stating that a completed *inter vivos* gift occurs when the donor intends to make a gift that will divest the owner of possession and dominion over the thing given and makes "a delivery of the subject of the gift in consummation of the intention").

14. In her letter to President Johnson dated July 14, 1951, Ms. O'Keeffe stated, "Would you like to consider letting me withdraw the Collection?" The reason for her request to "withdraw" the Collection was made apparent by the paragraph in the letter that followed:

> You do not seem to have anyone to take care of it or utilize it and you have written me nothing about air-conditioning or controlling dust and humidity. I saw the amount of dirt that settles down on a table top in the rooms over night, and with your humidity and changes of temperature it will soon be the ruination of the pictures. May I hear from you about this?

Considering the foregoing facts, including the express purpose of promoting the study of art by the public in Nashville and the South, that Ms. O'Keeffe made similar charitable gifts to several different charities when the gifts were made to the University, that there is no express divesting clause, and the legal principle that the courts favor finding a general charitable intent, . . . we have concluded that the gifts of the Collection to the University were motivated by a general charitable intent. . . .

Accordingly, we respectfully reverse the trial court's finding that the gifts were motivated by a specific charitable intent and the trial court's dismissal of the University petition for *cy pres* relief.

IS *CY PRES* RELIEF AVAILABLE TO THE UNIVERSITY?

Although we have reversed the trial court's summary dismissal of the University's petition for *cy pres* relief, we have not determined that *cy pres* relief is available to the University. It is premature to determine what *cy pres* relief, if any, the University may be entitled to receive based on the unique facts of this case because the University has not yet established all three prongs of the New York *cy pres* analysis. . . . At this stage of the proceedings, the University has not established whether the change of circumstances subsequent to the gift render literal compliance with the conditions impossible or impracticable. . . .

Accordingly, a determination of whether any form of *cy pres* relief is available must be held in abeyance unless and until the trial court, on remand, finds that literal compliance with the conditions imposed by Ms. O'Keeffe are impossible or impracticable. If *cy pres* relief is available to the University, then the trial court is to fashion a form of relief that most closely approximates Ms. O'Keeffe's charitable intent. . . .

IN CONCLUSION

We reverse the trial court's finding that the Georgia O'Keeffe Museum has standing. We also reverse the trial court's finding that the gifts to the University were motivated by a specific charitable intent instead of a general charitable intent, the finding that the University cannot establish that it is entitled to *cy pres* relief, and the order dismissing the Amended Petition of the University for *cy pres* relief. In furtherance of our decisions, we remand with instructions to strike all pleadings and motions filed by the O'Keeffe Museum, and its predecessor in interest the O'Keeffe Foundation, to dismiss the O'Keeffe Museum as a part to this action, to vacate all judgments entered in furtherance of the relief sought by the O'Keeffe Museum, including, without limitation, the trial court's order entered March 6, 2008, and for further proceedings consistent with this opinion. Costs of appeal are assessed against the Georgia O'Keeffe Museum.

Richard H. DINKINS, J., concurring.

I concur in the thorough and well-reasoned opinion authored by Judge Clement and write separately to express considerations I believe should guide the trial court and the parties as they determine the appropriateness and nature of any *cy pres* relief. . . .

The question for the court, the Attorney General and Fisk on remand is what "will most effectively accomplish its general purposes, free from any specific restriction, limitation or direction contained therein. . . ." N.Y. Est. Powers & Trusts Law § 8-1.1(c). As noted by Judge Clement, there is no indication in her correspondence with Fisk that Ms. O'Keeffe . . . did not intend for Fisk to have control over the artwork, subject only to its adherence to the general purpose of the gifts and the conditions imposed relative to its maintenance and display. The financial challenges facing Fisk are not unique and are shared by other educational institutions. . . . The trial court noted $17 million in deferred maintenance and other long-term financial challenges that Fisk faced at the time of trial as well as Fisk's recent fund-raising success in response to the Mellon challenge grant. I think it is appropriate, as the court and parties consider the question of *cy pres* relief, that the primary mission of Fisk as an educational institution be weighed as well, and that the extent and manner to which the Steiglitz collection may serve to attract revenue or donors to the university is not an impermissible area of inquiry in addition to issues related to modifying the conditions of maintenance and display of the art in light of the advances in technology as recognized by the trial court.

A doctrine closely related to *cy pres* is the doctrine of equitable deviation. Equitable deviation allows for the modification and administration of a charitable trust, as illustrated by excerpts from the following case.

In re Barnes Foundation

2004 WL 2903655 (Pa. Com. Pl. 2004)

Ott, J.

In this opinion, we consider the evidence presented at the second round of hearings on The Barnes Foundation's second amended petition to amend its charter and bylaws. In its pleading, The Foundation sought permission, *inter alia*, to increase the number of trustees on its governing board and to relocate the art collection in its gallery in Merion, Pennsylvania, to a new facility in Philadelphia. After the first hearings in December of 2003, we ruled that expanding the size of the Board of Trustees was appropriate in today's sophisticated world of charitable fundraising. We also determined that The Foundation was on the brink of financial collapse, and that the provision in Dr. Barnes' indenture mandating that the gallery be maintained in Merion was not sacrosanct, and could yield under the "doctrine of deviation," provided we were convinced the move to Philadelphia represented the least drastic modification of the indenture that would accomplish the donor's desired ends. . . .

DISCUSSION

After careful consideration of [the] evidence, we find that The Foundation met its burden of proof and the second amended petition should be granted. . . . The Foundation showed clearly and convincingly the need to deviate from the terms of Dr. Barnes' indenture. . . . [T]he three-campus model represents the least drastic modification necessary to preserve the organization. By many interested observers, permitting the gallery to move to Philadelphia will be viewed as an outrageous violation of the donor's trust. However, some of the archival materials introduced at the hearings led us to think otherwise. Contained therein were signals that Dr. Barnes expected the collection to have much greater public exposure after his death. To the court's thinking, these clues make the decision — that there is no viable alternative — easily reconcilable with the law of charitable trusts. When we add this revelation to The Foundation's absolute guarantee that Dr. Barnes' primary mission — the formal education programs — will be preserved and, indeed, enhanced as a result of these changes, we can sanction this bold new venture with a clear conscience.

Our conclusion that The Foundation should prevail does not mean all doubts about the viability of its plans have been allayed. Of serious concern are its fundraising goals. While Mr. Callahan was on the stand, we commented on his contagious optimism. It is clear The Foundation's Board will have to catch it. Mr. Callahan was only one of the many witnesses who acknowledged that The Foundation is raising the bar enormously above both its own fundraising abilities in the past and those of non-profits in general. "Ambitious" and "aggressive" were among the adjectives we heard to describe the target levels on which the Deloitte report is based. There is a real possibility that the development projections will not be realized, perhaps not in the first few years, but later on, when the interest and excitement about the new venture have faded. If that occurs, or the admissions do not meet expectations, or any of the other components of the Deloitte model do not reach their targets, something will have to give. We will not speculate about the nature of future petitions that might come before this court; however, we are mindful of the vehement protestations, not so long ago, that The Foundation would never seek to move the gallery to Philadelphia, and, as a result, nothing could surprise us.

We make a final observation about finances and the plans now being approved. The capital cost analysis prepared by Perks Reutter Associates contemplates renovations to the Merion facility to the tune of $1,600,000. In excess of $12,000,000 was spent upgrading the gallery during the world tour of some of The Foundation's works in 1993 and 1994. The irony of converting a state-of-the-art gallery into perhaps the most expensive administration building in the history of non-profits is not lost to us. Looking to the future, it is of the utmost importance that that Board of Trustees steer The Foundation so that another such irony does not surface ten or fifteen years hence.

In light of the foregoing . . . The Foundation's second amended petition to amend is granted.

Notes

1. The difference between equitable deviation and *cy pres* is further explained in G. Bogert, *Trust and Trustees* § 394 (2d ed. 1960) and in

Cy Pres and Deviation: Current Trends and Application, 8 REAL PROP. PROB. & TR. J. 391 (1973).

2. For additional information on the formation of the Barnes Museum, please read *Commonwealth of Pennsylvania v. Barnes Foundation*, 398 Pa. 458 (Pa. 1960), reproduced below in section C. Excerpts from the following article provide the reader with an overview of the issues facing the Barnes Foundation which led to the case above.

Jeffrey Toobin, The Battle for the Barnes

The New Yorker, Jan. 21, 2002, at 34

Before he died, in 1951, a Philadelphia businessman named Albert Barnes built what may be the greatest private art collection in American history. Like Henry Clay Frick, who filled his mansion on Fifth Avenue with Old Masters, and Isabella Stewart Gardner, who kept her eclectic collection in a Venetian-style palace she built in Boston, Barnes arranged for his paintings and sculptures to be housed and exhibited in perpetuity. But Barnes had grander ambitions than Frick and Gardner; he had a social agenda. He wanted to use his art to redress issues of inequality, particularly racial prejudice against African-Americans. He established a foundation to insure that his collection would be not so much a museum as a classroom, where blacks and whites would study together and learn that painting and sculpture could unite the most disparate peoples and cultures. "It wasn't really about the art for Barnes," Kimberly Camp, the executive director and C.E.O. of the Barnes Foundation, says. "It was about changing the society."

Barnes's priorities become immediately clear at the foundation complex he built in the nineteen-twenties on thirteen acres just outside Philadelphia, in the Main Line suburb of Lower Merion. The gallery building itself has an austere Renaissance-inspired design, but around the front door Barnes installed a ceramic-tile decoration modeled on artifacts from the Ivory Coast. Such juxtapositions — European art beside African art, the work of non-Caucasian people next to that of whites — continue inside the building. "The renascence of Negro art," Barnes wrote in 1925, "is one of the events of our age which no seeker for beauty can afford to overlook." Barnes, however, bought few works by contemporary black artists. He owned hundreds of examples of tribal and folk art, but the heart of his collection is French Impressionist and Post-Impressionist pieces, in astonishing profusion. Renoir (a hundred and eighty-one works), Cezanne (sixty-nine), and Matisse (fifty-nine) are among the artists represented, many of them by their best paintings. There are about two thousand works in all, by artists ranging from El Greco and Rubens to Miro and Modigliani. As Barry Munitz, the president of the J. Paul Getty Trust, puts it, "There are some of the most spectacular paintings that the world has ever seen." The collection is currently valued at several billion dollars. . . .

As such, the Barnes Foundation might be expected to thrive in an era more receptive to diversity in art and culture than Barnes's own time was. Instead, it is financially imperiled and perhaps mortally threatened. The story of Barnes's collection has turned out to be a lot like the story of his life, full of rancor, misunderstanding, and unhealed wounds. . . .

Because the collection was to be used only for educational purposes, Barnes banned "receptions, tea parties, dinners, banquets, dances, musicales or similar affairs" on the foundation grounds. The art was to be viewed on his terms or not at all. When T. S. Eliot asked to visit, Barnes told him, "Nuts." Le Corbusier and the sculptor Jacques Lipchitz, whose work Barnes collected, were similarly rebuffed. James Michener applied three times for admission when he was an undergraduate at Swarthmore and was rejected each time. Later, after he learned more about Barnes, Michener wrote to him and claimed that he was a poorly educated steelworker, and permission was promptly granted. (A wry appreciation of Barnes's peculiarities can be found in Howard Greenfeld's 1987 biography, "The Devil and Dr. Barnes.") . . .

Under the terms of Barnes's will, the art in the collection could not be sold or loaned to other museums; indeed, the paintings had to remain in precisely the same arrangement inside the galleries as they were on the day that Barnes died. Furthermore, an endowment of nine million dollars was shrinking and could be invested only in low-yield securities. [Richard H.] Glanton believed that the gallery needed millions of dollars for renovation, and, as he saw it, the Barnes's only marketable asset was the art itself. So, in 1991, he asked the Montgomery County Orphans Court, which supervises changes to wills, for permission to sell up to fifteen paintings to raise at least fifteen million dollars. . . .

In time, Glanton withdrew the request to sell off paintings, and came up with another plan to save the Barnes. He persuaded the Orphans Court to allow the foundation to send up to ninety of its French Impressionist paintings on a tour of seven museums around the world. The tour began in 1993, at the National Gallery in Washington, and over the next two years earned fees of approximately seventeen million dollars, most of which was used to renovate the building. *The Times* reported, "The Barnes exhibition was one of the most successful in museum history, ranking just behind 'The Treasures of Tutankhamen.'"

Notes and Questions

1. Toobin's article indicates Mr. Barnes' social agenda of desiring to redress issues of inequality, particularly racial prejudice against African Americans. How does establishing a museum address problems of racial inequality?
2. One of the challenges that many museums face is raising sufficient operating costs. Should museums, like the Barnes Museum, that become financially impoverished while remaining collection-rich, be permitted to sell part of their collection to raise operating costs?

2. The Corporate Form

A charitable or public trust should be distinguished from a charitable corporation. The trust is governed by common law as well as statutory rules for trusts, whereas the corporation is purely a creature of statute. The rules relating to a corporation's conduct will usually emanate from a state's not-for-profit corporation statutes, as interpreted by the courts of that jurisdiction.[2] A charitable corporation has been described as one "organized for the purposes among other things, of promoting the welfare of mankind at large, or of a community, or of some class forming part of it indefinite as to members and individuals and is one created for or devoted to charitable purposes."[3] The not-for-profit corporation is created by complying with the law of the state of incorporation.[4] Generally, the process requires the filing of articles of incorporation setting forth the name of the corporation, its duration, purpose, registered office, registered agent, directors' and incorporators' names and addresses, as well as a provision stating that, upon liquidation, any funds remaining after the debts have been satisfied must be turned over to a similar organization. Nevertheless, state laws are not consistent regarding the act that formally creates the corporation. In some, it is the act of filing the articles that commences the entity's existence.[5] In others, it is the issuance of the certificates of incorporation that brings it into being.

Once the entity is created, a state's not-for-profit corporation statutes generally require an organizational meeting or, in some instances, an action by the board in lieu of an actual meeting.[6] At this point, many of the formalities necessary to carry on the day-to-day work of the corporation will be addressed. It is typical to adopt a corporate seal, appoint officers, authorize bank accounts, and adopt bylaws.[7] The bylaws govern the internal workings of the corporation and may be thought of as the embodiment of non-statutory administrative procedures applicable to the corporation in question.[8]

Under the Revised Model Nonprofit Corporation Act (RMNCA), the organization must elect one of the three following classifications: (a) a private benefit organization (i.e., a low-cost housing development); (b) a mutual benefit organization (i.e., a professional association or club); or (c) a public

---

2. *See, e.g.,* N.Y. *Not-for-Profit Corp. Law* 35 (McKinney's 1992); Cal. Corp. Code §§ 5000 *et seq.,* §§ 5110 *et seq.,* §§ 7110 *et seq.,* §§ 9110 *et seq.* (West 1992).

3. *Lynch v. Spilman,* 67 Cal. 2d 251, 62 Cal. Rptr. 12, 18, 431 P.2d 636, 642 (1967).

4. *See generally* H.L. Oleck, *Nonprofit Corporations, Organizations, and Associations* (6th ed. 1994) [hereinafter Oleck]; M.E. Phelan, *Nonprofit Enterprises: Law and Taxation* (1989); M.E. Phelan, *Representing the Nonprofit Organization* (1987).

5. *See, e.g.,* Del. Code Ann. § 106 (West 1991); Or. Rev. Stat. § 65.011 (1987).

6. *See, e.g.,* Or. Rev. Stat. § 65.057 (1989).

7. *See generally* 8 Fletcher *Cyclopedia of the Law of Private Corporations* §§ 9-10 (perm. ed. rev. 1990).

8. For sample forms, *see* Oleck, *supra.*

benefit organization.[9] A museum is most likely to choose the third classification.

Notes

1. A helpful tool for the board governing a nonprofit is the American Association for State and Local History's AASLH Board Orientation Organizer, which can be ordered from AASLH at 530 Church Street, Ste. 600, Nashville, TN 37219-2325, (615) 255-2971. The organizer is meant to be combined with copies of the organization's own policies and procedures to create a handbook.
2. Another aid for directors is the Guidebook for Directors of Nonprofit Corporations, published by the American Bar Association, 1-800-285-2221. The Guidebook contains information on directors' duties and rights, committees, risks of directors, volunteers, and obtaining and maintaining tax-exempt status.
3. The National Center for Nonprofit Boards, 1225 19th Street, N.W., Suite 340, Washington, DC 10036 carries bibliographies and books on nonprofit boards and corporations.

3. Private-Governmental Partnerships

The Brooklyn Institute of Arts & Sciences v. City of New York

64 F. Supp. 2d 184 (E.D.N.Y. 1999)

GERSHON, District Judge.

The Mayor of the City of New York has decided that a number of works in the Brooklyn Museum's currently showing temporary exhibit "Sensation: Young British Artists from the Saatchi Collection" are "sick" and "disgusting" and, in particular, that one work, a painting entitled "the Holy Virgin Mary" by Chris Ofili, is offensive to Catholics and is an attack on religion. As a result, the City has withheld funds already appropriated to the Museum for operating expenses and maintenance and, in a suit filed in New York State Supreme Court two days after the Museum filed its suit in this court, seeks to eject the Museum from the City-owned land and building in which the Museum's collections have been housed for over one hundred years.

The Museum seeks a preliminary injunction barring the imposition of penalties by the Mayor and the City for the Museum's exercise of its First Amendment rights. The City and the Mayor move to dismiss the Museum's suit in this court, insofar as it seeks injunctive and declaratory relief, on the ground that this court must abstain from exercising jurisdiction in favor of the

---

9. RMNCA § 1.40 (1987).

New York court action, in which, they argue, the Museum may assert, by way of defense and counterclaim, its First Amendment claims. For the reasons that follow, defendants' motion is denied, and plaintiff's motion is granted.

BACKGROUND

An examination of the history of the Brooklyn Museum and its relationship to the City of New York will illuminate the current controversy.

I. The History of the Brooklyn Museum

The Brooklyn Museum traces its origin to the Brooklyn Apprentices' Library, founded in 1823, whose book collection was first permanently housed in a Brooklyn Heights building constructed in 1825, reportedly after General Lafayette laid its cornerstone on the Fourth of July. A successor entity, the Brooklyn Institute, incorporated in 1843, expanded its holdings of books, natural history specimens and, to a lesser extent, art objects during the ensuing decades of the nineteenth century. By the late 1880's, prominent citizens and public figures of the then independent City of Brooklyn conceived an ambitious plan to vastly expand the Brooklyn Institute's collections in a mammoth new building, which would rival the combined collections of New York City's Metropolitan Museum of Art and Museum of Natural History.

The City of New York had already established in the 1870's a relationship with the Metropolitan Museum of Art and the Museum of Natural History that would serve as a prototype for the City's relationship with other designated cultural institutions, and for the relationship of the Brooklyn Museum with the cities of Brooklyn and later New York. That relationship is described in the official "Procedures Manual for New York City's Designated Cultural Institutions," at 3, as "joint partnerships between the City and a group of private citizens." The Procedures Manual describes that state legislation was passed to incorporate those two museums, authorizing the City to construct the museums' facilities and to lease those facilities and the City-owned parkland on which they were located to the new corporations. The museums, in turn, "became responsible for programming the facilit[ies] and acquiring and exhibiting [their] collections. The leases . . . contemplate that the City will maintain the building[s] while the [museums oversee] the display of [their] collection[s] to the general public."

In keeping with this historical precedent, the New York State Legislature in 1889 authorized the City of Brooklyn to reserve a portion of Prospect Park as "building sites for museums of art and science and libraries," and to lease such sites at nominal rent for up to one hundred years to corporations "created for educational purposes," provided that "such museums and libraries shall at all reasonable times be free, open and accessible to the public and private schools of the said city, and open and accessible to the general public on such terms of admission as the said mayor and commissioners shall approve. . . ." L. 1889, c. 372, § 2.

The Brooklyn Institute was reorganized into the Brooklyn Institute of Arts and Sciences, the formal name of the plaintiff in this action (now known as the "Brooklyn Museum of Art" or "Brooklyn Museum" and sometimes referred to here as the "Museum"), by the New York State Legislature in 1890. The Act formally incorporating the Brooklyn Institute of Arts and Sciences, L. 1890, c. 172, designated by name approximately fifty private individuals as the original trustees of the Institute, and authorized the Institute to adopt its own constitution, bylaws, and all appropriate rules and regulations for its self-governance. *Id.* §§ 4, 5. Subsequent laws added public officials as ex officio members of the Board of Trustees, including the Mayor, Comptroller, Park Commissioner and Borough President. L. 1893, c. 579, as amended, L. 1934, c. 87 and L. 1949, c. 127. The 1890 Act further provides:

> Section 2. The purposes of said corporation shall be the establishment and maintenance of museums and libraries of art and science, the encouragement of the study of the arts and sciences and their application to the practical wants of man, and the advancement of knowledge in science and art, and in general to provide the means for popular instruction and enjoyment through its collections, libraries and lectures.
>
> Section 3. The museums and libraries of said corporation shall be open and free to the public and private schools of said city, at all reasonable times, and open to the general public on such terms of admission as shall be approved by the mayor and park commission of said city.

On December 23, 1893, as authorized by state law, the City of Brooklyn leased the land to the Institute for a term of one hundred years (the "Lease"), tracking the language of the 1889 Act as to the use of the property and the requirements for access by schools and the general public. The Lease further provides that "if and when such museums ... shall cease to be maintained according to the true intent and meaning of said act, and of this lease, then this lease shall be forfeited, and the said lands, and buildings thereon erected shall revert to the City of Brooklyn." Pursuant to other Acts of the New York State Legislature (L. 1891, c. 89; L. 1894, c. 577; L. 1896, c. 406), the City of Brooklyn funded construction of a building on the site designed by the noted architectural firm of McKim, Mead, & White (although only a fraction of the original ambitious building plan was ever completed), to be leased to the Institute.

Upon completion of construction of a wing of the new building, the City of Brooklyn entered into a building lease and contract (the "Contract") with the Institute, for a term coextensive with the Lease, to house the Institute's collections. The City of New York is the successor to the City of Brooklyn under the Lease and the Contract. The parties agree that, upon the expiration of the original term of the Lease agreement in December 1993, the Museum remained a tenant in possession of the land and the building on the same terms and conditions as contained in the Lease and Contract.

The Contract provides that:

> The Brooklyn Institute of Arts and Sciences ... shall place on exhibition in said Museum Building collections of paintings and other works of art and

collections and books representing or illustrating each and all of the Departments of the arts and sciences named in the constitution of said Institute, and shall cause to be properly arranged, labeled and catalogued all such collections and books as may be open to public exhibition or for public use, for the instruction and benefit of the residents of Brooklyn or the general public.

The Contract is unequivocal that the City has no ownership rights with respect to any of the collections in the Museum. It provides:

> That the collections of books and other objects in art and sciences placed in the Museum Building for purposes of exhibition, instruction, or to enable the Brooklyn Institute of Arts and Sciences to carry out its purposes as authorized in its charter, shall continue to be and shall remain absolutely the property of the [Institute], and that neither the [Mayor nor the City of Brooklyn] by reason of said property being placed in said building or continuance therein, have any title, property or interest therein.

The Museum established, as a branch, the first children's museum in the world in 1899. Throughout the first decades of this century, the Museum's collections greatly expanded, with Departments of Fine Arts, Natural Sciences, and a newly-established Department of Ethnology. The Museum decided in the 1930's to focus on its collections of fine art and cultural history, and to abandon its mission as a science museum. The Museum's natural history specimens were sent to other institutions. In 1934, the State legislature amended the description of the Institute's purpose quoted above, by adding reference to establishment and maintenance of "botanical gardens" and the provision of popular instruction and enjoyment through "musical and other performances." L. 1934, c. 87. In the 1970's, various components of the Brooklyn Institute of Arts and Sciences became independent institutions, including the Brooklyn Children's Museum, the Brooklyn Academy of Music and the Brooklyn Botanic Garden.

The Museum today describes itself as having the second largest art collection in the United States, with approximately one and a half million objects. Its collections are divided into the following departments: (1) Egyptian, classical and ancient middle eastern art; (2) painting and sculpture; (3) arts of Africa, the Pacific and the Americas; (4) Asian art; (5) decorative arts, costumes and textiles; and (6) prints, drawings and photography. The Museum also has two research libraries and an archive. The Museum's permanent collection includes secular as well as numerous non-secular objects. Materials submitted to the court confirm the following description by the Museum's Chief Curator: "The collections include Catholic and Protestant religious works of art, Jewish religious objects, objects representing many Eastern religions, African spiritual objects, native American tribal objects, pre-Columbian objects, Islamic religious objects, as well as religious objects from numerous other cultures." These include many paintings and other objects which are reverential of the Madonna and other figures and symbols important to Christianity.

In addition to displaying works from its permanent collection to the public, the Museum regularly mounts temporary exhibits, and has done so throughout its history. Some of these exhibits involve well-known artists and their works. Others display little-known artists or obscure or esoteric works. The current temporary exhibit, "Sensation: Young British Artists from the Saatchi Collection" (the "Sensation Exhibit" or the "exhibit") is not the first controversial exhibit the Museum has mounted. Past controversial exhibits include art and performance exhibits in 1990 and 1991, respectively entitled, "the Play of the Unmentionable: The Brooklyn Museum Collection," and "Too Shocking to Show," which, to judge from contemporaneous news articles and materials prepared by the Museum, were provocative responses to protests over exhibits and performances at other institutions. Neither party to this litigation is aware of any past objection by the City to any Museum exhibit, or any prior effort by the City to stop an exhibit because of the content of any works included.

Undisputed documentary evidence establishes the Museum's commitment, throughout its history and continuing to date, to extensive educational programs for children, teachers, families, members of surrounding communities, and the general public. The Museum's Education Division serves over fifty thousand children and thirty-five thousand adults each year, with a staff of twenty-six full-time employees, nine full-time paid interns, thirty-five part-time instructors, and forty volunteer tour guides.

II. City Funding of The Brooklyn Museum

The Contract provides that "[the City] shall pay to the [Institute] each year such sum as may be necessary for the maintenance of said Museum Building, or as may be authorized by law or be apportioned or appropriated by [the City]." The Contract specifically defines "maintenance" to include: (1) repairs and alterations; (2) fuel; (3) waste removal; (4) wages of employees providing essential maintenance, custodial, security and other basic services; (5) cleaning and general care; (6) tools and supplies; and (7) insurance for the building, furniture and fixtures.

Consistent with the applicable statutes, the Lease, and the Contract, as well as with historical practices, the City's Procedures Manual specifies that public funds are provided to designated cultural institutions to help meet costs for general maintenance, security and energy, and in some instances to support education programs. City funds generally "are not used for direct curatorial or artistic services." Procedures Manual at 12. The City also approves certain capital expenditures as part of its program "to protect and ensure the continued existence of New York City's most precious assets, its cultural institutions, for local communities, the general public and the artistic community." Id. at 14. The City's Fiscal Year 2000 appropriation of approximately $5.7 million to the Museum specifies that the funding contributes to "maintenance, security, administration, curatorial, educational services and energy costs." The City was not asked to fund the controversial exhibit giving rise to this action. The City's Fiscal Year 2000 appropriation to the Brooklyn Children's Museum is approximately $1.6 million.

Nothing in the City's lengthy annual final report and budget request form, which each institution must supply, asks for detailed information concerning the individual works in exhibits. Instead, the form is designed to determine, among other things: the general purposes and plans of the institution; "brief descriptions" (emphasis in original) of immediate past and future programming; accomplishments and plans for educational programs for children, educators and the general public; and detailed financial information. . . .

[The court's discussion of the controversy over the Sensation Exhibit is reprinted in Chapter 6, "First Amendment Rights." In this chapter, the focus is on the government's attempt to end a subsidy for a public museum.]

The City's motion to Dismiss is denied. . . .

Grunewald v. Metropolitan Museum of Art

125 A.D. 3d 438 (N.Y.: Appellate Div., 1st Dept., 2015)

Concur—Mazzarelli, J.P., DeGrasse, Manzanet-Daniels and Gische, Jj.

This appeal arises out of two separate actions in which members of the public seek to challenge a policy by the Metropolitan Museum of Art (MMA), in place since 1970, to have all visitors at all times pay an entrance fee. While the fee is currently "recommended" at $25, visitors may pay as little at 1¢, but they must pay something. Prior to 1970, MMA entry was free to all visitors, at least on certain days and times. Plaintiffs in each of these actions claim that they paid for tickets to enter the museum on days and at times that they allege admission was required to be free. In addition to other causes of action, each complaint alleges that MMA's policy of charging an entry fee, in any amount, separately violates both certain legislation and the lease by which MMA occupies its home in Central Park. In each action, plaintiffs seek a permanent injunction to enforce a free admissions requirement.

The narrow issue before this Court is not whether the legislation relied upon and/or the lease mandate free admissions to MMA, but simply whether plaintiffs have standing to raise the issue.

Plaintiffs lack standing to sue under the 1893 statute. The statute authorizes the Department of Public Parks in the City of New York to apply for up to an additional $70,000 of funds to keep, preserve and exhibit the collections in the MMA. As an express condition of the authorization, the MMA shall be free of charge for five days per week, including Sunday and two evenings per week. Clearly there is no express private right of action. Nor is there an implied right of action consistent with the legislative scheme (*see Sheehy v. Big Flats Community* 439*439 *Day*, 73 N.Y.2d 629, 633-635 [1989]). Regardless of whether the legislation is designated an appropriations bill or not, the plain language makes the two obligations of the bill interdependent. The Parks Department's authority to apply for the additional appropriations for MMA is expressly conditioned upon free admission. The plaintiffs in this case are not seeking to revoke the Parks Department's authorization to seek additional funds, but only to enforce the condition for that authority. No private remedy to enforce only the conditional portion of the statute is fairly implied. Nor would a private right of action to enforce only the condition be consistent with the mechanism of the statute (*e.g.* forfeiting the right to seek additional funds) (*see Rhodes v. Herz, 84 A.D.3d 1, 10* [1st Dept 2011], *lv dismissed* 18 N.Y.3d 838 [2011]). . . .

Plaintiffs also lack standing to sue under the MMA's lease with the City as third party beneficiaries because the benefit to them is incidental and not direct (*Burns Jackson Miller Summit & Spitzer v. Lindner,* 59 N.Y.2d 314, 336 [1983]). Government contracts often confer benefits to the public at large. That is not, however, a sufficient basis in itself to infer the government's intention to make any particular member of the public a third party beneficiary, entitled to sue on such contract (*see Fourth Ocean Putnam Corp. v. Interstate Wrecking Co., 66 N.Y.2d 38 [1985]; Moch Co. v. Rensselaer Water Co.,* 247 N.Y. 160 [1928]; Restatement [Second] of Contracts § 313). In order for the benefit to be direct, it must be primary and immediate in such a sense and to such a degree as to demonstrate the assumption of a duty to provide a direct remedy to the individual members of the public if the benefit is lost (*Moch Co.* at 164 [Cardozo, Ch. J.]). Neither the language of the lease nor any other circumstances indicate that the parties intended to give these plaintiffs individually enforceable rights thereunder (*see Oursler v. Women's Interart Ctr., 170 A.D.2d 407* [1st Dept 1991]; *Alicea v. City of New York,* 145 A.D.2d 315 [1st Dept 1988]).

4. Tax Status

In order to avoid paying income tax on money received for its charitable purposes, a museum may wish to obtain tax-exempt status. Such a status also serves to encourage individuals to contribute to the institution, as they may be able to take a charitable deduction for a percentage of the contribution. In order to obtain tax-exempt status, the incorporator should file an application for an advanced ruling with the Internal Revenue Service (IRS). This is accomplished by filling out Form 1023, which may be obtained from the IRS. Form 1023 is used by organizations claiming exemptions under Internal Revenue Code (IRC) § 501(c)(3) as charitable, religious, scientific, or educational organizations.

In addition to obtaining federal tax-exempt status, a museum should consider applying for an exemption from state and municipal tax laws. This is usually conferred automatically when the federal procedure is followed, although some states and municipalities may require an independent evaluation, making it necessary to consult the state and city tax statutes of the jurisdiction in which the museum is located.

If the taxing authorities believe that an institution is not complying with the law for tax-exempt entities, an investigation may be launched, which could culminate in revocation of a prior ruling. The entity, therefore, should be cautious about engaging in political or other activities that might jeopardize its favorable tax position. A museum may also lose its tax-exempt status if the state believes it lacks an educational or charitable purpose.

Georgia O'Keeffe Museum v. County of Santa Fe

133 N.M. 297, 62 P.3d 754 (N.M. Ct. App. 2002)

SUTIN, Judge.

. . . The Georgia O'Keeffe Museum, a private corporation (O'Keeffe), protested the assessment of property tax by the County of Santa Fe (the County), claiming an exemption for its museum property under New Mexico Constitution Article VIII, Section 3. The County Valuation Protests Board (the Board) upheld the assessment on the ground that O'Keeffe "failed to produce sufficient competent evidence" that "a substantial use, and the primary use, of the . . . property is charitable or educational." O'Keeffe appealed the denial, paid the assessment under protest, and filed a complaint for refund of the taxes it paid. After consolidation of the refund action with the appeal, the district court affirmed the Board on the exemption denial and dismissed the refund action upon the County's motion for summary judgment. We reverse and remand for further proceedings on the exemption issue. We affirm the dismissal of the refund action.

BACKGROUND

O'Keeffe is a New Mexico non-profit corporation and a tax exempt organization under the Internal Revenue Code, 26 U.S.C. § 501(c)(3). One of O'Keeffe's stated purposes is to "maintain property, including a building and museum collections, for the operation of a museum devoted primarily to the exhibition of the works of Georgia O'Keeffe." Another is to "promote and encourage public awareness of, interest in and appreciation of its collections and . . . engage in such educational programs as are consistent with the operation of a museum." O'Keeffe's museum is situated on Johnson Street in Santa Fe, New Mexico (the museum property). O'Keeffe has allocated about sixty percent of its annual budget for what it deems educational purposes.

O'Keeffe applied for an exemption from taxation of the museum property for the year 1999 under the "educational or charitable purposes" exemption contained in Article VIII, Section 3 of the New Mexico Constitution, which reads in pertinent part:

> The property of the United States, the state and all counties, towns, cities, and school districts and other municipal corporations, public libraries, community ditches, and all laterals thereof, all church property not used for commercial purposes, all property used for educational or charitable purposes, all cemeteries not used or held for private or corporate profit, and all bonds of the state of New Mexico, and of the counties, municipalities, and districts thereof shall be exempt from taxation.

The County Assessor denied the exemption application and O'Keeffe filed a protest with the Board. After a hearing, the Board entered a Decision and

Order upholding the Assessor's denial of the exemptions for educational and charitable use.

O'Keeffe's Evidence at the Board Hearing

O'Keeffe's director of education testified regarding its programs and activities, several of which are also illustrated in documents. We summarize this evidence which relates to the operation of the museum only during the period 1997 to 1999.

On-Site: The museum opened in 1997 and is open six days per week. O'Keeffe collects, houses, and publically displays artworks by Georgia O'Keeffe, and operates a retail gift shop. Over 665,000 persons visited the museum in the two years following its opening, the majority of whom paid an entrance fee.

In the museum, visitors receive a brochure that discusses significant events in Georgia O'Keeffe's life. Orientation tours for the general public are available thirty hours a week. Educational tours for school children are regularly conducted on Mondays when the museum is closed to the public. Student tours are given to about three thousand students each year. Less regularly, lectures are held, students from an elementary school visit the museum (three times per year) in conjunction with a primarily off-site art education program, tours are given for persons with disabilities, and teacher workshops are held for Santa Fe area teachers. O'Keeffe funds visits by students and teachers as exhibitions change at the museum.

O'Keeffe also provides pre- and post-museum visit educational material to give students "a richer and deeper experience." Further, O'Keeffe provides "hands on lessons in the galleries with teachers and students," and conducts a Saturday family program (once a month during the school year and twice a month during the summer) to encourage children to become lifelong museum visitors. The family program begins at the museum, teaching the children to develop critical thinking skills and to articulate what they have experienced, and continues at another location for practical lessons.

Off-Site: O'Keeffe conducts or participates in a substantial number of educational programs and activities that occur away from the museum property. For example, O'Keeffe, as part of its professional development program in art education: produces teacher lesson plans; conducts workshops and teaching programs for instructors in art education; offers professional development and art leadership experience programs for girls and young women; works with a city summer therapeutic recreation program for kids with disabilities; and conducts or is involved in various other educational and mentor programs. O'Keeffe also has office space on Grant Avenue in Santa Fe, where it often conducts educational programs.

Through several of its programs and activities, O'Keeffe reaches out to local communities around the state, conducting courses and workshops in conjunction with universities and schools. O'Keeffe also sponsors lectures; operates senior citizen programs; donates materials and supplies to schools, teachers, and libraries; and carries on a year-round university intern program, as well as a docent program that trains adults. For its plentiful programs and activities, O'Keeffe produces several types of resource materials and supplies for study in conjunction with artwork at the museum, for career development in the arts (*e.g.*, art conservation, art criticism, art education, art therapy), for instruction on how museums operate to use Georgia O'Keeffe's life as an educational tool (*e.g.*, as part of New Mexico history), and for use in art education generally.

Further, O'Keeffe has a resource library containing books about Georgia O'Keeffe and other contemporary artists, and donates books to repositories such as college and public libraries. In addition, O'Keeffe donates seventy-five percent of its one-day pass revenue to the Museum of Fine Arts and the Museum of New Mexico, and eighty percent of its four-day pass revenue to the Museum of New Mexico. Both of these museums are state owned and operated.

What Is "Use for Educational Purposes"?

Both parties rely on *NRA Special Contribution Fund v. Bd. of County Comm'rs*, 92 N.M. 541, 591 P.2d 672 (Ct. App. 1978), for the standard for determining whether the museum property is used for educational purposes:

> [W]e hold the phrase "used for educational purposes" to mean "the direct, immediate, primary and substantial use of property that embraces systematic instruction in any and all branches of learning from which a substantial public benefit is derived."

Id. at 548, 591 P.2d at 679. . . .

The Board's Decision

In the present case, the Board framed the issue before it as "whether a substantial use, and the primary use, of the subject property is charitable or educational, or a combination of charitable and educational." Using *NRA* as its guide, the Board found and concluded that the direct, immediate, and primary use of the museum property was the operation of a museum for which an entry fee is usually charged and the operation of a retail gift shop. Considering the whole record, the Board concluded that the educational uses of the museum property were not substantial and primary, as required by the *NRA* standard. . . .

O'Keeffe's Protest Appeal and Refund Action

O'Keeffe appealed to the district court pursuant to NMSA 1978, § 39-3-1.1 (1999), asserting the Board's decision was arbitrary, capricious, an abuse of discretion, not supported by substantial evidence, and otherwise not supported by law.... Almost simultaneously with its appeal to the district court, O'Keeffe filed an action in the district court pursuant to NMSA 1978, § 7-38-40(A) (1982) for a refund of the taxes O'Keeffe felt compelled to pay in order to prevent the accrual of interest and penalties it would have to pay if it were unsuccessful in its protest appeal. The protest appeal and the refund action were then consolidated.

The district court first resolved the protest appeal. Using *NRA* for guidance, the district court held that the Board's decision was supported by substantial evidence and in accordance with law, and was not fraudulent, arbitrary, or capricious. The court affirmed the Board's decision denying the exemption....

DISCUSSION

... The words "used for educational purposes" are very broad and are not defined in our state Constitution. As the County reminds us, virtually any aspect of the human experience can be considered educational....

The New Mexico Constitution drafters' use of the words "educational or charitable purposes" left for the courts the duty to interpret with no "line of demarcation." *Mountain View Homes*, 77 N.M. at 651-52, 427 P.2d at 15.... The words "used for educational purposes" are defined in *NRA* as "the direct immediate, primary and substantial use of property that embraces systematic instruction in any and all branches of learning from which a substantial public benefit is derived." *Id.* at 548, 591 P.2d at 679....

[W]e conclude that, while the Board did not err in respect to O'Keeffe's failure of evidence under the *NRA* standard as it was applied by the Board, the concept of a private museum as a tax-exempt property under the educational-use exemption should be viewed and evaluated through a somewhat different approach from that in *NRA*....

The traditional museum is an entity that collects and houses for posterity a permanent collection of notable items of public interest and presents those as well as perhaps other items of public interest to the general public for their education and enlightenment. A museum, according to *Webster's II New College Dictionary* 722 (1995), is "[a]n institution for the acquisition, preservation, study, and exhibition of works of artistic, historical, or scientific value." The *Encyclopaedia Britannica*'s description of an art museum is apropos:

> The public art gallery is a creation of the nineteenth century. Unconsciously, it is an assertion of the collecting instinct of the community; consciously, it has been designed to instruct the public, to educate artists, to encourage contemporary art by purchase, and to provide material for historical research.

15 *Encyclopaedia Britannica*, Museums and Art Galleries, at 994 (1947)....

There can be little question, however, that properties devoted primarily and substantially to traditional museum functions of: (1) the preservation and exhibition of significant aspects, artifacts, and works of our lives and history for the benefit of the general public's appreciation, study, and knowledge; and

(2) the carrying on of museum-related educational programs and activities such as lectures, studies, libraries, research facilities, publishing scholarly material, and creating instructional materials for teachers and school children, are properties with uses and purposes that ought to be considered for educational purposes exemption under Article VIII, Section 3 of our Constitution. . . .

It appears obvious that O'Keeffe's museum property is not meant to be used, and is not actually used, only as a gallery of Georgia O'Keeffe art serving little other purpose than simply to preserve her name as tied to her art. O'Keeffe presented evidence to show that Georgia O'Keeffe's life and art were not only a significant aspect of New Mexico's general and art history, but also a contribution to American art and art history. O'Keeffe has exhibited the artwork of contemporaries of Georgia O'Keeffe, and has shown that the museum opens the on-site doors to awaken tens of thousands of visitors, including thousands of children each year, to the world of fine art, art history, and a delightful aspect of New Mexico history. In addition, O'Keeffe provides opportunities for several segments of the New Mexico public to derive important tangible and intangible educational experiences. . . .

We recognize that a museum with on-site and intrinsic educational value and closely related on- or off-site programs and activities can be the type of property with a use that "embraces systematic instruction . . . from which a substantial public benefit is derived" as contemplated under the *NRA* standard. *Id.* at 548, 591 P.2d at 679. Because the Board did not consider the unique circumstances of a museum, we remand this case to district court for a further hearing before the Board, permitting further evidence, particularly on the issues of the extent of any intrinsic educational value the museum provides and of the relationship of O'Keeffe's off-site programs and activities to the museum. The Board is to then determine the exemption issue in conformity with this opinion. . . .

In the last analysis, an equation must exist showing the museum's educational component, that is, the educational benefit to the public, to be worth the public's grant of tax exempt status. . . .

B. Trustee/Director Liability

For all practical purposes, the public trust and charitable corporation have the same goals and are designed to benefit similar groups. Regardless of which legal form the institution adopts, it will be controlled by either a board of trustees or directors.

The trustee of a public trust and the director of a nonprofit corporation may have identical roles in a museum. Perhaps the most important distinction between the two relates to the duties and liabilities the law may impose on those persons in control of each institution. These duties are not uniform throughout the United States. Rather, each jurisdiction determines whether trust law or corporation law will be applied to define the individual(s) responsible for running the entity. Thus, the stricter trust standard may be used as a measure of nonprofit corporate directors' activities; similarly, the less demanding corporate standard may be all that a trustee of a public trust is required to follow.[10]

The trustee will be personally liable for any losses to the trust occasioned by the trustee's acts of mismanagement. The trustee is judged by the prudent person standard, unless he or she has greater skills, which will result in the trustee being judged by those higher standards.[11] The reasonably prudent and skillful person standard that the trustee must meet contemplates a person seeking objectives in property management similar to the purposes of the trust.

Historically, the corporate director has been said to be under the same duty to the corporation and its directors as the trustee.[12] The majority of jurisdictions have adopted a reasonable standard of care, similar to the New York State statute, which provides for "that degree of diligence, care and skill which ordinarily prudent men would exercise under similar circumstances in like positions."[13] This may be termed the "reasonable director" standard, although directors will not be held liable for mere errors in business judgment.[14]

1. Self-Dealing

The duty imposed on the trustee is that of complete and unfailing loyalty to the beneficiary. In the trust situation, self-dealing arises when the trustee is on both sides of a transaction personally dealing with the trust for which he or she is a trustee. While administering the trust, the trustee must refrain from placing himself or herself in a position where either personal interests or those of a third person may conflict with the interest of the beneficiaries. All conduct with any bearing on the affairs of the trust must be actuated by consideration of the beneficiaries only. The reason for this is that the trustee is in a position of such intimacy with those represented and has such control over property that a higher standard is established by the court of equity than would prevail for an ordinary business relationship.[15]

Situations involving self-dealing by a trustee do not require a showing of damage to the trust. In other words, just by the occurrence of the act, damage is presumed. Whether the trustee acted in good faith and with honest intentions is irrelevant. *Slay v. Burnett Trust*, 143 Tex. 621, 187 S.W.2d 377 (1945).

---

10. *See Stern v. Lucy Webb Hayes Nat'l Training School for Deaconesses and Missionaries*, 381 F. Supp. 1003 (D.D.C. 1974).

11. Restatement (Third) of Trusts § 227 (2003). *See also* Bogert, *supra*, at § 106.

12. *See* Marsh, *Are Directors Trustees? Conflict of Interest and Corporate Morality*, 22 BUS. LAW. 35 (1966) [hereinafter Marsh].

13. N.Y. Not-for-Profit Corp. Law § 717 (1970).

14. *See Ballantine on Corporations* § 63a (1946) [hereinafter Ballantine].

15. Bogert, *supra*, at § 95.

Justice Cardozo summarized the relationship a trustee should maintain in all of his or her dealings with the trust as follows:

> [M]any forms of conduct permissible in a workaday world for those acting at arm's length, are forbidden by those bound by fiduciary ties. A trustee is held to something stricter than the morals of the market place. Not honesty alone, but the [punctilio] of an honor the most sensitive, is then the standard of behavior. [*Meinhard v. Salmon*, 249 N.Y. 458, 464, 164 N.E. 545, 546 (1928).]

Corporate directors, in their relationships with the corporation and its board, are under a fiduciary duty of loyalty. *See* Marsh, *supra.*

One case of self-dealing occurred when the Brooklyn Museum used funds donated by the mother of the vice-chairman of the board to purchase several pieces of primitive art owned by that same vice-chairman.[16] The case was settled when the Attorney General entered into an agreement with the museum's trustees requiring that any transaction between the museum and its board members involving an interested trustee be approved by the Attorney General, and that the nature of the interest be disclosed. The agreement also called for the museum's board to suspend purchases, sales, and exchanges of pieces of the museum's collection pending the drafting and adoption of a code of ethics.

Another example of self-dealing occurred when the director of the Green-ville County Museum in South Carolina acted as an advisor and art purchasing consultant for one of the museum's patrons, receiving $80,000 for his services. The director believed he was owed such a sum as payment for convincing the patron to donate the collection to the museum. When the patron learned of the fees received by the director, he withdrew his support from the museum. The ensuing investigation revealed that the amount paid to the director constituted a commission rather than a consultant's fee; that is, the director was paid, not for his expertise, but for his ability to persuade someone to purchase works of art. Because of the danger of choosing a large commission over an advantageous price for the museum, the code of ethics adopted by the Association of Art Museum Directors specifically prohibits a director from accepting a commission on the sale of a work of art.[17]

2. Conflicts of Interest

Conflict of interest cases comprise the bulk of violations of the director's duty of loyalty in the corporate realm. For instance, in corporate opportunity cases, the duty of loyalty is breached when a director acquires property in which the corporation is interested or when a director takes advantage of an opportunity that is within the scope of the corporation's business.[18] Where a disinterested

---

16. *Lefkowitz v. Kon*, No. 40082/78 (N.Y. Sup. Ct., N.Y. County Jan. 3, 1983).

17. For more information on self-dealing, see DeMott, *Self-Dealing Transactions in Nonprofit Corporations*, 59 BROOK. L. REV. 131 (1993).

18. *Schildberg Rock Products Co. v. Brooks*, 258 Iowa 759, 140 N.W.2d 132 (1966).

majority of the board of directors rejects the opportunity after full disclosure, however, there may be no violation of the fiduciary relationship if the director then purchases the item.[19]

C. The Role of the Museum in Society

What is the purpose of a museum? Is the museum a sanctuary where the art lover can absorb the beauty of a work, or should it recruit an audience, perhaps by increasing the relevance of its collections?

If a museum compromises its standards and displays only those objects that the majority of the public believes to be relevant, it will merely mirror contemporary norms and will not aid in the education of its constituents. On the other hand, displays that only interest the scholar will result in the creation of an "ivory tower" institution and alienate the very individuals whose knowledge or appreciation needs expansion. Yet, quality is not necessarily different from relevancy. The two often coincide.

In general, a cultural institution's collection should be accessible to the public at reasonable times. Failure to provide such access may call the charitable or public-benefit nature of a nonprofit organization into doubt. The result may be termination of tax-exempt status or a charge of mismanagement by the trustees or directors for failing to carry out the purposes of the institution. A leading case in the area of accessibility of a charitable trust's collection involved the Barnes Foundation, a Pennsylvania nonprofit corporation.

Commonwealth of Pennsylvania v. Barnes Foundation

398 Pa. 458, 159 A.2d 500 (Pa. 1960)

MUSMANNO, Justice.

The Barnes Foundation in Montgomery County owns and possesses one of the extremely valuable art collections in the country. The paintings, numbering more than a thousand, include works by Renoir, Cezanne, Manet, Degas, Seurat, Rousseau, Picasso, Matisse, Soutine, Modigliani, Pascin, Demuth, Glackens, Rouault, and Afro. Among the old masters are works by Giorgione, Titian, Tintoretto, Paolo Veronese, El Greco, Claude le Lorrain Chardin, Daumier, Delacroix, Courbert, and Corot. The pecuniary value of this treasure ranges reputedly from twenty-five to one hundred million dollars.

Although the Barnes Foundation has been judicially recognized as an institution of public charity and, therefore, enjoys exemption from taxation, the public as such has been denied access to the gallery housing the canvases and other works of art. Because of that fact, the Attorney General of Pennsylvania filed on April 17, 1958, in the Court of Common Pleas of Montgomery County,

---

19. *See* W. Cary, *Corporations*, ch. 6, § 2 (1969) [hereinafter Cary].

a petition for citation calling upon the Barnes Foundation and its trustees to show cause why they should not unsheathe the canvases to the public in accordance with the terms of the indenture and agreement entered into between Albert C. Barnes, the donor, and the Barnes Foundation, the donee. The respondents made preliminary objections averring that the Petition failed to state a "cognizable cause of action," and that it did not specify "in what manner or to what extent or by what improper acts of the respondents any members of the public have been denied access." . . .

It is necessary here, with a few rapid strokes, to depict the background of this litigation. In 1922, Dr. Albert C. Barnes, a physician who had amassed a considerable fortune as the result of his compounding a chemical formula (argerol) which he kept secret and exploited by commercial manufacture and sale to the public, decided to offer to mankind a good portion of his riches, specifically his unique art collection and an arboretum as an:

> experiment to determine how much practical good to the public of all classes and stations of life, may be accomplished by means of the plans and principles learned by the Donor from a life-long study of the science of psychology as applied to education and aesthetics.

It was his expressed desire that, after the death of himself and his wife:

> the plain people, that is, men and women who gain their livelihood by daily toil in shops, factories, schools, stores, and similar places, shall have free access to the art gallery and the arboretum upon those days when the gallery and arboretum are to be open to the public. . . .

A corporation was duly organized under the laws of Pennsylvania to receive and administer the estate, works and property to be conveyed to it by Dr. Barnes. This corporation became known as the Barnes Foundation. On December 6, 1922, Dr. Barnes, by deed of trust, transferred to the Barnes Foundation (hereinafter to be referred to as the Foundation) his art collection, house, property, and the grounds known as the Lapsley Arboretum in Montgomery County together with certain sums of money represented in 900 shares of the common capital stock of A.C. Barnes Company, a corporation of Pennsylvania. By medium of an indenture, which eventually embraced 39 paragraphs, a code of procedure was formulated for the maintenance and operation of the Barnes trust.

In October, 1929, the Foundation purchased for $50,000 a property in Philadelphia. When city and school taxes were levied on this property, the Foundation claimed exemption on the basis that the entire Foundation was a public charity. The resulting litigation reached this Court which, through Justice Kephart, declared:

> "We have carefully examined the record and find that there was evidence to support the findings that appellee, [the Foundation] an educational institution, was a purely public charity. The foundation had its origin in a charitable impulse of its founder. It was the result of the generosity of Dr. Albert C. Barnes: all its real and personal property, including its endowment, was

donated by him." *Barnes Foundation v. Keely*, 314 Pa. 112, 116, 171 A. 267, 268.

Although the Foundation thus assumed indisputable status as tax-exempt public charity, its officers and trustees have consistently refused to the public admission to its art gallery. A painting has no value except the pleasure it imparts to the person who views it. A work of art entombed beyond every conceivable hope of exhumation would be as valueless as one completely consumed by fire. Thus, if the paintings here involved may not be seen, they may as well [not] exist. The respondents argue that the paintings may be seen, but only privately. However, that is not what Dr. Barnes contemplated and it certainly is not what the tax authorities intended. If the Barnes art gallery is to be open only to a selected restricted few, it is not a public institution, and if it is not a public institution, the Foundation is not entitled to tax exemption as a public charity. This proposition is incontestable. . . .

In the case at bar, the Attorney General, as *parens patriae*, seeks to ascertain why the Foundation as a public charity has closed the doors of its art gallery to the public. The respondents argue that the Foundation never intended its art gallery to be a public gallery, that the principal intendment of the trust indenture was to establish an educational institution, and that the art gallery is merely incidental to teaching. . . .

But there is nothing in the indenture which rivet-proofs that assertion. Dr. Barnes was, of course, concerned with education. Even enjoying the contents of an art gallery is a matter of education, but Dr. Barnes did not declare his trust estate to be exclusive a school.

In Paragraph 34 of the indenture, Dr. Barnes specifically stated that —

The Barnes Foundation is to be maintained perpetually for education in the appreciation of the fine arts and not as a school for instruction in painting, drawing, sculptoring or any other branch of art or craftsmanship.

Although the Foundation has been in Court at least three times,[2] it is not yet too clear just what constitutes the curriculum of the educational courses in the Foundation. At the oral argument, counsel for the Foundation did not know or would not say how many pupils were enrolled at the Foundation. He contended himself with saying merely that the school was "full." The Attorney General of this Commonwealth not only has the authority but the duty to ascertain what are the facts surrounding the school in the Foundation to determine if it should be insulated from the shock of taxation which hits all other citizens and enterprises in the land. . . .

A reading of the indenture will disclose that it contains many references to art gallery and works of art without mentioning education or school. . . .

The first sentence of Paragraph 5 of the indenture states specifically:

---

2. *Barnes Foundation v. Keely*, 314 Pa. 112, 171 A. 267; *Wiegand v. Barnes Foundation*, 374 Pa. 149, 97 A.2d 81, and the present litigation.

During the life of Donor and his said wife the art gallery of Donee shall only be open to the public on not more than two days in each week, except during July, August, and September of each year, and only upon cards of admission issued by or under the direction of the Board of Trustees of Donee.

There is nothing in this sentence or in the sentences which follow in Paragraph 29 which empower the Board of Trustees to exclude the public entirely. The mandate is that the gallery shall be open to the public on not more than two days of each week. Conceivably, under this provision, the visiting, for an explained and justifiable reason, could be limited to but one day or only part of a day a week, but the public cannot be forced to face sealed doors all the time. To deny the people any opportunity to look into the gallery is to make a mockery of the entire indenture with its emphasis on democratic principles and its absolute prohibition of special privilege. . . .

In *Barnes Foundation v. Keely*, 314 Pa. 112, 117, 171 A. 267, 268, this Court specifically said:

Its [Foundation's] property located in Montgomery county is open to the public which is admitted thereto in accordance with the provisions of the by-laws, rules, and regulations of the foundation.

The lower Court seeks to use the *Keely* case in supporting its decision dismissing the Commonwealth's petition by quoting from that decision as follows:

. . . the unrestricted admission of the public would be as detrimental to the works of the Barnes Foundation as it would be to the work carried on in the laboratories and clinics of the University of Pennsylvania.

But this limitation does not and cannot wipe out this Court's statement that the Foundation's property "is open to the public." Naturally, the general public cannot use the gallery at will. The general public cannot even use a public library at will. Orderliness requires that there be hours of opening and closing of libraries, that hours or days be set aside for rest of personnel, for taking inventory, for cleaning and repairing the property and facilities. But no library would be considered public if the public could be admitted only upon the caprice, whim, and arbitrary will of its administrators.

Similarly the trustees of the Barnes Foundation may not exclude the public from the art gallery without offering explanation as to why it ignores the expressed intention of Dr. Barnes that the gallery shall, within certain restrictions, be open to the public. The defendants will be required to answer the petition for citation and suitable discovery shall be allowed the Attorney General to the end that the rights of the public in the indenture, and in accordance with public policy, may be protected and assured.

Notes

1. For a discussion of museums' role in society, *see Exhibiting Dilemmas: Issues of Representation at the Smithsonian* (A. Henderson & A. Kaeppler

eds., 1997); S. Weil, *A Cabinet of Curiosities: Inquiries into Museums and Their Prospects* (1995); L. Roberts, *From Knowledge to Narrative: Educators and the Changing Museum* (1997).

2. For a discussion of the philosophy of a children's museum, *see* Richards, *No Untouchables in This Museum*, Or. J., Jan. 5, 1976, at 17, col. 1.

3. What choices should go into museums' decisions to curate certain shows? *See* Willette & Leach, *Between Choice and Context: Curating in a Post-Modern Age*, 25 J. Arts Mgmt. L. & Soc'y 310 (1993); Zolber, *Art Museums and Cultural Policies: Changes of Privatization, New Publics, and New Arts*, 23 J. Arts. Mgmt. L. & Soc'y 277 (1994).

PROBLEM 9-1

Corporate support of a museum may be from "tainted sources." How would you advise a museum that experienced receiving a gift of valuable paintings from a wealthy alumnus after the donor was convicted of fraud? Should it return the gift? Another cultural institution used a large gift from a wealthy businessman to underwrite an exhibition catalog. The businessman is currently serving a 20-year term in federal prison after pleading guilty to charges he swindled $80 million. Should it return the gift? *See* Gardner, *Tainted Money*, ARTnews, Apr. 1989, at 180. In such cases, donated funds may not legally be the donor's to give.

D. Acquisitions

Museums are confronted with numerous internal policy decisions, many of which involve practical problems as well as legal issues that are not easily resolved. This section considers some of the more difficult areas of a museum's internal policies and offers suggestions in an attempt to resolve some of the dilemmas museum personnel face.

While museums might be thought of as being free to acquire any item they desire, this is not actually possible, as there are many restrictions — both ethical and legal — on their acquisition activities. This section will review some of the constraints that have been imposed on museums with respect to these matters.

1. Determining Goals

One of the fundamental considerations that determines a museum's acquisition policy centers on the entity's role in the community. The museum must first establish an identity and then determine which displays will best serve its intended audience. As a practical matter, museums specializing in a particular type of art should obviously confine their acquisitions to that area. It would be a mistake, for example, for the Museum of Modern Art to start acquiring Greek or Roman antiquities, as it would have to deplete its treasury in this pursuit. In addition, it could not compete with the magnificent collection at the Metropolitan Museum, located only a short distance away.

Another factor to consider is whether the institution can afford to obtain and maintain a sizeable representation of the items it seeks to display. It would be tragic to acquire valuable works of art that run the risk of deterioration due to inadequate conservation measures. Some museums feel they are most effective when displaying works of contemporary local artists rather than archaeological or anthropological collections. Others have very broad selections. This is especially true of regional museums serving large communities.

2. Gifts

Museums frequently receive gifts from their patrons. By definition, a gift lacks the consideration necessary for a binding contract. Therefore, an unexecuted gift is unenforceable. Anyone may make a gift of his or her own property, as long as the donor is mentally competent, of age, and has a clear, unmistakable, unequivocal intent present to relinquish ownership rights and vest title in the donee. When this intent is present at the time of transfer, the gift is executed and the recipient owns the piece in the same manner as a purchaser.

Another form of gift, *donatio causa mortis*, is a gift of personal property made in contemplation of death. Because such gifts are not subject to the wills statutes, courts scrutinize them carefully. The donor may only transfer personally, the transfer must be in apprehension of death, and most courts require death from the illness involved. If the donor recovers, the gift may be revoked.

The vast majority of donations are unimpeachable, although occasional problems do arise, usually when an item is bequeathed. Thus, in *Redmond v. N.J. Historical Soc'y*,[20] the decedent's will read "if my said son shall die leaving no descendants, . . . the portrait by [Gilbert] Stuart shall go and is hereby bequeathed to The New Jersey Historical Society."[21] The child was fourteen and a half years old at the time of decedent's death, and perhaps for this reason, the executor delivered the painting in 1888 to the Society. Its ownership was unchallenged until 1938 when the son's heirs apparently realized the great worth of the painting and the institution's questionable title. The court, after examining the will and rejecting the Society's claim of adverse possession, awarded the portrait to the heirs. Obviously, the institution should have checked or discovered the nature of its holding when the picture was first delivered.

---

20. *Redmond v. N.J. Historical Soc'y*, 132 N.J. Eq. 464, 28 A.2d 189 (1942).
21. *Id.* at 191.

Valuable bequests are likely to be vulnerable to challenge and an institution may lose both the item and goodwill in any subsequent battles. Because this is undesirable, candor and caution should always take precedence over avarice. In addition to ascertaining the validity of a gift, a museum should observe any conditions attached to it, as the failure to do so may result in the loss of an item or liability for monetary damages. Frequently, donations will be made on the condition that they bear the donor's name, remain in the permanent collection in perpetuity or for a fixed period, or always remain on display. The request may be legally enforceable or merely precatory. In either event, it should be observed.

Another important consideration for a museum is whether it can legally accept the gift under its creating instrument. While this might appear to be a remote problem, it occasionally arises. In *Frick Collection v. Goldstein*,[22] the trustees sought a declaratory judgment as to the museum's power to accept gifts. The institution was created under the direction of a will segregating the testator's entire collection, residence, and a $15 million endowment for this purpose. It was alleged that the decedent had intended the museum to retain the same atmosphere in the display as his private collection, meaning that it could not accept gifts. The court, after analyzing the will, rejected this contention and held that the Frick Collection was free to purchase new items and accept donations.

3. Loans

Another means by which museums obtain pieces for display is by loan. The possession amounts to less than ownership. The museum in this situation is a bailee and is subject to the law of bailment. The loan is sometimes utilized for a single object and, occasionally, for entire collections.[23] Generally, the loan is for a fixed period of time, although it may, according to the loan agreement, mature into a gift.

The Museum Loan Network hopes to make artworks more available to museums through a database of objects and collections available for loan. The program was created by the John S. and James L. Knight Foundation and the Pew Charitable Trusts, to be administered through the Massachusetts Institute of Technology.[24]

a. Permanent Loans

Occasionally, collectors will place works from their collections in museums on a so-called "permanent loan." This may be for the purpose of ultimately donating the work when the owner feels that tax considerations warrant the

---

22. *Frick Collection v. Goldstein*, 83 N.Y.S.2d 142 (Sup. Ct. 1948), *aff'd*, 274 N.Y. App. Div. 105, 86 N.Y.S.2d 464, *appeal denied*, 275 N.Y. App. Div. 709, 88 N.Y.S.2d 249 (1949).
23. Hughes, *Riches From Russia*, Time, Apr. 2, 1973, at 66.
24. See *Lend-Lease for Museums*, ARTnews, Dec. 1995, at 47.

gift, or it may be because the collector is reluctant to relinquish outright ownership of the work. The term "permanent loan" is not only contradictory, but it also spells trouble for the receiving museum. As with all types of loans, a permanent loan confers no title. As a result, the museum, as possessor of the property, can only exercise a certain amount of control over it. Furthermore, unless the museum has entered into a carefully drawn loan agreement, the extent and duration of the museum's possession must be proven by implied contract with the lender.

Nevertheless, museums have a fiduciary obligation to provide reasonable care for works in their possession. Hence, both legal and ethical issues arise when objects on permanent loan have been damaged because of poor care, or have been lost or stolen. Therefore, a museum should never accept an object on "permanent loan," unless a loan agreement is carefully drawn specifying the duration and terms of the loan. The agreement should also be reviewed periodically.

b. Adverse Possession

Once a loan has been made to a museum, the institution may display the item for an agreed period or indefinitely, agreeing to return it on demand. When the time has been fixed in the loan agreement, it is the museum's duty either to return the piece to the bailor or to notify the bailor of its availability. In the latter situation, the lender should collect the object as soon as possible because the bailment will, from that point, be for the benefit of the bailor, rendering the museum liable only for gross negligence.

When the loan is for an indeterminate period of time or is considered a permanent loan, problems may arise. If the museum does not keep accurate records, the owner may have difficulty reclaiming the object on demand. While museums are multi-million dollar businesses, their recordkeeping is not always accurate and documents do get lost. The lender should always procure a receipt signed by an authorized official. This document should be kept with all important papers. It should spell out all of the terms and conditions of the loan and indicate that either the lender or the lender's authorized agent may reclaim the piece. The owner should apprise his or her attorney of the existence of the loan document so that the piece can be reclaimed in the event of the owner's death or illness. If this is not done, the piece may be lost forever, as in the case of Mitzi Briggs of San Francisco, who remembered that her late father had loaned important works of art to a California museum. Unfortunately, the institution had no record of this transaction, and her late father's papers did not make any reference to the loan. It was apparently either arranged orally or the receipt had been lost. In either event, Briggs was unable to establish title. Possession is considered *prima facie* evidence of ownership.[25] Briggs had no proof of bailment and so decided that litigation would be fruitless. Interview with Mitzi Briggs by Leonard D. DuBoff, Jan. 1, 1975.

---

25. *See generally Brown on Personal Property* (3d ed. 1975) [hereinafter Brown].

When a museum has possession without legal title, heirs can legally reclaim the piece at any time. However, as a practical matter, it may be difficult for heirs to establish their rights. The museum in this situation might rely on its presumption of ownership and later be sued for conversion when misplaced documents are found. Such is the dilemma: a valuable work of art requiring maintenance and conservation is in its possession, yet title is unclear. Technically, the arrangement began as a bailment but other facts may have altered it.

When a museum finds that it is in possession of art that was loaned years before, it should attempt to contact the owner in order to determine the owner's present relationship with respect to the item. This may alert the heirs to a possible claim but is preferable to later being sued for conversion when documents appear. In the event the museum is unsuccessful in its attempt to locate the lender, it should make every effort to give notice of its adverse holding. In this situation, the best constructive notice possible should be given. An advertisement in a newspaper circulating in the region of the lender's last known residence that runs for a reasonable period of time, perhaps several weeks, is likely to start the statute of limitations running for adverse possession. The notice, however, must be reasonably sufficient to apprise potential claimants of their rights. In *Bufano v. City & County of San Francisco*,[26] plaintiff/artist sued to recover works of art he had created years before while employed by the WPA. Defendants, successors in title to WPA art, claimed title to the sculptures in question. Plaintiff, however, was able to prove that these pieces were created during his free time and that defendants were, therefore, only bailees of the works in question by virtue of their succession, requiring them to establish ownership in some other way. It was also averred that title vested in the municipalities by virtue of their adverse holding. They introduced evidence showing both that plaintiff was a member of the local art commission and that a letter announcing the municipality's ownership was read at a commission meeting. Unfortunately, defendants were unable to prove that plaintiff was present and heard the letter being read. Plaintiff, therefore, won.

Some museums do not take precautions and act as owners after they have had possession of loaned items for a protracted period. The general counsel for one museum stated that his institution merely transfers the records from the loan to the ownership file when the bailor cannot be located and the museum wishes to sell the piece.[27]

As discussed in the previous section, many states have enacted legislation expressly dealing with the subject of converting a museum's ill-defined relationship to works in its collection into legal ownership.[28]

---

26. *Bufano v. City & County of San Francisco*, 233 Cal. App. 2d 61, 43 Cal. Rptr. 223 (1965).

27. For further discussion of the application of the adverse possession doctrine as it applies to art, *see* Webb, Jr., *Whose Art Is It Anyway? Title Disputes and Resolutions in Art Theft Cases*, 79 Ky. L.J. 883-99 (Summer 1991); Franzese, *Georgia On My Mind: Reflections on O'Keeffe v. Snyder*, 19 Seton Hall L. Rev. 1-22 (1989).

28. *See, e.g.*, Or. Rev. Stat. §§ 358 *et seq.*; Wash. Rev. Code. Ann. § 27.40.034; Me. Rev. Stat. Ann. tit. 27, § 601.

E. Collection Management

Guggenheim v. Lubell

569 N.E.2d 426 (N.Y. Ct. App. 1991)

WACHTLER, Chief Judge.

The backdrop for this replevin action (*see*, CPLR art. 71) is the New York City art market, where masterpieces command extraordinary prices at auction and illicit dealing in stolen merchandise is an industry all its own. The Solomon R. Guggenheim Foundation, which operates the Guggenheim Museum in New York City, is seeking to recover a Chagall gouache worth an estimated $200,000. The Guggenheim believes that the gouache was stolen from its premises by a mailroom employee sometime in the late 1960s. The appellant Rachel Lubell and her husband, now deceased, bought the painting from a well-known Madison Avenue gallery in 1967 and have displayed it in their home for more than 20 years. Mrs. Lubell claims that before the Guggenheim's demand for its return in 1986, she had no reason to believe that the painting had been stolen.

On this appeal, we must decide if the museum's failure to take certain steps to locate the gouache is relevant to the appellant's Statute of Limitations defense. In effect, the appellant argues that the museum had a duty to use reasonable diligence to recover the gouache, that it did not do so, and that its cause of action in replevin is consequently barred by the Statute of Limitations. The Appellate Division rejected the appellant's argument. We agree with the Appellate Division that the timing of the museum's demand for the gouache and the appellant's refusal to return it are the only relevant factors in assessing the merits of the Statute of Limitations defense. We see no justification for undermining the clarity and predictability of this rule by carving out an exception where the chattel to be returned is a valuable piece of art. Appellant's affirmative defense of laches remains viable, however, and her claims that the museum did not undertake a reasonably diligent search for the missing painting will enter into the trial court's evaluation of the merits of that defense. Accordingly, the order of the Appellate Division should be affirmed.

The gouache, known alternately as *Menageries* or *Le Marchand de Bestiaux* (*The Cattle Dealer*), was painted by Marc Chagall in 1912, in preparation for an oil painting also entitled *Le Marchand de Bestiaux*. It was donated to the museum in 1937 by Solomon R. Guggenheim.

The museum keeps track of its collection through the use of "accession cards," which indicate when individual pieces leave the museum on loan, when they are returned and when they are transferred between the museum and storage. The museum lent the painting to a number of other art museums over the years. The last such loan occurred in 1961-62. The accession card for the painting indicates that it was seen in the museum on April 2, 1965. The next notation on the accession card is undated and indicates that the painting could not be located.

Precisely when the museum first learned that the gouache had been stolen is a matter of some dispute. The museum acknowledges that it discovered that the painting was not where it should be sometime in the late 1960s, but claims that it did not know that the painting had in fact been stolen until it undertook a complete inventory of the museum collection beginning in 1969 and ending in 1970. According to the museum, such an inventory was typically taken about once every 10 years. The appellant, on the other hand, argues that the museum knew as early as 1965 that the painting had been stolen. It is undisputed, however, that the Guggenheim did not inform other museums, galleries, or artistic organizations of the theft, and additionally, did not notify the New York City Police, the FBI, Interpol, or any other law enforcement authorities. The museum asserts that this was a tactical decision based upon its belief that to publicize the theft would succeed only in driving the gouache further underground and greatly diminishing the possibility that it would ever be recovered. In 1974, having concluded that all efforts to recover the gouache had been exhausted, the museum's Board of Trustees voted to "deaccession" the gouache, thereby removing it from the museum's records.

Mr. and Mrs. Lubell had purchased the painting from the Robert Elkon Gallery for $17,000 in May of 1967. The invoice and receipt indicated that the gouache had been in the collection of a named individual, who later turned out to be the museum mailroom employee suspected of the theft. They exhibited the painting twice, in 1967 and in 1981, both times at the Elkon Gallery. In 1985, a private art dealer brought a transparency of the painting to Sotheby's for an auction estimate. The person to whom the dealer showed the transparency had previously worked at the Guggenheim and recognized the gouache as a piece that was missing from the museum. She notified the museum, which traced the painting back to the defendant. On January 9, 1986, Thomas Messer, the museum's director, wrote a letter to the defendant demanding the return of the gouache. Mrs. Lubell refused to return the painting and the instant action for recovery of the painting, or, in the alternative, $200,000, was commenced on September 28, 1987.

In her answer, the appellant raised as affirmative defenses the Statute of Limitations, her status as a good-faith purchaser for value, adverse possession, laches, and the museum's culpable conduct. The museum moved to compel discovery and inspection of the gouache and the defendant cross-moved for summary judgment. In her summary judgment papers, the appellant argued that the replevin action to compel the return of the painting was barred by the three-year Statute of Limitations because the museum had done nothing to locate its property in the 20-year interval between the theft and the museum's fortuitous discovery that the painting was in Mrs. Lubell's possession. The trial court granted the appellant's cross motion for summary judgment, relying on *DeWeerth v. Baldinger*, 836 F.2d 103, an opinion from the United States Court of Appeals for the Second Circuit. The trial court cited New York cases holding that a cause of action in replevin accrues when demand is made upon the possessor and the possessor refuses to return the chattel. The court reasoned, however, that in order to avoid prejudice to a good-faith purchaser, demand cannot be unreasonably delayed and that a property owner has an obligation to use reasonable efforts to locate its missing property to ensure that demand is not so delayed. Because the museum in this case had done nothing for 20 years but search its own premises, the court found that its conduct was unreasonable as a matter of law. Consequently, the court granted Mrs. Lubell's cross motion for summary judgment on the grounds that the museum's cause of action was time barred. . . .

New York case law has long protected the right of the owner whose property has been stolen to recover that property, even if it is in the possession of a good-faith purchaser for value (see *Saltus & Saltus v. Everett*, 20 Wend. 267, 282). There is a three-year Statute of Limitations for recovery of a chattel (CPLR 214[3]). The rule in this State is that a cause of action for replevin against the good-faith purchaser of a stolen chattel accrues when the true owner makes demand for return of the chattel and the person in possession of the chattel refuses to return it. . . . Until demand is made and refused, possession of the stolen property by the good-faith purchaser for value is not considered wrongful. . . . Although seemingly anomalous, a different rule applies when the stolen object is in the possession of the thief. In that situation, the Statute of Limitations runs from the time of the theft. . . .

In *DeWeerth v. Baldinger* (*supra*), which the trial court in this case relied upon in granting Mrs. Lubell's summary judgment motion, the Second Circuit took note of the fact that New York case law treats thieves and good-faith purchasers differently and looked to that difference as a basis for imposing a reasonable diligence requirement on the owners of stolen art. Although the court acknowledged that the question posed by the case was an open one, it declined to certify it to this Court (see 22 NYCRR 500.17), stating that it did not think that it "[would] recur with sufficient frequency to warrant use of the certification procedure" (836 F.2d, at 108, n.5). Actually, the issue has recurred several times in the three years since *DeWeerth* was decided . . . , including the case now before us. We have reexamined the relevant New York case law and we conclude that the Second Circuit should not have imposed a duty of reasonable diligence on the owners of stolen art work for purposes of the Statute of Limitations.

While the demand and refusal rule is not the only possible method of measuring the accrual of replevin claims, it does appear to be the rule that affords the most protection to the true owners of stolen property. Less protective measures would include running the three-year statutory period from the time of the theft even where a good-faith purchaser is in possession of the stolen chattel, or, alternatively, calculating the statutory period from the time that the good-faith purchaser obtains possession of the chattel (see generally Weil, *Repose*, 8 IFAR [International Foundation for Art Research] Rep., at 6-7 [Aug.-Sept. 1987]). Other States that have considered this issue have applied a discovery rule to these cases, with the Statute of Limitations running from the time that the owner discovered or reasonably should have discovered the whereabouts of the work of art that had been stolen (see, e.g., *O'Keeffe v. Snyder*, 83 N.J. 478, 416 A.2d 862; Cal. Civ. Proc. Code § 338[c]).

New York has already considered — and rejected — adoption of a discovery rule. In 1986, both houses of the New York State Legislature passed Assembly Bill 11462-A (Senate Bill 3274-B), which would have modified the demand and refusal rule and instituted a discovery rule in actions for recovery of art objects brought against certain not-for-profit institutions. This bill provided that the three-year Statute of Limitations would run from the time these institutions gave notice, in a manner specified by the statute, that they were in possession of a particular object. Governor Cuomo vetoed the measure, however, on advice of the United States Department of State, the United States Department of Justice, and the United States Information Agency (*see* 3 *U.S. Agencies Urge Veto of Art-Claim Bill*, N.Y. Times, July 23, 1986, at C15, col. 1). In his veto message, the Governor expressed his concern that the statute "[did] not provide a reasonable opportunity for individuals or foreign governments to receive notice of a museum's acquisition and take action to recover it before their rights are extinguished." The Governor also stated that he had been advised by the State Department that the bill, if it went into effect, would have caused New York to become "a haven for cultural property stolen abroad since such objects [would] be immune from recovery under the limited time periods established by the bill."

The history of this bill and the concerns expressed by the Governor in vetoing it, when considered together with the abundant case law spelling out the demand and refusal rule, convince us that that rule remains the law in New York and that there is no reason to obscure its straightforward protection of true owners by creating a duty of reasonable diligence. Our case law already recognizes that the true owner, having discovered the location of its lost property, cannot unreasonably delay making demand upon the person in possession of that property (*see, e.g., Heide v. Glidden Buick Corp.*, 188 Misc. 198, 67 N.Y.S.2d 905). Here, however, where the demand and refusal is a substantive and not a procedural element of the cause of action (*see Guggenheim Found. v. Lubell*, 153 A.D.2d 143, 147, 550 N.Y.S.2d 618; *Menzel v. List*, 22 A.D.2d 647, 253 N.Y.S.2d 43; compare, CPLR 206 [where a demand is necessary to entitle a person to commence an action, the time to commence that action is measured from when the right to make demand is complete]), it would not be prudent to extend that case law and impose the additional duty of diligence before the true owner has reason to know where its missing chattel is to be found.

Further, the facts of this case reveal how difficult it would be to specify the type of conduct that would be required for a showing of reasonable diligence. Here, the parties hotly contest whether publicizing the theft would have turned up the . . . gouache. According to the museum, some members of the art community believe that publicizing a theft exposes gaps in security and can lead to more thefts; the museum also argues that publicity often pushes a missing painting further underground. In light of the fact that members of the art community have apparently not reached a consensus on the best way to retrieve stolen art (*see*, Burnham, *Art Theft: Its Scope, Its Impact and Its Control*), it would be particularly inappropriate for this Court to spell out arbitrary rules of conduct that all true owners of stolen art work would have to follow to the letter if they wanted to preserve their right to pursue a cause of action in replevin. All owners of stolen property should not be expected to behave in the same way and should not be held to a common standard. The value of the property stolen, the manner in which it was stolen, and the type of institution from which it was stolen will all necessarily affect the manner in which a true owner will search for missing property. We conclude that it would be difficult, if not impossible, to craft a reasonable diligence requirement that could take into account all of these variables and that would not unduly burden the true owner.

Further, our decision today is in part influenced by our recognition that New York enjoys a worldwide reputation as a preeminent cultural center. To place the burden of locating stolen artwork on the true owner and to foreclose the rights of that owner to recover its property if the burden is not met would, we believe, encourage illicit trafficking in stolen art. Three years after the theft, any purchaser, good faith or not, would be able to hold onto stolen art work unless the true owner was able to establish that it had undertaken a reasonable search for the missing art. This shifting of the burden onto the wronged owner is inappropriate. In our opinion, the better rule gives the owner relatively greater protection and places the burden of investigating the provenance of a work of art on the potential purchaser.

Despite our conclusion that the imposition of a reasonable diligence requirement on the museum would be inappropriate for purposes of the Statute of Limitations, our holding today should not be seen as either sanctioning the museum's conduct or suggesting that the museum's conduct is no longer an issue in this case. We agree with the Appellate Division that the arguments raised in the appellant's summary judgment papers are directed at the conscience of the court and its ability to bring equitable considerations to bear in the ultimate disposition of the painting. As noted above, although appellant's Statute of Limitations argument fails, her contention that the museum did not exercise reasonable diligence in locating the painting will be considered by the Trial Judge in the context of her laches defense. The conduct of both the appellant and the museum will be relevant to any consideration of this defense at the trial level, and as the Appellate Division noted, prejudice will also need to be shown (153 A.D.2d 149, 550 N.Y.S.2d 618). On the limited record before us there is no indication that the equities favor either party. Mr. and Mrs. Lubell investigated the provenance of the gouache before the purchase by contacting the artist and his son-in-law directly. The Lubells displayed the painting in their home for more than 20 years with no reason to suspect that it was not legally theirs. These facts will doubtless have some impact on the final decision regarding appellant's laches defense. Because it is impossible to conclude from the facts of this case that the museum's conduct was unreasonable as a matter of law, however, Mrs. Lubell's cross motion for summary judgment was properly denied.

We agree with the Appellate Division, for the reasons stated by that court, that the burden of proving that the painting was not stolen properly rests with the appellant Mrs. Lubell. We have considered her remaining arguments, and we find them to be without merit. Accordingly, the order of the Appellate Division should be affirmed, with costs, and the certified question answered in the affirmative.

PROBLEM 9-2

> Compare *Guggenheim* to *DeWerth v. Baldinger,* which is discussed in the *Guggenheim* case. How much action must the true owner take before he loses his claim for replevin?

F. Deaccession

Collectors traditionally sold inferior pieces to upgrade their collections; museums stored less popular objects in vaults to await a return to favor. While these objects were stored, they were made available for study, loan, or perhaps to be exchanged for other pieces. Museums now frequently deaccession large numbers of works, for a variety of reasons, including the reduction of storage space, insurance, or restoration costs. A collection may have many duplicates (a repetition of similar themes in a similar medium), or there may have been a policy decision to specialize in certain types of art, thus restricting the scope of the collection and making retention of certain pieces undesirable. The sale of art may be necessary in order to finance the acquisition of an expensive masterpiece believed to have great public appeal. Finally, there may be a need to correct an imbalance between the collection itself and other museum activities. With operating costs rising, museums have been forced to reduce their present holdings and curtail acquisitions. This section will examine some of the criticisms leveled at museum deaccessioning in general and explore some of the problems that have arisen in the area.[29]

Critics decry deaccessioning collection pieces solely for the purpose of covering a museum's operating costs. Economic conditions have dictated that collections be sold, others made homeless, and many museums have been forced to curtail services or charge admission fees.

Administrative incompetence and inefficiency have been blamed for the economic dilemmas faced by many museums. While this may be true to a limited extent, higher prices commanded for art and declines in contributions, both monetary and in-kind, have led to financial hardship for many art institutions. Similarly, municipalities, as well as state and federal governments, have been forced to reduce museum support in order to provide other public

---

29. *See generally* Weil, *Deaccession Practices in American Museums,* Museum News, Feb. 1987.

services. As a result, some museums are left with little choice but to deaccession part of their collections when they cannot meet their current costs.

Critics of deaccessioning, on the other hand, believe that such a measure should only occur in special circumstances after much careful consideration and with close supervision.[30] Some believe that any trade or sale not to another museum should be outlawed.[31] Their rationale is that when an object is sold or transferred to another institution, it remains available to the public. This argument ignores the likelihood of a future purchaser lending the deaccessioned work to a museum for display and fails to consider the potential for transfers of partial interests or life estates.[32] An institution could thus obtain the necessary capital and still have possession of the piece when the term of transfer has expired. In addition, a conveyance specifying that the buyer will allow the art to be displayed periodically after the sale could be employed. Critics also ignore the possibility that a museum may have an item with no appeal for any other cultural institution.

Notes

1. The Shelburne Museum in Vermont raised $31 million by deaccessioning pastels and sculptures by Degas and Monet that were donated by the museum's founder. Proceeds from the sale of just one work ($11.9 million) brought in more than three and one-half times the museum's annual budget. Failing, *Shelburne Sale: Mixed Reviews*, ARTnews Jan. 1997 at 37. The museum intends to use the funds to create a "collections care endowment" to help offset operating expenses, including conservation and security. Failing, *Fading Impressions*, ARTnews Jan. 1996 at 106.

2. Sotheby's 1995 auction of works from the New-York Historical Society raised $8 million. *See* Kimmelman, *Should Old Masters Be Fund-Raisers?* N.Y. Times, Jan. 8, 1995 at Arts 1, for a critique of this sale. Despite the sale, the historical society remains in dire financial straits. *Id.*

3. For more information on deaccessioning, *see* Gibson, *Perspective: Cultural Patrimony or Overstocked Attic?* ARTnews, Jan. 1996 at 144; White, *When It's OK to Sell the Monet: A Trustee-Fiduciary Duty Framework for Analyzing the Deaccessioning of Art to Meet Museum Operating Expenses*, 94 MICH. L. REV. 1041 (1996).

30. *See* CAA Resolution, *supra*; Attorney General's Conference of Museum Representatives, held at the World Trade Center, in New York, N.Y., Oct. 19, 1973.

31. *See* Knoll, Museums—A Gunslinger's Dream (1975) (available from Bay Area Lawyers for the Arts) [now known as the California Lawyers for the Arts].

32. *See generally Miller v. Woodbury Trust Co.*, 2 N.J. Super. 497, 64 A.2d 634 (1949); *Guaranty Trust Co. of N.Y. v. New York Trust Co.*, 297 N.Y. 45, 74 N.E.2d 232 (1947).

PROBLEM 9-3

> A foreign prince wants to buy every Winslow Homer he can get his hands on for his palace. He makes a contract to purchase the entire collections of the St. Louis Art Museum, the Clark Art Institute, and the Nelson Atkins Museum (Kansas City). Based on the laws discussed above, analyze whether these museums can sell their collections.

ASSESSMENT

1. Artsy University (AU) was known for its wonderful art collection, which it opened to the public. One component of AU's collection included an exhibition which was donated by Dorothy Donor. Dorothy was an avid art collector and alumni of AU; her donation included several Picasso paintings that were worth millions of dollars. However, she never liked gifting her things, so she made AU promise that they would never put the exhibit in storage for any reason.

   Several years after Dorothy's donation AU needed to repair the roof of the building that held the Picasso collection, which meant they needed to put it in storage until the renovations were complete. When Dorothy's estate found out that her collection would be put in storage, directly against her wishes, they informed AU that they were entitled to get her collection back because AU had breached their agreement. Based on the court's decision in *Georgia O'Keeffe Foundation (Museum) v. Fisk University*, which of the following is the most accurate statement?

   (A) The gifting of the Picassos was charitable in nature, Dorothy had a general charitable intent, and there was a change of circumstances at AU, which would entitle AU to *cy pres* relief

   (B) AU will not be entitled to *cy pres* relief because Dorothy's gifting of the Picassos was made with a specific purpose in mind and had specific conditions attached to it, therefore she had a specific charitable intent

   (C) AU will not be entitled to *cy pres* relief because Dorothy did not like gifting her things and there was no evidence that she made any other charitable gifts to anyone else, therefore the gifting of the Picassos was made with a specific intent in mind

   (D) None of the above

   (E) Both (B) and (C)

2. Tracy Trustworthy is the director of a new museum in town called the Artsy Art Museum (AAM), which specializes in a rare collection of Banksy paintings. In order to grow their collection, Tracy asked a friend

of hers, Derek Donor, who has a wide collection of Banksy paintings as well, to donate some of his paintings to the AAM. Derek finally agreed, but only because Tracy is a good friend who makes him cookies on the weekends. When Tracy informed AAM that she acquired more Banksy paintings, they were happy until she said that she was entitled to a million dollar commission because without her help they would not have been able to get those extra paintings. Will Tracy be able to get the money she believes she is entitled to?

  (A) Tracy will be charged with self-dealing only if the AAM can prove that there was damage to the museum and that Tracy acted in bad faith

  (B) Tracy may be charged with self-dealing because requesting a commission for acquiring the Banksy painting positions her in a conflict between her personal interest and that of AAM

  (C) Tracy was not self-dealing because she deserves to be paid for the paintings she brought in since AAM would not have been able to get them if it were not for her friendship with Derek

  (D) Both (A) and (B) are correct

  (E) Both (A) and (C) are correct

3. Slinky Museum, a private corporation that displays colorful depictions of Slinkys, wants to claim a tax exemption for its museum property because it needs to save money. The museum believes it serves the public because there is some interest in seeing slinky paintings. However, SM does not provide activities for children and they do not provide any background information on the paintings. Based on the court's decision in *Georgia O'Keeffe Museum v. County of Santa Fe*, which of the following is the most accurate statement?

  (A) The Slinky Museum will not receive a tax exemption because it does not serve enough of a public benefit or have sufficient intrinsic educational value to qualify for educational purposes

  (B) Slinkys are important historical objects for a child's entertainment and education; therefore, the Slinky Museum serves an important educational purpose and benefit for the public and should be entitled to a tax exemption

  (C) The Slinky Museum has fun paintings and it is a museum, therefore it is automatically entitled to the tax exemption

  (D) Both (A) and (B)

  (E) None of the above

4. Which of the following statements are most accurate about adverse possession?

  (A) In a fixed loan agreement, museums must return the loaned piece of art to the loaner at the end of the agreement term even if not required to do so by the agreement

(B) Heirs can legally reclaim a piece of art that was loaned by a decedent at any time when a museum possesses it without legal title

(C) When loaning art to a museum it is best to obtain a detailed receipt of the loan signed by an authorized official so that the museum is unable to claim the piece through adverse possession

(D) Both (A) and (B)

(E) Both (B) and (C)

5. Mary Mortis became ill after a trip to South America. The doctors told her that she only had a week to live and that there was no chance of survival. On her deathbed, Mary decided to gift a painting worth $1,000 to the local museum. She wrote a letter stating her intent and sent it to the museum. When it received the letter, museum officials contacted Mary's heirs to obtain the art. However, Mary made a miraculous recovery and did not die from her illness. She decided to revoke her gift to the museum, and keep her art.

Which is the following is most likely to occur if the local museum tries to claim a breach of contract?

(A) The local museum will succeed and be able to claim the art because Mary already said that they were entitled to it and she is not allowed to take it back now

(B) Mary will be able to keep her art; however when she does die, the local museum will be able to then claim the paintings

(C) Mary will be able to keep her art because the gift was a *donation causa mortis*, which gives her the power to revoke the gift if she recovers

(D) Mary will be able to revoke her gift because she miraculously survived a life-threatening disease so she can do whatever she would like

(E) Both (A) and (B)

ASSESSMENT ANSWERS

1. Artsy University (AU) was known for its wonderful art collection, which it opened to the public. One component of AU's collection included an exhibition, which was donated by Dorothy Donor. Dorothy was an avid art collector and alumni of AU, her donation included several Picasso paintings that were worth millions of dollars. However, she never liked gifting her things so she made AU promise that they would never put the exhibit in storage for any reason.

Several years after Dorothy's donation AU needed to repair the roof of the building that held the Picasso collection, which meant they needed to put it in storage until the renovations were complete. When Dorothy's estate found out that her collection would be put in storage, directly against her wishes, they informed AU that they were entitled to get her collection back because AU had breached their agreement. Based on the court's decision in *Georgia O'Keeffe Foundation (Museum) v. Fisk University*, which of the following is the most accurate statement?

(A) The gifting of the Picasso was charitable in nature, Dorothy had a general charitable intent, and there was a change of circumstances at AU, which would entitle AU to *cy pres* relief

(B) AU will not be entitled to *cy pres* relief because Dorothy's gifting of the Picassos was made with a specific purpose in mind and had specific conditions attached to it, therefore she had a specific charitable intent

(C) AU will not be entitled to *cy pres* relief because Dorothy did not like gifting her things and there was no evidence that she made any other charitable gifts to anyone else, therefore the gifting of the Picassos was made with a specific intent in mind

(D) None of the above

(E) Both (B) and (C)

ANSWER: The correct answer is choice (A), because the university would most likely be entitled to *cy pres* relief under these circumstances.

2. Tracy Trustworthy is the director of a new museum in town called the Artsy Art Museum (AAM), which specializes in a rare collection of Banksy paintings. In order to grow their collection, Tracy asked a friend of hers, Derek Donor, who has a wide collection of Banksy paintings as well, to donate some of his paintings to the AAM. Derek finally agreed, but only because Tracy is a good friend who makes him cookies on the weekends. When Tracy informed AAM that she acquired more Bansky paintings, they are happy until she said that she was entitled to a million dollar commission because without her help they would not have been able to get those extra paintings. Will Tracy be able to get the money she believes she is entitled to?

(A) Tracy will be charged with self-dealing only if the AAM can prove that there was damage to the museum and that Tracy acted in bad faith

(B) Tracy may be charged with self-dealing because requesting a commission for acquiring the Banksy painting positions her in a conflict between her personal interest and that of AAM

(C) Tracy was not self-dealing because she deserves to be paid for the paintings she brought in since AAM would not have been able to get them if it were not for her friendship with Derek

(D) Both (A) and (B) are correct

(E) Both (A) and (C) are correct

ANSWER: The correct answer is choice (B). Choice (A) is incorrect because proving self-dealing does not require a showing of damage to the trust because the damage is presumed. Additionally, whether the trustee acted in good faith and with honest intentions is irrelevant. (C) is incorrect under the ethical rules adopted by the Association of Art Museum Directors, which specifically prohibits a director from accepting a commission on the sale of a work of art. (B) is the only correct answer, therefore (D) and (E) are incorrect.

3. Slinky Museum, a private corporation that displays colorful depictions of Slinkys, wants to claim a tax exemption for its museum property because it needs to save money. The museum believes it serves the public because there is some interest in seeing slinky paintings. However, SM does not provide activities for children and they do not provide any background information on the paintings. Based on the court's decision in *Georgia O'Keeffe Museum v. County of Santa Fe*, which of the following is the most accurate statement?

   (A) The Slinky Museum will not receive a tax exemption because it does not serve enough of a public benefit or have sufficient intrinsic educational value to qualify for educational purposes

   (B) Slinkys are important historical objects for a child's entertainment and education; therefore, the Slinky Museum serves an important educational purpose and benefit for the public and should be entitled to a tax exemption

   (C) The Slinky Museum has fun paintings and it is a museum, therefore it is automatically entitled to the tax exemption

   (D) Both (A) and (B)

   (E) None of the above

   ANSWER: The correct answer is choice (A). The Slinky Museum is unlikely to be used for educational purposes because not many people go to it, there are no educational activities for guests, and paintings of Slinkys do not have a historical or educational purpose, thus it will not be entitled to a tax exemption. (B) is therefore incorrect. (C) is also incorrect as having fun paintings does not have anything to do with serving an important educational public interest. (D) and (E) are incorrect because the only correct answer is (A).

4. Which of the following statements are most accurate about adverse possession?

   (A) In a fixed loan agreement, museums must return the loaned piece of art to the loaner at the end of the agreement term even if not required to do so by the agreement

   (B) Heirs can legally reclaim a piece of art that was loaned by a decedent at any time when a museum possesses it without legal title

(C) When loaning art to a museum it is best to obtain a detailed receipt of the loan signed by an authorized official so that the museum is unable to claim the piece through adverse possession

(D) Both (A) and (B)

(E) Both (B) and (C)

ANSWER: The correct answer is choice (E). Choice (A) is incorrect because museums are not required to return items loaned to them in a fixed agreement unless it is required by the agreement. If not indicated by the agreement, museums just have the duty to notify the loaner of the item's availability at the end of the agreement's term. (B) and (C) are both correct, thus, neither alone could be the correct answer. (D) is incorrect.

5. Mary Mortis became ill after a trip to South America. The doctors told her that she only had a week to live and that there was no chance of survival. On her deathbed, Mary decided to gift a painting worth $1,000 to the local museum. She wrote a letter stating her intent and sent it to the museum. When it received the letter, museum officials contacted Mary's heirs to obtain the art. However, Mary made a miraculous recovery and did not die from her illness. She decided to revoke her gift to the museum, and keep her art.

Which is the following is most likely to occur if the local museum tries to claim a breach of contract?

(A) The local museum will succeed and be able to claim the art because Mary already said that she would they were entitled to it and she is not allowed to take it back now

(B) Mary will be able to keep her art, however when she does die, the local museum will be able to then claim the paintings

(C) Mary will be able to keep her art because the gift was a *donation causa mortis*, which gives her the power to revoke the gift if she recovers

(D) Mary will be able to revoke her gift because she miraculously survived a life-threatening disease so she can do whatever she would like

(E) Both (A) and (B)

ANSWER: The correct answer is choice (C). Gifts *donation causa mortis* (made in contemplation of death) may be revoked if the donor recovers. (A) is therefore incorrect because Mary recovered and had the right to revoke her donation. (B) is wrong because once the donor has revoked his or her offer, it is then void. (D) is incorrect. Although it is correct insofar as it implies that Mary's survival is key to her revocation, it does not allow her to do whatever she would like, and is therefore irrelevant. (E) is incorrect because (B) is incorrect for the above reasons.

10 | INTERNATIONAL MOVEMENT OF ART DURING WAR

Since the earliest times, conquering armies have plundered those they defeated. "To the victor belong the spoils" appears to have been a rule of war throughout history. Ramses II, who is thought to have ruled Egypt for 66 years from 1279 BC to 1213 BC, led expeditions north into Mediterranean countries and south to the ancient kingdom of Nubia. As he built cities, temples, and monuments, Ramses II enriched his kingdom with treasures obtained from his military prowess. Homer's *Odyssey* catalogues many of the gems collected during the sack of Troy from 1194 BC to 1184 BC.

The Romans, in approximately 400 BC, glorified the plunder of art. They apparently believed collecting booty from a vanquished nation was a legitimate by-product of war. Property confiscated in accordance with the international rules of war is generally referred to as "booty" or "plunder."

It was this practice, established by the Romans during the height of their power, that the Visigoths adopted during the third century when they sacked Rome. Roman efforts to bribe the barbarians to prevent the Empire's ruin met with little success. In fact, bribes seemed to stimulate the invaders' appetite for Roman treasure, which — according to at least one historian — was so great that the accumulated wealth had to be removed by wagon trains.[1]

Thus, most of the great art works of the world — at one time principally within the dominion and control of Rome alone — were, by the end of the fifth century, to be found in such cities as Carthage and Constantinople; some were even spread among the transient dwellings of marauding Arabs. Many were lost forever in the sands of the Sahara and the depths of the Mediterranean as plundering parties were, throughout their travels, plagued by storms, desertion, and dissension.

Wars have taken place in every century, on every continent, and engaged every group of people. In the twentieth century when multiple countries became involved, we called them world wars. No matter the conflict, art

---

1. W. Trueue, *Art Plunder* (1961) [hereinafter Trueue].

and cultural property has suffered damage. This chapter presents cases and materials on the legal response to wartime looting. Historically, the world community did little to protect national patrimony from plunder and destruction. Fortunately that has changed.

Autocephalous Greek-Orthodox Church of Cyprus v. Goldberg

917 F.2d 278 (7th Cir. 1990)*

BAUER, Chief Judge.

Byron, writing . . . of the Turkish invasion of Corinth in 1715, could as well have been describing the many churches and monuments that today lie in ruins on Cyprus, a small, war-torn island in the eastern corner of the Mediterranean Sea. In this appeal, we consider the fate of several tangible victims of Cyprus' turbulent history: specifically, four Byzantine mosaics created over 1400 years ago. The district court awarded possession of these extremely valuable mosaics to plaintiff-appellee, the Autocephalous Greek-Orthodox Church of Cyprus ("Church of Cyprus" or "Church"). *Autocephalous Greek-Orthodox Church of Cyprus v. Goldberg & Feldman Fine Arts, Inc.,* 717 F. Supp. 1374 (S.D. Ind. 1989). Defendants-appellants, Peg Goldberg and Goldberg & Feldman Fine Arts, Inc. (collectively "Goldberg"), claim that in so doing, the court committed various reversible errors. We affirm.

I. BACKGROUND

In the early sixth century, A.D., a large mosaic was affixed to the apse of the Church of the Panagia Kanakaria ("Kanakaria Church") in the village of Lythrankomi, Cyprus. The mosaic, made of small bits of colored glass, depicted Jesus Christ as a young boy in the lap of his mother, the Virgin Mary, who was seated on a throne. Jesus and Mary were attended by two archangels and surrounded by a frieze depicting the twelve apostles. The mosaic was displayed in the Kanakaria Church for centuries, where it became, under the practices of Eastern Orthodox Christianity, sanctified as a holy relic. It survived both the vicissitudes of history, *see Autocephalous,* 717 F. Supp. at 1377 (discussing the period of Iconoclasm during which many religious artifacts were destroyed), and, thanks to restoration efforts, the ravages of time. . . .

Testimony before Judge Noland established that the Kanakaria mosaic was one of only a handful of such holy Byzantine relics to survive into the twentieth century. Sadly, however, war came to Cyprus in the 1970s, from which the mosaic could not be spared.

The Cypriot people have long been a divided people, approximately three-fourths being of Greek descent and Greek-Orthodox faith, the other quarter of Turkish descent and Muslim faith. No sooner had Cyprus gained independence from British rule in 1960 than this bitter division surfaced. Civil

---

* Most footnotes omitted.

disturbances erupted between Greek and Turkish Cypriots, necessitating the introduction of United Nations peacekeeping forces in 1964. (U.N. forces still remain in Cyprus.) Through the 1960s, the Greek Cypriots, concentrated in the southern part of the island, became increasingly estranged from the Turkish Cypriots, concentrated in the north. . . .

The tensions erupted again in 1974, this time with more violent results. In July, 1974, the civil government of the Republic of Cyprus was replaced by a government controlled by the Greek Cypriot military. In apparent response, on July 20, 1974, Turkey invaded Cyprus from the north. By late August, the Turkish military forces had advanced to occupy approximately the northern third of the island. The point at which the invading forces stopped is called the "Green Line." To this day, the heavily-guarded Green Line bisects Nicosia, the capital of the Republic, and splits the island from east to west.

The Turkish forces quickly established their own "government" north of the Green Line. In 1975, they formed what they called the "Turkish Federated State of Cyprus" ("TFSC"). In 1983, that administration was dissolved, and the "Turkish Republic of Northern Cyprus" ("TRNC") was formed. These "governments" were recognized immediately by Turkey, but all other nations in the world — including the United States — have never recognized them, and continue to recognize the Republic of Cyprus ("Republic"), plaintiff-appellee in this action, as the only legitimate government for all Cypriot people.

The Turkish invasion led to the forced southern exodus of over one-hundred thousand Greek Cypriots who lived in northern Cyprus. Turkish Cypriots living in southern Cyprus (and tens of thousands of settlers from mainland Turkey) likewise flooded into northern Cyprus, resulting in a massive exchange of populations.

Lythrankomi is in the northern portion of Cyprus that came under Turkish rule. Although the village and the Kanakaria Church were untouched by the invading forces in 1974, the villagers of Greek ancestry were soon thereafter "enclaved" by the Turkish military. Despite the hostile environment, the pastor and priests of the Kanakaria Church continued for two years to conduct religious services for the Greek Cypriots who remained in Lythrankomi. Hardy as they must have been, these clerics, and virtually all remaining Greek Cypriots, were forced to flee to southern Cyprus in the summer of 1976. Church of Cyprus officials testified that they intend to re-establish the congregation at the Kanakaria Church as soon as Greek Cypriots are permitted to return safely to Lythrankomi. (Thirty-five thousand Turkish troops remain in northern Cyprus.) . . .

When the priests evacuated the Kanakaria Church in 1976, the mosaic was still intact. In the late 1970s, however, Church of Cyprus officials received increasing reports that Greek Cypriot churches and monuments in northern Cyprus were being attacked and vandalized, their contents stolen or destroyed. (Such reports were necessarily sketchy and unverifiable as officials from the Republic and Church of Cyprus have been denied access to northern Cyprus.) In November, 1979, a resident of northern Cyprus brought word to the Republic's Department of Antiquities that this fate had also befallen the Kanakaria

Church and its mosaic. Vandals had plundered the church, removing anything of value from its interior. The mosaic, or at least its most recognizable and valuable parts, had been forcibly ripped from the apse of the church. Once a place of worship, the Kanakaria Church had been reduced to a stable for farm animals.

Upon learning of the looting of the Kanakaria Church and the loss of its mosaics (made plural by the vandals' axes), the Republic of Cyprus took immediate steps to recover them. As discussed in greater detail in Judge Noland's opinion, see 717 F. Supp. at 1380, these efforts took the form of contacting and seeking assistance from many organizations and individuals, including the United Nations Educational, Scientific, and Cultural Organization ("UNESCO"); the International Council of Museums; the International Council of Museums and Sites; Europa Nostra (an organization devoted to the conservation of the architectural heritage of Europe); the Council of Europe; international auction houses such as Christie's and Sotheby's; Harvard University's Dumbarton Oaks Institute for Byzantine Studies; and the foremost museums, curators, and Byzantine scholars throughout the world. The Republic's United States Embassy also routinely disseminated information about lost cultural properties to journalists, U.S. officials, and scores of scholars, architects, and collectors in this country, asking for assistance in recovering the mosaics. The overall strategy behind these efforts was to get word to the experts and scholars who would probably be involved in any ultimate sale of the mosaics. These individuals, it was hoped, would be the most likely (only?) actors in the chain of custody of stolen cultural properties who would be interested in helping the Republic and Church of Cyprus recover them.

The Republic's efforts have paid off. In recent years, the Republic has recovered and returned to the Church of Cyprus several stolen relics and antiquities. The Republic has even located frescoes and other works taken from the Kanakaria Church, including the four mosaics at issue here. These four mosaics, each measuring about two feet square, depict the figure of Jesus, the busts of one of the attending archangels, the apostle Matthew and the apostle James.

To understand how these pieces of the Kanakaria mosaic resurfaced, we must trace the actions of appellant Peg Goldberg and the other principals through whose hands they passed in 1988.

Peg Goldberg is an art dealer and gallery operator. Goldberg and Feldman Fine Arts, Inc., is the Indiana corporation that owns her gallery in Carmel, Indiana. In the summer of 1988, Peg Goldberg went to Europe to shop for works for her gallery. Although her main interest is 20th century paintings, etchings and sculptures, Goldberg was enticed while in The Netherlands by Robert Fitzgerald, another Indiana art dealer and "casual friend" of hers, to consider the purchase of "four early Christian mosaics." In that connection, Fitzgerald arranged a meeting in Amsterdam for July 1st. At that meeting, Fitzgerald introduced Goldberg to Michel van Rijn, a Dutch art dealer, and Ronald Faulk, a California attorney. Van Rijn and Faulk were strangers to Goldberg. All she knew about them was what she learned in their few meetings, which included the fact that van Rijn, a published expert on Christian icons (she was given a copy of the book), had been convicted by a French court for art forgery; that he claimed to be a descendant of both Rembrandt and Rubens; and that Faulk was in Europe to represent Fitzgerald and van Rijn.

At that first meeting in Amsterdam on July 1, 1988, van Rijn showed Goldberg photographs of the four mosaics at issue in this case and told her that the seller wanted $3 million for them. Goldberg testified that she immediately "fell in love" with the mosaics. Van Rijn told her that the seller was a Turkish antiquities dealer who had "found" the mosaics in the rubble of an "extinct" church in northern Cyprus while working as an archaeologist "assigned (by Turkey) to northern Cyprus." (Goldberg knew of the Turkish invasion of Cyprus and of the subsequent division of the island.) As to the seller, Goldberg was also told that he had exported the mosaics to his home in Munich, Germany with the permission of the Turkish Cypriot government, and that he was now interested in selling the mosaics quickly because he had a "cash problem." Goldberg was not initially given the seller's identity. Goldberg also learned that Faulk, on behalf of Fitzgerald and van Rijn, had already met with this as-yet-unidentified seller to discuss the sale of these mosaics. Her interest quite piqued, Goldberg asked Faulk to return to Munich and tell the seller — whose identity, she would eventually learn, was Aydin Dikman — that she was interested.

Faulk dutifully took this message to Dikman in Munich, and returned to Amsterdam the following day. Faulk returned from that meeting with a contract he signed as agent for van Rijn to purchase the mosaics from Dikman for $350,000. When Goldberg met with Faulk on July 2, she was not told of this contract, however. Faulk merely informed her that Dikman still had the mosaics (though he was "actively negotiating with another buyer"), and that, in Faulk's opinion the export documents he had been shown by Dikman were in order. Faulk apparently showed Goldberg copies of a few of these documents, none of which, of course, were genuine, and at least one of which was obviously unrelated to these mosaics. *See Autocephalous*, 717 F. Supp. at 1382.

The next day (all of this happening rather fast), the principals gathered again in Amsterdam. Goldberg, van Rijn, Fitzgerald, and Faulk agreed to "acquire the mosaics for their purchase price of $1,080,000 (U.S.)." The parties agreed to split the profits from any resale of the mosaics as follows: Goldberg 50%; Fitzgerald 22.5%; van Rijn 22.5%; and Faulk 5%. A document to this effect was executed on July 4, 1988, which document included a provision reading, "This agreement shall be governed by and any action commenced will be pursuant to the laws of the state of Indiana."

In those hectic early days of July, Goldberg contacted Otto N. Frenzel, III, a friend and high-ranking officer at the Merchants National Bank of Indianapolis ("Merchants"), and requested a loan from Merchants of $1.2 million for the purchase of the mosaics. She told Frenzel that she needed $1,080,000 to pay van Rijn and the others, and she required the additional $120,000 to pay for expenses, insurance, restoration, and the like. Merchants assured her that financing could be arranged, if she could provide appraisals and other documents substantiating the transaction. With Fitzgerald's and van Rijn's help, Goldberg obtained the appraisals (all three of which valued the mosaics at between $3 and $6 million), and sent them to Merchants. That done, she and Fitzgerald hurried to Geneva, Switzerland, for the transfer of the mosaics, which was to take place on July 5. After arriving in Switzerland, Goldberg learned that her requested loan had been approved by Merchants and the money would be forthcoming, though a few days behind schedule. Her financing secured, Goldberg proceeded to the July 5 meeting as scheduled. She could not yet turn over the money, but she wanted to get a look at what she was buying.

The July 5 meeting was held in the "free port" area of the Geneva airport, an area reserved for items that have not passed through Swiss customs. Faulk and Dikman arrived from Munich with the mosaics, which were stored in crates. Dikman introduced himself to Goldberg and then left; this brief exchange was the only time the two would meet. Goldberg then inspected the four mosaics. She testified that she "was in awe," and that, despite some concern about the mosaics' deteriorating condition, she wanted them "more than ever."

During the few days that Goldberg waited in Switzerland for the money to arrive from Merchants, she placed several telephone calls concerning the mosaics. She testified that she wanted to make sure the mosaics had not been reported stolen, and that no treaties would prevent her from bringing the mosaics into the United States. She called UNESCO's office in Geneva and inquired as to whether any treaties prevented "the removal of items from northern Cyprus in the mid to late 1970s to Germany," but did not mention the mosaics. She claims also to have called, on advice from an art dealer friend of hers in New York, the International Foundation for Art Research ("IFAR"), an organization that collects information concerning stolen art. She testified that she asked IFAR whether it had any record of a claim to the mosaics, and that, when she called back later as instructed, IFAR told her it did not. Judge Noland clearly doubted the credibility of this testimony, noting, among other things, that neither Goldberg nor IFAR have any record of any such search. (A formal IFAR search involves a fee and thus generates a bill that would serve as proof that a search was performed.) *Autocephalous*, 717 F. Supp. at 1403. Judge Noland also questioned Goldberg's testimony that she telephoned customs officials in the United States, Switzerland, Germany, and Turkey. *Id.* The only things of which Judge Noland was sure was that Goldberg did not contact the Republic of Cyprus or the TRNC (from one of whose lands she knew the mosaics had come); the Church of Cyprus; "Interpol," a European information-sharing network for police forces; nor "a single disinterested expert on Byzantine art." *Id.* at 1403-04.

However Goldberg occupied her time from July 5 to July 7, on the latter date the money arrived. Goldberg took the $1.2 million, reduced to $100 bills and stuffed into two satchels, and met with Faulk and Fitzgerald at the Geneva airport. As arranged, Goldberg kept $120,000 in cash and gave the remaining $1,080,000 to Faulk and Fitzgerald in return for the mosaics. Faulk and Fitzgerald in turn split the money with van Rijn, Dikman, and their other cohorts as follows: $350,000 to Dikman (as per Faulk and van Rijn's prior agreement with him); $282,500 to van Rijn; $297,500 to Fitzgerald; $80,000 to Faulk; and

$70,000 to another attorney in London. Along with the mosaics, Goldberg received a "General bill of sale" issued by Dikman to Goldberg and Feldman Fine Arts, Inc. The following day, July 8, 1988, Goldberg returned to the United States with her prize.

Back home in Indiana, Goldberg took what she had left of her $120,000 cut and deposited it into several of her business and personal bank accounts. After paying for the insurance and shipment of the mosaics, as well as a few unrelated art purchases, that sum amounted to approximately $70,000. Her friends and business associates in Indiana soon took quite an interest in her purchase; literally. For large sums of money, Frenzel, Goldberg's well-placed friend at Merchants, and another Indiana resident named Dr. Stewart Bick acquired from van Rijn and Fitzgerald substantial interests in the profits from any resale of the mosaics.

Peg Goldberg's efforts soon turned to just that: the resale of these valuable mosaics. She worked up sales brochures about them, and contacted several other dealers to help her find a buyer. Two of these dealers' searches led them both to Dr. Marion True of the Getty Museum in California. When told of these mosaics and their likely origin, the aptly named Dr. True explained to the dealers that she had a working relationship with the Republic of Cyprus and that she was duty-bound to contact Cypriot officials about them. Dr. True called Dr. Vassos Karageorghis, the Director of the Republic's Department of Antiquities and one of the primary Cypriot officials involved in the worldwide search for the mosaics. Dr. Karageorghis verified that the Republic was in fact hunting for the mosaics that had been described to Dr. True, and he set in motion the investigative and legal machinery that ultimately resulted in the Republic learning that they were in Goldberg's possession in Indianapolis.

After their request for the return of the mosaics was refused by Goldberg, the Republic of Cyprus and the Church of Cyprus (collectively "Cyprus") brought this suit in the Southern District of Indiana for the recovery of the mosaics. Judge Noland bifurcated the possession and damages issues and held a bench trial on the former. In a detailed, thorough opinion (that occupies thirty-one pages in the Federal Supplement), Judge Noland awarded possession of the mosaics to the Church of Cyprus. Goldberg filed a timely appeal.

II. ANALYSIS

[After analyzing jurisdictional, choice of law, and statute of limitation issues and concluding that it had jurisdiction, that Indiana law governed the action, and that the statute of limitations had not run, the court moved on to the merits of the Church's replevin claim.]

D. The Merits of the Replevin Claim

Under Indiana law, replevin is an action at law "whereby the owner or person claiming the possession of personal goods may recover such personal goods where they have been wrongfully taken or unlawfully detained." 25 I.L.E. Replevin § 1. "The gist of the action is the defendant's unlawful detention of the plaintiff's property. The issue litigated is the present right to the possession of the property in controversy, and the purpose of the action is to determine who shall have possession of the property sought to be replevied." *Id.* at § 2 (citations omitted). *See also State Exchange Bank of Culver v. Teague,* 495 N.E.2d 262, 266 (Ind. App. 1986). To recover the item sought to be replevied, (which is the primary remedy in a replevin action, *see Kegerreis v. Auto-Owners Insurance Co.,* 484 N.E.2d 976, 982 (Ind. App. 1985)), the plaintiff must establish three elements: "his title or right to possession, that the property is unlawfully detained, and that the defendant wrongfully holds possession." 25 I.L.E. Replevin § 42 (citations omitted). *See also Snyder v. International Harvester Credit Corp.,* 147 Ind. App. 364, 261 N.E.2d 71, 73 (1970).

Judge Noland applied these elements to the facts of this case and determined that Cyprus had met its burden as to each. *Autocephalous,* 717 F. Supp. at 1397-1400. Our review of this application of Indiana law to the facts convinces us that it is free of error: 1) the Kanakaria Church was and is owned by the Holy Archbishopric of the Church of Cyprus, a self-headed (hence "autocephalous") church associated with the Greek Orthodox faith; 2) the mosaics were removed from the Kanakaria Church without the authorization of the Church or the Republic (even the TRNC's unsuccessful motion to intervene claimed that the mosaics were improperly removed); and 3) Goldberg, as an ultimate purchaser from a thief, has no valid claim of title or right to possession of the mosaics. . . .

We note that Judge Noland again backstopped his conclusion, this time conducting an alternative analysis under Swiss substantive law. *See Autocephalous,* 717 F. Supp. at 1400-04. Briefly, the court concluded that the Church had superior title under Swiss law as well, because Goldberg could not claim valid title under the Swiss "good faith purchasers" notion having only made a cursory inquiry into the suspicious circumstances surrounding the sale of the mosaics. (Under Indiana law, such considerations are irrelevant because, except in very limited exceptions not applicable here, a subsequent purchaser (even a "good faith, bona fide purchaser for value") who obtains an item from a thief only acquires the title held by the thief; that is no title. 6 I.L.E. Conversion § 15.) As we state above, Indiana law controls every aspect of this action. Thus, Judge Noland's extensive (and quite interesting) discussion of Swiss law, as well as Goldberg's lengthy attack thereon, need not be reviewed. Cyprus adequately established the elements of replevin under Indiana law, on which ground alone we affirm the district court's decision to award the possession of the mosaics to the Church of Cyprus.

E. The Effect of the TFSC Edicts

Finally, Goldberg argues that several decrees of the TFSC (the entity established in northern Cyprus by the Turkish military immediately after the 1974 invasion) divested the Church of title to the mosaics. . . . Goldberg asks us to honor these decrees under the notion that in some instances courts in the United States can give effect to the acts of nonrecognized but "de facto" regimes if the acts relate to purely local matters. *See* Restatement (Third) of the Foreign Relations Law of the United States ("Third Restatement") § 205(3) (1987).... The TFSC decrees at issue, all propagated in 1975, are principally these: 1) the "Abandoned Movable Property Law," which provided that all movable property within the boundaries of the TFSC abandoned by its owner because of the owner's "departure" from northern Cyprus "as a result of the situation after 20th July 1974" now belongs to the TFSC "in the name of the Turkish Community" and that the TFSC "is responsible for the possession and control of such property;" and 2) the "Antiquities Ordinance," which provided that all religious buildings and antiquities, including specifically "synagogues, basilicas, churches, monasteries and the like," located north of the Green Line, as well as any and all "movable antiquities" contained therein, are now the property of the TFSC.... Because these decrees were enacted before the Kanakaria Church was looted and its mosaics stolen, the argument concludes, the Church cannot here claim to hold title to the mosaics....

What Goldberg is claiming is that the TFSC's confiscatory decrees, adopted only one year after the Turkish invasion, should be given effect by this court because the TFSC and its successor TRNC should now be viewed as the "de facto" government north of the Green Line. This we are unwilling to do. We draw on two lines of precedent as support for our decision. First, we note that, contrary to the New York court's decision in *Salimoff*, 186 N.E. 679, several courts of the same era refused to give effect to the nationalization decrees of the as-yet-unrecognized Soviet Republics. These courts relied on a variety of grounds, including especially the fact that the political branches of our government still refused to recognize these entities.... Similarly, as regards the Turkish administration in northern Cyprus, the United States government (like the rest of the non-Turkish world) has not recognized its legitimacy, nor does our government "recognize that [the Turkish administration] has functioned as a de facto or quasi government . . . , ruling within its own borders." *Salimoff*, 186 N.E. at 682 (relying on the fact that the U.S. government had so "recognized" the Soviet government).

Second, we are guided in part by the post-Civil War cases in which courts refused to give effect to property-affecting acts of the Confederate state legislatures. In one such case, *Williams v. Bruffy*, 96 U.S. 176, 24 L. Ed. 716 (1878), the Supreme Court drew a helpful distinction between two kinds of "de facto" governments. The first kind "is such as exists after it has expelled the regularly constituted authorities from the seats of power and the public offices, and established its own functionaries in their places, so as to represent in fact the sovereignty of the nation." *Id.* at 185. This kind of de facto government, the Court explained, "is treated as in most respects possessing rightful authority, . . . [and] its legislation is in general recognized." *Id.* The second kind of de facto government (is such as exists where a portion of the inhabitants of a country have separated themselves from the parent State and established an independent government. The validity of its acts, both against the parent State and its citizens or subjects, depends entirely upon its ultimate success. . . . If it succeed, and become recognized, its acts from the commence-ment of its existence are upheld as those of an independent nation."*Id.* At 186. (The Court held that the Confederacy was a government of the second type that ultimately failed.) Goldberg argues that the TFSC and its successor TRNC have achieved the level of "ultimate success" contemplated by this standard, because they have maintained control of the territory north of the Green Line for over fifteen years. We will not thus equate simple longevity of control with "ultimate success." The Turkish forces, despite their best efforts, did not com-pletely supplant the Republic nor its officers. Instead, the TFSC and the TRNC, neither of which has ever been recognized by the non-Turkish world, only acceded to the control of the northern portion of Cyprus. The Republic of Cyprus remains the only recognized Cypriot government, the sovereign nation for the entire island. Rejecting Goldberg's invitation to delve any further into facts and current events which are not of record in this proceeding, we con-clude that the confiscatory decrees proffered by Goldberg do not divest the Church of its claim of title.

III. CONCLUSION

. . . [W]ar can reduce our grandest and most sacred temples to mere "frag-ments of stone." Only the lowest of scoundrels attempt to reap personal gain from this collective loss. Those who plundered the churches and monuments of war-torn Cyprus, hoarded their relics away, and are now smuggling and selling them for large sums, are just such blackguards. The Republic of Cyprus, with diligent effort and the help of friends like Dr. True, has been able to locate several of these stolen antiquities; items of vast cultural, religious (and, as this case demonstrates, monetary) value. Among such finds are the pieces of the Kanakaria mosaic at issue in this case. Unfortunately, when these mosaics surfaced they were in the hands not of the most guilty parties, but of Peg Goldberg and her gallery. Correctly applying Indiana law, the district court determined that Goldberg must return the mosaics to their rightful owner: the Church of Cyprus. Goldberg's tireless attacks have not established reversible error in that determination, and thus, for the reasons discussed above, the district court's judgment is AFFIRMED.

Notes

1. Lest this result seem too harsh, we should note that those who wish to purchase art on the international market, undoubtedly a ticklish busi-ness, are not without means by which to protect themselves. When circumstances are as suspicious as those that faced Peg Goldberg, pro-spective purchasers would do best to do more than make a few last-minute phone calls. As testified to at trial, in a transaction like this, "All the red flags are up, all the red lights are on, all the sirens are blaring." *Autocephalous*, 717 F. Supp. at 1402 (quoting testimony of Dr. Vikan).

In such cases, dealers can (and probably should) take steps such as a formal IFAR search; a documented authenticity check by disinterested experts; a full background search of the seller and his claim of title; insurance protection and a contingency sales contract; and the like. If Goldberg would have pursued such methods, perhaps she would have discovered in time what she discovered too late: the Church had a valid, superior, and enforceable claim to these Byzantine treasures, which therefore must be returned to it.

2. In 2002, the United States and Cyprus agreed to a "Memorandum of understanding concerning the imposition of import restrictions on Pre-Classical and Classical archaeological objects." It was signed in Washington on July 16, 2002, and entered into force on July 16, 2002. The agreement was amended on August 17, 2006, and on July 16, 2007. Under the original memorandum, the U.S. imposed an emergency import restriction on Byzantine ecclesiastical and ritual ethnological material from Cyprus unless such material is accompanied by an export permit issued by the Government of the Republic of Cyprus. Subsequent amendments have extended the restriction many times.

A. International Law Guidelines

International law developed out of wars between and among European states, and between European states and the indigenous peoples they discovered on other continents. There are two individuals who, through their writings, can lay claim to being called the fathers of International Law. Francisco de Vitoria, who wrote *On the Indians Lately Discovered* in 1557, examined legal norms from a moral perspective. He put forth ideas on how Spain should approach the Indians in the new world; particularly, that Indians had rights and duties. Hugo Grotius published *De Jure Belli ac Pacis (The Law of War and Peace)* in 1625. The first major series of treaties, *The Peace of Westphalia*, were concluded in 1648 to end the Thirty Years War between the Holy Roman Empire and several European states, namely Spain, France, and Sweden.

Since that time, states have entered into bilateral (between two states), trilateral (between three states), and multilateral (between many states) treaties to not only end wars, but also address cultural heritage issues. In 1863, the United States attempted to incorporate such parameters in the Lieber Code, a set of army regulations for field activities in wartime. It was an early recognition of the need for the protection of cultural property by a conquering nation, and provided for a determination of ownership by treaty after war in the few situations where the code allowed the seizure of art objects. The instructions provided in part:

Art. XXXIV. As a general rule, the property belonging to churches, hospitals, or other establishments of an exclusively charitable character, to establishments of education, or foundations for the promotion of knowledge, whether public schools, universities, academies of learning or observations, museums of the fine arts or of a scientific character such property is not to be considered public property.

Lieber Code, Instructions for the Government of Armies of the United States in the Field by Order of the Secretary of War, Apr. 24, 1863, quoted in Friedman, *The Law of War* 158 (1972).

The Conventions of the Hague of 1899 and of 1907 constituted the first formal establishment of guidelines for the "Protection of Cultural Property in the Event of Armed Conflict and Protocol Conflict." Two provisions of the 1907 convention later became particularly significant.

Art. 46. Family honour and rights, the lives of persons and private property, as well as religious connections and practice, must be respected. Private property cannot be confiscated.

***

Art. 56. The property of municipalities, that of institutions dedicated to religion, charity and education, the arts and sciences, even when State property, shall be treated as private property. All seizure of, destruction or willful damage done to institutions of this character, historic monuments, works of art and science, is forbidden, and should be made the subject of legal proceedings.

See Convention with Other Powers on the Laws and Customs of War on Land, Oct. 18, 1907, 36 Stat. 2277 (1909), T.S. No. 539.

These guidelines set forth the basic principles that all interested parties hoped would govern situations that in the past had wrought such destruction upon many of the world's treasures. The rules were acceded to by all the major powers. Although the Hague Convention appeared responsive to the problem of destruction of cultural property during armed conflict with its creation of ethical guidelines, the convention was largely ineffectual when actually tested in the first major global conflict of the twentieth century.[2]

PROBLEM 10-1

Should countries anticipate that, if they invade other countries, looting will most likely take place by the local population and the invading soldiers? Should there be an international legal requirement to protect the invaded country's antiquities and artwork?

---

2. *Id. See also* Convention with Certain Powers on the Laws and Customs of War on Land, July 29, 1899, 32 Stat. 1803 (1902), T.S. No. 403.

Notes

1. For an excellent article discussing the protection of cultural property during times of war, *see* Jim Nafziger, *Protection of Cultural Heritage in Time of War and Its Aftermath*, 6 IFAR J. 56 (2003).
2. With the creation of the League of Nations following World War I came the Permanent Court of International Justice. That court was succeeded by the International Court of Justice, which accompanied the formation of the United Nations. In the ICJ case addressing a dispute between Germany and the Netherlands over art work, *Case concerning Certain Property (Liechtenstein v. Germany*, 20015 I.C.J. 6, the Principality of Liechtenstein sued the Federal Republic of Germany for the return of a painting by the seventeenth-century Dutch artist Pieter van Laer that had been lent by a museum in Brno (Czechoslovakia) to a museum in Cologne (Germany) for inclusion in an exhibition. This painting had been the property of the family of the Reigning Prince of Liechtenstein since the eighteenth century; it was confiscated in 1945 by Czechoslovakia. Germany raised six preliminary objections to the jurisdiction of the Court and to the admissibility of Liechtenstein's Application. The ICJ determined that there was a dispute between Liechtenstein and Germany and identified its subject-matter.
3. For an excellent article discussing the United States' legal approach to theft of art during times of war, *see* Katsenberg, *The Legal Regime for Protecting Art During Armed Conflict*, 42 A.F. L. Rev. 277 (1997).
4. On April 15, 1935, the United States and several other countries executed the Pan American Treaty on the Protection of Artistic and Scientific Institutions and Historic Monuments, 49 Stat. 3267 (1935), T.S. 899 (Roerich Pact) in Washington, D.C. This attempt to protect cultural property during armed conflict proved to be of little effect.

B. World War II: The Hague Convention Tested

World War II brought many challenges to the protection of art during a period when aerial bombing was deployed against enemies. In Adolf Hitler's desire to establish a German cultural center for the instruction and edification of the Aryan race, Hitler gathered treasures by the trainload. The Einsatzstab Rosenberg became the official department in charge of "protecting" the art of other countries. It was believed that after a German victory, these priceless items would be made available to the superior race. Not all masterpieces were to be preserved. Hitler believed that modern post-impressionistic works were "degenerate" and, as such, were to be purged from museums, galleries, and private collections. Ultimately, the Nazis hoped to trade the works for Dutch, Flemish, Germanic, and Italian old masters, which they highly prized, but the barn in which the works were stored was required for grain, and over 4,000 pieces of "degenerate" art were burned.

The German pillage of art in World War II is the most notable and documented of the many infamous examples of art destroyed by military action. Revelations at the Nuremburg trials of the extent of the plunder and destruction of art presented the modern world with its first comprehensive view of the effect of war upon the arts.

Immediately after World War II, the United States seized some 9,000 works of art that it feared might glorify Nazism. The German artists and their families protested and petitioned the United States for the return of their works. In 1978, President Carter signed legislation permitting the return of ten naval scenes.[3] In 1978, the U.S. Army held some 6,000 appropriated works.[4]

In 1982, Congress enacted Public Law 97-155, authorizing the Secretary of the Army to return to the Federal Republic of Germany certain works of art seized by the army at the end of World War II. Before any such transfer could take place, the act required the Secretary of the Army to establish a committee to examine the works of art to determine which were inappropriate for transfer and, thus, would not be returned.

Orkin v. Taylor

487 F.3d 734 (9th Cir. 2007), *cert. denied*, 28 S. Ct. 491, 169 L. Ed. 2d 340 (2007)

THOMAS, Circuit Judge.

Descendants of Jewish art collector Margarete Mauthner (collectively, "the Orkins") claim that their ancestor was wrongfully dispossessed of a painting during Hitler's Nazi regime, entitling them to ownership of the painting, which was later purchased by actress Elizabeth Taylor. In this appeal, we conclude that the Holocaust Victims Redress Act does not create a private right of action and that the Orkins' state law claims are barred by the statute of limitations. We affirm the judgment of the district court, dismissing the complaint.

I

Vincent van Gogh is said to have reflected that "paintings have a life of their own that derives from the painter's soul." The confused and perhaps turbulent history of his painting *Vue de l'Asile et de la Chapelle de Saint-Rémy* may prove the truth of his observation.

In 1889, a few months after cutting off the lower part of his left ear following a dispute with Paul Gauguin, van Gogh entered the Saint-Paul-de-Mausole asylum near the town of Saint-Rémy-de-Provence. During this period of his life, he produced over 150 paintings, including some of his most famous works, such as *The Starry Night*. In the summer or fall of 1889, he painted *Vue de l'Asile et de la Chapelle de Saint-Rémy*, which may have been

---

3. Pub. L. No. 95-517, 92 Stat. 1817 (1978).
4. The Oregonian, Oct. 27, 1978, § A, at 12, col. 6.

part of a series that he described to his brother Theo as "Sketches of Autumn." The painting portrays either the Church of Labbeville near the town Auvers, a few miles from the asylum, or a monastery that was part of the asylum. Within a year of completing the painting, van Gogh died from a self-inflicted gunshot wound.

Van Gogh sold only one painting during his lifetime. Since his death, however, his works have indeed had lives of their own. After Vincent's death in 1890, and his brother Theo's death six months later, ownership of *Vue de l'Asile et de la Chapelle de Saint-Rémy* passed to Theo's widow, Johanna. The German art dealer Paul Cassirer, an early promoter of the works of van Gogh and other post-impressionist artists, purchased the painting in 1906 or 1907. Shortly thereafter, Cassirer sold the picture to Margarete Mauthner, an early collector of van Gogh's works. The parties vigorously dispute the circumstances under which Mauthner parted with the painting, and that dispute forms the basis of the current controversy between the parties. We need not, and we do not, resolve those factual disputes in this appeal because the issues before us are purely legal in nature. However, a description of the general factual background of the case — highlighting where appropriate the factual disputes — is helpful to frame the legal issues presented.

One of the tools used by art historians to trace ownership is an artist's *catalogue raisonné*. A *catalogue raisonné* is an annotated, illustrated book of a particular artist's works, usually prepared by art historians, scholars, and dealers, which constitutes "a definitive listing and accounting of the works of an artist." *DeWeerth v. Baldinger*, 836 F.2d 103, 112 (2d Cir. 1987). A *catalogue raisonné* published in 1928, *L'oeuvre de Vincent Van Gogh Catalogue Raisonné*, shows Margarete Mauthner as the owner of the painting. J.B. de la Faille's *catalogue raisonné* of van Gogh, published in 1939, also identifies Mauthner as the owner.

From the time of Adolf Hitler's election as Chancellor of Germany in 1933 until the end of World War II, Hitler's Nazi regime engaged in a systematic effort to confiscate thousands of works of art throughout Europe. Hector Feliciano, *The Lost Museum: The Nazi Conspiracy to Steal the World's Greatest Works of Art* 3 (Basic Books 1997). Within Germany, the enactment of the Ordinance for the Attachment of the Property of the People's and State's Enemies and the Ordinance for the Employment of Jewish Property gave Nazi officials the authority to seize artwork from Jewish owners under color of law. Jonathan Petropoulos, *Art as Politics in the Third Reich* 190 (University of North Carolina Press 1996).

As the Nazis' persecution accelerated, Mauthner fled Germany to South Africa in 1939, leaving her possessions behind. She remained there until her death in 1947, at the age of 84. What happened to *Vue de l'Asile et de la Chapelle de Saint-Rémy* during that time is not clear from the record. A 1970 *catalogue raisonné* prepared by a committee of scholars in the Netherlands lists the next owner as Alfred Wolf, a Jewish businessman who left Germany for Switzerland in 1934 and ultimately relocated to South America. The auction catalogue prepared by Sotheby & Co. in 1963 lists the provenance, or chain of title, as including three owners prior to Wolf. The Sotheby's catalogue traces the ownership of the painting from Mauthner to Paul Cassirer, to Marcel Goldschmidt, and then to Alfred Wolf. The Orkins contend that this chain of ownership cannot be correct because Paul Cassirer had committed suicide in 1926, two years before the 1928 *catalogue raisonné* was published, listing Mauthner as the owner.

Notably, the Orkins do not contend that the painting was confiscated by the Nazis. Rather, they allege economic coercion, contending that Mauthner sold the painting "under duress." They note that laws promulgated by the Allied Forces after the conclusion of World War II established a presumption that any transfer or relinquishment of property by a persecuted person within the period January 30, 1933 to May 8, 1945 was an act of confiscation. Military Government Law No. 59 § 375(b).

Taylor contends that, at best, the record shows that the painting was sold through two Jewish art dealers to a Jewish art collector, with no evidence of any Nazi coercion or participation in the transactions.

In short, the parties agree that Mauthner once owned the painting and that it was later possessed by Alfred Wolf. At this point in the development of the case, the rest of what transpired with the painting during the 1930s in Berlin is clouded in uncertainty. Sometime in the early 1960s, the Estate of Alfred Wolf commissioned Sotheby's to sell by auction a number of Impressionist and Post-Impressionist paintings, including *Vue de l'Asile et de la Chapelle de Saint-Rémy*.

With the help of her father, who was an art dealer, Elizabeth Taylor began collecting art in the 1950s, acquiring works of Degas, Renoir, Pissarro, Monet, Cassatt, and other prominent artists. She had long wanted to acquire a van Gogh. While living in London with her husband, Richard Burton, Taylor learned that *Vue de l'Asile et de la Chapelle de Saint-Rémy* would be offered at a Sotheby's auction in April 1963. She authorized her father to bid for her at the auction, and he was successful in purchasing the painting on her behalf for £92,000.

Taylor's acquisition was publicized at the time. Subsequently, the 1970 *catalogue raisonné* referenced Taylor's ownership. From November 1986 until March 1987, the painting was exhibited publicly at the Metropolitan Museum of Art in New York, in an exhibition entitled "Van Gogh in Saint Rémy and Auvers".

In 1990, Taylor offered the painting for sale through Christie's auction house in London. The provenance for the sale lists Taylor as the current owner, with the prior owners being Alfred Wolf (of Stuttgart and Buenos Aires), Marcel Goldschmidt & Co. (of Frankfurt), Margarete Mauthner (of Berlin), Paul Cassirer (of Berlin), and Johanna van Gogh-Bonger (of Amsterdam). The work did not sell at the auction.

In 1998, Congress enacted three statutes pertaining to victims of Nazi persecution: the Holocaust Victims Redress Act ("Act"), Pub. L. No. 105-158, 112 Stat. 15 (1998), the Nazi War Crimes Disclosure Act of 1998, Pub. L. No. 105-167, 114 Stat. 2865 (1998), and the United States Holocaust Assets

Commission Act of 1998, Pub. L. No. 105-186, 112 Stat. 611 (1998). The Orkins allege that their inquiry into whether their ancestor, Mauthner, may have lost her art collection due to Nazi persecution began upon the passage of these acts. They retained a law firm in 2001 and claim that, until their attorneys completed their investigation, they did not discover the basis of their current claim. The Orkins allege that, before they began that investigation, they did not know that Mauthner had owned *Vue de l'Asile et de la Chapelle de Saint-Rémy*, that she had lost the painting as a result of Nazi persecution, that Taylor had bought the painting, or that there was a legal basis for recovering the painting. They also claim that they first learned of Taylor's ownership in 2002, through a rumor on the internet that Taylor was interested in selling the painting.

In December 2003, the Orkins wrote a letter to Taylor, demanding that she return the painting to them. After some discussion of settlement, Taylor wrote a response letter declining settlement and asserting that the Orkins' claim to the painting was untimely. Taylor then filed a complaint for declaratory relief to establish her title.

In 2005, the Orkins filed their First Amended Complaint for recovery of the painting under theories of specific recovery, replevin, constructive trust, restitution, and conversion. The district court dismissed the complaint, concluding that the state-law actions were time-barred and that the federal statute did not create a private right of action. Because there is complete diversity between the parties and because the painting is worth more than $75,000, the district court had jurisdiction under 28 U.S.C. § 1332. We have jurisdiction under 28 U.S.C. § 1291, and we review de novo the district court's dismissal of the complaint pursuant to Rule 12(b)(6). *Cervantes v. United States*, 330 F.3d 1186, 1187 (9th Cir. 2003).

Because the district court dismissed this case on a Rule 12(b)(6) motion, we must assume that all facts stated in the complaint are true and that they are provable by admissible evidence. Although the parties vigorously dispute whether the painting was effectively confiscated by the Nazis through forced sale or was legitimately sold through Jewish art dealers, we need not resolve that issue. We assume, for the purposes of our discussion, that the allegations of the complaint are true and that Mauthner was coerced into giving up the painting before she left Germany.

II

The district court properly dismissed the Orkins' federal claims on the ground that the Holocaust Victims Redress Act did not create a private right of action against private art owners. In determining whether a federal statute creates a private right of action, congressional intent is the cornerstone of the analysis. The Supreme Court has established a four-factor test for discerning whether a statute creates a private right of action. *Cort v. Ash*, 422 U.S. 66, 95 S. Ct. 2080, 45 L. Ed. 2d 26 (1975). Under that test, we must ask: (1) whether the plaintiff is a member of a class that the statute especially intended to benefit, (2) whether the legislature explicitly or implicitly intended to create a private cause of action, (3) whether the general purpose of the statutory scheme would be served by creation of a private right of action, and (4) whether the cause of action is traditionally relegated to state law such that implication of a federal remedy would be inappropriate. 422 U.S. at 78, 95 S. Ct. 2080.

The most important inquiry under *Cort* is the second factor: whether there is "any indication of legislative intent, explicit or implicit, either to create such a remedy or to deny one." *Opera Plaza Residential Parcel Homeowners Assn. v. Hoang,* 376 F.3d 831, 834-35 (9th Cir. 2004) (quoting *Cort,* 422 U.S. at 78, 95 S. Ct. 2080); *First Pacific Bancorp, Inc. v. Helfer,* 224 F.3d 1117, 1121-22 (9th Cir. 2000) (same). Indeed, the three *Cort* questions that are not explicitly focused on legislative intent are actually indicia of legislative intent, such that the *Cort* test itself is focused entirely on intent. *Touche Ross & Co. v. Redington,* 442 U.S. 560, 575-76, 99 S. Ct. 2479, 61 L. Ed. 2d 82 (1979). The four *Cort* factors, thus, are merely targeted inquiries to guide our central project of discerning Congress's intent. *Id.*

The plain text of the Holocaust Victims Redress Act leaves little doubt that Congress did not intend to create a private right of action. The Orkins rely on § 202 of the Act, entitled "Sense of the Congress Regarding Restitution of Private Property, Such as Works of Art." That section reads in its entirety as follows:

> It is the sense of the Congress that consistent with the 1907 Hague Convention, all governments should undertake good faith efforts to facilitate the return of private and public property, such as works of art, to the rightful owners in cases where assets were confiscated from the claimant during the period of Nazi rule and there is reasonable proof that the claimant is the rightful owner.

Act § 202, 112 Stat. at 17-18.

"Sense of the Congress" provisions are precatory provisions, which do not in themselves create individual rights or, for that matter, any enforceable law. *Yang v. Cal. Dept. of Soc. Servs.,* 183 F.3d 953, 958-59 (9th Cir. 1999). Although "sense of the Congress" provisions are sometimes relevant to our determination of whether other mandatory provisions create private rights of action, *id.* at 959 & n.4, the Orkins can point to no provision of the Act or of any of its companion legislation that can fairly be characterized as mandatory. There is simply no "right- or duty-creating language" anywhere in the statutory scheme, *Cannon v. Univ. of Chicago,* 441 U.S. 677, 690 n.13, 99 S. Ct. 1946, 60 L. Ed. 2d 560 (1979), and § 202's announcement of a "sense of the Congress" cannot, of its own force, imply a private right of action, *Yang,* 183 F.3d at 958-59.

Additionally, the Act's legislative history indicates that even its most ardent supporter did not intend for the bill to create a private right of action. Rather, the legislative intent was to encourage state and foreign governments to enforce existing rights for the protection of Holocaust victims. The sponsor and primary champion of the legislation, Representative Jim Leach (R-IA), believed that existing law would suffice to restitute Nazi-stolen artworks to their Nazi-era owners. At a hearing that occurred after passage of the Act, Representative Leach noted the possibility that new "domestic legislation" might assist in restitution of stolen art, but he went on to conclude that "Congress may have gone as far as it appropriately should on this subject in the Holocaust Victims Redress Act." Holocaust Victims' Claims, Hearing before the House Committee on Banking and Financial Services, 105th Cong., 2d Sess. (1998). That statement strongly implies, consistently with the precatory language of the legislation itself, that the Act was a limited bill, passed with an understanding of constitutional limitations on congressional power. The second *Cort* factor, thus, does not support the Orkins' claim; the bill simply did not intend to create a private right of action.

Examination of the remaining *Cort* factors buttresses this conclusion. With respect to the first *Cort* factor, although there is no doubt that the Act was focused on Holocaust victims and (in a colloquial sense) intended to benefit them, Holocaust victims do not constitute a "beneficiary class" within the meaning of the *Cort* test. The provision's focus is on "governments" rather than individuals, urging those governments "to facilitate" enforcement of preexisting property rights. Act § 202, 112 Stat. at 17-18. The statute, thus, does not "explicitly confer[] a benefit on" Holocaust victims; it merely expresses Congress's sense that Holocaust survivors and heirs should benefit fully from preexisting protections. *Cf. Cannon*, 441 U.S. at 693-94, 99 S. Ct. 1946 (concluding that the first *Cort* factor was met because the statute at issue "explicitly confers a benefit on" an identifiable class and because the plaintiff was a member of that class). The Orkins, thus, are not members of a class that Congress "intended to benefit," as that phrase is used in *Cort*.

With respect to the third *Cort* factor, the text and history of the legislation reveal that its overarching purpose was not to provide for private litigation. Rather, the general purpose of the statutory scheme was to fund research efforts and to declassify records, while simultaneously encouraging foreign governments, as well as public and private institutions, to do likewise. In other words, the motivating concern was not access to courts; it was access to information. In fact, throughout the committee hearings, witnesses testified that courts would likely do a poor job of resolving Holocaust victims' claims. Specifically, the committee heard testimony that the difficulties of tracing information would likely preclude effective judicial resolution of discrete claims, and several museum directors testified that alternative fora such as mediation and arbitration were preferable to litigation. Holocaust Victims' Claims, Hearing before the House Committee on Banking and Financial Services, 105th Cong., 2d Sess. (1998) (testimony of Philippe de Montebello, director of the Metropolitan Museum of Art). The general purposes of the statute, therefore, do not support the conclusion that Congress intended to provide a private right of action in this case.

Finally, with respect to the fourth *Cort* factor, there can be no doubt — as this case amply demonstrates — that state law provides causes of action for restitution of stolen artworks. Furthermore, the torts asserted here are undoubtedly causes of action that are traditionally relegated to state law. Implication of a federal remedy in this case, therefore, would be inappropriate under the fourth *Cort* factor. Representative Leach's statement that "Congress may have gone as far as it appropriately should" when it passed the Act strongly supports the conclusion that Congress did not intend to supersede traditional state-law remedies when it passed the Act. Holocaust Victims' Claims, Hearing before the House Committee on Banking and Financial Services, 105th Cong., 2d Sess. (1998).

In short, the Act does not satisfy any of the *Cort* factors; none of the relevant indicia of intent supports the conclusion that Congress intended to create an implied private right of action in this case. The Act is a precatory announcement of the "sense of the Congress," which neither confers rights nor creates duties. Given the absence of congressional intent to create a private right of action, the Orkins' assertion of a federal right of action must fail.

III

The district court also properly concluded that the Orkins' state-law claims were time-barred. California provides a three-year statute of limitations for any action arising from the "taking, detaining, or injuring" of any "goods or chattels." Cal. Civ. Proc. Code § 338(c). In 1983, the statute of limitations was amended to specify that a "discovery rule" governs accrual of causes of action for recovery of "any article of historical, interpretive, scientific, or artistic significance." *Id.* In other words, under the new law, an action for recovery of artwork accrues when the rightful owner discovers the whereabouts of the artwork. Before 1983, the statute did not specify when a cause of action for theft would accrue.

The Orkins do not argue that the 1983 amendment applies retroactively to their allegations of a 1939 theft and a 1963 conversion. Rather, they contend that the discovery rule applies even under pre-1983 law, citing an intermediate appeals court decision that so held. *Naftzger v. Am. Numismatic Soc'y*, 42 Cal. App. 4th 421, 49 Cal. Rptr. 2d 784 (1996).

> "The task of a federal court in a diversity action is to approximate state law as closely as possible in order to make sure that the vindication of the state right is without discrimination because of the federal forum." *Ticknor v. Choice Hotels Intern., Inc.*, 265 F.3d 931, 939 (9th Cir. 2001) (quoting *Gee v. Tenneco, Inc.*, 615 F.2d 857, 861 (9th Cir. 1980)). If the state's highest appellate court has not decided the question presented, then we must predict how the state's highest court would decide the question. *Id.* In doing so, we take state law as it exists without speculating as to future changes in the law. *Id.*

The California Supreme Court has never confronted the question of what rule governs accrual of pre-1983 causes of action for theft and conversion. The California Supreme Court has, however, specifically held that the discovery rule, whenever it applies, incorporates the principle of constructive notice. In *Jolly v. Eli Lilly & Co.*, the California Supreme Court held that, under

California's discovery rule, "[a] plaintiff is held to her actual knowledge as well as knowledge that could reasonably be discovered through investigation of sources open to her." 44 Cal. 3d 1103, 1109, 245 Cal. Rptr. 658, 751 P.2d 923 (1988). In other words, under the discovery rule, a cause of action accrues when the plaintiff discovered or reasonably could have discovered her claim to and the whereabouts of her property. In assessing California law, we conclude that it is highly unlikely that the California Supreme Court would abandon the *Jolly* rule, much less adopt a new rule that eschewed the concept of constructive notice.

Under *Jolly*, the latest possible accrual date of the Orkins' cause of action was the date on which they first reasonably could have discovered, through investigation of sources open to them, their claim to and the whereabouts of the van Gogh painting. From the face of the Orkins' complaint, it is apparent that Taylor's acquisition of the painting was certainly discoverable at least by 1990, when she held it out for sale in an international auction, and most probably as early as 1963, when she acquired the painting in a highly publicized international auction. In fact, the complaint alleges — and demonstrates by attachment — that Taylor bought the painting at a publicized auction in 1963, that Taylor was listed as the owner of the painting in a publicly available 1970 *catalogue raisonné*, and that Taylor publicly offered the painting for sale in 1990. Had the Orkins investigated any of those publicly-available sources, they could have discovered both their claim to the painting and the painting's whereabouts long before the 2002 internet rumor was posted.

We therefore affirm the district court's conclusion that the Orkins' state-law claims are time-barred. Even under the most generous possible rule for accrual of the causes of action, the claims expired in or before 1993 — three years after the last public announcement of Taylor's ownership. The district court correctly held that the Orkins' state law claims were untimely filed.

IV

Congress did not create a private right of action in passing the Holocaust Victims Redress Act, which merely reflected the sense of Congress. The Orkins' state law claims are time-barred. The district court was entirely correct in dismissing the complaint. We need not, and do not, reach any of the other issues urged by the parties. AFFIRMED.

Notes and Questions

1. In *Menzel v. List*, 49 Misc. 2d 300, 267 N.Y.S.2d 804 (1966), the jury declared the Menzels to be the sole and rightful owners of a Marc Chagall painting that the Nazis treated as "decadent Jewish art." The trial court denied a motion to set aside the verdict, finding that Mrs. Menzel never abandoned the painting, but that it was pillaged and plundered by the Nazis. When the Menzels, Belgian nationals, were

forced to flee the Nazi invasion of their country, they were forced to leave their art collection. The court determined that no title could have been conveyed by them as against the rightful owners. After Mr. List returned the painting to Mrs. Menzel, the lower court reduced the damages due him from the gallery from $22,500 to $4,000, List's original purchase price. 28 A.D.2d 516, 279 N.Y.S.2d 608 (1967). Dissatisfied with this outcome, List appealed. The New York Court of Appeals reinstated the original award over the gallery's objections.

2. In *DeWeerth v. Baldinger*, 836 F.2d 103 (2d Cir. 1987), Monet's *Champs de Ble à Vetheuil* disappeared from Germany at the end of World War II. Gerda DeWeerth, a German citizen, searched for the painting that had been in her family since 1908 following the war but ended her search in 1957. Unbeknownst to her, the painting was sold by a New York art gallery to Edith Baldinger in 1957. Baldinger kept the painting in her apartment, except for when it was displayed in public exhibitions in 1957 and 1970. DeWeerth learned of Baldinger's possession in 1981 and brought an action to recover it in 1983. The District Court adjudged DeWeerth had superior title, but the Court of Appeals reversed, holding that DeWeerth failed to exercise reasonable diligence when she did not search for her property between 1957 and 1981. Baldinger, as a good faith purchaser, thus had superior title to the Monet.

3. In *Toledo Museum of Art v. Ullin*, 477 F. Supp. 2d 802 (N.D. Ohio 2006), a museum brought a declaratory judgment action against a prior owner's heirs to quiet title to Paul Gauguin's *Street Scene in Tahiti*, which was sold during the Nazi era. The heirs of Martha Nathan, a Jewish woman born in Germany who sold the painting in 1938 to a group of European art dealers, who in turn sold the painting in 1939 to the Toledo Museum, filed a counterclaim alleging conversion and restitution. In ruling for the museum, the District Court held that the statute of limitations barred restitution and conversion claims, and that the museum did not waive the statute of limitations.

4. In many countries, appeals from seizures by foreign governments are limited or nonexistent. In the United States, confiscation due to violation of the Trading with the Enemy Act, 50 U.S.C. §§ 1 et seq. (Supp. 1990), is appealable only where a petitioner demonstrates that he or she is not an enemy or an ally of the enemy, and that the property was seized strictly because of the characterization of its owner as an enemy.

5. What happens if museums want to bring art work of questionable patronage into the United States for exhibition? Does the current owner run the risk of seizure from a former owner? The President may grant works of art immunity from seizure where they are brought into the United States for cultural exhibition. 22 U.S.C. § 2459 (1981).

6. The feature film *The Woman in Gold* (2015) recreates many of the facts in the case *Republic of Austria v. Altmann*, 541 U.S. 677 (2004), excerpted below.

Republic of Austria v. Altmann

541 U.S. 677 (2004)*

Justice Stevens delivered the opinion of the Court.

In 1998 an Austrian journalist, granted access to the Austrian Gallery's archives, discovered evidence that certain valuable works in the Gallery's collection had not been donated by their rightful owners but had been seized by the Nazis or expropriated by the Austrian Republic after World War II. The journalist provided some of that evidence to respondent, who in turn filed this action to recover possession of six Gustav Klimt paintings. Prior to the Nazi invasion of Austria, the paintings had hung in the palatial Vienna home of respondent's uncle, Ferdinand Bloch-Bauer, a Czechoslovakian Jew and patron of the arts. Respondent claims ownership of the paintings under a will executed by her uncle after he fled Austria in 1938. She alleges that the Gallery obtained possession of the paintings through wrongful conduct in the years during and after World War II.

The defendants (petitioners here) — the Republic of Austria and the Austrian Gallery (Gallery), an instrumentality of the Republic — filed a motion to dismiss the complaint asserting, among other defenses, a claim of sovereign immunity. The District Court denied the motion, 142 F. Supp. 2d 1187 (C.D. Cal. 2001), and the Court of Appeals affirmed, 317 F.3d 954 (C.A. 9 2002), as amended, 327 F.3d 1246 (2003). We granted certiorari limited to the question whether the Foreign Sovereign Immunities Act of 1976 (FSIA or Act), 28 U.S.C. § 1602 et seq., which grants foreign states immunity from the jurisdiction of federal and state courts but expressly exempts certain cases, including "case[s] . . . in which rights in property taken in violation of international law are in issue," § 1605(a)(3), applies to claims that, like respondent's, are based on conduct that occurred before the Act's enactment, and even before the United States adopted the so-called "restrictive theory" of sovereign immunity in 1952. 539 U.S. 987, 124 S. Ct. 46, 156 L. Ed. 2d 703 (2003).

Because this case comes to us from the denial of a motion to dismiss on the pleadings, we assume the truth of the following facts alleged in respondent's complaint.

Born in Austria in 1916, respondent Maria V. Altmann escaped the country after it was annexed by Nazi Germany in 1938. She settled in California in 1942 and became an American citizen in 1945. She is a niece, and the sole surviving named heir, of Ferdinand Bloch-Bauer, who died in Zurich, Switzerland, on November 13, 1945.

Prior to 1938 Ferdinand, then a wealthy sugar magnate, maintained his principal residence in Vienna, Austria, where the six Klimt paintings and other valuable works of art were housed. His wife, Adele, was the subject of two of the paintings. She died in 1925, leaving a will in which she "ask[ed]" her husband

---

* All citations to the record and most footnotes deleted.

"after his death" to bequeath the paintings to the Gallery.[5] The attorney for her estate advised the Gallery that Ferdinand intended to comply with his wife's request, but that he was not legally obligated to do so because he, not Adele, owned the paintings. Ferdinand never executed any document transferring ownership of any of the paintings at issue to the Gallery. He remained their sole legitimate owner until his death. His will bequeathed his entire estate to respondent, another niece, and a nephew.

On March 12, 1938, in what became known as the "Anschluss," the Nazis invaded and claimed to annex Austria. Ferdinand, who was Jewish and had supported efforts to resist annexation, fled the country ahead of the Nazis, ultimately settling in Zurich. In his absence, according to the complaint, the Nazis "Aryanized" the sugar company he had directed, took over his Vienna home, and divided up his artworks, which included the Klimts at issue here, many other valuable paintings, and a 400-piece porcelain collection. A Nazi lawyer, Dr. Erich Führer, took possession of the six Klimts. He sold two to the Gallery in 1941 and a third in 1943, kept one for himself, and sold another to the Museum of the City of Vienna. The immediate fate of the sixth is not known. 142 F. Supp. 2d, at 1193.

In 1946 Austria enacted a law declaring all transactions motivated by Nazi ideology null and void. This did not result in the immediate return of looted artwork to exiled Austrians, however, because a different provision of Austrian law proscribed export of "artworks . . . deemed to be important to [the country's] cultural heritage" and required anyone wishing to export art to obtain the permission of the Austrian Federal Monument Agency. Seeking to profit from this requirement, the Gallery and the Federal Monument Agency allegedly adopted a practice of "forc[ing] Jews to donate or trade valuable artworks to the [Gallery] in exchange for export permits for other works."

The next year Robert Bentley, respondent's brother and fellow heir, retained a Viennese lawyer, Dr. Gustav Rinesch, to locate and recover property stolen from Ferdinand during the war. In January 1948 Dr. Rinesch wrote to the Gallery requesting return of the three Klimts purchased from Dr. Führer. A Gallery representative responded, asserting — falsely, according to the complaint — that Adele had bequeathed the paintings to the Gallery, and the Gallery had merely permitted Ferdinand to retain them during his lifetime.

Later the same year Dr. Rinesch enlisted the support of Gallery officials to obtain export permits for many of Ferdinand's remaining works of art. In exchange, Dr. Rinesch, purporting to represent respondent and her fellow heirs, signed a document "acknowledg[ing] and accept[ing] Ferdinand's declaration that in the event of his death he wished to follow the wishes of his deceased wife to donate" the Klimt paintings to the Gallery. In addition,

---

5. Adele's will mentions six Klimt paintings, *Adele Bloch-Bauer I, Adele Bloch-Bauer II, Apple Tree I, Beechwood, Houses in Unterach am Attersee,* and *Schloss Kammer am Attersee III.* The last of these, Schloss Kammer am Attersee III, is not at issue in this case because Ferdinand donated it to the Gallery in 1936. The sixth painting in this case, Amalie Zuckerkandl, is not mentioned in Adele's will. For further details, see 142 F. Supp. 2d 1187, 1192-1193 (C.D. Cal. 2001).

Dr. Rinesch assisted the Gallery in obtaining both the painting Dr. Führer had kept for himself and the one he had sold to the Museum of the City of Vienna. At no time during these transactions, however, did Dr. Rinesch have respondent's permission either "to negotiate on her behalf or to allow the [Gallery] to obtain the Klimt paintings."

In 1998 a journalist examining the Gallery's files discovered documents revealing that at all relevant times Gallery officials knew that neither Adele nor Ferdinand had, in fact, donated the six Klimts to the Gallery. The journalist published a series of articles reporting his findings, and specifically noting that Klimt's first portrait of Adele, "which all the [Gallery] publications represented as having been donated to the museum in 1936," had actually been received in 1941, accompanied by a letter from Dr. Führer signed "'Heil Hitler.'"

In response to these revelations, Austria enacted a new restitution law under which individuals who had been coerced into donating artworks to state museums in exchange for export permits could reclaim their property. Respondent — who had believed, prior to the journalist's investigation, that Adele and Ferdinand had "freely donated" the Klimt paintings to the Gallery before the war — immediately sought recovery of the paintings and other artworks under the new law. A committee of Austrian Government officials and art historians agreed to return certain Klimt drawings and porcelain settings that the family had donated in 1948. After what the complaint terms a "sham" proceeding, however, the committee declined to return the six paintings, concluding, based on an allegedly purposeful misreading of Adele's will, that her precatory request had created a binding legal obligation that required her husband to donate the paintings to the Gallery on his death.

Respondent then announced that she would file a lawsuit in Austria to recover the paintings. Because Austrian court costs are proportional to the value of the recovery sought (and in this case would total several million dollars, an amount far beyond respondent's means), she requested a waiver. The court granted this request in part but still would have required respondent to pay approximately $350,000 to proceed. When the Austrian Government appealed even this partial waiver, respondent voluntarily dismissed her suit and filed this action in the United States District Court for the Central District of California.

II

Respondent's complaint advances eight causes of action and alleges violations of Austrian, international, and California law. It asserts jurisdiction under § 2 of the FSIA, which grants federal district courts jurisdiction over civil actions against foreign states "as to any claim for relief *in personam* with respect to which the foreign state is not entitled to immunity" under either another provision of the FSIA or "any applicable international agreement." 28 U.S.C. § 1330(a). The complaint further asserts that petitioners are not entitled to immunity under the FSIA because the Act's "expropriation exception," § 1605(a)(3), expressly exempts from immunity all cases involving "rights in property taken in violation of international law," provided the property has a commercial connection to the United States or the agency or instrumentality that owns the property is engaged in commercial activity here.

Petitioners filed a motion to dismiss raising several defenses including a claim of sovereign immunity. Their immunity argument proceeded in two steps. First, they claimed that as of 1948, when much of their alleged wrongdoing took place, they would have enjoyed absolute immunity from suit in United States courts. Proceeding from this premise, petitioners next contended that nothing in the FSIA should be understood to divest them of that immunity retroactively.

The District Court rejected this argument, concluding both that the FSIA applies retroactively to pre-1976 actions and that the Act's expropriation exception extends to respondent's specific claims. Only the former conclusion concerns us here. Presuming that our decision in *Landgraf v. USI Film Products*, 511 U.S. 244, 114 S. Ct. 1483 (1994), governed its retroactivity analysis, the court "first consider[ed] whether Congress expressly stated the [FSIA's] reach." 142 F. Supp. 2d, at 1199. Finding no such statement, the court then asked whether application of the Act to petitioners' 1948 actions "would impair rights [petitioners] possessed when [they] acted, impose new duties on [them], or increase [their] liability for past conduct." *Ibid.* Because it deemed the FSIA "a jurisdictional statute that does not alter substantive legal rights," the court answered this second question in the negative and accordingly found the Act controlling. *Id.*, at 1201. As further support for this finding, the court noted that the FSIA itself provides that "'[c]laims of foreign states to immunity should henceforth be decided by courts of the United States . . . in conformity with the principles set forth in this chapter.'" *Ibid.* (quoting 28 U.S.C. § 1602) (emphasis in District Court opinion). In the court's view, this language suggests the Act "is to be applied to all cases decided after its enactment regardless of when the plaintiff's cause of action may have accrued." 142 F. Supp. 2d, at 1201.

The Court of Appeals agreed that the FSIA applies to this case. Rather than endorsing the District Court's reliance on the Act's jurisdictional nature, however, the panel reasoned that applying the FSIA to Austria's alleged wrongdoing was not impermissibly retroactive because Austria could not legitimately have expected to receive immunity for that wrongdoing even in 1948 when it occurred. The court rested that conclusion on an analysis of American courts' then-prevalent practice of deferring to case-by-case immunity determinations by the State Department, and on that Department's expressed policy, as of 1949, of "'reliev[ing] American courts from any restraint upon the exercise of their jurisdiction to pass upon the validity of the acts of Nazi officials.'" 317 F.3d, at 965 (quoting Press Release No. 296, Jurisdiction of United States Courts Re Suits for Identifiable Property Involved in Nazi Forced Transfers (emphasis deleted)).

We granted certiorari, 539 U.S. 987, 124 S. Ct. 46 (2003), and now affirm the judgment of the Court of Appeals, though on different reasoning.

III

Chief Justice Marshall's opinion in *Schooner Exchange v. McFaddon*, 7 Cranch 116, 3 L. Ed. 287 (1812), is generally viewed as the source of our foreign sovereign immunity jurisprudence. In that case, the libellants claimed to be the rightful owners of a French ship that had taken refuge in the port of Philadelphia. The Court first emphasized that the jurisdiction of the United States over persons and property within its territory "is susceptible of no limitation not imposed by itself," and thus foreign sovereigns have no right to immunity in our courts. *Id.*, at 136. Chief Justice Marshall went on to explain, however, that as a matter of comity, members of the international community had implicitly agreed to waive the exercise of jurisdiction over other sovereigns in certain classes of cases, such as those involving foreign ministers or the person of the sovereign. Accepting a suggestion advanced by the Executive Branch, see *id.*, at 134, the Chief Justice concluded that the implied waiver theory also served to exempt the Schooner Exchange — "a national armed vessel . . . of the emperor of France" — from United States courts' jurisdiction. *Id.*, at 145-146.

In accordance with Chief Justice Marshall's observation that foreign sovereign immunity is a matter of grace and comity rather than a constitutional requirement, this Court has "consistently . . . deferred to the decisions of the political branches — in particular, those of the Executive Branch — on whether to take jurisdiction" over particular actions against foreign sovereigns and their instrumentalities. *Verlinden B.V. v. Central Bank of Nigeria*, 461 U.S. 480, 486, 103 S. Ct. 1962, 76 L. Ed. 2d 81 (1983). . . . Until 1952 the Executive Branch followed a policy of requesting immunity in all actions against friendly sovereigns. 461 U.S., at 486, 103 S. Ct. 1962. In that year, however, the State Department concluded that "immunity should no longer be granted in certain types of cases." In a letter to the Acting Attorney General, the Acting Legal Adviser for the Secretary of State, Jack B. Tate, explained that the Department would thereafter apply the "restrictive theory" of sovereign immunity:

> "A study of the law of sovereign immunity reveals the existence of two conflicting concepts of sovereign immunity, each widely held and firmly established. According to the classical or absolute theory of sovereign immunity, a sovereign cannot, without his consent, be made a respondent in the courts of another sovereign. According to the newer or restrictive theory of sovereign immunity, the immunity of the sovereign is recognized with regard to sovereign or public acts (*jure imperii*) of a state, but not with respect to private acts (*jure gestionis*). . . . [I]t will hereafter be the Department's policy to follow the restrictive theory . . . in the consideration of requests of foreign governments for a grant of sovereign immunity." *Id.*, at 1a, 4a-5a.

As we explained in our unanimous opinion in *Verlinden*, the change in State Department policy wrought by the "Tate Letter" had little, if any, impact on federal courts' approach to immunity analyses: "As in the past, initial responsibility for deciding questions of sovereign immunity fell primarily upon the

Executive acting through the State Department," and courts continued to "abid[e] by" that Department's "'suggestions of immunity.'" 461 U.S., at 487, 103 S. Ct. 1962. The change did, however, throw immunity determinations into some disarray, as "foreign nations often placed diplomatic pressure on the State Department," and political considerations sometimes led the Department to file "suggestions of immunity in cases where immunity would not have been available under the restrictive theory." *Id.*, at 487-488, 103 S. Ct. 1962. Complicating matters further, when foreign nations failed to request immunity from the State Department:

> "[T]he responsibility fell to the courts to determine whether sovereign immunity existed, generally by reference to prior State Department decisions. . . . Thus, sovereign immunity determinations were made in two different branches, subject to a variety of factors, sometimes including diplomatic considerations. Not surprisingly, the governing standards were neither clear nor uniformly applied." *Ibid.*

In 1976 Congress sought to remedy these problems by enacting the FSIA, a comprehensive statute containing a "set of legal standards governing claims of immunity in every civil action against a foreign state or its political subdivisions, agencies, or instrumentalities." *Id.*, at 488, 103 S. Ct. 1962. The Act "codifies, as a matter of federal law, the restrictive theory of sovereign immunity," *ibid.*, and transfers primary responsibility for immunity determinations from the Executive to the Judicial Branch. The preamble states that "henceforth" both federal and state courts should decide claims of sovereign immunity in conformity with the Act's principles. 28 U.S.C. § 1602.

The Act itself grants federal courts jurisdiction over civil actions against foreign states, § 1330(a), and over diversity actions in which a foreign state is the plaintiff, § 1332(a)(4); it contains venue and removal provisions, §§ 1391(f), 1441(d); it prescribes the procedures for obtaining personal jurisdiction over a foreign state, § 1330(b); and it governs the extent to which a state's property may be subject to attachment or execution, §§ 1609-1611. Finally, the Act carves out certain exceptions to its general grant of immunity, including the expropriation exception on which respondent's complaint relies. *See supra*, at 2245-2246, and n.5. These exceptions are central to the Act's functioning: "At the threshold of every action in a district court against a foreign state, . . . the court must satisfy itself that one of the exceptions applies," as "subject-matter jurisdiction in any such action depends" on that application. *Verlinden*, 461 U.S., at 493-494, 103 S. Ct. 1962. . . .

V

This leaves only the question whether anything in the FSIA or the circumstances surrounding its enactment suggests that we should not apply it to petitioners' 1948 actions. Not only do we answer this question in the negative, but we find clear evidence that Congress intended the Act to apply to pre-enactment conduct.

To begin with, the preamble of the FSIA expresses Congress' understanding that the Act would apply to all postenactment claims of sovereign immunity. That section provides:

> Claims of foreign states to immunity should henceforth be decided by courts of the United States and of the States in conformity with the principles set forth in this chapter. 28 U.S.C. § 1602 (emphasis added).

Though perhaps not sufficient to satisfy *Landgraf*'s "express command" requirement, 511 U.S., at 280, 114 S. Ct. 1483, this language is unambiguous: Immunity "claims" — not actions protected by immunity, but assertions of immunity to suits arising from those actions — are the relevant conduct regulated by the Act; those claims are "henceforth" to be decided by the courts. As the District Court observed, *see supra*, at 2247 (citing 142 F. Supp. 2d, at 1201), this language suggests Congress intended courts to resolve all such claims "in conformity with the principles set forth" in the Act, regardless of when the underlying conduct occurred.

The FSIA's overall structure strongly supports this conclusion. Many of the Act's provisions unquestionably apply to cases arising out of conduct that occurred before 1976. In *Dole Food Co. v. Patrickson*, 538 U.S. 468, 123 S. Ct. 1655, 155 L. Ed. 2d 643 (2003), for example, we held that whether an entity qualifies as an "instrumentality" of a "foreign state" for purposes of the FSIA's grant of immunity depends on the relationship between the entity and the state at the time suit is brought rather than when the conduct occurred. In addition, *Verlinden*, which upheld against constitutional challenge 28 U.S.C. § 1330's grant of subject-matter jurisdiction, involved a dispute over a contract that predated the Act. 461 U.S., at 482-483, 497, 103 S. Ct. 1962. And there has never been any doubt that the Act's procedural provisions relating to venue, removal, execution, and attachment apply to all pending cases. Thus, the FSIA's preamble indicates that it applies "henceforth," and its body includes numerous provisions that unquestionably apply to claims based on pre-1976 conduct. In this context, it would be anomalous to presume that an isolated provision (such as the expropriation exception on which respondent relies) is of purely prospective application absent any statutory language to that effect.

Finally, applying the FSIA to all pending cases regardless of when the underlying conduct occurred is most consistent with two of the Act's principal purposes: clarifying the rules that judges should apply in resolving sovereign immunity claims and eliminating political participation in the resolution of such claims. We have recognized that, to accomplish these purposes, Congress established a comprehensive framework for resolving any claim of sovereign immunity:

> We think that the text and structure of the FSIA demonstrate Congress' intention that the FSIA be the sole basis for obtaining jurisdiction over a foreign state in our courts. Sections 1604 and 1330(a) work in tandem: § 1604 bars federal and state courts from exercising jurisdiction when a

foreign state is entitled to immunity, and § 1330(a) confers jurisdiction on district courts to hear suits brought by United States citizens and by aliens when a foreign state is not entitled to immunity. As we said in *Verlinden*, the FSIA must be applied by the district courts in every action against a foreign sovereign, since subject-matter jurisdiction in any such action depends on the existence of one of the specified exceptions to foreign sovereign immunity. *Argentine Republic v. Amerada Hess Shipping Corp.*, 488 U.S. 428, 434-435, 109 S. Ct. 683, 102 L. Ed. 2d 818 (1989) (quoting *Verlinden*, 461 U.S., at 493, 103 S. Ct. 1962).

The *Amerada Hess* respondents' claims concerned conduct that postdated the FSIA, so we had no occasion to consider the Act's retroactivity. Nevertheless, our observations about the FSIA's inclusiveness are relevant in this case: quite obviously, Congress' purposes in enacting such a comprehensive jurisdictional scheme would be frustrated if, in postenactment cases concerning preenactment conduct, courts were to continue to follow the same ambiguous and politically charged "'standards'" that the FSIA replaced. *See supra*, at 2249 (quoting *Verlinden*, 461 U.S., at 487-488, 103 S. Ct. 1962).

We do not endorse the reasoning of the Court of Appeals. Indeed, we think it engaged in precisely the kind of detailed historical inquiry that the FSIA's clear guidelines were intended to obviate. Nevertheless, we affirm the panel's judgment because the Act, freed from *Landgraf*'s antiretroactivity presumption, clearly applies to conduct, like petitioners' alleged wrongdoing, that occurred prior to 1976 and, for that matter, prior to 1952 when the State Department adopted the restrictive theory of sovereign immunity.

VI

We conclude by emphasizing the narrowness of this holding. To begin with, although the District Court and Court of Appeals determined that § 1605(a)(3) covers this case, we declined to review that determination. . . . Nor do we have occasion to comment on the application of the so-called "act of state" doctrine to petitioners' alleged wrongdoing. Unlike a claim of sovereign immunity, which merely raises a jurisdictional defense, the act of state doctrine provides foreign states with a substantive defense on the merits. Under that doctrine, the courts of one state will not question the validity of public acts (acts jure imperii) performed by other sovereigns within their own borders, even when such courts have jurisdiction over a controversy in which one of the litigants has standing to challenge those acts. . . . Petitioners principally rely on the act of state doctrine to support their assertion that foreign expropriations are public acts for which, prior to the enactment of the FSIA, sovereigns expected immunity. Applying the FSIA in this case would upset that settled expectation, petitioners argue, and thus the Act "would operate retroactively" under *Landgraf*. 511 U.S., at 280, 114 S. Ct. 1483. But because the FSIA in no way affects application of the act of state doctrine, our determination that the Act applies in this case in no way affects any argument petitioners may have that the doctrine shields their alleged wrongdoing.

Finally, while we reject the United States' recommendation to bar application of the FSIA to claims based on pre-enactment conduct, nothing in our holding prevents the State Department from filing statements of interest suggesting that courts decline to exercise jurisdiction in particular cases implicating foreign sovereign immunity. The issue now before us concerns interpretation of the FSIA's reach — a "pure question of statutory construction . . . well within the province of the Judiciary." *INS v. Cardoza-Fonseca*, 480 U.S. 421, 446, 448, 107 S. Ct. 1207, 94 L. Ed. 2d 434 (1987). While the United States' views on such an issue are of considerable interest to the Court, they merit no special deference. *See, e.g., ibid.* In contrast, should the State Department choose to express its opinion on the implications of exercising jurisdiction over particular petitioners in connection with their alleged conduct, that opinion might well be entitled to deference as the considered judgment of the Executive on a particular question of foreign policy. . . . We express no opinion on the question whether such deference should be granted in cases covered by the FSIA.

The judgment of the Court of Appeals is affirmed.

Notes

1. The Foreign Sovereign Immunities Act became an issue in *Malewicz v. City of Amsterdam*, 362 F. Supp. 2d 298 (D.D.C. 2005). The city of Amsterdam filed a motion to dismiss a suit by heirs of a Russian artist whose 84 works of art were allegedly wrongly expropriated. Amsterdam claimed immunity under the FSIA, but the court denied the motion to dismiss and permitted the lawsuit to proceed. In 2008, both parties filed a joint motion to dismiss their appeal, which was granted in *Malewicz v. City of Amsterdam*, 2008 WL 2223219 (D.C. Cir. May 14, 2008).

2. For detailed accounts of Nazi theft of works of art during World War II and attempts made to secure the return of stolen art after the war, *see* Walton, *Leave No Stone Unturned: The Search for the Art Stolen by the Nazis*, 9 FORDHAM INTELL. PROP. MEDIA & ENT. L.J. 549 (Winter 1999); Decker, *A Legacy of Shame*, ARTnews, Dec. 1984, at 55-76; Decker, *Austria Will Auction "Heirless" Art*, ARTnews, Feb. 1985, at 96-99.

3. In many cases, governments are still attempting to locate art treasures that have not been seen since the end of World War II. The Amber Room is one such treasure. Crafted by the Prussians in the 1700s from six tons of amber, the spectacular room consisted of 22 ornate wall panels, carved in Baroque style. The panels were offered to Peter the Great by Prussian King Frederick William I. The panels were subsequently incorporated into the palace at Tsarskoe-Selo, later known as Pushkin. Hitler discovered the panels and had them transported back to Germany, where they were publicly displayed in Konigsberg. Just prior to the Red Army's invasion of Konigsberg in 1945, the panels of the Amber Room were again dismantled and secreted away. The Amber Room has not been seen since, despite valiant efforts by the Soviet

government to discover its whereabouts. Some speculate that those who knew the secret location of the panels were killed to guarantee their silence. *The Amber Room Mystery*, IFARreports, May 1991, at 3. Russian President Boris Yeltsin at one time indicated that he knew the location of the treasure, specifically somewhere in eastern Germany. Lowenthal, *The Amber Room Mystery*, Wall Street J., Jan. 13, 1992, § A, at 12, col. 1.

4. There is a feature film on the challenge of recovering work during World War II, *Monuments Men* (2014), that draws greatly from the wonderful non-fiction historical account by Robert M. Edsel, *The Monuments Men: Allied Heroes, Nazi Thieves, and the Greatest Treasure Hunt in History* (2009).

Dunbar v. Seger-Thomschitz

2009 WL 1911008 (E.D. La. July 2, 2009)

Ivan L.R. Lemelle, District Judge.

Plaintiff, Sarah Blodgett Dunbar, moves for partial summary judgment on the first amended complaint and for summary judgment on Defendant's counterclaims. Plaintiff alleges that she has acquired ownership of a work of art, a painting entitled *Portrait of a Youth*, and that Defendant's claims have prescribed. Defendant opposes the motion. After review of the pleadings and applicable law and for the following reasons,

IT IS ORDERED that Plaintiff's Motions for Partial Summary Judgment on her first amended complaint and for Summary Judgment on Defendant's counterclaims are GRANTED.

BACKGROUND

This case arises out of an adverse ownership claim made by Defendant, Dr. Claudia Seger-Thomschitz (Defendant), for the Oskar Kokoschka painting entitled *Portrait of a Youth* (Hans Reichel) (1910) ("the painting"). The painting is currently in Plaintiff's physical possession in New Orleans, Louisiana. While the painting has been loaned for exhibitions, Plaintiff has had continuous, uninterrupted possession of the painting since she inherited the painting from her mother in 1973.

Defendant is the sole heir of Raimund Reichel's estate, and she alleges that the painting was confiscated by the Nazis from Reichel's ascendants, in Vienna, Austria, in 1939. Prior to the painting's alleged Nazi confiscation and under duress, Defendant alleges Raimund Reichel's father, Dr. Oskar Reichel transferred ownership of the painting and four other paintings to Otto Kallir-Nirenstein (Kallir) in 1938. Kallir was a Jewish art dealer whose art gallery exhibited the painting in 1924 and 1933, for possible sale, at the request of the Reichel family. *The Museum of Fine Arts, Boston v. Dr. Claudia Seger-Tomschitz*, No. 08-10097 (D. Mass. May 28, 2009) (Zobel, J.). Defendant alleges that when Plaintiff's mother, Sarah Reed-Platt purchased the painting from Otto Kallir's Gallery St. Etienne in 1946 in New York, she knew or should have known that the painting may have been stolen from Jewish people in Europe, and therefore she had a duty to investigate the painting's ownership. Defendant further alleges because Otto Kallir did not have ownership of the painting, he was not capable of transferring ownership to Plaintiff's mother.

Plaintiff argues she has acquired the painting through application of a ten year and three year acquisitive prescription periods pursuant to Louisiana Civil Code arts. 3490 and 3491. Plaintiff further argues that even if Defendant has a claim arising out of quasi-contract for unjust enrichment, such a claim is subject to a ten-year liberative prescription period pursuant to Louisiana Civil Code art. 3499. Accordingly, Defendant's claims arising from quasi-contract have prescribed. Finally, Plaintiff argues there are no material issues of fact regarding her or her mother's good faith acquisition and possession of the painting.

Defendant argues that an action to recover a moveable based on quasi-contract may not be subject to liberative prescription. Defendant argues that when a person wrongfully obtains property, a duty to return that property arises in quasi-contract. Further, Defendant argues facts and circumstances at the time when Mrs. Sarah Reed-Platt purchased the painting warranted investigation as to the painting's history of ownership. Defendant argues that because Plaintiff's mother ignored these circumstances and failed to investigate, she was a bad-faith possessor who cannot obtain ownership, and thus cannot transfer ownership under Louisiana law. Finally, Defendant asks that if this Court finds employing Louisiana law would result in a ruling in favor of Plaintiff, that this Court should use its authority to supplant Louisiana law with federal common law. Defendant argues an adverse ruling would be contrary to the Holocaust Victims Redress Act passed by Congress in 1998.

DISCUSSION

.... B. Adverse Ownership Claims Under Louisiana Law

While there is some dispute as to the nature of Defendant's claims, actions seeking ownership of property or enforcement of rights thereof, whether movable or immovable are real actions. Yiannopoulos, *2 Louisiana Civil Law Treatise*, § 241, 476 (1991). Such real actions, otherwise known as "revendicatory actions," are expressly authorized by the Louisiana Civil Code. La. Civ. Code art. 526. As the official comments to the Code indicate, there are two kinds of revendicatory actions, depending on the object seized: (1) a "petitory action" for the recovery of immovable property, and (2) an "innominate real action" for the recovery of movable property. Yiannopoulos, *supra*, § 242, 477. It follows from this basic dichotomy that, as the Civil Code specifically provides, liberative prescription periods for all manner of personal actions, including delictual, contractual, and quasi-contractual would not bar real actions seeking to protect the right of ownership. La. Civ. Code. Arts. 3492-3502; Yiannopoulos, *supra*, § 249, at 487. The rationale for this distinction is that "[u]nder our Civil Code, ownership can never be lost by the failure to exercise it — only by the acquisition of ownership by another through possession sufficient to acquire it through acquisitive prescription." *All-State Credit Plan Natchitoches, Inc. v. Ratliff,* 279 So. 2d 660, 666 (La. 1972).

Pursuant to article 3491 of the Louisiana Civil Code, "one who has possessed a movable as owner for ten years acquires ownership by prescription. Neither title nor good faith is required for this prescription." It is well established that the burden of proof of establishing the facts of acquisitive prescription rests on the party who makes the plea. *Humble v. Dewey,* 215 So. 2d 378 (La. App. 3d Cir. 1968). However, the possessor is aided in this burden by a presumption that she/he possessed as owner. Louisiana Civil Code article 3488 provides:

> [A]s to the fact itself of possession, a person is presumed to have possessed as master and owner, unless it appears that the possession began in the name of and for another.

Louisiana Civil Code article 3421 defines possession as follows:

> Possession is the detention or enjoyment of a corporeal thing, movable or immovable, that one holds or exercises by himself or by another who keeps or exercises it in his name.

In the instant litigation, Plaintiff has established that she possessed the painting for well over ten years. Plaintiff acquired the painting as a bequest from her mother in 1973. Plaintiff's possession was open and continuous. Moreover, Plaintiff possessed the painting for herself as evidenced by her acts conveying ownership. In particular, Plaintiff accepted the painting as a bequest from her mother, Plaintiff displayed the painting in her home, and Plaintiff loaned the painting for exhibitions at local and national galleries, further publicizing its location and its ownership. Therefore, Plaintiff has acquired ownership irrespective of her good or bad faith pursuant to above-cited legal authorities.

C. Claims Arising in Quasi-Contract and Unjust Enrichment

Even if Defendant's counter-claims arise from quasi-contract and unjust enrichment, these claims have prescribed. The Louisiana Civil Code establishes the general rule that personal actions prescribe by ten years liberative prescription. *State of Louisiana v. City of Pineville,* 403 So. 2d 49, 53 (La. 1981); La. Civ. Code. Art. 3544. Actions in quasi-contract are governed by the general ten-year prescriptive term set forth by article 3544. *See also Minyard v. Curtis Products, Inc.,* 251 La. 624, 205 So. 2d 422 (La. 1967). Therefore, assuming arguendo that Defendant has a valid claim arising in quasi-contract due to unjust enrichment, such claims have prescribed.

The period for liberative prescription begins to toll when the claimant reasonably should have discovered the injury. *Jordan v. Employee Transfer*

Corp., 509 So. 2d 420, 423 (La. 1987). There are special considerations when the injury alleged is related to stolen works of art, antiquities, or cultural property. *O'Keeffe v. Snyder*, 83 N.J. 478, 493, 416 A.2d 862 (N.J. 1980). The court must consider whether the claimant used due diligence in recovering the art. In similar cases, claimants have been found to have exercised due diligence by notifying the Art Dealers of America, the International Foundation for Art Research, UNESCO, or similar national and international organizations. *O'Keeffe*, 83 N.J. at 494, 416 A.2d 862; *Autocephalous Greek-Orthodox Church of Cyprus v. Goldberg and Feldman Fine Arts, Inc.*, 917 F.2d 278, 283 (7th Cir. 1990). Other claimants whose property was confiscated by Nazis placed advertisements in international publications and pursued claims for monetary restitution in German courts. *Vineberg v. Bissonnette*, 548 F.3d 50 (1st Cir. 2008).

In this case, Defendant's ascendants, the Reichel family, sought compensation for the forced sale of their family home, a commercial property, and another art collection which were forcibly sold or transferred. The Reichel family never claimed compensation for any of the Kokoschka works that were transferred to Kallir for sale. Furthermore, the location of the painting at issue has been ascertainable since its sale. Plaintiff's mother recorded the sale and loaned the painting to local and national galleries for public exhibitions. Given this evidence, the Reichel family and its heirs had ample notice of any possible claim to the painting. Although Defendant accuses Kallir of dealing in stolen art as an agent of the Nazis, the Reichel family was aware of the early history of ownership, including the transfer, of this work of art, yet took no action to recover it after the fall of the Nazi regime. The inordinate delay in asserting claims prejudices Plaintiff because all witnesses to the sale to Kallir are now deceased. *Am. Pipe & Const. Co. v. Utah*, 414 U.S. 538, 554, 94 S. Ct. 756, 38 L. Ed. 2d 713 (1974); *The Museum of Fine Arts, Boston*, No. 08-10097 (D. Mass. May 28, 2009) (Zobel, J.). Therefore, Defendant's claims in quasi-contract and unjust enrichment have prescribed.

D. Holocaust Victims Redress Act

The Holocaust Victims Redress Act provides in pertinent part:

> It is the sense of Congress that consistent with the 1907 Hague Convention all governments should undertake good faith efforts to facilitate the return of the private and public property, such as works of art, to the rightful owners in cases where assets were confiscated from the claimant during the period of Nazi rule and there is reasonable proof that the claimant is the rightful owner.

Act § 202, 112 Stat. at 17-18. Defendant's assertion that this court may supplant Louisiana prescription laws in order to ensure the goals of the Holocaust Victims Redress Act will not be compromised is problematic for a number of reasons.

First, there is no "federal common law" cause of action created by this Act. The Supreme Court held Congress has no power to declare substantive rules of common law applicable to a state whether they be general, commercial law, or part of the law of torts. And no clause in the Constitution purports to confer such a power upon the federal courts. *Erie v. Tompkins*, 304 U.S. 64, 78, 58 S. Ct. 817, 82 L. Ed. 1188 (1938) (citing *Baltimore & Ohio R.R. Co. v. Baugh*, 149 U.S. 368, 401, 13 S. Ct. 914, 37 L. Ed. 772 (1893)). Second, the Holocaust Victim's Redress Act was not intended to give individuals a private cause of action. *Orkin v. Taylor*, 487 F.3d 734, 739 (9th Cir. 2007). Finally, the plain language of the statute indicates it was meant to encourage return of works of art where (1) the art was confiscated from claimant during the period of Nazi rule; and (2) the claimant has reasonably proven she is the rightful owner. Act § 202, 112 Stat. at 17-18. Undisputed evidence establishes that the Reichel family sought compensation for other works of art and property, but not this one. Further, the family twice loaned this painting to Kallir for exhibit and possible sale prior to Nazi occupation. Those with more direct knowledge about this painting within the Reichel family than Defendant never sought or petitioned for its return to the family. Moreover, Plaintiff has put forth considerable evidence which demonstrates she is the rightful owner. Defendant's suppositions to the contrary fail to create a material factual dispute over ownership by Plaintiff. Therefore, the Court will not supplant Louisiana's prescription laws in light of above undisputed evidence.

Accordingly, IT IS ORDERED that Plaintiff's Motions for Partial Summary Judgment on her first amended complaint and for Summary Judgment on Defendant's counterclaims are GRANTED.

Notes

1. Twenty-eight paintings taken by a retreating German soldier at the close of World War II were displayed in Paris in 1994, after twenty years of negotiations between the French and German governments. Because the original owners of the paintings are unknown, it was hoped that this exhibit would assist owners and their heirs to reclaim their lost artworks. *French Regain Art Pillaged by Nazis*, Oregonian, Oct. 26, 1994, at F6.
2. The U.S. Army also engaged in what some consider "questionable activities" at the end of World War II. In 1945, General Patton's Third Army at Merkers, Germany, confiscated masterpieces belonging to the Kaiser Friedrich Museum and the Nationalgalerie. The paintings were moved to Reichsbank, Frankfurt, and later to Wiesbaden, before being sent to the United States for "safekeeping." Upon arrival in this country, the art was entrusted to the National Gallery of Art in Washington, D.C. Many of the Monuments Officers of the Army bitterly denounced this movement in a "Wiesbaden Manifesto." Letter from Dr. Thomas Carr Howe to Leonard D. DuBoff dated May 19, 1975.

Von Saher v. Norton Simon Museum of Art at Pasadena

754 F.3d 712 (9th Cir. 2014), *cert. denied*, 135 S.Ct. 1158 (2015)

D.W. NELSON, Senior Circuit Judge:

This case concerns the fate of two life-size panels painted by Lucas Cranach the Elder in the sixteenth century. *Adam* and *Eve* (collectively, "the Cranachs" or "the panels") that hang today in Pasadena's Norton Simon Museum of Art ("the Museum"). Marei Von Saher claims she is the rightful owner of the panels, which the Nazis forcibly purchased from her deceased husband's family during World War II. The district court dismissed Von Saher's complaint as insufficient to state a claim upon which relief can be granted, and that dismissal is before us on appeal. We have jurisdiction pursuant to 28 U.S.C. § 1291, and we reverse and remand.

I. BACKGROUND

In reviewing the district court's decision, we must "accept factual allegations in the complaint as true and construe the pleadings in the light most favorable to" Von Saher. *Manzarek v. St. Paul Fire & Marine Ins. Co.*, 519 F.3d 1025, 1031 (9th Cir. 2008). We therefore hew closely to the allegations in the complaint in describing the facts.

A. Jacques Goudstikker Acquires the Cranachs[5]

For the 400 years following their creation in 1530, the panels hung in the Church of the Holy Trinity in Kiev, Ukraine. In 1927, Soviet authorities sent the panels to a state-owned museum at a monastery and in 1927 transferred them to the Art Museum at the Ukrainian Academy of Science in Kiev. Soviet authorities then began to arrange to sell state-owned artworks abroad and held an auction in Berlin in 1931 as part of that effort. This auction, titled "The Stroganoff Collection," included artworks previously owned by the Stroganoff family. The collection also included the Cranachs, though Von Saher disputes that the Stroganoffs ever owned the panels. Jacques

---

5. Image: Michael D. Murray, Cropped, revised, and resized thumbnail excerpts (2016) of exhibits depicting the two panels of "Adam and Eve" by Lucas Cranach the Elder (1530), at issue in *Von Saher v. Norton Simon Museum of Art at Pasadena*, 754 F.3d 712 (9th Cir. 2014).

Goudstikker, who lived in the Netherlands with his wife, Desi, and their only child, Edo, purchased the Cranachs at the 1931 auction.

B. The Nazis Confiscate the Cranachs

Nearly a decade hence in May 1940, the Nazis invaded the Netherlands. The Goudstikkers, a Jewish family, fled. They left behind their gallery, which contained more than 1,200 artworks — the Cranachs among them. The family boarded the SS Bodegraven, a ship bound for South America. Days into their journey, Jacques accidentally fell to his death through an uncovered hatch in the ship's deck. When he died, Jacques had with him a black notebook, which contained entries describing the artworks in the Goudstikker Collection and which is known by art historians and experts as "the Blackbook." Desi retrieved the Blackbook when Jacques died. It lists the Cranachs as part of the Goudstikker Collection.

Meanwhile, back in the Netherlands, high-level Nazi Reichsmarschall Herman Göring divested the Goudstikker Collection of its assets, including the Cranachs. Jacques' mother, Emilie, had remained in the Netherlands when her son fled to South America with his wife and child. Göring's agent warned Emilie that he intended to confiscate the Goudstikker assets, but if she cooperated in that process, the Nazis would protect her from harm. Thus, Emilie was persuaded to vote her minority block of shares in the Goudstikker Gallery to effectuate a "sale" of the gallery's assets for a fraction of their value.

Employees of the Goudstikker Gallery contacted Desi to obtain her consent to a sale of the majority of the outstanding shares in the gallery, which she had inherited upon Jacques' death. She refused. Nevertheless, the sale went through when two gallery employees, unauthorized to sell its assets, subsequently entered into two illegal contracts. In the first, the "Göring transaction," Göring "purchased" 800 of the most valuable artworks in the Goudstikker collection. Göring then took those pieces, including the Cranachs, from the Netherlands to Germany. He displayed *Adam* and *Eve* in Carinhall, his country estate near Berlin. . . . Miedl began operating an art dealership out of Jacques' gallery with the artwork that Göring left behind. Miedl employed Jacques' former employees as his own and traded on the goodwill of the Goudstikker name in the art world.

C. The Allies Recover Nazi–Looted Art, Including the Cranachs

In the summer of 1943, the United States, the Netherlands and other nations signed the London Declaration, which "served as a formal warning to all concerned, and in particular persons in neutral countries, that the Allies intended to do their utmost to defeat the methods of dispossession practiced by the governments with which they [were] at war." *Von Saher v. Norton Simon Museum of Art at Pasadena* ("*Von Saher I*"), 592 F.3d 954, 962 (9th Cir. 2010) (internal quotation marks and citation omitted). The Allies "reserved the right to invalidate wartime transfers of property, regardless of whether" those transfers took the form of open looting, plunder, or forced sales. *Id.*

When American forces arrived on German soil in the winter of 1944 and 1945, they discovered large caches of Nazi-looted and stolen art hidden in castles, banks, salt mines, and caves. *Von Saher I,* 592 F.3d at 962. The United States established collection points for gathering, cataloging and caring for the recovered pieces. *Id.* At a collection point in Munich, Allied forces identified the Cranachs and other items from the Goudstikker Collection.

In order to reunite stolen works of art with their rightful owners, President Truman approved a policy statement setting forth the procedures governing looted artwork found in areas under U.S. control. *Von Saher I,* 592 F.3d at 962. These procedures had two components — external restitution and internal restitution. Under external restitution, nations formerly occupied by the Germans would present to U.S. authorities "consolidated lists of items taken [from their citizens] by the Germans." *Id.* These lists would include "information about the location and circumstances of the theft." *Id.* American authorities would identify the listed artworks and return them to their country of origin. *Id.* The United States stopped accepting claims for external restitution on September 15, 1948. *Id.* at 963. Under internal restitution, each nation had the responsibility for restoring the externally restituted artworks to their rightful owners. *Id.*

In 1946, the Allied Forces returned the pieces from the Goudstikker Collection to the Dutch government so that the artworks could be held in trust for their lawful owners: Desi, Edo and Emilie.

D. Desi's Postwar Attempt to Recover the Cranachs

In 1944, the Dutch government issued the Restitution of Legal Rights Decree, which established internal restitution procedures for the Netherlands. As a condition of restitution, people whose artworks were returned to them had to pay back any compensation received in a forced sale.

In 1946, Desi returned to the Netherlands intending to seek internal restitution of her property. Upon her return but before she made an official claim, the Dutch government characterized the Göring and Miedl transactions as voluntary sales undertaken without coercion. Thus, the government determined that it had no obligation to restore the looted property to the Goudstikker family. The government also took the position that if Desi wanted her property returned, she would have to pay for it, and she would not receive compensation for missing property, the loss of goodwill associated with the Goudstikker gallery's name or the profits Miedl made off the gallery during the war.

Desi decided to file a restitution claim for the property sold in the Miedl transaction, so that she could recover her home and some of her personal possessions. In 1952, she entered into a settlement agreement with the Dutch government, under protest, regarding only the Miedl transaction. As part of that settlement, Desi repurchased the property Miedl took from her for an amount she could afford. The agreement stated that Desi acquiesced to the settlement in order to avoid years of expensive litigation and due to her dissatisfaction with the Dutch government's refusal to compensate her for the extraordinary losses the Goudstikker family suffered at the hands of the Nazis during the war.

Given the government's position that the Nazi-era sales were voluntary and because of its refusal to compensate the Goudstikkers for their losses, Desi believed that she would not be successful in a restitution proceeding to recover the artworks Göring had looted. She therefore opted not to file a restitution claim related to the Göring transaction. The Netherlands kept the Göring-looted artworks in the Dutch National Collection. Von Saher alleges that title in these pieces did not pass to the Dutch Government.

In the 1950s, the Dutch government auctioned off at least 63 of the Goudstikker paintings recovered from Göring. These pieces did not include the Cranachs.

E. Von Saher Recovers Artwork from the Dutch Government

In the meantime, Desi and her son Edo became American citizens, and Desi married August Edward Dimitri Von Saher. When Emilie died in 1954, she left all of her assets, including her share in the Goudstikker Gallery, to her daughter-in-law, Desi, and her grandson, Edo. Desi then died in February 1996, leaving all of her assets to Edo. Just months later, in July 1996, Edo died and left his entire estate to his wife, Marei Von Saher, the plaintiff-appellant. Thus, Marei is the sole living heir to Jacques Goudstikker.

In 1997, the State Secretary of the Dutch Government's Ministry of Education, Culture and Science (the "State Secretary") announced that the Dutch government had undertaken an investigation into the provenance of artworks recovered in Germany and returned to the Netherlands following World War II. Related to that investigation, the government began accepting claims for recovered artworks in its custody that had not been restituted after the war.

Around the same time, a Dutch journalist contacted Von Saher and explained to her the circumstances regarding Göring's looting of the Goudstikker gallery, Desi's efforts to obtain restitution and the Dutch government's continued possession of some Goudstikker pieces in its national collection. This conversation was the first time Von Saher learned about these events.

In 1998, Von Saher wrote to the Dutch State Secretary requesting the surrender of all of the property from the Goudstikker collection in the custody of the Dutch government. The State Secretary rejected this request, concluding that the postwar restitution proceedings were conducted carefully and declining to waive the statute of limitations so that Von Saher could submit a claim. Von Saher made various attempts to appeal this decision without success.

While Von Saher pursued various legal challenges, the Dutch government created the Ekkart Committee to investigate the provenance of art in the custody of the Netherlands. The committee described the handling of restitution in the immediate postwar period as "legalistic, bureaucratic, cold and often even callous." It also criticized many aspects of the internal restitution process, among them employing a narrow definition of "involuntary loss" and requiring owners to return proceeds from forced sales as a condition of restitution.

Upon the recommendation of the Ekkart Committee, the Dutch government created the Origins Unknown project to trace the original owners of the artwork in its custody. The Dutch government also set up the Advisory Committee on the Assessment of Restitution Applications for Items of Cultural Value and the Second World War ("the Restitutions Committee") to evaluate restitution claims and to provide guidance to the Ministry for Education, Culture and Science on those claims. Between 2002 and 2007, the Restitution Committee received 90 claims.

In 2004, Von Saher made a restitution claim for all of the Goudstikker artwork in the possession of the Netherlands. The Committee recommended that the government grant the application with respect to all of the artworks plundered in the Göring transaction, which the Committee deemed involuntary. The State Secretary adopted the Committee's recommendation.

Unfortunately, the Dutch government no longer had custody of the Cranachs. In 1961, George Stroganoff Scherbatoff ("Stroganoff") claimed that the Soviet Union had wrongly seized the Cranachs from his family and unlawfully sold the paintings to Jacques Goudstikker 30 years earlier at the "Stroganoff Collection" auction in Berlin. Thus, Stroganoff claimed that the Dutch government had no right, title or interest in the panels. In 1966, the Dutch government transferred the Cranachs and a third painting to Stroganoff in exchange for a monetary payment. The terms of this transaction, including the amount Stroganoff paid for the artworks, are not in the record before us. The Dutch government did not notify Desi or Edo that Stroganoff made a claim to the panels or that the panels were being transferred to him. In 1971, New York art dealer Spencer Samuels acquired the Cranachs from Stroganoff, either as an agent or as a purchaser. Later that year, the Museum acquired the Cranachs and has possessed them ever since.

F. Von Saher Seeks Recovery From The Museum

In 2000, a Ukranian art historian researching the deaccession of artworks from state-owned museums in Kiev contacted Von Saher. He explained to Von Saher that he happened upon *Adam* and *Eve* when he visited the Museum, and once he researched the origin of the panels, he felt compelled to contact her. Because Cranach the Elder painted 30 similar depictions of *Adam* and *Eve*, Von Saher could not be certain whether the diptychs in the Museum were the ones missing from the Goudstikker collection. She contacted the Museum about the panels, and the parties engaged in a six-year effort to resolve this matter informally, which proved unsuccessful.

In May 2007, Von Saher sued the Museum, relying on California Code of Civil Procedure Section 354.3. That statute allowed the rightful owners of confiscated Holocaust-era artwork to recover their items from museums or galleries and set a filing deadline of December 31, 2010. Cal. Civ. Proc. Code § 354.3(b), (c).

The district court dismissed the action, finding Section 354.3 facially unconstitutional on the basis of field preemption. The court also found Von Saher's claims untimely.

We affirmed, over Judge Pregerson's dissent, holding Section 354.3 unconstitutional on the basis of field preemption. *Von Saher I*, 592 F.3d at 957. Because it was unclear whether Von Saher could amend her complaint to show lack of reasonable notice to establish compliance with California Code of Civil Procedure Section 338(c), we unanimously remanded. *Id.* at 968–70.

Six weeks after this court issued *Von Saher I*, the California legislature amended Section 338(c) to extend the statute of limitations from three to six years for claims concerning the recovery of fine art from a museum, gallery, auctioneer or dealer. Cal. Civ. Proc. Code § 338(c)(3)(A). In addition, the amendments provided that a claim for the recovery of fine art does not accrue until the actual discovery of both the identity and the whereabouts of the artwork. *Id.* The legislature made these changes explicitly retroactive. *Id.* § 338(c)(3)(B).

Von Saher filed a First Amended Complaint. The Museum moved to dismiss, arguing that Von Saher's specific claims and the remedies she sought — not the amended Section 338 itself — conflicted with the United States' express federal policy on recovered art. The district court agreed. It held that the Solicitor General's brief filed in the Supreme Court in connection with Von Saher's petition for writ of certiorari from *Von Saher I*, "clarified the United States' foreign policy as it specifically relates to Plaintiff's claims in this litigation." The district court held "that the United States' policy of external restitution and respect for the outcome and finality of the Netherlands' bona fide restitution proceedings, as clearly expressed and explained by the Solicitor General in his amicus curiae brief, directly conflicts with the relief sought in Plaintiff's action." The court dismissed the complaint with prejudice. Von Saher timely appeals.

II. STANDARD OF REVIEW

We review de novo the district court's dismissal of Von Saher's complaint. *Manzarek*, 519 F.3d at 1030. As discussed, we must accept the factual allegations in the complaint as true, and we construe the complaint in the light most favorable to Von Saher. *Id.* at 1031.

III. DISCUSSION

We first must decide whether the district court erred in finding Von Saher's claims barred by conflict preemption. It did.

A. Applicable Law

"[T]he Constitution allocates the power over foreign affairs to the federal government exclusively, and the power to make and resolve war, including the authority to resolve war claims, is central to the foreign affairs power in the constitutional design." *Deutsch v. Turner Corp.*, 324 F.3d 692, 713–14 (9th Cir. 2003). "In the absence of some specific action that constitutes authorization on the part of the federal government, states are prohibited from exercising foreign affairs powers, including modifying the federal government's resolution of war-related disputes." *Id.* at 714.

"Foreign affairs preemption encompasses two related, but distinct, doctrines: conflict preemption and field preemption." *Movsesian v. Victoria Versicherung AG,* 670 F.3d 1067, 1071 (9th Cir. at 2012) (en banc). In *Von Saher I,* we found Section 354.3 unconstitutional on the basis of field preemption. 592 F.3d at 965, 968. Here, however, the Museum's argument focuses exclusively on conflict preemption. Specifically, the Museum contends that Von Saher's claims, and the remedies she seeks, are in conflict with federal policy on the restitution of Nazi-stolen art.

"There is, of course, no question that at some point an exercise of state power that touches on foreign relations must yield to the National Government's policy, given the 'concern for uniformity in this country's dealings with foreign nations' that animated the Constitution's allocation of the foreign relations power to the National Government in the first place." *Am. Ins. Ass'n v. Garamendi,* 539 U.S. 396, 413, 123 S.Ct. 2374, 156 L. Ed. 2d 376 (2003) (quoting *Banco Nacional de Cuba v. Sabbatino,* 376 U.S. 398, 427 n.25, 84 S.Ct. 923, 11 L. Ed. 2d 804 (1964)). . . . The question we must answer is whether Von Saher's claims for replevin and conversion, as well as the remedies she seeks, conflict with federal policy. We conclude that they do not.

B. Federal Policy on Nazi–Looted Art

We start by looking to federal policy on the restitution of Nazi-looted art. As discussed, the United States signed the London Declaration and subsequently adopted a policy of external restitution based on the principles in that declaration. In *Von Saher I,* we noted that the United States stopped accepting claims for external restitution on September 15, 1948, and accordingly concluded that the United States' policy of external restitution ended that year. 592 F.3d at 963. Thus, we held that California Civil Procedure Code Section 354.3 could not "conflict with or stand as an obstacle to a policy that is no longer in effect." *Id.*

It seems that we misunderstood federal policy. In a 2011 brief filed in the Supreme Court recommending the denial of a petition for writ of certiorari in *Von Saher I,* the United States, via the Solicitor General, reaffirmed our nation's continuing and ongoing commitment to external restitution. The Solicitor General explained that external restitution did not end in 1948 with the deadline for submitting restitution claims, as we had concluded in *Von Saher I.* Instead, "[t]he United States established a deadline to ensure prompt submission of claims and achieve finality in the wartime restitution process," and the United States has a "continuing interest in that finality when appropriate actions have been taken by a foreign government concerning the internal restitution of art."

Federal policy also includes the Washington Conference Principles on Nazi Confiscated Art ("the Principles"), produced at the Washington Conference on Holocaust–Era Art Assets in 1998. Though non-binding, the Principles reflect a consensus reached by the representatives of 13 nongovernmental organizations and 44 governments, including both the United States and the Netherlands, to resolve issues related to Nazi-looted art. The Principles provided first that "Art that has been confiscated by the Nazis and not subsequently restituted should be identified" and that "[e]very effort should be made to publicize" this art "in order to locate pre-War owners and their heirs." The signatories agreed that "[p]re-war owners and their heirs should be encouraged to come forward and make known their claims to art that was confiscated by the Nazis and not subsequently restituted." The Principles also provided that when such heirs are located, "steps should be taken expeditiously to achieve a just and fair solution, recognizing this may vary according to facts and circumstances surrounding a specific case." Finally, the Principles encouraged nations "to develop national processes to implement these principles," including alternative dispute resolution.

Additionally, in 2009, the United States participated in the Prague Holocaust Era Assets Conference, which produced the "legally non-binding" Terezin Declaration on Holocaust Era Assets and Related Issues, to which the United States and the Netherlands agreed. The signatories reaffirmed their support for the Washington Conference Principles and "encourage[d] all parties[,] *including public and private institutions* and individuals to apply them as well." "The Participating States urge[d] that every effort be made to rectify the consequences of wrongful property seizures, such as confiscations, forced sales and sales under duress[.]" In addition, the signatories "urge[d] all stakeholders to ensure that their legal systems or alternative processes . . . facilitate just and fair solutions with regard to Nazi-confiscated and looted art and to make certain that claims to recover such art are resolved expeditiously and based on the facts and merits of the claims and all the relevant documents submitted by the parties."

In sum, U.S. policy on the restitution of Nazi-looted art includes the following tenets: (1) a commitment to respect the finality of "appropriate actions" taken by foreign nations to facilitate the internal restitution of plundered art; (2) a pledge to identify Nazi-looted art that has not been restituted and to publicize those artworks in order to facilitate the identification of prewar owners and their heirs; (3) the encouragement of prewar owners and their heirs to come forward and claim art that has not been restituted; (4) concerted efforts to achieve expeditious, just and fair outcomes when heirs claim ownership to looted art; (5) the encouragement of everyone, including public and private institutions, to follow the Washington Principles; and (6) a recommendation that every effort be made to remedy the consequences of forced sales.

C. Von Saher's Claims Do Not Conflict with Federal Policy

Von Saher's claims do not conflict with any federal policy because the Cranachs were never subject to postwar internal restitution proceedings in the Netherlands, as noted in the complaint, the district court's order and the opinion of the Court of Appeals of The Hague.

Desi could have brought a claim for restitution as to all of the artworks Göring looted in the immediate postwar period, but she understandably chose not to do so prior to the July 1, 1951 deadline. Per Von Saher, the "[h]istorical literature makes clear that the post-War Dutch Government was concerned that the immediate and automatic return of Jewish property to its original owners would have created chaos in the legal system and damaged the economic recovery of [t]he Netherlands," and "[t]his attitude was reflected in the restitution process." Desi was "met with hostility by the postwar Dutch Government" and "confronted a 'restitution' regime that made it difficult for Jews like [her] to recover their property." In fact, the Dutch government went so far as to take the "astonishing position" that the transaction between Göring and the Goudstikker Gallery was voluntary and taken without coercion. Not surprisingly, Desi decided that she could not achieve a successful result in a sham restitution proceeding to recover the artworks Göring had looted. The Dutch government later admitted as much when the Ekkart Committee described the immediate postwar restitution process as "legalistic, bureaucratic, cold, and often even callous."

Moreover, the Dutch government transferred the Cranachs to Stroganoff fourteen years after Desi settled her claim against Miedl. The Museum contends that this conveyance satisfied a restitution claim Stroganoff made as the rightful heir to the Cranachs, but the record casts doubt on that characterization. As noted, the deadline for filing an internal restitution claim in the Netherlands expired July 1, 1951, and Stroganoff did not assert his claim to the Cranachs until a decade later. In addition, the Restitution of Legal Rights Decree, which governed the Dutch internal restitution process, was established to create "special rules regarding restitution of legal rights and restoration of rights in connection with the liberalization of the [Netherlands]" following World War II. The Decree included provisions addressing the restitution of wrongful acts committed in enemy territory during the war. To the extent that Stroganoff made a claim of restitution, however, it was based on the allegedly wrongful seizure of the paintings by the Soviet Union *before* the Soviets sold the Cranachs to Jacques Goudstikker in 1931 — events which predated the war and any wartime seizure of property. Thus, it seems dubious at best to cast Stroganoff's claim as one of internal restitution.

By the time Von Saher requested in 1998 that the Dutch government surrender all of the Goudstikker artworks within state control, the Cranachs had been in the Museum's possession for 27 years. Even if Desi's 1998 request for surrender could be construed as a claim for restitution — made nearly 50 years after the deadline for filing such a claim lapsed — the Cranachs were no longer in possession of the Dutch government and necessarily fell outside that claim.[1]

Though we recognize that the United States has a continuing interest in respecting the finality of "appropriate actions" taken in a foreign nation to restitute Nazi-confiscated art, the Dutch government itself has acknowledged the "legalistic, bureaucratic, cold and often even callous" nature of the initial postwar restitution system. And the Dutch State Secretary eventually ordered the return of all the Göring-looted artworks possessed by the Netherlands — the very artwork Desi chose not to seek in the postwar restitution process immediately following the war — to Von Saher. These events raise serious questions about whether the initial postwar internal restitution process constitutes an appropriate action taken by the Netherlands. . . .

Here, however, there is no Holocaust-specific legislation at issue. Instead, Von Saher brings claims pursuant to a state statute of general applicability. Also unlike *Garamendi,* Von Saher seeks relief from an American museum that had no connection to the wartime injustices committed against the Goudstikkers. Nor does Von Saher seek relief from the Dutch government itself. In fact, the record contains a 2006 letter from the Dutch Minister for Education, Culture and Science, who confirmed that "the State of the Netherlands is not involved in this dispute" between Von Saher and the Museum. The Minister also opined that this case "concerns a dispute between two private parties."

Von Saher's claims against the Museum and the remedies she seeks do not conflict with foreign policy. This matter is, instead, a dispute between private parties. The district court erred in concluding otherwise.

D. Act of State

We are mindful that the litigation of this case may implicate the act of state doctrine, though we cannot decide that issue definitively on the record before us. We remand for further development of this issue. . . .

We recognize that this remand puts the district court in a delicate position. The court must use care to "limit[ ] inquiry which would impugn or question the nobility of a foreign nation's motivation." *Clayco,* 712 F.2d at 407 (internal quotation marks and citation omitted). The court also cannot "resolve issues requiring inquiries . . . into the authenticity and motivation of the acts of foreign sovereigns." *Id.* at 408 (internal quotation marks and citations omitted). Nevertheless, this case comes to us as an appeal from a dismissal for failure to state a valid claim. The Museum has not yet developed its act of state defense, and Von Saher has not had the opportunity to establish the existence of an exception to that doctrine should it apply. Though this remand necessitates caution and prudence, we believe that the required record development and analysis can be accomplished with faithfulness to the limitations imposed by the act of state doctrine.

REVERSED and REMANDED.

WARDLAW, Circuit Judge, dissenting:

The United States has determined that the Netherlands afforded the Goudstikker family an adequate opportunity to recover the artwork that is the subject of this litigation. Our nation's foreign policy is to respect the finality of the Netherlands' restitution proceedings and to avoid involvement in any ownership dispute over the Cranachs. Because entertaining Marei Von Saher's state law claims would conflict with this federal policy, I respectfully dissent. . . .

Marei Von Saher and the Museum are both standing on their rights to the Cranachs. Their dispute spans decades and continents, and it cannot be resolved in an action under the laws of California or any other U.S. state. The United States has determined, as a matter of its foreign policy, that its involvement with the Cranachs ended when it returned them to the Netherlands in 1945 and the Dutch government afforded the Goudstikkers an adequate opportunity to reclaim them. This foreign policy decision also binds the federal courts, and it should end our many years of involvement with the Cranachs as well. I would affirm the judgment of the district court.

C. Challenges in Asia

The 1960s brought more instances in which art was brutalized in a time of armed conflict. One occurred during internal strife in Communist China, known as the Great Proletarian Cultural Revolution. The alleged purpose of the government-inspired chaos was the reconstruction of the country's educational system. Yet, the effect hoped for by government leaders, as viewed by one veteran China observer, was much more extensive: "Mao is bent on wiping out even the memory of Chinese culture." While few reports of the extent of the destruction occurring in 1966 (the primary year of this phase) filtered out, those that did evidenced the widespread ruin of ancient artistic properties.

Later, the situation in China changed, and the government began to take a hand in the preservation and conservation of works of art. One development derived from this change in philosophy was a worldwide tour of Chinese artifacts. The Chinese government also began to earmark resources for the excavation of ancient burial sites.[6]

The war in Southeast Asia also took a toll on the arts, although, as in China, the extent of the destruction was not easily determined. In December 1971, a committee that included leading authorities on Asian art was formed in the United States to lobby for the protection of important artistic monuments in Indochina. The committee, termed "The Committee on Monuments and Fine Arts in Southeast Asia," sent an appeal to the Defense Department requesting further action protecting these monuments. Gordon Washburn, the organization's head, explained that "hardly anyone knew what had happened to all the precious monuments in the Indochinese fighting zones."[7]

Numerous thefts by army troops were reported. Nguyen Ba Lang, director of Saigon's Archaeological Research Institute, stated that "[t]here is just no

6. *Chinese Discover a Potter 'Army' Buried 2000 Years*, N.Y. Times, July 12, 1975, at 1, col. 5.
7. Taubnian, *Greater Protection of Asian Art Urged*, N.Y. Times, Dec. 22, 1971, at 26, col. 1.

control over the theft of Vietnamese antiquities. . . . Some soldiers simply chop the last figures off a row of bas relief and then tote them around Saigon's antiquity shops."[8] Other reports comment that "wooden carvings and stone figurines on abandoned houses and temples in the country have often been stolen by troops on patrol. And even the museums, which are only casually-guarded, have been broken into."[9]

Two years after U.S. forces were withdrawn from Cambodia and Vietnam, both countries fell to the Communists. When collapse became imminent, South Vietnam's then-President, Nguyen Van Thieu, planned to ship 28 tons of his nation's gold reserves to North America for safekeeping. The United States agreed to help and flew in a cargo plane. Unfortunately, the harassed South Vietnamese officials were unable to accomplish the transfer, and the cargo plane was forced to take off empty. United States officials briefly considered seizing the gold before they fled Saigon but decided that such an action might be considered theft. The bullion was thus abandoned to the Communists. The 28 tons of gold left behind was worth approximately $29 million at the then-official U.S. rate, and approximately $110 million on the free market.[10]

Notes and Questions

1. What effect has increased terrorism had on the art world? The threat of terrorism has been said to be responsible for the postponement of a loan show of Florentine paintings on its way from Italy to Japan. *Naples Fights Art Terrorism*, J. of Art, Apr. 1991, at 4. In *Rubin v. Islamic Republic of Iran*, 637 F.3d 783 (7th Cir. 2013), a survivor of a terrorist attack sued the Islamic Republic of Iran claiming it provided material support to Hamas. The plaintiffs sought to attach property of Iran held in several U.S. museums, including the Museum of Fine Arts and Harvard University.

2. The Sainsbury Wing at the National Gallery in London was damaged when a bomb exploded in a museum bookstore in December 1991. The Irish Republican Army claimed responsibility for the attack, its first in which a museum had been the target. *Artworld*, Art in Am., Feb. 1992, at 144.

3. In 2015, the International Criminal Court (ICC) considered a case concerning the destruction of cultural heritage. The ICC Office of the Prosecutor charged Ahmad Al Faqi Mahdi with destruction of historical and religious monuments in Timbuktu, Mali, at a UNESCO World Heritage Site. In 2012, Al Faqi, a leader of Ansar Dine, an Al-Qaeda

---

8. *Vietnamese Plan Museum Revival*, N.Y. Times, Feb. 18, 1973, § 1, at 8.
9. *Id.*
10. *See The Gold They Left Behind*, Newsweek, June 30, 1975.

affiliated organization in Mali, allegedly ordered and oversaw the destruction of nine tombs and a mosque. He was charged under Article 8(2)(e)(iv) of the Rome Statute of the ICC, which defines "[i]ntentionally directing attacks against buildings dedicated to religion, education, art, science, or charitable purposes, historic monuments, hospitals, and places where the sick and wounded are collected, provided they are not military objectives" as a war crime in non-international armed conflicts. *See* "Situation in Mali: Ahmad Al Faqi Al Mahdi surrendered to the ICC on charges of war crimes regarding the destruction of historical and religious monuments in Timbuktu" (2015), *available at https:// www.icc-cpi.int/en_menus/icc/press%20and%20media/press%20releases/ Pages/pr1154.aspx* (Last visited March 26, 2016).

D. The Gulf Wars

"Stuff happens," Defense Secretary Donald Rumsfeld said when questioned about the pillaging of Iraq's National Museum of Antiquities after the end of major fighting in what came to be known as Gulf War II.

Secretary Rumsfeld's choice of words were most unfortunate, for history has shown that antiquities are more than just "stuff" and looting doesn't just "happen." Looting has become a predictable outcome of war since the Romans first glorified it in 400 BC, only to be sacked themselves in AD 455.

This section addresses the Iraqi plunder of Kuwaiti treasures in what lead to Gulf War I, and the theft of art items from Baghdad's National Museum of Antiquities during Gulf War II. The National Museum of Antiquities' collection contained artifacts that recorded history of ancient Mesopotamia, a culture more than 7000 years old that is the predecessor of modern Iraq. Looters stole several solid gold items, including a harp, sculpture, and jewelry from the Sumerian era, which began around 3360 BC.

Initially, regular Iraqis were suspected of having plundered their own museum. The United Nations Education Scientific and Cultural Organization (UNESCO) later confirmed that well-organized professional thieves stole most of the priceless artifacts and that they may have had inside help from low-level museum employees. One group of thieves had keys to the underground vault where the most valuable artifacts were stored after the 1991 Persian Gulf War. Eventually, in both Gulf War I and II, most items resurfaced and were returned.

1. Gulf War I: Iraqi Plunder of Kuwaiti Treasures

During the hostilities in the Persian Gulf in 1991, the director of the Kuwaiti National Museum issued an urgent appeal that the international art community be on the lookout for Islamic artifacts that might have been taken from the museum and sold by the Iraqis.[11] While it was rumored that Saddam Hussein's army had, indeed, looted the museum of its collections and had torched the remainder, Baghdad radio announced in April 1991 that the museum's collection had been removed "for safekeeping" by Iraqi archaeologists.[12] The Kuwaitis were fortunate that a portion of their collection, 114 pieces, was on tour in an exhibition entitled "Ten Centuries of Islamic Art and Patronage: Selections from the Kuwait National Museum." Other Kuwaiti art objects were, at the time, on display at the Virginia Museum of Fine Arts.[13] Beginning in August 1991, Iraq began to return to Kuwait property seized during the occupation. The Kuwaiti National Museum and the House of Islamic Antiquities received over 17,000 artifacts that had been looted by Iraq. The artifacts' return was prompted by several United Nations security resolutions.[14] Objects stolen from private collections have been less fortunate. Many have yet to be returned to their true owners and, in fact, some have shown up on the auction market.[15]

The United Nations Compensation Commission (UNCC) was created under the terms of the Gulf War cease-fire to compensate victims for war losses, including stolen art collections; however, thus far, few people have actually received compensation.[16]

Sherri L. Burr, The Acclaim and Hazards of Being an International Artist

Author Interview with Bill Arms, Copyright © 2004 by Sherri L. Burr

Internationally acclaimed sculptor and muralist Bill Arms was described by the Taos Arts School as "a master of capturing motion in line." Arms' early training set up what would eventually become an enriched international career.

After he graduated from University of Arizona, he received a one-year scholarship to study in Paris. To learn French, he slept with the radio, read everything he could whether he understood it or not, and attended classes at Alliance Française. Within a year he had mastered the language and he stayed three more years in France before moving to London to show his work for a year.

Of his European experiences, Arms says it provided him "a polish, a little different edge that I would never have had if I stayed in Tucson." He adds, "I met great artists who became my friends and influenced my work."

Arms has painted 50-foot and 100-foot murals in places as far flung as Kuwait, Singapore, London, Hawaii, and New York. Some clients change murals every five years when they redecorate their homes. It takes him weeks of

11. Arundel, *On the Trail of Kuwait's Treasures*, N.Y. Times, June 20, 1991, at D, § 4, col. 1.
12. J. of Art, Apr. 1991, at 8, col. 3.
13. *Front Page*, Art in Am., Nov. 1990, at 45, col. 1.
14. *U.N. Forces Return of Kuwaiti Loot*, J. of Art, Nov. 1991, at 4.
15. Rosenberger, *Plundered Kuwaiti Art Surfaces in London*, Art in Am., Mar. 1992, at 29-30.
16. *Model Tribunal Plagued by Cash Woes*, ABA Journal, Feb. 1995 at 30.

advanced planning to coordinate his international projects as he must build special cartons. He brings materials that can be rolled up, paints for retouching, and feels challenged to get it all through customs of a particular country.

When hired to do a mural, Arms often produces an initial maquette. He prefers to receive approvals of the design so that when it's finished, the hiring party receives what they want. Arms paints to the exact scale in his studio in Taos and subsequently hires wallpaper crew at the destination to assist in affixing the mural to a wall or ceiling. He works with acid free museum quality pigments. He says, "If you get good art pigments, they stand the test of time, supposedly 500 years."

"I'm always willing to travel for work," he says. "Sometimes they give me a swatch of colors and I have to work with greens and blues, specific colors that go with an environment. Sometimes they ask me to come up with the design. One client sent a poster and requested a similar 20 × 20 foot reproduction for his ceiling. I work on a product called Sanitas, which is a wallpaper liner, and it comes in various widths. It's like a vinyl. Once I apply paint, it becomes like alligator hide and is hard to destroy."

Arms is no stranger to the destruction of art associated with war. One of his works was pilfered during the first Gulf War. He says, "When Kuwait was invaded by the Iraqis, I had a mural stolen from a palace. I had installed a 50-foot jungle scene with giant carrots and enormous flowers in it, a very realistic painting. It was up in the prince's garden room. When the soldiers came in from the desert they saw an incredibly wet jungle and pulled it off the wall. The prince was so brokenhearted that he's never restored his palace."

The tragedy of 9/11 inspired Arms to produce a series that focused on the moment before the twin towers were hit. He says, "9/11 affected me so. I had a fascination with what people were doing the moment before the planes hit the building. A lot of people who died in the terrible tragedy didn't know what happened. Incineration was just instant. My series concentrated on the obliteration of matter as things exploded. I produced paintings in gold, silver, and copper metal. The metal is depressed and nothing looks real."

Arms thinks the world of art law is becoming more complex. Like many successful artists, he has had problems with people copying his work and passing it off as their own. He received a call one day that someone in Indiana had made an 18-foot copy of a painting he had produced in California. He decided against pursuing the artist because his work wasn't very well done. "I didn't want to bring attention to it," Arms says.

"Besides, it's hard to copy what I do. I take the anatomy of the body, and dissect it three times and put it back together in flat planes so that each figure shows six sides. It's very complicated work. I take my hat off to anyone who tries."

When asked what is the secret of his success, Arms says, "I love my work, I love people, and I love art." His advises other artists, "You have to be genuinely interested in your work and do it because you love it. You do what's right. You don't work for the dollar. You have to go with your gut feeling if you want to do the job."

For his legacy, Arms says, "I'd like my sculpture to be recognized around the world. I think my sculpture is unique."

Notes

1. Bill Arms's work can be seen at *http://www.taosguide.net/Ads/A1-arms.html* and *http://www.collectorsguide.com/ts/ts-g/g372_03.jpg*. His work has been exhibited in the Pasadena Art Museum, the National Gallery of Fine Arts in Washington, D.C., the Drain Gallery & Dembeck Gallery in England, and the Ventadour Gallery in Paris.

2. In Chapter 7, you saw several contracts. If you review them again, think about the additional terms that you would need to add to a contract to represent artists with international clients. Arms believes that there are several dimensions to international contracts that are important to artists, including currency exchange. Arms says, "You hope that you have a place to stay, food, transportation, and a guide if you don't understand the language, like in Kuwait. If they give you money while you're there, you need to be sure that you can cash the check. You want the contract to have a beginning, middle, and end with a payment scale. You can't wait for your money as a mural can take a year or a year and a half of work." What protections do artists who work in war zones need?

PROBLEM 10-2

> Analyze the potential United States' liability, if any, for its conduct during the Gulf War invasion, and further analyze the measures that should be undertaken to attempt to reclaim and preserve the cultural heritage items taken from the Iraqi National Museum by governmental and non-governmental organizations and entities.

2. Gulf War II: The Pillaging of the National Museum of Baghdad

After U.S. troops entered Baghdad the week of April 7, 2003, the National Museum of Iraq was reported destroyed 48 hours later when an estimated 170,000 artifacts were carried away by looters. The museum's 28 galleries, and vaults with huge steel doors guarding storage chambers that descend floor after floor into unlighted darkness, had been completely ransacked. Museum officials initially reported that nothing of real value remained. As examples of what was gone, the officials cited a solid gold harp from the

Sumerian era, which began about 3360 BC and started to crumble after 200 BC. Another item on their list of looted antiquities was a sculptured head of a woman from Uruk, one of the great Sumerian cities, dating from the same era, and a collection of gold necklaces, bracelets, and earrings, also from the Sumerian dynasties and at least 4000 years old.[17]

Three days after this *New York Times* story ran, the *Washington Post* reported that, according to the head of UNESCO, "well-organized professional thieves stole most of the priceless artifacts looted from Baghdad's National Museum of Antiquities last week, and they may have had inside help from low-level museum employees."[18] "Thousands of objects were lost at the museum, both to the sophisticated burglars and to mob looting," Koichiro Matsuura, director general of the United Nations Educational, Scientific and Cultural Organization, said in an interview. "Most of it was well-planned looting by professionals," he said. "They stole these cultural goods to make profits."

"Museum officials in Baghdad told UNESCO that one group of thieves had keys to an underground vault where the most valuable artifacts were stored. The thefts were probably the work of international gangs who hired Iraqis for the job, and who have been active in recent years doing illegal excavations at Iraqi archaeological digs, according to archaeological experts working with UNESCO. Matsuura said top museum officials tried to protect the institution, but the thieves may have succeeded in paying off guards or other low-ranking personnel. He said he doesn't blame the U.S. military, even though UNESCO had urged the U.S. government before the war to safeguard it and other cultural sites."[19]

"If I were to blame somebody, it would be those armed bandits who looted their own cultural treasury," Matsuura said. The museum was assaulted during "a power vacuum" following the collapse of Saddam Hussein's government, and "anything could happen in such confusion and turmoil," he said.[20]

On July 4, 2003, the Iraq Museum reopened, showing off the Nimrud collection for the first time since the 1991 Persian Gulf War. As it turned out, according to a *New York Times* report, the Nimrud treasures were not among those stolen after the war. They were found in June 2003 in a submerged bank vault. The initial reports of the looting proved to be exaggerated. Col. Matthew Bogdanos, a Marine reservist investigating the thefts, said that only about 12,000 items had been stolen, mostly objects primarily of archaeological significance like shards of pottery and individual beads of lapis lazuli. Bogdanos said that forty-two display-quality objects had disappeared and ten of those had been recovered. About 3,000 other items had been recovered, he said, but not the approximately 9,000 that had been stolen from a locked basement storeroom in what was apparently an inside job.[21]

---

17. *See* Burns, *Pillagers Strip Iraqi Museum of Its Treasures*, N.Y. Times, Apr. 14, 2003.
18. McCartney, *Expert Thieves Took Artifacts*, Wash. Post, Apr. 17, 2003, at A1.
19. *Id.*
20. *Id.*
21. *See* Shaila K. Dewan, *Iraq Museum Reopens with Assyrian Treasures*, N.Y. Times, July 4, 2003.

ASSESSMENT

1. During the Great War, a soldier named Frederick Finder came across an abandoned home decorated with several famous paintings. Since there seemed to be no one around to claim the paintings, Frederick assumed they were abandoned and decided it would be best to take them with him for safekeeping. Frederick brought the paintings back to the United States with him after the war and they stayed in his home until his death nine years later. After his death, his daughter, Francis Finder, inherited the paintings and began displaying them in a small local museum.

   Unknown to both Frederick and Francis, the paintings had belonged to a man named Larry Lost, who had been captured during the Great War. Larry thought about the paintings often, but he didn't try to find them because he thought they were lost forever. Ten years after Francis began displaying the paintings, Larry read about them in an article about the small local museum. He called the museum and demanded it return them to him. Based on the court's decision in *Dunbar v. Seger-Thomshitz*, what is Francis' best argument to reclaim the paintings?

   (A) Francis had the paintings in her possession for over ten years and she displayed them in a museum for the public to view

   (B) The paintings were abandoned; therefore Francis is now the rightful owner of them

   (C) Larry did not try to find the paintings or use due diligence in recovering the paintings

   (D) Both (A) and (C)

   (E) None of the above

2. Cleopatra Clumsy held an ancient painting for many years in her home. It was a famous painting, which she was very fond of. During the time that Cleopatra lived, there was a terrible war that brought many soldiers into her town. The soldiers ransacked the village where she lived, and all of her belongings were taken, including the painting. She was forced out of her home, and her home was eventually burned to the ground. The soldiers were very proud of their work, and thought that the painting would be an impressive gift to their leader. Lazy Leader kept the painting for twenty years before realizing that the painting was in fact famous. He then sold the painting to a museum for millions of dollars.

   Cleopatra's grandchild, Curious Carrie, knew of the painting, and that it was stolen several years ago. She saw that the painting was to be displayed in a local museum, and she verified that the painting was in fact that of her beloved grandmother. Will Carrie be able to successfully regain possession of the painting? Based on the court's decision in *Orkin v. Taylor*, which of the following is the most accurate statement?

(A) The painting was abandoned when Cleopatra allowed the soldiers to take it, therefore Carrie cannot now claim it

(B) Carrie would not be able to recover because the claim would likely be barred by the statute of limitations

(C) Carrie is entitled to the recovery of the famous painting because she sought to reclaim it immediately after she discovered she had a claim to the painting and the whereabouts of where the painting was

(D) Carrie cannot reclaim the painting because Lazy Leader possessed it for 20 years without a contest to its ownership

(E) Both (A) and (D)

3. In the article *The Acclaim and Hazards of Being an International Artist* by Sherri L. Burr, why does the interviewee, Bill Arms, believe that "the world of art law is becoming more complex"?

(A) Art is complex and it is difficult to keep his success a secret

(B) An artist has to keep pursuing copycats in order to protect their works of art

(C) It is too easy for other people to copy famous works of art and pass them off as their own

(D) Both (A) and (B)

(E) None of the above

4. When does the Holocaust Victims Redress Act Apply?

(A) When a piece of artwork is stolen during times of war, and the original owner seeks to reclaim it

(B) Where an original owner forgets to claim ownership over an artwork stolen during World War II, but now wishes to recover it

(C) When a person has owned a painting in their possession for over ten years, and a person from the Nazi era wishes to reclaim it

(D) Where assets were confiscated from the claimant during the period of Nazi rule and there is reasonable proof that the claimant is the rightful owner

(E) None of the above

5. Ian Importer wanted to bring a beautiful Picasso painting into the United States, but was aware that his great-grandfather had acquired it during World War II from a family he imprisoned. Ian wants to display the painting for everyone to see, but is afraid that it will be seized because of how his grandfather gained ownership over it. Will Ian Importer be able to protect his ownership over the Picasso Painting?

(A) No, if he brings the painting in, then it will be seized no matter what he tries to do

(B) Yes, if he brings the painting to the United States to be displayed in a cultural exhibition and is granted immunity by the President

(C) Yes, if Ian hides the fact that his grandfather obtained ownership over the painting during World War II

(D) No, but he will be able to appeal the seizure by the government, as long as his painting is seized because his grandfather was a bad soldier

(E) Both (B) and (C)

ASSESSMENT ANSWERS

1. During a Great War, a soldier named Frederick Finder came across an abandoned home decorated with several famous paintings. Since there seemed to be no one around to claim the paintings, Frederick assumed they were abandoned and decided it would be best to take them with him for safekeeping. Frederick brought the paintings back to the United States with him after the war and they stayed in his home until his death nine years later. After his death, his daughter, Francis Finder, inherited the paintings and began displaying them in a small local museum.

   Unknown to both Frederick and Francis, the paintings had belonged to a man named Larry Lost, who had been captured during the Great War. Larry thought about the paintings often, but he didn't try to find them because he thought they were lost forever. Ten years after Francis began displaying the paintings, Larry read about them in an article about the small local museum. He called the museum and demanded it return them to him. Based on the court's decision in *Dunbar v. Seger-Thomshitz*, what is Frederick and Francis' best argument to reclaim the paintings?

   (A) Francis had the paintings in her possession for over ten years and she displayed them in a museum for the public to view

   (B) The paintings were abandoned; therefore Francis is now the rightful owner of them

   (C) Larry did not try to find the paintings or use due diligence in recovering the paintings

   (D) Both (A) and (C)

   (E) None of the above

   ANSWER: The correct answer is (D). (B) is incorrect because one who is imprisoned during war and leaves behind property does not automatically abandon his property. (E) is wrong because she could potentially have an argument that the paintings correctly belong to her. (A) is correct because, in part, in order to claim adverse possession, a person must have possessed the property for over ten years and held it out openly and continuously. (C) is also correct because a claimant must have a claim if he or she knew or should have known about the adverse possession. Therefore, (D) is the correct answer.

2. Cleopatra Clumsy held an ancient painting for many years in her home. It was a famous painting, which she was very fond of. During the time that Cleopatra lived, there was a terrible war that brought many soldiers into her town. The soldiers ransacked the village where she lived, and all of her belongings were taken, including the painting. She was forced out of her home, and her home was eventually burned to the ground. The soldiers were very proud of their work, and thought that the painting would be an impressive gift to their leader. Lazy Leader kept the painting for twenty years before realizing that the painting was in fact famous. He then sold the painting to a museum for millions of dollars.

Cleopatra's grandchild, Curious Carrie, knew of the painting, and that it was stolen several years ago. She saw that the painting was to be displayed in a local museum, and she verified that the painting was in fact that of her beloved grandmother. Will Carrie be able to successfully regain possession of the painting? Based on the court's decision in *Orkin v. Taylor*, which of the following is the most accurate statement?

(A) The painting was abandoned when Cleopatra allowed the soldiers to take it, therefore Carrie cannot now claim it

(B) Carrie would not be able to recover because the claim would likely be barred by the statute of limitations

(C) Carrie is entitled to the recovery of the famous painting because she sought to reclaim it immediately after she discovered she had a claim to the painting and the whereabouts of where the painting was

(D) Carrie cannot reclaim the painting because Lazy Leader possessed it for 20 years without a contest to its ownership

(E) Both (A) and (D)

ANSWER: The correct answer is (C). Choice (A) is incorrect because one who is imprisoned during war and in the process leaves behind property does not automatically abandon his property. (B) is wrong because the statute of limitations does not begin to run until the claimant knew or should have known about the claim to the work of art and where the work of art is located. (D) is incorrect because there are more requirements than possession for over ten years to claim adverse possession. (C) is correct because Carrie brought a claim when she discovered the adverse possession. Therefore, (E) is incorrect.

3. In the article "The Acclaim and Hazards of Being an International Artist" by Sherri Burr, why does the interviewee, Bill Arms, believe that "the world of art law is becoming more complex"?

(A) Art is complex and it is difficult to keep his success a secret

(B) An artist has to keep pursuing copycats in order to protect their works of art

(C) It is too easy for other people to copy famous works of art and pass it off as their own

(D) Both (A) and (B)

(E) None of the above

ANSWER: The correct answer is (C). Arms' statement is solely based on the issue of others copying his artwork and passing it off as their own. Therefore (A), (B), (D), and (E) are incorrect.

4. When does the Holocaust Victims Redress Act Apply?

(A) When a piece of artwork is stolen during times of war, and the original owner seeks to reclaim it

(B) Where an original owner forgets to claim ownership over an artwork stolen during World War II, but now wishes to recover it

(C) When a person has owned a painting in their possession for over ten years, and a person from the Nazi era wishes to reclaim it

(D) Where assets were confiscated from the claimant during the period of Nazi rule and there is reasonable proof that the claimant is the rightful owner

(E) None of the above

ANSWER: The correct answer is (D). The Redress Act states these elements as required for it to apply. (A) is incorrect because it does not apply to just any war. (B) is incorrect because the original owner forgetting about his or her works of art is irrelevant. (C) is incorrect because adverse possession is not applicable in this instance. (E) is incorrect because (D) is the correct answer.

5. Ian Importer wanted to bring a beautiful Picasso painting into the United States, but was aware that his great-grandfather had acquired it during World War II from a family he imprisoned. Ian wants to display the painting for everyone to see, but is afraid that it will be seized because of how his grandfather gained ownership over it. Will Ian Importer be able to protect his ownership over the Picasso Painting?

(A) No, if he brings the painting in, then it will be seized no matter what he tries to do

(B) Yes, if he brings the painting to the United States to be displayed in a cultural exhibition and is granted immunity by the President

(C) Yes, if Ian hides the fact that his grandfather obtained ownership over the painting during World War II

(D) No, but he will be able to appeal the seizure by the government, as long as his painting is seized because his grandfather was a bad soldier

(E) Both (B) and (C)

ANSWER: The correct answer is (B). Under 22 U.S.C. § 2459 (1981), the President may grant works of art immunity from seizure where they are brought into the United States for cultural exhibition. Thus, (A) is incorrect. (C) is incorrect because individuals can possibly determine ownership even if Ian hides this fact. (D) is incorrect because his grandfather being a bad soldier is irrelevant. (E) is incorrect because neither (B) nor (C) are correct answers for the above reasons.

11 INTERNATIONAL PRESERVATION OF ART AND CULTURAL PROPERTY

Art teaches us about civilizations and periods of history that we otherwise would never know. The preservation of art not only ensures society's continued enjoyment of it, but also provides valuable insights into the development of humanity.

A. Disputes over Art and Cultural Property

Disputes over art and cultural property can take place within a country or between two or more countries. Consider the examples in this section of the dispute between Greece and Great Britain over the Marbles of the Parthenon and the case decided by the High Court of India. The episode of the Marbles illustrates the divergent attitudes that exist concerning the relocation of national treasures from the country that created them. While over two centuries have passed since the incident occurred, the issues raised by it still have vitality.

The Erechtheum of the Acropolis of Athens in 1997[1]

---

1. Image: Sherri L. Burr, Cropped, revised, and resized thumbnail excerpt of a Sherri L. Burr photograph of the Erechtheum of the Acropolis of Athens (1997).

1. The Marbles of the Parthenon (The Elgin Marbles)

In 1779, while French troops were appropriating art treasures of the world for the Republic, Lord Elgin — England's envoy to Constantinople — was engaged in a similar project, albeit on a smaller geographical scale. Elgin's activities were somewhat distinguishable from those of the French, as he initially acted without the consent of the British Crown to gain access to the sculpture works still intact at the Parthenon, which at the time was a conquered territory of the Ottoman Empire. When Elgin first arrived in Constantinople, he obtained permission from the Turks to record, catalog, and sketch Greek antiquities. Nevertheless, he quickly became dissatisfied with mere sketches and resolved to obtain the antiquities themselves. With acquiescence from the local Turkish officials, Elgin's agents began the systematic removal of the Parthenon's treasures on the Acropolis in Athens.

Elgin originally planned to use the marbles to decorate his mansion, although, after personal and financial reverses, the marbles were offered to the British government for purchase. Issues relating to the marbles debated in the House of Commons on June 7, 1816,[2] are the same ones debated in the art world today. The proper resolution of the problem remains dependent upon one's philosophical view of the function of art in society. Elgin claimed that a right of export was granted by the permit to carry on excavations. His opponents alleged that there had been an abuse of Elgin's diplomatic office in his obtaining legalized plunder. Had Elgin not been the British Ambassador, they believed it unlikely that he could have secured whatever permission was given. Because certain gifts had been received by the Turks at the time the permit was granted, bribery was suggested.

Even if the permit had been given voluntarily, how much excavation did it authorize? When the issue was considered by Parliament, some members of the House of Commons objected. They argued that no reasonable interpretation of the firman from the Grand Vizir of the Ottomans sanctioned removal of statuary on the grand scale employed by Elgin. Even had the firman been validly obtained and permission given to despoil the Parthenon, was the current governing body bound by the decision of the previous leadership? At the time the firman was granted to Elgin, the Greeks were fighting their war for independence. After the Greeks defeated the Ottomans, should they be bound to uphold the plundering of Greek monuments authorized by the Ottoman Empire? Still other members viewed Elgin's excavation as the pillage of a nation's patrimony and advocated the return of these monuments. Various schemes were proposed to compensate Elgin while returning the marbles to the Parthenon.

In the House of Commons, proponents of the motion to purchase the marbles were outraged. . . . The House divided, with eighty-two for the

---

2. Debate in the House of Commons, June 7, 1816, reprinted in B. Hollander, *The International Law of Art* 293, Appen. IX (1959).

original motion and thirty against it.[3] In the same year, the statuary was purchased by the government for the British Museum.

Notes and Questions

1. In 1983, the Greek government formally requested that the marbles be returned to Greece and, in 1984, the British government refused to do so. The issue of where the Elgin marbles should be housed heated up again in 1993 when internal borders among the members of the European Community (EC) were removed. The Treaty of Rome, the EC's founding charter, permits art works to be freely traded within the Community. One exception, found in Article 36, is for national treasures, which may be retained by owner countries. *Greece Turns to EC to Regain Marbles*, The Times (London), July 4, 1991, at 1, col. 8.

2. In late 1993, the UN General Assembly passed a resolution calling for restitution of cultural treasures to their countries of origin; however, the British government maintained the Elgin Marbles were legally obtained. *UN Move Adds to Clamour over Elgin Marbles*, Press Association Newsfile, Nov. 2, 1993.

3. At a May 1997 seminar given by Professor and co-author Sherri L. Burr on "Protecting Cultural Property and Cultural Heritage as an International Right," law students at the University of Thrace in Greece told her that Greece "would be so much stronger today" if the marbles of the Parthenon had never left their country. Do you think that artwork can have that much impact on a country's soul? What pieces of art do you think symbolize your country? How would you and your classmates feel if that artwork was removed to another country?

4. In 1991, Greece proposed the Acropolis Museum in Athens should include a climate-controlled building that is half underground, built into the side of the hill beneath the Acropolis. Planners of the museum hoped that the British would consider it a "safe home" for the Elgin marbles, and would be persuaded to return them to Greece. *Italian to Design Acropolis Museum*, J. of Art, May 1991, at 23, col. 1. In 2009, after the completion of the new Acropolis Museum, the British Government offered to lend the marbles of the Parthenon back to Greece if Greece would acknowledge the title of the British. The Greek government declined. *See http://www.cbc.ca/world/story/2009/06/12/parthenon-marbles-loan.html.* So far, all repatriation efforts on the part of Greece have been in vain.

5. By 2012, Greek Antiquities had become endangered by financial austerity measures that required the government to force experienced state archaeologists into early retirement as part of a 10 percent staff reduction within

---

3. *Id.*

the government's Ministry of Culture. *See* Randy Kennedy, *Greek Antiquities, Long Fragile, Are Endangered by Austerity,* N.Y. Times, June 11, 2012.

2. The Indian High Court

Sehgal v. Union of India

2005 WL 2205308, [2005] F.S.R. 39 (India High Court, 21 Feb. 2005)*

Pradeep NANDRAJOG, J.:

. . . The plaintiff's pleadings takes one back to the year 1957. A peep behind the pleadings would take us back to the early fifties.

India was a nascent democracy. The world was divided into two camps: the American camp and the Soviet Russian camp. Pt. Jawahar Lal Nehru, the first Prime Minister of this country, a man of vision, realised that to be non-aligned was the best policy. India, under the leadership of Pt. Jawahar Lal Nehru was a pioneer of the non-aligned movement. Fledgling India was asserting itself in the community of nations. International delegations were frequenting the territory of India. Conferences had to be held. Large numbers of delegates had to be accommodated. A building was conceived to be the hub of international and national conferences. It was named "Vigyan Bhawan." In the note to the Cabinet Secretary, V.N. Sukthankar recorded in file No. 2 (223)/48-PMS Jawahar Lal Nehru wrote:

> The Central Government as well as the State Governments are putting up many public buildings. Some of these buildings are big and imposing structures, like the building for the Supreme Court or the Theatre, or the big structure now on the point of completion which is meant for the expansion of the Central Secretariat.
>
> I think that all these major buildings should encourage Indian artists to function in some way. Sculptors, painters, designers, etc could be asked to cooperate. There might occasionally be woven tapestries. This will cost very little in comparison with the total cost of the building. But it will encourage Indian artists and would be generally welcome, I think, by the public.[4]

The brick, mortar, and concrete structure named "Vigyan Bhawan" may have been an architectural feat, imbibing the science of construction, but the building was too lifeless. It needed a soul.

What better soul could a building have other than being endowed with the cultural heritage of India. After all, Vigyan Bhawan was conceived to house international conferences and ought, therefore, to have reflected India's cultural heritage. [The plaintiff, Amar Nath Sehgal, received a communication from the Central Public Works Department offering him a commission. The plaintiff accepted and built a bronze mural sculpture, which he alleged acquired the status of a national treasure, representing the essential part of

---

* Most footnotes and all paragraph numbers deleted.
4. Refer to selected works of Jawahar Lal Nehru (2d series, Vol. 26, 1954).

Indian Art heritage. After the Indian government removed the mural from public view, the plaintiff sued claiming his rights were violated under Indian copyright law and cultural property law.] ...

It has to be noted that as originally enacted, § 57 of the Copyright Act 1957 was very widely worded because of the fact that the words "would be prejudicial to his honour or reputation" which found mention in subcl. (b) of subs. (1) of § 57 were not qualifying subcl. (a) of subs. (1) of § 57. Further, the words "any other action" which found mention in subcl. (b) implied that the action could be other than a claim for damages or a claim for injunction. .... [A]s the section stands effective from May 10, 1995, the legislature has restricted the right of the author to claim damages or to seek an order of restraint. Further, proof of prejudice to the author's honour or reputation has been made the sine qua non for claiming damages.

However, the various declarations by the international community in the conventions noted above, lift the moral rights in works of art if the same acquire the status of cultural heritage of a nation. India is a signatory to the conventions and it would be the obligation of the State to honour its declarations.

There would therefore be urgent need to interpret § 57 of the Copyright Act 1957 in its wider amplitude to include destruction of a work of art, being the extreme form of mutilation, since by reducing the volume of the author's creative corpus it affects his reputation prejudicially as being actionable under said section. Further, in relation to the work of an author, subject to the work attaining the status of a modern national treasure, the right would include an action to protect the integrity of the work in relation to the cultural heritage of the nation.

Under orders passed by this Court, the physical condition of the mural in question was directed to be reported. Shri B.C. Sanyal, an artist of international repute and Professor P.N. Mago reported that various parts were missing. Their report reveals a massive destruction of the mural. Ms. Kapila Vatsyayan, Academic Director, Indira Gandhi National Center for the Arts reported that she was pained to see an outstanding artistic composition dismembered in fragments which could not be put together even in part.

In view of the evidence on record, Ms. Jyoti Singh, learned counsel for the defendants did not even attempt to urge that the destruction and damage to the mural was debatable.

Issues No. 2 and 3 are accordingly decided in favour of the plaintiff and against the defendants. It is held that the plaintiff has a cause to maintain an action under § 57 of the Copyright Act 1957 notwithstanding that the copyright in the mural stands vested in the defendants. It is further held that the defendants have not only violated the plaintiff's moral right of integrity in the mural but have also violated the integrity of the work in relation to the cultural heritage of the nation. ....

I am of the opinion that the mural, whatever be its form today, is too precious to be reduced to scrap and languish in the warehouse of the Government of India. It is only the plaintiff who has a right to recreate his work and, therefore, has a right to receive the broken up mural. The plaintiff also has a right to be compensated for loss of reputation, honour and mental injury due to the offending acts of the defendants.

Suit is accordingly decreed in favour of the plaintiff and against the defendants as under:

(a) A mandatory injunction directing the defendants to return to the plaintiff the remnants of the mural within 2 weeks from today;

(b) Declaration is granted in favour of the plaintiff and against the defendants that all rights in the mural shall henceforth vest in the plaintiff and the defendants would have no right whatsoever in the mural;

(c) Declaration is granted in favour of the plaintiff that he would have an absolute right to recreate the mural at any place and would have the right to sell the same;

(d) Damages in the sum of Rs.5 lacs are awarded in favour of the plaintiff and against the defendants. If not paid within one month from today, the damages shall carry simple interest at 9 per cent per annum from today till date of payment;

(e) Costs shall follow in favour of the plaintiff and against the defendants. . . .

I would be failing if I do not put on record the assistance rendered to the court by Shri Praveen Anand, learned counsel for the plaintiff, who argued the matter virtually on first principles and enriched the court with material to understand the profound issue raised in the suit, which required a synthesis of personal rights vis-a-vis the cultural rights of the nation.

B. National Regulation of Cultural Property

Many concerned nations have enacted laws to control the flow of cultural property. This section examines national legislation enacted unilaterally regarding both the export and import of works of art.

1. General Export Restrictions

A vast majority of countries have some form of export restriction on works of art. While existing export restriction laws differ in many respects, they can, nevertheless, be divided into two categories: screening or selective enforcement and across-the-board or complete prohibition. These countervailing philosophies often appear on the face of the statute or occasionally are determined by the manner in which the law is applied.

2. Import Restrictions

In addition to export restrictions, another means of national control is the use of import barriers. Although many countries regulate the export of works of art, until recently most did not regulate their import.[5] The United States, as the largest art market in the world, has been particularly reluctant to place restrictions on the import of art or antiquities.[6] Such reluctance has been attributed to the perception that the result would be increases in both the price of art and black market trade.[7] The United States restricts the entry of works of art only where the specific provisions of a bilateral or multilateral treaty to which it is a signatory requires. Where no legal restrictions are in effect, there still may be economic barriers to the importation of works of art in some countries in the form of import duties. For example, until 1958, an import duty had to be paid on most works of art entering the United States.

An importing nation can refuse to admit works of art that have been illegally exported from another country. This approach requires only unilateral action. One example of this form of legislation is the Regulation of Importation of Pre-Columbian Monumental or Architectural Sculpture or Murals.[8] This U.S. statute not only denies entry to a prescribed category of art, but goes further to provide a means by which the country of origin can recover the object in question.[9] In 1978, the U.S. Customs Service amended its regulations on the importation of pre-Columbian art to clarify that unless specifically permitted, "no pre-Columbian monumental or architectural sculpture or mural which is exported (whether or not such exportation is to the United States) from its country of origin after June 1, 1973, may be imported into the United States."[10]

C. Pre-Columbian Art

In the Americas, the illegal traffic in pre-Columbian antiquities has stripped Central America, from Mexico to Peru, of countless artifacts from a culture that once flourished in that region. The pillaging of Central America is the work of thieves who feed a seemingly insatiable world appetite for pre-Columbian artifacts.

The looting and resultant destruction has seriously hindered the efforts of archaeologists seeking to unravel the mysteries of an ancient civilization. Not only do the Mayan articles lose much of their archaeological significance when removed from their sites, but many of the artifacts are sent "underground" to

---

5. *See* Jore, *The Illicit Movement of Art and Artifact*, 13 Brook. J. Int'l L. 55 (1987) [hereinafter Jore].
6. Antonio, *The Current Status of the International Art Trade*, 10 Suffolk Transnat'l L.J. 51, 72 (1986).
7. *Id.*
8. Regulation of Importation of Pre-Columbian Monumental or Architectural Sculpture or Murals, 19 U.S.C. §§ 2091 et seq. (1989).
9. *Id.* at § 2093(b).
10. 19 C.F.R. § 12.106 (1998).

private collections, which afford scholars no access. Often, those articles that can be studied are of little value.

Dealers in pre-Columbian art often use local peasants who are familiar with the jungle. In areas with minimal daily wages, it is not difficult to hire men to remove Mayan relics. Because a stela may have value exceeding $100,000 on the international art market, the incentive to locate ruins is significant. Efforts by local authorities to prevent looting are inadequate. There is simply insufficient economic power behind the efforts of these countries for them to succeed in blocking the illegal exportation of their artistic heritage.

United States v. McClain

545 F.2d 988 (5th Cir. 1977)*

WISDOM, Circuit Judge.

Museum directors, art dealers, and innumerable private collectors throughout this country must have been in a state of shock when they read the news if they did of the convictions of the five defendants in this case. . . . The defendants were indicted under the National Stolen Property Act, 18 U.S.C. §§ 2314, 2315, and were convicted of conspiring to transport and receiving through interstate commerce certain pre-Columbian artifacts (terra cotta figures and pottery, beads, and a few stucco pieces) knowing these artifacts to have been stolen. These articles had not been registered with the Public Register of Archaeological and Historical Zones and Monuments of the Republic of Mexico, or with any government register, and were exported without a license or a permit from Mexico into the United States. The district court instructed the jury that "since 1897 Mexican law has declared pre-Columbian artifacts . . . to be the property of the Republic of Mexico, except in instances where the Government" has issued a license or permit to private persons to possess, transfer, or export the artifacts. This instruction casts a cloud on the title of almost every pre-Columbian object in the United States. This Court, of course, recognizes the sovereign right of Mexico to declare, by legislative fiat, that it is the owner of its art, archaeological, or historic national treasures, or of whatever is within its jurisdiction; possession is but a frequent incident, not the sine qua non of ownership, in the common law or the civil law. The district court's instruction was erroneous. Not until 1972 did Mexico enact a law declaring all archaeological objects within its jurisdiction, movables and immovables, to be the property of the Nation. We reverse and remand.

I

The National Stolen Property Act (NSPA) prohibits the transportation (in interstate or foreign commerce (of) any goods, . . . of the value of $5,000 or more," with knowledge that such goods were "stolen, converted or taken by

---

* Footnotes omitted.

fraud." 18 U.S.C. § 2314. The Act also subjects to criminal liability "whoever receives, conceals, stores, barters, sells, or disposes of any goods . . . of the value of $5,000 or more . . . moving as, or which are part of, or which constitute interstate or foreign commerce, knowing the same to have been stolen, unlawfully converted, or taken. . . ." 18 U.S.C. § 2315. The case turns on whether the pre-Columbian antiquities in question, exported from Mexico in contravention of that country's law, were knowingly "stolen" within the meaning of the National Stolen Property Act.

Patty McClain, Joseph M. Rodriguez, Ada Eveleigh Simpson, William Clark Simpson, and Mike Bradshaw, the defendants-appellants, were all convicted by a jury of conspiring to transport, receive, and sell assorted stolen pre-Columbian artifacts in interstate commerce, in violation of 18 U.S.C. §§ 2314, 2315, and 371. The appellants were also convicted of receiving, concealing, bartering, and selling these items in violation of § 2315. Additionally, Rodriguez was convicted of the transportation of the items in interstate commerce (from Calexico, California to San Antonio, Texas) in violation of § 2314.

Many of the relevant facts are not in serious dispute. The evidence showed that all of the defendants except Rodriguez were involved in negotiations leading to the sale of various pre-Columbian artifacts to prosecution witness John McGauley, an undercover agent of the Federal Bureau of Investigation.

The government presented no evidence as to how and when the artifacts were acquired in Mexico, nor as to when the pieces were exported.

Mrs. Adalina Diaz Zambrano, an employee of the Mexican Cultural Institute in San Antonio, Texas, testified that Rodriguez had approached Albert Mijangos, the Director of the Institute, with a proposal to sell various artifacts. The Institute was an official arm of the Mexican government, a fact unknown to Rodriguez. Mrs. Zambrano identified, from photographs, artifacts later seized by the government from the other appellants as some of the artifacts shown to her and Mijangos by Rodriguez. In Rodriguez's attempt to sell artifacts to the Institute and in the other defendants' attempt to sell artifacts to McGauley and an informer, some of the defendants made statements showing that they were aware that Mexican law forbade the exportation of artifacts without permits from the Mexican government. After agreeing to a purchase price of $115,000 for the artifacts held in San Antonio, defendants Simpson and Bradshaw brought McGauley to Los Angeles to view other pre-Columbian artifacts. Bradshaw and Simpson told McGauley that they expected to realize about $850,000 for the Los Angeles artifacts. Before a final price was agreed upon they were arrested. The other defendants were arrested in San Antonio.

The defendants do not dispute that the artifacts involved in this case were illegally exported from Mexico. The government contends that the pre-Columbian artifacts were stolen from the Republic of Mexico; that Mexico owned these objects despite the probability or possibility that the defendants, or their vendors, acquired them from private individuals or "found" them e.g., by accident in overturning the soil or digging at archaeological sites on private property in Mexico.

The primary evidence as to the ownership of the artifacts under Mexican law was the testimony of Dr. Alejandro Gertz, a deputy attorney general of

Mexico. He was qualified as an expert on Mexican law without objection. Dr. Gertz had been instrumental in revising Mexican laws dealing with protection of the Mexican cultural heritage and, at the time of trial, his official duties included enforcing that law. Gertz testified that Mexico has had laws protecting its cultural heritage since 1897 and that the most recent modification of those laws was a 1972 statute. Gertz testified that the ownership of pre-Columbian artifacts has been vested by law in the Mexican government since 1897, . . . despite the fact that private individuals have been allowed to possess such items. Since 1934, individuals possessing pre-Columbian artifacts have been required to register them with the government. Export permits have been required since 1934, although since then only 50 to 70 permits have been issued. A check by Gertz of the records of the National Institute of Anthropology and History showed that the defendants had neither registered nor received permission to export the artifacts found in their possession in the United States. Finally, he testified that under Mexican law pre-Columbian artifacts which are removed from Mexico without permit are considered stolen.

Dr. Richard E. Adams, a Professor of Anthropology and Dean of Humanities and Social Studies at the University of Texas in San Antonio, Texas, testified as the other government expert on pre-Columbian artifacts. He testified that Mexican law with respect to pre-Columbian artifacts had not changed in two generations. As will be seen in Section III of this opinion, this belief was erroneous. He testified that some of the artifacts in question were from Guatemala, Honduras, Panama, and Costa Rica, and some were fakes.

The trial court declined to appoint an expert and also an interpreter, as requested by the defendant Rodriguez.

The trial judge instructed the jury that, before it could find any defendant guilty, it had to find beyond a reasonable doubt that the property described in the indictment was "stolen." The judge informed the jury that

> stolen means acquired or possessed as a result of some wrongful or dishonest act of taking, whereby a person willfully obtains or retains possession of property which belongs to another, without or beyond any permission given, and with the intent to deprive the benefits of ownership and use.

Basing his charge on Mexican law as explained by Dr. Gertz, the trial judge instructed the jury that

> since 1897 Mexican law has declared pre-Columbian artifacts recovered from the Republic of Mexico within its borders to be the property of the Republic of Mexico, except in instances where the Government of the Republic of Mexico has, by way of license or permit, granted permission to private persons or parties or others to receive and export in their possession such artifacts to other places or other countries.

This erroneous instruction is discussed in Section III of this opinion.

II

The apparent purpose of Congress in enacting stolen property statutes was to discourage both the receiving of stolen goods and the initial taking. . . . Such discouragement was, of course, intended to aid the states, which, because of jurisdictional limitations, could not prosecute the receivers or thieves of stolen property after that property moved across state lines. . . . The ultimate beneficiary of the law, of course, is the property owner who thereby enjoys greater governmental protection of property rights.

Sections 2314 and 2315 refer not only to interstate commerce, but to foreign commerce as well. It is no surprise, then, that the NSPA has been applied to thefts in foreign countries and subsequent transportations into the United States. *See United States v. Rabin*, 7 Cir. 1963, 316 F.2d 564, *cert. denied*, 375 U.S. 315, 84 S. Ct. 48, 11 L. Ed. 2d 50; *United States v. Greco*, 2 Cir. 1962, 298 F.2d 247, *cert. denied*, 369 U.S. 820, 82 S. Ct. 831, 7 L. Ed. 2d 785; *United States v. Hollinshead*, 9 Cir. 1974, 495 F.2d 1154. The Republic of Mexico, when stolen property has moved across the Mexican border, is in a similar position to any state of the United States in which a theft occurs and the property is moved across state boundaries.

First, the appellants contend that application of the National Stolen Property Act to cases of mere illegal exportation constitutes unwarranted federal enforcement of foreign law. They argue that the word "stolen" cannot include the pre-Columbian artifacts seized in this case, for there was no evidence showing that the artifacts had been taken without consent from private individuals or that the artifacts had been in the possession of the Republic of Mexico. Mexican legislative declarations of "ownership" of pre-Columbian artifacts are, the appellants say, not enough to bring the objects within the protection of the NSPA; "possession is the beginning of ownership." . . . This United States statute, the appellants argue, employs the term "stolen" to cover only acts which result in the wrongful deprivation of rights of "ownership" as that term is understood at common law.

Second, the appellants contend that, even if a legislative declaration of ownership would, with export restrictions, invoke the protection of the NSPA, the trial court erred in instructing the jury that Mexico had, since 1897, vested itself with ownership of all pre-Columbian artifacts.

Our consideration of the meaning of the term "stolen" best begins with *United States v. Turley*, 1957, 352 U.S. 407, 411, 77 S. Ct. 397, 1 L. Ed. 2d 430. There the Supreme Court was called upon to determine the meaning of that term as used in the Motor Vehicle Theft Act, . . . which prohibits the interstate transportation of "stolen" vehicles. The Court, pointing out that the word "stolen" has no accepted common law meaning and is not a term of art, . . . concluded that "stolen" does not refer exclusively to larcenously taken automobiles; instead, a vehicle that had been rightfully acquired but wrongfully converted by a bailee was held to be "stolen" within the meaning of the Act.

The Turley Court cited with approval two National Stolen Property Act cases that had also given the word "stolen" broad scope. *See Crabb v. Zerbst*,

5 Cir. 1939, 99 F.2d 562, 565; *United States v. Handler*, 2 Cir. 1944, 142 F.2d 351, *cert. denied*, 323 U.S. 741, 65 S. Ct. 40, 89 L. Ed. 594. . . . Both cases held that embezzled property was stolen within the meaning of the Act. In *Crabb*, we observed that "stealing" is commonly used to denote any dishonest transaction whereby one person obtains that which rightfully belongs to another and deprives the owner of the rights and benefits of ownership. Post-*Turley* cases have continued to give the term "stolen" a wide-ranging meaning. . . .

Thus, on one side of the argument we have a federal criminal statute that has been given an expansive scope. On the other side of that argument rests a doctrine of construction fundamental to a society in which governmental interest must be balanced against regard for individual liberty. It is not yet too ritualistic a practice to observe that, throughout our jurisprudence, the courts have considered that "ambiguity concerning the ambit of criminal statutes should be resolved in favor of lenity." *Rewis v. United States*, 1971, 401 U.S. 808, 91 S. Ct. 1056, 28 L. Ed. 2d 493. The rule that penal laws are to be construed strictly, is, perhaps, not much less old than construction itself. It is founded on the tenderness of the law for the rights of individuals. . . . This ancient precept has continued vitality.

Of course, the doctrine of strict construction is not absolute. "(T)he intention of the law-maker must govern in the construction of penal, as well (as) other statutes." *Id. See also Garrett v. United States*, 5 Cir. 1968, 396 F.2d 489, 491, *cert. denied*, 393 U.S. 952, 89 S. Ct. 374, 21 L. Ed. 2d 364; *United States v. Mikelberg*, 5 Cir. 1975, 517 F.2d 246, 252. We cannot accept, therefore, the appellants' initial argument by referring to the doctrine.

Nor can the issue in this case be resolved by suggesting that an affirmance condones unwarranted federal enforcement of foreign law. Congress chose to protect property owners living in states or countries hampered by their borders from effectively providing their own protection. The question posed, then, is not whether the federal government will enforce a foreign nation's export law, . . . or whether property brought into this country in violation of another country's exportation law is stolen property. The question is whether this country's own statute, the NSPA, covers property of a very special kind purportedly government owned, yet potentially capable of being privately possessed when acquired by purchase or discovery. Our examination of Mexican law leads us to reject the appellants' argument that the NSPA cannot apply to illegal exportation of artifacts declared by Mexican law to be the property of the Nation.

We do not base this conclusion on illegal exportation of the antiquities. Professor Bator correctly states the law applicable to violations of export laws:

> The general rule today in the United States, and I think in almost all other art-importing countries, is that it is not a violation of law to import simply because an item has been illegally exported from another country. This is a fundamental general rule today with respect to art importation. . . . This means that a person who imports a work of art which has been illegally exported is not for that reason alone actionable, and the possession of that work cannot for that reason alone be disturbed in the United States. . . .

This general rule has been qualified by congressional statute and by treaties. . . . But we cannot say that the intent of any statute, treaty, or general policy of encouraging the importation of art more than 100 years old was to narrow the National Stolen Property Act so as to make it inapplicable to art objects or artifacts declared to be the property of another country and illegally imported into this country.

III

The government's expert on Mexican law testified, and the trial court instructed the jury, that Mexico has, since 1897, vested itself with ownership of pre-Columbian artifacts. This testimony and the subsequent instruction, as we pointed out, were in error. Mexican law has been concerned with the preservation and regulation of pre-Columbian artifacts since 1897, but ownership of all pre-Columbian objects by legislative fiat, did not come until much later. When it did come, it came, not at once, but in stages. . . .

Article 1 of the Law on Archaeological Monuments, May 11, 1897, . . . did indeed declare that "archaeological monuments" were "the property of the Nation" and that no one could "remove them . . . without express authorization of the Executive of the Union." Archaeological monuments were defined to mean "ruins of cities, Big Houses (Casas Grandes), troglodytic dwellings, fortifications, palaces, temples, pyramids, sculpted rocks or those with inscriptions, and in general all the edifices that in any aspect may be interesting for the study of civilization and the history of the ancient settlors of Mexico." The class of objects involved in this case was covered by Article 6, which provided that

> Mexican antiquities, codices, idols, amulets, and other objects or movable things that the Federal Executive deems interesting for the study of the civilization and history of the aboriginals and ancient settlers of America and especially of Mexico, cannot be exported without legal authorization.

Nothing in this article constitutes a declaration of ownership. The 1897 law distinguishes between "antiquities . . . or movable things," which are subject to export restrictions, and archaeological monuments. Moreover, even with respect to movable artifacts ("antiquities, codices, idols, amulets and other objects or movable things"), the Federal Executive was obliged first to declare those objects "interesting" for studies of Mexican civilization and history for these objects to be subject to the export regulation under Article 6. We note too that the antiquities were not considered "immovables by destination," a category familiar to civilians.

The next major Mexican law pertaining to pre-Columbian artifacts was the Law on the Protection and Conservation of Monuments and Natural Beauty, January 31, 1930. . . . This law set up a more complicated system of controlling objects of "artistic, archaeological, or historical value." These objects, both movable and immovable, "whose protection and conservation may be of public interest" because of such value, were declared "monuments." Art. 1.

For an object to acquire status as a "monument," however, the object either would have to come into the care of the Secretariat of Public Education or be declared a "monument" by the Department of Artistic, Archaeological, and Historical Monuments, which was instructed to make the declaration "with precision." Art. 6. But the 1930 law implicitly recognized the right to private ownership of monuments and expressly allowed monuments to be freely alienated, subject to the government's right of first refusal. . . . Art. 16. Most significantly, ownership was not among the rights the government declared for itself in monuments. The 1930 law was the first to place export restrictions on all objects of the type here involved. The law prohibited the exportation of movables and immovables by destination which had been officially designated as "archaeological monuments," but permitted the exportation of other objects of archaeological value with official permission. Art. 19, 20. This law, therefore, is very different from the law of 1897.

The next relevant enactment came in the Law for the Protection and Preservation of Archaeological and Historic Monuments, Typical Towns and Places of Scenic Beauty, January 19, 1934. . . . Again, "monuments" were regulated and were defined as objects "of archaeological origin and . . . whose protection and preservation are in the public interest, owning to . . . historical value." Art. 1. The 1930 definition of monuments was significantly expanded, however, for the law declared that "all vestiges of the aboriginal civilization dating from before the completion of the Conquest shall be considered as archaeological monuments." Art. 3. The law then declared that

> [a]ll immovable archaeological monuments belong to the nation. Objects which are found (in or on) immovable archaeological monuments are considered as immovable property, and they therefore belong to the Nation.

Art. 4 (emphasis added). . . .

It is still clear that not all pre-Columbian artifacts were declared "owned" by the Mexican government. The 1934 law specifically recognized private ownership of archaeological movables. Article 9 required the "Register of Private Archaeological Property" to maintain a record of movable artifacts "that are the property of private individuals at the time of this law's entry into force and for those which they may legally acquire in the future." No records were maintained, therefore, before 1934. Article 10 recognized that "transfers of ownership: ("propiedad") may be made by the owners of registered objects, but required the transfers to be recorded. The artifacts found in or on immovable monuments form a subset of the set of all pre-Columbian artifacts; those artifacts not in the subclass were not owned by Mexico.

The next Mexican law in this area was the Federal Law Concerning Cultural Patrimony of the Nation, December 16, 1970. . . . This law again declared pre-Columbian archaeological immovables and movables found in or on . . . immovable archaeological objects to be the Cultural Patrimony of the Nation. Art. 52. Such objects could not be permanently exported. Art. 96. The law recognized private ownership of other movable artifacts, while continuing the scheme of registration established by the 1934 Act. Art. 54; Transitory Art. Fifth. Article 54 declares that movable artifacts which are not "unique, rare specimens or of exceptional value for their esthetic quality or for their other cultural qualities . . . can be the object of transfer of ownership." Article 55 creates a presumption that the unregistered movable archaeological objects are "the property of the Nation."

The statutory law shows, therefore, that Mexico did not assert ownership of all pre-Columbian artifacts in 1934. The same situation existed in 1970, when the next law was enacted. Even ethnological, anthropological, and paleontological pieces, which were defined as "articles of cultural value," Art. 3, and were ascribed to the "Cultural Patrimony of the Nation" were capable of being privately owned. See Arts. 17, 37. . . .

Finally, we come to the Federal Law on Archaeological, Artistic and Historic Monuments and Zones, May 6, 1972. . . . Article 27 provides that "[a]rchaeological monuments, movables and immovables, are the inalienable and imprescriptible property of the Nation." Article 28 then establishes that

> [m]ovable and immovable objects, products of the cultures prior to the establishment of the Spanish culture in the National Territory, . . . are archaeological monuments.

This law unequivocally establishes for the first time what Dr. Gertz testified had been the case since 1897. Only after the effective date of the 1972 law would the Republic of Mexico necessarily have ownership of the objects such as the artifacts involved in this case. This legislation "extended national ownership of the cultural patrimony to private collections and forbade absolutely the export of pre-Columbian items." . . . The law was adopted only after "a bitter constitutional debate" over the extension of public control over private property. . . . A grandfather clause protected pre-existing private ownership rights. Transitory Article Fourth. Moreover, Article 22 requires individuals to register monuments "of their ownership."

The Amicus states that this view is confirmed by the formal opinion of the Mexican Bar, which reviewed the 1972 statute prior to its enactment. See opinion de la Barra Mexicana Sobre La Iniciativa de Ley Federal Sobre Monumentos Arqueologicos, artisticos, Historicos y Zonas Monumentales (Opinion of the Mexican Bar on the Proposed Federal Law on Archaeological, Artistic, and Historical Monuments and Monument Zones), 5 El Foro No. 26 (Organo de la Barra Mexicana, Colegio de Abogados) 121, 124-25 (abril-junio, 1972): ". . . the Laws (prior to 1972) . . . established public ownership or general use only over archaeological immovable monuments and . . . movables found on them. . . . [I]t is of major relevance to point out that all this legislation permitted, recognized and protected private ownership over movable archeological monuments. . . ." (Translation from the Spanish, emphasis supplied.) . . .

We find as a matter of law that the district court erred by instructing the jury in accordance with Dr. Gertz's testimony. See Fed. R. Crim. P. 26.1 (Determination of Foreign Law); cf. First National City Bank v. Campania de Aguaceras, S.A., 5 Cir. 1968, 398 F.2d 779, 781-82.

The court's instruction that the Mexican government had owned the artifacts for over seventy-five years was highly prejudicial to the defendants. It could have been the decisive factor in the jury's inferring that the defendants must have known that the artifacts in question were stolen.

IV

This review of the relevant Mexican statutes demonstrates that the Mexican government has, since 1897, been staking out for itself greater and greater rights in pre-Columbian artifacts. Only in 1972, however, did the government declare that all pre-Columbian artifacts were owned by the Republic. We hold that a declaration of national ownership is necessary before illegal exportation of an article can be considered theft, and the exported article considered "stolen," within the meaning of the National Stolen Property Act. . . . Such a declaration combined with a restriction on exportation without consent of the owner (Mexico) is sufficient to bring the NSPA into play. . . .

We summarize, then, how these conclusions square with Mexican law as we understand it. In order to say whether any of the pre-Columbian movable artifacts were "stolen," it is necessary to know first when that artifact was exported from Mexico. . . . If the exportation occurred after the effective date of the 1972 law, the artifact may have been stolen but only if it were not legitimately in the seller's hands as a result of prior law. (Transitory Article Fourth.) If the exportation occurred before 1972, but after the effective date of the 1934 law, it would be necessary to show that the artifact was found on or in an immovable archaeological monument. If the exportation occurred before the effective date of the 1934 law, it could not have been owned by the Mexican government, and illegal exportation would not, therefore, subject the receiver of the article to the strictures of the National Stolen Property Act. Because the jury was not told that it had to determine when the pre-Columbian artifacts had been exported from Mexico and to apply the applicable Mexican law to that exportation, convictions of all the appellants must be reversed. . . .

The convictions are reversed. The cases are remanded for further proceedings not inconsistent with this opinion.

PROBLEM 11-1

> Escalating art prices spur the ambition of those who would acquire art without regard to its source. Would the advent of more restrictive laws or more effective protection of a country's cultural property merely increase the relative market price, or can such actions stop illegal traffic in stolen art? Prepare a one-page analysis of this question.

Another nation wrestling with export prohibitions is Peru. The Peruvian government, in 1929, passed legislation nationalizing most of the pre-Columbian artifacts found in that country. Further, it laid claim to collections of artifacts held in the United States.

Government of Peru v. Johnson

720 F. Supp. 810 (C.D. Cal. 1989)*

GRAY, District Judge.

The Government of Peru, plaintiff in this action, contends that it is the legal owner of eighty-nine artifacts that have been seized by the United States Customs Service from defendant Benjamin Johnson. The plaintiff charges the defendant with conversion of these articles and seeks an order for their return. Judgment will be rendered for the defendant.

Irrespective of the decision in this matter, the court has considerable sympathy for Peru with respect to the problems that it confronts as manifested by this litigation. It is evident that many priceless and beautiful pre-Columbian artifacts excavated from historical monuments in that country have been and are being smuggled abroad and sold to museums and other collectors of art. Such conduct is destructive of a major segment of the cultural heritage of Peru, and the plaintiff is entitled to the support of the courts of the United States in its determination to prevent further looting of its patrimony.

However, there is substantial evidence that Mr. Johnson purchased the subject items in good faith over the years, and the plaintiff must overcome legal and factual burdens that are heavy indeed before the court can justly order the subject items to be removed from the defendant's possession and turned over to the plaintiff. The trial of this action has shown that the plaintiff simply cannot meet these burdens.

1. THE PLAINTIFF CANNOT ESTABLISH THAT THE SUBJECT ARTIFACTS WERE EXCAVATED IN MODERN DAY PERU

The plaintiff has no direct evidence that any of the subject items came from Peru. It alleges, on information and belief, that they were taken from Peru or excavated from archeological sites in that country. The plaintiff's principal witness was Dr. Francisco Iriarte, who, according to the plaintiff's counsel, is Peru's foremost archeologist in Pre-Columbian artifacts. Dr. Iriarte examined each of the eighty-nine artifacts and in almost every instance asserted that he recognized it as an item of Peruvian style and culture, and he usually asserted the belief that it came from a particular excavation site or specific area in Peru. I have no doubt that Dr. Iriarte has seen artifacts taken from those respective locations that are very similar to the items that he was examining in court. However, Dr. Iriarte admitted that Peruvian pre-Columbian culture spanned not only modern day Peru, but also areas that now are within the

---

* Footnotes omitted.

borders of Bolivia and Ecuador, and many of the population centers that were part of the Peruvian pre-Columbian civilization, and from which artifacts have been taken, are within those countries. The fact that the subject items are identifiable with excavation sites in modern Peru does not exclude the possibility that they are equally similar to artifacts found in archeological monuments in Bolivia and Ecuador. Indeed, the evidence shows that at least one of the subject items is very similar to a figure depicted in a photograph that appears in an article concerning the cultural anthropology of Ecuador.

Moreover, Colombia also borders Peru, and customs documents that appear to pertain to some of the subject items assert Colombia to be the country of origin. Such an assertion is, of course, hearsay and, even though the documents may be business records kept in ordinary course, they should not be given great weight. However, they do further point up the difficulty that the court has in concluding that any specific one of the items concerned in this action originated within the present boundaries of Peru.

I was impressed by Dr. Iriarte's testimony. He doubtless is knowledgeable in his field and honest in his beliefs. He also has a genuine interest in helping his country recover artifacts that are such an important part of its patrimony, and this desire necessarily plays a part in his conclusions as to the origins of the objects at issue. In some instances, he admitted that an item may have come from Ecuador or Colombia or Mexico or even Polynesia, but nonetheless retained the opinion that it had been found in a particular area of Peru, due to its similarity to other objects taken from that site. Because of the many other possibilities, this court cannot base a finding of ownership upon such subjective conclusions. We are far from certain as to the country of origin of any of the artifacts here concerned. This unfortunate circumstance precludes an adjudication that they came from Peru.

2. THE PLAINTIFF CANNOT ESTABLISH ITS OWNERSHIP AT THE TIME OF EXPORTATION

Even if it were to be assumed that the artifacts came from Peru, in order for the plaintiff to recover them, it must prove that the Government of Peru was the legal owner at the time of their removal from that country. Such ownership depends upon the laws of Peru, which are far from precise and have changed several times over the years.

(a) 1822-1929

The plaintiff, in its Second Post Trial Brief, submitted for the first time copies of the statutes upon which it relies to establish that, from 1822 to the present time, Peru owned the artifacts located in that country. However, in its pleadings, its responses to discovery requests, and its pretrial memoranda, the plaintiff identified Law No. 6634 of June 13, 1929, as the earliest enactment that formed the legal basis for its ownership claims. Federal Rule of Civil Procedure 44.1 provides that "[a] party who intends to raise an issue concerning the law of a foreign country shall give notice by pleadings or other reasonable written notice." I find that initial presentation of these purported pre-1929 enactments after the case has been tried cannot constitute "reasonable notice," and I decline to consider them in rendering this decision.

In any event, the plaintiff's present reliance upon pre-1929 law is substantially undercut by the trial testimony of its expert witness on Peruvian law, Roberto MacLean, a former Chief Justice of the Supreme Court of that country. In response to a question regarding Peru's statutes concerning government ownership of pre-Columbian artifacts, he said: "even though there are several rules which have some academic importance but for all practical purposes the first law is from 1929; if I recall correctly from 13 of June of 1929."

The defendant's expert, Professor Alan Sawyer, whose qualifications concerning artifacts are comparable to those of Dr. Iriarte, testified that it is impossible to determine from examination of the items here concerned when they were excavated or left the country of origin, and that many Peruvian artifacts were brought into the United States before 1929. It follows that if any of the subject items left Peru before 1929, the plaintiff cannot claim ownership of them.

(b) 1929-1985

A written opinion by Professor MacLean asserts that what Law No. 6634 means "is that if a person found an archeological object before June of 1929 this object belongs to him; but if that person found the object after June 1929 it belongs to the State." Article 11 of Law No. 6634 provides that privately owned pre-Columbian artifacts must be registered in a special book "which shall be opened at the National Museum of History," and that any "[o]bjects which, after one year beginning on the day the book is opened, have not been registered, shall be considered the property of the State."

From the record at the trial, I cannot determine when the "special book" called for by Article 11 was opened or whether it ever has been opened. Interrogatory No. 9, propounded to the plaintiff by the defendant, asks for the date or approximate date upon which the special book was "opened"; the response was that "[t]his date is unknown." The plaintiff submitted a supplemental answer which said that the "so called 'book' is a card registry" that has been "adequately ordered since 1969 to date." The response further states that "[u]p to the year 1972 the books are found at the National Museum of Anthropology and Archeology, since 1972 to date, the books are found at the 'Museum of the Nation.'" The record does not show whether either of these named institutions is the same as the National Museum of History, where the special book was to be opened.

On January 5, 1985, Law No. 6634 was repealed and replaced by Law No. 24047. According to Professor MacLean's written opinion, "[a]fter that date there is also the obligation for private persons to register their archeological objects and if they do not comply with this obligation that could mean that the objects belong to the State." (Emphasis added.)

In undertaking to evaluate Peru's ownership claims in this confusing situation, I am assuming that none of the artifacts have been duly registered.

However, I do not know whether the repeal of Law No. 6634 nullifies the registration requirement therein contained. If it does, a private owner could have retained an unregistered item through January 1985 without losing his title. In any event, if the private owner caused his unregistered artifact to be removed from Peru within one year following the opening of the "special book" (whenever that may have occurred), title would not have been transferred from such person to the plaintiff.

(c) From January 1985 to the Present

As is mentioned above, on January 5, 1985, the 1929 law was repealed and replaced by Law No. 24047. Professor MacLean's written opinion states that under the latter statute "if a person finds after 5th January of 1985 an archeological object it can belong to him." The next relevant official document is a Supreme Decree of the President of Peru, dated February 27, 1985, which proclaims that Pre-Hispanic artistic objects "belonging to the nation's cultural wealth are untouchable," and that their removal from the country is categorically forbidden. This Decree does not clearly establish state ownership of any such art objects. However, on June 22, 1985, a new statute provided specifically that all archeological sites belong to the state. "So if a private person digs a site and excavates its objects [he] is taking somebody else's property," according to Professor MacLean's written opinion. Thus, it would appear that if any artifacts here concerned were privately excavated between January 5 and June 22, 1985, they would constitute private property, rather than being owned by Peru.

3. MICHAEL KELLY'S TESTIMONY DOES NOT ESTABLISH PERU'S OWNERSHIP

Mr. Michael Kelly testified that in August 1987 he brought to Mr. Johnson's home in California certain artifacts that he believed to have come from Peru. But all of his information as to the country of origin of these items was strictly hearsay. I am also skeptical of Mr. Kelly's ability to identify any of the specific objects here concerned as having been part of the 1987 shipment. Some of the subject items doubtless were in Mr. Johnson's home when Mr. Kelly was present, and he well may have seen them. However, Mr. Johnson submitted documents that quite clearly established his having purchased many of them in the United States well before 1987.

Despite Mr. Kelly's testimony, which was designed to show that Mr. Johnson was implicated in, or at least was aware of, the smuggling activities of Mr. Kelly and Mr. Swetnam, I am not satisfied that Mr. Johnson received any of the items here concerned with the knowledge that they were illegally removed from Peru.

4. THE UNCERTAINTY OF THE DOMESTIC APPLICATION OF PERU'S OWNERSHIP LAWS

Official documents of Peru long have asserted, in one way or another, the interest of the state in preserving its artistic objects as "part of the national cultural wealth," that they are "untouchable, inalienable, and inprescriptable," and that their removal from the country is "categorically forbidden." *See, e.g.,* Supreme Decree of February 27, 1985. Such declarations are concerned with protection and do not imply ownership. However, the law of June 13, 1929, does proclaim that artifacts in historical monuments are "the property of the State" and that unregistered artifacts "shall be considered to be the property of the State." Nonetheless, the domestic effect of such a pronouncement appears to be extremely limited. Possession of the artifacts is allowed to remain in private hands, and such objects may be transferred by gift or bequest or intestate succession. There is no indication in the record that Peru ever has sought to exercise its ownership rights in such property, so long as there is no removal from that country. The laws of Peru concerning its artifacts could reasonably be considered to have no more effect than export restrictions, and, as was pointed out in *United States v. McClain,* 545 F.2d 988, 1002 (5th Cir. 1977), export restrictions constitute an exercise of the police power of a state; "[t]hey do not create 'ownership' in the state. The state comes to own property only when it acquires such property in the general manner by which private persons come to own property, or when it declares itself the owner."

The second time that the case of *United States v. McClain* came before the Fifth Circuit, the opinion stated: "it may well be, as testified so emphatically by most of the Mexican witnesses, that Mexico has considered itself the owner of all pre-Columbian artifacts for almost 100 years. If so, however, it has not expressed that view with sufficient clarity to survive translation into terms understandable by and binding upon American citizens." 593 F.2d 658, 670 (5th Cir. 1979). Under all of the above discussed circumstances, I find the same comment to be applicable here.

5. CONCLUSION

Peru may not prevail in this action to recover the artifacts here concerned because:

   (a) We do not know in what country they were found and from which they were exported.
   (b) If they were found in Peru, we do not know when.
   (c) We do not know if they were in private possession in Peru more than one year after the official registry book was opened.
   (d) The extent of Peru's claim of ownership as part of its domestic law is uncertain.

Notes

1. After Benjamin Johnson died, the Ninth Circuit affirmed this case as *Government of Peru v. Wendt,* 933 F.2d 1013 (9th Cir. 1991). The court stated:

> Peru had the burden of proving that each of the objects came from within the boundaries of modern-day Peru. The testimony of

Dr. Iriarte was the only evidence offered to carry that burden. Peru incorrectly assumes that Dr. Iriarte's testimony must be accepted where it was uncontradicted. Cross-examination by the defense showed that some of Dr. Iriarte's testimony was contradictory, and the defense argued that all of the testimony was inconclusive. The district court determined that Dr. Iriarte's conclusions were "subjective" and refused to credit them. The court's credibility determination is not clearly erroneous merely because it was stated once in reference to Dr. Iriarte's entire testimony, rather than ninety times in reference to each artifact.

It concluded that, "Under any theory of recovery, Peru had to prove the artifacts originated in modern-day Peru. The district court's finding that Peru failed to carry that burden was not clearly erroneous." *Id.*

2. In *U.S. v. One Lucite Ball Containing Lunar Material*, 252 F. Supp. 2d 1367 (S.D. Fla. 2003), the federal district court ordered the claimant of a moon rock and plaque forfeited because they were introduced into the United States in violation of 19 U.S.C. § 1595a(c)(1)(A). Alan Rosen claimed he purchased the items from a retired Honduran colonel for $50,000. The initial asking price was $1,000,000, and Mr. Rosen told a NASA special agent that he planned to resell the items to a Middle Eastern buyer for between $5 and $10 million. The court concluded that the items were stolen from Honduras, which claimed the items as the patrimony of the government and people of Honduras under the 1984 and 1997 Honduran laws for the Protection of Cultural Patrimony.

Mr. Rosen cited Government of *Peru v. Johnson*, 720 F. Supp. 810 (C.D. Cal. 1989), for his contention that the United States had failed to show that the Republic of Honduras owned the moon rock and plaque. Further, the *One Lucite Ball* court distinguished *Johnson*, finding that the court reached its decision because (1) the court could not determine in what country the artifacts were found; (2) it could not determine when they were found; (3) it had no way of knowing whether the artifacts were the possessions of a private person; and (4) Peru's claim of ownership was not supported by its domestic law.

D. African and Asian Nations

Finds by archaeologists across the world have resulted in the filling of many gaps in our knowledge of history. In Egypt, the government has committed to the preservation of ancient monuments. Modern preservation techniques permit us to view Queen Nefertiti's tomb as it was originally completed.

Egypt's monuments and antiquities have also suffered enormous damage at the hands of the environment.[11] The gradual deterioration of Egypt's ruins over 4,000 years does not compare with the destruction that has resulted from pollution, development, and excavation in the last 90 years. The air over Cairo is full of sulfuric and nitric acids. Because of severe overcrowding in the city, villages have sprung up in outlying areas against the walls of ruins. The sewage generated by these villages accumulates, and fertilizers used by farmers leech into the soil. Each of these elements is eating away at the stone monuments. Groundwater, made more dangerous by its high salt content, causes humidity and decay in the monuments that it surrounds and permeates.

The Sphinx and the Pyramid of Khafre, Giza, Egypt

Experts, at one time, suggested the installation of a massive, climate-controlled tent over the Sphinx and the possibility of "sawing the monument at the base and lifting it from the step of limestone from which it was created so that a drainage and a ventilation system can be installed before putting the Sphinx back in its original place."[12]

United States v. Schultz

333 F.3d 393 (2d Cir. 2003), *cert. denied*, 540 U.S. 1106 (2004)
[Most footnotes deleted]

MESKILL, Circuit Judge.

Defendant-appellant Frederick Schultz (Schultz) appeals from a judgment of conviction entered in the United States District Court for the Southern District of New York, Rakoff, J., after a trial by jury. Schultz was convicted of one count of conspiracy to receive stolen property that had been transported in interstate and foreign commerce, in violation of 18 U.S.C. § 371. . . .

BACKGROUND

Schultz was a successful art dealer in New York City. On July 16, 2001, he was indicted on one count of conspiring to receive stolen Egyptian antiquities that had been transported in interstate and foreign commerce, in violation of 18 U.S.C. § 371. The underlying substantive offense was a violation of 18 U.S.C. § 2315, the National Stolen Property Act (NSPA).

---

11. Image: Sherri Burr, Cropped, revised, and resized thumbnail excerpt of a Sherri Burr photograph of the Sphinx and the Pyramid of Khafre, Giza, Egypt (1997).

12. *Giza News: Cleopatra No Beauty, Pyramid Builders Not Slaves*, J. of Art, Nov. 1991, at 68, col. 3 [hereinafter *Giza News*].

Schultz moved to dismiss the indictment, asserting that the items he was charged with conspiring to receive were not stolen within the meaning of the NSPA. Specifically, Schultz contended that the Egyptian antiquities he allegedly conspired to receive were not owned by anyone, and therefore could not be stolen. The prosecution asserted that the antiquities were owned by the Egyptian government pursuant to a patrimony law known as "Law 117" which declared all antiquities found in Egypt after 1983 to be the property of the Egyptian government. After an evidentiary hearing, the district court denied the motion to dismiss in a written memorandum and order. *See United States v. Schultz*, 178 F. Supp. 2d 445 (S.D.N.Y.2002). Schultz was tried before a jury in January and February 2002.

The following facts were adduced at trial.

In 1991, Schultz met Jonathan Tokeley Parry (Parry), a British national, through a mutual friend. Parry showed Schultz a photograph of an ancient sculpture of the head of Pharaoh Amenhotep III, and told Schultz that he had obtained the sculpture in Egypt earlier that year from a man who represented himself to be a building contractor. Parry had used an Egyptian middle-man named Ali Farag (Farag) to facilitate the deal. Parry had smuggled the sculpture out of Egypt by coating it with plastic so that it would look like a cheap souvenir, then removed the plastic coating once the sculpture was in England.

Schultz offered Parry a substantial fee to serve as the agent for the sale of the Amenhotep sculpture, which Parry accepted. Parry and Schultz discussed the problems that might arise if they were discovered to have the piece, and set out to create a false provenance for the sculpture, so that they could sell it. They decided that they would claim that the sculpture had been brought out of Egypt in the 1920s by a relative of Parry and kept in an English private collection since that time. Parry and Schultz invented a fictional collection, the "Thomas Alcock Collection," and represented to potential buyers that the sculpture came from this collection. With Schultz's knowledge, Parry prepared fake labels, designed to look as though they had been printed in the 1920s, and affixed the labels to the sculpture. Parry also restored the sculpture using a method popular in the 1920s.

Acting as Parry's agent, Schultz attempted to sell the Amenhotep sculpture to various parties, using the "Thomas Alcock Collection" story, but was unsuccessful. Eventually, Parry sold the sculpture to Schultz for $800,000, and Schultz sold it to a private collector in 1992 for $1.2 million. In June 1995, Robin Symes (Symes), who then owned the Amenhotep sculpture, asked Schultz to provide him with more details about the sculpture's origin, because he had learned that the Egyptian government was pursuing the sculpture. Schultz responded by asking questions regarding the Egyptian pursuit, but did not provide Symes with any additional information regarding the Amenhotep sculpture.

Parry and Schultz became partners, in a sense. They endeavored to bring more Egyptian antiquities into America for resale, smuggling them out of Egypt disguised as cheap souvenirs, assigning a false provenance to them, and restoring them with 1920s techniques. Parry testified about six items or groups of items, in addition to the Amenhotep sculpture, that he and Schultz attempted to remove from Egypt and sell under the false provenance of the Thomas Alcock Collection.

In 1991, Parry smuggled a sculpture of Meryet Anum (a daughter of Pharoah Ramses II) out of Egypt and performed extensive restorations on it. Parry brought the sculpture to New York and showed it to experts who determined it to be a fake.

In 1992, Parry sold Schultz a black top vase for $672, informing Schultz that the vase had been brought out of Egypt. Parry affixed a Thomas Alcock Collection label to the vase. Schultz and Parry acquired this vase because they believed that including some less valuable pieces in the imaginary Thomas Alcock Collection would make the Collection more believable.

In 1992, Parry wrote to Schultz from Egypt, telling Schultz that he had obtained a sculpture he called "The Offeror." Parry smuggled The Offeror out of Egypt and performed extensive restoration work on it. Parry believed the sculpture was authentic until testing revealed it to be a fake. Parry delivered The Offeror to Schultz without informing him of either the extensive restorations or the fact that the sculpture was not authentic. However, when Schultz discovered the sculpture was a fake, he returned it to Parry. Later, when Parry was arrested, The Offeror was confiscated by British authorities. Schultz contacted the authorities attempting to claim The Offeror as his own, eventually sending a forged invoice purporting to show that Schultz had bought the sculpture from a New York art dealer and had given it to Parry only for restoration. Schultz did not succeed in claiming The Offeror.

In 1992, Parry and Farag learned that someone had reported them to the Egyptian authorities for dealing in antiquities. Due in part to the assistance of Farag's father, who was a powerful Egyptian government official, Parry and Farag were able to get their names removed from police records by paying a bribe to certain corrupt members of the Egyptian antiquities police. These same corrupt police officers then entered into a deal with Parry and Farag, offering them a variety of antiquities in police possession in exchange for Parry and Farag paying off some debts owed by the police officers. Parry chose three items from the "bran tub"[13] full of items offered; he later sent those items to Schultz. Parry informed Schultz of how he had obtained the items. One of the items was marked with an Egyptian government registry number, which Parry succeeded in partially obliterating.

In 1992, Parry purchased the top half of a limestone sculpture of a striding figure, which he dubbed "George," from a group of Egyptian villagers. Apparently, when the sculpture had been found, it was in pieces, and the pieces were divided among rival groups of villagers. Parry wrote to Schultz telling him of the acquisition and informing Schultz that he was attempting to obtain George's bottom half. Parry also requested money to assist in the purchase of George and other items. Parry and Farag eventually succeeded in purchasing

13. A "bran tub" is a British term for a sort of "grab bag" selection of items.

the bottom half of the sculpture, and reassembled the whole thing. Parry then coated George in plastic, and in plaster, and painted it to look like a tourist souvenir so it could be taken out of Egypt. Parry kept Schultz informed of his progress and eventually brought George to New York for Schultz to sell. When George was offered for sale, it was treated with 1920s restoration techniques and represented to be part of the Thomas Alcock Collection. Schultz was unable to sell George, and Parry requested that Schultz send George to Switzerland, where Parry planned to retrieve it. For reasons that are not clear from the record, Parry was not able to retrieve George.

In June 1994, Parry was arrested in Great Britain, and Farag was arrested in Egypt. Each was charged with dealing in stolen antiquities. Schultz was aware of the arrests and communicated extensively with Parry after his arrest about Parry's legal situation. Parry and Schultz also continued to correspond regarding plans for new acquisitions.

In December 1994, Parry wrote to Schultz describing three limestone "stelae," or inscribed slabs, which had been discovered by builders in Egypt and were being offered for sale. Parry had an expert review photographs of the stelae, and the expert determined that the pieces were newly discovered and not listed in any of the catalogs of antiquities known to the Egyptian government. By 1995, there were ten pieces available from this find, and although Parry had been taken into custody in Great Britain, he continued attempting, with Schultz, to obtain the stelae. Schultz sent money for this purpose, and Parry directed that the pieces be shipped to Switzerland for Parry to retrieve in 1996. However, neither Parry nor Schultz ever actually obtained the stelae.

Throughout their partnership, Parry and Schultz communicated regularly; many of their letters were introduced in evidence by the government. Their letters indicate an awareness that there was a great legal risk in what they were doing. This awareness is reflected both in the content of the letters and in Parry's and Schultz's use of "veiled terms," code, or even languages other than English.

The jury found Schultz guilty on the sole count of the indictment, and on June 11, 2002, Schultz was sentenced principally to a term of 33 months' imprisonment. This appeal followed. . . .

DISCUSSION

I. Application of the NSPA to Cases Involving Patrimony Laws

In order to preserve its cultural heritage, Egypt in 1983 enacted a "patrimony law" which declares all antiquities discovered after the enactment of the statute to be the property of the Egyptian government. The law provides for all antiquities privately owned prior to 1983 to be registered and recorded, and prohibits the removal of registered items from Egypt. The law makes private ownership or possession of antiquities found after 1983 illegal. Schultz's primary argument is that the NSPA does not apply to cases in which an object was "stolen" only in the sense that it was possessed or disposed of by an individual in violation of a national patrimony law, as opposed to "stolen" in the commonly used sense of the word, for instance, where an object is taken from a museum or a private collection. The government contends that the plain language of the NSPA indicates that the NSPA applies to any stolen property, regardless of the source of the true owner's title in the property. The question, in other words, is whether an object is "stolen" within the meaning of the NSPA if it is an antiquity which was found in Egypt after 1983 and retained by an individual (and, in this case, removed from Egypt) without the Egyptian government's consent.

The NSPA reads, in pertinent part, as follows:

> Whoever receives, possesses, conceals, stores, barters, sells, or disposes of any goods, wares, or merchandise, securities, or money of the value of $5,000 or more ... which have crossed a State or United States boundary after being stolen, unlawfully converted, or taken, knowing the same to have been stolen, unlawfully converted, or taken ... [s]hall be fined under this title or imprisoned not more than ten years, or both.

18 U.S.C. § 2315 (2000).

This statute is unambiguous. It applies to goods that are "stolen, unlawfully converted, or taken." *Id.* Goods that belong to a person or entity and are taken from that person or entity without its consent are "stolen" in every sense of that word. *See, e.g., Black's Law Dictionary* 989-90 (6th ed. abr. 1991) (defining "stolen" as "[a]cquired or possessed, as a result of some wrongful or dishonest act or taking, whereby a person willfully obtains or retains possession of property which belongs to another, without or beyond any permission given, and with the intent to deprive the owner of the benefit of ownership (or possession) permanently"); Webster's Third New International Dictionary 2248 (1971) (defining "stolen" as "obtained or accomplished by theft, stealth, or craft"). Accordingly, Schultz's actions violated the NSPA if the antiquities he conspired to receive in the United States belonged to someone who did not give consent for Schultz (or his agent) to take them. That "someone" is the nation of Egypt.

In 1983, Egypt enacted Law 117. The law, which is entitled "The Law on the Protection of Antiquities," reads, in pertinent part, as follows:

> Article 1
>
> An "Antiquity" is any movable or immovable property that is a product of any of the various civilizations or any of the arts, sciences, humanities and religions of the successive historical periods extending from prehistoric times down to a point one hundred years before the present, so long as it has either a value or importance archaeologically or historically that symbolizes one of the various civilizations that have been established in the land of Egypt or that has a historical relation to it, as well as human and animal remains from any such period.
>
> ...
>
> Article 6
>
> All antiquities are considered to be public property-except for charitable and religious endowments. ... It is impermissible to own, possess or dispose

of antiquities except pursuant to the conditions set forth in this law and its implementing regulations.

Article 7

    As of [1983], it is prohibited to trade in antiquities.

    . . .

Article 8

    With the exception of antiquities whose ownership or possession was already established [in 1983] or is established pursuant to [this law's] provisions, the possession of antiquities shall be prohibited as from [1983].

Law 117 includes a chapter entitled "Sanctions and Penalties" detailing the criminal penalties to be imposed on persons found to have violated the law. This section provides, inter alia, that a person who "unlawfully smuggles an antiquity outside the Republic or participates in such an act shall be liable to a prison term with hard labor and a fine of not less than 5,000 and not more than 50,000 pounds." A person who steals or conceals a state-owned antiquity faces a prison term of three to five years and a minimum fine of 3,000 pounds. A person who removes or detaches an antiquity from its place, counterfeits an antiquity, or unlawfully disposes of an antiquity faces a prison term of one to two years and a minimum fine of 100 pounds. A person who writes on, posts notices on, or accidentally defaces an antiquity faces a prison term of three to twelve months and/or a fine of 100 to 500 pounds.

Schultz moved in the district court to dismiss the indictment on the ground that Law 117 did not vest true ownership rights in the Egyptian government, and, accordingly, the items he conspired to smuggle out of Egypt were not "stolen" within the meaning of the NSPA. In response to Schultz's motion, the district court conducted an evidentiary hearing regarding Law 117 pursuant to Federal Rule of Criminal Procedure 26.1. At that hearing, two Egyptian officials testified as fact witnesses for the government: Dr. Gaballa Ali Gaballa and General Ali El Sobky.

Dr. Gaballa is Secretary General of Egypt's Supreme Council of Antiquities, which is a part of the Ministry of Culture. The Supreme Council employs more than 20,000 people. Dr. Gaballa was asked: "Who owns all newly discovered antiquities?" He responded: "The Egyptian government, of course." Dr. Gaballa clarified that people who owned antiquities prior to the adoption of Law 117 in 1983 are permitted to continue to possess the antiquities, but they may not transfer, dispose of, or relocate the antiquities without notifying the Egyptian government. Dr. Gaballa testified that pursuant to Law 117, when the Egyptian government learns that an antiquity has been discovered, agents of the government immediately take possession of the item. The item is then registered and given a number.

In response to questioning by the court, Dr. Gaballa asserted that there are no circumstances under which a person who finds an antiquity in Egypt may keep the antiquity legally. The person who found the antiquity is not compensated for the item, because it never belonged to the finder. The only time compensation is paid is when a person owns a plot of land on which an immovable structure is located, and the government takes possession of the entire plot of land in order to possess the structure; in such a case, only the value of the land itself, and not the value of the structure, is taken into account in determining the amount of payment.

The court also asked Dr. Gaballa whether Law 117 had been used to bring legal actions against persons in Egypt who did not comply with the law, but did not attempt to remove an antiquity from Egypt. Dr. Gaballa responded that he was aware of cases in which Law 117 had been applied to persons whose violations of the law took place entirely inside Egypt.

The government's second witness, General El Sobky, is the Director of Criminal Investigations for the Egyptian Antiquities Police. General El Sobky testified that his department, which employs more than 400 officers, regularly investigates and prosecutes people for violating Law 117. General El Sobky testified that most of the Law 117 investigations and prosecutions conducted by his department are of people who are trafficking in antiquities within Egypt, as opposed to exporting them out of Egypt. Furthermore, General El Sobky testified, even when a person is acquitted in such a prosecution, if the person is found to possess an antiquity, that antiquity is seized and retained by the government.

Schultz called one expert witness at the hearing, Khaled Abou El Fadl, a professor of Islamic and Middle Eastern law at the University of California-Los Angeles (UCLA) Law School. Professor Abou El Fadl opined that Law 117 was at times ambiguous and confusing. He further testified that the language of Law 117 did not make it clear whether the law "intended to keep the antiquities inside of Egypt or actually was asserting governmental ownership over the antiquities." Professor Abou El Fadl asserted that "nothing in Law 117 prevents the Antiquities Authority from leaving physical possession of even an antiquity discovered after 1983 in the hands of a private finder, so long as the private finder promptly notifies the Authority of his find."

On cross-examination, Professor Abou El Fadl stated that he had never practiced law in Egypt, nor was he licensed to practice law in Egypt. He testified that he had never read Law 117 prior to being requested to do so by Schultz's counsel, and that he had been unable to locate any treatises discussing Law 117.

Schultz contends that in spite of its plain language, Law 117 is not a "real" ownership law, and that Egypt does not truly claim ownership over all antiquities, but merely seeks to restrict their export. The district court disagreed, finding, based substantially on the testimony and other evidence presented at the hearing, that the plain language of Law 117 accurately reflects its purpose and effect: to vest absolute and true ownership of all antiquities found in Egypt after 1983 in the Egyptian government. *See Schultz*, 178 F. Supp. 2d at 448.

"Issues of foreign law are questions of law," Fed. R. Crim. P. 26.1 (2003), and accordingly we review the district court's findings regarding Law 117 de novo. *See Curley v. AMR Corp.*, 153 F.3d 5, 11 (2d Cir. 1998) ("[A] court's determination of foreign law is treated as a question of law, which is subject to de novo review." (citing parallel rule Fed. R. Civ. P. 44.1)).

Schultz failed to present any evidence at the hearing or at trial that Law 117 is not what its plain language indicates it is, that is, an ownership law.

Professor Abou El Fadl's opinion that the law is ambiguous cannot overcome the combination of (1) the plain text of the statute, and (2) the testimony of two Egyptian government officials to the effect that the statute is a true ownership law and is enforced as such. Although Professor Abou El Fadl testified that he believed it would be possible for Egyptian authorities to leave antiquities in the possession of private individuals who discovered them, Schultz offered no evidence that the authorities ever actually had permitted an individual to retain an antiquity found after 1983. The Egyptian government officials testified that there was no legal way for a private individual to retain possession of an antiquity discovered after 1983, and that all such antiquities are seized by the government.

Law 117 defines "antiquity" and prescribes the procedure to be followed by persons in possession of antiquities at the time the Law takes effect, and by persons who discover antiquities thereafter. It sets forth serious criminal penalties for the violation of its provisions. It provides for licensure of certain foreign archaeological missions, and for circumstances under which antiquities may be donated by the government to foreign museums in appreciation of those missions' work. The Law's provisions are directed at activities within Egypt as well as export of antiquities out of Egypt. Law 117 makes it clear that the Egyptian government claims ownership of all antiquities found in Egypt after 1983, and the government's active enforcement of its ownership rights confirms the intent of the Law. Accordingly, we conclude that Law 117 is clear and unambiguous, and that the antiquities that were the subject of the conspiracy in this case were owned by the Egyptian government.

The question thus becomes whether Schultz's actions in conspiring to take antiquities owned by the Egyptian government pursuant to Law 117 out of Egypt violate the NSPA. Schultz argues that even if Law 117 does intend to vest true ownership of all antiquities with the Egyptian government, that sort of "ownership" should not be recognized by the United States for purposes of prosecution under the NSPA.

Schultz urges us to adopt a narrow reading of the NSPA. However, the Supreme Court and this Court have acknowledged that the NSPA has a "broad purpose," *McElroy v. United States,* 455 U.S. 642, 655, 102 S. Ct. 1332, 71 L. Ed. 2d 522 (1982), and that "the statute should be broadly construed." *United States v. Wallach,* 935 F.2d 445, 469 (2d Cir. 1991) (citing *Moskal v. United States,* 498 U.S. 103, 113, 111 S. Ct. 461, 112 L. Ed. 2d 449 (1990)). We have held that the language of the NSPA "is broad enough to justify the federal courts in applying the statute whenever they determine that the [property was] stolen in another country." *United States v. Greco,* 298 F.2d 247, 251 (2d Cir. 1962); *see also United States v. Parness,* 503 F.2d 430, 440 n.14 (2d Cir. 1974) (citing *Greco* with approval). Accordingly, there can be no doubt that if the antiquities involved in the conspiracy were stolen in Egypt and then shipped to the United States, the NSPA would be violated.

Just as the property need not be stolen in the United States to bring the NSPA into play, the fact that the rightful owner of the stolen property is foreign has no impact on a prosecution under the NSPA. *See United States v. Frazier,*

584 F.2d 790, 794 (6th Cir. 1978). . . . Furthermore, this Court has held that the NSPA applies to stolen property even where the person from whom the property was stolen may not have been the true owner of the property, and that the validity of the victim's title in the property is sometimes "irrelevant." *United States v. Benson*, 548 F.2d 42, 46 (2d Cir. 1977). Accordingly, it does not matter that the antiquities at issue here were stolen in a foreign country, or that their putative owner is a foreign entity.

Notwithstanding all of the above, Schultz insists that the antiquities are not "stolen" within the meaning of the NSPA because they were never truly owned by the Egyptian government. The leading opinion addressing this question was issued by the Fifth Circuit, over 25 years ago, in *United States v. McClain*, 545 F.2d 988 (5th Cir. 1977). The parties frame the question on appeal as whether the Second Circuit should adopt the reasoning set forth by the Fifth Circuit in *McClain*.

Schultz asserts that we should reject the holding in *McClain* based on existing Second Circuit precedent, which he reads as being hostile to McClain. Schultz then raises several additional arguments in support of his position, namely: (1) that *McClain's* approach conflicts with United States policy, (2) that the enactment of the Convention on Cultural Property Implementation Act of 1983, 19 U.S.C. §§ 2601-2613 (CPIA), "confirms that Congress never intended [the] NSPA to reach ownership claims based upon national vesting laws when the property has not been reduced to the possession of the foreign state," and (3) that the common law definition of "stolen" would not reach the property at issue here. We address each of these arguments in turn.

A. *McClain* in the Second Circuit

The *McClain* defendants were convicted of conspiring to violate the NSPA by importing artifacts from Mexico that were covered by a Mexican law declaring all such artifacts to be owned by the Mexican government. *See id.* at 992. The defendants claimed, as Schultz does here, that the NSPA did not apply to "stolen" objects that were taken in violation of patrimony laws. *See id.* at 994. The Fifth Circuit concluded that the NSPA did apply to such objects.4 *See id.* at 996-97.

The McClain Court cited precedent according an expansive meaning to the term "stolen" in the NSPA, including *United States v. Handler*, 142 F.2d 351, 353 (2d Cir. 1944), which held that embezzled property is "stolen" within the meaning of the NSPA. *See McClain*, 545 F.2d at 995 (citing cases). The *McClain* Court also cited *United States v. Bottone*, 365 F.2d 389, 393-94 (2d Cir. 1966). In *Bottone*, the defendants photocopied documents detailing secret manufacturing processes, and transported the photocopies across state lines. *See Bottone*, 365 F.2d at 391. The original documents were taken from the rightful owner only briefly for copying, and were never transported in interstate or foreign commerce. *See id.* at 393. The Court found that the transport of the photocopies violated the NSPA, and the fact that the photocopies were "never possessed by the original owner should be deemed immaterial." *Id.* at 393-94.

The *McClain* Court also distinguished between mere unlawful export and actual theft, holding that "a declaration of national ownership is necessary before illegal exportation of an article can be considered theft, and the exported article considered 'stolen,' within the meaning of the [NSPA]." *McClain,* 545 F.2d at 1000-01. The court engaged in a close study of the Mexican patrimony law, including its language, history and purpose, and concluded that the Mexican government had made a declaration of national ownership satisfying this standard. *See id.* at 997-1000. As discussed above, Egypt has made a clear declaration of national ownership through Law 117, and has enforced that law accordingly. . . . We agree that the Fifth Circuit reached the proper balance between these competing concerns in *McClain.* . . .

B. United States Policy

Schultz contends that it is United States policy not to enforce the export restrictions of foreign nations. Schultz offers no evidence in support of this assertion, but even if his assessment of United States policy is accurate, the outcome of this case is unaffected. We have already concluded, based on the plain language of Law 117 and the evidence in the record, that Law 117 is an ownership law, not an export-restriction law. Two Egyptian officials testified under oath that the law is used in Egypt to prosecute people for trafficking in antiquities within Egypt's borders. Law 117 provides for a minimum five-year prison term and a fine of 3,000 pounds for persons convicted of "[t]heft or concealment of a state owned antiquity." Persons convicted of smuggling an antiquity out of Egypt face "a prison term with hard labor and a fine of not less than 5,000 and not more than 50,000 pounds." Clearly, theft or concealment of an antiquity within Egypt is a different offense than smuggling an antiquity out of Egypt, and both are prohibited by Law 117. Accordingly, even if Schultz's interpretation of American policy is accurate, it is not relevant here. While Law 117 does restrict exportation of cultural objects, its scope is not limited to export restrictions. Law 117 is more than an export regulation-it is a true ownership law.

C. The CPIA

Schultz contends that the adoption of the CPIA shows that Congress did not intend the NSPA to apply to objects such as the ones he conspired to bring to the United States. The CPIA implements a United Nations convention that was ratified by the United States in 1982, the purpose of which was to achieve "greater international cooperation towards preserving cultural treasures that not only are of importance to the nations whence they originate, but also to greater international understanding of our common heritage." S. Rep. No. 97-564, at 21 (1982).

The CPIA provides a mechanism for the American government to establish import restrictions on "cultural property" at the request of another signatory nation and after a determination by the President that (1) "the cultural patrimony of [the requesting nation] is in jeopardy from the pillage of archaeological or ethnological materials of [that nation]," (2) the requesting nation "has taken measures ... to protect its cultural patrimony," (3) the import restrictions are necessary and would be effective in dealing with the problem, and (4) the restrictions are in the "general interest of the international community." 19 U.S.C. § 2602(a)(1)(A)-(D) (2003). . . .

The CPIA also bars the importation of items that have been stolen from a museum or other cultural institution in a foreign signatory nation. *See* 19 U.S.C. § 2607. Schultz argues that because only those items that are stolen from specified places are covered by the CPIA, Congress never intended in any way to limit the import of items "stolen" only in the sense that they were taken in violation of patrimony laws. This argument is unpersuasive. The CPIA does not state that importing objects stolen from somewhere other than a museum is legal. If, for instance, an artifact covered by the CPIA were stolen from a private home in a signatory nation and imported into the United States, the CPIA would not be violated, but surely the thief could be prosecuted for transporting stolen goods in violation of the NSPA.

The CPIA is an import law, not a criminal law; it is not codified in Title 18 ("Crimes and Criminal Procedure"), with the NSPA, but in Title 19 ("Customs Duties"). It may be true that there are cases in which a person will be violating both the CPIA and the NSPA when he imports an object into the United States. But it is not inappropriate for the same conduct to result in a person being subject to both civil penalties and criminal prosecution, and the potential overlap between the CPIA and the NSPA is no reason to limit the reach of the NSPA. *See, e.g., Hudson v. United States*, 522 U.S. 93, 98-99, 118 S. Ct. 488, 139 L. Ed. 2d 450 (1997) (holding that a person may be subjected to civil and criminal penalties for the same conduct without violating the Double Jeopardy Clause).

For the reasons set forth above, we conclude that the passage of the CPIA does not limit the NSPA's application to antiquities stolen in foreign nations.

D. Common Law Definition of "Stolen"

Schultz argues that the Court must look to the common law definition of "stolen" to determine whether the antiquities at issue are covered by the NSPA. Schultz cites *United States v. Turley*, 352 U.S. 407, 77 S. Ct. 397, 1 L. Ed. 2d 430 (1957), in which the Supreme Court considered the meaning of the term "stolen" in the context of the statute that served as the precursor and model for the NSPA. *See id.* at 410-11, 77 S. Ct. 397. The Supreme Court stated: "We recognize that where a federal criminal statute uses a common-law term of established meaning without otherwise defining it, the general practice is to give that term its common-law meaning." *Id.* at 411, 77 S. Ct. 397. Schultz contends that interpreting the NSPA to apply to items that are "stolen" in the sense that they are possessed by a defendant in violation of a foreign patrimony law would be in derogation of the common law. However, in Turley, the Supreme Court explicitly recognized that "'stolen' (or 'stealing') has no accepted common-law meaning." *Id.* If "stolen" has no common law meaning, we cannot look to the common law to assist us in interpreting that term.

The Supreme Court also stated in Turley that the term "stolen" included "all felonious takings ... regardless of whether or not the theft constitutes common-law larceny." *Id.* at 417, 77 S. Ct. 397. In other words, according to the Supreme Court, the precursor to the NSPA — and by extension the NSPA — covers a broader class of crimes than those contemplated by the common law. Accordingly, we find this argument unpersuasive.

E. Summary

In light of our own precedents and the plain language of the NSPA, we conclude that the NSPA applies to property that is stolen in violation of a foreign patrimony law. The CPIA is not the exclusive means of dealing with stolen artifacts and antiquities, and reading the NSPA to extend to such property does not conflict with United States policy. We believe that, when necessary, our courts are capable of evaluating foreign patrimony laws to determine whether their language and enforcement indicate that they are intended to assert true ownership of certain property, or merely to restrict the export of that property. In this case, the district court carefully evaluated the language of Law 117. The court also heard testimony from one academic expert and two Egyptian government officials. This evidence was sufficient to inform the court of the nature of Egypt's interest in the antiquities that were the subject of the conspiracy. . . .

II. Defense of Mistake of United States Law

Schultz argues on appeal that the district court erred in refusing to allow him to present a defense of mistake of law. Specifically, Schultz sought to argue to the jury that he did not know that importing antiquities owned by the Egyptian government pursuant to Law 117 violated the NSPA. The government contends that the district court was correct to bar this defense, relying on "the venerable principle that ignorance of the law generally is no defense to a criminal charge." *Ratzlaf v. United States,* 510 U.S. 135, 149, 114 S. Ct. 655, 126 L. Ed. 2d 615 (1994). . . .

A defendant charged with violating the NSPA may argue that he did not know a certain fact that made his conduct criminal, that is, that he did not know the objects in question were stolen. Schultz's "mistake of Egyptian law" defense goes to that issue. However, if a jury finds that a defendant knew all of the relevant facts, the defendant cannot then escape liability by contending that he did not know the law. . . .

In addition, the record demonstrates that Schultz's actions were not "innocent" or merely "negligent." This is not a case in which the defendant believed that he was doing something lawful, and was surprised to find that his conduct could result in criminal sanctions. To the contrary, Schultz was conspiring to smuggle antiquities out of Egypt and into the United States. He was defrauding (or attempting to defraud) potential buyers; the Thomas Alcock Collection story was invented by Schultz and Parry for the sole purpose of deceiving people as to the origin of the antiquities and when they had been taken out of Egypt. Schultz continued to do business in this manner even after his partners, Parry and Farag, had been arrested. Furthermore, Schultz and Parry demonstrated a keen awareness of the illegality of their actions by communicating in "code," forging documents, and even explicitly discussing the possibility that one or more of them might end up imprisoned.

We conclude that the district court did not err in denying Schultz's request to present a defense of mistake of American law. The jury did not have to find that Schultz knew what he was doing was illegal. As long as the jury found beyond a reasonable doubt that Schultz knew the antiquities were "stolen," the jury, following the law, would have been required to convict Schultz even if it believed he had misunderstood American law. . . .

CONCLUSION

We conclude that the NSPA applies to property that is stolen from a foreign government, where that government asserts actual ownership of the property pursuant to a valid patrimony law. We find the remainder of Schultz's claims to be without merit. Accordingly, the judgment of the district court is hereby affirmed.

Notes

1. Thirty-three hundred years after its creation, the Bust of Nefertiti remains a focal point of dissention. Jeevam Vasagar reported for *The Guardian*, "For more than eight decades, the serenely beautiful likeness of Queen Nefertiti's head has been the most celebrated exhibit in Berlin's Egyptian Museum, attracting thousands of visitors and resisting all attempts at repatriation. But a conceptual artwork involving the 3,300-year-old limestone bust and the body of a scantily clad woman has provoked outrage in the queen's homeland and the accusation that Nefertiti is no longer safe in Germany." *See* Jeevan Vasagar, *Egypt angered at artists' use of Nefertiti bust*, Guardian, June 12, 2003. Vasagar further reported, "[I]n Cairo the artwork is regarded as a calculated insult to Egypt's heritage and Islamic morals. We don't agree with this, that the head of Queen Nefertiti should be subjected to an experiment by unknown artists, and could possibly be put in danger."
2. In July 2003, Egypt launched a campaign for the return of antiquities taken from the country for an exhibition to mark Cairo's Egyptian Museum's 100th birthday. The BBC reported that at the top of the museum's list was the ancient Rosetta Stone, which is housed in the British Museum, and the bust of Nefertiti from Germany.

A British Museum spokesman said: "The trustees do not consent to the loan of what might be called "iconic" objects. To loan such pieces would result in our disappointing the five million or so visitors who come to the museum every year." . . .

The Rosetta Stone was discovered in 1799 at the mouth of the Nile and provided a key insight into hieroglyphics because it was accompanied by the Greek translation. The French yielded it to the British in 1801 and it has been housed in the British Museum since 1802. See *http://news.bbc.co.uk/2/hi/entertainment/3109065.stm.*

PROBLEM 11-2

Should Germany be required to return the *Bust of Nefertiti* to Egypt? There is controversy over how it was obtained. The intricately painted object was unearthed in 1912 by a German mission directed by Ludwig Borchardt, a German archaeologist working in Egypt. One report is that he took the bust to Germany under a law that allowed him take 50 percent of what had been excavated.

In 1992, one German group viewed the presence of the bust of Nefertiti in Berlin as "'a typical example of theft from the so-called Third World.'" *Nefertiti to Go, Say Greens*, Art Newspaper, Feb. 1992, at 1, col. 1 (quoting the Nordrhein-Westfalen branch of the German Green Party). In 2009, Egypt demanded the return of the Bust of Nefertiti from the newly reopened Neues Museum in Berlin. Germany again claimed that archeologist Ludwig Borchardt obtained Egyptian approval to take it to Berlin in 1913. *See* Michael Kimmelman, *When Ancient Artifacts Become Political Pawns*, N.Y. Times, Oct. 24, 2009.

Prepare an analysis of Egypt's request for the return of the *Bust of Nefertiti.*

United States v. One Tyrannosaurus Bataar Skeleton

2012 WL 5834899 (S.D.N.Y. 2012)
[Footnotes & record citations deleted]

P. Kevin Castel, District Judge.

The United States of America brings this in rem action seeking civil forfeiture of One Tyrannosaurus Bataar Skeleton, a/k/a lot 49315 listed on page 92 of the Heritage Auctions May 20, 2012 Natural History Auction Catalog (the "Defendant Property"). The government alleges that the Defendant Property is subject to forfeiture under three different federal statutes, each of which provides in general terms (and interaction with other federal statutes) for the forfeiture of property brought into the United States that is either stolen or introduced by way of false statements. 18 U.S.C. §§ 545, 981(a)(1)(C); 19 U.S.C. § 1595a(c). The amended verified complaint alleges that the Defendant Property was stolen in that it was taken out of Mongolia without permission from the Mongolian state and in violation of Mongolian law. It is alleged that under Mongolian law paleontological artifacts such as the Defendant Property are the property of the state. It is further alleged that the Defendant Property was brought into the United States by way of false statements concerning its value and country of origin.

Claimant Eric Prokopi moves to dismiss the amended verified complaint, arguing (1) that forfeiture of the Defendant Property violates due process because the public does not have fair notice of the predicate acts of illegality on which forfeiture is based, and (2) that the Defendant Property is not stolen property for the purposes of the forfeiture provisions invoked by the government.

For the reasons set forth below, the motion is denied.

BACKGROUND

I. Procedural History

On June 18, 2012, the government filed a verified complaint in this action. The following day, the Court issued a warrant for seizure of the Defendant Property.

On July 27, 2012, Prokopi filed a claim of interest in the Defendant Property pursuant to Supplemental Rule G of the Supplemental Rules for Admiralty or Maritime Claims and Asset Forfeiture Actions (the "Supplemental Rules") in which he stated that although he had consigned the Defendant Property to the Heritage Auctions for sale, he remained the owner of the Defendant Property.

On August 17, 2012, Prokopi filed a motion to dismiss the verified complaint. Following a conference held on September 5, 2012, the Court expressed several concerns regarding the sufficiency of the verified complaint and offered the government the opportunity to amend its pleading to cure certain actual or potential deficiencies. *See* Memorandum and Order of September 7, 2012.

The government filed an amended verified complaint dated September 21, 2012 (the "amended complaint"), and Prokopi moved to dismiss the amended complaint on October 5, 2012.

II. The First Amended Verified Complaint

The following facts are taken from the amended complaint and assumed to be true for the purposes of deciding this motion.

Within the Gobi Desert in Mongolia, there is an area known as the Nemegt Formation where fossilized remains of the Tyrannosaurus bataar ("Bataar") have been found since expeditions in the 1940s. Dinosaur fossils from this area have a distinctive color due to the soil composition of the Nemegt Formation.

Bataar remains have been found in areas other than the Nemegt Formation, although not as complete skeletons.

According to paleontological experts, the Defendant Property is a Bataar skeleton that almost certainly came from the Nemegt Formation and was most likely excavated between 1995 and 2005. This conclusion is based, among other things, on the distinctive coloring of the Defendant Property. Regarding the possibility that the Defendant Property is composed of pieces of multiple, distinct skeletons, some or all of which may have been found outside of Mongolia, three of the experts stated that "[w]hether a single skeleton or multiple skeletons were used to construct this specimen, we are virtually certain that all of the bones were excavated in Mongolia." Again, this conclusion was based in part on the "signature coloration that makes them easy to distinguish visually from fossils from equivalent age in neighboring countries (China, Kazakhstan, Russia)." Moreover, the experts opined that it is "unlikely" that the Defendant Property came from more than one specimen given that it is "60% grown" and such grown specimens make up only 13% of those recovered.

Prokopi, a self-described commercial paleontologist, has visited Mongolia on several occasions, including in 2008, 2009, 2011, and 2012. He has been seen removing fossils from the ground in the Nemegt Formation of the Gobi Desert. Prokopi consigned the Defendant Property to Heritage Auctions, Inc. ("Heritage"), which offered the Defendant Property for sale on May 20, 2012 at an auction in New York City. The Defendant Property sold for $1,052,500, contingent upon the outcome of any court proceedings on behalf of Mongolia.

The component parts of the Defendant Property entered the United States through as many as four separate shipments, including shipments on March 27, 2010, March 22, 2007, and August 29, 2007. The government alleges that the entry documentation for the Defendant Property contained several material misstatements regarding the Defendant Property's true country of origin (Mongolia) and value (approximately $1 million). First, in a March 27, 2010 Bureau of Customs and Border Protection Entry/Immediate Delivery form, the country of origin for the Defendant Property is listed as Great Britain and the value of the Defendant Property is stated as $15,000. The Defendant Property is also described in the Commercial Invoice for this shipment as "2 large rough (unprepared) fossil reptile heads;" "6 boxes of broken fossil bones;" "3 rough (unprepared) fossil reptiles;" "1 fossil lizard;" "3 rough (unprepared) fossil reptiles;" and "1 fossil reptile skull." Next, the importation documents for the March 22, 2007 shipment listed the items being imported as "fossil specimens" with a declared value of $12,000 and Japan as the country of origin. It appears that the country of origin for the March 22, 2007 shipment was first listed as Mongolia, but was changed to Japan after UPS received additional information from Prokopi. Finally, the documentation for the August 29, 2007 shipment listed the contents as "fossils" with a value of $42,000 and Japan as the country of origin.

DISCUSSION

I. Pleading Standards

The Supplemental Rules apply in "forfeiture actions in rem arising from a federal statute." . . . A claimant who establishes standing to contest forfeiture may move to dismiss the action under Rule 12(b)." . . .

II. Statutory Bases for Forfeiture

The amended complaint alleges three separate statutory bases for forfeiture of the Defendant Property.

a. 18 U.S.C. § 981(a)(1)(C) — Civil Forfeiture

The government alleges that the Defendant Property is subject to forfeiture under 18 U.S.C. § 981(a)(1)(C), because, in the words of the statute, it "constitutes or is derived from proceeds traceable to a violation of . . . any offense constituting 'specified unlawful activity' (as defined in section 1956(c)(7) of this title)." 18 U.S.C. § 981(a)(1)(C). The government alleges that Section 981 applies "because there is probable cause to believe that the Defendant Property is property, real or personal, which constitutes or is derived from a violation of Title 18, United States Code Section 2314 and/or Section 2315."

Sections 2314 and 2315 constitute the National Stolen Property Act ("NSPA"). *See Davis*, 648 F.3d at 87. Section 2314 states in relevant part:

> Whoever transports, transmits, or transfers in interstate or foreign commerce any goods, wares, merchandise, securities or money, of the value of $5,000 or more, knowing the same to have been stolen, converted or taken by fraud . . . [s]hall be fined under this title or imprisoned not more than ten years, or both.

18 U.S.C. § 2314. Section 2315 states in relevant part:

> Whoever receives, possesses, conceals, stores, barters, sells, or disposes of any goods, wares, or merchandise, securities, or money of the value of $5,000 or more, which have crossed a State or United States boundary after being stolen, unlawfully converted, or taken, knowing the same to have been stolen, unlawfully converted, or taken . . . [s]hall be fined under this title or imprisoned not more than ten years, or both.

18 U.S.C. § 2315. Thus, "[a]n NSPA violation consists of three elements: '(1) the transportation in interstate or foreign commerce of property, (2) valued at $5,000 or more, (3) with knowledge that the property was stolen, converted, or taken by fraud.'" *United States v. Portrait of Wally*, 663 F. Supp. 2d 232, 250 (S.D.N.Y. 2009) (citation omitted).

Because of CAFRA, forfeiture under Section 981 is subject to an innocent-owner defense, with the burden of proof on the claimant to prove he is an innocent owner by a preponderance of the evidence. 18 U.S.C. § 983(d)(1). A claimant may assert an innocent-owner defense where his property interest existed at the time of the conduct giving rise to forfeiture if he "did not know of the conduct giving rise to forfeiture," or, "upon learning of the conduct giving rise to the forfeiture, did all that reasonably could be expected under the circumstances to terminate such use of the property." 18 U.S.C. § 983(d)(2)(A). Alternatively, a claimant whose property interest was acquired after the conduct giving rise to forfeiture may assert an innocent-owner defense if he was "a bona fide purchaser or seller for value (including a purchaser or seller of goods or services for value)" and he "did not know and was reasonably without cause to believe that the property was subject to forfeiture." 18 U.S.C. § 983(d)(3)(A).

b. 18 U.S.C. § 545 — Smuggling Goods Into The United States

The government also alleges that the Defendant Property is subject to forfeiture under 18 U.S.C. § 545. Section 545 states in relevant part:

> Whoever fraudulently or knowingly imports or brings into the United States, any merchandise contrary to law, or receives, conceals, buys, sells, or in any manner facilitates the transportation, concealment, or sale of such merchandise after importation, knowing the same to have been imported or brought into the United States contrary to law — Shall be fined under this title or imprisoned not more than 20 years, or both.

18 U.S.C. § 545. The provision further states that "[m]erchandise introduced into the United States in violation of this section, or the value thereof, to be recovered from any person described in the first or second paragraph of this section, shall be forfeited to the United States." *Id.*

The government alleges that Section 545 applies "because there is probable cause to believe . . . that the Defendant Property was (1) introduced into the United States by means of false statements in violation of Title 18, United States Code, Section 542 and/or (2) imported into the United States knowing it was stolen or converted."

Section 542 states in relevant part that:

> Whoever enters or introduces, or attempts to enter or introduce, into the commerce of the United States any imported merchandise by means of any fraudulent or false invoice, declaration, affidavit, letter, paper, or by means of any false statement, written or verbal, or by means of any false or fraudulent practice or appliance, or makes any false statement in any declaration without reasonable cause to believe the truth of such statement, or procures the making of any such false statement as to any matter material thereto without reasonable cause to believe the truth of such statement, . . . [s]hall be fined for each offense under this title or imprisoned not more than two years, or both.

18 U.S.C. § 542. Thus, "[t]o be convicted for false statements under Section 542, a defendant must: (1) attempt to import merchandise into the United States (2) 'by means of a false statement (3) without reasonable cause to believe the truth of such statement or practice." *United States v. Avelino*, 967 F.2d 815,

817 (2d Cir. 1992). A violation of Section 542 may serve as a predicate for forfeiture under Section 545, provided that the misstatement is material. *See United States v. An Antique Platter of Gold*, 184 F.3d 131, 134–38 (2d Cir. 1999) (holding that misstatement as to country of origin was material where property may have been considered stolen under Italian patrimony law). A misstatement is material in this context if it would have "a natural tendency to influence a reasonable customs official." *Id.* at 138.

Presumably, a violation of the NSPA may also serve as a predicate under Section 545 as it may under 19 U.S.C. § 1595a(c), which uses the same "contrary to law" language. *See Davis*, 648 F.3d at 90 (holding NSPA violation may serve as predicate under Section 1595a(c)); accord *Portrait of Wally*, 663 F. Supp. 2d at 250 (analyzing claims under Sections 545 and 1595a(c) in parallel).

A forfeiture claim under Section 545 is subject to the same innocent-owner defenses as apply under Section 981. *See* 18 U.S.C. § 983(d).

c. 19 U.S.C. § 1595a(c) — Forfeitures and other Penalties

Finally, the government alleges that the Defendant Property is subject to forfeiture under 19 U.S.C. § 1595a(c). That section states in relevant part:

> Merchandise which is introduced or attempted to be introduced into the United States contrary to law shall be treated as follows: (1) The merchandise shall be seized and forfeited if it — (A) is stolen, smuggled, or clandestinely imported or introduced;

19 U.S.C. § 1595a(c). The requirements that the property be (1) introduced "contrary to law" and (2) "stolen, smuggled, or clandestinely imported or introduced" are separate and must both be satisfied. *See United States v. Broadening–Info Enters., Inc.*, 462 Fed. App'x 93, 97 (2d Cir. 2012) (summary order) (remanding to district court for consideration of second prong as distinct from the first).

The term "contrary to law" is not defined, but the requirement can be satisfied by proving a violation of another statute, including the NSPA or Section 542. *See Davis*, 648 F.3d at 90 (holding NSPA violation may serve as predicate for "contrary to law" requirement in Section 1595a(c)); *Broadening–Info Enters.*, 462 Fed. App'x at 96 (noting that "contrary to law" prong can be met by fraudulent or false statements in violation of 18 U.S.C. § 542). Although the "contrary to law" and "stolen, smuggled, or clandestinely imported or introduced" prongs are separate, the statutory language suggests that the same statutory predicate may satisfy both prongs in some instances, for example where property is introduced "contrary to law" in that it is stolen property or was introduced clandestinely in violation of a statute requiring disclosure.

Here, the government has not alleged a specific statutory predicate to meet either prong, but it has alleged that the Defendant Property was "(1) introduced into the commerce of the United States by means of false statement and/or (2) transported in foreign commerce knowing it was stolen or converted." The first of these two allegations could fall under 18 U.S.C. § 542 and the second under the NSPA, and in each case both prongs of Section 1595a(c) might plausibly be satisfied.

Unlike forfeiture under Sections 545 and 981 of Title 18, forfeiture under Title 19 is not subject to an innocent-owner defense. *See* 18 U.S.C. § 983(i)(2)(A) (excluding Title 19 from definition of "civil forfeiture statute[s]" subject to innocent-owner defense); *Davis*, 648 F.3d at 94–95 (noting the absence of an innocent-owner defense under Section 1595a(c)).

III. Fair Notice

Relying principally on the Supreme Court's recent decision in *Fed. Commc'ns Comm'n v. Fox Television Stations, Inc.*, 132 S. Ct. 2307 (2012), Prokopi argues that the amended complaint should be dismissed because fossil collectors have not been given fair notice of either Mongolian law or the country of origin and valuation rules relating to the importation of paleontological objects. As the Supreme Court stated in Fox, "[a] fundamental principle in our legal system is that laws which regulate persons or entities must give fair notice of conduct that is forbidden or required." *Id.* at 2317. . . .

a. Fair Notice of Country of Origin and Valuation Rules

As to the alleged misstatements concerning the country of origin and value of the Defendant Property, Prokopi's due process argument is misplaced. Prokopi contends that the failure of the government to provide regulatory guidance on determining the proper country of origin or value of fossils leaves importers "hard-pressed to respond to a customs broker's inquiry about the country of origin of a dinosaur fossil that existed millions of years before the emergence of Homo sapiens and even longer before the concept of a 'country' was established." This argument fails because the statutes in violation of which the Defendant Property is alleged to have been imported do not prohibit the importation of paleontological objects in contravention of certain regulations, vague or otherwise (and indeed, Prokopi submits that there are no applicable regulations). Instead, they prohibit importation by way of knowingly false statements. 18 U.S.C. § 542. The prohibition in Section 542 against importation by means of "any false statement" is not vague or ambiguous, and it does not make reference or in any way depend upon regulatory guidance concerning the proper country of origin or value of fossils. If Prokopi did not know that his statements were false, he may have a defense to forfeiture under Section 542 based on the absence of mens rea, or he may be able to invoke an innocent-owner affirmative defense, but these are factual question not properly before the Court on this motion. Prokopi's due process challenge fails because Section 542 gives fair warning that knowingly false statements are prohibited.

The amended complaint alleges facts that, drawing reasonable inferences in the government's favor, suggest that the Defendant Property was unearthed, not millions of years ago, but between 1995 and 2005, and that, based on its size and coloration, the Defendant Property came from the Gobi Desert in Mongolia. The amended complaint also raises a plausible inference that Prokopi's statements in connection with importation of the Defendant Property were knowingly false.

The amended complaint alleges that Prokopi erroneously listed the country of origin as Japan and Great Britain on importation paperwork when in fact the Defendant Property was from Mongolia. The amended complaint further alleges that Prokopi is a commercial paleontologist who had excavated fossils in Mongolia's Nemegt Formation himself before. These facts give rise to a plausible inference that Prokopi unearthed the Defendant Property himself in Mongolia, or, even if he did not, that he had reason to know that such fossils likely came from Mongolia. The inference of knowing wrongdoing is buttressed by the allegation that Prokopi changed the country of origin on the March 22, 2007 shipment from Mongolia to Japan. There may be an innocent explanation for this change, but on its face the allegation suggests Prokopi's awareness of illegality and his attempt to avoid detection.

The same goes for the value of the Defendant Property. Collectively, the three shipments identified in the amended complaint had a stated value of $69,000, whereas the Defendant Property was listed at auction as having a value between $950,000 and $1,500,000. While it may be the case that Prokopi's efforts in assembling the contents of the shipments into a single display piece constituting the Defendant Property significantly increased the value of the fossils contained in the shipments, it is not implausible that the declared values — which appear to have understated the value of the Defendant Property by more than an order of magnitude — constituted knowing misstatements, and it is reasonable to draw an inference of wrongdoing on these facts at the pleading stage.

b. Fair Notice of Mongolian Law

Prokopi's fair notice argument concerning Mongolian law also fails. It may be, as Prokopi contends, that "fossil collectors could have no fair notice of Mongolia's laws cited in the Complaint," as these are "not readily available to the general public," or perhaps that Mongolian law itself is impermissibly vague, but this does not appear on the face of the well-pleaded complaint and hence is not appropriate for consideration on a motion to dismiss. Moreover, the Second Circuit has stated that a defense based on the misapprehension of foreign law bears on the mens rea requirement under the NSPA. *See United States v. Schultz*, 333 F.3d 393, 411 (2d Cir. 2003) ("A defendant charged with violating the NSPA may argue that he did not know a certain fact that made his conduct criminal, that is, that he did not know the objects in question were stolen"). . . . Thus, Prokopi may ultimately prevail by demonstrating that Mongolian law is improperly vague or that Prokopi lacked the requisite knowledge of illegality, but neither defense is properly considered on this motion.

IV. Stolen Property

Finally, Prokopi argues that the Defendant Property is not stolen property for purposes of any of the statutory bases of forfeiture because the amended complaint fails adequately to allege that Prokopi knew the Defendant Property was taken from Mongolia without that state's permission, and further because Mongolian law does not make fossils the property of the state. Although this argument raises a question of foreign law that the Court could decide on a motion to dismiss, the Court declines to make a final determination as to the content of Mongolian law in this interlocutory order, finding it sufficient to hold that the amended complaint states a claim for relief under the Supplemental Rules.

The Second Circuit examined this issue in the context of the NSPA in *United States v. Schultz*, 333 F.3d 393, 410 (2d Cir. 2003), and held that "the NSPA applies to property that is stolen in violation of a foreign patrimony law" where the effect of the patrimony law is to "assert true ownership of certain property" as opposed to those laws that operate "merely to restrict the export of that property." In so holding, the Second Circuit adopted the reasoning of *United States v. McClain.* 545 F.2d 988, 1000–01 (5th Cir. 1977), in which the Fifth Circuit held that "a declaration of national ownership is necessary before illegal exportation of an article can be considered theft, and the exported article considered 'stolen,' within the meaning of the National Stolen Property Act."

The amended complaint sets out a number of provisions of Mongolian law in support of the allegation that fossils such as the Defendant Property have been state property under Mongolian law since 1924. Only some of these provisions are relevant here. First, the amended complaint alleges that the Defendant Property was unearthed between 1995 and 2005, so the law in effect before 1995 is not material. Second, only those provisions that purport to vest ownership in the state, and not those that merely restrict transfer or exportation, are relevant under Schultz.

The amended complaint alleges three provisions that warrant consideration. First, the most recent Mongolian Constitution, enacted in 1992, states that "[h]istorical, cultural, scientific and intellectual heritages of the Mongolian People shall be under State protection." Second, the 1924 Mongolian Rules to Protect the Antiquities, which, judging by the amended complaint, may still be in force, state that "all antique items and relics of the past found within the territory of Mongolia shall be owned by Mongolia," and further define "antiques and relics" to include "[p]aleontological items such as remnants of ancient plants and animals." Finally, the 2001 Mongolian Law on Cultural Heritage states that "[t]he territory and land bowels where historically, culturally and scientifically significant objects exist shall be under state protection and any such findings shall be a state property," and defines fossils and animal imprints as such objects.

Prokopi argues that the 1992 Constitution, when compared with earlier versions, effected a "radical shift from State 'possession' to State 'protection.'"

Even assuming arguendo that this is true, however, the 1924 Mongolian Rules to Protect the Antiquities and the 2001 Mongolian Law on Cultural Heritage would, if applicable to the Defendant Property, render it "owned by Mongolia" and "state property," respectively.

Even so, Prokopi argues that Mongolia must do more than simply decree by law that the Defendant Property is state property — it must actively enforce those laws. Prokopi relies on the statement in *Schultz* that "the government's active enforcement of its ownership rights confirms the intent of the Law" to claim government ownership of all antiquities found in Egypt after 1983. *Schultz*, 333 F.3d at 402. *Schultz* states that enforcement is probative of the intent behind a foreign law, but the opinion falls short of making active enforcement a pleading requirement. *See id.* at 410 ("[O]ur courts are capable of evaluating foreign patrimony laws to determine whether their language and enforcement indicate that they are intended to assert true ownership of certain property, or merely to restrict the export of that property"). If, at a later stage in this case, the Court is called upon to make a definitive determination as to the content of Mongolian law, evidence of Mongolia's active enforcement of its patrimony laws — or lack thereof — may be probative, but the government need not plead active enforcement of these laws in order to state a plausible claim for relief where, as here, the foreign statutes pleaded in the complaint appear on their face to vest title in the Defendant Property in a foreign state.

Little more need be said concerning Prokopi's argument that, even if the Defendant Property is stolen, the amended complaint fails to allege adequately that he had knowledge of its theft. As explained above, the amended complaint alleges that Prokopi is a commercial paleontologist who has excavated skeletons in Mongolia before. This, coupled with Prokopi's alleged attempts to obscure the Defendant Property's country of origin on importation paperwork, raises a reasonable inference that Prokopi knew the Defendant Property was stolen from the Mongolian state.

CONCLUSION

For the foregoing reasons, the amended complaint pleads "sufficiently detailed facts to support a reasonable belief that the government will be able to meet its burden of proof at trial." Rule G, Supp. Rules. Accordingly, Prokopi's motion to dismiss the complaint is DENIED.

Notes

1. Even where cultural links exist to particular objects, the desire to improve the contemporary standard of living has caused many individuals in underdeveloped nations to sacrifice their cultural heritage. The traffic in African art illustrates the complexities of the problem. In 1966, an African wood carving known as the *Afo-A-Kom* of Cameroon

was taken from its ancestral home and transported to a New York art gallery, where it appeared for sale. The events surrounding the transaction are cloudy, although members of the Royal Family of Kom are alleged to have been involved. The *Afo-A-Kom* is a statue that is said to embody the soul of the people of Kom. Its spiritual significance is such that it personifies the Kom belief in animism, through which the spirits and souls of the culture communicate with the present citizens of Kom. The effect of the statue's disappearance on the people of Kom was profound. An integral part of their spiritual life was gone. The Kom blamed all subsequent misfortunes on the loss of the *Afo-A-Kom*. When a Peace Corps volunteer located the statue in New York, Americans quickly registered their outrage. Some went so far as to threaten the dealer who had purchased the piece with physical violence, even though he had done so with no knowledge of its tribal importance. As a result of the efforts of the press, public opinion, a formal request from the Cameroon government, and numerous public contributions, the *Afo-A-Kom* was returned to its ancestral home in 1973. *See* Johnson, *Kom Statue is Back in Cameroon and its Kingdom Plans Biggest Festival of all Time*, N.Y. Times, Dec. 6, 1973, at 27, col. 1.

2. International efforts at urban conservation began to make an impact in 1964, at which time both the Venice Charter and the International Council on Monuments and Sites (ICOMOS) were established. UNESCO's 1972 Convention Concerning the Protection of World Cultural and Natural Heritage also provided international protection to 73 of the world's historically significant cities and towns. By 2016, the World Heritage List included 1031 properties, with 802 cultural, 197 natural, and 32 mixed properties in 163 States Parties.

3. Another route for preserving archaeological sites has been taken by the Archaeological Conservancy, which, like the Nature Conservancy, purchases privately owned sites in order to protect them. The Conservancy has purchased over 465 sites, including Powers Fort, Missouri, a Mississippian cultural-civic-ceremonial center dating to circa 1350, and Lamb Spring near Littleton, Colorado, a Paleo-Indian hunting and game-processing area that may be one of the earliest of its kind in the United States.

4. In 2016, the Islamic State, also known as ISIS or ISIL, destroyed some of the remains of a civilization that 2,000 years ago was a mix of Roman, Persian, and local cultures. The *New York Times* reported, "Where Palmyra's impressive Temple of Bel once stood, only a single stone archway was left to frame a rectangle of blue sky above the arid desert about 160 miles north east of Damascus, the capital." *See* Bryan Denton, *A Jewel in Syria Where 'Ruins have been Ruined' by ISIS*, New York Times, April 4, 2016, available at *http://www.nytimes. com/2016/04/05/world/middleeast/palmyra-syria-isis.html* (last visited on April 7, 2016).

ASSESSMENT

1. In *U.S. v. One Tyrannosaurus Bataar Skeleton*, the Court denied the defendant's motion to dismiss because it found the government's complaint was adequate, as it pled sufficiently detailed facts to support a reasonable belief that the government would be able to meet its burden of proof at trial. Which of the following reasons did the Court give in support of its decision?

   (A) The complaint set out several provisions of Mongolian law that vested ownership in the state over the defendant's property

   (B) It could be inferred that the defendant knew the property was stolen from the Mongolian state because he had excavated skeletons in Mongolia before and he allegedly attempted to obscure the property's country of origin on the importation paperwork

   (C) The complaint sufficiently alleged that the property was introduced contrary to law because the defendant's actions were allegedly in violation of several statutes

   (D) The distinctive coloring of the items was associated with Mongolian dirt

   (E) All of the above

2. The government of Birdlandia commissioned Mary Moral, a famous artist known for her elaborate chicken sculptures, to create one of her designs to sit in the center square of the capital. The sculpture was magnificent and stayed in the center square for over 20 years, however the government failed to clean it or protect it from visiting tourists. After some time the sculpture began to fall apart from the constant touching and climbing that it received from the tourists. Mary Moral came to know of the government's lack of care of her beautiful sculpture and wants to force them to restore her work. Based on the court's decision in *Sehgal v. Union of India*, what is Mary's best argument to get the government of Birdlandia to comply with her wishes?

   (A) The government of Birdlandia has to comply with her wishes because Mary is the artist of the sculpture, thus she is vested with the copyright of her work

   (B) As the artist of the sculpture, she has moral rights to her work and that includes the right to object to the distortion, mutilation or modification of her work because it is prejudicial to her reputation as a famous artist

   (C) The government has a duty to protect the works of art they commission

   (D) Both (A) and (C)

   (E) None of the above

3. Corey Collector was traveling across the border of Canastate when customs officers stopped him. In his possession were several beautiful miniature sculptures that appeared to be from the lost civilization of Jurassic Park, which was once located in present day Texacana, Georgiacana, and Sealandia. After finding these sculptures, the Canastate officials seized the items from Corey and Texicana now wishes to reclaim them. Based on the court's decision in *Government of Peru v. Johnson*, what are Corey's best arguments in order to regain possession of the sculpture?

   (A) There is no way to determine that the sculptures were from modern day Texicana; in fact they may be from any of the other countries where Jurassic Park once existed

   (B) Corey purchased the items in good faith

   (C) Both (A) and (B)

   (D) There is no way to know if the sculptures are not replicas

   (E) None of the above

4. What actions are hindering countries' preservation of their cultural histories found in historical sites and ancient artifacts?

   (A) The looting and illegal trafficking of artifacts because they lose much of their archeological significance when removed from their sites

   (B) The legal exportation or acquisition of art and artifacts, because excavation, legal or not, is inconsistent with the preservation of archaeological values

   (C) The housing of artifacts in underground private collections, which allow no access to scholars wishing to learn new knowledge of their country's cultural past

   (D) Both (A) and (C)

   (E) None of the above

5. Peggy Paleo, a French sculpture collector and an expert on Egyptian artifacts, had bought several Egyptian statues from a street dealer during her visit to Morocco. When she inquired into how he was able to find such valuable objects, he told her an elaborate story about how the objects miraculously appeared in his bag one day while visiting an ancient burial site near the Great Pyramid. Although she found his story to be a little silly, she did not think he had done anything illegal in obtaining the items because he seemed like a good person, so she bought the sculptures. A few years later, she moved to California; however, while transporting the sculptures to her new home, the United States government seized the items. Peggy is now being charged for the transportation of stolen Egyptian antiquities in violation of the National Stolen Property Act (NSPA). Which of the following would be Peggy's best defense to the government's claim?

(A) She did not know her actions were criminal because she was not aware the statues were stolen from Egypt

(B) She was unaware of Egyptian patrimony law or U.S. law prohibiting her actions

(C) If the statues were stolen, that illegal act did not occur in the United States and she is not a U.S. citizen, therefore the NSPA does not apply

(D) Both (B) and (C)

(E) None of the above

ASSESSMENT ANSWERS

1. In *U.S. v. One Tyrannosaurus Bataar Skeleton*, the Court denied the defendant's motion to dismiss because it found the government's complaint was adequate because it pled sufficiently detailed facts to support a reasonable belief that the government would be able to meet its burden of proof at trial. Which of the following reasons did the Court give in support of its decision?

   (A) The complaint set out several provisions of Mongolian law that vested ownership in the state over the defendant's property

   (B) It could be inferred that the defendant knew the property was stolen from the Mongolian state because he had excavated skeletons in Mongolia before and he allegedly attempted to obscure the property's country of origin on the importation paperwork

   (C) The complaint sufficiently alleged that the property was introduced contrary to law because the defendants actions were allegedly in violation of several statutes

   (D) The distinctive coloring of the items was associated with Mongolian dirt

   (E) All of the above

   ANSWER: The correct answer is (E) because it includes (A), (B), (C), and (D), which are all correct reasons given by the Court in support of their denial of the defendant's motion to dismiss.

2. The government of Birdlandia commissioned Mary Moral, a famous artist known for her elaborate chicken sculptures, to create one of her designs to sit in the center square of the capital. The sculpture was magnificent and stayed in the center square for over 20 years, however the government failed to clean it or protect it from visiting tourists. After some time the sculpture began to fall apart from the constant touching and climbing that it received from the tourists. Mary Moral came to know of the government's lack of care of her beautiful sculpture and wants to force them to restore her work. Based on the court's

decision in *Sehgal v. Union of India*, what is Mary's best argument to get the government of Birdlandia to comply with her wishes?

(A) The government of Birdlandia has to comply with her wishes because Mary is the artist of the sculpture, thus she is vested with the copyright of her work

(B) As the artist of the sculpture, she has moral rights to her work and that includes the right to object to the distortion, mutilation or modification of her work because it is prejudicial to her reputation as a famous artist

(C) The government has a duty to protect the works of art they commission

(D) Both (A) and (C)

(E) None of the above

ANSWER: The correct answer is (B) because the court held that an artist is entitled to the moral rights of his or her work, which includes the right to object to the distortion, mutilation or modification of that work because it is prejudicial to his or her reputation. Answer (A) is incorrect because the copyright of her work would have been vested by contract in the commissioning party, which here is the government of Birdlandia. Answer (C) is incorrect because no such duty exists. Answer (D) is incorrect because it references incorrect answers, and answer (E) is incorrect because there is a correct answer above.

3. Corey Collector was traveling across the border of Canastate when customs officers stopped him. In his possession were several beautiful miniature sculptures that appeared to be from the lost civilization of Jurassic Park, which was once located in present day Texacana, Georgiacana, and Sealandia. After finding these sculptures, the Canastate officials seized the items from Corey and Texicana now wishes to reclaim them. Based on the court's decision in *Government of Peru v. Johnson*, what are Corey's best arguments in order to regain possession of the sculpture?

(A) There is no way to determine that the sculptures were from modern day Texicana, in fact they may be from any of the other countries where Jurassic Park once existed

(B) Corey purchased the items in good faith

(C) Both (A) and (B)

(D) There is no way to know if the sculptures are not replicas

(E) None of the above

ANSWER: The correct answer is (C) because it includes both answers (A) and (B). When items have been purchased in good faith, the plaintiff has the burden of overcoming legal and factual burdens, including that the objects were from the plaintiff's country. Answer (C) is an incorrect statement of law. Answer (E) is the incorrect answer because there were two correct answers above.

4. What actions are hindering countries' preservation of their cultural histories found in historical sites and ancient artifacts?

(A) The looting and illegal trafficking of artifacts because they lose much of their archeological significance when removed from their sites

(B) The legal exportation or acquisition of art and artifacts, because excavation, legal or not, is inconsistent with the preservation of archaeological values

(C) The housing of artifacts in underground private collections, which allow no access to scholars wishing to learn new knowledge of their country's cultural past

(D) Both (A) and (C)

(E) None of the above

ANSWER: The correct answer is (D) because it incorporates answers (A) and (C), which are both correct statements concerning the issues countries are facing in preserving their cultural histories. Answer (B) is incorrect because archaeological interests can be completely consistent with export as long as the excavation is conducted properly, the piece's provenance is carefully noted, and the excavating or exporting party does nothing to contravene the laws of the state involved. Answer (E) is incorrect because there are correct answers above.

5. Peggy Paleo, a French sculpture collector and an expert on Egyptian artifacts, had bought several Egyptian statues from a street dealer during her visit to Morocco. When she inquired into how he was able to find such valuable objects, he told her an elaborate story about how the objects miraculously appeared in his bag one day while visiting an ancient burial site near the Great Pyramid. Although she found his story to be a little silly, she did not think he had done anything illegal in obtaining the items because he seemed like a good person, so she bought the sculptures. A few years later, she moved to California, however, while transporting the sculptures to her new home, the United States government seized the items. Peggy is now being charged for the transportation of stolen Egyptian antiquities in violation of the National Stolen Property Act (NSPA). Which of the following would be Peggy's best defense to the government's claim?

(A) She did not know her actions were criminal because she was not aware the statues were stolen from Egypt

(B) She was unaware of Egyptian patrimony law or U.S. law prohibiting her actions

(C) If the statues were stolen, that illegal act did not occur in the United States and she is not a U.S. citizen, therefore the NSPA does not apply

(D) Both (B) and (C)

(E) None of the above

ANSWER: The correct answer is (A). According to *U.S. v. Shultz*, a defendant charged with violating the NSPA may argue that he did not know a certain fact that made his conduct criminal; that is, that he did not know the objects in question were stolen. Answer (B) is incorrect because a mistake of law defense could be raised in order to show that a defendant charged with violating the NSPA did not know a certain fact that made his conduct criminal. However, here this would not be Peggy's best defense because she is an expert on Egyptian artifacts and therefore should have known about the Egyptian patrimony law. Answer (C) is incorrect because the fact that the property was not stolen in the United States and that the rightful owner of the stolen property is foreign has no impact on a prosecution under the NSPA. Answer (D) is incorrect because it incorporates incorrect answers, and answer (E) is incorrect because there is a correct answer above.

12 | NATIVE AMERICAN AND INDIGENOUS PEOPLES' ART

A. Historical Background

The United States enacted several laws to conserve the art and cultural property of its indigenous peoples. The Archaeological Resources Protection Act of 1979 (ARPA)[1] imposes stiff penalties on those who violate its terms. Specifically, the statutory prohibition reads:

> No person may excavate, remove, damage, or otherwise alter or deface, or attempt to excavate, remove, damage, or otherwise alter or deface any archaeological resource located on public lands or Indian lands unless such activity is pursuant [to an authorizing permit issued under the Act].
>
> No person may sell, purchase, exchange, transport, receive, or offer to sell, purchase, or exchange any archaeological resource if such resource was excavated or removed from public lands or Indian lands in violation [of the Act or any other applicable federal law].
>
> No person may sell, purchase, exchange, transport, receive, or offer to sell, purchase, or exchange, in interstate or foreign commerce, any archaeological resource excavated, removed, sold, purchased, exchanged, transported, or received in violation of any provision, rule, regulation, ordinance, or permit in effect under State or local law.[2]

The Act provides criminal penalties including fines of up to $100,000 and imprisonment for up to five years,[3] and authorizes federal land managers to impose civil penalties. The prohibitions contained in the statute are not retroactive; they do not encompass activities related to objects lawfully owned prior to October 31, 1979.

ARPA was drafted in response to widely perceived deficiencies in the Antiquities Act of 1906.[4] The Antiquities Act had been intended to curtail the

---

1. Archaeological Resources Protection Act of 1979 (ARPA), 16 U.S.C. §§ 470 *et seq.* (1990).
2. 16 U.S.C. §§ 470ee(a)-(c).
3. 16 U.S.C. § 470ee(d).
4. Antiquities Act of 1906, 16 U.S.C. §§ 431-33 (1906).

rampant looting and destruction of sites rich in American Indian artifacts. Throughout the nineteenth and into the twentieth centuries, treasure hunters resorted to excessive means to unearth the artifacts, including the use of explosives to clear sites. Unfortunately, the legislation subsequently enacted was quite narrow in scope. In *United States v. Diaz*,[5] an attempt was made to apply the statute to one-year-old Apache ceremonial masks. The court concluded that the law was unconstitutionally vague. Other courts reached the opposite conclusion, as in *United States v. Smyer*,[6] where defendants had excavated 800- to 900-year-old Indian potsherds and the 1906 law was upheld. In spite of the decision in *Diaz*, the government was successful in prosecuting archaeological vandalism in the Ninth Circuit as theft and depredation of federal property.[7]

The Native American Graves Protection and Repatriation Act (NAGPRA)[8] was enacted in 1990. According to *Thorpe v. Borough of Jim Thorpe*,[9] it was enacted "as a way to correct past abuses to, and guarantee protection for, the human remains and cultural objects of Native American tribal culture."[10] It was passed with two main objectives: "first, to protect Native American burial sites and to require excavation of such sites only by permit, and second, to set up a process by which federal agencies and museums holding Native American remains and cultural artifacts will inventory those items and work with tribes to repatriate them."[11] The Act was an attempt to respond to the looting and plundering of Native American burial grounds and the theft of cultural artifacts from Native American tribes that continued to pour salt into the many wounds that have been inflicted on Native Americans throughout the history of the United States. (The *Thorpe* case is excerpted in section C below.) At NAGPRA's core is the issue of "Who is Native American?"

B. Who Is Native American?

Bonnichsen v. U.S.

367 F.3d 864 (9th Cir. 2004)

GOULD, Circuit Judge.

This is a case about the ancient human remains of a man who hunted and lived, or at least journeyed, in the Columbia Plateau an estimated 8340 to 9200 years ago, a time predating all recorded history from any place in the

---

5. *United States v. Diaz*, 499 F.2d 113 (9th Cir. 1974).

6. *United States v. Smyer*, 596 F.2d 939 (10th Cir.), *cert. denied*, 444 U.S. 843 (1979).

7. *United States v. Jones*, 607 F.2d 269 (9th Cir. 1979), *cert. denied*, 444 U.S. 1085 (1980).

8. Native American Graves Protection and Repatriation Act (NAGPRA), Pub. L. 101-601, 104 Stat. 3048, codified at 25 U.S.C. 3001 et seq.

9. *Thorpe v. Borough of Thorpe*, 770 F.3d 255, 259–60 (3d Cir. 2014), *cert. denied sub nom. Sac & Fox Nation of Oklahoma v. Borough of Jim Thorpe, Pa.*, 136 S. Ct. 84, 193 L. Ed. 2d 207 (2015).

10. *Id.*; *see also* 173 A.L.R. Fed. 585.

11. *Kickapoo Traditional Tribe of Tex. v. Chacon*, 46 F. Supp. 2d 644, 649 (W.D. Tex. 1999).

world, a time before the oldest cities of our world had been founded, a time so ancient that the pristine and untouched land and the primitive cultures that may have lived on it are not deeply understood by even the most well-informed men and women of our age. Seeking the opportunity of study, a group of scientists as Plaintiffs in this case brought an action against, inter alia, the United States Department of the Interior, challenging various Indian tribes' claim to one of the most important American anthropological and archaeological discoveries of the late twentieth century, and challenging the Interior Department's decision honoring the tribes' claim. The discovery that launched this contest was that of a human skeleton, estimated by carbon dating to be 8340 to 9200 years old, known popularly and commonly as "Kennewick Man," but known as "the Ancient One" to some American Indians[3] who now inhabit regions in Washington, Idaho, and Oregon, roughly proximate to the site on the Columbia River at Kennewick, Washington, where the bones were found. From the perspective of the scientists-Plaintiffs, this skeleton is an irreplaceable source of information about early New World populations that warrants careful scientific inquiry to advance knowledge of distant times. Yet, from the perspective of the intervenor-Indian tribes the skeleton is that of an ancestor who, according to the tribes' religious and social traditions, should be buried immediately without further testing.

Plaintiffs filed this lawsuit seeking to stop the transfer of the skeleton by the government to the tribes for burial, and the district court held in favor of the scientists-Plaintiffs. The Secretary of the Interior and the intervenor-Indian tribes appeal. We have jurisdiction under 28 U.S.C. § 1291 and affirm the judgment of the district court barring the transfer of the skeleton for immediate burial and instead permitting scientific study of the skeleton.

I

In July 1996, teenagers going to a boat race discovered a human skull and bones near the shore of the Columbia River just outside Kennewick, Washington. The remains were found on federal property under the management of the United States Army Corps of Engineers ("Corps") and, at the request of the county coroner, were removed for analysis by an anthropologist, Dr. James Chatters, pursuant to an Archaeological Resources Protection Act of 1979 ("ARPA"), 16 U.S.C. §§ 470aa-470mm, permit. Because of physical features such as the shape of the skull and facial bones, anthropologists at first thought the remains were those of an early European settler. But the anthropologists then found a stone projectile point embedded in the skeleton's upper hip bone. The object's design, when viewed with x-rays and CT scans of the hip, resembled a style that was common before the documented arrival of Europeans in the region. Further study of the remains revealed characteristics unlike those of a European settler, yet also inconsistent with any American

---

3. We use the term "American Indian" because the definition of "Native American," as used in Native American Graves Protection and Repatriation Act, is a disputed issue in this appeal.

Indian remains previously documented in the region. A minute quantity of metacarpal bone was radiocarbon dated. The laboratory estimated the age of the bones to be between 8340 and 9200 years old.

The skeleton attracted attention because some of its physical features, such as the shape of the face and skull, differed from those of modern American Indians. Many scientists believed the discovery might shed light on the origins of humanity in the Americas. On August 31, 1996, Dr. Douglas Owsley, Division Head for Physical Anthropology at the Smithsonian Institution in Washington, D.C., made arrangements for Dr. Chatters to bring this important find to the Smithsonian's National Museum of Natural History for further study.

Indian tribes from the area of the Columbia River opposed scientific study of the remains on religious and social grounds. Four Indian groups (the "Tribal Claimants") demanded that the remains be turned over to them for immediate burial. The Tribal Claimants based their demand on the Native American Graves Protection and Repatriation Act ("NAGPRA"), 25 U.S.C. § 3001 et seq. The Corps agreed with the Tribal Claimants and, citing NAGPRA, seized the remains on September 10, 1996, shortly before they could be transported to the Smithsonian. The Corps also ordered an immediate halt to DNA testing, which was being done using the remainder of the bone sample that had been submitted earlier for radiocarbon dating. After investigation, the Corps decided to give the remains to the Tribal Claimants for burial. As required by NAGPRA, the Corps published a "Notice of Intent to Repatriate Human Remains" in a local newspaper on September 17, 1996, and September 24, 1996.

The scientists and others, including the Smithsonian Institution, objected to the Corps' decision, arguing that the remains were a rare discovery of national and international significance. In late September and early October 1996, several scientists asked Major General Ernest J. Herrell, Commander of the Corps' North Pacific Division, to allow qualified scientists to study the remains.

The scientists did not convince the Corps to permit them to study the remains, and commenced this litigation on October 16, 1996, in the United States District Court for the District of Oregon. In an opinion issued June 27, 1997, the district court denied the Corps' motion for summary judgment, finding that the Corps had "acted before it had all of the evidence," "did not fully consider or resolve certain difficult legal questions," and "assumed facts that proved to be erroneous." *Bonnichsen II*, 969 F. Supp. 628, 645 (D. Or. 1997). The district court vacated the Corps' earlier decision on disposition of the remains and remanded the case to the Corps for further proceedings. *Id.* at 644-45. The district court also denied, without prejudice, Plaintiffs' motion to study the remains and directed the Corps to consider, on remand, "whether to grant [P]laintiffs' request [under ARPA] for permission to study the remains." *Id.* at 632, 651.

On March 24, 1998, the Corps and the Secretary of the Interior entered into an agreement that effectively assigned to the Secretary responsibility to decide whether the remains were "Native American" under NAGPRA, and to determine their proper disposition. The Department of the Interior then assumed the role of lead agency on this case.

Almost two years after this matter was remanded, the Secretary's experts began to examine the remains in detail. The experts estimated that Kennewick Man was 5'9" to 5'10" tall, 45 to 50 years of age when he died, and 15 to 20 years old when the projectile point became embedded in his hip. The experts could not determine, from non-destructive examination of the skeleton alone, when Kennewick Man lived. However, analysis of sediment layers where the skeleton was found supported the hypothesis that the remains dated back not less than 7600 years ago and Kennewick Man could have lived more than 9000 years ago (the date indicated by the initial radiocarbon dating of the skeleton). Further study of the sediment was recommended, but the Corps' decision to bury the discovery site in April 1998 prevented completion of those studies.

The experts compared the physical characteristics of the remains — e.g., measurements of the skull, teeth, and bones — with corresponding measurements from other skeletons. They concluded that Kennewick Man's remains were unlike those of any known present-day population, American Indian or otherwise.

The Secretary's experts cautioned, however, that an apparent lack of physical resemblance between the Kennewick Man's remains and present-day American Indians did not completely rule out the possibility that the remains might be biologically ancestral to modern American Indians. Moreover, although Kennewick Man's morphological traits did not closely resemble those of modern American Indian populations, the Secretary's experts noted that Kennewick Man's physical attributes are generally consistent with the very small number of human remains from this period that have been found in North America.

Relying solely on the age of the remains and the fact that the remains were found within the United States, on January 13, 2000, the Secretary pronounced Kennewick Man's remains "Native American" within NAGPRA's meaning. And on September 25, 2000, the Secretary determined that a preponderance of the evidence supported the conclusion that the Kennewick remains were culturally affiliated with present-day Indian tribes. For this reason, the Secretary announced his final decision to award Kennewick Man's remains to a coalition of the Tribal Claimants. The Corps and the Secretary also denied Plaintiffs' request to study the remains.

Plaintiffs filed an amended complaint in the district court challenging the Secretary's decisions. The district court again ruled in Plaintiffs' favor. As pertinent to this appeal, the district court vacated the Secretary's decisions as contrary to the Administrative Procedure Act, 5 U.S.C. § 706(2)(A) ("APA"), on the ground that the Secretary improperly concluded that NAGPRA applies. *Bonnichsen III*, 217 F. Supp. 2d at 1138-39. The district court also held that, because NAGPRA did not apply, Plaintiffs should have the opportunity to study Kennewick Man's remains under ARPA. Defendants and the Tribal Claimants appealed, and we stayed the district court's order granting Plaintiffs-scientists' study of the remains pending our decision herein.

II

We first address an issue of jurisdiction. The Tribal Claimants argue that we lack jurisdiction because: (1) Plaintiffs' alleged injuries are not "redressable" by court action, and (2) Plaintiffs lack standing to bring claims alleging violations of NAGPRA because Plaintiffs do not seek to invoke interests within the "zone of interests" protected by NAGPRA. [The court concluded that it possessed jurisdiction because the Plaintiffs' injury will be redressed by a favorable decision on the NAGPRA issue, and thus Plaintiffs have constitutional standing. The court also concluded that it had jurisdiction over Plaintiffs' claims that NAGPRA was violated.]

III

Our review of the Secretary's decision to transfer Kennewick Man to the Tribal Claimants is governed by the APA, which instructs courts to "hold unlawful and set aside agency action, findings, and conclusions found to be . . . arbitrary, capricious, an abuse of discretion, or otherwise not in accordance with law." 5 U.S.C. § 706(2)(A).

NAGPRA vests "ownership or control" of newly discovered Native American human remains in the decedent's lineal descendants or, if lineal descendants cannot be ascertained, in a tribe "affiliated" with the remains. 25 U.S.C. § 3002(a). NAGPRA mandates a two-part analysis. The first inquiry is whether human remains are Native American within the statute's meaning. If the remains are not Native American, then NAGPRA does not apply. However, if the remains are Native American, then NAGPRA applies, triggering the second inquiry of determining which persons or tribes are most closely affiliated with the remains.

The parties dispute whether the remains of Kennewick Man constitute Native American remains within NAGPRA's meaning. NAGPRA defines human remains as "Native American" if the remains are "of, or relating to, a tribe, people, or culture that is indigenous to the United States." 25 U.S.C. § 3001(9). The text of the relevant statutory clause is written in the present tense ("of, or relating to, a tribe, people, or culture that is indigenous"). Thus the statute unambiguously requires that human remains bear some relationship to a presently existing tribe, people, or culture to be considered Native American. . . .

In the context of NAGPRA, we conclude that Congress's use of the present tense is significant. The present tense "in general represents present time." R. Pence & D. Emery, *A Grammar of Present Day English* 262 (2d ed. 1963). Congress, by using the phrase "is indigenous" in the present tense, referred to presently existing tribes, peoples, or cultures. We must presume that Congress gave the phrase "is indigenous" its ordinary or natural meaning. *Alvarez-Sanchez*, 511 U.S. at 357, 114 S. Ct. 1599. We conclude that Congress was referring to presently existing Indian tribes when it referred to "a tribe, people, or culture that is indigenous to the United States." 25 U.S.C. § 3001(9) (emphasis added).

NAGPRA also protects graves of persons not shown to be of current tribes in that it protects disjunctively remains "of, or relating to" current indigenous tribes. Thus, NAGPRA extends to all remains that relate to a tribe, people, or culture that is indigenous to the United States, *see* 25 U.S.C. § 3001(9) (defining human remains as Native American if they are "of, or relating to, a tribe, people, or culture that is indigenous to the United States").

Our conclusion that NAGPRA's language requires that human remains, to be considered Native American, bear some relationship to a presently existing tribe, people, or culture accords with NAGPRA's purposes. As regards newly discovered human remains, NAGPRA was enacted with two main goals: to respect the burial traditions of modern-day American Indians and to protect the dignity of the human body after death. NAGPRA was intended to benefit modern American Indians by sparing them the indignity and resentment that would be aroused by the despoiling of their ancestors' graves and the study or the display of their ancestors' remains. *See* H.R. Rep. No. 101-877, U.S. Code Cong. & Admin. News at 4367, 4369 (1990) ("For many years, Indian tribes have attempted to have the remains and funerary objects of their ancestors returned to them").

Congress's purposes would not be served by requiring the transfer to modern American Indians of human remains that bear no relationship to them. Yet, that would be the result under the Secretary's construction of the statute, which would give Native American status to any remains found within the United States regardless of age and regardless of lack of connection to existing indigenous tribes. The exhumation, study, and display of ancient human remains that are unrelated to modern American Indians was not a target of Congress's aim, nor was it precluded by NAGPRA.

NAGPRA was also intended to protect the dignity of the human body after death by ensuring that Native American graves and remains be treated with respect. . . . Congress's purpose is served by requiring the return to modern-day American Indians of human remains that bear some significant relationship to them. . . .

Our analysis is strengthened by contrasting the statutory definition of the adjective "Native American" to the statutory definition of the noun "Native Hawaiian." Under § 3001(9), "'Native American' means of, or relating to, a tribe, people, or culture that is indigenous to the United States." Under § 3001(10), "'Native Hawaiian' means any individual who is a descendant of the aboriginal people who, prior to 1778, occupied and exercised sovereignty in the area that now constitutes the State of Hawaii."

The "United States" is a political entity that dates back to 1789. *Owings v. Speed*, 18 U.S. (5 Wheat.) 420, 423, 5 L. Ed. 124 (1820). This term supports that Congress's use of the present tense ("that is indigenous") referred to tribes, peoples, and cultures that exist in modern times, not to those that may have existed thousands of years ago but who do not exist now. By contrast, when

Congress chose to harken back to earlier times, it described a geographic location ("the area that now constitutes the State of Hawaii") rather than a political entity ("the United States").

Our conclusion that NAGPRA requires human remains to bear some relationship to a presently existing tribe, people, or culture to be considered "Native American" is also reinforced by how NAGPRA defines "sacred objects." NAGPRA defines "sacred objects" as "specific ceremonial objects which are needed by traditional Native American religious leaders for the practice of traditional Native American religions by their present day adherents." 25 U.S.C. § 3001(3)(C). A literal reading of this definition reveals that any artifact to be deemed a "sacred object" must be connected to the practice of an American Indian religion by present-day peoples. This reading is consistent with our reading of "Native American"; that is, just as there must be a relationship between an artifact and a presently existing peoples for the artifact to be a "sacred object" under NAGPRA, there must be a relationship between a set of remains and a presently existing tribe, people, or culture for those remains to be "Native American" under NAGPRA.

Although NAGPRA does not specify precisely what kind of a relationship or precisely how strong a relationship ancient human remains must bear to modern Indian groups to qualify as Native American, NAGPRA's legislative history provides some guidance on what type of relationship may suffice. The House Committee on Interior and Insular Affairs emphasized in its report on NAGPRA that the statute was being enacted with modern-day American Indians' identifiable ancestors in mind. *See, e.g.,* H.R. Rep. No. 101-877, U.S. Code Cong. & Admin. News at 4367, 4372 (1990). . . . Human remains that are 8340 to 9200 years old and that bear only incidental genetic resemblance to modern-day American Indians, along with incidental genetic resemblance to other peoples, cannot be said to be the Indians' "ancestors" within Congress's meaning. Congress enacted NAGPRA to give American Indians control over the remains of their genetic and cultural forbearers, not over the remains of people bearing no special and significant genetic or cultural relationship to some presently existing indigenous tribe, people, or culture.

The age of Kennewick Man's remains, given the limited studies to date, makes it almost impossible to establish any relationship between the remains and presently existing American Indians. At least no significant relationship has yet been shown. We cannot give credence to an interpretation of NAGPRA advanced by the government and the Tribal Claimants that would apply its provisions to remains that have at most a tenuous, unknown, and unproven connection, asserted solely because of the geographical location of the find.

IV

Finally, we address the Secretary's determination that Kennewick Man's remains are Native American, as defined by NAGPRA. We must set aside the Secretary's decision if it was "arbitrary" or "capricious" because the decision was based on inadequate factual support. *See* 5 U.S.C. § 706(2)(A). We review the full agency record to determine whether substantial evidence supports the agency's decision that Kennewick Man is "Native American" within NAGPRA's meaning. Here, after reviewing the record, we conclude that the record does not contain substantial evidence that Kennewick Man's remains are Native American within NAGPRA's meaning.

The administrative record contains no evidence—let alone substantial evidence—that Kennewick Man's remains are connected by some special or significant genetic or cultural relationship to any presently existing indigenous tribe, people, or culture. An examination of the record demonstrates the absence of evidence that Kennewick Man and modern tribes share significant genetic or cultural features.

No cognizable link exists between Kennewick Man and modern Columbia Plateau Indians. When Kennewick Man's remains were discovered, local coroners initially believed the remains were those of a European, not a Native American, because of their appearance. Later testing by scientists demonstrated that the cranial measurements and features of Kennewick Man most closely resemble those of Polynesians and southern Asians, and that Kennewick Man's measurements and features differ significantly from those of any modern Indian group living in North America.

Scant or no evidence of cultural similarities between Kennewick Man and modern Indians exists. One of the Secretary's experts, Dr. Kenneth Ames, reported that "the empirical gaps in the record preclude establishing cultural continuities or discontinuities, particularly before about 5000 B.C." Dr. Ames noted that, although there was overwhelming evidence that many aspects of the "Plateau Pattern" were present between 1000 B.C. and A.D. 1, "the empirical record precludes establishing cultural continuities or discontinuities across increasingly remote periods." He noted that the available evidence is insufficient either to prove or disprove cultural or group continuity dating back earlier than 5000 B.C., which is the case with regard to the Kennewick Man's remains, and that there is evidence that substantial changes occurred in settlement, housing, diet, trade, subsistence patterns, technology, projectile point styles, raw materials, and mortuary rituals at various times between the estimated date when Kennewick Man lived and the beginning of the "Plateau Culture" some 2000 to 3000 years ago.

Dr. Ames' conclusions about the impossibility of establishing cultural continuity between Kennewick Man and modern Indians is confirmed by other evidence that the Secretary credited. For example, the Secretary acknowledges that the record shows that there were no villages or permanent settlements in the Columbia Plateau region 9000 years ago and that human populations then were small and nomadic, traveling long distances in search of food and raw materials. The Secretary's experts determined, and the Secretary acknowledged, that it was not until 2000 to 3000 years ago that populations began to settle into the villages and bands that may have been the antecedents of modern Indian tribes something like those encountered by European settlers and colonists. As the Secretary summarized, "[c]ultural discontinuities are suggested by evidence that the cultural group existing 8500-9500 years ago was likely small in size and highly mobile while the Plateau culture consisted o[f] larger, more sedentary groups."

The Secretary also acknowledges that "there is very little evidence of burial patterns during the 9500-8500 period and significant temporal gaps exist in the mortuary record for other periods." So, even if we assume that Kennewick Man was part of a stable social group living in the area, it still would be impossible to say whether his group's burial practices were related to modern tribes' burial practices. The Secretary also noted that "the linguistic analysis was unable to provide reliable evidence for the 8500-9500 period."

The Secretary's only evidence, perhaps, of a possible cultural relationship between Kennewick Man and modern-day American Indians comes in the form of oral histories. One of the Secretary's experts, Dr. Daniel Boxberger, concluded that modern day Plateau tribes' oral histories — some of which can be interpreted to refer to ancient floods, volcanic eruptions, and the like — are "highly suggestive of long-term establishment of the present-day tribes." . . . But evidence in the record demonstrates that oral histories change relatively quickly, that oral histories may be based on later observation of geological features and deduction (rather than on the first teller's witnessing ancient events), and that these oral histories might be from a culture or group other than the one to which Kennewick Man belonged. The oral traditions relied upon by the Secretary's expert, Dr. Boxberger, entail some published accounts of Native American folk narratives from the Columbia Plateau region, and statements from individual tribal members. But we conclude that these accounts are just not specific enough or reliable enough or relevant enough to show a significant relationship of the Tribal Claimants with Kennewick Man. . . . As the district court observed, 8340 to 9200 years between the life of Kennewick Man and the present is too long a time to bridge merely with evidence of oral traditions.

Considered as a whole, the administrative record might permit the Secretary to conclude reasonably that the Tribal Claimants' ancestors have lived in the region for a very long time. However, because Kennewick Man's remains are so old and the information about his era is so limited, the record does not permit the Secretary to conclude reasonably that Kennewick Man shares special and significant genetic or cultural features with presently existing indigenous tribes, people, or cultures. We thus hold that Kennewick Man's remains are not Native American human remains within the meaning of NAGPRA and that NAGPRA does not apply to them. Studies of the Kennewick Man's remains by Plaintiffs-scientists may proceed pursuant to ARPA.

We remand to the district court for further proceedings consistent with this opinion. AFFIRMED.

Notes

1. In 2015, according to the International Foundation for Art Research, researchers successfully sequenced the Kennewick Man's genome using

DNA analysis of a bone fragment and concluded that he is closely related to the Colville people, one of the five tribes that originally claimed him. Although some scientists questioned that interpretation, the Army Corps of Engineers began "documenting tribal affiliation under the stringent terms of NAGPRA so the Kennewick Man may be repatriated." *See http:// www.ifar.org/case_summary.php?docid=1179587769* (Last visited on April 20, 2016).

2. In 1976, a rare double human burial site was discovered on a La Jolla bluff, which happened to be the official residence of the Chancellor of the University of California, San Diego. After unearthing the remains, scientists determined they were between 8,977 and 9,603 years old, giving them great scientific value. Scientists sought to study the remains; however, the University, in an attempt to comply with NAGPRA, granted a request from the Kumeyaay Cultural Repatriation Committee (KCRC) to transfer them to the La Posta Band of the Diegueño Mission Indians, a federally-recognized Kumeyaay tribe. In response, several scientists sued the KCRC and the University, hoping to block the transfer and prevent the reburial of the scientifically valuable remains.

   In *White v. University of California*, 2012 WL 12335354, (N.D. Cal. Oct. 9, 2012), aff'd, 765 F.3d 1010 (9th Cir. 2014), the court reluctantly granted both the KCRC's and the University's motions to dismiss, stating "[s]uch a result is not reached lightly. It is, rather, compelled by tribal immunity, and admittedly, raises troubling questions about the availability of judicial review under NAGPRA." The court pointed out that, although NAGRPA does not limit jurisdiction to suits brought by American Indians or Indian tribes, the availability of judicial review by non-Indians is frustrated by tribal sovereign immunity. In other words, despite the holding in *Bonnichsen*, where the court held NAGPRA was not intended to protect the interests of Indians alone, non-Indians are easily blocked by tribal claims of sovereign immunity. The result is the right of "the tribes to claim the benefit of NAGPRA, without subjecting themselves to its attendant limitations."

Livingston v. Ewing

455 F. Supp. 825 (D.N.M. 1978), *aff'd*, 601 F.2d 1110 (10th Cir. 1979)

MECHEM, J.

This action is before the Court on cross motions for summary judgment by plaintiffs Livingston and defendants Ewing and the Museum of New Mexico. These parties are in agreement and I find that there is no genuine issue of material fact; intervenors oppose the motions for summary judgment, but I find that, on the basis of the law, affidavits, exhibits, and testimony submitted with these motions, it is proper to grant summary judgment in favor of the defendants.

This case involves the question of whether the Museum of New Mexico's policy permitting only Indians to sell their hand-made goods under the portal of the Palace of the Governors violates the Equal Protection Clause of the Fourteenth Amendment of the United States Constitution. Plaintiffs argue that the policy violates the Fourteenth Amendment because it is an unjustified classification based upon race. Defendants claim that there is a rational basis for the policy, and that they may constitutionally give a preference to Indians. Intervenors are Indian craftspeople who sell their wares under the portal; they argue that the Museum may undertake programs which enhance the ability of distinct cultural communities to maintain their self-determination and lifestyle.

FACTS

In 1909, the New Mexico Legislature established the Museum of New Mexico, giving its Board of Regents the responsibility for management and control of the property and policy of the Museum. The historic Palace of the Governors in Santa Fe, the oldest public building in the United States, was placed under the control of the Regents for the use of the Museum. The portal is the patio portion of the Palace of the Governors and is thus under the control of the Regents. When the Museum was created, it was dedicated to the presentation and preservation of New Mexico's multicultural traditions.

The Palace of the Governors has historically been visited and used for various purposes by several cultural groups. The Pueblo Indians occupied the Palace after the Pueblo Revolt of 1680-1693, and subsequent to the Reconquest by the Spaniards, the Indians sought justice from the governors in disputes over land, water, and personal rights. In addition, the Indians travelled to the Palace to sell food and miscellaneous wares. The plaza area was used as a market place by both Hispanos and Pueblo Indians after the Spanish conquest; later, Anglo traders and businessmen established shops in the plaza. Sometime prior to 1853, several ethnic groups began to use the portal as a public market place. By 1909, the non-Indian groups had largely abandoned the portal and only the Indian market remained.

The Museum's first director adopted a policy of incorporating the Pueblo Indians into the program of the Museum; they were encouraged to utilize its facilities to revitalize their native arts and crafts, for their own economic benefit, and for the benefit of the Pueblo communities as a whole. In addition, it was felt that by stimulating the native crafts, New Mexico's rich and diverse ethnic traditions would be highlighted and preserved. Finally, the presence on the Palace grounds of the Indians as they made and sold their crafts provided living educational exhibits, from which the public has benefited.

In 1935, the Museum began to permit only Indians to use the space in the portal for the sale of their arts and crafts. At that time, by agreement with the Museum, the New Mexico Association of Indian Affairs sponsored an Indian Market under the portal. It was discontinued during World War II but immediately thereafter the Museum permitted exclusive year-round use of the portal by the Indians. This practice has been in effect since that time, but was formalized as Museum policy by the Regents in 1972. In February, 1976, a written policy statement was issued to ensure that no vendors would be allowed to sell on Museum property, except the Indians.[1] There is no dispute that the Museum policy grants a preference to Indians not afforded to non-Indians.

The Indians under the portal are charged with the responsibility of allocating the space, maintaining a fair and orderly market, and guaranteeing that the articles offered for sale are genuine Indian handmade goods. It is not the policy of the Regents to operate an open market: the portal is to be used for the Indian program or not at all.

The program is not limited to New Mexico Indians, although few Indians from other areas of the country use the portal to sell their crafts. If there is a dispute, the director of the Museum or a member of his staff checks with the BIA office or the area office at the Reservation to determine whether persons claiming to be Indians are members of Federally recognized Indian tribes or pueblos. Most of the Indians who sell their arts and crafts under the portal live within the Pueblos of New Mexico, maintain their own native culture and remain unassimilated into the predominant American culture. They primarily speak their native languages and maintain strong ties with the traditional religious and social customs of their people.

It is undisputed that the viability and economic well-being of the Pueblos depends significantly upon the income which is produced by the sale of handmade goods under the portal. Thus, there is a direct link between the portal program and the self-determination of these Indians. If the market were to be opened to all vendors, the Indians would gradually retreat from or evacuate the Portal, fearing conflicts with the non-Indian vendors. Conflicts between the plaintiff, Paul Livingston, and one or two of the Indians selling under the Portal have already occurred. The eventual outcome would probably be that the Pueblo Indians would be largely dependent upon welfare instead of their own work, and the quality and production of traditional arts and crafts might suffer.

The plaintiffs have not established that their means of earning a livelihood is severely curtailed by the portal policy. They produce jewelry, some of which is fashioned after Indian designs. The Museum of New Mexico Foundation

---

1. The policy statement reads in part as follows:

WHEREAS, the presence of Indian artists and craftsmen at the Palace of the Governors has been an integral part of history, tradition, and function of the Museum of New Mexico for many years;

. . . NOW, THEREFORE, BE IT RESOLVED BY THE REGENTS OF THE MUSEUM OF NEW MEXICO that policy of the Museum with respect to the display and sale of merchandise on the grounds and areas of the Museum shall be as follows:

1. Other than during annually scheduled markets, no person nor group of persons will be permitted to display or sell merchandise on the grounds belonging to the Museum of New Mexico with the sole exception that the area directly under the portal in front of the Palace of the Governors may be used by Indians to display and sell arts and crafts produced by hand by Indian artists and craftsmen.

operates the Museum Shop in the Palace which accepts all kinds of art subject only to criteria for quality, authenticity, and the relationship of the art to the programs of the Museum. The plaintiffs can sell their handicrafts through various outlets, and have done so in the past, although the Museum Shop has rejected it as being of inferior quality and lacking in authenticity. There have been complaints from tourists that they had purchased from non-Indians under the portal, what they believed to be Indian-made jewelry, which actually proved to be something other than authentic.

The exhibits in the Museum are selected on a cultural basis, with the emphasis placed upon authenticity and the special historical relationship, if any, that such exhibits might have with the Palace itself. Each exhibit displays a discrete New Mexican cultural or ethnic heritage; it is felt that co-mingling the cultures is less instructive because this fails to clarify the lines of historical development within each culture. The portal program is authentic in that it presents what remains of a traditional market: there is no dispute that the Indians are the only remaining, relatively unchanged craftsmen of the original group who sold their wares under the portal. The portal exhibit presents one aspect of the Indian culture and allows the public to interact with it, which the Museum views as a substantial benefit to the public.

The Museum of New Mexico must, by its very nature, be culturally selective. The inclusion or exclusion of various exhibits is based upon the director's and Regents' view of the best way to present and preserve the historical cultures of New Mexico. The policy of the Museum to allow only Indians to sell their hand-made crafts under the portal is the expression of a choice made by the Museum based upon cultural considerations. The Museum, through this policy, seeks to foster native Indian arts, give impetus to the communities from which these arts arise, educate the public, and protect a unique tradition from assimilation so as to maintain, as best they can, its purity. The Museum's choice, therefore, is for the type of cultural style known as "traditional Indian arts and crafts"; items falling within this group must, by definition, be made by Indians. This was emphasized in one of the Intervenor's affidavits, and uncontroverted by the plaintiff:

> When we refer to ethnic arts we are not referring to a racial designation, but to a system of expressions shared by members of a self-identified cultural group that perceives itself and is perceived by others as having a unique esthetic tradition. While individual members of such groups usually have much latitude for creativity, the tradition itself defines the style and sets forth certain rules or approaches that distinguish it from other cultural groups. Indian and especially Southwestern Indian arts constitute a recognized ethnic artistic style. . . . Affidavit of Barry Toelken.

Thus, the policy of permitting only Indians to sell their hand-made goods under the portal is the means by which the Museum's decision to present and preserve the Indian culture has been effectuated. The prohibition of sales on Museum property operates against everyone except Indians because only Indians can produce hand-made Indian goods, and the Museum has determined that the most benefit would be derived by the public if only Indians were permitted to sell the goods that they or other Indians make.

LAW

The fact that the Museum is culturally selective does not in itself violate the Fourteenth Amendment, *McGowen v. Maryland*, 366 U.S. 420, 81 S. Ct. 1101, 6 L. Ed. 2d 393 (1961) and Justice Douglas' dissent in *DeFunis v. Odegaard*, 416 U.S. 312, 94 S. Ct. 1704, 40 L. Ed. 2d 164 (1974). In *New Orleans v. Dukes*, 427 U.S. 297, 96 S. Ct. 2513, 49 L. Ed. 2d 511 (1976), the City Council's ordinance barring certain vendors from the historic French Quarter, was aimed at "enhancing the vital role of the French Quarter's tourist-oriented charm in the economy of New Orleans." P. 303, 96 S. Ct. p. 2516. The Court stressed that it would defer to the judgment of the City Council on questions of the economy of the city and the preservation of the charm and beauty of an historic area, unless the classification "trammels fundamental personal rights or is drawn upon inherently suspect distinctions such as race, religion or alienage." P. 303, 96 S. Ct. p. 2516. In *Avins v. Rutgers*, 385 F.2d 151 (1967), cert. denied, 390 U.S. 920, 88 S. Ct. 855, 19 L. Ed. 2d 982 (1968), the Third Circuit upheld the right of a law review editor to exercise judgment as to inclusion of articles in the publication, noting that there was no constitutional right to publish one's opinions wherever and whenever one pleased.

The inquiry therefore, must be into whether the Museum's cultural selectivity has been exercised in such a way as to infringe upon the plaintiffs' fundamental rights or to operate against the plaintiff or for the Indians on the basis of race. If so, then a strict standard of scrutiny must be applied to the policy's reasonableness; if not, the policy need only bear a rational relationship to a legitimate state interest. *Loving v. Virginia*, 388 U.S. 1, 87 S. Ct. 1817, 18 L. Ed. 2d 1010 (1967); *Morton v. Mancari*, 417 U.S. 535, 94 S. Ct. 2474, 41 L. Ed. 2d 290 (1974).

A. Is the Museum Policy Based on Racial Preference?

The factual background of this case compels the conclusion that the Museum's policy excludes certain vendors on a cultural, not a racial, basis. Several U.S. Supreme Court cases and a substantial body of federal law would also permit no other conclusion.

Because of their unique cultural, legal, and political status, Indians have consistently received special or preferential treatment, from the federal and state governments. This treatment has been challenged as being violative of equal protection; however, the U.S. Supreme Court has found that, because these distinctions are not made on the basis of race, they need only be rationally related to a legitimate state interest, and the constitutional challenges have ultimately failed.

The Amicus brief details the historical and legal background that justifies the preferential treatment of Indians. Article I, Section 8 of the United States

Constitution grants special status to Indians by giving Congress the exclusive power to regulate commerce with the Indian Tribes. Title 25, United States Code, is entirely concerned with Indians; the New Mexico Constitution, Article XXI, Section 2, protects Indian lands, and Sections 73-31-1 et seq. establishes a state agency to encourage the preservation and development of Indian arts and crafts. Title VII, 42 U.S.C. § 2000e-2(i) exempts Indians on or near reservations from the equal employment provisions of that Title. The list of special laws, and cases giving preferential treatment to Indians is considerable, and the justification for all of this lies in the appreciation of the uniqueness of Indian communities, their wish to maintain a separate way of life, and the benefit that the preservation of such will confer upon society.

In the landmark case of *Morton v. Mancari, supra,* the Court denied a constitutional attack upon the preference for hiring Indians within the Bureau of Indian Affairs. In finding that this preference was not an invidious classification based upon race, but was rather a political preference, the Court relied upon the historical relationship between the federal government and the Indian people, and upon their definition of the alleged "racial group":

> The preference is not directed towards a "racial" group consisting of "Indians"; instead, it applies only to members of "federally recognized" tribes. This operates to exclude many individuals who are racially to be classified as "Indians." In this sense, the preference is political rather than racial in nature. Note 24, p. 553, 94 S. Ct. p. 2484.

The holding in this case makes clear that in any equal protection analysis dealing with Indians, the historical, legal and cultural context must be considered in determining whether an Indian preference constitutes invidious racial discrimination.

The reasons for this approach are fairly obvious. Because the federal government and the State of New Mexico are committed to insure the political separateness and cultural survival of Indian tribes, and because Indians who live on or near a reservation are members of distinctive cultural communities which would be gradually destroyed if some protection were not given against forced assimilation, Indians have gained a unique status in the law which no other group, racial or otherwise, can claim. As a result, traditional equal protection analysis falls grossly short of dealing in a fair manner with the question of Indian preference, unless it takes these factors into account.

In the present case there simply are no material uncontroverted facts which would give rise to a conclusion that this is a racial classification. On the contrary, the facts indicate a cultural basis for the Museum's policy: the basic nature and purpose of the Museum to present and preserve historical cultures, not races; the Museum's desire to provide an opportunity which will foster Indian arts and crafts; the fact that only members of federally-recognized Indian tribes may sell under the portal; the fact that at any one time the Museum displays, inside the Palace, not just Indian culture, but other historical New Mexico cultures as well; and the special recognition given to the

Indian cultures by the State of New Mexico in legislation designed to encourage traditional arts and crafts.

The requirement that the sellers of Indian hand-made goods be Indian does not make the Museum's preference one based upon race. It is the only logical way the Museum could carry out its cultural selectivity and still serve the Museum's educational purposes. The Museum is not in the business of sponsoring an open market, and to maintain its own standards of authenticity and historical relevancy, the Museum could not allow for the sale of imitation crafts by non-indigenous craftsmen.

The Museum has argued that the plaintiffs are not members of a suspect class, or a discrete and insular minority, so that the standard of strict scrutiny should not be applied. This type of equal protection analysis in cases involving Indian preference is singularly inapplicable. It is obvious that the plaintiffs are not members of a suspect class: the policy operates to exclude everyone in the world except Indians. This type of analysis overlooks the complexities which *Mancari, supra,* deems essential to a fair analysis of this type of case. Thus, having determined that the preference here is not based upon race, it is not helpful to determine whether it operates against a suspect class. It does operate for the benefit of many people, Indian and non-Indian, without regard to race.

B. Does the Museum Policy Infringe upon Plaintiffs' Fundamental Rights?

Even though the Museum's policy is not based on a racial classification, if it infringes upon one of the plaintiffs' fundamental rights, then the standard of strict scrutiny must be applied in the determination of the policy's reasonableness. It is clear that these must be rights which are guaranteed, implicitly or explicitly, by the U.S. Constitution, and plaintiffs have presented no evidence establishing such right. *San Antonio Independent School District v. Rodriguez,* 411 U.S. 1, 93 S. Ct. 1278, 36 L. Ed. 2d 16 (1973). The plaintiffs' exclusion from the portal does not deprive them of their First Amendment rights to freedom of expression since these rights are not absolute and do not guarantee every individual the exact forum he or she desires. *Nebbia v. New York,* 291 U.S. 502, 54 S. Ct. 505, 78 L. Ed. 940 (1974); *Avins v. Rutgers, supra; New Orleans v. Dukes, supra.* It would be absurd to hold that there is a fundamental right to be included in a Museum's programs under the circumstances of this case.

The conclusion must be, therefore, that there is no question of material fact and on the basis of the applicable law, the plaintiffs have failed to establish the violation of a fundamental right by the Museum's policy, and the result is that such policy will be upheld if it bears a rational relationship to a legitimate state interest.

C. Is the Museum's Policy Rationally Related to a Legitimate State Interest?

In *Morton v. Mancari, supra,* the Indian preference was found to be "... reasonably and directly related to a legitimate, nonracially based goal. This is the principal characteristic that generally is absent from proscribed forms of racial discrimination." 417 U.S. at 554, 94 S. Ct. at 2484. The undisputed facts of this case meet the *Mancari* standard.

The state has several interests or goals which are being furthered by the Museum's portal policy. Foremost amongst them is the preservation and encouragement of traditional Indian arts and crafts. Equally important, however, is the survival of certain of the Pueblos as cultural and economic entities. Education by interaction with Indian people is certainly a fundamental goal of the Museum. In addition, the state has further interest of promoting tourist trade by preserving the charm and beauty of the portal area in a manner consistent with its history, and attempting to prohibit the sale of reproductions or copies of Indian goods to unsuspecting tourists.

There is not, nor can there be, any question about the legitimacy of these state interests. It is also clear that these goals are not racially based. The final question, then, is whether the policy of permitting only Indians to sell their wares under the portal is reasonably and directly related to these goals.

The existence of a rational relationship does not require the Indians to have been the only people to have sold goods under the portal during the centuries of its use as a market. It is undisputed that the portal and the Palace of the Governors have a multi-cultural history, but the Indians were an integral part of that history and are the only remaining traditional craftsmen. New Mexico is fortunate to have living purveyors of the ancient cultures of this country, and is using this "natural resource" to benefit the Indians as well as the general public.

The possibility that there are other means of accomplishing the above-mentioned legitimate state interests does not indicate the lack of a rational relationship between such state interests and the Museum policy. The policy need not be set aside if any state of facts reasonably may be conceived to justify it. It is doubtful that opening up the market to all types of vendors and craftsmen would promote the goals of the Museum as well as the present policy does. On the contrary, it is likely that the abandonment of the portal by the Indians if other craftsmen were to be permitted access would serve to accomplish the opposite of the Museum's goals of fostering traditional Indian arts and crafts, and economic well being of the Indian people.

In *Mancari, supra*, the preference was approved because it bore a rational relationship to the goal of Indian self-government and determination. The uncontroverted facts in this case show a direct link between the portal policy and the economic survival of several pueblos. Indian self-determination is meaningless if opportunities for self-support are destroyed. Therefore, it is clear that the policy is intimately and directly related to this one very legitimate, racially neutral state interest. If, as *Mancari* holds, such an interest is legitimate, and a preference for Indians is constitutional for the federal government through the BIA, then the same must be true of a state government through one of its state-owned museums. *Bolling v. Sharpe*, 347 U.S. 497, 74 S. Ct. 693, 98 L. Ed. 884 (1954).

I therefore conclude that the Museum's policy in this case does not violate the plaintiffs' rights to equal protection under the Fourteenth Amendment; Now, Therefore, IT IS ORDERED that the plaintiffs' motion for summary judgment is denied, and the defendants' motion for summary judgment is granted.

C. Repatriation of Native American Art and Burial Goods

In November 1990, the Native American Graves Protection and Repatriation Act (NAGPRA)[12] became law. While the statute's primary impact is to require that museums and many institutions of higher learning inventory all Indian remains and grave pieces in their collections and notify the appropriate tribes in order that they might take steps to reclaim their possessions, it has permitted Native Americans more leeway in seeking return of their cultural heritage. One of its core questions concerns "What is a museum?"

Thorpe v. Borough of Thorpe

770 F.3d 255 (3d Cir. 2014)[13]

McKEE, Chief Judge.

I. INTRODUCTION

Jim Thorpe, multi-sport Olympic gold medalist ("Thorpe"), died in California in 1953 without a will. His estate was assigned to his third wife, Patricia ("Patsy"),[2] who eventually buried him in what is now Jim Thorpe, Pennsylvania ("the Borough"). Jim Thorpe, Pennsylvania was a newly-formed borough that had been created from the merger of the boroughs of Mauch Chunk and East Mauch Chunk. Thorpe was buried in this new borough over the objections of several children from his previous marriages. Thorpe was a Native American of Sauk heritage and a member of the Sac and Fox Nation of Oklahoma. Over the years, some of Thorpe's eight children have spoken out in protest of their father's burial, advocating that he be reburied on Sac and Fox tribal land in Oklahoma.

In 1990, years after Thorpe's death and burial, Congress enacted the Native American Graves Protection and Repatriation Act ("NAGPRA"). NAGPRA was intended to ameliorate and correct past abuses inflicted upon Native Americans and their culture and to protect Native American human remains and cultural artifacts. NAGPRA requires museums and Federal agencies possessing or controlling holdings or collections of Native American human remains to inventory those remains, notify the affected tribe, and, upon the request of a known lineal descendent of the deceased Native American or of the tribe, return such remains. 25 U.S.C. §§ 3003, 3005.

In 2010, John Thorpe, the son of Thorpe and his second wife Freeda, sued the Borough for failing to comply with NAGPRA. The District Court concluded that the Borough was a "museum" within the meaning of

---

12. NAGPRA, 25 U.S.C. §§ 3001 et seq.
13. Most footnotes and citations to the record deleted.
2. Patsy Thorpe is deceased. She and Jim Thorpe did not have children together.

NAGPRA and provisions of that law required the Borough to disinter Thorpe's remains and turn them over to the Sac and Fox tribe as requested by John Thorpe. This appeal followed.

We conclude that Congress could not have intended the kind of patently absurd result that would follow from a court resolving a family dispute by applying NAGPRA to Thorpe's burial in the Borough under the circumstances here. We therefore hold that the District Court erred in overturning the clearly expressed wishes of Thorpe's wife by ordering his body to be exhumed and his remains delivered to John Thorpe.

II. FACTS AND PROCEDURAL HISTORY

Thorpe died in California in 1953. Thereafter, Patsy, in cooperation with the Oklahoma legislature, made initial plans for him to be buried in Oklahoma. According to Plaintiffs, Thorpe had told family members that he wanted to be buried in Oklahoma. However, the parties agree that Patsy Thorpe had legal authority over the disposition of Thorpe's body and his estate. In any event, at some point following Thorpe's death, a bill was drafted by the Oklahoma legislature that would have provided funding for a permanent memorial near the contemplated site for Thorpe's grave. However, in what was a harbinger of difficulties to come, the bill was vetoed by the Governor of Oklahoma. This sad and regrettable posthumous saga took an even more ominous turn when Patsy, assisted by state law enforcement officers, intervened in Thorpe's ritual burial ceremony in Oklahoma, and caused Thorpe's casket to be removed and stored. After considering various sites for Thorpe's burial, Patsy arranged to have Thorpe buried at a location in Jim Thorpe, Pennsylvania. That municipality was to be formed by the merger of Mauch Chunk and East Mauch Chunk, and the resulting borough was to be named Jim Thorpe. This agreement was reached despite the objection of several of Thorpe's children. The agreement provided in part that Mauch Chunk and East Mauch Chunk would consolidate under the name "Jim Thorpe" "as a fitting tribute and memorial to the person and memory of the husband of [Patsy Thorpe] and that appropriately correlated to such designation of the name 'Jim Thorpe' the remains of [him] be laid to rest in the community so bearing his name." Patsy Thorpe intended that the Borough would be "the final and permanent resting place" for her husband. *Id.*

After the arrangements were made for the burial site in the Borough, Thorpe was first buried at the Evergreen Cemetery in the Borough while a mausoleum was being constructed for his remains. In 1957, he was interred in what was believed to be his final resting place. The agreement Patsy had reached with the Borough provides that the Borough is responsible for the maintenance at the burial site. However, family members have visited the site over the years and have worked with the Borough to conduct tribal ceremonies. The Jim Thorpe Hall of Fame has also worked to improve the site.

John Thorpe filed the instant Complaint in 2010, alleging that the Borough had failed to comply with NAGPRA. The Borough immediately moved to dismiss the complaint. The District Court dismissed John Thorpe's § 1983 claim but allowed him to proceed under NAGPRA. John Thorpe was also ordered to join all necessary parties in an amended complaint or submit evidence and briefing showing that joinder of any or all of the necessary parties was not feasible and that the action could proceed in "equity and good conscience" under Rule 19(b). App. 171. John Thorpe died the following year and the proceedings were stayed until his attorney filed an amended complaint naming as new plaintiffs John's brothers Richard and William Thorpe, the sons of Jim Thorpe and his second wife Freeda ("Plaintiffs").

Thereafter, the District Court granted Plaintiffs' motion for summary judgment based on its conclusion that "[t]he Borough of Jim Thorpe is a 'museum' under [NAGPRA] and subject to the requirements of the Act, including those provisions governing repatriation requests." App. 80. The Borough appealed that finding and Plaintiffs appealed the District Court's dismissal of their § 1983 claim.

III. JURISDICTION AND STANDARD OF REVIEW

The District Court had federal question jurisdiction pursuant to 28 U.S.C. § 1331, and we have jurisdiction pursuant to 28 U.S.C. § 1291. NAGPRA's jurisdictional provision vests federal courts with jurisdiction over "any action brought by any person alleging a violation of" NAGPRA. 25 U.S.C. § 3013. This Court exercises plenary review over the District Court's finding of law that NAGPRA applies to Thorpe's burial. *Pell v. E.I. DuPont de Nemours & Co.,* 539 F.3d 292, 305 (3d Cir. 2008). . . .

. . .

V. THE BOROUGH IS NOT A "MUSEUM" UNDER NAGPRA

NAGPRA defines the word "museum" very broadly, as:

> any institution or State or local government agency (including any institution of higher learning) that receives Federal funds and has possession of, or control over, Native American cultural items.

25 U.S.C. § 3001(8). The Borough is a local government entity that maintains Jim Thorpe's burial site. The parties agree that the Borough has "possession of, or control over," Jim Thorpe's remains, and that he is of Native American descent. Thus, the main question before the District Court was whether the Borough "receives federal funds." The District Court found that the Borough was a museum because the record showed that the Borough received federal funds after the enactment of NAGPRA. However, for the following reasons, we find that the Borough is not a "museum" as intended by NAGPRA. It is therefore not required to comply with NAGPRA's procedural requirement of providing an inventory of Thorpe's remains. Similarly, it is not subject to the statute's requirement that his remains be "returned" to Thorpe's descendants for "repatriation" at their request.

Ordinarily, we look to the text of the statute, rather than the legislative history, to interpret a statute or determine legislative intent as an aid to interpretation. *See Conn. Nat'l Bank v. Germain*, 503 U.S. 249, 253–54, 112 S. Ct. 1146, 117 L. Ed. 2d 391 (1992). . . . However, this rule of statutory construction is not an inviolable commandment that we must blindly enforce regardless of surrounding circumstances or the practical results of rigidly applying the text to a given situation. Thus, we have made exceptions in rare cases in which "the literal application of a statute will produce a result demonstrably at odds with the intentions of its drafters." *First Merchs.*, 198 F.3d at 402 (quoting *Griffin v. Oceanic Contractors, Inc.*, 458 U.S. 564, 571, 102 S. Ct. 3245, 73 L. Ed. 2d 973 (1982)). . . .

As the Supreme Court has explained, "[s]tatutory interpretations 'which would produce absurd results are to be avoided if alternative interpretations consistent with the legislative purpose are available.'" *Id.* . . . We conclude that we are confronted with the unusual situation in which literal application of NAGPRA "will produce a result demonstrably at odds with the intentions of its drafters." *Griffin*, 458 U.S. at 571, 102 S. Ct. 3245. We must therefore look beyond the text of NAGPRA to identify the intentions of the drafters of the statute, and that intent "must . . . control[ ] [our analysis.]" *Id.*

As we have explained, NAGPRA requires "repatriation" of human remains from "museums," where those remains have been collected and studied for archeological or historical purposes. 25 U.S.C. § 3005. It is clear from the legislative history we have recounted above that Congress was also concerned with returning to Native American tribes the human remains and artifacts that had been taken for profit, gain, exploitation, or rank curiosity without regard to the concerns of the Native American tribe whose legitimate and paramount interest should have been recognized. However, the definition of "museum" in the text of NAGPRA sweeps much wider than that. If interpreted literally, it would include any state or local governmental entity that "has possession of, or control over, Native American cultural items[ ]" regardless of the circumstances surrounding the possession. This could include any items given freely by a member of the tribe. Here, it would include human remains buried in accordance with the wishes of the decedent's next-of-kin. Literal application would even reach situations where the remains of a Native American were disposed of in a manner consistent with the deceased's wishes as appropriately memorialized in a testamentary instrument or communicated to his or her family. There is therefore no limitation that would preserve the final wishes of a given Native American or exempt determination of his or her final resting place from the procedural requirements of NAGPRA. . . .

Here, it is clear that the congressional intent to regulate institutions such as museums and to remedy the historical atrocities inflicted on Native Americans, including plundering of their graves, is not advanced by interpreting "museum" to include a gravesite that Thorpe's widow intended as Thorpe's final resting place. As we stated earlier, Plaintiffs do not maintain that Patsy was without authority to determine where Thorpe was to be buried. Moreover, as also explained above, the record is clear that Plaintiffs delayed bringing this suit until certain of Thorpe's survivors who favored his burial in the Borough died.

As stated in the House Report, "[t]he purpose of [NAGPRA] is to protect Native American burial sites and the *removal* of human remains." H.R. Rep. (emphasis added). NAGPRA was intended as a shield against further injustices to Native Americans. It was not intended to be wielded as a sword to settle familial disputes within Native American families. Yet, that is what we would allow if we were to enforce NAGPRA's repatriation provisions as written here.

Aside from the unusual arrangements between Patsy Thorpe and the Borough, and Plaintiffs' understandable desire to move Thorpe's remains to where they prefer for him to be buried, his burial in the Borough is no different than any other burial, except that he is a legendary figure of Native American descent. If we were to find that NAGPRA applies to Thorpe's burial, we would also have to conclude that it applies to any grave located in "any institution or State or local government agency . . . that receives federal funds and has possession of, or control over, Native American cultural items." This could call into question any "institution" or "State or local government agency" that controls a cemetery or grave site where Native Americans are buried, and would give rights to any lineal descendant or tribe that has a claim to a person buried in such a cemetery. The Amicus brief on behalf of Thorpe's grandsons, Michael Koehler and John Thorpe, makes this clear:

> Imagine a scenario where a deceased person is buried by his widow at the site of her choosing. But after the widow dies, the next generation — or even complete strangers in the case of a tribe — decides to dig up the body with court approval and move it somewhere else for any reason they desire. They aren't even required to bury the remains. This is not a "parade of horribles" conjured up by the Thorpe grandsons. That is their reality. If the district court's decision is allowed to stand, this scenario can repeat for funerals past and future as long as the deceased has any Native American ancestry.

Amicus Br. for Koehler and Thorpe, at 5. Accordingly, "based solely on the language and context of the most relevant statutory provisions, the court cannot say that Congress's intent is so clear and unambiguous that it 'foreclose[s] any other interpretation.'" *King v. Burwell*, 759 F.3d 358, 369 (4th Cir. 2014). . . .

Finally, NAGPRA requires that remains be "returned." 25 U.S.C. § 3005. This assumes that the human remains were moved from their intended final resting place. Thorpe was buried in the Borough by his wife, and she had the legal authority to decide where he would be buried. Thus, there is nowhere for Thorpe to be "returned" to. As the House Report explains: "[f]or many years, Indian tribes have attempted to have the remains and funerary objects of their ancestors *returned* to them." H.R. Rep. (emphasis added).

Thorpe's remains are located at their final resting place and have not been disturbed. We find that applying NAGPRA to Thorpe's burial in the Borough is such a clearly absurd result and so contrary to Congress's intent to protect Native American burial sites that the Borough cannot be held to the requirements imposed on a museum under these circumstances. We reverse the District Court and hold that the Borough is not a "museum" under NAGPRA for the purposes of Thorpe's burial.

V. CONCLUSION

For the foregoing reasons, we will reverse the judgment of the District Court as to the applicability of NAGPRA to the burial of Jim Thorpe in the Borough, and affirm the District Court's dismissal of Plaintiffs' § 1983 claim. We will remand the action for the District Court to enter judgment in favor of Appellant, the Borough of Jim Thorpe.

Note

1. In *Kawaiisu Tribe of Tejon v. Salazar*, 2011 WL 489561 (E.D. Cal. Feb. 7, 2011), the court held that privately owned real property on which a non-federally recognized Indian group claimed sacred to its group did not qualify as "tribal lands" for purposes of NAGPRA. The Kawaiisu Tribe of Tejon, a non-federally recognized Indian group brought a claim to challenge the authorization of a large construction project on private property. The Kawaiisu alleged that approval of the project violated NAGPRA and asked the court to declare that they were a "tribe" and that the historical Tejon/Sebastian Reservation was "tribal land." The court, however, refused, stating that there was no mechanism under NAGPRA to re-classify tribal groups or parcels of land. Ultimately, the plaintiffs' NAGPRA claim was dismissed with leave to amend to allow them the opportunity to bring a claim to recognize the land as an Indian Reservation, which would in turn trigger the operation of NAGPRA.

Pueblo of San Ildefonso v. Ridlon

103 F.3d 936 (10th Cir. 1996)*

GODBOLD, Senior Circuit Judge.

Appellant Pueblo of San Ildefonso ("Pueblo"), a federally recognized Indian tribe, filed an action under 25 U.S.C. §§ 3001-3013, the Native American Graves Protection and Repatriation Act ("NAGPRA"), to secure the return of a piece of Native American pottery from Appellees Daniel Ridlon and the Regents of the University of California. On cross-motions for summary judgment the District Court construed Ridlon's motion as a motion to dismiss for want of subject matter jurisdiction and dismissed the Pueblo's

---

* Footnotes and some citations omitted.

action pursuant to F.R.C.P. 12(b)(1). We vacate the judgment of the district court. . . .

I. FACTUAL BACKGROUND

In 1978 twelve-year-old Daniel Ridlon discovered a piece of Native American pottery while hiking on property owned by Los Alamos County, New Mexico. The pottery consists of two ancient bowls sealed together that contain a bundle of macaw feathers tied with yucca twine. Shortly after his discovery Ridlon turned the pottery over to the Bradbury Museum, a federally-funded museum operated by the Regents of the University of California. The Museum has continually possessed and displayed the pottery since shortly after its discovery in 1978.

In 1988 the Museum refused Ridlon's demands for return of the pottery and Ridlon successfully sued the Museum and Los Alamos County in New Mexico state court for conversion. *See* Opinion of the Federal District Court, No. 93-1467, at 2 (D.N.M. Sept. 14, 1995). However, the state court vacated its judgment and allowed the Pueblo to intervene asserting a right to repatriation of the pottery under NAGPRA. *Id.* Los Alamos County subsequently assigned its rights in the pottery to the Pueblo. The state court concluded that it lacked jurisdiction over the NAGPRA claim and dismissed the action without prejudice. *Id.*

Thereafter the Pueblo filed the present action seeking repatriation under NAGPRA, protection of its property interest under the Treaty of Guadalupe-Hidalgo, and declaratory relief pursuant to the Declaratory Judgment Act, 28 U.S.C. § 2201. The U.S. District Court, D.N.M., dismissed the action, finding that neither NAGPRA nor the treaty provided an adequate basis for federal subject matter jurisdiction. *Id.* at 4. The court also declined to exercise supplemental jurisdiction over the parties' state law ownership claims. *Id.* at 6. Because resolution of the NAGPRA issue is determinative of this matter, we do not reach the Pueblo's other grounds for appeal.

We exercise subject matter jurisdiction pursuant to 28 U.S.C. § 1291 and NAGPRA's jurisdictional and repatriation provisions, 25 U.S.C. § § 3013 and 3005(a) respectively. Section 3013 vests federal courts with jurisdiction over "any action brought by any person alleging a violation of this chapter." The Pueblo claims a violation of NAGPRA's repatriation provision, § 3005(a), which applies to "Native American human remains and objects possessed or controlled by Federal agencies and museums." Since the Bradbury Museum is a "museum" as defined by NAGPRA . . . and has possessed and controlled the pottery since shortly after its discovery, the district court has a basis for subject matter jurisdiction over the Pueblo's repatriation claim.

II. NATIVE AMERICAN GRAVES
PROTECTION & REPATRIATION ACT

Enacted in 1990, NAGPRA safeguards the rights of Native Americans by protecting tribal burial sites and rights to items of cultural significance to

Native Americans. *See* 43 C.F.R. § 10.1 (1995). Cultural items protected under NAGPRA include Native American human remains, funerary objects, sacred objects, and objects of cultural patrimony. . . . 25 U.S.C. § 3001(3)(1990). The Pueblo asserts that the pottery is an object of cultural patrimony and that the Regents had no right to possession of the pottery under NAGPRA. . . .

NAGPRA has two distinct schemes governing the return of Native American cultural items to tribes, with the analysis turning upon whether the item is presently held by a federal agency or museum or is discovered on federal lands after November 16, 1990, NAGPRA's effective date. First, the Act addresses items excavated on federal lands after November 16, 1990 and enables Native American groups affiliated with those items to claim ownership. *See* 43 C.F.R. § 10.1 (1995); H.R. Rep. No. 101-877, 101st Cong., 2d Sess. (1990), reprinted in 1990 U.S.C.C.A.N. 4367, 4368. Second, NAGPRA provides for repatriation of cultural items currently held by federal agencies, including federally-funded museums. *Id.*

The parties dispute the applicability of NAGPRA. The district court found that the Pueblo's claim fell short of providing an adequate basis of subject matter jurisdiction. The court relied upon NAGPRA's ownership provision which limits the effect of that section to ". . . Native American cultural items which are excavated or discovered on Federal or tribal lands after November 16, 1990." *Id.* (citing 25 U.S.C. § 3002(a)). Since "[t]he pottery at issue was discovered prior to the enactment of the NAGPRA on land owned by a county, not the federal government or an Indian tribe," the district court held that it lacked jurisdiction and dismissed the case. *Id.*

On appeal the Pueblo contends that the district court's reliance on the ownership provision was misplaced because the Pueblo brought its claim under NAGPRA's repatriation provisions, 25 U.S.C. §§ 3004 and 3005, which are not limited to items found on federal lands after November 16, 1990. . . . NAGPRA requires repatriation of items of cultural patrimony that are presently in the possession or control of federally-funded museums provided other requirements of repatriation are met. *See* 25 U.S.C. §§ 3004, 3005 (1990).

The Pueblo asserts that NAGPRA's express statutory language, administrative regulations and legislative history support the conclusion that the Pueblo's claim for repatriation of the pottery falls within the purview of NAGPRA and does provide a basis for federal subject matter jurisdiction. We agree and, therefore, vacate the judgment of the district court.

A. Statutory Language

As a preliminary matter, we note that by § 3013, NAGPRA explicitly vests jurisdiction in federal courts: the United States district courts shall have jurisdiction over any action brought by any person alleging a violation of this chapter [NAGPRA] and shall have the authority to issue such orders as maybe necessary to enforce the provisions of this chapter. 25 U.S.C. § 3013 (1990).

The Pueblo sought repatriation of the pottery pursuant to 25 U.S.C. §§ 3004 and 3005, which address repatriation of objects presently in the possession or control of federal agencies, including federally-funded museums like the Bradbury Museum. Nothing in the express language of these sections indicates that repatriation is limited by when or where the object subject to repatriation was found. Where statutory language is clear and unambiguous, that language is controlling and courts should not add to that language. *U.S. v. Thompson*, 941 F.2d 1074, 1077 (10th Cir. 1991); *Aulston v. U.S.*, 915 F.2d 584 (10th Cir. 1990), cert. denied, 500 U.S. 916, 111 S. Ct. 2011, 114 L. Ed. 2d 98 (1991). The language of the repatriation section supports federal subject matter jurisdiction in this case.

First, 25 U.S.C. § 3005(a) entitled "Repatriation of Native American human remains and objects possessed or controlled by Federal agencies and museums," provides

> If, pursuant to § 3004 of this title, the cultural affiliation with a particular Indian tribe . . . is shown with respect to . . . objects of cultural patrimony, then the Federal agency or museum, upon the request of the Indian tribe . . . and pursuant to subsections (b), (c), and (e) of this section, shall expeditiously return such objects.

25 U.S.C. § 3005(a)(2) (1990). As the title of § 3005 indicates, repatriation applies to items presently in possession of federally-funded museums, including items possessed on November 16, 1990, NAGPRA's effective date. Unlike the restrictive ownership provision, nowhere does the language of this section suggest that repatriation is limited to post-November 16, 1990 excavations on federal lands. Although the district court correctly concluded that NAGPRA's ownership provision only applies to items found after November 16, 1990 on federal lands, the court should not have imposed date and location restrictions on repatriation where nothing in NAGPRA's statutory scheme or language requires such limitations.

Second, the only section of the Act that expressly contains a limiting date is the ownership section, § 3002, which relates only to items excavated or discovered on federal lands after November 16, 1990. The district court concluded that, because the pottery was discovered in 1978 on non-federal land, the ownership provision did not apply to the pottery. However, the Pueblo did not sue under the ownership section. The Pueblo sued under § 3005, claiming a right of repatriation of the pottery. Because NAGPRA's express language does not limit repatriation to items found after November 16, 1990, NAGPRA applies to the Pueblo's repatriation claim as a matter of law.

B. Administrative Interpretations

Administrative interpretations support the Pueblo's contention that repatriation is not limited by when a Native American object was found. First, regulations issued to carry out the provisions of NAGPRA distinguish between ownership and repatriation. "An administrative agency's interpretation of a statute which the agency is entrusted to administer is entitled to considerable deference by a reviewing court." *Bernstein v. Sullivan*, 914 F.2d 1395, 1400 (10th Cir. 1990).

NAGPRA Regulations are subdivided into two distinct subparts that separately address repatriation and ownership. Subpart B concerns the disposition of Native American items discovered or excavated, either inadvertently or intentionally, on federal lands after November 16, 1990. 43 C.F.R. §§ 10.3(a) & 10.4(a) (1995). Subpart C addresses repatriation of Native American objects in possession of federal agencies and museums. 43 C.F.R. §§ 10.8-10.10 (1995). Regulations concerning repatriation do not contain a limiting date and, therefore, support the conclusion that the Pueblo stated a claim under NAGPRA to establish federal subject matter jurisdiction.

III. CONCLUSION

We VACATE the district court's judgment and REMAND for further proceedings consistent with this opinion.

Notes

1. In *Jensen v. United States Nat'l Park Service*, 113 F. Supp. 3d 431 (D. Mass. 2015), the district court held that a non-Native American plaintiff lacked standing to bring a claim under NAGPRA because she was not a Native American tribal member or a descendant of a Native American tribe, and the human remains were not discovered on tribal or federal lands. She also failed to identify the remains as Native American. Jensen initiated the suit after finding exposed human remains in a sewer drain at a National Historic Landmark on Nantucket Island. She claimed the situation caused "irreparable damage to American History," and caused her "two years of financial, mental, emotional, and physical stresses. . . ."

2. Several states, including California, Hawaii, and Kansas, have passed repatriation statutes. In 1989, Nebraska enacted a general repatriation statute requiring all state-recognized museums to repatriate "reasonably identifiable" remains and grave goods to the tribes of origin on request. Neb. Rev. Stat. §§ 12-1209 to 12-1210 (1990). In 1990, Arizona's legislature passed a statute to repatriate human remains, funerary objects, sacred objects, and objects of tribal patrimony held by state agencies. Remains that are not culturally affiliated with a tribe still must be reburied within one year nearest the place where the remains were discovered. Ariz. Rev. Stat. Ann. §§ 41-844 to 41-865 (1992). In 1991, California passed a law making it the policy of the state that Native American remains and associated grave artifacts be repatriated. Cal. Pub. Res. Code

§ 5097.99 (1991). For an article by several of NAGPRA's drafters, *see* Monroe & Echo-Hawk, *Deft Deliberations*, Museum News, July/Aug. 1991, at 55.

PROBLEM 12-1

Will the purchase and transfer ban on Native American artifacts effectively reduce illegal artifact hunting by reducing the value of these items? On the other hand, will the black market in protected items of Native American heritage soar? Prepare an analysis.

Idrogo v. United States Army

18 F. Supp. 2d 25 (D.D.C. 1998)*

KOLLAR-KOTELLY, District Judge.

Pro se Plaintiffs Michael Idrogo and the Americans for Repatriation of Geronimo bring suit to compel the United States Army and President William Jefferson Clinton to repatriate the human remains of Geronimo, to lift posthumously Geronimo's prisoner-of-war status, and to provide full military honors to Geronimo and celebrate his legacy with a parade through towns en route from Fort Sill, Oklahoma (where Geronimo's remains currently rest) to a point in Arizona or New Mexico. Pending before the Court are the Defendants' Motion To Dismiss or, in the Alternative, for Summary Judgment and the Plaintiffs' Opposition thereto. After liberally construing the Plaintiffs' Complaint and the materials that they appended to their opposition brief, the Court nonetheless concludes that the Plaintiffs lack standing to prosecute this action.

I. BACKGROUND

Plaintiffs predicate their claims on the Native American Graves Protection and Repatriation Act ("NAGPRA"), Pub. L. No. 101-877, 104 Stat. 3048 (1990) (codified as amended at 25 U.S.C. §§ 001-3013). Enacted "to protect Native American burial sites and the removal of human remains . . . on Federal, Indian and Native Hawaiian lands," H.R. Rep. 101-877, at 8 (1990), NAGPRA establishes a system for federal agencies and museums to inventory holdings of these remains and work with the appropriate tribes to repatriate such remains. *Id.* The Act mandates that a federal agency that possesses human remains of Native Americans expeditiously return those remains upon request from an Indian tribe. *See* 25 U.S.C. § 3005(a)(4).

---

* Footnotes omitted.

Geronimo was a Chiricahua Apache who lived the last twenty-three years of his life as a prisoner of war under the custody of the United States Army. . . . His remains are located at the Army's Fort Sill in Oklahoma. . . . Plaintiff Michael Idrogo is a resident of Bexar County, Texas. . . . In neither the Complaint nor the Plaintiffs' opposition, however, does Idrogo claim to be a member of any recognized (or unrecognized, for that matter) Native American tribe. Americans for Repatriation of Geronimo, of which Idrogo is a member, is "a group of concerned Americans who are eligible voters and residents of the various states of the United States. . . ."

II. DISCUSSION

A. Plaintiffs lack standing to prosecute this action

Parties that invoke federal jurisdiction bear the burden of establishing that there exists a justiciable case or controversy suitable for an Article III Court to resolve. *See FW/PBS, Inc. v. Dallas*, 493 U.S. 215, 231, 110 S. Ct. 596, 107 L. Ed. 2d 603 (1990). For this Court properly to exercise subject-matter jurisdiction, the Plaintiffs must satisfy the "irreducible constitutional minimum of standing." *Lujan v. Defenders of Wildlife*, 504 U.S. 555, 560, 112 S. Ct. 2130, 119 L. Ed. 2d 351 (1992). As this Circuit has framed it, "[t]o secure constitutional standing the plaintiffs must show injury in fact that is fairly traceable to the defendant's action and redressable by the relief requested." *Animal Legal Defense Fund, Inc. v. Espy*, 29 F.3d 720, 723 (D.C. Cir. 1994) (internal quotations and citations omitted). The first variable in this calculus, "injury in fact," means that the Plaintiffs must have suffered the loss of a legally protected interest that is (1) concrete and particularized, *see Allen v. Wright*, 468 U.S. 737, 756, 104 S. Ct. 3315, 82 L. Ed. 2d 556 (1984), and (2) "actual or imminent, not 'conjectural' or 'hypothetical,'" *Whitmore v. Arkansas*, 495 U.S. 149, 155, 110 S. Ct. 1717, 109 L. Ed. 2d 135 (1990). When challenging government action, the Supreme Court has consistently held that a plaintiff raising only a generally available grievance about government — claiming only harm to his and every citizen's interest in proper application of the Constitution and laws, and seeking relief that no more directly and tangibly benefits him than it does the public at large — does not state an Article III case or controversy. *Lujan*, 504 U.S. at 573-74, 112 S. Ct. 2130. . . .

Plaintiffs cannot demonstrate that they have suffered an injury in fact that is concrete and particularized. *See Warth v. Seldin*, 422 U.S. 490, 508, 95 S. Ct. 2197, 45 L. Ed. 2d 343 (1975). Under NAGPRA, where "the cultural affiliation of Native American human remains and associated funerary objects with a particular Indian tribe . . . is established," a federal agency that possesses those remains shall expeditiously return them "upon the request of a known lineal descendant of the Native American or of the tribe or organization." 25 U.S.C. § 3005(a). As Congress has structured the repatriation provisions of NAGPRA, only direct descendants of Native American remains and affiliated tribal organizations stand to be injured by violations of the Act.

Neither Idrogo nor Americans for the Repatriation of Geronimo falls within this class. As to Idrogo, he never so much as claims to be a member of any Indian tribe. While he "believes" that Geronimo is an ancestor of his, Idrogo offers nothing that remotely substantiates this claim. Specifically he bases his claim to patrimonial ancestry on two similarities that he and Geronimo supposedly share: (1) that Geronimo, like Idrogo, could speak Spanish and (2) that both men are approximately the same height. . . . Americans for Repatriation of Geronimo fares no better. NAGPRA clearly defines "Indian tribe" to mean "any tribe, band, nation, or other organized group or community of Indians . . . which is recognized as eligible for the special programs and services provided by the United States to Indians because of their status as Indians." 25 U.S.C. § 3001(7). Americans for Repatriation of Geronimo is not an organization that falls within the ambit of NAGPRA's reach. Moreover, it is well settled that "[w]hether a group constitutes a 'tribe' is a matter that is ordinarily committed to the discretion of Congress and the Executive Branch, and courts will defer to their judgment." *Cherokee Nation of Okla. v. Babbitt*, 117 F.3d 1489, 1496 (D.C. Cir. 1997) (citing *United States v. Holliday*, 70 U.S. (3 Wall.) 407, 419, 18 L. Ed. 182 (1865)).

Because NAGPRA does not vest any rights in Idrogo or Americans for Repatriation of Geronimo to repatriate or receive the human remains of Geronimo, they cannot claim any injury in fact even if it were proven that the United States Army somehow is violating NAGPRA by harboring Geronimo's remains at Fort Sill. In their opposition, the Plaintiffs make a series of cryptic and mostly incoherent arguments to establish standing. First, they write that "[t]he defendants violate 25 U.S.C. Chapter 32 — Native American Graves Protection and Repatriation and constitutional limitations." . . . At best, this grievance is nothing more than the same "generalized interest of all citizens" in seeing that the Army faithfully complies with the terms of NAGPRA. Such an interest is insufficient to confer standing on the Plaintiffs. *See Lujan*, 504 U.S. at 573-75, 112 S. Ct. 2130. Despite earnest effort to decipher the Plaintiffs' remaining arguments concerning standing, the Court simply cannot divine how the Plaintiffs attempt to satisfy the standing requirement. Reprinted in full, their arguments are: "plaintiff has suffered, or will probably suffer, violation of his 'Last Will' as what fraud has been complained of in this case. Violation on the basis of race. Violation of the Equal Protection. 'Fenced out' on the basis of member of a 'minority group.' . . ." Construed liberally, such incomprehensible statements cannot be fairly read to confer standing on the Plaintiffs.

Lastly, 25 U.S.C. § 3013 does not bestow standing on either of the Plaintiffs. Although they did not raise this argument in their opposition, the Court considers that it has a duty to explore all potential bases for these pro se litigants. Section 3013 provides: "the United States district courts shall have jurisdiction over any action brought by any person alleging a violation of this chapter and shall have the authority to issue such orders as may be necessary to enforce the provisions of this chapter." 25 U.S.C. § 3013. At first glance, this provision, by purporting to grant district courts jurisdiction to hear "any action brought by any person alleging a violation of this chapter," seems to save the day for the Plaintiffs. The Supreme Court's decision in *Lujan*, however, underscores the error in this argument. In *Lujan*, the Court reviewed a "citizen-suit" provision of the Endangered Species Act, which provided, in pertinent part, that "any person may commence a civil suit on his own behalf (A) to enjoin any person, including the United States and any other governmental instrumentality or agency . . . who is alleged to be in violation of any provision of this chapter." *Lujan*, 504 U.S. at 571-72, 112 S. Ct. 2130 (quoting 16 U.S.C. § 1540(g)). The Supreme Court rejected the Eighth Circuit's view that Congress could confer upon all persons "an abstract, self-contained, non-instrumental 'right' to have the Executive observe the procedures required by law." *Id.* at 573, 112 S. Ct. 2130. The Court reaffirmed the principle that although Congress may expand substantive rights through statute, it is a "different matter from abandoning the requirement that the party seeking review must himself have suffered an injury." *Id.* at 578, 112 S. Ct. 2130 (quoting *Sierra Club v. Morton*, 405 U.S. 727, 738, 92 S. Ct. 1361, 31 L. Ed. 2d 636 (1972)). Section 3013 of NAGPRA is the functional equivalent of the jurisdiction provision at issue in *Lujan*. . . . It attempts to confer standing on a class of individuals who need not demonstrate any injury in fact. Because the injury in fact requirement is constitutional, not simply prudential, see *Animal Legal Defense Fund*, 29 F.3d at 723, Congress may not augment the case-or-controversy requirement beyond what the Constitution permits.

B. The Claim in Plaintiffs' Amended Complaint must be Dismissed

Plaintiffs moved to amend their Complaint on March 26, 1998. Under Fed. R. Civ. P. 15(a), however, because the Defendants have yet to serve a responsive pleading, Plaintiffs may amend their Complaint as a matter of right. Nonetheless, the one additional claim presented is patently frivolous. As this Circuit has held, "[c]omplaints may also be dismissed, sua sponte if need be, under Rule 12(b)(6) whenever 'the plaintiff cannot possibly win relief.'" *Best v. Kelly*, 39 F.3d 328, 331 (D.C. Cir. 1994) (quoting *Baker v. Director, United States Parole Comm'n*, 916 F.2d 725, 726 (D.C. Cir. 1990) (per curiam)).

The Amended Complaint alleges that the United States Army and President Clinton violated 42 U.S.C. § 1981. . . . With respect to the Army, the doctrine of sovereign immunity completely bars the Plaintiffs § 1981 action. By now it is beyond peradventure that "'[t]he United States, as sovereign, is immune from suit save as it consents to be sued.'" *United States v. Mitchell*, 445 U.S. 535, 538, 100 S. Ct. 1349, 63 L. Ed. 2d 607 (1980). . . . Moreover, courts within this Circuit have expressly recognized that the Army enjoys sovereign immunity as an instrumentality of the federal government. . . . Accordingly, the Court dismisses the Plaintiffs' § 1981 claim against the Department of the Army based on principles of sovereign immunity.

Turning to their claim against President Clinton, the Court also dismisses the Amended Complaint's § 1981 count against the President under the well-recognized tenet of constitutional law that the Constitution affords absolute immunity to the President from civil damage actions challenging his official acts. *See Nixon v. Fitzgerald,* 457 U.S. 731, 749-56, 102 S. Ct. 2690, 73 L. Ed. 2d 349 (1982). Accordingly, the Amended Complaint must be dismissed pursuant to Fed. R. Civ. P. 12(b)(6) because "'the plaintiff[s] cannot possibly win relief.'" *Best,* 39 F.3d at 331 (quoting *Baker,* 916 F.2d at 726).

III. CONCLUSION

For the foregoing reasons, the Court finds that Plaintiffs lack standing to prosecute their NAGPRA claims. Additionally, the Court, *sua sponte,* dismisses the Plaintiffs' § 1981 claim against the Department of the Army and President Clinton.

Notes

1. In 2009, several New Mexicans filed a NAGPRA lawsuit seeking to rebury Geronimo's body in New Mexico. *See* Carlos Melendrez, *It's Past Time to Bring Chief Geronimo Back to His Mountain Home,* Albuquerque J., Oct. 10, 2009.
2. On the 100-year anniversary of Geronimo's death, twenty of his descendants filed a suit against President Barack Obama, Yale University, and the Order of the Skull and Bones. *See Geronimo v. Obama,* 725 F. Supp. 2d 182 (D.C. 2010). The claim arose from the alleged 1918 grave robbery of Geronimo's skull from Fort Sill, Oklahoma, by four members of the Skull and Bones Society at Yale University. The descendants sued under NAGPRA § 3002, seeking the return of Geronimo's remains and the payment of monetary damages. In *Geronimo v. Obama,* the court dismissed the complaint, stating the plaintiffs failed to establish that the United States expressly waived its sovereign immunity. The court also determined that the plaintiffs failed to state a claim because the allegedly wrongful removal of Geronimo's remains occurred in or around 1918, and NAGPRA § 3002 only permits claims of ownership to Native American remains or artifacts discovered after November 16, 1990.
3. For an interesting article on the Order of the Skull and Bone's grave robbery, *see* Terry Melanson, *Skull and Bones 'Crook' for the Tomb,* Conspiracy Archive (2009), available at *http://www.conspiracyarchive .com/2013/11/29/skull-and-bones-crook-for-the-tomb.*
4. In September 2007, the Smithsonian's National Museum of Natural History returned a lock of hair and wool leggings of Sitting Bull, leader of the Hunkpapa Lakota Sioux, to Ernie LaPoint, Sitting Bull's great-grandson and a representative of his four known living great-grandchildren. Sitting Bull was killed in 1890 while being arrested by tribal police. An Army doctor had obtained the hair and leggings from the body and sent them to the museum in 1896. Arts Briefly, *Smithsonian Returns Sitting Bull Relics,* N.Y. Times, Sept. 18, 2007.

PROBLEM 12-2

> Dr. Jones and Dr. Croft enjoy looting ancient Native American sites and archeological digs for artifacts so that they can bring them back to their world-famous research university for study and display. How might Dr. Jones's and Dr. Croft's conduct be regulated by the laws discussed above?

D. Theft of Native American Art

Tribal laws may also assist Native Americans by forcing the return of stolen cultural property.

Chilkat Indian Village v. Johnson

870 F.2d 1469 (9th Cir. 1989)*

CANBY, Circuit Judge.

The artifacts at issue in this case are four carved wooden posts and a wooden partition called a rain screen. They have been described as "the finest example of Native art, either Tlingit or Tsimshian, in Alaska." Emmons, the Whale House of Chilkat, in Raven's Bones 81 (1982). Art dealers and museums have repeatedly attempted to purchase the artifacts.

The Chilkat Indian Village Council is the governing body of the Village under the Village's IRA-authorized constitution. In 1976, the Council enacted an ordinance prohibiting the removal of artifacts from Klukwan:

> No person shall enter on to the property of the Chilkat Indian Village for the purpose of buying, trading for, soliciting the purchase of, or otherwise seeking to arrange the removal of artifacts, clan crests, or other traditional Indian art work owned or held by members of the Chilkat Indian Village or kept within the boundaries of the real property owned by the Chilkat Indian Village, without first requesting and obtaining permission to do so from the Chilkat Indian Village Council.
>
> No traditional Indian artifacts, clan crests, or other Indian art works of any kind may be removed from the Chilkat Indian Village without the prior notification of and approval by, the Chilkat Indian Village Council.

Chilkat Indian Village Ordinance of May 12, 1976.

On April 22, 1984, several defendants removed the four posts and the rain screen from Klukwan and delivered them to defendant Michael Johnson, an Arizona art dealer. When the Village discovered that the artifacts had been

---

* Footnotes omitted.

removed, it notified authorities of the State of Alaska. The State began a criminal investigation, located the artifacts in a warehouse in Seattle, Washington, and took custody of the artifacts.

The Village then filed suit, seeking return of the artifacts and monetary damages for their removal. The Village alleged that it was a federally recognized Indian tribe, and that (1) the artifacts belong to the tribe, and defendants removed them without permission; (2) defendants violated the ordinance prohibiting removal of artifacts; and (3) defendants violated 18 U.S.C. § 1163. The district court dismissed the Village's section 1163 claim, ruling that the statute did not create a private cause of action. *Chilkat Indian Village v. Johnson*, 643 F. Supp. 535 (D. Alaska 1986). In a separate memorandum and order, the district court also ruled *sua sponte* that it lacked subject matter jurisdiction over the Village's remaining claims. The court reasoned that (1) the Village's first claim was a simple conversion claim with no federal underpinning; and (2) the Village ordinance claim did not arise under federal law for purposes of 28 U.S.C. §§ 1331 and 1362.

[The court agreed that section 1163 provides no private right of action, and that the Village's first and fifth causes of action amount to claims for conversion, and thus do not arise under federal law.] . . .

IV

The most difficult question is whether the Village's claim to enforce its ordinance arises under federal law. For reasons to be explained, we believe that the answer depends upon the status of the defendants against whom the ordinance is sought to be imposed.

For its second "cause of action," the Village alleges:

> The Chilkat Tribe possesses paramount sovereign rights over the Whale House artifacts. Relying on the authority given to it by its federally-approved constitution and its reserved powers, the Chilkat Tribe has regulated the use and disposition of all tribal artifacts found within its borders.

It then goes on to allege that the Village's ordinance prohibited removal of the artifacts without permission of the Village Council, that the defendants violated the ordinance, and that the Village "can enforce the ordinance . . . with an action for equitable relief and damages pursuant to 28 U.S.C. § 1362."

The defendants and intervenor State of Alaska contend that this claim is merely one to enforce the Village's ordinance, and that it does not raise any issue of federal law whatsoever. They rely on *Boe v. Fort Belknap Indian Community*, 642 F.2d 276 (9th Cir. 1981), in which we held that no federal question was raised by Indian plaintiffs who sought to contest the results of a tribal election on the ground that tribal election laws had been violated. But to hold that this case is the same as *Boe*, we would have to ignore the foundation of federal law that the Village will clearly have to lay, and litigate, in order to enforce its ordinance against non-Indians. In *Boe* we said:

> Since plaintiffs' claims do not involve a dispute or controversy respecting the validity, construction, or effect of the IRA, they do not, in our opinion, arise

under federal law. "The federal nature of the right to be established is decisive — not the source of the authority — to establish it."

642 F.2d at 279 (quoting *Littell v. Nakai*, 344 F.2d 486, 488 (9th Cir. 1965), cert. denied, 382 U.S. 986, 86 S. Ct. 531, 15 L. Ed. 2d 474 (1986)). But *Boe* was an entirely internal dispute between a tribe and some of its members over the question whether a tribal ordinance of undisputed validity had been violated in an election. The complaint, in context, raised no federal claim. Although the matter is certainly not free from doubt, we conclude that the claims for enforcement of the ordinance against the non-Indian defendants does arise under federal law within the meaning of 28 U.S.C. §§ 1331 and 1362. In seeking to apply its ordinance to Michael Johnson and his corporation, however, the Village is not prima facie engaged in regulating its internal affairs. Instead, it is pressing "the outer boundaries of an Indian tribe's power over non-Indians," which "federal law defines." *National Farmers Union Ins. Cos. v. Crow Tribe*, 471 U.S. 845, 851, 85 L. Ed. 2d 818, 105 S. Ct. 2447 (1985). It cannot be said, as it was in *Boe*, that the Village's claim against Johnson and his corporation will not depend on any disputed interpretation or application of federal law.

Lying as it does on the boundaries of tribal jurisdiction, this case is far more like *Knight v. Shoshone & Arapahoe Indian Tribes*, 670 F.2d 900 (10th Cir. 1982), in which the Tenth Circuit held that a tribe's suit to enforce its land-use ordinance against non-Indians arose under federal law; the tribe's power under Federal law to regulate non-Indian use of fee land was a prime issue. Also comparable is *Confederated Salish & Kootenai Tribes v. Namen*, 665 F.2d 951 (9th Cir.), *cert. denied*, 459 U.S. 977, 74 L. Ed. 2d 291, 103 S. Ct. 314 (1982), in which we entertained a similar claim without discussing jurisdiction. In our case the state of the law is such that the heart of the controversy over the claim will be the Village's power, under federal law, to enact its ordinance and apply it to non-Indians. Indeed, the meaning of the ordinance is barely open to dispute, but the Village's power under the federal statute or common law to enact and apply it is open to immense dispute. The State of Alaska placed in issue in district court questions whether the Village was a federally-recognized tribe, whether it ever had or ever could qualify as one, and whether it had any legislative jurisdiction in general or over the artifacts and defendants in particular. Alaska also stated that it was prepared to dispute the Village's contention that its fee lands were Indian country; Alaska further asserted that, even if they were, the Village thereby acquired or retained no legislative powers. These issues are not before us now, but they are federal questions and they lie at the heart of the Village's claim to enforce its ordinance.

The district court was of the view that these federal issues were entirely defensive matter, and consequently had to be disregarded in determining whether the Village's claim arose under federal law. *See Louisville & Nashville R.R. Co. v. Mottley*, 219 U.S. 467, 55 L. Ed. 297, 31 S. Ct. 265, (1911); *Phillips Petroleum Co v. Texaco, Inc.*, 415 U.S. 125, 39 L. Ed. 2d 209, 94 S. Ct. 1002 (1974). The question is a close one, because some of the issues just listed are purely defensive. We conclude, however, that the Village's allegations of sovereign power, as a matter of federal statute and "reserved powers" (which could only be cognizable as a matter of federal common law), to apply its ordinance to Johnson and his corporation, bring this case within the rule of *Oneida Indian Nation v. County of Oneida*, 414 U.S. 661, 39 L. Ed. 2d 73, 94 S. Ct. 772 (1974). In that case, the Oneidas brought an action in ejectment, contending that they held aboriginal title to the lands in issue and that the conveyance by which the State or County held title had violated federal law. The lower courts held that the ejectment action arose under state law, and that the federal claims were purely defensive, negating jurisdiction in the federal courts. The Supreme Court reversed, holding that the possessory interest upon which the complaint depended — the original right of Indian occupancy — was a federally-founded interest upon which the complaint was fairly based. In our view, the Village's claim of the sovereign power to enact a valid ordinance, applicable to non-Indians regulating tribal artifacts on its fee lands is equally based on a disputed federal claim. The extent of the "reserved" power alleged by the Village is determined by federal common law, *see National Farmers Union Ins. Cos. v. Crow Tribe*, 471 U.S. 845, 85 L. Ed. 2d 818, 105 S. Ct. 2447 (1985), and the extent of the Village's power under the IRA depends upon the construction of that federal statute. These federal issues, in our view, inhere in the complaint. *See Oklahoma ex rel. Oklahoma State Tax Comm'n v. Graham*, 846 F.2d 1258, 1260 (10th Cir.) (federal question, though not pleaded, inheres in complaint because defendant is sovereignly immune tribe), *cert. granted*, 109 S. Ct. 53, 102 L. Ed. 2d 31 (1988). It would be too technical, we believe, to focus only on the ultimate ordinance, which is not federal, and to ignore the necessity for the Village to prove its disputed federal power to enact and apply it to those outside of its community. We conclude, therefore, that the Village's claim against Johnson and his corporation arises under federal law.

V

We reach a different conclusion with regard to the claim seeking to enforce the Village's ordinance against its own members or others whose Indian status may subject them to the internal jurisdiction of the Village. *See Duro v. Reina*, 851 F.2d 1136 (9th Cir. 1988) (amended opinion) (nonmember Indians subject to criminal jurisdiction of reservation tribe). It is true that in some cases enforcement of a tribe's ordinance against its own members may raise federal issues of tribal power. Indeed, this may well be one of those cases. But we cannot accept the view that these federal questions inhere in a complaint by a tribe seeking to enforce its ordinance against its own members. In the overwhelming majority of instances, a tribe's enforcement of its ordinances against its members will raise no federal questions at all. *E.g., Boe v. Fort Belknap Indian Community*, 642 F.2d 276 (9th Cir. 1981). Such cases primarily raise issues of tribal law, and they are the staple of the tribal courts. Nothing on the face of the Village's complaint tells us that this case is any different. We conclude, therefore, that the Village's claim for enforcement of its ordinance against its own members does not arise under federal law within the meaning of 28 U.S.C. §§ 1331 and 1362.

We also reject the Village's more sweeping argument that the ordinance itself was a federal law for purposes of 28 U.S.C. §§ 1331 and 1362. The Village's proposition is an exceedingly difficult one to uphold. *Boe v. Fort Belknap Indian Community*, 642 F.2d 276 (9th Cir. 1981), is sufficient authority that the federal courts do not stand ready to entertain every case arising under a tribal ordinance, when there is no inherent and disputed federal question about the tribe's power to enact it. Moreover, the Village's contention goes against the grain of *United States v. Wheeler*, 435 U.S. 313, 55 L. Ed. 2d 303, 98 S. Ct. 1079 (1978), in which the Supreme Court held that successive prosecutions under a tribal ordinance and a federal statute for the same offense did not violate the double jeopardy clause. That result could scarcely have followed if tribal ordinances were equivalent to federal laws. It is safe to say, therefore, that every claim based upon a tribal ordinance does not, ipso facto, arise under federal law.

VI

Having concluded that the Village's claim to enforce its ordinance against Johnson and his corporation arises under federal law, we reverse the district court's dismissal of that claim. Because the district court's dismissal of the pendent state law claims was based on its dismissal of all anchoring federal claims, we also reverse the district court's dismissal of those claims as to non-Indian defendants. We affirm the dismissal of claims against the Indian defendants and the dismissal of the entire claim based on 18 U.S.C. § 1163.

AFFIRMED IN PART; REVERSED IN PART.

Notes

1. In the follow-up case, No. 90-01 (Chilkat Tr. Ct. Nov. 3, 1993), Chilkat Indian Village Tribal Court ordered the return of the artifacts and the payment of expenses for the artifacts' return as well as costs and fees of the litigation.
2. The Council of Chiefs of the Onondaga Nation required twelve wampum belts, which they list on their website: *www.onondaganation.org/culture/wampum/* (lasted visited on April 15, 2016).
3. In *State v. Taylor*, 126 Hawai'i 205, 269 P.3d 740 (2011), the court held that a prior federal conviction for conspiracy to traffic in Native American cultural items under NAGPRA did not bar a subsequent state prosecution for theft in the first degree involving the same artifact. The court reasoned that statutory double-jeopardy did not apply because the theft offense under state law requires proof of facts that the property involved had a value in excess of $20,000, which the federal conspiracy act did not necessitate. Additionally, the two statutory

offenses were intended to prevent "substantially different harms or evils."

4. One of the most significant incidents involving a museum's return of an item of cultural importance to Native Americans occurred in 1978 when the Denver Art Museum voluntarily returned a War God to the Zuni people. Under Zuni law, no person is capable of owning such a War God, as it is tribal property. Rather, any person in possession of the War God would be a mere trustee for the tribe. For this reason, the Zunis believed that the War God was stolen. When tribal officials first demanded return of the War God, which was not to be seen by white men, the museum trustees issued the following release:

Press Release from the Denver Art Museum

The museum respects the sincerity of the Zunis and recognizes the importance of their religion to their people and the significance of War God sculptures to that religion, but is greatly concerned by the complexity of the issues involved. The museum is a public trust on behalf of the people of Denver and the nation, and as such, has fundamental responsibilities to collect important objects of esthetic and cultural significance and to assure their safekeeping for the growth of knowledge, cultural understanding, and artistic enjoyment of the public.

The museum is concerned by the fact and the principle of the proposal to give away an object from its collection, especially one which is believed to be the finest example of its type. As part of the museum's collection, the object is also communally owned by all the people of Denver.

The museum has held the object in good faith for over 25 years, exhibiting, publishing and protecting it for the benefit of the public throughout the world. Should the museum donate the object to the Zunis, it will be placed in an outdoor setting subject to the hazards of the natural elements of wind-blown sand, intense heat, cold, and certain, and in fact intentional deterioration and destruction. New War Gods are produced annually to succeed and supplement their predecessors; they are intended to "eat themselves up." The possibility of theft also exists. The Zunis have outlined plans to increase security measures at the several shrines which are near public roads, but acknowledge that a large number of more remote shrines also exist and are largely unprotected. The return of the object will assure its ultimate destruction.

One of the museum's greatest concerns is for the precedent that would be set by donation of the sculpture to the Zunis. The implications of that precedent can well lead to numerous claims by other Native American tribes and many other countries, cultures and religions, of objects in this museum's and other museums' collections. To our knowledge no legal precedent exists of a museum donating an object to any religious group on the basis that the object is of religious significance and should be presumed to have been stolen by virtue of having been communal religious property. There is concern that to set such a precedent can cause immensely complex problems for museums of many kinds throughout the nation.

The museum recognizes that cultural and religious attitudes of nations, religious, tribes and groups change from time to time, and that related objects are viewed differently by those entities at different times.

The museum, like most museums, contains a multitude of objects from virtually every major culture which have at one time or another been considered of great religious or cultural importance. Those include Christian, Buddhist, Hindu, Islamic, pre-Columbian, as well as Native American, religious objects. The museum is concerned about the consequences that could ensue should other groups assert that certain museum objects are of great significance to them, since the circumstances of the original acquisition of many ancient objects in any museums are undocumented.

Despite these concerns, museum officials ultimately agreed to return the War God. The trustees adopted the following resolution at their meeting on March 21, 1979:

1. Zuni religious leaders have informed the Board of Trustees of the Denver Art Museum that the Zuni War God, Ahayu:da, which has been in the Museum's collection for more than 25 years, is a religious deity which represents an object of continuing worship whose presence in the Museum, rather than its original shrine, is offensive to the religious principles of the Zuni people, and makes impossible the conduct of a part of their religion.

2. Zuni leaders have advised the Trustees that under Zuni law the War God constitutes communal property of a kind which cannot legally be sold or given away.

3. The Board of Trustees has been advised by qualified anthropologists and its own staff that in the Zuni religion it is true, as stated by the Zuni leaders, that the War God is a deity and a present, animate, object of worship, rather than a symbol or art object.

4. The Trustees have considered these facts in the light of all of the related interests and responsibilities of the Museum, as the art agency of the City and County of Denver. These include not only the Museum's responsibility for the preservation of its collection but also its interest in strengthening its relations with the Zuni people and other creative cultures as an institution which displays and preserves art objects from all cultures with sensitivity and appreciation.

5. In view of these and other considerations, it is the belief of the Trustees of the Denver Art Museum that it would be in the best interests of the Museum and the people of Denver to authorize the presentation of the Zuni War God, Ahayu:da, to the Zuni people. The Trustees therefore direct the proper officers of the Museum to meet with duly constituted representatives of the Zunis to arrange for its placement in a suitable shrine under appropriate security conditions, and further to discuss with such representatives other possibilities for enhancing the understanding between the Zuni people and the Museum with respect to matters of mutual concern.

After this release, Denver Museum officials categorically refused to answer questions about the incident and the propriety of their role in allowing this treasure to be destroyed by the elements. For more information, *see Zunis Seek Return of War God from Museum*, Straight Creek J., Feb. 15, 1979, at 1; *Zunis Rebut Museum's Statements on War God*, Rocky Mountain News, Feb. 20, 1979, at 4.

Notes

1. The sensitivity shown by the Denver Art Museum gave other institutions the impetus needed to resolve similar controversies related to human remains. In June 1989, after protracted discussions, Stanford University agreed to return the remains of over 500 Ohlone Indians to their descendants for reburial. Shortly thereafter, the University of Minnesota agreed to a similar return of remains. As a result of the decisions made by these three institutions, more than 80 years of precedent was reversed and a nationwide movement toward repatriation began.
2. Native American artists have also had their art stolen. Consider the following interview with famed Navajo painter R.C. Gorman.

E. The Life and Work of a Native American Artist

Sherri L. Burr, Conversing with the Picasso of Indian Artists

Author Interview with R.C. Gorman
Copyright © 2004 by Sherri L. Burr

When you walk through the front door of his home, you are greeted by a life-size sculpture of a full-figured woman sitting in a chair and wearing nothing but a lei. Navajo artist R.C. Gorman, who is also the author of the cookbook *Food and Nudes*, developed worldwide fame for his paintings of large Native American women in a whimsical fashion.[14]

On April 2, 2004, Gorman, now 72 and wearing a red, white, and black headband and Hawaiian shirt with jeans, welcomed my law students and me into his Taos, N.M., home to interview him for the cable television show *ARTS TALK*. He graciously provided a tour of

Jim Garton, Photograph of Gorman Poster from the collection of Sherri Burr (2010)

---

14. Michael D. Murray, Cropped, revised, and resized thumbnail excerpt of a Jim Garton photograph (2010) of an R.C. Gorman poster of a seated Navajo woman, from the collection of Sherri Burr.

his home and discussed his magnificent art collection, which includes four Picassos, a Miró, and an Andy Warhol painting of himself alongside paintings by dozens of other artists.

Gorman mostly displays the works of other artists in his home. He explains, "What do I want with my own work? They are for sale. Not these." Gorman says he collects because he can't live without a particular piece or he wants to take an item "off the market." He bought two of his Picassos after developing a friendship with Francine, Paloma's mom. He adds, "I bought the Miró from a gallery in Seattle when he was alive and now I have a treasure."

Alongside the art of prominent painters a visitor to Gorman's home will see water color paintings by his father, Carl Gorman, who was one of the Navajo code-talkers who received a Congressional Medal of Honor for his service during World War II. About his father Gorman says, "He didn't teach me that much about art, and he didn't encourage me, but he was just there. That means a lot. I'm self-taught."

Like many Navajos of his generation, Gorman received his formal education at religious boarding or day schools. "In the Catholic school," he says, "they used to punish us if we spoke our own language. In the Presbyterian school, they encouraged us to use our own language so we could preach the Bible." As far as art classes go he adds, "in the Catholic school they wanted us to emulate the traditionalists. In the Presbyterian school, I had a great teacher named Jenny Lind who wanted me to do everything. She was my most important teacher."

Gorman began drawing early in life. At the age of six, he drew a naked lady and his mother and grade school teacher whipped him. Now he draws and paints women who are large and covered. His models mostly come to him. When Gorman's work is described as elegantly simple in its lines, he says "It's because of my elegant models."

He says he likes to draw big women. "It saves me money, because I can use the whole page. With someone skinny I have to make up something to make them look larger." Gorman admires Flemish painter Peter Paul Rubens, who produced canvases of large naked women in the early 1600s. The word "Rubenesque" eventually became defined by The American Heritage Dictionary as "relating to, or in the style of painting of Peter Paul Rubens" or by the words "plump or fleshy or voluptuous. Used of a woman." About Rubens' paintings, Gorman believes that "sometimes he overdid it." He adds, "Too many dimples."

Gorman's paintings, which sold for $50-$60 in the 1950s, are now commanding $40,000 bids on eBay, the online auction company. Gorman sometimes repurchases his early work. He once paid $3,000 to buy back a $50 drawing. He says, "I sometimes think I can't believe I did that."

When asked whether artists are born or made, Gorman replays, "Who knows? I work very spontaneously. I sit down and just go to work. It's my models who inspire me." Gorman studied art in Mexico, where he visited galleries and saw how Mexican artists represented their own people. He then decided, "That's what I'm going to do." Gorman has sometimes followed in the footsteps of Mexican artists Diego Rivera and painted on huge canvases.

Even more renown in the art world for merchandizing his work, Gorman says he prepares derivative works "because why limit something that is very good. You might as well use it in every possible way, including sculptures. Keep it going." Gorman often takes an oil painting, which might sell for $30,000, and turns it into a lithograph series, posters, greeting cards, mugs, and even life-size sculptures. Gorman credits his success in the business of art to having surrounded himself with "brains. All the people who work for me are left-brained."

About some criticism of his work as having been over-merchandized, Gorman says, "I do what I do and whatever they think is certainly their privilege."

Like other famous artists before him, Gorman has also experienced problems with people stealing his work. An Austrian woman came to Taos and started copying and selling his work throughout the United States. Gorman says, "I got a phone call from New York City and they asked me if I knew this woman. She was copying my work and selling it. They sent her to jail."

The woman's mistake, according to Gorman, was to sell the work using his name. "That's a good lesson," he adds, "sign your own name for something you steal."

Gorman may be the most famous Navajo living. Arizona's Diné College will eventually house the R.C. Gorman Library Collection and display some of his work. Gorman says, "I've lived away from the reservation for over 60 years, but I've got so many relatives all of a sudden."

The *New York Times* once called him "the Picasso of Indians." Gorman says, "Picasso had a wide range. He didn't just start doing abstract. A lot of people do abstract because they can't do anything else. It's all art, but a lot of people can't do both."

Perhaps the ultimate test of Gorman's artistic legacy will come when the American Heritage Dictionary adds the word "Gormanesque" to refer to his type of art, or a hundred years from now an artist is called the "Gorman of Italians."

Note

1. R.C. stands for Rudolf Carl. He was born on July 26, 1932, and passed away on November 3, 2005. His work can be seen on the Internet at *www.rcgormangallery.com*. He told Nancy Gillespie in an interview for *Southwest Art* magazine, "I don't feel a bit different being rich and famous than I did when I was poor and wretched." Nancy Gillespie, *R.C. Gorman: Chinle to Taos*, Southwest Art, June 1988, at 40-47.

ASSESSMENT

1. One day while digging on Arizona Native American tribal land, Andy Anthro came across very old skeletal remains. After further analysis,

Andy discovered the remains dated back thousands of years. Additionally, to his amazement, he believed the skeleton was from a fabled tribe, whose culture now only existed through stories. If he could prove that the skeleton was from that tribe, it would be an unprecedented discovery and provide important information on early American culture.

Andy is very excited about this find and the important cultural implications it could lead to. Based on the court's decision in *Bonnichsen v. U.S.*, will Andy be able to continue studying the remains, or will he be required to hand them over to the Arizona Native American Tribe for proper burial?

(A) Andy will be required to turn over the remains because they were found on the Arizona Native American tribal land; therefore they are the rightful owners to them

(B) Andy will only need to turn over the remains if it is determined that they bear some relationship to a presently existing Native American tribe, people, or culture

(C) Andy will not be required to turn over the remains because they are from a culture that only now exists through stories

(D) Andy will not be required to turn over the remains because the study of them will provide valuable historical information on early American cultures

(E) Both (C) and (D)

2. In *Livingston v. Ewing*, the court held that the Museum of New Mexico's policy, which only permitted Indians to sell their handmade goods in an area that had been designated for the use of the Museum, did not violate non-Indian's equal protection rights. What reason(s) did the court give in coming to their decision?

(A) The non-Indian plaintiffs are not members of a suspect class, or a discrete and insular minority, so the equal protection standard of strict scrutiny does not apply and the policy is constitutional

(B) The non-Indian plaintiffs were not deprived of their First Amendment Rights to freedom of expression because those rights are not absolute and do not guarantee every individual the exact forum he or she desires

(C) The Museum's policy is directly linked with Indian self-determination through economic survival; therefore, it is rationally related to a legitimate state interest

(D) Both (A) and (B) are correct

(E) Both (B) and (C) are correct

3. During a class party, which was held in the backyard of the school's principle, a student came across what looked like an old Indian artifact. When she showed her teacher, the teacher suggested that she give it to the local museum so that more people could have the pleasure of viewing the

item. Shortly after giving the artifact to the local museum, the state Pueblo sued the museum under the Native American Graves Protection and Repatriation Act (NAGPRA), asking for it to be returned to its rightful place with the Pueblo. Based on the court's decision in *Pueblo of San Ildefonso v. Ridlon*, which of the following is the most accurate statement?

(A) The Pueblo cannot state a claim over the artifact because it was found on non-federal land and NAGPRA only applies to items excavated or discovered on federal lands after November 16, 1990

(B) The Pueblo will not be able to reclaim the Indian artifact because it is the property of the student who originally found it; therefore, she has the right to gift it to the museum

(C) The artifact will be subject to repatriation, even if it was found on non-federal land

(D) Both (A) and (B)

(E) None of the above

4. In *Thorpe v. Borough of Thorpe*, the court held that the "Borough of Jim Thorpe" created in honor of the famous athlete was not a "museum" subject to NAGPRA. What reason(s) did the court give in support of their decision?

(A) Based on the plain meaning of the text and Congressional intent, extending the definition of "museum" under NAGPRA to this borough would lead to absurd results

(B) Jim Thorpe's wife lacked the legal authority to decide where to bury her husband

(C) NAGPRA was intended to protect Native Americans from further injustices, not to be used as a way to settle familial disputes within Native American Families

(D) Both (A) and (C)

(E) All of the above

5. While looking through her purse, Rachel Ridiculous came across a gold Sacagawea dollar coin. Sacagawea was the famous Native American woman who helped the Lewis and Clark expedition. To Rachel's amazement Sacagawea looked just like her and, after further research, she found out they both were from the same area and were good with directions. With so many commonalities, Rachel was convinced Sacagawea must be her ancestor.

Based on the court's decision in *Idrogo v. U.S. Army*, if Rachel brought a suit under NAGPRA to repatriate the remains of Sacagawea, Rachel would probably be

(A) Unsuccessful, because only direct descendants of Native American remains or affiliated tribal organizations stand to be injured by the act, and she has no evidence to support her claim that Sacagawea is her ancestor

(B) Unsuccessful, because Sacagawea's remains have been in the United States possession since before NAGPRA was enacted; therefore, they cannot be repatriated

(C) Successful, because any person may commence a civil suit on his own behalf against the United States in order to assure it is in compliance with NAGPRA

(D) Successful, because Rachel researched Sacagawea's background who she believes to be her ancestor; therefore, she is entitled to her remains

(E) Both (A) and (B)

ASSESSMENT ANSWERS

1. One day while digging on Arizona Native American Tribe land, Andy Anthro came across very old skeletal remains. After further analysis, Andy discovered the remains dated back thousands of years. Additionally, to his amazement, he believed the skeleton was from a fabled tribe, whose culture now only existed through stories. If he could prove that the skeleton was from that tribe, it would be an unprecedented discovery and provide important information on early American culture.

   Andy is very excited about this find and the important cultural implications it could lead to. Based on the court's decision in *Bonnichsen v. U.S.*, will Andy be able to continue studying the remains, or will he be required to hand them over to the Arizona Native American Tribe for proper burial?

   (A) Andy will be required to turn over the remains because they were found on the Arizona Native American Tribe land; therefore they are the rightful owners to them

   (B) Andy will only need to turn over the remains if it is determined that they bear some relationship to a presently existing Native American tribe, people, or culture

   (C) Andy will not be required to turn over the remains because they are from a culture that only now exists through stories

   (D) Andy will not be required to turn over the remains because the study of them will provide valuable historical information on early American cultures

   (E) Both (C) and (D)

   ANSWER: The correct answer is (B), because in *Bonnichsen*, the court concluded that Congress intended NAGPRA to provide for the repatriation of only those remains affiliated with extant tribes. (A) is incorrect because whether NAGPRA applies is dependent on if the remains are found to be Native American and if they bear some relationship to a presently existing tribe. Where they were found was irrelevant to the court's decision in *Bonnichsen*. Choice (C) is wrong because, although the remains are from a culture that no longer exists, NAGPRA will apply if it is found that they bear some relationship to a presently existing tribe. (D) is incorrect because their value is insignificant to NAGPRA's intent, which is to protect the dignity of Native American remains, not to protect the interests of scientists. (E) is incorrect because (B) is the correct answer.

2. In *Livingston v. Ewing*, the court held that the Museum of New Mexico's policy, which only permitted Indians to sell their handmade goods in an area that had been designated for the use of the Museum, did not violate non-Indian's equal protection rights. What reason(s) did the court give in coming to their decision?

   (A) The non-Indian plaintiffs are not members of a suspect class, or a discrete and insular minority, so the equal protection standard of strict scrutiny does not apply and the policy is constitutional

   (B) The non-Indian plaintiffs were not deprived of their First Amendment Rights to freedom of expression because those rights are not absolute and do not guarantee every individual the exact forum he or she desires

   (C) The Museum's policy is directly linked with Indian self-determination through economic survival; therefore, it is rationally related to a legitimate state interest

   (D) Both (A) and (B) are correct

   (E) Both (B) and (C) are correct

   ANSWER: The correct answer is (E) because answers (B) and (C) are correct statements of the reasoning given by the court to determine that the museum's policy did not violate non-Indian equal protection rights. (A) is incorrect because the court stated that determining whether the plaintiffs are members of a suspect, or discrete and insular minority is an inapplicable type of equal protection analysis to cases involving Indian preference. (A) is an incorrect answer, making (D) incorrect.

3. During a class party, which was held in the backyard of the school's principle, a student came across what looked like an old Indian artifact. When she showed her teacher, the teacher suggested that she give it to the local museum so that more people could have the pleasure of viewing the item. Shortly after giving the artifact to the local museum, the state Pueblo sued the museum under the Native American Graves Protection and Repatriation Act (NAGPRA), asking for it to be returned to its rightful place with the Pueblo. Based on the court's decision in *Pueblo of San Ildefonso v. Ridlon*, which of the following is the most accurate statement?

(A) The Pueblo cannot state a claim over the artifact because it was found on non-federal land and NAGPRA only applies to items excavated or discovered on federal lands after November 16, 1990

(B) The Pueblo will not be able to reclaim the Indian artifact because it is the property of the student who originally found it; therefore, he has the right to gift it to the museum

(C) The artifact will be subject to repatriation, even if it was found on non-federal land

(D) Both (A) and (B)

(E) None of the above

ANSWER: The correct answer is (C) because the artifact will be subject to repatriation regardless of where it was found. (A) is incorrect because repatriation from a museum under NAGPRA is not limited by when or where the object of repatriation was found. (B) is incorrect because who found it is irrelevant to whether repatriation under NAGPRA is necessary. Since (C) is the only correct answer, (D) and (E) are also incorrect.

4. In *Thorpe v. Borough of Thorpe*, the court held that the "Borough of Jim Thorpe" created in honor of the famous athlete was not a "museum" subject to NAGPRA. What reason(s) did the court give in support of their decision?

(A) Based on the plain meaning of the text and Congressional intent, extending the definition of "museum" under NAGPRA to this borough would lead to absurd results

(B) Jim Thorpe's wife lacked the legal authority to decide where to bury her husband

(C) NAGPRA was intended to protect Native Americans from further injustices, not to be used as a way to settle familial disputes within Native American Families

(D) Both (A) and (C)

(E) All of the above

ANSWER: The correct answer is (D) because it incorporates answers (A) and (C). (B) is incorrect because it was undisputed that Jim Thorpe's wife had the legal authority to decide where to bury his body. (A) is correct because the court reasoned that it should use the ordinary meaning of the word "museum" and not interpret it so as to lead to absurd results. (C) is also correct because the court stated that NAGPRA was intended as a shield against further injustices to Native Americans, and it was not intended to be wielded as a sword to settle familial disputes within Native American families. (E) is incorrect because it incorporates (B), which is incorrect.

5. While looking through her purse, Rachel Ridiculous, came across a gold Sacagawea dollar coin. Sacagawea was the famous Native American woman who helped the Lewis and Clark expedition. To Rachel's amazement Sacagawea looked just like her and, after further research, she found out they both were from the same area and were good with directions. With so many commonalities, Rachel was convinced Sacagawea must be her ancestor.

Based on the court's decision in *Idrogo v. U.S. Army,* if Rachel brought a suit under NAGPRA to repatriate the remains of Sacagawea, Rachel would probably be

(A) Unsuccessful, because only direct descendants of Native American remains or affiliated tribal organizations stand to be injured by the act, and she has no evidence to support her claim that Sacagawea is her ancestor

(B) Unsuccessful, because Sacagawea's remains have been in the United States possession since before NAGPRA was enacted; therefore, they cannot be repatriated

(C) Successful, because any person may commence a civil suit on his own behalf against the United States in order to assure it is in compliance with NAGPRA

(D) Successful, because Rachel researched Sacagawea's background who she believes to be her ancestor; therefore, she is entitled to her remains

(E) Both (A) and (B)

ANSWER: The correct answer is (A) because only direct descendants of Native American remains or affiliated tribal organizations can sue in these circumstances, and she has no evidence to support her claim that Sacagawea is her ancestor. (B) is incorrect because repatriation under NAGPRA is not limited by when the object of repatriation was found. (C) is incorrect because a generalized interest of all citizens in seeing that the U.S. faithfully complies with the terms of NAGPRA is insufficient to confer standing. (D) is incorrect because it is irrelevant that Rachael believes Sacagawea is her ancestor based on the facts that led her to that conclusion. (A) is the only correct answer; therefore, (E) is incorrect.

TABLE OF CASES

Principal cases are indicated by italics.

INDEX

Contracts (*cont'd*)
  governing law, 545
  inspection period, 563
  insurance, 544
  loss or damage liability, 544
  mediation, 545
  nature, 543
  payment, 544
  portraits, 560-564
  price, 544
  public art contract, 553-560
  quasi-contract claims, 714-715
  satisfaction guaranteed, 562
  scope, 543
  statute of limitations, 581-582
Convention on Cultural Property
      Implementation Act of 1983, 771-773
Conventions. *See* Treaties and international
      conventions
Cooperative galleries, 519
Copyright, 31-158
  aesthetic or academic merit, 49-52
  architectural designs, 104-106
  attorneys' fees, 115
  author, defined, 31
  Barbie, 63-67
  Bratz Dolls, 91-92
  bundle of rights protected, 100-102
  choreography, 53
  common law, 238
  concepts, 35-36, 74-76
  copyrightable subject matter, 108
  costs, 115
  creation, defined, 36
  creativity and originality, 36-53, 108
  damages, 34, 114-116
  designs, 72-77
  dissection and filtration approach, 69
  division and transfer of individual rights,
      100-101
  doll faces, 63-67
  duration, 79-80
  expert testimony, 113-114
  expression and fixation, 33-34, 71, 108
  extrinsic similarity, 113-114
  fair use, 116-149. *See also* Fair use
  fictional characters, 115
  fixed and tangible, 53-57
  formalities, 81-83

functional works, 70-77, 109
historical overview, 31-32
ideas, 35-36, 45-47, 59-62, 108, 115-116
improvised performance, 54
indivisibility, 100
infringement, 106-116
  attorneys' fees, 115
  copyrightable subject matter, 108
  costs, 115
  creativity and originality, 108
  de minimis infractions, 110-114
  expert testimony, 113-114
  expression and fixation, 108
  extrinsic similarity, 113-114
  intrinsic similarity, 113-114
  protectable elements, 108
  subject matter, 107-109
  substantial similarity, 109-114
  work for hire doctrine as defense,
      98-99
international protection of, 81-84
intrinsic similarity, 113-114
lamp bases, 77-78
lectures, 53
limitations, 57-78
  functional works, 70-77, 109
  merger doctrine, 57-70
  scènes à faire, 57-70, 108-109
  useful articles, 70-77
live performances, 54
merger doctrine, 57-70
natural objects, 69-70
notice, 544
oral expressions, 53
original, defined, 36
ownership, 84-100
photography, 37-48, 128-129, 144-145,
      379-380
preemption of state law claims, 103-106
publicity rights, 362-363
reenactments, 54
registration, 34n14, 107
remedies, 114-116
rights in visual art, 100
scènes à faire, 57-70, 108-109
separability, physical, 74-76
Seventh Circuit Court of Appeals, 144-145
source countries, 84
speeches, 53